OPERA

as

OPERA

The State of the Art

CONRAD L. OSBORNE

PROPOSITO PRESS

Proposito Press, New York, N.Y.
First edition, third printing
ISBN 978-0-9994366-0-8
Library of Congress Control Number 2018935973

In memory of my father,

Clifford Osborne

1908-2001

TABLE OF CONTENTS

INTRODUCTION
AND READER'S GUIDE

This is a serious book about opera in performance. I open with this statement because most serious books about opera are not about performance. They are about text. Though presumably informed by performance experience (it is sometimes hard to tell), they speak of opera not as itself, but as literature, whether of the verbal or musical variety. Even Joseph Kerman's *Opera as Drama*, which has defined so much about the subject for my generation and those since, engages the form principally through analysis of musical text—it addresses opera as drama without much reference to opera as theatre.

Approaching opera through performance has two drawbacks. The first is that performance almost always falls short of the potential of a work as suggested in its text; we therefore resort to text to get a better sense of what could be there. The second is that performance is here and gone, leaving behind no object of contemplation save memory traces in those who were present, whereas text is itself such an object, always present to us.

Still, we have no choice. Performance is the *raison d'être*. Opera cannot come into being save through performance, nor drama save through theatre. To approach opera's problems without engaging its living reality would be, in our current predicament, almost fanciful. And so this book proposes engagement with performance, and what goes on in that engagement, as not only a serious way to consider opera, but the most serious of all.

I have mentioned a "current predicament," possibly to the annoyance of some who can say, with no lack of evidence, that opera is forever in a predicament and critics forever jumping up and down in excitement over it, and that the truth is that *plus ça change*, and so forth. But I believe this predicament is our very own, and special. Every generational adaptation to an artform involves disruption, but the ones that have occurred in opera over the past half-century have amounted to a repudiation unlike previous ones. While much of the pressure opera is under as institution and consumer good is quite recent and clearly related to demographic and economic developments, it has been at a loss artistically for a long time.

For over a century now (approximately since the eve of World War I, to which, as we shall see, our directors and designers return us with tiresome frequency), the form has failed to renew itself. Whatever their achievements in other artistic and intellectual spheres, the broad cultural movements we term Modern (operatically expressed most powerfully through musical language) and Postmodern (expressed primarily in visual production codes) have proved ill-adapted to opera. Moreover, the situation has progressively deteriorated. While the first half of the period in question produced at least a few works that are well-regarded and have, rather painfully, won a place, the second half has yielded almost nothing. Meanwhile, the presentation of the canonical repertory has lost much of its potency and authenticity. Groping for a way out of the creative *cul de sac*, we have blundered into an interpretive one. This is not due to any lack of talent, skill, intelligence, or even high-mindedness. All these have been, and are, abundant. But they now often lend themselves to practices that are not merely subversive of previous styles or schools, but inimical to opera itself. And since in this book opera will be taken as a given good (its four-plus centuries of beauties and truths being deemed ample evidence of its goodness), it is those practices that must now be examined, by opera's flickering light. If, as I have proposed, opera finds itself in a unique and potentially mortal predicament, criticism's most urgent purpose must be to present that predicament in the sharpest possible profile, and to analyze its causes. If one cannot define a problem, or even concede its existence, one has little hope of solving it.

In pursuit of such definition, several assertions will be advanced here. One is that to see a way forward, we need to deal more honestly and respectfully with our past—that we cannot continue to live off it while dishonoring it. Another is that the beauties and truths alluded to above are revealed primarily through performance (i.e., the sung and played actions of onstage characters in their musicalized world), and only secondarily through production (i.e., sets, costumes, staging); that we have lost sight of this; that pernicious and arrogant styles of production, justified by auteuristic and conceptualist presumption, have been especially destructive; and that a grievous erosion in the vocal techniques and interpretive freedoms needed to fulfill the requirements of the greatest masterworks of the past has at the same time effectively neutered the capacity of performers to counter these developments. Yet another is that the ascendance of a metanarrative (or, to use Morse Peckham's term, "redundant narrative"), derived from medieval sources, was the subliminal inspiration for the extraordinary Nineteenth-Century flowering of operatic creation under whose "anxiety of influence" (stealing from another great scholar, Harold Bloom) the artform now subsists.

Contentions like these cannot be left as generalizations. They must be argued through the realities, the seemingly small specifics, of performance experience. And since the only such experience about which one can confidently write is one's own, there is naturally a personal tone throughout most of this book. Forty-some years ago, after a dozen years of intensive performance and record reviewing, I decided to sharply curtail those activities. I had several reasons for doing so, but the main artistic one was that I had come to perceive the performance problems I was seeing and hearing more as systemic than as particular to given occasions and artists. To write about them regularly was to risk turning into a repetitive scold, a severely compromised temporizer, or an outright collaborationist of the "educative," "appreciative," or promotional sort. I preferred to turn to a mix of teaching, performing, and selective writing, and fortunately was able to do so. And though the critical habit, once cultivated, is never entirely shaken, this change also returned me to my original operatic status as devotee in search of sensory delight and emotional and intellectual nourishment—and, not at all incidentally, as paying customer of performance institutions and recording companies, in search of value for my limited time and money. For a writer, this dual identity as devotee and customer is quite a different starting point from that of reviewer on the opera beat, and in ways that I think can be salutary.

Over these past five decades, continuing a process already underway, the operatic world has grown more tightly integrated, thus facilitating more efficient distribution of the systemic problems mentioned above. During this time, the aesthetic ground has also shifted, and has now come set sufficiently to clarify its contours. The hostile takeover is on the books and the stealth candidates are out in the open. Still, nobody who is anybody will quite say so. Performance criticism (as distinct from the academic varieties) has been reduced, marginalized, and stuck in a lineup of popcult perpetrators, where it suffers the same woes as the artform on which it fastens. It is by far not enough for devotees to express exasperation and bafflement, or chuck everything into the Eurotrash bin. The dismemberment of opera is being undertaken by some of its most sophisticated, well-educated, and talented practitioners, and while their tongues are often in their cheeks, they don't seem to know it—they think they're chewing over something significant in there. Operatic true believers must show not that they don't understand, but that they understand all too well, and that they have reasons beyond the lazy pleasures of nostalgia for their dismay.

It was with this last conviction in mind, and given a final nudge by Robert Wilson's production of *Lohengrin*, that I undertook this book, which is an effort to present some of those reasons in a more complete and sustained form than is possible in articles and reviews. A few words about its organization may be of help to readers. Its aim is to present as complete a picture of the current state of the art as possible, considering all of opera's elements and how they relate to one another. But though these elements are all crucial, they are not of equal importance, and so are not assigned equal weight. The book starts with what I regard as the more peripheral (though still vital) ones and moves toward the more central ones. So it goes from thinking to doing, then from production to performance. This ascending progression is itself intended as a corrective to present practice. To some specific guidance:

Part I is a set of grounds rules—not a complete theory of opera in performance or critical practice, but a series of notes, in fourteen essayettes, toward such a theory. In keeping with this content, Part I's style is somewhat more abstract than that of the remainder of the book, and many would advise (indeed, some already have) that that's no way to start a book. When, though, would grounds rules otherwise be set?

Part II is concerned with production. It begins by contrasting the aforementioned *Lohengrin* with a production that, serendipitously, immediately presented its representational opposite—the Maryinsky's restoration of Tchaikovsky's *Mazeppa*. It then breaks down production styles into several groupings, and critiques examples of each. These examples, like those of performance later in the book, have been chosen not because they were in all cases the best imaginable, but simply because they presented themselves in the course of season-to-season operagoing; they are parts of everyday operatic reality. This section also discusses the impact of surtitles and amplification (largely negative, in the author's view) on the audience experience, and refers readers to the first of several Backstories for some historical background.

In Part III, the intellectual field on which the transformative changes in operatic presentation are being played out is surveyed. This has two aspects. The first is the body of thought contained in modern and postmodern critical theory, insofar as it pertains to opera. This chapter is supported by Backstory II, a bibliographical essay. The second is the plot-and-character metanarrative referred to above, whose sources are traced, and additional evidence of its determinative influence furnished in Backstory III.

Part IV concerns performance, and in accordance with my priorities is by far the longest and most detailed of the book's sections. It takes up first conducting and orchestral playing, then singing, and finally acting, with close attention throughout to the quest for the unification of these as artistic expression. Part V offers the book's only inclusive essay review (of the Metropolitan Opera's production of Borodin's *Prince Igor*), and then considers several topics that have either not been previously addressed (e.g., HD theatre transmissions, the *tragédie lyrique* genre) or that have presented substantive new development since their earlier discussion (such as eye/ear reception, or the atypical tenorial technique of Jonas Kaufmann). Finally, Part VI dreams about what opera rightly done, in the form of an imagined repertory company, would look like. It thus has an element of fantasy, but also engages with the real-world matter of money. The book ends with a brief note on the remarkable success of a new opera that not only embraces the old "redundant narrative," but returns to its medieval origins, and so brings that theme full circle.

Opera as Opera has been written chronologically in "real time" over an eighteen-year period, like a diary, and I have resisted all temptation to revise in hindsight. Inclusive dates are given for the chapters directly concerned with production and performance, and though not written quite on morning-after deadline, all have been completed (with the aid of in-the-moment notetaking) with the events fresh in memory. These dates in certain cases overlap, since productions are often considered for more than one element. I have avoided musical examples in favor of more generally accessible prose descriptions, sometimes quite dense with detail. I think readers will grasp the argumentative gist even when unfamiliar with the works and performances under discussion. But greater understanding of what's being driven at, as well as much pleasure, is always attainable through reference to texts (librettos and, for the musically literate, scores) and to the nearly endless profusion of audio and video documentation now easily at hand, which includes much of the material—live and recorded, recent and historical—discussed here. I strongly encourage such involvement.

And a note is in order concerning "apparatus"—the footnotes, endnotes, and Backstories that give the book something of a scholarly appearance. I should not want to mislead readers who are either in search of or in flight from such books, and in truth there is scholarship here. In some sections, especially late in the book, it is extensive enough to amount almost to a second narrative, though one always dependent on the first. Except for Part III, however, the scholarship is of performance. Performance is our text. My hope is that my main text will lead most readers through the arguments in a coherent and well-supported manner. But many disciplines are involved. Some readers will have passionate engagement in certain areas, and seek further elaboration in those, but only casual interest in others. Scholarly readers will have the knowledge and appetite to pursue in outside sources something that has piqued their curiosity or challenged a belief. But for the majority who are not scholarly by habit or inclination, I would rather provide the elaboration here than send them on unaccustomed searches, or simply leave them unsatisfied. And so the scholarly "apparatus" is chiefly for them, the unscholarly. The endnotes will be found immediately after the Chapters to which they refer—a rather unusual arrangement, but in this case preferable, I think, to stuffing them in a great wad at the end of the book.

Finally: though its subject is an artform that owes everything to Europe, this book is distinctly American, and I would suggest that this is no disadvantage, even for European readers. We in America can take little credit for the glories of the operatic past. On the other hand, we bear lightly its yoke, the fraught legacy that European artists, unable to replace or entirely disown, instead remain eager to transform beyond recognition. So perhaps—despite our own ill-arranged cultural, political, and economic priorities—the operatic future belongs here as much as anywhere else.

New York, May 23, 2016

PART I

FOURTEEN ESSAYETTES ABOUT THE ARTFORM

(As I noted in the Introduction, this is the theoretical part of my book. Readers impatient with theory may of course skip on to Part II. That wouldn't be my recommendation, though. These essayettes establish some of the critical principles to be employed and the themes that will recur in the pages to follow, and give the reader a general sense of my stance toward them. I might add that while extensive literatures exist on the subjects raised here, and I have some familiarity with them, my knowledge of these subjects and my opinions about them have come first and foremost from my practice as a performer and teacher, and my now-lengthy experience in performance criticism.)

1. OPERA'S ESSENCE

As fully developed, opera is civilization's most elaborate performance mode. It embraces all creative and interpretive disciplines. Its only indispensable components, however, are song and theatrical action. It needs only those to be itself, and to distinguish it from other artforms. It is theatre through song—action through song, song as action. It comes into being with one or more persons singing a theatrical action. This is only its essence, of course, but it helps us to see where our focus should be.

This sung action is a unity, the single, integrated act of a whole person, not an attempted assembly of separate acts. And opera itself is a unity, too. We have a habit of defining it as a synthesis of music and theatre, as if "music" and "theatre" were pre-existing entities from which opera has been cobbled together. There is no more justification for this assumption, logically or historically, than for declaring opera the pre-existing entity from which music and theatre have had the misfortune to come unattached, and so should be categorized as opera with one or more crucial components missing.

And it's odd: when we think of opera in this synthetic fashion, we define it one way but act in another. Whether we look in everyday dictionaries, in guides for beginners, or in more specialized sources, we find some version of the same definition: ... "a play having all or most of its text set to music..." (Webster Second Edition); "... a play set to music" (Edward J. Dent, *Opera*, 1940); or " ... simply and conveniently ... a sung play" (*International Cyclopedia of Music and Musicians*, 1964). The *New Grove Encyclopedia of Opera* (1992) says at one point " ... by definition a staged sung drama," and at another " ... a drama in which the actors and actresses sing throughout." However these definitions go on to elaborate, they start from one point only—"a play," "a drama." We would not find "play" or "drama" defined as "an opera in which the actors speak their roles," and we do not we find characterizations of opera as "a form of music in which . . ."—which is a very hard phrase to complete.

So if we define opera as a form of something else, it would appear that the something else would have to be theatre. Yet we treat it more often as a form of music, training for it in conservatories and music schools, entering it in histories, encyclopedias, and dictionaries of music, assigning music critics to review it in performance and musicologists to undertake its scholarship. The rationale for this is that, as Joseph Kerman put it, music carries " ... the final responsibility for the success of the drama," or, as Michael F. Robinson said of Gluck's *Alceste* in his *Opera Before Mozart* (1966), it " .. is good because its music is so." That seems incontestable. But it does not make opera a form of music. Rather, opera has given birth to musical forms unique *to* it, and the most important of those have to do with the expression of drama through song. We should think of opera as a form unto itself, unified, distinct, and "pure"—opera as opera.

To speak of sung theatrical action is to imply performance, and that presumes the presence of at least one person other than the singer/actor, namely, a listener/watcher. This second presence makes the performer's sung action public, and moves it beyond the realm of mere self-expression. The relationship of singer/actor to listener/watcher makes of the latter both communicant and critic—in short, an audience—and raises all the questions of belief and skepticism, engagement and distance, and many others, that are common to artistic discourse.

2. BELIEF

An artistic act may have an expressive use for the person who performs it, but beyond this it will have no significance unless it induces belief. Such belief must start with comprehension, but to have artistic value it must go well past that, to levels of recognition, assent, and discovery that are emotionally and intellectually nourishing. The most vital artistic encounters engender recognition and discovery at once. They are simultaneously familiar and strange. Sometimes, they win assent against resistance. They force recognition of some truth or beauty, and so become acts of conversion. Whatever their route to assent, if they are not finally believed, they have no use.

The nature of artistic belief is that of an agreement. The agreement is between the persuasive content of the act and the proclivities of the receptor. It is subject to all the bothersome arguments about the validity of personal response and the possibility of defining knowledge or truth that adhere to belief of any sort, as well as others concerning the nature and uses of taste. These arguments are the urgent and proper subjects of aesthetic contention and critical discourse.

Artistic belief must originate in the artist, as a conviction about a vision. This vision is not a reasoned construct (though the artist may build one for it), but an artifact of the imagination whose power creates a movement, a disturbance, in the artist's being and seeks to move beyond it. The artist may define this power and its sources any way he or she chooses, and others may do so as well—none of that matters to the creative act. The artist's imperative is to impart the vision. His victory comes with expanding the visions of others to include the artist's own, to believe as he believes. This applies to every artistic act, and to art as a whole. All must be believed, or nothing is gained.

Artistic belief is of the gut, the heart, and the intellect. The intellect may play an important and elaborate role, and may even initiate the quest for artistic expression, but in the moment of creative imagination, it stands to the side. Older, deeper forces stir, and must stir in the receptor as well. That's the nature of the agreement to believe: it's a spark of person-to-person connection before it's anything else. The pathways to it lie through the senses. Cultivation of the senses is, therefore, the precondition of artistic appreciation.

3. SKEPTICISM

Skepticism is the guard against an indiscriminate credulity. Many people believe many things. Often their convictions are strong and their persuasive talents advanced. The very qualities of sensory refinement and emotional availability so necessary to the artistic personality are also indicators of an easy suggestibility. Something must caution us against following the little man with the Napoleon delusion into battle.

Skepticism would seem to be a function primarily of the intellect, and indeed its practice consists mostly of marshalling arguments against belief. But no more than creativity itself does it originate in reason. Suspicion is not more rational than vision, and is just as primal. At the snap of a twig the ears prick. Then the reason goes to work.

The skeptical response is the beginning of the critical process. Criticism holds that matters of belief are too important to go unexamined. It seeks liberation not from belief, but from unexplored assumptions of belief. It relies on a willingness to adopt, at least provisionally, an alternative point of view, a perspective. The very being of the modern Western arts owes much to the search for such perspective, for a world-view that allows possibilities outside the church/state absolutes of Medieval Christendom. Certainly this is true of opera, born of a conscious, willed resurrection of the worlds of Greco-Roman myth and history.

But if art has become the instrument of perspective on religious and political convictions and has won its right to propose its own truths about these and other matters pertinent to the human condition, it must itself submit to critical examination. The acts and beliefs of artists cannot be presumed more worthy of credence than those of priests and kings, and a tyranny of art, with the cultish and slavish responses it so easily induces, and with its own sets of treasonous or heretical acts, is an improvement on one of state or church only in the relative mildness of the punishments it exacts. That is why criticism must exist, and why its function must not become "constructive" or promotional, as it is so often asked to be by artists and their devotees. The critical mandate extends not merely to scrutiny of specific acts or works within an artistic style or form, but to the risk of questioning the form itself, the belief system as a whole, together with all its institutions.

Skepticism also has an important task within the creative process, where it takes the form of self-criticism. That is where it is "constructive." It is also a crucial component in the makeup of an active, sentient receptor, whose predisposition to believe it insistently questions. The devotee in search of fulfillment trusts both his belief and his skepticism, and lives happily with the paradox.

4. ENGAGEMENT AND DISTANCE

The moment in which the person-to-person spark is struck is pre-rational, pre-critical. Assent to it or rejection of it by the receptor is instantaneous and reflexive, and this is true even when the assent sought is of an intellectual sort. The agreement may seem a reasoned one, but in fact it has preceded any reflection on its merits. The same is true of a rejection. The value of an artistic encounter rests in turning an initial moment of assent into a sustained engagement. As it proceeds, this engagement may prove a mixture of assent and rejection. Sustained, pure assent is rare, as is unqualified rejection. The spark will light not only the candle of belief, but the flame of conflict between the receptor's predispositions and alternative thoughts and feelings inspired by the encounter. This accounts for the disturbing quality that art of any complexity and depth holds for a receptor of any complexity and depth.

One distinction must be made between performance/audience intercourse and all other forms of artistic encounter. It is an obvious one, but no less crucial for that. Performance involves a direct transfer of creative energy between people. Moreover, this transfer continues as an active process for the duration of the performance. Before one spark has died, another is struck, and then another. The qualities and intensities of the individual sparks, as well as their collective density, are determined by the performer. The performer remains the initiator—the aggressor, if you will—throughout the encounter. The receptor's pre-rational response is extended, and becomes a state of being so long as engagement exists.

Clearly, this ongoing energy transfer is very different from other artistic experiences, those afforded by the fine arts or literature. Nothing insists like performance. The energy output and aggressive capacity of an *objet d'art* or a book are extremely low compared with those of a person. The creative sparks that shaped these objects have long since entered into paint or stone or paper. True, they are struck anew in the receptor. But an important shift has taken place. Because the *objet* or book cannot enter into a living interaction and can make no adjustments, file no appeals, it must perforce give itself over to its receptor. A painting may exert dominance, and the undertow of a novel may be powerful. But the quality of attention either receives, and the duration and timing of the attention, are entirely under the receptor's control. The receptor initiates the artistic encounter, provides all the energy for it and remains engaged (or not) of his own volition.

The nature of living interaction lends performance a unique power. But its insistent, aggressive nature, and its lack of the sort of contemplative space allowed by other artistic experiences, also engenders a unique resistance. Our skeptical tendencies do not easily accept an extended pre-rational state, and set off warning signals. Performers sense degrees of acceptance or rejection, and adopt strategies to influence them. The necessity of our ceding not only a duration of time, but the rhythms and tempos in which it passes, in the course of which assent is forever being freshly and directly sought by fellow beings, can be an exquisite tyranny. The oppressive potential of performance, all too often realized, far surpasses that of other artforms.

Because the artistic encounter enlists both belief and skepticism, passion and reflection, and because the aggressive appeal of performance engenders resistance, engagement is mitigated by distance. "Distance" is not meant here as disinclination (as with some affect of mood that destroys the receptor's predisposition), or as mere inattentiveness. Nor is it intended to describe simple artistic failure, the inability to establish or sustain engagement. The distance spoken of here is an active element in the artistic encounter, a part of what is assented to. It assumes several forms, and upon these depend the precise qualities of the engagement, and its intensity.

Distance can be established on either side of the performance encounter. On the receptor's side, it arises from the need to retain a measure of control over the terms of engagement, and to begin the task of fitting it into his or her framework of experience and belief. Choice is always open for the receptor: the choice of diving deep into the pool of the pre-rational moment, of dipping in a toe, or sitting at the edge to think it over. This last, the choice of thinking it over, is the essence of distance. It overlays the visceral, emotional response with a film of intellectualization.

The context of the choice is the entire life and being of the receptor. The more the elements of this context invade the receptor's consciousness, the greater the degree of distance. The crucial moments of a performance encounter are those that draw the receptor into emotionally or intellectually challenging territory, or into matters not customarily given assent in life. At these junctures, engagement and distance, pre-rational assent and intellectualization, tumble together in confusion, into the mixture of promise and threat inherent in all seductions. The effort to assess the experience and place it in context is underway even as fresh sparks fly.

Distance can also arise from the performer's side of the encounter. It can be built into a text or incorporated into a performance, or both. Its function is to encourage the choice of thinking it over, to move the engagement toward the intellectual and away from the visceral or emotional mode, and for this purpose it holds the receptor at arm's length. It still seeks assent, but in the form of agreement with an argument, acknowledgement of an apparently reasoned truth. When present in a performance text, it usually signals an effort to convey a philosophical, political, or social point with clarity and force. When incorporated into performance as an interpretive device, distance becomes a comment on the text by the performers, who hope the audience will share their perspective, and find it more useful or agreeable than other kinds of involvement.

The means for creating distance in performance are many. They include anything that removes the encounter from its continuity of pre-rational moments, anything that enlists the analytic faculties of the receptor. Thus, an emphasis on textual structure or presentational framework would tend to this purpose, as would the adoption of certain interpretive attitudes toward the material. Among these, irony and incongruity are outstanding contemporary examples.

Engagement and distance alternate and intertwine in all performance encounters. In opera, the play between the two is extremely complex, since either can be sought at any moment by any element of the elaborate creative and interpretive process. These elements need not be in agreement among themselves, and may be accepted or rejected in whole or in part by a given receptor.

5. MEANING

Like belief, meaning is a derivative of the artistic encounter, not an inherent quality of an object or act of art. Since each encounter is different from all others, meaning is not fixed. It begins with the striking of the spark and develops though the receptor's translation of it into the context of his or her entire life and being. As with engagement and distance, reception and translation are concurrent and interactive. Therefore, meaning is at once derivative and ascriptive.

If an encounter is of importance to the receptor, translation will continue afterward in a sort of half-life that consists of inner dialogue, the written or spoken opinions of others, and perhaps the demi-encounters afforded by the electronic media. (This process also can, and often does, precede an encounter, in the form of word-of-mouth opinion, reviews, background material, and so on—a partial pre-translation.) This ongoing translation is an extension of distance, in that it is analytic and reflective. It does not partake of the direct sensory contact of the encounter, but does bear its imprint, either in anticipation or recollection. It selects the elements of the encounter needed by the receptor and incorporates them into the peculiarities of his mind and heart, and that is where meaning, always in flux, will reside. Meaning is what survives, in whatever form it survives.

It is through the accumulation of these residues of meaning that a receptor may move from belief in an artistic moment to an investment in the artistic object or act, in an art form as a whole, in art as a way of life.

6. CREATION AND INTERPRETATION

Of all the terms under discussion here, these are among the most treacherous. Because it is hard to define the processes they stand for, they pose semantic problems in any context, and are easy targets for philosophic or linguistic challenge. And because they can confer dignity, these words are much abused by those wanting same. This is especially true in any nominally artistic or intellectual field, where creation and interpretation are by definition supposedly taking place, to say nothing of the "creative industries," where artistic processes are turned to non-artistic purposes but the hired hands are as much in need of self-esteem as anyone else.

Only people can be creative. Creativity is not a property innate in any mode of activity, including those named creative. The same is true of interpretivity. Furthermore, in the performance arts creation and interpretation are so overlapped that it is hard to confidently mark a boundary between them. Can any act or process of performance art be defined as creative and not interpretive, or the other way around? Even the purest strokes of authorial imagination are interpretive; they select objects from the potentially infinite field of consciousness as worthy of attention. Such selection is itself an interpretation. And there is no interpretive moment that is not also a creative opportunity, for although the presence of authorial instructions limits the interpreter's field in important ways, the range of response to any instruction or sequence of instructions is still broad. A successful performance encounter is one in which performer and receptor forge the crucial link in a chain that stretches from the first spark of authorial imagination into the residue of meaning in the receptor's life and being.

Experientially, the striking of the creative/interpretive spark is poorly described by the word "selection," since at whatever point it occurs, it has the quality of something that *presents itself* to the participant. It takes leaps across gaps in the rational sequence, or else seems to bypass it or precede it. We feel it as intuitive, sometimes mystical. This only means, though, that selection is taking place at a deeper level than it does for common transactional purposes. We have different ways of describing the spark, depending upon its location in the creative/interpretive chain. An author will think of it as an "idea" that comes to him, a performer as the moment of "connection to the material," a critic as the flash of "insight" in the search for meaning, and a receptor as that strange-but-familiar birth of belief, often with some strong affect attached to it. These terms certainly describe different perspectives and different nuances of experience. But they refer to the same sorts of events, and share a further similarity in state-of-being, involving raised levels of physiological excitation and receptivity at once.

Nevertheless, words are not arbitrary symbols, and the mere persistence of "creation" and "interpretation" suggests that some distinction is being described. Such a distinction is surely implied by the hierarchy of our everyday thinking, wherein creative acts are assigned a "higher" position than interpretive ones. This has to do with the extent to which the field of choice has been narrowed through previous artistic intervention. An act of "pure" creation is one for which no pre-interpretation has taken place. The "creative" artist selects from an infinite field, restricted only by the limits of his own responsive and inventive capacities, and by those of his primary choices: the medium in which he has decided to do his work and the techniques, tools, and materials with which he will carry it out.

The creator's process begins as an interior dialogue, a wrestling with inner objects to find an expressive form. This impels a first creative step. For operatic creators, the step may be a line of prose or poetry, a musical phrase or motif, or a fragment that combines these elements. It will be imagined as spoken or sung or played, perhaps even first expressed that way. But it will then be inscribed.

This expression and inscription, the end of one creative process, is the beginning of another. A unit of aesthetic material is now outside its creator, where it behaves quite differently than it did inside. The creator takes it in sensorily and responds accordingly, as would any other reader. He becomes its receptor, interpreter, and critic. As interpreter and critic, the creator remains at liberty to alter or expunge the now-expressed object, or to recapture it for further inner consideration. But with inscription, a line is crossed, a commitment made. A bias now exists to let the object stand and to move forward.

The expressed object has pre-empted a small portion of the previously infinite field, has begun to shape it and define its limits. It has become a first choice, and once assented to by the creator, it precludes all other choices. Nothing else may stand in its place, nothing proceed from it that does not take it into account. The incorporation and interaction with expressed objects will continue until the field is entirely defined, bound, and filled, at least insofar as the creator can envision it.

That inscription is not an inevitable step in the development of performance is attested to by the oral traditions of cultures that have done without it.

Indeed, this step marks a bifurcation of the creative and interpretive functions that have become a serious issue in the Western performance arts (see below). It makes the creator a writer, and thus subject to all the questions about the nature of writing and of languages, all the challenges to the notion of authorship, that are parts of the contemporary critical scene. So perhaps the uses of inscription are worth a moment's notice. The first is to keep track of a creator's discoveries so as to remember and, if desired, repeat them. Inscription is imprecise, and many of these discoveries—indeed, elaborate and subtle chains of them—can be remembered and repeated, possibly with greater imitative precision and interpretive force, without it. Which cannot? In music, those that involve complex interrelationships between the vertical and horizontal dimensions, together with the densities of harmonic and instrumental textures and the extent and variety of structures that result from those interrelationships; everything, in the creative process described above, that flows from the interaction of the creator's imagination with expressed (notated) objects, and from all relationships suggested or confirmed by the eye; everything that flows from the compilation of the creator's inscriptions to form a text, and from the compilation of texts to form a literature, which is in turn the referent for further creation. In other words, at the very least, everything since the advent of polyphony. In opera: all these things, plus their interactions with verbal content and stage action. The division between creator and interpreter forced by inscription is a form of specialization. While creative imagination and performance expressivity are often found to some degree in the same person, they only rarely co-exist at the highest level, and the technical perfection of each is usually best pursued independently.

The compilation of the creator's inscriptions—the text—becomes the interpreter's point of departure. Selecting from the field bounded by the creator's decisions, he initiates his own process of selection and invention in his own medium, with its range of techniques. The critic or commentator commences his analytic task (also selective and inventive) from this new, twice-interpreted point of departure. Indeed, the "practical" critic's steadiest employment lies in evaluating the tensions between the first and second layers of interpretation—that is, between text and performance. Finally, the receptor takes his step of incorporating the thrice-interpreted material. (It is always thrice-interpreted, for analysis is never bypassed, even when the receptor acts as his own critic.)

We might with some justice label the creator, the performer, the critic, and the receptor simply as First Interpreter, Second Interpreter, Third and Fourth Interpreters, and these terms will appear hereunder when emphasis on the interpretive function is intended. But this flattening-out does not serve all purposes. There is a validity to our ranking of creation, interpretation, analysis, and incorporation, even as we concede that all these take place simultaneously and continuously up and down the encounter chain.

For the First Interpreter has done something the others have not. He has struck a spark on his foray into the potentially infinite field of phenomena and made something of it. Upon this something depend the selections and inventions of all subsequent interpreters. It is because delimited selections are the most vexing ones, and because the First Interpreter has assumed the exhilarating but fearsome responsibility of making the first choice, that we at least loosely observe our hierarchical order along the encounter chain. It is also for this reason that we feel that interpretive artists, however gifted in their own right, have a degree of responsibility toward the results of the creator's work, by way of honoring the terms of the first choice.

It is true that any of the Interpreters may perform well or badly, creatively or not. Often there is more invention in a performance than in a text, or in a critique than in either. Indeed, receptors' acts of incorporation are sometimes the most ingeniously selective and inventive of any in the encounter chain.

It is also true that "honoring the terms of the first choice" does not mean mere obedience to the instructions of the text. It means using the field defined by the text as the territory for creative exploration. Determining the boundaries of this field is one of the heaviest obligations of the interpretive artist, and currently the most contentious.

But these observations do not alter the creator's status as First Interpreter, or contradict the uniqueness of his function. In practice, all they mean is that it is a good idea for interpreters to closely inspect the field the creator has defined for their work, and for creators to be well attuned to the realities of the performer/receptor encounter, where the fate of their selections will be decided. First choices remain first choices, always. But in any performance art, they are conceived for the performer/receptor encounter, where the "text" becomes the "work."

7. THE TEXT AND THE WORK

We speak of "a work" (for example, "*Otello* is a great work") as if there were no doubt that such a thing exists, or that it can be referred to with the same confidence of identification we have in speaking of common household objects or familiar features of terrain. But a work of performance is elusive of definition. It's not a fixed object, and its properties are not constant. What can be said of it?

Since the goal of performance is to leave a residue of meaning with the receptor, and it is with the receptor that the encounter chain reaches completion, perhaps the reality of "The Work" is best approached from his viewpoint. This viewpoint also offers commonality: We are not all creators or stage interpreters, but we are all receptors. We are of many sorts, but the sort that is of most interest here is the one who actively seeks the encounter, is alive to it and curious about it, hoping to extract nourishment and meaning from it, and who returns despite disappointments, having learned the potential importance of such experiences. In short, a devotee.

For the devotee, The Work is a living being, an incorporated organism. Since its meaning is within him, it alters with him, not only in relation to The Work or to art as a whole, but to all experience. So much could be said of any devotee of any art. The dynamic properties of performance, however, ensure that its incorporation is more volatile than that of other art forms. Changes occur in The Work, both during any given performance and from one performance to the next. Even if a piece is being experienced for the first time, the receptor is aware that such change is implicit and unavoidable: The Work itself is proposing new interpretations, new possibilities of meaning, while in progress. The performance devotee re-experiencing a work cannot be sure of where change has occurred, or what accounts for shifting balances between familiarity and strangeness. The viewer of an *objet*, on the other hand, can be fairly certain that apparent changes in the work, no matter now remarkable, are really changes in himself.

From the beginning of a devotee's experience of a performance work, he weaves about him and it a tapestry of personal associations. These associations are bound into the substance of The Work, and become parts of its living body. The tapestry is extended to embrace all performance works, the connections among them, and everything associated with them. This means not only the accumulated emotional, intellectual, and sensory experience of performance and its ancillary materials, but the everyday occurrences and relationships that surround it. The intermission drink, the smell of the cough drop from the row behind, are parts of the tapestry as surely as the treasured recording; the meeting with a friend or the argument with a loved one as much as the critical essay. The devotee tends the tapestry constantly, albeit often half-consciously, arranging and re-arranging the associations according to the flux of his life and being.

Many of these associations are the exclusive property of the devotee. The fanatical sort of devotee hoards such associations and guards their exclusivity. His life is lived vicariously through them, tapestry and devotee inseparable and virtually indistinguishable. Other associations, though, are shared. Performance encounters take place in public; they are social occasions. While there are important differences—contradictions even—in receptors' responses to the attempted striking of performance sparks, there are significant similarities as well. The differences fascinate from a critical standpoint, but it is the similarities that sustain the life of The Work. The usual assumption of performance activity, and of the gathering of receptors into an audience, is that something in common will be found. If that does not happen The Work will not make its way. The affects and effects that are widely and repeatedly found in common become the agreed-upon properties of The Work, the elements that render a statement like "*Otello* is a great work" understandable. Those that are more narrowly shared, or uniquely experienced, are the stuff of advocacy and debate.

The Work exists only during performance. The text, however, exists outside performance. It is itself a work—a work of literature. It can be directly incorporated and interpreted, without the services of a Second Interpreter. Such incorporation does not constitute an interpretation of The Work, but only of the text. It is simply a reading. As such, it has the advantages of any reading, including the possibility of devising an imaginary "ideal" interpretation, of initiating and discontinuing engagement at will, of mentally pursuing argument and pondering meaning, or of contemplating the physical attributes of the text as an *objet*.

But since the texts of stage works are notations for performance, whose essential properties emerge only under performance conditions, they are notoriously elusive and misleading with respect to their qualities and meanings. This is especially true of operatic texts. The verbal portion of the text is at least accessible on some level to any literate person, though because it is intended for singing and structured for some convention or other of the musical stage, it is far less helpful than a playscript with respect to an imagined realization. And it is subsumed by the musical text, usually of sufficient complexity to demand far more than basic musical literacy for a reading of much interpretive value. Even for a reader of experience and expertise, many surprises are in store en route from text to work, and from one realization of The Work to the next.

That a text should exist at all, that a First and Second Interpreter should be separately embodied, tells us that an important step has been taken beyond the operatic essence, beyond the sung action and the spark between performer/creator and receptor. It tells us that a need, or in any case a desire, has arisen for something more than momentary excitements and empathies. Beyond the creator's own need to control his materials, this desire has to do with coherence, with shape, with a sense of destination, with closure—with a gathering of the sparks, we might say. It also has to do with the need to record things of importance and preserve things of value, to remember ourselves.

At the same time, we must note that a dichotomy has arisen. The performer's sung action must now be fashioned from notations that track—imperfectly—the imaginings of someone else, somewhere else, sometime ago. This suggests not only the probability of slippage between the creator's vision and the performer's interpretation, but the threatened loss of the creative component in the interpretive act, which is the component that strikes the spark in the first place. It is this dichotomy that has been commonly defined as the most persistent problem of performance: how to make the creative and interpretive visions appear as one, to fashion the illusion of fresh, living creation from the stuff of premeditated interpretive actions. Only if this problem is solved can the receptor's belief be unreserved and engagement sustained.

8. SINGINGACTING AND WORDS

The rather clumsy construction that begins the heading for this section is on loan from the late Robert Lewis, the noted American theatre director and acting teacher who worked with opera on occasion. Run together this way, his term reflects the fact that we have no word for opera's unique and essential mode of communication. This fact in turn raises the prospect of a second dichotomy at the very core of operatic expression, a split between vocal and verbal behaviors on one hand, and bodily behaviors on the other—or, to state the difficulty from the receptor's viewpoint, between signals received by the ear and those received by the eye. This second dichotomy, this falling-apart of the sung action itself, has been addressed by some of opera's most talented and observant artists, yet has proved extremely stubborn.

The reason the second dichotomy has been perceived as increasingly troublesome is that the gap between the physical and emotional commitments of operatic singing on one hand, and the behavioral language deemed believable on the other, has widened appreciably. The mobilization of energies associated with singing, once not far removed from those demanded by theatrical styles more rhetorical and presentational than ours, have remained more or less the same. But those associated with acting have been radically transformed. The reasons for the changes are at bottom sociocultural, but have found theatrical expression in physical and verbal behaviors of progressively lowered rhetorical profile and projective energy. In contemporary popular culture, camera acting and microphone singing set the standards of credibility for most potential receptors. Both substitute mechanically controlled electrical energy for human vitality to transmit performing intent over distance. The state-of-being necessary to effective operatic singing remains highly charged and focused on the direction of energy into aesthetically determined physical acts whose demands are absolute. It is like no other condition in life, though it somewhat resembles that of a dancer or athlete. The state-of-being required by most contemporary acting, on the other hand, is a kind of alert receptivity, responsive but physically casual and intimate. The gap between these states is experienced as a contradiction by the performer in search of an integrated singingacting technique.

Such integration is desirable onstage for the same reason it is desirable in life: actions that are dis-integrated, at odds with themselves, are difficult to trust. They do not seem unreservedly committed, and so do not win unreserved assent. Efforts to resolve the problem have served mostly to exacerbate it. Musicians have tended to burrow ever deeper into their texts, while theatre workers have brought to bear a mélange of contemporary training techniques, many of which purport to restore the performer's creative integrity by "freeing" him from the text. This contradiction is carried through in the ways creators prepare their texts. Composers have tended toward ever more elaborate micromanagement of interpretive choice in their scoring, while playwrights, on the whole, have moved toward carte blanche. In perfect consistency with this, performing musicians periodically raise the bar on reproductive precision with notations and articulations, while actors proscribe as overly restrictive stage directions, intonational suggestions, even scansion and punctuation. In opera, this bifurcation of the text is now almost routine, with close (though, in truth, often quite selective) observation of musical instructions on one side, and a willful ignorance of theatrical instructions on the other.

Theatre workers deserve credit for at least recognizing the dichotomies as artistic problems, and providing some energy for attacking them. But they have failed to take singing itself—classically structured singing of theatrical format—as the central component of operatic action. Instead, they have either attempted to re-define singing to avoid the rigors of the classical model, or to hope that this model can somehow be reconciled to the contemporary actor's state-of-being. Neither approach nurtures an environment in which great singing in any of its traditional definitions is at all likely to take place.

Words are central components of nearly all sung actions. Of course it is possible, even in opera, to commit actions wordlessly, either through music or through physical behavior. Generally speaking, though, opera is a form that doesn't do that. "Singing" implies the presence of words, without which it is vocalization, an instrumental expression.

The relationship between words and notes is not simple, and is not fixed. Either can constitute a bounded field for the other; either can be a first choice the other must interpret. In opera, it is more often than not the case that the librettist's choices impel those of the composer, that the words suggest the actions while the music suggests how the actions are carried out. But there are many exceptions to, and complications of, this usage.

What is important from the singingacting standpoint is that both words and notes are bound into the actions. They are a unity in the service of dramatic intent. The singingactor's basis for carrying out actions is not the same as the theatre actor's. The difference between the two is more than a "heightening." Much of it has to do with the state-of-being already discussed. And much else has to do with the word-note relationship. Words convey meaning in two ways. The first, usually called the denotative, is through identification of an object or function for which the word has become the agreed-upon symbol. We can codify such meanings, then look them up. In the present context, the second level of verbal meaning is best called inflective or intonational. Contained within it is everything that can be conveyed through melody, rhythm, timbre and stress or accent: everything we can't look up, and everything we call musical. This is the level on which interpretation takes place. While it is theoretically possible to deal with words in their purely symbolic function, in practice words (even when read silently) cannot be detached from some inflectional quality, and therefore from interpretation.

Relative to spoken usages, singing emphasizes the inflectional at the expense of the denotative. This does not mean the inflectional is always more completely realized in singing than in speech. Indeed, certain nuances of spoken expression are coarsened or even foreclosed by singing. Moreover, the singingactor operates within a field where interpretive choices the theatre actor would regard as his essential creative property have already been assigned. The singingactor's "line readings" are roughly in place in the text: melodic rise and fall, dynamic contour, rhythmic pulse and tempo, even details of accent or timbral shading, are specifically and concretely present (not merely implied), and he is obligated to them in a way the theatre actor is not.

But though the singeractor cedes this interpretive ground to the creator, he acquires in exchange vast expressive territories, all lying within the domain of inflection and intonation. These are in turn dependent on the two innate advantages of the singing voice over the speaking voice: its wider pitch range and its capacity for sustained tone that can be elastically shaped. Together, these attributes carry the technically proficient singeractor into a realm of expression that incorporates abstract elements of color and intensity. These are the elements of voice in its purely musical function, of voice as an instrument—an instrument whose color range is an extension of vowel formation.

This new expressive range explores the entire spectrum of affect beyond words, where sparks can be incorporated and interpreted by a receptor, but not verbally defined. We think of it as the range of the inexpressible, but this is not true, for music expresses it. Yet, in singing, expression seldom makes a clean escape into the abstract. It is tied to the word, to the denotative, and in fact contains the denotative within it. It is distinct from speech in its pull toward the musically abstract and its adventurous exploration of the inflective; it is distinct from instrumental music in its pull toward the verbal and its persistent recollection of the denotative. Some singing pulls far in one direction, some in the other. But without these distinctions, there would be no reason to sing anything.

In singingacting, singing is put to dramatic purpose. Strings of wordnotes carry out dramatic actions. Although the singeractor's state-of-being and expressive range differ from those of the theatre actor, his essential task is the same. Walter Felsenstein, seeking to define the dramatic function of music and singing, put it well: (it is) "to transform an action through music and singing into a theatrical reality that is unreservedly plausible." Yet no operatic action can render satisfaction without placing singing itself at its core, and granting it full inflectional freedom.

9. THE CHARACTER

In opera, sung actions seek two kinds of credibility. They ask first to be trusted as expressive messages from performer to receptor, and second as the purposive undertakings of an inhabitant of the stage world, a dramatic character. Since actions do not exist in a vacuum, but are the expressions of a character's drive toward fulfillment, the first kind of credibility depends on the second. When a receptor finds it plausible that if the conditions are as represented, the character's actions will be as represented, the receptor will assent to them at least provisionally. When he finds this not only plausible but inevitable and urgent, he will assent unreservedly.

Like The Work, The Character is all too easily assumed to exist and to be generally knowable. This assumption is pernicious both for performance creativity and for critical discussion. Obviously, there is no such objective and enduring entity as The Character, somehow immanent in the world. Therefore, nothing can be known of such a creature, and nothing stated. Stage characters are the offspring first of the engagement between the First and Second Interpreters, and second of the interactions among all the interpreters embarked on The Work. Thus, The Character is no more a fixed reality than The Work itself or the word-note relationship. It changes with every new interpreter, every performance, every new interaction.

Nonetheless, The Character has an offstage half-life, in much the same sense as The Work itself. As with all aspects of The Work, The Character assumes its first form in the imagination of the creator. There, the glimpse of a person is caught, a sense of a certain way of being, a certain story to be told. In opera, these glimpses and senses have customarily originated on the literary side of the process. Nearly all operas have been derived from literary or theatrical works or from "real life" situations whose narratives have surfaced. Often, in fact, they have been taken from literary or theatrical works that are in turn derived from "real life" narratives. The characters and their stories, at least in outline, have thus passed through two or three pre-interpretations before reaching their musical creator, the composer. But this is not an inevitable sequence. A character can arise from a musical wisp—a melodic or harmonic fragment, or a characteristic color.

In any case, the composer works on his interpretation in the manner of all creators. He makes choices, each of which stands in the stead of all others. He generates a progression of such choices, until he has realized as fully as he can the story and way of being of the person glimpsed at the outset. Much about this realization will be surprising, for though the creator pursues the original vision, each choice presents unforeseen consequences that cannot be ignored. Creators often speak of a moment in their process when characters begin leading independent lives, dictating their own fates to the creator. This means that the chain of choices, of expressed character objects, has generated a logic that can lead in only one direction. The sense that this direction is determined from the outside is an illusion, but one that is experientially real.

No matter how skillfully and meticulously the librettist and composer have done their work, The Character of the text is incomplete in relation to their vision. Words fall short, notes fall short, wordnotes fall short, and no excess of musical articulation, inflectional instruction, or stage direction will make up the shortfalls. An unexpressed differential remains. To a reader of the text, this differential is unknowable. The Character is his to interpret from the text. And operatic characters are as open as those of a novel or playscript to interpretation and incorporation into a reader's inner life, free of interpretive intervention. But, as with everything about The Work, the reader of these characters must be literate in the language of wordnotes and their musical environment, and conversant with the soundworld the notations evoke. For this reason, operatic characters lead their textual lives in narrowly restricted circles, and when devotees speak of operatic characters as if they were known, they are usually referring to the attributes found in common among interpreters of the role.

Among the receptors attempting to incorporate The Character are the performers themselves, whose task it is to embody their interpretations. They go about this in two stages. The first involves examination of the text for all the suggestive interpretive evidence it can be made to yield. The second embraces interaction with the other interpreters in rehearsal. The second is actually more important for the general vitality of performance, but the first has much to do with how complete and individual the performer's version of The Character will become.

The manner in which character is presented in music has undergone much variation in opera's 400-year history. So has the relationship between character and the rest of the musical setting. Sung character actions take many forms. But all these forms have two conditions in common. The first is that they are committed in the singing state of being, and must reflect that reality behaviorally. The second is that their vocal component is expressed through song, through strings of wordnotes with their expanded inflectional range. As we have observed, this range is peculiarly adapted to the expression of otherwise-inexpressible emotional and sensory nuance. Indeed it lingers with such nuance, exalts it, and does so in a band of color, accessible only through singing, that is streaked with abstract descriptive hues. Opera proposes that it is within this emotional and sensory sphere that we most truly and urgently live, whatever the appearance of reality may be, whatever the denotative meanings of words uttered. It is by its power to bring this sphere to the fore and—through the relationship of word to note, of sung line to musical environment—show its ongoing centrality, that opera, for all its evident artificialities, stakes its claim to artistic honesty and profundity.

Operatic characters and their actions, therefore, must believably occupy a stage world wherein their emotional and sensory lives, animated and described by music, are asserted as truths that override other considerations, and generate the conflicts that are essential to drama. Operatic drama, as a rule, does not hold these truths to be separate from everyday reality; it rather acknowledges their importance within it. Its conventions are attempts to penetrate through the everyday to levels of greater, not lesser, "truth" and "reality." An oft-cited example is also a useful one: the convention of presenting the thoughts and feelings of character simultaneously in groupings ranging from the duet to the massive ensemble finale—something that, as Victor Hugo ruefully noted, is far beyond the reach of spoken drama. This is an "impossibility" in strictly naturalistic terms, yet is also undoubtedly what is "really" taking place all the time, everywhere, with all of us. In opera, this reality is expressed through the music even as the everyday reality and the denotative level of meaning never quite slip from view.

Beyond the word, yet born of the word and containing the word within it. Dwelling with inflectional extravagance, but tethered to the denotative.

Transcending the world of the everyday, yet happening within it. These are the dichotomies to be resolved, in the person of the singeractor.

10. DRAMA

The entrance of this term and its adjectival form, which the reader may have already noticed, should not pass unremarked. At the outset, we defined opera as theatre through song, and noted that so long as any kind of theatrical action and any kind of song were present together, opera could be said to exist. Opera has developed around the same theatrical form as have its sister stage arts: the drama. Conflict is the essence of drama, and generates its action. But theatre does not have to be drama. It is possible to envision, and aspire to, a life without conflict, and to represent such a life and aspiration theatrically, and therefore operatically.

The difficulty seems to be that when life has been cleansed of conflict, we cannot recognize it. Such a life is a vision, a fantasy, that can be imagined as a fixed moment, but not as an ongoing reality. We don't believe in it and frankly aren't interested in it on a sustained basis. We are interested in, excited by, drama. We believe in a life that contains conflict, and cannot in all honesty say that a life without it would be functional or desirable. Of course, we strive to resolve our conflicts, and on a case-by-case basis we do so. Each drama ends in resolution, agreeable or not. Then it is time for the next drama to begin, for conflict to assert its survival. It is because conflict's survival is undeniable that drama is the dominant form of stage representation. Even the rituals and pageants that do not present dramatic action in an overt and immediate way are traceable to dramatic origins or are meant to show the resolution of a conflict.

Music is better suited than theatre for evasion of conflict. It can flee into the purely lyrical, the descriptive, for fairly extended periods in the hands of a master who is so inclined (Bellini or Berlioz, Delius or Messiaen). Its abstract and sensory elements make the ascription of meaning treacherous, and thus yield at least the potential for non-dramatic interpretation. Even so, very little Western music is not suggestive of drama in harmonic tensions seeking resolution, in structural dialectics to be worked out, in color variations and contrasts tending toward coherence of design.

On the stage, conflict is embodied by characters whose objectives are at odds, and its progress is shown through actions undertaken by the characters in pursuit of their objectives. It is important to understand that in dramatic terms, "action" refers not merely to physical behavior, but to any means employed by a character to further an objective. Dramatic characters are never *not* in action. Since conflict is usually present within individuals as well as among them, there is an inner and an outer aspect to their actions, and their courses toward their objectives are seldom simple and direct.

Operatic music accomplishes its mission by setting forth character conflict in theatrical terms, and its integrity lies in that. While it has incorporated at one time or another most of the structures known to "absolute" music, these must remain subordinate to dramatic purpose in opera, where scene structures and the arcs of character action must determine the musical progression. Opera has therefore contrived its own techniques of musical conflict—for the presentation of opposing actions, inner and outer actions, action and description, action and emotional state—either in alternating or overlapping structures, or in perfect simultaneity. These techniques, and the psychological realities they reflect, are available to no other art.

Operatic singing, too, must possess a dramatic vitality that goes beyond pure lyrical expression. This is true partly because it must project in large spaces over an orchestra, but more importantly because it must convey urgency of action and intensity of emotion. A struggle to overcome, a striving to fulfill passionate needs threatened by denial, is inherent in operatic vocalism. It might be said that feeling, action, and obstacle must all be present in the tone itself. Like all arts that subscribe to classical precepts, operatic singing seeks to contain the conflict within the form, to show grace and mastery of execution, so that the character's struggle is not perceived as the artist's dysfunction. And operatic voices must be capable as well of the transcendent, triumphal gestures that crown so many of the form's most powerful moments. But they must convey the ongoing impression that the issue is in doubt. Their tensions must evoke the atmospheric essence of all drama, suspense.

It is because of drama, of the stories of characters in conflict, that operatic music comes into being. Music that does not find a means of dramatic fulfillment is not good operatic music, whatever its other qualities. And the same is true of its performance.

11. CONCEPT

A concept is a thought or idea that gathers a set of particulars into a general notion. Since the term is used glibly and vaguely with reference to the performing arts, a few distinctions are in order. A concept is not the same as a subject, topic, or theme. True, these terms share with "concept" a concern with the meaning, the aboutness, of a work. But "subject," "topic," or "theme" imply something to be addressed, developed, discoursed upon; they suggest a dynamic potential. "Concept" has a fixed quality. It stands for the attempt to pin down "the-thing-that-it-is" in idea form.

Because of this fixed quality, the concept of concept would appear to be applicable more to the fine arts than to performance. Indeed, the several varieties of art categorized as "conceptual" are unified in their attempts to be about idea, rather than about their materials or processes, or their putative "content" or "meaning." They aspire to create images of concepts. Whether or not they actually do so is debatable. The shifty nature of creativity, with its endless sorting through its fields of choice, would seem to argue against the likelihood of directly rendering even the simplest, most tightly bound concept into an expressed object. In terms of the artist/receptor encounter, though, this problem is of little importance. It is certainly possible to create an art-work that instructs the receptor to search it for its idea, and that refuses the viewer satisfaction if seen in any other way. It will either be "thing-that-it-is" (simultaneously derivative and ascriptive, like meaning), or will be deflected by the receptor, and therefore nothing to him.

In performance, the concept of concept as an image of an idea is inher-ently antidramatic. If the separate elements or particulars have been gathered up in a general notion that can be represented, then conflict has been subsumed as well. In painting or sculpture, conflict can be shown representationally in the subject matter, or abstractly in tensions that can be perceived by the eye. But it cannot develop, it cannot play out. We sometimes call a skilled artwork "dynamic"—it seems *almost* alive. But it isn't. It is arrested. In the sorts of "conceptual" art that include performance elements (living mannequins, television images, and so on), a suspended quality is always evident, and is part of its nature by design. Drama is nei-ther a goal nor a possibility. Leaving drama aside, theatre is a poor venue for visual conceptualization. It involves people, and people get in the way of the images. Even when an image is fascinating and a person not, the person tends to draw attention, especially with the passage of time. And when people attempt to embody concepts, there is failure all around: the idea disappears in the person, and the person loses all reality and interest pretending to be an idea.

Thus, although in the stage arts "concept" is now almost universally assumed to be an enormous improvement on the absence of concept, its very pres-ence, to say nothing of the peculiarities it has spawned, should not be taken for granted. Nor should the modern understanding of the roles of conductor and director. In our practice, these are Second-Interpreters-in-Chief, inter-posed between both the performers and the text and the performers and the audience, given authority over interpretive decisions that would otherwise fall to the performers, and deemed responsible for an overall shaping of the text and the gathering of performance particulars into a unified interpretive statement—hence, a concept. But the functions of conductor and director may also be considered as purely co-ordinative. At the historical extreme, those duties have been reduced to a few tempo indications from the orchestra leader (keyboard player, concertmaster), some cues and rough blocking from the stage manager. In this view, conceptualization is assumed to be the province of the creators, and present in their texts, while interpretation is the prerogative of the performers.

Production concepts can be determined in many ways. Actually, no competent performance of a reasonably crafted text is without concept. The executant skills of the performers, supplemented by their conditioned expressive responses, will convey enough of the structural and thematic properties of the text to at least suggest a conceptual statement. In current usage, though, a "conceptual production" is usually one that does not entirely accept the assumptions of the chain of encounter outlined above, and does not derive its viewpoint solely from the close inspection of internal evidence. The bounded field of choice left by the creator's text, despite its large territories of unexpressed differential, is viewed as too restrictive, and its conceptual content as somehow insufficient, to constitute an appropriate basis for interpretive work. Conceptual authority is therefore shifted from the creator to the Second-Interpreter-in-Chief of drama, who changes one or more of the text's premises to arrive at a new version of The Work. Now the text is expected to reconcile to the new premises, as are the performers' choices, whose fields have new boundaries.

Among the frequently encountered sorts of conceptual production are: Change-of-Venue, in which time and/or place are altered; Point-of-View, in which some framing device (e.g., production-within-a-production, production inside a character's head) intercedes between Work and receptor; Anachronistic/Localistic, in which time and place are left nominally intact, but character psychologies and social attitudes are contemporary and parochial; and Change-of-Style, in which the scenic environment and/or behavioral manner are removed from that indicated in the text, as with an abstract setting and stylized behavior in a realistically conceived work.

But the most provocative contemporary conceptual genre is the Adversarial, in which the conceptualizing Second Interpreter takes the occasion of presenting The Work to conduct a critique of it. There is a prosecutorial aspect to such efforts. The aesthetic principles of the text, and the philosophical and socio-political viewpoints associated with them, are put on trial and a guilty verdict urged upon the jury (audience) in the very act of supposedly advocating The Work. The creator's text is used to reverse his victory. The Second Interpreter assumes not only the conceptual authority of the First, but the critical authority of the Third, and instructs the audience as to how

The Work is to be received and incorporated. This extraordinary and unprecedented notion has recently won widespread acceptance.

As suggested earlier, these manifestations of revisionism, rebellion, and authorial denial on the theatrical side of operatic production have proliferated at a time when the authority and integrity of the text have been insistently re-asserted on the musical, ostensibly restoring conceptual privileges to the creator. At first glance, this is puzzling. But as we look into the case, we shall discover a logic to it.

12. EYE AND EAR

Performance in the stage arts consists of energies intended for eye and ear. Its effect depends on how these energies are distributed and how they are received. The eye and ear have strong similarities in their reception and routing of sensory information, and in the processing of this information in the brain. This is an active, selective process. The afferent nervous system is not a passive conveyer; it assorts, searches, edits. Much of this selection takes place below the threshold of awareness. What interests us in terms of performance encounters, however, is the sensory intake that reaches at least the dimmer reaches of consciousness. Once there, it is subject to the rather mysterious focusing of awareness we call attention. Our selection is now experienced as a matter of choice, though one that is heavily influenced by the thoughts and emotions that are parts of our response.[1]

Sensory awareness can be rapid, flexible, adaptive. It can even accommodate polysensory input, and divide itself by automatizing some of its responses. But true attention has its limits. By its very nature, it fixes on an aspect of the available sensory information and relegates the rest to background status, or excludes it altogether. We can focus the eye on a point in the visual field, shift among such points, follow a particular movement, or let in the wider field. We can do the same with the ear with respect to sound, and we can shift between eye and ear, putting one in the foreground and the other in the background. We can even turn attention inward, placing all messages from the outside on hold. We *decide* to do these things, unless interrupted by an external or internal stimulus of some urgency. Each decision conditions the experience as a whole and forecloses many other possibilities. The performance receptor's most basic discriminations consist of selecting certain stimuli to eye and ear as objects of attention.

All the stage arts exploit our capacities for focusing attention on eye and ear signals, for maintaining attention or shifting it, and for using eye and ear to confirm each other. Each stage art proposes its own set of balances between eye and ear. More than the others, opera is *ear-led, eye-confirmed.*

Its world of light and color is summoned by its world of sound and timbre. When its sound is physically present but its light visible only to the mind's eye, a rich operatic experience is still possible. But when the inverse is true, only an ill-conceived dumbshow remains—the mind's ear, however educated, cannot eliminate the deficit. This does not mean that the eye is anything less than crucial. The music of an opera is the music of an opera, not an opera.

The taking in of sensory energies from the outside induces responsive energies in the receptor—the striking of the spark. These internal energies are passed along by a selective process similar to that involved in response to outer stimuli. When they reach the consciousness threshold, we experience them as emotions. Whether they generate return signals (and if so, which) or are internally contained (and if so, how), depends on individual temperament and social code. In the case of an audience, most of the responsive process remains internal most of the time; an audience is a community of private response. The quality of response varies from receptor to receptor. What is shared is response *per se*, and the agreement to express it at specified times in specified ways, which is part of the performance understanding.

Eye and ear each convey important information about space and time. However, they differ in their specificities. It is their complementary and confirmative interplay that gives us our time/space orientation. For instance: the ear takes in a much wider field than the eye. Sound can reach us from any direction without our turning towards it. It can move around, under, over and through light-blocking barriers. But the ear requires eye confirmation as to exact location. We know the crow is up in those trees somewhere, but which tree, and how high up, cannot be determined without visual aid, which requires turning the head, searching the field, and focusing. The eye is more space-precise than the ear. On the other hand, the ear adapts much more rapidly than the eye to changes in intensity. Sudden, extreme shifts in light levels can require minutes for adjustment, whereas equivalent swings from loud to soft, from massiveness of texture to an isolated line, are accommodated almost instantly. To these events in time, one following another, the ear's response is quicker than the eye's.

Eye and ear can incorporate sensory messages on more or less equal terms, and combine them in a single psychological reality, so long as neither is searching its own field too intently. As soon as closer inspection is required in one sensory field, the other is transferred to background status—still present, but perceived in a vague, semiconscious way. The same is true within either field: to follow a particular sound through an aural environment, or to focus on a detail within the visual field, entails the peripheralization of the surrounding texture. The more subtle the detail sought the more concentrated the attention must be, and the more complete the blocking-out of competing signals. When attention is turned inward—as in daydreaming or thinking—sensory input from all sources is shut down to a barely perceptible level. The purest experience of either sense demands the absence of the other: silence is the ideal aural environment for the art museum or the library, and darkness the best viewing condition in the listening room.

Operatic performance leads its receptors through broad perspectives of attention in both sensory realms, shifting from wide-field to narrow focus, from one element of primary attention to another. It is the richest of all stage forms in the range of options it presents to a receptor at any given moment, and while it certainly makes strong suggestions as to where the center of attention should be, the choice is always the receptor's. The vibratory energies of sound have a stronger visceral impact than the radiatory energies of light, and are harder to close out. Opera exploits this fact to induce its range of ear-led, eye-confirmed response. It uses the ear to guide the receptor through a stretch of rhythmically organized time that is marked by a series of vibrationally induced emotional events, whose qualities are determined by selected combinations of pitch, intensity, and timbre. The precise locations of these events are specified by the eye, and their qualities confirmed by light-conveyed messages regarding spatial relationships, movement, and color.

In opera, vision and hearing are used as they are in their evolutionarily derived, survival-directed functions, that is to say in a complementary, mutually confirmative way. Artistically intended disturbances (the inner and outer conflicts of drama) are generally conveyed not by oppositions between the two sensory fields, but by oppositions within each, whose coincidence reinforces the coherence and power of the situation portrayed. This is also true of their resolutions. Of course, complex messages of the "Your lips say no, but your eyes say yes" variety, or the apparent resolution that is not really a resolution, can be conveyed by eye/ear juxtapositions in opera, just as they are in spoken theatre or in life itself. These are artifacts of the stage world, of which the characters apprehend only parts, but the receptor the whole. From the receptor's perspective, the lack of eye/ear confirmation in the stage situation is precisely what alerts him to its "real meaning." But if the stage world's overall light and sound realities are detached from each other and put into a non-confirmative relationship, the result is to undermine the receptor's time/space orientation in a way that suggests an incipient threat to the organism. That is very hard to reconcile with any artistically useful purpose.

Two uniquely operatic eye/ear conditions merit brief mention. The first concerns physical distance within an enclosure, which affects sights and sounds quite differently. It is our customary belief that the farther removed we are from the stage world, the "less well" we see. But this is not literally true. The throw of light, and the eye's receptiveness to it, is not appreciably weakened from the first row of the orchestra to the last of the top balcony. What is lost with increased distance is subtlety of non-verbal expression, and therewith our sense of being in intimate contact with much of the texture of human interaction. But something is gained, as well: a wider perspective, an overview from which patterns of movement and the composition of the stage world as a whole is effortlessly absorbed.

For the ear, though, distance within an acoustically adequate enclosure is almost pure gain. This is especially true of vertical distance—being "up in the house." Here, the only "loss" is an extreme degree of spatial separation, a dubious merit in most musical circumstances. Distance is an acoustical advantage in all other respects: the richness and warmth of timbres; the blending of orchestral and vocal choirs and of individual voices with retention of "space" around each; the balance between voice and orchestra; the gut impact of massed forces. Even the "presence" of musical sound is enhanced: extremely soft dynamics register with a closeness that transcends distance— a distance that is verified by the eye. This sense that the ear is in intimate contact with the subtlest sound events of a measurably far-off stage world creates one of the most compelling varieties of operatic experience. These eye/ear differences in distance perception exist because the reflection of sound waves off interior theatre surfaces constitutes an acoustical gathering and enrichment of tone (which does not happen with reflected light), and because the reflected sound wave is inseparable from the aural image it carries, whereas reflected light is only reflected light, and bears the image not of its source, but of the reflective surface. These are among the reasons that opera must be understood as ear-led, eye-confirmed.

Finally, we must note eye/ear distinctions in the reception of language. We have already outlined the characteristics of wordnotes, and asserted the indivisibility of their verbal denotations from their musical properties of pitch, intensity, and timbre. In the eye/ear context, we should note that performed wordnotes activate the same sequence of reception and response as do all sounds. This includes the emotional reaction to the vibrational impact of the wordnote, whose precise properties have been calculated by the operawright. The wordnote's denotative verbal meaning is always an aspect of its impact. But the significance of this aspect varies radically. At times, the word meaning is clearly of primary importance. But at others, including those intended as emotionally climactic in most kinds of writing, it plays almost no part in the immediate effect, which is purely sound-induced within the framework of a generally understood dramatic situation. The wordnote's aural impact and inflectional meaning assume the expressive burden in such moments.

Regardless of its centrality or lack thereof, the sung wordnote's verbal meaning is apprehended and responded to instantaneously and without any special effort of attention, as one part of the overall sonic experience. But written language—the kind that is captured by the eye—involves the analysis and translation of visual symbols. Even when practiced and expert, such translation is a more complicated process. It is by definition conscious and active. It requires that our attention place eye-information to the fore and ear-information to the rear, and that thought processes be interjected into visceral, emotional ones. When introduced as a performance element, it becomes an eye-led, thought-screened intervention.

13. TIME

There is, first, the displacement of time inherent in all performance. When we consent to the performance encounter, we enter into a bargain concerning time. We agree to substitute the psychological time of the performance for "real" time. Indeed, we seek this substitution, and in exchange cede to the performers control over the ordering of time.

This substitution of performance-rhythm for life-rhythm lends us the sense of an event taking place outside time, and therefore not leading toward death. If there is no time, we will never arrive at death. For this purpose, it does not matter if the performance is experienced as fast or slow, whether The Work is an hour-long life celebration or a six-hour meditation on mortality. To be sure, the psychological experience of time is illusory. Exactly the same amount of "real" time passes as otherwise would. But the illusion can be salutary. This imposture of immortality can be stimulating, rejuvenating to our beings. That is why we seek the bargain, and want to believe in the world of the performance. To believe unreservedly is to be immortal, for a while.

"Real" time passes. The inexorable deterioration of our bodily selves continues. But during performance it does not continue as usual. The sensory stimuli of performance affect our respiration, our pulse. They affect peristalsis and glandular secretion, the rhythm of every inner movement. They probe to the sources of emotion. Returned to the flow of time and therefore once again mortal, we nonetheless recognize that our inner selves are in a different place, positioned at a different angle, and that this difference would not have come about in the "real" time of "real" life. Perhaps *that* was reality— the performance. Perhaps we were more authentic, more ourselves, there and then than here and now. If so, time has suffered a defeat. Its wasteful drainage, the spillage that haunts us with the awareness of time expended *without difference*, has been stanched.

Opera time is like no other. It is most evidently musical time, and as such presents the same problems of the relationships among musical materials and time's passage as does all music. These include debates over the interpretation of meter and tempo, as well as our attempts to explain the presence or absence of "movement" in performance (why rhythmic life seems to come and go, why a longer performance can seem quicker than a shorter one). It also invites exploration of the tension between musical ideas and structure, of the density of musical substance within a time period, and of the distribution of vertical information (harmonic, timbral) along a horizontal axis (melodic, rhythmic).

But opera time is also drama time. This has two aspects. The first involves the decisions made by creators and interpreters as to the variations of time that will most effectively generate the dramatic events of character actions, scenes, and the arc of the work as a whole. The second concerns the time-frame proposed by the dramatic style of the piece, which can extend from the examination of the contents of a few minutes to the span of lifetimes or generations, or to non-sequential treatment of linear time.

In opera, the rise and fall of dramatic action, the pace at which scenes are played, the building of dramatic tension and its release, the location of significant events or turning points within scenes, are structured into the time values of the music. These values are, in fact, meant to fulfill those dramatic necessities. But there is always an uneasiness in the relationship between dramatic structure and musical form, and this uneasiness is about the progression of time. Even in musical settings that are conceived as real-istic, where sung conversation and its orchestral commentary are meant to proceed "naturally," the melodic, harmonic, and rhythmic devices of music take on lives of their own, with their own needs for closure.

And of course, most operatic writing does not adhere to a strictly realistic style. Formally, two of the most important differences between opera and spoken theatre are time-related. One lies in music's capacity for creating a sense of time's compression or expansion during the action, or even evoking the passage of time between action sequences. The other lies in music's "ver-tical" dimension, which makes feasible the presentation of simultaneous or overlapping dramatic actions and intentions, made comprehensible through the music. In spoken theatre, dramatic action can certainly be overlapping and simultaneous, sometimes in subtle and complex ways. But the ear-receiv-able portion of it (the inflected verbal text) must for the most part be laid out in linear sequence. Actions must alternate; time must pass. Non-verbal char-acter behavior that suggests meaning beneath the text, or even contrary to it, or that shows characters in simultaneous independent or conflicting action, must be tracked by the eye. This is also the case in everyday life, and that is one of the reasons we generally regard spoken theatre as the most "realistic" of the stage arts. In everyday life, the eye can scan a roomful of people engaged in conversations and activities, and with sufficient perspective can summarize the overall situation. It can also identify the activities, and characterize the tone of certain interactions. The ear can detect the atmospherics of the gathering as a whole. But the actual subjects and intentions of the conversations, the real content of the interactions, can be determined only by separating them and following them by ear in linear fashion. That is how spoken theatre is obliged to present them.

Opera transcends this obligation. It is able to present with clarity the simultaneity of independent or conflicting actions and intentions even when denotative meaning is lost. As already noted, it is able to expand a moment and freeze the outward appearance of reality to examine the inner lives of its characters, to express everything that is being thought and felt. While the horizontal dimension of its music carries the receptor all the way from freeze-frame to fast-forward and charts the progress of moments, its vertical dimension stacks the emotional and psychological content of the passing time. Individual strands stand in relief or meld with the texture. The private and public, the individual and the social, co-exist in their full realities, together in time.

Despite this capacity for expanding moments and thus slowing or even suspending the passage of time, opera observes the general theatrical practice of conflating time. That is, the presumed time of the work as a whole is, almost without exception, greater than that of the performance's duration. Opera time is a series of expansions and suspensions within a conflation; its action is accordion-like. Thus, the receptor outlives the characters, takes in their lives whole with but a minor expenditure of his own, yet experiences crucial moments of these lives with a surreal intensity and depth.

All this depends on music's unique capacities for organizing events in time, and is received by the ear. That is an essential difference between opera and dance. Dance also has music time and drama time, and a vertical dimension that transcends the sequential requirements of verbal expression. But dance characters are silent. They lead lives of rhythmic movement in space, and that must be tracked by the eye. Dance is eye-led, ear-confirmed.

Only in opera do the characters themselves make music. Only in opera are both music time and drama time essentially ear time.

14. OPERA AS OPERA (A SUMMARY)

Opera is theatre though song. Its theatrical form is drama, the theatre of conflict. It is nothing without belief, but belief must always be challenged. Its life is in performance. Performance is a chain of encounter involving engagement and distance, a successive transfer of energies from creators to interpreters to receptors. Each link of the chain is both creative and interpretive, but the chain is also a hierarchy, defined by the boundaries of fields of choice. Through performance, texts become Works, living organisms whose meanings reside and change in the minds and hearts of receptors.

Opera's basic unit of expression is the vocalized wordnote, which embraces its own verbal content while transcending it by musical means. Its central interpreter is the singeractor, who embodies the drama's characters, and can alone vitalize the wordnotes. Conductors and directors, Interpreters-in-Chief with various degrees of conceptual authority and differing attitudes towards it, are also extremely important to the form as it has developed. The former, it should be noted, are themselves performers, the latter not.

Opera guides its receptors on its ear-led, eye-confirmed way through a unique ordering of psychological time. It induces in its devotees an especially intense and complex quality of engagement.

Opera is not an amalgam of other forms, but only itself: opera as opera. Time now to examine some living specimens.

NOTES

1. For some grounding in the subjects discussed in this section, I would recommend: Drew Westen: *Psychology: Mind, Brain, & Culture* (Second Edition), John Wiley & Sons, 1999, a well-regarded textbook. Chapter Four, "Sensation and Perception," is especially relevant here. The book has a glossary and an extensive list of references. An older text I have long found useful is: Frank A. Geldard: *The Human Senses* (Second Edition), John Wiley & Sons, 1972.

   Also of interest to musicians because of its implications for the relationship of tones to colors is the condition known as synesthesia, a sort of cross-wiring of sensory pathways. For a nice introduction to the subject, see "Composers Who See Color, and the Meaning of Synesthesia," by Andrew Quint, *The Absolute Sound* 113, July/August, 1998.

PART II

PRODUCTION
(DIRECTION AND DESIGN)

1

BOB DOES DICK

(March–June, 1998)

As noted in my introduction, it was Robert Wilson's production of
Richard Wagner's *Lohengrin* for the Metropolitan Opera (March,
1998, and retained in subsequent revivals) that proved the last-straw
impetus for the writing of this book. Wilson's early reputation was built on
a series of extraordinary original theatre-pieces, done in collaboration with
composers and his own troupe of performers. He then began applying his
aesthetics and techniques to works of the operatic canon. This *Lohengrin*,
severely abstract and objectified in style and adversarial in stance, raises
several of the questions that must be confronted in any assessment of the
current state of operatic art.

In the Wilson *Lohengrin*, the dominant design elements are bars, strips,
and panels of light, sometimes fixed but often in slowly moving patterns.
Occasionally these patterns arrange themselves in ways that could be connected to a theme of the drama (e.g., a cross), but any direct interpretive
suggestion (as by timing such connections with an event in the action or
the music) is avoided. The geometric impression is sharp and angular, the
textures flat, the color spectrum cool (white to silver to blue to black, with
a contrasting splash of red in Ortrud's costume). There is no set in the ordinary sense, hardly any set pieces (a wobbly little platform for the King being
the main exception) or props. There is one emblematic piece: a small, rather
lovely blue cutout of a swan's wing.

The production's behavioral language is a form of mime, executed with
a slowness that matches that of the lighting events. Hand positions are presented with studious gravity, and indeed the performers are more concerned

with their hands than with one another. Transactions among the characters (even ones of seemingly unavoidable vitalization, like the Lohengrin/ Telramund combats) are never carried out save through the filter of this slowed, mimed language. The chorus is kept in a line and stationary, except during its necessary entrances and exits.

I want performance experiences to be as immediate and unmediated as possible. So I don't read program notes, interviews, or press releases before attending an event. Afterward, though, I'll look at whatever's at hand, particularly if anything out of the ordinary has occurred. In this case, two items were of some help. One was a "Critic's Notebook" article in *The New York Times* by Mel Gussow (a longtime theatre critic and editor for the paper) that included phone-interview comments by the auteur, the other a Met program feature on Wilson by Holm Keller, a dramaturg who has written a monograph on Wilson and collaborated with him on some of his ventures.[1]

In Mr. Gussow's piece, Mr. Wilson is at pains to assure us of his respect for Wagner and his work, saying that his abstract design had been inspired by the composer's own drawings, that he wished to keep the production simple so as not to diminish the music, and that he wanted to make the singers comfortable. He also says he believes the story must be "timeless" and "present." With respect to the violently negative response from part of the audience, he observed that "With Wagner, there's a society that's very closed. They regard *Lohengrin* as 19th-century romanticism and want to guard it." (The misguided bounders! Who will these Germanophile Romanticizers seize upon next with their wild-eyed claims? Heinrich Heine? Franz Liszt? Where will it end?)

While Mr. Keller's article (translated by Douglas Langworthy) includes no direct quotations, its author clearly has close familiarity with Mr. Wilson's process and philosophy. These seem to me to be his key points: Wilson considers each production, whether of new material or old, "an opportunity for an independent creative act"; he creates a visual world that follows its own laws, and in which each theatrical discipline is treated as an independent element rather than as a contribution to a unity; and his work does not seek to educate, instruct, resolve psychological issues, or explain itself—Wilson is going for truth and beauty, and we must sort it all out for ourselves.

Soon after my visit to the *Lohengrin* production, I received a postcard from the New York Theatre Workshop, a venue for exploratory work. On its face was a photo against a black background. The photo showed the head and shoulders of a youngish man, viewed from behind. The man had a very nice traditional haircut, wore a light jacket, and appeared to be holding a tall glass of milk, which was visible over his right shoulder. "What is it? Who is it?" asked some white dropout type against the black of the postcard's upper half, and below came the answer, "It is Bob . . ."—this in black type against the light jacket, with a contrasting splash of red for "Bob dot dot dot."

Sure enough, as the card's verso disclosed, this was a Wilson-connected affair, advertising a theatrepiece based on the sayings of Bob himself, and directed by Anne Bogart, a highly regarded cutting-edge director. It sported a provocative quote from Bob, as well as a blurb promising exploration of such topics as "family, art, and American culture" and a "creative crisis in the making, where American pop culture and high culture collide," all addressed to "everyone who has ever been challenged by society in an effort to achieve their goals." Since each of these topics is of genuine interest to me and I am certainly a person who has been so challenged (so are you, I daresay), and since "what is it?" and "who is it?" were the very questions I was asking, I resolved to head down to East 4th Street to check it out.

But before I tell you about *Bob*, I should confess: even before *Lohengrin*, I knew a few things about Bob. Since I follow both music and theatre, I knew Bob by reputation practically from the start. My interest in his work grew beyond casual curiosity through Basil Langton. Basil was an actor and director I'd known of for many years, and I had seen his effective productions of Büchner's *Woyzeck* and Dallapiccola's *Volo di notte* at the Manhattan School of Music, where he worked with singers on their acting. Around that time (the late Sixties) I met Basil and his wife, the excellent actress Nancy Wickwire, through a mutual friend, and spent a long evening chatting with them about theatre and opera. I found Basil to be urbane and knowledgeable, and full of artistic appetite.

I ran into Basil on two or three subsequent occasions, and on one of them he told me enthusiastically of an overwhelming experience he'd had recently over in Iran. It sounded like the Mother of all Happenings. It had gone on for days and taken place all over a mountain, with the audience hiking from one "scene" to another, like pilgrims to the Stations of the Cross. Basil thought the creator/director of this event, an American named Robert Wilson, was a genius. "Oh yes," I was able to mumble, "I've read about him." I was about Happeninged out. I'd attended only a few, but it gets late early for me with this whole idea. Still, I had to admit this sounded a bit different, or at least more.

Not long after that, I picked up a copy of *The Drama Review*. It was labeled "Visual Performance Issue," and it contained pieces on artists I was interested in, as well as a couple I felt I should at least know something of. And *voilà*, here were two articles about Robert Wilson and his Iranian adventure, one a lengthy descriptive analysis by Ossia Trilling, the other an experiential recounting by Basil. The articles included many photos, excerpts from the event's program and daily schedule, fragments of the text, and extracts from an interview dialogue between Mr. Wilson and Mr. Trilling.[2]

Wilson's creation was called *KA MOUNTAIN and GUARDenia* Terrace. It began with an overture and went on for 168 hours. It was performed by Wilson himself, 30 members of his then-company-in-training, the Byrd Hoffmann School of Byrds, plus 20 Iranian participants, and was a presentation of the Shiraz Festival. Financial constraints forbade some of the intended effects (such as blowing the entire top off the mountain of Haft Tan or, alternatively, painting the whole peak white, like snow), but even so quite a lot took place.

After a prelude in a Persian garden, the performance began at the base of the mountain near the graves of seven Sufi poets and proceeded upward through sites suggestive of prehistoric, Biblical, mythological, American folkloric and suburban, and other themes. It culminated in apocalyptic events at the mountaintop, including the burning of models of the Parthenon and New York City. Along the way certain events took place (an Old Man telling a tale, or a solo daylong Knife Dance—"movements similar to T'ai Chi, but at a much slower pace," according to a picture caption).

My response to the descriptions of *KA MOUNT*, etc., was a mixture of the empathetic and the skeptical. I was attracted to much of the cultural material, and in particular had a longstanding interest in Middle Eastern influences (including Sufiism) on the birth of Western Romantic culture. I had some respect for Basil's opinions, and he claimed to have been personally and artistically transformed by his Wilsonian encounter. Other Western theatreworkers were being drawn toward these cultural sources, and they included significant ones like Peter Brook, whose own *Orghast* had nearly busted the Royal Exchequer at the Shiraz Festival a year earlier. The a-technological, treehouse-out-back feel had some appeal for anyone overdosed on slick theatre mechanics, and this too was in the air—Jerzy Grotowski, with his Poor Theatre philosophy, was at the height of his American influence. Finally, I am temperamentally sympathetic to quirky, gargantuan projects that want to change the world, and to artists in search of a stance toward both their contemporary surroundings and their artistic heritage.

Against all this was my deepset distrust of anything cultish, my suspicion of sudden conversions or an eagerness to leap into other cultural skins, and my aversion to the enigmatic pose. All these diseases were raging unchecked, and I believed I detected some of their symptoms in *KA*. Nonetheless, this was clearly a case of you-hadda-be-there. These were only articles. I felt that while I might not discommode myself to check out the world of Wilson, if a reasonably convenient way presented itself, I would take it. I missed one or two chances, but before long the planets aligned: *Einstein on the Beach*, production by Robert Wilson, music by Philip Glass, Nov. 21, 1976 at the Metropolitan Opera House, New York—my own neighborhood in all senses. So I was there.

The atmospherics of the evening were, by Met Opera standards, quite extraordinary. Over the five-hours-and-counting of the service, members of the congregation rose and drifted about, some in somnambulistic mode (the fragrance of smoldering hemp wafting down the corridor by the press office might have had something to do with it). I recall a widespread bemusement, numerous early departures (including, around Hour Three, my companion), and grins and bumps from assorted cool types made giddy by setting foot inside the main uptown club and loosening the joint up. It was all mildly pleasant, if you had nothing that needed doing.

From the production itself, I retain a few hazy images: Lucinda Childs standing on one leg, Einstein fiddling, the couple singing the counting duet on the train's observation platform, each of these for a very long time. Some of the stage pictures were striking. The technical command of both the performing company and the crew was impressive. Glass's music was like sausage extruding from some unstoppable grinder; every so often, there'd come a little crimp to tell you that one superlong link had just slid by, and this next stuff was another link. Its instrumental textures whined, twanged, and doodled. The score's overall feel was that of an electrified raga with incidental vocal parts.

Since *Einstein* had been in the news and "Minimalist" music had been on the scene for a decade or so, I'd had some idea what I was in for, and had made a pact with myself to stay the duration and allow myself to be bored, to see if some door would open beyond boredom. No go. Instead, I found my wretched Occidental, linear mind doing what it always does when sufficiently detached from its surroundings: trying to figure things out, trying to uncover some meaning, a purpose in the proceedings. I turned up nothing I thought could be of use in my life, but I did come away with some observations. The people onstage were living lives of stasis and repetition. They evidently had no wills; their behavior came from outside themselves. Their environment had its beauties, but within it every inch of space, every second of time seemed absolutely determined. In this world there might be movement, but no destination; there might be actions, but no consequences. Further, both the work's content and its mode of presentation suggested that surrender to this state of affairs, or at least acceptance of it, was the wisest course open to us. To me, this smacked more of psychological alienation than of philosophical wisdom. I checked off to pure research the time and money spent and resumed seeing if I could make any sense of the admittedly less orderly world of reality.

And so, a couple of decades later, to *Bob*. I enjoyed myself hugely. I'm always happy in the presence of a fine performer, and Will Bond was remarkable. What he and Ms. Bogart had done was to fashion a script from Bob's writings and sayings, and an action scenario of Boblike moves, and create a sustained hour-and-a-half of public life for "Bob." "Bob" of *Bob* was not intended as an impersonation of Bob, but he was a fully elaborated character whose surface peculiarities seemed the outcome of a complicated psychology, grounded in a biography. What I admired most in Mr. Bond's work was that he not only commanded both the verbal and mimish disciplines of the piece (rare enough), but made both seem to proceed from the inside out. The techniques of *Bob* were tightly disciplined and thoroughly styled, yet I believed in "Bob." This was different from my experience of Bob's own work—Mr. Bond had created a credible artistic unity from disparate theatrical elements. I do not know, of course, precisely how the performer/director relationship played out for *Bob*, but Ms. Bogart is credited with "Conception/Direction," and Mr. Bond with "Creation/ Performance," and so I presume that Mr. Bond was responsible for most of the moment-to-moment invention, with Ms. Bogart providing basic ideas, a critical eye and ear, some shaping, and supervision of the technical elements. These last (sound and lighting) were of superior quality, and were integrated with the script, not separate from it. The appearance of *Bob* was Wilsonian, but the effect was not.

All right, "Bob" was not Bob. Still, his verbal self consisted entirely of Bob, and his physical self of Bobish invention. Certainly there were clues here to Bob himself. Bob plus Will and Anne, of course: selected Bobparts as interpreted by others before we may interpret. I found "Bob" good company. A highly autonomous person, and comfortable thus, full of interesting insights and witty commentary, idealistic and intellectually passionate. He seemed quite in charge of himself most of the time, but late in the show there was an episode of crisis. "Bob" grew flustered at being pressed on personal matters. He momentarily lost his verbal acumen, then embarked on an extended mime sequence, dashing back and forth on the diagonal, accompanied by sound and light disturbances and teetering dangerously at the borders of his space, including the lip of the apron. But then, quite suddenly, he returned to his normal slow-signing, cool-speaking state. I took from this that he had undergone a panic concerning the relationship between his personal and artistic selves, but had transcended it by returning to his customary mode of observation and abstraction. These moments felt very lonely, and I was sad for "Bob."

As for the substance of *Bob*, I could not derive much from the mimed scenario. Since the text included some remarks about the tensions that exist along and between planes (horizontal, vertical, diagonal), between parts of the body (hand and face, for example), and between the body and space, I gathered that these ways of seeing were important, even dramatic, for "Bob." I had some familiarity with this vocabulary as expressed through certain systems of movement work. But there, meaning is dependent on analysis according to a particular code of definitions, such as Laban's.[3] Here, I had no key to the code; besides, "Bob" kept insisting *he* didn't know what his work *meant*, in a tone that implied that if that was O.K. with him, why wouldn't it be O.K. with me?

The glass of milk I'd spotted on the postcard was the central prop. It rested on a plain table. Several times, Mr. Bond approached it with fierce concentration along one of his tensed diagonals, slowly inclined on one leg toward the glass, and grasped it. Three or four times, he actually drank the milk, straight down. No Parsifal with his Holy Grail has ever given a piece of glassware such wholehearted devotion, to say nothing of quaffing its contents. I thought of several possible messages: that any object given sufficient attention will take on significance, for the significance depends on our investment in the object. Or simply that we would do well to be more aware of the everyday things and acts of our lives. I also caught memory-glimpses of my Mom, in Denver, Colo., and then in Mt. Vernon, N.Y. in the 1940s, telling me to be sure to drink my milk, and figured "Bob's" own Mom down in Texas was telling him something similar a few years later, and that the importance of the glass of milk for "Bob" might be found in this area. But I didn't know. This was a fragment of a private iconography. The only thing I could say for sure about any of "Bob's" physical actions was that they had to do entirely with an isolated individual in a strictly bounded world of space, light, and sound.

I gleaned more from *Bob*'s spoken text. It consisted, after all, of words, and words stubbornly go right on depositing their residues of meaning. There is even a certain constancy in these residues, despite differences in context and interpretation. "Bob" made a number of provocative statements about theatre and its uses, for instance that he thinks "naturalism is a lie," and that what he wants is a theatre of clarity in which the audience is left free to think "without all this—emotionalism." (The dash is my transcription of the performer's delicate pause before the word "emotionalism." I don't know if it appears in the text.) He also said that whereas most theatre tries to speed up time, he wants to slow it down. Also, that instead of binding together the elements of sight and sound so that they are constantly interfering with each other, he prefers to separate them, even oppose them. Then, he hopes, each element will be seen more clearly, and the observer will have time and space to think. Finally (well, "Bob" said much more—this is my selection, for my critical purposes), he said something I gather is of particular importance to "Bob" and possibly Bob, since it's reproduced on the address side of the promotional postcard and echoed in the lines that caught my eye on the photo side: "The reason we work in theatre is to ask, 'What is it?', not to say what it is. . . Interpretation is for the public so they can interpret the work. . . We invite them to get an exchange of ideas. We don't say, 'This is it.' Instead we say, 'What is it?' And people will have many different interpretations."

These ideas begin to suggest a coherent artistic philosophy, a sort of Bobthink. Since aspects of this philosophy are shared by other influential artists, and present themselves repeatedly in the world of performance, they merit consideration independent of reaction to a specific production. Certainly the questions of time, of separation of elements, of interpretation, and of what-is-itness deserve such attention.

Bob's attitude toward time, as articulated by "Bob," is mighty appealing. What *is* the hurry, after all? Any artistic practice that might help us settle and calm down, that might detain the rush of half-digested images and "information," might counter the frenetic passing-on and passing-by of our existences, has something going for it.

As Bob points out and we have already noted, there is a conflation of time in all theatre. But this compression is in relation to the time span suggested by the work itself. It occurs within the performance framework, and has nothing to do with how the time values of a work, or of a specific moment—squeezed or stretched?—are experienced. Further, theatre-time's conflation of real time is generally a function of the writing, not of the speed at which actions are committed. But this last, true slo-mo, is what Wilson is up to.

And what happens in slo-mo? At least three things: detachment, ritualization, reality shift. Detachment, because the slowing of action invites us to study, to inspect, to remove from the viewing experience its visceral, reactive element and replace it with an analytic one. Ritualization, because actions take on the quality of being executed for their own sakes, with extra care and intent; even accidental, uncontrolled actions appear purposeful and formed. They are aestheticized. Reality shift, because our attention is directed to details that are otherwise unnoticed, though perhaps subliminally received. New material is drawn into awareness, and a new sense of significance is created—a new level of reality, in short, comprising elements already present in the old.

In this last regard, *Bob* repeats an excerpt of the Trilling/Wilson interview published in *TDR*. In it, Wilson speaks of collaborating with an unnamed anthropologist to shoot and study film of mother-infant intereactions: the baby cries, the mother picks up and comforts the baby. Then Wilson and his collaborator stop down the film and study it frame by frame. (In *Bob*, amusing illustration of successive frames by Mr. Bond.) Wilson in *TDR* says that 300 such instances occurred in the films, and that "in eight out of ten cases" the collaborators observed that whereas at normal speed the sequence seems a simple matter of the mother lovingly picking up her baby and comforting it, the stopped frames disclose something quite different: the mother lunging and the baby reacting with fear. Wilson goes on to say that this shows how much we unconsciously communicate on a nonverbal level, and how unlike the apparent reality this communication can be. He believes that slowing down or arresting theatre action is a way of suggesting the content of these other levels.

Let's take Bob's word that there are 300 such pieces of film, of which 240 show something like what Bob describes. It's still a slippery business. We first of all have to assume that this particular anthropologist and artist are interpreting their stopped frames usefully. The last time I looked, there remained considerable indecision about which facial expressions or gestures or postures represented which emotional states or personality traits, and considerable skepticism about efforts to get them into an agreed ranking. One thinks of the often unsettling histories of such efforts, as with the sculptures of Messerschmidt or, in theatre, the plastiques of Delsarte.[4] One also thinks of all those psychological tests that show the range of response to a particular image, whether representational or abstract. Beyond this, we are asked to agree that reality minus one of its important components—energy flow, motion, intention being carried through—is somehow truer than reality with it. And that is the implication. Bob records (a bit gleefully, I think) the distress of the mother, who is clearly allowed to assume that what she is seeing on the stopped frame is *really* real, realer than her plain old everyday perception of it.

I have no doubt that what Bob and his partner saw was *interesting*, and that it adds something to our awareness. I am also sure that you can stop any film at any point and get something interesting and apparently revelatory, but that exactly what it might be is a matter of interpretation. Also, that if you pick up your crying baby 300 times, something other than pure milk of humankindness will be flowing on some of those occasions. Knew that already.

Besides: what has this to do with theatre slo-mo? Whatever value the films have lies in their Candid Camera nature. They are little chunks of reality. Frozen chunks, and lab reality; nonetheless, they are supposed to represent unrehearsed, unedited sequences from the relationship between an actual mother and baby. Anything we may learn from them depends on accepting them as real. Bob, though, creates an avowedly artificial world. The people who inhabit his world behave in choreographic patterns. They create controlled shapes, space-sculptures, whose elaborately slow execution is perfected through rehearsal. We will certainly learn nothing about them they don't want us to know, and the only thing they share with the movie stills is the coolness with which we observe them.

Then there's Bob's idea about the separation of elements. This seems to take two forms. One involves the going-on of unrelated action sequences within a space, and the other (more important here) the detachment of eye-information from ear-information. "Bob" explained this entertainingly. I can only paraphrase him, but the gist of it was that instead of allowing these sensory channels to get tangled up like crossed wires, let's put one over *here* and the other over *there*. Then we can take in each on its own terms. This reminds me of arguments I used to get into as an adolescent with contemporaries who thought of themselves as defenders of purity in art. According to them, each artistic discipline had its own integrity, and to combine one with another (words with music, acting with design, even instrumental with vocal music) was to create a hopelessly corrupt mishmash. There goes opera, for sure.

This purification, though, is not Wilson's main point. He's trying to create clarity through juxtaposition. Keller, in his Met program piece, calls the effort "mutual strengthening," and observes that it cannot be achieved through what he terms "parallel illustration, i.e., by representing the same idea through different media... Instead, Wilson builds on the theatrical dictum that says when a Coke can is set on a baroque dresser, both objects can be seen more clearly."

What theatrical dictum is that? We might find things in the writings of postmodern theorists that are suggestive of it, but as stated, this isn't a theatrical dictum at all. It's a fine-arts dictum, a way of *looking* at *things*. Its home territory would be sculpture or still-life painting or architecture or installation. Even there, it's a special view. It assumes that "more clearly" is synonymous with "in opposition to" or "decontextualized from," and that this is a desirable form of clarity. Well, sure, it's a new arrangement. It's not the Coke can in the Coke machine, or in the cooler. It's not the baroque dresser with a gilded hand-mirror on it, or a little flagon of cologne, or as part of an entire baroque boudoir.

You can't *argue* with the Coke can on the baroque dresser. There it is. It's entirely valid observation. If it makes you stop and look and think, good. When the Coke can on the dresser becomes a theatrical principle, however, argument is in order. In any kind of theatre I value, to say nothing of life itself, even Coke cans and dressers aren't just objects. They're things people use in the course of pursuing their lives, and it's from that pursuit that their associative meanings for both characters and audience are derived. And theatre actions, even theatre design elements, do not merely "illustrate" or "represent". . . "ideas." They seek to evoke, to embody, a life. Furthermore, while it's possible to view cans and furniture purely as objects, an analogy between such objects and the elements of living theatre is extremely tenuous. Movement, language, music—*objects*? Severed from one another, like the lobes of a brain whose corpus collosum has been cleft? Why would we want that?

Bob's conception of interpretation, like his theory of separate elements, is grounded in fine-arts thought. It assumes a fixed object and a direct relationship between object and viewer. And it's true that when I encounter an *objet d'art*, I may interpret it as I please. There is a wonderful freedom in this. I'm not reliant on any intermediary, and don't have to answer to any authority. I can form a relationship to the work that is entirely my own, and of the moment. It is also true that my perception of the work, my relationship to it, will change with context, and that I am a part of that context.

Equally true, though, is the observation that the work has a certain unchanging essence. Unless it or I is actually destroyed or defaced, it remains its recognizable self. In the long run, this enduring essence is at least as important as the contextual changes. Over time, we often seem much altered, the work and I, and often much the same. But here we still are, in any case. I can choose to create context for the *objet*. Usually, I do. It's called learning about it, and includes a curiosity about how others have interpreted it. But I don't have to do this. I can own this as an exclusive relationship, *l'objet et moi*.

But in performed art, where The Work is realized through the intervention of Second Interpreters, this is not so. So what in any given moment (like that of a stopped frame, say) might be taken for an *objet* springs to life. Many more changes, a virtual infinity of them, are introduced, and the paradox of ceaseless change/unchanging essence is even more miraculous. The performance work simply is not a fixed object, and there is no such thing as an uninterpreted transference of it.

These points may seem elementary. If so, I am sorry to belabor them. But here's a fellow—an intelligent, talented fellow—who designs stage spaces, puts people in them, and sets the people in slow motion, then disavows interpretation. He wants you to believe he's only asked a harmless question or two and left you free to interpret. His main question, "What is it?", is a superb one, but it doesn't belong exclusively to Bob. It's what any creative interpreter asks. Still, Bob is right to emphasize it, because too often it is asked in only a token way, almost a hypocritical way, then left in the dust.

Exactly how, though, are we going to ask "What is it?", yet disclaim interpretation? When we come down to it, Wilson's effort to get his non-interpretive-theatre-artist contraption off the ground rests with the "it" of "What is it?" He asks to be held blameless of interpreting by being granted the ultimate interpretive freedom: that of fashioning a stage work that will be considered a free-standing creative act. Components of this act may include the verbal and musical texts of, for example, Wagner's *Lohengrin*, which are to be viewed as found materials to be used, along with any others, as the new author may wish. Once more we encounter a stance associated with the visual arts, in this case collage. See what I came across! I found this old refrigerator, a whole bunch of twine and some tar, and this stuff called *Lohengrin* that somebody threw out! Wouldn't it be neat to patch it all together, light it up, and install it somewhere—like maybe, a few of the world's leading opera houses?

Now we have a new "it." Bob cannot be accused of misinterpreting *Lohengrin* any more than he can be accused of misinterpreting the refrigerator. Both have the same value as objects of cultural detritus from which a new reality may be fashioned—"and people will have many different interpretations."

Certainly Wilson is correct in saying that an artist's approach to a preexisting work must be creative, not reproductive. To assume that a work is already "known" is lazy and uninteresting. It is also his artistic "right" to reinterpret as he chooses. And it is ours to ask not only of the work itself "What is it?", but of the interpretation "Is it a good idea?"

For the devotee, *Lohengrin*, like other works of the operatic canon, is a living being. Its music is associated with moments of spiritual exaltation and clarification. Its characters and their conflicts, as expressed through the music, arouse the noblest and darkest energies within us. They bring the sad reminder that the darker ones are all too comprehensible and familiar, while the nobler are somehow mysterious and unattainable, a beauty we can't quite grasp. We learn this through the palpable, sensory experience of performance, in no other way.

Each performance is different from all others. Each trip on the journey brings us to landscape features, even fine details, that are known in a profound sense, for they have been not merely often seen and noted, but deeply felt. Yet we never know exactly what's around the corner or how it will affect us this time, because we are guided by the interpreters, and their maneuvers are not predictable. Besides all this, our tapestry of private associations with The Work changes and grows. Each re-experience of The Work constitutes a report to ourselves on the standing of these associations. To check in with *Lohengrin* is to check up on the mind, the heart, the memory.

It is habitual for devotees who are offended by productions like Bob's *Lohengrin* and forthright enough to say so to complain that the director has no understanding of The Work, and that his production has nothing to do with it. It is clear that Bob and the devotee do not have the *same* understanding of *Lohengrin*. Bob does not seem to have incorporated it, really, but to have deflected it. It is also quite possible—and this would be the devotee's suspicion—that Bob, an eye man, is not responsive to the musical content of the piece. Aesthetic philosophies aside, that would explain Bob's apparent indifference to the events of the score, and his willingness to proceed as if Wagner's music were just so many links of Phillip Glass's sausage.

I don't impute such exculpatory ignorance to Bob. I think Bob is intelligent, artistically talented, and culturally aware, and therefore fully responsible for his work. I think he understands *Lohengrin* in at least one important sense: he knows what it stands for, and is clear about his relationship to that. He opposes it. His opposition is conscious and willed, and is expressed with specificity and consistency in his production. Here are a few particulars:

· In *Lohengrin*, Wagner wrote of an exact time in the history of the Germanic peoples, which he wished to associate with a dawning awareness of German identity. In the world of The Work, myth is giving way to history, Norse polytheism to Christianity, tribal enmities to national unity. Tangible specifiers, inserted in detail by the operawright, are required for belief in this world. We believe in what is there. But Wilson does not want us to believe in the world of The Work. He wants us to believe in his world, "timeless" and "present"—*Anonymous, 20ᵗʰ Century*, in the architect Luigi Ricci's phrase. Of course, in that world, Wagner's music and drama have no reason to exist. That would be the point. "Timeless" and "present" mean, "Detached from time and place, from past (history) or future (destination)." True, we can consult the program, which continues to say, "Antwerp, first half of the tenth century." But it could as well say, "The surface of Io, early Pleistocene." It would make no difference. Wilson believes it *should* make no difference, and sees to it that his opinion is determinant.

· Wagner envisioned a musical drama embracing certain rituals. Wilson envisions a ritual incorporating the narrative of the drama—but the narrative only. Through the power of Wagner's musical dramatization, the meanings of these rituals (of state and church) are re-discovered, made emotionally alive, and re-affirmed. Through the power of Wilson's ritualization, the meanings of the drama are re-interred, rendered emotionally inert, and denied.

The ritualization is imposed on the audience through the forced dominance of eye-information. The design, though abstract, is far from neutral. It is in fact the leading performer, moving and changing more than the characters themselves, and offering much more of visual interest (Wilson is no slouch at what he does). The characters are absorbed into the design, caught in its patterns. A receptor has the choice of trying to follow the design and ascribe meaning to it, or of giving up on meaning and surrendering to the design's rhythms and atmospherics. This creates a free-floating state detached from any specifics, and therefore from the drama. If one tries to re-focus on the characters, one finds them in slow-motion study of themselves, under a spell in which their actions are automatic and dreamlike. Any behavioral distinction between the public scenes, where the characters are under the constraints of the rituals, and the private ones, where in the course of "being themselves" they decide the course of the drama, is obliterated. They all act the same, all the time. They thus resemble the poor suspended pawns of *Einstein*, and they seem terribly alone, like "Bob" of *Bob*.

Because the behavioral language is not Western-looking, it has the further effect of re-contextualizing the material. It introduces a literally foreign tone and a set of associations that sit incongruously on The Work. Of course, *no* variety of mime would be a comfortable fit with *Lohengrin*. Any would constitute commentary. But the Wilsonian idiom is particularly remote. It owes nothing to any of the Western mime traditions, and is not even very like the Japanese and Chinese theatre languages we have made nodding acquaintance with. T'ai chi is certainly suggested. But the strongest association, at least for me, is with Merce Cunningham, particularly a piece from some 30 years back called *Second Hand*. Merce. Carolyn Brown. Hands that are claws, jerking, twisting. Stasis. John Cage (score) on a sputtery connection with some engineers in the basement. Indeterminacy. In the BAM balcony, more of that aromatic smoke, and a mustachioed bravo in a cowboy hat, yelling "You bug me, Cage." Above it all, to and fro across the false proscenium ("decor" by Jasper Johns), a creeping bar of fine white light.

Yet another tone and chain of association is introduced by Wilson's realization of Ortrud. From the start of Act I (during which she is silent until the final ensemble), she prowls the perimeter, sending bad vibes with witchy hand signals and preposterous mugging (I'm not criticizing the performer—Deborah Polaski did it with conviction). Since her makeup and costume strongly suggest the fashion tsarina Diana Vreeland (or more precisely, the actress Mary Louise Wilson doing her evocation of Diana Vreeland), at least three incongruous, unwelcome worlds are evoked in a single stroke:

fashion design, silent-movie vampdom, and downtown camp.* It's trendy, it's Ridiculous, it's hilarious. Couldn't it just be coincidental? We mustn't rule it out, I suppose. It's possible that Bob is so encapsulated in his own aesthetic universe, so secure in the prerogatives of his auteurship, that he innocently replicates himself wherever he goes. But I doubt that. Bob has an eye. He knows what he's up to.

No likelier accidents are the choices that undercut the authority or dignity of the characters. Henry the Fowler carries on his own dinky royal platform, like an invalid with a walker. The portly happy couple is made to display full embonpoint, in profile and in silhouette against a white screen, as Bridal Chamber bliss impends. Bits of operamock, for us to savor if so inclined, or else overlook if we can.

· Wagner dreamed of the *Gesamtkunstwerk*, the total stage-artwork, wherein all the sense-affecting devices available to all the creative and interpretive artists involved would coalesce in a unified statement of overwhelming emotional force, resulting in a sustained engagement that would allow of no distance whatever and induce the receptor to surrender to the experience unconditionally. He dedicated his life and being to pursuit of this particular artistic ideal, and achieved something like it with impressive frequency. If one were to tug at a single brick in the Wagnerian edifice which, if extracted, would bring the entire structure down, it would be this idea of the *Gesamtkunstwerk*. And that, of course, is what Wilson has done. The separation of elements, the "mutual strengthening" without all this—emotionalism: These are precisely, elegantly Anti-Wagnerian. Let's put this over *here*, and that over *there*, and when we're through, there won't be a blessed thing left, will there? And when we put a strong visual design into motion, drawing the eye's attention, the music will recede, not advance. These are additional things that Bob, philosopher-auteur of imagocentric theatre, surely knows.

Altogether, it's quite a set of associations Wilson invites the receptor to patch into his *Lohengrin* tapestry. Other receptors' would be different from mine. The point is that they will be from outside The Work's cultural framework, because Bob's choices are leading questions, and are too strange to ignore. He'll have you thinking about them as you watch and try to listen. And while you're doing all that thinking, you won't be feeling much.

---

* One person I spoke with at intermission, not familiar with *Lohengrin* but conversant with the New York arts scene, was shocked to discover, when Polaski began to sing in the Act I finale, that this figure on the fringe of the scene was not a man in drag.

There are other areas of opposition we could discuss—the very notion of abstraction vs. illusionistic realism, for example, or of Bobtime (eye-rhythm) vs. Wagnerian time (ear-rhythm). But these will do. They represent, to say the least, fundamental disagreements over the handling of cultural material. These disagreements intrude in most contemporary opera productions, irrespective of the stylistic labels attached.

Look! Someone's set a Coke can down on top of that lovely old piece! I'll bet it was Bob, lonely guy from Texas with a tall glass of milk, who still wants to burn down the Parthenon.

NOTES

1. For the former, see: "A Director Who Dares, And Takes The Heat," by Mel Gussow, *NYT*, March 16, 1998; for the latter, see "The Geometry of Magic," by Holm Keller, *Stagebill* (Metropolitan Opera Program edition), March, 1998.

2. See: "Robert Wilson's 'Ka Mountain'," by Ossia Trilling, and "Journey to Ka Mountain," by Basil Langton, *TDR*, Vol. 17 No. 2 (T-58), June, 1973.

3. Rudolf von Laban (1879-1958): Austro-Hungarian dancer, choreographer, teacher and movement theorist, influential in the development of modern dance. Probably still best known in the U.S. as the inventor of the widely used system of dance notation called "Labanotation," he also elaborated a method of observation of posture, gesture, and bodily relationships which became the basis of a school of movement therapy ("Effort/ Shape" work).

4. Franz Xaver Messerschmidt (1736-1783): German sculptor, lavishly gifted but mentally disturbed, whose primary legacy is a series of busts (49 survive), which graphically portray emotional states. Physiognomic interpretation was heavy in the air at the time, and admiring contemporaries attached descriptive labels to the busts, pinpointing the affect and station of each ("A Surly Old Soldier," "The Ill-Humored One,"etc.). See Ernst Kris: *Psychoanalytic Explorations in Art*, International Universities Press, 1952, and Schocken, NY, 1964. This volume includes biographic and analytic material, and illustrations of over half of the surviving busts. See also: Maria Potzl-Malikova and Guilherm Scherf (eds.), *Franz Xaver Messerschmidt*, Louvre Editions/Neue Galerie, 2011. This is the splendid catalogue of the Messerschmidt exhibition shown at the indicated museums—probably the best current reference on the artist.

   François Delsarte (1811-1871): French teacher and founder of the eponymous training system that had an almost incalculable effect on all branches of performance (acting and oratory, singingacting, mime and dance) for over a century. Among his direct pupils were Rachel, Barbot, Lind, Carvalho, Sontag; those strongly influenced by his ideas include virtually the entire line of descent of modern dance: Wigman, Duncan, St. Denis and Shawn, et al., not to mention the above-noted Laban, and through him, Jooss, Leeder, Holm, Graham. He had many disciples in the U.S. (beginning with Steele Mackaye), through whom his methods were widely taught in American theatre. His meticulously detailed system, based on categorization of body parts and their movements and a somewhat mystical set of correspondences between these and certain intellectual and spiritual categories, rests on the assumption that a precise reproduction of physical attitudes and movements will result in meaningful expression in performance. For further, see p. 584, n. 3.

2

A RUSSIAN STYLE NOTE

(June, 1998)

Among all the sayings of "Bob" and Bob, only one that I've come across has seriously bothered me. It's an anecdote about *Death of a Salesman*. In it, Bob tells of a performance he attended (from the timing, I would judge it to have been during the run of the 1984 Broadway revival) and his reaction to Linda Loman's grief over Willy late in the play. "Take it easy, lady," Bob says he thought, "it says right here on the ticket—'*Death of a Salesman*.'"

Bob got a nice laugh with this, but I took umbrage. Bob is showing us how distanced he is from this scene, this grief, this kind of emotional engagement in the theatre. He's implying that to be moved by the scene is to be taken for a chump. He's condescending to Miller's writing, the audience, the actress. As one who happens to believe that on the cosmic scales of art, Robert Wilson's entire lifework will not hold balance with any one of several Arthur Miller plays, I think this comes with small grace.

Well, it's only a crack, a sliver of attitude. But I put it together with another of Bob's opinions: "I think naturalism is a lie." He cannot be using the term in its narrow, initial-cap meaning. He is trying to dismiss out of hand the entire set of illusionist conventions, to belittle as naïve and outmoded any connection between theatrical representationalism and belief.

But however narrowly or broadly intended, the statement "naturalism is a lie" is absurd. It is impossible for a theatrical style in itself to be truthful or untruthful. It can only constitute a set of limits within which interpretation may take place. Interpreters and receptors either agree to engage within those limits, or they do not. They believe, or they do not. Their belief will depend on whether or not the set of limits strikes them as not only appropriate and sufficient to the aesthetic content of the work, but as necessary to it, the natural means of conveying it. Then engagement, and belief, will be sustained. Belief held in common will be named "true." The rest of the matter lies in our arguments over difference, our reasons for holding that a particular view of the engagement is deeper, richer, more interesting than another. Although Bob's logic is spavined, the issue he raises needs to be addressed. He has plenty of company in his effort to wave away theatrical realism, and the easy acquiescence in this effort by critics and practitioners—as if persons of intelligence could entertain no reasonable doubt about the matter—is a source of bemusement. The case for the continuing validity of illusionist production styles does not rest entirely on audience naïvete and lassitude.

The most powerful argument against theatrical realism is that it constricts the imagination. According to this view, the more the visual instructions from the stage specify—the more they fill in the details and limit us to literal representation—the less free are our imaginations to soar, as they may in response to well-chosen visual metaphor or abstract suggestion. But the issue isn't whether or not the imagination is "free." It's where we want the imagination to run: into the Work, or away from it. Into the lives of the drama, or toward other considerations.

I thought about this matter on the occasion of the most recent New York visit of the Maryinsky Theatre of St. Petersburg, on the heels of the Wilson *Lohengrin*, and the contrast was instructive. These quaint folk are still stuck with parallel illustration. They seem to not feel the imperative for independent creative acts. They tolerate—even espouse—historicism. Time for a confession of faults and a reply to welcome criticism, which the demands of globalization will doubtless bring forth soon enough.

Meanwhile, the Maryinsky is affording us valuable experiences. Of pertinence here is its production of Tchaikovsky's *Mazeppa*. Both the balletic and operatic wings of the Maryinsky have been mounting restorations of old productions, bits of Illusionist Repro. This is one such.

The Maryinsky's *Mazeppa* was the best night I've had in an opera house for many years. It gave me an experience I'd given up on ever having again: the full, first-time impact of an authentic grand-opera masterpiece in a committed, idiomatic performance. I hadn't much known *Mazeppa*. At a time when I did some discographic work on Russian opera, I was unable to locate the old Bolshoi performance, then the only extant recording save for a pirated edition of Italian provenance. A thoughtful retired record dealer in Columbus, Ohio later sent me a copy from his remainder stock, but I listened to it only casually, and never found my way back. I'm glad: I discovered the piece in the theatre, and subsequent hearings of the recordings (there have now been four, plus that Italian pirate) have confirmed its stature. It belongs in the repertory of every company with the forces to do it justice.

There are many reasons for *Mazeppa*'s triumph in New York. Here, I'd like to focus on how certain elements of this style of physical production influence the direction imagination runs. We must understand the dramatic situation. Reduced to the poverty of brief prose description, here it is: the young Maria, daughter of the magistrate Kochubei, is in love with Mazeppa, the 70-year-old Ukrainian hetman. Because of this infatuation, she disarms the advances of her childhood friend, Andrei. When Mazeppa asks Kochubei for Maria's hand at a celebration, Kochubei refuses, despite his longstanding comradeship with Mazeppa. After forcing Maria to publicly choose between her family and himself, Mazeppa carries her away by force of arms. Devastated by the loss and urged to action by his wife, Lyubov, Kochubei resolves to betray to Tsar Peter Mazeppa's plans for Ukrainian independence. Andrei is sent as courier to the court. But the Tsar doesn't believe him, and turns Kochubei over to Mazeppa, who has him tortured by his henchman Orlik.

Maria knows nothing of these developments, but she reproaches Mazeppa for distancing himself from her in the time since their marriage. Mazeppa re-affirms his love for her, and explains the reason for his preoccupation: the time for independence has arrived, and he will ally with the Swedes against Peter. Maria, her hero-worship revived, is ecstatic. However, her mother arrives with the news of her father's torture and imminent execution. At first incredulous, Maria is finally convinced. She and Lyubov rush to the field where Kochubei and a companion are to meet their fate before a roistering crowd, but they arrive just as the axe falls.

We have come to the opening of Act III, and the sequence I should like to explore for "production values." The act opens with a substantial orchestral entr'acte describing the Battle of Poltava. Considered on its own, the music of this interlude is just a merry battle symphony à la *1812* or *Wellington's Victory*, though well-crafted and relatively short. But of course it isn't on its own. It has a dramatic function. It is descriptive narrative for the ear of a crucial event that cannot be made plausible to the eye. It tells us that the battle is extensive and fierce, and (as the tune of the *Slava* peals forth) that Peter has won: the Swedes are repulsed, Mazeppa's rebellion is crushed.

The Poltava sinfonia also serves as suspense. We have been led on arcs of rising tension and heightening emotion generated by the private conflicts of the characters. Tchaikovsky builds the horror to an almost unbearable intensity by the end of Act II—I was left shaken by the scene of the execution, and I was not the only one. Now the portentous historical events that have so far been the story's background (the birth of Peter the Great's New Russia,

Mazeppa's failed Ukrainian revolt), are brought briefly to the fore. The battle is almost a relief, except that we await its outcome for the fateful role it will play in the end of the story.

Many possibilities present themselves for the theatrical handling of this sequence. Poltava could be staged. But if so, how? In realistic manner, with supers popping blank rounds and toy cannons going off? In choreographed style, by a cohort of dancers or acrobats? In slo-mo, very grave, with slow bayonet thrusts, slow dying falls? With slides or film? Assuming you're beyond the age of eight, have you ever seen a stage battle you believed?

Poltava could be left alone, played as a concert piece with the curtain down, as was formerly customary with overtures, entr'actes, and intermezzos. One of the joys of the Maryinsky's stand for me lay in the fact that of the formal overtures to operas boasting same (*Mazeppa*, *Prince Igor*, *Ruslan and Lyudmilla*), three out of three were rendered in this fashion. And between Maryinsky performances, I had slipped down to Wilmington, Delaware, to see *Der fliegende Holländer*. Once again, the overture was left to its own devices. As it played, I felt the great pleasure of sitting before a theatre curtain, listening. And I thought of the many uses of an overture. For this kind of listening is a complex experience involving choices of both outer and inner attention, and memory, and anticipation.

The Wilmington Grand Opera House is one of many auditoriums around the country that originated as a Masonic hall. It has a companionable warmth. While its basic feel is intimate, it has just enough size and aspiration in its design to suggest opera-house grandeur. The house was new to me, and since I arrived close to curtain time I had only moments to take it in. So as the overture began, I let my eye roam in the half-light. Under such circumstances, there is plenty to look at, but none of it demands attention, for one is led by the ear. In this case one is led down a well-worn path—*Holländer* (unlike *Mazeppa*) is a work I have seen and heard many times, and so it presents a tapestry that is already richly woven. Each of the overture's motifs carries me forward into the performance: I know what each foreshadows, how each will reach its dramatic realization, and what effect that is apt to produce. Each carries me back, to old performances or old moments, to the time of discovery: to the wartime recording under Krauss and the Met broadcast under Reiner, which between them first took me into the complete score; to my first live performance that same season; to the 78-rpm recording of the Dutchman's monologue by Joel Berglund, which I played a hundred times; to *Captain Video*, the superbly tacky TV series of those years that plundered the overture for theme music. At the same time, each of these motifs continues to serve its original purpose: to catch the ear with something that is fascinating and premonitory in itself, and whose development prepares one emotionally for the drama about to unfold. With the light from the pit, the conductor's silhouette, and the apron of the stage before me, I also recapture, childlike, some of the suspense the overture is meant to engender: what lies behind the curtain? What world will be disclosed? *What's going to happen*? I know, but I don't know.

The most important thing the overture tells me is that my ear must be engaged with the music. The eye will be important, and sometimes dominant, but this experience will slide by if my ear is inactive. So long as my eye roams while the overture plays, I may register any and all things without disengaging my ear from the music. Only the conductor (and whatever I may see of the orchestra) actually confirms the music, but nothing else contradicts it, and everything confirms the facts of hall, audience, impending performance. The objects remain in place; my eye moves. It absorbs the objects into the inner space that melds this sensory moment with past and future. However, if my attention is caught by moving objects with intentions of their own, the balance is changed. This is true whether or not the movements are intended as confirmatory. Granted, there's a difference between some disturbance in the hall and purposive movement onstage. The former may actually break off the ear's engagement, while the latter is more likely to shift it to the background. But either pulls loose the thread of time, and knots it up with spatial events. Either steps onto the path down which my anticipation and memory and imagination were leading me into The Work, and begins to re-route it with pre-interpreted instructions. Either breaks the intensity of listening. Even intelligently selected interpretive movement undercuts the listening imperative by suggesting that all can be explained for the eye. All this happens when a prelude or interlude is staged, irrespective of the nature and quality of the invention.

So I would not at all have minded if the Battle of Poltava had gone without visual commentary, even though the music is highly programmatic and serves as dramatic narrative. The Maryinsky's stagers and designers went one better: they found a simple, powerful visual solution that left the ear in charge, the eye to roam and confirm. They raised the act curtain (the Maryinsky's visiting-team-color blue, in place of the Met's home gold) to disclose a forecurtain in the style of an old battle tapestry, filled with the ghastly details of combat events. The eye might well have spent the interlude's duration in contemplation of this scene while the music played, but the production made one more move: it brought the brass battery out before the curtain.

These were magnificent fellows. Clothed in stunning blue uniforms with shoulder capes (the Class-A's of the Preobazhensky Regiment band? I don't know, but they looked mighty historical) and convincingly military in carriage, they deployed before the tapestry in a skirmish line that stretched the width of the apron, raised their gleaming instruments, and just about blew the back wall off the theatre to proclaim Peter's victory. Once in place, they did not move.

From my seat near the front of the Met's balcony (the best location in the house for the sound-sight relationships of grand opera), my eye flitted across the visual field. At moments it focused on figures in the tapestry. At others, it scanned the line of players, and from time to time dropped down to the pit and podium, or widened focus to take in the scene as a whole. Everything seen was incorporated into my sense of progression, design, and balance through unpremeditated sensory selection, always enveloped in sound, carried with me through time by the music. The binding of sight and sound inside my brain constituted my interpretation of that theatrical encounter, visceral, pre-analytic. The memory of it and of the response it aroused (and memory is another selective, interpretive process) is what I can struggle to articulate. It is all that can be talked about.

The overture to *Der fliegende Holländer* (unstaged) is an ear-dominant event whose only visual components direct the receptor back to the music. The Battle of Poltava (as staged by the Maryinsky) is a tableau: an ear/eye event that leaves the ear in charge of narrative, of time, while using the roaming eye to confirm the nature of the event and heighten its sensory effect. Except for the moments of disclosure of the tapestry and the entrance of the stage band, it leaves the receptor's attention uninstructed. In both the overture and the tableau, the visual stillness—the *absence* of movements the eye must follow, of patterns it must interpret—is of the engagement's essence.

With the rise of the curtain on Act III of *Mazeppa*, we are returned to the lives of the characters, and so to opera's habitual ear/eye relationships. The action of *Mazeppa*'s brief final act is simple and stark. It takes place where the opera began, on the grounds of Kochubei's estate overlooking the banks of the Dnieper. But the site is much changed: the house, terrace, and garden are now charred ruins. Remnants of the hetman's troops and their Swedish allies flee across the scene, pursued by a detachment of Peter's forces. Among the latter is Andrei, who has vainly searched the battlefield for Mazeppa. Hearing approaching hoofbeats, he conceals himself. The arrivals are Mazeppa himself and Orlik. Andrei steps forward and challenges Mazeppa, who tries to avoid confrontation by pleading his age and ill fortune. But Andrei rushes upon him; Mazeppa fires and mortally wounds Andrei. A figure moves in the trees. The moonlight brightens and discloses Maria, in a demented state. Mazeppa tries to elicit a response from her, but she does not recognize him.

Mazeppa and Orlik confer briefly, then leave. Now Maria discovers the
dying Andrei. He recalls their childhood games, but she takes him for her
infant and places his head in her lap. The opera closes as the crazed Maria
sings a cradle song to her now lifeless "child," in the moonlit ruins of her
family's home.

As in most of the great 19th-Century operas, the action is only the framework for the emotional heart of the sequence, which lies in its lyrically
elevated expanded moments: Andrei's aria, drenched in an unfulfilled longing; Maria's recounting of the execution, which she experiences as a recurrent dream; her scene with Andrei and concluding lullaby. The fairly standard devices (characters homing back to their story's starting-point over
long stretches of time and distance; the mad scene for soprano; the Death
Scene duet for soprano and temporarily revived tenor) become powerful
psychological inevitabilities if the music takes us there, as Tchaikovsky's
assuredly does.

Throughout the act's duration, the set and the stationary objects on the
stage constitute emotionally reinforcing points of reference. The objects
include an abandoned cannon and the bodies of a Cossack killed in the opening skirmish and (soon) the apparently lifeless Andrei. With a dramatized
scene now underway, eye and ear are asked to re-enter the opera's world
and follow its events. Since the plot sequences are short but the expanded
moments long, the findings of fact quickly grasped but their implications
only slowly absorbed, the eye is again free at moments to roam the space
while the ear remains engaged through time. It may flit from the soliloquizing Andrei to the fire-blackened doorway of the once-splendid house and
back, or from the vanquished Mazeppa to the cannon in the garden.

We are encouraged to inspect the setting by the characters themselves.
Both Andrei and Mazeppa are given entrance moments that include recognition of the place and characteristic response to it (nostalgic or bitterly ironic).
The fact that Maria does not recognize her own house, and responds as if
somewhere else, keeps the significance of place before us. In a sense, the act
is *about* being back in this place, under tragically altered circumstances. Here
women sang and wove garlands and Cossacks danced a Hopak, flirtations
were held, secrets confessed aloud and overheard, ardent pleas painfully
rejected and a bitter confrontation held. The lived-in house, the lushness
of the garden, the spreading shade trees, the paths for strolling—we saw all
these things. Not ideas of things, or symbols or emblems of them, but the
things themselves. We saw how they were used and what they meant in the
lives of the characters, and that these uses and meanings were much the
same as those of our own lives. And now each glance about the scene recalls

the aspirations of these lives, and throws us back to their present condition as their journey approaches its bleak conclusion.

The strength of these representational devices lies in their directness. They seek immediacy of engagement and a minimum of distance. Thus, they involve no translation, no thought about what or why, no solving of puzzles while The Work is in progress. True, they do not "free" the imagination to explore the interpreters' philosophy, The Work's place in history or its contemporary relevance, the nature of Art or of theatrical experience. There will be plenty of time for that. Instead, they free the imagination to run into The Work as far as it can go, to explore every inch of its bounded field, to take in everything within it in all its sensory richness—a much more important kind of freedom, artistically speaking. The scenic objects leave imprints that immediately evoke the associations we have with them in our own lives and histories, and set up an interplay of such associations in each receptor. That is an entirely different process than that initiated by emblematic forms which refer us not to life but to other art and to generalized concepts.

Still, could not a production that is more abstract or essentialist, or that presents the stage world as psychologically experienced rather than as "objectively" perceived, establish engagement with The Work as well or better than this rather old-fashioned, literal approach? Long acquaintance with performance teaches at least one thing: never say "couldn't." Too much depends on the specifics of execution, on sheer interpretive talent. And what interpreters start out to do, how they define the boundaries of their field, does not necessarily set the terms of engagement for a given receptor.

Nonetheless, I'd be surprised to find a non-representational production engaging as powerfully with *Mazeppa* as this one did. What abstract distillate, what concept, would serve to intensify the experience? One approach was suggested by an old colleague of mine who didn't care much for the Maryinsky production, and thought a more conceptual stylization might work better. "After all," he said, "those are pretty crazy people."

So it would seem: crazy and dangerous, Mazeppa first, but all of them, really. When we plot out the narrative and contemplate the characters' decisions, we can easily see how their ill-considered actions, their morally flawed choices, mix into a compound that blows their world to smithereens. We can observe and label their failure to make any connection between actions and consequences, their head-in-the-sand obtuseness that allows them to pursue their desires in a limbo of ethical deferments. Craziness all around, craziness on the rampage.

I think it's not so simple, though. If we inspect these actions and choices in full context, in the light of the social understandings of that time and place and the psychologies they encourage, the actions acquire a certain logic and the choices begin to resemble compulsions. Mazeppa is unsympathetic, monstrous. But his course is set by a guiding star of post-Enlightenment ethic, the unquestioned right to choose a love and marriage partner across lines of age, family, class. He is the very template of the loose-cannon individualist (and this would have been a given for his intended audience, nearly all of whom would have had familiarity with some of his historical and literary pre-existence), with bottom-line ethics to match and an impressive track record. By this standard, what is he *supposed* to do with old friend Kochubei, who tried to betray him to the Tsar and is now remanded into his graces? And if the choice is between your life and the woman you may have loved, but who is now beyond reach and most probably cannot be saved, is the choice so terribly clear?

By contrast, Maria is sympathetic, loveable. Unlike Mazeppa, she has the decency to go mad when confronted with the consequences of her actions. Still: she followed that same guiding star. Her choice in Act I is an agonizing one, but it is hers, left to her until the last. In Act II, she hides from the truth until it is too late: three times (the key raised each time) Lyubov must hammer home the situation (a swooning episode for Maria along the way); only twice, and the execution might have been stayed. The other principals, too, have their ethical ambivalences. The point is that these arise from genuine moral dilemmas, conflicts between love and family, between friendship and responsibility, between personal and patriotic loyalties. It is not easy to disentangle them or to invest this one with moral authority, that one not.

It would all be less complicated if we could get rid of the context, lift all these messy choices out of their life circumstances into an abstract realm where we can pass judgments in a more confident manner. That is exactly what Tchaikovsky will not allow us. His music keeps us immersed in the emotional lives of the characters. We are forced to acknowledge the power of their compulsions before we may evaluate and pigeonhole them. Tchaikovsky grants us no sense of superiority to his characters, or any surety that our own responses to such situations would be more admirable or effective than theirs. Under the sway of the music, the clarity we thought we had when we inspected the narrative is gone. That is one of the troubles with parsing narratives and thinking we are deriving meanings therefrom. Of course matters are clearer when we omit the affective qualities of the music. But it is a false clarity.

There are, I think, two reasons why *Mazeppa* has not quite achieved the international canonical status finally won by Tchaikovsky's other two operatic masterworks, *The Queen of Spades* and *Eugene Onegin*. These reasons are interrelated; in fact, one is an expression of the other. The first is its unforgiving nature. The second is its de-emphasis on tunefulness of the direct, instantly memorable sort.

It is hard to think of another pre-World War I opera as unconsoling as *Mazeppa*. It employs all the devices of a standard Romantic opera to arouse certain expectations, then refuses to fulfill them. An unconventional opera is hidden inside a conventional one, and that is always more forbidding than a piece that announces its unconventionality. In the first two acts, the holiest themes of the 19th Century lyric stage—the flight and bonding of defiant lovers and the stirring of nationalist sentiment—are sounded as expected. But the excited approbation they normally seek, while still present, is strongly laced with suspicion of motives. Apparently noble causes and principles are actually personal compulsions, and these themselves elicit conflicted sympathies.

In Act III, we longingly anticipate some release from the horror, not by means of a happy end, but through recognition and transcendence. Neither is granted. Mazeppa is given a final chance at recognition, as he stands between Orlik's urgings to flee and the hallucinations of Maria. In a moment of devastating emotional emptiness, he mutters "*Idyom*" ("Let's go") and departs to a subdued echo of the "Riding Music" theme first stated, aggressively, in the overture. Maria, as already noted, recognizes nothing, save perhaps her deep and unacknowledged need to nurture, to mother. When the wounded Andrei (the only principal to behave consistently in accordance with an accepted code of honor) revives, we are primed for the soaring duet that will bring a tragically belated recognition, the sense of redemption peculiar to doomed operatic romance. But as Maria rocks her childhood friend to sleep with her hauntingly simple lullaby, she does not know whose head she cradles. Andrei dies without the comfort of a moment's acknowledgement. The scene looks like a *Liebestod*, and even sounds like one of a sort. No one is transfigured, though, and nothing is transcended. It is merely the hopeless end. The act is an apotheosis of desolation, which is not what we sought.

The absence of big-tune arias does not, in my opinion, represent a shortfall of inspiration on Tchaikovsky's part. It is a reflection of ambiguous feelings that are never quite resolved. The most obvious examples are Maria's arioso in the opening scene and Mazeppa's monologue and arioso at the beginning of Act II. The soprano solo, in which Maria enumerates Mazeppa's cherishable attributes (attributes that remain mysterious to us, particularly his alleged wit), has a lovely vocal line and a softly bedded accompaniment. However, it stays safely within its standard form. There is a tenderness in it, but slightly distanced, as if Maria were examining her feelings, then reciting them—drawing the expected sentiments from within. In Mazeppa's monologue (sung while the torture of his old comrade and father-in-law proceeds downstairs), he apostrophizes the Ukrainian night in a manner common to many nocturnal Russian romances, only with a strong strain of guilt: the very stars and poplars seem to accuse him, and he fears Maria's reaction when she learns her father's fate. The following arioso is a love song to Maria, a confession of all this vibrant young woman has meant to an old soldier in decline. It is a beautiful piece with the undulating cantabile feel and repeated after-the-beat entrances typical of the composer's vocal writing, and it carries the baritone up to a sustained G-flat, then A-flat, territory not otherwise invaded by the role. Its instrumental and harmonic colorings and nearly constant dynamic variation lend it an unsettled mood.

These are songs of people who are certainly experiencing feelings, but cannot quite define them. They grope for self-awareness, but don't attain it. Emotions well up inside them, but just when they threaten to take over, they subside. I think we must assume that if Tchaikovsky had wished to assign these characters wholly felt outpourings of unconflicted sentiment he could have done so. No composer was ever better at it. Indeed, he finds instantly recognizable motifs of the martial sort to remind us of the unambiguous forces that are slowly gathering, and when his characters are directly in touch with themselves they arrive at urgent, uncomplicated melodic expression: Kochubei's eloquent prison solo about his three treasures, Lyubov's desperate pleadings with Maria, the latter's final cradle song. Tchaikovsky is working on something else.

It seems to me that the patterns of behavior and expression we have been discussing are all too recognizable. These characters have familiar desires, ambitions, limitations. They differ from ordinary folk pursuing ordinary lives in that they have the power to affect events on a cataclysmic scale, and are placed under extreme circumstances. Their anguished and distorted responses create a stage world that does, indeed, look crazy. But it surely looks no crazier than the one we live in often does when power and circumstances come into unhappy convergence—especially if, like an audience at a performance, we are able to step back and see it in perspective.

To represent the stage world as crazy, to signal its craziness, therefore seems worse than redundant. It seems evasive. It identifies the stage world as something other than our own, something that belongs in the overheated imaginations of people separate from ourselves. What might appear to take us into their world actually keeps us at a safe remove from it. What seems to draw us into their psychological reality only deprives us of our perspective on reality itself, the one we share with the characters.

Mazeppa shows terrible things happening in our world. It tries to make us understand, emotionally, how these things can happen. Like *Onegin* and

The Queen of Spades, it makes a particular point of setting up, and making us feel, the safety of the benign quotidian—the customs and etiquettes of daily social and personal life—then blowing them apart. It also sets up, and makes us feel, all the aspirations to transcendence of the then-prevailing Romantic ethos, then brings them sickeningly to earth. We will find no comfort in them, the piece says. This is what they really are, this is what happens to them in our very own world. *This is the truth.*

That, I believe, is what The Work is trying to tell us, and it is more or less what the Maryinsky gave us. I don't mean by this that everything in the Maryinsky performance was all that one might hope. Indeed, it should be emphasized that by the historical standards set for its singing and staging conventions, there was nothing extraordinary about the evening. Of the performers, only Larissa Diadkova, the mezzo who sang Lyubov, would bear comparison vocally with the leading Russian artists of earlier generations. The sets, picturesque in design and serviceable in execution, were also old and somewhat faded. There was one disastrous staging decision: Lyubov was brought into the scene of Kochubei's imprisonment and torture. Apart from the improbability of her having gained admittance, this turned Kochubei's despairing monologue into a scene with his wife—easier to play, no doubt, but far less intense, allowing the character to externalize feelings and thoughts that should be turned inward, and introducing a measure of comfort where there should be none.

But these are shortcomings not of style, but of execution. They occur not because the production is realistic, but because it is not realistic enough. The evening was wonderful because the performers sang and acted with theatrical and passionate commitment, and because the conductor, Valery Gergiev, and his splendid orchestra dug into the piece in the same spirit. That is all *Mazeppa* (and many another opera) needs—a solid, idiomatic repertory performance by some dedicated people.

The stylistic assumptions of this production were for many decades so pervasive in both the operatic and spoken theatre as to relegate all others to the categories of the outmoded or experimental. They are made with far less frequency now, and with noticeably weakened interpretive conviction. To see them once again forcefully endorsed is to feel the shock of the strange in an oddly familiar way.

3

THE ENHANCEMENTS

(Nov. 1999–Mar.2002)

"Repertory" means works that are ready to be performed. A repertory company is an institution that stands ready to perform such works on an ongoing basis. These works are sorted into lots according to their repeatability. Repeatability is just that. Its congruence with quality as defined by musicians and critics is haphazard, but it is at the heart of the agreement between a repertory institution and its audience. Absent a body of repeatable work, repertory forces have no reason to convene.

For interpreters, repeatability is determined by the ease with which a work falls within reach of their cultural understanding and technical skills. For the audience, it depends on how well the work meets its needs for re-affirmation and renewal. Re-affirmation occurs when something continues to appear true and important with passing time and changing conditions. Renewal happens either when something not previously held to be true and important appears so (is "discovered"), or when something previously held to be true recovers its importance through re-formulation (a "fresh understanding"). Finally, audiences have a way of imposing a third requirement on a performed work: that it be pleasurable. They have no cause to repeat an experience they have already found disagreeable.

Over the past four hundred years, opera has generated a substantial body of repeatable works, works of renewable re-affirmability. That has given it legitimacy as a form of cultural continuity in Western civilization, and made feasible its great repertory institutions. While creators are ultimately responsible for renewal of the form as a whole, they cannot negotiate directly with receptors, for opera's decisive agreement is between audience and interpreters.

Interpreters hold life-or-death power over the works of all creators, past and present—over what may be renewed and re-affirmed, and how. There are only two restraints on this power. The first is supply (interpreters can choose only from what creators create). The second is demand (the assent of an audience must be obtained).

Two alarming developments, and fear of a third, constitute opera's artistic predicament now. The first is that the birthrate of repeatable works has plummeted over the past century. The second is that the cultural understanding and technical skills of interpreters have moved away from the requirements of the most repeatable works. The feared third is that the sort of audience needed to sustain repertory institutions—a pool of semi-automatic repeater receptors—has diminished, or soon will diminish, to a level at which the institutions cannot sustain themselves. While this fear smacks strongly of projection (I know I'm guilty, *ergo* I'll soon be caught), it is the predictable end of an art form's terminal stage: first, the creators dry up; a generation or two later, the interpreters lose touch; a generation or two after that, the audience drifts away. Supply and demand both fizzle out. Of course, it is upon the solution of the first two problems that the future of opera depends. But since they are very hard and can only be solved by artists themselves and not by institutions, it is not surprising that the institutions have vigorously addressed the third, as if it were causative.

Some of our institutions' efforts to ensure themselves of an audience (advertising and promotion; various forms of outreach, education, and audience development) affect the performance engagement only subtly and indirectly. But others affect it directly and radically; in fact, they alter its very essence. These are the enhancements. "Enhancement" is the sublime euphemism that stands in place of "amplification." In New York it is most often associated with the New York City Opera, which outed itself on the subject in 1999 (our sampling period, in fact, crosses from the company's starkly unenhanced past into its blissfully enhanced present), but the phrase "acoustically enhanced" had murmured about our theatres, concert halls, and opera houses for at least a decade before that. In this discussion, the word will cover alleged aids to both eye and ear, a/k/a surtitles and amplification.*

The stated purpose of both these interventions is intensification of the engagement. They are meant to bring performers and audience closer together through easier reception and greater understanding. They share one obvious achievement: the extension of technological control into the

---

* The enhancements were not born in the theatre, but in the home and at the movies. For a chronology of the ear/eye electronic media and some commentary on their implications for live performance, see Backstory I, p. 749.

auditorium. Projections of light and sound no longer emanate exclusively from the stage, but from points in the audience area. There, they change both the direction and quality of attention. They create a new audience/performer relationship through revision of its fundamental sensory elements. But this relationship is not at all the intended one. It is looser, more casual, more distanced than the one it replaces, and far less emotionally potent.

The enhancements address perceived defects—defects that went undetected during opera's flourishing centuries, but are now seen as grave, and correctible by technological means. Amplification addresses a defect in performance: the failure of the performers to project their voices, with a resultant lack of sonic impact in the theatre. But since it is embarrassing to admit to such an elementary professional shortcoming, this defect is imputed to the "new" audience, whose ears are held to be irretrievably conditioned to electronic communication, their eyes to lissome bodies incapable of fat-lady sounds. Or it is ascribed, even more disingenuously, to the auditorium, which mysteriously resonates with only half the force it did a few years back. Titles seek to compensate for another presumed defect in the contemporary receptor: an inability to acquaint himself with an opera's plot, characters, and words ahead of time. Like other handicaps, this one isn't spoken of as such, but is accepted as a natural, unchangeable state, to be rendered discreet remedial assistance. Together, the electronic megaphones and flashcards flag again the issues of engagement and distance, of what kinds of understanding are important and when, and of control over the performance encounter.

This last matter was raised to some point not long ago by *New York Times* critic Paul Griffiths.[1] I disagree with Paul Griffiths daily, but in this case I am with him all the way. Much of his column concerned itself with the problems of accuracy and tone that afflict most surtitle texts, but in good time he got to the fundamental difficulty: "... that somebody is addressing us, literally, over the characters' heads. . . The titles, flashing us news about the opera, invite us to collude in a feeling of superiority over the characters. Instead of bringing us closer to what the characters are expressing, the titles take us farther away." In a rejoinder to Griffiths' piece, Jonathan Dean (the English captions co-ordinator for the Seattle Opera), found this ". . . incomprehensible. We've all had the experience of feeling inferior when we don't understand a foreign language, but does comprehension then imply superiority?"

Well: if incomprehension makes one feel inferior, then I guess comprehension *does* imply superiority. Either you understand or you don't, you're in or you're out. But that sort of comprehension (word meanings of the denotative kind), that sort of inclusion, is not the nub of the issue, nor is it the nature of the control Griffiths was writing about. He is talking about the distance of the magnifico from the crowd—the receptor as magnifico, the performers as rabble clamoring for attention. The latter expend their precious energies and talents in pursuit of a stage life. The surtitled receptor, though, puts them on background to peruse the "captions." The function of these captions is not analogous to their use in any other form. They cannot function as they do with still photos, for when we return to the picture with our new information, it has moved on. Nor do they operate as do Brechtian signs, announcing the event of a scene, then remaining in place to remind us of it (as in the Met's *Moses und Aron*). A closer comparison is to film subtitles. They, too, draw attention from the acted life to translate verbal content, and constitute an everpresent, everchanging choice for the eye.

There is no point in questioning the practical necessity of film subtitles, but we should be aware of what we are missing. The shift of attention they require has three aspects. First, the eye must focus attention on the part of the screen that contains the caption, effectively cropping out everything else. Second, the ear must be placed on background, so that while sound effects of the more general sort (the overall mood of the music, the basic tone quality of a voice) still register, subtler varieties of inflection are only half-apprehended, and the simultaneity of vocal and bodily behaviors is shattered; instantaneous word recognition by ear is replaced by time-sequenced comprehension by eye. Third (and most important), the brain must move from a receptive, sensory mode to an active, intellectualizing one. It must move, in short, to reading, to an essentially literary experience for which the performed work is providing a more or less supportive sensory environment, and in which both eye and ear are subordinated to the higher brain function of symbol translation. Of course, we learn to do this quickly, to take in impressive amounts and miss surprisingly little. And since the significance of the missing elements will vary according to the verbal density of the script, the distraction is not always severe. There is in any case no remedy for the problem short of fluency in the language being spoken, so we accept the tradeoff: the loss of some of the beauties and meanings of sight and sounds for the gain of a rudimentary verbal understanding.

In opera, this tradeoff is far less acceptable. The beauties and meanings of sights and sounds, and their unmediated sensory reception, are of supreme importance, while the rudimentary verbal understanding is available to anyone with the slightest interest in the operatic experience, for unlike most new film or play scripts, nearly all opera libretti are easily and inexpensively obtained. Suppose, however, that we were to posit a receptor who *hasn't* the slightest interest in the operatic experience, but might be a customer for some other experience, one that more closely resembles his idea of an entertainment option? What might that idea be? Evidently, this potential customer needs to be stroked and flattered, not inspired or challenged. So we need something upscale (he's being charged good money) and painless (he can't be bothered). Since he may be threatened by classical music and made to feel inferior by a foreign language, it might be wise to help him mute the former by giving him the illusion of transcending the latter. Above all, he must be placed in the driver's seat, made to feel in charge in his accustomed unruffled and casual way, and in the presence of his accustomed technotoys. To be sure, these toys are comparatively crude (he has cooler ones in his pocket, on his belt), so his sense of superiority remains intact with respect to them, as well. He is the New Audience Magnifico—let's christen him the Nam.

The relationship between Nam and performance is much clearer at the NYCO than at the Met for two reasons: the City Opera is cultivating an audience of Nams, and its titling system is more primitive and more public than the Met's.* As a devotee, I have generally tried to ignore both titles and Nams. I have never succeeded entirely, particularly at comedies, but in recent NYCO seasons I have felt overrun by Nams, and so have for the first time attempted the Nam experience. Everyone at this party's taking the stuff and the atmosphere in the room has definitely changed; should I be the only square? So for long stretches of several performances, I tried to follow the talk of the titles, to live the life of the Nam.

The Nam cruises above the operatic engagement. He surfs it. His relationship is not so much to the performance as to the news-strip above it, from which he may glance down to the picture below, the thing-sort-of-going-on that can be zoomed in or out for occasional confirmation of what he's reading. The visual split alone is enough to short his circuits—up and down, squinting to re-focus, timing always off, continuities always out of register. But that is nothing to the muffling of the music, which burbles along below, breaking the surface now and then only to re-submerge.

Comedy is especially revelatory of any audience/performer relationship, owing to the openness of audience response. In opera, at least in this country and in my experience, this response has usually had a strained quality. Not being in on the joke, I should say, induces an even sharper feeling of inferiority than the sound of a foreign language, and more quickly. Certain comic situations and characteristics can play independent of language through sight gags and pantomime, and earn an honest response. But they are generally of the broadest sort. The richer the writing, the subtler the playing,

---

* As Griffiths observes, the Met's seatback missives are more in the nature of private communication than the NYCO's blinking proscenium billboard. They are also individually controlled.

the more tightly bound the comic and serious elements, the more elusive the experience will be for anyone not thoroughly familiar with the work or acquainted with its tongue. A perceptive audience following a fine comedy laughs selectively and holds its amusement underneath. To keep the bubble afloat, sustained attention is important. For the majority in any American audience, there is no hope of keeping up with the detail of comedic elaboration or, in opera, of recognizing the interplay between shades of verbal inflection and small points of musical emphasis that constitute wit in wordsetting.

Besides, in opera there is rarely anything funny. Comedy is hard to play, period comedy even harder, and period comedy in repertory (repeatable comedy) harder yet. Period comedy in repertory for an audience that answers to only the broadest points is an invitation to public embarrassment that is seldom declined. Frantz falling down has never been and never will be funny; Frantz falling down in twenty out of twenty-five seasons is unendurable. Count Almaviva uncovering Cherubino in the chair may be funny the first time (the musical set-up is perfect, and double-takes are among the easiest of tricks for a performer with any hint of timing); but with many repetitions it will need to be truly dexterous. In place of something funny we have things that are reputed to be funny or to have been funny once upon a time, things whose funny pictures are now being drawn by the performers.*

All this puts our audiences on the spot, and so our laughter has had a discomfited tone compounded of the inappropriately hearty (as at the boss's stale joke), the cheerlessly obligated, and the wishfully in-the-know. It's had a tentativeness, too, due in part to elementary politeness (don't make noise while the music's playing) and in part to some awareness that the music contains much delight and many clues to the comic progression—that if we *listen*, we'll come near the soul of the work.

Since the advent of surtitles, this situation has deteriorated. I first appreciated the extent of this at a Met *Don Giovanni*, during the Act I, Scene 3 quartet. There are certainly elements of the comic—even of the ridiculous—in this sequence. But there is also a perilous game being played beneath its punctilious social observance, and an undercurrent of suspense which finally finds outlet in the ominous double-bass-and-cello entrance that launches the accompanied recitative wherein Anna tells Ottavio she has recognized her father's murderer. This is one of the most commented-upon recitatives in all opera. As usual in the Mozart/Da Ponte operas, the scene preceding

---

* The artistic benefit that was, preposterously, prophesied for surtitles—the performers would no longer have to resort to gestural illustration, to mugging and winking, to make the audience understand—has of course not materialized. On the contrary, the same devices now compete with the titles.

it leads us there in a series of playful and innocent steps—we don't know where we're going till we're suddenly there.

In American performances, the scene has always contained two reliable laughs. The first is at Elvira's re-entrance (*"Ah, ti ritrovo ancor, perfido mostro!"*)* The second is on Giovanni's line, *"La povera ragazza è pazza, amici miei."*† Elvira's moment, often wrecked by soprano posturing and/or pantomimed appeals to the audience by the Don, nonetheless contains genuine situational humor. Elvira, having just snatched Zerlina from her fate worse than death, returns to find the Don professing courtly obeisance to Anna. The moment is intensified by our awareness of Elvira's mission to disrupt all of Giovanni's schemes with women and her desire to have him back. And it is nailed down by a bit of verbal wit: Giovanni's recitative protestations to Anna, elaborate but in prose, are finished off as a rhymed couplet by Elvira (*"del viver vostro"*. . . *"perfido mostro"*). Her unexpected re-appearance is also a punch line. The brief solo with which Elvira now opens the quartet (*"Non ti fidar, o misera"*)—firm, calm, and orderly, anything but *pazza*, is the turning-point of the scene, for with it she plants the first suspicion in Anna and Ottavio. The quartet's suspense lies with the question of whether or not Anna will recognize the truth the audience already knows. If honestly played and intelligently received, the Don's line might earn a grim chuckle or a disturbed murmur, but not an outright laugh. And a laugh at this juncture is all the more inappropriate because, whereas Elvira's line steps on the end of a recitative, the Don's is a fragment of a developing set piece: real music is happening, telling us things about the Don's strategies and the progress of the scene. The line usually gets a laugh, though, because the Don usually takes extraordinary measures to secure one, exploding his "p" on *"pazza,"* circling his ear with his finger (I've seen it), or stepping right out of the scene to pop the word into the house. Or all three. I didn't notice what this one (Thomas Hampson) did, because as he sang the syllables *"La po—,"* I was startled by a lusty roar from the house: HAHAHA. The word *"pazza"* had not yet been sung, and whatever behavior that went with it for any of the characters had not yet occurred, but the Nams in the audience had read their joke and taken the moment away from everyone, onstage and off.

In Act II, Scene 1 of *Falstaff* Ford, disguised as Mister Brook, offers Falstaff a filled purse as inducement to seduce Ford's wife, Alice. Falstaff, at once wary and constrained by his remembered manners, stares at the sack for a moment, then says: *"Prima di tutti, senza complimenti, messere . . . accetto il*

---

* "Ah, I find you once more, wicked monster!"

† "The poor girl's crazy, my friends."

sacco."* Verdi writes the timing right into his setting—formal and grand at the opening, then a rush after the pause as Falstaff plucks his prey—and any competent singing-actor can score a nice passing point with it. At City Opera Mark Delavan, like Hampson with his "*povera ragazza*," got as far as "*prima di-*" HAHAHA. First the laugh, then the gag; first the effect, then the cause.

Performance in English brings no surcease. Titles are still deemed necessary. At the NYCO's presentation of *Central Park*, the audience yukked from the start at some feeble Wendy Wasserstein one-liners despite the fact that we were ten or twelve minutes into the first piece (*Festival of Regrets*) before Margaret Lloyd entered and uttered the first comprehensible line. We translate from our own language to cadge ill-timed laughs for tired jokes. The very premise of direct communication by musical-theatrical means is dispensed with.

These are not isolated anecdotes. The playing of operatic comedy is now regularly conditioned by this eerie separation between what much of the audience is following and what is actually taking place on the stage and in the music.† It's the last step in shaping receptors into a participant studio audience—but the wretch with the cue cards holds them up too soon. If anything comic were to occur onstage, the reader would either receive it out of synch with its verbal part, or miss it altogether. In none of these cases did anything comic in fact take place, so the disconnection was complete: laughter at the wrong time at the mere idea of something amusing, an instruction about something that would be funny if funnily done—but it wasn't.

To a devotee the Nam state is intolerable, for he knows the potential of the engagement and understands that there is no way to harvest it under these conditions. He is apt to assume that no sane person can feel otherwise. But that is clearly not the case. The Nam is simply re-creating his habitual

---

* "First of all, without formalities, good sir . . . I accept the sack."

† And not only comedy, unfortunately. Another point made by Griffiths is that even when surtitles are well done, the contrast between their flat, condensed quality and the extravagance of operatic action (to say nothing of the music) creates its own comedy, incongruous and reductive. To cite one instance: every melodramatic turn of plot in *Simon Boccanegra* (there are several) occasions audible amusement from the Met's entitled audience. And another: Ford's "*È sogno? O realtà?*" in the Met's *Falstaff*. The centrality of this monologue is evident (it is the most highly elaborated solo in the score, and the only one whose ending invites applause in conventional aria manner), and there is nothing faintly comic about it—it is a portrait of raging male sexual paranoia, whose jagged outbursts and semi-coherent mutterings tell us that the pranks could turn ugly at any moment. It got three major laughs, the loudest of which buried the powerful ascending line to the upper G-flat at "*Due rami enormi crescon sulla mia testa!*"—the line that sets up the whole piece. This is laughter that comes from outside any possible experience of the music, and from above and beyond the character—presumptuous and emotionally impervious, like most Nam response. It could not occur without subtitle invitation.

arrangement with audiovisual infotainment gadgets: click, zoom, extract the wanted information, surf on by anything that doesn't fit the mood, maintain multi-tasking mastery, and stay tuned to classical easy listening. It is true that he has no idea of what it means to enter The Work, or the intensity of experience available in there. But he has his own set of expectations and evaluations, and can enjoy himself to the extent that they are met. At *Falstaff*, two thirtysomething, casual-smart, good-natured men sat behind me. They laughed, clapped, and commented on the story being told by the titles, and did fairly well at keeping track of the major sight gags. "Oh, no!" sang out one near the end of Act II. "They're gonna dump him out the window!" And the other: "That's the river!" As it happened, the lid on the hamper wouldn't open, so the big curtain gag fizzled ignominiously. Laughter, all the same.

I can say these fellows didn't have a clue about the opera *Falstaff*, or about the nature of any opera. I can say they were unmannerly. And I can say that I itched for the ejector button that would launch them back through the roof and into the Lincoln Plaza fountain. What I can't say is that they weren't having some sort of good time. So, perhaps, were the *Giovanni* revelers and the Wasserstein yukkers. But God help anyone trying to follow Da Ponte's scene through Mozart's music, or the interchange among characters through the inflections of the performers, or the way the singers met the vocal challenges. God help anyone hoping to experience the exalting emotional content of the music Verdi wrote in *Boccanegra* for his father/daughter recognition, or the disclosure of Paolo's villainy, or Fiesco's belated discovery—to follow a great, solemn drama in music, not a silly story in captions.

The studio audience is learning quickly. The laughter at *Central Park*, in particular, was laugh-track laughter, in sharp, mechanical bursts with sudden cut-offs. I don't know what sort of good time it may represent, but all the possibilities I can think of are depressing.

The acoustical enhancement installed at the New York State Theatre has not so far had an impact on engagement equivalent to that of surtitles. Its benefits—if any—have been hard to discern, while certain drawbacks have been easy to spot, so its principal effect has been to engender a state of nervous alertness, suspicion, and bafflement in anyone who cares about the quality and integrity of operatic performance. Like the term itself, though, some of enhancement's effects enter by stealth on both sides of what used to be the footlights, and in opera, its transformative potential is far greater than that of any eye device.

The reason that proponents of this measure feel justified in calling it "enhancement" is that if it works properly, it appears to leave intact the relative loudness levels of sound sources. It is a fixed system ("electronic architecture" is another of its aliases) that, once in place, operates on the rising-tide-lifts-all-boats theory.[2] But it is still amplification. It still reinforces sounds electronically, picking them up with microphones and transmitting them through loudspeakers, passing them through an amplification stage en route. Acoustics are acoustics, electricity is electricity.

Theatre amplification is still young. Its use in boosting the general sound level of a performance (as opposed to its employment for sound effects) is less than fifty years old. Nearly all the "classic" works of American musical theatre (both popular and operatic—a number will be discussed in the next chapter) were written for acoustical performance, and originally presented that way. The theatres that housed them did not change, though some vanished. They no more required amplification in 1970 than they had in 1950. Yet they got it.

Many reasons are advanced for this change. It isn't my present purpose to adjudicate them or to sort the artistic from the economic, except to note that they are complex and that their underlying assumptions are well worth questioning. The most obvious—that the mere availability of a technology creates a pressure to use it in all practicable circumstances, whether appropriate or not—seldom enters the discussion. Others, whatever their merits may have been in the commercial theatre, are not germane to the situation at the City Opera. These would include the wish to introduce new musical styles (rock and its derivatives) that are inherently electronic;* the wish to build larger theatres without paying much attention to the acoustics (like the Uris/Gershwin, the Minskoff, the Marquis, the Ford); and the wish to employ orchestral arrangements dominated by brass, heavy reed, and percussion instruments (or, latterly, their synthesized equivalents) with which no voice can compete. These factors unquestionably accelerated the transition to amplified sound. But they did not cause it, because its first uses antedated them. And those uses arose from one last wish: for the freedom to cast performers with undeveloped singing (or even speaking) voices in important roles and, as corollary, to downsize instrumental and vocal ensembles, filling the latter with the now-familiar "triple-threat" performer, whose voice is seldom his principal threat.

Amplification fulfills these wishes. Sounds that would not of their own nature be audible under prevailing acoustic conditions can be made audible, while those that would be audible but weak can be made strong, and those

---

* Electronic composition has of course been experimented with in opera. But it has not, to date, generated works that demand acceptance into the repertory.

that would lose in competition with others can be reinforced and given their desired place in the texture. When these gains are combined with the economic advantages of amplification, it is not surprising that it made rapid headway in our commercial theatre, first for musicals (for which it has become the norm), and more recently for many plays. It has troublesome consequences, though, and on Broadway these were evident from the start. The first is that the quality of the sound is changed, in ways that are often artistically undesirable: for most kinds of music, edginess and distortion, poor balance and distribution, are not considered improvements. The second is that an eye/ear detachment occurs. It takes two forms, geographic and energetic. In the first, location is off; sound does not seem to originate with the performer. In the second, sound carries in a manner unjustified by its tonal properties or by visible performer effort. In both forms, the receptor is asked to leap a belief barrier of the most primitive kind—an eye/ear contradiction. He is asked to bear witness to a miracle of sorts, a magical transcendence of space. But to be deemed authentic, even a miracle requires the testimony of sensory evidence: I saw with my own eyes, heard with my own ears, and so I believe. If my eyes tell me one thing and my ears another, I don't.

Because of these consequences, which strike at the heart of the operatic engagement compact and carry the stigma of artistic betrayal, operatic institutions have been reluctant to adopt amplification. They have waited for technical advances to improve sound quality and overcome the location problem. They have waited for amplification to not sound like amplification, to reach a state of refinement best demonstrated locally by the Lincoln Center Theatre's revival of *Carousel* (1994), which overcame an acoustically unfortunate space (the Vivian Beaumont) and the lack of "legit" voices on the male side without distortion or displacement, without a detectable evening-out among stronger or weaker voices, without upsetting balances, and without any sense of manipulation or highlighting.[3]

It cannot be denied that the New York State Theatre has been acoustically peculiar from the start. Its first operatic evening (Rossini's *Cinderella* by the Metropolitan Opera National Company, Nov. 3, 1965) occasioned many complaints and donnish devotee jokes, and the company resorted to amplification later in its run. At the City Opera's Lincoln Center opening night (Ginastera's *Don Rodrigo*, Feb. 22, 1966), certain frequencies from stage and pit (the piece also featured antiphonal brass from the balconies) seemed to emanate from points midway up the proscenium, left and right, like early ping-pong stereo. Since mikes had already been used in the theatre, some of us were suspicious.

Such artifacts came and went subsequently, and no one ever professed real satisfaction with the hall's sound, but the issue faded for a couple of decades. Acoustical tweaking effected slight improvements in resonance and distribution. With so many possible causative factors involved (scoring combinations, orchestral seating, stage position, seat location, set designs and materials), the occasional rumors of discreet electronic boosting were impossible to verify short of an industrial spying operation. The crude noises-off amplification attempted from time to time at the Met (from the Boogie-Man mess that has disfigured the Act III Dutchman's Crew chorus in *Fliegende Holländer* since the 1960s to the impenetrable sonic mud that represents a distant uprising in the *Giulio Cesare* of the '90s, or the boomy reverb for Aegisth's murder in the *Elektra* of the aughts) and at the City Opera (such as the miking of the off-stage choruses in *Dr. Faust*, which dashed any hope that this music might make its points), not to mention the ongoing example of Broadway, left no reason to suppose that anything elegant might be going on.*

I cite this history by way of acknowledgement that the State Theatre is a tough room to play. But like the older Broadway theatres, it is the same room it has always been—a little better, in fact. And the primary reason the issue of acoustics moved to the back burner is that when the City Opera moved into the house, with substantially the same company that had been playing the City Center (itself no acoustical paradigm), it became apparent that the house, though far from ideal, was perfectly playable.

A listing of principal artists of the New York City Opera for one season to either side of its move to Lincoln Center (1965-67) would include sopranos Beverly Sills, Patricia Brooks, Anne Elgar, Rita Shane, Elizabeth Carron, Joan Patenaude, Donna Jeffrey, Ellen Faull, Patricia Neway, Brenda Lewis, Jeannine Crader, and Eileen Schauler; mezzo-sopranos and contraltos Beverly Evans, Frances Bible, Claramae Turner, Ruth Kobart, Beverly Wolff, Tatiana Troyanos, and Maureen Forrester; tenors Placido Domingo, Michele Molese, Jon Crain, Richard Cassilly, Enrico di Giuseppe, and John Alexander; baritones John Reardon, Dominic Cossa, Richard Fredricks, David Clatworthy, Sherrill Milnes, Walter Cassel, Chester Ludgin, and William Chapman; bass-baritones and basses Norman Treigle, Donald Gramm, Thomas Paul, Spiro Malas, Herbert Beattie, Ara Berberian, and Malcolm Smith.[4]

This is not a complete roster. It includes only those singers I heard repeatedly, in principal roles, in more than one house, in similar vocal estate. In

---

* Rumors of unacknowledged amplification at the Met, usually involving specific singers, are very persistent. But in the absence of company confirmation or journalistic exposé, they must be left in the hearsay category.

some cases (e.g., Milnes, Cassel, Domingo) I heard these voices in all four New York opera houses of the era (the old and new Mets, the City Center and State Theatre); in many others, in two or three of them, plus other venues. All other artistic strengths and weaknesses aside, these singers (and most of their colleagues, including supporting artists) penetrated the orchestra and reached the seats of the State Theatre with operatically satisfying tone—of some richness and body, and of weight appropriate to the roles they undertook. While their voices often sounded marginally better in other halls (Domingo's and Milnes', for instance, took on more bloom at the Met), there was no essential difference in their quality or impact from one theatre to another, and audibility was never an issue. If it's an issue now, the cause is not the house. It's the singers.

In addition to its difficulties with the auditorium, the company advances as an argument for amplification its wish to present works from the pre- and post-Romantic repertories that are best appreciated in a less-than-grand-opera setting. This point has some merit. Many fine pieces do not belong in a large house, and many others, performable there, reveal themselves differently in more intimate surroundings. For over a century, New York's clearest operatic need has been an acoustically warm theatre with a decent pit and good stage facilities for just this purpose. Still, the works themselves are not in most cases the limitation, nor even those works in this house. Handel's *Giulio Cesare* did not prove a problem in 1967, and neither did Monteverdi's *Il Ritorno d'Ulisse in Patria* in 1976, and both productions were extremely successful with the public. Despite its chamber orchestration and children's roles, Britten's *Turn of the Screw* has worked powerfully, unenhanced, in both the company's homes. The operas themselves are not the issue, but rather the wish to perform them according to a particular aesthetic currently in fashion, with singers that suit a particular taste. That may indeed be unrealistic, but the suiting of a work's mode of presentation to the performing space available has always been one of the producer's basic responsibilities. If you want to do the work, find the singers; if you don't have the singers, don't do the work.[5]

Since the amplification system's installation, performance at the City Opera has proceeded through long stretches without incident, orchestral timbres and balances not definably altered, and voices familiar from pre-enhancement performances or from other halls seeming more or less themselves in quality and loudness. Most of the time, live opera has still sounded like live opera. But not all the time. The standard set by *Carousel* has not been met, and when problems have intruded they have taken several forms:

Peaking. This is not breakup or overload distortion of the traditional hi-fi sort, but the occasional crossing of a threshold by solo and choral voices, creating a boomy aura around the sound, often for just a single note. Several of Delavan's top notes in *Falstaff* triggered this effect, as did some of Kishna Davis' high notes in *Porgy*, and choral climaxes in the same piece. These were clearly "unnatural" moments. While this peaking is less bothersome on the ground floor than in the upper tiers, Delavan hit it again, even from an orchestra seat, in the generally low-lying role of Tabor in *Baby Doe*. As is always the case with amplification, the voices of larger format (the ones with the most potential for authentic excitement) are the most heavily penalized. On Broadway this is accomplished out front by monitoring and mixing, squeezing the real voices down while puffing the non-voices up. Here, the bigger voices are just made to sound weird and unpredictable at infrequent but crucial junctures. At this level, the old City Opera roster would have blown the system half the time.

Equalizing and flattening. This is easy to sense for anyone with a good basis for comparison, but hard to describe. I encountered it first at *La Clemenza di Tito*, whose closing ensemble was unlike anything I'd ever heard, loud but unfulfilling, with a glassy sheen and an improbable evenness of distribution around its stage space. Similar phenomena cropped up at *La Bohème*. In the Act II ensemble the decibels seemed to be there, but not the satisfaction of voices and instruments filling the hall; it was very odd. There was again a strange spatial smoothing-out: although the voices were connected to the bodies, positioning to either side of the stage, and more particularly upstage or down, somehow made no difference—the acoustic was flattened into two dimensions. In the *Tito* finale the sound, though not one that would normally be associated with a stage of any depth, at least had some eye confirmation, with the performers strung out in a vaudeville line. In *Bohème* it was bothersome in Act II, and ruinous in Act I. Voices off right or left, from the rear or below, all registered the same, and the Bohemians' lines from the bottom of the stairs or the street, Mimì's lines outside the door, and the melting away of Marcello's "*Trovò la poesia*" under the opening of "*O soave fanciulla*" (one of Puccini's most fragrant little moments) completely lost their effect.

According to a diagram of the amplification system published by the *New York Times*,[6] a number of speakers are actually in the stage area, presumably to help the singers hear the orchestra. (Difficulty hearing from the stage is another recently diagnosed performance ailment for which treatment is suddenly available.) I don't know whether these speakers transmit only orchestra sound or a mix of stage and pit sound; the latter would surely help to account for this solid-color-painting impression. Another first in my experience was the sound of falling snow at the ends of Acts I and III (do you recall the music's mood?): it slapped on the deck like hail on a creosote roof.

Coasting. I can't prove coasting's happening, but I believe it is. And if it's not happening yet, it will be soon. For I am certain of this: Musicians are in continuous, interactive contact with their acoustical environment, and are affected by sound levels during performance. In the case of a singer, the loop that runs from what is sung to what is heard to what is sung next is entirely internal, an afferent/efferent circuit that literally incorporates the instrument. The singer monitors the sound and calculates energy requirements accordingly. Differences in impact may be considerable, but under most performance circumstances the singer's adjustments are relatively subtle, and the monitoring goes on at a subliminal level. By trusting the "feel" of their singing, experienced artists learn to minimize the range of adjustment to maintain consistent, economical function. But the loop is always in operation, and always has some effect on singers' projective efforts.

When musicians hear themselves well, they tend to let up a bit. They shouldn't, they don't mean to, a few of the best don't. But the tendency is there, especially with singers and players who might have to go past their level of comfort or endurance to sustain the desired sonic presence. Thus, coasting is to be expected as a byproduct of "enhancement;" indeed, it is almost the point. The orchestra's too small for the score—never mind, it's enhanced. The singer's voice is too light for the role, the technique too fragile—but no need to force!

I first came to believe in enhancement-induced coasting at the very same Nam-infested *Falstaff* referred to above. It was at that performance that I first had the perception, beginning as a suspicion and ending as a conviction, of something different from the sort of dull, underdone run-through we put down as just another off-night. The orchestra, smaller than we'd really want for this work in this hall, played along casually, never sharp or zestful, never digging in, never alert to dramatic situations or seemingly even mindful of them. Except for the Falstaff and Pistol every singer was, as the English put it, overparted: The Mistress Ford (Amy Burton, a nice singer with a secure technique) would have been well cast as Nannetta, but that role went to a voice too light for the house and, at least on this evening, precarious at the top. The Meg disappeared altogether, the Quickly had a mushy middle voice and unreliable top, the Ford showed a pleasant, narrow baritone of roughly the right sort but small-sized, and the Fenton a tenor with a bland, grainy middle and an upper voice that could not withstand even the pressure that would produce a clear leggiero resonance. Collectively, they chirped and pecked at the music. Yet I could not call the performance sloppy or musically inattentive. It was above all comfortable, as if unaware of its inadequacy. From neither stage nor pit came any sign of response to a "down" night—only an unearned sense of ease. These were pros who believed they had things well in hand, and weren't about to force or push.

I received much the same impression from parts of *Bohème* (also very lightly cast) and *Baby Doe*. But of course, once one is alert to the possibility, one begins to anticipate it. Many factors affect a receptor's impression of a performance's commitment and energy, and there is no way to compare an amplified performance with its unamplified self, or with what it might have been without performers' and receptors' awareness that "enhancement" is in place. Would the *Falstaff* have been equally featureless quite on its own merits? I can't rule it out. Did Act II of *Bohème*, the slackest I've ever encountered, get that way in part because of amplification? I think so, but truly, it's anyone's guess. Would Delavan have sung through the role of Tabor with the same smooth prettiness and softness of attack, the same lack of drive and toughness, without electronic assistance? I don't know. In fact, I don't know for sure that he didn't, for the City Opera now admits that its sound system isn't always left strictly alone, that it isn't always even on.[7] In short, we don't know what we're hearing—not just critics or others professionally interested, but anyone alive to music and its effect, to artistic communication, to the non-virtuality of live performance, or simply to the honest labeling and packaging of a consumer product. That should be the cue for an old-fashioned theatre riot, followed by sustained boycott.[8]

NOTES

1. *NYT,* Nov. 1, 1999.

2. For a description of the State Theatre's system, see: Tommasini, Anthony: "Meddling With Opera's Sacred Human Voice," *NYT,* Aug. 3, 1999. And further: Tommasini, Anthony: "Enhancing Sound in a Hush-Hush Way," *NYT,* Aug. 18, 1999. And finally: Tommasini, Anthony: "Visionary of the Opera Inspires a Turnaround," *NYT,* May 16, 2000.

3. The *Carousel* production was directed by Nicholas Hytner, with musical direction by Eric Stern and sound design by Steve Canyon Kennedy. The care and taste of their work is highlighted by comparison with other musical productions in the Beaumont—the aggressively orchestrated and amplified *Anything Goes* (1987, antedating the existence of the theatre's pit and thus necessitating an onstage orchestra) and *Parade* (1998), which used the pit but returned us to the worst sort of pumped, dislocated Broadway sound.

4. For readers interested in the vocal level of the NYCO during the 1950s and '60s, there are recordings. I would especially recommend three: Moore's *Ballad of Baby Doe* (Sills, Bible, Cassel, Joshua Hecht); Ward's *The Crucible* (Bible, Brooks, Ludgin, John Macurdy); and Handel's *Giulio Cesare* (Sills, Wolff, Forrester, Treigle, Cossa, Malas). Further NYCO recordings of that era: Moore's *Carry Nation,* Blitzstein's *Regina,* Beeson's *Lizzie Borden,* Ginastera's *Bomarzo* (a City Opera production, despite its Washington premiere). The City Opera principals that made Floyd's *Susannah* go (Phyllis Curtin, Treigle, Cassilly, Keith Kaldenberg) are together in fine form in a 1966 New Orleans performance on the VAI label. Original-cast recordings of Menotti's *The Consul, Saint of Bleecker Street,* and *Maria Golovin* included NYCO regulars Patricia Neway, Gloria Lane, Cornell MacNeil, Leon Lishner, David Poleri, Richard Cross, and William Chapman—yes, all on Broadway—and the first complete *Porgy and Bess* stars Camilla Williams and Lawrence Winters. Archival digging will turn up many more groupings and individual performances, and of course the international stars—Sills, Domingo, Milnes—recorded extensively, though only their earliest records represent their City Opera form. Many of the company's important artists recorded little or not at all. Records are deceptive with respect to vocal format. But I think the overall difference in size, richness, timbral individuality, and vocal personality between these singers and those of the present roster will be apparent to any listener. For further observations, see the chapters on singing, acting, and the rhetorics in Part IV.

5. The problem of these singers in this house is related to the more general one of the availability of able-bodied singers at all professional levels. It is also much involved with the City Opera's production-sharing arrangements, chiefly with Glimmerglass Opera. These arrangements mitigate some of the company's production problems, and the fact that these are largely economic and logistic does not mean that they aren't real and serious. For a fair summary of the company's perception of the matter, see Tommasini's extended interview with its director, Paul Kellogg (*NYT,* May 16, 2000). I will return to these questions later. My only concern here is that artistic issues be seen for what they are.

6. See Tommasini, *NYT,* Aug. 3, 1999.

7. See Tommasini, *NYT,* May 16, 2000.

8. Subsequent performances (*Mikado* from orchestra front, *Capuleti e i Montecchi* and *Fliegende Holländer* from the Second Tier, fall of 2001; and *Don Giovanni* Act I from the Second Tier, spring of 2002) have displayed the same artifacts and settled none of the questions. At the Bellini and Wagner performances I was encouraged to find little evidence of coasting, and peaking seemed to have resolved into an intermittent rim around the sound. But at the *Don Giovanni*, an edgy boominess on the male low voices was very unpleasant in Scene 1. Then it settled down, I don't know why. Even with my previous experiences, I was stunned by the title-fed boorishness of the audience—an ongoing uproar of chatter, laughter like ack-ack, and general unsettlement, right through arias and ensembles. Occasional reference to the titles revealed a rib-nudging panhandle for laughs (Leporello's "*No, tutto va male!*": "No, everything stinks!"). According to Anne Midgette's review of *Agrippina* ten days later (*NYT*, Apr. 9, 2002), the titles summed up the characters' fates with updates in the style popularized by *American Graffiti*, and "the final words of the optimistic Long Live Rome chorus were drowned out by the audience's hearty laughter."

4

HERE AND NOW

(Mar. 1998–Mar. 2000)

Treacherous terrain, the here and now. Time and again we set out across it, curious and stubbornly openminded. We feel out the engagement for minor adhesions that tell us something is going to cling, or a faint pulsing that confirms life inside us, the possibility of growth. And often we find something. But it is seldom enough to banish, even temporarily, the hunch that Liù's demise was also opera's or (at the farthest stretch) that opera's dying reflection was left in the Countess' mirror at the close of *Capriccio*. If all that was opera, what has followed is not. Something went off in the lab, and odd life forms are about.

And the conditions for life are forbidding. In opera, we haven't merely a canon. We have a repertory, and the repertory is sustained by its institutions, with their needs for repeatable works and repeator receptors. We like to think the repertory is infinitely expandable, that it has room for untold riches. But this is not so. Performance venues are limited in number and capacity, and bound by economic factors. Their administrators must choose one work instead of another, instead of a hundred others. Everything is in place of something else. The canon is ever-present, and comparison with it is not merely implied but asserted and re-asserted, because that is one of the things performance does, especially in a repertory context. The canon's standard is by no means unfair (it did not descend with Moses from the Mount, but was sweated into being by quite mortal operawrights), but it is intimidating.

For the receptor, too, everything is in place of something else and each choice is instead of another, a hundred others. Life contains only so many years, weeks, evenings, and attention is finite. Each engagement has its uses and limits. Each receptor must decide how much of himself to allot to this or that. In trade parlance, the receptor is called a consumer. Nothing could be more inaccurate. It is true that the institutions of opera have customers. But it is upside-down to think of the devotee as a consumer, even in his customer transactions. He does not consume the opera company, the record conglomerate. It consumes him. It consumes his time and money, his energies of body and mind and heart, to say nothing of the vast inner territories occupied by the collected Works, by the tapestry that is never finished. And even these are finite, though we have not learned to measure them.

His status as a customer notwithstanding, the devotee does not approach the performance engagement in search of anything so insignificant as a product or service, a "consumable." He approaches it to participate in The Work, and The Work can only grow thereby. Each engagement is an accretion to it, not a consumption of it. The devotee seeks to give himself over to The Work, to be consumed by it, because he derives nourishment from it. But he gains this nourishment without consuming a morsel. He *is* the morsel. Art has its own Book of Miracles.

Items of operatic custom (tickets, recordings, scores) are entry passes into a realm. But they are temporary and, in a sense, revocable, for an engagement can refuse to yield the expected nourishment, and nothing is more disappointing than a Promised Land without milk and honey. Because of this, and because everything is in place of something else, unfamiliar works bear a heavy burden of proof, and as we encounter them we ask if they are repeatable, if we are willing to be consumed by them in large portion—in short, if they are candidates for the repertory. If not, they aren't merely off someone's Great Books list like literary works, or excluded from some department's curriculum. They're off the shelf altogether and not to be found. And so a special anxiety attends the introduction of a work into a repertory institution.

During the period under discussion here, four 20th-Century operas were presented for the first time at the Metropolitan Opera House. One, John Harbison's *The Great Gatsby*, was actually a new piece, receiving its world premiere (December 20, 1999). Another, Sergei Prokofiev's *Betrothal in a Monastery* (1940), was a Maryinsky production. The remaining two were new/old works with contrasting claims to attention: Arnold Schoenberg's *Moses und Aron* (1932 or never, depending on your view of its unfinished state) and Carlisle Floyd's *Susannah* (1955). This pair's short and simple story—at least in the U.S.—is that the former is of high critical reputation though seldom produced, the latter of modest repute but often produced. Taken together, as at the Met, they embrace an odd polarity according to which the canon and the repertory seem mutually exclusive.

A century has passed since Arnold Schoenberg began to move away from the early practices found in pieces like the *Gurrelieder, Verklärte Nacht*, or the downright *gemütlich* unnumbered D-Major Quartet (which would charm any Dvořákian), and eighty years have gone since he proposed his "method of composing with twelve tones that are related only to one another" as a new basis for generating musical structures. As has been the case with so many 20th-Century master artists (and no musical professional doubts that Schoenberg was a master), he has found fierce and influential champions. The victory of the non-tonal musics has been declared periodically but rather emptily, for these idioms have never found broad acceptance. For the general musical public—and certainly for the operatic portion thereof—Schoenberg's "mature" music has remained in question, not just as a matter of temperamental preference or political stance, but for its very validity as artistic expression. With recent turns in other compositional directions, the banishment of serialism and other non-tonal procedures is now proclaimed. But this is vacuous, too: Schoenberg's music will survive, though there is still little evidence of any wide accommodation to it. Even in the context of the now-familiar division between "advanced" art and the general understanding, it's an unusual case.

The debate about Schoenberg's later music concerns the relationship between its emotional content and its intellectual argument—"feeling" and "thought"— and whether or not the nature of twelve-tone technique in itself (or of post-tonal writing in general) separates one from the other, usually at the expense of "feeling." Schoenberg himself addressed the question (see his essay *Heart and Brain in Music*), and it remains alive among thoughtful, non-doctrinaire musicians.[1]

For me, the issue is not whether Schoenberg's music does or doesn't, should or shouldn't, "contain" feeling—or thought. I'm in favor of both. But feeling and thinking are done by people; they aren't "in" the music. And since "feeling" and "thought" are very broad terms, the questions become: which feelings? Which thoughts? What emotional and intellectual places does Schoenberg guide me to, and what meaning can I derive from being there? What is the relationship between engagement and distance in the encounter? And I am fairly certain of this: it is impossible to feel intensely and think straight at the same time. Scraps of feeling and thought may fly about together in a vague, free-association manner. But to give in to deep feeling, or to organize a coherent thought, a choice must be made. My preference is to feel intensely during the encounter, and try to think straight afterward. If the former process doesn't occur, the latter one will be barren. The reverse is unworkable altogether.

When I hear music of the "mature" Schoenberg (the third and fourth string quartets, or the Piano Concerto, Op. 42, would be good examples), I am certainly aware of intensity in the writing, of gestures and structures that suggest emotional behavior. The music is highly volatile. Episodes are brief, and change direction and color quickly and often violently, jerking their affects along with them. The difficulty is that while I hear these things and recognize them as instructions for emotional response, the feelings they signal belong to someone else. I can tell that this other person is having a complicated and often rather terrible time, and I am there for him, so to speak, but my empathy is of an obligated sort. The predicament is *interesting*; I examine it and reflect upon it. While I don't mind being in this place from time to time, and concede that it evokes a category of human experience, the emotional life of the music seldom meshes with my own.

Schoenberg said that he believed the principal obstacle to acceptance of his music was not serialism per se, but the thematic density of his writing, the profusion of "aphoristic" (Schoenberg's term) ideas in the music. This begs the question, I think. It seeks to deny that while according to a theoretical logic serialism may be represented as a continuation of previous harmonic language, in sensorily immediate terms it is a radical break from it. A profusion of aphoristic themes with some reference to tonality (however chromatic or modal, however fleeting—think of the Scherzo of Mahler's Fifth, for example, or of *Pelléas*, or for that matter the *Falstaff* of Verdi) is different from a profusion with none, and it is surely this difference, in combination with the music's departure from recognizable forms of such rhetorical devices as repetition and variation, that leaves many listeners stranded. Retrograde inversions of tone rows, user-friendly as they may become to performers of the music or to harmonic analysts, do not leap to even an accustomed ear in quite the same way.

My experience of *Moses und Aron* since my first live exposure to it (the Boston Opera Company in late 1966, its American premiere production) has been of the Platonic sort described above. I feel excited involvement with it as metaphor, before and after the fact, but only an alert, detached interest during actual performance. As idea-piece, thought-piece—concept—the Work is a true monument. But it is not on concept that its theatrical life depends. For that, it must answer the same questions asked of any opera, however high or low its aspiration: how well does its music serve the demands of character and action, of the progression of theatrical scenes, and of expression through singingacting? Can it be satisfactorily realized in performance?

I still don't know the answers to these questions. The Met's production did not fail for lack of effort or skill. In thoroughness of preparation and sharpness of execution, it represented the highest level of professionalism, and that must never be undervalued. Interpretively, though, it was ingeniously removed from anything that might give the opera a fighting chance at dramatic life.

The "ingeniously" is not merely snide. Graham Vick, the production's director, is a brilliant visual entertainer on the grand scale.* His *Lady Macbeth of Mzensk* for the Met (a kind of production I ordinarily resist—updated, technologically exhibitionistic, postmodernly emblemized) was still grounded in the lives of its characters, friendly to the fine acting of its principals, and aware of the piece's stylistic inconsistencies as opportunities rather than as obstacles. As seen on video, his Maryinsky staging of *War and Peace* (note that we're speaking of notoriously problematic operas) actually pulls together the work's second half into a powerful, coherent act. But in *Moses und Aron*, Vick's theatrical sophistication leads into a stylistic *cul de sac*. Among the work's many needs, increased distance would be last on the list.

The agon of the brothers is the through-line of *Moses und Aron*. It is clearly set forth in Scene Two, but for it to spring to life Moses must first descend from Mt. Horeb filled to bursting with his Call. That is the event of Scene One. If we don't believe in Moses' belief, share in his life-or-death investment in the *necessity* of his mind-altering new idea of a single God who is "eternal, omnipotent, imperceptible and inconceivable," nothing in the work will make dramatic sense.

This opening scene is hard. It is brief but slowly paced, and subdued until its last few pages. It makes immediate demands and offers no concessions. Its principal playable element is Moses' resistance to his Call, and he must play that against offstage voices. The scene also presents musical usages that can prove troublesome, and these do not end with the score's "pantonal" harmonic and melodic devices. Against open, transparent textures, Moses declaims his *Sprechstimme* in regularized rhythms, one syllable per note, predominantly eighth notes, often in triplets or quintuplets, with an occasional dot or tie by way of nuance. The indicated "line readings" are predictable enough according to normal spoken inflection, but are stretched all the way through the bass-baritone singing range by the suggested pitches, so that the utterance is not "natural" as either speech or song. The Voice from the Burning Bush is taken by a speaking chorus whose treble includes boys' voices, but the same text (the words of God) is also sung by six solo voices from the pit.

In Scene Two Moses, having reluctantly accepted his Call and the designation of Aron as his spokesperson, traverses the wasteland. Here (true to God's

---

* Can be, at least. The case of his *Il Trovatore* will be taken up later.

word) he encounters Aron, who already knows what their meeting is to be about. The tension in their bond is immediately apparent. Aron descants fulsomely on the oneliness of God (it solves the messy problem of all those other gods, with their potentially different points of view) and Israel's imminent deliverance. But scarcely is a thought out of his songful mouth before Moses jumps in to correct him with his spokesong wordnotes. ("*Gn—*", sings Aron, and Moses is already there to make sure he knows what "*Gnade*"—grace— is about.) God's oneliness, eternalness, and omnipotence are all right with Aron, but he's not so sure about the rest of it. In a bar of recitative whose held rests must be determined by actor's timing, Aron sings: "Invisible." (Pause.) "Inconceivable." (Pause.) Now in tempo: "Folk chosen by the only God," (slowing down) "can you love what you dare not conceive?" "DARE?" answers Moses, dragging his unsinging voice slowly and loudly up the seventh from low D to middle C-sharp. And Moses begins a monotone chant of his adjectives—trust me, He is that He is. Aron never does buy it. The brothers are united in mission but separate in vision. Like summit politicians who have agreed on little but must now issue their joint communiqué, Moses and Aron go forth to carry their message to the people.

Here is what Vick and his designer, Paul Brown, showed us in these opening scenes:

Scene One: Moses, semirecumbent on the side of a triangle that is meant to read as "mountain" in the system of angular forms and flat, pure colors that has become the vulgate of smart-set theatre designers. Blue against red. At the summit of the triangle, a spangly metallic thing that quivers under light—the Burning Bush. From time to time, Moses hooks the crook of his staff around the trunk of the bush and pulls himself an inch or two higher. There is nothing else for him to do.

Scene Two: Moving sidewalks with undulating cutouts. Moses and Aron walk in place while singing and reciting. The walking is energetic but has a dreamlike quality. The brothers come into proximity, but remain separate.

In both scenes, artfully "handwritten" signs announce Schoenberg's titles for his scenes: "The Calling of Moses," "Moses Meets Aron in the Wasteland."

It's *interesting*, isn't it? And all these design and staging decisions can be defended if one believes the Work finds its life on the metaphorical plane, and that receptors should be involved with the ideas of the piece rather than the lives of the characters. There is the idea of a mountain, clean and pure. There is some idea, however cheesy, of a burning bush. Moving along, here is the perfect symbol of Moses and Aron working hard to get nowhere, talking past each other. And the undulations suggest the passing dunes, the triangle motif can carry over into pyramids, and the moving sidewalks will serve for the next scene transition, where Schoenberg calls for the brothers to be seen approaching in alternating perspectives. As for the signs, they fleetingly interrupt, they set you thinking, they funnel your attention to an idea of the scene, label the scene and put it (and you) in a little box. Altogether, these devices ensure the victory of distance over involvement. The scenes are fixed images, frozen in their concepts, unactable—*objets*. Like Second Empire roués, we fidget and wait for the dancing girls and bleeding nuns to come.

And if we want engagement, belief, dramatic life? First, we need a move-able Moses and a shrub. We need a rocky, sandy, scraggly place, and a big bush that burns with a leaping holy flame, yet is not consumed. We need a Moses who has turned aside at this miraculous sight, who circles the bush warily and starts at the sounds of voices that speak from within it and sing from the surrounding air. Now he can actively play his resistance to the Call, his wonder at the sights and sounds, and his encounter with the bush (beautiful and seductive, but hot and repellent). The voices mount; Moses surrenders to them; they fade to a whisper; the flame flickers out; black.

New scene: The Wasteland, not filled with prettymodern light and color and helpful to its voyagers, but desolate, parched, endless, and forbidding. Aron's there first, with his skittery flute obbligato, but after a moment Moses arrives, obsessed. Aron sees the situation—it is what he awaited—and he addresses his brother: "Thou son of my fathers, has the almighty God sent you to me?"

To play this scene for the separateness of the brothers (or worse, as at the Met, to merely represent that symbolically) is to fall into a trap. Actors of a certain persuasion call it playing the obstacle instead of the action. The scene is about *trying* to be *together*, about conflict within intimacy. For the brothers are true intimates. They know each other deeply, and so anticipate each other, divine each other, touch each other at the quick. They share a desperate mission, and so know the pain and awkwardness of their divergent understandings of it. They need each other, and are bonded in their need, and so yearn for freedom from each other, and struggle for the power to define. All this is in the verbal and musical text of the scene, but none of it can be played while walking and counting, counting while walking. The opera's over before it's begun.

Schoenberg's preferred theatrical style was realism. We have no direct evidence concerning his production intentions for *Moses und Aron*, since the opera did not even reach the pre-production discussion stage during Schoenberg's lifetime. But we know from his own writings and other accounts that he disliked stylization ("what style?", he asked, and it's an excellent question) and wanted the physical production of his operas to be illusionistic. He wanted a real forest for *Erwartung*, recognizable objects and set pieces for *Die Glückliche Hand*—works far more amenable to abstract or surreal treatment than *Moses und Aron*.[2] It will not do to ascribe his views to the limitations of his time and place—the German theatre of the '20s was a maelstrom of experimentation, and he had plenty of choices. Schoenberg's own musical leaps and his interest in analogous developments in the visual arts had nothing to do with innovation for its own sake. He saw them as the search for a necessary next step in a continuity of artistic development. He despised trendiness, fashion, the grasping after the new. His opera *Von Heute auf Morgen* (the very first twelve-tone opera) is about exactly how much he despised all that. It's a rather clumsy satire on open marriage *à la Moderne*, and a thoroughly ugly little piece. It directly preceded *Moses und Aron*.

Many commentators (including Schoenberg "adherents"—quotation marks his) find a contradiction between his musical style (progressive!) and his theatrical vision (regressive). But perhaps that is their problem. *He* did not see the contradiction, and while it is easy to dismiss him as a theatre naïf, I think it's always advisable to take a creator's recommendations seriously (they grow, after all, from the same root as his text) before deciding what's good for him. I think Schoenberg hoped people would believe in his opera, would be drawn into it emotionally. I think he perceived that there is a connection between the style of a setting and the kind of acting that can be done on it. If the forest in *Erwartung* is not real, he pointed out, and the woman seen always in it, it won't be possible for her to be truly afraid of it. That is neither naïve nor regressive. It's simply a plea for belief, both ours and the performer's.

With respect to *Moses und Aron*, the score itself asks for belief of the same sort. I am not referring to Schoenberg's stage directions, which in any case leave no doubt about his illusionistic wishes, but to his construction of scenes and setting of text, both of which bespeak the play-set-to-music philosophy of so much post-Romantic operawrighting. Aron rhapsodizes, but in the same one-to-one syllable/note relationship evinced by Moses' *Sprechstimme*. There's no room for inflectional embellishment, for sostenuto or portamento (Moses' "DARE?" is an exception) or beyond-the-word vowel shades or swell-and-diminish effects. The composer has mandated an entirely naturalistic wordnote progression, distinguishable from that of a play only by its pitch range and the frequency of overlapping lines.

I doubt, though, that Schoenberg heard his music as plain or parched. Here is the sample cast he offered for *Von Heute auf Morgen*, whose voice setting is similar to that of *Moses und Aron* and whose libretto calls for everyday, naturalistic stage behavior: Marie Gutheil-Schoder, Lotte Schöne, Hans Duhan (but no objection to Michael Bohnen, a very different singer*), and Richard Tauber or Franz Naval.[3] Gutheil-Schoder's records are few and primitive, but suggest a substantial voice, a good technique, and considerable freedom with the music. Naval discloses a heady, well-controlled lyric tenor, probably not very large but lovely in quality. The remaining four, better documented, had voices of blandishing beauty and temperaments of size, vivacity, and charm—not a "modern-music" singer or "serious musician" among them. Superimposed on Aron's requirements, these suggestions would imply a tenor of the *Jugendlich Heldentenor* or strong lyric variety—Helge Rosvaenge or Fritz Wunderlich—allied to a major theatrical presence. They assume an instrument of *inherent* color and excitement to bring sensory interest to the writing. Philip Langridge, the Met's Aron, has a clear, well-equalized voice. He is a fine musician, and can count and walk with the best. But of the qualities desired for the part, he offers the merest hint.

Except for a few bars that have the composer's permission to be sung, and some others set to noteless stems (indicating greater freedom of pitch, but not of rhythm), the part of Moses is written in *Sprechstimme*. This carves the role in relief against the music and, as has often been noted, contrasts Moses' articulatory frustrations with Aron's sung eloquence. The performer is enjoined to avoid singing the indicated pitches for fear that they will not correspond to the rows. This means that to fulfill his obligation of declaiming text over an octave and a fifth in a large theatre, the unsingingactor must not only forego all the expressive niceties denied Aron, but must drain his voice of overtone and vibrato as well—both have harmonic implications and bring the voice to the border of song. The Met's Moses, John Tomlinson, was criticized for an overly *cantabile* approach, but his problem is real. Performers of the role are left with a choice between glottal vehemence (Moses as ranting fanatic) or a flattened bellow (Moses as loud, didactic bore). Booming classical actors and the usages of *mélodrame* (speech over underscoring) and spoken choral recitation would have been more familiar to Schoenberg than to us, and the conventions he sought to establish no doubt seemed more plausible in prospect. That doesn't mean they can be made to work.

If the performer may not sing the pitches, why suggest them at all? Because the composer wishes to assume control over every detail of the line readings, while denying the performer any of the inflectional advantages of singing. This wish to control performance through notational micro-management,

---

* So different it makes one wonder about the composer's perspicacity on such matters: Duhan, a warm high lyric baritone of a sort suggested by the writing for the role of The Husband; Bohnen a booming, wide-ranged basso and outsized divo personality. Bohnen as *Moses*, perhaps—there's a thought.

to leave the performer no choice but to interpret exactly as the composer wishes, is evident in much Twentieth-Century scoring. It is argued that it is necessary for the conveyance of musical thoughts of greater complexity and precision, and there is some validity to this. In the layout of the overloaded piano reductions of the Schoenberg vocal scores, for example, it certainly makes sense to indicate where a particular line is intended as a principal voice and where a secondary, and Schoenberg often does so. With respect to the vocal line, though, most of the increased complexity and precision consists simply of the transfer of nuance from performer to composer. *Von Heute auf Morgen* (self-published and hand-inscribed—no problems with fonts or editors) is downright oppressive in this regard. As in much modern writing, rhythmic groupings are suffocatingly elaborate. They do not allow for the smallest freedom; except at points specified as "free" or "recit.," rubato is out of the question. Dynamic markings are profuse and precise. For long stretches, virtually every note is articulated as a stronger or weaker syllable, irrespective of its place in the measure. Staccatos, spiccatos, and trills abound, so the line often resembles a transcription of a coloratura showpiece (where, however, many of the articulations would originate with the singer). Few phrases pass without affective instruction; in the space of one eight-bar sequence the singer is enlightened by "*schmelzend*," "*pathetisch*," "*schwungvoll*," "*klaglich*," "*recit.*," and "*lacht.*"[4] Every line bespeaks the creator's desire to retain control over interpretation in every particular. The score of *Moses und Aron* is somewhat less obsessive in appearance. But of course it was printed. Fonts and editors.

All this, mind you, in the service of belief. Schoenberg hears how it will all sound just right, and how the smallest event fits into that. He hears many traditional vocal effects as falsities. They would not seem truthful, *real* in the context of his writing, and so he eliminates them, though he still wants voices whose formats and colors depend largely upon them. Since he is the creator, interpreters must respect his vision and attempt to fulfill it, to induce emotional engagement and belief. Unfortunately, Schoenberg has bound their field so narrowly it is very hard to see wherein, vocally and musically, the interpreters' creative contribution might consist, even under ideal rehearsal conditions. For interpretive freedom, the sense of something creative happening in the moment, we must turn to acting as tracked by the eye. And here Schoenberg, like most opera composers, indicates little—there is no "Moses raises left arm, scowls fiercely" or "Aron staggers two steps left, stunned." This, at least, is the performer's province. And this is what the Met's production refused to explore. I have doubts as to the workability of Schoenberg's vision, but there is nothing to lose by giving it a try: passionate, realistic acting on spectacular illusionistic sets. It might even carry over into the music-making.

There is a parallel, appropriate but unpleasant, between the nature of Schoenberg's vocal settings and his interpretation of his subject. The lack of creative space allowed the performer, combined with the frequent sense that the singing line exists more to realize structural aims than to express character action, lends the writing a deterministic feel. The characters' actions and sayings often seem to originate outside themselves. They are parts of an expressive order on which they appear to have little influence. And this mirrors the stageworld of the opera, wherein the outside force generating the action is God. The performer struggles for creative independence within the composer's ironclad, encoded system, just as the people of Israel yearn for freedom, but may hope for it only through unquestioning obedience to the inconceivable God's detailed and often inscrutable commands. The parallel is accurate, therefore appropriate. It is absolutist and tyrannical, therefore unpleasant.

As the completed portion of *Moses und Aron* ends, the people follow the triumphant Aron and the pillar of cloud on the long road toward Canaan. Moses, left alone, sinks to the earth in despair with his famous last line, "O Word, thou Word, that I . . . lack." In the unset third act, the tables have been turned. Aron is dragged before Moses in chains. He protests that he only served God by translating Moses' idea into image for the people to see, and both idea and image into miraculous acts to win their trust. But Moses berates him: this God cannot be shown as other gods are. The idea cannot be expressed by image or action; instead, the images and actions assume lives of their own, and the idea is lost. Having made his point, Moses orders Aron unbound, so that he may live if he wishes. Set free, Aron falls dead. Moses announces: "But in the Wasteland thou shalt remain unconquerable and strive toward the goal: to be one with God." Curtain.

This is all of Schoenberg's choosing. In the Pentateuch, both brothers are denied the Promised Land for their disobedience in striking the Rock to bring forth water. (Schoenberg assigns all the guilt to Aron by shifting the act itself from Moses to Aron.) But both die peacefully and full of honor at God's command.[5] Why does Schoenberg reduce Aron to the condition of a prisoner being brainwashed? Why does Schoenberg's Aron fall dead? (Of the two possible answers—that he is stricken by God or that, allowed to live *if he wishes*, he gives up the spirit in a sort of ritual suicide—the second is more probable. But both are unpalatable.) Why is Moses shown as so impenetrable that, with his brother dead at his feet, he can only assert that the Promised Land for which his people long is itself merely an image, a screen for the mystical union with an only, invisible, inconceivable God?

I do not know why Schoenberg was never able to set this act. But I know I am glad he didn't. It is too horrible to contemplate, however these questions are answered. I like to think the composer felt this himself. Wherever one looks in the music and prose of Arnold Schoenberg, one encounters a formidable mind and artistic sensibility. But one also meets that odd creature, the authoritarian humanist. He is generous with all who seek his guidance, but does not handle polytheism well. Writing to Kokoschka of the death of Galka Scheyer, Schoenberg remarks: "But I'm afraid it was a bit of a similar case to my adherents, who all rank Hindemith, Bartók, and Stravinsky if not above me at least on a par with me: she had *too many gods. . .*" (Schoenberg's emphasis).[6] The Chosen must not merely place one god ahead of all others, they must admit of no others.

It was Schoenberg's pupil Alban Berg, Aron to Schoenberg's Moses, with his sharp instinct for the theatre and his willingness to allow tonal references into twelve-tone practice, who won the hearts of the people, in consequence whereof *Wozzeck* and *Lulu* hover around the repertory while Schoenberg's operas belong to a shadow canon. In an addendum to Schoenberg's first essay on composition with twelve tones, there is a hint of concession, quickly withdrawn. Noting that Berg had contended ". . . that as an opera composer he could not, for reasons of dramatic expression and characterization, renounce the contrast furnished by a change from major to minor," Schoenberg continues, "Though he was right as a composer, he was wrong theoretically. I have proved in my operas *Von Heute auf Morgen* and *Moses und Aron*, that every expression and characterization can be produced with the style of free dissonance."[7]

Every expression and characterization? Proved? This is an outlandish assertion, more than could be claimed for the collected operas of Verdi or Wagner or Mozart, or all three taken together. *Right as a composer, but wrong theoretically*—the idea, perfect in itself and inexpressible, must never be betrayed. Let us grant Schoenberg's operas their theoretical perfection, and their composer his unity with God. Let us also agree with him that pure idea, concept, cannot be expressed through images and acts; the idea becomes something else in the process. But this does not mean that theatre betrays idea. Idea betrays theatre. In the theatre, musical or not, acts and images are the essence. In the theatre, Aron must always win.

And curiously, in the *Moses und Aron* we have, he does.

The operas of Carlisle Floyd seek their place in place of something else on grounds quite different from those of Schoenberg. No one proposes Floyd as a master theoretician, or dreams that statues will be unveiled, speeches recited at the point where he turned off the way to break a new path. He's never done so. He has, though, created a body of work that includes at least two appealing and touching operas, *Susannah* and *Of Mice and Men*. And now that we have traversed the rough high trail marked by Schoenberg and his hardy party, with its glimpses of exhilarating vistas and its *Allees* to imposing mansions whose livability we wonder about, we descend to rejoin the road at an ordinary country junction. Looking to left and right, we cannot quite tell if we have come farther along or are back somewhere we have already passed. But there's a sweet smell in the air, we hear the sound of running water, and across the road behind an indifferently well-tended lawn is an unassuming house that looks like the old Floyd place. Nothing grand, but it has a homey feel.

Susannah and *Of Mice and Men* are about characters living in privation on the margins of society. These people are simple but eloquent. They find poetic ways of expressing basic needs. There is something of the artist about them, of the artist's aspiration to transcend, and it is this artistic quality and aspiration that sets them off from those around them. Their powerful longing for the freedom to live as they choose does not preclude a need for inclusion, or at least acceptance. Susannah yearns to leave her valley and see the world of elegant folks and tall buildings, the cities beyond the mountains. But then she wants to come back, to be content with her community and with nature. George and Lennie dream of rising above their harsh lives as migrant ranch-hands to live in their own home and work their own land.

These are dreams of an independence which, once won, will be exercised not to perform deeds of renown, or to accumulate power or wealth, but to simply settle down—dreams of peaceable freedom. In the juxtaposition of the open road and the little white house that is at the heart of the American romantic myth, it's the little white house that stands for freedom here. The men of the road are traveling slaves; they cannot choose home. This is true not only for George and Lennie, but for Olin Blitch, the itinerant preacher who creates his own transcendence in his revival meetings, but is finally trapped by his loneliness and rootlessness. In both operas, cruelty and violence are done, and people die. But in the end, we are left with the image of a survivor numbed by the act he or she has been forced to commit. Tragedy inheres not in death alone, but in life without the dream.

As a piece of operatic composition, *Of Mice and Men* is more surefooted than *Susannah*, subtler and more sustained, its musical structures more thoroughly integrated into scenic progressions. *Susannah*, though, is apt to remain the more popular piece. This is because of the tunes. I use the term "tune" advisedly and respectfully. I mean by it a piece of melody—not necessarily in traditional four- or eight- bar segments, but beyond the motivic or "aphoristic" stage—that seeks to lodge in the memory at first hearing, with the most casual listening effort. And a casual effort will suffice, because a tune reaches and delights the child, both the child that was and the one that lives within. Some musicians (Steven Sondheim is one)* maintain that a hit tune is merely one that is repeated a sufficient number of times, almost irrespective of merit. And in the contemporary media-saturated world, there may be some truth in this. When it comes to undifferentiated product, some will be sold and some not, and there are masters of this craft. But *"La donna è mobile"*— to take a famous example of a real-world tune—is not memorable because it was sung a lot; it was sung a lot because it was memorable, instantly and persistently.

In opera, tunes offer the advantage of not only pleasurably engaging the ear, but directing the ear toward the sole musical means by which a stage character can directly express himself, the melodic line. They can earn the ear's trust in following melody into more declamatory rhetoric and more complicated relationships with other musical elements, with some hope of reward. They can tag aspects of character, then be employed motivically. They can plunge the listener into the character's feeling or action, and enlist the listener on his or her behalf. Because of their childlike property, they can do all these things quickly and viscerally. When they are well suited to their theatrical usages, they also act as instant-dry cement for the components of singingacting. Finally, tunes have an outreach function. They sprout from the performed text into The Work, and become the most immediate element of its call for return. They assume lives of their own (as recordings, recital excerpts, items for study and audition, tokens shared among receptors) which all lead back to the work. While other musicodramatic elements may also be in an opera's call, and may eventually sink deeper, none can substitute for the love-at-first-sound chemistry of an apt tune.

Susannah has several excellent tunes, "composed folk" melody-memes. Most of them are placed at points where music would occur in the lives of the characters—a reel for a country dance, a hymn for a revival meeting, an old song sung to oneself or between brother and sister. They have fulfilled for *Susannah* all the uses suggested above, and surely help account for the opera's success; I well remember their invitation at first hearing, in the mid-1950s. But they are also a part of what has made the piece dismissable among the musical intelligentsia. What is really being objected to is Floyd's failure to move into realms of abstraction, of idea, to grapple with issues of artistic

---

* See Robin Pogrebin: "Songwriter's Independence Isn't Easy to Hum," *NYT*, May 12, 1999. "Hummability," says Sondheim, "has to do with how many times you hear something... It's as simple as that."

philosophy. Instead, he plunks along telling a linear story about common folk who sing of their strivings and feelings without irony or self-consciousness, and with an earnestness that can border on naïveté and sentimentality. Withal, he touches spots not accessible by more sophisticated routes, and so raises the possibility that true, artistic sophistication does not have to reside in ideational rarefaction or structural complexity or stylistic invention. Beyond this, Floyd's writing suggests that intellectually passé ideas of relationships between content and technique, between substance and form (e.g., that if an artist actually has something to say, he will find the ways to say it, that "style" will emerge from "content") may yet be valid.

These are now subversive notions. But since it is hard to oppose emotional openness, and curmudgeonly to attack simplicity, Floyd is usually picked on for unadventurous harmonies and thin orchestrations. Since I subscribe to the old-fashioned views of style and content, form and substance, I don't think the harmonic critique carries much weight. Floyd's harmonic idiom is a natural fit with the settings and atmospheres of his stories. It has a supportive and unobtrusive relationship with stage events and with the melodic line. These are strengths, not weaknesses, in the sort of opera he is writing. His orchestration, I admit, has its limitations. Inner moments or lyrical exchanges often draw evocative colors from Floyd, but elsewhere there is an over-reliance on snare/cymbal/tambourine garnish, as well as the drift from lower, string-based sonorities toward the upper woodwind-with-trumpet shrilling so often favored by composers of the century just past. These tinny tints have their uses, but are dramatically limited and tiring. In opera, particularly in combination with percussive rattlings, they fight the voices.

In any event, Floyd's harmonizations and orchestrations would have to be much less capable than they are to constitute serious drawbacks. He's an operawright, not a symphonist. An issue that *is* of some technical interest in Floyd's scores is word-setting. The subject is so barren of reward for musical analysts that it is seldom discussed save among the working stiffs who must come to terms with it in practice: singers, teachers, coaches. But it is the field on which the operawright must join battle with the prime element of his art, the wordnote expressions of his characters.

The most vexing kind of word-setting is prosification. I mean by this the setting into a through-composed context of all dramatic materials once assigned to dialogue, *mélodrame*, or recitative. It thus includes everything expositional and everything conversational; by extension, everything that emphasizes denotative rather than inflectional meaning. The *parlando* usages just cited correspond to levels of theatrical reality. The stylistic devices for moving among these levels have gained the status of conventions in the European past, but have been prevailingly a source of irritation in American musical theatre. This is most easily seen in the corny song-cue clichés of the garden-variety musical. But it also accounts for painfully clumsy moments in more ambitious pieces of the non-through-composed sort (*Street Scene, Regina, Porgy*).

Mainstream American opera (operas of some repertory standing) consists almost entirely of through-composed works modeled on naturalistic theatre. Prosification is its usual expressive mode. The principal task of the American operawright has been to locate the means whereby ordinary characters in everyday circumstances may believably sing through their stage lives. It's difficult. The wordnote tensions of the prosification mode pull in two directions. In one, the vocal expression seeks to impassion the everyday. In the other, it resolves into a "heightened" interpretation of speech patterns. There is ample precedent in the classical canon for solutions in both directions, and indeed for subtly melding the two. But these precedents are not easily adapted to the American realist temperament. Impassionisation is awkward and sometimes embarrassing; endless melody and the kitchen sink are uneasy partners. Heightened speech assumes that a relationship will be found between voice and orchestra that suggests an inner life beneath the verbal surface powerful enough to generate the sung actions and condition them emotionally. That, in turn, requires an acute sensitivity to both the refinements of verbal expression and to the precise nature of the complex inner events that are their source—the gifts of the actor, deployed in the creator's score. American composers have not often shown these gifts.

In *Susannah*, Floyd's word-setting difficulties have to do mostly with impassionisation, and they emerge in their usual forms: a conflict between the low pitch range of everyday speech and the elevated tessitura of the classical singing voice, and a conflict between the relatively flat, clipped nature of American vernacular and the undulating, sustained contour of European melodic models. Susannah's "Ain't It a Pretty Night" is a highpoint of the score, yet it contains famously nasty spots for sopranos hoping to keep the words clear. Where longer note values or broader tempi might help, the music specifically presses on. Important portions of Susannah's scenes with Sam and Little Bat are even more problematic: bunches of short notes at agitated tempi to build excitement, tough country diphthongs and contractions (ain't, say, git, scairt, etc.) and the hard American "R", all on the upper G, A, and B-flat of the voices' respective octaves. These are the patterns of heated "natural" conversation, an octave and a half above the pitch levels of speech. But people don't talk at these altitudes, even under duress. They sing, but they don't talk. This observation has carried the force of natural law for four hundred years, through many styles of vocal writing, because it is grounded in physical function: in the upper range of any voice type, tissues stretch and hold for vowel formations and modifications; breath compression increases; articulatory actions are under greater stress. The law can be violated (at some cost to the singer) to introduce distortion or caricature, but that is not the intention in this writing.

In *Of Mice and Men*, written fifteen years after *Susannah*, the tessitura strain is eased. The writing is more accommodated to the heightened speech mode. The set pieces (like the fine "We just might swing 'er" trio), the sustained arioso sections (like Slim's "Ev'ry ranch hand I ever knew" or George's answer, "You bet it's gonna be diff'rent!"), and the shorter, "aphoristic" figures that are used motivically (like Lennie's "Just give me the word, and I'll strike out alone" or Curley's "Damned good-for-nothin' ranch-hands!") grow more easily from their conversational roots. Except for an offstage ballad singer's ditty, nothing is occasioned by "real-life" singing moments. There are fewer tunes.

At first glance, this opera's score has a faintly Schoenbergian look (no key signatures, lop-sided meters that change from bar to bar). And it begins to show Schoenbergian word-setting symptoms, marked by a scattering of the stemmed x's and noteless stems that indicate pitched and pitchless *Sprechstimme*. Some of Floyd's spokesong touches are interesting. In Scene One Lennie, trying to explain to George his urge to touch a girl's dress that's sent them on the lam once again, says "I just wanted to stroke the cloth; it was yellow and looked so soft." The line is elegantly set, with an eighth-note rest between "the" and "cloth," in a halting ascending line that carries the tenor up to an A-flat on "so." This is all in *Sprechstimme* marked *stentato*, which I assume is meant to convey Lennie's struggle to express himself. Then the line drops a half-step and releases gently into a sung G for "soft," the word we might take as Lennie's keyword, the keyword for the tragedy that will ensue when he accepts the invitation of Curley's Wife to stroke her hair. This is not easy for the performer, but if well executed is a lovely effect. In the final scene, when Slim is heard offstage ordering the search to spread out and head west, his call is given a suggestive spokesung curlicue (triplet sixteenths tied to an eighth) in the resonant baritone middle C territory—an unusual sort of embellishment on *Sprechstimme* practice.

These are nice moments. Others, where the line falls to *Sprechstimme* to indicate generic, throwaway exchanges, are at least defensible. But there seems little to be lost, and perhaps something to be gained, by simply singing most of these lines. And there is another sort of spokesong usage to which Floyd sometimes resorts. This is the sudden breaking into speech at a climactic juncture, as if music could no longer withstand its own tensions. (George's

"Dammit, Lennie, I said I want you to stay!" in Scene One is an example.) This has become a favorite evasion of American composers and performers, and is quite simply counter-operatic. If music cannot bear the full weight of an action or event, if it builds its suspense only to fizzle into speech at the moment of culmination, why fuss with opera?

Actually, Floyd has handled these problems more adroitly than many composers. His line readings, if not often brilliantly insightful, usually make rhythmic and melodic sense. He has even written the only passages of American *mélodrame* I know that have not proved ruinous in performance: the spoken portions of Blitch's revival sermon in *Susannah* and George's reading of the ad for the homestead in *Of Mice and Men*. But perhaps it is time for a moratorium on all varieties of *Sprechstimme*. Schoenberg and Berg had strong, High-Concept rationales for their use of the technique for the characters of Moses and Wozzeck: the former struggles to translate his thoughts into speech, the latter to translate his feelings into thoughts, and both to transmit to others some sense of what they mean. Still, we accept the results only provisionally. (And what about the other characters—talking choruses, even—of these and derivative operas? All in the same difficulty?) Between the 1930s and '50s, these advanced European practices were grafted onto our own humble, populist spokesong usages, our regional pageant dramas and *Ballad for Americans* and choral recitations of Sandburg and Lindsay and Benet. Perhaps the prototype of such efforts is Kurt Weill's *Down in the Valley*, a friendly little folk opera that had an influence far out of proportion to its genuine but modest merits.

The resulting hybrid must have seemed promising at the time, but it hasn't proved hardy. For us, the objective of spokesong has been to bridge the gap between realistic drama and opera, between plain talk and lyrical effusion or elevated declamation, and it has nearly always failed in practice. In the American context, spokesong ends up not in smoothing the transitions between the spoken and sung worlds, but in reminding us of the distance between them, and of the distinctions between their premises for belief. This is pointless in through-composed works. Face the music; find singing solutions.

In these two operas, Floyd overcomes his occasional struggles with word-setting, his passing disappointments of harmonisation or orchestration, by persuading us that he takes his characters seriously and writes from the heart about them. But because these characters and their actions stand only for themselves, they seem pre-modern as artistic figures, parts of a world that antedates Freud and all the symbolisms and abstractionisms of our artistic philosophies. They are not merely unfashionable now, but have been so for a century or more. Nonetheless, this unfashionable, pre-modern quality also makes Floyd's characters well suited to clear, direct dramatic action. It makes them easily recognizable as people we know from life, if not from contemporary art. It connects them to basic understandings that are also deeply felt, and reminds us in our cleverness not to pass them by. Confessing a fondness for Floyd's work in the artistic world can be faintly embarrassing, like introducing a sweet, slow relative to smart and trendy friends. But the survival of his best operas, no thanks to the operatic *haut monde*, is a sign of health.

Both these pieces were given fresh New York mountings during the 1998-99 season. Although *Susannah* found the Met playing its now-accustomed role of guest host (the production having originated at the Chicago Lyric Opera), the event per se must have been gratifying to the composer. In fact, though, it was an occasion of the most insidious sort, whereupon a work is set forth in what appears to be the best possible light but its guts left untouched, and the work held responsible for the failings of the interpreters. "The piece had its shot," the cognoscenti say.

No, it didn't. As with *Moses und Aron*, the physical production spoke in honeyed tones with forked tongue. It was designed by the gifted and omnipresent Michael Yeargan. Its style was faux-Realism, its execution impeccable, its look pretty and pristine. Its emblem, filling the proscenium opening during the prelude and returning later, was a painting in the American folkish style usually called Regionalist. Its figures evoked those of Thomas Hart Benton, whose *Susannah and the Elders* presumably (though I've never seen it acknowledged) suggested setting this tale from the Apocrypha in the Tennessee hills, first to Jerome Moross and John LaTouche for their ballet, then to Floyd for his opera. This forecurtain was splendidly executed, and its sardonic edge brought a grin.

An enjoyable painting in an appropriate style, on the very subject and setting of the story: what could be the problem? The problem was the grin. The painting was a hoot. Its cornlikker hicks took us closer to Dogpatch than to New Hope Valley. They had a kind of cartoon menace, but none of the real-world hypocritical meanness the opera tries to convey. The same eye-ear correspondence and choices as those of the *Mazeppa* tapestry were set in motion, but in places where no visual distraction is called for. The music is intended to set the tone, and it's not this one.

The sets themselves moved on past Benton or even Al Capp, into a territory somewhere between Norman Rockwell and Maxfield Parrish. The Polk Place was just lovely. Sweet little cottage, great location, new paint, move-in condition. It was aster yellow with a roof in perfect repair and neatly tended geraniums in the winnder. It nestled beneath tall, slim trees that cast mighty peculiar shadows: As the sun set on our left, dark stripes slanted down from the right; ditto when the moon came over the mountain.

The real Polk Place is a dump. It's overgrown and shabby, the roof's patched but still leaks, and the weathered siding has seen no paint in years. There's an old sink and a rusty boiler out back, some faded washing on the line, and an overturned wheelbarrow in the yard. The property's owner, Susannah's brother Sam Polk, is a goodhearted but weak-willed alcoholic trapper, often absent, who couldn't keep the place up even if he had the money. If, in the midst of this devastation, there are signs of Susannah's struggle to maintain a household, to see some of the beauty she finds around her reflected in her home, that is appropriate. But it's a losing cause. "They be pore as chitlins, them two, bare able to live," says Elder Gleaton—shanty poor. And at the real Polk Place, shadows would fall where Nature puts them.

Into the Met's Designer Appalachia stepped Renée Fleming, an attractive woman with an attractive voice who might well embody the Susannah described by the text—". . . a young girl of uncommon beauty," flushed by the dance, ingenuously open and effortlessly the center of attention, the cut of whose dress occasions comment from the Elders' wives. She was perversely costumed in a frowsy, shapeless house smock that exaggerated her one physical demerit for this character, her well-fed look. Thus clothed and with no special-evening do for face and hair, she melted politely into the ensemble.

A wrong dress is actually more bothersome than vagaries of sets and lights. The forecurtain of Bentonesque Elders, the sweet little cottage and the goofy shadows (unlike the triangles and moving walkways of *Moses und Aron*) do not prohibit acting. They alter tone, but they needn't influence performance. A dress, though, affects behavior and comments on character. The performer keeps wearing it, we keep watching. Some statement was undoubtedly intended, possibly in reinforcement of Susannah's identity as innocent victim: in the utter absence of provocation, the men still act like swine. The point, though, is not that Susannah is modest and frumpy and therefore blameless, but that she is bold, sensuous, and even flirtatious, and still blameless. She creates a genuine, perfectly normal sexual disturbance that the pious rigidity of the community cannot accommodate and Blitch's defenses cannot resist. The underlying political point, important to Floyd at the time of the composition, is parallel: it's not that there weren't leftists about, but that it's all right to be a leftist unless one commits treasonable acts, the evidence for which is supposed to be weightier than that provided by excitable snoops with fevered imaginations.

The performance had its merits. The conductor, James Conlon, brought rhythmic vitality and some dramatic bone to his reading. It was a pleasure to hear the score's fullest moments realized by an orchestra and chorus of this size and quality, though the silky timbres and musicianly sophistications were not exactly what the music needs—that was a mighty sweet violin solo at the top of the show, but it wasn't a country fiddle at a square dance.

Of the principals, Samuel Ramey was the best, more honestly grounded in his character than I've ever seen him, and singing handsomely save for occasional shakiness in the middle. Fleming had vocal moments that could be called exquisite in an abstracted way, and summoned some spirit in Act II. Her warm soprano did not ride the orchestra at the climaxes, however, or project well in the lower-middle range. Except for a few low phrases, her words were indecipherable. The interpretation had a prevailingly detached quality, underlined by peculiar staging in "Ain't It a Pretty Night." This aria is not a monologue. It's the core of a scene between Susannah and Little Bat. She: the one soul from whom he can expect kindness and understanding. He: the one soul to whom she can safely confide her depth of feeling, her aspirations. She sings to him; he feels the comfort of her nearness. Twice, her dreams soar beyond the valley, beyond Little Bat. At these points ("And be one o' them folks m'self," "When I see what's beyond them mountains"), the vocal line sails out ecstatically, but the accompaniment (beautifully orchestrated, by the way—variations on the titular theme in ominous brass chords with shrewdly selected percussion) colors the thrill with foreboding. This dark foreshadowing in the music does not belong to Susannah alone, for when she leaves, Little Bat will lose her. If the characters' closeness and mutual need is not made compelling here, then both Little Bat's betrayal of Susannah and her vengeful sexual teasing of him at the close lose their emotional force and even their logic. In this staging, Fleming climbed up on the roof (not at all like a country girl used to such things) and sang to herself while McVeigh lay down and waited for her to finish. Later, she carefully lowered herself and headed down center, but with no stronger reason than the delivery of her final money notes. This crucial sequence, the heart of Act I, had no event, no content beyond soprano sounds.

In situations like this, it's impossible to know from the outside where things have gone wrong. Here was a talented production team in evident sympathy with the piece (Robert Falls, the director, is an experienced theatre man of high reputation), and equally talented principals who were devoted to their roles and who pushed for the project. Without knowing what went on in rehearsals and production meetings, one can only go by the names in the program. Somehow, it added up to the worst-acted *Susannah* of my experience. It also demonstrated that the turn-of-millenium Metropolitan Opera could not cast a single principal role as effectively as the New York City Opera of mid-Twentieth Century.

It was that company that Floyd had in mind when he wrote *Of Mice and Men*. Specifically, he intended the roles of Lennie and George for Richard Cassilly and Norman Treigle, two world-class singers then in their vocal primes who fit with uncanny exactitude the character descriptions of the novel and play (Lennie: ". . . a huge man, shapeless of face, with large pale eyes, with wide, sloping shoulders . . . dragging his feet a little, the way a bear drags his paws." George: ". . . small and quick, dark of face, with restless eyes and sharp, strong features . . . small, strong hands, slender arms, a thin and bony nose."), and who had teamed with the original Susannah (Phyllis Curtin) to form the cast of choice for Floyd's first success. But Floyd had followed *Susannah* with two poorly received pieces (*Wuthering Heights* and *The Passion of Jonathan Wade*). The City Opera found itself with elevated production costs in its new theatre at Lincoln Center, and had experienced a fiasco with Hugo Weisgall's *Nine Rivers to Jordan*. Cassilly had left for Hamburg, to sing great roles and earn a steady living. So the premiere of Floyd's new opera occurred in Seattle, in January of 1970.

The most heartening aspect of the City Opera's recent *Of Mice and Men* was not that the opera finally received a definitive production, but that it registered strongly with a merely decent one. The work has always seemed fragile. During its premiere run in Seattle, the variance in impact between the first and second casts was disproportionate, even when differences in talent, experience and rehearsal time were taken into account. When the piece eventually arrived at the City Opera in 1983 with only its director (Frank Corsaro) and Lennie (Robert Moulson) remaining from the premiere, it held little of the heat and tension that Corsaro, conductor Anton Coppola, and their cast had created in Seattle. Though there was clearly theatrical vitality and emotional force in the opera, it seemed that these qualities could not survive the sort of mid-level professional effort the work was apt to receive. That made its future questionable.

This time around, *Of Mice and Men* survived just such an effort. There was nothing outstandingly bad in either the cast or the production, but nothing outstandingly good, either; yet the piece "landed." The most authentic presence belonged to Julian Patrick, the baritone George of the Seattle premiere, now in the bass part of Candy at an age when most singers are angling for a comfortable faculty pension. Candy is not really his role either vocally or temperamentally; it was simply good to hear a sound with operatic size and core.

The other leading voices were all light for their roles: Nancy Allen Lundy's a pretty *Hochsopran* for Curley's Wife (she was a pleasing Sophie a few seasons back); Anthony Dean Griffey's a mellifluous, heady tenor without the bite in the timbre or strength at the top required for Lennie; Joel Sorensen's a high-set, overly bright tenor for Curley; and Dean Ely's a warm, mid-sized baritone better suited to Slim than the role he sang, George. (Without the high options written for Patrick's fine upper range in Seattle, the part could well be sung by, say, Ramey—and in fact needs that weight in its lower octave.) All these nice voices were drowned by the orchestra at key points, and neither the writing nor the conductor, Stewart Robertson, was to blame.

Under Rhoda Levine's direction, the cast worked with commitment, and had effective moments. Ely was the most consistently successful, and Griffey the farthest off-track—physically implausible as the man who maniacally bucks wheat, who crushes Curley's hand (Griffey is big only in a friendly chubby-boy way, utterly unthreatening), he pled his case as lovable, innocent victim every step of the way. In general, there was too much demonstration, too little trust and groundedness in the acting.

Of Mice and Men's most problematic sequence remains the first bunk-house scene. After a strong opening (Curley cussing out the ranch-hands, the arrival of George and Lennie), this consists of two episodes: the intrusion of Curley's Wife and the shooting of Candy's dog. On the evidence to date, the writing for Curley's Wife in this scene is Floyd's one failure of character setting in either of these operas. In his effort to capture her tartiness (slithery midrange runs, wide upward leaps at the ends of groupings), he misses her lonely ache. The writing stays outside her, commenting and disapproving, and no soprano I've seen has been able to overcome this difficulty.

The matter of the dog is dangerously close to bathos. In the play, this scene rolls on into the ongoing life in the bunkhouse. Candy curls up against the wall, there's a little entrance for the stable buck Crooks, a few lines about Curley's Wife, and then conversation about visiting Suzy's parlor of ill repute. Floyd turns the dog's death into a scene-ending mood piece, complete with offstage ballad singer and humming ranch hands. It becomes the most obvious instance of a lyricizing, softening tendency in the score, which the drama does not need. In this production, it had a vague animal-rights feel, and the tension waiting for the offstage shot didn't quite hold. These sequences come early enough to throw us off-course. If they can be solved in production, the opera will climb over a big hump.

The mise en scene (by John Conklin) had a basic feel that was right, though it didn't give us much to go on (no hay in the hayloft, for instance, with all its sensory properties—a smell, a softness, a kinship to the tresses Curley's Wife is brushing out, a sexual suggestiveness). The set for the first and last scenes caught a sense of open country. This can't be open country, though. For in the opera's first scene, unlike the play's, the search party is in hot pursuit—we hear the sirens, we see the searchlights. George and Lennie must have a place to hide ("A clearing full of dense undergrowth in a woods," according to the score; a brake of tall rushes, according to the original production). But here they are, in plain view. They and the searchers must play a kiddie game of pretending to be hidden, pretending not to see. We're under way on false pretenses.

Despite the half-successes of the production, the quality of audience attention in *Of Mice and Men*'s final scenes was of a sort rare in our opera houses. It was quiet, intense, receptive. The exit mood was subdued and thoughtful. First comes feeling, then comes thought. Someday this opera will find its cast, as *Susannah* did early on, and a production team that goes for all the toughness and bleakness to be found in it. When that happens, it will find its place, in place of something else.

Beyond these Floyd revivals, I was able to attend fresh productions of eight American operas (ten, really, since *Central Park* is a trio of one-acts) and see telecasts of two more. They divided neatly into two groups. Five were new (*Gatsby, Summer, A Streetcar Named Desire, Emmeline,* and *Central Park*) and five old (*Porgy and Bess, The Mother of Us All, The Consul, Lizzie Borden,* and *Postcard from Morocco*). They have all been born of high aspiration. But the realistic context for them is our Little American Canon, the dozen or fifteen native works that have pleased audiences and cleared the first generational hurdles.

Among the newer operas, arguments about levels of inspiration and craft can be supported to a degree, as can speculation about the extent to which production and performance affect the first impression of a given work. I will not do justice to these matters here, because in considering these operas as a group, I am struck by something else, and that is how little the differences among them matter. There is a sameness in the quality of engagement with them, a sense of being brought to a familiar place where no discovery will be made. They are more alike than unalike, and more alike than those of the older group. While some of these likenesses can be found in the attributes we call "style," there is something more essential in it, too.

Certain similarities present themselves immediately. A narrowness of locale (except for *Streetcar*, southern New England and Greater New York— virtually commuting distance) is no doubt coincidence, though an odd one and a bit stultifying in tone. There is also a commonality in subject matter and enlistment of sympathies. Ill-treated women are the protagonists of all these pieces except for *Gatsby* and the first third of *Central Park*, and their predicaments in a patriarchal order the central concern. The men are oppressive, abusive, morally cowardly, or simply ineffectual. This was not of course a group decision on the part of the operawrights, but it suggests an understood obligation to the socially safe and virtuous. Broad similarities among these works can also be noted in their musical language, which is where we are accustomed to look for the defining characteristics of an opera. While variations in compositional character can be defined—Picker more rhythmically perky, Paulus more lushly lyrical, Previn more Southern/urban and sensual, and so on—these scores can all be classified as Modern Lite. All are tonal but not tuneful, moderately "advanced" harmonically but seldom astringent, accessible but not alluring. All are also middle-of-the-road orchestrally (the customary complements are used in customary ways) and vocally (their usages are derived from classical models, avoiding the experimental or "extended"). Structurally, they are all fully integrated, their episodes bound into the through-composed texture, with word-setting that proceeds through stretches of prosification into passages of sustained lyricism.

These likenesses add up to a centrist harmlessness. We trudge across an oft-tilled stylistic field whose boundaries are all too quickly discerned. Yet there is nothing *wrong* with the harmonic and orchestral idioms employed, or with the voice-setting and singing techniques used, or with suffering heroines and mean males as dramatic material. All these have been made powerful and true in the past. Nor can any of them, or all taken together, be at the root of the sameness. Operas cluster together by the dozen in terms of vocal and musical style, yet retain their profiles as individual works. And narrative redundancy is often a mark of well-being in an art form, an indication that it has appropriated—perhaps even discovered—something of importance to its time and place. This has certainly been true of opera in its most fertile periods.

Nonetheless, something is askew here in the relationship between subject matter and music. In opera, it's music that specifies any differences that matter among versions of a narrative. But since opera is a dramatic form, such musical specification must have to do with how a story can be told theatrically. And all these operas are dramas of character. Their stories are not controlled by divine machination or pre-determined by a tragic destiny, and their characters are not figures blown by the cosmic winds or caught in an apocalypse; rather, it is they who generate the drama. Therefore it is to the qualities of the music as character action that we must look to explain the sameness.

In this regard, I believe that three generalizations may fairly be made about these operas. First: there is a forced quality to their prosification. This is in part a performance problem, and I will return to that aspect later. But it's there in the writing, too. It is often impossible to determine why highly developed, acoustically complex voices should hoist themselves up into full latterday operatic mode for the simplest of conversational exchanges; why a given note should be emphasized when it bears no special emotional burden, carries no urgent action; why the voice should make an intervallic leap here or dwell at the inflectional extremes there. The line-reading implications of the word-setting are sometimes arbitrary and nearly always neutral; they seldom illumine.

Second, sustained lyrical passages fall into generalized rhapsody. This rhapsodic writing is surely intended to reveal the hearts of the characters. It accounts for the prettiest, audience-friendliest moments in these operas—pastoral-idyll love duets in *Emmeline* and *Summer*, a reflective quartet in the opening scene of *Gatsby*, or Mitch's arioso about the nature of true love in *Streetcar*. But the loveliness remains generic. With very minor stylistic adjustments, these passages could be moved from one opera to another with no loss or gain, like Handel arias or Rossini overtures.

Third, in these scores it is the orchestra, not the singing line, that holds most of the musical interest. At times this is because the orchestra is organizing structure or setting forth musical argument that has some independent merit and at others because it is setting momentum or direction or signaling for attention by dramatizing itself. And sometimes it's simply because orchestral variety of timbre, movement, and texture is the only aesthetic pleasure to be had. Except for an occasional descriptive passage, it is almost never for the reasons an operatic orchestra might legitimately dominate: to represent an outer environment (natural or supernatural forces, overwhelming events, rigid social structures) against which the singing characters must struggle, or an inner one (subtextual, intrapersonal) that impels the singing or establishes a counterpoint to it. The orchestra's centrality in these scores is usually by default, vague in dramatic purpose or detached from it. The incidental is more intriguing than the essential, yet it remains incidental.

These habits of vocal prose and rhapsody and of orchestral gesticulation produce a language that is at once puffed-up and flattened out. We note the descriptive gestures and announcements of import, but they have a token quality. We hear the oath music, love music, shattering-turn-of-events or shocking-disclosure music, but it sounds unearned and oversold. Bludgeoned with the alleged importance of it all, we are unable to sort out what might have real emotional weight. It would be easy to assume that this language had exhausted itself, or simply that these composers were not sufficiently talented or original to freshen it for us.

But I believe there is a particular element, central to the creative process of all great operawrights, that has somehow been peripheralized. The element is specificity of character intent. Behind the forced prosification is a failure to pin down the qualities of particular actions in particular circumstances, and to judge where they belong in the arc of a character's journey. Behind the generalized rhapsody is a failure to define the nature of a character's inner life and the emotional uniqueness of exchanges between developed, complex characters. The inflated importance of the proceedings hides a failure to identify and musically delineate the crucial event of a scene or sequence, while the disproportion in musical interest between orchestra and voice conceals a failure to determine the orchestra's role in relation to the stage action in general.

Without character action at the core of the creative process, even the sharpest compositional tools are rendered gratuitous in opera. Thus, the music sounds as if it were written from the outside in, from a series of general notions into which the specifics of moments are asked to fit. And over these generalities the tonal-but-not-tuneful harmonic and orchestral language lies like a blanket, carefully decanting its affects, indicating the emotional life of the drama but seldom expressing it directly.

Under these circumstances, it is not surprising that the characters themselves are unshaded and anonymous. This is especially true for the male figures, most of whom seem present only to assume their subsidiary but necessary places in herstory. The antagonists among them (Lawyer Royall in *Summer*, Maguire in *Emmeline*, and even—in a sort of masterpiece of sustained uninflected writing—Stanley in *Streetcar*) are nearly as interchangeable as the rhapsodic ariosos, and so are the *pas de deux* partners (*Emmeline*'s Lucius, *Summer*'s Matthew, supporting roles in the first two *Central Park* pieces, and *Streetcar*'s Mitch, improbably transformed into a sweetly tenorizing New Age guy).

In the entire array of characters on offer in these works, only one exerted a real grip in performance—that of The Woman in *The Food of Love*, the final portion of *Central Park*. A committed realization of the role by Lauren Flanigan was partly responsible. But the heroines of *Streetcar*, *Summer*, and *Emmeline* were surely not so poorly cast (Renée Fleming, Margaret Lattimore, and Patricia Racette, respectively) as to conceal any strengths in the writing, and even the finest performance can't be coaxed from nothing. Terrence McNally's libretto for *The Food of Love* places us immediately in a situation of dramatic urgency: a homeless woman who hangs about the Central Park Zoo, unable to care for her infant son, tries unsuccessfully to give him away to passersby. The woman's love for the baby, the pain of her inability to provide for him, and the desperation of her search fuel the emotional intensity needed for vocal writing of operatic heat and reach.

The same premise, though, could easily yield just another hour of bleeding-heart goo. At moments in the piece this prospect is on the verge of fulfillment, and I am not sure if a trio encounter with a bitter elderly couple or the odd choral finale, reminiscent of the Expressionistic scenes in *The Hairy Ape* or a Marxist *Lehrstück*, can be made to work. Robert Beaser's music, though, is authentically operatic. Its structures audibly delineate scenes. Its word-setting conveys the relative emotional importance of events. There is a touch of wit, for which McNally's knack for social observation must receive some credit. Most importantly, two extended monologues for the protagonist, the first *La Valse*-ish, the second more Sondheimesque, actually dig into her predicament, and lift us there with her. At these junctures, the clouds of sameness momentarily part.

If we are ushered to a familiar psychological space by the scores of these operas, we are led to a literal, physical one by their production teams. It's not that all the productions look alike.[8] And though, as is so often the case nowadays, the designers seem less concerned with evoking the life of a work than with emblemizing it (e.g., *Emmeline*: this life is plain and hard, its boundaries are tight, its women and children are down in the pits; *Gatsby*: this life is pretty but *triste*, it has no boundaries, it can blow away in a second), none can be accused of not responding to specific qualities in the works. Indeed, the point is that in doing so they have located a sameness, an anonymity, analogous to that of the scores. Just as with the scores, the settings' differences of style, tone, and technique are real, but not finally significant. And the reason again has to do with the lives of the characters.

Behind the nominal places of these settings is another place, a sort of common room. This is the place they really take us to, and if you have seen many productions of contemporary opera you have visited it often, though its variations of décor may have made it hard to pin down. It cannot possibly be a place where people live in any fully believable sense. It's open and public, sterile and uncluttered, like a gallery or museum of contemporary art, or perhaps one of those lofts that is rented out for small celebrative occasions. It is in fact an exhibition space, for the arrangement and display of selected aesthetic objects. Performers promenade and sing among the objects, and are themselves objectified. We examine them, curious and detached, as we do the strangers at real-life events in similar spaces, and wonder forlornly if we shall ever get to know them. In sum:

Singing characters trying to assert their individualities and emotions through music whose forms are devised to convey ongoing life but whose content does not do so, in spaces that gesture toward the realities of such a life but do not conjure them. The whole effort seems displaced and distanced. One is forced toward the conclusion that distance is the true, unacknowledged goal, the unconscious choice. It's *as if* we all cared about these people, these lives, these issues.

And here is *Gatsby* (music and libretto, John Harbison), whose very nature embraces distance. In the novel, everything is seen through the eyes of Nick, the narrator. We observe the characters, but are left to infer what's going on inside them. Nick himself is so closely guarded that we cannot say we come to know him. He is also remote from his story in time, and we in his audience are at a yet farther and sadder remove. One detects in Harbison's music an attraction to this melancholy distance, as well as a congruence between the novel's writerly virtues (economy, elegance, descriptive precision) and Harbison's own. He retains Nick, attempting to integrate this non-character into the action, where Gatsby himself remains inscrutable, finding no definition in the music.

A novel that bathes its lost, desperate people in a cool, clear light while shining none within, set by an orderly and polished craftsman of lyrical, not dramatic bent—altogether, it's a peculiar piece of goods for the operatic stage. And it landed there with a soft plop, stirring passions neither for nor against and affording passages of mildly pleasant listening, but coming to noticeable life only in brief passages that also evoked the most vivid performances: Mark Baker seizing on Tom's pugnacity with vocal and bodily presence, and Lorraine Hunt Lieberson giving us hot, painful moments in the tragic Myrtle's single scene.

Gatsby is brand-new, a Metropolitan Opera commission—something true of only six other operas between 1950 and 2000. Among the revivals, Jack Beeson's *Lizzie Borden* (based on the notorious 1892 axe-murder case) is most like the current works. There is a special family resemblance between *Lizzie* and Tobias Picker's *Emmeline* in the brooding New England atmosphere, the grinding work routines (albeit domestic in *Lizzie*), the heroine trapped in the masculine social order. Both works enjoy librettos (Kenwood Elmslie's for *Lizzie*, J.D. McClatchy's for *Emmeline*) of high professionalism—strong scenarios, scenes that make their points clearly and economically, language that is literate and musically suggestive, and still reasonably lifelike. *Lizzie* also presents several now-familiar symptoms: the dogged stringing-together of dialogue whose intensity is not specifically motivated; the resort to a smoke-screen of general musical clamor in dramatic climaxes; and the overuse of metallic-alloy orchestral textures compounded of higher strings, woodwinds and brass, with lots of cymbal. In the sustained solos for Lizzie's father and sister, and above all in the extended monologue of derangement for Lizzie herself that closes Act I (an ambitious scene), there are striking touches, but not, finally, quite the structural logic that would put them across as "arias" or the brilliance of moment-to-moment invention that would make them fully satisfying as veristic scenes.

Nevertheless, *Lizzie* has much in its favor. For one thing, it sticks to its guns. Its harmonic idiom (conservative by pan-tonal standards, but quite acerbic compared to the younger composers') is not immediately appealing, but Beeson insists on its applicability, and this lends the score a toughness, some courage of its own convictions. *Lizzie* is one of the very few American operas to never turn mushy or beg for sympathy on behalf of its protagonist. A second virtue of this score is that often the voices take the lead, the characters call the tune. Here, the contrast with *Emmeline* is telling. Picker begins each of his first three scenes with a short promising prelude, evocative of either a mood or an activity. Then the scenes begin. Our attention should shift to the stage, and of course the eye leads us there. But in each instance, the ear quickly recognizes that the continuation of the orchestral conversation holds more interest than the singing; we're at a sensory standoff. In *Lizzie*, on the other hand, nearly all the moments of sharp musical profile are found in the voices. This is true not only of the "real-life" singing or reciting moments (a children's choir, Abigail at the piano, a harvest-of-wishes parlor game), but the above-cited solos, the lyrical scene between Lizzie and her sister Margret, or the rather ingenious quintet that leads into the parlor game. And it is true of several recurring "aphoristic" motifs that derive from wordsetting (Andrew's "Make it do, wear it out/use it up or do without," or Lizzie's "Two old ladies in a childless house"). Even when the writing does not entirely achieve its goals, one hears the effort to keep the dramatic focus on the characters, to keep the orchestra responsive to their inner lives. At the least, *Lizzie* is consistently aspiring to the operatic condition.

Postcard from Morocco (here produced by the American Chamber Opera) is the most recent of the older operas, but it feels far away now. It's a period piece in three ways. Musically, it dabbles in "aleatoric" usages and pastiche. Attitudinally, it has an ironic/nostalgic, passive/aggressive stance toward European cultural tradition, and some of the love-not-war sweetness, that marks the trail of the domesticated hippie, circa 1970. Dramatically, it belongs to a still older lineage of American theatre, one whose dates would approximate 1925 to 1950. In plays of this genre, a group of oddly assorted people are held in an isolated or exotic spot by *force majeure* (transit breakdown, political upheaval, outlaw incursion, mysterious time-space anomaly) and come to disclose their hidden desires, the secrets of their pasts, or their true identities. *Outward Bound, Hotel Universe, Idiot's Delight, Lost Horizon, The*

Petrified Forest—there were dozens of these plays, all informed by the sense of repressed souls wandering through the world in displacement, finding outlet with the removal of social constraints. The model's potential for operatic expression is obvious.[9]

Postcard's setting is a North African railroad station ("hot and strange, like the interior of a glass-covered pavilion or spa," say the stage directions), which lends it a fringe-of-empire, Cook's Tour feel. The year is 1914, the eve of World War I. Theatrically, *Postcard* makes use of cardboard cutouts (as "extras"), puppets, and mime. It proceeds by using these children's-play devices (John Donahue, the librettist and first director, ran a noted children's theatre, and the motto at the head of the libretto and score is from Robert Louis Stevenson's "We Built a Ship Upon the Stairs") to intersperse onstage entertainment sequences with the scenes in which each traveler describes a secret, concealed in a valise or instrument case, a cake box or hat box. The score is of chamber distribution, for seven singers doubling or tripling roles and eight to eleven players, depending on whether or not the string trio is doubled. The instrumentation includes guitar, keyboard, and sax with a selection of more delicate sorts of percussion. It is executed with technical expertise and a subtle ear, and has some captivating bars.

Almost everything in *Postcard* having to do with the play elements is fatuous or jejune. But the "secrets" scenes often catch an eccentric charm and a whiff of mystery. They culminate in a long and splendid sequence in which the Cake Lady sings of the lover she claims to carry about in her cake box, and then fends off suggestions of Mr. Owens, a man with a paint box, that they have met before. The passage tastes of the Austro-Hungarian twilight. In the foreground, the Cake Lady's arioso might be an early Berg song or another soprano solo for a Schoenberg string quartet; in the background, two operetta singers soar in the manner of a palm-court arrangement of Lehár or Kálmán. When foreground and background mesh, the music drips like Korngold, and there is suspense and menace under the lushness. Regrettably, just as *Postcard* seems to have forsaken its silliness for something dark and grown-up and to have turned its pastiche to real dramatic use, it collapses into a sentimentality all the more offensive for its sophisticated tone: Mr. Owens' closing monologue is a pre-adolescent fantasy of the effete artist transcendent, hoisting anchor for his lonely voyage through life. It is just possible that a tenor with a convincing upper-middle range (the role is a Pelléas-like baritenor) and the ability to suggest a man coming into maturity before our eyes might make this scene palatable. But he would have to be remarkable.

Among these pieces, *Postcard* also happens to be the one to make elaborate use of pastiche. One hopes that this technique has attained its grand climacteric in the Corigliano/Hoffmann *Ghosts of Versailles*, wherein it actually substitutes for life on a fulltime basis. But it has proved too influential for its implications to be ignored, and *Postcard* lays out these implications clearly.

By "pastiche" I do not mean the use of old music simply to fix a scene in period, as Tchaikovsky, Massenet, Giordano and many others all did to good purpose, and Harbison, for that matter, with his '20s pop music in *Gatsby*. Nor do I refer to mere incorporation and development of folk or pop forms and materials in a "high art" context, or the quotation of one composer by another with serious intent and respect for the eloquence of the original, as Shostakovich does with Wagner in his 15th Symphony. I mean, rather, the re-contextualizing of old music as a means of cultural argument. Doing this in opera is not the same as doing it in a purely musical form. In the latter, there is always considerable leeway with respect to derivation of meaning. Even when we feel that Mahler must have meant this or that Shostakovich's intent was unmistakably that, our proofs are less than absolute. In opera, the evidence is less open to dispute. Words specify. Character action and word-note interpretation specify. Design specifies.

So in opera, pastiche can exist not only in the music, but in staging practices, acting styles, pre-existing characters (like the ones in *Ghosts of Versailles*), or in design. It can exist for the eye and not the ear, and vice-versa. It can be imposed at the interpretive level. And there is one more difference between the uses of pastiche by masters of early modern music and those of our recent operawrights. When Mahler or Shostakovich used a dance or folksong or march, when Schoenberg wrote cabaret songs, when Stravinsky or Milhaud or Gershwin composed in jazz idiom, the idea was to make something *more* of the source. In *Postcard,* it is to make something less. I refer in particular to the show-within-a-show called *Souvenirs de Bayreuth.*

Argento and Donahue would, I assume, disavow any effort to make something less of Wagner. But then, so does Robert Wilson with his anti-*Lohengrin*. We must examine their deeds. In *Souvenirs de Bayreuth*, the assembled travelers are offered an entertainment. The puppet stage's curtain is drawn and a comedy enacted. The action of the show is Kukla-Fran-and-Ollie slapstick and sideshow acts; later it turns violent. Its music is a cocktail-orchestra arrangement of Wagnerian scraps. Among these, Argento accords centrality to the Spinning Chorus from *Der fliegende Holländer.* He posits *Postcard* as a prequel to that opera, one that shows the origin of the outcast's endless voyage ". . . not launched by supernatural forces at all, but by very human ones, by people who fail to show charity or pity, love or understanding for a fellow creature."[10] (The travelers, harassing Mr. Owen to paint a group portrait, knock open his paintbox, which is seen to be empty. This motivates his closing monologue, and the launching of the "ship upon the stairs.")

This may strike those whose familiarity with Wagner is only casual as just jolly-tacky irreverence. For those of us with tapestries, it raises some questions. If the Dutchman's voyage is being evoked, why the Spinning Chorus instead of his own motif or the storm music? Why the insertions from other Wagnerian sources, like the Valhalla motif, presented fairly intact from Scenes One and Four of *Das Rheingold*, or the barroom-piano sendup of Wolfram's Ode to the Evening Star, or the rushed snippets of the *Lohengrin* Bridal Chorus to resolve the whole sequence? And why, later, does one puppet smash the other and "send him home?"

I think I have some answers: All these quotations represent bits of Wagner's work comfortably absorbed by the "bourgeois" culture, put to use in church, school, and home. They are emblematic of domestic virtue. Women spin and sing in Daland's workshop. The noble and heroic Valhalla theme (here, mock-noble and -heroic) announces the completion of hearth and home and the fulfillment of Wotan's obligation to his wife, the protectress of home and "family values." The murdering of "*O du, mein holder Abendstern*" is very close to the bathetic out-of-tune clatter that inspires Jake's "*Das ist die ewige Kunst*" in the Brecht/Weill *Mahagonny*—thus, a comment on the consolatory sentimentalisation of culture. The Bridal Chorus is *the* Bridal Chorus (after all, no one's going to pick on Mendelssohn). The vanquished puppet is Fasolt, the victorious one Fafner—cartoon brutality is the logical outcome of this Teutonic farrago.

Any of these associations might be fortuitous. But not all. And the context itself is reductive: a childish and, finally, nasty little show accompanied by cheap music, performed for an audience of self-absorbed buffoons and mannequins. It's not that Wagner, or his audience, or the social uses made of Wagner, should be held immune to satiric commentary. But *belittlement*? By right of what alternative vision? Our attention is directed to Wagner's powerfully sounded tale of an actual captain of an actual ship, who curses God while in mortal danger on a real ocean and is condemned to eternal wandering unless redeemed by the unconditional love of a woman (specifically that—not, as Argento puts it, "a stranger's act of compassion and love"), only to see it turned into an anecdote about a would-be artist waif who's pushed around a bit and dreams of sailing away on an imaginary ship, in charge of an imaginary crew. And there we have the contemporary use of pastiche: to vitiate the power of the borrowed cultural material (to "de-valorize" it, in the wonderful postmodern locution) by repositioning it at a level we can easily handle—where we, not it, seem in charge—while taking full advantage of its familiarity and remembered impact, because we have so little of our own to offer in its stead.

The remaining revivals take us back another generation or two, and will be at least somewhat familiar to devotees. Their qualities can thus be discussed more in the context of their productions, as we normally do with repertory pieces. Before taking leave of *Lizzie* and *Postcard*, I should note that both productions served their works quite respectably. As seen on television, the NYCO's *Lizzie* had much the same tone as that of its original production—somber, bleak, and spare, like the life it contains, with enough in the way of furnishing and props to allow its performers to pursue that life. It featured more bleached planking and white light, with the peculiarity that the interior walls seemed to have been finished in white siding, as if the house had been built inside-out—something about how the life inside shuts out the world, I assume. As always, there were plusses and minuses in the staging and performances, but nothing that was in any way sloppy or unintelligent. *Postcard* was presented by a small company that performs intermittently on a tiny budget, staged simply in sets and costumes that had none of the splashy gloss of the Minneapolis premiere. It was pleasing to see the work exert much of its spell under these conditions, and to observe once again that the depth of the New York operatic milieu is such that a very decent cast and instrumental ensemble can be assembled for such an occasion.

I didn't take much from *Porgy* (at the NYCO) this time around. This was a routine professional performance in a production that has seen many, and presumably better, days. It barely stayed above water, though that is more than can be said of *Porgy*'s last local outing, at the Met, where it foundered like one of those overloaded ferries we read sad stories about once a year or so.

Porgy raises questions I've never seen resolved. Many have to do with deciding what to include—here, for instance, was the Jasbo Brown pantomime at the top of the show. It's all right in itself, but I don't think it belongs. First, it's a red herring: it seems to be setting up a recollected-life framework for the story, then doesn't follow through. Second, it deprives us of the move straight from the overture into the gentle sway of the intro to *Summertime* and Clara's entrance on the upper F-sharp to sail her lullaby out into the theatre—one of the knockout opening curtains in all of opera. On the other hand, there was only a single verse of the Buzzard Song, and that is incomprehensible. Not only is it a fine song that shows us something in Porgy not found anywhere else, *it has two matching verses, with a bridge, that tell a story.* The message here was, "We'll start it off for you, but then what the heck, you get the idea." I sure don't.

Can the sequencing of scenes and songs, particularly in Act II, be made to seem organic, to seem something other than a succession of loosely related numbers, each with its little button at the close? Can the divorce scene be made charming and touching rather than cornpone-cute and condescending to the characters? Can this scene, and the intrusion at the burial, be acted with tang and force, some edge, but without snarling and shouting to set up the white folks? Should Maria be given her *Sprechstimme* number,"Oh, I hates yo' struttin' style," and the stature of a major character, a counterweight to Sporting Life, or does that pull too much focus from the main story line? Do we need all of the extended choral prayers in the hurricane scene, beautiful but so similar to that in the burial scene that the two seem like the same communal event? All the score's often perfunctory connective tissue?[11]

For many years, the answer to these and other questions was deemed to be "no," and substantial cuts were made. The evidence for mass restorations is so far not overwhelming. Performance solutions may be possible, and the opening of certain cuts justified, but *Porgy* will remain awkward and flawed, a source of impatience. It will also continue to be performed with frequency, and is the only one of all these operas of which that can be confidently said. That's because of its moving story, appealing characters, and its picture of folk life, fascinating and commonplace at once. But above all, it's because of its tunes. Granted, they're more highly developed than those of most musicals (and some operas); also granted, the rhythms *are* infectious. But neither compositional development nor rhythm, nor anything else about *Porgy*, would amount to much without the stream of irresistible melody—sung melody for operatic voices—that catches us from first hearing and compels our investment in these people and their tale.

The remaining two operas were much affected by their productions, one substantially helped, the other not. *The Consul*, which I had not seen for many years, packed more of a wallop than I'd supposed it could. To be sure, its faults were not entirely overcome. Its verbiage is sentimental and melodramatic, like that of radio dramas of the time then ending, and is often stuffed into patches of breathless wordsetting that reinforce its naïveté. The Magician wears out his welcome quite promptly. The bargain-basement symbolism of Magda's dream scenes is easy to laugh at. And there is nothing in the composer's Italian-American verismo style and technique that will serve as a paradigm of operatic subtlety, complexity, or originality.

In Menotti's operas, the emotional expression is uncoded and raw. His best work has an unguarded earnestness. His efforts at irony are either of an obvious dramatic sort or by way of lampooning intellectual, artistic, or social pretentiousness (notably in *Maria Golovin* and *The Last Savage*), and would have been better left unattempted. There is a lovely (because so accurate) passage in the diaries of Sir Peter Hall, on seeing a production of O'Neill's early sea play, *The Long Voyage Home*. He terms O'Neill ". . . the greatest *bad* writer among world-league dramatists. His dialogue is a string of clichés, but what power and authenticity of emotion. . . . Don't let it happen . . . don't let the poor Swedish sailor who has saved his wages during two years of voyaging be made drunk, drugged and robbed. But he is."[12]

And so with Menotti, though admittedly he never developed into an operatic equivalent of the mature O'Neill. In *The Saint of Bleeker Street*, he spends the first act establishing Annina as a candidate for sainthood (literally—she has the stigmata), her brother Michele as an embittered and confrontational skeptic among people for whom belief is both necessary and easily threatened, and the relationship between brother and sister as one of peculiar intensity. The act ends as, under cover of the passing procession of the Festival of San Gennaro, a group of community youths beat Michele and leave him tied by the wrists to a wire fence. And now Menotti introduces the voluptuous Desideria (yes, that's her name). Dressed in red with a carnation in her hair, she crosses the empty stage, unties Michele, and kisses him as he sobs uncontrollably. The strings attack a big tremolando, *sforzando*. Curtain.

Well, it's corny and hamhanded. But if you ever see *Saint*, I think you will have trouble dismissing it, because it's also chilling. And you are apt to feel a similar ambivalence toward *The Consul* from the start. The dramatic situation is strikingly like that of the Carol Reed/Graham Greene *Odd Man Out*, except that after the opening scene we follow the journey of the wounded freedom fighter's wife, rather than that of the fugitive himself. John Sorel's desperate plight, the family's dire circumstances (sick baby, old grandmother bewailing the fate of the world, no money, no escape), the menace of the police agent in hot pursuit—all this is flung out in the first few minutes in dialogue and *mélodrame*, accompanied recitative and a few arioso passages, much of it requiring outstanding performance to mitigate its crudeness. Nevertheless, you are, without quite realizing it yet, caught up with these people in their life-or-death predicament. As the scene ends with the opera's first formal number, the haunting trio "Lips, now say goodbye," you're probably on the hook. If not, it may happen with the quintet ("In endless waiting rooms") that closes Act I, or with the Grandmother's lullaby (just when you, a devotee, were mildly annoyed that her game of peekaboo with the baby so clearly mimics the children's scene in *Boris*). In all the major lyrical moments, capped by Magda's "To this we've come," Menotti meets the challenge with something that makes you care about his characters. Without ever losing consciousness of the work's weaknesses, or suspicion of being manipulated, at some point you give in, and remember that opera's *supposed* to be emotional. Even the dream sequences and the Magician's hypnotism demonstration pay off at the end, when the Magician as a dream figure coaxes Magda back to her place in front of the oven as the phone from the Consulate rings unheard. I think at that point you'll be where Sir Peter was with the sailor Olson: "Don't let it happen—don't let her inhale that gas." But she does.

The Berkshire Opera's presentation of *The Consul* was extremely success-ful by the only measure that is meaningful: it realized in performance terms everything that's important in the opera. It was staged by the company's then-resident director, Mary Duncan. I have been able to see three of her productions (besides this one, *Summer* and the Handel masque *Semele*). In each case, she has taken her material at face value and met it on its own stylistic terms within the limits of her production situation. Her work has taste and intelligence, and shows signs of empathy with her performers. She and the company's artistic director, conductor Joel Revzen, cast consistently well. *The Consul*, despite its problems, is eminently playable as a realistic the-atrepiece, and she followed through with it meticulously. So did her set, light, and costume designers (David P. Gordon, Eve Conwall, and Helen E. Rodgers, respectively). There was a detailed but uncluttered interior for the dim, shabby Sorel flat. When the set swung around to reveal stacks of gleaming black file cabinets with their rows of white knobs, settling into place as the orchestral interlude faded to little blips under the sound of the Secretary's typewriter (a rare moment of understated suspense from Menotti), we knew we were in good hands. And here, in the Secretary's suit, was a costume that did everything Susannah's dress did not. It was a dark suit with white but-tons and piping. Besides giving the performer (Emily Golden) an appropriate look, chic and severe, it had an emblematic function in the good sense, carry-ing out the visual motif of the cabinets to which she will so often turn while maintaining perfect plausibility: the Secretary might well be the sort who fashion-co-ordinates with the office décor. The role of Magda was given a well-sung, truthful performance by Beverly O'Regan Thiele.

The Mother of Us All at the NYCO was baffling and irritating. This lovely, witty little opera, which I had never before not enjoyed, emerged as a sour, tendentious clump of camp.

In terms of irritation, one could well begin with the anonymity of the casting or the noise of the "enhanced" snaredrum, wind, and brass jammed into our ears like Q-tips dipped in hot sauce. But as is so often the case, a directorial bias (in this case, Christopher Alden's) was the principal irritant. The fact that the bias was gay is really incidental—the grounds for objec-tion to it would on principle remain the same whatever its origin. Still, in this instance it was derived from misplaced gay advocacy. Stonewall, not women's suffrage, was the campaign of the evening, most egregiously in the scene of Jo the Loiterer's wedding to Indiana Elliot, where, according to Alden, Jo plants a big, wet smacker on the mouth of his Civil War buddy, Chris the Citizen. The wedding scene, given position as the Act I finale and bearing that importance, is entirely undone by this interpretive raid on the text. The digressions from the wedding that are meant to be there (the courting of Angel More by Daniel Webster and of Constance Fletcher by Samuel Adams), which are both fragrant and amusing and thematically related to the scene, are effectively obliterated. The objections to the marriage by Indiana Elliot's brother (that Jo might be a bigamist, a grandfather, an uncle, a refugee) are made to seem code for closeted queer—you know about those Civil War boys, Walt Whitman and all. The kiss and its aftermath (Jo and Chris, dazed and disturbed, dealing with their self-realizations) becomes the central event of the scene, the only believable event. The actual truth of the moment (that the wedding takes place in an atmosphere of silly-sweet romance, and that Susan B. blesses it and carefully explains why) is lost, along with her apologia for her own single status. Even the tag line of the act—Susan B.'s prediction that Jo and Indiana's children, women and men, will have the vote—is overshadowed.

Throughout this production, the only characters accorded any dignity and sincerity were the gay/lesbian/feminist ones. All the others—the whole grand collection of 19th Century American figures, large and small—were presented as idiots, their actions and sayings mere struttings and gabblings, their every scene a spectacle of chaos. Yet in Thomson and Stein's *The Mother of Us All* there is not a messy moment. Its little scenic and musical cells, though presented in pageant form and often at first glance unrelated, are in themselves models of simple clarity. The character relationships appear in fragments, but have clean through-lines and perfect logic. The words mean exactly what they say, and are serious about it. I know of no stage text more in need of being taken literally. The playfulness of Stein's style arises from the perception that all utterances, no matter how passionately conceived, contain their own linguistic contradictions, their own semiotic critique. Thomson's score grounds this in a warm, commonsensical lingua franca of hymns, marches, and parlor songs, caught in wisps and snatches. Every word, every tunelet must tell, must sink in. Every character, every action and relationship must be sharply defined and played at face value.

The authorial attitude toward the characters of *The Mother of Us All* and their way of life is manifest in the verbal text, the authors' suggested stage scenario, and above all the music. It is very much that of the central character. It combines an unswerving dedication to equal rights and powers for all with an awareness that these rights and powers will probably not be more wisely used for being more liberally distributed; an amused exasperation at the posturings of politics and romance with a resigned tolerance and even affection for same; a recognition that real battles must be fought with the acknowledgement that antagonisms arise principally from fear, and do not negate the common humanity of those caught in them. It digs at the roots of American experience and finds much to change, much to love.

There is no doubt that to be gay is to occupy a particular place in the world, and that the view from that place offers a perspective of potential value to us all. I believe that Stein and Thomson understood that though their commentary might be keen, this value could be realized only through an engagement that is essentially inclusive and invitational, and therefore socially practicable. When performed in that spirit, *The Mother of Us All* tweaks our brains, expands our vision, and entertains us mightily. That's not because its authors were gay, but because they were artists.

None of these revived works is an operatic masterpiece. America has no operatic masterpiece. But each of them shows a compositional self-confidence, an individuality of voice, a vitality that is lacking among the recent premieres. They are not much like one another, and the productions they inspire do not induce a sense of sameness. If we add to them the Floyd operas, *The Ballad of Baby Doe* (Moore/La Touche), *The Crucible* (Ward/Stambler), *Regina* (Blitzstein/Hellman), *Street Scene* (Weill/Rice), *Vanessa* (Barber/Menotti), one or two other Menottis, and a few quasi-operatic musicals (*The Most Happy Fella, Carousel, Candide,* perhaps *Sweeney Todd*—all at least as operatic as *Porgy* or *Street Scene*), we have a fairly complete roster of the American operas that have shown some rate of return.

Porgy dates from 1937, and *Sweeney* from 1979. Otherwise, all these works, including all those unequivocally operatic, were born in the quarter-century after the end of World War II, with a very heavy concentration in the first half of that period. That stretch of time produced far more viable American opera and near-opera than the two centuries that preceded it or the three decades that have followed. It was the only time, I think, when we felt that an American operatic culture was starting to thrive, that an American operatic masterpiece might be just around the corner. It was the only time American opera had momentum.

Most of these composers would be considered semi-educated primitives now—indeed, they were so then—by prevailing academic and critical standards. Even the exceptions (Barber and Weill, later Beeson and Argento) wrote in "conservative" styles, and Weill, rigorously trained and technically "advanced," forsook his early direction to write in populist modes. The conditions under which their operas were written and produced were not at all the same as those we complain about these days. By our usual standards of measurement, they were much worse.

I point this out with some hesitation, for fear of lending aid and comfort to those who believe that funding for the arts should be removed altogether from the public sector. In the current political climate, they are comfortable enough. But the fact is that the time of flourishment and promise for American opera predates Federal and state support for the arts, the development of the regional opera network, and the elephantiasis of our performance-oriented conservatories and music schools. Of the contemporaneous works mentioned, one (*Vanessa*) was premiered by the Metropolitan and one (*The Crucible*) by the New York City Opera. Two were first produced by universities, *Susannah* at Florida State, Tallahassee, and *The Mother of Us All* at Columbia, a school with a strong composition department but no other operatic aspiration. The others were produced on Broadway, under commercial circumstances, running like any other show, except for *Baby Doe*—and it was originally meant for Broadway, too.

To re-create the anticipatory sense of the time, therefore, it is not necessary to imagine oneself at the Metropolitan suddenly in the presence of an American *Otello* or *Meistersinger*, but rather in one's seat at the Barrymore for *The Consul*; if not there, the 46th Street Theatre for *Regina*; if not there, the Music Box for *Lost in the Stars* (all these in the same season, 1949-50); if not there, at the City Center for any of the thirty-six American works presented by the opera company between 1949 and 1965, when it moved to Lincoln Center; if not there, in the living room, tuning in the NBC-TV Opera Theatre, which along with its other repertory offered the occasional new American opera, live in real time, from the studio, on the commercial network.

In other words, composers had a theatrical world to live in and write for. They were building an American form of operatic theatre that comprised folk elements, Broadway theatre practice, and the musical language of the interwar American symphonists in approximately equal measure—all assimilated, of course, to the European models crafted of such long experience. We felt ourselves passing through our version of the developmental stage in which the Germanic countries, and later the Eastern European ones and Russia, had reconciled their folkish musical ways with the formal examples of Italian and French opera to establish the basis of a national repertory. Surely, we thought, one of these classically trained composers writing for our theatre, or one of our theatre composers reaching toward classicism, would make a breakthrough. As Leonard Bernstein (himself one of those composers) observed some years later, we assumed that any minute now someone was going to do for the American musical what Mozart had done for the *Singspiel*, and American opera would be off and running.

That world has vanished, and that momentum is long gone. The reasons for this are in good measure economic, political, and demographic, compounded by a thousand little failures of nerve. But let us stick, for the moment, to the creative dilemma. The effort to lay the cornerstone for American opera was squeezed from above and below. Above lay the cloudland of the pantonal hegemony, seeing to the proper upbringing of the composers that would follow the Moores and Wards, the Menottis and Floyds. Below lay the quicksand of the new Broadway, rendered inhospitable to serious sung theatre by an aesthetic that can be summed up in three words: mikes, rock, dance. In its eight decades, Cloudland has produced a number of scores respected by musicians, but only two (by Berg) that approach repertory status. And that's its global record. From the Great White Quicksand nothing has emerged for forty years save a piece or two of Sondheim's.

By the time of *Postcard* and *Mice and Men* (1970-71), all these and related phenomena (e.g., electronic composition, theatrical improvisational techniques) had run headlong into the counterculture. If *Postcard* stirs memories of some of the goofier aspects of that confrontation, it should also remind us that there was, briefly, a creative energy in it. And the circumstances of both premieres* recall the largely unrealized artistic potential of de-centralization, which lay not in mere dissemination, or even in the founding of civic institutions, but in the establishment of opportunities for artists and audiences to approach the form anew. That energy and those opportunities, riding the tailwind of the Great Society initiative with its bracing gusts of public and private funding, characterized the last "moment" for American opera to date.

While the unsameness of the older works is inevitably expressed in their music, I doubt that we could demonstrate a significantly wider range of musical style in the earlier generation than in the later. What the older works display is conceptual freedom, alternative definitions of what an opera can be and how it should go on, of what stories bear telling and how. We can see this breadth (as we saw its obverse in the recent operas) in choices of locale and milieu and how these are used to present a stage world of some interest. It is evident in the greater variety of characters and a more balanced, nuanced approach to relationships between the sexes. And it is apparent in

---

* *Postcard* was commissioned and written for the Center Opera of Minneapolis, a small resident company with a specific theatrical vision and working method; *Mice and Men's* route to Seattle has already been traced.

the way causes are advocated and appeals to our sympathies entered: *Lizzie* and *The Consul* put forward strong female protagonists without a hint of special pleading; *Mother* advances its powerful heroine and indubitably political stance in full acknowledgement of human contradictions, and with a strict avoidance of moral superiority.

Finally, the relative openness of the older pieces is present in their theatrical construction—their layouts or scenarios. How the fit between content and form was arrived at in each case—whether it grew from a musical idea, a verbal one, or a scenic structure—is an interesting question, particularly in the cases of solo operawrights like Floyd and Menotti, but finally doesn't matter. What matters is: what releases music? What structures and progressions help pull it out? What forces an urgent dramatic response?

In Menotti and Floyd, in Thomson and Ward and Moore, in Weill and Gershwin and Blitzstein, even Beeson and Argento, we had composers formed by the higher culture contending with materials and energies that pushed in from the sides, bubbled up from below. The more recent work has the feel of a down-from-the-top imposition, straining toward a "relevance" the earlier pieces come by more naturally. Now that our ragtag but feisty native rebellion here below has bogged down in the quicksand, now that the neo-Schoenbergian clouds have dispersed aloft, we seem adrift between. We mean to move forward, but seem to float back.

For as we follow the integrated, prose-to-rhapsody progressions of the recent operas, we trace the outline of the North-European, late-Romantic model given its last coat of finish by Richard Strauss. And it isn't only the shape that shows through: the lingering, high-arching lyrical line that crops up often when emotional pay-off is sought is suggestive stylistically as well. It's as if we hoped the Countess' reflection could be coaxed back through the mirror to walk and sing once more. That is a longing any devotee can share, but not one apt to be requited. If picking up the pieces is our current job, perhaps midcentury America is a better starting-point than Europe *avant le déluge*.

On the same Maryinsky visit that brought us a powerful 19th-Century operatic tragedy in *Mazeppa*, the company introduced us to a fragrant, scintillant 20th-Century comedy, *Betrothal in a Monastery*. Whether or not *Betrothal* is (as I think) the best comic opera since *Ariadne auf Naxos* and the best of its particular kind since *Falstaff*, this much can be safely said: it shows us the happy state to which our own operawrights aspire, the very one our midcentury culture strove to approach. By the time Prokofiev took up this subject (Richard Brinsley Sheridan's comedy-with-music, *The Duenna*), he was in full command of a style perfectly suited to it—one that reconciled the hard-edged gestures of his youth to the lyricism that had always been an important part of his gift. The resultant language is fresh and surprising, yet tugs at the heart in a simple way. In *Betrothal*, it shifts with every turn of the volatile, convoluted stage situation, wraps it in mysterious and sensuous hues and saturates it with an ache for romantic fulfillment that is finally released in the exhilarating resolution. Besides all that, it's genuinely funny, crackling with a wit that is ironic but never cynical.

Betrothal has every qualification for repertory status. But its demands are considerable. Deft renditions of Sheridan plays are in themselves rare collectibles for American theatre connoisseurs. In this case, the comedy must be played by a large cast (over twenty roles, including eight principals) of technically adept, musically accomplished operatic singers. And in full raiment, the piece is big: maskers, dancers, full chorus, large virtuosic orchestra plus offstage sideband; nine scene locations, interior and exterior; period costumes with many disguises and variants. The two male leads and the Duenna herself are character roles that call for real voices (if you imagine good casting for King Dodon, the *Siegfried* Mime, and Mistress Quickly, you'll have them about right). The remaining parts are for standard romantic voice types (lyric soprano, mezzo, tenor, two baritones), and are expected to dispense romantic magic.

Fortunately, *Betrothal* is written with such expertise that it will play and please without ideal realization of all its elements. It has in abundance what we have found missing in our glances at works by several talented composers: specificity. The characters' desires and actions are vivid in the music. So are the events of scenic progression ("beats," in acting terminology). Their rhythms, colors, and gestural qualities are nearly always unmistakable. Thus, the interpreters are given a clearly defined field of work without being subjected to an interpretive regime of the Schoenbergian sort; there is plenty of playing room left, plenty of creative work to do. The theatrical devices and themes in *Betrothal* (deception and disguise, interlocking plots and counterplots over love vs. money, authority vs. rebellion, male schemes vs. female) are common enough to comedies of generational intrigue. But because the work is an original, it can (like *Mazeppa*) defeat our expectations. From whichever direction we approach it (Russian opera, earlier Prokofiev, Sheridan, opera buffa, etc.), it sits at an angle; it's a strange new amalgam of things we think we know. I particularly cherish the way scenario and music make us feel sleek, sable romance gradually enveloping brittle, brilliant scheming. At the opening (a plaza in Seville, night, carnival time), Don Jerome and Mendoza (the aforementioned character tenor and bass, roles that singers of those descriptions should covet) gleefully plot a marriage alliance that will seal their commercial one, a fishing monopoly. The music prances and gloats and illustrates (delightful undulating swimming-fish melody for Mendoza, delightful ascending wriggling-fish figure for violins), but quite without rancor or judgment. In the plaza, maskers flit about. Enter Ferdinand, baritone lover and son of Don Jerome with a few lines to his absent beloved, a bit of chromatic melody that has an obsessive undertow, like one of the darkling Porter or Arlen songs. It starts, is interrupted by a servant, then resurfaces in fuller arioso form. Enter Antonio, tenor lover, aspiring to Louisa, the daughter/sister of the Jerome/Ferdinand household. Spanish guitar chords. He sings an enchanting serenade that recalls so many others, yet is very much itself; from inside the house Louisa soon joins in. Jerome interrupts. The romantic spell is broken, and the rest of the scene goes in an entirely unanticipated direction, alternating Don Jerome's sputtering laments about fatherhood with sardonic comment from the maskers and their silent, shadowy dances, the last of which ends the scene. Elderly scheming and youthful romance have both declared themselves, but neither holds the stage. As in *Falstaff*, we are ready for the women to take over with their counterplots—and they will win, because they are so much better at this sort of thing than the greedy older men or the testo-macho-besotted younger ones.

As the piece proceeds, the plotting is accompanied by an orchestral spicing of trumpet and clarinet, snare and cymbal that reminds us of both the sources of these now-common combinations and their most appropriate uses. Through this run the richer, string-based textures and cantabile vocal line of the lovers' longings, fleetingly at first, then unanswerably in the heart-stopping quartet that ends the first tableau of Act III and the musk-scented convent garden scene, with its passionate mezzo aria. Throughout, Prokofiev's harmonies tug and twist, always bringing us home, but by devious routes. The finale incorporates everything in the opera's idiom and adds a last surprise in a sprightly song with chorus—somehow rueful and self-congratulatory at once—for Don Jerome, who accompanies himself on the musical glasses. The spirit of the carnival, absent since the first scene, returns at the close.

Another odd fragrance is captured in this score, one that recalls the very origins of the Western romantic spirit. Through all the sneaking and peeking, the cavorting and hand-rubbing, drifts the figure of Don Carlos. He is an impoverished old nobleman sunk to the condition of trophy errand boy to Mendoza, his chief duty being that of courtly escort to Louisa. In the play, he is given only a few lines of dialogue but prominence in the music—two extended solo songs and a shorter air, and parts in two trios. He is in no way essential to the plot, and could easily have been reduced to functionary status or even eliminated. But Prokofiev and his collaborator, Mira Mendelson, retain him as relic of a lost code and griever for lost love who finally can't resist doing some peeking himself. His warm baritone legato over halting little figures and his lyrical regrets in the quartet haunt the central portion of the work, and make this character one of Prokofiev's loveliest achievements.

There is much more awaiting discovery by newcomers to *Betrothal in a Monastery*; these are a few of its aspects I find worthy of attention. For another I feel constrained to address, please see the end-of-chapter notes.[13]

The opening-up of the Russian repertory, and of Prokofiev in particular,[14] to our audience is the most heartening development on our operatic scene for the past several decades. This is true for the works themselves, for since World War I, only three composers have added to the Straussian *oeuvre* bodies of work that hold some claim on the international repertory: Janáček, Britten, and Prokofiev. And it is true for the possibilities suggested. While artistic styles are never wholly autonomous, it's fairly clear that musically these three all fall outside both the German Romantic progression that ended with Strauss and the post-tonal reaction to it. Theatrically, too, they embrace a range of subject, style and structure that lifts our sights beyond our habitual prose-to-rhapsody continuities, the vague, distanced cool of our exhibition common rooms, our collation of differences that do not matter.

Essentially, I had known *Betrothal* only on records. The Maryinsky performance was a fine enough ensemble effort to remove any doubt about its stageworthiness. The orchestra, which in this score must stay alert as a dramatic participant in a rather unconventional way, played with rhythmic snap and coloristic splash under Gergiev. The sets, beautiful to look at and warmly, subtly lit, were based on a side balcony structure, carnival lanterns and hangings, nicely painted perspective backdrops and tapestries, and a big, lovely fan, translucent when backlit, that folded down to become a secondary apron. They met the considerable scenic demands and playing requirements quite resourcefully. The costumes were lavish and in period, the dance and mime sequences well choreographed.

The casting was superb on the female side, a bit less than that on the male, where only the winning Mendoza of Sergei Aleksashkin was fully satisfying. I was also disappointed in some of the comic shtick resorted to, and the obvious, elbow-in-the-ribs handling of the Duenna-disguised-as-Louisa sequence. But the personalities were engaging, the playing always alive and released. This was a true company performance.

NOTES

1. See, for instance, Charles Rosen in *Harper's Magazine*, March, 1998, and Russell Sherman in his beautiful little book, *Piano Pieces* (Farrar, Straus & Giroux, 1996). Both these writers hear Schoenberg as an almost extravagant emotionalist. *Heart and Brain in Music* (1946) has been re-printed several times. My source is *Style and Idea*, revised edition, ed. Leonard Stein, trans. Leo Black (Univ. of Calif. Press, 1984). The theme recurs in Schoenberg's writings.

2. See: *Arnold Schoenberg: Letters*, ed. Erwin Stein, trans. Eithne Wilkins and Ernst Kaiser (Univ. of Calif. Press, 1987, pp. 139-40).

3. *Letters*, p. 133.

4. "Melting; pompous; spirited; lamenting; in the manner of a recitative; laughs." See Schoenberg: *Von Heute auf Morgen*, vocal score, Edition Benno Balan, Berlin, pp. 22-23, Bars 199-207.

5. See *Numbers*, 20, and *Deuteronomy*, 34.

6. *Letters*, pp. 242-243.

7. *Style and Idea*, pp. 244-45.

8. At least not exactly. *Summer* (David P. Gordon, des.): three rising terraces marked off by bellied tiers of wooden slats, like a rolltop desk; the scenes defined by set pieces and scrim effects, with projected slides at the rear and lighting levels necessarily low. The effect was of a display case in front of a diorama. *Emmeline* (Robert Israel, des.): a bleached plank deck with sunken pits used for burial and workplace scenes; border lights at the front lip and a three-panel wall upstage, the lighting flat and white. *Central Park* (Michael Yeargan, des.): a plain, open box, sparsely dressed (bench here, potted tree there), minimal lighting definition, some mood only in the *Food of Love* segment. This set bore the marks of keep-it-cheap, keep-it-simple constraints. *Gatsby* (Yeargan, des): gauzy and open, silhouettes and projections, just the necessary furnishings. Black-and-white for a couple of scenes, pale lovely luminosities (peach, aqua) for the rest. *Streetcar* (Yeargan, des., as seen on video): this set does show us the cramped Kowalski household in lifelike detail. Even here, though, the rooms are set into a revolving unit (convenient for exterior/interior) that floats in a dark surround. On video we are taken into the rooms, but in the theatre the open perspective would be constant. Williams asked for a neighborhood; this gives us Space. The feel is more easily associated with *Glass Menagerie* (a memory play) than with *Streetcar*.

9. But oddly, it hasn't been much used. *Postcard*, an original work and a deliberate throwback, is the only opera I can think of to adopt the pattern. In theatre, the form reached a noir-ish apotheosis with Williams' *Camino Real*. There, though, the entrapment itself is the point, a fixed condition of life with the hope of release only a tease, and the protagonist's destruction the dénouement. Of all Williams' plays, it seems the most inviting operatically—certainly more so than those thus far attempted (*Streetcar* and *Summer and Smoke*). Its closest operatic equivalent, *The Consul*, actually preceded *Camino Real* by three years.

10. See the composer's note in the booklet accompanying the *Postcard* recording. See also Donohue's note in the same source, and in *Showcase* (Twin Cities program magazine), Vol. I No. 2, Oct., 1971.

11. For a sensible evaluation of cuts and restorations in the *Porgy* score, see David Hamilton's review of the Maazel recording (*High Fidelity*, May 1976, reprinted in *Records in Review*, Wyeth Press, Gt. Barrington, MA, 1977), as well as Jon Alan Conrad's chapter on the opera in *The Metropolitan Opera Guide to Recorded Opera* (W.W. Norton & Co., NY, 1993).

12. See *Peter Hall's Diaries*, ed. John Goodwin, Harper & Row, NY, 1984, p. 417.

13. Not quite literally. In the 1960s there was a production by the Bel Canto Opera, and before that (1948, just two years after the world premiere in Prague), by the Lemonade Opera. The former effort, in workshop format, was plucky but seriously overambitious. I did not see the earlier version, but the Lemonade was a nice little company. Its production was staged by Max Leavitt and conducted by Sam Morgenstern, both well-regarded professionals, and ran for 53 performances. Note to small companies: The vocal score published by Leeds (New York) contains the English translation apparently used in those performances, a feasible-looking one by Jean Karsavina. Orchestral parts may exist for a reduction (the Lemonade production used a few instruments), but since many of the score's captivating passages are for instrumental solos or small groupings, an extraction should not be difficult in any case. The full score was published by State Publishing, Moscow, 1967.

14. Unfortunately, anyone recently making first acquaintance with this opera is apt to encounter an obstacle in the form of an anti-Semitism alert that is as unnecessary as it could be off-putting. This subject usually makes its operatic appearance in relation to Wagner. In that connection, an eminently sensible statement can be found in the Appendix of Bryan Magee's *The Tristan Chord* (Metropolitan, N.Y. 2001); the matter is also touched on below (pp. 345-347) in relation to *Tannhäuser*. With respect to *Betrothal*, the question is raised first in the Prokofiev entry in the *New Grove Dictionary of Opera* by Richard Taruskin, which is cited in turn by Bernard Jacobson in the booklet accompanying the Maryinsky recording *and* by James Oestreich in his *New York Times* review of the Maryinsky production (April 28, 1998). The concern centers on the character of Isaac Mendoza, the fish merchant. This much is true: in Sheridan, Mendoza is identified as a Portuguese Jew who has recently renounced his Portuguese citizenship and converted to Christianity. These facts are briefly discussed as they relate to Mendoza's suitability as a husband for Louisa (*The Duenna*, Act I, Scene iii). It's the sort of discussion that might still take place in traditional Christian families (or traditional Jewish ones, for that matter), though of course in our theatre the lines would be carefully allotted to unsympathetic characters to whom we can feel morally superior. Savvy members of Sheridan's audiences might have found resonances with the case of Roderigo Lopez (Portuguese Jewish physician to Elizabeth I, executed for treason on fabricated charges), to Shakespeare's Shylock, or to the singer Leoni, who stood before them in the role of Don Carlos (more prominent in the play—especially in the songs—than in the opera), an Italian Jew. Eighteenth-Century London is in any case a very different context. For a balanced discussion of that, see Fintan O'Toole's fine biography of Sheridan, *A Traitor's Kiss* (Farrar, Straus & Giroux, NY, 1999, pp. 106-113) or, better yet, simply read the play, hear the opera, and consult the latter's libretto. (O'Toole also discusses the play's anti-[Catholic] clericalism, occasion for more tsk-tsking by Taruskin because Prokofiev has a fine time with Sheridan's corrupt, drunken monks.) For here's the thing: whatever one feels about Sheridan's Jewish characters, the only trace of them left in Prokofiev/Mendelson is Mendoza's first name. As Taruskin admits, all other references to Jewishness have been removed. In the music, there is no hint of commentary. Indeed,

Don Jerome is the one who could be heard as stereotypically Jewish—there is nothing in Mendoza's music that comes as close to that as Jerome's whining over his daughter or gloating over his ducats. One could easily take it as part of the opera's fun that Christian characters behave in accordance with the Jewish comic stereotype. The Duenna herself, ill-favored but Christian, aims for Mendoza and his money from the outset. Granted, there is still the matter of stage behavior: Mendoza *could* be portrayed in an offensive manner. Oestreich detected this in the makeup of the Maryinsky performer (Sergei Aleksashkin), and while I did not pick up on it from my seat in the first row of the Grand Tier or from the souvenir program photos, the video (different performance but same production, same performer) does disclose a big prosthetic hooked nose. Diadkova, as the Duenna, is also given a heavy makeup job to emphasize the character's ugliness, and both these performers are drawn into a fair amount of mugging. This is imitation-Restoration stereotyping of the comic-grotesque figures, historically probably defensible but in my opinion artistically objectionable and in poor taste. It is, however, a production choice, not an ingredient of the work. Anti-Semitism is certainly to be deplored, but only where it exists. This utterly benign, joyous opera should not be put in its shadow.

15. Until its presentation of *The Gambler* in the Spring of 2001 (thanks to its working agreement with the Maryinsky), the Metropolitan had produced nothing of Prokofiev's—an astounding record of neglect, for all the practical difficulties. Prior to the Maryinsky's recent stands with *Flaming Angel, Betrothal* and *Semyon Kotko*, the Bolshoi brought to the house Boris Pokrovsky's impressive production of *The Gambler* in 1975 (it sold so poorly that one of its scheduled performances was replaced by a repetition of *Eugene Onegin*), and its strongly cast *War and Peace* in the same year. A dull ENO *War and Peace* visited in 1984. Otherwise, New York has relied on the NYCO (*Flaming Angel* in 1965, *Love for Three Oranges* in 1949 and several subsequent seasons) for its taste of the operatic Prokofiev. And, of course, The Lemonade Opera.

5

THERE AND THEN

(Mar. 1994–Mar. 2002)

ACTUALISM

Most of the critical tests applied in this book are by now familiar to the reader. But as we begin to consider productions of canonical works, one of these tests merits emphasis. It underlies the reactions of all receptors, but is seldom confessed. Connoisseurs and critics are ashamed to admit to it. A furtiveness surrounds it. I call it Actualism because it holds the artist accountable for actually doing what he says he's going to do—not indicating it, but actually doing it. With respect to a production, this means following to the letter its own rules: whatever it states to be the case must continue to be the case. That in turn dictates that all its parts agree with one another, which is another way of saying that the production is fully integrated. It also asks that this integration aim for a perfect fit with that of the work itself, thus creating an Actualism of the Whole.

So Actualism is not the same as realism. It is not, in itself, a style. It is, however, a kind of literalism, and it is a horror of the literal that makes people furtive and ashamed. I think literalism is natural and crucial, and should be proclaimed the first principle of performance criticism. This is because of all the little brain barriers. That is how I think of the steps we take away from theatrical literalism, the leaps and assumptions we ask of our imaginations. It's not that we can't take these steps. Of course we can. The engagement is an agreement, and assent is ours to give or withhold.

But a price is paid. At each brain barrier a toll is exacted, in the currency of belief. Sensory impressions that were headed straight for our oldest and deepest parts are sent on longer, more complicated routes. We can still believe, but the nature of belief has changed, however slightly and surreptitiously. It has taken on more the quality of considered assent, and less that of spontaneous surrender. With the passage of each barrier, the receptor moves closer to an engagement consisting *exclusively* of considered assent. He is distanced in a particular direction, and probably feeling self-congratulatory. He is quite the sophisticate. His brain has overridden all barriers to belief, as if they did not exist. At each one, he's reassured himself: "Yes, of course, I understand. It's not a problem." He's in full, conscious control of the engagement. But in exchange, he has lost his capacity for giving himself over to the emotional, visceral aspects of the experience. He has relinquished two vital parts of himself. One is the child, the same child reached by the tune. The other, paradoxically, is the skeptic. For it is the skeptic who says, "No, I don't believe that. It *is* a problem." It is the inner being formed of these two parts—the skeptical child—who insists on actualism.

Wherever it is applied along the interpretive chain, Actualism necessitates pickiness and doggedness. It pursues detail in a way that can seem petty to those with a more relaxed attitude. We have already had examples in *Susannah*'s unnatural shadows, frumpy dress, and prettied-up house. Those belong to different orders of transgression (the first contradicts the laws of the physical universe and could not happen under any circumstances, while the others depart from given circumstances of the work), but all are Actualist violations. All concede that something stated to be the case isn't the case, after all.

To the Actualist, these are not small things. Each non-observance sends a message, and while not all the messages are consciously noted, they are absorbed at some level of attention, and nudge the receptor farther from unreserved belief. If there are many of them, the receptor shifts into neutral. *Unreserved* belief is no longer even an issue. This state of neutrality, of tacit agreement, is frequently misread as a loss of interest in the there-and-then repertory, a proof of its "irrelevance." I believe it's almost entirely due to deficiencies of performance. If the operatic engagement repeatedly fails to deliver what it seems to imply, what grounds has the receptor for asking more of it? Only a sense of something missing that is all too easy to mistake for something missing in oneself. And among the receptors, setting a certain tone, are the aforementioned sophisticates and connoisseurs, who have reified and re-reified their experiences so often that they stand permanently on the other side of all these barriers, quite out of touch with their basic operatic reflexes. We who criticize are leading candidates for membership in this group, and so have a particular obligation to embrace Actualism and nurture the skeptical child.

Because Actualism involves a clear definition of the interpretive field, an accountability for everything inside it, and an uncompromising enforcement of behavioral laws within it, it is vital to the success of any performance style. In fact, in opera Actualism is most often encountered well away from the mainstream. There, a passionate commitment to the very idea of what is being done and the necessity of doing it, and an intense devotion to visionary auteurs of strong personality, give enterprises the energy and focus demanded by an Actualist approach. *Einstein on the Beach* was an Actualist production. It asked: are they really going to go on counting? Is the train really going to move imperceptibly until it's gone? Is she really going to stand on one leg until you think a statue's replaced her? Actually, yes. Furthermore, the execution of these actions will be thorough. The interpreters are not going to merely suggest these things or ask you to assume them, they're going to carry them out. So, while one might eventually reject the entire engagement, as I did, by not agreeing to its stipulations, one could only envy it as a specimen of Actualism.

With respect to the physical production, the same could be said of Wilson's *Lohengrin*. But as I have tried to show, this production represented an Actualism that was adversarial in concept, that created an opposition between eye and ear (the "strengthening of elements"), and that proposed itself as an eye-led experience. Thus, it embraced one major internal contradiction, induced another in the receptor, and turned upside-down the sensory balance of opera itself. At issue here is whether or not these are good things for interpreters to be doing. The obvious alternative is an Actualism of the Whole, and in this regard it is worth noting that when functioning as creators, contemporary auteurs do not find it necessary to disassemble or contradict their own work. *Einstein on the Beach* is Actualist as creation and interpretation, a true *Gesamtkunstwerk*. Eye and ear confirm each other endlessly. The eye is nearly always dominant, but that is embedded in the work itself, part of what it states to be the case. I think it's reasonable to suppose that if we were to re-interpret *Einstein* through adversarial commentary, assigning the counting duet to heavy-breathing Italian *veristos*, giving Lucinda Childs thirty minutes of Romantic ballet choreography, substituting Jack Benny with his fiddle for Einstein with his, and transferring the action to 9th Century Ireland—changes not a bit more radical than those often imposed on classical repertory operas—Wilson would protest. He would explain that while it is all right to strengthen Wagner's elements, we should leave his alone. He would claim consistency of style and literalness of detail as integral to the creative concept. He would insist on Actualism of the Whole.

The question of which actions can be made to fit which music is of course an open one. One of the successes of recent directorial conceptualization has been to show that at least on a moment-to-moment, de-contextualized basis, nearly anything will go with anything. Such moments defy critique. "It works" is the sole criterion, and nearly anything *can* "work" if it doesn't have to be attached to anything else. Nearly anything can even be eloquent. But that requires two things: an emotionally apt place in the context of the work, and room in the receptor's tapestry. *Bob* afforded an example. It appropriated Wagner's music, and in that sense must be categorized as pastiche, like the Bayreuth show in *Postcard from Morocco*. But the *Bob* sequence, unlike that in *Postcard*, did not leave an aftertaste of rip-off or belittlement. To the contrary, it made the point that Wagner's music can make a drink of milk into an overwhelming dramatic event. It took a substantial section of the Act One *Lohengrin* prelude and used it to build "Bob's" final grasp of the iconic glass: it was as this music waxed and glowed that "Bob" slowly approached and bent, then seized and raised the brimming glass. It was exactly at the stroke of the climactic chord with its cymbal crash that "Bob" greedily gulped. Ecstasy, transfiguration! Anything can go with anything! It doesn't have to be about the Grail, only a tall Texan tumbler! Not the blood of Christ, just some milk.

Note, however, the artistic care with which Wagner's music has been reset. The glass of milk has been previously established as something of great, though mysterious, importance in the life of the character—a life sufficiently rounded and intense for us to invest in. The analogy between the glass and the Grail chalice is sensorily clear, not a barrier but an instantaneous connection. So is the relevance of the particular musical passage, and the function of the music for the real-life Bob, who has recently staged this very opera. And the music's power is not undercut, as in *Postcard*, but given rein, performed as written by a full orchestra on an excellent audio system, shaking the theatre with deep, undistorted sound. That was a moment of ear-led, eye-confirmed Actualist fulfillment made central and resonant by the context of the work. To fully receive it, however, Wilsonians in the audience had to know a lot about *Lohengrin*, Wagnerians a lot about Wilson. And for both, surrender to the music was imperative. In a predominantly eye-led work whose ear-content was almost exclusively verbal, this moment relied on the primacy of music. Whether or not Bob honored Wagner, Wagner honored "Bob," lending him dignity and depth.

Professionally skillful though it may be, an Actualist realization of an adversarial concept does not encourage belief in a creator's work, but in a critique of it; not in any version of a work's thesis, but in some proposed antithesis. It asks receptors to accept the resulting confusion as The Work. But it remains confusion, however intellectually agile the justifications for it are. Its ruling idea has originated either from outside the boundaries of the interpretive field, or from a process of metaphorical reduction that has crossed so many brain barriers as to have left all life-giving specifics far behind. Therefore, it cannot account for many of the phenomena within the field, which now present themselves as inherent implausibilities. It will not lead receptors' imaginations deeper into the life of the work, but guide them elsewhere. In short, such an interpretation cannot be an Actualism of the Whole, which requires interpreters to work from internal evidence and account for all of it.

It is in the light of an Actualism of the Whole that the works and productions to follow will be considered.

To engage with productions of operas of the classical canon is to focus on the powers and limitations of interpretation. This is particularly so with standard repertory works, those that have instructed us in their constant qualities through long experience, repetition, and interpretive variance. With them, we feel we know what may fairly be ascribed to interpretation, a knowledge we cannot so confidently assert with respect to new work.

These are the operas that have earned a place in place of others. The reasons why are among the points of interest here, especially at a time when significant shuffling of the classical repertory has taken place, and interpretation itself has assumed a new and problematic role. Our predicament is not entirely a matter of the here and now; it is equally a question of the there and then. If the latter is found to be at once indispensable but culturally incommodious (as it is), and its interpretation largely a means of criticism into which creative energies are displaced (as it has), it is clear that the creative frustrations of our present are at one with evasions and dishonesties about our past.

The productions discussed below are sorted according to their governing elements. While production teams usually aim for balance and unity in their collaborations, their work has to start somewhere, and this usually means that one of the elements becomes determinant in shaping the production. In some cases, this element is design, in others a choreographic language, in still others a thematic concept. Regardless of how a production develops or whose choices eventually rule its fate, the director must in all cases be held responsible for the whole, and that will be the working assumption here.

Since there are many productions to consider and most are of only routine interest, they will be commented upon piecemeal, as they relate to their determinant elements or other issues argued here.

TIME TRAVEL: UPDATING

Of all the contemporary revisionist approaches to production, updating is the oldest and still the most commonplace. In our theatre, money limitations mothered this invention—a spare production style and clothes off the rack or, often, out of the closet—were and are its hallmarks, and costume its main delineator. "Modern dress" was in fact its customary appellation. In our major opera companies, though, money is not usually the point, and not much of it is saved. Updating is an artistic choice. Its ostensible purpose, like that of the enhancements, is to bring interpreters and audience closer together by placing them on common cultural ground where the understood rules of dress, behavior, and attitude are followed and social distinctions can be effortlessly recognized.

Updating can serve this purpose, and that is surely preferable to an in-period production whose specificities have not been addressed. Currently, though, updating is usually used as a lazy shorthand, the boilerplate of an audience-appeasement pact. It has its own specificities, and production teams tend to address the convenient ones, leaving the rest as loose ends. For directors, updating involves some stretching and straining, for it requires them to search for cultural parallels for character relationships and behavior, as well as in the "production values." It is hoped that such parallels will clarify or illumine; often this hope inspires the production concept. At the least, the parallels seek to "justify." They try to make the original motivations and actions believable in their new context, usually through substitutions. This can work in certain instances, but overall it is a hopeless errand: those parts won't fit, no matter how hard we try. Though one often cannot help but admire the inventiveness of these justifications and substitutions, they generally succeed in solving peripheral problems while bypassing or even exacerbating the central ones. And since our response begins with acknowledging their ingenuity—"getting" them—they are inherently amusing: whatever the originally intended affect of a given moment may have been, it is now also a little joke. The engagement takes on gamelike qualities. Its value as theatrical entertainment may be reinforced, but its standing as dramatic event is weakened.

Since everything is in place of something else, the gains and losses of updating must be evaluated on a case-by-case basis. For the moment, I shall set aside productions I call "pan-dated" (a jumble of elements across several periods) or dis-dated (e.g., everyone in white on an abstract set), as well as those in which updating is one element of a deconstructivist concept or other general postmodern commentary, and consider those wherein a forward time-shift (or, sometimes, a time-and-place shift) is the primary interpretive technique.

One of these was the NYCO *La Bohème*, directed by James Robinson. Having heard a few things about the production (that its time had been advanced by eighty-some years, to the eve of World War I, and that it sported home-front military artifacts), I smiled on my way to the theatre for reasons purely personal that are, however, relevant. In the late 1960s, the tenor John Stewart* and I worked on the brief opening scene (Rodolfo and Marcello in the garret, working) in Frank Corsaro's operatic acting class. For some of the behavioral reasons alluded to above, which coincided with the objectives of the class, we decided that Rodolfo and Marcello were American ex-G.I.'s who'd participated in the liberation of Paris in 1944, then returned there at war's end for the arts scene, the cafés, and the women. Two or three years later (don't know if John and I planted a seed), Frank devised a *La Bohème* set in the ex-pat community of post-World War I Paris, with an English-language adaptation by Anne Bailey that allowed for the necessary textual adjustments. It raised some questions (all updates do), but answered them rather plausibly.† And now, here was a *Bohème* with a First-World-War milieu, and I felt myself a particle of its atavistic past.

In Robinson's production, the attempts to work out the implications of its chosen period grew more grotesque from scene to scene. I liked the first-act set, a life-sized little whitewashed studio with a ladder to its roof (though its perch in an open surround may have contributed to the acoustical difficulties alluded to earlier), and there was nothing egregious visually or behaviorally in this scene. Act II brought an invention for Parpignol that at first seemed charming and lively: the fact that the toy seller's lines are sung offstage before his entrance allowed for the casting of a mime for the vending scene. The note sounds nice overtones—of Parisian street performance, of the French mime tradition, and of the Pierrot-ishness that was in the air of the time, though musically most often in Germanic or Russian expressions. It is even a reasonable character choice (he's learned a few mime bits to help attract the children), though for this purpose the performance was too expert. But Parpignol's brief stand was not the mime's destination. The war has begun, its grand strategy being to cast a long symbolic shadow of historical hindsight over early Puccini operas. In the finale, the tattoo is manned by *poilus*,

---

* Who sang several seasons with the NYCO, and many more in Europe, most of them based in Frankfurt during the Gielen/Zehelein/Berghaus years. He then became head of the opera department at Washington University, St. Louis.

† In Act II, for instance, the Café Momus showed us the *Moveable Feast* crowd, and the Barrière d'Enfer of Act III was a grimy factory district with workers changing shifts through the chain-link fence—this desolate scene worked particularly well. The adaptation was commissioned by the Southern Regional Opera in Atlanta and was later franchised to other American regional companies. I saw it at the Lake George Festival.

its sergeant-major ("*Di Francia è il più bell'uom,*" sing the chorus women) is off to Flanders' fields, and across the apron, outside the frame displaying the festive scene to the audience, marches the mime as Death the Commander, straight out of the old Kurt Jooss ballet *The Green Table. Schaden,* but no *Freude.*

Act III featured a locomotive. It emitted a belch of steam over the sharp opening chords, and the rest of the act was hoist on this pétard. I expected the engine to do something, perhaps creep on apace in Wilsonian fashion or, for symmetry's sake, obliterate the answering chords at act's end. But it remained strictly decorative, and the setting—at a railhead, with no gate, no tavern—left whole scenes not only without a playable place, but without a playable action (the opening sequence, for instance, is literally about passing a physical barrier), and nothing was done to carry through the life of the new setting as background to play against.

My anticipatory dread concerning Act IV—what would they do with the byplay leading up to Musetta's entrance?—was vindicated several times over. Of the libretto's many Second Empire references that must be fudged to accommodate updating, none are more bothersome than all those to the King, to Guizot, to travestied formalities of duel and quadrille, to the "noble assembly" and the "manners of a lackey," and so on.* Since, unlike the Corsaro/Bailey adaptation, this one is left in the original language, the solution is to sing the words as written but misrepresent them in the titles, relying on the audience's Namish ignorance and uninterest to cram it all down their throats. And so, it is not "Il Re," Louis-Phillippe, but "The General" who summons Colline to the "War Ministry." Schaunard is actually in the army, home on leave and in uniform. The friends' adolescent mock-aristocratic bowings and scrapings, their silly gavotte and minuet must somehow overlook the real war, or else embrace it and set up an unresolvable conflict with the music and the spirit of the actions that inspire it. The duel carries the scene into the realm of the unthinkable: Rodolfo and Marcello, Schaunard and Colline playing at trench warfare. The spectacle of the Marne, the Somme, and the Ardennes Forest is evoked—gas attacks, machine guns, finishing off with bayonet—these are the Bohemians' jolly, giggly games.

It's not merely that prominent elements of the production are "out of style" (true enough) or in execrable taste (true again), or that many details must be blurred or twisted to fit. It's not even that *La Bohème's* story and music will not bear the weight of worldwide slaughter and the disintegration of European civilization, though that's getting closer. It's that the characters' ability to dismiss politics, economics, and the scorned bourgeois quotidian,

---

* In 1914, these would be the fantasies not of Bohemians, but of nostalgic royalists, the society's arch-conservatives.

and to live instead in their art-for-art's-sake world, with the ways of friendship, love, and death that are of that world, is the necessary precondition for story and music, and our willingness to sympathize with their aspirations the prerequisite for accepting the premise. To ignore World War I, however, is not to be an idealistic, hopeless romantic, but a self-absorbed idiot. There is nothing sympathetic about that.

More problematic than any of the things that are done in productions like this are the things that are not done. Many of them have to do with singing, acting, and singingacting, and will be dealt with later on. But the thinking here seems to have gone wrong from the start, to judge by Robinson's program note.[1] It opens with the false assumption that if the production team cannot find something ". . . to say about *La Bohème* that has not been said before," they are helpless ("perplexed," actually) before their task. Following a paragraph descriptive of the Parisian social and artistic scene circa 1914 (in effect, a list of reasons why this opera could not take place in that time), Robinson concludes with the question, "Is Rodolfo's final outburst a mournful cry over the death of the doomed Mimì or rage against a world that would never be seen again?" The answer is: the former.

"Jonathan Miller: he's so bright, why can't he direct?" So reads the opening of a performance journal entry I made in 1996. It's unfair, of course, but I was exasperated. Here's a droll and intelligent fellow who's not an adversarial conceptualist or deconstructionist. I've been predisposed in his favor ever since *Beyond the Fringe*, and want to like his work. But most of the time, I don't. With only one exception in my experience, he dances out around the edges of pieces, full of invention but reluctant to dig into characters or music, and ends up seeming just another of the English cleverists. And his use of updating, to which he frequently resorts, is part of the problem.

This was true of Miller's *Rosenkavalier* for the NYCO, which prompted my little journal outburst. He had brought the time forward to the date of the premiere (1911—again, the eve of World War I), a favorite updatist move. It made no sense. It was just a look, and a chance for some joke-on-joking that, if you thought about it for even a second, turned very sour. Take the setting for Act II, the reception hall of Faninal's *Stadtpalais*. In a traditional interpretation, this room helps show us how the elegance of aristocratic taste is passing into a degraded, inflated mimickry in the relatively untutored hands of the rising middle class, just as the Marschallin is giving over her noble young lover to a daughter of that class, and that something genuine is lost with these presumably desirable and inevitable changes. The *mise en scène* thus needs to convey something of the nouveau pretensions of its owner, a *bourgeois gentilhomme* whose pomposity and servility are unmistakable in the music. Yet (as the music also tells us), the Faninalish aspirations of the time produced a certain magnificence. There must be a genuine splendor to the Presentation of the Silver Rose. And while we are surely intended to smile ruefully at Faninal's flounderings, we aren't meant to smirk in contempt. He's in a predicament, after all, and it is important to the work's resolution that we feel some empathy with Sophie's father.

Miller had to stretch for 1911 parallels in these class relationships, and so his Faninal lived in a house whose gallery displayed a rank of gilded heroic archers, indicative (at the parody-skit level) of the very worst taste in early 20th Century decorative monumentalism. Indeed, their Mussolini-esque cast suggested a proto-Fascistic Faninal, and this not only takes the comment on the character to an almost savage pitch, but brings us up against the underlying unfeasibility of the update: these relationships, these customs and social assumptions, in that Vienna? Never mind, for a moment, that we have thrown out the fantasy of the late Baroque that Strauss and Hofmannsthal crafted for us—it's only the wellspring of the passing beauty and shining renewal that is the heart of the work. And what is to be in its place? The Vienna of Mahler and Schoenberg, of Klimt and Kokoschka and Schiele, of Freud and Herzl, of the end of the Habsburgs, the rise of Karl Lueger and anti-Semitism? *That* city? Only if you turn off your brain. Only if your sensibilities are numb.

With your brain off, you may not notice that Miller's picturesque cultural-reference parallels function as decoy targets, pulling focus from the emptiness of core relationships and scenes, and that they are usually drawn not from the life of the period in question, but from other cultural representations of it, often movies. His celebrated Mafia *Rigoletto*, set in New York's Little Italy in the 1950s, was inspired by *The Godfather* and *Some Like it Hot*,[2] his *Mikado* by black-and-white film comedies (*Grand Hotel, Animal Crackers,* Busby Berkeley musicals). In *Der Rosenkavalier*, the Marschallin posed for us with her cigarette in holder, a world-weary sophisticate off a fashion page or an aperitif ad.

For his *Pelléas et Mélisande* at the Met, Miller and his designer, John Conklin, place the action in a decaying dirty-white house with flaking gold trim, propped up by scaffolding. A jumble of loosely related rooms, it revolves from position to position during Debussy's eloquent scene-change interludes. The doorways gape, the turntable creaks. The light is white, the costumes white-and-black, the servants white-in-black, padding about silently like the albinos in Nicholas Hytner's ENO production of Handel's *Xerxes*.[3] Altogether, the spectacle is reminiscent of a ruined upper-class London club—the creepiest place an Englishman knows, I guess. The black-and-white scheme recalls other Miller productions (*Mikado, Káťa Kabanová*), and the scaffolding turns up again in his *Nozze di Figaro*. The time would appear to be around that of the work's composition, which would make it . . . let's see, here . . . the eve of World War I!

It would be one thing if these changes gave the performers something to work with. At his best (for me, in *Káťa*, whose essentially veristic nature he concedes, and for which his timeshift does not really disturb the pressures necessary to the drama) Miller does this. But here, the production not only is of no help to the performers, but stands in their way. If you are Mélisande, forever displacing your emblems of sex and status in watery depths, and you must play with your crown and your ring not over a forest pool or the Blindmen's Fountain, but a boarded-over sump, you and your audience have some barriers to leap.

It's only honest to concede that the set has atmospheric value, and is a plausible alternative to the castle (*très noir et très profond*) in the interior scenes. It avoids some of the old *Pelléas* humiliations, like Mélisande's flaxen *chevelure* tangled in a plastic vine on a pasteboard wall. But consider some of the possibilities foreclosed:

- Variety of locale, beginning with the basic indoor/outdoor distinction—stony halls, cloistered rooms, and dank subterranean vaults on one hand; tangled forest, dappled park and fountain, moonlit grotto or seaview terrace on the other. For all these, the production must pose substitutions. Some of these "work" (the scaffolding as stand-in for the vaults) and some do not (the sump). All stretch.

- Any feel of sea and sky or the lights and colors thereof, lost to the dark surround.

- The pull of legend, of storybook daydream, together with the variations on Medieval-ish tone they suggest (e.g., grim Gothic, lush pre-Raphaelite, Book of Hours Provençal). This tone is explicit in the text because of what is implicit in the text: the belief world of the characters. In that world the sense of decaying matter, the pull toward death, is present not because an era is dying, but because all human existence is seen as a trap from which the soul must free itself. Its events of light and color are chosen not only because they are picturesque, but because they represent an interplay between planes of existence and mark the stations of a predestined journey.

- Beauty, both of this world (all the more ripe and intense for being illusory) and of the beckoning beyond, for this revolving pile is no prettier than a set for *The Caretaker*. Indeed, with a sagging couch and a sprung chair or two, it could *be* a set for *The Caretaker*. Which leads our summation of losses to its final item:

- Any hint of French, or even Continental, identity. The damned show looks English. *This show is not English*. Conceivably, it could be Matter-of-Britain ur-English—Avalonish mists, emerald gleams—but anything post-Arthur is *out. Not everything is about the fall of empire*. The whole world is not black and white, and the clock is not stuck at one minute till World War I.

The *Bohème, Rosenkavalier,* and *Pelléas* productions are all approximate examples of the era-of-composition update. That is not the only kind. The Met's *Capriccio* of a few seasons back, faced with the impossibility of the date of premiere (1942—Occupation Paris? You see the problem) settled for the 1920s. It didn't help a bit. The incongruities of updating were still evident—*tout Paris* atwitter in the '20s with the *Guerre des Bouffons*, dropping the names of Gluck and Piccinni, of *"den alten Goldoni,"* of Pascal, the Countess musing over Couperin and Rameau, Flamand with his sonnet—who, onstage or off, can buy any of this? Yet, the performers were no less constrained by these attitudes and poses and costumes than by those of the original, so we had at once the contradictions of an update with the obligations of period, both unsolved. Even more foolish was the City Opera's *Capuleti e i Montecchi* ("around 1910"—what conflict looms?). With Romeo in preppie jacket, vest, tie and haircut, and Giuletta prim in a Gibson do and white dress, this looked like a date to a rumble between the great houses of Eton and Harrow, until the fighting factions emerged in contemporary cammo fatigues to make nonsense of even that conceit.

More thoughtful updates than these have their rationales, sometimes plausible. But such rationales are as easily set aside as invented. The date-of-composition update can be sensibly defended as a search for unity of tone. Sir Peter Hall is fond of saying that however a historical opera is staged, it should "look like the music." That sounds fine. It's on the side of eye/ear confirmation (and so against the "mutual strengthening of elements"), and seems to respect the boundaries of the creator's field by taking his soundworld into account. But what does music look like? Which of its attributes are being selected for visual representation, and whose ears are doing the selecting? Is that the Holy Grail, or a glass of milk? Besides, by this reasoning nearly all standard repertory operas would have to be set in the mid-to-late-19th Century, always excepting those set on the eve of World War I.

A plea for time-and-place shifts in general (and especially for fully contemporized, localized productions like Peter Sellars') is frequently entered in the name of universality or timelessness, the idea being that the essential content of a great work holds true in all times and places, and that freeing the work from the fetters of its original setting will convey its universal and eternal nature. This argument betrays the very faith it professes. It is only if a work is *not* seen as eternal and universal that such basic elements as time and place of setting would require transposition. Universality is not reinforced by pretending that the there-and-then was just like the here-and-now; on the contrary, we see it best when the enduring essence of a work, its "timeless" human meaning, shines through a clear definition of its differences. "Universal" usually turns out to mean merely generalized.

And yet: my two favorite *Don Giovanni* videos are both updates. They are Hall's and Sellars' own, the former brought forward to date of composition or a little beyond, the latter to the South Bronx, circa 1990.[4] Their theatrical vitality (far beyond that of any of the productions considered above) is owed not to the fact of updating, but to their directors' use of it to pursue detailed, moment-to-moment character action in the framework of precisely defined social conditions. The same could be said of Vick's *Lady Macbeth of Mzensk* or the Corsaro *Bohème* adaptation, and the one thing the directors of these productions (otherwise so different in taste, temperament and working method) have in common is their appetite for that pursuit, for an Actualistic rendering of a singingacted life. Fortunately, talent and hard work trump rationale every time; Aron still comes out on top.

The relative merits and failings of particular productions notwithstanding, it is important to note, finally, that like all revisionist production styles, updating requires the substitution of the interpreter's judgment for the creator's. Regardless of what all these composers and librettists thought they were writing about, we think we know better. We think this only because we are beyond the work. We can fix it in its time, and assign to it a new set of associations and assessments. These associations and assessments can have their own interest and meaning. But these are about the work, not of it. Rather than conveying the work directly to us, they locate it by triangulation. "No great opera can escape its period," says Hall (its period of composition, that is, not its indicated setting). Not escape, perhaps, but—and here is what the universalist plea is trying to get at—transcend. Such transcendence is, in fact, a standard measure of greatness, sorting the works that are renewable and re-affirmable from those that are time-bound. What Hall's statement comes down to is that *we* have escaped the great opera's period, and choose to view it from a perspective rather than go back inside it.

The creators had no such perspective. They stood inside their fields, looking out. Among the things they saw, or imagined they saw, was the life of the period they were writing about. It was before them as they wrote. It penetrated their words and music. Its influence in a given work may seem to us quite marginal, or to represent not the period itself, but a romanticization of it. We may judge it naïve or dated, or simply inadequate. But these observations are valid (when they are) only so long as our perspective is maintained. From there, it becomes convenient to ignore everything in the words and music that might spring from the creators' imagining of the original period of their work. That is why perspective—any perspective—is disastrous to an Actualism of the Whole, according to which it is not the director's job to assign and assess, to fix and triangulate, to objectify or dialecticize, but to attempt to be at one with the creator, enter into his subjective state, stand in the field with him and see what he saw. It is to *eliminate* perspective, not maintain it.

Our muddleheaded assertion that the creative element of interpretation is co-equal with creation itself is our true confession of creative impotence. We are badly in need of something new to put in place of the old, and we don't have it. So we pretend. The worst of our pretense is not the claim to have made something new, but the claim that the old is still available within it, the pure metal easily extracted from the alloy by those who want it. And that is not true.

THE EYE OF A GOD: CHOREOGRAPHY

In Act III of Glinka's *Ruslan and Lyudmila*, Prince Ratmir is lured from his quest for the abducted bride Lyudmila to an enchanted castle conjured by the scorceress Naina. Wearied by his arduous travels and feeling himself back on his native Khazar soil, he has seen visions of voluptuous maidens, and heard their singing. In a long double aria (gorgeous cavatina with clarinet obligato followed by a captivating waltz-song), he begs the maidens to come to him. And at the Maryinsky performance even the eyeless knew the lovelies were on the way and had then arrived, for on they thundered on pointe, in what I assume were historically authentic toe shoes carved of hardest oak, a leggy battery of untuned percussion. They did not await the aria's conclusion—they just barged on in.*

The momentary shock of this *entrée* started me thinking in several directions about the relationship between dance and song, ballet and opera. It reminded me, for one thing, that the Maryinsky remains an institution of a nearly extinct type, the resident ballet/opera company whose components share an orchestra and have access to each other's artistic resources. Such institutions reflect the view of ballet and opera as the twin lyric arts, closer to each other than to the spoken theatre. This view must be taken seriously. It has been dominant through long stretches of theatre history, and its implications

---

* For some reason, the noise is not audible on the Maryinsky's live recording of this production, taken from St. Petersburg performances, but trust me: it was there. Was the stage floor miked at the Met?

are embedded in opera's performance language and in the formal nature of many of its works.

Ruslan is one of these works. It incorporates dance as *divertissement*, pantomime as narrative, and, in this scene, an intermixing of dance and song. Indeed, the enchantress corps goes on to act out an elaborate scene among Ratmir, his abandoned beloved Gorislava, and then Ruslan, the dancers acting in ballet language, the principals answering with singingacting and whatever pantomime skills may be at their disposal. From our perspective, the scene can look forward to Parsifal with the Flower Maidens or even Alberich with the Rhine Maidens, or back to the true opera-ballets of the French Baroque, like Rameau's *"Ballet-Buffon" Platée*.

Platée came to the NYCO in a production directed and choreographed by Mark Morris, whose own company provided the dance component. I think it's possible that a spectacle of value to heart and brain is in the piece, though with expectations based on my previous experience of Rameau operas (*Castor et Pollux, Hippolyte et Aricie*—not comedies), I was disappointed in the score when I first came to it via the recording. But for all of us non-specialists in the period, there is a great deal of burrowing to do in the material before all but the most obvious qualities of characters and scenes begin to come clear. The music's gestural and timbral idiom (and, therefore, the nature of its theatricality) is entirely different from that of Handel or Gluck, and for lovers of singing there is a lot to get past in two well-filled CDs featuring predominantly special-team vocalists doing their period "character work"—it's like a whole evening of Papagena as the Old Woman and Gianni Schicchi as Buoso Donati. *Platée* is also one of the pieces for which that smaller, warmer auditorium would be most welcome.

Given the nature of the performing forces, it was obvious that no period reconstruction would be undertaken. The production was given an updated framework that embraced a now-familiar sort of mixed-period comment. It was good to see splashy color on the State Theatre stage. The costuming had a goofy theatricality, and some of it wit. In this hall, and with singers generally prettier of sound but less grounded in language and style than those of the recording, the score registered as a sequence of mild incidental pleasures— several nice little airs, a catchy *orage* or two, some charming color. And then, of course, Ye Baroquey Dances: we have the Jiggety-Jog, the Joggety-Jig, the Tiddely-Pom, and the Dumpitty-Dump, all rendered here as cheerful variations on polymorphous perversity. The dancers were not very successful as lip-synching actors, mugging and posing for the singing chorus down in the pit, but they were engaging enough as dancers, in their contemporary classical-pops way. The difficulty was that there are only so many moves to make and bits to play in illustration of the two or three jibes about sex and fashion that were the actual content of these many sequences, all of which are finally in the service of a tale about a repulsively ugly, deluded frog-woman who is mercilessly baited by superior creatures and then sent back to her swamp. It was all perfectly amiable—there was nothing to get upset about until afterward, when the question arose: this in place of what, exactly, and why?

The fundamental questions about an effort like *Platée* have to do with the physical language of performance, for which I must refer readers forward to the chapter on singingacting, and with the nature of the piece. It is an opera. The singing characters clearly carry the burden of its action and its emotional life. Dance embellishes and diverts, and can be made to respond and comment, but it does not impel. Still, there's no doubt that *Platée* is heavy on dance, and that there is at least an argument for attempting to resolve its staging issues choreographically. This solution was also proposed for the *Orfeo*s of Gluck and Monteverdi, both presented in New York in the season of 1998-99, and both entrusted to directors whose orientation is choreographic: Martha Clarke and Trisha Brown.

With the late operas of Gluck in total and inexplicable neglect at the Metropolitan (we used to get *Orfeo* with regularity, and *Alceste* at intervals of a decade), one feels obligated to the City Opera for occasionally reminding us of these works, so musically powerful and, one would think, more dramatically accessible than those of Handel or Rameau. And in fact the company's productions of *Alceste* (1982) and *Iphigénie en Tauride* (1997) conveyed enough to keep hunger alive, if not to satisfy it. But the *Orfeo* was a calamity—visually depressing and musically feeble, with no discernible point of connection between Clarke and Gluck. It had little effect beyond dismissing the opera for another generation or so.

Brown's Monteverdi was more interesting. It started with the advantage of close collaboration with early-music forces of quality and experience and stylistically familiarized soloists, and without the disadvantage of fitting into a repertory season. This gave it a specificity and unity of tone to the ear which found a stage parallel, for the choral participants and principals had been well integrated into the movement language of Brown's own company. This cleverly blended performing unit peeled, wrapped, and then cleared for the one-on-one scenes in patterns that were often striking and responsive to the music. In the physical production, too, there were some simple, beautiful things—the crisp bifurcation of the stage between bright light and nearly impenetrable dark as Orpheus encounters Charon at the river, or the black-and-deep-aqua cutout for the Pluto/Prosperina dialogue.

Against these virtues, and against the ultimate impact of the evening, must be set the feel of an abstract group-body-work project-in-process. As *L'Orfeo*'s opening brass-and-drums toccata sounds from the side boxes, we embark on a thrill ride to the source, to the earliest full stagework of opera's first master creator—and opera's response to Harold Bloom's brief for Shakespeare as the originator of the very idea of character in the modern sense, for while the personages of *L'Orfeo* are not as individualized as those of *Il Ritorno d'Ulisse in Patria* or *L'Incoronazione di Poppea*, they are certainly on the way. And here, at the birthplace, is more of our unisex discourse. The dancers ("We are loose, we are free, we have no hang-ups") pad and patter about the stage in their loose, free, undifferentiated costumes of white, occasionally overdressed with anonymous panels of dingy brown or landlord green that have an institutional look at times medical, at others sacramental—the vestments of our clergy of androgyny.

Also assisting at the service is The Tumbler. The brass give way to melting strings, the praises of La Musica ascend from (yes) the pit, and here she comes, an acrobatic young woman on wires turning somersaults across the disc-shaped cutout in the forecurtain. She's fun to watch, but my associations jump quickly to Cirque du Soleil videos and to the Prologue of *Ghosts of Versailles*, wherein another young woman on wires performed the identical stunt in the identical manner. Her presence there is no mystery, for Debra (not Trisha) Brown was choreographer for both Cirque du Soleil and *Ghosts*, and there's some attitudinal similarity there. But what is she doing here? She seems simply a stray effect given a home for the night. Even granting that the character of Music be split between a singer and some celebrative visualization, why The Tumbler, with her oddly memorable, culturally specific set of references?* Quite possibly, there is a contemporary dance-world loop I'm out of, or a thread in the work of Trisha Brown I can't follow. This suspicion is

---

* Such images, originating outside the world of the work, set in motion free-associative culture loops; they are loose-cannon elements that form random attachments in the receptor's mind. In mine, for instance, this one runs on from *Ghosts of Versailles* and Cirque du Soleil to *Columbo* (an episode in which men at a bar stare through a window of miniaturizing glass at a young woman tumbling on wire, looking like a small creature in an aquarium or terrarium—*strikingly* similar), and re-connects with opera in the Prologue of Morris' *Platée*, set in just such a bar with terrarium, through which the action of the main play is supposedly viewed. I wonder: Do T. Brown and Morris both watch *Columbo*? Are T. Brown and D. Brown related? Are the Browns and Morris all in cahoots? If so, to what purpose? You may object that Trisha Brown isn't responsible for my private chain of associations. Yes, she is—she set it in motion with this image dragged in by the hair from contempo popcult, rather than trying to lead me into Monteverdi's *L'Orfeo*. In some postmodern practice, this is held to be precisely the point. Since meaning is the residue of the encounter, surviving in the receptor's mind and heart, my chain of association *is* the truth of the work for me. And that's a fact, for the Prologue of *L'Orfeo* is now in a section of my tapestry that includes a camp operatic pastiche, a circus video, a detective series, and the frog-woman. The interpreters of *L'Orfeo* led it there. If they did so by intent, it can only be that they want Monteverdi to take his place on the passing entertainment scene and not put on such airs. If it happened by accident, they were awfully sloppy.

reinforced by a biographical note in the program, which explains that Brown likes to work in cycles of three, and that *L'Orfeo* is the third piece in a "music cycle" that included dances set to Bach and Webern. And so, assuming that the word "cycle" has any meaning as applied to artworks (as: a grouping of works that constitute a narrative, or that are thematically interrelated), what we are seeing is one-third of a Trisha Brown cycle (not, say, a Monteverdi cycle, or an Orpheus cycle), and what the audience is asked to make sense of is the progression of the director's imagistic thinking, which seems to incline toward abstraction and androgyny, and may for some reason include The Tumbler. We're dealing, in short, with tripartite choreographic auteurship, to one fragment of which Monteverdi contributes his cool old music.

Things missing? The lyre. Orpheus doesn't have one, according to either Clarke or Brown. The lyre, given him by Apollo himself; the lyre whose sound enchants both man and beast; of which Orpheus sings in both these operas; that is heard in the orchestra as Orpheus entreats the Furies (Gluck) or Charon (Monteverdi)—the lyre that he cannot possibly ever be without. Choreographers don't much like props, I suppose, and when they must have them wish them emblematic rather than practicable. This one is practicable in the awkwardest way—it must be played, it must be carried wherever Orpheus goes. It leads us away from the abstract toward reality, where things have to be dealt with. I know: we're meant to take it on faith. It's an air-lyre, a lyre of the mind. For an air-opera, an opera of the mind.

When we move beyond the realm of early-opera-as-modern-dance-makeover (all these productions are, by virtue of their dance styles alone, either updated or "timelessly" pan-dated), we encounter a peculiar contradiction: while the role of formal dance is at an irreducible minimum, choreographic thought governs the staging of many episodes, or even entire works, where it is substituted for acting or made to fill in dreaded pauses in the endless bombardment of visual information—for eye-people, the equivalent of dead air. At the Met, balletic participation has been reduced both by the lessened performance frequency of works calling for significant dance contributions (e.g., *Faust, La Gioconda, Orfeo*) and by the elimination or token treatment of some of the remaining possibilities (examples: there is no longer dancing at either of the *Lucia* celebrations, and the rich potential of the Brocken Scene of *Mefistofele* was barely hinted at—an expectable consequence of a widely shared production). No effort has been made since the middle Bing years to give the ballet wing any standing of its own, and while the company's dancers handle their remaining assignments with what seems to me surprising competence, it has fallen to the Maryinsky to show us again, in all four of its

1998 presentations, how invigorating the ballet component of opera can be when danced in appropriate style by a world-class ensemble.*

Meanwhile, choreographed behavior is everywhere. It rules the world of stage fighting. Opera fights have always been infuriating. Very few singers learn how to handle a sword or carry a gun. Few even have the modicum of athleticism that would enable them to carry out informed instruction or direction. There are concerns for safety and breath that must be respected. In recent years, the old tactics of the token wave, the random flail, or total neglect have been replaced by pro moves under the supervision of a stage-fight specialist (in New York it is most often B.H. Barry, highly regarded in the profession). This should be an improvement, and if one thinks a good stage fight is a more or less orderly sequence of obviously arranged pugnacious maneuvers following which no one will have to run for the stage manager's first-aid kit, so it is. But if one thinks it should be a scene in which it looks as if someone might be in danger, and after which complaints of injury or approaching death might be comprehensible, then the pros are no better than the amateurs.

A choreographed move is always symbolic and stylized. It is the representation of an action, not the action itself. In the languages of metamovement we call dance styles, the relationship of action to ordinary behavior is analogous with that of singing to ordinary speech. Except in formal dance pieces, however, fights are supposed to *be* ordinary behavior, however extreme. Crown is supposed to kill Robbins; Cassio's supposed to wound Montano; the Capulets and Montagues are supposed to mix it up—and they are all meant to look as if they could and did do these things. But they don't. Particularly jarring among these was the *Porgy* sequence, written as a vicious little encounter that grows out of naturalistically detailed street life. This was elaborately staged with leaps and tumbles that didn't look necessary, and heavy falls in reaction to blows that never landed—a series of showy moves that mimic reality, at exactly the same level of belief as those of Schaunard and Colline, musician and philosopher, playing at dueling. On a level yet farther removed were the exhibition wrestlers of Vick's *Il Trovatore*. These were two big shaved-head lugs who took phony swats at each other, with step-right-up-folks backflips as the pretended outcome, during what used to be the Anvil Chorus. These *pas de deux* take us right out of their respective scenes and into worlds of visual indication. The gratuitous *Trovatore* bit comes from the world of the carnival, the macho sideshow around the corner from The Tumbler's

---

* Admittedly, the Polovtsian Dances of *Prince Igor* were conceptually of a piece with the rest of that ill-begotten production. But the dancing itself had high finish, and even excitement.

tent, or else from animation—Popeye blams Bluto over the wall. The *Porgy* moment—not gratuitous, but mandated and important—seemed to want to be an action-movie fight. Onscreen, camera angles can cheat, sounds can be looped, and timing can be edited to perfection. But for all that, we don't *believe* those fights; we enjoy them. Onstage, however, it has to look like life, not martial arts, and if it's any good, we don't enjoy it at all.

In the ballroom scene of *War and Peace* we were again taken to the movies. In charge of this joint Maryinsky/Met production (which in St. Petersburg replaced the one by Vick that looks so effective on video) was the noted Russian film director Andrei Konchalovsky, who, one guesses, passed some of his youth in thrall to American movie musicals. In this exquisitely written scene, against the background of a formal ball amongst the Frenchified St. Petersburg aristocracy, Natasha and Andrei discover each other. To her dismay, Natasha is the last of her group to be asked to dance. When Andrei finally escorts her to the floor, it is to a lovely but subdued and melancholy little waltz that perfectly conveys feeling held under, then takes on a stronger pulse as the mutually anticipated discovery unfolds (and finally returns, to devastating effect, in the deathbed reconciliation late in Act II). The limits of stage reality perfectly serve the scene, with its closely regulated social ritual and gossipy commentary, its restrictions on what can be said or shown. Konchalovsky did not accept these limitations. He wanted movie P.O.V., leading to the Hollywood fantasy dance sequence at its corniest. To accomplish this, he choreographed Natasha and Andrei into a jawdroppingly silly Private World ballet, complete with scampery chases and falling to the floor, helplessly giggling, at the close. In a movie, the surrogate eye of the camera can take us into a private world by any of several devices. Onstage, this could be achieved by lowering lights and freezing action around the couple (a cliché, but at least a stage cliché, and still workable if delicately done), or by melting the other dancing couples away into open rooms at side and rear, which is what the stage directions specify. Konchalovsky simply trooped everyone off on group cue, whereto and wherefore we shall never know, then on again for the scene's conclusion, the movements made slow and awkward by George Tsypin's famous roundtop set. But in any medium, by any means, to propose this soapy nonsense as the essence of the tragically flawed but very deep love we read of in Tolstoy and hear in Prokofiev is inadequate as aspiration, never mind realization.

However fervently we may wish for a more rigorous distinction between the fighting and dancing that might occur in life from that dreamed up for soundstages, stage fights and dances clearly require the services of specialists in those techniques. More broadly damaging is the intrusion of choreographic thought into the staging of undanced scenes—the arrangement of stage life into patterns patently not generated by the characters in pursuit of their objectives, and/or the imposition of choreographed behavior on individual performers in the absence of a stylistic framework for it. There are two important facts about such thought. First, it displaces ear-attention with eye-attention. Second, it makes it inescapably clear that character action is under control from above. A few examples:

- In the Met's new *Die Frau ohne Schatten*, the part of the Emperor's hunting falcon was split in two: the usual offstage voice, and another Tumbler. The bird, in the person of a mime in vermilion plumage, flopped intriguingly about the stage, lying still at times, then twisting, rolling, jerking in imitation of the crush-notes that festoon the falcon's music. The falcon's wound, his wariness at returning, his distress at the Emperor's impending fate, his pull back to the master he loyally serves—all these were suggested, at times touchingly, in the mime's movements. Indeed, the mysteries and misfortunes of the falcon became the subject of each scene in which he appeared, first among them the Emperor's anguished Act II monologue outside the forest cottage, wherein the singer must be dominant and the audience's attention ear-led. And precisely because the illusion was a good one, its means became a preoccupation—how's he doing that? Like most such devices, it first pulled focus, then wore out its welcome.

- In Act I of the City Opera's *Fliegende Holländer*, Daland and the Steersman were made to play with a length of rope stretched the width of the stage. This was of course an emblematic activity, not a part of actual shipboard life. It hinted at tying up a ship, winding the capstan, or making perilous way along the deck, but wasn't any of those things. The rope's tautness came and went, suggesting slacker stagehands in the wings. A couple of times, Daland went skittering along the rope in dainty steps with odd pelvic swivels, as if the ship had suddenly pitched—but of course the stage and everything on it remained perfectly flat. It was a distracting, silly-looking exercise, and since it came early it threw the question of how the production intended to show physical life into unnecessary confusion.

- Strauss' *Intermezzo*, given its local stage premiere by the NYCO, concerns a crisis in a marriage when the husband (a conductor) is absent—the wife's ambivalent flirtation with an impecunious young Baron, a misdirected backstage letter to the husband, a visit to the divorce lawyer, eventual explanation and reconciliation. Its tone is often light and there are charming genre scenes set at a toboggan slide, a ball, and a skat game, but the threat to the marriage is real, and the music goes far into the emotional lives of the couple, especially that of the wife.

The opera is constructed as a series of scenes separated by symphonic interludes. The interludes serve to cover set and costume changes and to set the tone and pace of each new scene. But that is not their primary function. Into them Strauss poured his characters' feelings and thoughts, everything not expressed in the everyday interchanges of the scenes. In a fine working of the prosody-to-rhapsody model, the richness and depth of these mini-tone poems gradually invades and impassions the vocal line. Music wells up from below to overwhelm life's gabble of evasions, flatteries, quarrels, and conventions with its emotional truth. The Act I interludes belong to the wife: they carry us through her excitement at liberation, her fun at a ball and almost *Lerchenauisch* exultation at the attentions of the Baron, her melancholy longing as she tries to sort things out (an especially beautiful passage, after Scene 5, pregnant with the sense of a whole life awaiting resolution), and her desolation as she faces the end of her marriage at the close of Act I. The Act II interludes are more the husband's, as he realizes the seriousness of the matter (inner and outer storms on the Prater, a wonderful noise) and hurries back to straighten it out (horns and cymbals, the full *Don Juan* treatment).

Our reception of *Intermezzo* as anything more than an anecdote is dependent on an unconditional surrender to the interludes, something that should give no listener trouble, for they are vintage Strauss. The City Opera turned them into underscoring for furniture-moving and Downstairs bustle: scene-changing and other business for the domestic staff and assorted extras, complete with arch interrelationships, in-jokes among the men, invented bits like one boy starting to play the piano and being shushed, etc., etc. The storm on the Prater became a pantomime of blown-out umbrellas, as if the husband's life problem were a recalcitrant bumbershoot.

In each of these instances, choreographic meddling cuts the legs from under a scene, a series of scenes, or an entire work. In all of them, the ear is sacrificed to the eye. And as always in such usages, music is trivialized, its content made to appear something less than it is.

In the moment, execution is always an issue. In the long run, however, execution cannot rise above the value of the idea behind it, which is determined by its appositeness to the stage world being shown. It happens that the presentation of the *Frau* falcon was highly skilled, that of the *Intermezzo* interludes reasonably so, that of the *Holländer* hawser (the only one foisted on a principal singer) not very. But what if they had all been impeccably performed? We'd be appreciative, of course. But we'd still be left with a bird act, a cute dumb show, and a Norwegian Rope Trick in place of (respectively) a monologue that's crucial and painful, interludes that are deep and beautiful, and a small, tangy slice of natural life. To illustrate further: amid the incessant choreocartooning of the Met's *Barbiere* and *Cenerentola*, one performer was consistently amusing: Alessandro Corbelli, as Dandini in *Cenerentola*. He showed the relaxed physical deftness, delicate stylistic awareness and ease of timing to carry off well-worn bits like the old sprung-couch routine and make them aspects of his character's way of dealing with life's surprises. Consequently, small character-action ideas that looked pushed and generalized in the hands of others made for nice comic points in his. Taken individually, such ideas stand or fall on their execution. A stageful of Corbellis would surely make for an unprecedentedly enjoyable evening of Rossini. But unless one truly believes that the composer wrote nothing more than perky accompaniments for the sitcoms of his day,* when it's all over one will still have the hollow, hard-to-define feeling that comes of having seen something apparently well done that doesn't satisfy, and leads one to suspect that the great comic classic in question (for all its jolly music) isn't all it's cracked up to be.

The great comic classics are irresistible to the choreographic mind, since they nearly always show groups acting in concert against transgressive individuals, or in factions against one another, and the structural patterns that reflect this in both scenario and music are usually clear. Translating these patterns into arrangements of space and time that illustrate the plot is by no means always easy, but it's far easier than the alternative, which is to define and develop the characters and track their journeys, so that any pattern is a result of their actions, rather than a template for it. That is the belief test of any staging, and *Falstaff* is a perfect crucible for such a test, inasmuch as it retains the traditional devices and structures of Italian comic opera but makes them serve the purposes of continuous action. Until the concluding fugue, which moves outside the frame for a moral-drawing ending in the

---

* An excusable impression. In the 55 years since my first *Barbiere*, I have twice seen its story enacted with fair wit and appeal. But one occasion was Beaumarchais' play (by the Comédie-Française), the other Paisiello's modest but playable opera (by the Piccolo Teatro Musicale di Roma). In Rossini's setting I have heard some fine singing of different sorts and seen some good moments, but never a sustained playing of the piece for its character-grounded comic and romantic values.

older *vaudeville* tradition, it can be played straight through in full accordance with the character-action principles of stage realism. The City Opera's *Falstaff* was a tidy group show with lots of co-ordinated moves, people popping up in unison from behind cutout hedges, etc. The individuals who made up the groups had nothing in the way of characterization beyond little logos (Falstaff flipping out his hair, Quickly shaking her ample bosom) that were used as sign-offs in a cute staged curtain call of the sort that seems smug even after a memorable performance. In the absence of characters leading their lives in ways that might inevitably and amusingly coincide or conflict, there could not be an honest playing of situations, only a series of drill-team maneuvers. Over at the Met, in one more sad go-round for a production that was once the pride of the (old) house,* there was a prancing quality—groundless jumping and skittering for Bardolfo; Alice genteelly bopping to *"Quand' ero paggio;"* the otherwise faceless Meg doing a Lucy dizzywalk on an exit; girl-group rhythm moves in place of stage life.

The mechanical quality of both these productions ("inevitability" in the wrong sense) could certainly have been mitigated by better singing and conducting, by more vivid stage personalities. From even such concealments, however, the truth will eventually emerge: these characters cannot possibly be generating their own actions. For all their bustlings, they are no more in charge of their destinies than Robert Wilson's deadly becalmed creatures. Some outside force or person, the eye of some god, determines their comings and goings. Can such a stage world ever be justified? It can: by a work intended to show humanity robbed of its will, or by parts of works that show this as a temporary condition (e.g., "sudden blow" ensemble finales, or choral scenes portraying concerted action by a mass). Are any of the works or scenes here discussed of such a nature? No, none.

In part, all this *ballet mécanique* is an aspect of the contemporary compulsion to view staging purely as a matter of visual style, to ensure that no musical gesture or structure will pass unencumbered by its physical imitation. But mostly, it is a substitute for the re-examination of the operatic training and production systems that would be necessary to re-awaken the creative element in interpretation. Anything to resolve all issues from the top down rather than working them from the ground up. Anything but people to fill the void.

---

* The Zeffirelli/Bernstein *Falstaff*, strongly cast, theatrically conducted and beautifully played, was also the best of Zeffirelli's work for the Met. His designs, meticulously pictorial and eminently practicable, were finished with his extraordinary eye for light on paint. His direction, while not entirely free of shtick and convention, actually created an illusion of individuals arriving at destinations through a behavioral logic a fair proportion of the time, making it unique in my experience of comic opera stagings.

EYEDEOLOGIES: DESIGN

In contemporary operatic practice, design has claimed the right to define the interpretive field. And while earlier efforts to elevate spectacle over music and action have been associated with frivolity and decadence, ours is asserted to be serious and advanced: *meaning* is embedded in design. This is most clearly the case in avowedly "conceptual" productions, since design is the theatre's best bad hope of representing a concept. But most current design, of whatever stylistic cut, partakes of this seriosity and advancement. The *mise en scène* that does not aspire to meaning, to some commentary or declaration of its own, is a curio.

It is partly because of the presence of such curios—"meaningless" settings that have no purpose beyond their theatrical ones—in a number of the Met's standard-repertory productions that New York is considered a backward city amongst the operatic capitals. This view is exaggerated, and can be irritating when expressed by Anglo-European commentators or by the director of the latest poorly-received production. For every patella-reflex boo-the-newer, there's a this-is-the-coolest standing-ovationist, and there is no ground for supposing that either has better motives for display than the other. Nonetheless, there's no doubt that if cutting-edginess as defined on Continental stages or by the international fashion industry is the test, we flunk. Here's the Twenty-first Century, and here are we in our shameful bourgeois comfort, applauding floods of wattage thrown on the culinary, consolatory representations of the likes of Schenk with Schneider-Siemssen, Gian-Carlo Del Monaco with Michael Scott, or the incorrigible Zeffirelli with Zeffirelli.

Despite our local reputation for stodginess, fewer than a third of the there-and-then productions encountered here are of traditional representational design. Among them, the one best qualified, through consistency with its own premises and freedom from upkeep problems, to fairly argue its stylistic case is the *Simon Boccanegra* of the Del Monaco/Scott team. Its sets and costumes, though not strictly reproductions of old designs like some of the Maryinsky's, have the same ambition: to pull us into the life of the work by direct representation. They show period buildings and rooms and streets, with the people and furnishings that inhabit them, in colors that are vivid but not glossy. Like *Mazeppa*'s, they are sensory lures into the "how it really was" of romantic historical fiction, a world that demands an accumulation of details that, however aestheticized, will testify persuasively for it. Unless its small realities withstand scrutiny, its fantasies cannot survive.

Light is the particular success of the *Simon* production. We have grown used to light as creator of its own reality without much reference to the "natural" world in which most dramas supposedly take place—light as a sculptor of space, as isolating device, as symbolic colorist, as audience-assault weapon, light for beauty and mood in themselves. But in illusionistic theatre, every element must defend the receptor's right to be *made* to believe, as opposed to being given the option to believe by virtue of overlooking what he sees. With respect to light, this means that whatever fealty it owes to beauty and mood (in this sort of drama, much), it must seem natural. In strength, angle, hue, and transparency, the light must appear to be that, and only that, that would fall on the scene from its actual sources.

One might assume that this principle and right would be enforced as a matter of course, but even apart from such oddities as the *Susannah* shadows, that is far from the case. It is the case, though, in this *Boccanegra*: the hours of day or night with their changes, the locations and qualities of light sources, work powerfully to keep us within specific times and places, especially in the Prologue (the plebeian conspiracy keeping to the shadows in the square on a moonlit night) and Act III, Scene 1 (the cut-down-to-lifesize apartment in the Doge's palace, where the credibility of overheard conversations and unde-tected presences is crucial to plot and suspense). This is a physical production that shows what representation can do for the playing of a drama, and for audience surrender to it. The rest depends on performance.

Even among lesser or outworn examples of representational production, it must be said in their favor that they try to allow the work to speak; they are not of their nature adversarial. Two productions of *Carmen* illustrate this. One is Zeffirelli's at the Met. There is nothing distinguished or even interesting about it. Acts I and IV are built on one common shape, II and III on another, in both cases poorly disguised despite lots of dressing. The outer acts convey openness and height, which seems wrong, and don't truly make present (but only indicate) the tobacco factory, guardhouse, bridge, and bullring. Thus, the climactic events of each scene (Carmen's escape at the end of I, her efforts to get inside the arena in IV) lose much of their pressure. The sets do not condition them, much less force them. The whole has the air of a touring-show grand-opera *Carmen*, trying to fool us on the cheap.

Still: gripping performances of *Carmen*, embracing a wide range of inter-pretation, could take place on these sets. Even an updated or pandated per-formance could be staged with, at most, a tweak or two. So, while they may contribute little to the drama beyond atmospherics with color correspon-dences to the music, these sets do get out of the way. They *say* nothing. The only sort of interpretation they would inhibit would be one that contradicts the atmospherics or seeks to dictate the interpretive focus.

But this last is of some relevance, because just such contradictions and dictations are taken for virtues in today's world of polemical design, and such design is never more tyrannical than when making a show of getting out of the way. The second *Carmen*, brought to BAM by Stockholm's Folkoperan, is an example. It asked us to look at a fixed rectangle in dirty white with a high back wall. No on-the-cheap opulence or badly masked set changes here, but real cheapness, cheapness as message: we put on no pretty show, we purge all allure, we bring you down to the squalid truth.* In their austere definition of performing space and semi-abstract blankness, such sets appear to abjure aesthetic seduction. But in fact their appeal to the smartness of counter-interpretation and their invitation to pass judgment on the characters and the work itself according to a certain socio-political standard, is as flattering and comforting to the sensibility being sought out as any piece of illusionistic beautification. Through the increasingly customary technique of eye-for-ear substitution it clears the ground for its adversarial gloss, in this case one involving military fatigues, wet suits, banks of women's shoes and combat boots, plus assorted staging wisecracks, all in sophomoric ridicule of the brutal, impotent, fetishistic male characters.

In the score and libretto of *Carmen*, a drama about the shared, chosen dark fate of two outsiders takes place in social settings of great variety and vivacity, into which the brilliant, full-hearted music pulls us by evoking all of it at face value, without judgment. If Zeffirelli's production fails to second the score with fullest conviction, the Folkoperan's makes it lie outright, and asks for our cynical, smug assent.

Madama Butterfly offers another standard repertory pairing that may be instructive. The Met's version was by Del Monaco and Scott, but on a level far below that of their best work. This was a rep revival in the worst sense—a weakly conducted, feebly performed run-through of a piece whose impact is taken for granted and whose essentials are assumed to be the stock-in-trade of any credentialed interpreters available. Its design was naturalistically detailed, but merely picturesque rather than dramatically logical, "lovely" but not magical, and surprisingly clumsy in its traffic accommodations. (The Bonze episode, for example, was entirely about not tripping on the set, with an *exeunt* worse than the *War and Peace* ballroom scene's—choristers queuing to shamble off well into the mood change into the next scene for "*Bimba, non piange.*") As with Zeffirelli's *Carmen* though with greater effort, one could imagine an evening on which performers might rise above this production, but not one on which the production might help them to do so.

At the NYCO, meanwhile, an actively supportive production was on display. I almost didn't go, The *New York Times'* capsule review having spoken of

---

* And, of course: we have no money, we are of the people.

"vividly abstract" settings and of rescuing the opera from "Oriental exotica and verismo cliché," and I having long since learned that words like those usually mean contemporized attitudes in a vague, antiseptic setting. But this was a satisfying evening. The physical production (sets by Yeargan, costumes by Constance Hoffmann) *was* abstract, but in the old-fashioned sense: a compacting and sorting of elements in search of simplicity and clarity. The set, an open deck built up by a stage-wide stair unit, gave the feel of a height overlooking water. A disc projection took turns as an emblematic Rising Sun, a natural dawn sun, and the lovenight moon. Screens functioned as scrim and as the house itself, which after all is usually no more than a decorated version of such screens. The set took light extremely well, a fact nicely exploited by lighting designer Robert Wierzel.

Against this plain, cool-toned environment the props, furnishings, and costumes stood out sharply. While much had been eliminated that could be present in a fully naturalistic production, the objects used were all real and all really used in Mark Lamos' thoughtful, thorough staging. The little ceremonies associated with the objects (tea set, prayer chimes, flowers) registered as moments of gravity and dedication, their meaning for those engaged in them beyond doubt. Costume colors were beguilingly co-ordinated with each other and the set, yet looked like things being worn. Cio-Cio-San's nuptial dress remained on permanent honored display, its emotional power as an emblem of doomed hope and loyalty exponentially increased by its truth to character—it's something this Cio-Cio-San would actually have done. The production's only emblem that failed (a fleet of toy ships hung in our faces like a crib mobile) did so because it had no such character truth—it was a bit of outside preachment à la *Pacific Overtures*. With that sole exception, the NYCO *Butterfly* admirably illustrated the role of design in fulfillment of a directorial vision derived not so much from opinions about meaning as from the lives of the characters, which were realized with far more realistic intensity than in the elaborately illustrative settings at the Met. Good design leads and suggests; it establishes physical conditions and atmosphere. But it leaves performance as the interpretive determinant, and the receptor as construer of meaning.

I cite these *Butterfly* productions in part to make clear that I am not proposing representationalism as a guarantor of artistic validity, even for those works that were conceived in its spirit, like most of the operatic standard repertory. Indeed, until a certain line is crossed (we shall come to this Rubicon presently), style per se is not the issue, for it has always been assumed that some congruence is sought between the physical setting and the manifest content of the work, and that interpretation proceeds within that framework. One of the most effective designs I've seen recently was for Louis Gruenberg's *Emperor Jones* (after O'Neill) at Operaworks, an operatic techno-boutique on the Upper West Side. Operaworks is as close as we yet come to virtual opera, opera as simulacrum: the orchestra is synthesized (all there, though, painstakingly programmed) and the visuals embrace mixed-media techniques. On the other hand, the singers are unmiked and there's no surtext in the way, so in some important respects the goings-on are more actual, less virtual, than those a half-mile South. The *Emperor Jones* set, by Patrick Casey, took two steps away from strict naturalism, according to which only an outer, "objective" reality would be represented. The first was into the Expressionism O'Neill was exploring in his play, in which inner and outer worlds interpenetrate and the nature of reality is thrown into question. The second was to an abstraction of that style, for Expressionism can still incorporate "real" elements—trees trying to look like trees, vines like vines, etc.; recall Schoenberg's view on style in *Erwartung* (pp. 89-90), commonly considered an Expressionist work. Thus, this setting comprised strips and sheets of painted scrim that formed a maze of some depth, enhanced by mirror panels at the sides and a turning mirror within, a few lights from the front and a few more strategically placed inside the maze. In the tiny upstairs space used by the company, this set served all the staging necessities of the piece (the shifting jungle locations for the Emperor on the run; the jumbling of hallucination and reality; accommodation of the choreographed apparitions), and did so atmospherically and ingeniously—it was fun to watch. Although this style could be described as an abstract Expressionism, it is not Abstract Expressionism, for here the set elements operate by metaphor and metonymy—they still stand for real objects and recognizable phenomena, not for pure color or form.

In its use of undisguised materials and its exploitation of the materials' own textures and reflective properties while maintaining their function as symbolic representation, the *Emperor Jones* set would fall under the broad artistic category of The Modern. Very few recent productions could be so classified—they are almost as out-of-fashion as representationalist mountings. A few more are hardcore Conceptualist. The rest—the great majority—sound some variation on mainstream eclecticism, a set of styles I shall group under the rubric Postmodern Lite.

Postmodern Lite is freestyle. In it, scenic elements and staging devices of any fashion may be drawn upon. In the forms that we recognize them, these elements and devices originated as ways of using the technological advances that followed on electrification and the evolution of scenic materials. Relative to the techniques that preceded them, such advances are in themselves transformative, and any succeeding efforts to reinstate the older usages would constitute a conscious aesthetic retrogression. Once in broad practice, however, these devices and elements are at the service of any style. In themselves, they are artistically neutral.

But their uses are not. Those were closely associated with theories of art, color, staging, of the very purposes of performance, proposed by successive generations of the aesthetic, intellectual, and political counterculture. (I resist the term "avant-garde," with its implied progressivist claim.) I will use one example familiar to all experienced theatre- and operagoers and already part of our discussion: the planks-and-white-light look. While it was not invented by Bertolt Brecht or his usual designers (Teo Otto, Caspar Neher), it will never shake its association with the kind of theatre they sought (a theatre that aimed at intellectual clarity and suasion through the impact of purely theatrical energies, not at sentimental empathy or illusionistic seduction), or with the political thrust behind it. New York has seen this look with its political connections intact in productions of plays by Brecht and writers who followed his lead, in imported operatic offerings from the Soviet Union (Molchanov's *The Dawns are Quiet Here*) or Finland (Sallinen's *The Red Line*), in the Met's own *Mahagonny* or the NYCO *Soldaten*, and, in probably its purest form (*nothing* but planks and white light), the production of *Acropolis* by Grotowski's Polish Laboratory Theatre. It has been introduced into works that could be argued into the "Epic" category in whole (for example, the Hamburg Opera's *Mathis der Maler* and *Jacobowsky und der Oberst*, the Met's current *Boris Godunov*) or in part (the scene in the Streltsy Quarter in the Met *Khovanshchina*; the refugee scene in the company's old *Macbeth*).* It leads directly to productions like the Folkoperan's *Carmen*, and is an ancestor of not only the Common Room, but all design that deals in bare essentials of space and light and in the unmasked use of theatrical materials and techniques. However softened and cooled down, however removed from its social context or employed as mere tone, it trails its message along behind, like skywriting. Should we glance up a moment too late, we nonetheless know the little puffets said something just now. What was that? Epic Something, can't quite make it out...

---

*   Both Mussorgsky operas were directed by August Everding in settings by Ming Cho Lee. *Macbeth* was designed by none other than Neher (Carl Ebert, dir.—an echo of the early Verdi revival begun in interwar Germany). Neher also designed the first Met *Wozzeck*. Unless we count the economically forced season unit set by Leo Kerz for the NYCO's brief Leinsdorf regime, I believe these late 1950s productions represent the first operatic uses of this look in New York.

So it is with all such stylistic markers, each originally attached to the works and manifestoes of its cultural-political school or to a more specifically theatrical creed (think, for instance, of Craig and Appia, of Wieland Wagner, of Robert Wilson), but in time deemed free of them on statute-of-limitations grounds, and thus available for incorporation into the vocabulary of mainstream eclecticist production. In this form they are usually stylistically modified, to keep up appearances. But they continue to comment. Decorously mixed in with other markers, they become parts of a polyglot lingo of codes, public and private, to which no single receptor can possibly hold all the keys.

Such codes may be sent and received mindfully or heedlessly, and in many cases there is no way to tell which. Sometimes it is clear that a comment is intended, nearly always of an extraneous nature—a message that beeps insistently in the inner ear of the director and must perforce be beamed our way. More often, we are just left in a state of unease—not the salutary kind caused by the impact of disturbing material, but the quizzical, dissatisfied sort that comes of an uncertainty about intent. Such unease can pervade an entire production. To wit: the much-traveled *Mefistofele* is by no means empty-headed, but what is its ruling design idea meant to do for the piece? Its structural logic seems clear. There are visual constants that tie together Faust's experiences and the parallel roles of the hosts of the spheres (Heaven, Hell, Elysium). There is a persistent element of show that reminds us of both the provisional nature of Faust's compact and the Faust legend's medieval theatrical beginnings. There is an ongoing rose motif that blooms into striking imagery at the end of the Classical Sabbath and again in the finale.

But during the performance, the design's tone kept bothering me. With its splashy colors and rococo over-embellishments, it evoked not quite the cherubs and seraphs, the frescoes and triptychs of the great Italian church sculptures and paintings, but their kitschy imitations—stereotypes of Catholic bad taste. Possibly, I thought, this was mindful, and meant to draw a touching contrast between the lofty aspirations of the subject and its everyday meaning to the humble. But at moments the look would come into focus with one of Boïto's tunes, and I'd think: these are loveable tunes, catchy and even eloquent, overwhelming in their choral investiture. But it can't be denied that with their string or trumpet doublings and ungainly transitions, they can sometimes be heard as ticky-tacky pop inflated to monster proportions. Could it be that our director and designer (Robert Carsen and Michael Levine) have actually picked up on this dashboard-Jesus tint, on the occasional failings of the ambitious score, as the basis for their design concept? Could the feel of their Heaven/Hell confrontation (Our Lady of Little Italy vs. a night in a crummy disco) be deliberately reductive? Is their intent affectionate or condescending, or an attempt at both? Have they gone to all this trouble only to express conflicted opinions about their material?

Such worries can arise over even a subsidiary design idea, an apparent incidental. Take the Magritte men of *La Cenerentola*—I mean the pale little fellows in charcoal suits with derbies, white gloves, and orange ties, clone-like and mechanical in movement, who here stand in as the gentlemen of the Prince's entourage. I've never met such a person, for these are figures of performance. If I did meet one, he would still be only that. They are close relatives of Chaplin and all vaudeville tramps, of Richard Foreman characters, and of the black-tie snoot-symbol swells who have become one of the clichés of postmodern production (they crop up here in *Capuleti* and *Mefistofele*). But these are specifically Magrittish, and I can only guess why. Admittedly, my knowledge of Magritte is not much beyond the cultural-literacy level (surely this is true of many others in the audience?), but then, I've never considered Magritte necessary preparation for Rossini comedies. Would each character kindly wear a sign on each change of costume, bearing the signified thereof? "*Ceci n'est pas un opéra*," the signs might say.

Cenerentola is a comedy based on a fairy tale. From the time of the earliest *intermezzi*, operatic comedies have brought us down to earth. The tragedians could have their superb heads in the clouds, but the comedians showed us ordinary people in an everyday perspective, flawed and foolish, but finally coming to their senses. Plots might be contrived, characters purloined from *commedia* stock, but stage and music made life of the former, flesh and blood of the latter. This is expressly the case with *Cenerentola*. It's for grownups. For reasons both practical and temperamental, Rossini and Ferretti disposed of everything fey and magical in the tale to explore whether or not true qualities can be discerned beneath imposture, whether or not meanness can be resolved in forgiveness. Because the answer to both questions is "yes" the piece is a comedy—but unless its propositions are taken seriously and its stage life given a reality, a meaningless one. With its sprouted golden wings for an otherwise ill-defined Alidoro (I trust the surtitles spelled out the wordplay), its bridal couple as the little figures atop the wedding cake, and a dozen other design messages, this production announces its refusal to take anything or anyone seriously for a moment—there never was a problem, really, and that sadness you thought you heard was just pretend. After all, it's a comedy, it's a fairytale, and we *love* jolly old Rossini.

We love Donizetti, too. We just have strange ways of showing it, none stranger than those of the last two Met productions of *Lucia di Lammermoor*. The first was a scandal, the next a void, and between them they evinced every appearance of an institutional snit: didn't care for that one? All right, we'll give you nothing—see how you like that. And they must have known they'd get nothing, because that's what they'd got from the same design team's *Il Trovatore*. Advised by this experience, *they still brought them back.*

The first of these *Lucia*'s, the scandalous one, was directed by Francesca Zambello in sets by John Conklin. I demurred over the very point cited by the director in her program note: P.O.V.[5] Zambello told the tale from inside Lucia's head, currently a common directorial feint. So on the set buildings teetered, coffins hung in the air and sloshed blood. The wedding guests danced a simian dance and flung gold glitter about while the chorus sang from the pit. Only Lucia's reality counted.

What about the others? What about us? With respect to the former, Zambello offers that "The Lammermoor men . . . are sinister, stiff-backed Victorian silhouettes." (Director to baritone and bass: "Here you are, my good fellows—a pair of sinister, stiff-backed Victorian silhouettes for you to play. Do make it interesting.") This leaves Lucia as the opera's only human being. And this solitary human being is more than ever a loony victim, not responsible for herself or her plight in even the smallest degree. All her troubles come from without, from those beastly male silhouettes. Zambello, following Catherine Clément,[6] tries to salvage some dignity for Lucia by asserting that ". . . as she moves from passive pawn to active assassin, she also takes control of her life and fate." Some control.

This approach is sometimes termed "psychological realism," but I don't detect an interest here in either realism or psychology. Not even the heroine's psyche is explored (showing us how crazy her world looks doesn't do that), for that would entail examination of her temperament and choices, and admit of the off-chance that they may play some part in her downfall. The Lammermoor stiffbacks have no psyches. Edgardo, our male protagonist and a Ravenswood, presumably does, but his reality is not shown on a footing with Lucia's, so he is hard-pressed to let us in on it. Clément, concluding her précis of the plot: "She dies. Later, so does Edgar, but it is less important." That is, to be sure, the effect of many productions, and there's no doubt that the Mad Scene, even in its most modest form with respect to keys, interpolated *acuti*, and cadenzas, is the big eleven-o'clock number. But there are other factors to consider. Lucia's story is enclosed within the last chapter of the Ravenswood/Lammermoor feud. The opera's opening scene is given to the antagonist, its closing one (a funny spot for a "less important" event) to the hero's death. The final act is shaped the same way, with one big scene for the soprano sandwiched between two for the tenor. Structurally, the heroine's story—her life—is locked inside the iron container of the male quarrel about political power, property, and clan pride. As conceived by its creator and received by its early audiences, Edgardo's death scene is no afterthought, and though to us his two splendid arias seem less challenging than the Mad Scene, their first voicings (not to mention those of the Wedding Scene malediction or the swirling upward divisions of the Wolf's Crag Scene) from the throat of Gilbert-Louis Duprez, the first "from-the-chest" tenor, surely seemed as startling and adventurous to their hearers as any of the soprano's excursions, for which there was ample precedent.[7]

As for us, her audience, Zambello revokes our most basic privilege, that of deciding where our empathy belongs and where justice lies, of viewing the matter through our own eyes with the evidence fairly argued. *Enrico has a case*, and so does Raimondo. Let them make it, as strongly as possible. Let them at least momentarily cast the issue in doubt, make us see how men may reason thus, under what conditions, and with what consequences. Of course nothing exonerates them, and there is no possibility that we will decide in their favor (unless, perhaps, we are made to view the action from Enrico's P.O.V., or as Raimondo's dream). For the strange thing is that even though it was written by men a long time ago, *Lucia di Lammermoor* already draws the conclusions Zambello tries to force upon us, and with considerable emotional force. If the artists would only play fair with it, we'd have a drama, not a support group. Why would any director not prefer the drama?

From the scandal to the void: the newer *Lucia* (Nicolas Joel, dir., Ezio Frigerio, des.) is as close to a non-production as a theatrical enterprise can come. A bare, shiny deck. Spare, faintly Gothic units ranked along the sides, with throws of light to define the unfurnished space—the all-purpose contemporary set, taken to zero as a limit. We are in another Common Room, the antique wing of the exhibition hall frequented in the here and now. Lonely individuals, seated or standing, again float in the vacuum—I have seen few more miserable sights than that of Lucia in the person of Ruth Ann Swenson, first revealed to us sitting for her portrait-in-profile far, far upstage in a sort of gazebo, whence she was expected to transfix us with her tale of the fountain phantom. We need no placards here. Our recent museum experience acquaints us with the kind of thing they would say, to pre-empt any thoughts of our own about meaning: "Note the pose of the female subject, rigidly obedient to social structures;" "Observe the isolation of the figures, occupying a common space but incapable of genuine contact." And we know our place in relation to these figures: remote and superior, Nams without portfolio.

With *Trovatore* we reverse direction from a void to a scandal, from the Melano/Frigerio/Squarciapino production (preserved on one of the unhappiest of opera videos) to that of Vick and Brown. Vick is always worth taking seriously; he's so obviously of superior talent and intelligence. Here he is, for instance, discussing German direction and design in the context of German culture:

> ". . . it's an 'ideas-based' culture. It doesn't matter that you should believe, it doesn't matter that it should look beautiful or ugly, as long as you get the point of the set; it doesn't matter if it sounds ugly, because the language is visual largely. And the danger is that the combination of that approach, the belief that acting is largely histrionic, and the very strong arrival of supertitles on the scene, has turned opera into a very, very visual art form, which is an absurdity. As a result, I feel we're breeding an audience that doesn't listen. . ."[8]

I couldn't put it better, or agree more. In fact, I agree with almost everything Vick says in the course of this interview. What, then, were he and Brown up to with their *Trovatore*? I regret I can't give you a full report. Although I saw the production early in its run, Joseph Volpe (the Met's GM) had already intervened to strip out universally derided bits and pieces. As previously recounted, we did still have the extreme wrestlers of the gypsy camp and the big Bessemer pot in the same scene, and we still had the Count di Luna running through "*Il balen*" in a pointedly inelegant pose astride an altar, backed by a big crazy moon, in the Convent Scene. But much else that one had read of or heard about was gone.

I find this objectionable and cowardly. Once again, someone is making up my mind for me, and this time it's not even the director. Vick and Brown are artists; Volpe isn't. Volpe hired Vick and Brown, and not without precedent. Either Vick and Brown have a free hand or they don't, and if they don't there is time to intercede in the planning or rehearsal stages. Once the curtain rises, the administration should go down the line with its artists. Besides, as one of the consumed, a customer, I had contracted (at a price) to see the *Trovatore* of Vick and Brown, whether or not others think it's awful. If it *is* awful, I'm entitled to see it in all its awfulness.

It was awful. It was ideas-based. It didn't matter whether it looked beautiful or ugly (mostly ugly, though, and I think it matters) so long as we got the point, and the point was not invariably clear. Oh, the panels sporting positive/negative black-and-white Rorschach blotches, that's easy—the good/bad flipside bros; also Depth Psychology. I suppose the moon suggested Romantic excess, and that Di Luna's stance aimed for the shock effect felt by some in a mid-19th-Century audience at blasphemous intrusions on an induction ceremony in a holy sanctuary (Verdi was worried about this scene on that account). I don't like these ways of showing these things, and I don't believe them, but I guess I get the point. But as to why the soldiers were done up as Hussars (are we in Hungary or Bulgaria? Has Verdi's Manrico turned into Shaw's Bluntschli? Or—God, I'll bet this is it—have the civil wars of Aragon become the Balkan mess, leading us yet again to the origins of WWI?), and why they should enfile in freeze-frame slo-mo like the dream chorus in Von Trier's *Dancer in the Dark*—about these things I have no clue. I know only that they are more items of code, that in Vick's case they are mindfully sent, and that their effect is incongruous and comic.

I suspect it's no accident that these two operas, *Lucia* and *Trovatore*, recently and consecutively account for four of the very worst productions seen in New York since WWII (I'm sticking to what I can personally attest to). These works show an even stronger narrative redundancy than most matched pairs from the there-and-then:* an opening scene in the brother/antagonist's camp; an early narrative of the dispossessed hero's appearance, sung by the heroine; the stunning, providentially timed crashing of a wedding (for that is what a nunnery induction is) by the hero; the hero's tragic misunderstanding and accusation; a late tower scene; the deaths of first the heroine and then, not at all less importantly, the hero. And each of these works can stand as the paradigm of Italian Romantic opera in its strongest, simplest form, one that can be evaded only by particularly convoluted conceptualization or by declaring it null and void. So that is what we do.

The scandals and voids should give us pause. Clearly, there is greater vitality and ambition in the scandals, but taken with the voids they confirm that even the smartest directors and designers of contemporary mindset, sometimes capable of compelling work, have no way of approaching this repertoire. Productions like those of Zeffirelli, of Del Monaco and Scott, or the *Rigoletto* of Schenk and Zack Brown (nothing special, but a decided improvement over the dreary Dexter/Moiseiwitsch effort that preceded it) are doubtless uncool, but they at least betray a feel for the cultural texture of the work in question, a willingness to work within its aesthetic field, and an accommodation to a range of character interpretation.

Progress, though, lies in other directions. The Vick and Zambello scandals bring us to the border of High Concept, the land that lies beyond Postmodern Lite. This is not entirely new territory for us. We've had glimpses of it at least since 1976, when the Paris Opera (Rolf Liebermann at the helm, as he had been

---

* Both libretti are by Cammarano, and though he died before *Trovatore* could be finished, the scenario was firmly in place.

of the Hamburg company at the time of its visit) brought its productions of *Faust* (Jorge Lavelli/Max Bignens) and *Otello* (Terry Hands/Josef Svoboda) to the Met. Not until the last few seasons, though, after years of prep by productions like those I've been discussing, by Dexter and Ponnelle and Moshinsky and BAM importations, by our videos of Harry Kupfer and Willy Decker and the Chéreau *Ring*, our Syberberg and Losey movies and our illustrated periodicals from abroad, have we had High Concept in purest medicinal strain and in a good, stiff dose. This form, the true German *Regietheater* ("Director's Theatre") that holds sway from the major Continental companies and festivals down through the "B" and "C" houses of the smallest German cities, came to us in the new Met productions of Wagner's *Tristan und Isolde*, Busoni's *Dr. Faust*, and Strauss' *Die Frau ohne Schatten*. The *Tristan*, with its succession of alternately hilarious and infuriating visual images and dainty feints in the direction of performance, evinced what was probably the widest gap in my experience between the known content of a work and what was actually extracted from it. Musical aspects of it will be taken up in Part IV, Chap. 1. I will comment on the other two here, and for good measure add one video example: David Alden's Munich *Tannhäuser*, a famous provocation.

The first thing to be said about current *Regietheater* with big money and top talent behind it is that it looks amazing. If you are interested (as any theatre-lover must be) in the full range of effects made possible by contemporary stage techniques in the hands of master craftsmen, you can do no better than to attend such productions in a major opera house. They are the ongoing industrial art exhibition-cum-fashion show of the theatre world, seasonally revised and updated. Their amazingness is of a particular sort. It embraces a strangeness and mystery. This rests in part on the same foundation as Postmodern Lite's jumble of ironic codes: an incongruity of elements drawn from realities that do not appear to belong together, but which possess referents somewhere in the cultural universe. These, though, have a numinous quality, a visual weight, that goes far beyond the accommodations of Postmodern Lite. This numinous, weighty amazingness, this unreal reality of many realities, must surely be profound, and thus unlike any amazingness achieved by the benighted representationalists, who deal only in the unreal reality of a single reality that is fatally unmysterious, instantly recognizable, and hasn't a single social, political, spiritual or philosophical thought in its head. This particular amazingness, this massive assemblage of emblems standing for many thoughts however obscure, is itself enough to persuade many that High Concept is the realm of deep significance.

Further things to say about such productions are that they are design-dominated—by design that is about itself, design designed to overwhelm, all design and nothing but design; that as Vick observed, this design is derived from ideas and consists primarily of representations of ideas; and finally that (through practices already familiar here) these idea-generated, design-dominant productions are almost invariably at pains to establish points of transfer from the creators' *Zeitgeist* into our own. They thus imply lost connections, meanings that cannot be understood unless explained by visual analogies, which themselves constitute codes to be cracked.

While the above generalizations hold true for all these productions, the details of realization naturally differ. These details can usually be shown to originate through a kind of contact with the work—a contact that is undeniably intelligent, but always at this level of idea and analogy. The opening scene (Prelude I) of *Dr. Faust* is made up wholly of such details. According to Busoni's scenario, the scene takes place on Easter Sunday in the forenoon, in Faust's study (". . . a high Gothic room, half library and half alchemical kitchen, lost in an unclear distance; somewhat dilapidated."[9] In this production, however, the scene is within Faust's mind. (Director Peter Mussbach's program note: "Faust's journey is an autistic one . . . a virtual journey taking place solely inside Faust's head. . ."[10] There goes our P.O.V. again.) What is in there? Well, there's a dream landscape that looks like a Depression-era hobo jungle, laced with sets of rails on which handcars move and among which men in belted trenchcoats, gloved and hatted, sit. There are fires around which bums can huddle, slow-walking students and slow-walking devils whose tails burst into flame. Faust and Mephistopheles are there, as near-identical twins. Some might see them as Beckett's Gogo and Didi, but more folks will peg them for Richard Widmark and Bogie or their German knock-offs, all the way from Brecht's Chicago mobsters to Wim Wenders' playful use of Peter Falk (Columbo again!) in *Wings of Desire*, and to the latest in German-style Messiaen, from San Francisco to Berlin.[11] We're back in the movies, and back with the bums. But this is Heavy, not Lite, so we can't have Jonathan Miller's references to goofball comedies, let alone Konchalovsky's to gummy musicals, and our men in hats can't be from Magritte or Chaplin. This is *dark*.

And amazing, of course. There were captivating images (mostly in the sets) and foolish ones (mostly in the costumes). But truly, if one grants the premise that anything from anywhere and any time may be put into Faust's head, what grounds remain for accepting one or rejecting another? Only one's taste in fashion. Further, though all this *looks* heavy, is it, really? What weight can we assign the journey of a philosopher whose head is filled with Guy Noir woolgatherings? Continental semioticians manage to take this sort of thing seriously; I can't. It was all fine and scary and romantic from the balcony of RKO Proctor's in one's adolescence, and is lovely now in memory.

That's where it belongs: the balcony, adolescence, memory. On the scales of adulthood or of the real (not filmic) world, it doesn't weigh much of anything, however tricked up with tech.

It's not that the images, or their sequencing, are arbitrary. It's that their connection to the work is entirely through the director's analysis of meaning. Like the choreographers who lead their characters through patterns to destinations, he decides on meanings, then devises a series of images that make sure we arrive at those meanings, rather than pursuing actions derived from characters' needs and seeing where they bring us out. The individual is not the subject; the meaning is, somehow separate. (Mussbach's notes: "Busoni. . . adapts the Faust legend in order to reflect on himself. Therefore the play must be depersonalized.") Mussbach proposes a "Mr. X" as the fantasist whose dream we are watching, with the character of Faust as the enacter of the dream. But both, it turns out, are Busoni himself. (Mussbach: "'Mr. X'/ Faust/ Busoni perishes, and thereby overcomes himself.")

But isn't it clear that Mr. X is neither Faust nor Busoni, but Peter Mussbach? Isn't X just a fabricated front man for the auteur? My inner skeptical child thinks so. And his suspicion, I believe, is a variation of the feeling reported by Andrew Clark, who reviewed this production at its point of origin, the Salzburg Festival.[12] He was impressed by it, saw the idea-connections at work in it, and could register only minor reservations about it. Yet he concludes his review by confessing that he cannot ". . . understand why, despite this production's stylistic sweep, it made me feel more ambivalent than ever about *Doktor Faust.*" This is so often the bind we're put in by our best and brightest: it looks amazing, its arguments are all in place, it's hard to fault— why am I not convinced? There seems nowhere to place blame except upon the work. Like *Susannah*, *Dr. Faust* appears to have had its best shot. And it is a problematic opera. As Mussbach says, it's episodic. Its harmonic and orchestral languages are rich, complex, and often fascinating, but its vocal writing, while sometimes ingenious, seldom sounds instinctive. Its musical elaboration can get in the way of dramatic clarity. But since this production, though on a far higher plane of execution than the City Opera's attempt, left me feeling scammed by a fast-talking pitchman whose style I admired, I'm not quite ready to chuck the piece in the Noble Failure bin.

One of the production's images moved me, and stuck to the ribs: Faust cradling his baby's body in the final scene. That was in the action itself. It showed a relationship in a decisive moment of recognition, and was very beautiful.

In *Die Frau ohne Schatten*, everything we saw was the work of Herbert Wernicke.[13] He designed the sets, costumes, and lighting, and directed as well. His command of High Concept's High Tech was total. He achieved remarkable transformations of light, color, and space. The finish on these transformations—a cleanly defined block of space suddenly plunged into a pure, trim, uniform color; a magical fringe of golden light—is owed to recent advances in lighting technique and to the complete control and flexibility afforded by sheer riches. (At the end, in a display that would give any small theatre director fits of envy, at least a hundred instruments dangled over the scene—and those were the unlit ones.)

In accepted auteur manner, Wernicke had his own *Frau* narrative. Indeed, the auteur onstage was also the author out front: in a tiny but indicative departure from established Met practice, Wernicke wrote the story synopsis in the program—not a director's note like Mussbach's for *Dr. Faust* or Zambello's for *Lucia*, and not the analytic essay, but the synopsis itself. While its narrative corresponded for the most part to that of the libretto, it also contained unacknowledged shifting points from Hofmannsthal to Wernicke. These occurred at spots where an accurate account of the libretto would have contradicted the spectacle on view: in Act I, where ". . . the Nurse and the Empress appear on the *staircase* connecting the *Empress' glass* world with the abyss of the human world," and in Act III, where the libretto's fountain of golden water becomes a "*body* of gleaming golden water" (emphases mine).[14] The effect of the former change will be examined momentarily. As to the latter, it is important both symbolically and practically, for a fountain that springs up, subsides at a particular point for a particular reason, springs up again and subsides again, is an entirely different matter from a pond abstracted into light. In a work as symbol-laden as this we do not need symbols of symbols. We need representations of them. And with a writer of Hofmannsthal's stature, such choices are central, not marginal.

Opening scenes often tell much of the conceptual story, and so it was here, though since any staging of this opera must concern itself with passage between higher and lower realms, a glance at the first two scenes will give us a fairer sense of Wernicke's narrative. According to Hofmannsthal's suggestions, Scene One shows the rooftop terrace of the Imperial palace, with the royal bedchamber to one side. This place is often assumed to belong to the spirit realm, and Wernicke's set and synopsis could easily leave that impression. But as Andrew Porter fortunately points out in his program note, that is not the case: the spirit kingdom of Keikobad, the *Geisterreich* from which the Messenger comes and to which the couples gain admission in Act III, is in the beyond. Here we are in the Emperor's neighborhood, admittedly a rarefied upper-class, Orientalist-fantasy one that is intended as an intermediate "upper sphere," but not a spiritual one. It's below Heaven, but above

Earth. Only a few of its basic features are specified in the text of the work.[15] Apart from Alfred Roller (designer of the *Frau* premiere, Vienna, 1919) and Robert O'Hearn, who designed the Met's first (highly effective) production in 1966, the designer always in my mind's eye for these and similar sightscapes is Joseph Urban, whose firm architectural base, strong lines, and lush colors would sweep us straight into a vision like this one. (A fine exhibition of his work at Columbia University's Wallach Gallery in the fall of 2000[16] had freshened him for me.) Urban never designed *Frau*, but a good selection of other designers' realizations is contained in Rudolf Hartmann's valuable book on the production of Strauss's operas.[17] They make clear that the architecture of the palace, the Imperial gardens and the lake, the landscape that lies beyond, the changing light of the dawn hours, and above all Strauss's music are powerful, almost hallucinogenic stimulants to visual imaginations of many stylistic bents.

What Wernicke finds is mirrored glass and obliterative light. On an otherwise bare stage, the glass forms the walls of the set; the light flashes and beams off of it and out at us, especially when panels open and close for entrances and exits, setting up in-your-face angles of glare. These walls of mirror reflect all onstage objects, back and forth in a kind of infinite regress. The only such objects, however, are the singers and the floppy falcon. Since the former, as staged, exhibit no behavior save for a baffling spread-legged exit caper by the Messenger—it looked like a bladder emergency—the sole beneficiary is the falcon, whose floor acrobatics are replicated many times over by the mirrors.

Referents for glass can be found in the words and music. When the Nurse assures the Messenger that the Empress still casts no shadow, she sings: "Through her body/passes the light/as if she were of glass." The clear, tinkling textures of the instrumentation that accompanies the Empress' entrance music (harps, celeste, high woodwinds, solo strings) and the vocal writing itself, with its altitudinous tessitura, its modest roulades, a trill and a glancing stroke off the high D (like a reflection?) can certainly be heard as glassy.* The Emperor has caught, and fixed in his high-human world, a transparent being of spirit whom the Emperor's servants may not even look upon—though in one of those transubstantial miracles known only to students of mysticism, this woman whose body casts no shadow nonetheless *has* a body, and evidently some thoroughly satisfying sex with her husband.

---

* Hartmann also refers to "the lofty, glass-like sphere of the Emperor" and to "the milky, glass-like quality of the atmosphere on the terrace." This appears to be his own interpretation, however.

Wernicke takes this identity of the Empress as an airy brilliance awaiting substance and does a nifty sidestep with it: he creates his "Empress' glass world," a world of narcissistic emptiness in which people cannot see beyond their own reflections, and in which apparently external forms are only illusory extensions of their vacuous insides. This isn't just beside the point. It reverses the point. The Empress has not transformed her surroundings in her image; on the contrary, she has lost her transformative powers and finds herself in a world of solid buildings, flora, geographical features, and people that is external to her consciousness and belongs to someone else ("legally," the Emperor). She's *not* in her own world. *That's her problem.* She moves through the Emperor's realm in her special, shadowless light, isolated save for Nurse and husband, living a romantic dream. But now, warned by the falcon, she finds that to spare her husband a living death and continue her life with him, she must become completely of the lower world: solid, earthbound, fertile. To pretend that the world of the first scene is a projection of the Empress' self, its reality and the other characters incorporated within it, is perhaps the sneakiest of all the P.O.V. switches we've encountered.

Had an acquaintance of *Die Frau* read Wernicke's synopsis before the curtain's rise, he or she might have tripped over its mention of a staircase—Dyer's huts do not usually have second storeys. This one, though, was a multilevel metallic construction, at the bottom of which the Dyer and his family were shown to live and work in contemporary technosqualor, like squatters in an abandoned factory building. Its considerable naturalistic detail (overhead factory lamps, a sink with a spray nozzle, a fridge stocked with beer) certainly allowed for the playing practicalities of the scene, and though this was not turned to much advantage by the performers, that was not the fault of the set. The staircase was not a problem in itself. It "worked." But we should note the sort of connection it represents, and between what and what. "Then downward with us!", sing the Empress and Nurse as they prepare to plunge into "the abyss of Mankind" at the end of Scene One, and the orchestra takes on the description of their flight to Earth, a miraculous flight like the magic carpet excursions of *A Thousand and One Nights*.*[18] Part way through Scene Two, an evanescent shimmer of light heralds their sudden appearance in the hut, without having passed through the door. In Wernicke's interpretation, no magic is required. You just walk down the stairs, out of the Empress'

---

* Hofmannsthal was concerned that this journey be a flight through the air, not a sinking through the earth via a trapdoor.[21] No doubt it is futile to suggest that these magnificent interludes, like those of *Intermezzo*, might better be returned to the ear, however impressive the sights of machinery on the move. Nonetheless, that's what I'd recommend.

glassy self into the downrent urban here-and-now. Here we are on our journey again, an "autistic" one, solely inside someone's head: the director's.

At least it's not the movies.

The 1994 Munich Festival *Tannhäuser* of David Alden* became a provocation because of the way it used the opera to jam the Bavarian audience's finger into the socket of its connection to Wagnerism, to German Romantic artism in general and the role retrospectively assigned to it in subsequent European history. It happened that I first viewed the video of this production not long after seeing an edition of Bernard Pivot's *Bouillon de Culture* featuring George Steiner, Gottfried Wagner, an Israeli Palestinian author whose name I'm afraid I didn't catch, and the actor Roberto Benigni. As you have probably guessed from this cast list, the show's principal subject was Wagner's anti-Semitism and its consequences, and *Tannhäuser* found its way into the discussion. G. Wagner asserted that a direct line could be traced from R. Wagner to Auschwitz, and Steiner agreed. Yet, Steiner went on, the world would be the poorer without R. Wagner's music. And the affair can get pretty complicated: it was at a performance of *Tannhäuser* that the young journalist Theodor Herzl first envisioned a Zionist state in Palestine. And so in addition to the "direct line" from Richard Wagner to Auschwitz, there's another from Wagner to Israel—"... *la même musique!*", as Steiner noted. The same music, yes, and more than that, drama, since *Tannhäuser* is an opera. Exactly where, I wonder, did the thought flash into Herzl's mind? Was it Tannhäuser's great cry of "*Allmächt'ger, dir sei Preis!/Gross sind die Wunder deiner Gnaden!*",† when he finds himself in the Valley of the Wartburg with the shepherd and pilgrims, sprung from the lair of Venus? Or the end of Act II, when he lifts himself from despair to depart for Rome? Or (most likely, I think) the pilgrims' return in Act III to re-embrace their homeland with their much-loved chorus? Whichever it was, it was a uniquely operatic (not just musical) moment, striking into the mind and heart of Herzl from without with the full energies of performance, courtesy of Richard Wagner.

That the lines defined by Gottfried Wagner, Steiner and many others exist is not at issue; they do. All that I know for certain about them, though, is that they run from many points in the here and now to many points in the there and then, and that they have been drawn backward. However interpreted, they still leave us with the only important question, which is how to deal

---

* Not to be confused with his brother Christopher, of the NYCO *Mother of Us All.* D. Alden's career, a significant one, has been principally in Europe and the U.K.

† "Almighty, be thou praised! Great are the wonders of thy mercies!"

honorably with Wagner's works in performance. The nation-state envisioned by Herzl has its answer: ban them. As we have already seen, Robert Wilson has his: an anti-Wagnerian aestheticism. Alden's response is more complicated, and in a sense more courageous. He faces the work and, from a certain P.O.V., digs into it.

His P.O.V., though, shares key assumptions with the High Conceptualism of Mussbach or Wernicke. It is design-dominated and, in Mussbach's sense, "autistic." (This term will now be discontinued. It is a clinical word that refers to a grave condition not suffered by any character in any of these operas. Mussbach's use of it is of course a coercive exaggeration. Since I believe the true subjects in the case are the directors themselves, I will henceforth use a more accurate and less prejudicial term, "auteurial subjectivity.") Alden is admirably open about his embrace of this approach. "I can't really direct something until I feel that what I have to say personally I can say through this piece," he says. He describes his productions as "... deeply felt rather than deeply thought... very much about my inner emotional life... all instinctive, a chemical reaction."[19]

Alden's chemical reaction to *Tannhäuser* begins with staging the overture. (Like so many operatic auteurs, he asserts his deep attachment to the music, then hands the music over to the Eye Force.) The story we're about to see is the dreamlike reminiscence of an aging, worn-down musician (no lyre, but a suitcasefull of his music) who seeks admission to first one realm, then another (doors in walls), finds a home in neither, and shakes his fist at both. As we move into the Venusian bacchanale, the images proliferate, and they aren't pretty: masked women, bareskulled leathery men (one brandishing a sword as he vogues past the camera), a man lugging a heavy stone (his "*Sünden Last*"—this image recurs), a black knight, some bondage, much slow walking, a green man, a topless babe writhing in the jaws of a crocodile and evidently enjoying it—there's a "perverse element to modernism," observes Alden.

The compulsive piling-on of "perverse" images is numbing. But it's more interesting to watch than, say, Wilson with his distaste for "all this . . . emotionalism," and it does represent involvement with the music's febrile side, though not its sensuous one. Any mind's-eye devotee can spare a moment of empathetic recognition for the goings-on that give rise to such fantasies. You should have seen my *Tristan* Act III! In early adolescence, especially when home sick (a heavy chest cold and raging fever lay an excellent base for this scene), I'd put the Melchior/Janssen 78s on the old console turntable and act out the whole thing, leaping to my feet for Kurwenal, dropping to the floor as if shot for Tristan, mopping the brow while changing record sides. Committed work, let me tell you. Both my deaths were unbearably moving.

Then there was the shooting scenario for my *Otello* movie, mainlined straight from the Toscanini recording. The Storm Scene haunts me yet, the faces...*

But while acknowledging this comradely bond, I still wonder why it is we are supposed to accept the director's inner emotional life in place of the field defined by a work's creator(s), not to mention the huge philosophical assumption (shared by all these productions) that the world itself is but a projection of that life, that no reality exists outside it. And if the stage world is only a representation of that assumption, how is it that the director's projections are determinative, rather than those of the conductor or the performers, who might with equal justice assert the same imperative? As for us receptors, not only does *Regietheater* force meaning upon us at every turn, it determines our fantasies for us while overtures play.

None of this, though, is what stirred controversy at Munich.[20] That was due chiefly to the scene of the song contest in Act II. Here, in a continuation of the themes and modes established earlier, the Thuringian court and its Minnesingers assemble in slo-mo under a giant stone inscription that reads, "GERMANIA NOSTRA." The motto has not only its general cultural resonance and connection back to Tacitus and to the roots of Germany in the barbaric post-Roman past, but (as Jane Kramer noted in the *New Yorker*), a specific reference to the City-of-the-Thousand-Year-Reich dreams of Hitler and Speer.[21] It serves as ongoing comment on the spectacle below it; in this function and in its purely theatrical effect, it inevitably recalls Brechtian usages. Its employment by Alden is an evident exception to his chemical, emotional way of work, for such choices are arrived at by calculation.

Brecht reasoned that if he threw in the audience's way a bit of something to read, a different sort of engagement would result, and that if he kept it in view the audience would have to return to it and keep its commentary under consideration. He frequently put such signs above his sets. He also often put signs in the hands of performers, where they continued to serve the same distancing purpose even when "realistically" justified, as with picketers, beggars, et al. (Operatically, both kinds of signage are familiar from the Brecht/Weill collaborations.) If we can imagine this scene in a production by Brecht, the superscription might be just a tag ("THE SONG CONTEST AT THE WARTBURG"), but would more likely have a twist intended to extract the Marxian lesson from the stage event—viz., "TANNHÄUSER DISCOVERS THE LIMITS OF CHRISTIAN COMPASSION AMONG THE ORPHIC BRETHREN". Down on the stage, he might show two or three loners brandishing slogans

---

* "It is such a high to be paid to work on *Tristan* for a couple of years, to listen to a thousand recordings..." says Alden in Clements' profile, bearing witness to the birth of auteurial subjectivity out of the spirit of the mind's-eye devotee. See Backstory I, p. 749 and ff.

like "FOR ALL THE VARIETIES OF LOVE," while a phalanx responds with "FOR GOD AND COUNTRY" or "AGAINST THE PROFANATION OF THE HOLY VIRGIN."

Brecht knew exactly what he was about. I'm not so sure about Alden, because it doesn't sound as if distance is really what he wants. But there it is: "GERMANIA NOSTRA." It combines with the costuming of the assembly as fingerpointing, but I am more interested in it as undercutting. Live, it has to have been inescapable throughout. On video the camera gives it the slip for significant stretches of time, though we never lose our awareness of it or our curiosity about what will happen to it—its function as a distraction and a restraint on belief is ongoing. At the act's end, there's almost a great moment. At the cry of *"Nach Rom!"* René Kollo, who troupes through all this with admirable professionalism, struggles over a makeshift drawbridge onto the upper gallery where, silhouetted against a blue-white background in an image established earlier, he heads off in pursuit of the pilgrim band. The full orchestra sounds the swelling theme that dominates the latter part of the finale. For a second, eye and ear make the heart beat quicker, close to bursting. Then here comes the damned sign, yanking us back from Tannhäuser's hope and desperation. The building moment collapses on the instant, and the act flops to an end.

The idea that design should embody meaning, that a set is supposed to say something, is quite recent. Here's a nice little paragraph on the purpose of theatre design:

> "The designer creates an environment in which all noble emotions are possible. Then he retires. The actor enters. If the designer's work has been good, it disappears from our consciousness at that moment. We do not notice it any more. It has apparently ceased to exist. The actor has taken the stage; and the designer's only reward lies in the praise bestowed on the actor."

The paragraph was written not by a Method director, or a star performer, but by Robert Edmond Jones, considered by some the greatest American stage designer of the first half of the Twentieth Century.[22] I cite Jones for the sense of proportion inherent in his view of the artistic calling. He believed in the hierarchy of the chain of engagement, and saw that the importance and urgency of an artist's work is in no way diminished by an awareness of where it begins and ends. That contribution is part of a large collaborative enterprise, exalted in nature, to which the creator's vision is central.

The paragraph above conveys this with respect to design. Surely Jones did not devote his life to ambitious, innovative work in the belief that his gifts and efforts were insignificant. But he accepted that even masterful design, though absolutely crucial, has its limits: it's still just an environment.

Let's concede that Jones was stretching his point. He cannot have meant that once a performer steps on the stage we crop out the surroundings, utterly and permanently. He did mean that since drama is about people our focus should be on them, and that the surrounding enters consciousness, leaves, flits about the edges in accordance with the needs of the drama, dominating only when called upon to do so.

Jones was not alone in his view of design's portion. For example:

> "... the scenic designer must assert himself to ensure that the action remains unhampered by visual elements of subsidiary importance. Every resource employed has to be subordinated to the unfolding of the work's meaning, great though the temptation is, in certain scenes, to emphasize points of purely mechanical virtuosity."

That is Rudolf Hartmann, writing of *Die Frau* but obviously cleaving to a principle.[23] Note that he refers to meaning as something that *unfolds* in the course of performance, not as something adumbrated by a set. Another formulation:

> "The substance of an opera. . . cannot be made visible simply by following the prevailing rules of taste of the period but only by meeting the internal requirements of the work itself. All genuine music dramas contain their own laws of realization and these laws... grow out of the relevance of the drama to the human being..."

That is Rudolf Heinrich.[24] He re-entered my thoughts at a performance of *Werther*. It is an old production that I had not seen for many years, and until an intermission glance at the program I had quite forgotten that Heinrich had designed it. That is because his now-fading but lovely romantic-realist sets (that church, that inn—yes, it could be Wetzlar, I can imagine the life) were utterly different in style from the work I remembered him for, the *Salome* and *Elektra* mounted for Nilsson in the 1960s. I liked the former, didn't care for the latter—that's not the point. The point is Heinrich's stylistic adaptability. Not a "visual theatre artist," perhaps, but a true stage designer.

We have seen in this chapter how far we have come from the lofty yet humble philosophy of Robert Edmond Jones, or of designers like Hartmann and Heinrich. But to give the newer attitudes a verbalization beyond the apologias of program notes, here are two more brief citations:

> "Design and casting provide about 60 percent of the necessary preconditions for success. But the central issue is the collaboration between the producer and the designer. . ."

> "Designers of opera productions fall into two broad categories: those making interpretive work, with proper dramaturgical foundations, whose designs encapsulate the concept and philosophical message of the production; and those who are using history or current fashion merely to provide a pleasing and realistic (or approximately realistic) environment."

These passages are from *Believing in Opera*, by the English critic Tom Sutcliffe.[25] This is a useful book for anyone in search of solid descriptive accounts of Anglo-European production practices of the past quarter-century (different from those discussed above only in their range of personal idiosyncrasy, which is considerable), and the thinking behind them (ditto). I support its underlying premise—that opera must be taken seriously as a theatrical form, and that it's supposed to engender belief. As to the sources of theatrical validity and belief, however, it is as far from the views presented here as it's possible to get. The quotes above are from a chapter entitled "The Design Matrix." That in itself is telling, for it presupposes that it is decisions about design that will determine the reach of interpretation, rather than (let us say) parameters set by agreement between the director and conductor for the discovery phase of rehearsal, in the course of which the designer (whatever his preliminary ideas might be) will find out precisely what's needed. Like most of the book, it buys into the current assembly-line model of production. It not only describes contemporary S.O.P., it endorses it. I will return to this subject later.

Note that (apart from the silliness of assigning percentages to production elements) the conductor is not included in the collaboration that is called "the central issue." The central issue is all-eye. And all-idea, for dramaturgically proper design must "encapsulate the concept and philosophical message" of the production. These will not be derived from the "internal requirements" or "laws of realization" mentioned by Heinrich, but from the moilings of auteurial subjectivity, whether emotional like Alden's or depersonalized like Mussbach's. And they are apt to be adversarial, for:

> "Interpretation is an act for the present context: criticism in action."[26]

This is misleading purely on grammatical grounds: that colon (similar to the one I just used) suggests that in order to qualify as "an act for the present context," interpretation must consist of the "criticism in action." That's not so. More important is the substance of the statement, the assertion that interpretation *is* criticism. In light of the examples of direction and design I have already discussed, it would be disingenuous to feign shock at the openness of this claim. It is, nonetheless, outrageous. For the "interpretation" meant here is not that of a Third or Fourth Interpreter (a critic or receptor) but that of the Second Interpreters—and the ones in charge of only the visual aspects of the performance, at that—while "criticism" is not the self-examination we hope artists apply to their work as it develops, but analysis and argumentation from an outside perspective. So the lawyer appointed to defend the interests of you, the creator, or of you, the receptor, is in fact the prosecutor and judge as well. Now let the work's fair trial begin.

Where could such an idea have come from? Sutcliffe of course refers back to the unavoidable Craig and Appia, but frequently to Roller, too. In fact he goes so far as to include as an Appendix the whole text of Roller's 1909 essay, "*Bühnenreform.*"[27] And that is a service, for it's a marvelous little article, quite as easily quotable in support of my arguments as of Sutcliffe's own.* Roller would, I am sure, be astounded at finding himself enlisted in support of the varieties of amazingness we now encounter. His designs have been often reproduced, but quite by chance (as with the Urban exhibit) a number of the original renderings recently wandered my way.[28] Certainly they are highly concentrated, focused on key dramatic elements and on mood, rather than on elaboration of naturalistic detail. But they consist entirely of representational elements, and nothing in them suggests reference to anything outside the boundaries defined by the creator. Near the end of Roller's essay, though, we do find this:

> "It [theatre reform] is a matter of resolutely turning our backs on frivolity and our accustomed vulgarity (known as 'tradition') in order to achieve a theatre that will live once more, where what happens onstage frankly signifies, rather than being, or pretending to be."

Ah, there we are: "*signifies.*" Now we're getting close.

---

* For instance: ". . . people concerned with the theatre now give more attention than they should to its secondary aspects. To design, for example. . ." Or: "Production is. . . an altogether secondary thing, ineluctably taking its principles and rules from the work itself. . ." Or: "Gordon Craig looks forward to a time when painters and designers will write their own plays; I would be satisfied if the writers of today's works would simply think in terms of a particular stage and its requirements." See? He's on my side.

NOTES

1. See: James Robinson: "Director's Note," *Stagebill* (NYCO Edition), March 2001.

2. For further discussion of that production and its subsequent recording, see my "A Long Night at Riguhlettuh's," *Opus*, Feb. 1985. For a time, it seemed that the title character had entered an operatic witness-protection program, never to reclaim his true identity—this was the third English-language update of the opera I had seen, each involving a change in milieu and a substitute identity for Rigoletto. Each also illustrated my point about solving small problems while sidestepping big ones. In a 1971 San Francisco Spring Opera Theatre production (director, Gilbert Moses; translation, Ruth and Thomas Martin), Rigoletto was an Afro-American funnyman in a contemporary "corrupt court." This version had the strongest enactments I've seen of the Countess Ceprano interlude and the humiliation of Monterone's daughter. At Eastern Opera Theatre (NYC) in 1980 (Nicholas Muni, director; Donald Westwood, conception and translation) the jester became a freak attraction in a traveling American sideshow, circa 1850 (time of composition). It solved the seldom-credible abduction scene, with Rigoletto sent into a trance by the circus mesmerist's swinging watch. Miller's production (for English National Opera as seen at the Met, 1984, translation by James Fenton) gave us the courtiers as midlevel mobsters, fun with dances and jukeboxes, some underworld glam and newspapers blowing prettily down the street in the storm scene; Rigoletto was bartender to the mob. But none of the three came any closer than a traditional production to the central scenes and characters of the opera—the singers just wore different costumes.

3. Available on video from Kultur and Pioneer. Another date-of-composition update, set in the Vauxhall Gardens of 18th-Century London, though embellished with Persian scenic motifs. The indolent aristos rage and flirt; their zombie-like servants set out chairs.

4. Both available on video, the former from VAI, the latter from London. Hall's suffers from lighting levels too low for video purposes, and must surely have been more effective in the theatre; it is nonetheless consistently absorbing in this form. Sellars' is also less impressive than in the theatre (as seen at Pepsico Summerfare, SUNY/Purchase, in 1987), but a fair measure of its effect comes through. Neither offers memorable singing (the Sellars, indeed, is vocally quite rough), but both play well. Sellars', of course, does not "look like" Mozart, and Hall's looks rather more like Beethoven, I should say, or like some great early *Ottocento* English composer, had such a creature existed.

5. See *Stagebill*, Metropolitan Opera program edition, for any performance of *Lucia di Lammermoor* during the seasons of 1992-93 and 1993-94.

6. See Clément, Catherine: *Opera, or the Undoing of Women* (Betsy Wing,   trans.), Univ. of Minnesota Press, Minneapolis, 1988.

7. It could almost be said that the modern tenor (and for that matter, baritone) model, in which the upper range extension and associated head-mix graces are sacrificed to the ability to drive the head voice against a stronger chest-voice hold as high as the upper B and C, emerged in response to the need to deliver the Wedding Scene curse and other expressions of frustrated male rage, oaths of vengeance, etc., in tones of sufficiently scarifying vehemence. (See further discussion in Pt. IV, Chap. 3.) As this model became established and the writing of Verdi, Puccini, and others pushed from the repertory all

earlier "serious" Italian operas save *Lucia* and *Norma*, the standard performance version of *Lucia* took huge cuts in the stiffbacks' roles—the entire Nos. 7 (Raimondo and Lucia) and 11 (Wolf's Crag—Enrico and Edgardo), the Mad Scene trio that shows Enrico's belated remorse, and a bridge section and repeat in the cabaletta of Enrico's aria. Except for the last, these are now customarily restored. But what is the point, if the men are not to be made whole?

8. See Della Couling: "Opera Directors: Graham Vick", in *Opera Now*, July/August, 1999. Vick also contributes to "Which Direction Now? A Directors' Symposium" in *Opera*, August, 2002. In this article 21 directors, including many under discussion here, address questions posed by the editors. Nearly all of them have thoughtful things to say. But as with Vick and his *Trovatore*, it is often impossible to reconcile the talk and the walk.

9. See Ferruccio Busoni: *Doktor Faust*, piano/vocal score, "Breitkopf & Härtel, Wiesbaden, 1922," Sc. 1.

10. See *Playbill*, Metropolitan Opera program edition, for any performance of *Dr. Faust*, season of 2000-2001.

11. See Alex Ross: "Sacred Monster," *The New Yorker*, Oct. 28. 2002. Reporting on Nicolas Brieger's production of Messaïen's *St. François d'Assise* in San Francisco (a generally enthusiastic review) he notes: ". . . the decision to dress the chorus in trenchcoats and fedoras . . . lent a curious film-noir flavor to the final scene of death and resurrection. . . Evidently, a lot of Bogart impersonators will be standing around when the saints go marching in." And on Daniel Libeskind's production of the same work in Berlin: "Here, too, were many men in coats, scurrying around like pigeons in Trafalgar Square."

12. See Andrew Clark: "Salzburg at the Crossroads," *Opera*, November, 1999.

13. Wernicke, one of the most prominent European designer/directors, died unexpectedly shortly after the premiere of this *Frau*, which marked his New York debut. There is an affectionate tribute by Peter Jonas, Intendant of the Bayerischer Staatsoper, in *Opera*, July, 2002.

14. See *Playbill*, Metropolitan Opera program edition, for any performance of *Die Frau ohne Schatten*, season of 2001-2002. In Met programs, synopses are usually anonymous or "Courtesy of *Opera News*." Flipping back through recent seasons and the memory file, I find one more attributed to a director: John Cox's, for *Capriccio*. It contains no special pleading. There is of course no reason why a director should not discuss his thinking, and we're used to hanky-panky with scenarios from, say, Peter Sellars. This is the first time, though, that the Met has acceded to presenting details of a director's concept as if they were "authorized" by the text.

15. See Richard Strauss and Hugo von Hofmannsthal: *Die Frau ohne Schatten*, study score, Verlag Dr. Richard Strauss GmbH & Co., KG, Vienna, 1996, for this and all subsequent references to the text. This score is distributed by Boosey & Hawkes, London, as is a piano/vocal score.

16. See Arnold Aronson: *Architect of Dreams, The Theatrical Vision of Joseph Urban*, Univ. of Washington Press, Seattle (distr.), 2000. This is the catalogue of the Columbia exhibition, containing several informative essays and a wealth of beautifully printed reproductions. Urban, rooted in the same cultural soil as Strauss and Hofmannsthal, spent the latter half of his life in New York, where, though many of his architectural plans went unrealized, he was among the most important stage designers of the interwar years. Several of his productions were still in use (in much-deteriorated condition) at the Metropolitan when I began my operagoing in the mid-1940s.

17. See Rudolf Hartmann: *Richard Strauss, the Staging of His Operas and Ballets*, Oxford University Press, N.Y., 1981. Set and costume designs from a dozen productions of *Frau* are reproduced, including two of Roller's originals. Among them are six versions of Scene One, three in color. Hartmann himself directed three Strauss premieres as well as many other Strauss productions at his home house (the Bayerischer Staatsoper, Munich) and elsewhere. See also Hartmann's essay, *"Die Frau ohne Schatten* as a Problem of Scenic Design," in the booklet accompanying the Deutsche Grammophon recording of the 1963 Munich production of the opera.

18. Ibid, pp. 125-26, quoting the Strauss/Hofmannsthal correspondence.

19. See Andrew Clements: "David Alden (People: 217)," *Opera*, Feb., 1996.

20. For a report on the production and its initial reception, see Rodney Milnes' review in *Opera*, Festival Issue, 1994. And on the fallout, see Jane Kramer: "Opera Wars (Letter from Europe)," *The New Yorker*, Aug. 20/27, 2001. Kramer's article focuses on the Thielemann/Barenboim dustup in Berlin, but chronicles some of the doings of the Jonas era in Munich as well, including the political implications of Alden's *Tannhäuser*, complaints about its "chaos" from tenor protagonist René Kollo, and Thielemann's later refusal to conduct its revival. A sympathetic chapter on Alden in Sutcliffe's *Believing in Opera* (see 28, below) also includes commentary on this production.

21. See Alexandra Richie: *Faust's Metropolis*, Carroll & Graf, New York, 1998, pp. 470-474, for a concise description of the Germania plan.

22. See Robert Edmond Jones: *The Dramatic Imagination*, Theatre Arts Books, NY, 1941, a book that is still required reading for theatrical literacy. Note that this statement has nothing to do with style, and in fact Jones was a modernist, opposed to photographic realism; more than anyone else, he translated the theories of Craig and Appia into working American practice, collaborating along the way with Reinhardt, Diaghilev, O'Neill, and many others. With Kenneth MacGowan, he co-authored the classic *Continental Stagecraft*, Harcourt, Brace & Co., NY, 1922.

23. See the Deutsche Grammophon recording essay referenced above (note 18).

24. See Rudolf Heinrich: "Set Designer for the Music Theater," in *The Music Theater of Walter Felsenstein*, Peter Paul Fuchs, trans. & ed., W.W. Norton & Co., NY, 1974. This brief essay first appeared in *10 Jahre Komische Oper Berlin*, 1957. Heinrich was one of the Komische Oper's principal designers in the Felsenstein years.

25. See Tom Sutcliffe: *Believing in Opera*, Princeton University Press and Faber & Faber Ltd., London, 1996, pp. 84-86. The book includes thorough reports on many auteurs, including several (e.g., Ruth Berghaus, Hans Neuenfels) little known outside the Germanic countries.

26. Ibid., p. 44.

27. Ibid., p. 427. Roller's essay first appeared in *Der Merker*, 1909-10. The translation is by Meredith Oakes.

28. At the Williams College Museum of Art in an exhibition on Hitler's Vienna, part of a multi-institutional project on that city and its art. Roller's renderings for productions of *Der fliegende Holländer*, the *Ring*, and *Parsifal* were included, some in the original and some in digital reproduction.

PART III

THE INTELLECTUAL BACKGROUND

1

MERCI À TOUS, MAIS ÇA SUFFIT, JE CROIS

It's a superspecial edition of the late, lamented *Bouillon de Culture* (and I do hope you caught at least a few of the American cable showings of this program or its predecessor, *Apostrophes*, both hosted by the redoubtable Bernard Pivot). This episode transcends all boundaries of art, language, space, and time. No lens can frame it, no eye supply its missing dimensions, find its center, or fix a given moment among its perpetually drifting, morphing objects and figures. But if, like Faust, we could cry out to some devil *"Verweile doch! Du bist so schön!"* and freeze the whole reality of it, we'd have a stupendous, phantasmagoric mural. I'd install it above a lovely old bar where people are polite and long drinks served. There, we'd have time to contemplate the many personages on display. These would include a sixty-year crop of postwar, postmodern, poststructural, postFreudian, postExistential French philosophers, semioticians, sociologists, and psychoanalysts. English and American literary and media critics are sprinkled generously among them (Marxists and Deconstructionists jostling rudely or stepping daintily), as are specialized thinkers on art, feminism, and queer theory, and representatives of clusters found in places like Geneva, Sw., and New Haven, Conn. Behind all these, the pioneers of linguistic and anthropological structuralism and of artistic modernism (in a smoky corner of this middle distance, the Existentialists), and the champions of the ancestral critical theories in all these fields. Behind *them*, receding as far as the lines of perspective will take us, generations of German philosophers and sociopolitical analysts, from Habermas to Heidegger, Husserl and Hegel, even to Kant (Nietzsche looming along the way), and from the Frankfurt School back to Marx. Here, right down front, under a blinking *Cinémathèque* sign, a merry band of film-ists—the founders of *Cahiers du Cinéma* and a dozen other journals, at whose feet lie prostrate the grateful directors of a thousand movies B now anointed films noir.

If we touch the scene to life, the apparently aimless movement is constant and the Babel of tongues deafening. (The deplorers of the phono- and logo-centric are the loudest and wordiest of all.) And front and center, poor Pivot—damp, touseled, and hoarse, his spectacles now up, now down—attempting to sign off. "*Merci!*", he cries. "*Merci à tous! Merci à tous et bon soir!*" But in vain.

I don't mean to imply intimacy with all these thinkers and their works. Some years back, at the flood tide of deconstructionism here in the U.S., a journalistic report on Jacques Derrida took the occasion to deride his dense, neologistic style as mere bad, obscurantist writing (and so, by implication, thinking). A reader wrote in to protest that the author of the article was in no position to make such a judgment: a lifetime of study, she advised, taking in the whole of the Western philosophic tradition and all its terminologies, would be prerequisite to a proper understanding of Derrida's usages. This respondent was unquestionably right. It *would* take a lifetime of study (not mine, I have decided) to acquire a true mastery of the intellectual background to the arguments of these writers, and so with some confidence contend with them in their own spheres.

Fortunately, nothing of the sort is to the purpose here, which is only to define and evaluate the effect of these theories on opera. That effect has been murderous. It is also ongoing, despite the whiff of mould detectable in its disciplines of origin. Some familiarity with the principles and arguments of these modes of thought—at least of those that are clearly related to the tales I've been recounting—is therefore in order.* It's not that our modern *philosophes* "invented" or "discovered" all these concepts (which often surfaced first in artistic representation, and were felt before they were thought), but they have articulated and promulgated them, and so enabled us to see them for what they are. By seepage and slippage, these same concepts have become the premises for most artistic working and thinking. Indeed, seepage and slippage have themselves been validated as principles of artistic process.

Some of the germane concepts question the most basic assumptions of artistic tradition, e.g., that there are such things in art as content, author,

---

* For this reason, I have taken some trouble to expand my own patchy knowledge of them, and rather than concern myself here with acknowledgements, attributions, chronology, etc. (the ideas themselves are all that matter), I refer the reader to the bibliographical essay in Backstory II, p. 759. All citations of this literature in this and subsequent chapters refer to works listed there.

meaning, and so on. But perhaps I can best begin to illustrate their entanglement with opera by an example that at least accepts the proposition that an artwork *has* a content, whose nature is subject to interpretation. We have already encountered this example. It is Herbert Wernicke's set of mirror for the opening tableau of *Die Frau ohne Schatten*. As I have already pointed out, this choice uses references in the libretto and score (thus giving it an apparent grounding in the text, an alibi against the charge of arbitrariness) to turn the creators' stipulation on its head: instead of a transparent woman in a solid, objective world, we have a woman of solid flesh in a world of flitting reflections. Yet, unlike the campy men of Magritte or the risible Tumbler/terrarium shtick, there seems no question that this is seriously, meaningfully intended. It has seeped in from somewhere in the meaning-world of a contemporary German auteur.

The mirror as artistic metaphor (mirrorness—"specularity," "reflectivity") has a long history to which opera has contributed little beyond a few occultish incidents and the fairly elaborate example (Madeleine's *Spiegelarie*) that brings the There and Then to a close, and so serves its audiences primarily as reflection of, and on, a lost world. But in the literary and film criticism of our time, in psychoanalytic writings and cultural theory, specularity is all over the place. The deconstructive semiotician Jonathan Culler uses M.H. Abrams' *The Mirror and the Lamp* to trace a literary line that touches on Coleridge and Wordsworth, on Georgian poets and Yeats. Film theorists (e.g., Spellerberg and Metz—see Backstory II) have worked up an "ideology of specularity," and not illogically, since that quality is constitutive of the medium itself (projected images in reflected light—though of course the true mirror's main object of fascination, the observer's own image, is not present). It's but a tiny slip from here to a wider specularity, to the universe of the virtual, the ideal, the simulated and the simulacrum, that receives so much attention from such thinkers as Gilles Deleuze and Jean Baudrillard. The latter, for whom (following McLuhan's lead) television, not film, is the culturally dominant medium, eventually concludes that because the distinction between the real and the reflected no longer obtains, the specular has disappeared, lost in what he calls the "precession of simulacra." At any of these "sites," we are at a considerable remove from the old thoughts of art as a mirror held up to nature or the poet as a mirror of truth. And from any of them—or from Rudolf Hartmann's notes or a chance encounter with *Alice Through the Looking Glass*—the specular may have seeped into Wernicke's vision.

But by far the likeliest source of Wernicke's idea is the psychoanalytic concept of the Mirror Stage in ego development as elaborated by Jacques Lacan, through whom it seems to have undergone the alchemical conversion, common to many Freudian or Jungian formulations, from empirically derived therapeutic theory into all-purpose cultural-critical tool. Lacan's theory about a Mirror Stage is not apt to have escaped the attention of a culturally informed European. It is also just the sort of symbolic importation favored by Regietheatrists. It describes the developmental sequence whereby a child learns first to recognize his mirror image as himself, then to differentiate this self from other images. The idea is entirely absent from other influential theories of child psychology, but for Lacan it is a cornerstone in the construction of the "I," and his presentation of it has been powerful enough to make it a frequent resource in several fields (it crops up here, for instance, in Culler, Spellerberg, and Metz). The analogy is obvious: the Empress (less than a year reborn in human form, after all, and unable to conceive) is at her own Mirror Stage, barely able to distinguish Self from Reflection or from Other.

I hope that Wernicke's mirrored stage reflects Lacan's Mirror Stage. That would at least address the Empress' psychology, and have an intellectually serious tone. The difficulty remains that since it does not respect the boundaries of the interpretive field set by the creators, and actually reverses the relationship between the character and her environment, for any believer in the integrity of an artwork it is not *operatically* serious at all. Operatically, it is frivolous and hubristic.

The integrity of the artwork, however, is precisely what is at issue. It is called into question by the principle of intertextuality, especially when that principle is theatrically fused with the filmic theory of the auteur. Intertextuality goes far past the tracing of common themes or stylistic markers from work to work, creator to creator. It proposes that interpretation of an artwork (or of any element thereof—a single word, for example) is best approached through study of its relationship to an ongoing cultural discourse. Indeed, it suggests that this is the *only* valid approach to interpretation. This relationship inheres in an interplay of signification from text to text, the pursuit of which is itself the interpretive imperative. Further, since there is (so it is claimed in deconstructive usage) always a slippage (*glissement*) among the signifiers and signifieds that make up the semiotic universe, and the signifiers wind up evoking not their referents, but other signifiers (and texts other texts) in an endless chain, the relationships are never fixed—"meaning" is always deferred.

Intertextuality is a child of language, and therefore of literature, of "text" and "writing" in the common understanding of these words. It provides a way of examining the codes, the ruling metaphors, of a culture through its literature(s). It therefore considers individual works primarily as bearers of these codes and metaphors, whether the purpose in so doing is to uncover meaning through structural analysis or to demonstrate that meaning is forever deferred. Moreover, since in the general semiotic understanding anything may serve as "text" to be "read" for its signifying value in the ongoing discourse (a household appliance, the presentation of food on a plate, a face, a body), the associative play of intertextuality may be infinitely extended—it is no longer confined to writing or even to art. Or, as some would have it, "writing" takes in everything, and anything can be "art." Finally, this theorizing includes a strain in which the identity of the author, the existence of authorship, is itself effaced (see Barthes and Foucault, who will in turn refer you further back).

Which brings us to the *politique des auteurs*. In relation to the Death-of-the-Author hypotheses just mentioned, it is hopelessly old-fashioned, for its whole purpose is to argue just who is an author to whom an *oeuvre* may be attributed, and who is not. In the popular understanding, auteurism still seems to be identified with the designation of the director (not the writer) of a film as its author, or simply with a strong personal stamp on a film that seems to be the director's. *Somebody* has to be so attributable, or the whole business is obviated. Either way, the identification appears justified by the unexampled power of the film director to manipulate his medium and thereby micro-control the work of all other Second Interpreters, to define and fix the overall shape and texture of a performed work. Yet many directors wield this power without qualifying as auteurs. Power, however great, is not the same as creativity. Here auteur theory comes to the rescue through intertextuality or, rather, a reductive adaptation of it, in the interplay of directorial tropes throughout the works of a given director. The "signature" of a director, discoverable only when his films are considered in relation to one another, is taken as a token of merit, as grounds for distinguishing him as an *auteur* rather than a mere *metteur en scene*.

The power is a fact. There's no gainsaying that, or the convenience of auteuristic intertextuality for movie critics—most movies are hardly worth a second thought in themselves, and many a director is brought into the realm of the ponderable only by assigning importance to his habits.* Regardless of whether or not this validation has proceeded satisfactorily in the filmic world, when it is transferred to the operatic one we encounter two *glissements* of mudslide proportion and character.

One: *the "valorization" (the vocabulary does come in handy) of the director as "author," i.e., of an interpreter as creator, a Second Interpreter*

* "The task of validating the auteur theory," said Andrew Sarris in his influential 1962 essay on the topic, "is an enormous one, and the end will never be in sight." Happy Days!

as First. In many film instances this is entirely defensible. But that is because auteurs *have* taken important First Interpretive steps (conceiving the scenario, plot, characters; writing the screenplay) and closely supervised others.

In a handful of cases (Richard Wagner, Gian-Carlo Menotti, Robert Wilson when librettist, Peter Sellars when collaborating on a new work) this could also be said of operatic directors. *In no other instance* does the elevation of opera director to auteur have a leg to stand on. Yet it is the prevalent contemporary practice, and while the stage director's power has in any event grown steadily over the past hundred years, it has taken auteuristic thinking to name him creator and free him from the responsibilities and limitations of the interpreter.

This freedom corresponds well with that of the choreographer, who alone among stage directors comes by auteuristic powers legitimately, creating roles "on" dancers and determining their physical behavior in detail. That's a leg to stand on, but in opera it's a wobbly one.

Two: *The unleashing of the director, so valorized, to range across a limitless field both horizontally (through contemporary cultures and subcultures) and vertically (through time, the cultures of historical periods) in search of pillage to "create" (assemble) his productions.* Intertextual pursuit is the intellectually respectable referent for this, but it is part of a wider effort to erase standing categories and hierarchies, ostensibly to do away with categories and hierarchies altogether with all their rigidities and traps, but in reality to install new ones with theirs—that is to say, disempower certain people and empower others.

In this process, intertextuality slithers from the works of true creators (authors, composers, et al.), to the productions of auteurs. In the former the signifiers are usually unconsciously embedded, to be rooted out by linguistic and philosophic critics. In the latter they are deliberately planted.

Often these tropes have an in-joke character, and are passed from one of the auteur's productions to the next, or Tumbled around a community of auteurs and their devotees. From a single instance, it is impossible to know if a particular sign is playing a role in this intertext of productions. (Seeker: "Are there mirrors in *all* Wernicke productions?" Mentor: "Then you haven't *followed*

Wernicke?" Seeker: "Uh, I was trying to follow Strauss." Mentor (pityingly): "Child, your road is long and hard.")

While the most intelligent directors are careful to select signs that can be tagged as items of cultural discourse, they're really offering us glimpses of their personal tapestries. Some glimpses may strike a receptor as self-indulgent or tasteless (D. Alden's Venusberg), others as proper or high-minded (the mirror), but in principle they are all the same. In terms of fidelity to the work Alden's choice is actually the more plausible of these two: the Emperor's palace does not have walls of mirror, but the Venusberg does have sex.

From all the above follows the single rule of "advanced" operatic production: *whether a sign is drawn from the cultural discourse, the auteurial psyche, or some other source, it must in any event come from outside the creator's boundaries, and so displace them.*

"Only a few opera producers from the United States have real individual signatures," says Tom Sutcliffe.[1] To the extent that this may be true,* it reflects not only the complacency and systemic restrictions Sutcliffe mentions but, more positively, a set of beliefs about performance. According to those beliefs, just as the very best actors (singing or not) disappear into their roles and the greatest conductors into their music, so the best designers and directors have no signatures, because they seek to discover and work by the internal rules of the work at hand, to become "invisible" in Jones's sense. Thus, their personal styles, histories, opinions, faiths are beside the point; they give themselves over to the work—that particular work, different from all others—and do everything possible to delineate its particularity. *It* becomes their faith, until the next time.

To what extent the caves and cellars of Europe may yet harbor adherents of this now-heretical credo, I can't say. It is by no means uniquely American, having been adapted from Russian and German sources, and has never been consistently honored. But it remains not only our finest performance ideal, but our most productive performance practice—in the qualitative, not quantitative sense. It is derived from stage performance work by stage performance workers, and so is the best bastion from which to defend stage

---

* And it's a dangerous generalization to make. For instance Sutcliffe, obviously working largely from hearsay, goes on to quite mischaracterize Corsaro's best work at the NYCO, and even to leave the impression that it was associated with a performance-in-English policy, which is not true. For further on this, see the *Acting* chapter in Part IV.

performance itself from the misappropriated strategies that seep and slide from literature, philosophy, the visual arts, the electronic media.

Gladly granting that much can be illumined by skillful intertextual examination, I would still ask: of what value is the grand critique of the discourse if the individual works of which it consists are not allowed to fulfill themselves? How can the "ruling metaphors" be honestly derived? In the context of poetry, Harold Bloom complains of ". . . the anti-humanistic plain dreariness of all those developments in European criticism that have yet to demonstrate that they can aid in reading any one poem by any poet whatsoever." But Bloom, in poetry, still has resort to the works themselves. We, in opera, do not. They are not before us. Of discourse we have plenty, but of opera very little.

And this is owing to a final *glissement* that goes beyond mudslide to freefall—the simple, puzzling failure to acknowledge the in-kind difference between performed art and other art. This is nothing less than the failure to distinguish between an act and an object. The modern *philosophes* are not directly to blame for this. They are, on the whole, an unlyrical and untheatrical bunch whose sensibilities are elsewhere, with language and literature. They have things to say from time to time about the fine arts and, as noted, quite a lot about film and television. But concerning theatre or music, their offerings are scant, and as to opera, nonexistent. Opera is irrelevant to them, and they could be safely held irrelevant to it had not their ideas, indigestible though they are, been swallowed whole by the operatic maw.

It's not a question of defacing a work, as one might a painting or statue, or destroying its stock as one could a film's, or even of burning a book. It's a question of not allowing the work to come into existence at all, let alone to shine forth with its own light, its own truth. Until an opera is vivified by performance energies, and in the process necessarily interpreted, it does not exist. A thing exists (the text), but not an opera, not a work. To my considerable surprise and infinite wariness, it is Martin Heidegger who offers philosophic help on this point. Heidegger's essay *The Origin of the Work of Art* is knotty, meaty, and problematic. Some of its problems lie in the very area under discussion, in the non-distinction between Arts of the Object and Arts of the Act. It is couched entirely in language of the former, glissing occasionally into the domain of the latter in the wish to be inclusive about "art." Nevertheless, in the essay's central effort—which is to define what a "work" is, and thereby to see what art is, since "Art essentially unfolds itself in the artwork"—Heidegger speaks eloquently for the imperative integrity of the individual work in a way that certainly applies to Arts of the Act, so long as we remember that the work has its being only in the act. After leading us through his division of all beings into three sorts (things, equipment, works) in order to separate "workliness" from other modes of essence, he writes of how a work opens up a world. "The work belongs, as work, uniquely within the realm that is opened up by the work." It creates its world by clearing space in an "open region"—which, in my reading, is by definition a region unoccupied by anything else, including other artworks. "The work as work sets up a world. The work holds open the open region of the world." In doing so, it brings about an "unconcealment" of beings. It is ". . . a distinctive way in which truth comes into being, that is, becomes historical."

Like all philosophic language, Heidegger's takes some getting used to and needs its context to settle in. But to many creators, interpreters, and devotees—art-ists—these definitions will feel familiar, even re-assuring. They are philosophical formulations, finished articulations, of a particular art-istic sense about the worth of art and artworks—a worth that can be realized only through the "holding open" and "shining forth" (this usage, complete with Biblical echo, is Heidegger's) of each work, unique. True it is, that works can be seen as belonging to discourses, or as playing political, social or religious roles. Truer, that each fully accomplishes itself only by standing over against the discourse and subsuming such roles. This accomplishment is (or, rather, would be) a triumph not of art for art's sake, but for ours, for the world's.

Though Heidegger belongs to the post-Nietzschean era, the aesthetic views of his essay are in sympathy with an older cultural tradition, and it is artists of that tradition who will most easily recognize and take comfort from them. From their P.O.V., Heidegger stands as corrective to the views of his successors and deconstructors—not the other way around. And he shows a responsiveness to art, a taking-in of art, an *acknowledgement of engagement*, that with a few exceptions is not found in the successors. Among them, it is as if one must be rendered impervious to the engagement before proper analysis can begin. And among artists themselves, the older tradition withers; the more talented and ambitious are children of the successors' discourse. The masterworks cannot shine forth.

Aporia is a word often encountered in postmodern critical literature. It is from the Greek term for "unpassable path," and is used to identify a "self-engendered paradox" in an argument, beyond which thought cannot pass (Norris, discussing Derrida and De Man—again, see Backstory 2). Such a place in a text is the common entry point for deconstructive analysis. But aporia is also taken as existential fact, the ground condition for life and the starting-point of artistic endeavor, in much cultural analysis: art *as we have known it*, philosophy, history as we have known them, are held to be at an end, or to have collapsed into one another. As constituted they can go no further. Whatever follows (if anything can follow) must take some radically other form. In music, all the developments of pantonality have sprung from the perceived aporia of tonality. *Waiting for Godot*, the seminal play of our time, is a dramatization of aporia, with its central inaction of not going on. As for opera, its forward thinkers and doers have seen it at an impasse since (yes) World War I, and in the progressively feebler strugglings of creators and interpreters in the generations since there is little to contradict them.

If creativity and interpretivity lose their energy, their will, what replaces them? Criticality. It is not simply that there is more or better criticism, less or worse creation and interpretation. It is that criticality *invests* creation and interpretation, occupies their spaces and assumes their forms, and that creators and interpreters become critics even while creating and interpreting. Thus, it turns out that criticality is itself the radically other form, in which creation and interpretation are enmeshed.

The definition of "aporia" in my dictionary reads: "... in rhetoric, an *affectation* of being at a loss where to begin, or what to say" (italics mine). The lecturer, the minister pauses, in professed awe of the problem he has just hypothesized. Dear me, where to begin? How to approach the incommensurable? Perhaps one might venture this humble beginning...

I am not trying to suggest that all contemporary criticism is affectation, or that the notion of aporia is sheer invention. Creation *has* faltered, has left a vacuum into which some nearby thing will be drawn. Still, this is also true: the acceptance of aporia is what makes certain forms of criticism possible, just as the acceptance of auteuristic intertextuality is the enabling concession for Sarris's endless task of validation. And such acceptances perpetuate themselves. Let's announce an aporia; with creation declared dead (and with each declaration, more likely to remain so), criticism goes freely forward, and becomes our primary way of dealing with art. Everything is assimilated to criticism, and by that route to literature, to text. This criticism claims everything for text. Anything that threatens to escape from text is, therefore, outside its laws.

What threatens to escape from text? Live performance. Not film, or recorded performance of any kind. Such performance is inscribed, like text; fixed, like text; analyzable and available for reference, like text—thus, fair game for textual criticism, a material form of text with fragments of past performance preserved inside. Live performance is none of those things. It relies on presence and authenticity in the performer—presence and authenticity that vanish with the moment and may be vouched for, but never conclusively demonstrated, by criticism.

In the vocabulary of deconstruction (and, by seepage and slippage, much semiotic analysis that is not, strictly speaking, deconstructive), the words "presence," "speech," and "voice" mean more than they do in their performance applications. They refer to rhetorical elements of writing that seek authenticity in language as if spoken by a present speaker, and thus reflect what Derrida and others maintain is a "phonocentric" bias in all Western thought—a presumption that speech antedates writing, and that the speech of a present person is more direct, immediate, and (hence) authentic than the mediated symbolic inscriptions of language called writing. Through extended and complex argumentation, deconstructive and allied schools of thought seek to expose the distortions introduced by phonocentrism and the "logocentrism" of which it is an aspect. Metaphors of speech and voice (so the argument holds) are bits of flim-flam that serve to disguise the aporias of thought, to persuade by "presence" whenever the pursuit of fugitive meaning is turned aside on the unpassable path. So they are to be uncovered and, to the limited extent possible (for we are always inside our structures of language, and must perforce employ the very means we acknowledge to be incomplete), discarded.

These pervasive modes of critical thought have sought a science of language (a "grammatology"), a science of signs, for the purpose of addressing purported distortions in other modes of criticism and in philosophy. As ways of addressing art itself, though, they seem patently inadequate. Artistic analysis can never approach the truly scientific; it can aspire only to the *manner* of science, a sort of scientism. And even if it were possible, such an effort would be desirable only if the goal were to strip art of its artness, for when it comes to works of art, the metaphorical "distortions" turn out to be an inventory of content. Even granting that the outing of presence, speech, and voice in a philosophical tract may be productive, what's left of a poem? The experience of the poem *depends on* presence, speech, voice—performance. That is, on its music. Performance is the embodiment and celebration of the phonocentric, of sounded presence's escape from text.

Of all the stage arts' escapes from text, opera's is the most definitive and irreversible. This is due in part to its sheer ear-led, eye-confirmed sensory overload. Even if the initial visceral response to sound could somehow be laid aside, ear and eye ganged into separate-but-equal analytic modes in search of a Semiotics of Immediately Present Energies, and then some species of narrativity cobbled up therefrom, exactly which of the thousand candidate signifiers in any of a thousand fleeting moments, in what combination and set of inter-relationships, are to be pursued? The enterprise is clearly absurd. Presence(s), voice(s), energies block its very conception. And even more: opera devours text. It takes the sounded word (which, sounded, has already escaped from text), binds it into the wordnote, swallows and digests it for what sound/sense nourishment it may provide, then spews it forth among myriad phenomena of its own and other sorts. Transcendence of text is its *mission*.

By its non-engagement with live performance generally, music particularly, and opera most particularly, the literary and philosophical discourse tacitly acknowledges all this. It also acknowledges its own fear: that if the power of the phono-celebrative, presence-authenticating, text-transcending Arts of the Act is allowed, text loses its centrality and criticality its hegemonic position. Textual criticality, having only recently come by this position by default, won't stand for that; it can no longer see itself as other than definitive. Aporia must be preserved. The rise of academic critical schools that claim the disciplines of musicology and dramaturgy for the philosopho/politico/literary line, and the simultaneous tug-of-the-forelock, backing-out-the-door retreat of art-istic performance criticism, are helpful but insufficient for this purpose, for performance can at any moment rally and brush their musings aside. Criticality must somehow encapsulate performance, push its visceral element, its energies and actions, into the background and cause it to be read like text. There are no grounds in opera, music, or theatre for doing this, and so the operating principles must be enlisted from the Arts of the Object, from film, and from literary criticism, then projected with the domineering force and clinical clarity of contemporary industrial technology, science's forward strike force into the realm of art.

Since the present *is* the aporia, its creativity cannot menace aporia. At its smartest, it rejoices in it. The creativity of the past, however, is always latent in the works of the canon. The only way it can be suppressed is to absorb it into the critical discourse, and the only way that can be accomplished is to subvert its interpretive fulfillment by means of a wholesale betrayal of interpretation to criticism. Here is another analytic process that happily will never be at an end; it can spin critical straw from creative gold to the crack of doom. But, though never complete, the seemingly impossible betrayal project has been remarkably successful. Its basic move is desperate but ingenious: with creativity stuck in our throats and performance turning into a loop of ever-paler mechanical recitations, we simply shift the meaning of "interpretation" from advocacy of the work to comment on it, contextualization of it. The spirit of the critic is injected directly into the bodies of performers, the clothes they wear, the worlds they inhabit. This done, the injectors call themselves creators.

The transformations wrought by auteurial, intertextual, critical, hi-tech production are impressive: a shift of sensory attention from the ear to an eye that reads and analyzes; a shift in representation from the real to an abstract that does not intensify or essentialize the phenomenal world, but hides from it; a shift in interpretive focus from psychology to philosophy, from personal specifics to generalizations of discourse; a dulling of emotional response in favor of a distanced, intellectualized one; the absorption of past understandings into contemporary ones. These are species of torture visited upon the work, upon the past, upon the audience, and they end in the death of performance itself, if by "performance" we mean an occasion on which all efforts are bent to make manifest and alive the workliness of an individual work, to make that work truly present, and to engage the audience with its world.

In the place of performance is set a mock-performance event that asks its audience to observe a brand-new principle of engagement: the willing suspension of belief. Belief belongs to the past, to the old understanding of engagement. In exchange for suspending it, initiates get to play their intellectually fashionable games and non-initiates may drift in the haze of the Great Deferred Whatever, in the knowledge that they at least belong to the moment. With belief left behind to mourn over the corpse of performance and creativity still back there at the aporia, the project of assimilation to critical discourse nears completion.

NOTES

1. See Sutcliffe, op. cit., p. 167.

2

THE FLIGHT FROM E-19

The assimilationist project and the conceptualist project are closely bound. According to the former, creation's true purpose is criticism, while interpretation *is* criticism. According to the latter, an individual artwork's true purpose is the conveyance of an Idea. As we have seen, however, its ideas generally have to do with disunification (of the artwork), delegitimation (of narrative, of representation), and deferral (of meaning). These in turn require a severance from longheld working hypotheses about unity, narrative and representation, meaning, and continuity itself.

Obviously, we can't have art without ideas. But Idea in the conceptualist sense, as the thing-in-place-of-everything-else at an artwork's center of attention, is another matter. What does it displace? Most recently: form, materials, structure—the foci of the modern. And before that? Content (or, if you prefer, substance), to whose expression forms, materials, and structures were bent, and *from which* concepts would be derived. In shorthand: to go from Idea to Form to Content is to journey back from the Postmodern through the Modern to the Premodern—to the eve of World War I, aporia's onset and opera's sunset. Thus, the process of opera's removal toward the cultural margin dates to the turn away from content. This turn from whatness to howness was much more than a style shift. As intended by its champions, it was a radical break. (To cite the most obvious musical cases, Schoenberg and Stravinsky had very different stylistic responses to it, but after their early Premodern periods, both settled on howness as the central creative issue.) So, too, with the subsequent turn away from Form to Idea. This could be seen as a return to content, but in nothing like the old sense—it is an intellectualized, depersonalized, abstracted content, an essentialized substitute for content.

These breaks were of course charged with energy—with the promise of revolutionary change, progressivist assertion, and the urgency of perceived necessity. Nonetheless, here we are, our art assimilated to criticality, collapsed into philosophy. It therefore behooves those of us who would like art to go on being art to stick up for content as content. And opera is a favorable battleground, since both the modern and postmodern aesthetics have failed it so miserably.

With respect to the stage arts, there is no mystery to the whereabouts of content: it is to be found in plot (narrative), and character. In opera, it is tempting to add description as a third essential component. Certainly description is what the orchestra is up to much of the time and often to great effect, and when we add to this the descriptive element in singing, which by means of embellishment, timbral shading, and other rhetorical devices goes so far toward determining the emotional quality of the performance engagement, the case seems strong. However, most of what the orchestra describes really belongs to either plot (physical environment, atmosphere, passage of time or change of place) or character (emotional climate, mood, suppressed feeling, the unconscious itself) as conditions of them, while vocal description (even as narration) belongs by definition to character. In any case, this is a short list—two or three "items" only, though rife with interpretive possibility even given a strict observance of the boundaries of the creator's field. And it's all right out in plain sight. In fact, it is so transparent that the turn away from content on the pretext that it can't be located reeks of evasion. This supposedly progressive, supposedly principled move begins to look more like a flight from a certain *kind* of content, one or more conformations of plot and character that, together with all their musical and theatrical elaborations, cannot be countenanced.

Let me recall briefly my earlier discussion of the canon and the repertory, of the works of renewable re-affirmability that sustain our operatic institutions (p. 65), and the related matter of narrative redundancy. And let me recall as well that though the availability of performance may expand or contract, it remains finite, made up of certain works chosen over others. Over the past half-century, the composition of the repertory, though in comparison with other periods virtually frozen with respect to new work, has changed considerably in regard to old. A handful of post-World-War-I operas have found some repertory status. The operas of the young Verdi, those of the early Italian Romantics, of Monteverdi and Handel and the Baroque, and most recently of 19th-Century Russia, have come up for re-examination, all given impetus by the modern industries of musicology and recording, and all disclosing greater performability than had long been granted them. But if we were to sort all these works into categories according to frequency of repeatability, as our real-world impresarios must, we would find that most of this activity has occurred in the lower categories. The cumulative presence is impressive and the aesthetic variety alluring, but our index of indispensables still begins with the mature Mozart and ends with Puccini and Strauss. Movement within this core repertory has been due primarily to the lessened repetition of a few former perennials, to be replaced not by individual works of comparable viability, but by a dozen each from a tasting menu. I reiterate that I am not arguing here the merits of particular works or genres, or trying to account for all that has been of importance at one time or another, but only to consider what remains of importance, and what this says about the nature of the engagements we seek, and those we shun.

I call the stretch from Mozart though Strauss the Extended Nineteenth Century, or E-19 for short.* At its early boundary, Mozart stands somewhat apart from the succeeding era's typical content, but in an interesting juxtaposition to it. At the late one, the operas of Puccini and the verists are transforming that content, though still infused with it, while those of Strauss move some distance from it. The century between opens with roughly thirty years (the years of Rossini and the early Bellini, of Cherubini and Spontini, Auber and Boieldieu, and of Weber and Lortzing and Marschner) that are the least represented in live performance of any such period since Mozart. These three decades can be seen as the response of emotion to reason (the rebound from the Enlightenment) or the quarrel between the early Romantics and the holdout Classicists, or—as I am suggesting here—as the time of the search among character types and plot elements for those that would build the engine of E-19 Proper. Once that gets going in the 1830s, a single plot-and-character conformation generates the central action of virtually every work still regularly performed today. This conformation is typical only of E-19, and is the period's principal identifying mark.

I am aware that this last claim is open to challenge. We are accustomed to thinking of artistic works and eras in terms of themes that determine our sense of what they're about and qualities that seem to account for their effects, and of regarding such themes and qualities as being fundamental to content, rather than merely belonging to it. When it comes to opera, we are also in the habit (even when speaking of it as "drama"!) of looking to music rather than theatre for our definitions. But the fact that music is strongly implicated in the conveyance of plot and character and of themes

---

* I employ this slight variation on Eric Hobsbawm's more-or-less co-extensive "Long Nineteenth Century" because I wish to confine the discussion to operatic eras, not broad cultural or political ones. The synchronicities are close, but not exact.

and qualities, the fact that opera is ear-led and eye-confirmed does not free it from its status as a stage art, an Art of the Act. In any stage work, themes and qualities (whether transmitted musically or otherwise) emerge from the progress of its central action, and operatic eras are more accurately defined by the natures of the actions they represent than by either their musical or theatrical innovations. The latter do not spring up as mutations in search of a story. The reverse, though reductive if presented as simple cause-and-effect, would be far closer to the truth.

Over the course of E-19, startling musical transformations occur. Among these are the increasing prominence and complexity of orchestral writing; marked changes in the conventions of voice distribution and the nature of vocal gestures; the harmonic push toward chromaticism and then free dissonance; and the pull of musical narrative toward a seamless, flexibly responsive continuity. A pronounced development also takes place with respect to the wholeness and lifelikeness of character, both in the relationship between inner life and outer action and in the presentation of the individual as free and responsible agent.

Yet through all these changes, any of which could be advanced as defining, the typical plot-and-character conformation keeps right on going. Thus, it appears that a particular dramatic circumstance is the common element, indeed the enabling element; that the need for the story spurred the increases in its telling; and that the need for the story to work itself through brought both the story and its telling to eventual maturation. It is true that the story has many variants, some of which may act as disguise. It is also true that the stereotypical progression of the story's events and personages does not invariably correspond to what is most compelling in the music and hence most worthy of belief. This, too, can distract us from what in fact happens. But all eloquence notwithstanding, what happens still happens, and when it happens over and over I think we must take it as an interpretive key.

In skeleton form, the E-19 story is this:

> By reason of dispossession or other disconnection, a male protagonist cannot assume his "rightful" place in the social scheme. This injustice is the flashpoint of the plot; it drives the action even when our attention is on a female predicament. The outcast/hero falls instantly and obsessively in love with a woman identified through family or title with the very situation from which he is excluded. This forbidden woman returns his love. An antagonist opposes the fated couple by reason of his station (which is often that claimed by the protagonist) or his own attachment, romantic or familial, to

the woman. The decisive clash between the male claimants, in the course of which the woman's fate is determined and in which she usually plays a catalytic role, is the dénouement of the plot. In the handful of comedies among these operas, the conflict ends in a social accommodation. In the far more numerous tragedies, it leads to the death of one or (usually) both members of the protagonist couple.

For a "protagonist couple" is what we are dealing with: a man and a woman who unite against the antagonist and the established order he represents—falsely, from the couple's P.O.V., which we are persuaded to share. And it is specifically this situation that is the E-19 marker—not love, or romantic rivalry, or even unrequited love in general. The elements of unjust dispossession, of the lovers' instant attraction to each other and their "right" to this attraction, are essential. So, in the tragedies, is the sense of doom hanging over the characters.

The template for E-19's enabling conformation is late-Medieval. It was stamped in the 12th and 13th Centuries, an era often thought of as a proto-Renaissance, even a proto-Reformation. This was a time of constant, brutal conflict occasioned by the push from feudal toward centralized monarchical systems of governance; of the Crusades, with their East/West cultural crosscurrents; of the flourishment of courtly love and its poet-singers, the troubadours; and of the ascendance of several powerful heresies that openly defied the hegemony of Rome. The birthplace of the troubadour/courtly love culture lay in Southern France (the old Languedoc, far more extensive than the province that now bears that name, and tied not to the North, but to the Kingdom of Aragon, across the Pyrenees), which also spawned the most significant of the anti-Rome religious movements, the Cathar (or Albigensian) Heresy. So widespread was the threat of this faith, and so strong its hold on its followers, that it required for its eventual suppression the invention of the Inquisition, the founding of the Dominican Order, and the launching of the horrendous Albigensian Crusade.

As part of the Mediterranean rim, the old Languedoc was in a constant and lively interchange with not only the rest of Southern Europe, including Muslim Spain, but the Middle East and Orient as well. Its culture was more open and varied, more sensuous, more cultivated and sophisticated than that of the North, and under its mantle of orthodox Christianity it preserved in its religious observance beliefs and practices whose sources lay in early Christian or pre-Christian faiths—Gnosticism, Manicheism, even the ancient bull-worship of Mithra. It was ideal soil for both courtly love and religious unorthodoxy.

The extermination of the Cathar Heresy entailed the crushing of the Provençal culture. But the flourishment of the courtly love ethos in Western artistic and intellectual life (to say nothing of its "real-life" role as a model of social conduct) was just beginning, and since it has a direct bearing on the ascendancy of E-19, its primary attributes are worth a moment's attention. It is not my concern to separate history from legend, or to adjudicate among the many theories of origin of the chivalric stories and symbols. All that is a delicious entanglement, but not of much consequence here, since our subject is the life of these elements in the artistic imagination. As with the E-19 operas themselves, whenever a myth is needed, its propagators seek to authenticate it historically. The fact that this authentication is often spurious does not delegitimize the myth; on the contrary, it speaks all the more strongly of the need for it.[1]

In the artistic tradition of courtly love, a poetic knight (or knightly poet) declared himself to a chosen lady, highborn and usually married. (Marriage among the highborn, it should be recalled, was nearly always a matter of pre-selection for the purpose of political alliance or social and economic advancement—a duty, not a choice. Any coincidence of love and marriage was fortuitous, and indeed the courtly ethic went so far as to proclaim them incompatible. For this reason the taking of a lover was deemed acceptable, though in carefully regulated stages and according to a strict etiquette.) To this lady the knight/poet pledged his devotion, his feats of valor, and if necessary his life. His verses sang of an anguished, worshipful longing for his lady's favors, a yearning and suffering that was close to mortal even as its object was extolled as the fount of purity and virtue. Those sentiments were projected in a profusion of poetic and musical forms whose language was elaborately figurative, and often coded for political and religious comment.

Three aspects of courtly love merit emphasis here. The first is its elevation and exaltation of woman, the surrender of ultimate power to her. Obviously, this was in spite of patriarchal dominance in both the secular and religious spheres, though we should note that women's legal standing was stronger in this era (and especially in the South) than subsequently—as the centralized state and the papacy strengthened their grip, restrictions on women tightened. The second is its assertion of the right to choice of personal affection and allegiance. This too has a rebellious aspect: the man declares himself vassal to the woman but in legal fact owes fealty to his feudal lord, and the woman accepts the man's declaration but is really bound by oath of marriage to *her* lord. (In the most archetypal of courtly love romances, that of Tristan and Iseult, these lords are one and the same and the hero's uncle to boot.) And the third is a foreordained sublimation of passion. For despite the permissive courtly code, adultery remained for the orthodox the gravest of transgressions, and marriage between the lovers was excluded by the very nature of the configuration.

Catharism was a dualistic, neo-Manichean faith, by which is meant that it held not only that the world is locked in a struggle between good and evil, light and dark, but that the material world is inherently evil, the creation of a malevolent god. Thus, the only goal of worldly life is to transcend it in preparation for the next one. For this reason, the Cathars rejected such central doctrines as the Incarnation and the Resurrection,* as well as all the sacraments of the worldly (Satanic) Church, including marriage. In fact marriage, permitted to the Cathar rank and file, was forbidden to the Perfect (the Cathar term for high initiates). It should also be noted that women were equal in status to men among the Cathars at a time when orthodox Catholicism granted them no standing. The Perfect had many women, some highborn, among them, and it is not too fanciful to suppose that these included at least a few to whom the troubadours had once addressed their lays.

It can be seen that on several of these points there is an odd sort of agreement between the spiritual world of the Cathars and the very worldly culture of courtly love, which in general tone seem so incompatible with each other. The exact extent of the interpenetration of Cathar and courtly love beliefs and practices, and of the relative importance of religious and political motivations, is much argued. At a minimum, I think we may say that their co-existence in this time and place means that the modern Western arts have from their beginnings had about them a whiff of the heretical as well as of the politically rebellious, and that although (or perhaps because) their creators have been predominantly masculine, both these aspects have been associated with an exaltation of the feminine.

The Albigensian Crusade had profound political as well as religious consequences, and from these emerged the figure of the faydit. This term, etymologically related to words meaning "sworn enemy," "persecuted one" or "banished one," was applied to Cathar nobles and knights who were dispossessed of their estates by reason of their heretical allegiance. Many of these were executed or killed in defense of their lands, but others who escaped or recanted were nevertheless deprived of title, possessions, and noble rights—which is to say everything, since outside these rights there was no citizenship, only subjecthood. The patrimony of the faydit in this original context was frequently awarded to one of the Crusaders who had sided with the papacy; the persecutor himself now occupied the faydit's ancestral castle and ruled over his domains. Later,

---

* A god made flesh would be fallen into the evil world; a god not so fallen is not in need of resurrection. By the same logic, transubstantiation and the Eucharist itself are rendered nonsensical, and indeed the Cathars rejected these central beliefs as well. Not coincidentally, the Incarnation was made official Church doctrine only at the Fourth Lateran Council (1215), convened by Pope Innocent III in large part to define and strengthen orthodoxy against the spread of heretical beliefs.

"faydit" was used to describe any noble dispossessed in the course of shifts of political power or by disputations or other irregularities of inheritance. Such a malfortunate was left with the options of becoming a penitent pilgrim or hermit, taking leadership of a marauding band, joining forces with any emergent faction that might hold promise of redress, or turning soldier of fortune. His makeup (or that of any figure of fiction or drama modeled on him) would add to the courtly elements of his romantic life a central motivating grievance over unjust dispossession. And with respect to fictional or dramatic characters, this sense of unjust dispossession may extend to any we are made to feel deserving of rights or social inclusion denied them by the society shown in the work. Any such character stands in the faydit position.

The faydit and his lady are the protagonist couple, the twin muses of E-19, and their joint fate is its overriding preoccupation. It is their social dilemma, presented in personal, individualized terms and erotically charged, to which our canonical operawrights repeatedly turned, and which drew from them their most compelling work. Devotees will have no difficulty spotting the hardcore faydit cases: Edgardo, brooding in the ruined Wolf's Crag while the stiffbacks occupy his ancestral properties; Manrico, freelance knight and troubadour (an "unconscious" faydit—he doesn't know he's the Count's brother, but senses a connection and instinctively follows the chivalric code); Alvaro, despised halfbreed unfit for "good family," but really a faydit Peruvian prince; Ernani, bandit chieftain but actually Don Juan II of Aragon; Tannhäuser, outcast minstrel and "real-life" trial-by-song combatant (1207, Heinrich von Ofterdingen vs. Wolfram von Eschenbach), et al. The cases of Don Carlo, Gabriele Adorno, Enzo Grimaldo and their ladies, while slightly more complex, are no less obvious. For each of these proscribed or outcast heroes, the lady in question offers hope for legitimation and re-connection. He in turn offers her hope of release from a domestic trap, for which purpose he performs deeds of daring on her behalf, and otherwise behaves in chivalric manner.

E-19 opera is, I believe, unequalled for narrative redundancy.* En route to E-19 Proper we encounter important pieces that are partial exceptions (*Fidelio, Der Freischütz, Norma*—operas that contain most of the E-19 elements, but are not perfect fits), and we find such among the lesser Verdi and Donizetti as

---

* Is any other important body of stage work (or literary work, for that matter) comparable in this respect? I think not. Certainly not the plays of Shakespeare, or of the ancient Greeks. Other operatic or theatrical groupings, by period or by nationality? Not that I can see. Perhaps the other lyric stage art of the same era, E-19 ballet, would come closest. And perhaps (as Joseph Kerman has argued with respect to the instrumental concerto) an analogous case can be built for the era's "absolute" music, whose developments in vocabulary are so similar. Such a case would remain analogical, though, an assignment of actions and roles.

well (but there we are: they are lesser). But of true exceptions I can think of only two, *Parsifal* and *Boris Godunov* in its original version. The former, though it takes as its hero a perfect Fool who is certainly a kind of faydit, is drawn not from the Tristan/Iseult-Lancelot/Guinevere story line with all its projections forward into both fiction and life (Romeo and Juliet, Paolo and Francesca, Dante and Beatrice, Petrarch and Laura, Berlioz and his *idée fixe*, et al. ad inf.) but from the other face of the Matter of Britain, the Christian (Grail) Quest, otherwise ignored by E-19. And the original *Boris*, with its almost exclusive focus on the title character's psychological progression, was early on displaced by a revision whose most important change is to bring the courtly romance onstage, giving it a central position and a seductive musical setting—as if no opera could reasonably be expected to get along without it.

To verify E-19's narrative redundancy, it is necessary only to keep one's eye on what happens. This can be harder than it seems, however, for even beyond its thematic twists and turns, opera is an artform of many distractions. Formerly, these distractions were chiefly aesthetic and emotional. They arose from the impact of works in performance. Now, as we have seen, they tend toward the intellectual and analytical, and have to do with meanings visually conveyed, themes critically pondered. Beyond these, we have the diversions concocted by the E-19 operawrights themselves, which enabled them to produce work of such extraordinary range and quality from the singing of a single story—work that is uniquely redundant but not monotonous, and that bores only in feeblest performance. A sampling of these diversions may be found in Backstory III. Here, I shall note only that even when the protagonist couple's tale is disguised, inverted, or moved off-center, it is the force that drives the action, and even when we feel it isn't at the heart of what an opera's about, it's what enables it to be about whatever it's about.

"Aboutness" returns us to the matter of the themes and qualities that belong to works, and which we often take for fundamental content. "Individualism" would surely be the great thematic catch-all for the aboutness of E-19, choice in love the nearly inevitable vehicle for its expression, and the faydit/ protagonist couple its nearly inevitable dramatic embodiment, its onstage advocate. And we have seen that for this conformation the era's operawrights reached back to the late-Medieval time of the West's cultural re-awakening.[2] But "individualism" is much too general. For one thing, we may well take all the arts of the West (since the Renaissance and before the aporia, at any rate) as an expression of that -ism, and inseparable from it. For another, this "individual," the singular human as subject and agent, has many parts, and can stand in many relationships to a community, to conformative social assumptions and worlds of belief, and can accordingly act in many ways. A more articulated under-standing is needed to give us a handle on the question of content, and on what it is that the Critical Assimilationists, Conceptualists, and Anti-Metanarrators are turning our attention away from. To the themes first.

Marriage, and the alternative. Marriage—the attainment, preservation, or replacement thereof—has been opera's central concern from the beginning, as Monteverdi's three surviving masterpieces show. The question for us is its relation to the faydit narrative. Choice in love, yes—but to what end?

Well, the ends are of two kinds: happy and sad. And apart from the cen-trality of the faydit story itself, the greatest difference between E-19 operas and those that came before is the prevalence of sad endings as opposed to happy ones. There are many reasons for the often tacked-on happy ends of earlier styles and eras (it was social convention; the King made them do it, etc.), but these whys don't alter the what. The fact is that before E-19's advent most operas, both comic and serious, turn out well, whereas thereafter only comedies do. Further: though the protagonist couple's actions are rebellious, they are directed at the terms of inclusion, and this inclusion is represented by marriage. Marriage is the promised outcome, and sooner rather than later: rings have been exchanged, a priest awaits, the organ sounds. Everything is at stake for both partners (for the man, that the dispossessed shall be restored, the outcast taken in, the blasphemer forgiven; for the woman, that the patriar-chally oppressed shall be delivered, the domestically imprisoned freed)—and always through marriage.

Marriage is the only conceivable happy end, and in the comedies it is achieved. But E-19 comedies are exceptions; we must consult the rule. What is the alternative to marriage? It is death, nothing less. The choice is not between *love* and death. You may have both of those, in quick succession or all at once, as if they were the same thing: lovedeath. But you may not have love and *marriage*. They prove incompatible. Comic mask or tragic mask, marry or die—that is the choice.

This pre-occupation with getting married does not extend to the matri-monial state itself. That is left almost completely unexamined, as if getting married would settle everything. And though this is a departure from the courtly-romance model, wherein the obstacle to the lovers' alliance is the fact that the lady is already married, even Wagner's setting of the Tristan story tells us nothing of the marriage itself beyond Marke's allusions to his illu-sions in his Act II monologue.

Fathers, mothers, and inheritance. The reason getting married would settle everything is inheritance. On the individual level inheritance means personal fortune and standing: the marriage bond, sacrosanct and legally permanent, determines the lifelong status of the couple, and this status transfers by right to their progeny. On the societal level, it means succession—the patrilineal order of generational transfer, long held as natural law but now thrown into serious question by political and social democratization, and hence a source of deep unease. When a woman is the connection to inheritance, it is because of a displacement in the patrilineal succession, i.e., she is the temporary link in the chain. Fathers ultimately control inheritance, and therefore are nearly always present in these operas. They are not necessarily ill-intentioned. Indeed, they often occupy the ethical high ground in their societies, upholding codes of honor, protecting family and property, and defending social stability. For these very reasons, though, they are usually impediment to the marriage of true minds. If a father is not around, a surrogate fills the bill.

In the *ur*-faydit operas, inheritance carries with it all the appurtenances of nobility or even royalty. Through marriage, the man hopes to reach equality with the elevated woman, whereupon he (not she) will assume the rights of succession. But the increasingly fluid class atmosphere of E-19 frequently requires inversion of the status of the man and woman, while somehow preserving the faydit conformation. The appellant male is now rendered faydit not by dispossession but by possession: his very aristocracy makes him an outsider under suspicion. It thus falls to the father to defend against the feared predations of the aristocrats an "inheritance" consisting solely of his family's honor and his daughter's virtue, the money and property being on the other side. The suitor must still honor the daughter as lady, the father as patriarch. Ways to play the old courtly drama are found, even when the economics are upside down.

For most of E-19's duration, mothers play only marginal roles. Save for a few instances in operas not much performed—Lyubov in *Mazeppa*, Fidès in *Le Prophête*—Azucena stands alone as a dramatically important character who is the mother of another dramatically important character (as is not the case with Norma or Medea). This certainly seems peculiar. All our heroes and heroines had mothers as surely as fathers, sisters as well as brothers. But since the subject is marriage as an end, not married life itself, there is no occasion for domestic drama in which the mother might be central. And since mothers do not usually hold the power to grant permission for marriage or to withhold an inheritance, they do not figure prominently in the faydit conformation.

Toward the end of E-19, mothers and their surrogates emerge. This is part of a more general shift in gender focus, whose ramifications will be considered farther on.

Destiny. What can we call the unrelenting bad luck that befalls the protagonists of E-19? It is with them from birth and has a fateful quality, often dominant in the music. It seems to hold the characters fast, to drive them down a road not of their choosing. That is how they themselves experience it. Manrico's first words are the key scripture: "*Deserto sulla terra/col rio destin in guerra.*"* But for these self-proclaimed self-determinists, this poses a question of belief. They do not belong to the pre-Christian world of the old *opera seria*, and so can no longer appeal to the classical gods and fates. Yet they are not quite free-thinkers, and are reluctant to finger their Christian God as the perp.

The perception of a ruling fate, of a book already written in which the characters' ends are inscribed, is a form of predestination belief, and as such counter to the Christian doctrine of free will. Further, it posits a mystic realm, also unaccounted-for in Christian orthodoxy, outside the jurisdiction of both God and Satan. This theological contradiction, descended from the uneasy co-existence of medieval beliefs described above, does not bother the characters. Except for those of *Pelléas* (a world of High-End mysticism) and the *Ring* cycle (a world outside the Christian belief system), they live it out in fairly mundane ways—the shuffle of cards, the roll of dice, the telling of fortunes—which they often invest with the weight of supernatural governance.

Occult force is also presumed to inhabit the curses or oaths that shadow the plots of many of these operas. In E-19, while these maledictions occasionally take the form of religious anathemas or of the spells and enchantments cast by wizards, witches, or fairies so commonly encountered in legendary sources, they are usually the personal swearing of one character (most often a father) at another. This character is altogether human and not possessed of otherworldly powers. But because he has been wronged in a way that strikes at social code, his oath or curse takes on such moral authority that it must be either realized or lifted. It fulfills Fate's function.

Finally, "destiny" underlies the instances of dramatic coincidence in which these works abound, and is present in the heroines condemned from the start by sickness or fragility. In short, it becomes the stand-in for any intervention in life that is beyond human control. And it is the force to which characters may ascribe actions of their own for which they do not wish to assume responsibility.

---

* "Forsaken upon the earth/with evil destiny at war".

The meeting, the bond, and trust. Many of the protagonists' love affairs are well advanced as these operas get under way. But when we do see the lovers' first meetings, or learn about them as the story proceeds, they have this quality: that life is, in an instant, utterly changed, its central purpose transformed. The moment is understood as recognition of a mutual destiny and as surrender to a power so overwhelming as to neutralize the issue of responsibility. It is based on a purely intuitive response that has knowledge only of itself, not of the other person.

The bond thus formed has the strengths and weaknesses of love-at-first-sight at its most extreme. The strengths are: a two-against-the-world togetherness, and the moral force of its claim to choice based on attraction rather than arrangement, with strength of feeling itself taken as a kind of sanctification. The weaknesses are that in the absence of any other sanctification the bonded couple is subject to social disapproval or even ostracization, and that the lack of knowledge can not only lead to some nasty surprises, but make trust abnormally difficult. Hence the proliferation of crises of trust marked by fateful misunderstandings, to which the women respond by going insane or nobly sacrificing themselves, the men with torrents of unjust accusation followed by belated remorse.

To give oneself over to an instant call based solely on intuitive knowledge is to exalt that kind of knowledge above any other. It makes blind trust the central moral test.

The political is the personal. "Nationalism," during E-19 a progressive movement directed at the unification of peoples into nation-states and independence from foreign tyranny, is the usual name for this theme. It is often cited in attempts to demonstrate the significance and highmindedness of certain works (standing o's, even encores, for the certified profundity and nobility of "*Va, pensiero*"), and is equally useful for those drawing lines backward from what turned out as nationalism's worst-case scenario. And Wagner and Verdi most certainly were, at important stages of their lives, political men associated with the nationalist movements of their countries. The nature of political power is a strong theme in some of their operas. What these operas say about political power, however, is that it comes down to some very personal matters. The bond of the protagonist couple, the love between parent and child, the struggle to trust, the longing of the ill-favored for intimacy, or of the outsider for inclusion—upon such emotional imperatives do the fates of nations turn.

These things are true of much earlier opera, as well. The differences in E-19 are two. First, the aforesaid personal matters, which in earlier operas had been reconciled among the concerned parties and accommodated to the social order, now end in death; social accommodation is out of the question. Second, the acting-out of the personal drama takes place against a far more active and portentous social background, which has the effect of setting it in relief. This background is represented by the chorus, much augmented in size over previous practice and far more dramatically active. The chorus brings the community into the action as a massed force, in blocs according to class or political faction. Later, this community is sometimes more highly individualized and the lives of the principals interwoven with it. It remains a background, though, a field of humanity against which the principals pursue their destinies. The demos has been brought onstage, all its latent power made visibly and audibly present. But the claims of selected individuals on our attention is all the more sharply highlighted by its arrival.

The artist as faydit. Who are these individuals so pointedly selected for our sympathy, so often seen as painfully separated from birthright and community, and whose struggle for inclusion on their own terms comes to a tragic end with such regularity? Whose position in society is so in question, of such urgent concern to artists, as to suddenly displace all other protagonist pretenders and generate E-19's still-dominant body of work? Who *is* the faydit? Many people, surely, but first among them the artist himself. So it is that when our protagonist is not a "professional" or aspiring artist (a troubadour or minstrel, poet or painter), he is still a singer of serenades or aubades or courtly-dance duettinos, or spinner of flowery romantic conceits or apostrophiser of nature, or at the very least has on him the mark of aesthetic sensibility or artistic temperament. This quality, as much as his chivalric bravery or fiery rebelliousness, draws his lady to him and induces her to share his outsider fate. So it is also that a question often raised in these operas is whether or not the high artistic temperament is compatible with the community. As with the congruent question of the compatibility of true love and marriage, the answer is usually no.[3]

Transcendence. If the problems of the protagonist couple have no worldly solution, one dream remains: to rise above this world to another. There, those who have loved truly, who have suffered unjustly, who have followed their destinies to the end, who have seen what others could not or dare not and have been faithful to their visions, shall at last soar free of the soul-crushing weights and bonds of society, the endless strife of tribes, classes, nations. They shall transcend. Of course in many instances it could be said that they have lived in a state of transcendence from their first meetings—the "out-of-this-world" state of romantic love. But that "out-of-this-world" is still in this world. It is the second transcendence, the transcendence of the sad ending, that takes them beyond.

Sometimes, the sad-end transcendence has a clear religious identity and, as repeatedly noted in our contemporary discourse, it is frequently achieved first by the female protagonist, as if her intercession were required. Just as the elevated woman is the dispossessed man's hope of earthly salvation, so is she the guide to the heavenly kind. As E-19 matures, the language of transcendence is still employed, but not so often in the service of religious meaning. The operawrights are in a quandary analogous to their characters': the old religious model is less and less credible, but is the only brand of transcendence commonly recognized. And we love our sad endings, we rejoice in them, because transcendence is so satisfying. Thus, there arises the question of what the recently holy transcendence can be about. E-19 proposes several possibilities—ashes to ashes, unity with the All, fulfillment of the mysterious mutual Destiny, and for the artist, union with the Muse—before eventually concluding, with a bit of a vengeance, that there isn't any transcendence: lives end, that's all, while Life goes on.

Comedies deal with the resolution of worldly problems in the world, and so have never required transcendence. They do require celebration (of marriage), and during E-19 the musical expression of this celebration often partakes, once again, of transcendental qualities. Since E-19's comedic problems are worked out by the characters without godly or fateful interventions, this suggests that the only real transcendence is from one worldly state (single) to another (married), and that its attainment is entirely up to us.

These are the principal themes attached to the story of the faydit and his lady. Readers who wish to fill out their picture of how these themes interact with the faydit narrative and with the diversions are referred to Backstory III. For instructive contrast that shows how radical the E-19 departure really is, we need glance back no further than the four great Mozart comedies: there isn't a faydit in sight; baleful Destiny plays no role; inheritance crops up only as an amusingly out-of-kilter incidental (Figaro as Bartolo's heir); the artist's predicament is not an issue; the demos is well to the rear and content with rubber-stamp endorsements and celebrations; and of course transcendence is beside the point, these being comedies. Marriage is certainly the central issue, and trust the central issue of marriage. But these operas are also very concerned that the right people marry one another, and while rightness is presented partly as individual attraction and partly as mental affinity (romantic idealists should marry romantic idealists, witty schemers witty schemers, old fools old fools, etc.), it is fundamentally a matter of class. In terms of marriage suitability, distinctions of class (by birth, not merit) are assumed.

This assumption also informs the faydit narrative, which does not at all suggest that the elevated lady marry beneath her station, but rather that her lover is in truth entitled to the status that would qualify him as her marriage partner. And no more in E-19 than in the Mozart comedies is the social structure altered by the characters' actions. It doesn't budge, in fact. It's just that whereas in Mozart the problems of love and marriage, trust and rightness, work out within the structure and we are asked to feel good about this, in E-19 they generally don't, and we aren't.

Granted, the effect of Mozart's happy ends can be debated. Do they really settle everything? Aren't there undercurrents? We seem to hope so, and here we touch on a contemporary discomfort. We aren't at all sure we should feel good about these happy ends, but they are full of genuinely uplifting music, so dammit, we do, and would like to find in them something that gives us permission to feel that way or, failing that, some grounds for dismissal. In *Le nozze di Figaro*, by far the most conventional and comfortable of these works, that's practically impossible. Mistrust has been overcome; the men have prostrated themselves; the women have extended forgiveness (the Countess from her social and moral altitude, in best "sublime" fashion with suitably reverential communal response); one marriage has been restored and two more achieved; and the celebratory coda, though brief, is hearty and unequivocal. No undercurrents to swim in here, so the best we can do is recite the meagre ingredients on the "revolutionary" label and pretend the piece is proto-democratic, which is far from the case.

The remaining two Da Ponte operas do contain revolutionary elements, but not in the political sense. In *Don Giovanni* (no, "*Viva la libertà*" is not the Carmagnole or the Internationale), it is the presence of the scoundrel hero. Not anti-hero, but hero: among the men of the audience he arouses envy; among the women he arouses arousal.* A great deal is made of the Don's supposed sexual futility or other antiheroic qualities (he is given no extended solo aria, therefore has no inner life, etc.), but in an actualist light these are strained and flimsy ratiocinations. We simply have no reason to discount his history of successful seductions—they are why there's an opera about him to begin with. Of course he encounters obstacles onstage—dramas are about the moments of such encounters. *Of course* he has no extended aria—lacking

---

* Contemporary women forthright enough to confirm this would include Marthe Keller, the fine actress who directed the most recent Met production of *Don Giovanni*,[4] and the *philosophe* Julia Kristeva.[5] I doubt that either can be accused of counterfeminist softheadedness.

both conscience and self-doubt, he has nothing to work through, no one to impress or assuage. The cause of elaborate vocalization in others, he has no need of it himself. He is entirely the man of action and appetite, and has to show for it three short but superb action arias (a party song, a seduction serenade, a dupe-the-doltish-peasants piece), a duet that's been a seduction cliché for over two centuries, and finally one of the Western theatre's greatest scenes of cosmic confrontation. This confrontation occurs not simply because Giovanni conquers, deceives, and abandons women, but because he specifically violates the proprieties of class and the sanctity of marriage, and above all because he kills a worldly father, then defies the call for repentance when this same father returns as emissary of the otherworldly one.

So, herowise, what's Don Giovanni's problem? None whatever, save that the hero is also a scoundrel, and actually that's our problem, not his: our ethics conflict with our responses, as they often do. In any event, it is the power of this confrontation that has led so many to feel that the subsequent happy-end scene with fugal sextette is anticlimactic, perhaps even insincere, and should be cut as it was in its second (Viennese) production and regularly thereafter in the 19th Century.[6] I thought I felt that way myself when young (adolescents are often disappointed to see social order restored), but of course I had never seen (and still haven't) a production without the final scene. I must say that on the page the prospect is not inviting, either musically or dramatically: those few bars of rushed crescendo in D minor under an empty stage (Leporello's still under the table), with the other characters (as was evidently the case) reappearing for a second for an ensemble scream of horror over the fermata in the last bar—as an ending, it looks unsatisfying, even ridiculous. Against this, a scene in which all characters are accounted for; the class lines (sorry) cleanly re-drawn; the projected marriages put back on track; the narrative and harmonic loose ends tied up, as Mozart invariably did; and a last ensemble that is, if strongly sung, brilliant and restorative in its effect. That a feeling of disturbance, of a chaotic spirit loose in the world, may linger does not render the restoration false. Life disturbs us often; we do our best to return to normal and carry on.

In the case of *Don Giovanni*, the 19th Century cut the final scene. In that of *Così fan tutte*, it cut the whole opera. *Così* simply wasn't done, or was presented in radically re-written versions rivaling the most excessive depredations of contemporary directors. The work's theatrical artifice, extreme refinement of musical style, and extended development by ensemble, all quite foreign to E-19 taste, partially account for this aversion, but thematic incompatibility was surely the main problem. *Così* pulls women down from their pedestals, so that men can neither be saved nor damned by them. It puts on a reality show with Don Alfonso as Executive Producer to prove that women (we already knew about men) will, as a matter of natural inclination, enter into marriage commitments in all apparent solemnity and then, at first opportunity (though with due allowance for "process"), agree to switch off and marry other partners. It cheerfully draws the moral that foreknowledge of this is a much better basis for an alliance than E-19's intuitive, Destiny-ridden sort. Unforgivably, it reaches this conclusion before E-19 has even gotten underway. E-19 goes on to protest that marriage is being mocked, but that is hardly so. *Così* argues that marriage must go forward at any cost and despite any contrary witness, which must be reconciled to the marriage convention. Like the other Mozart operas, it clinches this argument in a celebratory ensemble finale that is musically as convincing as anything else in the opera. We may not *like* the message, either because of what it implies about the human capacity for loyalty and the validity of "all noble emotions," or because of its very resolution into conventionality. Too bad.

If the authenticity of this resolution into conventionality is hard to swallow in Da Ponte's Mozart operas, it is all the more indigestible in Schikaneder's. *Die Zauberflöte* is the ultimate patriarchal "just trust us" opera, whose message the most scholarly exegesis on the development of its libretto cannot mitigate, nor the most prejudicial feminist polemic exaggerate.[7] It unequivocally states that for its protagonist couple to marry, all trace of maternal influence must be harrowed out and replaced by unquestioning acceptance of paternal wisdom and benignity, supposedly legitimized by some solemn initiatory hoo-hah cooked up by the forefathers. It does this in both symbolic and highly personal terms: *That's Pamina's mother* who's cast into outer darkness, along with the three charming ladies who saved Tamino's life and their clownish but dangerous little North African co-conspirator—all the night people, the moon people, swept away. Thirty seconds later the people of the light sing the father's praises. The right people marry each other and the happy couples assume their proper class positions, apparently on terms of mutual personal respect and "equality," but within the strictest of patriarchal, monarchical rules. (True, the prince and princess must earn their enlightenment. But it is their prince-and-princessness that pre-qualifies them for their trials.) There is no lack of clarity, no attitudinal doubt in the piece, nor any question that we are meant to find its conclusion other than wonderful.

In its initial premise, *Zauberflöte* has more in common with the scenarios of E-19 than with those of Da Ponte. Its hero is an almost-faydit, a prince without standing in either of the realms he enters. He falls in love even before first sight—not with a living, breathing woman but with her image, like Faust with the vision of Marguerite or Hoffmann with the sleeping Olympia in the alcove. Like those images, Pamina's is summoned by forces of darkness, these female and, famously, to all appearances with us, not against us. The Queen of this Darkness proclaims the prince the destined rescuer of her abducted daughter; he accordingly sets forth on a chivalric quest to deliver the princess from her circumstances. She returns his love, but with even less foreknowledge than he possesses: the only thing she knows is that she wants to be rescued, and he might do it. But then, instead of pursuing their defiant destiny to a tragic end, they learn that their true destiny is to pass the fathers' trials, get married, and inherit the kingdom—happy end!

The more persuasive we find the explanations about the notorious switch of P.O.V. (in playing terms, I've always thought it a red herring—the progression makes perfectly sound theatrical sense), the more we must conclude that Mozart very badly wanted the opera to turn out this way, saw to it that it did, and was inspired to write some of his greatest, most heartfelt music for it.* Our opinions and reactions notwithstanding, the work is what it is, says what it says. That is its clearing in the world.

I trust that the thematic distinctions between Mozart's operas and those of E-19 Proper are sufficiently clear. They would be even sharper if extended back to Gluck, the Baroque and beyond. Now let us look at the disposition of all this subject matter—the faydit-protagonist-couple narrative itself and its associated themes—as E-19 draws its final conclusions. In this respect, there are a few generalizations that can be made about the entire bundle of late-E-19 work. I will come to them presently. We must first take account of the era's most significant development, the loosening of narrative redundancy. Just as a particular dramatic conformation is E-19's identifying mark, so is its weakening the mark of its dissolution.

This weakening is much less pronounced in the operas of Puccini and the verists (I'll define this term in a moment) than in those of Strauss. For one thing, the faydit motif remains intact in the majority of their works, and so, often, does its identification with an artist protagonist, now in a milieu in which nearly everyone has become an artist, and nearly everyone is

---

* "Inspired," "heartfelt": I very much believe in the relationship between creator and material represented by these adjectives. Wasn't Mozart simply a great composer, always inspired and heartfelt? Yes to the former, no to the latter. Listen again to *La Clemenza di Tito*, written at the same time—a nobly attitudinizing preachment set to yards of well-crafted, generically beautiful music that only occasionally approaches the level of the better Handel operas, to say nothing of the Mozart Big Four, or even of *Entführung*. This is no reason to disrespect it or deny it the occasional revival. But the pretense that it deserves a place alongside the Da Ponte operas and is merely a different *sort* of opera (yes, much worse) is ludicrous. I am again with Dent (op. cit. pp. 213-215), whose fair assessment is, in sum, that the composer's heart just wasn't in it.

dispossessed.* In these reduced circumstances, our heroes and their ladies continue to imitate chivalric models, and their stories to end unhappily, though among these operas there is occasionally the serious piece that ends in celebration (*Fanciulla, Turandot*) or the lighter one that ends in a bittersweet mode, as with the renunciatory conclusion to *La Rondine*, a story rightly enough compared with *La Traviata's* but even closer to Massenet's *Sapho*, based on the then-popular novel of Daudet. We are back, of course, to the Parisian demimondaine and the Provençal youth (see the discussion of *La Traviata* in Backstory III). The faydit conformation, if no longer quite a *sine qua non*, nonetheless continues to flourish.

There are marked changes, though, in the handling of several major themes. They add up to a desanctification. Except in the still-rare happy-end operas, marriage is no longer presumed to settle everything—or, indeed, anything. The texture of married life does finally come in for some attention (*Pagliacci, Tabarro, Butterfly*, the parents in *Louise*), but is found to be unhappy or illusory, and the unmarried protagonist couples either declare themselves openly for free love or simply ignore the question. Among the matters no longer settled by marriage is inheritance. Save in the comedy *Gianni Schicchi*, which satirizes the subject, and the nice reversal of *Fanciulla* (Dick Johnson's inheritance is his late father's band of highwaymen, which he must *renounce* to win the lady), the new protagonist couples are either unconcerned with inheritance or parental legacy of any sort or, like Louise and Cio-Cio-San, struggling to escape it. Destiny is seldom invoked, and then in the sense of being true to oneself (Chénier professes belief in "an arcane power which, for better or worse"— doesn't sound very God-the-Fatherlike—"guides our steps along divergent ways" and has dubbed him poet), or in a generalized way that sounds more like a rhetorical habit than an article of belief.†

All these are important shifts in P.O.V. But the surest indicator of E-19's desanctification is the capitulation of transcendence. It stays on in its in-the-world, emotionalistic sense, in the defiant transport of free-love couples, the

---

* Consider, in various combinations of fayditry and artistry, the characters of *La Bohème, Tosca, Andrea Chénier, Louise, I Pagliacci*. Other faydit-protagonist-couple scenarios: *Manon Lescaut, Madama Butterfly, Il Tabarro, La Fanciulla del West, Turandot, Cavalleria Rusticana, L'Arlesiana, L'Amore dei tre re*.

† For a neat summary of the evolving attitudes toward these themes, see the scene of the lovers' first encounter in the Puccini/Illica setting of the Manon story, and contrast it with the version of Massenet and Meilhac/Gille (see Backstory III). In Puccini, words about destiny and a Road of Life are still employed, and the instant bond still sealed. But Des Grieux is not passing through on his own road (he's part of the local student scene, playing the field and waiting for lightning to strike), and so the metaphor is not played out onstage. And neither in this episode nor subsequently is there any mention of a Des Grieux *père*, his blessing or his money, or any talk of Manon becoming a Mme. Des Grieux.

rage of the socially oppressed, the feverish fantasy of the abandoned wife, or the fury (no longer a misapprehending one—Nedda, Fiora and Lola *are* faithless) of the betrayed husband. The transcendence of the sad ending, however, is gone, with all its promise of female souls ascending and wretched males redeemed. When this violent life is violently over, it's over. When a daughter flees into the Parisian night, we have no idea what's to become of her, and are left with her embittered, dying father.

The veristic creed is articulated by Tonio in the Prologue to *I Pagliacci*. The author, sings the Prologue in part, will once more set forth the "ancient masks," take up again the well-worn customs. But "... not to tell you, as of old: 'The tears we are shedding are false ones! At our writhings and sufferings, do not alarm yourselves!' No! No. The author has instead sought to paint you a slice of life. His only maxim is that the artist is first a man, and that for men he must write, inspired by truth."

The truth to which Tonio as Prologue refers is that for most of our fellow men life is a bitter struggle for gratification and dignity against circumstances that are harsh and oppressive; that under such circumstances their actions seldom rise to the level of the heroic or noble; and that our empathy with them should not depend on heroism or nobility (much less a presumed "right" of birth), but on the struggle itself. In this world, the good-and-evil dualism represented by the protagonist and antagonist tends to resolve itself either into the inner conflicts of characters who are neither or both, or into the fight of the individual against a social system, a set of conditions not reducible to a single character. If there is a God-the-Father or a mystical Destiny, He or It is not available for transcendental or redemptive purposes. Of course, none of this precludes *attempts* at heroism or nobility, or wishes for transcendence and redemption. It is not that aspirations and emotions have changed. It is the perception of the world and one's place in it that is different.

If we think of *verismo* as the term was originally applied to "slice-of-life" works of the younger school of Italian operawrights or, as it came to pass, to a loosely defined compositional style associated with them, it gives every appearance of having done a quick fade after its initial excitements. But if we look at verism as neither a verbal nor musical style, but rather as a theatrical philosophy founded on Tonio's truths, it emerges as a dominant and vital influence in 20th-Century opera. Further, it carries forward with it the E-19 conformation, albeit in changed circumstances—the faydit protagonist couple in *petit-bourgeois* suffocation or downright squalor. Seen in this light, verism accounts for much more than a handful of post-Verdian Italian works plus a scattering of French and German ones (*Louise, La Navarraise, Tiefland . . .*) that seem to have lost their hold. Janáček's two most successful operas (*Jenůfa* and

Kat'a Kabánova) are veristic, as is his *In the House of the Dead*. Shostakovich's *Lady Macbeth of Mzensk*, both of Berg's operas, Britten's finest one (*Peter Grimes*), and of course the sturdiest of the American pieces discussed earlier (*Porgy and Bess, The Consul, Susannah* and *Of Mice and Men*, as well as a host of lesser works), are all decidedly veristic in the sense I have proposed.

Irrespective of how we evaluate this body of work vis à vis other post-aporia operas (e.g., those of Ravel and Poulenc, Stravinsky and Schoenberg, Henze and Tippett, Berio and Ligeti, Thomson and Barber), it is clear that at the least it constitutes a fair portion of the past century's viable repertory. With just one or two exceptions, it also keeps before us the E-19 conformation: Jenůfa and Laça, Kat'a and Boris, Katerina and Sergei, Peter and Ellen, Porgy and Bess, Blitch and Susannah, even Lennie and Curley's Wife, are surely faydit protagonist couples, while the Berg operas show what we might term the conformation's neurotic afterlife. (Lulu has no inheritance or social elevation to offer—quite the reverse—but is still on her pedestal, entertaining serial replications of faydit behavior from her hapless suitors. Wozzeck is the very *Untermensch* embodiment of the married faydit, like Canio and Michele or, more remotely, Otello—men who, at least in their own eyes, have fulfilled their courtly duties and are rewarded by betrayal.) This continuance, added to the sharing of theatrical philosophy with what we more narrowly think of as the *verismo* school, confirms verism as the extension of E-19, cutting (like E-19 itself) across an array of disparate musical styles.

Needless to say, these later operas do little to resurrect transcendence or redemption. Most are bereft of these to the point of denial, and those that attempt celebration still leave us with an ache. Will Jenůfa and Laça life happily ever after? Will Porgy find Bess up in New York, and if so, what will happen to them? In *In The House of the Dead*, one of many prisoners is reprieved and a wounded eagle set free, but prison life grinds hopelessly on. *Makropoulos* ends in countertranscendence, the voluntary surrender of the dream of eternal life to mortal reality. All told, verism takes up transcendence where Giuseppe Verdi left it.

Verdi's sad-end transcendence music generally has one or more of these three associations: the ascendance of souls (salvation); the arrival of a destined moment (fulfillment of an oath or curse or, in the case of *Don Carlo*, the recognition of a calling); the granting of forgiveness. Except in two or three of his early operas, notably *I Lombardi*, Verdi was not a Christian triumphalist. It is true that in his subsequent portrayals of souls ascendant (as with Gilda, the two Leonoras, and possibly, according to one's interpretation, Violetta), transcendence is a function of the religious faith of his character, an assumption of the stage world they inhabit. Our emotional involvement, though, requires only our identification with the characters (both those departing and those left behind) and their lives in that world—with their longing for salvation, not our belief in it. Similarly, while in these operas forgiveness perforce presents a Christian aspect because it takes place in a Christian stage world, sometimes with specifically Christian referents (Arvino and Pagano, Stiffelio/Aroldo and his wife) and sometimes not (Boccanegra and Fiesco, Riccardo/Gustavus and all concerned), it is hardly exclusively Christian, and we need not consider it such to feel its cleansing power. The single element that unites most of these death scenes, and might arguably be identified as specifically Christian, is the presence of a sacrificial act whose selfless nature is discovered too late to avert a tragic conclusion. Sacrifice, seen as a virtue and an imperative, is certainly a point of Christian emphasis.

It should be noted that with Verdi, transcendence never has the last word. It occurs near the end, but not at the end. The end either jerks us back with a precipitous exclamation of horror (rather in the tradition of the Vienna *Don Giovanni*), or comes to a contemplative resolution under a tableau of survivors. Either way, we are remanded to the stage world's here and now, as if on the way back to our own.

In his last three operas, Verdi lovingly shows transcendence the door. The lofty, glowing final duet of *Aïda* takes us with two souls sweetly ascending (together, for a change)—Catholic salvationism crossed with Redemption Through Love, the sacrificial element still intact. It's a fitting apotheosis of religious transcendence, but discretely distanced by its location within an ancient and exotic rite in which no one has actually believed for 2,500 years, and for which the operawright is not recruiting. Dabbing our eyes, we can still conjure visions of an ancient light from above, and feel consoled. Then comes *Otello*, offering no consolation at all. We would like to believe that Desdemona's prayer will prove stronger than Iago's Credo, that her innocence and bravery, and Otello's dying recognition, will somehow waft them skyward with her last "Amen." But at the close the music gives us none of that—just those heavy, darkling chords, like shovelfuls of earth. We dab our eyes once more, but see nothing but the dark ahead. And finally there is *Falstaff*, a comedy entirely in and of this world and life, a life lived without a moment's piety, in which the romance of faydit and lady is seen as either ridiculous (Falstaff and Alice, Falstaff and Meg) or thoroughly domesticated (Fenton and Nanetta), a benign social convention of the benign bourgeois community. The exhilarating finale celebrates being alive and being a fool: to be alive is to be a fool; therefore, to be a fool is to be alive, and nothing more is needed or desired.

Richard Strauss was almost exclusively a writer of musical scenarios. He composed principally operas, ballets, songs, and programmatic tone poems. So when he expressed a desire to turn away from Romanticism and to shed the "Wagnerian musical armor"[8] (talk about an anxiety of influence!), he was in effect speaking of new sorts of dramatic subject. At one point he proposed to devote himself wholly to comedy, and while he did not quite do that, he did devote himself wholly to the happy end: after *Elektra*, every one of his operas, comic or not, has one, and these operas' actions and settings, though not their music, have much in common with pre-E-19 practice.

It's not a surprise, therefore, that the faydit circumstance is either de-emphasized or given a twist in most of his operas. It is present as a set of varia-tions on a half-forgotten theme. *Der Rosenkavalier* depends on it, through layers of ironic class-reversal comedy: the count Octavian first sings the authentic troubadour lay of praise and despair to his married mistress, then enacts the courtly romance as social ritual in the Presentation of the Silver Rose, and finally contends with the Falstaffian Baron Ochs for the hand of the pointedly ordinary, sentimental daughter of a nouveau-riche haut bour-geois. In *Arabella*, Mandryka certainly bears the faydit traces, but though there are rival suitors and impediments of understanding to his marriage with Arabella, there is neither a true antagonist nor any element of dispos-session. (Quite the contrary: Mandryka's holdings are vast if provincial, while Arabella's parents are comic-pathetic versions of familiar E-19 types, the father at once an updated Magnifico and a count at the edge of ruin who runs to the gambling table, the mother a client of Dame Fortune at her silli-est—though as always, the Dame's prophecies come true.)

The Artist as Faydit can be spotted in the Composer of *Ariadne* or in Henry Morosus of *Die Schweigsame Frau*.* Strauss's last operatic statement, *Capriccio*, brings back the troubadours in pristine reproduction: poet vs. singer, vying with their arts for the highborn lady. But Olivier and Flamand have nothing about them of the heretical or rebellious, and are not dispossessed—they are ensconced in the old world of aristocratic theatre patronage, just as Storch of *Intermezzo* is within its Wilhelmine/Weimaraner equivalent, the closest the real world has come to the Sachs/Stolzing aspiration. For the rest, Strauss's lover protagonists (Bacchus and Apollo) are gods who unite with mortal

---

* In a change from the Ben Jonson source, Henry is here an opera singer. With assistance from his troupe and a Figaro-esque barber, he and his Norina/Adina-esque wife, Aminta, perpetrate a *Pasquale*-esque masquerade marriage on a Pasquale-esque uncle to ensure an inheritance. *Schweigsame Frau* and *Rosenkavalier* are the only Strauss operas with faydit/inheritance story lines, though in both our deepest emotional engagement lies elsewhere. (See below, p. 223).

women, whom they rescue from contradictory but equally repugnant predicaments (in the case of Ariadne, male abandonment and social isolation; in that of Daphne, male attention and social participation; in both, with transformative effect and without any hint of knightly dedication or humility).* All these, as well as the secondary figures of Narraboth, Da-Ud, Matteo, and Leukippos, show the faydit imprint, sometimes weak, sometimes bold, but with the exceptions already noted, not determinative in the action. It is an influence, but it is not central to Strauss's work.

Marriage is, for a time. But for one so fervently dedicated to the exaltation of married love, Strauss brings it to a strange end. After his string of six connubial-bliss-and-problem operas (*Rosenkavalier* through *Arabella*, all save *Intermezzo* to Hofmannsthal librettos), he plays the theme out thusly (I leave aside the seldom-produced *Friedenstag*, wherein marriage is not the central issue):

Die Schweigsame Frau. After the raucous tortures of the masquerade marriage, poor old Uncle Morosus concludes that a silent woman is the most miraculous of blessings, and even more so when married to someone else. Henry and Aminta, whose only kindness has been to cease their cruelty (get that inheritance!), join hands with him as he drifts off peacefully in a cloud of pipesmoke, unmarried. Some of Strauss's loveliest music, warm and tender but suffused with melancholy, concurs.

Daphne. The hypersensitive, nubile heroine rejects all aspects of human and godly life known to her (the wishes of her parents, the pleadings of her devoted pastoral suitor, the revels of Dionysus and the lustful advances of Apollo) in favor of eternal vegetation—life as a tree, wordlessly rustling, again to bewitching strains.

Capriccio. The endless, pointless chatter about the operatic primacy of word or music is a screen for the real dilemma: should the Countess Madeleine re-marry, and if so, with whom? Concerning the artistic question, she finds the right answer, which is that since it's impossible to have one without the other, the question itself is a non-starter. As to the men, however, she can't have both—gain here, lose there, everything being in place of something else. She's inflamed, no doubt about that, but doesn't know where the fire is struck. She consults her mirror. A bit of irony there, perhaps, but no answer—just that

---

* Perhaps we should also take note of bass-baritone lover-god Jupiter, whose attempted predation has the unintended effect of transforming his goldthirsty prey into the contented wife of a muleteer, leading the simple life. But his opera, *Die Liebe der Danae*, has not proved even marginally stageworthy.

state of in-loveness. She wonders if an end for the opera of Olivier and Flamand can be found that will not be *trivial* (the libretto's last word, my emphasis). Still no answer. Come morning, poet and singer will meet each other in the library, but the Countess will not be there. Madeleine goes in to supper alone, still in love, still without an answer, and contented to be so. For one last time, surpassingly lovely music, profoundly settled at last, concurs.

The writer of musical scenarios was also a secular humanist.* All the stirrings that might be termed spiritual or sacramental, with their hymnic, rhapsodic musical manifestations, he poured into varieties of strictly worldly transcendence. In *Salome* and *Elektra*, transcendence is in the ecstasy of bloody vengeance for passion unrequited or marriage and motherhood betrayed. From *Rosenkavalier* through *Arabella*, it exults in the marriage of true lovers, in the reconciliation of the already married or in the attainment of full humanity within marriage. But in the three late examples just cited, it becomes a peace beyond transport: a lone individual's recognition of his or her deepest, truest longing—which is to say, the acceptance of oneself, and of the questions without answers. *All* answers are trivial; the acceptance alone is not. Like the verists, Strauss concludes that marriage doesn't settle everything, after all. Unlike them, he doesn't find this tragic. He even fashions from it a kind of happy end. It's a sad kind, though, full of wistful farewell and reminiscent pining.

In terms of dramatic content, then, Strauss's operas are distinct from the rest of Late E-19 and its veristic continuation in three ways: a more pronounced weakening of the faydit scenario, an avoidance of contemporaneous settings, and (after *Salome* and *Elektra*) an insistence on the happy ending. They share, however, Late E-19's desanctifying thematic alterations—the end of sad-end transcendence and of Destiny as an extrahuman force, and the almost total disappearance of the political into the personal. Musically, of course, they belong to E-19 right through to the end. As operatic composers, Strauss and Prokofiev, each writing more "conservatively" than in his youth, are E-19's last holdovers.[9]

Throughout late E-19, a marked shift in gender focus goes hand in hand with these thematic changes. With deadly dispute over patrilineal succession no longer the most pressing issue, the heroine's role need not be restricted to that of partner to the faydit hero. But that restricted position was also a special one, and by the end of E-19 it was gone. A desanctified, transcendenceless world has no need of the pure, exalted lady who clears the path to Heaven, and a world of free love does not need the unattainable highborn mistress or the repressed

---

* As disclosed by his work, not his personal belief or conduct—though they appear to have been in general agreement.

passion of her long-suffering vassal. And so, like the Empress in *Frau*, women descend into the abyss of mankind. Here, in exchange for their lost status, they will be allowed their common humanity, including the right to be bad. In effect, they are returned to the place Da Ponte and Mozart brought them in *Così fan tutte*, the opera E-19 could not abide. The world they find themselves in, though, is not one of an encapsulated aristocracy where elaborate love-lesson games are played. It is in one part the Straussian farewell to that world, in another that of Tonio's truths, and in a third that of the break from E-19, the world of the Modern and beyond. Whereas in the faydit-protagonist-couple conformation the heroine—though frequently as highly developed a character as the hero and the object of our strongest sympathies—is seldom the initiator of the central action (at most, fully complicit in it), she is now often the impeller of the action while the men, however important *their* roles, become accessories to it. As corollary to this, the texture of womens' lives, the nature of feminine psychology and of peculiarly feminine concerns (first among them motherhood and the female P.O.V. on married life) move to the center of many of these works. In short, we would say that Late E-19 undergoes a radical feminization, except that this term is so laden with implication (of sentimentalization or loss of virility in Strauss and Puccini *vis à vis* Wagner and Verdi; of the presence of hidden signs or suppressed voices in their scores, etc.) that its usage would require the understanding that something different is meant here, namely, the re-positioning of female characters of a new wholeness and reality in a world of greater wholeness and reality. In their new position, women are more dominant but less exalted. Perhaps the right word for this re-positioning is "womanization," and the right adjective for the new view of the world "existential," lower case advisedly employed.

The operas of Strauss are foremost in this womanization, followed by those of Puccini, Massenet, and Tchaikovsky. The tendency is less pronounced, but still strong, in the rest of the veristic continuation, as the characters of Santuzza, Louise, Rosa Mamaï (*L'Arlesiana*), the Janáček heroines, Katerina Ismailova, and Lulu attest. Any attempt to pinpoint on a timeline the turn of E-19 Proper toward a womanized, existential world is obviously subject to exception. Nonetheless, if we were to look close to the median, at the years 1875-76, we'd be in a hotspot on the treasure map. There, we would discover Verdi with his final transcendences (*Aida* and the Requiem) just behind him and only *Otello* and *Falstaff* to come. We would find also the first performances of *Carmen* and the complete *Der Ring des Nibelungen*.

The contrast between these works, so effectively exploited by Nietzsche in his contra-Wagner essay,[10] is sharp in several important ways. But with respect to the issues under discussion here, *Carmen* and the *Ring* converge.

Both show lives ruled by Fate, and identify this Fate with occult female forces that undermine masculine order, masculine understanding. Both lead us toward transcendence, then repudiate it. Both bring us to the brink of a womanized, existential world.

The conceptions of Fate presented by these two works are not identical. But they have the same determinative effect. They show Fate as ". . . not a power that governs, but an order that exists."[11] In the *Ring*, this order is neutral in the battles of the creatures who inhabit the world, but will not be altered by them, and in the end imposes itself upon them. The creatures have struggled murderously against one another throughout the cycle only to find that their true antagonist is the natural order itself. That order is female, represented by Mother Earth in person, Erda, seconded by the Norns and the Rhine Maidens. She/it is in place long before the cycle's action begins, before the advent of the gods, from time immemorial. It is pointless to question or seek authentication for her laws. She is simply the "order that exists." The aspirations of men and the vaunted power of the gods—the structure of known civilization, in other words—are of indifference to her: "How to stop a rolling wheel?" asks Wotan (*Siegfried*, Act III, Sc. 1), and Erda's answer is a sleepy shrug—go ask Brünnhilde. It is Brünnhilde who knows, finally, what must be done. She knows without being told, for she is Erda's daughter, and through fire and flood will guide our way back to her.

The character of Carmen, unique among operatic figures in its penetration of the popular culture, is usually taken nowadays as the embodiment of female sexual emancipation and freedom of action. Her full-disclosure, warning-of-side-effects declaration of free-love rights in the *Habañera*, her cry for the "*liberté*" of life without borders in the Act II finale, her defiant "Free I was born, and free I shall die!" at the mortal moment, her boldness and bravery, have turned her into a role model for women as much as a sex fantasy for men. And all this is certainly present in her makeup, though it must be said that in the eagerness to discover and celebrate these qualities, ethical questions—surely as germane to Carmen as to, say Don Giovanni— have gone largely unaddressed. That, in turn, is because her core belief in a Fate that has predestined her lot, and what such a belief implies for individual responsibility, is not taken seriously enough. Her assertions of independence, while perfectly "sincere," are parts of how she wishes to see herself and be seen by others. Only in the Card Scene does she look into herself and tell us what she thinks she knows, which is that "if in the book on high your page is a happy one" you may shuffle and cut without fear, but that if you're meant to die, if the dreaded word is written by Fate, the pitiless card will always read "Death."

Everything in the musicalization of this passage—the way it is set off as monologue from the frivolous trio that brackets it (it is Carmen's only "private" utterance); the low tessitura that evokes dark, blended vocal colors; the inexorable progression of eighth notes over dirge-like brass chords, leading to the weighty climax on the upper F at "*vingt fois;*" the concluding chesty repetitions of "*Encore! Encore! Toujours la mort!*"—mark this as Carmen's own, personal moment of truth.* This truth is disclosed by a Fate derived from the malevolent side of a goddess-worship tradition that traces to the Gypsies' pre-migration Indian origins. Itself female, it is also invariably contacted in occult practice through a female medium.

It is not merely the case that a hostile female destiny lurks, awaiting its moment. It is also the case that Carmen is the agent of this destiny, and whereas in the *Ring* the central action is set in motion by men but completed by women, in *Carmen* it is womanized from the start. At every juncture that binds the protagonist couple closer (coincidence playing its role, as always), the first step is taken by the woman over the ostensible resistance of the man. This womanized initiation of action reverses romantic custom. Its previous operatic associations are with such definitively unpleasant sorts as Abigaille or Lady Macbeth. But Carmen, like Don Giovanni, *attracts* us; she is a heroine, and while the opera certainly intends us to feel the full force of both Carmen's belief in the book above and the protagonist couple's fateful bond, its progression of action leaves no room for doubt that from an objective P.O.V. (ours), Destiny is nothing more than the accumulated decisions of the characters, plus a dash of happenstance.

The final element in *Carmen*'s womanization has to do with Late E-19's emergence of the mothers. It has two aspects. First: the title character is apt to *sound* maternal, owing to her migration, early in her performance history, to the mezzo-soprano or even contralto voice category. The more complete such a voice is, the more it suggests the maternal and the seductive at once, and exploits the combination of the two. In Carmen, this threatening confusion is present not in an Other Woman antagonist, like Eboli or Amneris (or, let us note, Erda, Wotan's Other Woman), or a misapprehended royal mistress like Léonore (*La Favorite*) but in our heroine.† Second: José's mother is a strong offstage presence throughout the opera. Those of his actions that are not determined by his obsession with Carmen are determined by his feelings toward his mother, compounded of genuine devotion and filial obligation

---

* So does what is not present: the "Fate Motif." This theme occurs only at points of confrontation between Carmen and José, and belongs to them as a couple. It would more accurately be named The Fateful Bond.

† The implications of voice categories will be taken up at greater length in Part IV.

reinforced by an expiatory need. In fact, *Carmen* suggests not only the dominance of maternal influence in its hero's psychology, but that the violent, macho qualities of that psychology may owe something to that influence.[12]

This last suggestion points to the observation that, as we might expect in a world of greater wholeness and reality, the emergence of the mothers changes, but does not necessarily improve, the balance of power in it. Indeed, after the charming family-values example of *Falstaff*, the news is not good. There are sympathetic mothers or mothers-to-be who are to be pitied by reason of male betrayal or the old patriarchal religious oppression (Santuzza, Butterfly, Suor Angelica, Kat'a), and at least one (Rosa Mamaï) whose suffocating and nearly incestuous love is at least catalytic in driving her son to suicide. Strauss offers two monster mothers (Herodias, Klytemnestra); then an opera (*Frau*) that is all about the desirability of motherhood without getting down to its realities, as if it is now motherhood that will solve everything; and then an opera (*Daphne*) in which the words of the mother (Gaea, a/k/a Erda in worldly guise) seem to urge her daughter to accommodate herself to men and their gods, but can as easily be taken to mean union with the female earth-spirit, which is what in fact happens. Then there are mother-surrogates (Puccini's Zia Principessa, Janáček's Kabanicha and Kostelnicka) who step in to enforce the standing code of sexual guilt on younger women. They are harsher and more meddlesome than the fathers they replace. For an apotheosis of wretchedness, there is finally the ill-equipped and hopelessly trapped Marie of *Wozzeck*. The mothers of Late E-19 bear two messages: 1) The lot of the mother, especially the single mother, is a difficult one, often made more difficult by men, and 2) Power comes in many forms, and someone brings up all those men.

That the operatic world of Late E-19 is a womanized one is, I submit, evident. To say that it is also "existential" is to say that it cannot be transcended. It cannot embrace otherworldly forms of salvation or damnation, triumph or redemption. It cannot rise above itself. The harder it tries, the harder we fall. *Carmen* takes us to the peaks of passion and the vales of Destiny with its unprecedented protagonist couple, and its final scene carries to the level of transport "That love which is war in its means, and at bottom the deadly hatred of the sexes!" (Nietzsche's apt formulation.) But when its sad tale is over we're left where we began with the soldiers and onlookers. The opera returns us to our world, our own conclusions, as surely as do its veristic successors. So does the *Ring*. The Immolation Scene soars as high as humans can fly, but "Redemption Through Love" is a preposterous piety—no one redeems anything or anybody. While the magnificent theme that for so long passed under that bad old name* first sings out, then fragments, then settles, as the flood recedes and flames obscure our last glimpse of the gods, the mortal survivors huddle at the front of the stage. Only they and the Earth remain, men and women in fear and wonder on the edge of a world that has reasserted its feminine essence but is otherwise defined only by its natural features and elements—an existential world that will be what people make of it.

Between Nietzsche's poles, his twinned masterpieces of '75-'76, the path does seem to have taken a turn. But not all can follow it. Some even turn back, and—disheartening as this is in terms of social progressivism—we must note that of E-19's five grandmaster operawrights, three recant their beliefs in their final testaments, while a fourth attempts to move on, but with only partial success. Consider:

- Mozart: After the Da Ponte operas, which lead successively toward a womanized, existential world *avant la lettre*, he takes it all back with *Die Zauberflöte* (see pp. 216-217, enough said).

- Wagner: He spends a lifetime trying to escape the maximum-security facility of Christianity, and in his late works actually contrives a breakout. Then he writes *Parsifal*, wherein sex is a sin, the evil mother-seductress is eliminated as surely as was the Queen of the Night, and the ancient, sanctimonious all-male order is restored, complete with transcendence and redemption. We can go on about pre-Christian origins, Buddhism, alchemy and the Philosopher's Stone, and many other matters, but when the whole affair is presented via Christian symbolism and soaked in the Dresden Amen, what's the point?

- Puccini: He gives us his Manon, his free-love artist-Bohemians, his prima donna who kills for her Voltairean lover, his heartbreakingly wronged mothers, his scamp from Dante's Eighth Circle of Hell, his love triangle on a barge on the Seine, his card-cheat Minnie and her bandit chieftain, and then, for Pete's sake, the Unknown Prince who will sacrifice anything and anybody to conquer his ultimate Belle Dame Sans Merci, marry her and inherit the kingdom!

---

* It has, of course, sounded only once before, sailing on the ecstasy of the expectant Sieglinde in Act III of *Die Walküre*. It is thus identified most personally and immediately with the joyful glow of impending motherhood, and more broadly with the continuance of the species against all odds. And this is an *exclusive* identification—there is no other usage, no variation to cloud the message.

- Strauss: The fourth, and more complicated, case. Had he died in 1920, he would fit the same pattern, ending with a mythic, numinous, weighty work in which all the characters (but especially the women—it is they who have problems in this regard) struggle through to the realization of where they belong in the order of divine descent (Keikobad still rules). They are thereby humanized and redeemed, and may proceed to celebrate the preserved marriages of the right people to one another, the higher and lower classes of the participating couples being carefully specified. However, Strauss did not die in 1920. He went on to compose seven more operas, arriving, as we've seen, at his own womanized and existential resting place. But there's a catch: while some would mark the Straussian *summa* at *Frau*, and others, impatient with the bloat or obscurity factors, would put it earlier, no one would place it later. And with some reason, for however fond we may be of the glorious pages of the late scores or even of certain works in their entirety, and however resistant to the arrogant whilom view of Strauss as an enfeebled has-been because he wouldn't pipe the pantonal untune, the fact remains that none of these pieces attains the musical and dramatic consistency of the earlier ones. But then, he was attempting something very difficult. With his rich but conservative idiom, he was exploring a reality that is philosophically as modern as any, and finding it beautiful. By virtue of his music, this reality is radically different from older ones but audibly evolved from them. The works have their flaws. The project, which Strauss continued through the *Four Last Songs* and *Metamorphosen*, is mature and constructive. He was no mere revolutionary.

- Verdi: The Fifth, the exception. An artistic life that comes to a bracingly sane, world-loving conclusion with what turns out to be perfect logic, yet has surprised at every step along the way. The dark horse that finishes at the head of the pack.

I have discussed the redundant narrative that is, in my view, E-19's interpretive key, and the recurrent themes that constitute so much of its aboutness. There remains the matter of the qualities that account for its effects. We would not much care about the stories or themes if effects, describable only in qualitative terms, did not first move us. In performance they are what we hear, see, and feel first. Because they are received sensorily, bypassing the analytic filter and requiring no tracking, they are absorbed more quickly than narratives or themes. For the same reason, they are more elusive of definition—the same words can be employed to describe quite different orders of experience. Nonetheless, such description is all we have in trying to convey our sense of a work's or a moment's qualities, and this sense is in turn our most basic connection to the work.

In opera, qualities are experienced most vividly when the drama heard in the music is bonded with the action seen onstage. And just as, when seeking to define the qualities of an individual work, we would look for those that belong to it alone, so with a body of work we must look for musical effects and theatrical actions found in it and not in others, at least with the same emphasis. Among the qualities that could be so ascribed to E-19, one stands out: suspense. Something of life-and-death significance, its outcome unknown but foreshadowed, hangs in the balance and holds us in tense anticipation. This building of suspense and release from it (through the fateful confrontation, the fulfillment of the oath, the disclosure of the secret, etc.), accounts for E-19's most characteristic effects. Might this not be said of all operas? It might, but not very accurately. Suspense is certainly present in the two greatest pre-Mozart operawrights, Monteverdi and the Gluck of the reform, but is probably not what anyone would select as the defining quality of either. It is comparatively weak even in composers of such accomplishment as Handel and Rameau, whose operas are structured so as to actually diffuse suspense, not intensify it.

This suspenseful quality is closely related to two things: melodrama, and a through-line of action centered on the principal characters. "Melodrama" is here intended in two senses: that of its original derivation (a dramatic action that is sung, or recited over music), and that of a theatrical event whose effect is so disproportionate to its cause or so reliant on improbable coincidence that it approaches credibility only in the irrational realm of music. All opera embraces the first definition. E-19 not only embraces the second, but puts it forward *as reality*. It proposes melodrama as part of life—particularly of life at decisive moments. Theatrical exaggeration, the heightening of the improbable, is therefore not something to be avoided, but the thing to be most believed, and thus crucial to the work and its performance. This is not the way of modernity, let alone postmodernity. Take a famous case we have already encountered: Fitzgerald's *The Great Gatsby*. What!? On the *very evening* that Gatsby and Tom have had their ghastly confrontation over Daisy at the Plaza, and Tom, with contemptuous bravado, has sent Daisy home with *Gatsby himself* in Gatsby's *own car*, which Gatsby has let *Daisy* drive to steady her nerves, and then, at the *very bend* in the road that marks Wilson's garage, Wilson's wife, the *very woman* with whom Tom has had a longstanding affair, rushes despairingly into the road at the *very moment* Daisy is rounding the bend—there's enough melodramatic coincidence here for half a dozen Verdi operas and a few two-reelers into the bargain. It's all foreshadowed, too. But, with the exception of a single melodramatic line melodramatically placed ("So we drove on toward death through the cooling twilight," given its own paragraph at the end of a narrative sequence), Fitzgerald has done all he could by way of indirection and deflection (Nick's observant, recollective tone; breaking off the narrative so that we back into the accident scene by way of a minor figure's testimony at the inquest—also a subtle suspense device) to de-emphasize the extreme improbability of it all so that we may have the cool, coincidental facts and note that yes, it's true—life is crazy like that, there's some weird connection at work here. Words can give us this cool deniability, if we want it, but opera is simply unsatisfying without underlined suspense, a heightened theatricality embedded in its music. E-19 ennobled melodrama, and melodrama raised E-19 to a new level of emotional intensity.

Melodrama is personal. One cannot melodramatize thematic arguments, concepts, or structural perceptions, because the excitements of intellectual discovery do not penetrate into the realm of personal emotional engagement. Melodrama depends on identification with imperiled characters. That's what the suspense is about, and why the quality of suspense is, almost as a matter of course, reinforced by E-19's concentration on an increasingly lifelike thrust of narrative—lengthening arcs of through-written action—carried forward by characters conceived as whole, present persons even when they carry an archetypal weight.

As for qualities other than suspense, it is not so much that E-19 introduces new ones while minimizing others (e.g., the contemplative affect of the pastoral) as that it presents the whole range of qualities with new vitality and forcefulness. All its themes and qualities are lent greatly intensified impact in performance. This impact is primarily sonic, owing to the growth in the size of musical forces and in the sonority of both vocal and orchestral instruments, but visual, too—more light on the stage, less in the auditorium; a more massive, layered spectacle. Unprecedented impact and impetus are the salient characteristics of the E-19 engagement. We are drawn in and on in a new way, and the receptor who wishes to maintain a skeptical distance must guard his emotional responses, his insides, as never before.

One quality is notably missing from E-19. That is irony of the contemporary sort. There are ironies of other sorts—of the belated discovery, of extreme coincidence, of hope dashed on the verge of fulfillment or of the reunion that comes a moment too late. These are ironies of positive expectation unrealized or reversed, bitter and deeply felt. They can arise only when such an expectation has been entertained in the first place.* Contemporary irony, on the other hand, is attitudinal and *a priori*. It is set in place in advance as proof *against* any positive expectation, whose unrealization or reversal will therefore not only not be bitter and deeply felt, but taken for the new expectation itself, the thing we should have known all along in this worst of all possible worlds. It sometimes appears sophisticated and sometimes cynical (think of Bob's *Death of a Salesman* crack). But a stance that puts hope in quotes, that precludes the very possibility of being swept away, is sadder than that. It's a barrier of brain and heart, both. Its presence means that receptors can't respond to E-19 honestly, or interpreters present it honestly, or creators write anything of comparable qualities. Critics, of course, are in business with a vengeance.

Some people don't want to be swept away. They equate the experience with a loss of self, and wish to remain in rational control of the performance engagement. Consequently, there has arisen the tribe of Skipovers, closely related to that of the Nams. What the Skipovers skip is E-19. Some skip from Mozart Lite to Stravinsky in Neoclassical mode, and others from the Baroque to the interwar sassy-perky French, while a few clear everything from medieval chant to the Mystic Revivalism of Pårt or Taverner or Messaïen, or the treadwater burbling of Glass. Not much opera to be found in any of these landing places, but they don't mind. They've skipped all this emotionalism, and stayed on their feet.

They have their reasons. Some, looking at the (ironic) juxtaposition of 19th-Century art and 20th Century history, see fascistic potential in an emotionally engulfing engagement, as if we could not choose to be swept away and somehow recover; as if we could not distinguish between a performance, with its closure, containment, and afterthought, and a mass rally or demonstration, with its openendedness and spur to action. But most Skipovers have nothing so heavy in mind. Their *goal* is to have nothing heavy in mind. The precise extent of Skipover influence is a matter for conjecture, but its cultural presence is certain, in testimony whereof I call two expert witnesses, one of whom writes from a "cultural criticism" viewpoint, the other from a specifically operatic one. In a nice bit of Skipover autobiography, Michael

---

* It can be argued (and I do) that such ironies are endemic to tragedy. To take a prototypical example: Oedipus finds that the man he killed at the crossroads was *his own father*, the woman to whom he has been married *his own mother*, the source of the city's woes he has been pursuing *himself*. These discoveries are ironic with a capital "I," are bitter and deeply felt, and inseparable from the work's tragic nature. They are also melodramatic, and we are again reminded that the Greek tragedies were, literally, melo-dramas. Comedies begin with their characters in apparently irremediable predicaments which are then resolved, while tragedies begin auspiciously, in an atmosphere of promise that is then progressively destroyed—ironic, that all that should come to this. For further examples, see Backstory III.

Lind recounts his temperamental turnaround from a college-years affinity for the religion of art, as represented by primetime Thomas Mann, to a more recent preference for Dryden and Pope and their milieu of "clubbable poets and scribbling polemicists."[13] He observes that ". . . we live in an age of political pamphleteering, popular drama—and coffeehouses . . . closer to 1699 than to 1899 or 1799." Perhaps that's right (must remember to look for Addison and Steele the next time I'm in Starbucks), but is it *good*? Lind thinks so. He's happy to see those upstart artists put back in their "correct" place, and even implies that the late Mann is to be preferred to the earlier. Now, I got a kick out of *The Holy Sinner*, too, and the unfinished *Confessions of Felix Krull*, for that matter. But to rank them with *Dr. Faustus* or *The Magic Mountain* is like claiming that those last Strauss operas should stand with *Salome*, *Elektra*, and *Rosenkavalier* because we approve of the way they come out. Intellectual maturation and artistic inspiration are not the same thing.

Barry Emslie, *Opera*'s regular Berlin correspondent, is probably not a thoroughgoing Skipover, at least all the time. But his Inner Skipover runs riot in his article about presenting and receiving Handel operas.[14] He fashions a serious, though debatable, argument about the centrality of the *da capo*, and makes one other cogent point, which is that our contemporary concept of stage characters as integrated, "real" people whose pursuits generate a coherent through-line in a work's plot rests uncomfortably on the *opera seria* form, and that we might look elsewhere for staging solutions.* But he extends his argument far beyond these observations. Wagner is, as we have come to expect, the bogeyman. His ". . . narcotic of the darkened theatre has conquered, and reality . . . is hidden." His devotees are escapists from the quotidian, "nocturnal Peeping Toms" seeking to lose themselves and put their problems ". . . pathetically and briefly, aside." These notions are current, and they are daft. Anyone who understands the modern theatrical compact knows that a darkened auditorium sharpens and concentrates the attention on the stage; that this results in an alert, active engagement in which emotional and intellectual responses are heightened, not a passive one in which they are dulled; that forsaking everyday reality for theatre reality can bring one up against concerns more fundamental than those left outside; and that to lose oneself in this way is really to find oneself, to be in touch. It's true that this entails a giving-over, a choice to go inside something and stay there, until it's over. That is a willed act. It makes sense only if the self is augmented and refreshed, not diminished and enervated.

Or one can choose to not give oneself over, to avoid. Emslie wants house lights up, scene-change mechanics on display, the audience in a looser, more

---

* Though I am more than a little puzzled by his designation of this view of character as a "post-Leavisite lit. crit. value." It's a lot older than that, and its origins are theatrical, not literary. Character presentation will be taken up at greater length Part IV.

socially oriented relationship to the stage—all as in Handel's day. He wants a "theatrical erotic" that is more "virile" (this must mean distanced, in charge of oneself, *not giving in*) and "heterogeneous" (this seems to mean "pansexual"). His dream encounter is between a stage event reminiscent of Mark Morris' *Platée* and an audience like that for *Einstein on the Beach*. And it is not merely that he endorses this sort of encounter for Handel's operas. He recommends it as a *better sort* of operatic experience—"more attractive and intellectually radical"—than the E-19 alternatives.

What sort of investment do these Skipover preferences imply? An extremely cautious one. Relieved that the creators have been, as Lind would have it, "defrocked," we enter the theatre unburdened of awe or dedication, unthreatened by temporary loss of self, and free of the "linear drag" (Emslie) of a story with consequences. We sample the decorative objects and mood moments on offer, safe in the awareness that even when we're affected, we'll snap out of it soon enough, and that likely as not we'll never again savor this evening's collation of tidbits. Sustained attention is a waste of effort, belief beside the point. Onstage and off-, we share our Common Room while charming music plays—not so much pathetically putting our everyday problems aside as pathetically pretending we haven't any deeper ones. If this is "modern" or "radical," it can only be in the sense that it consorts comfortably with an avoidance of emotional commitment.

Let me summarize our current situation as I read it. We are in full flight from E-19, which is to say from opera's central body of work. This flight is not, and never has been, a popular movement. It is an expedition of the intelligentsia (a class to which very few of opera's creators or interpreters had previously belonged), outfitted by theorists, fed and housed en route by the academy. In fact, it could quite properly be dubbed theory's triumph over creation and interpretation.

The flight has occurred in two stages. In the first, the center of creative attention shifted from content to materials—from what it's about to how it's made. This involved a re-definition of howness, away from structure in the old sense (musical, literary, and theatrical forms) to the eye-and-ear building materials themselves.* The move was not only from what it's about to how it's made, but to what it's made *of*, and thence to the notion that what it's made of *is* what it's about. It was a little revolution within structure; we might call it Structural Materialism. In my opinion, this is not in the long run a very

---

* Again: these shifts are changes of emphasis, not wholesale substitutions, except in the most extreme instances (e.g., aleatoric music, an attempt to eliminate form). They're no less important for that—changes of emphasis determine the directions of artforms.

interesting direction for any artform to take, but what is certain is that it's an unproductive one for opera. Opera has to be about something other than materials, and the something has to be expressed through character action. Wordnotes signify meanings far beyond their materials, and for the receptor who derives them those meanings are not endlessly deferred. They register as emotional and intellectual specifics, on the spot.

In theatre, the focus on materials took forms, expressed through design and stagecraft, of which we have already noted contemporary examples. In music, it had three aspects. The first was a new harmonic language, at first glance "free" from tonality, but quickly gathered into a new system strongly inclined to structural determinism. The second was the unleashing of rhythm, giving it greater dominance and complexity. And third was an extended definition and exploration of instrumental timbres and sound combinations from many sources, eventually including electronic usages. Harmony, rhythm, instrumental timbre: the missing element is melody, the element on whose line the voice sustains the utterance of the individual, and proclaims his survival amid the hubbub. The voice was not freed by these developments, but imprisoned. The new harmonic system, despite the claims made on its behalf, has not proved itself capable of wide emotional range or of sympathetic character expression. The rhythmic unleashing is more apposite to dance than to song. The timbral explorations are, in opera, largely by way of embellishment, however elaborate and, on occasion, descriptively or atmospherically useful.

For reasons just cited, the new harmonic, rhythmic, and timbral ideas proved more adaptable to instrumental music than to opera, and most of the viable operas written since the shift away from content have come from composers who used them sparingly and selectively. But the harmonic system was intellectually challenging and infinitely manipulable, the rhythmic unleashing accorded well with cults of the body and with philosophical and anthropological fascinations (with the Dionysian, the primitive), and the timbral tinkering was aurally seductive and suggestive of lab work with both mystical and scientific implications. Thus, they were naturals for the teaching and research functions of the university, which mentored, then cloistered, most potential operawrights. And so this initial stage of flight proved operatically impoverishing not only because it produced so few renewable operas, but because it put so many talents to work on problems of operatic expression the wrong way round, diddling with how instead of considering what, if anything, they had to say. It is synchronous with the creative aporia.

But materials are, after all, material, still dangerously close to outer reality and suggestive of representation, even when abstractly employed. They represent at least themselves, and palpably. So the flight's second stage was on beyond materials and structure, to idea and poststructure. This was part of art's forcible "collapse" into philosophy. The "collapse" was of course a shove, courtesy of the European *philosophes* and their American followers, again inescapable in the halls of higher learning that now incubated the new generation of Second-Interpreters–in-Chief. Compositionally, it is best typified by the minimalist influence, with its de-emphasis on structure, narrative, and dualistic oppositions such as protagonist/antagonist (drama, in other words) in favor of conceptual imagery for the eye and an Easterly preoccupation with time instead of matter for both eye and ear. This carried opera from a difficult creative position to an impossible one. Arts of the act can contain ideas and concepts, but they cannot become idea or concept, and of them all opera is probably the least suited to philosophical contemplations and ideational arguments. Therefore "concept" can express itself only through interpretation, and the flight's second stage has brought us beyond creative aporia to interpretive self-mutilation.

The shove into philosophy was also a shove into politics, so that art, philosophy, and politics were "collapsed" into a single wondrous tangle, surely requiring the services of culturecrit theorists to unsnarl. Most of the shoving came from the left, as is usually the case in the arts.* In the politics of the Old Left (roughly contemporaneous with Flight Stage One), High Art was accommodated, even honored. It was held as an aspiration of the Common Man, part of the rights and riches to which he was entitled. Since history was seen as dialectic on the verge of a new synthesis, the old culture was not something to be repudiated, but something to be incorporated and made more widely available—democratized, in short.† But the New Left is less a unified mass movement than a stapled-together coalition of congruent minority causes, originally those of Terry Eagleton's "triplet" of class, race, and gender (see Backstory II), more recently mutated into a still-disunified alliance embracing human rights, environmentalism, and an increasingly beleaguered secularism—the New Triplet. The New Left's goal has been less the extension of cultural privilege through political change than radical cultural change itself, a

---

* This is natural, since the arts (once freed of political or religious servitude) are constitutionally liberalizing, seeking a broadening of vision, a more inclusive understanding of humanity. Complaints from the right about leftist "domination" of the arts are analogous to assertions of liberal bias in the media: assuming their rough, street-level truth, they would mean either that liberals are more interested in artistic exploration and public affairs to begin with, or that those so interested become liberalized in the learning process. Either way, were I on the political right I would be ashamed to advance such self-damning arguments.

† And, though neither faction would concede it, this view of the role of the arts was quite compatible with ideas of intellectual, spiritual, and cultural uplift for the masses long entertained by what we might call the educational/evangelical tradition of American Conservatism.

goal that has found its mirror image (literally "reactionary") on the right. Since to this mindset the cultural and the political are co-extensive, and since the system of alliances is in truth somewhat forced, there has been little tolerance on the New Left for artistic expression that does not accord its political values centrality, and an absurd indulgence of any that does. And since history is no longer something to be synthesized, but something to be untold or "paralogized," culture identified with historical narrative (especially recent historical narrative) is suitable only for similar processing. However, the visions of art that belong to liberal humanism cannot be cut to fit a political ideology. They subsume the political, not vice-versa, simply because the individual human, to whose full realization they are dedicated, is much more than a political or economic self, and a civilization much more than its political or economic structures. Nor do those visions reject the past or seek to misrepresent it, but rather to learn from it and build on it, which in turn means searching it for its values, not ours. Thus there has for some time been a state of tension between the liberal-humanist artistic tradition and forms of social progressivism that would seem to be its natural allies. Of course, that tradition has always been under suspicion from the right, though that bears more heavily on the place of the arts in society than on their intramural atmosphere. Between the triplet politics of a Left that is not liberal and the free-market, evangelical politics of a Right that is not conservative, there's not much room for arts and humanities that are politically independent.

Speaking broadly and roughly: Flight Stage One was Marxist in political tone, Modernist in artistic attitude, and Structuralist in critical stance. In these respective areas, Flight Stage Two has been Tripletist, Postmodernist, and Poststructuralist/deconstructionist. Since Stage One thought is still reliant on a dualistic play of forces, drama remains a possibility within it, however changed in aesthetic. Stage Two, seeking to move beyond dualism, necessarily moves beyond drama as well.* It goes without saying that these stages and categories are not cleanly separated, and that for most persons, including artists, they make up a grab-bag of available ideas and convenient solutions to immediate problems, with consistency not required or necessarily desirable.† But I submit that as general characterization of the reaction to E-19, these stages and categories are accurate enough.

---

* I hope it is clear that "dualism" is here meant in its broad sense of the tendency to define any situation or development in terms of oppositions, rather than in its narrower theological sense.

† A handy example: Peter Sellars' Mozart/Da Ponte cycle was Stage One makeover—still tied to narrative, character, and representation, all seen from a P.O.V. on the Old Left/New Left cusp. But his more recent "*Tristan* Project" collaboration with Bill Viola is from all reports (it had not come to New York as of this writing) very much Stage Two—intertextual in concept, dominated by visual imagery that is only metaphorically related to the action.

The challenge posed by the working-through of the E-19 narrative and its associated themes was this: now that we find ourselves in a desacralized, existential, womanized world in which getting married is less the problem than being married and female predicaments are as urgent as male; in which inherited title and privilege have given way to brutal "revolutionary" totalitarianisms and the inequalities of industrial capitalism as the chief obstacles to individual fulfillment; in which the artist's place is not only indeterminate but slipping from view; in which Destiny is not in our stars, and otherworldly transcendence is not an option—what is opera to be about? And this is where the flight began. As noted earlier, those who did not take part wrote nearly all the operas that have subsequently proved repeatable, and did so by either accepting the challenge outlined above or continuing to write from the E-19 conformation. Those who did take part, and thereby succeeded in establishing a musico-intellectual fashion, declined the challenge. They took up instead the modernist causes of language, structure, and abstraction. Of course, all operawrights contend with these matters and always have. And most try to come up with something unconventional and personal in the process. Janáček, for instance, was certainly dealing very directly and consciously with howness in his efforts to ground an operatic style in the inflectional and rhythmic patterns of his native language. So was Strauss in his struggles to reconcile what he saw as the prosody/impassionisation difficulties of his late comedies. But these are attempts to solve *dramatic* and *theatrical* problems—problems of how characters are to express themselves, scenes to play, acts to arc—in the context of new subject matter, a new P.O.V., and new standards of theatrical believability. That is quite different from inventing a new musical structural order, then imposing it on whatever dramatic material is selected. And which of these approaches should be seen as progressive? In the case of that oft-contrasted pair, Strauss and Schoenberg, the supposed rearguard conservatism of one and radical progressivism of the other rests on taking their musical languages (defined for most listeners in harmonic terms, though in fact strict serialism applies to all elements of music) as determinative. Yet while Strauss employed his highly evolved but recognizable, invitational E-19 idiom to propose existential acceptance, Schoenberg, after a brief fling with psychoanalytic drama used his then-new-fashioned, in-your-face system to prop up the old Moses claim and wag a moralistic finger at sitcom marital transgressors. The former loves his characters, the latter judges his. Which of these shall we call progressive?

That's a genuine debate. But, as I have argued throughout this chapter, I believe it is properly joined on the grounds of dramatic aboutness, of plot-and-character content, rather than those of musical language and structure. It is certainly plausible (standard wisdom, in fact) to see Strauss as an artist in retreat from the horrors and oppressions of his time—into the personal and private, into the happy end—and Berg, let us say, as one who contended with these and recognized their tragic nature. I see both composers as offering valid humanistic responses to their situations, and count both as progressive, since I define progress as that which carries forward liberal humanism in the face of all else. By that standard, to step away from E-19's aboutness challenge toward materials and abstraction, and into forbidding languages—first of music, then of criticism—is no step forward.

The second leg of the flight was necessitated by the belated observation that the leaders of the first were marching in place and rallying few followers. In fifty years, they had added nearly nothing to the E-19 repertory, and the anxiety of E-19's influence had only heightened. The creative revolutionaries having faltered, the auteurial interpreters took up the wand. Their assignment—to exploit E-19 while suppressing it, display it while concealing it, to hide it out in plain sight—was formidable. But they are bright and well-educated, and have been fully up to the task. First explaining that E-19 had, alas, become irrelevant, they unveiled the tactics earlier discussed (the shift from ear to eye; adversarial conceptualism; intertextual tropes; auteurial subjectivity, etc.) to undo E-19's coherence and blunt the impact of its engagement while preserving deniability—there it is, right in front of us, now we see it, now we don't, and remember, we *love* E-19.

There are a thousand worldly reasons for both stages of opera's flight from itself. Europe has had powerful incentives to disengage from its cultural past. Who, of any artistic prescience whatever, would not have sensed in the Europe of 1918 that the individual as responsible agent was already in a bit of trouble, owing not only to war's mass devaluation of life, but to the unnerving re-definitions of reality, both inner (with the birth of modern psychology) and outer (with the birth of modern physics), all scientifically and technologically gotten up, but still feeling suspiciously like Dame Fortune in a new outfit? Or consider, amid the material and spiritual ruins of 1945, the condition of narrative, especially any that evokes a past of folk, nation, faith, so recently used as validation for a delusional present. Even for those who had emerged from the delusional or had never succumbed to it, the extrusion of its authentic elements, the unrewriting of its history, appeared an insurmountable task. Besides: narratives *are* selective, histories *are* constructs, and everything *is* in place of something else. Better, then, to cut the cord with all narratives. Better the tireless exposure of their falseness and the hopeless but merry play of endlessly deferred meanings. The story of the faydit, of the protagonist couple, is mere collateral damage in this purge of narrative. So much the worse for it, though, that it is redundant—there's a tyranny.

And who, by 1968, would have failed to notice that all these histories were now shadowed by yet another, annihilative form of Fate, for which mankind could hardly escape responsibility but over which the individual exerted no more influence than he formerly had over god or king? And that the response to this was turning to impotent rage, a fragmentation of social purpose, a severance from and denial of history *per se?* In this country, opera was again incidental road kill, for America had no operatic patrimony to disown, and beyond some adolescent truculence associated with trying to establish one, no apparent need to cast Europe's aside. To whatever extent culture might be culpable in Europe's catastrophe, and opera in culture's, it certainly didn't land us in *our* mess. Nevertheless, opera became as entangled here as in Europe with the countercultural energies of the first postwar generation, with that churning of moral authenticity with hypocrisy, dialectical flux with juvenile rebellion, cultural populism with commercial manipulation.

Fine. Art is in the world; we are all complicit. The question isn't whether or not these conditions exist, but what the artist's answer should be. Conditions and causes notwithstanding, artists are responsible for art, and unless one believes the artist to be nothing more than pure social fabrication, his contribution has to be something more than the propagation of *Zeitgeist* artifacts, the ratification of fashion. It must have to do with the assertion of art's clearing in the world, of each artform's clearing distinct from others, and with the individual artist's clearing, also distinct. It must have to do not only with the arts as necessary components of anything that can be called a civilization, but with the *Bildung*esque wholeness of each person, beginning with the artist himself.

Opera's creative aporia, against which contemporary operawrights continue to struggle with admirable tenacity but meagre success, cannot possibly be passed by further picking over the fields of language and structure, much less those of abstract idea or style. It does not matter whether those fields are bound tightly (as in serialism) or broadly (as in Worldish eclecticism or pastiche), because they are barren to begin with. The field to explore is the field of content, wherein characters and plots are to be found—which is to say people and their stories, to which the inner life of the artist is connected in some personally urgent way, as in any intimate relationship. Where stories are involved, narrative is by definition indispensable. And narrative cannot escape linearity—it's a journey from a point of departure to a destination, which it is the creative artist's privilege to designate. That this designation may be perceived as arbitrary from some (imaginary) perspective at the edge of eternity or infinity does not relieve the artist of his responsibility. He undertakes to show precisely that his designation is not arbitrary, by reason of its lifelikeness and its aesthetic properties, from which receptors may derive meaning and solace. Stories have beginnings and ends because people do. That is the fourth-dimensional truth of each and every life, and the well-spring of both the tragic and comedy-of-fools sensibilities. To designate these and the episodes they embrace as more than arbitrary is to bring the artist's effort at illumination and definition to selected samples of experience. Be he genius or journeyman, that is his job.

Finally, we must remind ourselves that characters in stories (again like people in life) strive toward different destinations, and by crossed paths, and thus that drama is also indispensable. Drama's nature is inherently dualistic. Perhaps, as some religious and philosophic thinkers have urged, we should learn to rise above dualism. Perhaps, one day, we will. We'll do without drama then. Meanwhile, human experience slogs along its linear, contentious way, and artists may choose to grapple with it or render themselves superfluous. Granted that there may be no redundant narrative available to us (but then, E-19's was surely not recognizable as such to its creators), it is still something of a mystery why our operawrights have had so little luck identifying stories and characters they can inhabit.*[15]

But then, the aspiration to live in the subject, the willed loss of perspective—I'd call it an assumed subjectivity—that allows the artist to become part

---

* To make a distinction: I refer to those who are actually trying to do so. There are a number of contemporary music-theatrepieces whose goal is otherwise, e.g., Birtwistle's *Mask of Orpheus* (return to mythic ritual), Messaïen's *St. François d'Assise* (return to religious ecstatic contemplation), Ligeti's *Le Grand Macabre* (depiction of chaotic de-evolution ruled by dark powers), Saariaho's *L'amour du loin* (origins of courtly love as entropy), or of course the *tableaux mourrants* of Glass/Wilson (mankind as specks of foam on the space/time tide). Each gestures in a postoperatic direction, toward a theatre of state-of-being rather than of dramatic action. Available recordings and descriptions do not whet the appetite for this hereafter (though Messaïen and Ligeti at least arouse curiosity), but theatre-pieces are proved or disproved only in the theatre. In any case, the discussion here concerns not postopera but opera. That the latter requires a dramatic element may seem so crashingly obvious as to not bear repeating, but consider this paragraph on Philippe Boesmans' *Julie*, based on Strindberg and premiered in the summer of 2005 at the Salzburg Festival: "His [Boesmans'] aim, he explains in a program interview, is to *reconnect music to emotions through narrative* [emphasis added]. 'The beauty of some contemporary music often resides in a search for light,' he says, 'but it is divorced from human feelings. An opera must be based on the alternation of emotions and on an interplay of tension and release from tension.'"[15] That operatic music should stand in need of "reconnection to emotion through narrative," and that a prominent, veteran composer should feel obliged to report this discovery (partly, I gather, as explanation for his apostasy from atonality) is explainable only in some variant of repressed-memory theory. The crashingly obvious, it seems, is in need of recovery.

of the story he is telling or to assume the subjective consciousness of each of his characters and so write from inside them, is the very thing targeted by the coolness and distance, the concentration on structures and concepts, that characterize the modern and postmodern attitudes toward creation: the subject becomes an object, and so by definition loses any potential for development as a living, lived-in individual. The audience, too, loses its most precious privilege, that of its own empathetic identification with the characters, which alone makes its perspective on events—*its* "objectivity"—meaningful.

I believe that these habits of thought, and the techniques associated with them (how one handles a dramatic moment, a character action, a musical idea), have become so pervasive all along the chain of engagement that they influence the work of not only those creators who espouse them, but those who sincerely wish to "reconnect music to emotions through narrative." This is unprovable, of course, but it's a conclusion, not an assumption, drawn from the evidence we have been reviewing. On one hand, we have the ongoing presence of venerable masterworks that in retrospect emerge as examples of a redundant narrative, yet are experienced as freshly conceived and sharply differentiated. On the other, there is a now-lengthy series of virtuously intended newer pieces that, irrespective of subject matter, we experience as redundant even when new, as if a screen were in place between creators and subjects—a screen finely wrought from the intellectually rich, emotionally impoverished tooling of the modern and postmodern creationists. No such screen is innate in the artist. It has to be installed according to instructions.

The operawrights of the verismo continuation carried the E-19 conformation on into 20th-Century circumstances—those of the protagonist couple in socially or politically pressured marriages, or of the individual existentially alone, or in the older romantic position of yearning for connection. Their best operas embrace all the themes of the triplets. They bear the marks of labor on materials and structures. They're light on ideas, though. Their subjects were not selected *because* of their themes or because they posed ingenious structural questions, or even because they embraced noble thoughts or philosophic insights. They were selected because the creators sensed they could live in them, and understood that that was the task.

The artist's answer? The answer to the individual disappeared is the individual emergent. The answer to chaos is coherence. The answer to false narrative is honest narrative. Opera, the medium of sung stories, is the ideal artistic champion of these causes, but only if it remains true to them, and to itself. For while new creation is at the heart of our predicament, creators require a theatrical world to write for, and it is hard to envision a future for opera unless it gets straight with its past. That means restoring integrity to interpretation.

Our present stance, at once parricidal and parasitic, cannot hold for long. Sooner or later, the father's decaying body ceases to nourish, and the parasite dies with the host. Scavenging the graves of more remote ancestors for cheering adornment and harmless engagement distracts only momentarily.

And what an embarrassment! After all the grand ideas, the thrill of leaving the old world behind and below, the seductive sophistries of an aboutness of materials, an aboutness of abstraction, of concepts and images; after the ringing declarations of ends and collapses, of aesthetic futility and infinite deferral; after the triumphs of irony and parody and pastiche, what still matters to the operatic public (enough of it, at least, to sustain repertory institutions) is the old-world body of work dependent on linear narrative, dualistic drama, and un-ironic passion that sings of the struggle for an individual fulfillment to which love, marriage, and aesthetic experience are presumed to be crucial. Disguised, disfigured, held up for mockery—no matter what's done to it, its identity cannot quite be obliterated. It remains European, heterosexual, and premodern. It comes complete with transcendence, the artist as faydit, art as religion, and all the rest of it. It depicts the attitudes of its time toward nation, family, gender, and class, toward codes of loyalty and honor, and toward certain emotional states (e.g., romantic love, male jealousy, female madness) that we try to censor. It does not endorse or celebrate these attitudes. In fact, it generally deplores them. But it acknowledges them as real, and allows them powerful representation. It makes receptors experience them in a way that leaves a deep emotional imprint, like a brand on the spirit.

In reply, we have only arguments. They may be excellent arguments, but they don't fare well in the presence of the experience, which we intuit as more authentic and inclusive. And so the experience itself is feared. It must either be given corrective instruction to bring it in line with our arguments, or be shown as irrelevant to them. The problem, of course, is not that it is irrelevant (why would one fly from that?), but that it remains relevant in unwelcome ways. And so we treat it dishonorably, finding only ourselves in it and learning nothing from it.

In this regard, I would like to propose a code of ethics for Second-Interpreters-in-Chief. It is not aimed at moral improvement, but at the coherence and integrity of artistic process. The code has only three brief articles:

1. The interpretive artist should consider himself bound by the hierarchy of the chain of encounter (see pp. 8-14).
2. He should proceed according to the principles of actualism (see pp. 131 ff).
3. If he wishes to be thought of as a creator, he should write something.

That's it. It's short and simple, but its implications, if pursued, would be momentous. They would include that concepts must be derived from internal evidence, above all the progression of action in words and music. That, in turn, would mean an end to adversarial productions, to the intertextuality of productions, to the puerilities of camp and pastiche. It would mean restoration of the proper relationship between content and style. It would not in principle mean an end to the abstract, but would hold abstraction to the test of essentializing what is most real, most urgent in a work. Nor would it in principle mean an end to shifts of time or place, but would hold them to the test (severe, but just) that they contradict nothing in the work. It would return to the Interpreter-in-Chief a measure of artistic humility, which is also the source of any pride he can come by honestly. And it would mean that the matrix is not found in design, but in the needs of performance itself, to which we now turn.

NOTES

1. Like other operaphiles of my generation, I am sure, I was first drawn to the "Matter of Britain" (childhood brushes with Tennyson aside) through Wagner, led thither by two books: Jessie L. Weston's *From Ritual to Romance* and Denis de Rougemont's *Love in the Western World*. The former was first published in 1920 and is still a cornerstone in Grail legend studies, though its central thesis locating the origin of the Grail in pre-Christian fertility myths is not today's standard wisdom on this much-debated subject. Part of its influence in intellectual life is owed to T.S. Eliot's mining of it for symbolic imagery in *The Wasteland* (see Eliot's notes to the poem). De Rougemont's famous study of the Tristan legend is considered eccentric by some ("weird and tendentious," one medievalist said to me recently), and no longer surfaces with any regularity as a point of reference. Doubtless it claims too much for Cathar influence on subsequent artistic and intellectual developments, and perhaps its many intuitive connections and insights are more appealing to artists than to scholars. Still, his overall assessment of the nature of Western romantic love and its debt to a peculiar compound of Christian, Islamic, and Jewish mystical elements (orthodox and "heretical") remains stimulating and often persuasive, and I expect opera devotees who read it will experience at least a few of the flashes of recognition I felt on first encounter with it. De Rougemont nailed the E-19 conformation dead center, even if he was aiming at other targets.

   The literature on the Grail, Tristan, and other medieval myths and their sources is as extensive as it is contentious, for the body of work we call "Arthurian" is a mingling of Provençal, French, German, Celtic and British tellings in overlapping and conflicting versions, and it presses many ethnic, national, and religious hot buttons. There is little point in an intrigued layman like the present author attempting discriminations; as with the philosophical and critical material discussed in the last chapter, readers can follow bibliographies as well as I. An excellent starting point, though, would be Richard Barber's splendid *The Holy Grail: Imagination and Belief* (Harvard Univ. Press, 2004).

   On the Provençal courtly love culture and its relationship to the troubadours, there is also a wealth of material beyond de Rougemont, beginning with translations of troubadour poetry and recordings of their lays. Some recent authors are persuaded that the courts of love were entirely figments of the literary imagination—see, for instance, Alison Weir: *Eleanor of Aquitaine* (Ballantine, N.Y., 1999, pp. 175-76). More to the point, though, is the romantic belief in the courts of love during the 19th Century, and a good source on that is: John Rutherford: *The Troubadours* (Smith, Elder & Co., London, 1873).

   With respect to the Cathars and the Albigensian Crusade, the problem is not the quantity of material, but its reliability. There are classic studies by Runciman and Le Roy Ladurie, but most of the widely circulated literature is taken with the siege of the castle of Montségur and the nature and whereabouts of the "treasure" reputedly smuggled therefrom on the eve of the immolation of the Perfect in 1244. Calling all Grail romancers and inquirers into initiatory cults and societies (the Templars, the Rosicrucians, the Freemasons, the Theosophists—Skull and Bones, for all I know), cryptographers of the mystical and diggers for buried treasure anywhere from the banks of the Indus to the shores of Nova Scotia. *Da Vinci Code*-ists welcome here. Among recent and easily available volumes, Sean Martin's *The Cathars* (Thunder's Mouth Press, N.Y., 2004) seems to me reasonable and responsible; it includes a decent, though far from exhaustive, bibliography. For a sober, concise accounting that also places the events in longer perspective, I would refer readers back to Friedrich Heer's *The Medieval World* (World Publishing, 1961, Janet Sondheimer, trans., Chaps. 7 and 8), and the same author's *The Intellectual History of Europe* (World, 1966, Jonathan Steinberg, trans., Chap. 7).

Finally, Marina Warner's *Alone of All Her Sex: The Myth and Cult of the Virgin Mary* (Alfred A. Knopf, 1976) remains a *sine qua non* on female elevation/subjugation in Western Christianity (Chap. 9 is devoted to the time and place at hand); and I can recommend Mark Girouard's *The Return to Camelot* (Yale Univ. Press, 1981) on the English chivalric revival of the 19th Century, and its impact on social custom.

2. Naturally, this does not mean that they all consciously modeled their characters on figures of the courtly tales, or their plots on the story of the *ur*-faydit. Beyond the Wagner/Wagner and Maeterlinck/Debussy teams and a few secondary examples (e.g., Chausson's *Le Roi Arthus*, Massenet's *Esclarmonde*, and Mascagni's *Isabeau*, in which the banished Ethelbert d'Argile presents himself as a "Cavaliere Faïdit"), we would probably be hard-put to demonstrate any great intimacy between E-19 operawrights and the origins of the faydit conformation or its associated legendary sources. But as De Rougemont observed about Wagner, great composers do not set "ideas" to music. Rather, they carry within a pulsating need to express something of immediate, personal significance, sharpened in the air around them, for which an idea provides an articulation. (See *Love in the Western World*, Doubleday Anchor, N.Y., 1957, Montgomery Beligion, trans., p. 239. I have paraphrased and expanded here to fit my broader operatic context.) And the courtly material was certainly circulating. In the 19th Century there was an explosion of interest in Arthurian and other mythic (e.g., Nordic) literature. It manifested itself in fresh retellings, intensive research, translations from old language forms into modern ones, and cross-translations among the modern languages. There was a passion for locating the historical sources of the legends and tracing them to real or imagined folk roots, and this was closely connected to movements toward political self-determination and unification, as well as philosophical and religious freethought. Great Britain saw a renewed interest in the chivalric codes of honor and conduct, in tournaments and other neo-Medieval observances. In France, there was a revival of the near-dead Occitan language and fascination with the old Provençal culture, led by Alphonse Daudet and the circle of writers known as the *Félibrige*. Operatic and musical works derived directly from this movement would include Gounod's *Mireille*, Cilea's *L'Arlesiana* (and, of course, Bizet's score for the Daudet play on which it is based—see n. 13, below), and Canteloube's *Chants d'Auvergne*.

3. For a well-argued presentation of the development of this artistic plight in a literary context, to which my discussion here is indebted, see Gene H. Bell-Villada: *Art for Art's Sake and Literary Life: How Politics and Markets Helped Shape the Ideology and Culture of Aestheticism, 1790-1990* (Univ. of Neb. Press, 1996).

4. See Cori Ellison: "Reaching the Top of the Opera World by Accident" (interview with Marthe Keller, *NYT*, Feb. 29, 2004).

5. See Julia Kristeva: *Tales of Love*, Columbia Univ. Press, 1987 (Leon S. Roudiez, trans.), Chap. 5. Her observations on *Don Giovanni* are in the context of a broad examination of love and desire, and the thrill of Mozart's Don for women is certainly not a point of advocacy or even emphasis in her presentation. It is simply acknowledged as fact, and that is my point.

6. It's rather surprising—to me, at least—to see the final scene still being wished away or apologized for. For instance, Michel Poizat, in *The Angel's Cry* (Cornell Univ. Press, 1992, Arthur Denner, trans.) contends that "Far from being 'obtuse,' nineteenth-century directors—Mahler notable among them—were actually quite perceptive in understanding the superficial character of this rehabilitation and in continuing the tradition of the Vienna production by generally omitting the final scene." This remark is, again, in a

context (the book's eponymous central argument), and I intend no blanket dismissal here. But little *glissements* slither around this point, and they are typical of contemporary critical discourse. First, Poizat takes the fact that the scene was dropped in Vienna as evidence that Mozart ". . . undertakes this moral rehabilitation more or less reluctantly." Without further documentation, this is pure supposition, nicely hedged by that "more or less." I suspect that Edward J. Dent was much closer to the truth when he observed many years ago (see his *Mozart's Operas*, 2nd Edition, Oxford Univ. Press, 1947) that with the addition of the "*Mi tradì*" and the "*Per queste tue manine*" scene and with very little time saved by the substitution of "*Dalla sua pace*" for "*Il mio tesoro*," a long two-act opera had grown even longer, and that the last scene was cut for this most ordinary of theatrical reasons. Dent also points out that the opera was absorbed into the German theatre system at exactly the time that system's resources were being turned to (apologies to Polonius) the romantical-historical-tragical—hence the tradition. It's not a question of "obtuse" v. "perceptive," or even of preferring one version to another. (I'd love to see a full-blown production of Vienna, complete with detailed settings, heavyweight cast, Mahlerian orchestra and conductor. In fact, I'd love to see such a production of *any* version.) It's a question of making poorly founded assertions about the nature of a work for the convenience of an intertextual critical argument. Later Poizat, again for the sake of a distinctly special litcrit point, claims that Molière's *Don Juan* ". . . served as *the* basis for Mozart and Da Ponte's *Don Giovanni*" (op. cit., p. 142, my emphasis). So much for Bertati and Gazzaniga, not to mention several others! But if you think that's dubious, try Catherine Clément on the Supper Scene (*Opera, or the Undoing of Women*, p. 34): "Before the eyes of Elvira, begging her seducer to repent, and the terrified Leporello, the statue talks with Don Giovanni." No, he doesn't: Elvira has exited, with one of the screams (a note, actually—an A-flat) Poizat expatiates on. Farther down the page, Clément invents an enactment of the Giovanni/Zerlina offstage encounter "A brutal Don Giovanni, presses with all his weight, as inexpert in love as he is gifted in leading up to it."—punctuation in original). She wants the opera to be all about rape, but while it is one of the refreshments of her book that it is personal and impassioned rather than scholarly, you can't just make things up, then offer them in evidence.

Nicholas Till, in his *Mozart and the Enlightenment* (W.W. Norton & Co., 1993), offers irony as the saving grace of the final scene. Till's critical procedure is a good deal more rigorous than Poizat's or Clément's, and his book is a major contribution to the literature on Mozart's operas (his *Don Giovanni* discussion is especially strong on the violation of marriage). I supposed the last scene, if reduced to a verbal slogan—"*Quest' è il fin di chi fa mal*"—can be seen as "trite" (Till's word), and irony a possible undertone for it. But how can anyone hear the music that way?

7. Clément, in fact, is good on this aspect of *Die Zauberflöte*, and insists on seeing it plain (see *Opera, Or the Undoing of Women*, pp. 70-76). Of course, much else in her presentation—Tamino and Pamina as children; Sarastro as Pamina's father, seeking custody; the Queen's coloratura as incomprehensible madness; Mozart seeking vengeance on his parentally mandated prodigy childhood—is interpretation informed by her thesis. However ingenious and plausible one may find it, it must not be confused with established fact. For a more extended discussion of the opera's character relationships and symbolic background in the light of this distinction, see my "The Mouth-Honored Prophets: Stanislavski and Felsenstein" (*The Musical Newsletter*, Vol. V, Fall 1975).

8. See, for instance, Strauss's letter to Hofmannsthal of early September, 1916 (*A Working Friendship*, trans. Hanns Hammelmann and Ewald Osers, Random House, N.Y. 1961, p. 262). Creatively speaking, the date falls between *Frau* and *Ariadne* and, of course, in the middle of WWI. But the impulse goes back at least to the conception of *Rosenkavalier* (1909). With respect to individual projects, Strauss's librettists customarily took the lead.

But he assented to only those that engaged him, those he knew would call forth his music. The choice was always his.

9. As Strauss, hunkered down at Garmisch while the great civilization he had been a part of commenced its self-destruction, began work in a spirit of defiant hopelessness on what he knew would be his last opera, Prokofiev, sequestered far to the East across the battle lines, had just completed *Betrothal in a Monastery*, his pure E-19 marriage masquerade-inheritance comedy, complete with obsolescent courtly knight (see pp. 124-127). These two exquisite works, atmospherically quite different but both brushed with the bittersweet and the nostalgic, seem to have written *finis* to operatic comedy; certainly there's been nothing comparable since. Prokofiev had ahead of him, operatically, only his *Story of a Real Man* (an example, though a strong one, of the faux-verismo subspecies of Soviet Socialist Realism) and his titanic struggle with *War and Peace*.

10. See Friedrich Nietzsche: *The Birth of Tragedy* and *The Case of Wagner*, (trans. and with commentary by Walter Kaufmann, Vintage, N.Y., 1967).

11. The phrase is Helmut Ringgren's. See his "Fatalistic Beliefs in Religion, Folklore, and Literature" (symposium of Sept. 7-9, 1964, Åbo, Sweden, Almquist and Wiksell, Stockholm).

12. It should be emphasized that no good understanding of *Carmen*'s plot and characters is possible without consulting the full text of the original libretto. It is contained in *Théâtre de Meilhac et Halévy*, Vol. VII, Calmann-Lévy, Paris, 1901. The Oeser/Felsenstein version of the full score (Alkor-Edition, Kassel, 1964) is another source, but one must be wary of its troubling brand of scholarship, cause of much contention. My own views of the opera, lightly sketched here, are grounded in a much longer study, conducted over thirty years ago, which explores in some depth the opera's mythic background (Gypsy religious beliefs and moral codes, the survival of bull worship and sacrifice in the bullfight ritual, etc.); the progression of relevant themes through the work of Mérimée and thence into the opera's libretto; the positioning of *Carmen* in Bizet's lifework (especially *vis à vis* Daudet's *L'Arlésienne*, whose plot-and-character conformation forms a perfect interlock with *Carmen*'s, and which drew from the composer his only other score of comparable passion, tone, and depth), and much else. Its bibliography includes the Ringgren item cited above. Bits of the material found their way into an essay review of the Solti/London recording (*High Fidelity*, Dec. 1976, reprinted in *Records in Review*, Wyeth Press, Gt. Barrington, 1977) and into the aforementioned Stanislavski/Felsenstein essay (see n.7 above).

13. See Michael Lind: "Defrocking the Artist," *NYT* Book Review, Mar. 14, 1999. Lind is concerned mostly with the admittedly excessive sacralization of artistic genius that is one aspect of the E-19 mystique, and attributes its decline to an outbreak of "common sense" that I confess myself unable to detect, especially in the presumed sphere of the authentically sacral, religion.

14. See Barry Emslie: "Let's Misbehave," *Opera*, Vol. 54, No. 12, Dec., 2003. But also see Winton Dean's rejoinder, "Why Misbehave," in the Feb., 2004 Issue. Emslie is the best source of stimulating reportage on opera in Europe known to me—an entertaining writer, alert to all the issues. From his references to F.R. Leavis and Barthes and his use of such terms as "univocal" and "free-floating signifier," we also know that he is on speaking terms with the litcrit background sketched earlier. He and Dean, our Handelian elder statesman, rather talk past each other in this exchange, but in doing so define a gap in assumptions and understandings.

15. See Alan Riding: "Modern Opera Shines in Mozartland," *NYT*, July 18, 2005.

PART IV

PERFORMANCE

1

PERFORMANCE AND NOTPERFORMANCE

(Jan. 1999–Jan. 2007)

As devotee and customer, my only motive for returning to a production like Wernicke's *Frau ohne Schatten* would be starvation—a long-unassuaged hunger for the music in that space instead of my space. I would return reluctantly, resenting my need. But if the Met's cast from the Sixties (Rysanek, Ludwig, Dalis; King, Berry, Dooley) were announced, I'd be there, and my vexations over mirrors, floppy falcons, fountains, and blinding lights would recede to the status of real but minor irritations. Performance can transcend production. In opera, this usually happens when the ear transcends the eye and the living human elements transcend the material ones. Sometimes an individual performer's presence and will is momentarily sufficient. Production is meant to serve performance, not the other way around. So performance, not production, is the key. But what is it, really?

To perform something is to fulfill it (the verb comes from a root meaning "to consummate"). This implies that there *is* a something (a "work") that we can define, and whose fulfillment we can recognize. If we cannot at least roughly agree on what the something is, we have no basis for declaring it consummated or not. Performance then has no meaning beyond a display of skill for its own sake. And that would dispose of any coherent notion of performance, since a skill is usually developed with a particular task in mind. Earlier, I suggested that with respect to opera we have come close to just such a disposition. Reluctant as I am to join the ranks of prophets proclaiming the death of this or the end of that, and so able to describe a present state only as the aftermath of a previous one, I have to concede that we do seem to be sliding from an era of performance into one of something that closely resembles, but is not, performance. Whatever it is runs its course but consummates nothing, and so is not even a "performance" in the dictionary sense cited above, let alone in the meaning I have proposed, which I now take the liberty of repeating for emphasis: "...an occasion on which all efforts are bent to make manifest and alive the workliness of an individual work, to make that work truly present, and to engage the audience with its world."

Baudrillard would probably peg this new sort of event as a simulacrum, or Walter Benjamin as a mechanical reproduction sans aura, and they would be onto its essential quality. Derrida might have noted its absence of presence and Barthes its substitution of pure signification for drama, and would perhaps have approved. I call it a Notperformance, for want of a better word. ("Antiperformance" isn't right—the participants aren't *against* performance. "Postperformance" falls in too easily with current all-purpose usage, while "unperformance" sounds like the undoing of something already achieved.) The term is not facetiously intended—I am in earnest, and the phenomenon is real. The perception of Notperformance starts with an unexplained feeling of emptiness. It takes time, perspective, comparison with other events, and the reactions of others, and considerable self-questioning to merely verify its existence. For myself, all doubts have been erased on that score. For you, I can only counsel you to trust the unexplained emptiness.

A Notperformance is not the same as a bad performance or a routine performance, and does not necessarily coincide with a mischievous production. In those, an educated receptor can discern qualities of badness, routine, or mischief that are clearly attributable to the representation, and therefore not to the work, whereas the Notperformance entails the seemingly appropriate deployment of high professional skills. It gives every appearance of having rendered the work. *It is blameless,* and the worst thing about it is that the perplexed receptor, whether a tyro or a dyed-in-the-wool devotee, has nowhere to place the blame except on the work or himself, or the relationship between the two. Has he outgrown the work or tired of it, or even of opera itself? Does he simply not appreciate it? Or was he formerly a chump to have liked it, and only now sees how empty it really is? No, the problem is the Notperformance, whose nature is subtractive: it actually deducts from the receptor's awareness of the work, loosens his connection to it, and by so doing shrinks the work's clearing in the world. It is most insidious, and therefore of keenest critical interest, when it is excellent in its Notness. The "better" the Notperformance, or the greater the work being Notperformed, the emptier the occasion.

In illustrating Notperformance, we mustn't stack the cards. Apart from ignoring events in which production usurps interpretation before we even arrive at performance considerations, like Wilson's *Lohengrin* (whose slo-mo *is* a kind of antiperformance) or the Dorn/Rose *Tristan* (stupefying in its all-round Notness), we must also avoid selecting some undercast dud of a revival and setting it up against the best on offer. The fairest contrast is between two roughly comparable occasions, one of which promises the best on offer but devolves into a Notperformance, while the other appears ordinary enough but turns out to be a performance. Such a contrast is afforded by two recent Verdi presentations at the Met, the home company's *Ballo in Maschera* and the Maryinsky's *Macbeth.*

I attended these productions out of starvation and curiosity in approximately equal measure. Since everything is in place of something else and I try not to throw away time and money, I had chosen with some care. The *Ballo* cast (Deborah Voigt, Lyubov Petrova, Larissa Diadkova, Marcello Giordani, Carlos Alvarez), though certainly not of the calibre the Met could once field with regularity, was about as strong as could presently be gathered. I was interested to hear Giordani in the sort of role to which he would seem best suited (I'd seen him in *Manon, Il Pirata,* and half of *Benvenuto Cellini*), and the baritone Alvarez, of whom I'd had favorable reports, in anything at all. I consider James Conlon one of the Met's strongest conductors. The production has some silly touches and is of no positive help, but could certainly be waved aside by the right performers.

Prospects for the *Macbeth* were murkier. I'd seen nothing of the Maryinsky's Verdi, which had been poorly received in London and elsewhere. In the true repertory fashion still practiced by the Maryinsky (at least on its New York visits), the announced casts for the few performances were significantly different. A few years back, Lady Macbeth might have been a role for Guleghina or even Gorchakova, but I was not familiar with any of the scheduled sopranos. So I had selected a performance whose Macbeth was to be Nicolai Putilin, reasoning that his short, burly baritone at least has the requisite thrust and color for this relatively low-lying role. However, this announced performance was withdrawn, and Putilin's immediate successor was Vassily Gerello, a pleasant high lyric baritone whose local appearances—a nice Don Ferdinand in *Betrothal* and Tomsky in *Queen of Spades* (but Yeletsky is surely his role), Napoleon in *War and Peace,* and especially a lackadaisical, stylistically clueless Marcello in *La Bohème*—had disclosed neither the vocal nor the expressive qualifications for the part. So I moved on to the final performance, featuring Valery Vaneyev, with Olga Sergeyeva as his Lady—both unknown quantities to me, as was the conductor, Mikhail Sinkevich.

From the first bars of the prelude, I had a fine time at this *Macbeth*. I haven't heard the Met's orchestra tie into a Verdi score this way for many, many years—the auditorium was filled with suspense and dark propulsion, and every bar sounded important. With the company's splendid chorus singing out, the wonderful ensemble finales registered their full impact. The witches sang not in the cartoon cackle that has been our embarrassing norm, but in grave, rich tones pregnant with premonition. The two leads proved vocally capable, temperamentally mettlesome, and dramatically alert. The production, though not of my favorite sort (stark, abstract in a Modernist manner), nevertheless had mood, and there were some emotionally apt connections made in the restored sections of the ballet (here more of a pantomime) after the Apparition Scene.

I don't wish to suggest that this *Macbeth* enters the Great Verdi Performances pantheon. As Gennady Bezzubenkov, one of the Maryinsky's serviceable character basses, pushed valiantly into the sustained D on the second syllable of "Duncano" in Banquo's aria and came up with a closed, straight tone that was immediately covered by the orchestra, or as Yuri Andreyev nursed his glinty tenor precariously through Macduff's potentially heart-tugging recitative and aria, there was no avoiding the 39th Street echoes of Jerome Hines, then Giorgio Tozzi, as Banquo, or of Carlo Bergonzi as Macduff. That's another standard, another level of experience, altogether.

The two leads came closer to sustaining such comparisons. Sergeyeva showed a beautiful, limber voice that was at once satisfying in size and color and adept with articulations, runs, and trills. She sang fearlessly, with headlong rhythms. Her behavior, somewhat standard and generalized in the early scenes, became specific, inventive, and personal in the Sleepwalking Scene, which left a deep impression. She's a reasonably slim, well-proportioned person with good carriage, who establishes an immediate theatrical presence. The same is true of Valery Vaneyev, a well-set-up man not at all implausible as a battlefield leader. I already knew that I'd made the right choice from his work a few days earlier as Shaklovity in *Khovanshchina*, though he'd sung the part rather thickly. But then Shaklovity is a role, like Escamillo, that never seems to bring out the best in a baritone's voice. What's needed is a roomy bass-baritone with good line and controlled command of the top (George London, to dream on), the trouble with this being that there's already such a preponderance of male low voice in the piece that one longs for some brightness and upper-voice ring from this role. As Macbeth, Valery Vaneyev sounded better, the Italian language and Verdian legato lighting up the voice to a degree. He even created some nice *piano* effects, though here his technique wasn't consistent. The top notes had substance, though no real ring or core. I was disappointed that he was not allowed Macbeth's death scene from the early edition, to which he might have brought emotional power. (They dragged in the body for the final laud—feeble!)

These two protagonists played well off each other, and along with the production's other virtues made for a stirring evening. Still, in terms of vocal format and excitement and, in Valery Vaneyev's case, technical finish, they, too, are not sensibly equated with the soprano and baritone of the old Met production (Leonie Rysanek, Leonard Warren) or its revival (Birgit Nilsson, Cornell MacNeil). So this was not what anyone but PBS would call a Great Performance. But it was a performance: the available energies and talents were going directly into dramatic realization, and the work's sanguinary grip took hold. On a night-to-night basis, that's all the devotee asks.

The *Ballo* clicked along smartly. There were two distractions early on, the first caused by an orchestral musician arriving, with some displacement, a page or two into the Prelude, then fussing over a document unrelated to the musical proceedings;[1] and the second by Alvarez jumping in a bar early, then sheepishly withdrawing, for the B section of "*Alla vita.*" But apart from these momentary incidents, everything was shipshape, and since *Ballo* is itself shipshape (unlike the other sprawling, much-reworked Verdi operas of this period), there was almost a surfeit of shipshapeliness. What there wasn't was the emotional fulfillment of a single scene or major section of a scene, of the many that *Ballo* affords for chills and thrills. There were hints, most of them dropped by Giordani, but except for one or two of his sustained passages, they quickly vanished into the shipshapeliness.

Words like "blameless" and "excellent" refer to this shipshapeliness, to agreements about text and traffic patterns, and an orderly rendition of same. They mean that there is nothing in the execution of these agreements that one can point to as a source of notness except, perhaps, blamelessness itself. That includes even the energy level of the rendition. This *Ballo* was not lazily traversed. Conlon led a crisp, sharply played reading in well-proportioned tempos and well-defined rhythms. Though the singers were staying so well within themselves that one was grateful, once again, to Giordani for an occasional effortfulness, they weren't really coasting; their voices were engaged. Neither precision, proportion, nor energy were lacking.

Were the rendition to become a performance, it would no longer be blameless or excellent—there would be things to find fault with. This is true in two senses. First, something untoward might happen—an excitable conductor might push a stretto to the scrambling point, a singer might force a big phrase in search of a climax, a histrionic actor might go over the top, some combination of these might leave little messes here and there. Second, in the presence

of a performance, faultfinding would serve a purpose, that of defining where
the performance falls short and could be improved, of locating an absence
when something is actually present. Evoking past standards in relation to the
Maryinsky's *Macbeth* seems *à propos* not only for the purpose of identifying
its weaknesses (thereby reminding ourselves that there is more to be gotten
from the music and drama) but for that of acknowledging its effectiveness as
well, and the reasons for that. A personal fragment will illustrate. Amid the
ups and downs of *Ballo* performances and broadcasts of the 1950s and '60s,
a youthful encounter with W.J. Henderson's review of the Met's performance
of Nov. 22, 1913 was a source of some wonderment to me. "Mr. Caruso alone
stood forth as the artist commanding the respect of the connoisseur," wrote
Henderson, Caruso's literally unmentionable colleagues that evening having
been Emmy Destinn, Frieda Hempel, Margaret Matzenauer, and Pasquale
Amato, with Andrès de Segurola and Marcel Journet as Sam and Tom. (The
conductor, Toscanini, does get Henderson's approval.)[2] Feeling the passions
of *Ballo* at least sporadically stirred in the here and now, one contemplated
how different a profile the piece must have presented in the there and then
and what a different set of expectations the critics and operagoers of that
time brought to it. One's imagination of the work's potential was expanded.

Thus, in a performance context, we might note that Voigt's blond, mid-
calibre soprano is hardly an ideal Amelia instrument (we want something
fuller and warmer, informed by a more passionate personality and a more
theatrical presence); that in the line of Met Riccardos since the 1940 revival,
Giordani barely makes the cut;* that Petrova's pretty little voice, though it
has the lightness and flexibility for Oscar, doesn't have the flash and bite that
really brings his music to life or the strength to lead out in the quintet; etc.,
etc. But those are shortcomings of performance. They cannot account for
Notperformance. After all, is Karita Mattila's Northern Lyric soprano, with its
almost total negligence of chest voice, any better suited to middleweight Verdi
than Voigt's? Certainly not. Yet as the other Amelia (Boccanegra-Grimaldi),
she gave a consistently absorbing and moving performance of the sort she
is able to give. To go even further afield: was the heady lyric tenor of Sven-
Olof Eliasson, who succeeded Ragnar Ulfung in Goeran Gentele's famous
Stockholm production of *Ballo*'s Swedish adaptation, a better fit for the role
than Giordani's? On the contrary, it suggested useful employment in the
music of Britten, or that of Bach and Handel in the pre-performance-practice

---

* Without summoning the spirit of Caruso, or those of the tenors who would have sung
the part had the Met mounted *Ballo* between his era and 1940 (e.g., Gigli, Martinelli in his
prime, perhaps Lauri-Volpi), they include: Bjoerling, Peerce, Tucker, Bergonzi, Domingo,
and Pavarotti.

days. Its weight, timbre, and linguistic set were all wrong for Verdi. Still, he too gave a performance, a rather interesting and involving one.

In short, while these singers' voices are not the stuff of a *Ballo* enthusiast's dreams, they are by no means disqualified for their roles, and the same is true of the remaining principals. Alvarez's baritone turned out to be a firm one of decent size, Latin coloration, and no basic technical glitches—a perfectly plausible Renato instrument. As was anticipated from her previous local appearances, Diadkova was a vocally and musically solid Ulrica. So we cannot say that this cast, conductor, or orchestra were at any point lacking the essential requirements for a satisfying—even hot—repertory performance of this opera, or that they were not applying themselves with high professionalism to their work as they understood it. The difficulty must, therefore, lie with the understanding itself—not with the ability or willingness to do the artistic job, but with how the artistic job has come to be defined.

I don't mean to suggest that Notperformance has become the invariable rule. There are still performances, even good ones, and there are individual artists who transcend their Notperformed surroundings. The *Ballo* revival was, in fact, a rather unusual bonding of surface gleam with interior emptiness, the opera safely sealed inside. What is disturbing are the indications that the Notperformance is becoming the accepted goal. In that case, the map *does* precede the territory. We follow the map but see and feel nothing of the countryside's beauties, surprises, and terrors, then tell ourselves what a fine trip we've been on. The distinction between map and trip will be the central subject of the rest of this book.

NOTES

1. This kind of annoyance is recurrent at the Met, less so at the NYCO. By coincidence, in one of the Inside Info letters he posts with such regularity that one wonders if he's not really a Special Correspondent embedded with the Met orchestra, violinist Les Dreyer spoke to the situation around this time (see his letter to the *NYT*, Feb. 27, 2005). "In the darkness of the pit," Dreyer writes, "we opera musicians can read a magazine or book . . . sneak out to the bathroom, change a string or make a quick phone call." With an air of collegial joviality, he goes on to describe the many variations in footwear and lower-body attire (clogs, bedroom slippers; black ski pants, fish-net stockings, etc.) pit players can get away with undetected. What peek-a-boo fantasy is this? With the Met's Grand Canyon of a pit yawning before us, music stands and conductor's desk lit (much more brightly than of old), these supposedly darkly cloaked doings are plainly visible from any seat above orchestra level. It happens that I saw both the *Ballo* and *Macbeth* (no such goings-on, by the way, from the Maryinsky players) from Dress Circle boxes fairly close to the stage—one of a couple of thousand seats from which the attention, attitude, and discipline of every member of the orchestra is clearly discerned. Even from the Family Circle, pit entrances and exits are detectable. I'm sure no one objects to a discreet move during a scene break or the applause for a number, but nothing signals blatant disrespect more clearly than the sort of thing here described. If symphonic musicians can sit attentively for a Bruckner Seventh or a Mahler Ninth, why can't opera players have enough respect for the music, the drama, and the audience (not to mention the conductor) to hold it together for the duration of an act?

2. See Henderson's *New York Sun* review (presumably of Nov. 23, 1913—reviews were out the next morning in those days), as reprinted in *The Metropolitan Opera Annals*, W.H. Seltsam, ed. (H.W. Wilson Co., N.Y. 1947).

2

THE PIT AND
THE PODIUM

(1998–2010)

I have said that in today's operatic world too much territory is ceded to the realm of the eye; that even within this realm too much attention is paid to physical production and not enough to performance; and that auteuristic privileges claimed by directors and designers have too often been flaunted in irresponsible ways. On the musical side, first appearances are quite different. To begin with, conductors, unlike directors and designers, are themselves performers, participants in the unfolding of The Work. And while over time there have been changes in instruments and voices that certainly affect performance, there has been nothing like the technological transformations on which superintendents of the visual have been able to capitalize, with the dubious exception of audio enhancement when it is used. Nor can conductors be lumped with directors and designers as flagrant flouters of text. On the contrary, they have become evermore the enforcers of text, and of what is sanctioned as authentic in text. From the original-intent P.O.V. they usually appear as restorationist holdouts against the revolutionary chaos visible across the apron. While some are active collaborationists, the worst that most could be accused of is a see-no-evil deference, as if their efforts were entirely detached from onstage events.

As intimated earlier, there is nothing novel in a cleavage between the musical and theatrical elements of performance. What is new is the agreement to embrace it, of which the Wilsonian Coke-can-on-the-dresser manifesto is but one articulation.* Since performance is alive and fluid, this cleavage is no mere sundering of inert objects, but a pulling-apart of living tissue, a purposely inflicted wound whose edges are torn aside even as we watch and listen. The theatrical elements of text—set descriptions, period references, behavioral instructions—are granted no authority; the musical, ultimate. As between theatre and music, eye and ear, presumptions about what is authentic and what is creative are not only different, but opposed. The performance is a vivisection.

And yet there is agreement. With the occasional principled objection (like Thielemann's over the D. Alden *Tannhäuser*), the motion to dismember is passed with the signatures of all parties. It's a sort of face-saving pact, or (recall Sutcliffe's description of the "matrix" discussions from which the conductor is excluded) a pre-nuptial separation agreement stipulating that the musical spouse may keep the old manse and the family name in exchange for his or her meek endurance of nightly public repudiation.

If this forced parting of the primary elements that interpretive artists once sought to unite is really an agreement, what is its essence? It's clear enough why hubristic directors and designers would espouse the split: it grants them auteurial license. But what of the conductors? Apart from those who are conscious enthusiasts for the semiotic and deconstructive, or those simply trying to make a given situation work (that director from the rock-porn video industry?—he's really *intensely* musical), one doesn't hear much from them. But their otherwise puzzling, even shameful deference must at its best have to do with their faith in the power of music and its supremacy in opera, their belief that music will finally carry the day. The work lives in the music; the music will transcend; the work will survive.

On a primitive subsistence level, this is true. In the mere act of drawing the bow across the string, placing the reed to the lip, drawing breath to attack the wordnote, of following the score and observing its articulations, professional musicians cannot fail to summon some of the work's presence. But beyond that, this is a misplaced faith unless opera is allowed to be its ear-led, eye-confirmed self. To what extremes would conductors have to resort to counter the attention-compelling ploys of their nominal colleagues on the visual side? What would be the aural equivalents? Re-assigning the voices to parodic effect, or amplifying them at rock-concert volume? Ignoring the

---

* And a consistent one. Once again disavowing the imposition of an interpretation, Wilson says of his Paris *Ring*: ". . . with a work that is already full of overwhelming emotions, a production that is equally moving and emotional makes no sense"[1]—as if these overwhelming emotions could somehow register their impact independent of performance and of production choices.

composer's articulations and substituting contradictory ones? Scrambling the orchestrations? Playing the music out of sequence, backward, upside-down? Expanding Les Dreyer's prerogative (see n. 1, p 260)—the musicians will now perform in the nude, and may come and go on whim? In the instances of a number of the productions examined earlier, something along those lines would be needed.

And of course musicians don't do that sort of thing. Instead, they counter-pose the integrity of their portions of text, trusting (to give their intentions the benefit of every doubt) that virtue will be rewarded. As already noted, that can happen in cases of transcendent performance. But the chances for transcendence are limited not only by the thinness of fully developed talent or the split between the musical and dramatic elements, but by the agree-ment itself. Its nature is this: to bring the onstage performers under ever-stricter conceptual control, thereby reducing their areas of interpretive free-dom, responsibility, and creativity, while obligating them to simultaneously embody the schemes of both the theatrical and musical conceptualizers, contradictory though these may be. The conductors' territorial claims may rest on adherence to the text and scholarly authentication, and the direc-tors' on independence from these, but so far as performers are concerned the result is the same: the restriction of interpretive choice.

To be clear, lest the following mislead: I am not arguing against the final-decision authority of either director or conductor, or of the two together in shaping production and performance. The campaigns against the laziness of received tradition and sloppy execution, against the egocentric willfulness of some performers, the struggles toward the goal of fully integrated produc-tion—these tough engagements, fought by conductors like Toscanini, Mahler, and Beecham, by directors like Stanislavski, Reinhardt, and Felsenstein, are ones I happily support, and they cannot be undertaken without an order of battle. Nor am I challenging the practice of close and respectful examina-tion of text, or the value of musicological and dramaturgical scholarship when properly employed. But we have reached a point at which it is entirely legitimate to question not only the uses to which the powers of auteurship and authentication are often put, but whether the extent of their present distribution is in our best artistic interests. This applies to conductors and their forces as surely as it does to directors and designers and theirs.

There is an opinion, almost unanimous among critics and connoisseurs, that the quality of orchestral participation in operatic performance is at an all-time high. Here in New York, one regularly hears this with reference to the Met's orchestra as developed over the now-lengthy span of James Levine's regime, and similar endorsements of other international-level opera ensembles and their music directors are easy to come by. In some ways (the ones most easily identified) I can agree. These ways have to do with sheer skill—precision and ease of execution, sharpness of mechanics—and its instant adaptability to at least the surface aspects of a widened range of musical styles and technical difficulties. These are the common measures of musicianship as professionally defined, and at their highest development are everything we mean by "virtuosity." Certain aesthetic qualities, whose outlines will emerge as we proceed, are also represented as virtues, and indeed are such in some kinds of music under some circumstances.

The trouble for me, though, is that my evaluation of operatic musicianship rests on the extent to which the orchestra becomes a vital participant in the drama being played. The skills are only tools to dramatic ends, while the adaptability is useful only if it penetrates below the stylistic surface, and the aesthetic qualities only if dramatically and theatrically pertinent. Absent such purpose, they are of no *operatic* value whatever. Indeed, the more they command attention in the forms of technical brilliance, stylistic mimicry, and aesthetic seduction in and for themselves, the more of a distraction and distortion they become. For the opera orchestra, failure to dramatize is graver than technical imperfection, and an excess of theatricality more forgivable than musical purity for its own sake. It's a *theatre* orchestra.

To dramatize is: to search out units of action when these are represented in the orchestra; to locate them within a broader arc of action and movement toward a dramatic destination; to depict the conflict engendered by these actions; to understand accompaniment as furtherance of characterization and embrace it as a crucial function; to delineate the textures and colors of dramatic episodes; to vivify passages of description and mood; and to maintain suspense.

To theatricalize is: to project these dramatizations with a profile and energy that lends them unmistakable presence for the audience and to maintain an intense, unbroken interaction with onstage events.

The opera conductor's job is: to co-ordinate, guide, assist and inspire all performers in the enthusiastic and dedicated execution of these efforts within a conceptual and stylistic framework agreed upon with the director, and answerable to the hierarchy of interpretation.

As is true in any aspect of any of the arts of the act, it is to be hoped that the interpreters will locate both whatever is authentically dramatic in the material and the most appropriate means of theatricalizing it. To theatricalize the undramatic (either because the creator has neglected to provide any drama, or the interpreters to find it) is to produce an empty vitality. Even that, however, is a step up from the abstract—it acknowledges a superficial awareness of operatic responsibility. Effects without causes are still effects, and there is always the chance that one of them will bump into a cause while running backwards, so to speak.

The actorly language I have just used is not always welcome in musical circles, where it is often seen as an attempted usurpation or as a looming threat of job creep. But to describe an opera orchestra's function in purely musical terms is to evade the central issue, because the drama "contained" in the music must be animated not as general qualities or abstract structures, but in small, specific, concrete ways, and in opera these ways are always tied to the stage. Stage language is therefore both appropriate and accurate in speaking of the opera orchestra, and actor's language in speaking of its players. In any case, it's not so much a question of language as of something in the blood. Instances: At least since his Leipzig Gewandhaus days, we think of Kurt Masur as an exclusively symphonic conductor. But before that he was in East Berlin working with Felsenstein at the Komische Oper, and at least one reason he has conducted no opera for many years is that under the prevailing conditions of operatic training and rehearsal, the opportunity for fruitful stage/pit collaboration does not in his opinion exist. Valery Gergiev and his Maryinsky (then Kirov) predecessor, Yuri Temirkanov, both studied under Ilya Musin at the St. Petersburg State Conservatory. Musin's particular fascination was with the relationship between gesture and orchestral sound—an actorly pursuit of the mimetic sort—and for formal theatrical guidance he drew on the work of Stanislavski.[2]

Beyond these contemporary examples, we should recall that with only a few important exceptions (e.g., Mravinsky, Munch), the great conductors of the 19th and 20th centuries were theatre men. In the Austro-German and Central European traditions, they began as orchestra players or assistant conductors in theatres that performed a popular repertory of operas, operettas, ballets, and plays with incidental music. In Italy, they played and conducted in the opera houses. Regardless of whether or not they chafed under their early assignments, or of where their interests and ambitions later led them, their professional grounding was in the requirements of music for the stage, music that succeeded or failed as stage events succeeded or failed, and as its dramatic and theatrical content was or was not animated.[3] Of Mahler himself as conductor, Bruno Walter wrote: ". . . no matter how foreign a sentiment might be to him, how contrary to his character, his imagination would enable him to place himself inside the most opposite person and in the strangest of situations"—the actor's task, precisely defined. Walter continues: "Thus, Mahler's heart was on the stage when he sat at the desk. He conducted, or rather, he produced the music in accordance with the drama."[4] Roller accounted Mahler *as director and producer* the greater of the two geniuses with whom he had worked, the other being Max Reinhardt.[5] I am not citing Mahler to summon godly authority—I cannot know what I might have felt and thought about either his conducting or his directing. It's the lineage of an ideal I'm hoping to convey, and the passion for that ideal.

This drama-in-music, music-for-drama paradigm, held in common by all the artists mentioned above, has been shattered by the stage/pit divorce agreement. What might we expect to hear from an orchestra that is party to the agreement? Playing, I would venture, whose beauties and refinements are increasingly ends in themselves, playing that calls attention to its own importance while receding from its role in the drama. Since the agreement is a postmodern artifact, the aesthetic properties of the playing would likely reflect qualities prized by modernist and postmodernist creators in other artistic disciplines. Since it is a separation agreement, it cannot spring from the sung actions committed onstage, whose own connection to the dramatic progression that gave birth to the music has been severed. And since the agreement's sole provision for mutuality is on the point of conceptual control, the playing would be apt to exert a constraining effect on the autonomy and presence of the stage performers. All this is, in my perception, our situation with sufficient frequency to be considered the norm.

Despite their discomfiture with thespic definitions of their duties, most conductors and musicians will concede (how could they not, after all?) that the opera orchestra must have about it something of the dramatic and theatrical. They will even profess that the search for this something is just what they are up to, and some of them, I'm sure, do so honestly. It is important to ignore these protestations. We must keep in mind the many directors and designers who assert their love of the scores and reverence for the composers while consigning both to perdition; perhaps also the luminaries of sports, politics, movies and TV who learn early in their professional grooming to always pronounce the disarming word. It's only acumen—pay no attention. Listen to the musicmaking.

Most of the discussion here will focus on the two major New York opera orchestras, and that will inevitably settle on the influence of Levine at the Met. Bearing in mind that some of the aesthetic tendencies under review may therefore present a different balance than they would elsewhere, and that in defining a norm it is essential to take careful note of exceptions to it, I will try to avoid wild generalizations from local particulars. I don't think, though, that Levine and his orchestra are by any means out of the contemporary mainstream; I think they *are* the contemporary mainstream, a summation of qualities I first began experiencing several decades back in the work of other conductors and (mainly on recordings) other orchestras. As suggested by my *Ballo/Macbeth* observations, Gergiev and the Maryinsky will more than once prove handy by way of comparison.

In measuring orchestras and conductors, it's natural to turn one's thoughts first to scores of size and complexity. Two of my most rewarding recent experiences have been with the *Frau* of Thielemann and the *Kat'a* of Jiří Belohlávek. In my only previous encounter with Thielemann, he had failed to bring Pfitzner's *Palestrina* to more than widely separated episodes of life for me—but then, I am not among this opera's acolytes, and the visiting Covent Garden production, visually dreary and prosaically sung, cast a pall. I thought his *Frau* was marvelous. It had all the music's implied weight and depth of sonority, but was not ponderous; it had transparency but coloristic cohesion as well; it fulfilled the lyrical moments without losing the architectural grasp necessary to bring us through the long evening. This didn't prevent me from reflecting from time to time that some of the old cuts made by Böhm (among others) might not always be to our disadvantage, especially in the absence of Böhm's casts; but I don't think any failing of Thielemann's was responsible for this. In *Kat'a,* Belohlávek's crackling reading, dramatically alive at every step, made the Met's previous offerings under Charles Mackerras—well played though those were—seem temperate by comparison. In recent years, most of the performances I have found orchestrally satisfying have belonged either to this category (i.e., big 20th-Century works) or to that of the Skipovers, with Monteverdi or Rameau or Handel at one end, Britten and the contemporaries at the other.* These occasions are always welcome, but of course they leave out most of the works we hear most often. I have proposed that the insistent problem in the playing of those works is the substitution of an aesthetic exhibition for dramatic action, so perhaps I should identify the most common qualities of this exhibition before proceeding. The first, already mentioned, is shipshapeliness, technical and musical proficiency carried out with such dispatch that it becomes an expressive characteristic in and of itself. What it expresses is proficiency, and what we listen to is proficiency, just as in *Regietheater* we watch amazingness. A second is hyperclarity. This

---

* It's always possible that this impression is due in part to the unfamiliarity of some of these works relative to those of the standard repertory. One sometimes hears this thought put forward with an insinuation of Jaded Reviewer Syndrome—one has heard too many *Bohèmes,* etc. But this argument could as easily be reversed: if we'd heard as many *Platées* or *Midsummer Night's Dreams* as we have *Bohèmes,* their performance faults would be equally apparent. I think the strongest explanation is the simplest: our orchestras and conductors are most at home, technically and temperamentally, in these kinds of scores.

means a clean profiling of horizontal lines, much attention to inner voices, and meticulous balancing of dynamics up and down the pitch range, with minimal tonal decay or overtone spillage, so that the music is laid out in nice, shiny parts. Corollary to this is a separation and purification of colors, as in much modernist painting—no thick impastos or dark, heavy blends, but sharp edges and bright, distinct bands. Graphics, not oils. In orchestral conducting of modernist persuasion, this approach to spatial considerations (separation of lines and colors) is allied with a structuralist view of temporal ones—the pursuit of musical structures and architectural shapes (close reading of the map) in the belief that if their progressions are carved in bold relief, meaning will stand out. But except for a few highly formalistic works, this way of thinking is a very rough fit in opera, where musical structures are at the service of scenic ones. The result is usually an unrewarding standoff.

A third quality is moderation of dramatic accent, as if the theatrical functions of musical gestures (active and descriptive) either pass unnoticed or are unwanted. They are *observed*, of course, they are indicated; their purely musical, textual imperatives are obeyed, but with discretion and poise. We might, in fact, say that they are signified. And this plays into a fourth quality—which is a kind of unruffled ongoingness, a smooth connectivity that mediates all transitions, conflicts, or potential interruptions—and finally into a fifth, which is a particular timbral exquisiteness, silky, luminous, and soothing—Feng Shui in sound.

Though contrasting examples in close proximity are desirable in distinguishing between good and bad, performance and not, they don't always pan out as advertised. We had three avowedly different *Bohèmes* in town not long ago, courtesy of the Met, the NYCO, and Baz Luhrmann on Broadway, but not only was it the case that half a presentable *Bohème* could not have been stitched together from the tattered remnants of all three, but that the usable swatches didn't even turn out to be complementary. As with our recent operas of Here and Now, one could discern among them distinctions of intent, but scarcely of effect. Sometimes, however, the differences are genuine and instructive, and with respect to conducting and playing, this was true of the NYCO and Met *Butterflys*.

At the City Opera, an improvement in orchestral standards has been the chief success of Paul Kellogg's artistic directorship, soon to end as this is written. After a long period of decline, the playing in most of the repertory has returned to a level at least comparable with that of the Rudel era. It has been generally alert and crisp in pre-Romantic music under several conductors (Jane Glover, Harry Bicket, Daniel Beckwith) and in Sir Arthur Sullivan under Gerald Steichen and Gary Thor Wedow (a special pleasure to hear these delicious instrumentations given some bright, singing tone and lively but un-pushed tempos). There was even a successful early Romantic excursion— a warmly played, idiomatic *Capuleti e i Montecchi* under Joseph Rescigno. Among contemporary works, Stewart Robertson's reading of *Of Mice and Men* was strong, and *Dead Man Walking* sounded well realized under John De Main, though here I had nothing to compare it with. Obviously, this overall improvement must be credited to the company's Musical Director, George Manahan, who has also conducted a healthy plurality of the NYCO performances I've heard in recent years. It was his taut reading of *Macbeth* that first persuaded me better things were happening in the State Theatre's pit. (This same performance, however, also first aroused my suspicions of enhancement—the balances in the *a cappella* quartet section of the Act I finale were *exceedingly* strange). Under Manahan, the orchestra has often thrived, and sometimes in scores (I'm thinking of Strauss and Wagner) of a size and complexity one does not expect it to quite fill out. Where Manahan and company have tended to fall down is either in operas that need extra help (e.g., the thinly instrumented *Baby Doe*, which needed not only more rhythmic bone and incisive attack, but some touch-up augmentation to reach critical mass) or on evenings of standard-rep coasting (*Falstaff, Bohème,* and *Don Giovanni*). I was particularly happy, therefore, to encounter a *Butterfly* that not only sounded good (positively lush at times), but had a sense of destination and co-ordination with scenic events. It was led by a maestro I haven't encountered before or since, Guido Johannes Rumstadt.

The playing of *Madama Butterfly* by the City Opera's orchestra was less exquisite than the Met's, which I regret to say was under the late Marcello Viotti—"regret" not only because of Viotti's untimely death, but because through his handling of the uneven but thrilling *La Juive* and an enjoyable evening of Ibert, Saint-Saëns, and Respighi with the New York Philharmonic (all unusual sympathies nowadays) I came to regard him as a valuable musician. His *Butterfly*, though, incorporated all the aesthetic tendencies cited above except the one that could have helped, the modernist pursuit of structure. Impressionistic atmospherics were well enough served—solo woodwind or violin over a muted string cushion, etc., lovely in an *Après-midi d'un faune*-ish way. But the music just sat there being exquisite, its sonic presence tasteful and modest, the shapes of episodes smoothed into the overall texture rather than defined within it.

This last is make-or-break in a Puccini reading, because it goes to the heart of his genius. While Strauss was worrying to death the problems of prosification and impassionisation, Puccini was solving them. His pairing of a technique for the interweaving of musical development with scenic progression into a seemingly natural, inevitable flow and a melodic imagination that served both the transcendent (with his big, sweeping tunes) and the sensory everyday moment (with his instant-imprint motivic and descriptive figures) remains unique—he alone took the post-Verdian step with complete assurance.

Around the time of these *Butterflys*, I was pleasantly jolted by a re-hearing of Tullio Serafin's mid-Sixties recording of *Bohème*. At this stage of his long and distinguished career, Serafin's recorded output, spread among several orchestras, labels, and recording teams, was unpredictable. But I had fond memories of this set for its high-powered grand-opera cast of Met familiars and for its rich, lucid sound and Serafin's conducting. Still, after all the *Bohème*s of the intervening years and the slow, sometimes subliminal erosion of expectation, I was unprepared for the rediscoveries of this one. Act I's sequence of introductions was like a reunion with classmates whose personalities I'd forgotten. Obviously the singers, who in a contemporary context sound like interplanetary visitors from an impossibly advanced operatic civilization, are the principal agents of the encounter. But their musical circumstances are important, too: The self-dramatizations of Rodolfo and Marcello trying to work, trying to get warm; Colline's entrance with its wonderful horn announcement over the burning of the playscript and the dying of the fire; Schaunard bursting on the scene with his coins, his provender, his tale of the parrot and his call to the streets of the Latin Quarter; the intrusion and expulsion of Benoit; and at last the fateful, love-at-first-sight meeting of the lovers—each of these given its particular tempo and color, treated as important and present for dramatic purpose and energetically projected, all without any sense of choppiness or forced highlighting. The performance continues in kind.

Serafin's *Bohème* is only a convenient example; there is, of course, no just comparison between live performances and studio recordings or between the levels of talent, experience, and cultural background available to each of these conductors.[6] For that matter, the performance problems of *Bohème* and *Butterfly* are not identical. *Butterfly* presents longer passages of subtly varied slow tempos and exotic atmosphere, and its technique of scenic continuity is if anything more finished than *Bohème*'s; for these reasons, its continuity is more of a trap. Nevertheless, one *Butterfly* conductor fell into the trap and the other avoided it, and while Rumstadt had the advantage of collaborating on a carefully considered new production and Viotti did not (see pp. 157-158), the chief difference between them was that Viotti and his executants played the music almost entirely for its descriptive qualities, Rumstadt and his for its actions and events. The more modest group was, on this occasion, the better opera orchestra.

Either Viotti's tempo selections were on the whole slightly slower than Rumstadt's, or seemed so owing to their inactive properties. Whichever way this works in a given instance, inertia is naturally associated with slowness. But even the slowest tempo cannot of itself kill suspense or flatten dramatic profile. The question is never how long a moment takes, but whether or not it holds. What slowness will do is expose other factors: sonic presence or absence, accent and attack, timbral contrasts and mixtures, weight distribution. At slow speeds the need for destination in the music, which I believe is best understood as keenness of dramatic intent and for which driven tempos are so often mistaken, is all the more urgent. If I have a bias, it is on the slow-to-moderate side. I like melodic gestures to fully develop, sustained notes to either intensify and enrichen or else declare their changelessness, sonorities to bloom and harmonies to simultaneously blend and clarify. In bigger, thicker scores—and especially in opera, where voices must clear the orchestra—I like the center of gravity to be low. Thus, Barbirolli's *Butterfly*, distinctly gradual but for the most part tensely held and built, is an old favorite of mine, and my preferred Wagnerians are the likes of Furtwängler, Knappertsbusch and Goodall (usually recalled as prevailingly slow, though I think it is more a matter of unfolding the music rather than pushing it, and of sonic depth) or Walter, Kubelik, and Kempe (prevailingly moderate or, in Pierre Monteux's usage, *tempo juste* conductors).[7] I will tolerate even an obstinately slow reading of the sort that allows no unmarked quickening no matter how intuitively right or stylistically sanctioned, if it at least makes the music *sound*. Mark Elder's *Mefistofele* was of this kind. It set up perhaps two dozen emotional roadblocks that made me squirm, but the courage of its rhythmic convictions did eventually accumulate the color and weight that bring this work home; the interpretation finally earned its keep.*

Because "too slow" or "too fast" is the easiest thing to say about a reading that doesn't feel right, tempo is frequently the scapegoat for undramatic musicmaking. For the same reason, *tempo juste* performances are the ones that force us to look elsewhere for the problem. Conlon's *Ballo*, though a bit on the lively side of *juste*, could be taken as a high-end example. Two others are the *Zauberflöte* of Mackerras and the *Boris* of Semyon Bychkov, highly regarded musicians whose presence would seem to indicate an effort to do well by repertory revivals of these works. On both evenings, it didn't take

---

* Elder, for many years the Musical Director of ENO and a Verdian of high reputation in England, was the conductor of the Jonathan Miller *Rigoletto* (see p. 180, n. 2), which displayed this same gradualism in a piece that cannot sustain it. More recently, though, he surprised me with a mettlesome *Otello* that achieved great intensity with an unstarry cast.

long for the dreaded Drama Cancellation Effect* to take hold. Tasteful moderation of tempo sometimes goes hand-in-hand with tasteful moderation of everything else. During *Flute*, by way of mitigating my annoyance at time and money wasted, I reminded myself of All We Owe Sir Charles—in my case, his orchestrally splendid Met *Orfeo* of 1974, the good Janáček performances, and the bracing recording of Handel's *Music for the Royal Fireworks* I still take off the shelf from time to time. Could this be the same fellow? With an orchestra certainly capable of being brought up smartly and a cast much in need of it, all we got was a dull shipshape shine on the routine inspection: nice balances, sensible tempos, mediation of all accents (like the *sforzandi* near the end of the overture) and tremolando effects, and for the singers, a sprinkling of slippery little ornaments of a sort that do not etch, emphasize, or reinforce, but only soften or evade. And again, as with Viotti's Puccini, the sense that dramatic points aren't even being recognized, much less animated, and that the sheer sonic energy isn't quite enough for the hall.

My hopes were up for Bychkov (younger than Gergiev or Temirkanov, but another Musin pupil), who had made splashes here and there and was embarked on a well-received series of Shostakovich symphony recordings. Perhaps he and a few onstage compatriots would bring a charge to the *Boris* revival. A knowledgeable friend who had heard him live several times described him to me later as something of a flailer, more given to the emotion of a moment than to structure. A not altogether unpromising impression, but not at all what I'd heard. I was stunned by the flatness of the proceedings, and neither tempo nor impulsiveness was the culprit. Maybe misplaced rectitude was involved. Since its premiere in 1974, this production has employed Mussorgsky's original orchestration.[†8] As an act of faithfulness to authorial intent, this is an admirable decision. But it poses significant performance difficulties, at least with this orchestra in this house. The idea would be to bring up a chilly steelpoint print from the duns and greys of hue, a sinewy toughness from the asbestos textures, an astringency from the harsher harmonies of the original, and to drill into the score with strong accents and attacks. Not a bit of that happened. The music was overmodulated and underplayed throughout. Did Bychkov simply miscalculate the auditorium? Did his perfectly appropriate tempos indicate a mollifying stance toward everything in the score? What did he believe was being achieved? I don't know, but while

---

* Or, for that Brechtian ring that only the German language can sound, *Dramadurchstreichungseffekt.*

† Rimsky-Korsakov's, once ubiquitous, has not been used by the Met since the days of Ezio Pinza. In the 1950s the instrumentation of Karol Rathaus, billed as "Mussorgsky's original" and indeed closer to it, was employed, and for some seasons thereafter that of Shostakovich.[9]

"purity" as banishment of Rimskian sweetening sounds like a good deed, "purity" as banishment of all color, strength, and theatricality is only punishment. The original needn't be *this* dead—in the production's early days Conlon found more urgency and drive in this scoring. But I must admit that whenever Rimsky has returned to one of our theatres with a visiting company I have wallowed in it, not because I prefer it on principle, but because it has made the spaces tingle. It has made the music present.

Most often these days, the Drama Cancellation Effect occurs at brisk tempos. The briskness usually goes hand-in-hand with a weightlessness, creating a lite, brite, fleet quality that skims over the music. One version of this is the Rossini Retro sound, offspring of devoted scholarship. It has its charms but some serious limitations as well. It's one thing in a theatre of modest dimensions, or in the stage/pit/auditorium conformation that was customary in early 19th-Century Italian houses, with the orchestra higher and the singers farther forward. But it's quite another under our performance conditions. I recall first being aware of this when the current Met *Barbiere* production was new (1981), and the performance scholarship first of Alberto Zedda, then of the Rossini critical edition supervised by Phillip Gossett, was just beginning to take effect. Andrew Davis was the conductor. He's no routinier, and the playing was very nice, but *where was it*? From my seat (rear orchestra but in front of the overhang, auditorium right—an area whose acoustical properties I know) it chattered away just over the aural horizon, where any points it might have registered were of slight consequence.

I have ever since tried to sit higher and closer, even at a sightline disadvantage, for Rossini, Handel, Mozart—any composer threatened with the lite, brite, brisk makeover. That helps some. And some of the recent Rossini performances have been led by a real theatre conductor, Bruno Campanella. Campanella's recording of *Don Pasquale* (live, Torino, 1988) is the best example I know of Italian Romantic comedic style traced to its theatrical roots. Every pit decision sounds like a stage decision, and a decision more felt than thought. The reading is not notably brisk, because Campanella knows that briskness *per se* has little to do with musical or theatrical vitality. His teasing treatment of tempo (the stretch, hold, and release that builds a hundred little moments of comic suspense) and of dynamics (especially his delightful way of using the orchestra as set-up, leading us by ear through the accompanied recitatives) is not merely performance practice observed; it is the orchestra turned actor, just as Walter recounts of Mahler. At the Met, with its internationalized casts, orchestra, and repertory rehearsal habits, he has not been able to achieve the same level of idiomatic understanding or stage/pit specificity, but has still brought unusual profile, point, and projection to these scores and to Bellini's *Il Pirata*. The textures and balances of the cleaned-up instrumentations, too, are nearly always refreshing—at the start. But soon, the lack of dimension and richness in the sound, its failure to ever quite fill out the space so that one can sit back and receive it, grows a little tiring. The incessant "fwee" of the piccolo and "ting" of the triangle, piquant at first, starts to nag. The many string tremolandos, intensely rendered but still lacking in sonic oomph, can evoke a sneaky yearning for reinforcement, even for a nip of trombone here and there or a whack on the old bass drum at Basilio's "*Come un colpo di cannone.*" The truth is that even with a favorable seat and the right conductor, Rossini Retro doesn't finally do the job. It aims for period authenticity but does not attain it, because the first requirement for that would be the originally intended presence of sound, which is out of the question in our performance circumstances. I expect we will soon be told that the orchestra needs enhancement, and indeed it does—in the form of more instruments and bolder playing.

Unsatisfying as this light, lean approach is for Rossini comedies, when it is transferred to works of greater weight the results are truly calamitous. Short of Wagner and Strauss, no composer is safe. To conduct the last repertory run of *Trovatore*s in the pre-Vick production (another unenviable assignment) came Jun Märkl, well spoken-of by those familiar with his work in Germany. His solution was to push along all tempos from *andante* up as if wishing to dispatch the music before we could take note of anything about it, but to then insert from time to time an expressive slowdown that took everyone, onstage and off, by surprise. Two examples of this were the climactic bars of both verses of Ferrando's opening narrative and the brief orchestral interlude between the verses of "*Tacea la notte.*" The former is a notorious trouble spot that is often blurry in live performance, the latter a normally unproblematic moment.[11] Both went seriously awry, after which Märkl opted for fast idle all the way to the last-scene trio, which milled about aimlessly. During the "*Il balen*" I felt badly for the baritone, a newcomer named Sulvarán. He had a secure voice of sympathetic timbre, perhaps of good use in a role like Silvio in *Pagliacci*, but underpowered for all but the most lyrical passages of Di Luna's music. His only hope of making much of his big moment lay in a moderate basic tempo with some comfortable broadening at the tops of phrases to allow his tone to bloom, and comparable allargandos around the F's in the cabaletta. He seemed to have something of that sort in mind, but Märkl cranked through at an organ-grinder allegro, while the orchestra took yet another view of the matter. Not shipshape!

Worse than Märkl's *Trovatore* (which at least featured an occasional choral and orchestral loudness) was Carlo Rizzi's *Lucia,* sloppy enough to ruin the point of its quick tempos (that would be a crisp liveliness) and possessed of so slight an orchestral presence—tinny and faraway—as to trivialize the whole score. And this was for the newly mounted *Lucia* of the void (see pp. 164-165), completing its strategic retreat from the *Lucia* of the scandal, which had been led with at least some sense of the music's importance by Nello Santi, anchored onstage by the firmly declared expressive intentions of Mariella Devia, and made musically eloquent at times through the shared understanding of these two.

I do not assume that any conductor of high professional standing actually looks down on the music of Donizetti or middle-period Verdi, or is simply trying to be rid of it as quickly as possible. I sometimes suspect it, but I don't assume it. Nor do I assume bad orchestral attitude, though I know it can be a factor. But there is a dismissive quality to readings like these, the excuse for which (doubtless influenced these days by the Skipover aesthetic) is that these scores are best rendered with a light touch, lean textures, fast tempos, and little tolerance for vocal expansion. There's an analogous theory at work in the French repertory. Here the rationale is derived partly from the general contemporary notion that if the music's French it should be airy and elegant, and partly from awareness of the *opéra comique* origins of several popular French works. These ideas could indicate a fruitful approach in the right place with the right advocates. At the Met, with Bertrand de Billy as their proponent, they have worked out poorly.

I first encountered de Billy at the revival of Zeffirelli's *Carmen*. Musically, it bore a strong resemblance to Märkl's *Trovatore* or Rizzi's *Lucia*—the same feverish dash through all sections of more than moderate tempo, the same lack of weight and richness, the same belittling effect—with a few of the slow lyrical passages (the *Fumée* Chorus, the Act III entr'acte) or accompaniments (Micaëla's aria) evocatively rendered. Clarity and sprightliness are certainly qualities to be prized in this score. As the Met reminded us with its last previous production of the work under Levine (ironically, while trying to present a fairly inclusive edition of the *comique* version, and with the aid of a real director, Peter Hall), *Carmen* can founder and head straight for the bottom quite early in the evening. We don't need more of that. But clarity is effectively negated if the music sprints past before the ear can sort it out; likewise sprightliness if there is no counterweight to it, no depth in the orchestral sound. And of course this was not the *comique* version in a *comique* theatre, but the grand opera one in a grand opera house—surely the plausible choice for this company, though here undercut by niggling cuts and an undersupply of grand-opera vocalism.

If you are in search of lucid textures, elegant phrase shapes, and springy rhythms, you have no better resource than Sir Thomas Beecham. These qualities were always present in his conducting, whether of French music (for which he was justly renowned—try his Franck D Minor), of Haydn, Mozart, or Schubert symphonies, or for that matter the operas of Verdi, Wagner, and Strauss. They are also what enabled him to render uncommonly enjoyable the music of that descriptive lyricist nonpareil, Delius. If you listen to Beecham's well-engineered 1958 studio recording of *Carmen*, you will hear them, as you will his melting, songful treatment of the purely lyric episodes, marked by the distinctive wood and brass timbres of his French orchestra (that of the Radiodiffusion Française). You will also hear the nuance and rubato of his collaboration with a Carmen (Victoria de los Angeles) who knows what she's up to at every moment. But if you are listening with anything resembling de Billy's *Carmen* in your ear, you will be struck first by the reading's spaciousness, its symphonic grandeur and dramatic bite. Those are immediately apparent in the overture—the opening announcement of something about to happen that is both important and exciting, the vigorous build-up to the recapitulation of the Toreador theme, the chilling tremolando and the sforzando attacks of the "Fate" motive and then its suspenseful development to the sudden cutoff before the muttering opening of the scene on the square. And they are present throughout in moments like the sweeping orchestral figures that are coda to the factory women's brawl in Act I (a vista opens up here) or, soon after, the single plosive chord after Zuniga orders Carmen to prison. With Beecham, these gestures are sharp, even startling. Yet they are always proportionate, as are his tempo selections, which allow ample room for the music's flavors and fragrances to emerge. It is in such a context that rhythmic bounce can lend its life and lightness truly sparkle—and so they do.

The foregoing examples are representative, not exceptional. For the past quarter century, sonic presence and dramatic intent have been in retreat from the Met's pit and podium. In the canonical works of the French and Italian repertories, their absence is now a general condition. I have been trying to figure out why this should be so and, even more baffling, why it is not the object of continual critical censure and devotee outrage. Dramatic intent, I will grant, can be heard in many ways. It can lead the ear and reach the heart at almost any tempo, almost any dynamic. Descriptive detail—since it is a kind of specificity—can be mistaken for it, especially when aesthetically seductive. But sonic presence is more objectively determined. And as *tempo juste* means not merely plausible but right, as dramatic specificity means not merely possible but inevitable, sonic presence means not merely audible but unavoidable and constant. It's supposed to be an ongoing state, not an intermittent occurrence. Unless it is established and maintained, nothing, including the subtlest of nuances or the most delicate of evocations, can find its proper place. It is the receptors' most basic right and the performers' first responsibility. Yet its absence is seldom remarked, even on those occasions (Rossini Retro, Bychkov's original Mussorgsky, Rizzi's toy-music *Lucia*) when it is clear that no performance is going to happen without it. Bare audibility, *the fact that the music can be detected*, is being settled for.

Since this absence of presence, a kind of casual withholding, occurs repeatedly under many conductors, it must be asked whether the orchestra itself hasn't something to do with it. I've long been persuaded that it does, though as its default mode has congealed over the seasons, the self-doubts and questionings of sense memory mentioned earlier have more than once assailed me. I have used my experiences with other orchestras and with recordings to keep a grip on my sonic perceptions. But these other orchestras play in other halls and, except for concert opera presentations* in orchestral repertory, while recordings are particularly unreliable with respect to sonic presence. So although these comparisons have often had the effect of confirming my sanity, they aren't exact enough to be definitive. Repeated exposure to another opera orchestra in the same auditorium is required. That's where Gergiev and his Maryinsky come in, bringing with them two sets of useful comparisons: two orchestras playing opera in the same hall, and often under the same conductor.

Three Met performances in a single week firmed up my convictions on this matter. The first of these was the new joint Met/Maryinsky *Mazeppa*. With the same conductor (Gergiev) and three of the same principals (Guryakova, Diadkova, Putilin) in the same hall, it had, to be generous, half the impact of the earlier production (see pp. 54 ff) and seemed twice as long. Much of this loss was attributable to onstage shenanigans that mocked Mazeppa's cathartic scenes, and some to the weak casting of two important roles, Andrei and Orlik. But at least as important (it's hard to prioritize in the coolth of the moment) was the playing. Relative to the Maryinsky's, the Met orchestra's sound was a little lighter and brighter, at some spots slightly more transparent. The score was rendered with high proficiency. Tempos at times seemed marginally quicker than those of Gergiev's Maryinsky reading or its recording, but this may have been a *trompe d'oreille* traceable to the lighter/brighter textures. And at no point did the playing have the intensity, the resounding quality, the sense of engagement with the piece the Maryinsky players had shown from beginning to end. To raise the obvious objection:

---

* Such as: the CSO/Barenboim *Tristan*; the NYPO/Masur *Tristan* excerpts; the NYPO/C. Davis *Béatrice et Benedict*; the BSO/Haitink *Pelléas*; the LSO/C. Davis *Peter Grimes*, all heard in connection with the present study.

Mazeppa is Tchaikovsky, Russian stuff for Russian players. There's something to that, and the same observation could be entered with respect to Gergiev's *Khovanshchina* with both orchestras (the Maryinsky's playing was markedly more urgent and full-blooded), or the St. Petersburg National loading into the State Theatre with *Boris, Golden Cockerel,* and *Queen of Spades* and, whatever the other qualities of their work, making the room sound as it hadn't in a couple of decades. All Russian stuff. But then, *Macbeth* is Italian stuff, and from the first bars of the Maryinsky orchestra's prelude I'd sat up with the thought: *"That's Verdi!"*

Verdi was the composer of the week's other two performances. The operas were *La Forza del destino* and *Luisa Miller,* in repertory revivals much dependent on a spark from the pit. It happens that these operas are preceded by Verdi's two finest formal overtures, extended and elaborately worked *sinfonias*, and thus afford opportunities for listening without distractions from the stage for either ear or eye. With neither conductor (Gianandrea Noseda for *Forza,* Maurizio Benini for *Luisa*) up to anything special, and without the extra rehearsal and extra adrenalin attendant on a new production, there was nothing out of the ordinary about either of these occasions. And that is to my purpose, which is not to single out exceptions, but to account for the ordinary, the playing of habit that whiles away most of a season's auditor-hours. The clearest examples involve the strings.

From the outset, the *Forza* overture was smoothed-over and underaccented. The opening brass chords—the three blasts whose repetitions here and in the opera's first scenes lead us to suppose Verdi is up to something *Flute*-ish, till he suddenly drops the idea—were there, and sort of *forte,* but they were routine announcements, not commands. The entrance of the violins and 'cellos with the obsessive figure we think of as the destiny theme was, as marked, *pianissimo,* but had none of the keeping-the-lid-on quality that makes it electric, and the little swell into the downbeat of its fifth bar, where it's reinforced by the woodwinds, carried no suspenseful charge. Once this treatment of the motive (observed but not animated) had been established, it naturally carried over into its subsequent employments, when it wells up from below as antagonist to melodies associated with peace, mercy, and deliverance (premonitions of Alvaro's *"Le minaccie, i fieri accenti,"* Leonora's *"Deh! Non m'abbandonar, pietà"* and *"Tua grazia, o Dio sorride"*), all very tame in their effect. The theme's final appearance clinched the case. This starts at the beginning of the overture's closing development (letter N of the Dover full score, for anyone checking up). Here, the violins in octaves launch a chattery pattern of eighth-note triplets (*pp, staccato e leggiero*) while the violas, 'cellos, and bassoon reply with repetitions of "destiny." This merry but edgy figure is not taken from any of the score's sung melodies, and is not about peace and mercy. I associate its tone with the forced gaiety of the inn and camp scenes, but this is entirely subjective. What's important is that this is one more effort, in a new mode, to rise above destiny—and the last, as the overture whips up its concluding excitements. The upper strings must bite; the lower with bassoon must burrow. They didn't.

The following evening, the playing of the *Luisa* overture left a similar impression. From the insufficiently brooding introduction of its keystone theme (this piece is not an assemblage of hit tunes, like *Forza's*), it was weakly dramatized. But the defining moment for me was again a violin gesture, a vigorous four-bar descending pattern first introduced at Bar 44, with subsequent repetitions and development. Julian Budden speaks appositely of this overture's similarities in tone and development to that of *Der Freischütz*,[10] and this figure is of a particularly Weberian caste. It has a churning motion suggestive of imbroglio; it tells us the drama of intrigue is underway. As the Met's strings tossed off this figure—impeccably, as usual—I heard no hint of imbroglio or intrigue. I heard insouciance, and taken with the events of the evening before, the matter seemed quite clear: these fine musicians were playing on the surface of the music, as if their idea of what it's about were something far cooler, far less extreme, than it really is. Worry-free—*that's not Verdi!*

Sonic presence has two elements. One is sheer loudness. There are 873,000 cubic feet of air to be moved in the Met's auditorium[11]—far more than in any other musical venue in New York—and though the hall's acoustics are good, it simply takes a heightened output of energy in the form of sound waves from the pit to keep them stirred up. In this space, all dynamic markings need upward revision. The second element, especially important at lower dynamic levels, is what Paul Jackson, referring to the conducting of Dmitri Mitropoulos, calls "kinetic tension,"[12] a term I like because it locates a musical quality in the physical act of playing. But since efforts to make music kinetically tense are likely to produce only an imitative tightness (as with any attempt to evoke a quality for its own sake, in any performance discipline), I return to specific dramatic intent as the source of this element, and in the performances I have been discussing, over a range of E-19 styles under several conductors, I could detect no appetite for searching it out. Among them, Elder's *Otello* stands alone for any fervency of belief, for a measure of emotional consummation. Yet the playing is usually blameless: all is observed, the execution is skillful, aesthetic niceties are present. It's as if the playing were meant to confirm the music's obsolescence—as if the playing were an alibi for ineffectiveness.

To judge by the word on the street and most of what is often written, Gergiev and the Met orchestra have been at loggerheads. Around their collaboration hangs an atmosphere of free-floating complaint: the beat isn't clear, everyone's left swimming, he shows up late and then doesn't address the issues—no less a pejorative than "fraud" has escaped the lips of some who have played and sung with him here. I don't think all this grousing can be dismissed outright, and being late is no good, for sure. Gergiev will never be crowned champion of the clear, consistent beat. Even in complex passages, he leaves many bars more or less at the discretion of his players. He does creepy-crawly things with fingers, hops and bounces, and signals expression with his elbows, shoulders, and face. Stick technique, in short, is not the key to his method (indeed, more often than not there is no stick), and from what one hears of his rehearsal practice, he trusts more in the response of the moment, less in the pre-determined result, than do many conductors. We could say much the same, however, of the loosey-goosey Furtwängler, the jazz-dancing Bernstein, or the converted-cellist Soul Man Rostropovich. We debate their qualities, but no one calls them frauds.[13] And it's odd: not only does Gergiev's own orchestra usually play intensely for him, but excellent and demanding Western ensembles like the Vienna Philharmonic, Rotterdam Philharmonic and, most recently, the London Symphony have responded to him artistically and found his methods compatible enough to sustain productive relationships.

With the Maryinsky, I've heard Gergiev approach the Notperformance threshold only once, with a soggy, thinly sung Berlioz *Roméo et Juliette* at Avery Fisher Hall. Shortly thereafter, I heard a splendid Tanglewood evening (Rachmaninoff's *The Bells* and the Tchaikovsky 6th—the latter substantially more powerful than an Ozawa/BSO traversal in the Shed three seasons earlier, which was by no means shabby), and most recently some terrific Shostakovich with the Rotterdam. Between these, his readings of several operas during the Maryinsky's Met visits.

With the Met's orchestra, on the other hand, I've heard Gergiev lift the level and hold it only twice, once in *The Queen of Spades* when the production was new (a revival performance was still solid, but the edge was off) and once in *Lady Macbeth of Mzensk* (Shostakovich clearly a Gergiev strength, with the orchestra clearly eager to engage). In his Wagner (*Parsifal* and *Die Walküre*) I have heard some fine passages (a really eloquent *Walküre* Act III), but have not been consistently persuaded of his ear for melodic line or depth of color. His *Salome* struck me as rather pushed and unsensuous, not unlike some of Böhm's late Strauss and Wagner performances, and his *Otello* somewhat the same.* Even that great mass of Russian stuff, *War and Peace*, was not as sharply pointed as I had hoped, or the tensions of its personal scenes (like the Natasha/Ahrosimova confrontation) quite driven home. I enter these reservations by way of conceding that I don't necessarily think that Gergiev's affinities extend across the whole repertory, or that failings in his performances are invariably the orchestra's fault.

I muse on Musin, whose ideas (from what we can learn of them) so directly address the lacks I often feel. There's a gap between such ideas and those of our technically splendid players. Temirkanov, whose work I have liked on the few occasions I've heard it (once with the Baltimore Symphony, twice with the NYPO, once with his own St. Petersburg Philharmonic, and most recently with Rome's Santa Cecilia) has not conducted at the Met, and whatever Musin's influence may have been, his technique is in any case more conventional than Gergiev's. But our view of him as "famously difficult to predict" (see n. 2) describes the same gap. And might that not also account, at least in part, for the puzzlement of Bychkov's Met *Boris*? I cannot say, but for me two things are clear: the Maryinsky orchestra—formerly Temirkanov's, now Gergiev's—plays E-19 opera with more full-blooded sound and keener dramatic intent than the Met's; and despite all the caveats entered above, in certain non-Russian stuff (Wagner, for sure) the Met's own ensemble under Gergiev sometimes reaches heights neither attained nor striven for in the measured, rational aesthetic of James Levine.

Levine's dominance at the Met is bound to lessen from now on. But his influence, like that of deconstruction on production, will endure for many years to come. In any case, he is of interest here less as an individual personality or interpreter (I find him elusive in these capacities, in any case) than as a summation of the aesthetic qualities enumerated earlier and their acceptance as a standard. I would not dream of questioning his work ethic, his musical command, or his impact on the technical capacities of his orchestra. But it has been many years since anything in his work excited me, moved me, or surprised me.† He is, for me, the shining knight of the blameless

---

* I saw the *Salome* early in the run, and should note that a friend given to clocking performances (the same friend who'd filled me in on Bychkov) reported that by the end of the run, six minutes had been added to the reading. Whether or not this made the performance correspondingly better he neglected to say. But performances do change, and if the added minutes meant increased expansiveness and lushness without slackened suspense, then this one improved.

† I do not mean that during this time I have never been excited or moved at a performance led by Levine (look at all the music that would take in), but that I have not been so affected by anything attributable to him—that the emotional experience of the music has been weakened, not strengthened, by his presence.

Notperformance. And since the Met orchestra is by now his creation in as full a sense as this can ever be said of a conductor and ensemble, he is inescapably the fashioner of the predilections I have been discussing. Yet over a span of thirty-five years in this allegedly tough-minded, foul-mouthed city, scarcely a harsh word has been spoken or written about him and his players. New York critics have formed an honor guard around him, their responses ranging from routine small-arms salutes to the occasional panegyric rocket. Amongst the audience, the postperformance pep rally is a nightly drill; dissenters skulk silently into the night. I am forced to the conclusion that blameless Notperformance is the operatic event of choice. People (at least the tastemakers and tonesetters among them) *like* it. I am nonplused.

Here I must enter a confession: I'm not an unreserved fan of the Cleveland Orchestra. I admire it tremendously—superb musicians, a crack ensemble, et cetera. I just don't find its way with the music I care about deeply to be as satisfying as the ways of a number of other American and European orchestras, including some of lower standing. This has been true as long as I can remember. While this doesn't take us back quite to the Ohio sojourns of Rodzinski or Leinsdorf, and I am not an orchestra omnivore like my Bychkov/*Salome* informant, I've heard the Cleveland from time to time under all its music directors from George Szell on, and the characteristics that hold my engagement to admiration level have remained remarkably close to constant. My latest encounters with the Cleveland were under Christoph von Dohnányi (his New York farewell as its music director) and his successor, Franz Welser-Möst. Dohnányi's program comprised Strauss's *Metamorphosen* and Beethoven's Ninth Symphony. In shorthand, I would term the performances quick and dry—beautifully articulated, but the Strauss missing the undertow that draws us deep and the Beethoven lacking suspense and weight in I, and the urgent striving that would have made IV more than a neat speedthrough. The Welser-Möst concert left me glum. Roy Harris's tough, assertive Third, one of my favorite American symphonies, sounded nice and reasonable—in other words, useless. And around it were sounded well-ordered retreats from Beethoven's second and third piano concertos. Radu Lupu, installed at the keyboard with the infuriating unruffled-guru physicality he has perfected, played them like cocktail music, tickling the ivories for your listening pleasure. I suppose one can get away with an argument about the Second concerning its classical balance, its Apollonian qualities, and so forth. An argument, not a performance in Carnegie Hall, any attempt at which would need bounce and bones. And I know the cadenza is a strange piece of writing, but it must be up to *something* more than doodling. And the *Third*? And the *Fourth*, to which Lupu had administered the same treatment with Maazel and the NYPO a couple of seasons earlier? This isn't a "view" of Beethoven or of the stylistic progression through the concertos; it's a restraint on the music, passed off as a virtue. The orchestra provided an accompaniment well mated with the solo playing—discreet, balanced, and lovely—once again, useless.

The Cleveland Orchestra has never been more celebrated than on the occasion of these Welser-Möst concerts, in both the major reviews and a *New Yorker* article by Charles Michener.[14] Most of the qualities extolled are ones I can recognize, elevated to the status of objects of veneration. ("Effortlessness," "ease and naturalness," "velvety smoothness, pristine intonation," "elegant," "extraordinary precision, transparency, and balance," with Pierre Boulez's "crisp, understated style . . . much favored by the orchestra." Also noted are the band's versatility and adaptability, its readiness to take on anything. With the exception of the Boulez characterization (I can go along with "crisp," but "understated" is way off) all these attributions are, I think, just. One other, though, puzzles me, and that is a view of the Cleveland (widely held, according to Michener) as "the most 'European' of the American orchestras." On this matter, it would appear, I have an ally: Les Dreyer, who calls the notion "questionable."[15] Dreyer, though, frames the issue purely as one of ethnic composition, which isn't quite what Michener is driving at.* Michener proposes that of the American Big Five, the Cleveland ". . . is the only one with a collective identity . . . a sustained consistent approach . . . that illuminates whatever they happen to be playing . . . whoever happens to be conducting them . . . the only one that is distinctive and refined enough to stand alongside the two preëminent European ensembles: the Berlin Philharmonic and the Vienna Philharmonic."

Refined? Certainly. A consistent approach and collective identity? In a sense, yes—that would relate to the historical constancy I've noticed. Distinctive? Exactly not. Even in the Szell era, the Cleveland was where one went for an objective view, a sort of neutral corner one could retreat to after a few rounds with the BSO of the Koussevitsky/Munch years, the Stokowski/Ormandy Philadelphia, the Reiner/Solti CSO, or the Mitropoulos/Bernstein NYPO. Nevertheless, under Szell the orchestra's string texture was sinewy, contrapuntal gestures strongly limned, rhythmic structures sharply profiled. There was a boldness, a sometimes severe clarity. All that has been softened. That leaves a collective identity consisting of the sum of the press descriptions quoted above, which really equal the *absence* of a recognizable characteristic, an identifiable sound or orchestral personality. Of the Big Five, the Cleveland

---

* It is, however, to the point in the case of Dreyer's own orchestra. The presence of many Continental musicians in the Met's pit of forty and fifty years back assured a core of players brought up in the European theatre tradition, and familiar with the repertory in native-language renditions.

is the most anonymous, the one that's pinned down only by elimination. *European*, as from Vienna or Berlin? I have not heard the Vienna Philharmonic live recently enough to be sure, but at last hearing the Berlin Philharmonic under Rattle played Sibelius and Schubert with a deep-throated string sound and burnished brass that belong to no American orchestra, least of all the Cleveland (in my experience, the Chicago under Barenboim, and sometimes the NYPO under Masur, would come the closest), yet had all the brilliant edge, lucidity, and precision in Heiner Goebbels' *Aus einem Tagebuch* that the great American orchestras bring to such pieces. Any other Continental or British group? Not (to stay with orchestras I've heard in the past few seasons) the Rotterdam or St. Petersburg or Maryinsky, the Oslo Philharmonic or London Philharmonic or London Symphony. Going back further, to include others? None that I can think of.

It is the anonymity that is being praised, like the colorlessness or "purity" of audiophile loudspeakers, as if an orchestra (or any interpretive entity) were supposed to be a transparent medium through which artistic matter passes untouched. Let this ideal not be confused with the interpretive humility of which I have spoken. A willingness to work within interpretive bounds does not imply extinction of personhood. The great conductors named earlier *all* strove to render music in the spirit of its composers, but all left their stamp on it, the "*com'è scritto*" proponents no less than others. That is because they committed *their selves*, as men in full, to the task. They were wholly present in the music, not at an "unbiased" remove from it. And they took their orchestras with them. The idea that if an orchestra gets out of the way, something called "the music" will come through is absurd. All that happens is that the music gets out of the way, too.

In any case, it is impossible: absolute transparency does not exist. Nor can character or color be washed clean away. The Cleveland has its astonishing ease and elegance. But the only music in which ease and elegance come first is the sort for which one lights a candle and pours a glass of wine, not the sort for which one buys a ticket and climbs the balcony stairs. And the Cleveland is not truly colorless, either. It is tan, a very light tan.

The qualities of the Cleveland would be of no consequence here were it not for the fact that it was to that orchestra that the young James Levine, deemed a prodigy by all who'd worked with him, was attached as Associate Conductor at the outset of his career, appointed to the post by Szell. Levine had other teachers and mentors, of course, and was already a developed talent; caution with respect to influence is in order here, as with Musin and his pupils. Nonetheless, it's undisputed that Levine shared important musical sympathies with Szell, and that these were reinforced by his contact with the older master. Szell had a deep and detailed knowledge of how to make things work in an orchestra, and of how to apply such knowledge to problems of musical balance and structure. He was a great believer in arriving at interpretation on purely musical terms— i.e., without much use of story lines, imagery, dramatization, illustrative analogy, or emotional personalization, to list a few "extramusical" incitements— and of achieving his musical aims through technical exactitude. He strove above all for clarity, both spatial and temporal, and laid great emphasis on chair-to-chair, choir-to-choir listening, in the manner of chamber musicians. (His views were admirably summarized in an extended conversation with Paul Henry Lang, the only writer of the time I can call to mind who was qualified by background and working knowledge to conduct such an interview.[16])

The chamber-music paradigm has been a guiding star for Levine, attested to by his own declarations and those of his players.[17] And who will argue against clarity, against mutual responsiveness or intimacy? It's a question of priorities, and actually it strikes me as strange that this ideal of the "sensational, huge chamber group" should be given primacy with the pit orchestra of a grand opera company. In that setting, what is most often needed is either the firm impelling support of relatively uncomplicated accompanimental gestures and textures, or unified, massive (but controlled) sonorities to underpin dramatically charged passages and big ensembles. Not every orchestral note should be heard for itself, or every linear strand teased out, or every vertical texture rendered sheer; it's the singing that's meant to stand out. It might seem (and the case is often made) that chamberish playing will help the singing stand out. But that isn't what happens. What happens is that ear-concentration is drawn toward interplay *within the orchestra*, toward *its* elucidations and refinements, which sound lovely and deferential, but in their demure way coax constantly for attention.

It is true that Szell and other conductors of his time and place had chamber playing and listening in their musical upbringing. (Walter, for instance, played and wrote chamber music in his early professional years.) But this cannot possibly have been as formative for most of them as their operatic experience, their day-to-day work in the theatre. Lang and Szell discuss this in their conversation. Noting that Szell ". . . like practically all great conductors . . . grew up in the opera pit," Lang wonders if the talented young conductors Szell has mentored (Levine soon to be one of them) will be able to acquire ". . . the ultimate in technical finish without that hard but priceless schooling of the opera house?" Szell guesses not, and the two go on to agree about the things that can be learned in an opera pit and nowhere else. They define these as accompanimental flexibility and ". . . a readiness for any emergency in fractions of a second." Observing that a symphony orchestra is "less yielding" because the players know "they are the protagonists," Szell says that ". . . every pit orchestra knows that they are basically subordinate. They have to go with what is happening onstage."

Szell and Lang, then, have no difficulty recognizing the benefits of opera experience, even for symphony musicians and conductors. What their "pure music" credo will not acknowledge is that for both players and conductors, growing up in an opera pit means far more than acquiring accompanying skills and rescue-squad chops; it means that all those anathematized "extra-musical" story-and-character-related tropes are bred in the bone as ways of thinking, feeling, and working. Some conductors will embrace them for life in the making of any music, and others disavow or re-name them. But no one can sensibly proscribe them in opera.

In the U.S. the symphony orchestra, not the opera company, is in most cities the central performing-arts institution, both artistically and socially. Practically no one grows up in the opera pit, or looks to it for either financial stability or artistic satisfaction. Theatre usages are ill-learned, and tend to be thought of as (in Szell's unfortunate terminology) "subordinate." Few aspire to that. The young Levine was something of an exception—he *wanted* to conduct opera. It was just that at the time of his Met debut he had not had much opportunity to do so, and that he came to it from a place and time in which "pure music" orchestral habits of mind had been formed, and modernist musical aesthetics, with their emphasis on structural and coloristic lucidity, were in the ascendant. A place and time in which "absolute-music" assumptions were taken into the world of opera, rather than operatic assumptions into the world of absolute music.

Chamber-music listening and response is not, I am sure, intended to compromise the presence and solidity of the orchestra's sound—"huge" and "sensational" are meant to see that it doesn't. But a huge ensemble concerned first with chamberlike interplay and precision plays differently—less hugely— than one that doesn't, and the tonal ideal comes to mean something different, too—something exquisite. These qualities were not new to the Met orchestra. Karajan, in particular, had worked for them in the two completed installments of his projected *Ring*, and with notable results: in my hearing, the sheer beauty of the Met orchestra's playing had never been equaled before and has been only once since,* while the relative subtlety of the sound always had a

---

* In *Cavalleria Rusticana* under Bernstein, a couple of years later—very slow and lingeringly descriptive, not unlike Karajan's own take on the same score with La Scala, but more sustained and a bit less rarified. *Cavalleria* holds an attraction for some conductors one might not associate with it. Bernstein took it on while leaving *Pagliacci* in other hands; Mahler thought highly of it, too.

sense of dramatic latency, and there was no lack of sonic presence when the full forces were summoned. But of course Karajan's version of the paradigm was informed by his own ear, cultivated on the darker colors, more cohesive textures, and stronger gravitational pull of Austro-German and Central European orchestras (first and foremost Furtwängler's Berlin Philharmonic, inheritance of which he coveted and won) and guided by long theatre experience. Levine's ear is quite different. If it had an antecedent, I suppose it would be Szell's, but its soundstage has no ancestry. "Soundstage" is another audiophile concept,* appropriate here because as soon as Levine began to have a recognizable effect on the Met sound, the image that recurred for me as I tried to place it came not from any previous experience of live performance, but from recordings: the orchestra began to sound like '60s stereo, and not the very best of it.

When, in what has long been one of my favorite bits of characterization, Hans Keller proposed as Furtwängler's epitaph: "He was the opposite of a gramophone record,"[18] he was referring to the record's changelessness, its representation of interpretation as something fixed and repeated. He was also, at least by implication, joining Furtwängler in attacking the idea of interpretation as something that could be perfected, made blameless. Changelessness and blamelessness are, in part, what I'm speaking of when I invoke '60s stereo, but though Levine well represents them, they are hardly unique to him. I am referring primarily to the orchestral sound itself. It inclined toward the clean, bright coloration favored by the "hi-fi" ear. Its frequency center was shifted from the lower midrange to the upper, where there was a bit of a blare. The texture, too, was similar to that of a multi-miked heavily highlighted recording designed to show what stereo can do—a sort of exposé of the score's workings. Sometimes this had the desirable effect of undoing textural knots or penetrating thick orchestrations. More often, it reduced sounds of some complexity and mystery to pure, simple components which, because they could now openly declare their pure, simple selves, gave listeners an illusion of "seeing through" the music, and so "understanding" it. All told, this ear for color and texture reminded me less of Szell's or Karajan's than of Erich Leinsdorf's, especially as conveyed on his RCA Victor recordings with the BSO or the Roman opera orchestras.[19]

To the stereophonic soundstage, the parsing of the vertical dimension, and the color separations of Levine's orchestral ear, we must add his particular sense of the exquisite. It is heard mostly in the strings, though woodwind

---

* It refers to the dimensionality of sound, beginning with its horizontal channel distribution and sense of "air" around instruments, and proceeding to perceptions of depth and height.

lyricism also partakes of it, and is most easily recognized in Wagnerian guise: contemplative, softly singing passages like the *Lohengrin* prelude, the Good Friday Spell in *Parsifal*, the opening of the final scene of *Siegfried*, or the slow ascent through the string choirs of the *Meistersinger* Act III prelude, pull us into a shining cloud, as if to hold us there. The Levinian exquisite is closely related to the silken sound Karajan cultivated, but is brighter and cleaner, and does not give one the creeps as Karajan's did when the rhythmic bone went out of it. At first, it can seem the ultimate realization of the exquisite sought by all good orchestras in such passages, but in time its gradations of refinement become too much the point, a sort of aesthetic preening that, once recognized, engenders grudging surrender or outright resistance.

These modernist ways of hearing texture and color—even this dwelling on the exquisite in descriptive moments—do not necessarily render music inactive. That happens in the horizontal dimension, in time. Here tempo again rears its head, and must again be dismissed. "Too slow" is the sole demerit occasionally entered for a Levine reading. But though some Levine performances (*Parsifal, Les Troyens, Faust,* parts of the *Ring*) do feel as if they'll never end and are in fact slow, tempo is not the primary cause of the embalmed effect he creates. It's his infernal ongoingness.

In the years immediately following his impressive Met debut (*Tosca*, 1971), Levine's rhythmic drive and sharp ear for articulation and balance spruced up the orchestra. Among his own readings, the best results came in Verdi (e.g., *Vespri*, the early *Otello*s), but in terms of the playing there was also an overall uptick in alacrity and élan. Yet within a dozen years or so, the roots of blameless Notperformance had taken hold. They were hard to trace, for many virtues were intact; all was shipshape. But the more Levine brought his work and his orchestra under control and the more comfortable everyone grew with one another, the more the music failed to register. It went by, but it didn't happen. I searched for clues in rhythmic slackness or structural vagueness, but didn't find them there—things were moving, the structure was clear. Then, one *Meistersinger* evening, a subliminally awaited moment turned up missing. By "subliminally awaited" I mean the sort of moment we take for granted—not one of the obvious testing points in a score, but one of the transitions that keeps the ear/eye story going and, whether subtly or crudely, to charming or irritating effect, always occurs because it's so elementary. About an hour into Act I, Walter concludes his first stab at a trial song ("*Am stillen Herd*") with what he hopes is a persuasive flourish. All hangs in suspense: what do the mastersingers think? Beckmesser puts a leading question ("What do you make of the effusion?") and Vogelgesang (tenor) ventures "Well, it's nervy," which can be interpreted pro or con. Otherwise, baffled silence. The bassoon sticks its head in with a cranky low A. Two beats of total silence, one plunk of string pizzicato, then Nachtigall (bass) with his throat-clearing *"Merkwürd'ger Fall!"* ("Remarkable case!"). As he lands on the downbeat with *"Fall!"* there's a change of meter (from three to four—we're in march rhythm now) and note value. Violins and violas begin a steady holding pattern of staccato eighths (*"Gemessen"*—"measured"—reads the marking), and a bar later the doublebasses sneak in from below, also staccato, with the ascending second half of the mastersingers' motif. Kothner rises to restore parliamentary order. A new beat, a new scenic movement, has begun.

Many elements, visual and aural, go into the making of this moment, but their final effect must be of a pregnant pause followed by a new action. It was only a few bars later, during Beckmesser's self-introduction as Marker, that I realized that the pause had not been pregnant, and no new action had begun—we were merely farther along. Inattention was not the problem: in my unease with yet another performance whose faults did not account for its neutrality, I'd been scanning closely with eye and ear. Yet we'd still slipped through. Neither stage nor pit had played its role, let alone together. We were missing not only the illusion that must always be sought in the theatre (that the music is actually being generated by the stage reality), but its more commonly encountered second-best obverse as well (the stage action dictated by the music, from the podium). No version of the moment had taken place.

I began tracking Levine performances with such moments in mind. A subsequent *Meistersinger* confirmed the original's musical shortfall: the bassoon blew a good note, but with nothing cranky or intrusive in it; the pizzicato didn't tell; the staccatos had no tension, and the doublebass entrance was insufficiently assertive. A close comparison of Levine's *Parsifal* with other readings for videographic purposes[20] revealed a genius for smoothing all wrinkles—the music flows like cooling lava. Here are a few of my notes from the *Tristan*, compiled in hot blood (mine) from theatre and video impressions, somewhat resequenced to focus on orchestral performance, and with explanatory commentary in brackets: [Opening of Prelude]: "Sounds are so sweet, how could one object? L. luxuriating—almost a Mantovani sound, 'lyrical,' discreetly throbbing. Upward rush of strings: not a chance. [This refers to the repeated string figure that begins at the third bar of p. 13 (Dover orchestral score) and leads into the prelude's climactic fortissimo (final bar of p. 18). The "upward rush" is created not by pressing on the tempo* but by overlapping repetitions of triplet thirty-seconds that gradually mount in pitch; by a

---

* Felix Mottl, the editor of this score, who certainly knew Wagner's wishes and had the advantage of lengthy performance experience to guide him, enjoins broadening, not quickening.

controlled buildup of volume that finally lets out; by allowing each phrase to crest at the top; by string playing that dives into the meat of the tone; and above all by a rhythmic sweep to the gesture that releases its soaring, surging quality. Levine and his players are fine with overlapping and containing, but not with cresting, diving, soaring or surging.] [At the end of the prelude]: "Nothing." [Literally. The five wonderful bars in the low strings that capture both the sway of the ship and the tension of the situation as the curtain goes up were not just *pp*, they were all but inaudible in the theatre—not present, not setting the scene. This is even detectable on the video. A singer would call the sound "unsupported."]

Then, in Act I: "Sforzandos under *"Hört meinen Willen, zagende Winde!"* etc. don't burn . . . the violins' *'Sehr feurig'* doesn't guide into Isolde's *'Er schwur mit tausend Eiden'* . . . this all just rattles on . . . *these tempos not slow* . . . (emphasis added) L. doesn't find the character of a given episode, for instance, Brangäne's plea after the Curse, and then her *'Wo lebt der Mann'* [where the] orch. has none of the wheedling, coaxing quality to support her . . . or the [sense of] warning, foreboding in the woodwinds at *'Kennst du die Mutter Künste nicht?'* . . . Beginning of Sc. 5 [this is Tristan's entrance]: Strings a strange timbre, not beautiful, trying to be 'savage,' but not biting in a meaningful way, just steely, while brass and winds fail to burn through . . ." A comment overheard at the first intermission: "There's no line, one thing doesn't connect with the next." It's only an anecdote of anonymous hearsay, but the hearsayer was listening well: musical line and dramatic throughline are not always the same, and neither is the same as ongoingness.

My notes on Acts II and III include observations on an exquisitely shallow sounding of the Act III prelude and a rendition of the famous English horn solo that recalled the country fiddle of *Susannah*, that is, aesthetically irreproachable but entirely innocent of its dramatic purpose as a call, a message on a shepherd's horn, keening across the open air. There's nothing to be gained from extending the list; it is best summarized as a record of abstraction and extraction, of careful delineation of the outlines of events in endless succession, none of which is allowed its full impact. *Tristan* sweet and lovely, smoothly joined at every juncture, evened-out and tamed—the last things *Tristan* should be. Or, as another skulking dissenter muttered afterward, "No part of the *Tristan* experience."

This ongoingness, this passing-along of the music like a length of rope, each of its little twists noted (you will never catch Levine unobservant) but never grasped and felt, is for me the definitive Levinian frustration, by no means confined to Wagner.[21] Because ongoingness and exquisiteness are reifications of virtues prized by all musicians and receptors, namely, legato line and tonal beauty, they come closest to explaining why Levine is so easy to praise, so hard to blame, and why the feeling of emptiness is so hard to account for.

There is, finally, his artistic relationship to onstage performers, most of whom love working under him. Like orchestral musicians, they appreciate his clarity and exactitude; they also find him an understanding, supportive accompanist, sensitive to rubato and attuned to the singer's state. This is doubtless often to the good of a performance. As with his ongoingness and exquisiteness, Levine's accompanimental sensibility is congruent with a genuine virtue, and one that mustn't be undervalued in a time when few upscale maestros display any intimacy with voices or willingness to bend with them. There's a difference, though, between a sympathetic collaboration with an artist of like temperament and the Mahler/Walter aspiration of putting one's heart onstage, of inhabiting "the most opposite of characters," of being an actor while conducting; between musical collaboration and dramatic leadership. Levine's accompanimental tendencies first crystallized for me on an occasion when he was actually playing the accompaniment, for Christa Ludwig's 1976 traversal of Schubert's *Die Winterreise* at the Met. Ludwig is surely one of the two or three best female *Lieder* singers of the past half-century. At this time, though, she had recently pulled back from her high-mezzo/dramatic soprano forays and, in this hall of huge, sensational unsuitability, was singing a demanding cycle written for male voice[22] rather cautiously, in contralto-ish keys. To have any hope of registering with these songs, she needed an accompanist who either would encourage her to sing out more boldly, more operatically, and possibly in higher keys or (if that were really too risky) to search out every sharpness of accent, impel every rhythm, project every decided-upon articulation (and there are many to decide, the markings being so few) to draw us into the world of the music. Instead, he just fitted in and purled along, always refined and tasteful, sometimes (as at the opening of *Frühlingstraum*) exquisite—like, come to think of it, a more genial twin of Lupu. As with his conducting, his technical capacities were never in doubt.

From many potential examples of Levine's singer/conductor collaborations (chosen, I must stipulate, with special attention to ongoingness), two will serve. As with Notperformance, I've selected instances involving highly gifted singers capable of carrying out their intentions, so that the performances involved "succeed" on their own terms. The first is Mephistophélès' serenade, "*Vous qui faites l'endormie,*" as rendered by René Pape. To Levine's somnolent, spiritless trek through Gounod's score, Pape provided the occasional hotfoot. But the serenade, taken as *some* sort of opportunity by generations of bassos, passed without notice—the *Meistersinger* Moment, expanded to aria form. Pape is the one bass on the current international scene with the upper-range poise and dynamic control, the well-oiled legato, to insinuate the song in the *basse chantante* manner, along with the size of voice to make such an approach present in the Met auditorium. And it's fine with me if we forego the imitation histrionics that, in imitation, sound so hollow. Pape vocalized well, of course—smoothly, effortlessly, stretching nothing, point-ing nothing, as if to say "No big deal." Levine's accompaniment agreed: no derisive cut from the woodwind staccatos, no threat or giggle in the scurry-ing string pizzicatos, or suggestive pulse in the bowed accompaniment. From big deal to no deal. Why bother?

The Pape/Levine *Faust* excerpt illustrates an ongoingness wherein an entire number (indeed a "highlight") is passed over by sleight-of-ear. My second example is of internal ongoingness, wherein the features of a number are blurred. It affords a recorded comparison, and refers us back to a live per-formance already spoken of: Reneé Fleming's Susannah. Susannah's second song, "The Trees on the Mountains," makes the distinction that interests me here. It is a strophic piece in 6/8 with modest variations, in the style of an Appalachian folk ballad on the abandoned-maiden theme. Everything about it, from its plaintive C-minor melody to its spare but suggestive accompani-ment (lute-like harp arpeggios at the start, with prominent woodwind colors later), urges a direct, unsophisticated rendition. The sole peculiarity in its layout is a recurring pattern of pauses (commas for the slight ones, fermatas for the more decisive), contrasted with continuation through the normal line breaks of the text in the following measures. Of these pauses, the fermatas (six, all told, of this sort) are by far the most important. They linger mourn-fully just before upbeats; then the motion of the song picks up again and the voice sings on through. This device, together with the other logical resting points (sentence endings in the words, quarter notes in the music) alters the otherwise predictable scansion of the stanzas, so that (taking the first eight bars as example) instead of:

> The trees on the mountains are cold and bare.
> The summer jes' vanished an' left them there.
> Like a false-hearted lover jes' like my own
> Who made me love him, then left me alone.

we have:

> The trees on the mountains are cold and bare.
> The summer jes' vanished,

An' left them there like a false-hearted lover,
Jes' like my own,
Who made me lo-ove him . . . (beat)
Then left me alone.

The eight-bar repetitions give the piece the ritualistic feel of an old song often sung; the frequent breaks create the short-breathed phrases characteristic of folk song; the little scansion device lends a slightly irregular feel; and the fermatas provide the sort of simple narrative effect—tarrying for a bit of suspense, then pressing on with a refrain—that the singers of such songs delight in.

Fleming's recording of the song with Levine and his orchestra is full of misplaced ongoingness and exquisiteness. Intrabar rubatos abound. The fermatas are very prettily suspended on their vowels, then given little nudges just before their final consonants and deftly *carried over* into the upbeats. Descending intervals are almost invariably caressed with gentling portamentos. The pore baby fox whose mama jes' left him is commiserated with in the brush of whisper that has become the all-purpose *effetto* of the contemporary female singer. Except for the range-stretching flights of "Come back, o summer," etc., the voice is never let out. It's a really high-quality supper-club styling of a folk song arrangement, by a singer whose voice has the classical extension. Levine's accompaniment is hand-in-glove. The basic tempo, though slow, would be *juste* if the implication of "andante" (that we do, after all, proceed) were adhered to; but the stylings are so accommodated that the piece loiters. The woodwind flavors are soothingly folded into the creamy string batter. Shore is a pretty night (yawn).

My comparison comes from a 1962 live performance by the role's creator, Phyllis Curtin. Here, phrases are not fussed over. There are no downward portamentos; the line is etched, not pampered. "Pore" occasions not a whisper, but a passing moment of bleak straightness. And every fermata is a brief full stop—a bar is broadened, a note is held, and then a poised pause before the pickup, with the pungent final consonants (n, m, the American r) binding off those lengths of rope before moving on.

There's the piece, there's the woman. She's never been in a supper club, and hasn't heard *"Ah, non credea"* or *"O quante volte."* Curtin's interpretation isn't a styling because it's inside the style, heartfelt but plain. It has less subtlety than the Fleming/Levine version, but sharper profile. Though less ongoing, it moves better, owing to its stronger definition and its relative freedom from expressive dawdlings. The voice itself is firmer and more boldly projected; it hasn't all the lyrical warmth of Fleming's, but more spine.

The accompaniment is by the New Orleans Opera Orchestra under Knud Andersson, whose tempo, no quicker than Levine's, is less rubato-prone. The woodwinds stand out, plangent and (to borrow a word from the text) sere, and the strings, leaner than the Met's, don't luxuriate around them. Recording circumstances can account for some of the differences in tone and balance, but not in movement or in overall feel, less plush than Levine's and far better suited to the piece and the character singing it.

In none of these cases (Ludwig/Levine, Pape/Levine, Fleming/Levine) do I have any knowledge of how agreements were arrived at. They sound easy and natural, in the manner of couples with like leanings who have become each other's enablers—everything's too comfortable and too much is taken for granted to stir anything up. In this connection there are two interesting paragraphs in Fleming's appealing vocal memoir.[23] One concerns Levine, the other Gergiev. In the first, Fleming speaks of discussing with Levine ". . . the difference between a performance upon which interpretive elements and emotions are placed and a performance in which those elements are relayed to the audience in a way that feels natural and organic." Apart from observing that the Fleming/Levine "The Trees on the Mountains" surely belongs to the first of these categories, what strikes me about the passage (the quote is an excerpt) is its tone—respectful but neutral, noncommittal, and abstract.* The Gergiev paragraph, in contrast, is downright electric: ". . . virility . . . that I find gutsy and exciting . . . I'll sing more passionately . . . a much more strongly rhythmic reading than what I'm used to . . .", etc. She terms their artistic sensibilities (hers and Gergiev's) "complementary." It's as if she knows that though her propensities fall in easily with Levine's, she becomes a more engaged performer when challenged by a stronger, wilder temperament. That certainly squares with my observation.

James Levine's ear for the clarity of structures, for color separations—for the transparency of all sonic materials—marks him as a modernist. The composers he has chosen to champion with the Met orchestra in concert, and now with the BSO (Schoenberg, Carter, Wuorinen, Babbitt, Harbison), further reinforce this definition. (Indeed, except for Harbison, these are creators from the intellectually gnarly side of modernism.) It could also be said that Levine's ongoingness bespeaks a postmodernist sense (rather Glassish, in fact) of musical continuity as a flow of minimally differentiated events, of

---

* Unless I've missed something (there is no index), it's also the only mention of Levine in the book. I don't want to read too much into this, but in a volume devoted specifically to its author's artistic development and replete with generous comment on teachers, conductors, directors, coaches, and colleagues she has worked with, it's more than slightly odd.

moments always becoming, of meanings forever deferred. As for the Levinian exquisite, it unquestionably betrays an aesthetic concern that would seem to be a premodern artifact. But it presents not a beauty of sensual excitation or emotional conquest, but a loveliness that poses for aesthetic admiration; it falls not into a sentimentality of feeling, but into one of sensory refinement. This sounds like a strangely shaped ear, attuned to the modern in space, the postmodern in time, sweetened by a susceptibility to the dulcet accord. But of course it's not strange at all. It's the stereotypical contemporary high-culture ear, which is what I meant when I termed Levine and his orchestra "mainstream."

And is there something *wrong* with this contemporary ear? In opera, plenty, for hardly any of opera's renewable works (least of all E-19's) benefit from the abstraction, objectification, and anonymity, the dramatic and emotional reticence it favors. In its fashion, such an ear loves music as music and opera as music, but does not hear opera as opera. And it's happy that way.

As for the orchestra this ear has groomed, it is indeed superior in many ways. Like the Cleveland, it stands ready to take on anything, to make light of any musical or technical problem. Even in its standard-repertory Notperformance groove, it executes well most of the time—misadventures like the *Trovatore* and *Lucia* are less frequent than they once were. But since presence and dramatic awareness are so often lacking, this advance is on many evenings only a formality. The encomiums rain down, but (to compare best with best) does this band truly improve on the old in *Salome* or *Tosca* under Mitropoulos? *Tannhäuser* or *Rosenkavalier* or *Meistersinger* under Kempe? *Wozzeck* or *Fidelio* or *Holländer* under Böhm? *Samson* or *Faust* under Monteux? Verdi or Mussorgsky under Solti? Is everybody crazy?

NOTES

1. As quoted by Alan Riding: "Audiences Love a Minimalist 'Ring' Cycle; Critics Aren't Sure," NYT, Nov. 2, 2005.

2. See the NYT's unsigned obituary of Musin, June 14, 1999; also John Ardoin: *Valery Gergiev and the Kirov*, Amadeus Press, 2001, especially pp. 20-22 (on Musin) and pp. 166-167 (on the Musin/Temirkanov/Gergiev connection). Caution is called for in ascribing teacher/pupil influence in any artistic discipline. And it's true that for nearly a century Stanislavski has been appealed to as the acting authority by performers and commentators who hadn't the slightest idea what it would mean to actually pursue his ways of working; they have only wanted to appear serious about acting. Musin, however, does appear to have had distinct notions about conducting to which Stanislavski's techniques were relevant, and to have conveyed them strongly to a loyal "school" of students that has included some major maestros. He wrote a book on conducting and a memoir, neither of which I have seen. For reasons evidently related to his Jewishness and political nonconformity, he lost out to Yevgeni Mravinsky for conductorship of the Leningrad Philharmonic, and his long teaching career represents both an artistic and a political unorthodoxy. (For a faint echo of this, see Temirkanov's remarks on Mravinsky in Anne Midgette: "A Russian Conductor Famously Difficult to Predict Comes to Carnegie Hall," NYT, Sept. 29, 2005.) To anyone interested in the milieu from which Musin sprang (he arrived in St. Petersburg in 1919), I can commend two fascinating volumes. The first is Sergei Levik's *The Levik Memoirs: An Opera Singer's Notes* (Symposium Records, 1995, Edward Morgan, trans., with accompanying CD). Levik was a baritone who sang in St. Petersburg and the Russian provinces in the prerevolutionary decade and a few years beyond, and remained involved in the Soviet musical scene for many years following his relatively short career. His lengthy, detailed account, based on diary notations, is one of the few singers' memoirs to incorporate professional knowledge, acuteness of observation, and freedom from self-glorification in sufficient measure to be of use. The second is Oliver M. Sayler's *The Russian Theatre*, 2nd Ed., Brentano's, NY, 1922. (See also n. 8 below—Sayler was an important chronicler.) Sayler traveled to Moscow and St. Petersburg in the winter of 1917-18(!) to report on the extraordinary theatre scene of that time and place—not only the companies of Stanislavski and Meyerhold, but others representing a wide spectrum of artistic attitude. Expert and well written, the book contains many fine illustrations. The excitement of creative ferment, of the fashioning of art, jumps from the pages of both these volumes, as does the spirit of close involvement of all the arts and their practitioners with one another, in a highly theatricalized atmosphere. For some notes on the extensive literature by and about Stanislavski, including his abiding passion for opera, see Part IV, Chap. 4, and Notes 00—00.

3. Readers interested in verifying these observations can easily do so by reference to full-length biographies or to the relevant entries in Grove's or other reference works. Another excellent source is the series of "People" profiles, tributes, and obituaries in *Opera* Magazine. A quick run through the '50s and early '60s, for instance, turns up solid background on Igor Markevitch, Arturo Toscanini, Clemens Krauss, Eric Coates, Karl Böhm, Wilhelm Furtwängler, Rafael Kubelik, Erich Kleiber, Sir Thomas Beecham, Rudolf Kempe, and Walter—many of these stressing the importance of their early theatre experience and their understanding of music as drama.

4. Walter's remarks are from his *Gustav Mahler* (James Galston, trans.), here as quoted in Michael Kennedy: *Mahler*, Oxford Univ. Press, N.Y., 2000 (orig. pub. 1974). On Walter's own grasp of the music as embodiment of dramatic character, see remarks by Parry Jones, Friedrich Schorr (as quoted by Jones), and Regina Resnik in tribute to Walter, *Opera*, April, 1962), of which Schorr's "what an amazing actor" is the quickest summary.

5. See Roller's contribution to *Max Reinhardt and His Theatre*, Oliver M. Sayler, ed., Brentano's, N.Y., 1924, p. 132. We do need to consider the repertory theatre milieu of the time and place: how many other creative directors might Roller have encountered, given that the director's standing was traditionally not much above that of glorified stage manager, or what we would now call an Assistant Director? Still, Roller worked with many of the top theatre men of his day, and sought the most progressive among them at a time when this role was being revolutionized. His evaluation surely carries weight.

6. Serafin's cast for this recording: Renata Tebaldi, Gianna d'Angelo, Carlo Bergonzi, Ettore Bastianini, Cesare Siepi, Renato Cesari, and Fernando Corena, all of whom sang these roles regularly in the theatre. The orchestra and chorus were those of the Accademia di Santa Cecilia, Rome—not a great symphonic ensemble, but a solid orchestra of good Italian operatic stock, often used for opera recordings of that era. Since I have cited this recording and will be citing more, and since I think it is important to maintain the distinction between opera as opera and operatic music as recorded, perhaps this is the place to acknowledge the limitations of such citations where conductors and orchestras are concerned (singers will be taken up soon). The only way a recorded/live comparison is of any use is as an imaginative exercise, that is, a projection of what the effect of the performance would be if heard and seen live. Beyond the mind's-eye leap over the gap between eye and ear (see Backstory One), this entails assumptions about both the progress and the acoustical presence of the music. I make such assumptions with some confidence because I trust my ear and my extensive experience in shuttling back and forth among recordings, broadcasts, and live events. Still, the possibility of misjudgment remains, and while readers may check their own impressions of recordings against mine, they cannot, except in rare cases, do the same with respect to live performance. (Using broadcasts to verify life performance reports is, I might caution, particularly treacherous.*)

    Thus, when I refer to Sir Thomas Beecham's readings of Verdi, Wagner, and Strauss, I must concede that to supplement critics' and musicians' reports of his ways with these operas we have only aircheck and in-house recordings of Wagner chunks and one complete *Aida* from Covent Garden in the 1930s, plus the 1947 BBC *Elektra*, in broadcast mono, and that the sound quality of these ranges from tolerable downward. Performance-practice information, and even some thrills, can certainly be extracted

---

* And getting more so. Presence and balance are not merely equalized, but reversed. With recorded radio programming, Mahler symphonies and Strauss tone poems have one leaping from the easy chair or reaching for the dashboard to boost the gain; then, a harpsichord/recorder morsel of Telemann's or a bit of Bach for unaccompanied violin or 'cello rattles the brainstem. The Baroque is near and opened up, the Romantic far and compressed; all proportions are *faux*. With live performance one is at the mercy of the broadcaster's "helpful" distortions. A fresh example: in the theatre on a Tuesday night, the bustling orchestral opening of the *Don Pasquale* overture is bracingly present; then the 'cello entrance with the "*Com'è gentil*" tune is lovely in tone but lacking in thrust and ardor. Over the air five days later, the tutti is chattery and faint, the 'cello suddenly overbearing, like an amplified instrument. This happens all the time, with voices and instruments, voices vs. instruments—an unceasing misrepresentation. Airchecks of the '50s and '60s have more integrity, convey a better sense of what registered and what didn't: At least the equipment reported more honestly on its own limitations.

from these (the *Aida*, with Caniglia, Stignani, and Gigli at or near the height of their powers, is particularly fascinating, and the *Elektra* is riveting), but with respect to orchestral depth, breadth and color they are seriously deficient. Similarly, when I list some of my favorite Wagner conductors (p. 271), I should note that I am referring almost entirely to recordings (studio, in-house, and broadcast), Kempe being the only of those mentioned I heard live in Wagner. I grew up with the generation of Wagnerians who, for all their differences, shared key aspects of a modernist aesthetic (faster, brighter, clearer): Reiner, Szell, Mitropoulos, Böhm, Schippers, Leinsdorf, Steinberg, Solti, to name the most notable among them.

In referring to studio recordings, I have tried to choose ones that I think were well-made, and that at least do not contradict my live recollections. Anent the Serafin *Bohème*, I suggest as dissertation topic: "Opera Recording in Rome, 1950-1970." For most of this time, the venues and resident forces of both the Santa Cecilia and the Rome Opera were steadily employed by several major labels with various matchings of producers, engineers, and conductors for recordings of virtually the entire standard Italian canon, with many mono/stereo remakes and rival versions. In 1962, RCA Victor opened studios on the Via Tiburtini and began recording there with the "RCA Italiana" Orchestra, a high-quality ensemble of auditioned players, including some from the above-named orchestras, as well as that of RAI, Rome. Among the issues to be explored: the recording philosophies of the producers; conductorial tastes and styles; equipment used and its characteristics; the acoustical spaces and their conformations; mike positioning; staging; editing and other postproduction practices; schedules and accommodations to soloists. Of course, Rome is but a single city; the rest of Italy, Europe, and the U.K. (the U.S. having pretty much priced itself out of the operatic recording business) offers rich material for parallel studies.

7. *"Tempo juste"*: ". . . the speed neither too fast nor too slow at which a piece of music is not just plausible but *right*." See *Samuel Lipman: Music and More*, Northwestern Univ. Press, 1992, p. 164. "Right" is an awfully subjective term; from my P.O.V., any tempo that keeps alive the dramatic movement and qualities of music can be "right". Monteux was advocating a search for tempos that avoided the ponderous or inert on one hand, or a whipping-up of surface flash on the other—a search his own conducting exemplified. This chapter of Lipman's book is an affectionate and much-deserved appreciation of Monteux.

8. The Rathaus version was used on the Metropolitan Opera Club recording of the late 1950s. Shostakovich's clangier re-write, which I recall as powerful, has not been recorded except in bits and pieces. There is an aircheck of a 1944 NYPO concert under Reiner whereon Alexander Kipnis, in surprisingly good voice for the date, sings the standard title-role extracts up till the choral entrance in the death scene (this was apparently the world premiere of any of the Shostakovich orchestration, a peculiarity of the wartime situation), and in 1970 Berlin Classics recorded an excerpts disc, in German, with Theo Adam and several colleagues under Herbert Kegel. Its sound is of course more immediate than the '44 broadcast and so conveys a bit more of Shostakovich, but to my ear overdoes the harshness of the overall effect. In the opera house, the Shostakovich seems to have fallen out of use. For an informative description of it and a comparison with Rimsky, see the Metropolitan Opera program for *Boris* performances of 1962-1963, which presents S. Ostrovsky's translation of an article by A.M. Veprik, originally published in *Sovietskaya Muzyka*, July, 1959. I never cared for the plain-sounding Rathaus, but can testify that under their conductors in the old Met (Mitropoulos and Solti, respectively) neither it nor the Shostakovich lacked for presence. For a thorough sorting-through of the various editions of Mussorgsky materials (to which the orchestration choices are incidental), see Richard Taruskin: *Musorgsky*, Princeton Univ. Press, 1993, Chap. 5.

9. In Ferrando's solo, "*Abbietta zingara*," the basso must scurry his way through a series of ascending flourishes, difficult for low voice, to attacks on the upper E-natural (also difficult) that, for both vocal and dramatic reasons, call for a broadening for emphasis before returning to tempo with another flourish, where the vocal line is doubled by the violins. The exact timing of the broadening and the return is seldom precise in live performance, but this instance was especially un-coordinated, and since I have never known the singer (the veteran Paul Plishka) to have a wayward musical moment, I'm not inclined to blame him. About the simple little passage in Leonora's aria, I haven't a clue as to what went wrong.

10. See Julian Budden: *The Operas of Verdi* (Vol. 1, from *Oberto* to *Rigoletto*), Praeger, N.Y., 1973, pp. 424-425.

11. See Herman E. Krawitz: *An Introduction to the Metropolitan Opera House*, Metropolitan Opera/Saturday Review, N.Y., 1967. Krawitz, Assistant General Manager of the Met, oversaw the building of the Lincoln Center house and the company's transfer from the old one. This guidebook, long out of print, is the best source of factual information on the structure.

12. See Paul Jackson: *Sign-off for the Old Met*, Amadeus Press, 1997, p. 240, discussing the 1956 broadcast of *Manon Lescaut*. "Tempos," says Jackson, that ". . . might be considered leisurely were it not for the kinetic tension in them."

13. For absorbing eyewitness testimony on these and other conductorial matters, I strongly recommend a pair of videos: *The Art of Conducting/Great Conductors of the Past* (BBC/IMG Archives, Teldec Classics) and *The Art of Conducting/Legendary Conductors of a Golden Era* (Teldec Classics). These discs offer historical footage, in some cases fragmentary but in others quite extended, of 22 of the 20th Century's leading conductors, plus commentary from players, conducting colleagues, and other analysts. From such material, evidence can be extracted in support of any aesthetic, technical approach, or physical style. On the points I have raised, I'd direct attention first to Furtwängler and Klemperer, with their relatively slovenly beats, their disavowals of precision as their primary aim, and insistence on remaining open to the moment in performance. Opera conducting, unfortunately, receives no attention apart from a couple of overtures; it has yet to receive its proper video due. But for any music lover, these are fascinating volumes.

14. See Bernard Holland: "Elegance of Steel, Elegance of a Flower," *NYT*, Feb. 4, 2005; Jeremy Eichler: "An Illusion of Effortlessness for Musical Time Travelers," *NYT*, Feb. 7, 2005; and Charles Michener: "The Clevelanders," The New Yorker, Feb. 7, 2005.

15. See Les Dreyer: "Orchestral Composition," letters column, *The New Yorker*, Feb. 28, 2005.

16. See George Szell and Paul Henry Lang: "A Mixture of Instinct and Intellect," *High Fidelity*, Jan., 1965, also anthologized in *High Fidelity's Silver Anniversary Treasury*, Wyeth Press, Gt. Barrington, 1976. Lang's *Music in Western Civilization* was the required reading in music history for several generations of American students. He was one of the founders of musicology as a recognized discipline in the U.S., and later succeeded Virgil Thomson as chief music critic of the *New York Herald-Tribune*. He started his professional life, however, as an orchestral musician in Budapest (operatic pit experience included), and was fond of saying that "before I was a critic, I was a working stiff." He was very much in accord with Szell's "purely musical" views on interpretation—neither man, one suspects, would have had much patience with Musin's ideas. Szell is also among the subjects of the Teldec discs (see note 16 above), but the segment is not very illuminating. It does end, though, with a neat splice out of a Cleveland performance of the Beethoven Fifth into a continuation by the Berlin Philharmonic under Karajan—a contrast in timbre and texture, if not in attack, that would still hold roughly today.

17. For a sample, see Anthony Tommasini: "Cheers from the Pit Accompany a Coda," NYT, May 18, 2000, a nice *pièce d'occasion* on the retirement of Raymond Gniewek, longtime concertmaster of the Met orchestra, whose tenure went back well into the pre-Levine years. Tommasini writes: "This intuitive way of working has been essential to Mr. Levine, whose goal has been to make the Met orchestra sound 'like a sensational, huge chamber group.'" Whether the quote is from Gniewek or Levine himself isn't entirely clear. It's authoritative enough in either case.

18. See "Furtwängler—An Appreciation by Hans Keller," *Opera*, Feb., 1955. There is so much in this article that is germane here that I would urge anyone interested in the subject to read it in its entirety.

19. When two-channel recording came in, the horizontal distribution of "stereo separation" and the capacity for highlighting that came with it became important debating points in the home listening experience. Where was the listener to be placed in relation to the sound? Some producers favored a close-in, multi-miked perspective that placed the listener at front row center, up on the podium, or even (as one excitedly told me at a gathering in the dawn-of-stereo days) inside the orchestra—in ascending order, the three worst places from which to make sense of music. Others (most famously the Mercury team with its "Living Presence" method that used three mikes hung farther out) sought to put the listener back and up. Obviously, the former approach de-emphasizes a hall's (or studio's) acoustics while the latter attempts to reproduce them, securing a "deeper," "roomier" sound. Splendid recordings were made all along the P.O.V. continuum, and some of the '60s RCAs with the Chicago and Boston orchestras still hold the status of audiophile monuments. At less than its best, though, this technique, especially when combined with RCA's characteristically "brilliant" sound (also that of so many postwar concert halls—the "hi-fi" ear and the contemporary acoustic are a perfect fit) was now strung out from side to side in a perspective that favored width over depth, detail over cohesion. And somehow, even from its pit and heard from well back in a not particularly bright auditorium, Levine's orchestra began to suggest this. Whereas recording had once sought to capture the woven tonal fabric of a good hall's acoustics, live performance now suggested the unraveled threads of stereo "spread" and "air."

20. See the *Parsifal* entry (pp. 448-452) in *The Metropolitan Opera Guide to Opera on Video* (Paul Gruber, ed. (W.W. Norton, 1997).

21. In Mozart, for instance, Levine goes on at tempos *juste* or quick. The points at which the Count and Countess bring each other up short in the *Figaro* Act II finale (Count: "*Non so niente!... Va, lontan dagli occhi miei*, etc.; Count: "*Vel leggo in volto!*"..."*Mora, mora*" etc.; Count: "*Rosina!*" Countess: "*Crudele! Più quello non sono,...ma il misero oggetto*," etc.) are examples. One partner puts a foot down, the other takes it in, then the action resumes. These are acting momentinos, and can happen very fast; but they must happen, and cannot unless the conductor is fully with it. The genius of this finale lies not in the fact that it is a perfectly proportioned continuous structure whose sections are ingeniously crafted, joined, timed, and fitted to scenic events, but that this structure bristles with emotional small-arms fire that threatens at any moment to pull it apart. Levine just sends it along without a trouble in the world; we smile faintly and nod at the predictable arrival. In two performances of the Zeffirelli *Don Giovanni*, the first in the theatre (see p. 710) and the second on video with a different cast, the tempos are pushed, scenes and numbers slam up against each other, the orchestra slashes and bangs. It's an effort, no doubt, to light a fire, but it's really more ongoingness, and the effect is merely brutalizing. In the new production of 2005, scenically dull but more thoughtfully staged, the reading is calmer and graver (an improvement), though quite predictable.

22. I make this observation not from the gender-identity P.O.V. (though of course that is an important consideration for the performer) but from the vocal. In their original keys,

these settings are intended to exploit the unique set of tensions and balances available to technically proficient low tenors and high baritones, for which other voice types can find only approximations. This does not mean that these other voices can't sing the cycle effectively (two of my favorite recorded versions are by Lois Marshall in her late mezzo-soprano incarnation, with Anton Kuerti, and Hans Hotter in his late low bass one, with Erik Werba). But it does mean that a female voice singing it in relaxed low keys will have extra difficulty locating and projecting many of its dramatic effects. In a hall like the Met, the possible compensations of deep, intimate expressions are lost.

23. See Renée Fleming: *The Inner Voice, the Making of a Singer,* Viking, N.Y. 2004.

3

ONSTAGE I: SINGING

(1902–2008)

In my introduction I said that my book would proceed from periphery to center, and in my first chapter I located that center in the sung theatrical action. Accordingly, we have made our way past Second Interpreters-in-Chief who wish to be deemed creators or, for some reason, critics; aspiring creators stuck at the aporia and auteurs who try to sneak them past; encoders for the eye and pacifiers of the ear who have agreed to live together but apart; and *philosophes* who have made all these socially and intellectually presentable. So we are now ready to consider the present condition of those responsible for making singing and acting into "a unit in the service of dramatic intent," for transforming "music and singing into a theatrical reality that is unreservedly plausible." But we find that their position in the interpretive hierarchy is much reduced, and that among those who fancy themselves serious about opera, there is even an element of condescension toward singing and the love of singing—"melomania"—as if the love of any performing art were grounded anywhere save in the allure of those who give it life. Melomanes, balletomanes, thespomanes, fellow gullibles all, hooked on singing, dancing, acting: be suspicious to the point of prejudice of anyone first drawn to our art by any other means, or who seek to install anything else at its center.

In turning our attention back from pit to stage—this time not to the objects on it or the ideas they may signify, but to the people who populate it—honesty dictates that we begin by recognizing that something essential to operatic singing has been lost, and that although other somethings have taken its place, they cannot serve the same purposes or provide the same

satisfactions. Among devotees and professionals there is a widespread awareness of this. But it struggles against an inertia compounded of the natural
wish to savor the expensive meal on one's plate without being reminded that
there is or was more toothsome fare, a spitting-into-the-wind helplessness in
the face of sociocultural context and intellectual fashion, and a mixture of
outright ignorance and denial. Since the absence of something can always
be countered with the presence of something else (as if the somethings were
equal) and one generality with another, we need particulars. For a start,
"*Ombra mai fu*" will do.

"*Ombra mai fu*" comes to mind because it has just surfaced in somewhat
surprising surroundings—the very paragraph in Renée Fleming's book that
refers to her discussions with Levine about "placed" interpretive elements vs.
"natural and organic" ones. "I am so often haunted," she says, "by the difference between Beniamino Gigli singing '*Ombra mai fu*,' which is the simple,
thrilling deployment of a great voice, and the interpretation of singers like
Dietrich Fischer-Dieskau and Elizabeth Schwarzkopf, who performed with
highly detailed, intelligent, and imaginative artistry. Who can say which
approach is best?"

It's a strange juxtaposition, the "approach" of having a great voice vs. the
"approach" of interpretive intelligence. One would not seem to preclude the
other, but obviously the first approach is open only to singers who in fact have
great voices, and the second does often appear as a compensatory alternative
to it. It's also peculiar that of all the great-voiced singers who have left recordings of "*Ombra mai fu*" (Enrico Caruso, Heinrich Schlusnus, Pavel Lisitsian,
Ezio Pinza, Dame Clara Butt, Maria Olszewska, et al.), Fleming would cite
Gigli; and that instead of any of Gigli's wonderful recordings of E-19 repertory, she would pick "*Ombra mai fu*," to which his singing is inappropriate in
every way except one, i.e., having a great voice. This is probably just serendipi-
tous—she happened to hear Gigli's version and not the others—but whether
by accident or design, she is getting at a real and important distinction about
singing and how we receive it. And if we open up the little box labeled "*Ombra
mai fu*," we will discover many of the issues we need to engage: what it means
to "have" a "great" voice or to aspire to great-voiced singing as opposed to
other kinds; the E-19 temperament vs. the Skipover temperament; voice types
and their implications; sexuality; style and authenticity; and the shifting
place of the piece itself.

"OMBRA MAI FU" AND THE MODERN MEZZO

I can't remember when I first heard *"Ombra mai fu."* It's as if I've always known the tune. It must have been early 1940s, in the living room around the piano, in elementary-school music class, or over the radio. In those days it was one of perhaps threescore items such as Martini's *Plaisir d'amour,* Lully's *"Bois épais,"* a few Bach and Handel arias, and other selections from the G. Schirmer volumes of *arie antiche,* that constituted the standard vocal repertoire from the mysterious Antemozartean Era. As such it took its place as a student piece and in the opening group of many a chronologically planned recital. These were free-floating songs, detached from their original contexts and available to all voices. *"Ombra mai fu"* could be heard in arrangements for string trio or concert band, or as an organ prelude at church. For Handel, like Bach, was for the general public an almost exclusively "sacred" composer (*Messiah* was Handel, and Handel was *Messiah*), and under its usual title of "Handel's Largo" or even "Largo Religioso," *"Ombra mai fu"* had a distinctly churchy association, sung and listened to with all due solemnity.*

Several decades into the Handel opera rebirth, all operaphiles know that *"Ombra mai fu"* is the knockout opening number (every bit as good as "Summertime") of the composer's late Italian opera *Serse* (that's Xerxes, king of Persia); that it was originally sung by a castrato, Caffarelli; that the botanical references are to a plane tree to which the king is obsessively attached; and that the "theatre erotic" it represents embraces much that is sensual and playful. Under the erotic, however, are emotional strivings and ethical vexations (the opera is an elaborate fantasy-fable), and this brief, almost spare solo, while having nothing to do with Christian worship, does have about it a reverential gravity which, whether for the sake of a mock-chivalric parody or of any "serious" purpose the interpreters manage to discover, must be realized in performance.† That is why Gigli's rendition, with its many intrusive h's, slurpy downward slurs, and overall treatment indistinguishable from that given a song of De Curtis or Di Capua, verges on the ludicrous. There is still the voice, though—refulgent, ringing, addictive and, to complete the

---

* As recently as the early 1960s Winton Dean felt constrained to point out, in his notes for the first recording of *Serse* (on the Westminster label), that the aria is neither *largo* nor *religioso*. One wonders what grown-up Italians like Caruso, Gigli and Pinza could possibly have told themselves about the text's apostrophe to the "fronds tender and lovely" of the "vegetable dear and amiable" as they played along with the devotional pretense.

† Dean, following an apology in the 1738 libretto for the "imbecility" of Xerxes' "being deeply enamour'd with a plane tree," states that the aria "...is clearly meant to begin the opera almost on a note of parody." In her first lines from the summerhouse soon after, Romilda pokes fun at the king for a passion whose only requital will be the rustling of leaves. But see n. 2.

insult, dripping with sex of the movie shipboard-romance variety. That'll pop a few buds on your *platano amato.**

For the two centuries Handel's operas lay dormant, the closest "*Ombra mai fu*" could come to its intended effect was in the female alto voice, and since the best of these (such as those of Butt or Kirkby-Lunn, Ernestine Schumann-Heink or Louise Homer or Sigrid Onegin) also bade us rest in the Lord and tell good tidings to Zion as the dowager-contraltos of oratorio, the aria's cultural mission was best fulfilled in such voicings. A singer of just this type, Maureen Forrester, assumed the role in the Westminster recording. In its original key of F, however, the piece lies ineffectually low for most sorts of tenors, especially in the old tuning, which lowers it by a full half-step. So Gigli sings it in G at modern concert pitch. The reason he and many other tenors do this (for this became the standard high-voice key) is not so much that in F the lowest notes may be weak (though in some cases this would be true) but that the highest ones will not take on a characteristic upper-range ring. By transposing it up to G in the modern tuning, the tenor is able to upend the Christa Ludwig/*Winterreise* dilemma and turn it to advantage, for whereas the main coloristic effects of the original key as heard in a low female voice depend on the descent of a presumably deep-throated, head-dominant voice into the rich register-blend area a note or two above middle C, Gigli's revels in the capacity of his balanced, chest-grounded tenor to play with the springy tensions, the colorations of open and closed vowels and registral border-crossings of the *passaggio,* and the tingle of the pitches just above it. These are the same notes crucial to the alto voicings, but for the tenor they fall in the upper-middle, not lower-middle, part of the voice's range. This results in transitions and emphases quite different from (we could almost say the opposite of) those written into the piece, but immensely satisfying as

---

* The slurs and slides are the postRomantic remains of the concept of *portamento,* here quite heedlessly applied. As understood by the early generations of Handel singers (they *did* use it), *portamento* implied a firmly guided smoothing of both ascending and descending intervals (to avoid angularity) bonded with the *messa di voce* (the swell and diminish, to avoid dynamic monotony and establish vocal poise) as the basis of all *cantabile* movement. Caruso's interpretation also makes regular use of the downward glide, but is far more dignified and musically pure than Gigli's. And I wonder which version of Gigli's interpretation Fleming heard (she sings Handel, after all, and in a stylistically informed way). The audio and film versions both emanate from Kingsway Hall, London, in the Spring of 1933. The released audio recording is accompanied by a studio orchestra supplemented by organ (Barbirolli, cond.) while the film, minus the recitative, has only organ, and concludes with a little nod from Gigli, as if approving a test runthrough for the take with orchestra. (The dates given, though, are two weeks apart.) Aside from the considerable difference in impression made when eye-attention is added (Gigli looks so calm, centered, and businesslike), the singing itself in the film is more straightforward and less objectionable from a performance-practice P.O.V.

vocalism, and thus impressive as musical statement. It is the functional basis of the thrilling deployment.

The original key and tuning of *"Ombra mai fu"* are restored in contemporary recorded versions, e.g., those of Andreas Scholl, David Daniels, or Lorraine Hunt Lieberson. But of course none of these is an alto-ish dame. Scholl and Daniels are "countertenors," and Lieberson a mezzo-soprano.

Following a memorial service not so long ago, a group of us were gathered at an old haunt. In my conversation circle the topic was, "What's *happened* to all the mezzos?" I answered that while I could think of several voice types that had up and gone missing (deep basses, true contraltos, dramatic voices of all categories), it seemed to me we had nothing but mezzo-sopranos, and that so far as I could tell mezzo-sopranodom was now the aspiration of all young singers of both sexes. But of course I knew what they meant. They were talking about *real* mezzo-sopranos, the grand-opera dramatic mezzos of their young years (like Stignani, Minghini-Cattaneo, Besanzoni, and Castagna; Klose or Thorborg) and mine (like Elmo, Barbieri, Simionato and Gorr, or such Americans as Thebom, Resnik, Madeira, Dalis, Rankin, Bible or Turner). They were recalling those instruments' presence, set, calibre, and color, which for them were constitutive of the operatic mezzo-soprano sound. By that definition, the mezzo-sopranos *have* vanished, though singers who can be called nothing else are all about us. Consider this list:

Conchita Supervia
Giulietta Simionato
Teresa Berganza
Frederica von Stade
Cecilia Bartoli

Devotees will recognize this as a chronological ordering of singers (c. 1920-2000) celebrated in the Rossini mezzo-soprano roles. It has a glaring omission—Marilyn Horne, of whom more later—but is otherwise a fair representation of the historical progression. It shows a radical reduction in vocal calibre—from two singers of E-19 vocal type (though very different technical set-up) at the top to two Modern Mezzos at the bottom, with Berganza a bridge over a smoother-running but ever-narrowing stream. What it does not show is the exponential widening at the base that would be necessary for an inclusive list. For most of the Supervia-to-Simionato time, one would be hard put to add a competitive Rossinian name to theirs—Gianna Pederzini's, perhaps, but to judge from recordings there's a steep fall-off in execution there.

To the names of von Stade and Bartoli, on the other hand, we could easily append another fifteen or twenty at a comparable level of technique and stylistic grasp. These pleasing, slender voices, usually indistinguishable in weight and timbre from the fuller types of lyric soprano, are capable of fluent execution in Rossini or Bellini, Handel or Vivaldi, but are not at all suited for the dramatic roles Simionato sang, or even the leading French mezzo parts (Carmen, Charlotte, Mignon) taken by Supervia. If we were to look to those roles, the chronological pyramid would be inverted.

Of the new-style mezzos, Lieberson was for me (and many others) the most treasurable. From my first sighting of her as Donna Elvira in Peter Sellars' *Don Giovanni*, she was one of the handful of contemporary singers I gladly went out of my way and out of pocket to see. She's the ideal exemplar of the art of the modern mezzo, and many of her finest qualities are evident in her "*Ombra mai fu.*" It could fairly be said that, not having quite a great voice of either contralto or mezzo (let alone tenor) persuasion, she requires an approach. What we really mean by this is that the voice in and of itself, as deployed with general musicality on this music, would not constitute a consummation. A special interpretive contribution is needed. Gigli isn't an apt comparison here, because he "interprets" incessantly, as noted above. A better one is Lisitsian. In 1960, he opened what remains the finest evening of baritonizing I've heard with this aria. He also recorded it—in E-flat, a minor ninth down if we take the tuning differential into account, and thus hanging on the Southern edge of the registral divide.* Here, once his rather ponderous version of the recitative is out of the way, Lisitsian's voice rolls through the piece settled, seamless, and unimpeded, the legato so effortlessly sustained we can take it for granted. He applies no colors—the only shadings are those reflected by the instrument itself as it moves through pitches and vowels—and does nothing to alter the spin of his vibrato. As with Caruso, the only ornament is a solitary trill, on the second syllable of "*amabile*" at bar 32.[1] His singing does, however, superbly represent true *portamento*. There is no movement, intervallic or verbal, that is not smoothly steered, no phrase not fully formed and finished. The swell-and-diminish, latent throughout, is exploited at the outset (a slow, natural crescendo—like the growth of a tree or the creep of its shade—on "*o-o-o-mbra*" and at the end, where the tone builds through the climb on "*so-a-ve*" into the juiciest of E-flats on "*più,*" first leaning into, then easing off the note with a perfect (but not prolonged) concluding diminuendo. Every beat of the rendition is in perfect balance and proportion, yet nothing sounds like an intellectual decision; the controls and "choices"

---

* Fortuitously, it is exactly the pitch at which it was originally sung—but down an octave.

are coming from the Greatsingingland within. The interpretation seems unselfconscious and self-contented, as if it would never occur to either singer or listener that anything beyond voice and music might be desired.

Lieberson's account, though reflective of performance-practice scholarship, is as sparsely decorated as Lisitsian's (plainer in fact than Forrester's, which is festooned with pretty trills). But it leaves an entirely different impression, not only of vocal category and quality but of interpretive intent, of the sort of interest we are meant to take in it. Lieberson searches the music. As usual, she is searching for the right thing—a deeply felt connection. But she *is* searching, and asks that we follow. After a recitative much more sharply pointed than Lisitsian's, she opens the aria as he does, with a *messa di voce*, starting with one of those rare pianissimo attacks, most readily available to poised female voices, that seem to magically materialize out of silence and hang suspended. From there, she swells the tone steadily through the next bar into the downbeat of the following one, where the descent of the hit tune's signature phrase begins. Always with restraint (she doesn't fuss or pile on detail), she subtly alters her vibrato, her timing, her dynamics to keep the music "in the moment." She is equally subtle and spare with vowel shadings, with a single exception: on the word "*cara*," she opens and lightens the "*a*" to the whitening point. She does this three times, once in the recitative (where the "*a*"s in "*platano amato*" receive similar treatment) and twice in the aria, all in the A-to-B vicinity (modern tuning), and the sound jumps out each time. It's a device so often used to finesse this vowel in the fourth above the break that the technically wired listener is immediately alert.* But even if this consideration contributed to the choice, Lieberson would never have left the effect expressively unjustified or, in the theatre, unconnected to her physical behavior. It is a product of her search, in a sense that none of the effects created by Lisitsian (or Gigli, or Caruso) are, and since it is in each instance descriptive of the singer's feelings toward the tree, we must take it as a deliberate and specific interpretation.

Lieberson's choices are perhaps most striking in the recitative, if only because it comes first and calls for more naturalistic treatment than aria or arioso. The ears prick up as early as bar three, where the "tender" and "beautiful" leaves (these adjectives given their normal shadings) turn out to

---

* The open Italian "*a*" is treacherous in this part of the female voice; even technically adept singers can encounter difficulty with it. Strong pressure on the tone tends to evoke an intrusive chest mix and/or constriction. In all but functionally perfect voices, the safety solutions range from singing the vowel "open" (but thinned and lightened) to "covered" (but often fuzzy and poorly projected). When the word "*cara*" sits higher, Lieberson sings the vowel with full, round tone.

belong to . . . "my beloved plane" (special "*a*" treatment). Then declamatory mode reigns through the thunder, lightning, and tempests that must not outrage . . . "your dear peace" ("*cara pace*"—again special treatment, before resuming the declamation). These spots are marked as with highlighter, then underlined again in the aria, like a recurring motif. Lisitsian also does a little something with the word "*cara*"—once. On the A-flat that is sustained for three beats in bars 34 and 35, he drops down to *mezza-voce.* In the context of his uncomplicated voicing it's a blandishing nuance, because the texture of Lisitsian's *mezza-voce* is so beautiful, and because he employs it with such discretion. But it does not become a motif. Though I wish Lisitsian had sung the recitative with clearer intent and greater fluency, the introduction of a usage like Lieberson's "*a*" would have sounded ridiculous in his voice. And what would have been the need? For in the aesthetic governing his singing, the entire color spectrum is inherent in the *chiaroscuro* of his voice, and its relation to interpretation wholly reflexive. Anything beyond that would be in the province of the character singer.

Lisitsian's "*Ombra mai fu*" comes out at us—magisterial, stately, expansive, unitary, inevitable. Its few variations feed directly into its central statement; they are not qualifications. Lieberson's draws us in and along through a progression of events and moments, entirely logical and formed, but suggestive of changeability. Its overall tone is more inward, pensive, and a little sad. The baritone's voicing is celebrative and public, the mezzo's contemplative and private. Both performances speak directly, but to different parts of us. We would ordinarily say that Lieberson's is (to borrow Fleming's adjectives once again) the more "intelligent" and "imaginative," but there is more than one kind of intelligence, and more than one route to the imagination. Lieberson's way of reaching us is rare, now and always. It's Lisitsian's, however, that represents the essential something we've lost, the hunger that cannot now be appeased.

Since we are talking about operatic performance, not concert singing or sacred soloizing, we cannot fail to consider "*Ombra mai fu*" as dramatic action and character expression, and while we would cast Lieberson in one sort of dream *Serse* without a second thought, we could not so employ Lisitsian.* Certainly many of the differences between their interpretations

---

* Not quite. For the right performer, I'm entirely open to the now-proscribed practice of octave transposition. We are drowning in a sea of head voice here, from which the characters of Ariodate and Elviro provide only brief and unrewarding surcease, and Serse has only a few bars of true duet (with Amastro, Act Two, Scene XIII) where intervallic inversion is of any (very slight) consequence. Still, though an in-key "*Ombra mai fu*" sits well for baritone, much else in the role is too high, even in old tuning—it would have to be a tenor. You may say it would be the rare tenor who would qualify. But Lieberson aside (or, to think in another direction, Podles), which of the Modern Mezzo multitude will hold you breathless through the many arias and recits of this lengthy role?

come down to the fact that whereas it is doubtful that Lisitsian had more than a passing acquaintance (if that) with the action, the character, and the questions of musical style and theatrical practice attached thereto, Lieberson was immersed in them and temperamentally attuned to them. Her singing of the aria reflects study and performance of the entire role, and her recording of another of Serse's arias—the more elaborate "*Se bramate d'amar*," of which she makes far more than Forrester or Ann Murray (the Xerxes of Hytner's ENO production)—confirms how compellingly she invested the part: the mind's eye can see the scene play out, both in the rage Serse works up at Romilda ("I want to despise you") and in the daringly long fermatas (time for the emotional turnabout to happen) before each adagio repetition of "*Ma come, non so*" (". . . but how, I don't know). The behavior is audible in the singing.

In context, then, if Forrester's intoning of "*Frondi tenere*," etc., evokes (as it does) a warm, possibly motherly, closeness, and Gigli's his first move on the girl at the rail, what is suggested by Lieberson's colorings of "*cara*" and "*platano amato*"? A special attachment, surely, implying a touch of preciosity—the tone of the connoisseur with a prized *objet*, or even the babytalk of owner to pet. Either is plausible as a part of the king's makeup. Whether either is "right" or not depends on what direction the character is being taken on his journey through the role, and whether or not that direction proves convincing—not just that it "works," but that in singing and playing it is made to seem the strongest one the artist could have chosen. The question can't even be sensibly debated on the basis of one number, much less a recording of same. Nor can the "rightness" of Lisitsian's rendition (adjusted for vocal category) be ruled out. It's not at all hard to imagine such a voicing sending both opera and character off to a splendid start. It is only necessary to take the plane tree, and Xerxes' attachment to it, seriously.[2]

The talents of Lisitsian and Lieberson would have remained obvious under any performing conditions, but neither would have done well with the other's approach to "*Ombra mai fu*." In Lisitsian's case the lack seems mostly a matter of what we call "style," and in Lieberson's of sheer voice—Fleming's Gigli-vs.-Schwarzkopf/Fischer-Dieskau distinction again, which I have tried to refine by citing on one hand a great vocalist with a more straightforward interpretive bent than Gigli's, and on the other a great interpretive artist less given than Fischer-Dieskau to affects that sometimes feel daubed on. But "voice" and "style" are not so easily separated. Concerning this, I have two propositions to advance. First (and this will be argued further): If either of these singers had been acculturated in the other's time and place, he or she would not only have sung, interpreted, "styled" differently, but would have done so *with a different voice.* Second (and this can't really be argued, though its implications are about to be): the most important distinction between them, however culturally modified, cannot be erased—that one is male, the other female. Here's "theatre erotic" in its most literal sense.

Even before the latterday revivals of operas of the 17th and 18th Centuries, the tradition of female singers in male roles was alive and well—indeed, Strauss gave it a good booster shot in the early 20th. Like any eye/ear contradiction, this convention strains belief—it's a brain barrier. But its capacity for suspension of disbelief benefits from opera's ear-led, eye-confirmed nature. With the ear in the lead, if voice and music are well enough matched and the spectacle not too preposterous, belief can survive in the typical cases, which involve youth trembling at the brink of adolescence.

Strauss gave the convention a stiff test, though. Octavian is no Cherubino with his suggestive but decorous little love poem, or Siébel with his bouquet and holy water; and *Rosenkavalier* is no *opera seria*, with its protestations tied up in lovely packets of aria form. It's a through-written, play-like scenario. And in that context, is the Marschallin really supposed to be making love to a boy whose voice has not yet broken? With Strauss's music and a good adult mezzo voice, we can suppress incipient queasiness if the sound is not too lushly female, and its owner able to fill in the lower range without resort to a sharply defined chest voice. For that would be fatal to the aural pretence. It would remind us that in both men and women, the emergence of this sound is a sure mark of sexual maturity, and that the singer in question, with her few notes of that quality at the bottom and her octave-and-a-half of another quality above, is no adolescent male, but a fully grown female.

In discussing voice, there is no statement one can venture about its internal acoustics ("resonance") without becoming entangled in controversies about "placement," "ping," "*squillo*," etc., or about its respiratory engagement without encountering arguments about "support," "*appoggio*," "breath control," and so on. I have views on these matters, but to elaborate them here is not to the present critical purpose. However, when it comes to the subject of mezzo-sopranos of both sexes singing "*Ombra mai fu*" (and by extension, much else), there is no getting around this question, already alluded to, of range-related timbral groupings, usually called "registration." Even here, I shall try to simply trace what I consider an outline of vocal reality, and to describe it in language as free as possible of technical or "scientific" baggage.

Anyone with a Westernized musical ear (others too, I think, but I'm restricting myself to conservative statements) can hear that the human voice produces two families of sound. These are extended families, to be sure. They embrace many variations, including some that suggest cross-breeding, but there are only two of this primary-color sort. However different any of the many sounds of the voice may be from others, no difference is as stark as that between the two families. It is also plain to hear that one of the families occupies the lower half of the total human voice range, the other the upper, and that while both are much strengthened and enriched by the passage from childhood to adulthood, the lower of the two does not make an appearance at all, in either sex, until puberty. With maturity, the upper/lower division becomes sexually defined, female voices being pitched approximately an octave higher than the corresponding male categories. The reasons for this have long been understood: women's vocal cords are less massive than men's, allowing them to vibrate at the faster frequencies we hear as high pitches, while the longer and thicker male bands vibrate at the slower ones. In addition, the cavities responsible for the voice's amplification are also smaller in women, and so more accommodated to reinforcement of the higher pitches and partials, and less to the lower. Thus, whether one believes the origin of the two sound families is primarily vibrational or bio-acoustical, or any proportion of the two in interaction, the outcome is the same.

As far back as we can trace an historical record—with any reliability the late Renaissance, when the gradual mutation of the dominant vocal usages from those of church and chamber to those of theatre began in earnest, and Italian pedagogues began to publish their observations—the disparity in strength and quality of the two families has been remarked, as has the desirability of uniting and equalizing them. Indeed, the difficulty of this last has been the central technical issue of Western vocal culture for at least 400 years, and most of the ensuing controversy has involved the precise pitch location of the transitional point between the two families (the "break" or "*passaggio*"), and how to negotiate it—a question much complicated by the fact that the upper family, on its own, is far weaker than the lower in the vicinity of the "break." But if we hew to this single distinction between major sound families, and keep the entirety of the human vocal range in view, there's no question that this transitional area centers around the E above middle C. From there it can slide up or down somewhat, but as practitioners and theorists have repeatedly observed, the farther away from this center the transition is pushed, the more symptoms of physical malfunction and aesthetic imperfection emerge. So consistently does this observation prove out in practice that we might call it the Displacement Rule, following which the transitional center is defined as the fulcrum of the voice, located toward the top of the male range and the bottom of the female—we have already noted the effects of this in the Christa Ludwig/*Winterreise* case and in the male/female contrasts of *"Ombra mai fu."* This definition will be an important point of reference for the remainder of this discussion.*[3]

The traditional, though misleading, names of the two families are "chest register" and "head register." Since they're so common and I have done my best to indicate what I mean by them, I'll use them here. They could as well be called "low" and "high" or "thick" and "thin." Or, just as accurately, "male" and "female," for these are sexually determined artifacts grounded in anatomical reality, not cultural preference. Nevertheless, in our time there have been two efforts to substitute preference for reality. One is located in the popular culture, predominantly among women; the other is found in the high culture, exclusively among men. Each is, functionally and aesthetically, the flip side of the other, and each attempts to take as its own the defining characteristics of its sexual opposite—in effect, to swap families. One is the "belt," the other the "countertenor" falsetto.[†]

The Displacement Rule holds only so long as two related assumptions about "the voice" are in place. The first is that voice is an expression of Western musical aesthetics, and the second that it is self-amplified, a strictly acoustical instrument. If voice is cut loose from either or both of these assumptions, then the historical body of aesthetic and functional understanding is cast aside, and the Displacement Rule is effectually nullified in very much the same sense that juries sometimes nullify laws—that is, the laws are still in force but the juries, for reasons of their own, have decided to ignore them. Since the "belt" departs from both assumptions, it falls outside consideration here except in the functional sense already indicated: in extending the range of the chest register upward, it is the obverse of the "countertenor" project of drawing the head downward into the chest territory. While these usages

---

* Colleagues and technically aware singers will have concluded that the above account of vocal phenomena marks me as "a two-register, fixed-break" man. That is true, but I don't want pedagogical disputes to interfere with critical integrity. My only wish here is to be clear. For some further explanation and translation of terminology, see n. 3.

† "Falsetto" is another term of confusion and dispute. Some of the early Italians considered it synonymous with *"voce di testa"*—"head voice." Later, it was used to define the middle range of the female voice. Since it stands for a range of sounds ("pure," "mixed," "reinforced," etc.), the boundary between male falsetto and full voice can be disputed—as is true toward the lower end of the female range, of the boundary between "pure" or "raw" chest and the blended varieties thereof. That is true no matter where the boundary is placed. As used here, the meaning of "falsetto" is simple: in the male voice, any sound that falls into the upper-family timbral grouping. Yes, there are "tweener" tones—perhaps 2% or 3% of the total—just as there are with blended tones in the female voice. They define the boundary area. Except for these, there is no more difficulty determining when a male voice is in falsetto (as here defined) than when a female one is "in chest"—though of course one encounters some peculiar notions about that, too, some of which are acknowledged farther on.

fall into separate aesthetic orders, one virilizing the female voice in the name of countercultivation and the other de-virilizing the male in a manneristic hypercultivation, they are twinned examples of vocal displacement. And each is a regression: the "belt" returns the female voice to its untrained state—it is simply the sound of the raw speaking voice yelling as high and loud as it can be coerced to do—while the falsetto returns the male to its prepubescent one.[4]

Neither of these misappropriations makes one sex sound like the other. For that, an appropriate female voice (low and strong) would be the natural candidate. Functionally, there seems to be no reason why such an instrument could not be trained like a tenor's, integrating the head register with the right admixture of chest "hold" in the transitional area. Given female anatomy, such a voice would extend higher than a male tenor's, and might bring to the stratospheric *bel canto* tenor parts excitements undreamt-of by Rubini. Granted, the stars of physique, musicality, and temperament would also have to align; it would be a nervy project, but not an implausible one. It would be more promising, in fact, than that of attempting to construct a tonally complete male voice dominated by the head register, so much weaker than the chest in the transitional area and so subject to distortion when integrated at any distance from it.*

Many readers must have noticed that I place the word "countertenor" in quotes. This is not meant to disparage the singers so categorized, many of whom are splendid musicians and, within the limits of their chosen vocality, expressive artists. It is meant to indicate that the word is being misused. It's a euphemism for the accurate term, "falsettist," and a tacit admission that that term would imply a lack. A true countertenor is a voice whose compass lies between those of tenor and contralto. It is recognizably male (though of "high," "heady" timbre) throughout most of its range, and still subtly different from the female sound at the upper range limit. Its high extension is reached

---

* To the best of my knowledge, the closest we have approached my female tenor model was in the person of Ruby Helder, who sang in concerts and musicales in the late teens and twenties of the last century. She recorded at least four 78-rpm sides—excerpts from Benedict's *Lily of Killarney* and Balfe's *The Bohemian Girl*, a song called *Thora* by one S. Adams (the coloratura Suzanne Adams?), and Flotow's "*M'appari*"(*Martha*). The voice is clean, well-balanced and tuned. She sings with beautiful line and pure vowels (her Italian pronunciation is poor, but not because of ill-formed vowels), the voice properly gathered at the *passaggio*, and is in no way distinguishable from the better male recital and salon tenors of her day. According to what I've been able to learn of her, she was not a hormonal anomaly—that is, she "had" a soprano voice, but chose to train at the Guildhall School as a tenor. While her range was apparently limited (a rather pinched B-flat at the end of the *Martha* aria is the top shown on the discs) and agility untested, there is altogether quite a lot in her singing to support my speculations.[5]

without artificial lifting of position or thinning of the vowels. Its pitch center in speech mode is higher than normal, and "naturally" so.* Such voices are rare, and presumably rarer than of yore, since body size has increased and anatomical proportions are consistent more often than not.

The true countertenor would sing with all his given equipment in balanced co-ordination.† The falsettist does not. He suppresses his primary sound family (the chest register) to favor his secondary one. While sincere congratulations are due the talented singers and teachers who have made this imbalance work as well as it does for the best of the falsettists, such a registral distribution cannot produce a tonally complete voice, as comparison with any reasonably accomplished female mezzo or contralto will instantly verify. Our *"Ombra mai fu"* singers, Daniels and Scholl, illustrate this. They are among the finest contemporary falsettists, and both render Serse's ode in key and in admirable style. I happen to prefer Daniels' timbre—slightly breathy, but warmer than Scholl's and not so prone to straightness of tone as it approaches the upper E and F. But neither voice can settle into the piece as Lieberson's or Forrester's can, and neither can risk digging into the tone or incising the words into the line, for fear of a Dame Edna-with-a-cold accident. Thus, neither can allow a recognizably male timbre to intrude until far below the Displacement Rule's line, and then only gently. (This necessity does not arise in *"Ombra mai fu"*). Neither can declaim in recitative with effective force. Each suggests the *messa di voce* (a crescendo at the song's opening, a

---

* This is often called "optimum" pitch—the area in which the speaking voice sits with the greatest ease of emission and gathering of resonantal properties. It is usually calibrated at about one-quarter of the distance up the total range of the voice, though it is sometimes unclear what this is being measured against. By "naturally" I mean: in a highly efficient relationship to the anatomy of the individual voice and what I call the Hardwired Complex—the responses and co-ordinations habituated so early on (as with the acquisition of language) that they might as well be anatomical. This relationship is not infrequently distorted by personal issues of communication, identity, or self-presentation—distortions which can run deep, notwithstanding that they are overlays.

† I regret that I cannot cite a convincing, currently active example. In daily life I have encountered a handful of speaking voices that seemed to indicate the type, and in the studio a very few more in states of partial development. But I know of no technically finished case, unless one decides to declare tenors with usable high D's or E-flats (e.g., Kraus, Gedda, Kozlovsky, Rosvaenge) to be countertenors. The American tenor Enrico di Giuseppe, in the role of the Astrologer in Rimsky's *The Golden Cockerel*, ascended without a break to an E-natural, and used at least part of that extension in other roles. (A pirated recording of *Cockerel*, from a 1972 performance, has circulated. I heard Di Giuseppe as The Astrologer three times in the theatre; the extreme *acuti* were reliable and strong.) But most of his career was devoted to the standard lirico-spinto repertory, and the overall quality of his voice did not set him apart from that category. Failure to recognize and correctly train high male voices may contribute to the scarcity, and market considerations as well; but at best, the voice type is exceedingly uncommon.

diminuendo at the close), but it is indicated more by control of vibrato than of loudness—indeed, the dynamic range of these voices is narrow, and as limited on the soft end as on the loud. Except in florid passages (again not involved in this aria) all interpretive selections, however ingenious, must be of the subdued, "sensitive" sort, lending the piece a grey, abstract, and slightly spooky feel. What has that to do with the character or the situation? And what, therefore, makes it any more "authentic" than Gigli's romantic tenorizing or Lisitsian's baritonal peroration?

What is supposed to make it more authentic is its resemblance to castrato vocalization. And we should recall that in the time of the castrati, anatomically normal falsettists (a Spanish school was especially prominent) competed with them and occasionally "passed." But they lost out, being judged as on the whole inferior. They hadn't the tonal brilliance or the wider pitch range of the *evirati*. And note: our falsettists are all "mezzos" or "altos," with little timbral distinction between these types. A few can reach, in passing, soprano high notes—so can some male rockers—but none that I have heard can sustain true soprano tessitura with anything like acceptable tonal quality. Some of the castrati, on the other hand, are reported to have sung higher than any female soprano, and that is not an unreasonable claim, since after castration the vocal cords and associated apparatus of the boy sopranos would not have lengthened and thickened to the same degree as an adult female's.

Obviously, we have no castrato model before us, even on recordings (certainly the hooty quaverings of the aged Moreschi, last of the Sistine Chapel castrati, as heard on a few very primitive discs, teach us little). Perhaps a clue can be traced in the singing of the jazz vocalist Jimmy Scott who, owing to a hormonal condition known as Kallmann's Syndrome, never attained sexual maturity. In some of his upper notes, particularly on his earlier recordings, one can detect a touch of the *clarino* brassiness that was said to have outvied the trumpet. From the classical P.O.V. Scott's voice is governed by a foreign aesthetic and almost completely undeveloped. His practical range is not more than an octave and a third or fourth, of which the lower half is very weak, and if he ever sang without a mike, it must have been in the tiny clubs of the "Chitlin' Circuit" at the outset of his career. Nonetheless, his sound gives a glimpse at the raw material of a castrato instrument.[6] That is different from all others, including that of the falsetto "countertenor," and whether or not a modern ear would find the finished product appealing is, I think, questionable.

It is certainly a matter of curiosity that, nearly 200 years after the final waning of a taste for the sound of mutilated males, we should be cultivating one for imitation mutilated males. This is unquestionably due in part to the postmodern dalliance with the blurring or transgression of boundaries, including sexual ones, and derives much of its energy from the feminist/gay/lesbian quest for validation. In this light, the falsettist is the drummerboy of Difference, claimed for the transgendered or androgynous Other. This last is surely wrong, though. The falsetto voice isn't feminine; it's merely unmasculine. And it isn't androgynous; it embraces the characteristics not of both sexes, but of neither. The only sexual taste it serves would be that for the prepubescent boy. Ironically, it is in the fully-developed E-19 voice that each sex incorporates the qualities of the other, and in which (particularly in the transitional range area) the truly "androgynous" can be heard.* The catch, of course, is that even as it achieves this yin/yang completion, it embraces heterosexual vocal definition, confirms its grounding in anatomical reality, and declares it normative.[7]

To attribute the re-emergence of the operatic falsettist solely to sexual politics would be a serious overreach. This re-emergence is only the most obvious peculiarity of a more general shift in vocal usage—a shift that is at one with the tempered, elucidated, exquisite, anonymous sounds emanating from the pit. It is also the male sacrifice at the altar of contemporary mezzo-ism, to an upper-range vocality that's limber, slender, pleasing—never rugged, granitic, or threatening. It is, in other words, a part of the voice's own flight from E-19.

THE DUPREZ MOMENT

The thing that separates the E-19 vocal model from those that preceded it is this: a new emphasis on the masculine sound family, and exploration of what that can accomplish for voices of *both* sexes. As Paul Robinson aptly observes about vocal equality in general, "... those operatic characters unambiguously identified by their singing as female nonetheless sing as loudly and assertively as do their male opposites. Dramatically women in opera suffer every known form of sexist depradation, but vocally they enjoy absolute parity with men."[†] This parity is in a way a comedown from the near-total hegemony of the feminine sound family that obtains in Handel, where the

---

* These arguments have nothing to do with an aversion to falsetto per se. Many teachers, myself included, make extensive use of falsetto adjustments in the development of male voices. There, however, the purpose is to strengthen, integrate, and properly balance the role of the upper family in a structure dominated by the lower—not to isolate it and give it, so to speak, the upper hand.

† See n. 7, p. 408. From the general context of his discussion, but especially an earlier paragraph on the athleticism of operatic singing, with its requirement of projecting a two-octave range with "... enough volume to carry—without electronic assistance—over the assembled forces of a full symphony orchestra and into vast auditoriums", it is clear that Robinson is speaking of E-19-style opera.

masculine is relegated to truly subservient status. But in another way it's pure women's lib: with the emergence of a more aggressive male vocality, the female meets it on its own terms and fights to a draw.

The birth of what we now think of as the operatic tenor voice, represented by the triumph of Duprez, is usually taken for the tipping-point into E-19 singing. That is undoubtedly an oversimplification. For one thing, a school of singing that embraced greater tonal vitality than that allowed by the French emphasis on gradations of head mix and inflectional delicacy already existed in Italy, where the reigning idol, Adolphe Nourrit, went in search of a technique with which to combat his younger rival. For another, the more refined head-voice effects remained in use, at least among the French, for many more years. Still, Duprez clearly established a usage not attained by even other heavier-voiced tenors like Donzelli, and as a marker his Moment is accurate enough. So, in best postmodern manner, I shall take Duprez the individual to signify "Duprez" the event, auteur of E-19 voice. The story is well-known: Duprez was desperate to find the means by which his evidently then-smallish tenor could conquer the role of Arnold in Rossini's *Guillaume Tell,* with its vaultings to accented high notes, its high tessitura, and its repeated climbs to the top C. To succeed as he did, he cannot have simply forced the active chest register a fifth above the *passaggio*—that would produce an impossibly laborious adjustment that would not work on even a temporary basis. Instead, what he located in his body was the feel for using his awareness of chest action to create a greater resistance against the head register, allowing only enough head participation to carry his voice to the C without shading away from the male sound family, and re-arranging the register transition in the process. To judge from descriptions of his singing and the relative brevity of his subsequent career, he did this imperfectly (he had neither model nor guide, after all). But he did it.[8]

This was a genuine advance, whose full implications have not, I feel, been widely understood.* While its initial impact—the one that swept audiences before it—was felt in the upper reaches of the male voice, it also created a new sonic model for all voice types, throughout their ranges. Duprez did not just stack a suddenly loud, ringing upper fifth on top of his existing lower range; that makes no sense functionally or aesthetically. By "leaning into" his

---

* In speaking of an "advance," I don't mean to imply that nothing was lost, or that passage of time equals progress. To repeat myself: everything is in place of something else. The best of the old-style tenors must have been capable of ravishing effects, and there is no question that a number of the Italian and French early Romantic roles were written to those effects, and cannot be sung as intended by tenors of the modern model. For the tally of gains and losses that add up to what I mean by "advance," read on.

upper range with newfound stress he fashioned a whole new voice, fuller-throated and more deeply grounded. In so doing, he enabled many things, not all of them feats of performance. We think of changes in performance styles as "responses to" new ways of writing, but that is only one side of the symbiosis between interpretation and creation. Certainly the need that Duprez felt for a transformation in his singing must have been stimulated by a sense of change in the dramatic requirements of the music, but in fact the roles to which his new method was first applied (in operas of Rossini, Halévy, Meyerbeer, et al.) had already been sung to acclaim by tenors of the older type. Once heard, the new model became creators' muse, now indispensable to their imaginings of musical gesture, emotional effect, and dramatic character. Without its presumption of crescive top notes, overall sonic thrust, and broadened color spectrum, E-19 opera is inconceivable.

For women's voices, the changes seem to have been less clearcut—we have no record of a Duprez Moment for women. But then, female voices were not in the same need of completion as the male, the chest range being already present and, however modulated by aesthetic and social cultivation, unavoidable owing to its natural proximity to the speaking voice. Nor was a decibel boost of Duprezian magnitude required, given the female voice's natural superiority in altitude (high voices carry more easily) and its acoustical separation from other voices and instruments. Still, it is clear from the internal evidence of E-19 scores that a settling took place; that while high range extension, extreme agility, and delicacy of affect were still valued in certain roles, what the new heroines needed to match their new heroes and their ever-intensifying orchestral environment was a more engulfing, proclamatory sound and a richer, deeper sonority.

Now the sound families were roughly equal in extent* while retaining their defining timbral and behavioral characteristics, and both set into a more powerful format; these are the voices of assertive, grown-up men and women. A by-product of this development is, unquestionably, a sharp (hetero) sexual profile. Paul Robinson terms this an exaggeration. I call it a completion, a maturation. *It is the strongest physical integration, the fullest realization of sonic and athletic potential and therefore of artistic expression, that Western vocality has achieved.* Like all artistic developments brought to maturity (dance would provide the closest parallels), it presses toward the human limit. In so doing, it enhances, sets forth—or as Heidegger would have it, "unconceals"—the properties inherent in it. That's not an exaggeration; it's a consummation.

---

* "Roughly" because female voices remain, on average, slightly "longer" than male—a natural consequence of their greater elasticity.

One immediate dividend of the new masculine integration—a male empowerment, we'd call it now—was its incarnation of male rage, the voice of malediction and vengeance. Another, as Robinson notes, was its capacity for sexual excitation, not solely in moments of transport but as an ongoing presence, especially in the upper range. And though sex has always been among singing's pleasures, this was different, a new kind of climax. But the E-19 voice in its prime conveyed much more than rage and sex, and was not given to men alone. Behind the rage is anguish: the curses of Edgardo, Manrico, José, or Otello are born of perceptions of betrayal, as are Isolde's curse and Brünnhilde's oath on the spear. All are voiced, not with bursts of fast little notes, but with sustained, crushing force. Beyond the sex is love itself, usually E-19's defiant, fatally destined love, of which sex is only the fevered bodily expression. In brief, these voices carried with them the tragic burden of the protagonist couple and their antagonists—a weight the earlier usages could not have borne.

A TURN TO THE RIGHT

There is an inescapable element of speculation in any discussion, including mine, of vocal practices that predate the E-19 masculinization. In the absence of sounds we can "prove" nothing; however extensive our knowledge, however close our reading of evidence, our arguments remain inferential to a degree. That is not the case, though, with the flourishment of E-19 voice, or with our retreat from it in recent decades. The sounds of the former are available on recordings, and those of the latter both recorded and live. True, E-19 singing is not utterly extinct. But as a culturally pervasive force it is spent. Its era ended around 1970, with the passing of the generation that matured in the post-World-War-II years. That is the last time casts of what had come to be understood as international quality for the masterworks of the repertory could be assembled by major companies (though even then, in not more than two or three houses at a time for the weightier works) and the supply-side trickle-down benefits of that standard could be detected throughout the operatic economy.

As with the other aspects of operatic culture already considered, this sea-change in singing is only one measure of social currents that run broad and deep. The softening of sexual definition, the weakening of cultural identity (ethnic, national, linguistic), the frequently noted loss of vocal individuality or personality, and the less commonly remarked migration of whole vocal types toward one another in a smooth-textured upper-midrange cluster (with near-total loss of the lower extremes in both sexes as corollary), are all examples of this. They are specific, demonstrable artistic realities easily seen as byproducts of such irresistibles as globalization, multiculturalism, or the corporatization of yet another workforce. But as always, I prefer to reason from the artistic realities, for which artists bear responsibility and over which they have some control, toward the irresistibles, which they must seek to humanize. Voice is something we do, not just something we have, and singing is a form of selective behavior. We are best off examining the disappearance of E-19 singing at the working level.

If the Duprezian era began with a new use of the chest register, with the result that the old Italian ideal of balanced registration now had to be pursued in the context of a heavier calibration, then it follows that a suppression of the chest action and a lightening of calibration is implicated at its end. And so it is. But beyond this question with its unavoidable functional P.O.V., we need language that is accurate without being technical—that is, a set of terms that describe without assigning causes. I suggest these opposing pairs:

bright vs. dark
lean vs. plump
taut vs. loose

The three in the left-hand column belong together, as do those on the right. These are not lists of virtues vs. faults—voices from either column can be big or small, beautiful or ugly, fleet or slow. They do, however, classify both virtues and faults. Adjectives of virtue that we would apply to left-column voices would include "brilliant," "focused," or "springy;" faults would be described as "edgy," "shrill," or "constricted." On the righthand side we would praise with "round," "velvety," "relaxed," and condemn with "shaky," "mushy," or "slack." While higher voices incline toward the left and lower to the right, the spectrum cuts across each type, too, and for this reason comparisons of individual voices must stay within a given category to be very meaningful. Behaviorally, voices to the left tend to be more mobile and precise, those to the right more stately and massive.

The more complete the voice and the finer its technical control, the harder it is to assign to either column. The ideal is a voice that embraces the virtues of left and right and is capable of throwing emphasis to either side without losing its balance—where would one put Caruso or Ponselle? Most singers, though, even great-voiced ones of both span and speed, can be placed at least a tick to the left or right. Lisitsian, for example, belongs left of center, and his baritone contemporary Leonard Warren on the right. By way of further illustration, here are a few more pairings, all of very high-quality vocalists, selected for left/right comparison within their voice types:

Luisa Tetrazzini/Joan Sutherland
Lucrezia Bori/Anna Moffo
Giovanni Martinelli *or* Lauritz Melchior/Jon Vickers
Alfredo Kraus/Léopold Simoneau
Heinrich Schlusnus/Dietrich Fischer-Dieskau
Fyodor Chaliapin/Cesare Siepi

Even if, as is likely among my younger readers, these voices have been experienced only on recordings, I think the contrasts will be sufficiently clear.

While the withdrawal from E-19 vocalism has displayed several characteristics, I think that at the structural level these come down to two: an overall reduction in format, and the damping of a tonal element I will call "core." "Format," I suppose, is fairly obvious. While linguistic set and temperamental color enter into this, its main ingredient is size or calibre—assuming that this is achieved with poise and relative ease and is combined with the tonal completeness alluded to earlier. It implies the many uses beyond mere loudness to which the melding of calibre with color can be put. "Core" means the meat of the tone, and this differentiates it from clarity, which can be on the surface. Call it "deep clarity." It takes in an imagistic concept like "bite," as well as a clinical one like "Singer's Formant"—the overtone territory said to account for the ringing quality of great voices. By it I also intend a sense that the voice is centered in the singer, that its visceral component can reach into the listener in an unimpeded energetic connection. Finally, core is the tonal element that allows voices of smaller format to capture and guide the listener's ear. It is more often prominent in left-column voices than in right. To say, then, that singing has misplaced something of both format and core is to say not only that it has foregone a measure of presence and of a particular aesthetic quality that may be much prized by some and less by others, but that it has lost some of its directness and urgency, and grown modest in its demands on our emotional response. If it is not taking the trouble to resound and make public its confessions, how important can it be? And to say that is to say, in turn, that opera has shriveled from the inside out, and while this is most clearly the case with E-19 opera, it is also true of the art form as a whole.

The final stage of E-19 vocalism and the withdrawal from it has occurred in my operagoing lifetime. I can testify to it on the evidence of live performance, with recordings used only to refresh my memory or to guide the curious. This last is important because, as with orchestral performance, recorded impressions of singing can be quite misleading. It requires a fair knowledge of singing and of the history of recording techniques, plus extensive and ever-renewed comparative listening to voices recorded and live, to advance informed propositions about the evolution of vocal behavior, and the farther back we reach the more problematic such propositions become. This doesn't mean that recorded evidence, even when skewed by technological differences, is inadmissible, or that plausible arguments can't be constructed around it. Indeed, with respect to important aspects of singing they will be necessary. But with these basic matters of format and core, live comparisons are far preferable to recorded ones. And since I am asking you to trust my ears, and ears are bent by time's passage and memory, these comparisons should be contemporaneous and their conditions as similar as possible. Here's one:

In the fall of 1968, I attended a performance of *Adriana Lecouvreur*, with Franco Corelli as Maurizio. Less than two weeks later I returned for Plácido Domingo's Met debut in the same part. Having seen Domingo in several roles with the New York City Opera, I was sure the debut would be successful, and so it was: smooth, warm singing with a fine glow, and quite sufficient resonance for the house. Still, here was a comparison of the two-*Mazeppas* sort—same role, same hall, same sets, same orchestra and conductor, all heard from the same seats and only a few days apart—and I was left with this equation: 1 Domingo = 2/3 Corelli. In literal, decibelic terms this cannot have been quite true, but as an overall impression—voice, theatrical presence, command of idiomatic effect—it was. Fairness would demand observing that Domingo was near the beginning of his career while Corelli was at the peak of his, with long experience in this, one of his best roles. True, and that accounts for some of the differences. But most of it lies with format and core.

An unusual thing about Domingo's vocal history is that at an early stage of a career already underway he moved across the center line, from right to left. In his NYCO seasons his voice had ample size and bloom in lyrical parts like Alfredo and Pinkerton, but when he pressed for the sinew wanted in *Tabarro*, *Pagliacci*, or the late scenes of *Carmen*, it tended to tighten and recede, and in his admirable traversal of the daunting title part in Ginastera's *Don Rodrigo* a slow quaver sometimes invaded sustained tones in the lower range, where there was often a huskiness betraying an imprecise phonation. These are indicators of peril for a voice seeking to move into the spinto or dramatic-tenor repertory. But Domingo adjusted. His vocal usage became leaner, tauter, more highly compressed. This gave his tone more metal, his breath management more economy. It enabled him to sing with security, safety, and endurance through a career whose cumulative stats are virtually unprecedented.[9]

It did not, however, make him into a *tenore di forza,* or even the type of spinto* voice previously considered capable of filling out such roles as Radamès, Canio, or Alvaro. His voice added core, but not format. Yet he sang these roles—and Otello, Samson and Siegmund besides—repeatedly, and for nearly the entire duration of his career was on merit the tenor of choice for them. That's the point: for thirty years, the best interpreter of the central dramatic protagonist parts of the E-19 repertory (the only one, in fact, to survive them with consistent technique and singing tone) has been a singer of noticeably smaller calibre and narrower dynamic span than the earlier norm.

Perhaps you don't consider this anecdotal comparison indicative of much, or even quite believable. Here's another: Flaviano Labò. I first heard him in 1957, as Alvaro, and was pleased to make his acquaintance: a sturdy Italian voice in good balance that sang a good Verdian line in good Verdian style with excellent *pronuncia* and which, as was apparent right from the first ascending line to B-flat at *"Il mondo inondi al suo splendore,"* had an exciting lift at the top. The going Met standard for this role, however, was then set by Del Monaco, Tucker, and Bergonzi, with Corelli soon to come—all voices and personalities of somewhat greater assertiveness and individuality. So while Labò was certainly to be preferred to certain other tenors of this repertory (Ortica, Baum), and offered high competence in lighter parts as well (Alfredo, Edgardo—but there was plenty of competition there, too), he was Italianate Tenor No. 6 or 7 on the roster, never No. 1. He often sang better than more illustrious colleagues, and gained more prominence in Europe and South America. But at the Met he settled into the repertory routine, a reliable "second cast" tenor, never selected for premieres and seldom for broadcasts.

Labò recorded very little. A 1961 *Don Carlo* for DG, which does not show him to much advantage, is his only commercially recorded complete role. On pirated live-performance recordings, there is a *Forza* from Fidenza in 1961 (in harsh sound and unfortunately lacking the Act III Carlo/Alvaro scene, but well sung, with Labò's Alvaro much as remembered), and a *Tosca*

---

* I really don't care for this term—the "pushed" lyric tenor—according to which Corelli is usually classified as a "big spinto" and Del Monaco a true *tenore di forza,* whereas their voices were nearly identical in format—but it's too handy to forego. Corelli's voice actually often seemed the bigger of the two owing to its freedom and control of dynamics; Del Monaco's sometimes had a greater impact through its projective intensity. The difference is more in handling and temperament than in calibre. We could say, though, that Domingo is truly a *"spinto"*—a lyric voice successfully worked up into a functionally stronger category. His format is closer to Richard Tucker's, with Domingo's voice a shade more malleable and lovely, Tucker's slightly the richer, with meatier *acuti.* To extend my rough-play quantitative comparisons: a Domingo is to a Tucker as a Corelli is to a Del Monaco.

(Vienna, season of 1963-64) with Rysanek and Bacquier, conducted by Argeo Quadri—a wildly theatrical performance, and if your Italian Tenor receptors are in working order, you'll be thrilled by Labò's Cavaradossi. There are also several discs of live-performance excerpts in Bongiovanni's *Mito dell'opera* series. For a well-recorded approximation of this voice as it first emerged, however, you will have to listen to the material from two LPs made in his early years—an aria recital for Decca/London and some *Manon Lescaut* excerpts with Moffo for RCA Victor. (They have recently become available on CD.) On the aria record is a memento of my *Forza* first hearing, Alvaro's scene "*O tu che in seno agl'angeli*," and I think you won't have to listen too closely to agree that there is no tenor now active who can approach, let alone match, Labò's singing of this demanding piece. So Met tenor No. 6 or 7, circa 1960, is markedly superior to Met tenor (and, so far as I'm aware, world tenor) No. 1 of the '00s.*

To adequately document the overall diminution in format across all vocal categories would entail dozens of citations of the Corelli/Domingo/ Labò variety, and probably still would not satisfy anyone prone to disbelief. So, with other aspects of singing, acting, and singingacting yet to be considered, I'll not undertake that task. (For a sketch of what such documentation would look like, see Note 36.[10]) But I can vouch for this: performance power is in brownout. And crude as the observation may seem, its importance can hardly be overstated, for only big, free voices can offer visceral impact, sing softly to magical effect in big theatres, and keep beautiful voices of smaller calibre to their appointed rounds. Night to night, and season to season, the sheer sound energy coming off the stage—which is the ground requirement for the conveyance of information, the projection of character and personality, and the stirring of emotions—putting on an opera, in short—has settled to a nice, containable level.

There are large voices still about, a few of excellent quality and solid technique. But here, too, there have been changes. In the left-right pairings shown on p. 323, there is a clear generational divide: with one exception, the

---

* And who would that be, after all? Licitra, perhaps—flashes of a potentially great voice and a slightly heftier format than Labò's, but nowhere near the latter's technical control, stylistic finish, or sense of musical shape and proportion. Alagna? A well-drawn line and command of phrase in lyrical roles, but his top has dried and he's grown depressingly careful. Giordani? Tonal substance comparable to Labò's, and the clang of good coin on top. But he rams foursquare through the music, sharps persistently, and has a shaky-baritone lower octave—darkness with no core. Labò is an Old Master by comparison with any of these.

left column singers are by some thirty to fifty years the older.* This is not, I confess, a coincidence. But while the list does illustrate a general proposition (that, in most categories and with some exceptions, prewar singers leaned to the left, postwar to the right), the particular selections are the results of an often futile search. Could I, for instance, find among postwar lyric sopranos strong enough to hold the stage as Mimì, Nedda, Fiora, and both Manons with high-powered singers (howevermuch by contrast with them) a voice with the centered purity, steadiness, and vowel clarity of Bori's? I could not.† Could I, on the other hand, name a great prewar dramatic tenor who sang with the cushioned, loosely held tone, derived from a soft attack, that was Vickers' vocal profile? Again, no. Either voice (i.e., either way of singing) would have been deemed an oddity in the other's time. And here we are speaking not so much of calibre (Bori's voice was probably not bigger than Moffo's, and certainly not bigger than Freni's, nor Vickers' smaller than Melchior's or Martinelli's) as tautness and tonal concentration—of core.

This left-to-right, prewar-postwar shift applies to all the chosen pairings, with the single exception noted. I will be using the pairings to illustrate. The first of these (Tetrazzini/Sutherland) will be the most extensively analyzed and documented, partly because the left/right, chest/head dualities are so clearly heard in this voice type and partly because some of the salient points, once made, need not be proven out at length for the remaining categories. And since this pairing not only raises the issue of live vs. recorded singing, but introduces into evidence singing as heard on some of the earliest recordings, caveats are necessary. I am keenly aware that many of my readers will not have heard any of these singers—at least in anything resembling their best vocal condition—save on recordings.‡ I am also aware that many listen-

---

* This exception is in the lyric tenor category. Kraus sang so long, more or less intact, that one thinks of him as belonging to a later generation than Simoneau, but in fact the latter's life and career began only a few years sooner. They perfectly typify the left-right qualities. While Kraus' exquisitely balanced, shrewdly graded voice carried well, it remained slender and a bit dry, and impinged on large spaces only at the top. Simoneau's fatter, lovelier sound bloomed warmly into the reaches of Carnegie Hall and the Met, but was so relaxed as to sometimes seem placid; and he did not have Kraus' high extension.

† Bidú Sayão and Dorothy Kirsten would come closest. But Sayão was an interwar-wartime singer whose career extended a few years beyond 1945. She shared many roles with Bori, and took some coloratura assignments Bori would not. But Sayão stayed away from such roles as Fiora, Nedda, or the Puccini Manon. Kirsten did essay some of these heavier parts effectively, but without quite the cited qaulities of Bori's, or the alacrity for Bori's *leggiero* roles.

‡ Item of disclosure: of the left-column singers to be discussed, I heard only Kraus and Melchior in person, whereas I saw all the right-column singers with regularity from their youthful primes onward, with the exception of Hotter, whom I saw only once in his brief Metropolitan career.

ers are impatient with, or even dismissive of, early recordings. This is a big mistake with respect to the understanding not only of the history of style and performance practice, but of singing itself, of the physical capacities and interpretive range it once possessed, and how these served musical and dramatic ends. The caveats, therefore, are entered not to discourage, but to suggest their cautionary place in an enjoyable and artistically enriching pursuit. For anyone professionally involved in any capacity, familiarity with early recordings is indispensable. Knowledge of the possibilities of the operatic voice is too incomplete without it.

Beyond the rather puerile beginner's complaints about surface noise and tinny accompaniments (are you interested enough to focus your ear, or not?) and the more substantive problem of distortions introduced by incorrect playing speeds—both much mitigated in the hands of the best contemporary restorers—there remain some genuine difficulties in the evaluation of early recorded performances. They have to do primarily with aural perspective and recording conditions, and are at their most pernicious with high voices. To start with, the frequency range of at least some early acousticals (dependent as it was on the sensitivity of the system's diaphragm) was limited at the upper end, and this means that on notes of high pitch, and particularly on certain vowels, overtones are missing, making it hard to judge the fullness and color, and even the intonation, of some of these notes. An even graver problem was that of blasting—the distortion caused by the inability of the acoustical apparatus to accommodate the impact of loud high notes. Again, high voices, and big voices, are those most severely penalized. To avoid this distortion, singers were often either positioned at a distance from the horn that disadvantaged the lower range and softer dynamics, required to step back from the horn for climactic passages, or to "pull the string" for loud high notes, reducing their effect. Finally, we must remember that the recording process and everything incidental to it—indeed, the very idea of submitting one's art to a mechanical device—was new, and that while some singers took to it others found it intimidating, unfriendly, or at least uninspiring; that each recording was a start-to-finish take without benefit of editing, piecing together, or post-production sweetening; and that at the beginning there was no accumulated technical wisdom or standardization of equipment to render comparisons of one time and place with another at all reliable.

This sounds daunting, and for all these reasons there is general agreement among the artists themselves and those who heard them live that many of the era's indisputably great singers were so unsatisfactorily recorded as to render them virtually unrecognizable. (Lillian Nordica is perhaps the most notorious example. But there are still extraordinary things to be heard on her discs.) *On the other hand*: because of these very limitations, we can at least be sure that for an aria's duration, were are hearing the piece exactly as the artist sang it, and as the energy of his or her voice, unaided, activated the recording mechanism,[11] and that (as opposed to the situation today) few of these voices can have been made to sound *better* than they did in life.

After the first primitive years, most voices were well enough accommodated, and in the finest of recent re-workings are presented with astonishing presence and, in many respects, more honesty than is preferred by contemporary "studio product." In any event, while there are aspects of tonal quality and sonic presence that may elude absolute certainty, there is much about a voice's behavior that can be extracted from even the poorest recordings—its basic color range, how it moved and connected, how it formed vowels and articulated words, how it attacked and released tone and—to some purpose here—how it negotiated between the sound families. All these are closely related to core, and that relationship is, I think, easy to hear in the singing of my chosen high sopranos. The left/right contrast between Tetrazzini and Sutherland is stark: considering that they are both great singers of the same category, they are as far removed from each other as any pair could be in terms of functional technique.*[11]

THE HIGH END DARKENS

The difference between Tetrazzini and Sutherland is well represented by the characteristic colors of their lower and middle ranges: the former's bright and open, sometimes glaring; the latter's dark and covered, sometimes gummy. Both instruments are of commanding size, especially for their range category, but their structures are not at all the same. Tetrazzini's voice has a compact strength—it drills into the centers of wordnotes and incises them into the line as if etching in glass. It leaps, quickspoken, over the widest intervals and through the most elaborate passagework. Its staccati are sharply stroked, its trills vigorously warbled. Its attacks on sustained forte notes have a palpable laryngeal impact equaled among voices of this sort only by some

---

* "Functional technique": I use this term to distinguish between a voice's underlying structure and its executional capabilities, and to emphasize that the former, though in sum the attributes we often ascribe to "having a great voice" or a "natural gift," nonetheless belongs to technique, and in fact ultimately determines everything else in a voice's sound and behavior. Most singers of the quality under discussion here begin with a basic structure in place, needing at most some tinkering, and so think of "technique" almost entirely in executional terms. Major functional re-adjustments would be disavowed as not "belonging" to the voice in question, and most singers would not describe their own techniques in the analytic terms used here. But these structural concerns, which account for any voice's essential impact and "message" before we even arrive at finer points of execution and interpretation, are what is presently under examination.

of Marcella Sembrich's. The "normal" soprano high notes (through the top B and C) are round and full-bodied, the high extension, to the sustained E, clean and strong. Never does the voice relax—even the pianissimi have a tensile, "on-the-voice" quality.

Sutherland's magic lay not in sounding on the voice, but in sounding released from it. Her executional technique was fully the equal of Tetrazzini's, except at the bottom (an important exception to which I will return below), and her tone soared with an unprecedented freedom and ease. Its size was of the full-bodied, voluminous sort, its accustomed emission too effortless to be called an "attack." Recorded comparisons show her sustaining legato at least as well as Tetrazzini, often for longer stretches and almost always at slower tempos. But her tone floats above the furrows ploughed by Tetrazzini's; there's an unearthly quality, the wordnotes a bit abstracted and aestheticized, as if to be kept discreet. Whereas Tetrazzini sounds of good cheer and in excellent health even in mournful passages, Sutherland tends to sound elegiac even in joyful ones.*

Both these singers were inimitable. I once wrote of Sutherland that in my operagoing experience, no other singer had sung "... that high, that loud, that fast, that beautiful," and that remains the case forty-some years on. Observe that in my format catalogue (see n. 10) Sutherland is alone in her category, and she would have been so for many years preceding and following the period in question. She would be now. Tetrazzini is more representative of her era. For all that there was no one just like her, there were many whose singing showed the same structural characteristics: bright, open voices with strong lower-to-middle-range connection, displaying the long range extension and executional alacrity of the fully mastered high-soprano voice type. I have chosen Tetrazzini because she recorded extensively at the height of her powers and the discs (leaving aside the early Zonophones) are of high quality, generally held to have been among the most successful of their time in capturing this sort of voice. But I could have picked Sembrich or even the post-retirement Patti; Galli-Curci; any of the many Marchesi-trained sopranos, from Melba on down; such Russians as Nezhdanova or Lipkowska; or, despite their somewhat rounder midranges, the German Margarethe Siems or the Austrian Selma Kurz. For all their many differences with one another

---

* For recorded representation of both women in their prime years, those interested should seek out Tetrazzini's HMV (now EMI) London recordings of 1907-1914—overall familiarity recommended, but for a sampling try the "*Ah, non giunge,*" "*Io son Titania,*" and *Carnevale Veneziana*—and Sutherland's recordings of the late 1950s and early '60s, among which her *Acis and Galatea, Lucia di Lammermoor, La Sonnambula,* and the "Prima Donna" album are perhaps the best, along with the live performances of *Rodelinda* (Sadler's Wells, 1959), *Lucia* (Covent Garden, 1959), and *Gli Ugonotti* (La Scala, 1962).

and with Tetrazzini, these (and other) high-soprano voices of pre-World War I cultivation all show the qualities mentioned. They all have core. It's not unreasonable to suppose that some of this impression is owed to the acoustical process, which undoubtedly tended to minimize a voice's aura, leaving nothing *but* a core. The best way to satisfy oneself on this count is to listen to some of the singers who began recording in the acoustical days and continued, with representative repertoire, into the electrical before vocal deterioration set in. A few examples would be sopranos Ponselle and Rethberg; tenors Gigli and Martinelli; baritones De Luca and Stracciari; basses Chaliapin and Pinza. Certainly one hears a change in immediacy, but little in timbre and none in technical impression. The voices gain a richness, but do not lose core, in the acoustical/electrical transition.

Speaking of deterioration, it is always instructive to observe what form this takes, for whether it happens early or late, it usually metastasizes from the point of greatest structural vulnerability.[12] Thus, while there can be no fair complaint about Sutherland's longevity,* there can also be little surprise that as time went on, her voice became not harsher and squallier, but looser and more opaque, and that the reticence of her lower range revealed itself as a lack of grounding. This is manifest on the 1976 *Trovatore* recording (see n. 38). The Act I double aria still shows much beautiful tone, well controlled line, and ease with passagework and ornamentation. The lower-middle area, though, is by this time not merely gentle but hollow, and the longstanding reluctance of the voice to speak clearly and straightforwardly in recitative is almost comically clumsy. In Act III, the weaknesses take over, despite some lovely effects higher up. The "*D'amor sull'-ali*" and "*Tu vedrai,*" built on ascending arcs from the now-unstable low range, both suffer (especially "*Tu vedrai,*" which proceeds upward from the middle C and needs impetus and thrust); and the *Miserere,* requiring strong low D-flats and E-flats and direct, clean intervals, is not successful.

For Sutherland did not engage the chest register.† She and her teachers, operating entirely within the upper sound family, succeeded in extending her mezzo-ish midrange upward into the "normal" soprano top, then the coloratura extension, in the process freeing it from any weight that might have

---

* I hope it's understood that "longevity" refers not to the interval between debut and retirement, but the span during which a voice retains its essential qualities and capabilities. Sutherland's was extraordinary for neither length nor brevity; it was approximately the expectable norm. Her decline was gradual, not precipitous.

† Only toward the end of her singing days (as in her 1980s Lucias, with some downward transpositions) does she venture an occasional defined chest note, and here we cannot be certain how much is technical choice and how much hormonal fate.

clung to it and training it in all the classical uses of limberness. That the voice was in hindsight a soprano all along, and the mezzo coloring a snare and a delusion, does not in the slightest detract from their achievement. In avoiding chest, however, they departed from the practices of all the pre-Great War high sopranos named earlier, even such light "pure coloraturas" as Maria Barrientos, not to mention other, more dramatic, voices. Those singers did not all handle the transitional area with Tetrazzini's sturdy openness, but they all had chest registers, ready to fire and equalized with the midrange notes just above.* Exceptions to this are extremely rare.[13]

Sutherland's first recording for English Decca was a recital of Donizetti and Verdi arias. This was my first impression of her voice, and is unlike any singing subsequently heard from her. While there's a silvery hue overall, the difference is especially apparent toward the bottom of the range, where the Italian vowels are clear and open, if sometimes on the shallow side. To hear this intoning of "*Alfin son tua*" in the *Lucia* Mad Scene against that of the first complete studio recording (1961) or the opening of her "*Ah, non credea*" in the *Sonnambula* of 1962, is to assume the singer had switched teachers. She hadn't, but in an early biography there's this:

> ". . . somehow her voice was also below par. Deliberately she and Richard [Bonynge] sat down to analyse the cause—and finally decided that, by applying to the Sutherland voice the special tones and colouring of singers like Galli-Curci and Tetrazzini . . . they had taken Joan beyond the limits of her own technique. . ." [Bonynge is quoted:] "'. . . one day you'll want to sing roles that aren't coloratura. Then you'll need that middle voice . . . faking it to sound like other people's only strains it.'"[14]

And so they set about working on her middle voice, to "warm it and round it." Now, this is reported as having transpired just before Sutherland's departure for Vancouver to sing Donna Anna in the summer of 1958, so it would appear that the warming and rounding had at least begun before the sessions that produced that first LP recital, in April of 1959. Nevertheless, the contrast it affords with recordings made only two or three years later certainly suggests "special tones and colouring of singers like Galli-Curci and Tetrazzini"—but

---

* Singers of Germanic culture usually treated the chest less brashly than Italians or Spaniards. Kurz, who of all those named is probably the most like Sutherland (still not very) and who also began as a mezzo, had a rich lower register into which she could dip in a legato blend or define more sharply. The low phrases in her recordings of "*Qui la voce*" offer an excellent example of the former; at the same places in her beautifully floated rendition, Sutherland just sings very quietly.

without the pre-requisite chest-register connection. Sutherland's infrequent attempts to summon vigor at the bottom (as at *"ognor m'insegue"* in the recitative to *"Ernani, involami,"* reveal a virgin territory whose borders are being skirted.*

We think of the chest register first as a source of vitality, of open-throated sound, and of positional depth (all good) or of raw, rough power and destructive imbalance (bad). Fear of Bad Chest, whose consequences are from time to time displayed in spectacular crash-and-burn cases that even the minimally informed can diagnose, leads to an exaggerated caution (often masked as snooty disdain—there are issues of taste and class here, too) with respect to any engagement with the lower sound family in high female voices. However, it was precisely the healthy participation of the chest register (defined at the bottom, balanced at the break, and blended into the lower middle) that gave singers like Galli-Curci and Tetrazzini not merely the ability to descend with strength, but to sing quietly and conversationally with pure, penetrating tone and verbal clarity, to sculpt phrases firmly, and to deploy a full expressive range throughout the lower octave. Thus, any effort to imitate their "special tones and colouring," to brighten and open the vowels, in the absence of a properly melded chest register was foredoomed; it could only lead to a shallow, blanched adjustment that faded ignominiously toward the bottom. So of their immediately available options, Sutherland and Bonynge did well to restore the more complex and full-bodied "mezzo middle," however artificially darkened it sometimes became. As for Tetrazzini, we cannot definitively judge the quality and presence of her sound, or know whether or not we would have preferred it aesthetically to Sutherland's (surely not always). But we can hear the workings, and marvel at the flex and strength of a champion athlete, the top-to-bottom structure of a completed high soprano voice.

---

* Even more pronounced is the distinction between her studio *Lucia* of '61 and the broadcast of February, 1959—the premiere release in the Royal Opera House "historic" series. Here, there are many moments in the lower midrange where she could easily be mistaken for an old-school Italian soprano, the bright vowels (like the *"i's"* in *"felici"*) and the open ones (*"a's"* and *"e's,"* as in *"Edgardo"* or *"ne separa"*) all noticeably clearer and purer, inflected with a more typical Italian affect, and even some use of "baby chest," as at *"'Porgimi la destra.'"* The singing in general has more rhythmic bone and stronger accenting, more flash in the sudden leaps to the top, than in any later version. One also hears passing moments where the low notes sound not fully prepared to receive such energies, particularly at phrase endings. Part of the excitement is live-performance adrenalin and heightened dramatic intent, but the actual vocalization, especially with regard to vowel formation, is also radically different. Sutherland had prepared the role in detail with Serafin, and rehearsed it with Zeffirelli, and it is certainly their influence that is being heard. By April in the recording studio, she had already pulled back to safer ground, but much of the vowel set remains, never to be heard again.

Among all voice types, Sutherland's represents the one that would seem least likely to require chest register engagement. Indeed, she is proof that without it, construction of a large-format high soprano voice of superior quality and executional technique is still possible. But the fact that she remains alone among singers of her category in her lifetime, whereas Tetrazzini had plenty of company in hers, suggests that the procedure is not a high-percentage play. And if that's so for her voice type, it would seem even more so for those below it. Yet, in the years following WWII, this chest-shy, loosely held, "relaxed" model did not merely reinforce upper-family dominance in female voices: it made its way downward through the male range. And so, leaving further consideration of the lower female voices aside for the moment, I propose a look at this new aesthetic for the male voice. I call it The Easy Plush, and it is recognizable in all my right-column male singers.

THE EASY PLUSH AND THE DEMISE OF DUPREZ

If there is a general observation to be made about the difference between the dramatic tenors* of Tetrazzini's time and those of Sutherland's, it would be that the later ones sound darker. In the singing of such Mediterranean dramatics as Tamagno, the young Zenatello, De Muro, Viñas, and Escalaïs—and, by and large, continuing with Martinelli, Lauri-Volpi, Cortis, Fleta, Vezzani, et al.—one hears clear, open vowels in the lower octave, gathered in but not overtly covered in the *passaggio,* and constant striving for tonal brilliance. At least on records, this last can be wearing, but of these singers' ability to sustain a continuity of vocal presence, maintain the musical line, project words clearly, and create upper-range excitement there can be no doubt. While they fully form the darker vowels, and sometimes use their coloration to induce upper-family participation in lyrical passages, we never hear a prevailing darkness of tone, looseness or lack of core.† When a voice is more fully rounded, as with the great Dutch heroic Jacques Urlus or the splendid French dramatic Paul Franz, there is still clean focus and firm grounding.

---

* That is, the Duprezian tenor, expected to extend full voice to B-flat, B, and if possible beyond. This to distinguish the term from both the older *"dramatique"* with mixed-voice extension and the *Heldentenor,* not to mention other categories such as the Bach/Handel/Mozart tenor or the Broadway baritenor, all of which agree on an upper limit of A-flat or A. In my "dramatic" category I include strong spinto voices capable of fulfilling dramatic roles.

† A partial exception would be Aureliano Pertile, so admired in Italy as musician and singing-actor. His progressively looser hold on the line and mealier tonal texture are the primary markers in the gradual unraveling of his fine instrument. The voice is still a bright one, however.

Caruso and Melchior are often cited as models for a baritonal sort of tenor voice—the former because of the obvious contrast between his way of singing and that of "older school" tenors like Marconi, De Lucia, and Bonci (or, for that matter, the more heroic Tamagno and Slezak), and the latter because of his baritone origins and his eventual specialization in the slightly lower Heldentenor repertory.* Certainly both these were deep-set instruments. The broadness and richness of Caruso's tone is still without parallel, as is the closed-in power and bedrock grounding of Melchior's; between them, they represent the apogee of the Duprezian tenor voice, insofar as we have aural evidence. Melchior stands a half-step to Caruso's left, but neither voice is ever far from the midline. They are neither prevailingly bright nor dark; they are both. Their tone is never dull in color or slow in action, and never lacks for core.

After World War II, there are still some dramatic and spinto tenors—Corelli, Bergonzi, and Tucker foremost among them—whose singing reflects the earlier modeling of balance and chiaroscuro, as well as the continuing example of Bjoerling, a lyric tenor whose vocal structure, like an exquisitely balanced system of springs and counterweights of strong, light metals, could support all but the heaviest roles. But previously undiscovered species come to light as well. Mario del Monaco exemplifies one: a powerful, visceral instrument whose position is pinned down by force, the *passaggio* kept low, and the line firmly but stiffly maintained. Its "a" and "e" vowels are usually turned in, not opened out, so that the lower range's darkish hue does not always seem entirely natural. In this Del Monaco differs sharply from his predecessors, among whom only Francesco Merli, famed *tenore di forza* of the 1930s, bears a similarity. But his technique influenced many a short-lived tenor voice to come, especially among Italians and Russians.

For all their deep set and dark vowel formation, there is core aplenty in the voices of Merli and Del Monaco, and laryngeal excitement in their tone. Not so with the other breed of postwar heroics—thick, pressurized, pharyngeal voices like those of Ramón Vinay, Ludwig Suthaus and, to a degree, James McCracken, through whose sounds the ring of true coin glints only fitfully. Whereas by earlier standards Del Monaco's vocalism would have been deemed technically primitive but tonally valid, these would have been found aesthetically wanting altogether.[15] And then there is Vickers. Like

---

* Baritonal color in tenors has little to do with baritone origins per se: it's a question of where the voice really belongs and how the re-positioning is done. Set Svanholm and Carlo Bergonzi began as baritones, but their voices bore scant traces of the fact. For that matter, Melchior's own early recordings as a baritone sound as "tenory" (though nowhere near as good) as those of his more familiar tenor self.

Sutherland, he stands in solitary splendor, the sole successful representative of his *Fach*. To name it is to define the structural contradiction within it: the Easy Plush Heroic Tenor. It sounds less like a big, ringing instrument into which the gentler ways have been introduced than a soft-textured, grainy one from which the metallic properties rather cautiously emerge—a voice built up from the *piano* rather than tamped down from the *forte*. Under Vickers' idiosyncratic guidance, it made unique sounds and created unique effects. It was the vocal aspect of a performing identity most unusual among opera singers: a strong, silent type, almost mystical, a presence at once impressive yet somehow withheld.

Vickers' vocal structure gave him access to an assortment of roles that crossed the boundaries of several categories without fully embracing any— that is one reason I've placed him opposite not one, but two left-column partners, Martinelli and Melchior. Certainly the roles in which he was fully satisfying (in my experience: Grimes, Florestan, Siegmund, Parsifal, Saint-Saëns' Samson, and—not a left-handed compliment—Vasek) make an intriguing group. So do those he consummated only in part, gener- ally owing to a reluctance to cut loose in defining moments (José, Canio, Ghermann, Alvaro) and those he dropped early on or never assumed (most famously, Tannhäuser). The suspicion that there was a vocal component in his distaste for this and other long, tenorcidal roles that pound on the notes just above the *passaggio* is consistent with the unease one often felt over the voice's ability to withstand a vigorous attack on a high note. (His perfor- mances of Otello and Alvaro in the '70s were marked by "junk" in some of the B-flats and Bs, and not-infrequent cracking.*) It is also at one with the singer's increasing reliance on a dreamy half-voice.

The uses of the *mezza-voce*—its presence or absence in a singer's technique, and its precise quality when present—have much to tell us about left-to-right

---

* An entire chapter devoted to the *Tannhäuser* episode will be found in Jeannie Williams' *Jon Vickers—a Hero's Life* (Northeastern Univ. Press, 1999, pp. 210-225). There is also an interesting recounting in: Peter G. Davis: *The American Opera Singer* (Doubleday, 1997, pp. 526-29). Both sources emphasize Vickers' religious convictions in his role selection process, but also speculate on vocal difficulties that may, consciously or not, have affected his decisions. In the Davis book, Vickers speaks of a proneness to cracking as a problem he had to overcome early on. With respect to this role-shyness, I think a struc- tural comparison of Vickers and his contemporary Wolfgang Windgassen is revealing. Like several other tenors I am about to mention, Windgassen sang an open "a" in the E-F# area. But he did so in the context of a left-column technique that kept the tone clear, steady and ringing, with the other vowels closed in the typical German manner. With a voice of neither the size nor quality of Vickers—and less sheer substance than those of Vinay, Suthaus, or McCracken—he nonetheless sang hundreds of highly credit- able Tristans, Tannhäusers, and Siegfrieds from the late 1940s into the '70s.

drift and the erosion of core and format. The half-voice is best defined as the midpoint on the swell-and-diminish, a hovering at the moment when the tonal texture begins to change from that of the *piano* to that of the *forte* (on the swell) or back again (on the diminish). Needless to say, in a voice of either sex the sound families must be balanced and knit to accomplish this. That's why the *messa di voce* is a classical test in vocalization, and a sure *mezza-voce* a mark of technical sophistication. In both sexes, the effect of the half-voice is greatest in the upper or upper-middle range, and since in male voices this places it close to the transitional center, it takes on an interfamilial aspect open to the female only in lower-middle blending, where it tends to attract less attention. Since in order to swell evenly from *piano* to *forte*, the kernel of the full voice must be present from the beginning, a genuine half-voice (among dramatic tenors, Caruso's is the best example) has the same tensile quality I have already identified in Tetrazzini. It carries easily, makes word-notes present, and draws the ear along in suspense. Because its tensility is derived from its physical reality—not so much a release as an elastic inter-play of opposing forces—it is inherently dramatic.

When we think of the tenor half-voice, we naturally recall exquisite moments from essentially lyrical singers. On records there are countless examples from such artists as Smirnoff, Bonci, Anselmi, Schipa, Tauber, or McCormack; French *voix-mixte* adepts like Clément or Villabella; more recently, from Valletti or Kraus—all wonderful, all capable of the half-voice as special effect. It is quite another matter, though, to integrate the *mezza-voce* into a voice of heavier calibre, and into music more reliant on chest-voice proper-ties. And so we find that among post-WWII tenors of dramatic format, only Corelli had a convincing command of the swell-and-diminish, and could draw on the tensile *mezza-voce* for remarkable effects. Except for him, we must turn to the records of much earlier singers to hear these usages from a comparable instrument.[16]

With the microphone came the croon. In popular music, the croon became the basis for whispered sweet nothings for the boys and mini-baritone bur-blings for the girls. Among male classical singers, it fostered the detached headvoice, useful for avoiding the trouble of full-voice high notes or of a gen-uine *mezza-voce*. Though the earliest example of the classical croon known to me is actually in the plenteous, long-ranged bass-baritone voice of Michael Bohnen (Spoliansky's "*Ich habe heimweh*," a film song, 1930, and a captivat-ing, if somewhat weird, three minutes), it usually made its appearance in the upper midrange of the tenor. Gigli and Ferruccio Tagliavini cleaned up with it in Italian films, and Richard Crooks on American radio. In the cases of Gigli and Crooks, it became a form of assisted living for senior-citizen tenors; in

Tagliavini's, it was his way of singing softly from the start, as if he had picked up on Gigli's practice of the late '30s.[17] (Tagliavini's half-voice stands in relation to Gigli's almost exactly as Crooks' does to McCormack's.)

Among the unique moments created by Vickers, many involved his version of the half-voice. It differed from the crooning of the lyric tenors just mentioned. In the context of Vickers' larger, darker instrument, it was a deeper sound than theirs, and avoided their syrupy quality. It could be touching and tender, but there was also a strangeness about it, and it was in that mode that it was most memorably employed. No one who heard it can forget the rapt eeriness with which he intoned "Now the Great Bear and the Pleiades" in *Grimes*, especially the gradually filled-in "who's" of "who can turn skies back and begin again?"—the masculine voice born in agony of the feminine, our genderistas would say, and an affect available to no one else.

Certainly not to Martinelli or Melchior. The former, a far leftwinger among front-rank tenors (if you want to hear core, he's your man), had superb control of line and dynamics. He could shave down the high B-flats in the *Aïda* tomb scene, play freely with the *passaggio* in songs, and ease the leash on the voice toward the bottom. But as for employment of a texture we would describe as a heady mix, or anything recognizably derived from the upper family, there are the merest hints on a few of his earliest recordings. From Melchior, though, there are many examples, including his perfect entry on the upper G-flat and subsequent arc over high B-flat in the *Meistersinger* Quintet; the weaving upper-middle line of "*Wie sie selig*" or long stretches of the Love Duet in *Tristan*. These are textbook demonstrations of upper-family inclusion in a heroic voice.* Melchior's singing, in fact, rides on the swell-and-diminish as surely as the earlier singers' do, and his half-voice, while less prodigally used, is of their tensile sort.

Vickers resorted more and more to the softer side as his career progressed, especially when collaborating with Karajan, who loved getting big voices (Vickers, Ruggero Raimondi) to sound dainty while pushing lyrical ones (Freni, Carreras) to sound muscular. But his predilection for it was clear from the start. A striking example is in his treatment of Otello's monologue, "*Dio mi potevi*," on his 1960 recording under Serafin. No other singer approaches the opening section of this in Vickers' gentle manner—not even the *lirico-spinto* Gigli. In principle, Vickers' approach has two virtues, one positive, one

---

* These examples refer to his recordings of 1929-31, including the abbreviated *Liebesnacht* duet with Frida Leider, where the blend is at its headiest. As one would expect, this extraordinary head-voice integration diminished with age. But it remains surprisingly available on broadcasts of the 1940s and some of the commercial recordings of that decade for Columbia; it is surely a strong factor in this singer's genuine longevity.

negative. The positive lies in observing Verdi's dynamic indication of *pppp*, the negative in avoiding the tenoristic accents usually hung like emotional pennants on the horizontal line of the writing, which, if literally rendered, does little but shift between A-flat and E-flat in the tenor's lower octave. Now, I don't know what sound Verdi had in his mind's ear when he wrote his quadruple *p*—surely this is one of his admonitory exaggerations. Nor do I care, actually, provided the alternative is convincing. But it cannot have been anything like the sound made by Vickers, because no tenor of Verdi's time would have conceived of such a sound as part of this (or any other) opera—it wouldn't have been deemed "legit." However softly sung, these phrases would have been on the voice; they would have had core. Vickers' half-voice is loose and easy, floating on a free vibrato, pretty and almost casually quiet. It's *soothing*. And nothing happens to it; it doesn't develop, it just goes along. He enunciates fastidiously, but the words carry no weight. I recall waiting in the opera house for this aural zephyr to waft itself up to the middle C at "*al volere del ciel*," where it could be heard, aware from the singer's comportment that he intended to convey something of urgency (knowing, even, what that was) and yet unable to track it in the moment—a frustration I encountered more than once with this artist. Even on the recording, these lines hide behind the *pianissimo* violin figure. The monologue is built on sand.

How different are Martinelli and Melchior. I don't mean their specific interpretive choices. I mean the underlying vocal ones, the technical constructs that, for all practical purposes, describe the singer's imaginative limits. Martinelli took on this role only in the late years of his career, when his voice had stiffened and its inclination to a lean-and-mean straightness and penetrating but somewhat sour timbre ("*aspro*, like lemon," as Del Monaco said of his own early efforts to sing lyrically) had turned into habit. On the ascent to G at "*l'anima acqueto*," in lieu of *mezza-voce* he can only squeeze down to a controlled but ugly *mezzo-forte*. The opening section, however, presents no such issues. Martinelli sings it at a firm mid-volume level—which, he knew, is the softest that can tell in this tessitura. His absolutely continuous line is drawn tight; his crystalline Italian sounds hewn, chiseled. The moment is material and visceral, not ethereal and incorporeal.

Melchior is even better.* He sings at about the same loudness as Martinelli in a more beautiful, shaded timbral mix, as observant of textual purity as

---

* I again refer to his early (1930) versions of the monologue and death scene. These are in German, but the disadvantage is mostly theoretical, so expressively are they rendered. Melchior later recorded extended excerpts in Italian with the baritone Herbert Janssen. These are not to be sneezed at, but German was his operatic language, and the voice fresher at the earlier sessions.

Vickers but to far greater effect. (Martinelli employs a number of the tra-ditional tenorial accents, though always with expressive logic and in the best musical taste.) Throughout the monologue and death scene, Melchior's command of the swell-and-diminish keeps the temperature, tension, and shape in proportions that seem inevitable; yet he never exaggerates its use or shows it as a technical effect—it simply informs the line. If you will listen to Melchior's voicing of the very G that proves troublesome for Martinelli, or better yet, to the same pitch at *"Or, morendo"* (*"Nun, im sterben"* in translation) in the death scene, you will hear a true half-voice, perfectly integrated into this most clarion of dramatic tenor instruments.

One can spend many hours with records of pre-WWII *Lieder* baritones without hearing anything like Fischer-Dieskau's *mezza-voce*. One will hear soft singing, of course, and much of it beautiful, from such artists as Demuth and Duhan, Hüsch or Rehkemper or Janssen, or even more remarkably in the *Lieder* recordings of Josef Schwarz, a full-ranged operatic dramatic baritone. But none of it will much resemble F-D's, which can only be described with adjectives that are becoming familiar here: "loose," "silken," "exquisite," or even "crooned." I first heard it on the word *"Ha!"*, late on a rainy afternoon in the old Record Hunter shop on upper Lexington Avenue, in the days when one auditioned potential purchases in a listening booth at the back. LPs were taking over now, and one was spinning on the turntable up front, where the proprietor and a couple of habitués listened, chatted, and smoked. *Tristan*, Act III, and as I heard the low strings well up with an especially dark pre-monition (it was Furtwängler) and an unfamiliar tenor voice intone *"Die alte Weise"* (it was Suthaus), I knew from my many private enactments that Kurwenal's cue was coming up—two *"Ha's,"* first softer then louder, and then the joyous full-voice leaps into the top for *"Diese Stimme! Seine Stimme!"*

I was used to Janssen's Kurwenal—I'd heard the Columbia album at least fifty times—and his combination of sufficiently heroic tone with a warm legato that could convey a touching tenderness had modeled the role for me. From seeing him as Gunther and Telramund, I also knew that his sound was ample, and from the old Bayreuth *Tannhäuser* set that it had once had a firmer center and greater ring. I knew, too, that his voice was then considered at the lyrical extreme for the part. My first live Kurwenal had been the rock-like Ferdinand Frantz, who with Hans Hotter was a leading Wotan of the time, and who sang both bass and *Heldenbariton* roles. On records I'd heard Rudolf Bockelmann, and over the air Joel Berglund—both magnificently steady bass-baritones with full command of Kurwenal's high tessitura. And at the Met, Hotter and Paul Schöffler were taking the part. In his prime,

Friedrich Schorr had sung it. These deeper, heavier voices, I realized, were probably "righter" for the character, the music, the contrast with the tenor, than Janssen's, devoted as I was to his way with the music.

But now came "*Ha's!*" lighter yet than Janssen's; then, instead of joyous leaps, a kind of easing into the top, as if slipping through the moment. Certainly the voice sounded fresh, freely emitted, and unbothered. Phrase after phrase, though, was softened at the corners, lyricized. When a more proclamatory accent was unavoidable, as at "*Nach Kornwall! Kühn und wonnig*," a choppy barkiness stood in for tonal solidity. The top of this voice sounded clear but rather thin, like a transparency with nothing underneath it, and the overall timbre seemed oriented toward the brightness of German closed "*ih*" and "*ee*" sounds. This was Kurwenal?—gruff, rough, blindly loyal old dog, inexcusable manners toward helpless upper-class women, overscale music to match? This sounded like a man of considerable delicacy. "Who's *that?*", I asked. One of the habitués removed the cigarette from between his lips, crooked it alongside his cheekbone, and fixed me with a look. "That's Dietrich Fischer-Dieskau," he said. "He's the coming German baritone." I nodded and said nothing. But I was perplexed.

My perplexity was eased in months and years to come as I heard much more of Fischer-Dieskau on records, over the air, and in person, and came to a fuller realization of his virtuosity, his range of musical and verbal imagination, and the depth of expression he often reached in the masterworks of the German song literature. As descriptive colorist, he has had few peers. And though his voice was light in weight, it was by no means small. It filled large halls without pushing. Its plump midrange sat in the ear even at soft dynamics and dipped to easily audible low notes most baritones only wave at as they pass by. He made big spaces intimate, and cast a spell.*

In sum, Fischer-Dieskau created a new paradigm for the baritone voice. He did it by the same means used by Sutherland and Vickers—incorporation of an unprecedented proportion of upper-family action, drawn yet farther down on the human voice chart. No baritone of whom we have aural tracings had succeeded in doing this without severely limiting the reach and strength of the voice. (The best of the French recitalists, like Barthes' hero Panzéra or Fischer-Dieskau's contemporary Gérard Souzay, perhaps came closest, but their instruments were small in format and of almost no operatic utility.) It was this extraordinarily heady adjustment that gave F-D's vocalism its honeyed tone, its suppleness, its pinpoint articulation, much of its color

---

* Since Fischer-Dieskau never sang at the Met, I heard him only in recital and concert settings: Town Hall, Hunter Auditorium, Carnegie Hall, and Avery Fisher Hall. Two of these appearances were with the New York Philharmonic; the rest were piano-accompanied.

spectrum, and above all its unique, purling half-voice. It is also responsible for that thin transparency in the upper range, and for the whitening and flattening-out (in quality, not pitch) that overtook the transitional notes from midcareer forward. In terms of the established E-19 categories, this was an odd vocal structure indeed, despite its range and size. Whereas earlier recitalists had sounded like opera singers singing *Lieder,* F-D sounded like a *Lieder* baritone singing opera.[18]

One hears and reads little about Heinrich Schlusnus these days. But in terms of vocal weight and quality as well as technical mastery, comparisons with Battistini, De Luca, or Lisitsian are not far-fetched.* His signature role was Wagner's Wolfram, of which he left an unsurpassed recording made when he was past sixty. But in the interwar years he was the foremost lyric baritone of the German Verdi revival, and his wartime performances, though sung in German and marked by stylistic peculiarities, show him still in full command of this repertory. He gauges dynamics superbly in this music, but always in operatic proportion, and so for demonstration of his consummate skill with *mezza-voce,* one turns to his *Lieder* recordings. Even here, he resorts to heady refinements far more selectively than Fischer-Dieskau. Nonetheless, his song recordings afford dozens of examples, from which I choose an illustrative few: the perfect ascent (legato, piano) to the F on "*Nur Liebe im erklingen*" at the close of Schubert's *An die Leier;* the shadings of Ds and E-flats (just under the *passaggio,* the most difficult area for piano "on the voice" singing) in the same composer's *An die Dioskuren*; the suspended top F at "*In den Frieden*" in Strauss' *Freundliche Vision*; or—most stunning of all—the softly taken, melting-yet-ringing Fs, F-sharps, and single high G-sharp scattered throughout Mahler's *Lieder eines fahrenden Gesellen,* always with a full-voice connection clearly behind them and alternated with hefty, biting fortes in the same tessitura. Clearly, Schlusnus' instrument—like Tetrazzini's when juxtaposed with Sutherland's or Melchior's with Vickers'—is strung on a sturdier framework than Fischer-Dieskau's. Its half-voice variants possess

---

* In one area of technical mastery—the display of bravura *fiorature* and ornamentation—Battistini stands unrivalled among baritones. But this is more a matter of the execution called for by different singing styles than of functional capability. By virtue of repertoire, generational custom, and personal taste, Schlusnus and Lisitsian had far fewer obligations of this sort than did Battistini. But that does not mean their voices weren't of comparable suppleness and alacrity. In his New York recital, Lisitsian played with melismatic flourishes while swelling and diminishing on the *passaggio* notes in an Armenian song, *The Crane*; on records, the echoed flourishes in the "Song of the Venetian Guest" (*Sadko*) give a glimpse of this expertise. In his recording of the Rossini *Figaro* aria, Schlusnus shows a true trill and a fine, dashing descending run, sung legato (whereas Fischer-Dieskau's, in his singing of Mozart, Bach, and Handel, achieved definition via the choppy articulation already alluded to, as if the notes were all *marcato* or even *martellato*).

(once again) greater tensility and core, and are heard in a different context: even the daintiest of Schlusnus' efforts are at one with the voice as a whole, whereas much as one admires Fischer-Dieskau's skill in suggesting dramatic weights, colors, and inflections, there is frequently an imitative quality to these efforts, the feel of an add-on that doesn't quite match, and whose seams widen at points of stress.

So it is that, while Fischer-Dieskau's "approach" to Verdi and much other operatic material seemed to require (and certainly received, for better and worse) the "highly detailed, intelligent, and imaginative artistry" spoken of by Fleming, one is quite content to hear Schlusnus just sing the music—it's more direct and natural, less of a stretch. Even his voice, though, is emphatically of a lyric, high-baritone set—it had not the calibre of such Italian dramatic baritones as Magini-Coletti, Amato, Ruffo, Stracciari, et al. (this list is long), or of his Berlin colleague Schwarz. Or of Leonard Warren, the first Easy Plush heavyweight baritone.

Warren accomplished for the dramatic baritone voice what Fischer-Dieskau had for the lyric. Before him, no one had brought such pillowy mellowness of texture and lightness of touch into a large, long, dark baritone voice of the first quality, capable of both the highest and heaviest roles of the Italian repertory. (His only predecessors who could accurately be described in loose, right-column terms were Carlo Galeffi—esteemed in much the same way as was Pertile among tenors, and evincing the same range of strengths and weaknesses—and Mariano Stabile, properly categorized as a very fine character baritone.) And with this structure came a unique *mezza-voce*, released and buoyant, yet fat and full-throated. With it, Warren would launch into the *passaggio* and beyond many a phrase—seductive, tender, recollective, or consoling—that sounded in one's ear at the farthest reach: "*Ah! Deh, non parlare al misero,*" "*Un nido di memorie,*" "*Vieni meco,*" "I'll go no more a-rovin'." The same headiness in the mix contributed to the soaring *forte* top notes that so often brought down the house.

Like Vickers, Warren relied more and more on soft options as his career progressed, and while his singing remained effective to the end of his abbreviated life, his voice drifted ever rightward. Its midrange not infrequently turned shuddery when loud, breathily husky when soft, its overall tone less informed by solidity and bite ("fudgy," as my former colleague Roger Dettmer once put it). Warren's immediate successor, MacNeil, had much of the same roominess and release in his singing, and a similar float to his *mezza-voce*. However, whereas Warren's voice had tended toward a "covered" looseness, (hence the fudginess), MacNeil's inclined to an "open" looseness (hence a timbral blandness), and when his voice showed an earlier and more worrisome midrange instability (a slow waver, rather than the shuddering), his technical answer was to introduce a raw, straight tone—an extreme leftward switch, and an aesthetic trajectory one cannot imagine Warren ever having taken, even in old age.

The singing of the third great American baritone of the immediate post-war years, Robert Merrill, was more grounded and straightforward (a focused brilliance in the upper range, no fussing with *mezza-voce*), and while the top gradually eroded, his midrange remained rich and secure to an advanced age—a more traditional sort of vocal decline. These three singers, with the addition of Milnes (whose technique suggested an effort to combine Warren's *mezza-voce* with Merrill's top), came to define the American baritone sound.

Yet that is much changed from the tonal model that had obtained only a few years earlier. Or, I should say, models, for there were two—a brighter and a darker. The former is best exemplified by John Charles Thomas: hefty and biting; steady and true, sometimes to the point of straightness; bright, with touches of nasality, and ascending with little manipulation into a ringing, dramatic-tenory top. This is the voice type most commonly thought of as American Baritone in the pre-WWII years, the sound heard from concert platforms, over the airwaves, on records, and in the movies from such singers as Thomas himself, Reinald Werrenrath, Nelson Eddy, Igor Gorin, countless church soloists and Community Concert recitalists. Its basic qualities are also those of the American show baritone from the Herbert/Friml/Romberg operetta days to the musicals of Kern, Rodgers, and Loesser. Of all these singers, only Thomas and Robert Weede did more than dabble in opera.

The darker edition of this American model is shown by the voice of Tibbett, similar to the others in its steady-and-true emission, but deeper-toned, more akin to those of the Italian dramatic baritones of the time. Compared with the best of those, his primary technical weakness was in his approach to the top, which was often impressive but seldom free-sounding.* On the other hand, Tibbett had at his disposal a tensile, old-style half-voice that stood in relation to Warren's approximately as Schlusnus' did to Fischer-Dieskau's. He used it to greatest effect in the upper midrange, where it sounded like a call from afar, beckoning from songs by Arlen or Gershwin or Speaks, from Handel's "Where'er You Walk," from the broadcasts of Wolfram, Germont or Boccanegra (my favorite—hear that death scene benediction, with its

---

* With a voice of heavier calibre and darker coloration, Tibbett sang as "open" as Thomas up to the *passaggio*, where he adopted a "cover and drive" system for the remainder of his range. For a cruder version of the same technique in a voice of similar format, listen to Tito Gobbi.

heart-catching piano attack on F at "*Cangia le spine in fior.*" Warren's *mezza-voce* is a balm; Tibbett's haunts.

Of all the remarkable things about Fischer-Dieskau's art and career, none was more remarkable than his sheer pervasiveness—the omnipresence of his voice in all music that could be made to fit within its compass, and the omnipresence of the resulting interpretations around the world on records. One aspect of this pervasiveness is that, with a voice that could without malice be described as suitable for only the most lyrical operatic roles (he himself characterized his young instrument as "a gentle oboe"), he in fact sang many of the heaviest, including assignments once considered strictly the province of the true *Heldenbariton*, bass-baritone, or Italian dramatic baritone. The employment in some of these parts of a voice of F-D's natural lightness of weight and color and of such persistently lyrical guidance was, so far as I am aware, without precedent. Even among voices whose weights and hues fit the traditional heroic baritone profile more closely, a more loosely knit structure is evident as we move through the generation that bridged WWII to the one that followed. There are hints of this in the singing of such admirable artists as Schöffler, whose large, warmly shaded bass-baritone voice was sometimes given to unsettlement; of Hermann Uhde, whose slightly higher baritone, also warm and large, could turn hollow in timbre and dodgy of pitch; and of the young George London, whose big, round sound suggested mushiness in its lyrical mode. (He later made a leftward adjustment similar to Gedda's, and under the same teacher's supervision.) These were singers whose tone was still of heroic substance. Their right-column attributes are perhaps not immediately apparent unless compared with those of Frantz, Otto Edelmann, Berglund, and Hans Hermann Nissen, not to mention (working our way ever leftward) Wilhelm Schirp, Emil Schipper, Josef von Manowarda, or—particularly on his later recordings—Wilhelm Rode. No refined distinctions are required, however, in the case of Hans Hotter.

Among the important voices of all categories mentioned herein, Hotter's is the farthest to the right—an imposing mass, but so loosely agglomerated (Sutherland's or Vickers' or Warren's are fiercely gripped by comparison) that the wonder is that it stayed together for a career of normal duration. His full voice had reasonable firmness and center in the *Heldenbariton* tessitura for a few years early on, and again much later in bass roles. But for most of his singing life in the roles for which he was noted, his full voice tended toward a spread, chewed-over sound whose center was hard to locate. At worst, it had a blown-through-the-nose quality, the consonants sloughed over. This peculiarly fluffy adjustment was, to be sure, an antidote to the tonal rawness, expressive stolidity, and adamantine manner too often associated with this voice type. Even at its slackest and most approximate, Hotter's voice retained expressive pliability and, when not too hard-pressed, an inimitable enfolding sound. It also embraced a calm *mezza-voce*—Easy Plush of the deepest pile—with which he communed movingly in *Lieder* and his operatic characters' inward moments.

Hotter was the pre-eminent Wotan, Holländer, and—with Schöffler—Hans Sachs of the postwar decades, the singer of choice for those bellwether roles (especially as Frantz relinquished them in the mid-Fifties) everywhere except the Metropolitan. As such, he stood in the place left vacant by Friedrich Schorr. Schorr, the son of a prominent Hungarian cantor of markedly similar vocal characteristics, was by no means a far left-winger. Indeed, it is the nappiness of his tone, its autumnal color range (browns, maroons), and the *bel canto* ductility of his legato—all unusual among Wagnerians—that are most apt to strike a first-time listener. By contrast with Hotter, however, it is the firmness and sturdiness, the centered pitch (which once in a while hangs slightly flat—a fact that is instantly detectable precisely because of the tonal center), and a pealing, brassy sonority that are evident on his primetime recordings of the late Twenties and early Thirties.* And, once more, a tensile, on-the-voice *mezza-voce* of extraordinary beauty that informs the Dutchman's "*Wie aus der Ferne*," Strauss' *Traum durch die Dämmerung*, the tender spots in Wotan's Farewell, or, most famously, the piano E natural at "*Johannisnacht!*" in Sachs' *Wahnmonolog*. Like Schlusnus in his *Lieder* or Lisitsian in "*Ombra mai fu*," Schorr finds the need to create special moments with his *mezza-voce* less frequently than some of his right-column successors, and although we all have our favorite ones evoked by this artist or that, on the whole we do not miss them in Schorr, because we sense the possibility ever-present in the conduct of the line, the pose of the tone. When the softer effects come, they seem truly special, the gentle or introspective or poetical aspects of a person of unquestioned strength and self-containment, secure in his trust of self, voice, music.

I'm sure the pattern is clear by now. Among non-Italians in the postwar generation of male singers, from tenor down to low baritone, there rose to prominence several whose voices were still of grand-opera format, but whose textures were headier, more loosely woven, and of lower compression than those of the preceding generations. Their techniques embraced an enviable

---

* According to an early mentor of mine, the baritone Hugh Thompson, Schorr's voice sounded through the house "like a trombone." Thompson's Met career overlapped Schorr's for a few seasons; as the son of the New York critic Oscar Thompson, he also knew Schorr's singing from its prime years. I found him an acute listener.

fluency and ease in *cantabile*, but not the thrust, attack, and core of their elders'. Their soft singing conveyed more in the way of comfort than suspense. Surely, though, this structure would not be found even farther down, in the lowest (and, by definition, chestiest) of categories, the bass? Or amongst those authors of *squillo* and guardians of pure, clear vowels, the Italians?

On March 5, 1948, Ezio Pinza sang his final performance at the Metropolitan, in the title role of *Don Giovanni*. Since even the irreplaceable must be replaced, the most successful of the younger Italian basses soon appeared. One, Italo Tajo, had a voice of mellifluent beauty and considerable substance (his later reputation as a no-voice wonder was poorly founded), but lighter than Pinza's and given to tremulousness under pressure. Another, Nicola Rossi-Lemeni, had a bigger sound, also of basically fine quality, that leaned toward wooliness. Both were theatrically gifted, artistically imaginative singers, but with their relative lack of tonal center and weak low notes did not have the vocal vitality and authority of Pinza or the other notable interwar Italian bassos, Tancredi Pasero and Nazzareno de Angelis. The third and youngest import, Cesare Siepi, had what remains the most complete and highly finished Italian bass voice since Pinza's. I wonder if a largish instrument ever sat with such cushy roominess on the extended bass range (low C to the high F-sharp, to my certain knowledge). Once again the texture of the *mezza-voce* is a key: smooth and buttery, flowing across Giovanni's *"Deh, vieni alla finestra"* or over the first top E of Filippo's *"Amor per me non ha,"* or moving suavely, at the merest touch, through the midrange in Freire's *Ay, ay, ay.* Siepi's full voice, quite voluminous in the singer's prime, seemed a natural outgrowth of this softness—pliant and rich, never forced, and steered along the line with a patrician elegance. And yet: the profile of this large, beautiful voice was somehow indistinct, its features lacking the ultimate contrast. In the great Verdi roles, as Boris or Mephistophélès, his voice always had amplitude and fine quality, but not always the core that would have translated presence into dominance, or the quick, direct movement from the center of one note to the center of another that would have conveyed the greatest immediacy and urgency. His Mozart singing was always sprightly, pleasing, and reassuringly easy. But it did not have Pinza's flash and bite, or the sense of danger wrapped in the Latin velvet of his *mezza-voce*—at *"E là, gioello mio, ci sposeremo"* he offers Zerlina a life of sensuous luxury where Pinza promises thrills, and the difference is again in the tensility of the tone, Pinza's light and caressing but suspenseful, Siepi's so relaxed as to verge on the casual. When I used to hear Siepi's renditions of Cole Porter criticized for being "too much like opera," I thought "No, his opera singing is too much like Cole Porter." And like Warren's, Siepi's voice slid rightward over the years, its grounding (firm at the outset) softening underfoot and midrange pitches sometimes hazing over, until, to attain the required tension for high notes, he had to resort to an uncharacteristic thinning.

Pinza's singing certainly affords a contrast with Siepi's. So does that of many earlier basses, like the Pole Adamo Didur, the Spaniard Jose Mardones, the Frenchman Jean-François Delmas, the Italian Navarrini, to say nothing of the Germanic and Scandinavian Wagnerians—almost any prominent bass of the 1900-1930 period, in fact, including those of a more bass-baritonish sort like Bohnen or Journet. All these voices were of tauter structure, a more resounding sonority, than Siepi's. But if we are in search of vocal core and the tensile half-voice, especially among higher basses (for he was not a deep, "black" bass in either range or timbre), Chaliapin is surely the exemplar. Apart from his Living Legend status in the cultural history of his nation and era, Chaliapin is so complete an embodiment of the E-19 male performing personality—and that spirit, in turn, so removed from us, so disruptive of our rules and regulations—that it is not easy to train a cool gaze on the workings of his voice. Nor does he give the matter close attention in any of his reminiscences. He had after all sung such roles as Ferrando, Mephistophélès, Oroveso, and Brogni before reaching 20, without anything much we could identify as training. It does not matter how he sang them, or under what provincial conditions. The mere fact that he did so shows that the vocal structure (range, volume, basic quality) was present before tinkering—and there wasn't a lot of that, either. It's noteworthy, though, that the few bits of technical commentary he offers have to do with respiratory control. I think it likely that if he learned anything of functional importance from his only real teacher, Usatov, it was in the area of breath resistance, which would in turn have lent the voice a more penetrating focus.[19]

It is this penetrating quality of his full voice—lean and gathered, compressive, and (for a bass) quite bright—that jumps out from his recordings, no doubt at the expense of the rounder, more velvety textures often noted by those who heard him in person. The more powerful he wanted the sound to be (the "*Ave Signor*" in the *Mefistofele* Prologue offers several instances, including the attacked high F at "*Ah! Si, Maestro divino*"), the more compacted and "against the air" the emission becomes. His unique *mezza-voce* is the perfect companion to this sound. Its most extraordinary deployment (or at any rate, the most quickly and commonly noted one) is in his pianissimo, teased like a single strand out of the knit of his voice. In songs, he used it to bewitching effect in the highest range (try No. 9 of Rubinstein's *Persian Love Songs*, where he wings it to the high G); in opera, he holds us with the seemingly endless, barely audible middle B-flat ("*ot ikusheni*") that concludes the prayer in Boris' Farewell. Remarkable as these isolations are of themselves, the singer's access to their source (upper-family, but neither feminine nor boyish) is also what enables the blended half-voice in which he swaddles the recollection of the tsaryevna in Boris' monologue, or the modulation and balance of the voice through the long sustained phrases of "In the Ocean of the Air" from Rubinstein's *The Demon*, which for beauty of tone and purity of legato (the "*bel canto*" virtues) is among his finest recordings.

When I term Chaliapin's half-voice "unique" and "bewitching," I do not mean that it was suited to all purposes better than anyone else's. For one thing, it didn't always work. In his early recording of the *Don Carlo* aria, for instance, he obviously wishes to avoid the *cupo* sound so often heard on the D's at "*sotto la volta nera*," but his solution—a denuded open *mezzo-piano*—is not at all convincing; Siepi is certainly preferable here. For another, varieties of floated-yet-connected soft singing in the upper range constitute something of a tradition—perhaps inspired by Chaliapin's example, but obviously accessible to others—among Russian and East European basses. The best of this that I have heard live came in a Chicago *Khovanshchina* in 1971, when Nicolai Ghiaurov offered a stunning demonstration in the scene of Khovansky's farewell to the streltsy. On recordings, Alexander Kipnis (a deep bass), Boris Christoff, Mark Reizen, and Boris Gmyrya all create remarkable half-voice effects; in another of Rubinstein's Persian songs (No. 2), the last-named ends with a feathery high pianissimo quite like Chaliapin's. Quite, yet not quite: Gmyrya's is ever so slightly more wispy and released, Chaliapin's ever so slightly more held in, its thread of tone strung a half-turn tighter and in consequence a shade more precise. The English critic Neville Cardus observed that "His [Chaliapin's] *pianissimi* were, so to say, resonance turned down," and it is that sense of a mighty force held in check, latent in even the finest tracings, that to my hearing belongs to Chaliapin alone among basses.[20]

The Easy Plush men I have been discussing were not typical of their time in a proportional-representation sense. Each loomed large at least in part because of his *unlikeness* to both his forebears and his contemporaries. Yet what was atypical about them was also what was new, and when the new finds such champions it becomes the stamp of the age; it re-sets the compass. Technically, the male Easy Plush proposes the retention of large format but a reduction of core. *Within the structure of the tone itself*, it expresses a preference for ease over struggle, for relaxation over tension. And from this grows a Not-a-Problem concept of legato, a guidance of the line that strives for an impression not of overcoming obstacles, but of encountering none. But since struggle, tension, and the overcoming of obstacles are necessary to drama, and drama necessary to opera, it is by no means a stretch to suggest that it points toward an aesthetic that is inherently less dramatic and thus less operatic that the one(s) it replaced. It also sets forth a new model of masculinity, and thus of the stance of male characters toward one another, their female counterparts, and us.

THE LOW END VANISHES

"What has happened to the contralto species?", Giulietta Simionato once asked, taking my interlocutor's query about mezzos one step deeper. ". . . It went two octaves from F to F. Now all mezzos are taking on the contralto repertory, but they must resort to chest tones." (Rasponi, *The Last Prima Donnas*, p. 341). A pertinent question, though her way of posing it raises several more, and for clarity's sake they mustn't be skipped. To start: what can she mean by "chest tones?" As a mezzo of high accomplishment, *she* must know what she means, and I know what *I* mean—but these seem not to be the same thing. In interviews, Simionato more than once asserted that she never used chest voice. What manner of tone was that, then, that she employed at the end of the "*Condotta*" in *Il Trovatore*, and in numerous other spots in roles like Amneris or Santuzza (or Quickly!—those "*Reverenzas*" and "*Povera donnas*" aren't in chest?)—whenever lower-range strength was called for? Granted, hers was not a raucous chest, like Supervia's, and she didn't break into it sharply, lean as hard on it as Elmo or Barbieri sometimes did, or drag it in above the transition area, as others have been known to do. But if we can't term these sounds—distinctly lower-family ones, however nicely blended—"chest tones," then the term has no meaning save one known only to the singer, possibly based on her reading of bodily sensations.[21]

And to which contraltos could she have been referring? If we take her F-to-F measurement literally, these must have been among the oratorio dowagers. But what operatic repertory could they have undertaken? Orfeo, in the most austere of versions, and so some did. But even La Cieca and Madelon must have Gs (La Cieca an A in ensemble), and Erda an A-flat. So Simionato is really speaking about the "sit" of the voice—tessitura, not compass—and its overall color. For indeed contraltos once assumed certain roles now always taken by mezzos, including some (Brangäne, Adalgisa, Siébel, et al.) originally designated for soprano. But did they do so without resorting to chest tones? Who? Sigrid Onegin? Schumann-Heink or Arndt-Ober or Matzenauer? Marie Delna or Jeanne Gerville-Réache? No, none of those. Simionato's earlier compatriots Eugenia Mantelli and Armida Parsi-Pettinella? Hardly. Even those models of English concert-and-oratorio dowagerness, Louise Kirkby-Lunn and Dame Clara Butt, boomed in chest when the time arrived, as it often did. (Dame Clara's traversal of Orsini's Brindisi from *Lucrezia Borgia*, camp-prone but impressive, is a famous example, but there are many others.)

It is true though (and this is certainly what Simionato was driving at) that many of these contraltos, especially among those of Anglo-American and Northern European origins, cultivated the *"Ombra mai fu"* sound—a dark-toned, open-throated one that kept upper-family timbres dominant in the transition area and brought in tinctures of chest only as the voice settled deeper in the range. It was their version of the "seamless scale" ideal of regis-tral unification, and in the best of these voices resulted in tones of matchless beauty and gravity throughout the octave centered on the *passaggio*. Indeed, F-to-F would imply a half-and-half voice comprising precise equalization of the families *as the natural state* of instruments so disposed, and this, I would suggest, accounts for the deep, assured calm regularly conveyed by this voice type and not quite by any other—though it is approached, at times, by the best of the deep basses.

Now, a voice that extends from the low F through the high G or A-flat with sophisticated control of large-format, aesthetically gratifying tone is as fully realized, as greatvoiced, as one of any other conformation. There is no more fin-ished a singer than, for instance, Sigrid Onegin. Her deep, lovely tone moves through the vocal setting of Chopin's Op. 29 A-flat impromptu or Arditi's *Leggero invisibile* with a gestural ductility and play of color that bespeak total command. In *"Ah, mon fils" (Le Prophète)* she sends a mezzo-piano line curling over the top A-sharp in a kind of wail that is angelic and eerie in equal mea-sure. In the flashing divisions of *"O prêtres de Baal"* (same opera) she can (like Schumann-Heink in that passage or in the allegro of *"Parto, parto"* from *La Clemenza di Tito*) send her voice hurtling through the same territory in per-fect order. But these examples are either of passing notes, or else of phrases to which a soft, heady sound are appropriate. Among all these singers, it is difficult to find a persuasive example of a sustained forte note higher than A-flat, and that means that complete as their voices are in and of themselves, and as satisfying as they are in the alto writing of Handel or Bach or Gluck, in certain Rossini hero roles or such Donizetti parts as Orsini and Léonore, or in Wagner, when he really specified *"alt,"* their sit are not right for the dramatic mezzo or alternate-*Fach* roles that became the E-19 norm—and at boosted concert pitch, at that. Thus, the indubitably greatvoiced Homer leaves us still waiting for Amneris's knockout punch in the boudoir and judgment scenes of *Aïda* (opposite Gadski and Caruso, respectively), and the similarly equipped Olszewska does a ladylike fadeout with the loftier outbursts of Octavian or Ortrud. And thus, certain arias (*"O don fatale"*) and convenient throughwritten passages (Ortrud's *"Entweihte Götter"*) were frequently transposed downward to accommodate these otherwise potent voices.

Heard in E-19 perspective, many of the F-to-F-plus, seamless-scale contraltos violated the Displacement Rule by doing precisely what Simionato congratulates them on—carrying a head-dominant blend too low—and were therefore punished in accordance with the Rule's decree: she who violates it at the bottom shall suffer the consequences at the top.[22] And so, as the late E-19 repertory became standard and the oratorio culture faded, contraltos were almost entirely displaced by mezzos, who brought the defined chest up toward the transition center not only to project the lower-middle range more forcefully, but to provide a launching platform, so to speak, for the more propulsive top now preferred. This major readjustment enabled some very exciting performances of Amneris, Azucena, and Eboli, of Ortrud and Santuzza, but has also meant at least three less desirable things. One: The upward extension of chest in many of these low voices has made equalization more treacherous, the "seamless" ideal harder to attain; it is also easily abused. Two: Some fine instruments have gone underused, or altogether unemployed, while many more that could—and in some cases should—sing the contralto's two-octaves-plus have instead been trained to negotiate the mezzo's. Three: the embrace of the deep female voice, with its range of suggestion, has been withdrawn. And before we follow the upward migration of certain aggressive properties in the female voice, we should pay our respects to the uses of that banished sound.[23]

When onstage role-playing falls out of compliance with the real-life kind, the onstage variety conforms. People will not pay to see and hear themselves represented in ways that contradict their idealized self-images. Thus, a vocal culture willing to do away with the contralto is also willing, perhaps even eager, to dispense with the qualities uniquely hers. These would seem benign enough: I have spoken of a deep, assured calm and of an embrace, to which we can add evocations of devotion and contemplation, funerary grief, and motherly solicitude. Granted, there is also a conceivably authoritarian kind of grandeur that, doubtless helped along by the deliciously imperious contralto concoctions of Gilbert and Sullivan, became inseparable from an oft-ridiculed social stereotype. There's masculinity, too: in an instrument that can plummet an octave-and-a-half into lower-family regions (Schumann-Heink intones a sepulchral low D to end *Der Tod und das Mädchen*; one of the Butts intrudes on her sisters a-Maying with a pedal-point contra-C), that is natural and inevitable. But even these seem hardly worth the cluck of a tongue any more.

It's hard to resist the conclusion that on some level, we don't want women to sound deeply calm and embracing, devotional and contemplative, grieving and motherly. Or, simply, mature. Still not trusting any voice over thirty, we first of all reject the equation of maturity with wisdom and authority. Not only is ripeness not all, it's nothing. But even if we still held those female virtues dear, we would have trouble hearing in the old contralto sound two qualities that late E-19 audiences seem to have assented to unquestioningly: sexual allure and male pubescence. Certainly low female voices can sound languorous and smoky, and as the foregoing examples illustrate, given technically superior guidance they can move with quick athleticism. But the old contraltos did not usually sound languorous and smoky. They sounded matronly. And even when they bounced through the dashing-youth measures of Orsini or Urbain or the boyish couplets of Siébel or Stephano, they went on sounding matronly. Yet evidently no contradiction was felt. In roles like Carmen, Dalila, Kundry, and Venus, and by extension such romantic-rival mezzo parts as Amneris, Eboli, Laura, and Contessa di Bouillon—even sexpot supporting roles like Maddalena and Lola—the contralto sound in all its maternal stateliness, its very dowagerness, was accepted as irresistible to otherwise defiantly autonomous heroes, and served as well for cheeky pageboys and male tweeners on their first sexual adventures.

The proto-Freudian and –Jungian implications of all this, including those of mother-son incest and a Pagan goddess-religion rebellion, would suffice to accomplish a psychoanalytic Restoration. And while other, more everyday operaworld factors surely contributed (e.g., the availability of contralto voices owing to their more general employment, including the male heroic roles once assumed by castrati; the necessity of matching in format while contrasting in color with other grand-opera voice types; and the influence of particular individual interpretations[24]), the fact remains that the late E-19 moved contraltos into these roles, and we have moved them out. Reminding ourselves that the deep contralto species is native to Northern habitat and seldom found in the South,* we could speculate that for Victorian and Edwardian receptors, it was exactly the matronliness in sound and look of these singers, and the fact that it was the same woman who enticed José or Samson of a Friday night who emerged, to everyone's relief, singing of redemption on a Sunday afternoon, that allowed these meanings to be either ignored or secretly reveled in. There's nothing like the vicarious violation of a major taboo, especially when the music's good.

---

* Though some Italian and Spanish voices of the late E-19 are categorized as contralto (even Minghini-Cattaneo is sometimes listed that way, and later, with better cause, Elmo), their sound is invariably brighter and more open—more mezzo-ish—than that of their Northern sisters. They never resort to "pure head," and are generally less concerned with from-the-top-down blending. They would rather sound harsh than hooty.

Or we could ask ourselves why we have such difficulty hearing sex and youth in the low female voice. As for sex, we don't have to be Freudians to recognize the maternal element of Other-Womanly allure in the psychologies of these characters. And as for youth: while the contemporary pattern is to prolong adolescence indefinitely, it was once an ambition to look, sound, and act like a grownup as soon as possible. Life was shorter, for one thing, and adult responsibilities assumed earlier. Operatically, this is faithfully reflected in both the onstage lives of the characters and the career patterns of the singers who depicted them. It's one of our conceits that youthfulness is properly conveyed by light, "fresh" voices—the inadequacies of entire *Bohème* casts are excused on the grounds that they are "believably young." Yet, if one were to average out the ages of the Serafin *Bohème* cast listed earlier (see p. 270) when they sang these roles together in the 1950s, it's unlikely there's a year's difference from Baz Luhrman's or the NYCO's in the '00s. The Bohemians of yore sounded like lusty, vigorous, life-to-the-fullest young adults. They also sounded like opera singers.* Earlier, the pattern of very young singers, including our contraltos, in major roles was if anything more pronounced. The instance of Chaliapin has already been cited, but in addition: Ponselle, the *Forza* Leonora at 21; Johanna Gadski, Agathe at 17; Schorr, the *Walküre* Wotan at 23; Schumann-Heink, Azucena at 17 (admittedly, a one-shot—but by age 28 she was singing Carmen, Fidès, and Ortrud), etc., etc. Until WWII, these examples are closer to the rule than the exception. In this context, the issuance of deep, matured female tone from the throats of young males is not such an incongruity.

When the real mezzos took over contralto duties in addition to their own, the displacement was at first not too severe. Their lower extensions had enough depth and strength, their higher ranges enough darkness and body, to meet the basic tonal requirements of the major roles formerly assigned to contraltos. But as the first post-WWII generation faded, the upward pull continued. This was not an elevation of pitch—the mezzo range remained as it had been. It was, rather, the cultivation of an increased brightness, openness, and youthfulness in timbre; of a more soprano-ish balance in handling; and of a leaner format—a move, in short, to the left, as if the descent of the Easy Plush to the floor of the male range had sprung a counterweight on the female side. It included a tendency to carry the defined chest voice higher in the range, and led to an overall adjustment almost indistinguishable from

---

* Tebaldi made her debut at 21; Bergonzi at 22 (as baritone) and 25 (as tenor); Bastianini at 22 (as bass) and 28 (as baritone); Siepi at 18. All were international stars within three or four years, sounding very much like Tebaldi, Bergonzi, Bastianini, and Siepi, respectively.

that of a spinto or "young heroic" soprano. Living on the upper edge of the mezzo spectrum, these voices still possessed strength and drive, and so were capable of handling (though often roughly) the high dramatic mezzo parts and borderline roles like Carmen and Santuzza, but sat unhappily on the contralto range. Typical among these voices were those of Grace Bumbry and Shirley Verrett—who eventually migrated to soprano repertoire—and, a few years later, the yet-lighter-and-leaner Agnes Baltsa. But the most intriguing was Marilyn Horne's.*

If Berganza is the bridge between the real mezzos who sang Rossini parts and the modern mezzo model, Horne is the singer who drew elements of the earlier dramatic mezzo and contralto adjustments into a new technical structure uniquely suited to bighouse renderings of the major Rossini and Handel roles. She achieved this through a remarkable combination of keenly tuned agility with projective strength that ranged over the combined mezzo/contralto compass. She had more of the agility than any mezzo since Supervia, more of the strength than the modern mezzos who have followed her. Her career was launched in soprano roles (Marie in *Wozzeck*, Nedda in *Pagliacci*, even Marzelline in *Fidelio*), and she shared the general timbral characteristics of the other soprano-ish mezzos I have named. But she did not share their tendency to push the chest upward and drive from there into the top; her technical configuration is quite different. Horne refers to this configuration as "like an hourglass," and that accurately delineates the unusual structure of her voice in its prime: a narrow, focused midrange (she even uses the terms "squeezed" and "tight" to describe this area) that widened downward into the chest and upward into a full soprano top. In effect, she and her teachers created their own version of the three-register distribution, keeping the "middle register" slender so as to blend with the lightened upper notes of her long lower extension and avoid weighting the tone as she approached her "upper *passaggio*."[25]

This was an ingenious re-working of the triune concept, and since Horne was a technically meticulous singer she used it consistently and preserved it well. At the time when Callas, Sutherland, and Caballe were opening up the possibilities of the early *bel canto* and Handelian revivals and Berganza was bringing an unprecedented fluency to the lighter roles of these repertoires, it made Horne a uniquely plausible mezzo partner for the heroic ones, and it

---

* Contralto/mezzo/soprano crossovers and conversions are by no means new, as the vocal histories of (among many) Olive Fremstad, Edyth Walker, Margaret Matzenauer and later Rose Bampton, Margaret Harshaw, and Regina Resnik show. The difference, though, is that the voices of the earlier generations tended to sound and behave like mezzos and contraltos even when singing soprano repertory, while the more recent ones show the opposite tendency.

is in that context that she can legitimately be considered a great vocalist. At the same time, this conformation imposed certain limits. The narrowed mid-range possessed neither the dark, open-throated beauty of the old contraltos nor the full-bodied punch of the dramatic mezzos. Her sound remained that of a bright American soprano with a startling lower extension. Further, hourglass structure or no, the ends of the range had to be kept in reasonable equalization with the middle, so while the voice's overall presence was more than sufficient in what became her home territory, it wasn't dominant enough to be fulfilling in the Real Mezzo standard rep: Verdi, Wagner, the verists. Though vocally proficient and musically intelligent (I never heard her singing when it was not), her Amneris and Eboli were tame, and she sensibly left Wagner pretty much alone.*

In the 1970s, Horne took on two of the great low-voice challenges—Orfeo and the mother of all mother-contralto roles, Fidès—and dispatched their display aspects impressively. But the sit and coloration of the voice were not quite right in these roles, either. With the anchored depth of the older contraltos in one's ear, the bland openness, girlish edge, and excitable vibrato of Horne's "Ah, mon fils" sounds out of kilter with the lie of the music, missing some of its wonted dignity and sorrow.† These qualities were also lacking in her Orfeo, though here there was an interesting corollary. For Horne chose to end Act I with the elaborate aria interpolated for the high tenor Legros in 1774. She pluckily churned her way through this in a parched, crimped tone that verged on a thinned-out belt. It occurred to me that she might actually be attempting to imitate the presumed registral mixing of the pre-Duprezian tenor. But the unlovely sound neither took on the heady ring of my imagined female tenor nor stayed within the range limits observed by Ruby Helder. A voice so adjusted is not going to settle down for rich intonings of "Che puro ciel" or the "Che farò."

The accomplishments of Horne and her contemporaries outline two developments of her time in the lower female voice categories. First, the range of roles that could plausibly be assumed by them under modern performance conditions and according to modern musical manners was extended to some long-neglected repertory. Second, the tessitura of such voices rose. Their

---

* Temperamental, stylistic, and histrionic factors were of course significant in the effect Horne made in such parts—but I am speaking here strictly of her vocal conformation and its inherent expressive capacities. The interplay of all these factors is the single most enticing question in the formation of a singing personality.

† This judgment is based on a recollection of live performance combined with listening to recorded performance—the latter done via CDs of the 1977 Met broadcast (not the contemporaneous studio recording), the former of the 1979 revival of that production.

collective center of weight and strength, and thus of the ear-attention they commanded, shifted from the lower-middle to the upper-middle pitch range, their coloristic and behavioral ranges adjusting accordingly. Abandoned almost entirely (except in Horne's own case) was the bottom end, and we must note that it is not only among women that we have chosen to forego the grave, the settled, the parental—not to mention the sheer, scary excitements of loud subterranean noises. That has happened in both sexes. As with the contraltos and dramatic mezzos, the true basses and heavy baritones have been directed upward, structured to feature effective high notes and the Not-a-Problem handling exemplified by Pape's *Faust* Serenade, effectively squeezing off the low end. In the sixty-some years since the declines of Kipnis and List, only Kurt Moll has offered the sort of low-end "money notes" once flaunted by the deep bass.[26] Looking at the human voice as a choir in its traditional double-mixed SSAATTBB alignment, we have removed the Second Alto and Second Bass from the balance. There's no longer a ground.

THE LEADING LADIES SETTLE DOWN

One Category of large-format, E-19 voices is yet unaccounted for. Here's a final trio of groupings:

	A.	B.	C.
TIER I:	Johanna Gadski	Félia Litvinne	Celestina Boninsegna
TIER II:	Frida Leider	Germaine Lubin	Rosa Ponselle/ Giannina Arangi-Lombardi/ Claudia Muzio
TIER III:	Kirsten Flagstad/ Helen Traubel/ Eileen Farrell Birgit Nilsson	Régine Crespin	Renata Tebaldi

To present these fourteen singers as a single category is to cast a wide net over roles ranging from *Hochdramatisch* to *lirico-spinto*. The unifying concept is: top-of-the-line sopranos with big voices and solid functional techniques. Read vertically, these lists are in chronological progression, covering roughly the last half of the Duprezian era. Read horizontally, they also allow in some measure for the linguistic and "cultural ethnicity" factors that are among the variables in vocal comparison. We must once more be aware of the influence of variations in recording techniques, and of the very great difference between recorded and live listening experience, especially in matters of tonal presence and "aura."* In this regard, the dramatic soprano is the most difficult of all voice types to confidently assess, for reasons already stated.[27,28]

Extended technical commentary on all these singers being neither possible nor necessary here, I'll make some general observations augmented by a few comparisons. Further elaboration may be found in the endnotes. When due allowance is made for mitigating factors, it remains clear that between the top and bottom of each of these groupings, major changes have occurred. The top "lateral cut" (Tier I) shows singing whose power is of a lean, thrusting type, combined with tonal brilliance and a technical alacrity we no longer associate with voices of dramatic calibre. Like Tetrazzini, all three of these exemplars (Gadski, Litvinne, and Boninsegna) anchor their techniques in highly developed, defined chest registers, and though Boninsegna exploits hers with what can seem like an unseemly eagerness (she loves to "snap down" into chest with no concession to blending), they obey the Displacement Rule to the letter and keep their lower and middle ranges in balance. The singers in the bottom category (excluding, for the moment, Nilsson, who is a sort of appendix to Column A) are distinctly to the right: big, plump voices, more loosely held, with less pronounced chest activity. And those in the middle are—in the middle. Some of the changes are less marked among the Italians of Column C than in the other two, but they are noticeable throughout. In short, we see over the course of the 20th Century something analogous to the Easy Plush movement among the men. And we see some of the properties once possessed by the contralto voice—particularly its settled, embracing quality—vaulting over the mezzo-soprano's territory to land in the soprano's, as if they had fled the bodies of the mothers and the Other Women to land in the arms of wives and girlfriends.

Gadski's repertoire comprised a spectrum of light and heavy parts that have long since been considered mutually exclusive. She did not quite intermix the weightiest Wagner roles with those requiring a high extension and scintillating *colorature*, like Lilli Lehmann in her *"Marten aller Arten"* (in key), or Nordica in her *"Je suis Titania"* (down a half-step), along with their Liebestods and *"Ho-jo-to-hos."* But she regularly performed Mozart's Pamina, Countess, and Elvira; the lighter Wagner heroines; big Verdi (*Aïda, Trovatore*); and the ultimate dramatic soprano challenges of Isolde and the Brünnhildes. With

---

* Disclosure: of the singers named above, I heard in live performance Traubel, Farrell, Nilsson, Crespin, and Tebaldi—obviously, all Tier III singers.

reservation for some (not all) Bs and Cs that sound narrow and straight,* her records show consistent control of all the techniques required for satisfying these roles. The voice is always true, firm, and mobile. It was obviously powerful. No one, at any time, has triumphed as Isolde and Brünnhilde in the world's major houses without plenty of strength and stamina. This may seem self-evident. But it can use reiteration, because there is enough misreading of evidence by people who should know better to feed the belief that everyone sang lighter in the old days. Crespin, for instance, generalized that "they" (19th-Century female singers) ". . . had such little head tones and not a big voice" (see Hines, *Great Singers on Great Singing*, pp. 84-85—she blames corsets). This is just ill-informed, and puzzling from someone of her heritage (see the discussion of her singing below). The issue isn't big vs. little; it's right vs. left. Shaw, reporting on the Brünnhildes of Lilli Lehmann at the 1896 Bayreuth Festival, says: ". . .a bright soprano voice, brilliant at the top, but not particularly interesting in the middle—just the wrong sort of voice for Wagner . . . I should like to hear her as Marguerite in Gounod's Faust."[29] And on Lehmann's records, made in her twilight and recording's dawn (that is why she is not my exemplar), one can hear some justice in GBS's complaint. But note that this is not a complaint about audibility. Shaw isn't talking about size; he's talking about timbre and structure. What his observations really say is not that he expected much less of his "Brynhild" than we would, but much more of his Marguerite. So, too, of Gadski's Pamina or Countess: a far stronger voice than we are used to, but with the purity, evenness, and dynamic control needed for Mozart.

Still, for all their fortitude, these voices seem not to have had quite the massiveness and voluminosity we grew accustomed to in the 1930s and '40s. Leider carries us toward these last-named qualities. Her tone is rounder and broader than Gadski's, but still firmly centered, and quickened by a touch of vibrato that lends extra excitement to the top Bs of her *Abscheulicher!* or *Walkürenruf.* In the latter, she shows the truest, tautest trill of any High Dramatic. However, along with these attributes Leider shows one functional departure from the practice of Gadski and her other predecessors (Lilli Lehmann, Nordica, Fremstad, Sedlmair, et al.) or for that matter her fine contemporary Helene Wildbrunn. This is at the voice's lower end. She only occasionally sings a recognizable chest note, when an open vowel and strong intent make it practically unavoidable. When she does it is clear and slender, and kept well below the border. Most of the time, she stays on the Upper Family side or with the most discreet of blends, and the voice's presence can

---

* But this is not corroborated by earwitness report—see n. 28.

suffer in the lower-middle area, even on recordings. For the first time that I know of, we have a major dramatic soprano voice whose shape resembles only the upper two-thirds of Marilyn Horne's hourglass—but with its crimped neck poking down below the point of transition.

Throughout the interwar decades, Northern dramatic sopranos of the older model continued to flourish alongside Leider. Apart from Wildbrunn (who, on records, sounds like the structurally soundest of them all), perhaps the most illustrative were four of Anglo/Aussie provenance: Eva Turner, Florence Austral, Marjorie Lawrence, and Florence Easton. There were temperamental and musical differences among them, and vocal ones as well (Turner's, for instance, seems to have been the most solid and thrusting of these voices, Austral's the most compact, Easton's the most consistent and enduring, and Lawrence's the boldest and most volatile). What they shared was commanding format, tonal purity, firm line, and a reach that convincingly embraced both range extremes, including clear chest definition at the lower one. All sang the heaviest of dramatic soprano parts, yet embraced a wide range of roles. Only the foreshortened career of Lawrence could be described as principally Wagnerian. Into this field stepped Flagstad.

The biggest soprano voices I have heard in person belonged to Traubel and Farrell.* Since through a series of mischances I did not hear Flagstad, I must take the unanimous word of professionally qualified listeners who did that her sound was, at the least, of similar amplitude. It is just conceivable that some earlier soprano (Fremstad or Wildbrunn, both converted contraltos, would be candidates) produced tone whose sheer breadth and depth was comparable, but that cannot be concluded from their recordings. All the evidence supports the view that Flagstad re-configured the *Hochdramatisch* voice type in a way Shaw would have approved of—less brilliance at the top, but more "interesting" in the middle—and that Traubel and Farrell essentially sustained this conformation. Its crucial element was a flood of beautiful tone, freely emitted and handled in a manner less concerned with reach and quickness, and more exclusively with sustainment of horizontal line. The result was a new monumentality, tone that was at once denser and more expansive, rendered all the more magisterial by its lyrical guidance and apparent ease of birth.

There were naturally differences among these voices, too. Bearing in mind once more that no singer of such accomplishment is far off center, they

---

* I speak of instruments of first quality, released action, and full calibre throughout the range. I thus omit singers as important as Jessye Norman, whose resplendent sound was of High Dramatic mass in the lower and middle ranges but never at the top, or Martha Mödl, an artistically intriguing singer whose voice was huge, but under constant pressure induced by excess weight, and so endured in soprano mode for only a few seasons.

delineate a gradual rightward succession. Flagstad—albeit that her sound has plenty of bite, at times a glacial core—is by virtue of her tonal span and "relaxed" onset already to the right of her predecessors and leaner contemporaries. Traubel, given her even rounder, warmer timbre, the settled presence of her low notes, and the loosening of her later years, is another notch over; and Farrell yet another—cumulous billows of tone, and the best movement of the three, though not the precise velocity or ornamental capacity of earlier generations. Still: in overall structure and handling, as well as basic tonal aesthetic, these three were of a kind.

They were also of a kind with respect to their developmental arcs. After fifteen to twenty years spent in various less demanding pursuits (Flagstad in lighter repertory in Norway; Traubel in concerts, recitals, and musicales in St. Louis; Farrell in radio and concert work), each came to the High Dramatic repertory only when approaching her fortieth year. (Hence the now-common view, impossible to dismiss owing to the easy splendor of these voices but unsupported by earlier precedent, that such instruments must grow "naturally" and slowly, to emerge only in midlife.) Finally, they presented in common a quite different profile with respect to the ends of the range from the sopranos of Shaw's day. At the bottom, there was now not merely the slender, seldom-used chest voice of Leider, but no sharply defined chest at all; at the very top (B and C), there was some shyness that for Flagstad and Traubel turned into a shortfall soon after their assumption of heavy Wagnerian duties. (Farrell seems to have had somewhat better fortune. But then, she never took up those duties—or, indeed, the week-to-week, season-to-season burden of any operatic repertory for a sustained stretch of time.)[30] Of the hourglass, only a neckless upper bowl remains. But its volume equals that of the entire older piece.

That conformation describes even more exactly the voice of Régine Crespin. She is the loosest, the rightmost of all these greatvoiced sopranos. So the distinction between her singing and that of her Tier I predecessor, Félia Litvinne, is the keenest of any in this category, and all the more intriguing by reason of the cultural, personal, and pedagogical connections that run directly from Litvinne through Lubin to Crespin.[31] Of the truly beautiful and well-disciplined soprano voices I've heard, I believe Crespin's was the most voluminous save only Traubel's and Farrell's. When she and Nilsson, as Sieglinde and Brünnhilde respectively, alternated their vaulting lines in Act III of *Die Walküre*, the complementary contrast was of core, not format—Crespin's warm, lush tone gushing into the house, Nilsson's cold, compact one lancing through it, and Crespin's if anything the larger of the two. Yet Crespin, so satisfying in the light-heavyweight roles of Wagner and Verdi, Gluck and

Berlioz, never joined Nilsson as a reigning Isolde and Brünnhilde, let alone an Elektra or Turandot—the size fit, but not the quality and structure. As with Sutherland and Tetrazzini, the Crespin/Litvinne comparison vividly illustrates the trade-offs between easy luxuriance and sculptured radiance in greatvoiced sopranos. And despite my frustrations with her recordings, I am confident that Lubin belongs at the median between them: less chiseled, brilliant, and extended than Litvinne, but more solid and gathered than Crespin.[32]

We can't assert, on the basis of old records, that Litvinne's singing was always expressively superior to Crespin's. I doubt that the melting beauty of Crespin's voice in music like *Les Nuits d'été*, *Shéhérazade*, or Desdemona Act IV has ever been surpassed. But Litvinne's technique had greater reach. The young Crespin sang Marguerite and the *Figaro* Countess, but the young Litvinne sang Violetta and even Gilda. Granted, we can't hear *how* she sang them ("*Sempre libera*" in key?—I imagine so. Gilda's traditional high options? I imagine not), but it is hard to envision Crespin attempting them at all. While in midcareer Crespin tiptoed up to Brünnhilde (with Karajan, naturally), then tiptoed away, Litvinne incorporated Brünnhilde and Isolde into her repertory fairly early on and for many years sang them concurrently with her Marguerites, Donna Annas, and *Trovatore* Leonoras. And whereas a bit farther along Crespin turned to such interchangeably soprano/mezzo assignments as Charlotte and Carmen with only partial success, Litvinne undertook Carmen, Gertrude, Chimène, and Dalila—again maintaining these mezzo and contralto parts alongside her soprano ones.

Of this late phase of Litvinne's career (roughly age 40 forward) we have a generous recorded sampling, and the differences in functional technique between Litvinne and Crespin are not hard to discern—as with Sutherland's opened and covered vowels, the presence or absence of a defined chest quality originates with the voice, not the recording apparatus. For one clear illustration, take the *Carmen* Habañera. Technically, Litvinne's approach to this is nearly identical to Calvé's (see n. 24), combining some of the depth and color of the old contraltos with the smoky chestiness of the Real Mezzos, these qualities held in classical balance in the lower area of what were actually big soprano voices. And so Litvinne is able to carry the chromatic line smoothly and evenly downward into a clear, projective low range on every descent, while Crespin must gently decline, thus depriving her of the primary source of expressive effect built into the piece.* And this declination underlines not only the often mushy grounding of Crespin's low notes, but the absence of

---

* Crespin recorded *Carmen* at 47, in 1974, but age and career mileage do not figure into this comparison. Litvinne's Habañera is from 1910 or '11, making her at least the same age (birthdate claims range from 1860-63), and she had sung for slightly longer.

underpinning that accounts for her frequent inability to mold the line and keep the voice present at moderate volume. She floated heartstopping pianissimi, but in the span between mezzo-piano and mezzo-forte—the middle ground that establishes a norm—her voice habitually dropped into a lovely-lazy softness (at times almost the microphone croon) and let the line fall slack, so that interpretation turned neutral through long stretches of music. In recital, this was arguably *à propos* in rare instances like Poulenc's *Hôtel*, but not as a means of clearing a path through Schumann or Fauré, let alone Bizet or Verdi or Wagner.

Virtually any comparison of Litvinne and Crespin recordings ("*D'amor sull'ali*" is a particularly clear example, I think) will serve to make the structural distinctions and demonstrate their influence on interpretation. But to show the deployment of these distinctions not simply for virtuosic display or even for purely musical colorization but as tools of dramatization, I prefer a byte of Wagner that has become something of a test pattern for me: the opening of Sieglinde's Act I narrative, "*Der Männer Sippe.*" The section encapsulates the paradox of this role, which is that although it calls for a more lyrical, feminine sound than does Brünnhilde, it lies lower. Its layout is similar to Wotan's Act II narrative and the *Todesverkündigung* scene (or, for that matter, Otello's monologue), keeping the voice near the bottom of its range and reined back in tempo for many bars before ascending and quickening to its climax. At the outset, it's essential that it draw us into the scene of the wedding feast gathering and the appearance of the grey-clad stranger with a palpable feel of suspense, of impending high import. For personification of this, Litvinne is not available, for though she sang the part of Sieglinde and we can in mind's ear reconstruct how her voice must have moved through it, she recorded nothing from it. So I am obliged to enlist another soprano, Lotte Lehmann.

Both in format and in certain aspects of executional technique, Lehmann was a lesser singer than either Litvinne or Crespin. But after three-quarters of a century, her substantially complete recordings of two roles—Sieglinde and the Marschallin—remain the gold standard. This owes largely to her deep identification with the characters, manifested in the personal inflections of word and phrase, the audible "insights" she brought to her interpretations. These owe in turn to the vowel foundation on which they rest. Without that, the same identification and insights must needs have relied on other, weaker choices, on clever artistic compromises. For Lehmann's vocal structure is perfect for these roles—slightly short on top (which does not matter in this writing) but otherwise solid, meaty and filled-in throughout with Young Dramatic tone that is both warm and pungent. I hope it is by now unnecessary to note that this perforce includes a well-soldered entry into Lower

Family territory, blended when desired and without a crude break or lower-middle hole. And so it is that when Lehmann begins to etch for Siegmund (and for us) the moment of the stranger's entrance, she has at her disposal an expectant tension and range of color that quite eludes the majestic, deep-seated tones of Flagstad or Traubel or Norman. She can capture the suspense even while hanging on the low B on closed vowels at "*tief hing ihm der Hut*" ("low hung on him his hat"—I'll preserve literal word order here), then carve the line back and forth across the break at places like "*traf die Männer sein mächt'ges Dräu'n*" ("met the men his threatening looks"), or—after tugging the heartstring with the "*ä*" of "*Tränen*" ("tears"), then guiding us with portamento through "*und Trost*" ("comfort")—landing conclusively on a strong, perfectly blended E for the last syllable of "*zugleich*" ("at once").[33] These recitational events, these instinctive vocal "insights," are simply unavailable to any voice, however beautiful, that has not defined and balanced out the transitional area. That is why Lehmann, like Martinelli in "*Dio mi potevi*," is able to build the opening of her narrative so that the passions to come will follow as if inevitable. She creates a *tableau vivant* while greatvoiced others sit for imposing portraits.

Among these last is Crespin's. Sieglinde was one of her greatest roles—in my live experience, only Rysanek's would be competitive. The stately, open-throated sound she brings to this passage is lovely in itself, and was ample in the theatre. But from this calm Easy Plush tone with its merest hints of chest blend, nothing leaps or flashes; nothing rivets the attention. The line is smooth but doesn't lead on—just half of what is meant by "legato." All is softened, all is lyricized. The same thing occurs in the *Todesverkündigung*, where in her rendition Brünnhilde's part of the scene doesn't really start to happen till the line mounts and the voice is compelled to gather its forces, or in "*Ich sah das Kind*," studio or live, with Prêtre or Knappertsbusch—yes, the passage is seductive and evocative, but the story does have to be told, and Parsifal does have to stay awake. A more extended comparison of the Crespin and Lehmann Sieglindes or Marschallins will repeatedly present the listener with the same choice—between an impressive and bewitching voice, a "heavenly" voice that alternately catches us up and lets us drift off, or an attractive but distinctly worldly one that pulls us willy-nilly through the drama. I succumb as easily as anyone to the former, but must advocate for the latter.

As I have already suggested, the left-to-right downward slant is less pronounced in Column C than in the other two. In part, this is because greatvoiced Italian sopranos (or Italianate ones, like Milanov) did not relinquish their hold on the defined chest register, with all that that implies for the structure of the voice as a whole. In that respect Renata Tebaldi has more in common with her Tier I or II ancestors than with contemporaries like Farrell or Crespin. Nevertheless there are changes, the most obvious being that whereas none of the earlier singers would have hesitated to term herself a dramatic soprano, Tebaldi insisted that she was a *spinto*. "I, a spinto, recorded *Don Carlo, Ballo,* and *Trovatore* [she might have added Santuzza], but never dared sing them in the theatre, for these operas are written for dramatic sopranos, and only they can really honor the scores," she said (see Rasponi, *The Last Prima Donnas,* p. 249)—this despite the fact that she successfully assumed several roles as "heavy" as those she named (e.g., Aïda, the *Forza* Leonora; later, Gioconda), and the format of her voice was certainly equal to them.

Still, I think Tebaldi assessed herself correctly. She was not a true dramatic soprano, but the world's biggest lyric; the 20th Century's most vocally satisfying singer of Puccini's heroines, but not (with the debatable exceptions of Desdemona and Amelia Grimaldi) Verdi's. If size and beauty of voice do not account for this, what does? And why, despite her Mediterranean brightness of tone and active chest register, is she perfectly at home in Tier III? As with several of her male Easy Plush contemporaries, the key to these distinctions lies in the quality of her *mezza-voce*.

Tebaldi's *piano* singing was of incomparable warmth and, owing to the voice's large format, unique immediacy—it could permeate the largest hall with tender, feminine intimacy. In her early years, she could float this soft sound almost to the top of her range, *vide* the B-flats in the Tomb Scene of her 1952 *Aïda* recording. Even in her late seasons, she retained its essential quality in the midrange. I'll offer two examples of it, recalled from theatre performances and verifiable on a live recording. The first is from a purely lyric role that Tebaldi's voice filled out as no other had—Mimì. We cannot capture the sound in words (for that you must listen), but we can trace the contours: first her slow descent (in *"Mi chiamano Mimì"*) on the words *"e in cie-e-lo,"* then an expectant lingering on the last syllable of *"cielo,"* than a beckoning little glide up to *"ma,"* then the gradual warming and intensification of *"quando vien lo sgelo,"* then (and only now a fresh intake of breath) the blooming of the rich full voice for the ecstatic greeting to the first sun and April's first kiss.

These few bars of *Bohème* lie in the lower-middle range, where projection is an issue for so many voices. Tebaldi's ability to lead the ear along in this area in spite of her predilection for slow tempos and teasing *tenuti* (for, unlike Crespin's, her soft singing was never inactive), and with tone always round and relaxed, was a singular gift. But the floating *piano* attracts more

---

* Translation: "[I look out over the rooftops] and to the sky/but ... when the thaw comes ..."

attention higher up—at the upper G-flat, for instance, where Butterfly's "*Un bel dì*" begins. Many sopranos have launched the aria with lovely soft attacks, but not to Tebaldi's effect. I first heard it from the top row of the Carnegie Hall balcony in 1955, and again when she sang the part at the Met. Since it depends on a soft tone coming (as the eye will confirm) from a great distance, yet giving the illusion of a confidence in the listener's ear, the effect can only be suggested on recordings. The suggestion is strongest, I think, on the live broadcast pirate of an all-Puccini concert featuring the 1950s' most beautiful Italian voices of their types—those of Tebaldi, Di Stefano, and Taddei. After the lustrous opening phrases of this "*Un bel dì*," Tebaldi's full voice first asserts itself at "*romba il suo saluto. Vedi? Egli è venuto!*"* Here there's a bit of bite in the tone. It's an exciting sound, solid and proud, and there may seem nothing remarkable, let alone alarming, about this textural change as the full voice emerges from the *piano*. Indeed, both the floated *piano* and the "bite into the tone" are oft-prized qualities. Their juxtaposition, though, is directly to my point, and its significance becomes clear by comparison with the same passage as recorded just five years earlier, in 1949. Here, as the voice lifts and strengthens, it takes on volume and brightness without the bite. And here, the full weight of "*È venuto!*" glides without a pause into a girlish lightness for "*Io non gli scendo incontro. Io no,*"† the changes of volume, color, and intent carrying us forward with the kind of transport that only great operatic voices can create. In later versions, Tebaldi separates the *forte* "*venuto!*" from the *piano* "*Io*" with a breath—still very well executed, but nothing like the same moment. It could be argued that this difference is simply a matter of interpretive choice. It could also be argued that the hints of edginess at *forte* in the later versions are the inevitable result of five more years of performance, even at this early stage. Yes, but: there's a technical issue involved—namely, that the midrange *mezza-voce*, for all its blandishments, was not engaged quite firmly enough to buttress the voice for the increased tensions that by definition come with higher pitches. Thus, as seasons passed Tebaldi was obliged to grip the upper range more tightly (there's the bite), slowly increasing the undertow on the top and decreasing the voice's freedom of play—overall, the route taken by this extraordinary instrument. With this slight constriction on the sound, effecting the diminuendo and vowel changes from "*venuto!*" to "*Io,*" while surely still possible, would have run the risk of sounding pinched. Better to take a bit of breath and re-set.

This combination of lower and slacker, higher and tighter goes along with the natural ratio of tension and compression up and down the voice,

---

* "[The ship's cannon] roars its salute. See? He has come!"

† "I do not go down to meet him. Not I."

but overdoes it. Tebaldi sounds slightly right of center in the lower middle, slightly left above, and as with all such tendencies, this one becomes more pronounced as performance energy is directed against it over and over. Tebaldi sensed (and/or discovered) that the roles she fought shy of demand more heft in the middle and release at the top, and that the shortfall of tautness also limited the mobility and precision needed for such seemingly logical assignments as Norma or the *Ernani* Elvira. The imbalance may seem slight in so big and beautiful a voice—but it comes clear when heard alongside Tebaldi's dramatic soprano predecessors. As always, Tier I (Boninsegna or, if you prefer, Ester Mazzoleni*) affords the greatest contrast, and Tier II splits the difference. Thus, whereas Boninsegna habitually carries chest right up to the Displacement Rule's limit in the click-stop manner we usually associate with higher sopranos of her era, then enters a midrange that, though not weak or "unsupported," is quite ordinary in quality, Ponselle and Arangi-Lombardi define the chest but use it less aggressively, allowing an equalized transition into a solid, tonally enriched midrange that will bear considerable tonal weight. None of these has Tebaldi's sensuous, floating *mezza-voce* in the middle octave, but their tighter rein on the midvoice frees them from the need to clutch the tone farther up; their voices are in truer balance. Boninsegna and Ponselle both had far greater facility and accuracy in florid passages. All three had freer action and better centering of pitch at the very top (at least at the start—Ponselle's adventures in this area have already been touched on in n. 52), and high *pianissimi* whose set-in quality is not necessarily aesthetically preferable to Tebaldi's, but more convincingly poised. Any matching of recordings from these singers' prime years will show these distinctions, and any lover of singing should know these artists well. But for easy reference I would recommend *Trovatore* (complete from Tebaldi, substantial excerpts from the others) and *Aïda* (complete from Arangi-Lombardi and Tebaldi (the 1952 version), major excerpts from Ponselle).

Tebaldi was a soprano of the *spinto* variety and her forerunners of the dramatic by reason of vocal structure, not size. She belongs in Tier III because of that structure's emphasis on ease and relaxation in the midrange, its preference for sensuous dalliance over dramatic tension. It's undoubtedly true that the reasons for this lie more in individual temperament and cultural context

---

* Mazzoleni is perhaps the best reference point for any reader wondering if Boninsegna, with her idiosyncrasies and peculiar career parabola, is sufficiently representative. She's not my Tier I model because her recordings are of neither the quantity nor quality of Boninsegna's, and her intense vibrato will probably blur the picture for many listeners. But in functional terms—the bright, open timbre; the defined chest; the firm line; and the ringing top—this legendary Italian dramatic soprano clearly seconds the Boninsegna patterns.

(i.e., fashion) than in conscious technical choice. The fact that the last voice Italy produced with the quality and format of a great dramatic soprano sang instead as a *lirico-spinto*, and that in the three singing generations since, opera's motherland has yielded nothing at all in that line, is not wholly a matter of technique. But it is technical in part—the part artists and teachers can address provided the functional issues are correctly analyzed. Suppose, for instance, that Tebaldi had sung more like Claudia Muzio, also correctly defined as a *lirico-spinto*? This comparison would be an Italianized version of the Lotte Lehmann/Crespin pairing, and similar temperamental differences are immediately apparent; but I should again like to focus here on the technical aspect. Muzio and Tebaldi are alike in some important ways. Both show a typically Italian defined chest, used with increasing boldness as years pass. (For an interesting late example, hear their voicings of *"Esser madre è un inferno,"* from *L'Arlesiana*, a verismo mezzo aria often taken up by older sopranos.) Both were renowned for the *mezza-voce*; indeed, Muzio is often credited with originating the "floated" *piano*. But even early on, Muzio brought the chest in higher and with greater confidence than did Tebaldi. Her tone is more vibrant, less lush than Tebaldi's. In the lower-middle range, her vowels are clear and open, Tebaldi's darker and rounder, so that Muzio's words dig into the pitches, rather than gently wafting across them—very like the difference between Tetrazzini and Sutherland, or for that matter between Schlusnus and Fischer-Dieskau, Martinelli and Vickers. Higher up, Muzio's floated *piano*, though certainly free, has a touch of the same held-back quality I spoke of in Chaliapin's case, giving it a feel of suppressed emotion.* At times, Muzio's control of the line in the upper range even has the listener wondering about her capacity for a forte top—until she suddenly releases it, as when she leaps to the high B at the close of *"Ebben, ne andrò lontana" (La Wally)*.

I think it is reasonable to assume that Tebaldi's full voice was more massive and voluminous than Muzio's, as we assume of Flagstad's or Traubel's in relation to Gadski's. Yet once again, its overall strength cannot have been that much greater. Muzio sang her Aïdas, *Trovatore* and *Forza* Leonoras, Toscas, Santuzzas, and Maddalena di Coignys opposite the big guns of her day; and on the same night that Florence Easton was "creating" her Lauretta and Geraldine Farrar her Suor Angelica, Muzio was giving first life to Giorgetta. Her voice, especially in the crucial lower-middle area, had the "carrying sound that's going to pierce through" touted by Horne, but with no hint of a squeeze. It was not an hourglass, but a crystal vase with the slightest flare

---

* I love Lauri-Volpi's description of "... that unique voice of hers, made of tears and sighs and of restrained interior fire." We would not choose quite the same words for Tebaldi. Her tears and sighs and fire were more overtly expressed; Muzio's were embedded in the tone.

at top and bottom. And what might we have had if Tebaldi's voice been so proportioned? A little less, I imagine, of the pearly midrange softness that held us spellbound. But quite possibly, the greatest Italian dramatic soprano we have heard, and for a longer time.[34]

At the very end of the E-19 vocal age, extending her prime a few seasons beyond my 1970 limit with a functional technique that afforded a backward glance, was Birgit Nilsson. By fine measurements, her voice was slimmer and taller than Traubel's or Flagstad's. She did not define the chest register as clearly as Gadski or Wildbrunn or the Italians, using instead a strong mix (not always ingratiating) that cut through. The lean, gleaming thrust of her sound, her easy command of the top and pliancy of line in high tessitura, and the mobility that afforded her access to Lady Macbeth and even Donna Anna—all these are suggestive of the best pre-Easy Plush dramatic sopranos. They enabled Nilsson to maintain her Turandots, Aïdas, and Toscas alongside her Brünnhildes, Isoldes, and Elektras. In her international phase she sang no purely lyrical roles, but her voice had the ease and dynamic control to have done so. Like all the other Tier III sopranos, however, Nilsson has been without successors.

In tracing E-19 singing to its end, I have been concerned with vocality itself—with the structure, texture, behavior, and above all the presence of voices, and how these determine what is available to their owners for interpretive purposes. As I have tried to show, the Duprezian polarity, with its strong chest-register engagement, deep positional grounding, and vigorous laryngeal vitalization, was significantly redirected by the exemplars of the E-19 endtimes. But no greatvoiced line cut to their pattern has followed. Instead, a new vocality has emerged.

THE NEW VOCALITY

Replication notwithstanding, the world of performance is still finite. Everything is still in place of something else. And though, as I noted at the beginning of this section, anything can be made to stand in place of any other, the two cannot be made equivalent. When my fellow *Tristan* survivor complained that the Met's recent take on that work had contained "no part of the *Tristan* experience," I think he meant that in the course of tending to his *Tristan* tapestry—productions seen, recordings heard, a conductor's reading here, a soprano's Isolde there—he had discovered what is emotionally alive, intellectually meaningful, and spiritually rewarding in the performance potential of the work. Once made, this discovery becomes the sought-after essence of the work. It is of course subjective. But if he's found what's in there for him, and then finds it missing, it's not there for anybody. No one is having *that* experience, no matter what they call the experience they are having—even if, for instance, they use the same words to describe it. And in amongst this *Tristan*'s offerings for the eye (the predominantly satirical metaphors of the physical production, the empty signaling of the behavior) and ear (the exquisite ongoingness of the Levinian orchestra, the professionally virtuous but utterly harmless vocalism), he detected no traces of what he knows to be there.

So it is with all devotees with all operas, and with singing itself. And so it is that night after night, the masterworks of E-19 pass before us unconsummated altogether, or in such small part as to arouse only frustration. Singing, the only thing that could rescue ear-attention from eye captivity, then draw the ear from orchestral notperformance to the passions of the drama, fails to do so. The new vocality isn't up to it.

A vocality is an aesthetic order, and like all such (see n. 4, p. 406) it trades gains for losses. When a new one displaces an older one in general use, it expresses a cultural preference. The questions become: what is the nature of the new order? What's gained and what's lost? And what is the nature of the preference? The first thing to be said of the new vocality is that its expressive habits are congruent with the orchestral practices previously discussed, and that in this congruence is heard opera's contemporary sonic aura. The second is that it has perpetuated the Domingo/Corelli 2:3 ratio pretty much across the board. The third is that within its two-thirds-of-the-formerly-normative framework, a bias toward headvoice dominance, represented at the extreme by the outright registral inversion of the male falsettist, has gradually asserted itself. A fourth—that singing is evermore detached from its oral traditions and evermore glued to text, and thus evermore delimited by the selections of the Second Interpreters-in-Chief thereof—is primarily a topic for the coming chapter, but cannot be ignored here as a factor in how voices are made to work.

To examine individual representatives of the vocality as I have my E-19 exemplars—that is, for the tonal significance of the instruments themselves, and thus for their basic qualifications as vehicles of dramatic expression—would be pointless. With a handful of exceptions, the voices would not withstand such scrutiny. This is not so much because they are lesser specimens of older types (though some of our better singers are that) as because they are not of those types at all, and ask to be evaluated on their own merits, which have to do mostly with a wider distribution of movement skills (velocity, floridity) and a narrowing of focus that yields cleaner tuning. These are of course Skipover preferences, groomed to the requirements of our reconstruction of pre-E-19 performance practices and some kinds of post-E-19 writing. They are the principal virtues of our many Modern Mezzos, and of the "lyric" tenors and baritones who partner them, and as virtues are genuine enough in certain repertory under certain conditions—I am sorry, for instance, to have not been in Pesaro for some of the Rossini revivals of the '80s. The trouble is that though most of our repertory is still not Skipover repertory and is not presented under such conditions, most of our voices have substituted these virtues for the older ones. From their early ear-modeling and categorization through their training and on into employment, few voices now escape the downsizing and tidying-up of the Skipover ear.

The new vocality's shortfall is most obvious in Wagner and Strauss, Verdi and Puccini, or among the straggling survivors of the verismo or French grand-opera repertories. But it affects everything. It extends, for instance, to Mozart and Gluck and Handel. Take *Die Zauberflöte*, and in particular its casting of the protagonist pair. When I remarked a few pages back that Nilsson might well have sung (and might have sung well) purely lyric roles, Pamina was one I had in mind. Her voice at its best, like Gadski's, had all the tonal purity, the balance of dynamics and evenness of line of the best latterday Paminas Lite, with exponentially greater presence and authority. She could have been paired with Vickers: imagine the effect of his big, pliant tone, predominantly soft-textured but possessed of metal when called for, to say nothing of his dominant/restrained physical self and air of spiritual quest—all perfect for this role—and tune your mind's ear to the effect of these house-filling voices weaving through Mozart's music. That would have done for *Zauberflöte* what Tebaldi & Co. did for *Bohème*. There is plenty of precedent, though none recent, for such casting. When Gadski was singing Pamina at the Met, her most frequent Tamino was Urlus. Alternate Paminas included dramatic sopranos Emmy Destinn and Melanie Kurt, and the strong lyric (or light dramatic? a vanished category) Emma Eames; other Taminos were Slezak, Karl Jörn, and lesser lights like Andreas Dippel and Thomas Salignac—all singers of roles ranging from *spinto* to *Helden*.

Instruments of grand-opera calibre have long been absent from these works. But the post-E-19 decades have brought true miniaturization. Once again restricting myself to singers I heard live in the same acoustical environment (the Met), and proceeding from the latest *Zauberflöte* production (the "Julie Taymor *Flute*") back through the previous one ("It's a Hockney!") and the one before that ("It's a Chagall!"), the Pamina/Tamino casting reads thus: Dorothea Röschmann/Matthew Polenzani; Dawn Upshaw/Paul Groves; Kathleen Battle/Francisco Araiza; Benita Valente/Stuart Burrows; Judith

Raskin/George Shirley; and Pilar Lorengar/Nicolai Gedda.* Adding the protagonist pair of the last production in the old Met gives us Lucine Amara and
Brian Sullivan. Once past the first-named duo (for Röschmann and Polenzani
turned up the gain a notch), and considering only vocal calibre, not all-round
artistic quality (I loved Valente's Pamina; I preferred Araïza's clean, centered
vocalism to Burrows' puffy right-column sort; I never much cared for Gedda
in Mozart, etc.), this sequence shows a continual, incremental increase in
vocal presence as it moves back in time, and with no loss at all in technical control or tonal quality. Over the full century span, Amara and Sullivan
stand at the midpoint both temporally and vocally: while Amara, a full lyric
soprano, sang some roles of dramatic scope, she certainly did not do so with
Gadskian command, let alone tackle Brünnhilde and Isolde; and though
the full lyric tenor Sullivan sang Tamino and Lohengrin concurrently and
later essayed heavier repertory, his attractive voice hardly evoked a Slezak
or Urlus.

Or, take Gluck. Back in Gadski's day the Met revived first his *Orfeo*, then
his *Armide* in consecutive seasons. Toscanini conducted both, and both had
settings by Puvis de Chavannes. The cast of *Orfeo* was led by Homer (followed by Delna and Matzenauer), with Gadski herself, then Marie Rappold,
as Euridice. In *Armide*, the principal roles were taken by Fremstad, Homer,
Caruso, Amato, and Dinh Gilly. Later, there was a German-language revival of
Iphigénie en Tauride in Richard Strauss' edition, led by Artur Bodanzky with
an all-Wagnerian cast. Since these productions antedated modern old-music
scholarship, they could not benefit from its scholarly reconstructions. There
was undoubtedly awkwardness with the idiom—in fact, this was noted at the
time. But think of how the music must have resounded! Think of the beauty,
richness, and amplitude of those voices, and of the stature such voices must
have lent, *a priori*, to the characters of these dramas. That is a radically different perspective from which to consider the desirability of performance-
practice niceties, and while one is at liberty to fantasize such voices bent to
Skipover purposes, the fact is that once a very short distance along that road
has been traveled, one no longer has such voices.[35]

Indeed, the Met's 2007 restoration of *Iphigénie* is a textbook example of
reduction in format and concentration in the upper-middle pitch-and-color
range. In the title part was Susan Graham, a good Modern Mezzo of French
inclination, responsive to the musical idiom and directorial suggestions. She

---

* The last two pairs alternated in English- and German-language versions in the first
season of the new Met, Gedda assuming the part when Fritz Wunderlich died. Other
Paminas of the early new-Met years included Adriana Maliponte and Teresa Zylis-Gara,
whose instruments easily met or surpassed those of Amara and Lorengar in calibre.

did admirable, enjoyable work, but with an instrument that by comparison with the dramatic sopranos and mezzos who sang this role a generation and more ago (Crespin, Gorr, Horne, Callas, Borkh, and others of lesser quality but similar format) is quite restricted—cool in color and moderate in size. The Pylade was Groves, a musicianly light tenor with a limited top not much tested in this music; he sang with more confidence and commitment than I had previously heard from him. It's a role that in the '50s and '60s belonged to tenors like Simoneau, Gedda, André Turp, Roberto Ilosfalvy, or sometimes, in German theatres, to Wagnerians who had vocal substance but probably did not treat the music very kindly.

The other two important roles, Oreste and Thoas, are of particular interest. Though their ranges are almost identical, the former makes its best effort with a high baritone, the latter with a lower one, or even a bass-baritone if he can surmount the tessitura of his aria, "*De noirs pressentiments.*" Oreste has sometimes been cast with a singer of the *Martin* sort—for example, Pierre Mollet, a well-known Pelléas, sang it at the Aix-en-Provence Festival in 1952 and on the subsequent recording. But this tends to cheat the more forceful utterances, and while a close blend with the tenor is called for at times, differentiation is also necessary. So throughout the 20ᵗʰ Century, the part was generally taken by a heftier baritone with access to the top, e.g., Martial Singher (who despite his beautifully sung Pelléas, preserved in a 1945 broadcast recording, was a *baryton grave*, not a *Martin*), Ernest Blanc (a Bayreuth Telramund), and Robert Massard, who moved up from Thoas at Aix to become the almost universal choice for Oreste in the 1950s. Thoas, a shorter role, is seldom strongly cast, but an exception would be Louis Quilico, a typical Verdi baritone of dark coloration.[36]

At the Met, this picture was somewhat re-arranged, largely to accommodate the presence of Domingo, now returned to his original baritenor status, as Oreste. This wasn't altogether arbitrary, for when *Iphigénie* was first performed in Vienna, Gluck created his own German-language version (not to be confused with Strauss') two years after its Paris premiere for the singers of that city's company. Among his revisions were some upward adjustments for Oreste, making that more of a low tenor part, and a lowering of Thoas' music for Ludwig Fischer, the original Osmin and thus undoubtedly a *tiefer Bass*. These revisions were incorporated at the Met, though French was still the language used. In his Met program notes, Andrew Porter observes that this makes for a wider spread for these two roles, lifting (and, presumably, brightening) Oreste while "deepening and darkening" Thoas. If that was the point, the Met missed it. As of Dec., 2007, Domingo still had metal in his sound, and as always brought energy to his work. But in this range (for the changes from the baritone setting are not radical), his voice is actually darker than that of many a contemporary baritone—for instance, that of the NYCO's Oreste, Gary Lehmann, now a *Heldentenor* but then an effective high baritone with a healthy "ping" in his sound. Nor does even a strong tenor voice create the impact of the tortured "*Dieux qui me poursuivez*" as a good baritone's can (the repeated *passaggio* crossings create quite different stresses in the two voice types), or the warmth and gradual settling of "*Le calme rentre dans mon coeur.*" Meanwhile, the potential "deepening and darkening" for Thoas was squandered by casting a welterweight baritone of nondescript coloring. With that voice at the bottom, a cool mezzo on top, and two tenors in between, we had an evening of unrelieved upper-middlish color from voices of middlish calibre, their sincere efforts at individualization further constrained by rules of good taste.[37]

As to Handel, much has already been said here of his writing in relation to the new and old vocalities. He is, however, a more extreme case than the Gluck of the reform operas or the Mozart of the mature masterpieces. This has to do with two factors in combination: the preponderance of setting for Upper Family voices—for their behavioral patterns and associated tonal characteristics—and the demands of the *opera seria* form, with its almost unbroken reliance on the *da capo* aria. In the latter respect, neither "*Ombra mai fu*" nor the opera it's from is altogether typical. But *Rodelinda* is. It's a fully elaborated *opera seria,* and one of the composer's strongest scores, displaying at its height his genius for finding dramatically powerful variations within the A-B-A form. It is also among the Handel operas that come closest to supporting what we now think of as an emotionally compelling through line, or spine. In fact, it was this work's first recording (1964, again on Westminster, and again with Forrester in the "male" lead) that first persuaded me that Handel's weightiest operas might be theatrically viable for us. And some of them are, though the forced staging conceits and campiness of many productions, the utter dullness of others, and obstinacy about cuts often make it appear otherwise.

The biggest obstacle to vivification of these operas, however, is vocal. It would appear that Handel and the new vocality are made for each other, and as with the Rossini mezzos and their accomplices, it's true that in certain areas of technical execution and stylistic grooming there are many more singers able to give acceptable accounts of themselves in this music than there were a generation or two back. But, finally, to what effect? *Rodelinda* is long. There are lots of arias and not much else. The more fluent the singers become with their bursts of little notes and ornaments and the more expert and consistent their re-enactments of old-music practice, the more these are taken for granted and seen for what they are—just another set of mechanical conventions, within which the endless search for "variety," for an illusion of improvisation and spontaneity, in itself grows tiresome. Variety *becomes* the convention. That is, unless one or both of two things is true: that the singer's feel for the dramatic sources of the musical gesture is so deep as to seem entirely personal, natural, and of utmost urgency (as with Lieberson at her best); or that the singer's voice is so tonally compelling and its action so liberated that "variety" and "spontaneity" are already present in the very act of singing, and the gestures merely a continuation of that (as with Sutherland at her best). But of course both these sorts of accomplishment are uncommon, and Sutherland's sort not to be found within the new vocality—it belongs to E-19. Further, we need not just one or two such singers, though Sutherland as Rodelinda, Lieberson as Bertarido, would be an excellent start. We need, at minimum, three or four.

The six singers of the Met's *Rodelinda* were all among the current best of their type. Unlike *Serse, Rodelinda* does afford some respite from Upper Familyness in the extended tenor role of Grimoaldo, who of this opera's characters is the one we would now say has the "most interesting journey." Indeed, though the protagonist couple is awarded most of the score's musical highpoints, the moral problem of the piece rests with Grimoaldo. A powerful, psychologically plausible representation of his inner conflict and its eventual resolution (our bridge to the happy end) is the dramatic key to the work. At the Met the role was taken by Kobie van Rensberg, whose voice falls somewhere between Lyric and Character in *Fach*. On the René Jacobs-led recording of *Nozze di Figaro* he sings the important supporting part of Basilio, complete with his last-act song, and within the stylistic framework of that performance does it extremely well. He's a good artist. But the case is the same as that of Philip Langridge's Aaron—an admirable effort that on purely professional grounds can't be faulted, but which only hints at what is really required. Who, in a big opera house, with a voice of quality and agility, might evoke a dangerous, tortured character and make believable his redemption? Vickers, of course, again comes to mind, or George Shirley. More recently Domingo, or possibly Neil Shicoff in his agonizing antihero mode. But not a new-vocality tenor, however artistically virtuous. It does not suffice.

I have explained above why I also think falsettists do not suffice. In the *Settecento* their insufficiency was clear next to the castrati; now, alongside any of fifty mezzos, preferably the least Modern available. In *Rodelinda* we had two of our "countertenor" best (Daniels as Bertarido and Behjun Mehta as Unulfo), but that only served to underline the unsuitability of the whole proposition. With half the cast thus limited, it was left to the other half to provide some of the wanted vocal substance and texture. Not that the warm, nicely groomed light bass of John Relyea suggested much of Garibaldo's edge, or the hearty contralto-designate of Stephanie Blythe (see comments on her Fricka, below) a full measure of genuine alto hue. But these voices at least approximated the categories and technical capabilities called for by the writing. And we had the Rodelinda of Fleming. Because of the ripe loveliness of her sound and her personal default setting of mild melancholia, she is widely admired for a supposed *Innigkeit*. But I have liked her best when she has lots to do—clear musical structures, overt physical actions. Or, to put it another way, in writing whose emotional life is easily externalized. The times she has moved me (Imogene's Mad Scene in *Il Pirata*; the last act of *Manon*, where the mannerisms of her "styling" are replaced by direct, heartfelt expression; moments of her Violetta; some of her Thaïs) have all been of this nature, and far more persuasive than such abstracted, stillborn creations as her Susannah or Arabella. Thus, there was much to enjoy in her Rodelinda—not quite a Sutherland on one hand or a Lieberson on the other, but some of the strengths of each, presumably aided by the vigorous musical leadership of Harry Bicket and the directorial collaboration of Stephen Wadsworth, which in my experience has been generally positive in terms of *Personenregie*. And this time, her costuming allowed her allure.

Flute, Iphigénie, Rodelinda: all three evenings had attributes of the Upper-Middle-ish, Skipover kind. The Gluck came off best, partly because apart from its ravishing score, it is the most workable of these operas dramatically, and in part because it did not suffer from weak casting at the range extremes (as did *Flute*) or from the Upper Family monotony of *Rodelinda*. For Handel and Gluck, the Met's orchestra was reduced to the Studies-approved allotment of players. They looked lonely down there with all that lowland acreage around them, but they played with the incisiveness of attack and clarity of texture this music does need. And why not? They're Skipovers themselves. Still, there they were, in the same nicely balanced upper midrange and the same dynamic span of *pp* to *mf* as their onstage new-vocality colleagues—just enough lovely sound to afford aesthetic pleasure at arm's length.

A day or two before the *Rodelinda* performance (and again afterward, to re-confirm and restore) I listened to stretches of my old LPs, not of the Westminster recording, but that of London's Handel Opera Society, performing at the Sadler's Wells under Charles Farncombe in 1959, the Handel bicentennial year. It's in English. On it is the young Sutherland spoken of earlier, and three female mezzos: Margreta Elkins as Bertarido, Janet Baker as Eduige, and Patricia Kerns as Unulfo, also all in fresh estate.*From their throats emerges a far broader Upper Family tonal palette, a far richer filling-out of the music, than the Met performance could offer. The Garibaldo is Raimund Herincx, a potent dramatic baritone. And—in retrospect, perhaps most startlingly—the Grimoaldo is Alfred Hallett, a tenor who has left few traces, but whose stylish singing has a strength of tone and depth of shading that makes it immediately more interesting than a tenor of Van Rensburg's kind. One can argue about interpretive choices, about physical presence and personal qualities, and even, at moments, about execution. But with one debatable exception (the Baker/Blythe comparison), every voice in the Handel Opera Society's cast is a stronger presence—more "truly 'operatic'"—than its Met counterpart, and no less adept. As Sutherland tops off the final ensemble with her full-throated elaborations *in alt.*, we feel a Handelian consummation, a happy end we can believe in.[39]

I have thus far spoken of the new vocality in relatively congenial surround-ings. When it comes to the E-19 masterworks, it naturally gives us some events that are better than others, and occasionally one (like the blameless *Ballo*) that is preferable to certain better-forgotten occasions of yesteryear. It also contributes from time to time to strikingly effective individual per-formances, though of a kind whose qualities are more appropriately defined in the chapter to come. On the whole, however, it leaves us well short of "the E-19 experience." To show how, I am once again in need of performance spe-cifics and, if possible, a worthy exemplar.

ERNANI, HAMPSON, AND THE "VERDI BARITONE"

In choosing objects for critical examination, I have tried to play fair by selecting those with plausible claims to artistic excellence, where the issue is not so much skill or even quality per se as the uses to which they are put. The Met's 2008 revival of *Ernani* does not meet that test. It was a put-in of an old and lame production, and under Roberto Abbado received the most perfunctory sort of text-rendition runthrough. It gave off the stale odor of a piece that "needs lots of help," and though it's one of the stronger early Verdi operas, it's true that it doesn't survive indignities as easily as a *Rigoletto, Traviata,* or *Aïda.* But in a way, this *Ernani* was an eminently fair critical object, for it was neither better nor worse than most of what

---

* "Another truly 'operatic' mezzo," said Andrew Porter of Elkins in his review of the performance. He was distinguishing her and Baker from the altos and mezzos of the English oratorio tradition—but the contrast with today's falsettists (and even most modern mezzos) is yet more pronounced. [38]

one of the world's foremost opera companies is setting before its public on "repertory" evenings throughout the season. And on those evenings there's no knockdown on ticket prices.

Besides, there have been times within living memory when, depending on your P.O.V., *Ernani* either has not needed lots of help or else has received it. It was quickly dismissed at the time of its Met premiere—1902, when the early Verdi operas were considered outdated and trivial. But it established and maintained a toehold through the 1920s, when Ponselle, Martinelli, and Mardones were nearly invariable in their roles while De Luca, Ruffo, and Danise alternated as Don Carlo—all told, quite a bit of help of the greatvoiced kind. When Rudolph Bing brought the early Verdi revival to the Met in the 1950s, Milanov, del Monaco, Warren, and Siepi made a success of *Ernani* under Mitropoulos, and when that production was revived in the '60s with Price, Corelli, MacNeil, and Hines under Schippers, it was a genuine hit. On the work's earliest complete recording (Cetra, 1950), the principals are Caterina Mancini, Gino Penno, Giuseppe Taddei, and Giacomo Vaghi—big, fat Italian voices. The high excitement of those performances were of the late E-19 sort, with less of the elegance and old-school technical finish we can hear on the best early recordings of the work's famous solos. But they were real; *Ernani* seemed fresh and hot. If it is floundering now, the fault is not in itself, but in its stars.

Chest-voice chastity is today the besetting problem of soprano voices of all types. While I think contemporary vocal theories play an important part in this, I also think that in the last analysis teachers work more by ear than by theory. Regardless of what they profess, they wind up adjusting voices according to what they hear—and would like to hear. Sounds come first; then theories arise to explain them. So sound models are extremely significant. And as I have tried to demonstrate, the soprano exemplars of late E-19 established a model in which a defined chest voice was de-emphasized, and in a few cases virtually eliminated. This happened concurrently with (and probably in response to) fairly widespread devastation among sopranos and mezzos of veristic inclination, whose reckless impassionisations frequently included an element of chest abuse (too raw, too high) that was held responsible for vocal imbalance and early demise. This Bad Chest/No Chest contrast seems to have led to a broad agreement that chest voice per se is best left alone, or else approached so cautiously as to have no chance of exerting any appreciable effect, negative or positive, on the voice as a whole.

Thus, we were left to contemplate not merely pure coloraturas whose high extensions solicited tolerance for weak low notes (viz., Lily Pons, Mado

Robin, Rita Streich); or Northern Lyrics whose heady loveliness faded or flattened out as they grew older and took on heavier assignments (e.g., Lisa della Casa or Irmgard Seefried), or even the bigger voices that, for various lengths of time and with various degrees of instability, made do with a lower range that was either vaguely formed and only intermittently reliable (like Leonie Rysanek's), or else weak and huskily phonated (like Leontyne Price's). Instead, we were (and increasingly are) dealing with voices of smaller format and little or no chest engagement, which nonetheless undertake parts of greater-than-*leggiero* weight. Anna Moffo's was the first soprano instrument of world-class quality I encountered that was so disposed, and while it would be presumptuous to ascribe the whole blame for her voice's early, precipitous implosion on a single cause, the major technical factor was surely the absence of any Lower Family development. Oddly, "head abuse" (or, more correctly, "chest nullification"), though every bit as pernicious as its opposite, is seldom cited as a source of ruination. That's reflective of the contemporary prejudice.[40]

Allowing for minor variations, this low-range weakness sets a limit on the effectiveness of young lyric voices in regional companies as surely as it does on bigger ones attempting heavier repertory at the international level, though it is in the latter context that it usually becomes obvious.* It is shared by many of our most talented singers—Frittoli, Mattila, Gheorghiu, Netrebko and, arguably, Dessay are all prominent examples. Of them, it cannot even be said that Georghiu is two-thirds of a Dorothy Kirsten, or Frittoli of a Gabriella Tucci, or Mattila of a Lotte Lehmann, because the voices of Kirsten, Tucci, and Lehmann were sonorously present throughout their ranges. So not only is it the case that Frittoli shouldn't be taking on Verdi's Requiem or *Trovatore* Leonora, Georghiu Tosca or Carmen (!), or Mattila Fidelio or Salome, but that they are often only partially gratifying in roles to which their fine voices and considerable expressive gifts should entitle them.[41]

In *Ernani* the Elvira was Sondra Radvanovsky, who had worked her way up through Micaëlas and Antonias—roles for which the size and quality of her voice (round, well-focused, with a touch of quiver) are apt. I had enjoyed her Roxane in Alfano's *Cyrano*. But the Elvira *Ernani* is another proposition altogether. Like the *Trovatore* Leonora, it was once upon a time sometimes sung by sopranos best described as "dramatic coloratura." Sembrich, in fact,

---

*   Among the more egregious examples to have recently surfaced at the Metropolitan would be Adrianne Pieczonka and Nuccia Focile, trying to sing Sieglinde and Nedda, respectively, without a trace of chest quality or any other form of low-range strength. That can't be done in any setting, let alone the Met.

sang it at the Met premiere, and even Patti essayed it, though not often.* I think it's doubtful that, were we to hear Sembrich today, we would find her voice larger than Radvanovsky's in the upper octave of the latter's range. But Sembrich was a Tier I soprano, and Radvanovsky is post-Tier III, so their voices are structured quite differently. Sembrich's had a strong but unabused chest register; a firm penetrating middle; a brilliant top with a high extension; the tensile type of swell-and-diminish; and chiselled trills and *acciaccature*, along with strong attacks and a general alacrity comparable to Tetrazzini's. These attributes would have carried her across the range and through the passage work of the double aria without weakness or compromise, and would have enabled her to penetrate the ensembles in a musically incisive way without thickening their textures. When Ponselle assumed the role, she created an Elvira that must have been as different from Sembrich's as was Flagstad's Brünnhilde from Lilli Lehmann's, and this dramatic soprano type, modeled by Ponselle in the U.S. and Arangi-Lombardi in Italy, held for the role through the 1960s. Accustomed as we grew to anticipating this voice type in the role, we should keep in mind that only the very best such singers (perhaps a half-dozen in their fifty-year ascendancy) came very close to the virtuosic finish of the earlier school. The possibility that a voice of smaller calibre might offer welcome satisfactions in this writing should not be discounted—it's not hard, for instance, to imagine the middle-period Scotto doing well by the part.

But the voice must be properly conformed to the music. Radvanovsky sailed over the lofty divisions and C-C leaps of the aria in good form, though without any real tonal éclat, and all in all sang two-thirds of a very pretty lyric-soprano Elvira, the missing third being the bottom one. For all its ensemble-topping flights at the upper end, the role cannot be fulfilled with such a set-up. In this writing beginnings and endings—fierce attacks and conclusions that leave no room for doubt—are crucial, and from the opening recitative (think of Sutherland's "*ognor m'insegue*") through the aria, continuing with the fiery ripostes to Carlo's advances and beyond, there are too many strongly accented phrases that descend to the low range, and ascending ones launched from there, to allow for low-end shyness. On its own two-thirds of the two-thirds terms, the performance was entirely competent—no ugly or

---

* Sembrich left two recordings of "*Ernani, involami*" (1906 and 1908), interesting for both her vocalism and her choices of variants and of tempo—the latter, despite the 78 rpm time limitation, slower than now customary. She can also be heard briefly in a Mapleson cylinder live-performance extract (from the 1902 run) of the Tomb Scene finale, where Scotti's is the most prominent voice, but those of Sembrich and De Marchi emerge clearly on the high line of the ensemble. Bear in mind that all Sembrich's recordings are from the final phase of her operatic career.

out-of-tune notes, no unmusical phrases, sloppy rhythms, or messy runs. We can say of it, "That was nice." But nice is hardly enough.

Giordani was the Ernani. It is a difficult role to bring off, not because it's full of virtuosic challenges, but because it isn't. After his opening aria, he has flashes of vocal opportunity in duet, trio, and ensemble numbers, but doesn't really re-assert his centrality, musically speaking, until the opera's closing scene. Yet he is the protagonist, an original faydit hero, and must hold the stage in that capacity. Del Monaco and Corelli scored in the part, the former through his brooding intensity and smoldering tone that adapted so easily to Accursed Sufferer coloration, and the latter with his physical dash and tingling vocal release. Giordani cannot count these among his assets. Nor does he have Pavarotti's tonal glamor or Domingo's clarity, consistency, and drive. So that first scene (opening chorus for Ernani's bandit band; double aria with choral interjections) becomes even more critical, for it is the only one that belongs to the tenor.

Yet while the aria ("*Come rugiada al cespite*") can be effective when brilliantly sung, it is less distinctive than those accorded Elvira, Carlo, and Silva, and was clearly not written for the modern dramatic or spinto tenor. Its andante is a languishing song of romantic pining whose effect relies on a soulful rendering of typical graces, and the following allegro responds more to sharp execution of staccato and off-beat accents than to sheer volume or clarion *acuti* (the highest written pitch is an A). "*Come rugiada*" has never been a recording favorite, so while there are multiple early versions by important singers of the soprano, baritone, and bass solos to give us some feel for late 19th-Century style (still, we can be sure, changed from that of the first *Ernani* generation), for the tenor's we have only Fernando de Lucia's disc of the andante. It is sprinkled with deftly touched variants, oldstyle mezza-voce tenuti, and shrewdly paced rubatoes that lend it a High-Romantic feel; the rapid tremolo that obtrudes on the delicate side of De Lucia's singing is also present.* The young Martinelli's version (again of the andante only, 1915) is at least approximately what Met audiences were hearing in the '20s. It is suave and finely shaped, with a cleaner line than either Del Monaco or Corelli commanded, but it's distinctly a modern dramatic tenor voicing, tonally strong and vibrant, and thoroughly purified of De Lucia's liberties.

---

* Collectors interested in De Lucia tend to focus on his connection to an older *di grazia* style, and to group him with Bonci and Marconi as a "pre-Caruso" singer. With some allowance for range limitation at the top, he could be another of my strong-but-flexible exemplars. However, his greatest successes were in then-modern repertory of the veristic kind, and on records it is in full-throated music that his voice sounds best and the tremolo is minimized. Still, his mastery of the graces can't be doubted, and the *Ernani* aria is an emphatically different piece in his hands.

Among postwar Verdi tenors, it was undoubtedly Corelli who was the best Ernani, and Bergonzi who most successfully wedded textual obedience to stylistic finish. But perhaps Penno came the closest to showing the interpretive possibilities of the *tenore di forza* in this music. Though his singing life was short, at the time of this recording he seemed poised for a career as important as Del Monaco's, and artistically more interesting. His voice was famously (one could almost say notoriously) big and penetrating. In reviews of his singing from the early '50s, one encounters complaints about intonation and "throatiness," and his rendering of *"Ah, la paterno mano"* on the live 1952 La Scala *Macbeth* (one of the most persuasive Callas documents) betrays a couple of constricted A-flats along with impressive tone and phrases that are movingly shaped and colored.[42] On the *Ernani* recording he is in freer form. His delivery of the opening scene shows both the brassy ring of his full voice and a poignantly shaded legato—an admirable realization of both sides of the writing, much aided by the collaboration of the conductor, Fernando Previtali. (Here, in fact, and in the immediately following *"Ernani, involami,"* can be heard the work of a fine theatre conductor who understands not merely how to accommodate a singer's comfort, but to bring out the strengths of the particular voices at his disposal as they relate to the task at hand. It's one of the lost operatic arts.)

Among contemporary tenors, Giordani seems a reasonable candidate. The part is too vigorous for any of the new-vocality tenors, with their over-equalized compasses, who might charm us with textually delimited versions of oldstyle effects. Licitra would be the logical *di forza* postulant if only his technique were at least reliable enough to ensure an ongoing supply of undisturbed tone, and Alagna the lyrico-spinto one if there were more swash to his buckle and release to his high notes. It's one of many parts for which Domingo was the last good choice. Giordani's voice has some heft, some metal in the top, and some consistency of emission; these alone put him near the head of the bedraggled class of the '00s, and while he's been given some surpassingly strange assignments (e.g., *Il Pirata*, for which his opaque midrange and squealy high extension are almost uniquely unsuited), medium-weight Verdi is sensible enough. But, in especially grey voice and with no spark or lift from the pit, he barely registered, feeling his way dutifully through the many little turns around the passaggio, and once freed from those unable to unleash Duprezian fireworks in compensation. The opening scene, meant to leave us in excited anticipation, was a throwaway, and the rest of the role just rattled along.

It was Furlanetto's Silva that, in prospect, held the most promise of adding an attractive medallion to my *Ernani* tapestry. This role's primary solo, the cavatina "*Infelice, e tu credevi,*" is the opera's most recognizable hit tune and, along with "*Ernani, involami,*" its most frequently performed and recorded extract. It is also atypical of the role. Except for his brief, touching meltdown ("*Ah, io l'amo*") late in Act II, this song of mourning and bitterness intermixed is the only moment of softening allotted an antagonist otherwise trapped between impotent jealousy and ancestral honor codes. The singer of Silva must own timbral beauty and a well-oiled legato for the aria; tonal depth, steadiness, and solidity to convey the man's implacability; and a largeness of format that sustains the bottom line against presumably potent higher voices. Mardones, whose huge, wideranging bass rolled up and down the left/right midline with nary a kink, must have been close to perfect, vocally speaking. During the '30s, when Pinza and Pasero were at their peaks, *Ernani* was out of the Met repertory.

In recent outings as Brogni and Fiesco, Furlanetto had shown a voice of large calibre and a satisfying "sit" on the bass range, as well as a strongly limned line that served well for "*Si la rigueur*" and "*Il lacerato spirito.*" Though his top Es and Fs did not make good on all the promise of the instrument (and to appreciate the difference, listen to Pinza in *his* confrontations with Tibbett's Boccanegra), they were secure, and I found myself wondering why, with all this at his disposal, he had expended so much vocal capital on Mozart and Rossini buffo parts, which served to draw out the drier and plainer qualities of his voice. But along with the size and sit of the sound, his singing in *La Juive* and *Simon Boccanegra* had shown something else that interested me: something in the texture that sounded suspiciously like a core, and set him apart from his colleagues and competitors.

Among contemporary voices I am familiar with, all those that are of genuine dramatic calibre and in happy operating condition fall into the lower voice types in both sexes. I cannot think of a single soprano or tenor ready and able (though many are willing) to fulfill E-19 dramatic roles. From my technical P.O.V. this is not a mystery, but rather further corroboration: today's head-heavy, warm-and-fuzzy preferences fare somewhat better when plugged into deeper voices (where the Lower Family inevitably awaits them) than when overlayed onto lightly anchored higher ones. Even in these lower categories only four in addition to Furlanetto have been recently active hereabouts: Dolora Zajick, Stephanie Blythe, Bryn Terfel, and René Pape. So oceanic is one's sense of relief and gratitude upon encountering a voice that fills the house, sounds good, and doesn't trip over itself that it seems only prudent to humbly accept these gift horses and move along to more pressing critical concerns. And that is what I propose to do, noting only in passing that while format and general tonal aesthetics are not at issue with these singers, their vocal structures nonetheless yield qualities of texture, sit, and color that do not give full satisfaction in many of their assignments. They often leave an impression of "Very good, but not the right kind of very good." And to feel unsatisfied in the presence of plenitude is a serious aggravation.

Recall that in the heyday of the Easy Plush, as the softening texture, darker color, rounded format, and loosening grip of Upper-Family dominance made its way down the male vocal ladder, the lower female voices ran in countermotion, thrusting up and out. Zajick and Blythe are a synthesis of that dialectic: daughters of the bright-and-open American mezzo-soprano/soprano-mezzos like Bumbry and Verrett (or even, in timbral terms, Horne), buffed and blended to restrain crude utterance and tone down sexual aggression. On the male side, Terfel and Pape are direct descendants of the Easy Plush low voices via the long line of heavyish baritone and lightish basses that have succeeded them. They are large vocal animals, certainly, but thoroughly domesticated, their voices distinguished by warmth, ease, smoothness, and uncontested access to the top notes of their chosen roles. It was by contrast with them that I looked forward to Furlanetto's Silva. (Pape would, of course, be the first alternative for the role.) In the event, he was not quite at his best. There was some grit and sputter in his tone, and he didn't sustain the line of "*Infelice*" quite as I'd hoped. Even so, owing to the factors already alluded to (calibre, texture, color, and sit), his was the evening's most authentic vocal presence. We could at least say of him, "there's a Verdi bass."[43]

All is not yet lost. The most workaday *Ernani* can be salvaged by a front-rank Verdi baritone, for Carlo is the opera's best role. While the others sing their introductory numbers and then become entangled in confrontations and ensembles, Carlo traces an ascending arc through a series of captivating arioso passages ("*Da quel dì che t'ho veduta,*" "*Lo vedremo, o veglio audace,*" "*Vieni meco, sol di rose*") to the great set pieces that dominate Act III ("*O de' verd'anni miei;*" "*O sommo Carlo*"). This scene, *La Clemenza,* in which Carlo is elected Holy Roman emperor and then, at Elvira's intercession, pardons the regicidal conspirators, is the musical denouement of the work. It shows us what the morally transformative, happy-end ensemble finale would be, with Carlo's blessing granting the rebel couple what they truly seek and seem to have attained (inclusion through marriage), were it not for the feudal code and the power of the oath to which that primitive trumpet motif returns us in Act IV. Carlo's progression of highlighted solos carries the character on an ennobling journey up and out of the opera, and a superior baritone can just about take the evening with him, with an act yet to go.

Here the Met's casting had at least curiosity value, for the Carlo was the gifted and versatile Thomas Hampson, who in terms of the variety, importance, and frequency of his assignments has become the Met's leading baritone. I don't wish to pretend that I anticipated deep satisfaction with Hampson's Carlo, because while his singing always shows musical intelligence and diligence, stylistic awareness, and a pleasing timbre, and while I've seen him in roles as apposite as Bellini's Riccardo, Rossini's Figaro, and even Verdi's Posa, I still do not consider him a Verdi baritone. But the question then arises: why not? Is the category "Verdi baritone"—or for that matter any of the categories I've been tossing about, any of these efforts to define "authenticity" or the "right kind of good"—a valid one? Isn't good singing just good singing? These are fair questions, and Hampson himself has articulated them in the context of his Verdi singing. Indeed, he has made himself a spokesperson for the new vocality's interface with E-19 voice types and singing traditions. So in both capacities—singer and spokesperson—he is my final exemplar.

No artist can be blamed for wanting to sing Verdi's music and embody his characters. But it's one thing to perform and another to proselytize; one thing to honestly give what value one can, and another to represent that value as equivalent, or even superior, to proven ones it seeks to replace. The former contributes, to the best of the artist's ability, to our art. The latter blurs our understanding of it. There's no question that Hampson has done serious listening and reading. When he sang Werther in the baritone revision Massenet wrote for Battistini, he did so in full awareness of the precedent, and he speaks with an appreciative familiarity with the artistry of some of his predecessors (especially among art-song singers) that is uncommon among contemporary performers. As to reading, he once cited Fritz Noske's *The Signifier and the Signified* as a favorite reference on Don Giovanni (he's ahead of me there, and shall probably remain so), and his comments often show that, like many of our directors, he is engaged with the idea-content of works, scenes, and characters. But as we also see with the directors, there can be *glissements* between words that seem to address important artistic issues and the consummation of a performance reality. (What relationship would there be, for instance, between Hampson's capabilities and those of Battistini, without which Massenet would certainly not have re-written—and re-set into Italian—the role? Or between semiotic analysis and the actual singing and playing of any part, let alone Don Giovanni?) And this can happen with regard not only to interpretive matters, but to the voice itself. Here Hampson's reasoning follows on that of one of my previous exemplars, Fischer-Dieskau, who could on occasion resort to special pleading when venturing beyond native habitat.[44] I think it can be justly said that both as singer and apologist, Fischer-Dieskau is in fact the enabler of Hampson as Verdi baritone.

In advancing his qualifications for this repertory (for the references used here, see n. 45), Hampson seeks to deconstruct "Verdi baritone" as a category. He has gone so far as to call the whole notion "a silly cliché," complaining that "certain perceptions just hang in there." But I think the "cliché" is not altogether silly, and that the perceptions hang in there for a reason. Hampson argues that not all Verdi baritone roles are vocally alike, and that their psychological individualization is the most interesting thing about them. Neither of these assertions, in itself, gets any argument from me. But with respect to the first, I would observe that the roles do fall into two broad groups, distinguished mostly by tessitura, and that some fine voices are more comfortable in one group than in the other. Further, the distance between these groups notwithstanding, many singers over the years (the ones we would call "great Verdi baritones", beginning with those of Verdi's own time—Ronconi, Cotogni, Varesi, et al.) have assumed virtually the entire canon to notable effect. And with respect to the second, the real question is, "How are these individualized characters to be dramatized?" My answer begins: "With voices whose presence, color, and weight are *of themselves* impressive in the music, and whose structures support the expressive range of the music, allowing in particular for emotionally stirring renditions of its key gestures." In the role of Carlo V, what sort of presence, color, and weight are desirable, and what are the key gestures?

In the *Ernani* chapter of his study of the Verdi canon, Julian Budden notes that "This is the opera in which Verdi defines most clearly his male vocal archetypes," and that of these the baritone combines the "granite-like, monochrome" coloration of the bass with the "lyrical, ardent" accents of the heroic tenor into an instrument "now zephyr, now hurricane" that became "the greatest vehicle of power in Italian opera."[46] Like most such statements, some exceptions could be taken to this one.* But in general, it holds. To it we can add Shaw's observations about Verdi's upward extension of baritone tessitura, which—though also subject to exception—are generally true of at least the higher Verdi baritone roles (e.g., Di Luna, Miller, or Ford, as opposed to Boccanegra, Macbeth, or Amonasro).[47] Taken together, what these changes add up to *vis à vis* the already expanded baritonality of such roles as Bellini's Riccardo or Donizetti's Alphonse is not heavier weight and darker color in

---

* It could be maintained, for instance, that in a few of his last tenor parts (Alvaro, Radamès, and especially Otello) Verdi created vehicles of equal power for the upper male voice. Even in these operas, though, the baritone holds his own, and the sheer force of his intent, well represented by his vocality, drives the action.

themselves, or higher tessitura in itself, but the combination of the two, i.e., greater weight at higher pitch. And since a singer sustaining greater weight at higher pitch is going to sound louder, an increase in calibre is also implicit. As with the Duprezian tenor born only a few years before Verdi wrote *Ernani*, this higher/weightier, louder voice is still meant to obey classical precepts of registral integration and balance. Therefore it is expected to show control of the swell-and-diminish, to negotiate the *passaggio* gracefully, and to emerge therefrom into climactic high notes that seem to grow naturally from below, a tenorial brilliance sprouting from the basso-esque darkness.

And what are the "key gestures" by means of which Verdi asks such voices to dramatize and characterize? I should say they are marked by three tendencies: 1) The persistence with which the crest of an arc occurs directly on, or passes through, the *passaggio* notes of E and F; 2) The use of dynamic contrasts, frequently sudden (requiring clean, decisive attacks) or sweeping (melding the cresting arc with the swell-and-diminish capability); and 3) A proliferation of accents and other articulations, often to bring emphasis and point to an otherwise smooth cantabile, but just as often to indicate explosive force. These tendencies are present in all of Verdi's writing for the baritone voice, and in combination with the requirements of format and weight they pose great challenges. No other composer tests the baritone like Verdi, or so rewards him when the test is passed. Early though *Ernani* is, the role of Carlo is already a fully elaborated example of the type, and for a century and a half has been considered a showcase for Verdi baritones, whether of the leonine sort (Ruffo) or the more lyrical (De Luca), of left-column (Battistini, Ancona, Stracciari) or right-column (Warren and MacNeil) persuasion.

To anyone at all familiar with these voices, it will be instantly clear that Hampson's does not belong among them. Its overall sound is neither dark and voluminous nor brilliant and ringing; thus, there is little room for play between these timbral families. Its tonal impact is noticeably less than that of any major Verdi baritone of the late E-19. (To call him 2/3 of a Warren, MacNeil, Merrill, Taddei, Bastianini or Milnes would be generous. In my last-wave format rankings [see n. 4, p. 410], he would fall at the end of the baritone category.) Note that I speak of "tonal impact," rather than size per se. That is because while the higher/weightier/ergo-louder format is the most obvious characteristic of the "Verdi baritone" category (Hampson himself defines the "cliché" in terms of tonal weight and size), it remains true that just as a relatively light soprano voice of proper structure and superb executional technique (like Sembrich's) might well provide fulfillment as Elvira, so might a baritone equivalent as Carlo. Such an equivalency would presuppose the same kind of lean, poised, penetrating tone and the same consistent firmness throughout the range (most particularly in the transitional area) as Sembrich's. But these qualities would now be distributed over a compass approximately an octave and a third below the soprano's, and with its transitional area three-quarters of the way up, not three-quarters of the way down—characteristics that suggest the baritone of whom I spoke near the beginning of this chapter, Pavel Lisitsian.

Lisitsian's voice was not huge. I think it's possible that its decibel count in midrange was no greater than Hampson's. But in quality, behavior, and impact it was different from both Hampson's and those of the big Western Verdi baritones of the time. In his Carnegie Hall recital, it sounded to me like a throwback—a way of singing I had heard only via recordings of earlier baritones like Battistini, Schlusnus, or perhaps John Charles Thomas. I had been excited by the bits and pieces of his singing that had made their way through the Iron Curtain (e.g., the *Sadko* song, the Prince Yeletsky). But to experience his voice live in a large hall was to recognize the same immediacy of communication that Tebaldi's first lines in *Otello* had established: "*Mio superbo guerrier, quanti tormenti . . .*"—midvoice phrases, sung at moderate volume, but jumping into the ear with that "directly beamed" quality described by James Hinton.

It so often happens at recitals that the most memorable singing comes during the encores. The singer, having met his or her pro forma obligations (in the old days, to stylistic groupings of time and place, now to thematic conceits) is at last at liberty to sing what he or she most wants to sing, and the audience to hear. So it was at Lisitsian's recital. After a bow to the worlds of *Lieder* and *mélodie* (good, but not the right kind of good) and a splendid sequence of Rachmaninoff, there were some unprogrammed songs and arias. And among the latter, the capstone of *La Clemenza*, "*O sommo Carlo.*" Lisitsian necessarily offered only the solo line of this number. However, the solo line is in itself very beautiful and vocally rewarding. In the recital setting, Lisitsian was sole arbiter of musical choices, free to shape the melody exactly as he felt it and as it led his voice to bloom, and free to interpolate for maximum effect. After stating the section's opening midrange theme, which Lisitsian traced with the same legato and refulgence that distinguished his "*Ombra mai fu,*" the line rises to a sustained E-flat at "*delle tue gesta imitator.*" This happens twice. The first time, the note (held on the first syllable of "*gesta*") is completely in the clear, and articulated with a swell-and-diminish. The singer is, by longstanding oral understanding, allowed to treat this as if marked with a corona—a special moment leading toward the conclusion of this opening section, before the brief *declamato* passage wherein Carlo pardons the conspirators and unites Ernani and Elvira. The second time, the entire ensemble jumps in fortissimo after the first beat, *ergo*, the baritone must sustain the note at forte and, unless there is an extraordinary concession, stay in tempo.

Among baritones with long reach on the high end, there is, again, an old tradition of taking the first of these E-flats up to the high A-flat, then coming back down to linger, perhaps with discreet ornamentation, over the phrase's conclusion on the word "*imitator.*" The tradition apparently originated with Antonio Cotogni; at least, it is attributed to him by Luigi Ricci, who did us the favor of notating variants and cadenzas introduced by great 19th-Century singers he had heard.[48] It's one of many such interpolations that might or might not have had the composer's sanction and that in the wrong hands become tiresome bits of bluster but which, once heard from a great voice under masterly guidance, create an emotional, almost physical hankering in the listener. Lisitsian not only made this ascent, with ideal smoothness and perfect intonation, but then executed the complete *messa di voce*, flawlessly even and centered, on the high A-flat—a stunning effect, especially from the throat of a center-left baritone. Then, unconstrained by ensemble or conductor, he swept up to the A-flat again the second time around, now at a full, ringing forte as he launched the quickened tempo that carries the scene to its end. This wasn't just thrilling vocalism. It was Charles the Fifth assuming full manhood and empire at once.

On musical grounds, it is unlikely that Hampson would attempt these feats; on technical grounds, equally unlikely that he could execute them, and inconceivable that they would produce anything like the same effect. His midrange does not prepare the voice for them. As I have said, in terms of calibre this part of his range is at least comparable to Lisitsian's. But in timbre and texture, it is not. Instead, it suggests a light baritone version of the grouping whose bass and low-baritone types we have met in Pape and Terfel, and which has many other representatives among current "lyric" baritones. And this is yet another type that did not emerge, operatically speaking, until the tail-end days of E-19. Among baritones of that time, Hampson most clearly resembles Theodor Uppman. Uppman was a fine singer and a valuable artist. His greatest successes came as Billy Budd (he created the role) and Pelléas, supplemented by such assignments as Eisenstein, Paquilo (*La Périchole*), and the lighter Mozart parts (Papageno, Guglielmo, Masetto). So long as Uppman's voice remained within that framework, its size was ample and its range well-equalized, topping off quite satisfactorily with A-flats and A-naturals when required. But in the context of more dramatic repertory (and even the lightest of Verdi is that), the texture of his voice seemed overly heady and lyrical, more typically French than Italian, and his attack lacking in punch. The top notes, though easily accessed and never in peril, now sounded anticlimactic. So, although he sang some of the standard baritone arias in concert and on broadcasts, he did not assume roles much heavier than those indicated above. That was a matter of commonly held artistic judgment—to have proposed Uppman as Macbeth, let's say, or even Di Luna, would have been regarded as peculiar, if not downright perverse.[49]

For voices like Uppman's or Hampson's, it is the relationship of the midrange to the top that is most problematic when they are confronted with dramatic material. They are forced to deal with the male version of the "a" dilemma, i.e., how to manage open vowels on the *passaggio* notes and come out on the other side with a dominant high range. Many singers of Verdian weight sing the midrange "open" and the transition notes more closed or "covered" (see the previous discussion of some of those singers, pp. 344-345). Very occasionally one encounters a baritone able to sing F or even F-sharp "open" without loss of quality or vocal seating, e.g., Gino Bechi (but his prime was short), de Luca (but G was his upper limit), or—most remarkably in this particular—Thomas. But true center-line masters with good core in the middle voice (Battistini, Stracciari, Schwarz, Schlusnus, Lisitsian) can make the transition smoothly, almost imperceptibly, and with a supple control of dynamics, yet still "lean into" the *passaggio* notes for emphasis and accent, and top off the cresting phrases with freely ringing *acuti*.

It is to this last condition that Hampson as Verdi baritone would logically aspire. If, from his warm, nappy midrange he were able to soar fearlessly into the top in the manner of any of the above-named singers, and to ring the changes in color and accent that come with that capacity, the relatively light weight of his instrument would be of little consequence, especially for the higher Verdi roles. The proportions would then be right, the key gestures accessible. But you can't get there from here, if the "here" is Hampson's midrange. The nappiness of that timbre—a velvety or silken quality, so apposite to art song and quite adaptable to the light operatic and operetta repertory—tells us why: it lacks the necessary bracing. Without this, the singer must treat open vowels with such caution that they lose all force and bite, and never take on their wonted resonantal glow. The sound families are, in effect, turned upside down: in the midrange, a heady, closed-in tone that for Verdi-baritone purposes must be loaded to capacity; above, a chestier, more open one that, if pushed, would migrate toward the "male belt" of Broadway baritenor notoriety.

Hampson, being smart and cultivated, generally manages this situation in a way that makes the best of it. But it is precisely this managed quality that is, in the context of this literature, often disappointing. The basic presence and weight of the voice are at one moment adequate, at the next moment not, and many of the key gestures can only be indicated, rather than fulfilled. From *Ernani*, a few examples from the "power" side of the writing for Carlo must suffice.[50] The first is from "*Lo vedremo, o veglio audace*," the passage in which Carlo threatens Silva with "the vengeance of your king" and a "lightning bolt upon you" if he is concealing Ernani in his castle. After the vicious impetus of the heavily accented opening tune with its swirling accompaniment, the music drops back for a moment to pianissimo—a held-back, ready-to-pounce pianissimo—at "*essa rugge sul tuo capo*," then bends upward through the *passaggio* on the words "*pensa pria*".* This is one of those cresting arcs, legato but *con forza*, whose impact depends on the combination of rising pitch, swelling volume, and a vowel change (from "*i*" to "*a*") as the voice crosses into the upper register on an accented F-sharp. It is followed by a succession of accented, stomping sixteenths that brings the voice back down to midrange. Though unmarked, some broadening of this bar is advantageous, to give the F-sharp time to intensify and the following accents to hit home. All of the true Verdi baritones I have named have achieved versions of this moment; it is fully realized on the recording of Battistini or, even more impressively, that of Stracciari. It is the crowning effect of the aria, recurring in a slight variation on the words "*il tuo capo, o traditore*" just three bars before the mini-cadenza (once again carrying up to the F-sharp) that brings the section to its crushing close. Hampson, with his nicely controlled line, carefully husbanded F-sharp, and barely suggested accents, could not crush; he could only reprove.

My remaining examples are from the second half of "*O de' verdi'anni miei*." They can be heard as no more than vocal effects (though stirring ones, if consummated), but collectively they also carry crucial dramatic import. Francis Toye, writing in a time and place of early-Verdi eclipse (England, 1930) and contrasting the character of Charles in Hugo's play with the Carlo of Piave's libretto, calls the latter "... a mere puppet who, for no apparent reason, turns from a lecherous and frivolous Prince into a humane and statesmanlike Emperor".[51] And it is true that the libretto, written in melodramatic operatic shorthand, only states the reasons, without allowing them any credible depth of development. But they are not really so mysterious, and are two in number. The first is the dawning in Carlo of a tragic sensibility, coupled with awareness of his imperial destiny and his wish to rise to it—his Prince Hal/Henry V moment, represented in this aria. The second is the compassion aroused in him by Elvira's plea for clemency, which tempers power with love and leads directly into the "*O sommo Carlo*" finale.

---

* "It [the royal vengeance] roars above your head ... think first (*pensa pria*), think first before it all descends," etc.—here is Budden's "hurricane" in one of its most literal representations.

In place of Hugo's verbal depth (or, at any rate, length) stands Verdi's musical conviction, which lives or dies by its voicing. In opera, we do not believe in such transformations for "reasons"; we succumb to song. And in this case, four similar vocal gestures determine our willingness to do so. The first is the phrase that quite specifically marks the turning point in Carlo's life-direction; the second and third build enthusiastically upon that; and the last is the cadential conclusion to the aria. They are all set to variations of the same words: "*e vincitor de' secoli/il nome mio farò*".* As the aria's first part, built around the lingering *gruppetti* with which Carlo bids farewell to his youthful illusions, reaches its close, the voice holds a moment to gather its forces on the middle C with the word "*Ah!*", then springs up to the E-flat for the "*e*" that launches the big phrase—a famous one, sometimes called "The Grand Phrase." And this is a true born-again moment: a new tune, a fresh impetus ("*con forza, legato*" and "*con un po' più di moto*"), with a brightened harmony and the entry of full orchestral forces, exultantly doubling the voice, after the chamberish, meditative accompaniment of the opening section. And above all, a palpable opening-out from the singer's throat. For a good Italian baritone, D and E-flat on an open vowel are particularly favorable notes, not because they belong to his high range but because they are at the very edge of it, where a unique combination of vibrant tension, intense coloring, and fatness of format can be assembled. Verdi knew this and wrote to it (think of Amonasro's "*Suo padre!*" or the *Forza* Carlo's "*Finalmente!*"), and so have Verdi baritones from the start (recall the traditional interpolated E-flat at Rigoletto's "*Un vindice avrai!*"). The *Aïda* and *Forza* moments dramatically arrest forward movement; Rigoletto's puts it in suspense before setting a new momentum, as in the present example. Battistini, whose command of vowel-color extremes that somehow stay in balance remains unparalleled, creates the most startling effect here, but Stracciari is close behind, and De Luca and Ancona realize the moment as well. In the continuation of this phrase ("*il nome mio farò*") we recognize the domineering pattern set in "*Lo vedremo*" of a sustained high note (here an F, on the second syllable of "*nome*"), followed by stomping downward accents, and this applies once more on the next cresting arc, this time carrying from E-flat up into the G-flat on the first syllable of "*secoli*," before again descending in like manner.

Thus, three rising phrases carry the baritone to and then through the transition center. Each is higher than the one before it; each is voiced on the vowel "*e*" as it takes on progressively greater tenorial ring; and each

---

* The complete thought is:["Lifted by virtue as on an eagle's wings,] my name shall conquer the centuries."

returns to midvoice with heavily accented emphasis. Two more bars bring us to the traditional spot for a closing cadenza. None is written. Instead, after a presumably well-exploited fermata on the D ("*Il nome mi . . . o . . . farò*" one more time), the aria's "down" ending leads directly into a soft, haunting orchestral recollection of The Grand Phrase as Carlo enters the bronze door of Charlemagne's tomb to await both his election and the conspirators. But at least so far as I know, no baritone has ever gone without some sort of cadenza for this, his defining solo scene. Battistini and De Luca use the C as the jumping-off point first for a proud flourish that ends on the lower C, and then for a leap up to the high G on "*nome*," taking the following fermata on the E-flat ("*Fa--*") before settling down to the tonic A-flat to finish ("*—rò*"). Modern singers usually omit the run, proceeding directly up to the G and then either returning to the lower tonic or—as did Warren, MacNeil, and Milnes—taking one route or another up to the high A-flat.

From a greatvoiced throat, these high endings are memorable theatre events—and again, once heard, they seem not only dramatically justified but virtually imperative.[52] Ambition, pride, and intimidation can be heard in them (and certainly belong to this character), but nobility and revelation as well. The born-again moment is physical, emotional. It is something felt.

Could the close of this aria be sung and staged in keeping with the score's suggestions, and thereby find musical and dramatic values at least as important as those conveyed by a greatvoiced cadenza? Possibly. However, that isn't what Hampson attempted, despite his predominantly lyrical predilections and his keen awareness of text. He presented the cadenza in its modern simplified form, with the high G, the held E-flat, and the low ending. His G, though, hadn't enough sheer mass or timbral tingle to be more than a token effect, and the E-flat, instead of intensifying the concluding bar, withdrew on a dulcet diminuendo, as if intended to lead directly into the orchestra's soft postlude. That would at least have been a musical effect of some atmospheric use. But with Hampson having made cadenza-like gestures and his audience well aware of its end-of-aria responsibilities, there was the customary break for applause, as everyone concerned must surely have anticipated. So we had neither one sort of effect nor the other. In the supreme moment of his life Carlo is first interrupted for no compelling reason, then slips discreetly away.[53]

Was there still not something of value in Hampson's Carlo? Certainly, for the role has its zephyr side, and in the smooth, soft line with which he intoned "*Da quel dì*" and "*Vieni meco*" were to be found the evening's only eloquent moments. Even this eloquence, though, was restrained first by the croony nature of his *piano*, and second by the narrow color range available to him.

He can play beguilingly with dynamics so long as they don't approach hurricane force, but whether louder or softer, his tone's chiaroscuro hardly changes—it stays suede-ish in texture and brownish in hue. And for an alternative to my usual terminology of right- and left-column voices, of core and tensility, etc.—for language that describes without assigning cause—I can do no better than borrow the E-19 words of Ernest Legouvé, as quoted by one of the ur-Verdi baritones, Jean-Baptiste Faure:

> "Someone . . . who has no metal in the voice will never become a colorist reader. This metal can be gold, silver or bronze because each of these metals corresponds to a different sonority . . . but one of the three qualities is necessary . . . Last [there is] the voice of velvet. But this does not work without one of the three others . . . Without metal, a velvet voice is no more than a voice of cotton."[54]

I would hesitate to call Hampson's a voice of cotton. But in it there is no trace of metal—not the sparkle of gold, the sheen of silver, or the clang of bronze. On the occasions when he rubs through the nap in search of something harder, we glimpse wood, not metal.* These occasions are infrequent, but invariably important.

For suavity and tenderness of the right sort—the sort that, however delicate and intimate, still belongs to a voice of power, a voice of coloristic (and therefore emotional) extremes that remain integrated—we must turn back a half-century and more. Hampson's instrument hasn't the combination of greater weight and darker color at higher pitch that would make it "of itself impressive in Verdi's music," or the structural strength and balance to allow for "emotionally stirring renditions of the writing's key gestures." It hasn't the core and metal of the left-column voices or the plump format and heady release of the right-column ones that have, in many individual variations, consummated these great roles. Even its softness is not of quite the right sort. Whether one believes (as I tend to) that his voice's technical structure is what separates it from that of a Lisitsian or Schlusnus, or that Hampson simply "has" a lyric baritone voice that is "naturally" suited only to lighter repertory, one thing is, I think, self-evident: he's not a Verdi baritone. He's a new-vocality substitute.

---

* An instance fresh in my mind: the forceful open F of *"Je te hais,"* in Athanaël's *"Voilà donc la terrible cité" (Thaïs)*. At times like this, he has no resource but a vehemence of attack—the predicament Uppman avoided by staying "in *Fach.*"

If the arrival of the new vocality were a matter of augmentation pure and simple, of adding one set of capabilities to another and thereby broadening our aesthetic embrace, there would be no cause for concern. But that is not at all what has happened. Instead, the Skipover/Crossover ways of singing have displaced the E-19 ways of singing, and the losses far outweigh the gains. Even if one embraces the dubious proposition that on one end the many operas of Handel, Gluck, Mozart, and the comedic Rossini, and on the other the scattered few of Britten, Ravel, Stravinsky and Poulenc are better served by the new than by the old; even when one allows that it has been edifying and sometimes exhilarating to make close acquaintance with the happy-end erotic of the Baroque; and even if one grants that interpretive brilliance can sometimes be more compelling than greatvoiced vocalizing, one is still left with the nightly neutralization of Beethoven and (on rare occasions) Weber; of the grander Bellini, Rossini, and Donizetti; of Verdi and Wagner, Puccini and Strauss, the Italian verists, and all French opera from Meyerbeer and Halévy through Massenet. That is one of the worst cultural deals ever struck. And while adversarial productions, technological alienations, Notperformance, the hyper-refinement of the orchestra and the Drama Cancellation Effect have certainly figured in the negotiations, it is the suppression of E-19 vocality that has sealed the bargain.

WE GO TO SCHOOL

By 1970, operatic singing faced an aporia. We all sensed it. The grace period had expired: the symbiotic flex between creation and performance, by means of which compositional styles and vocal usages evolve to shared artistic purpose and mutual benefit, had come to a virtual standstill because the creative side of the flex had long since ceased to provide any impetus. Now, it neither reinforced established practices nor supplied the energy for an evolutionary step. Its creative mind baffled, opera flapped on like a bird on one wing, trying to sing. It certainly did not help that this came to pass amid the sociocultural churning of the time, and was bound up with it. But I believe that singing's aporia was due in any case, as natural sequel to the creative one. And, as always, that artists are obliged to address artistic problems in artistic terms. Along with the loss of tonal format and core, a certain homogenization and blandification of expression—a mechanical quality—is the most commonly recognized demerit of the new vocality. Many partial explanations are offered. They include today's highly pressurized travel and rehearsal schedules; the accelerated commercialization of the profession, with its attendant entrepreneurial and promotional aspects and its tendency to push for short-term career moves as opposed to selective, long-term decision-making; and the necessities of remaining camera-cool and mike-focused for the sake of the virtual identity that is rapidly shoving aside the real one. Though I have no way of evaluating their relative importance, these factors clearly have the cumulative effect of commending a safety-first, preventive-maintenance discipline—a stopping-short of full physical and emotional commitment—to smart young singers. But they have to do with the singer already embarked. I would like to focus on three additional factors I think are more formative. Each is related to a development we would in most respects consider an advancement, and whose negative aspects tend, on that account, to be overlooked.

The first is the acceptance of the integrated production as a norm— doubtless a good thing, but one that does tend to transfer decision-making from singers to Second-interpreters-in-Chief and to tamp down individual extremes of personality and interpretive choice. The implications of this will be more productively considered in the chapter to come. The other two are: 1) the diversification of the repertoire and 2) here in the U.S., the immense wartime and postwar expansion of the university/regional opera complex. The synchronicities between these are striking, and they have created new symbioses—between profession and academy, scholarship and performance—and a new definition of the singer's job. They are, again, good and welcome things in many ways, but ones that have exerted reductive pressures on greatvoiced singing.

This is not the place for a detailed history of the American regional opera system. Suffice it here to say that, like the regional theatre system, it came into being in its present form in the 1950s and 60s, and continued to grow into the 1980s.* It supplanted both the old touring troupes that had by then become economically unworkable and the "civic" or "municipal" opera companies that for decades had, in many cities, mounted a handful of performances of a few standard-repertory works with a couple of visiting stars, rented sets and costumes, and barely enough rehearsal to rough in the staging. Stoked by the postwar prosperity, by the money and initiative of the newly founded governmental support agencies and major private foundations, and by the same civic ambition that fueled the arts-center building boom, it multiplied several times over the national totals of opera productions and performances, and of

---

* The Santa Fe Festival (founded in 1957) and the Tyrone Guthrie Theatre in Minneapolis (1963) are often taken as the flagship institutions of the "regional" movement in opera and theatre, respectively. Santa Fe, however, is a summer seasonal operation, whereas the ultimate vision behind regional development was of year-round resident companies based in metro areas, and serving their surrounding territories—hence "regional." A better example might be the Seattle Opera, founded in 1962 (the World's Fair of that year providing a civic push and an appropriate facility) in a city with almost no history of opera performance.

audience attendance.[55] It put down roots for the artform in many locales. It promoted the model of the well-rehearsed, integrated production presented not in repertory but in a brief single-production run, and de-emphasized the star system. It created a market for a kind of performer that had previously been of little use: the mid-priced, middle-class pro.

It was during these same years that university opera programs and vocal departments also saw exponential growth in size and number—a reflection of the expansion and democratization of higher education overall. To the long-established major conservatories, small independent music schools, and modest sideline departments of most colleges were added dozens, if not hundreds, of programs, many of imposing scope and reach, housed in facilities that often surpassed those available to professional companies (for campuses had their own arts-center building boom). In this movement's prehistory (the late 1930s and 1940s), these nascent departments and workshops were usually guided by European conductors, coaches, directors and designers of the same generation that soon furnished the artistic directors and coaching staffs of many of our opera companies and the private teachers and coaches with whom American singers trained. They carried in them some of the same bred-in-the-bone knowledge of repertory and working theatre practice that Szell, Walter, and the other great conductors of that time and place possessed, not to mention an intriguing attitudinal mix of Old World traditionalist, New World frontiersman, and operatic colonialist.*[56] By the 1970s, though, their ranks were as thin as those of the last Duprezians, and a new army of American educators marched in their place.

These two systems—regional opera and academic opera—bonded as they grew. Their bonding comprised the same circulation of personnel as characterizes the more widely noted flux between, let's say, banking and government, or legislating and lobbying, and by more or less the same means: recommendation by reputation or personal acquaintance from one sphere to the other; the recycling of careers from one to the other; and, of course, graduation from one to the other—not only of artists of all descriptions, but

---

* Note that these artists and teachers were almost exclusively of German/Austro-Hungarian origin. Both the traditions they sought to uphold and the "making new" spirit they brought to their adopted land derived from ways of thinking cultivated in the theatre systems of those countries. Speaking broadly, their influence waxed as the Italians' waned in American operatic life, and was in turn later displaced by a new-fashioned Anglo-American one. (The French, so important earlier on, had already faded.) These successive shifts, defined not only by generations but by national cultures, had significant vocal implications with respect to linguistic and stylistic cultivation, technical training, and understanding of the singer's status in the production system, the operatic world, and society.

of administrators as well (for arts administration and development were now academic subjects). While there had always been some preferential intercourse between the few major conservatories and the few major opera companies (most notably, that between Juilliard and the Metropolitan in the late 1930s), there was now such intercourse among many and many. And from this interchange there emerged a new bottom rung on the professional ladder—that assigned to the apprentice or associate artist, who received further training in a professional environment in exchange for choral, comprimario, cover, and "outreach" duties. A new marathon course had been marked for the aspirant singer, with thousands herded annually at its trailhead and dozens, at least, still running at the finish line six to eight years later: undergraduate school, graduate school, apprentice-to-associate artist, and finally freelance seeker of midpriced, middle-class employment. Each year, a small minority of finishers would establish actual careers of some duration and stability. Of the remaindered majority, some revolved directly back into the academy as teachers and gatekeepers, but most, sooner rather than later, found other lines of work. Whether the academy was becoming more professionalized or the profession more academized is hard to say. Either way, a system had been established where, really, there had been none before, and like all systems it tended toward agreed-upon criteria for accreditation and certification—in other words, toward standardization.

The third synchronous development to influence operatic singing (and one not confined to North America) was the diversification of the repertoire. It has had five components. In rough chronological order, they are: 1) The "*bel canto*" revival, involving primarily the resuscitation of works by Bellini, Rossini, Donizetti, and the young Verdi; 2) The Handel revival; 3) The Baroque revival; 4) attempted Here-and-Now startups, which have added little to the repertory but much to the training and preparation mindset; and 5) the changing nature of Crossover, and its acceptance as "legit."[57] The second and third of these are crossbred with the early-music, original-instrument movement; the last four together make up the Skipover menu, whose technical practices bear a deceptive tangential relationship to the requirements of the *bel canto* repertoire, viz.: though they cannot fulfill it, they can render it to the satisfaction of Skipover ears, or those of people unaware of what fulfillment would feel like.

Concurrent with everything I have spoken of has been the growth spurt in the field of musicology, which is by definition a scholarly, research-oriented pursuit whose natural goals are critical analysis, editorial correction, and rediscovery, and whose natural home is the academy. Although the academy does not often initiate artistic movements (it absorbs and canonizes them, and so directs student minds—and in this case, voices—toward its intellectually ordered versions of them), musicology has exerted generative force on the professional opera world. Its rediscoveries and corrections have provided a badly needed measure of repertory refreshment for professional companies and of display of scholarly findings for academia (and in an art of the act, publication of findings will not suffice—performance is required).[58] That this refreshment stands in place of creative renewal is not exactly the scholars' fault (though I sometimes wonder: in its absence, would more creation have taken place?), and that it consists almost entirely of audience-friendly entertainments with no power to disturb or provoke is apparently a great relief to all concerned. In any event, the performance requirements of Skipover repertory proved more compatible with the artistic and economic resources of most educational institutions than did those of E-19 opera, and Skipover singing models fit more easily into the early career steps dictated by the new system than did ambitions toward greatvoiced singing. The impact of all this on vocal training and career preparation has been profound.

I think often of our wartime generation, the American singers who debuted sometime between the late-Depression years and the end of the Second World War. Prominent among them were sopranos Traubel, Varnay, Harshaw, Farrell,* Steber, and Kirsten; mezzo-sopranos Stevens, Thebom, and Resnik; tenors Peerce and Tucker; baritones Warren, Merrill, and Weede; and bass Jerome Hines. They varied widely in musicianship, stylistic sophistication, and stage skills. They had only three things in common: first, they were Americans; second, they were authentic grand-opera singers; third, at the time of their arrival on the scene they were by present-day standards remarkably uncredentialed and inexperienced. Most of them studied exclusively with private teachers.[59] They did not progress through the university/regional complex, or learn the many things to be learned there, because it didn't exist. Nor could they (except for Stevens, briefly, in Vienna) gain stage experience and repertoire—as did many of their postwar successors—by working their way up through the German and Austrian system, for it was closed off by the war and the events leading up to it. They sang in churches and synagogues and Borscht Belt resorts, at musicales and movie theatres (Radio City Music Hall is on several of these resumés) and over the radio. They received no study grants or Fulbrights; their progress depended on private patrons and their teachers' contacts. Then, with little or no stage experience, they made their

---

* I think it's fair to include Farrell here despite her delayed operatic career—these were her early performing years. See pp. 360-361.

debuts, usually at the top. Without benefit of anything like the formal education of today's singers, or the opportunities of their stepwise career progression, the older singers somehow "knew," somehow incorporated into their
performing selves, the elements of greatvoiced singing: a voice of sufficient
size and quality to consummate leading roles of the standard E-19 repertoire;
an instinctive musicality compatible enough with the musical styles of
those roles to learn them; and adequate command of the foreign languages
in which they sang. They also found the nerve (call it confidence, chutzpah,
blissful ignorance, even arrogance—but not "self-esteem") to step directly
onto major stages and make a mark, as had some of their illustrious interwar
predecessors.* So it is not unreasonable to ask: is there actually an inverse
relationship between our training and career development system and the
cultivation of great voices?

I believe there is. Naturally, that was not the intention. Whatever the
motives of some of the individuals and institutions involved, our system was
created in a constructive spirit. For cities and regions, it proposed an end to
dependence on imported opera in favor of permanent companies responsive
to, and largely supported by, their communities. For singers and other artists,
it held promise of a democratization of educational opportunity, an expanding job market, and more clearly defined progression to professional status.
Indeed, although it soon ran up against some serious limitations, it achieved
those things to a degree. And in defense of the system, it must be said that the
young folks now assembled at the trailhead, talented and dedicated as some
of them are, are very different people from a Traubel or a Warren—let alone
a Ponselle or Tibbett—at the same life moment. Vis-à-vis their European
counterparts, American singers have always suffered the disadvantage of not
having been born and raised inside a native operatic language and culture.
But once, they customarily grew up in families and communities only a step
removed from European origins, and their voices came to maturity in daily
use without electronic assistance or the electronic tone in the mind's ear.
The pop culture's hegemony and the commodification of its content were
less advanced, and a distinction between pop and high culture, however
invidious to the latter, was recognized. Now, even these rudiments of cultural
and vocal identity fall into the realm of acquired skills. *Everything* must be
taught. So while our young singers would appear to have every advantage,
they really don't.

---

* The great majority of the interwar Americans (like most American singers before them)
  had gone to Europe for study and/or performance experience. But the two greatest, Rosa
  Ponselle and Lawrence Tibbett, had not.

This is not to say, however, that there are not some in their midst who could in a few years' time emerge with E-19 vocal structures and singing habits. There most certainly are. I know this both from long personal observation and participation and as a matter of simple sense. Ask: is it remotely conceivable that year after year, so many aspiring young artists enter our system, and that among those who exit there is not to be found a single voice of true dramatic format, without concluding that something happens to winnow out, suppress, re-direct, or simply fail to recognize such voices? That even if the yearly crop of entrants includes only a handful with the potential for dramatic singing and a predilection for it (and the predilection is a part of the potential), all of them have fallen by the wayside despite every encouragement? Not to me. They have been led in other directions.

The diversification of repertoire and the Skipover/ Crossover aesthetic influence all training, everywhere. No teacher, whether inside or outside the university/regional complex and irrespective of his or her personal preferences and standards, can simply override cultural leanings already present in students, or in conscience ignore the realities of the marketplace. And the "facts on the ground" with respect to early employment now dictate readiness not for some fifteen or twenty expectable roles in one or two closely related grand-opera styles, but any number in several very different ones, each of which implies its own vocal identity but any of which may prove to be the path of least resistance and first opportunity, and among which an E-19 dramatic assignment is the least likely to provide entry-level work. Instinctive musicality is of less use than a broadly applicable quick-study musicianship, and a deep familiarity with one or two foreign languages of smaller account than a good-to-go, "lyric-dictionized" acquaintance with a half-dozen. What's called for is not the confidence and preparation to make a sudden bold leap over the crowd, but the conformability and survival smarts to run the marathon in the company of many others and come out a little ahead.

Private instruction is not necessarily better or worse than academic instruction. There are within the system many fine, knowledgeable, well-motivated teachers, at least some of whom are well aware of the problems under discussion here.[60] And since a voice's development is an accumulation of thousands of little day-by-day choices regarding everything from admission procedures to audition and casting decisions, and juried recital judgments to counselling conferences and recommendations, and since the most significant of these choices occur one-on-one in teaching and coaching studios, it's difficult to pinpoint what's determinative in an individual case, let alone the general one.

Think, though, what would be required for an E-19 dramatic voice to flourish in its passage through the university/regional complex. It would mean, first, that the potential for such a voice (which is often, at an early stage, very much a diamond in the rough) be quickly spotted, and then that its development be given the highest priority at every step of the progression sketched above. That in turn means an intensity and continuity of vocal training seldom encountered now, and the close co-ordination of all other aspects of artistic development with it. It means that all this would proceed under guidance of the Duprezian ear—and though, to repeat, the model is more important than the particular technical method—that inescapably implies a rebalancing toward a Lower Family orientation and a reawakening of the wider timbral range and more sharply defined categories (including the lowest voice types of both sexes) that would accompany that. Throughout the process, the developing voice would have to be exempted from the Skipover curriculum and somehow given repeated opportunities in its intended repertoire.

Never say never, I suppose, but I think the odds on this are about the same as those on Megamillions, and that is the first of the two particular problems of our system as a system. The second is that as the prescribed route into the operatic profession, it is for all practical purposes a closed shop. To independently structure a program of private studies in acting, dance and/ or movement, languages, musicianship, and stylistic training, and integrate these to a defined performing self, requires levels of autonomous drive, judgment and discipline (to say nothing of financial support) well beyond most teenage aspirants.[61] Further, were such a course to be successfully completed and the singer embarked on the entrepreneurial, free-lance enterprise of establishing a career, he or she will find the early professional levels of the system, with its sequence of credential requirements, age limits, etc. almost impossible to penetrate.

Educational primetime for singers—the years during which an emerging voice should be correctly categorized, its format drawn out and its basic technical structures set in place, and when the singer's vocal personality and confidence should be established—extends from the midteens through the early twenties, female voices running perhaps two to four years ahead of male, and lighter ones the same ahead of heavier ones. After that, discoveries can still happen, development can occur, and course corrections can be made, but they become progressively more difficult from both the learning and career-launching standpoints. For the reasons given above, for a young singer to do other than enter the system during those years would seem foolhardy, and for those offering guidance to recommend otherwise, irresponsible. The

university/regional complex cannot be bypassed except in the most extraordinary cases—so extraordinary, in fact, that I can't think of one among recent
American singers of any prominence.

The system works well by its own lights. It produces a goodly number of
capable Young Artists.*They are adaptable, well-coached, co-operative, and
musicianly, with a wide range of stylistic recognition. They sing in reduced-
calibre versions of the traditional formats, the right-of-center majority never
risking the management problems of the voluminous Easy Plush voices,
or the left-of-center minority the stress of a Duprezian core. The working
theory seems to be that once past the Young Artist stage, a fair proportion of
these singers will "grow into" the dramatic repertoire. Indeed, a fair proportion of them do eventually assume such roles. The more technically oriented
and self-contained among them survive, giving performances whose effect
is . . . technical and self-contained; while those who push for the actual vocal
and temperamental requirements of the music with voices not prepared to
withstand such demands come to an early, ugly end, thus reinforcing the
view that technical and self-contained is the way to be, and that big, emotional singing is dangerous. For them, it is. Modern Mezzos do not "mature"
into Azucenas, or "lyric" baritones into Macbeths. From young Young Artists
come old Young Artists.

In summation: our education/early employment system takes in nearly
all available talent, including all that would be commonly recognized as
highly promising, and retains it through the crucial years of growth and
cultivation. Yet it produces no great voices. I can think of only three possibilities. One: despite the general trend toward increased body size and in health-
and-fitness awareness, the vocally relevant parts of the raw human material
that presents itself are at some deep, undetectable level (hormonal? cellular?)
weaker than formerly. Two: Owing to the cultural changes I have touched on
and their influence on early vocal habituation, the potential of this material
has already been suffocated beyond revival before formal training begins—
and *there are no exceptions.* Three: The potential is still present in at least some
cases, but goes unrealized in its passage through the system. I don't discount
any of these as a likely factor, but I do discount the hypothesis that in the
space of two generations, One and Two have rendered Three utterly moot. At
the very least, there *are* exceptions (lots of them, in my opinion), and for them
Three is determinant.[63]

---

* Altogether too goodly, for though regional development did furnish some jobs, academic
  development furnished many more candidates for them, and so far as I can ascertain
  the always-grim supply/demand ratio is worse than ever. Were there twice as many jobs
  and half as many schools, our operatic life would be healthier both as to quantity and, I
  think, quality. [62]

Even if I am only partly right about this, or wrong in my emphasis, this suggests either that the system needs not just a tweak but a fundamental shift in how it identifies, categorizes, and trains vocal talent, or that we must search for solutions outside the system without sacrificing the richness of a liberal arts education or toying recklessly with life prospects. It's obvious that the kinds of greatvoiced singing we hear on century-old recordings will not return. That confidence of cultural identity, that time-and-place authenticity, that eagerness of expression in a still-creative tradition, cannot be restored, and imitation is perilous. However, the recordings do keep before us the models of the Duprezian engagement, and the survival within it of older technical usages, in voices of all types. That engagement, stylistically modified to our own sense of emotional truth, would bring with it the essential vocal vitality required for musical realization of the E-19 repertory. Beyond that, as the term "emotional truth" and the example of some gifted performers suggests, there are other ways of tapping opera's beauty and power. They come from the theatre.

NOTES

1. All references to the *Serse* score are taken from the piano/vocal reduction based on the Bärenreiter-Handel Gesellschaft Urtext: Series II, Vol. 39, BA 4076a (Bärenreiter, 2006, Terence Best, ed.).

2. There are ample grounds for doing so. First, there is the music. While Handel does sometimes kid his characters for their pomposities and lovelorn extravagances, and Xerxes would be a handy target for this, the composer generally leaves clues in the tone of his writing, and there is not a hint of such intent in "*Ombra mai fu*," whose tone is deeply dedicatory. That, after all, is why it survived so long in anthem guise. Second, there is the very sort of response cited by Dean and others (the "imbecility," etc.), which really argues that we are apparently being asked to take the scene seriously—if it were parodic, why would it have been criticized as ridiculous? (Romilda's teasing is no evidence. It's the comment of a character with a motive.) Third, there is Herodotus, whose *History* provided the background for the old libretto Handel worked from. In Book Seven, 26-31, Herodotus relates the following: Xerxes, on his way to Greece with overwhelming force to avenge the defeat of his father, Darius, at Marathon, has arrived at Celaenae. While there, he and his men are feted by a wealthy Lydian named Pythius, who also pledges financial support for the great undertaking. Upon inquiring, Xerxes is told that this Pythius is the same man who had presented his father with a "golden plane tree and vine" under identical circumstances, a decade earlier. Soon after, on the road to Sardis, Xerxes comes across another plane tree, of such extraordinary beauty that he vows to defend it, orders it adorned with gold, and places it under the keeping of "one of the Immortals." He then marches on to Abydos, where the libretto places the garden in Act I, Scene 1, with Romilda's summerhouse and the tree. In all this I discover nothing parodic. By decorating and sheltering the tree, Xerxes honors the memory of his father and celebrates, as favorable augury, the coincidence in place and circumstance of its discovery. To him, the tree is nothing less than holy. And so, in a lush garden dominated by a magnificent golden tree, the Great King of Persia, about to lead the largest army yet then assembled on its perilous crossing into Europe, renders thanks to his beloved plant and pledges to protect it from all peril. He sings out fervently and simply in Lisitsianesque tones, alto or tenor as the case may be.

3. The scientific search for the causes of voice, begun (at least emblematically) with Manuel Garcia's invention of the laryngoscope, soon followed by the early discoveries in the science of acoustics (both 19th-Century events) and almost infinitely extended by more recent technological advances, has yielded a body of intellectually fascinating and medically useful information. It has also tended to overwhelm the common sense of the ear, and to replace a musical aesthetic with one that is "elegant" in the scientific meaning of that term. To me, the two-family model of the voice, as outlined in the text, is an open-and-shut case. I have used the word "family" in hope of avoiding the inevitable reactions to "voice" (as in "head voice" or "chest voice," the early Italians' purely imagistic terms) or "register" (Garcia's more cause-oriented one—"a series of homogeneous sounds produced by one 'mechanism'") [my internal quotes] or "mode," which is currently modish among revisionists of the classical aesthetic. I think that if one steps back and listens for *primary* groupings of "homogeneous" sounds and divisions between them, one cannot fail to hear the two families (and only two) and the single *major* transition area. And by

the simplest definitional logic, if those groupings are given a name (any name), it makes no sense for subsidiary groupings that fall within them to be given the same name. Nor is the point only semantic. Sounds have physical causes, and technique depends on function. If a theoretical model fails to recognize the relative importance of sounds, it will also fail to correctly identify their origins in functional processes. This has profound implications for the development and technical training of voices. Of course, a theoretical model is only that—an acute ear (the teacher's) and quick singing intuition (the singer's) may find a path irrespective of the model. That's how the old Italians started: with a theoretical model based on the ear, and intuition. I would be remiss if I did not acknowledge that many of the voices I will be citing, especially female ones, were trained according to a three-register system ("chest," middle," "head"," following the model proposed by Garcia and his successors), and that this remains a common way of interpreting the distribution of timbral groupings among teachers and theorists who deal with registration at all. The fact that many good-to-great singers were so trained (so, of course, were many bad-to-mediocre ones) can be advanced in favor of such interpretation. Or it can be taken—as from my P.O.V.—as more likely accounting for some of the deficiencies of these same singers, notably the relatively weak, colorless upper extensions of some as they passed over the supposed *secondo passaggio* from "middle" to "pure head," or else adopted an exaggerated vowel modification to "cover" the same transition. When we add to the three-register hypothesis the fact that in these systems of training, as recorded in their written codifications, the voice's range was built from the bottom up or else solidified in the middle and then extended to either side, it's small wonder that a bit of an aporia would be encountered upon arrival in the upper-middle area. Nonetheless, although according to me these approaches get an important thing wrong in the upper third of the voice, they get something more important right in the lower—namely, the necessity of establishing the chest register and giving it dominion over the low notes, even in high soprano voices. For discussion of the uncertainties of assessing high notes on early recordings, see the main text, pp. 328-329.

The truth is that the entire lexicon of the vocal *lingua franca* should be packed off to the *philosophes* and quarantined "under erasure," as necessary but inadequate. In reverting to the bad old terms "head register" and "chest register," I do so with the proviso that by "register" I mean primary "family," and that "head" and "chest" are employed purely in "as if" manner; they do not refer to extralaryngeal sources of sound or its amplification ("resonance").

4. It must be granted that aesthetics are not fixed. Aesthetic orders are after all systems of triage, preferential accountings of expressive gains and losses. In singing, the ordering revolves around an everpresent tension between a given tonal model and the behavior of which it is capable. It is impossible to change one without changing the other; mutations in vocal aesthetics come down to adjustments in this tonal/behavioral tension. And since the adjustments are responses to psycho-social energies in the culture at large, it is impossible to comment on them without at least implicitly engaging those energies. That engagement is where most of the emotional heat is generated by such discussion. So I am aware that when I employ the E-19 operatic model as a measure according to which other vocal usages are found lacking, and observe that these comparisons inevitably touch on highly politicized matters (sexual, ethnic, cultural), I may arouse resistance on grounds that are not strictly artistic. But I can't help that: bearing in mind that no model is all-inclusive, I submit that E-19's demonstrably offers the best combination of tonal completeness with behavioral range of any we can experience or reconstruct. It's the one we use when we speak of deploying "a great voice."

Although the questions of exactly what Western musical aesthetics comprise and whether or not they should be honored are too gnarled to be tackled here, I think that with respect to voice they can at least be rendered comprehensible. Any Western vocal aesthetic has to start with the presumption of the Western system of tonality. This means not that the voice must sing tonal music, but that the instrument itself is developed and regulated according to our tonality's laws, especially with respect to incorporation of the overtone series into its tonal structure. Schoenberg, let us recall, wanted rich, beautiful voices for even his fiercest pantonal writing, and when we use adjectives like "rich" and "beautiful" we are referring to tone that is harmonically balanced and complete, and to the range of color made available thereby. The realization of this tonal model, in both voices and mechanical instruments, was E-19's signal sonic accomplishment; it contributed at least as much as sheer loudness or increased numbers to the heightened impact of E-19 musicmaking, and created a new context for the assessment of the classical behavioral virtues of range extension, agility, control of dynamics and of vibrato, etc.

My second presumption about "the voice"—that it is an acoustical instrument—can no longer be counted on as part of the general understanding. Microphone usages have become so pervasive, and have so elaborated their own orderings of expressive gains and losses, that the "classical sound" is now widely heard as another among them—and an odd one at that, since there is no call for it if the voice does not need to project. Indeed, the removal of this need renders any further comparisons nonsensical, whether they are for the purpose of valorizing new sounds (many of which are by classical standards failings, malfunctions, and discontinuities) or of finding a pretended equivalence to classical virtues. (John Rockwell's pleas on behalf of Frank Sinatra and Linda Ronstadt are perhaps the best-known examples of the latter.) The disposition of the respiratory system and allocation of energy throughout the body for acoustical projection are so much more demanding than those required in miked singing as to constitute an entirely different order of accomplishment. Even if the best microphone singers surpassed the best acoustical ones in, let's say, breath sustainment or legato or agility (they don't), the removal of the primary test of audibility would still render the achievement moot. I can win next year's marathon, too, if only I am allowed to ride a jet-propelled scooter and take a few shortcuts.

The modern music-theatre/jazz/pop/rock belt (it has antecedents in folk, vaudeville, and café vocalisms) was born in pre-enhancement days. In its early form, represented by singers like Ethel Merman or Celeste Holm, it was an uncomplicated, mono-affective mode, authentically loud in a pitch range corresponding to the tenor's upper register. More recently, some fairly intricate twistings and turnings with mixes and patched-up segments have lent the usage greater timbral variety and range extension, and when intelligently employed have somewhat reduced its threat to vocal health. But these improvements have been made possible only through use of the mike, and do not hold together under the requirement of acoustical projection. For a more detailed discussion of the belt and associated phenomena (though obviously not inclusive of the most recent developments), see my "Just Singin' in the Pain," (*High Fidelity*, Jan. and Feb., 1979).

5. My information on Helder is derived from entries in the splendid annual auction catalogues published by Lawrence F. Holdridge. In particular, see the 2007 catalogue, p. 77.

6. The best easily-accessed source on Jimmy Scott is Joseph Hooper's article "The Ballad of Little Jimmy Scott" (*NYT Magazine*, Aug. 27, 2000), which thoroughly documents his life and career struggles and belated recognition. I am indebted to singer/songwriter Jeffrey Paul Bobrick for directing my attention to this article, as well as to his own tribute, "The Triumph of Jimmy Scott," privately published, and for providing a sampling of Scott's recordings (many still hard to obtain) from 1951 to 1992. In my strictly jazz-amateur opinion, Scott is an inventive and often touching singer well worth the attention of aficionados. Hooper is deceived, however, when he characterizes Scott's voice as abnormally "high" or "pitched well up in the conventionally female range." Scott's singing stays within normal tenor territory, topping out around B-flat in the octave above middle C, or B natural for a passing note—also the approximate upper limit of the pure belt range. As with the female countertenor, there seems to be no obstacle to

training such an instrument along classical lines. However, it's my understanding that effective medical interventions now exist for Kallmann's Syndrome, so the opportunity will probably never present itself.

7. This is an emotionally fraught area, and thus often an intellectually confusing one. For the sake of critical coherence, one would hope that a distinction could be maintained between matters of artistic and aesthetic concern and those of social and political urgency, but in much of the commentary on the topic this has proved impossible. There is now a large body of feminist/gay/lesbian critique on opera and singing, and as with the Grail studies, my knowledge of it is less than comprehensive. I can, however, suggest a few points of entry. Among works devoted in whole or in part to such critique, I am familiar with those of Carolyn Abbate (her *Unsung Voices*, Princeton Univ. Press, 1991, and *In Search of Opera*, Princeton, 2001); Susan McClary (*Georges Bizet: "Carmen,"* Cambridge Univ. Press, 1991); Sam Abel (*Opera in the Flesh*, Westview Press, 1996); the anthologies *Reading Opera* (Princeton, 1988, Arthur Groos and Roger Parker, ed., *Musicology and Difference* (Univ. of Calif. Press, 1993, Ruth A. Solie, ed.), and *The Work of Opera* (Columbia Univ. Press, 1997, Richard Dellamore and Daniel Fischlin, eds.), in addition to Catherine Clément's volume, previously referenced. *Opera, Sex, and Other Vital Matters*, by the always-stimulating Paul Robinson (Univ. of Chicago Press, 2002), contains much of interest; of direct pertinence to my discussion here is the essay "The Opera Queen: A Voice from the Closet," which addresses exactly the questions of vocal sexuality and identity I have raised. Just as Clément's book informs almost all feminist discourse on opera, so Wayne Koestenbaum's *The Queen's Throat* (Poseidon Press, 1993) hovers behind the gay literature. It is insightful and highly readable, but its subjective orientation makes it fuel for criticism, not criticism itself. As for identifying, sorting, and evaluating the issues of this field as a whole, by far the most acute and critically responsible effort I have encountered is Thomas McGeary's "Gender, Sexuality, and Method in Musicology," in *Current Musicology #65* (2001). An essay-review of two volumes (*Queering the Pitch: The New Gay and Lesbian Musicology*, Routledge, 1994, Philip Brett, Elizabeth Wood, and Gary C. Thomas, eds.); and *Cecilia Reclaimed: Feminist Perspectives on Gender and Music*, Univ. of Illinois Press, 1994, Susan C. Cook and Judy S. Tsou, eds.), McGeary's piece surveys the principal arguments of this literature, and brings some much-needed toughmindedness to them.

8. For a well-documented recounting of this episode and its cultural context, see Henry Pleasants: *The Great Tenor Tragedy* (Amadeus Press, 1995). This volume focuses on the last two years of Nourrit's life, but necessarily includes material on Duprez, Rubini, and the singing scene of the time. With respect to the passaggio, it is interesting to note Duprez' obstinate refusal to sing the G-flats in *"Asile héréditaire"* (he substituted F's), complaining that they "bothered" him. (Pleasants, p. 158, as reported by Berlioz.) The older-style tenors obviously had the means of smoothing the area of transition, but with a co-ordination that would carry only to A or B-flat, where the headier mixes took over. Since both these transfers had to be accomplished subtly, and calibrated to the strength of the reinforced falsetto high notes, the power of the lower and middle ranges had to be held in check, and the laryngeal position doubtless fixed rather high. When Duprez found the means of engaging chest hold and a lower position all the way to C, he eliminated the problem of the upper transition, but threw more weight against the lower one, and could not quite figure out how the new registration could be ideally balanced. As many a contemporary tenor will attest, F can be stabilized in the lower co-ordination under most conditions, but this renders G-flat/F-sharp an awkward balance-point, especially on open vowels. (Note that this is consistent with the "a" difficulty in the lower-middle area of the female voice, here approached from the other side, and that in *"Asile héréditaire"* the "bothersome" pitch embraces open vowels: F-sharp at *"J'apelle, il n'entend plus ma voix!"* and G-flat on the word *"voir."* (My colleague Will Crutchfield thinks the "bother"

was to Duprez' ear, that is, a harmonic discomfort. He may be right. My Tenor Passaggio Radar still inclines me toward physical "bother," or at least a combination of the two.)

9. The technical adjustment made by Domingo was in the area of breath control, usually called "support"—a term almost as treacherous as "head" or "chest"—and is a documented part of his vocal history. (See the descriptions in Jerome Hines: *Great Singers on Great Singing*, Doubleday, NY, 1982, pp. 99-108; Cornelius Schnauber: *Plácido Domingo*, Northeastern Univ. Press, 1997, trans. Susan H. Ray, especially pp. 22-28; and Plácido Domingo: *My First Forty Years*, Alfred A. Knopf, NY, 1983, pp. 46-47.) These accounts agree on all essentials, Domingo's own being the briefest and least enlightening, and Schnauber's the most credible. Unfortunately, the latter's tiny bibliography includes no references to works of vocal pedagogy, and his own credentials ("literature and language psychology") do not establish technical expertise. Yet, though I have a few quibbles with the presentation, its description of respiratory and resonance issues in voice is actually fairly accurate—most unusual in a book of this sort. Domingo began work on the new adjustment in 1963, while in Tel Aviv, for the purpose of securing the high notes. (His early adult singing had been baritenor in range, largely in zarzuelas, though by this time he was unequivocally a tenor.) With the basic range and timbral properties of the voice already in place, such a change is to the ear more subtle and gradual than the recounting makes it appear—a drift from right to left that consolidates over time. For me, the difference was most noticeable after a four-year gap between a 1970 *Ballo* and a 1974 *Vespri Siciliani*, wherein the voice clearly showed more iron and less suede. The change cannot be marked clearly on recordings, the earliest of which already postdate the re-working; but its general nature can be illustrated by comparison between those records (aria recital LPs released in the U.S. in 1969) and any of his late-'70s or early-80's discs—say the *Louise* of 1976 or the *Aïda* of 1981.

A similar change, though not arrived at by the same technical route, was effected in the higher, more lyrical voice of Nicolai Gedda, and is easier to hear on records. The sweet, heady timbre evinced on his first recording of the part of Dmitri (on the Dobrouwen *Boris*), that of Vincent in Gounod's *Mireille*, or the tenor solos in Karajan's Bach B Minor Mass is the sound he brought with him to his debut in New York (*Vanessa*, 1957), where he soon began intensive study with Paola Novikova and rather quickly moved from right to left. Gedda refers sketchily to this process in his memoir (*My Life and Art*, "as told to" Aino Sellemark Gedda, Amadeus, 1999, trans. Tom Geddes, pp. 83-85), speaking primarily of mask placement and equalization of the scale. While I think his assertion that his timbre grew more beautiful is open to argument, there's no question that his voice gained in strength and security. Gedda's early training had been with Carl Martin Oemann, a Swedish tenor of the heavier Italian and lighter Wagnerian repertory, whose records show a warm timbre, a strong disposition for a heady half-voice that is often quite captivating, and a slight shortness of range that makes his approach to the top overcareful. Shifts like Domingo's and Gedda's are nearly always ascribed to the passage of years or the influence of heavier repertory, and these can indeed have their effect. But in both these cases, the mini-Duprezian changes occurred early in the singers' vocal histories, and with study applied to the purpose—they are 90% technical, 10% temporal.

10. Here is another list:

High soprano	:	Joan Sutherland,
Soprano	:	Eileen Farrell, Birgit Nilsson, Régine Crespin, Leonie Rysanek, Inge Borkh, Leontyne Price, Ingrid Bjoner, Gabriella Tucci, Gladys Kuchta, Aase Nordmø-Løvberg, Raina Kabaivanska.
Mezzo-soprano	:	Rita Gorr, Mignon Dunn, Giuletta Simionato, Biserka Cvejic, Ruza Pospinov.
Contralto	:	Lili Chookasian.
Tenor	:	Franco Corelli, Jon Vickers, James McCracken, James King, Jess Thomas, Sándor Kónya, Flaviano Labò, Eugenio Fernandi, Bruno Prevedi.
Baritone	:	Cornell MacNeil, Thomas Stewart, Morley Meredith, Geraint Evans, Mario Zanasi, Mario Sereni, William Dooley, Anselmo Colzani, Gabriel Bacquier, Norman Mittelmann, Kostas Paskalis, Nicolae Herlea.
Bass and Bass-baritone	:	Nicolai Ghiaurov, Nicolai Ghiuselev, Gottlob Frick, William Wildermann, Ezio Flagello, Bonaldo Giaiotti, Justino Diaz, John Macurdy, Ernst Wiemann.

These singers all made their Metropolitan Opera debuts (or, in a couple of cases, first assumed leading roles) within a six- or seven-year period in the late 1950's and early '60s. They constitute a Met generation, the last wave of large-format, grand-opera voices to hit the house. They had prewar childhoods, and most had started their careers five to ten years before their Met debuts. (A few had been singing longer: Simionato and Frick, and Farrell as well, though largely in concert and on radio.) It was they, intermixed with surviving older stars (another list, somewhat briefer and thinning from year to year) and a few more who were strictly Europe- or U.K.-based, who carried the possibility of a full-scale E-19 occasion forward another dozen years or so.

Within each range category, these voices are ranked in roughly descending order of calibre, though adjacent names could often be transposed. I have omitted from the list the purely lyric voices, and those I may have heard only once and either do not remember clearly (e.g., Anita Välkki as Kundry) or heard in what I gathered to be an uncongenial role that did not bring out the best in the voice (such as Kim Borg as the *Figaro* Count), or did not hear at all in person. There are names here that do not echo loudly through the halls of fame; they nevertheless belong to singers whose voices were of large size and acceptable singing quality, who could plausibly assume major roles in major venues.

In the seasons immediately following this influx, a sprinkling of new contenders turned up. They included sopranos Gwyneth Jones, Martina Arroyo, and Montserrat Caballe; mezzo-sopranos Marilyn Horne, Fiorenza Cossotto, Shirley Verrett, and Grace Bumbry; tenors Domingo, Pavarotti and Carreras; baritones Sherrill Milnes, Peter Glossop, and Matteo Manuguerra; basses James Morris, Ruggero Raimondi, and Samuel Ramey. (I am again omitting strictly lyrical voices, and limiting myself to singers of whom I had in-house experience.) These fine talents all quite properly occupied important positions in the years to come. With respect to the heavy-calibre roles of their categories, however, only the often-troubled voice of Jones could be ranked with those of her predecessors in terms of size with quality. Price became the leading *spinto* soprano of her time, and is now frequently invoked as exemplar of the old-time prima donna. Yet when her voice—properly positioned at the median in her category—was in its best balance its calibre was noticeably lighter than those of such immediate ancestors as Tebaldi, Milanov, and

Stella; and when it put on weight around the middle, it receded at the top. Even Milnes, exciting as he was in his early seasons, was of lighter format than MacNeil, Robert Merrill, Leonard Warren, Giuseppe Taddei or Tito Gobbi.

The feel of this era at the Met, and of its general qualities relative to what came before and after, are well conveyed by the second volume of Paul Jackson's broadcast study, previously referenced. Of course, acoustical presence is the aspect of singing most easily misapprehended in over-the-air listening, and of my own disagreements with Jackson's assessments—surprisingly few, given the differences in ears and tastes—a fair proportion seem due to live vs. broadcast impressions. (For instance, I think Jackson misses the plangency around what he calls the "narrow focus" of Fernandi's voice, and takes the warm, thickish texture of Herlea's tone—he compares it to Alexander Sved's—for massiveness, whereas it actually carried rather poorly. However, Jackson listens closely, offers both detail and context, and is so experienced an auditor that he is seldom misled.

If, for orientation to present-day realities, we were to place a few of our best voices—instruments of good quality that essay major roles—in the format rankings, Voigt would belong between Borkh and Price; Heppner in the Thomas/Kónya vicinity; Hvorostovsky between Paskalis and Herlea; and Diadkova and Borodina behind Simionato and most, if not all, of the "real" mezzos cited earlier. For further comment, see the main text.

11. When I first entered collectors' circles some fifty years ago, it was still possible to receive agitated lectures on the Great Fall from acoustical to electrical recordings—echoes of the reservations sometimes entered by commentators like Herman Klein or P.G. Hurst (for the former, see *Herman Klein and the Gramophone*, W. R. Moran, ed., Amadeus Press, 1990; for the latter see *The Golden Age Recorded*, Second Edition, Oakwood Press [U.K.]—the culmination of a very long listening and writing life). Before dismissing such observations, we should recall that Klein and Hurst (and a few of my older collector acquaintances) had seen the singers they were talking about, and that their argument was not that acoustical records sounded better than electrical ones, but that they represented solo voices more realistically—that, so far as voices were concerned, they were for all their limitations more lifelike. (For two especially clear but by no means uncharacteristic statements, see "The Gramophone as a Vocal Instructor" [Klein, op. cit., pp. 346-348] and, in the same volume, "Vocal Recording . . . Then and Now" [p. 380]—these entries date from 1932-33. While noting that in pre-electric days recording often made voices sound distant, Klein says in part: "Yet of the two systems, as has been so frequently declared, it was the older that yielded the truer result, the greater beauty of timbre when the voice had beauty, the greater clarity of execution when the technique was flawless." It's still just an opinion, of course, but note the "as has been frequently declared," and the fact that Klein's piece was a follow-up to one by Compton Mackenzie, editor of *The Gramophone*, to much the same effect.)

So, while we must keep in mind that comparing a Tetrazzini record with a Sutherland one is to compare a slightly desiccated apple to a puffed-up orange, the desiccated apple may be the more authentic artifact. I thought of this recently in listening to two recordings of *Il Trovatore*, one recorded by Pathé in 1912 (a French version, featuring singers of the Paris houses) and the other by English Decca in 1976, featuring Sutherland and Pavarotti. I heard both on CD, the former in a typically meticulous restoration by Ward Marston on his own label, and the other on Decca's CD transfer of its original analogue recording. For the 1912 *Trouvère*, I must stretch my ear and imagination, travel a distance to it; that can tire the ear after an hour or two. With the '76 *Trovatore*, on the other hand, I soon want to run away. It seizes all the ground between us like a Panzer onslaught. Of course its sounds are more complete and, initially, more satisfying. But between its close miking and cathedral-echo reverb (no good cutting the volume—you lose the quiet passages), supplemented by what I take for a layer of digital zing (I don't have the LPs to compare), it's more fatiguing than the Pathé, and phony and coercive besides. I've seen these singers often, so I hear what's going on. But on the basis of the recordings alone, I would feel more confident about assessing Pathé's cast of 1912 than Decca's of 1976.

12. Speaking of "structural vulnerability," I am sure that in this discussion of high, large-format soprano voices, the name of Maria Callas will be on many protesting lips. And it is true that in addition to the expressive intensity, interpretive insight, and personal mystique that made her magnetic, she possessed many of the purely vocal attributes of the "dramatic coloratura": calibre, pitch range, and agility, as well as a unique color span. What she didn't have, unfortunately, was the perfection of functional technique that would have allowed her to fulfill her limitless repertoire aspirations or sustain a career of normal duration. The connection between Callas' technical flaws and her voice's rapid disintegration is so direct and logical as to make a cause/effect assumption almost inevitable, whatever else may have been involved; so, with all due admiration and affection for her unique artistic achievement, I cannot include her in a discussion of model voice types, save as cautionary example. (For further on Callas, see n. 58.)

I will be making further observations about what I perceive as structural deficiencies and the shelf life of voices. But though Callas' case seems clear, in general the relationship between technique and longevity must be approached with care, because of the "whatever else." Each situation is unique, and without intimate knowledge it's hard to separate technical issues from the many others (health, temperament, lifestyle, personal circumstances, etc.) that are always involved. The testimony of interested parties needs careful evaluation. Consider the Tetrazzini/Sutherland comparison in two of its aspects: longevity and vocal power. Like many singers of her time, Tetrazzini made her debut at an early age (19), sang only in concerts from age 43 on, and made her final recordings (of songs) in her early 50s. Sutherland, after a protracted period of mezzo-to-soprano conversion, began in small roles at Covent Garden at 26 and moved into her home repertory only in her early 30s. Thus, age's role in longevity (which in any case varies greatly from one individual to another) is skewed by a good dozen years. Furthermore, while Sutherland's later years are thoroughly documented in sound, with Tetrazzini's we must piece things together as best we can. Thus, any suspicion that she withdrew from opera because of vocal decline must be set in the context of the outbreak of the war (she sang many fundraising benefits), her ever-increasing girth and attendant difficulties, and the general custom of the time for female singers of a certain age to gracefully retreat from anything deemed unbefitting, such as pretending to be a fifteen-year-old innocent or a dangerous twentysomething babe. (Or, to reduce the question to its biological basis, to wrestle publicly with the effects of menopause with the medical palliatives then available and the attitudes then prevalent.) Then, there are her last records—excellent late (1922) acousticals. These do not repeat the astounding achievements of her most ambitious earlier recordings. But the voice sounds firm, quick, and fresh, there isn't a hint of "ceiling" or drag in the upper midrange, and in the occasional bursts of agility or the sudden high excursion (one sustained top D, and a good one), I can hear no loss at all. Finally, there is earwitness testimony. Some of it comes from singers who were important high sopranos in their own right: Frieda Hempel and Lina Pagliughi. In both cases, there are strong personal ties to be considered. Still, when an artist of Hempel's stature is involved, even such vague expressions of taste as "she was my ideal" or "I admire her art above that of Sembrich and Melba" must be granted some standing. And when technically specific remarks are made, we are on even surer ground. So when, with respect to longevity, Pagliughi says that "Until the very end [of Tetrazzini's life], she could tackle Es and E-flats with a security and roundness that left me gasping;" or when Hempel reports that late one evening at the time of Tetrazzini's last New York engagement (at the Paramount Theatre, 1932, singing "'Caro nome' and other arias" four times daily between movies—she was 61) "She took a high C pianissimo, swelled it like a fireball, and then diminished it to a whisper;" further, that she "... trilled on a high D in a way that was incredible" and that "Her voice had no tremolo, no quiver. . . never breathless, and always on pitch," I find no reason to reject the testimony. (The quotation from Pagliughi is taken from Lanfranco Rasponi: *The Last*

Prima Donnas, Knopf, N.Y., 1982, pp. 166-167; those from Hempel from Frieda Hempel: *My Golden Age of Singing,* Amadeus Press, 1998, pp. 271-278.) Pitts Sanborn, a champion of Tetrazzini's but not an uncritical one, also characterizes Tetrazzini's voice during the Paramount run as "Doubtless . . . not quite what it had been 30 years before, but . . . still large, limpid, voluptuous, unworn. . ." (See the thorough and knowledgeable notes by Michael Aspinall in the booklet accompanying EMI's two-CD set of Tetrazzini's London recordings, CH 7 638022; the quote is taken from an article uncertainly dated as 1913. For a longer Sanborn assessment of Tetrazzini, with comparisons to Melba and Sembrich, see Henry C. Lahee: *The Grand Opera Singers of To-Day,* L.C. Page & Co., Boston, 1912, pp. 128-141. Finally, another excellent source of Tetrazzini reportage is: John F. Cone, *Oscar Hammerstein's Manhattan Opera Company,* Univ. of Oklahoma Press, 1966.)

As to vocal power—a topic of some importance with early recordings in general, since the uninitiated frequently mistake the distance for smallness of voice—I am willing to take some grains of salt with Hempel's assertion that "She had strength of voice as no living Isolde had it. Her high B natural and C were bigger than any Isolde's . . ." (see Aspinall again, quoting the Hempel of 1940) without at all rejecting her claim that this was a powerful voice, or her more general claim that in the turn-of-century decades there were many voices that combined agility and range extension with power in a way not encountered since. With all due allowance for the natural propensity of aging singers (and auditors) for sanctification of their own lives and times, there is too much commentary to similar effect from too many sources to be ignored. Besides, while the "proof" of live experience is far behind us, the recorded evidence is very persuasive to a practiced ear, as is common sense about casting requirements.

13. Interestingly, these exceptions include both Hempel and Pagliughi (see above). Again interestingly, we note that neither of these lovely voices achieved as much or endured as well as Tetrazzini's; even Hempel, for all her tonal purity, *agilità,* and artistic sophistication in working around her weaknesses, discloses the occasional rawness on top, instability on sustained notes in the upper-middle, and reluctance to attempt a full-throated *forte* in the high extension. And interestingly once more, Hempel and Pagliughi both report being urged by Tetrazzini to develop their chest registers. Both demurred.

14. See Russell Braddon: *Joan Sutherland,* St. Martin's Press, 1952, p. 93. This is very much an early-opportunity book from an entourage member. (Flap copy: "The author admits that he knew nothing about music when he set out to write the Sutherland biography. After two years in the company of the Bonynges, however, there is little he does not know. . ." etc. There's nothing in it, in other words, that hasn't come through the subject couple, including the obviously reconstructed dialogue. Still, on a matter like this, why would they lie? In Sutherland's autobiography (*Joan Sutherland, A Prima Donna's Progress,* Weidenfeld & Nicolson, London, 1997), there is a brief acknowledgement of the episode. Throughout this book, though, the singer keeps her studio door securely shut; there are actually more clues about her early development in Braddon's volume. In his foreward to the autobiography, the veteran English critic Edward Greenfield, who was on the scene for Sutherland's early appearances, recalls disappointment at her first recordings, feeling that they did not capture her distinctive timbre. That's quite possible (though I like the L'Oiseau-Lyre *Acis*), but it doesn't account for the differences noted here: it's not the microphone that's opening or covering her vowels. Between 1959 and 1961, a marked technical change was made.

15. Item of disclosure: whereas I saw Vinay and McCracken often in a range of roles, I know Suthaus only through his recordings of Wagner, mainly under Furtwängler. Of those, I am most favorably impressed by the extensive *Tristan* excerpts (most of Acts II and III) from Berlin, 1947, with Erna Schlüter, where all concerned go deep. His singing is always secure, substantial, and musically shaped, and his voice endured far longer than Vinay's tenorial adjustment. Its tone, however, even as early as the 1943 Bayreuth *Meistersinger,*

was opaque and shadowed. (Of his first seasons, when he sang non-Wagnerian parts, there seems to be little or no documentation.) McCracken had more success than either Vinay or Suthaus in obtaining some upper-range brilliance, particularly in Italian music in the years of his international emergence. Still, his sound was prevailingly dark and—owing to his laborious method of breath management, rather overblown.

16. In the WWII-and-after generations, tenors of even the lyric (e.g., Peerce or Poggi) or spinto (Tucker or, I must admit, Labò) categories simply didn't bother cultivating it. Bjoerling, with his near-ideal registral integration, produced many blandishing mezza-voce moments—but his voice was no *robusto* or *tenore di forza*. Bergonzi executed some beautiful high diminuendos, and controlled dynamics in the *passaggio* very well; however, his voice narrowed toward the top and was, all told, of lesser format than Corelli's or Del Monaco's. The latter made valiant efforts, and later on Giuseppe Giacomini occasionally shaded off nicely. But only Corelli offered the combination of ringing, top-to-bottom full-throated tone with true mastery of the swell-and-diminish and the half-voice. Examples that can be verified on recordings: the concluding B-flats of "*Celeste Aïda*" and "*Ah, lève-toi, soleil*"; the tapered A-naturals of "*Solenne in quest'ora*"; the lingering *messa di voce* phrases just above the break in the *Adriana Lecouvreur* arias. Of the tensile, old-style special effect *mezza-voce* in the dramatic tenor voice, a celebrated example is Leo Slezak's recording of "*Komm, o holde Dame*" (Boieldieu's *La Dame Blanche*). This is a beautiful record, and certainly remarkable from a famous Otello, Radamès, and Lohengrin, though Slezak's is a headier voice than most such. Among Italian dramatics, Tamagno's "*Sopra Berta*" (*Le Prophète*) shows mastery of the technique even at the end, and Caruso offers some examples, of which "*Magiche note*" (Goldmark's *Reine de Saba*) is a good one.

17. There is usually an association between the crooned headvoice and singing the full voice "too open"—i.e., carrying the chest voice too high and then widening and lifting its position to compensate. The Met's broadcasts of *Faust* through the 1940s disclose a succession of tenors singing the title role "too open": Crooks (1940), Raoul Jobin (1944), and Giuseppe di Stefano (1949). In all three of these cases, the overly open tendency was present from the start and accelerated with time, resulting in loss of gathered ring in the sound. Jobin's voice was of dramatic format (he sang Canio, Samson, Julien, as well as more lyrical roles) and he really had no way of handling softer dynamics. The other two, though, had lyrical voices of great beauty, with both their top notes and their *piano* effects on display and, at the outset, reasonably well integrated. (Di Stefano's diminuendoed high C in "*Salut, demeure*" is commonly cited, and there are other examples on the early studio recordings of both singers.) Both suffered premature loss of the top and an increasing detachment of the soft headvoice, and while other issues were involved (health in Crooks' case, reckless role selection and lifestyle in Di Stefano's), the importance of the technical factor is clear. In other words: the separation of loud from soft and of "chest" from "head" are parallel parts of the same process. Gigli was of course a greater singer than Di Stefano or Crooks. For some twenty-five years he displayed an exemplary registral balance, often marked by superb *mezza-voce* effects. However, when his voice at length did start to wear down (around 1940, age 50), it presented similar symptoms: an increasing reliance on mouthy, overly sweet crooning together with a widened full voice that rather quickly lost its ringing and liquid qualities.

18. Of course, the vast majority, then as now, *were* opera singers first, concert and recital singers second. But even those noted almost exclusively for their recital work (always excepting the more rarefied French specimens) sang in a stronger, more settled framework than is now the custom. Returning recently to some of Elena Gerhardt's Schubert and Wolf records, I was startled by the almost steely strength of the midrange and the neatly soldered downward transition. In the extraordinary rendition of *Am Meer* made at the age of 71 by Gustav Walter—a student of Vogl's, and the nearest we come to

the sound of an "original" *Schubertabend*—there is a wealth of full, steady tone and of expertly graded half-voice, without a hint of crooned preciosity. Among the pre-WWII baritones named in the text, Rehkemper most resembles Fischer-Dieskau in his use of the headvoice, his treatment of vowels, and, on occasion, his interpretive approach. But his full voice is more solid and centered (more "operatic") and his top notes, though narrowly focused, more convincingly connected to it—we "view" the tone itself, not the transparency.

19. The primary autobiographical sources in English are: *Pages from My Life* (H.M. Buck. trans., Katharine Wright, ed., Harper & Bros., 1927); *Man and Mask* (Phyllis Mégroz, trans., Knopf, 1933); and *Chaliapin: An Autobiography As Told to Maxim Gorky* (Nina Froud and James Hanley, trans. and ed., Stein & Day, 1969). There is also: Victor Borovsky: *Chaliapin, a Critical Biography*, Knopf, 1988, valuable for its thorough consideration of materials, its sensible efforts at evaluation and perspective, and its readability. Apart from these, the most extended and informed artistic commentary is to be found in Levik, especially pp. 346 ff. In all these sources, Chaliapin's relatively brief period of study with Usatov in Tiflis (1892-93) is the only section to touch on the "how" of Chaliapin's singing, and that only lightly. Indeed, a single incident is all that is given us to go on—but it does have to do with "support." *Pages from My Life* presents it thus: "If he detected that a pupil's voice was weakening, Usatov used to hammer the singer on the chest and shout: 'Sustain it, the deuce take you! Hold it!' It was a long time before I comprehended what he meant by 'sustaining.' . . . that it was necessary to support the sound on one's breathing and concentrate it." Gorky's Chaliapin has it this way: "If he heard a pupil's voice weakening he immediately began thumping his chest, exclaiming loudly, 'Press down, you fool, press down.' It took some time for me to realize that this indicated to the pupil that he must concentrate the sound." In *Man and Mask* (and this is the version Borovsky chooses to paraphrase) Chaliapin says of Usatov's precepts: "Sound should, in fact, rest lightly but firmly on the breath and be able to freely run up and down, like the bow over the strings of a 'cello . . . all the instructions given to the student of singing are to the end that he may make the bow glide over the strings—that is to say, control the vocal cords." This last, of course, is only a goal, like good intonation or legato, that no singer or teacher would fail to endorse. On the other hand, "Press down, you fool" is a scrap of method. Though only a scrap, it hints at a fairly compressive way of approaching "support," and this hint is seconded by the talk of "concentrating" the sound. The fact that this is the only area of technique spoken of by Chaliapin confirms that the essentials of range and volume were already in place—as they would have to have been for the roles Chaliapin had already sung. Like many great "natural" singers, Chaliapin tended to belittle the importance of technique. (For instance, in Jean Goury's monograph *Fédor Chaliapine* (Sodal, Paris, undated but evidently 1950s), he's quoted thusly: "*Je me rappelais alors des conseils techniques 'appuyez sur la poitrine, tenez la voix dans le masque . . . etc., et je me disais, est-ce là vraiment tout l'essentiel de l'art?*" ("I've sometimes recalled such technical advisories as 'Lean on the chest, place the voice in the masque,' etc., and asked myself, 'Is that truly the whole essence of art?'" And of course it isn't. But that is not to say that what Usatov conveyed to Chaliapin about breath management did not fill a crucial chink in his vocal armor. That is often the case with talents already substantially formed, and is one reason great singers tend to fare poorly teaching others whose voices may have different chinks, or are perhaps mostly chink and not much armor. My own interpretation is that the young Chaliapin was overblowing a bit, and learned from Usatov to find a more efficient balance between breath pressure and vibratory resistance. That accords well with what one hears on his recordings: a powerful, concentrated tone, capable of quite startling plosive effects and color contrasts, yet of a smooth, even, "bow across the strings" legato as well.

20. The Cardus quote is taken from the booklet accompanying the Chaliapin disk in Angel's "Great Recordings of the Century" LP series (COLH 141, 1964), which in turn reprinted it from the magazine *Records and Recording.* The booklet also contains an evocative reminiscence of the singer by his longtime accompanist, Ivor Newton.

21. In the video *Opera Fanatic,* replying to questions posed by Stefan Zucker, Simionato even asserts that chest voice "*non esista*"—"doesn't exist." In view of her complaint about mezzos in contralto roles, she can't really mean this. She seems to believe that if she "places" a tone "in the mask" it can't be chest voice, just as Barbieri (in the same video) apparently thinks that if a tone (and she demonstrates in a fierce post-retirement chest) is "*sul fiato*" ("on the breath") it mustn't be a chest tone. The soprano Leyla Gencer effects a partial escape from these absurdities by noting that in both these voices, the difference in tonal quality between the low notes and the midrange is "*molto evidente,*" and entirely natural to the mezzo-soprano range. Zucker seems to agree; but he has in fact contributed to the confusion by framing the question in terms of "chest *resonance*" (my italics), an eminently deniable concept. Misunderstanding reigns.

22. Intentionally or not, these low-transition contraltos wound up with a particularly illogical version of three-register distribution: a couple of notes in recognizable chest at the bottom, a couple more in "pure head" at the top, and everything else in "Middle Register." Schumann-Heink, who could certainly blend head downward but generally brought the chest in close to the transition center, has interesting advice in some remarks she left on technique and practice. She speaks of carrying "middle voice" to (the upper) D or E-flat, then bringing in "what is termed the head tone," by which she clearly means the "pure head" that produces the sort of upper range exemplified by Onegin, Homer, and Olszewska. She counsels: "Female singers [sic—note that she does not refer only to contraltos] should always begin the head tone on this degree of the staff and not on F and F#, as is sometimes recommended." Schumann-Heink, of course, had an unusually low extension that took in over an octave of for-the-public chest, and claims to have had easy access to the top C. This last we must take on faith, but if we do, we arrive at a much more balanced three-register system. Consistent with this is her use of "ah" as her basic practice vowel. She notes that "oo and ue [ü]" are often recommended for contraltos (that would not only encourage a dark, sometimes hooty timbre, but would assist in the downward overlay of head), but that ". . . ah secures natural color by means of the most open vowel sound"—and would, incidentally, encourage the entry of chest. (See James Francis Cook: *Great Singers on the Art of Singing*, Theodore Presser, Philadelphia, 1921, pp. 245-247.)

23. Note that in my Met listing (see n. 10, above) the contralto category, like the high soprano's, has only a single occupant—Lilli Chookasian, who was confined almost exclusively to supporting roles. Of the lower-voiced female singers then still active and sometimes cast in E-19 leading roles (e.g., Carmen, Azucena, Klytemnestra), only Jean Madeira could arguably be termed a contralto—her voice had the size, darkness, and reach, if not the technical polish, of some of the earlier singers. The last of those was the excellent Karin Branzell, who came out of retirement to sing Erda in the *Ring* cycles of 1950-51. (She had passed 60, and the lower octave had coarsened—but on the broadcast recordings she is still mighty impressive.) More recently, the Handel and Rossini revivals have given some life to the contralto, but not in combination with the dramatic mezzo repertory. Stephanie Blythe has found an alto-range niche at the Met; but her open, bright, and often hectic sound has little in common with the traditional contralto hue. There is of course Podles, with her fascinating transitional mix and admirable coloratura facility— F-to-F, she does offer the genuine contralto set, though to my ear without the roomy format of a Schumann-Heink, Onegin, or Homer (or—and here I am on sure ground— Madeira). At the top she matches Schumann-Heink's stretch, not with the "pure head" adjustment, but by narrowing and lifting the tone, and though there have been good

reports of her Azucena, I find myself wondering how satisfying this technique can be in this and similar roles; perhaps the fact that she made only a few late-career ventures in this direction speaks for itself. In the best of cases, she would bring to a total of one the number of E-19 leading contraltos recently before the public.

24. Emma Calvé's Carmen is a typical example of this. When in my early adolescence I first heard Calvé's 1908 recording of the Habañera, I assumed she was a contralto and (since she had been considered definitive in the part) Carmen a contralto role—this last no doubt reinforced by the fact that my first live Carmen (Winifred Heidt) was so classified. I soon learned better on both counts. But my young ears were not entirely deceived: Calvé's voice on her *Carmen* recordings does suggest contralto colorings, and however classified, it's a fully matured sound. Carmen has always been more of a "personality" role than a virtuosa one, and no single vocal type has ever established exclusive claim to it. Following Calvé, though, and notwithstanding the success of Farrar and Garden, the part gravitated downward, away from the sopranos and comique-style mezzos who had owned it. Genuine contraltos took it (Onegin and Schumann-Heink, for instance, both sang it). So did propulsive dramatic mezzos like Aurora Buades and Gabriella Besanzoni, who made interwar Italian-language recordings of the opera, and by the time Ponselle undertook it (1935-36) her voice was nearly indistinguishable in timbre and balance from that type. These last, of course, do not sound matronly in the Northern-alto way, but they are emphatically deepset and powerful.

25. See Hines, *Great Singers on Great Singing*, pp. 134-43 (an interview devoted exclusively to technical concerns); also Davis, *The American Opera Singer*, pp. 520-22, which provides corroborative material and a fair artistic assessment. In the Hines book, Horne describes her early training process of first extending the chest to a remarkable depth; then using swell-and-diminish exercises to shed its weight as she approached the transition area; then "squeezing" or tightening the midvoice up to around D. In her outline of registration and insistence on "ah" as the basic exercise vowel, there is a great deal reminiscent of Schumann-Heink (see n. 22, above). The latter, though, certainly did not "squeeze" the midvoice, and Horne did not release into "pure head" for the top segment of her range. In the first phase of Horne's mezzo career, the squeezed middle wasn't squeezed enough to be displeasing. It had great clarity and a modest warmth, and with it the singer sustained a superbly even line. With time, however, it took on the sort of shallow quality often termed "mouthy," and as this crept upward the top notes lost their "opening-out" bloom. Her literally tenorial foray aside (see the main text), it sometimes sounded more like the upper range of a rather constricted tenor than the midvoice of a mezzo or contralto—and interestingly, it's most often in the context of training the *passaggio* of a tenor or high baritone that one hears of "keeping it slender" or "narrow." Horne's teacher during her first years of study, when the structural wiring gets done, was William Vennard, whose writings comprise perhaps the most sophisticated modern presentation of three-register theory. (See his *Singing: the Mechanism and the Technic*, Carl Fischer, N.Y., 1967. He would not have agreed with Horne's opinion that registers are primarily "areas of resonance"—a surprisingly tenacious 19th Century view.) Obviously, the technique was expertly adapted to Horne's young instrument, and it can hardly be sensibly argued that it didn't "work." Still, from a two-family P.O.V., it can be seen as illustrating what always seems potentially worrisome about positing a "middle register" (invariably defined as a mixture of the other two), which is that it tends to tolerate an excess of chest function disguised in its blend, which must then be thinned to avoid weighting the upper-middle range; and that it sets the "upper *passaggio*" on an equal footing with the lower, when there is no basis for doing so. Horne leans a lot on the Garcia school, and on the assumption that her training was similar to that of the "early gals." But that is highly speculative. Theory aside (and despite the copious literature left by Garcia, Viardot, Marchesi, De Reszke, and their influential critical followers like

Klein and W.J. Henderson, their theories of registration and placement were far from universally held or taught), we just do not know how the great contraltos and mezzos of pre-recording times (Alboni, Viardot herself, Ravogli, Scalchi, et al.) actually sounded—the intensity and color of their tone, their format and depth of core. Did they squeeze the midrange? Intuitively, that seems unlikely. Did they sound more like Horne, or more like the contraltos and mezzos of whom we have our earliest recorded evidence? That, too, is speculative, but since in the memoirs and critical or pedagogical commentary I have encountered (admittedly, often sadly reticent on such specifics) there is nothing to support the notion of any sudden or major change, I'm inclined to the latter view. Still, I am in general agreement with Horne that the "Golden Age" singers strove for "a carrying sound that's going to pierce through," as opposed to "a big fat sound"—in my terminology, they were more left-wing and possessed more core. Curiously, the observation applies less to contraltos than to any other voice type.

26. Among the basses of Siepi's years and those immediately following (see the list and discussion in n. 10, above), Jerome Hines came the closest to the true basso color, with core in the sound and satisfying low notes. Even he, though, was not an old-school deep bass, while several of his contemporaries (e.g., Tozzi, Ghiaurov) were notably weak at the bottom relative to the calibre and quality of their instruments. Today, we are grateful for the rare throat (Furlanetto's or Robert Lloyd's) wherefrom the occasional low note of a Fiesco, Inquisitor, or Sparafucile can emerge with decent presence; Sarastro or Osmin cannot be effectively cast. Especially disappointing of late have been the Russians, whose traceable line of low-rumbling bassos, from Sibiriakov in the early 1900s to Krasovsky in the 1950s, seems to have come to an end. The last Russian bass voices to combine fine singing quality with large format—Petrov, Shtokolov, and Nesterenko—were of the *cantante* variety. The current Maryinsky contingent, though stocked with some viable material, has neither a front-rank singing bass nor a true deep one.

27. I am often bemused by the certainty with which connoisseurs assert that voices they cannot possibly have heard in person were the biggest or richest of their era. After many years of critical listening to voices, and nearly as many of practical work with them, I must allow that while I have a better basis than most for making such assessments, I can't be *altogether* sure of them. To mitigate the uncertainty, I have chosen my early dramatic sopranos at least in part because of recorded legacies that are of adequate scope and quality, and in reasonable agreement with the reputations of the artists involved.

If we read the lists on p. 357 horizontally, they fall into these groupings by recording method: Tier, I, acoustical; Tier II, early electrical; Tier III, late electrical/stereophonic. In addition to the problems of recording high, loud voices, only the bottom grouping escaped the time constraints of the 78 rpm record side, which often had a distorting effect on both the musical intentions and actual sound of the singer—a subject whereon Ponselle was especially eloquent. (See James Drake: *Rosa Ponselle, a Centenary Biography,* Amadeus, 1997, pp. 266-274, also drawn on for the notes by John Ardoin for *Rosa Ponselle On the Air*, Vol. 1, Marston 52012, 2 CDs.) "If you want to hear what I truly sounded like," says Ponselle, "listen to my radio broadcasts," and Drake adds interesting testimony from the memoirs of André Kostelanetz, conductor for the *Chesterfield Hour* broadcasts of the 1930s, on the solution arrived at for capturing the power of Ponselle's voice for the microphone. There was indeed a marked advance in the impression of calibre, tonal completeness, and expansiveness of phrasing on these broadcasts over that of Ponselle's studio recordings of just a few years earlier. This is also true of her late Victor song recordings, not to mention the post-retirement recordings made at Villa Pace. Microphones were getting better. I suspect that for the most part Ponselle was right, and that the broadcasts do put us in the closest touch with her true sound. Yet her sound also changed, and fairly significantly. It deepened in both range and timbre, and by the later '30s had acquired a rather unattractive leatheriness in its lower-middle range. From the onset of her broadcast career (1934, taking in both her many studio programs and her Met broadcasts of *Traviata* and *Carmen*) she sang, in effect, as a mezzo-soprano. Unless I've missed something, she never sang a high C or B-natural over the air. Meanwhile, the lower range grew stronger and richer, with the chest increasingly prominent. The standard interpretation of this would be that Ponselle sang too heavy a repertoire from an early age, and this eventually pulled the voice lower. Could be. But see the remarks of Max de Schauensee, a veteran critic who, like Levik, listened with a singer's ear, and who had heard Ponselle throughout her career. (See Drake, p. 264. The interview dates from 1977.) De Schauensee thought that Ponselle had lightened her voice to the detriment of her singing, first for Norma (1927), then for Violetta (1930), and that after the Violetta her voice "was never the same." In other words (my interpretation now), she subtly lifted and thinned the vocal position, only to discover that this hurt, rather than helped, the top notes, and then simply gave in to the lower adjustment. I should add that de Schauensee was a De Reszke-ite whose technical bias was toward high, forward placement and "nasal resonance"—hardly an advocate of vocal heaviness. So the observation is particularly interesting coming from him.

There's a lot of sifting to be done, even in so well-documented a case as Ponselle's.

28. *Recording sources, Column A dramatic sopranos:* Johanna Gadski's discs (1903-1917), all for Victor except for Met Mapleson cylinder snippets, are complete on Marston (Vol. I, 52002-2; Vol. II, 53015-2). They show virtually no change over that 14-year period, technological improvements notwithstanding. In his notes for Marston, Harold Bruder quotes W.J. Henderson as reporting that when Gadski returned to New York in 1929 (she would have been 57), her voice was in "astonishingly good condition," with upper notes of special "brilliance, resonance, and power." She was still trouping at her death three years later.

Leider began opera recording for Polydor around 1921, when with the Hamburg opera company, and continued when she moved to the starry Berlin ensemble. These are late acousticals, including much of her non-Wagnerian repertory, and often rather dim and narrow-sounding in transfer. In the late '20s she signed with HMV and recorded electrically with somewhat better results. A lengthy Preiser/CD series is from my sampling decent; but the most convincing re-recording I know is still an LP in Odeon's *Goldene Stimme* sequence (83 386), which also includes spoken reminiscences by the singer and uncommonly informative notes by Klaus Laubrunn. Her last recordings were of songs, made during WWII. Fortunately, there is a live transmission of a Covent Garden *Götterdämmerung* Act II, now on Guild CDs with improved sound. Though late for Leider (1938), it conveys a good measure of performance life, and presents her in the best possible context—Beecham, cond., with Melchior, Janssen, and Schirp. Pieces of her Isolde and Brünnhilde (Met and Bayreuth, 1934 and '36, under Bodanzky and Elmendorff) have also surfaced. They are extensive (three CDs' worth) but fragmentary, and in variable, aficionado-only sound. But, though only a few seasons older than the Covent Garden transmission, they show Leider in slightly fresher voice, and convey plenty of performance heat.

Among my Tier II old-stylers, Easton and Austral were generously documented on studio recordings (and in very broad repertory), but Turner and especially Lawrence, less so. The output of all four—complete or substantially so—has circulated on CD, though not always widely or for long. There is some supplementary broadcast material: For Turner, a Covent Garden *Turandot*; for Lawrence, a Met *Götterdämmerung* and Teatro Colón *Walküre* and *Parsifal*, plus a 1940 San Francisco *Carmen* Act II—the performance is an unholy mess, but it does show Lawrence's strong low-to-middle integration. And Easton's long recording career concludes with a 1942 aircheck of English-language *Tristan* excerpts with the tenor Arthur Carron that affords yet another (and more verifiable) example of changed expectations of Shaw's Brynhild/Marguerite sort. Is Easton's Isolde (the voice still fresh and full at 60, only marginally fattened over the years) different from Flagstad's or Traubel's? Yes, certainly, and none of us, I suspect, would prefer it to theirs. But how much more different is her "*O mio babbino caro*" from any recent soprano's—and it was Easton who "created" Lauretta in 1918, shortly after the *NYT* critic Richard Aldrich pronounced her ready to assume "the Brünnhildes, Isolde, Kundry," as indeed she did when the Wagner operas returned to the Met following WWI.

29. See: George Bernard Shaw: *Musical Criticism*, Dodd, Mead & Co., NY, 1981, ed. Dan Laurence, Vol. III, pp. 373-4.

30. The recorded evidence I have considered is as follows: For Flagstad: All her studio operatic recordings (and some of the song literature) made for RCA Victor between 1935 and 1941; her broadcasts of 1936 (Met *Tannhäuser* and Covent Garden *Tristan*), 1937 (Met *Siegfried* and *Lohengrin*, Covent Garden *Walküre* Act III and *Fliegende Holländer* highlights, San Francisco *Walküre* Act II) and 1941 (Met *Tannhäuser*, *Tristan*, and *Fidelio*); and postwar, the complete La Scala *Ring* (1950), plus the Met *Walküre* and Covent Garden *Parsifal* of 1951. For Traubel: All her operatic studio recordings (and, again, some of *Lieder*), 1940-1947, for Victor and Columbia; broadcasts of 1941 (Met *Walküre* and NBC Symphony *Walküre* I, 3); 1942 (Met *Tannhäuser*); 1943 (Met *Tristan*, Teatro Colón *Tristan*), 1944 (Met *Walküre*); and postwar, the Met *Tristan*, *Siegfried*, and *Götterdämmerung* (1950-51), plus her *Voice of Firestone* video (1950). Though both singers made many studio recordings in the late 1940s and '50s, I have left them aside because tape, with all its new possibilities for insertion of individual notes, etc. (of which the Flagstad/Furtwängler *Tristan*—that of the Fischer-Dieskau "*Ha!*"—with its interpolated Cs by Schwarzkopf, is a notorious example) was now the recording medium. Though some of these discs are wonderful and can tell us much, for present purposes they are too far short of conclusive. I have also passed over Flagstad's post-retirement appearances—the 1955 Symphony of the Air "farewell" concert and the Oslo *Götterdämmerung* of 1956 (the fact that a 60-something Heroic Soprano's top is gone tells us little), as I have the pop, jazz and musical comedy excursions of Traubel and Farrell.

As for my interpretation of this evidence: first, Flagstad is much harder to get a handle on than Traubel. Neither in critical assessment nor earwitness report have I ever encountered a suggestion that her prewar singing was other than consistently magnificent. Yet her recordings of this period, both studio and live, contain many moments that give rise to uneasiness about the security of the voice's upper range and its support at soft dynamics. Indeed, only the 1936 and '37 broadcasts show her fully in command in these respects, the voice eager to leap to the top. By 1941, B natural is trouble more often than not and her habit of "melting away" after attacks in the upper-middle leaves the listener unsure as to intent and effect. Even in the studio-recorded Kundry/Parsifal scene (1940) she is clearly backing away from the ascending figures in the demanding closing pages. There are possible mitigating circumstances. 1940 and '41 were trying years for her personally. Perhaps she was instinctively microphone-shy in the studio. Perhaps, in *Lieder*, she was afraid of overwhelming the music, as with the disappointingly timid A and B of her Strauss *Cäcilie* (1937). Such factors can't be ruled out, but I don't believe they are determinative. Taking her recorded work as a whole (still not the same, of course, as hearing her live night-to-night), I think it's evident that her top (or her confidence in the top—same thing) was eroding rather rapidly within a few seasons of her Met debut. Most instructive, as always, are like-to-like comparisons, i.e., *Tannhäuser/Tristan* '36 vs. *Tannhäuser/ Tristan* '41, and they certainly support this conclusion. After the war, things are decidedly better. The 1950 La Scala Brünnhildes are in some important ways Flagstad's most convincing legacy—live broadcasts, the sound cramped but untinkered-with, the artistry fully matured, the phrase-making more decisive, and the upper range firmer and more focused than it was a decade earlier. She stays on A-flat rather than taking the C at the end of the *Götterdämmerung* duet; but throughout this complete *Ring* her B-flats are solid and her B naturals, while not big and ringing, are clean and reliable.

She's in slightly less glorious voice in the Met *Walküre* later that season, but the general impression is the same, and in the '51 London *Parsifal* she attacks the top (even risking an ugly one for the B on "*Lachte*") with a vigor not heard since 1937.

Meanwhile, the Traubel of the early-to-mid 1940s presents none of the Flagstad problems—the contrast, in fact, is telling. Recording at the same time by the same methods (in the cases of the Met broadcasts and the Victor recordings, presumably on the very same equipment) her comparably voluminous higher range arouses no doubts as to its assertiveness. Indeed, in the '41 *Walkürenruf* her Bs sail out with more zip than any of Flagstad's. They are still in fine shape in the '43 Met Isolde, only a little less so in the Colón performance a few months later. (There's a poor one—as bad as Flagstad's in '41, in the '42 "*Dich, teure Halle*"—but she's disgracefully rushed by Szell.) By 1944, she has lowered her Battle Cry a half-step; but everything up through B flat/A sharp is well integrated and imposing. This remains substantially true in the 1950 *Tristan*.

In sum, my impression is this: within four or five years of regular Wagnerian use from age circa 40, both these torrential voices lost a half-to-full step at the top. In addition, Flagstad grew tentative, at least on some occasions, with respect to the higher range in general, while Traubel did not. Then, Flagstad took a war-enforced hiatus of four years—vocal rest, vocalizing, and almost no public singing—during which the voice settled and re-grouped, emerging with the top B re-aligned and the entire upper fourth firmer. Traubel, however, kept singing through the comparable stretch (ages 45-50), and simply dealt with the gradual lowering as best she could, which was rather well. This is not merely a matter of voice-fan top-note obsession. It's true that, thrilling though it is to hear the top Cs of Isolde and Brünnhilde confidently popped out, there are only a few of them, and except for the *Götterdämmerung* duet their time values are short—it's not a crucial note. B, though, is important—Wagner writes to it at key points (like the two just before Isolde's Curse), and only the ones in the Battle Cry can be lowered without major disruption. Even more important is solidity and dynamic control of the upper-middle range. Shaw was essentially right: an Isolde or Brünnhilde without a C, and even with only on-pitch indications of B, but with all else rich, beautiful, and technically in hand, can still give utterly compelling performances (Traubel's '44 *Walküre* and '50 *Tristan*, and to a slightly lesser degree her '51 *Siegfried* and *Götterdämmerung*, are excellent cases in point),but insecurity in approaching the top seriously undercuts the music.

Farrell's is a case that cannot be adjudicated on these same terms, since she never took on complete Wagner roles, and her career in Italian dramatic repertory was neither long nor intensive. It's impossible to say how she would have fared had she moved into what seemed her proper place as Traubel's immediate successor. Based on my recollections of live performance (starting with two between-movie renditions of "*Pace, pace*" at the Roxy Theatre with Mitropoulos and the NYPO—you could stay for continuous showings in those days—and ending with a Met Santuzza in the spring of 1964) and familiarity with most of her classical discography (from airchecks of songs and arias and the soundtrack of *Interrupted Melody* in mid-1940s to her Elisabetta in *Maria Stuarda*, 1970), I think it's fair to say that her voice, extending to strong and well-integrated Bs and Cs, was reliably refulgent in the period leading up to her Met debut, and less consistently so thereafter, when the top sometimes thinned and spread. Her best discs, such as the late-'50s aria recordings with Max Rudolf and Thomas Schippers, or the Wesendonck/Immolation pairing with Bernstein, are as greatvoiced and technically impeccable as any ever made. But, though the evidence is admittedly anecdotal (she was, for instance, in much better voice for the *Forza* Leonora of 1963 in New Orleans than the one of 1965 in Philadelphia), I cannot trace either in memory or on broadcast hearings a complete role, sung live, that upholds quite that standard; probably her fine broadcast Santuzza comes closest. This is not entirely a matter of the inevitable imperfections of live performance: greatvoiced singers quite often equal or transcend their studio recordings in live performance, even from a purely technical P.O.V.

Let us stipulate that it isn't common for High Dramatic sopranos of any technical persuasion to fully incorporate the top B and C—that is, to sing these notes as a true continuation of the rest of the voice, complete with its vibrato pattern, a sense of "room" above the pitch, and the climactic "topping off" of the range implied in the writing. In my theatregoing experience, Nilsson was unique in consistently peeling off exciting, sustained *acuti* (honorable mention to Margaret Harshaw, Rita Hunter, and on occasion Varnay), while on records the only other singers who are to my ear convincing in this respect are Leider, Wildbrunn, Lawrence, and Turner. (For the reasons given above, Farrell must in my opinion be set aside.) While these were surely powerful voices, they were neither of the "big, fat" Flagstad/Traubel/Farrell variety nor the Horne "hourglass" configuration. They were tall and big-boned but relatively trim, firm and filled-out in midsection—in other words center-left, up and down.

Regarding the natural-growth, late-emergence theory of development, which has gained near-mythic standing as the recommended procedure for this voice type, I am a confirmed skeptic. Its central notion is that it is dangerous to place High Dramatic demands on young voices, and so it is best to let them slowly mature, gradually acquiring the security and endurance needed for such repertory. This sounds plausible, and the careers of these three women, all of conservative temperament and domestic inclination, happened more or less that way. But were they better or longer as a result? In the case of the Americans, the question is almost moot: short of the international level represented by Chicago, San Francisco, and the Met, the U.S. afforded no place for voices of this sort to gain stage experience and explore repertory. Were they really building strength and endurance with their concerts, recitals, and radio work, or only getting older? Were their voices truly not ready for the grind in their physically prime years? Their own written accounts are replete with equivocations, rationalizations, and lacunae. (See: Helen Traubel, with Richard C. Hubler: *St. Louis Woman*, Duell, Sloan & Pierce, 1959; and Eileen Farrell with Brian Kellow: *Can't Help Singing*, Northeastern Univ. Press, 1999. See also Conrad L. Osborne: "American Valkyrie," *Opera News*, Apr. 2003.) Of Traubel, we have nothing to listen to from her early years, but all indications are that her vocal development (size, quality, range) was substantially complete in her twenties. Many of Farrell's early tracings are of pop or musical-comedy material, but a 1945 "*Il va venir*" (*La Juive*) certainly sounds like a major voice ready for prime time, as did those 1950 "*Pace, pace*"s, and as do her Toscanini Beethoven 9th (1952, live) and Marie in *Wozzeck* (1952, under Mitropoulos). Above all, there is her *Siegfried* final scene with Svanholm under Leinsdorf (1949—she was 29). This is a recording often belittled by connoisseurs for Farrell's somewhat generic interpretation, but it shows a voice fully capable of encompassing anything in the High Dramatic literature—nothing approaching it has been heard for forty years now. When finally launched, Traubel did adapt to the demands of the stage and operatic life to put in some ten-to-twelve years of reliably great singing. Farrell, for all the vocal plenitude of her best performances, never really did.

The years that can be credited to Flagstad's account, once she was launched on her world-class Wagnerian way, really total no more than Traubel's. Nonetheless, given the overall length of her stage career, she remains the best argument for the late-bloomer philosophy, which otherwise stands in contradiction of all precedent we know of. Unlike Traubel or Farrell, Flagstad was able to make an early stage debut (at eighteen, as the childlike Nuri in d'Albert's *Tiefland*) and spend more than twenty years working her way toward heavier repertory in Norwegian theatres. She sang hundreds of performances in operetta (Planquette, J. Strauss, Lehár, Kalmán, et al.) and in roles like Micaëla, and gave recitals, while continuing studies in voice, movement, etc. In this respect, she certainly fits the "natural growth" pattern, and there is no gainsaying the benefits of year-to-year stage experience in a home environment for the maturation of an opera singer. It is not synonymous, though, with the growth of the voice itself. From the outset, Flagstad made studio recordings. Since the early ones seem to have been exclusively of song literature, they do not reveal everything about the voice—particularly in its response to dramatic demands and stress on the top.* They do, however serve as a corrective to any notion that the young Flagstad's voice was light and girlish. As early as her first recording of Grieg's *Vaaren*, one hears a completely formed voice, full and solid, already hinting at the maternal. She was nineteen. By her mid-teens, she had studied (not sung in public, but studied—one can imagine the scarification this would induce in today's pedagogical climate) the roles of Aïda, Elsa, Senta, Tosca. At age 25, she sang Desdemona opposite Slezak's Otello, and the *Ballo* Amelia, with its high Bs and Cs. As with Chaliapin, it matters less how or where she did this singing than the fact that she did it. And through her recordings, we get some sense of how she sounded.

These women sang differently from all the others cited herein. The systems of registration that governed the training of most E-19 singers, and the hypotheses about resonance that were so influential in the late 19th and early 20th centuries, seem not to have been important to their learning processes. From their highly advantageous starting points, the voices of Flagstad and Traubel were worked from the middle outward. (In Flagstad's case I base this assertion primarily on her recordings, supported by her vocal history and the secondary written evidence, which from a technical P.O.V. is scanty; in Traubel's, on her own testimony regarding her study with Vetta-Karst. See Traubel, *St. Louis Woman*, chap. 4.) Farrell's process with her principal teacher, Eleanor McLellan, is not quite so clearcut. (See Farrell, *Can't Help Singing*, pp. 53-57—she speaks of breathing techniques, but also of adding notes at the top and of a "no registers" approach to negotiating the range. When she began work with McLellan, her radio career had already been underway for several years; she had previously studied with contralto Merle Alcock.) But the overall picture is similar.

These three singers are the only successful exemplars of the late-to-launch, slow-growth theory of dramatic soprano development. Flagstad and Traubel, these tonal estuaries, are as historically isolated among Wagnerians as Sutherland in her *Fach* or Vickers in his (all right, not quite: they are two instead of one). Their predecessors (and such contemporaries as I have cited) started earlier, sang far more varied repertory (because they could—how was Traubel to have sung an Aïda, either she or Flagstad a Donna Anna or Lady Macbeth, without the requisite reach and alacrity?), and (except for Lawrence, and she for health reasons) sustained these assignments longer. Strength, energy, elasticity, and fast recuperation are attributes of youth. My own belief is that if circumstances had been right for any of these three, trained as they were, to set a High Dramatic course some five to ten years earlier then she did, her singing prime would have been correspondingly longer. (Farrell's is, as always, the most elusive case: would her relatively relaxed hold on her "no-register" instrument have held up?) It certainly matters what one sings and how soon one sings it; but it matters far more how one sings it. My argument here is not aesthetic (anyone protesting, "Fine—give me back my decade of Traubel or Flagstad" will get no argument from me), but structural. For its continuation, I now return you to the main text.

---

* Over the years, I have heard a few of Flagstad's early 78s. However, these observations are based mostly on the sequence in Vol. I of the 13-CD centenary edition on the Simac label. These are relatively undoctored transfers, evidently from best available copies, not original metal parts—there is some surface noise, but the voice sounds unfiltered. The booklet has a memoir by Arne Dørumsgaard and a chronology by Per Dahl, to which some of the above detail is indebted. For a comprehensive rundown of her early career, see Bernard Miles' article in *Opera*, June, 1950.

31. Crespin's principal teachers in her Conservatoire years were the soprano Suzanne Cesbron-Viseur (to whom she ascribes little influence) and tenor Georges Jouatte (to whom she ascribes a lot). Later, she worked in a corrective way with Rudolf Bautz, and also studied with Milanov. In truth, much of the most important work on her voice seems to have occurred before she entered the Conservatoire, with a certain Madame Kossa in Nîmes, who evidently brought out the size and true quality of her previously high, light instrument. She studied with Lubin during the winter of 1957-58, while preparing Kundry for Bayreuth. (Lubin also states that Crespin worked with her on the Marschallin, but Crespin makes no mention of this.) This was undoubtedly coaching on role interpretation; but that always has technical implications. Lubin, in turn, seems to have studied with every prominent ex-singer-cum-pedagogue in her vicinity, including De Reszke, Lilli Lehmann, and—over a period of ten years—Litvinne. And yet structurally, these voices are all quite different from one another. On the basis of technical analysis, one could not ascertain that any was the pupil of any other, and whatever the teacher/pupil influence amounted to, it did not forestall the rightward migration. However, if we were to extend the line another generation back, we would arrive at the person of Pauline Viardot-Garcia, with whom Litvinne trained. And here, for all that we have not even an echo of Viardot's voice, we can discern more clearly a functional connection. For we know from Viardot's instructional remnants that the fundament of her method was to firmly establish the lower family ("*Voix de potrine à pleine voix sans forcer*"—"Chest voice at full voice without forcing") and then, with F (possibly a lower F than we now tune) as the point of transition, to bond it evenly with the "*fausset*" (falsetto—the then-current term for the midrange). As her exercises progressively rise in pitch, eventually to the upper B natural, they give no comparable instruction concerning a "*secondo passaggio*" from *fausset* to *voix de tête*, leaving us to conclude that she must not have considered it an issue of any importance. And this is very much the distribution heard in the singing of Litvinne.

    (See Viardot-Garcia: *Gesangsunterricht, Übungen für die Frauenstimme*, Bote & Bock, Berlin, undated. This is a 19th-Century bilingual edition of her *Une heure d'étude*, originally published by Heugel. In my copy a previous owner, presumably a contemporaneous German female student, has crossed out the chest-voice instruction and substituted "*Mittellage*" ["middle position"]. She has also changed the indicated vowel from an "a" to "u" and "o." In effect, she was trying to use Viardot's patterns for precisely the reverse of their purpose, probably at the behest of a "*Kopfstimme überall*" teacher. On Crespin, see her *Onstage, Offstage: A Memoir*, Northeastern Univ. Press, 1997, trans. G.S. Bourdain; also the previously cited chapter in Hines, *Great Singers on Great Singing*, [p. 359]. There, she discusses at some length her working-out of the transition to and from chest voice, and as we are tempted to ask Simionato what she can mean by asserting she doesn't sing in chest, we are tempted to ask Crespin what she means by saying she does. Finally, on Lubin see Rasponi, *The Last Prima Donnas*, esp. pp. 94-95. Litvinne left an autobiography, *Ma vie et mon art*. I have not seen it, but it is summarized at length in Levik, *Memoirs*, pp. 308-315.)

32. *Recording sources, Column B dramatic sopranos*: Litvinne's records were made in Paris between 1902 and 1922, for several labels. They have surfaced at numerous CD sites, including the Symposium series, whose Harold Wayne Collection has done so much to document the sequence of early recording in Paris. Once again, we are fortunate to have from Marston *The Complete Félia Litvinne* (52049, two CDs). Even on this exemplary set, the earliest G&Ts are hard to listen to and evaluate; but the later sessions show marked improvement. The main hurdles, as expected, are with the highest pitches at full voice, notably in the *Walküre* Battle Cry and the "*D'amor sull'ali,*" where they sound glaring and straight. So it's good to be able to turn to Levik, who has this to report on Litvinne:

"... after hearing a single act, you forgot all other excellent voices: you had never heard another voice like Litvinne's, for fullness of the sound itself, for the enchanting timbre, for the softness and richness of the range of colourings or for such music in the sound itself and its overtones. It wasn't the range, although this covered with equal ease the soprano heights, the firmness of the mezzo-soprano and contralto depths in different roles: powerful voices with a range of two and a half octaves were quite common in those days ... in every sound was the music of a particular character. Irrespective of the tessitura and language in which she was singing, the articulation of every word was clear and somehow transparent." (Levik, *Memoirs*, pp. 307 ff.)

The "enchanting timbre," "softness and richness," etc., are obviously shortchanged by the recordings, but the strength and firmness are easily confirmed, as is the almost uncanny pan-*Fach* adaptability. Geoffrey Riggs, author of some of the commentary in the Marston booklet, rightly points to the contrast between the dusky, deep-seated set of Litvinne's Dalila to the bright, shining timbre of the prayer from the *Faust* Church Scene, where the powerfully soaring high line, including the climactic B, is for once captured and contained. Both excerpts unquestionably sound like the singer's "natural" voice. The impression is not of "adjustments" (though the singer must have made some), but of an instrument that simply embraces the full range of pitches and colors. If one adds to these excerpts her single most comprehensive interpretation—Suleika's "*A mes genoux*" (*L'Africaine*), with its twisting, ornamental line—one begins to comprehend a level of vocal command unheard for many decades.

Most of Lubin's operatic recordings were done in Paris in the late 1920s and in 1930; a few more, including a rather bumpy German-language *Liebestod*, date from 1938. I am familiar with them exclusively via LP and CD re-releases, principally Qualiton 150052. This includes eight of the 1927-30 excerpts (Weber/Wagner, all in French), a few songs from the 1938 sessions, and a few more from private sources, 1954, when the singer was in her mid-60s. On the whole, I find these records frustrating. Though electrical, their technical standard is not high and Lubin's voice does not take kindly to it—as with the Traubel/Flagstad case, the records of Lawrence from the same time and place present her voice much more convincingly. On Lubin's discs one hears a large and beautiful voice, artistically managed, but feels quite certain that its scope and quality are only hinted at. There's a vagueness to the sound. Nevertheless, in the matter of core vs. plush, they leave little doubt that Lubin occupies almost exactly the midpoint between Litvinne and Crespin. The late privately recorded items make the same impression as those of Ponselle and Easton: the voice may no longer have its full reach, but the listener feels more in touch with its authentic quality and calibre.

As for Crespin, I heard her so often in critical listening mode that I have relied first and foremost on my live-performance recollections bolstered by a lookback at some of my old reviews. But I have also refreshed my acquaintance with a number of her recordings: the early aria collection with Otto Ackermann; the "Voice of Wagner" album with Prêtre; the extended *Les Troyens* excerpts (also with Prêtre); her Sieglinde under Solti and Brünnhilde under Karajan; and finally with a more recently acquired CD of live Paris performances, 1955-circa 1962 (Laserlight 14 263). This last contains what is for me the most complete realization of her voice as a dramatic soprano, an "*Abscheulicher!*" with Klemperer. In this magnificent performance she allows her voice its full profile, weight (in the good sense), and deeply rooted low range. She spurs the line along and binds off the words, never slacking off. Had she always sung like this (in the theatre she came closest in Italian roles—Tosca and the *Ballo* Amelia—Brünnhilde and Isolde would have been well in hand, and she would not occupy her far-right position.

33. For a brief excursion into the world of tiny variants that make up the ground level of operatic interpretation, compare a dozen or fifteen renderings of the single word "*mächt'ges*" as it occurs in this sequence, in voices of both the *Hoch-* (Flagstad, Traubel, Norman et al.) and *Jugend-* (Bampton, Mueller, Ljungberg et al.) dramatic types. The word takes the singer from the high end of the Lower Family (at D) up to the B in midrange, then back down to D, en route to the phrase's endpoint (C sharp) on the word "*Dräu'n.*" The phrasings invariably revolve around two related sets of choices, whose effect depends in turn on the registral colors available to the artist. These choices are, first, between two- or three-syllable versions of the word (that is, with or without the contraction) and, second, on the use or non-use of an upward portamento through the break from D to B. I am not concerned here with textual "authenticity" (I have seen librettos and scores printed both as "*mächt'ges*" and "*mächtiges*," and while I've not seen a score without a slur on the upward sixth, scholarly research might turn one up), but with vocal structure as a factor in interpretive choice. Some sopranos, including Crespin and others not in a defined chest on the D, use the three-syllable version: "*mäch-*" on the D, then "*-ti-*" on the B. The vowel change helps ensure that the singer will not drag weight upward, but it makes for a square, literal effect. It also virtually rules out the portamento, since after gliding upward on "*mä-*" the singer would be forced to divide the quarter note allotted to the B in order to sneak in the conclusion of "*mäch-*" before thudding out the "*-ti-*". Even if gracefully done, this would amount to the awkward sort of rewrite often done to accommodate translations. A clean interval is therefore preferable with the trisyllabic variant—but the effect of the portamento is lost. Lehmann's ability to roll up out of the chest onto a still-firm Upper-Family B on the open "*ä*," unaided by a vowel change, then cleanly back down, welding the bunched consonants of "*-cht'ges*" onto the D before dipping to her low C sharp for "*Dräu'n,*" creates an entirely different effect—at once more natural and more dramatic—than any of the other possibilities. This effect (and this is what I mean by "ground level of operatic interpretation") cannot be verbally defined; nor does it depend on understanding the word "threatening," although such understanding adds to it. Its impact as sound event trumps its meaning as a word. Yet it is also not abstract—it registers as part of the way the drama moves forward. I will return to this subject below.

34. Debut to retirement (1944-1976), I think of Tebaldi's career in five stages, allowing a few months' wiggle-room on the dates:

   1. Early prime (1944-53)
   2. Late Prime (1953-62)
   3. Collapse (1963)
   4. Recovery (1964-68)
   5. Final decline (1969-76)

Tebaldi is a much-documented singer, and these stages are quite accurately reflected in her recordings, with preference always to be given to live over studio versions with respect to the voice's condition. According to the chronology in Carlamaria Casanova's *Tebaldi: The Voice of an Angel* (Baskerville, Dallas, 1995, trans. and ed. Connie Mandracchia De Caro), the Puccini concert emanated from RAI's Rome auditorium (with an audience) on Nov. 29, 1954. I first encountered Tebaldi live three months later, as Desdemona, having previously heard several of her early complete opera sets. That was also exactly the experience of James Hinton, Jr., the best American opera critic of those years, and his acute, evocative description of the occasion rewards attention, particularly with respect to the voice's impact in the house:

> "The first vocal impression was . . . startling, for the voice on records has so essentially lyric a quality that it seems unnatural to think of it as being of any great size. In a house the size of the Metropolitan the perspective was

quite different, and, used in full, the voice sounded huge . . . not so much filling the whole house with sound as seeming to be beamed directly at the listener." (See *Opera*, Apr. 1955, pp. 239-240.)

Hinton goes on to discuss ". . . the continual process of dynamic modulation, the continual almost instrumental play of color . . . that made the line breathe and pulsate and contract and expand." *À propos* the nip in the tone I have noted in my "*Un bel dì*" comparison, he also detects ". . . top notes, mezzo-forte and above, [that] were hard enough to be called so". This was roughly the state of the voice—with a progressively more granitic quality and loss of play in the upper range—until her vocal crisis and withdrawal from performance for rest and re-study in 1963. Upon return, she was at first tentative, reluctant to put any pressure on the voice; but as she regained confidence, she sang out effectively in a few of her old roles (though never again with the warmth and freedom of her early years), and had a deserved success as Gioconda in 1966-67. After that, the pitch problems at the top that had always nagged her and the stiffening of the vocal action increasingly took their toll.

For listeners unable to track down the RAI Puccini concert, comparisons of any of her early '50s opera sets with their late-50s-early-60s stereo remakes will serve approximately the same purpose. I chose the '54 broadcast because it's live, and the '49 arias because of my general rule about studio recordings: the earlier the date, the less funny business likely. A few live La Scala performances from Tebaldi's early prime, under Toscanini and De Sabata, have survived, for those intrepid enough to seek them out. For Muzio/Tebaldi elucidations, I think it's best to listen to a generous selection of each singer, to accustom the ear to differences in both vocal set and recorded sound. Several representative excerpts afford direct A/B possibilities: the *Mefistofele, Chénier, Adriana,* or *La Wally* arias, or the Desdemona/Otello scenes. But the *Bohème* passage cited in the main text is especially clear for Muzio's word-etching and active narrative impulse, both inseparable from the strong registral bonding in the voice. Muzio does not linger over tonal seduction or atmosphere: she takes a measured retard on "*cielo*," uses the portamento up to "*ma*," then breaks for the timed rest and starts anew with "*quando vien lo sgelo.*" Muzio breaks the line where Tebaldi carries it over; yet it is Muzio who moves the action more urgently forward. There is a similar contrast in the treatment of the top A-flat on "*di primavere*": Tebaldi creates a moment of suspended magic with her *mezza-voce* while Muzio, for all her vaunted floated *piano*, sings out with a bright, healthy *forte*, before refining down on the G. This, incidentally, is how it's marked. (N.B.: Muzio recorded "*Mi chiamano Mimì*" three times. Her late electrical disc for Columbia has the fullest sound and demonstrates these points, but on balance the best of the three is the 1921 Edison version, well reproduced on Romophone's CD collection [81005-2].)

As to Ponselle and Arangi-Lombardi: Ponselle's early (1920-23) Columbia acousticals are narrow-sounding, but they do show the voice at its most mobile. Among them are the most finished of all "*D'amor sull'ali's*," in key and with the high D-flat, and the superb *Trovatore* duet with Stracciari. Her late-'20s Victor electricals are certainly richer in sound. They include the *Aïda* arias and duets with Martinelli, the re-do of the *Ernani* aria, and the famous *Norma* extracts. And Arangi-Lombardi: after starting as a contralto, she had a dramatic-soprano career of only a decade or so, accepting a pedagogical position while evidently still in full command of her powers. She seems not to have had the florid capability of Ponselle, but is in all technical respects easily the best of the interwar greatvoiced Italians—tonally preferable to the edgy Scacciati or the rather cloudy Pacetti, and far more solid and consistent than such exciting but soon-frazzled veristas like Cigna and Caniglia. In addition to her aria discs, she left decently recorded versions of several complete roles (Aïda, Santuzza, Gioconda, and the *Mefistofele* Elena), each a plausible nominee for best-ever ranking.

Granting Tebaldi her *spinto* status and Ponselle her Italian heritage, we must account Ponselle and Arangi-Lombardi the last great Italian dramatic sopranos, and Milanov,

428 · OPERA AS OPERA

who chronologically would fall into a Tier IIa, the last great singer of any nationality in that line. Her voice, at least from the time I heard it upon her return to the Met in 1950-51, was not larger "in full" than Tebaldi's, and indeed did not have Tebaldi's "beamed directly at the listener" focus—nor all the core of her predecessors' (it was softer in texture and creamier in quality), nor yet all of Ponselle's technical address for *Norma* or *Ernani*. But Milanov was a true dramatic soprano, and for the very reasons I have been discussing. Her lower-middle range was ample and filled-in; the *forte* top freer than Tebaldi's if sometimes erratic; and the high *pianissimi* always poised on the *messa di voce*, ready for a crescendo. Owing to this sturdier structure, her voice lasted longer in good running condition. All her commercial recordings date from the final third of her career, and of the earlier airchecks, not many are in more than marginally acceptable sound, her Met *Ballo* of 1940 and *Gioconda* (1946), the Toscanini *Rigoletto* Act IV, and the 1936/NYPO Verdi *Requiem* under Toscanini, as restored on Immortal Performances, being among the most listenable. Taking sound and singing together, I would recommend that *Requiem,* her studio *Trovatore* of 1952, and the live New Orleans *Forza* of 1953 as her most complete statements.

Of course Callas presents herself once again, and now at least in proper context, for in my opinion she *was* a dramatic soprano. That, in any case, is how her voice was structured, and the repertory to which it had conformed, until the fall of 1948, when Serafin, desperate to find a soprano to step into the role of Elvira in *I Puritani* on short notice, persuaded Callas to learn and rehearse the part while still fulfilling her engagement as the *Walküre* Brünnhilde in Florence. It is what one hears on her (mostly live) recordings of 1949-52 (the Naples *Nabucco;* the Mexico City *Trovatore* and *Aïda;* the La Scala *Macbeth;* plus her 1949 studio 78s and complete *Gioconda* for Cetra). Serafin heard a coloratura facility unusual for a voice of big format, a temperamental and musical predilection for Italian Romantic style, and a compass that took in the soprano high extension. What he evidently did not hear, or else overlooked, were the technical distortions (the hot-potato, "hooded" quality of the lower-middle; the not-infrequent harshness and "gripped" sound of those high notes; the occasional oscillation) that could only be aggravated by lifting and—inevitably—thinning the set of the instrument. This project of hoisting her voice, unreconstructed, into a tessitura and behavioral pattern for which it was not designed almost immediately began to erode its stability and tonal integrity. That process was undoubtedly sped along by her precipitous weight loss and her many professional and personal agonies and distractions. But it was already underway. As with her frequent partner Di Stefano: had the voice been rightly structured, it might have embraced some of the roles to which she aspired, as well as others (Salome? Elektra? Wagner?—that's a beautiful early *Liebestod*). On the other hand, if with its flaws it had kept within sane bounds, it would surely have sounded better and lasted longer.

35. For critical summations of the Met's Gluckian efforts during this period (1910-16), see Irving Kolodin: *The Metropolitan Opera,* Alfred A. Knopf, NY, 1953, pp. 245-46 (*Orfeo*), 297-98 (*Armide*), and 309 (*Iphigénie*), and the reviews (principally by Richard Aldrich and W.J. Henderson) on which they are based. Those include plenty of reservation with regard to both stylistic comfort and vocal suitability. Nonetheless, while *Orfeo* had the greatest success, all three operas clearly left deep impressions. Judging from recordings, the *Orfeo* casting sounds wonderful; that for *Armide* fascinating but weird (a few of Hammerstein's singers—Dalmorès for Caruso as Renaud, Maurice Renaud for Amato as Hidraot, and perhaps Gerville-Réache for Homer as La Haine—would have made for far greater stylistic integrity without losing much vocally); and, except for the baritone Weil, that for *Iphigénie,* in German, rather grisly. All this is quite apart from such musical issues as Toscanini's interpolations from other Gluck scores in *Orfeo* or Strauss's apparently significant revisions of *Iphigénie.*

36. Since the Gluck operas are not repertory standards, their casting lines of descent cannot be traced step for step, as I did locally for *Zauberflöte*. The names cited here are culled from European and Mexican *Iphigénie* productions of the 1950s and '60s, except for that of Singher, who sang Oreste in Paris in the 1930s, with Lubin as Iphigénie. He had a large, essentially dark voice. By the time I heard him as Oreste in the 1950s (in a concert performance with Simoneau, Quilico, and the gifted *lirico-spinto* Gloria Davy), his upper range had dried, though his singing still carried authority. His prewar recordings take searching out, but they include extracts from his Hamlet, Telramund (with Lawrence as Ortrud), Zurga, the Father in *Louise*, and even Boris, as well as a complete Amfortas. In a greatvoiced context, Lisitsian or Schlusnus would have been exemplary in this role; a German-language recording of the two big solos by Willi Domgraf-Fassbänder gives a good idea of the effect created by such singers.

    Gorr, Gedda, Blanc, and Quilico can all be heard on an *Iphigénie* highlights disc under Prêtre, circa 1961. The complete *Iphigénie* derived from the Aix production, conducted by Giulini, offers the peerless Pylade of Simoneau (a real "lyric tenor"); Mollet's lightvoiced but expressive, impeccably declaimed Oreste, and Patricia Neway as Iphigénie, just two years after creating Magda Sorel in *The Consul*—she's uneven, but her vocal quality and stylistic command may surprise you. Massard must have done a makeover, for his Thoas bears little resemblance to the very respectable recordings he made a few years later. This performance also crowds its male voices into the upper midrange (where they are further squeezed by the recording's thinnish quality), and it suffers thereby.

37. The Vienna version of *Iphigénie* has been given a few postwar revivals in German-language houses. It would be interesting to hear it in a strongly cast performance, e.g., Voigt/Heppner/Domingo/Pape. I know nothing of Strauss's edition, but wonder if he may not also have adjusted Thoas' keys for the Met. The thought of the huge, hardcore bass of Carl Braun (a much-admired Hagen and Wotan), with its straight upper tones, powering across the repeated F-sharps and Es of the aria, is not a happy one.

38. See *Opera*, August 1959, pp. 549-51.

39. These were Handel singers of the late E-19, as were those of the first major full staging of a Handel opera in New York, the NYCO's musicologically horrific but theatrically spellbinding *Giulio Cesare* in 1966. Except for Sutherland in London and Treigle in New York, these weren't the voices that would have undertaken the dramatic roles of the standard repertory. Yet they were constructed on E-19 models, so they sounded dominant in Händel.

    From the earlier generations of E-19 singers we have less direct recorded evidence of the operatic Handel than we do of Mozart or even Gluck: the multiple "*Ombra mai fu*'s" aside, there are duplications of a few of the more popular oratorio pieces and a sprinkling of opera arias from the years of their concert-selection half-life. We must extrapolate from other repertoire, and assume stylistic and linguistic retrofitting. Still, I think we can take from them two lessons. One is that the Duprezian voice in full cry is not necessarily incompatible with quite astonishing feats of floridity and embellishment, which are far more thrilling when executed by such voices than by new-vocality instruments. The second is that the presence of great voices, sensitively guided, obviates the need for much embellishment. Lesson No. 1 has, I believe, been adequately demonstrated so far as the female voice is concerned: I think it is obvious that high sopranos like Tetrazzini and Sembrich, dramatic sopranos like Lilli Lehmann and Gadski, and altos like Homer, Onegin, and Schumann-Heink could have done anything contemporary Handelians do, and with half again the sonority. And how about the young Ponselle, say, as Rodelinda? In male voices, this melding of power and agility is never as common as among females, regardless of technique. And as I pointed out in regard to Schlusnus and Lisitsian, many earlier 20th-Century male singers show florid capacity only in little patches because that's all their repertory called for. Still, for those interested in making the effort of imagining greatvoiced Tier I male singers applying their technique to the Handelian challenges of fully ornamented da capo arias, here's a starter list of suggestive recordings. They are all collectors' touchstones, and should suffice as a feasibility study:

Barbiere di Siviglia: "*Ecco ridente*" or *Idomeneo:* "*Fuor del mar*"	:	Hermann Jadlowker, tenor
I Puritani: "*Ah, per sempre;*" "*Bel sogno beato*"	:	Mattia Battistini, baritone
Le Caïd: Air du Tambour-major	:	Pol Plançon, bass

From a purely vocal standpoint (allowing, that is, for a wider stretch in aesthetic and stylistic applicability), one could supplement these among higher male voices with such examples as Escalaïs' rendition of the Sicilienne from *Le Prophète* or Kozlovsky's of the "*Ecco ridente.*" Among lower voices, the florid singing of some of the Anglo/Austro oratorio and concert basses and bass-baritones (Peter Dawson is a good starting-point) is obviously applicable to Handelian opera, though none that I know of are comparable to Plançon for lightness of touch and deftness with the graces. Nor should we overlook the great cantors. Somehow, first in Russia and Poland, later at points West, older Jewish liturgical practice and Romantic-era singing techniques came together in the *chazanut* tradition, of which there is a rich recorded legacy. Most of these voices are tenor or baritenor, though the occasional baritone or bass (like the older Schorr) sneaks in. A few singers of such background, from Schwarz and Jadlowker to Kipnis and on down to Tucker and Peerce, made their way in the operatic world and are known outside the Jewish community for that. Some, like Sirota, Rothstein, and the elder Rosenblatt, cultivated tone that would be recognized as beautiful in any cultural context, and employed old-school falsetto mixes for extreme high notes and *piano* effects. Others, like Hershmann, Kapov-Kagan, or David Kusevitsky, developed a high-compression technique and full-throated top notes of a brilliant, sometimes edgy timbre. The highly emotive, exhibitionistic styles of some of these singers, and the tendency in this literature toward high cantillation and much word repetition in the upper-middle range, creates a quite stressful set of vocal conditions, and a fair amount of nasal, straight, or constricted tone can be encountered in their work. But many of them show impressive skills in florid passages, in trilling and other ornamentation, as well as a wide coloristic span, in combination with a format which in the operatic world would be categorized as dramatic or *spinto*. The pairing of strength with flexibility is, in fact, the technical hallmark of this tradition.

Lesson No. 2 has already been taught, I think, by Lisitsian, but one could also cite such pre-Revival recordings as Dorothy Maynor's "O Sleep, Why Dost Thou Leave Me?" (*Semele*); either Pinza or Kipnis on "*Si, tra i ceppi*" (*Berenice*); or Lawrence Tibbett's "Where'er You Walk" (*Semele*). In none of these wonderfully satisfying performances is any expressive burden carried by variation or ornamentation. It is borne instead by E-19 resources, by the expanded dynamic and color range of the greatvoiced singers whose instruments instantly establish a visceral, emotional connection to the melodic line. That is a connection embellishment would more likely weaken than secure.

40. It's always easier to blame aggression than restraint—the former sounds dangerous, the latter safe. But Moffo's distressing history also affords us an intriguing instance of how differently the same aural phenomena are explained by different technical beliefs. Paul Jackson reports that Beverly Johnson, the teacher with whom Moffo tried to re-work her voice, defined the problem as one of "no breath support," and that both Johnson and another (anonymous) singer acquaintance unhesitatingly blamed Eufemia Giannini-Gregory, Moffo's early teacher at the Curtis Institute, claiming that this lack of breath support was endemic to her student population. (See Jackson, "Start-Up at

the New Met," p. 85. Moffo also studied with other teachers before the collapse.) And certainly her breath was not efficiently employed. In the theatre, one was aware that the seductive bloom of her tone trailed down to nothingness at the bottom, and that in more energetic passages (of her Violetta or Manon, for instance) it sometimes hosted a telltale threat of leaking air. On records from her prime years, the latter symptom is not much in evidence, but the former is easy to hear: listen to her "*Deh, vieni non tardar*" on the early Mozart recital with Galliera and the New Philharmonia—not only the notorious (among sopranos) descent to A at "*notturna face,*" but the one only to middle C for "*amoroso foco.*" Without any chest engagement, there is simply nothing to pick up the tonal load. It is true that the result is "unsupported." But of what does support consist? Many teachers and singers define this exclusively in terms of operational strength in the nether regions of the respiratory system, i.e., the diaphragm and its associated muscular network, the action of the ribcage, etc.—all of unquestionable importance. But this bypasses the other end of the system, where the valve action of the larynx monitors subglottal air pressures with the very muscles that bring about phonation and therefore, through the controlled variation of their mass, are at the basis of "registration." In other words, in my view, proper breath support and correct registration are inseparable. And since the vocal range is a continuum of elastic co-ordinations, the weakness of any part affects the whole. Working on support, therefore, without defining and strengthening the missing register, is in this view a foredoomed procedure.

To restore the broken voice and shattered confidence of a singer who has experienced past success is the hardest job a teacher can face—in the setting of international-level performance and judgment, it is close to impossible. So no blame attaches to the very partial results of the work undertaken by Johnson and Moffo, which are probably most favorably heard in the 1976 recording of *L'amore dei tre re*. With due allowance made for the great differences in the challenges posed by Lucia (the vehicle of the 1969 broadcast disaster) or Thaïs (which Moffo also recorded around this time) and Fiora, some improvement is still noticeable in tonal firmness, and there are patches of effective singing on this set. But the voice's structure has been scarcely touched, and the lower range is still weak. Fiora is usually considered a *spinto* part: at the Met, Ponselle and Muzio were among its interpreters, followed by strong lyric voices with full lower ranges (Grace Moore, Kirsten); on the Cetra recording that dates from the last days of the opera's popularity, it is well taken by Clara Petrella, a veristic *lyrico-spinto*. Nonetheless, the singer most identified with Fiora at the Met is Bori. And the biggest difference between Bori and Moffo is the former's strong, tensile chest register, welded to a penetrating midvoice. Thus, Fiora's many stonewalling lower-midrange replies to Archibaldo and Manfredo, which Moffo could not have projected to any dramatic purpose in the opera house, would have been present and pregnant in Bori's voicings. In many of the same roles (and their repertories were almost identical), Bori sang as a slender-but-strong lyric soprano with a good lower range and some limitation at the top, and Moffo as a warmer-voiced lyric-coloratura with (at the outset) good high notes, some tonal fuzziness, and no chest register. Despite her early-career nodes (following which she seems *not* to have lightened her voice or avoided chest), Bori lasted. Moffo didn't.

Another soprano I would indict for head abuse is Gwyneth Jones. The size and quality of her voice, her radiant presence, and her compelling interpretive gifts earned forgiveness from critics and devotees for the tonal distortions, wobbliness, and poor intonation that often afflicted her singing. But when she first emerged her voice was large, lovely, and steady, the vowels clearly formed. It disappeared at the bottom, however, and in the house the tone was at times slightly diffuse. (Her debut recital record, for Decca/London, was released in the U.S. in 1967; the voice's early estate can also be heard on the 1964 Covent Garden *Trovatore* in the Royal Opera House broadcast series. I first heard her live as Fidelio in Vienna in 1968.) The difference between this vocal condition and that of her recorded Kundry and Ortrud (1970 and '71, respectively, the former a live Bayreuth performance) was a shock. As my colleague David Hamilton reported in his review of the *Parsifal*, "Jones . . . in the space of a little more than five years, has apparently managed to almost completely ruin a splendid natural endowment" (see *High Fidelity*, Nov., 1971). And that was no exaggeration. Her situation was not as dysfunctional as Moffo's, and Jones recouped sufficiently to continue her career. As always, other factors were undoubtedly involved (in Jones's case, recovery from injuries sustained in an accident), but the functional one cannot be overlooked: she blew big tone over a structure that had no underpinning. The standard-wisdom complaint is "oversinging," but that's like talking about a baseball pitcher "overthrowing". The point isn't how much force is directed into an action, but whether the co-ordinations that perform the action have the strength and balance to respond efficiently and accurately.

41. To pursue the argument to its present state among these soprano voices: Just as Duprez's *"ut de poitrine"* was not simply a matter of stacking one registral block atop another in the high segment of the tenor range, so the drawing-out of defined chest voice is not merely pinning a tail on the low segment of the soprano's. If successfully balanced and integrated, this process re-aligns and braces the voice's positioning, adds core to its timbre and tensility to its softer dynamics, and enlarges its format throughout the range. In other words, these same voices would be stronger, more brilliant, and better equalized if so developed. But the balancing and integrating can constitute a hard, time-consuming project, prone to missteps. So it seems safer to finesse the whole subject and take the course of least resistance. (But see n. 40, above, on "safety.")

All these voices were trained in different places and, presumably, according to at least somewhat different precepts. So it is all the more peculiar that the one technical principle to meet with general agreement is this dainty avoidance of the Lower Family. For it should be no onerous task to "draw out" chest register response from today's bigger, more assertive women. Few of them speak in the polite, modulated tone of their cultivated forebears, and they grow up among pop belters and screaming rockers, not operetta songsters or salon sopranos. Yet their singing makes a timid showing alongside the dominant vocalism of E-19's supposedly constrained ladies. Willful neglect and evasive technical compromises are required to have produced this across-the-board enfeeblement.

Among the singers named in the main text, it is probably Mattila who affords the best material for assessment: she's been around the longest (at least for New Yorkers) and has pushed furthest into dramatic repertory. She is one of my favorite performers, and not solely for extravocal reasons—her Eva, her Lisa, and her Janáček heroines were beautifully sung, their low-range requirements sometimes finessed, but successfully so. When it comes to Salome or Fidelio, however, her vocal structure is a serious misfit. The former's thunderous orchestration and extensive lower-midrange parlando (from Mattila, much of it inaudible and the rest in a thin, brittle mix) and the latter's wide-roaming High Dramatic writing shoved her upper octave into a hollow, overblown adjustment that had little of the clarity and shine of her lyrical singing. Dispiritingly, this condition carried over into a breathy Jenůfa (though the role still "worked" for her) and a withdrawn, ineffectual rendering of Strauss's "Four Last Songs" that sounded like a singer "marking" so as not to hurt herself. Equally unsuitable for her was the Puccini Manon—"straight" tones at the top; shallow, raucous ones at the bottom (a kind of chest perforce emerging, but only to be exposed as something never musically developed or incorporated into the instrument); and frequently cloudy ones in between.

Mattila has reached a certain age, and has used her voice hard. But, as with others previously cited, what's informative is not only when a voice enters decline, but how. And that is what will be of interest with the younger sopranos, as well. I call Dessay's membership in this group "arguable" only because she belongs to the "pure coloratura" type. Like Robin, she has combined a strong upper reach (initially, all the way to A³) with more tonal body than is normally heard from this kind of voice—though hardly the fullness of Sutherland. She also shows some of the midrange slackness heard on Robin's recordings, and the same tendency to touch chest lightly (as if by accident) or not at all when descending below the transition center. It can be contended (as I do, and as did Tetrazzini) that even (or perhaps especially) this sort of instrument would benefit from the buttressing influence of a properly strengthened and integrated chest voice. But clearly, the tide is out on this view.

42. Penno cancelled the only one of his performances (a Manrico) for which I held a ticket, and did not subsequently return to the Met, so I didn't hear him live. But as to the voice's impact, Hinton—who clearly did not consider him a mere bellower—had this to say: "...not, I would think, as big as Mario del Monaco's...but it sounds like Gabriel's trumpet...the effect is rather like being hit on the ear with a length of resonant gas pipe." He speaks of "spectacular moments" alternating with "painfully straight" ones. (See *Opera*, May 1954, p. 282.) On hearsay I have not been able to verify, it's my understanding that deterioration in hearing contributed to Penno's early retirement from singing. That would make sense: hearing problems interfere not only with pitch perception, but with the sensory/motor loop that governs everything involved in a singer's aesthetic self-awareness and consequent physical effort.

43. Normally, one would assume that mere chance encounters between voices of such amplitude and quality and the settings of the master operawrights would hit the thrill button and leave a satisfied afterglow with some regularity. Yet even these instruments do not achieve those effects as often, or with the same impact, as the best of E-19's. The reasons are multiple. They involve issues of musicality, interpretive imagination, temperament, and ethnolinguistic identity, some of which I shall return to. They are the ones usually cited when dissatisfaction is acknowledged, because to go beyond them is to venture into technical analysis. But after all, none of these artists is unmusical, and among the earlier dramatic singers of all categories some were interesting interpreters and some not; some had fiery temperaments or intriguing personalities and some not; some were native to their repertories and others foreign. And the fact is that all these qualities taken together can neither entirely explain nor replace the more primal ones of texture, sit, and color, whose roots lie deeper, in the place where body and mind organize their energies to create vocality at its foundational level, and so cannot be discussed in any terms *other* than technical. Thus:

Zajick sings as a dramatic mezzo. Her voice's overall sound and action are if anything bigger and freer than Bumbry's or Verrett's. At her peak, her vocal mechanics were extremely impressive. Indeed, from a purely executional standpoint, I doubt there has been so inclusive a run-through of Eboli's music since a younger Stignani than the one we hear on the postwar Cetra recording. But her timbre is insistently bright, more so than most true dramatic sopranos'. It hasn't the depth and darkness, the three-dimensional mass, of the real mezzo. The voice's soft texture and easy size most readily suggest the high-mezzo-or-soprano Wagner roles like Brangäne or Venus, or possibly Sieglinde en route to a Brünnhilde/Isolde conversion (Harshaw's is the earlier voice that comes most easily to mind). Big French roles (Charlotte, Didon) might work well. But she has hewed to the major Italian dramatic mezzo parts and a couple of Russian ones (Marfa, Tchaikovsky's Joan), and in that repertory her voice's color is too transparent, its flavor insufficiently meaty, to sound emotionally bonded to the music. Lately Zajick has begun to define chest more strongly in her lower range, and this has given her Azucena moments of greater intensity. As often happens, though, this has been accompanied by a weakening of the notes just above the chest range, seriously compromising some important effects—e.g., the long trills on middle B in "*Stride la vampa.*"

Blythe's case is similar, a step or so down the scale. Though she has to date sung almost exclusively as a contralto and has been by no means ineffective in that capacity, in truth her ample sound has little of the old Northern Contralto coloration, its profound beauty. It is still essentially of Modern Mezzo hue, registering as marginally deeper than Zajick's owing mostly to the lie of her roles. If she's a contralto, Blythe needs a deeper set and darker, rounder color. If a mezzo, she needs more at the top than she's shown. As of this writing, she is declaring intentions toward some of the real mezzo parts, and with her impressive *Walküre* Fricka her voice seemed in its intended groove and at its proper tension. But Fricka is an anomaly. It's a role once commonly taken by contraltos, but it benefits from a good mezzo's cutting midrange and (like Brangäne, Venus, and Kundry, but unlike the *Rheingold* Fricka) was originally designated soprano. Yet it extends to only the same upper limit as Erda's: G sharp/A flat. The big real mezzo roles lie higher. If Blythe can encompass them without on the one hand thinning her tone or on the other overweighting the high tessitura, the results could be exciting.

As to the men: how can Terfel sing so well to such slight effect? A Falstaff that just didn't take hold; a Carnegie Hall recital that left an impression of Lieder Lite. He is sometimes compared with George London, and perhaps that reference offers some clues. For though with respect to pitch range and approximate format the comparison is apt, Terfel is nothing like London. London's tone sat firm in its low-baritone range. Its texture (which, as noted earlier, underwent some right-to-left change) had point and bite along with its roundness, solidity under the velvet overlay. While his breath management was not as compressive as, say, Chaliapin's, or as stiffly resistant as Frantz's, it was never loose, and his softer dynamics sounded "on the voice." His timbre was dominated by chocolate and charcoal hues, shot through with brighter gleamings. It was a dramatic voice, capable of heroic utterance, with more lyrical capacity than most such. Terfel's voice, by contrast, glides across its range with no hint of pressure from below. Its sit is cushioned, and its texture evokes not metal or stone or even wood, but fabric in thick, cuddly folds, with traces of starch out at the edges. Its color is predominantly wheat, lightly flecked with darker and brighter shades, and his *mezza-voce* is pure Easy Plush, ingratiatingly crooned and nicely woven into the loose-knit, freely flowing full voice—the Siepi/Cole Porter syndrome redux, but farther advanced. In sum, a friendly, lyrical voice, with enough substance and thrust to give it some dramatic value in writing that isn't too heavy.

Pape is, of these four singers, the most fully satisfying. In his Gurnemanz, the Good Friday music flooded lyrically forth, and the Act I narratives were effortlessly present. He brought us the liveliest, most specific Leporello since Corena and Evans, and sang it more beautifully and fluently than either. As Marke, he allowed us to close our insulted eyes and listen for a while. And despite the benignity of his tone, he even built the *Faust* Church Scene to a dominant enough climax to momentarily wrest attention from the Priapic absurdity of his costume. (The old devil get-ups were silly, too, but they didn't try so hard.) Is anything missing? After a while, yes. In the low bass parts, blackness, depth of seating, buzzy low notes. In higher ones (Chaliapin and Journet territory, where Pape's voice more properly belongs), some bite into the language and (as in that Notperformed *Faust* serenade) a sense of effects recognized, striven for, and achieved. Tensility and core.

44. The new baritone paradigm personified by Fischer-Dieskau contained an internal tension. He seems to have had a perfectly realistic view of his own voice—the "gentle oboe" at the outset, and in maturity a hybrid of "lyric baritone" and "character baritone," as these terms are understood in the German *Fach* system. Yet his artistic ambition was all-inclusive—pancultural, transepochal, embracing all song save pop and all opera short of rock—and so subsumed at least a half-dozen of the established male voice categories. He proposed, in effect, that his formidable interpretive powers should sweep aside all considerations of vocal appropriateness, and he would express mildly offended surprise were anyone so untactful as to raise the subject. There's a typical vignette, fortuitously concerning a Verdi aria, in the absorbing video *Autumn Journey*. In this retrospective

documentary, Fischer-Dieskau demonstrates repeatedly and to illuminating effect his search for specificity of inflection, what he calls "the right character" of a singing moment. Yet, having been taken to task for singing "*Il balen*" "like a Schubert *Lied,*" he self-contentedly professes himself "*sehr geschmeichelt*" ("very flattered"). Granted that many a baritone has roared and hacked his way through this lyrical aria in a manner that might well send us back to F-D, we are still being asked to believe that this ultimate musical sophisticate, whose singular gift lay precisely in his acute awareness of which sounds seem "right" in which context, cannot detect the difference between his silken, chamberish *piano* singing and the opera-house mezza-voce of a Verdi baritone. Or that "right character" can extend to a voice as a whole, or a role as a whole. (As Hampson himself observes, the rest of the writing for Di Luna is nothing like "*Il balen*.) Fischer-Dieskau just didn't think expectations about vocal types should apply to him, and wanted an artistically virtuous reason why they shouldn't. Nowadays, we'd call that spin.

With his extraordinary gift for vocal mimesis and his functional resilience, Fischer-Dieskau was often able to make his case for pushing established norms in performance—even (at least on records) in some of his Verdi roles. It's always exciting when that happens. Still, the value of such exceptions is exactly that they are exceptional, that they direct our attention to alternative possibilities—not that they in turn become the norm. They leave too many basic needs unmet for that. Besides, beyond a certain point even a Fischer-Dieskau can alter his sound only on its surface, not at its core, and when that point is passed we become conscious of a cosmetic effect. In any case, Hampson isn't at all that sort of singer. His expressive range is far narrower and his temperament much less demonstrative. And whereas Fischer-Dieskau's purely personal, self-defensive rationalizations accidentally anticipated the postmodern project of blurring boundaries and dismantling interpretive hierarchies, Hampson has grown up comfortable with the project's attitudes and vocabulary, which he can proffer in a more disinterested tone.

45. Hampson has been the subject of many articles and interviews. The ones I have drawn on here are: Rodney Milnes: "Thomas Hampson (People, #221," *Opera,* June 1996, also reprinted in "Baritones in Opera," Jan. 2002); Matt Dobkin: "Thomas Hampson, Techie Baritone" (*Metropolitan Opera Playbill*, Jan. 2007); David J. Baker: "Homecoming" (*Opera News*, Nov. 2007); George Loomis: "The Cliché-Busting Baritone" (*The New York Sun*, Apr. 4, 2008); and Zachary Wolfe: "Baritone and Big Thinker," (*The Observer* [NY], Apr. 15, 2010).

46. See Julian Budden: *The Operas of Verdi,* Vol. I, Praeger, NY, 1973, p. 147.

47. See Shaw/Laurence, *Shaw's Music,* Vol. II, pp. 852-ff. Shaw beat this drum persistently, often with the amused exaggeration he enjoyed using *pour épater,* and usually in the context of defending Wagner's vocal writing. In that respect his arguments are not exactly airtight: some of Wagner's roles (e.g., Kurwenal and Telramund for baritone, Brünnhilde and Isolde for dramatic soprano) range as wide and hang as high as any Verdi wrote for equivalent types, and that's to say nothing of orchestral textures, the sheer length of roles and of unrelieved stretches of singing, etc. And while it is true that Wagner's writing for tenor is, as Shaw points out, much closer in tessitura to that of Handel and Mozart than it is to Verdi's (and is on this account more "considerate"), the difference in the calibre of tone required puts it under a very different stress. Shaw knew this—he was just annoyed at the *idée reçu* of Wagner as voice-wrecker, and the failure to recognize that the problem lies more with how Wagner is sung than with the concededly heavy demands of his writing. Despite these *glissements,* Shaw's observations in this passage, devoted primarily to the baritone voice, are in themselves entirely accurate; his specific example (the role of Di Luna) is apt; and Verdi was indeed the man responsible. We must remember that Shaw wrote at the noonday of E-19 voice development, and could not have foreseen later adaptations, for which his perhaps overly fixed view of vocal categories did not sufficiently allow.

48. See Luigi Ricci: *Variazioni—Cadenze—Tradizioni per canto, Vol. II, Voci maschili*, p. 16 (reprinted by Jos. Patelson Music House, NY, 1986). Note also a second variation in this number attributed to Cotogni, embellishing the line and interpolating a high G, on the repeat of the melody that leads the closing concerted section. Slightly altered versions of this variation can be heard on the Battistini and De Luca recordings.

49. Uppman did little or no recording for major labels. He can be found on the Metropolitan Opera Club's abridged versions of *The Magic Flute* and *La Périchole* and made a fine recital LP for the small Internos label. To the best of my knowledge, none of this material is yet on CD. However, his Billy Budd, taken from broadcast sources, has had some distribution, and a good selection from mid-Fifties Bell Telephone Hour broadcasts was released by VAI. Several operatic arias, including three by Verdi, are among the items, and all are well sung—indeed, I imagine that listeners new to Uppman's voice will be impressed by its quality and "legitimacy" when compared with today's "lyric" baritones. However, they will also surely hear how much closer a fit of voice with music is revealed in the songs, particularly those on the Internos disc.

50. All citations from the *Ernani* score refer to: Giuseppe Verdi: *Ernani*, vocal score, based on the critical edition of the orchestral score, Univ. of Chicago Press/Ricordi, 1995, Claudio Gallico, ed.

51. See Francis Toye: *Giuseppe Verdi, His Life and Times*, Vintage, NY, 1959, p. 239. Originally published in England in 1930 and the U.S. in 1946, Toye's was the first "life and works" to take the pre-*Rigoletto* Verdi operas as objects of serious critical examination, and though the picture has become much fuller and clearer since, his succinct, witty evaluations are still worth reading.

52. No one who heard them in the theatre will forget Warren poising on the E-flat, then sailing up to the A-flat, or MacNeil climbing the ladder from the lower G to the upper one, his tone waxing chubbier at every rung, then holding at the leading tone before releasing into the A-flat—an exact copy of Cotogni's version as reported by Ricci, and a hair-raising effect. (Broadcast CDs of both these performances circulate.) Equally astonishing, on records, is Stracciari's stampede through the entire cadential sequence, normally taken as two or three separate phrases depending on the choices made, in a single breath. In all these cases, of course, the presence of greatvoiced tone is a *sine qua non*: it's not just what's being done, but who's doing it.

53. The closest approach to a *come scritto* conclusion I have come across is in the La Scala performance conducted by Muti. Given Muti's usual insistence on textual fidelity, it's surprising that the baritone (Renato Bruson) does insert a cadenza: first a run *à la* De Luca or Battistini, then an ascent to a held upper F, as if beginning the Cotogni/MacNeil ending but stopping short, and finally the held E-flat and lower A-flat to close. The Milan audience being trained to hold its applause, Carlo enters the tomb as the lovely postlude plays through uninterrupted. It's as much an acting moment as a singing one. For it to make its point, the performer must convey his internalization of the Grand Phrase's repetition—his call to destiny echoing within him—and must do it without wordnotes. Bruson does not quite bring that off, but he has sufficient presence and dignity to at least avoid a serious letdown. On video, the production gives him some support: a regal costume, a tolerably imposing tomb, and a background which, though eccentric (the electors gathered in a sort of parliamentary gallery above the scene), shows awareness of the need to create an impression. At the Met we had nothing but the little shack plunked down in the center of the unit set, from which Hampson re-emerged in a casual stroll at "*Carlo Quinto, o traditor!*"—a regular guy, much too cool to go all dramatic on us.

54. See Francis Keeping and Roberta Prada: *The Voice and Singing*, Vox Mentor, NY, 2005, p. 213. This is the first English edition of Faure's *La voix et le Chant*, originally published in Paris in 1886. Generally considered the most important 19th Century French baritone (a

generation elder to the earliest recorded ones—Lasalle, Melchissédec, Maurel), he created, among many other roles, that of Rodrigue in *Don Carlos*, and later became an influential teacher. The Legouvé quotation appears in a section entitled "Coloration," and is also cited by W.J. Henderson in the course of entering reservations about Ponselle's Violetta (see *The Art of Singing*, Dial Press, N.Y., 1938, p. 403).

55. There's no question that expansion during this period was rapid and dramatic. But precise, reliable figures are hard to come by. Opera America, the field's primary support organization, keeps track of company, production, and performance numbers (for which see their annual field reports)—a function earlier fulfilled by the Central Opera Service in its bulletins—and for some impressive stats for the years 1962-87, see John Dizikes: *Opera in America, a Cultural History* (Yale Univ. Press, 1993, p. 510), though the source of his figures is unclear. However, there are many problems with even these numbers. Dizikes, for example, notes that during the period cited the number of companies with budgets exceeding $100,000 grew from 27 to 154, but that hundred grand (and consider, for a moment, just what kind of opera, and how much of it, can be done for that) has evidently not been adjusted to real-dollar value, which in the quarter-century's time would have markedly declined. What would that 27-to-154 growth look like in real-dollar numbers? Something a great deal less bullish, I suspect. Similarly, Opera America cites some fine-looking statistics on the establishment of new companies by the decade (e.g., 13 in the 1950s, 16 in the '60s, 29 in the '70s, etc.), but they are gross, not net: they don't account for the attrition represented by companies founded in the '60s, say, only to go under by the '80s, or by any former operatic activity that may have been replaced by the new organizations. I think particularly of the number of performances (and attendance at them) lost with the death of touring companies like those of Fortune Gallo, Charles Wagner, Boris Goldovsky, or the Metropolitan itself (both its main company and its short-lived "national" company of the mid-Sixties)—which among them might very well equal, or for all I know exceed, the comparable numbers for new companies founded in those years. (For an idea of the number of performances given and customers served by these touring entities in the late 1940s, see Herbert Graf: *Opera for the People*, Univ. of Minnesota Press, 1951, pp. 69-71.) That's a lot of opera.

With respect to opera in academic settings, there is literally nothing by way of statistical documentation (how many programs and departments, productions and performances, etc., and which operas chosen), though a hint is offered by the fact that along with its professional membership, some 100 university programs are now included on Opera America's rolls, and these are producing entities with their own constituencies.

We must bear in mind that the very incomplete figures we have are compiled for a purpose—that of explaining to people whose support it needs (foundation and corporate executives, politicians, monied private individuals) that despite its high-culture status, opera has economic and redeeming social value, and can thus be charitably accommodated as a minority special interest. That is entirely legitimate, but it is different from a set of figures assembled to give a complete and rigorous accounting of American opera's development and present condition—a large job waiting to be done. When and if completed it will still tell us only how many times certain kinds of encounters happen. It will say nothing about what meaning, if any, the encounters have.

56. For a sense of how the American scene looked to one of the most prominent of the European missionaries, see an earlier book of Herbert Graf's, *The Opera and Its Future in America* (W.W. Norton & Co., New York, 1941), especially Chapters 10, 11, and 12. His overview of the seedling stage of grassroots professional development and the embryonic one of academic opera convey both the excitement of an envisioned potential and the very primitive state of affairs outside the three or four major cities with international-level grand opera companies—the state our postwar system has tried to address. And for a thoroughly researched look back at the same scene from a more recent perspective,

see Victoria Ernier Villamil: *From Johnson's Kids to Lemonade Opera* (Northeastern Univ. Press, Boston, 2004), particularly its stage-setting opening chapter.

57. "Crossover" is a coinage of the Skipover era, necessitated by the fact that the gap between vocal usages of the classical and popular cultures has widened. The operetta ariettas, concert ballads, and leading-man and –lady musical comedy songs that constituted the "popular" excursions of late-E-19 classical singers required a bit of stylistic cosmetic, but no significant technical adjustment. On radio and recordings, the model of the pop singer "with a real voice" co-existed with others through the 1950s, and even the strictly mike-enabled pop singers cultivated sounds not entirely incompatible with classical aesthetics. "Crossing over" to anything that can properly be called rock, though, implies embracing a kind of anti-aesthetic, and along with it technical structures that aren't just different, but physically contradictory. Wherefore, the Crossover repertory consists largely of songs from Back Then, supplemented by a few from contemporary neo-Romantic musicals.

58. I am speaking here of only one department of the musicological store—the one responsible for the valuable critical editions of the operas of Verdi, Rossini, Mozart, Handel, et al.; the reconstruction of performance materials for earlier operas; and the books and articles from such authors as Budden and Philip Gossett. But we should not forget that the store has several other departments of theory and analysis, in often quarrelsome competition with one another, and that their ideologies spill into the operatic conversation as well; or that the academy that nurtures these efforts is the same one that placed the arguments of the litcrit *philosophes* at the center of its arts and humanities studies, and to a remarkable extent adopted countercultural attitudes toward those studies as its own. Such the atmosphere and these the priorities impressed on the developing mentalities of most of our young singers in recent decades. Their effects may have been only indirect on some narrowly focused students. But they would, naturally, reward and advance those most responsive to them—the intellectually and musically curious, the ambitious, but not necessarily the most vocally gifted, and certainly not those culturally resistant to them.

59. Stevens, Steber, and Harshaw attended leading conservatories (Juilliard, New England, and Curtis, respectively). Resnik went to Hunter College and Hines to UCLA, but both studied voice privately. Otherwise, this group had little or no formal education beyond high school, and counted among them none of the degrees now considered pre-requisite to an operatic career. The greatvoiced trios of Traubel/Varnay/Farrell and Tucker/Warren/Merrill are among those with no higher education. Very few schools had an opera program as we now understand it. There were many places, some of excellent quality, to study voice and music, but only a handful offered even elementary stage instruction or production experience. For thumbnail background sketches of just about all the American singers of that generation, see the biographical appendix in Villamil: *From Johnson's Kids to Lemonade Opera*. Davis: *The American Opera Singer* also gives biographical background, and one can consult individual singers' biographies or entries in the standard musical references such as Grove's.

60. For an informed exploration of this self-awareness at the highest levels of the system, see Anne Midgette: "Endangered Species: Big American Voices," *NYT*, Nov. 13, 2005. One would suppose that this issue would be repeatedly to the fore in journalistic opera criticism. Instead, Midgette's article startles us by paying some substantive attention to it, and her quotations from well-placed teachers and administrators ("There must be something wrong with what we're doing," "I think it's us, somehow," etc.) reflect the frustration that arises from the consciousness of knowledgeable, well-intentioned professionals working with what seems to be promising material, but finally to so little effect in this regard.

61. A glimpse of what it means to try to put together such an independent program is afforded in Villamil: *From Johnson's Kids to Lemonade Opera*, pp. 153-55: "Private voice teachers routinely assigned their students to outside teachers for drama, dance, theory, fencing, and languages, as well as to various coaches . . . the serious student studied and memorized operatic roles in their entirety, fine-tuned them with a musical coach, and learned the scenetics of the roles with a dramatic coach." She goes on to describe the curriculum prescribed by William Pierce Herman, one of the "in" teachers in New York in the 1940s and '50s, who specialized in coloratura soprano voices. Ironically, the singers cited by Villamil were among those that might well have been better off in today's system. But it was from such courses of private instruction that the great singers of the time also emerged. As Villamil notes, however, "Such private preparation was hardly available to everyone," and on financial grounds alone, that is even truer today.

62. Without data of the sort described in n. 55, above, there is no way to even approximate the supply/demand predicament of American singers. Actors' Equity compiles annual figures for work-weeks under contract for its members, and publishes them annually in its newsletter, complete with categorical breakdowns and some quite objective statistical analysis. But AGMA, the solo singers' union, does not. Even if it did, those numbers would have to be measured against the total of those seeking work in the field, which by definition would include many not yet in the performers' unions, and then measured against the comparable (non-existent) historical figures. So we have only our subjective impressions and observations. Mine are that despite the "expanded opportunities" of the regional system and the Young Artist programs, the ratio of competing aspirants per available job has not grown more favorable (and a job is only a job, not a career). The ratio is unquestionably worse for women than for men, there being many more of the former than of the latter who seek entry. One might also assume, for the same reason, that it is worse for lyric voices than for dramatic—but that is probably not true at the entry and early-career levels, since operas calling for dramatic voices are simply not done. As Graf observed in 1951 (*Opera for the People*, p. 128), ". . . the limited repertoire of most of the smaller companies . . . excludes the performance of demanding works like Wagner's operas or Verdi's *Aïda* and *Otello*. In consequence there is almost no opportunity for the development of new *dramatic* voices . . ." We now have many more small companies not doing the demanding works, and so develop no voices for the few that do. We've just gone in a wider circle.

63. Of course, all three of these factors could be contributing to the problem. I used to treat the first (which I termed the "deterioration of protoplasm theory") as a joke, but I do no longer—reports of environmental pollution affecting animal (and now human) genetics force us to take it seriously. See, for instance, Nicholas Kristof's *NYT* column of May 3, 2012, wherein he summarizes the evidence for endocrine disruptors (i.e., certain chemicals present in combination in agricultural pesticides and industrial compounds) as suspects in increased observations of hermaphroditism in amphibians, male fish displaying female characteristics, and genital deformities in newborn boys. Note that these disruptors act as "weak estrogen," and that though they affect both sexes, males have a heightened sensitivity; and then think about the gender-related aspects of the vocal phenomena I've been examining—admittedly a speculative leap, but not at all an illogical one. (There is followup on Kristof's blog of June 27, 2009, with links to the published scientific evidence.) As to the second factor (the broad cultural changes), I have no doubt that it's the principal influence. But even taken together and given all possible weight, these influences cannot conceivably mean that there are no voices now susceptible of Duprezian cultivation.

4

ONSTAGE II: ACTING

(1890–2005)

To many devotees, it doubtless seems that the last thing opera needs is more theatrethink. Isn't it theatrethink of a sort that has produced much of what I've been complaining about? It is. That has replaced an essential something with a less essential something else? That, too. That has bollixed up our sensory wiring by giving the eye dominion over the ear? Guilty again.

But before passing sentence, we must inquire how this came to pass. For, as with the founders of our university/regional complex, it was surely not the intention of the theatrethinkers to undermine opera's foundations. Nor was theirs, at the beginning, a hostile takeover. Their participation was solicited by an artform that had lost faith in itself. They thought they were coming to the rescue. And just as our university/regional system developed in response to a genuine need, so it was manifestly true that some theatrical reform of opera was required, reform that would go beyond the usual generational adjustment in perceptions of credible behavior to a more fundamental way of getting at the "unreservedly plausible." It also seemed clear that such reform would involve at least some realignment in opera's eye-ear flux.

At first, theatrical reform consisted mostly of trying to reconcile the requirements of opera with modern acting practices. It was directed at how people behave onstage, usually within an entirely traditional scenic environment. It aimed at training singers to rely less on the reproduction of received histrionic effects, and on conditioning receptors to follow new patterns of character action and its fusion with music, and so register its emotional logic. Inevitably, these efforts confronted all the divisions and apparent contradictions outlined in Part I (see especially the sections "Singingacting and Words" through "Drama," pp. 14-21), and in consequence were sporadic and often ill-fitting. Not infrequently, though, they at least suggested a way of going forward, and once in a while brought the sting of real discovery. Since this was occurring concurrently with the promising creative developments alluded to in "Here and Now" (pp. 121 f.), we entertained a vague but insistent hope that the aporias of creation and interpretation might find a common solution—that an American repertory would emerge, and our way of performing it might direct us toward that new-yet-restorative way of approaching the classics.

But then three bad things happened. The first was that the creative momentum died. Though we have added many works, we are really no closer to an American repertory today than we were forty years ago. The second was that along with a few successes, the attempts at acting reform led to too many productions and performances that strained for "originality," whether grounded in the work or not; that attempted to simply paste contemporary behaviors and attitudes on characters and actions; that distracted ear-attention with endless eye-clutter; or that showed willful ignorance of or disdain for the dramatic implications of the music. These gave the whole project a bad name, and helped drive musicians back behind their stockades of text. Then came the postmodern theatrethinkers with their semiotic abstractions and auteurial, often adversarial conceptualizations, giving directors near-total interpretive control and glueing the receptor's eye to the "design matrix" with its interplay of signs and ideations. Reform was now off the rails, and opera with it. That doesn't mean, though, that the singingacting ideal should be abandoned. It argues, rather, for its reassessment.

Let us recall that according to this ideal, the sung action is an indivisible whole. It is not supposed to consist of parts (a vocal part, a bodily part; a part for the ear, a part for the eye) that must be put together. It's supposed to *be* together. But we fall willy-nilly into speaking of parts. This isn't arbitrary. We do it because we observe that in practice it often *is* in parts, and because in training and rehearsing we are frequently obliged to work on it in parts. Having so worked, we may proceed in either of two ways. We can seek to assemble the presumably finished parts (the "coached" vocal interpretation, the "staged" physical one) into an integrated whole. Or we can search for a common inner source that will generate a unified voice/body action. Either way, we are in quest of sung action that seems authentic, true, and compelling. While either way can lead toward that happy end, I believe that in general the second is the more fruitful. It's part of the modern psychology of acting, and I continue to believe that it is crucial to our search.

There's a catch, however. If, as I have insisted, opera is ear-led, eye-confirmed, it follows that operatic acting is at its heart acting for the ear—something that happens within the music, to be received by the audience through its connection to the music. It is "acting with the voice"—a once-commonplace expression that is seldom heard anymore because very little of what it's meant to define is done anymore. This is especially true of E-19 interpretation, for the ways of "acting with the voice" associated with the great interpretive artists of that era were inseparable from the evolution of singing technique outlined in the previous chapter. E-19 technique arose to recount the E-19 story, with all its attendant actions and feelings. Its power-ful, prismatic tonal format drove the story forward with increased urgency and with a widened, emotionally saturated descriptive range. It ensured that despite grand-opera augmentations of sound and spectacle, the actions and emotions of individual characters would continue to command attention through their voicings.

And there's the catch of which I spoke. Because this voice-to-ear primacy has in our time been misplaced, our efforts at acting reform, though to a degree productive insofar as physical behavior is concerned, have tended to evade the central truth of operatic interpretation, which is that the vocal gesture is the wellspring of the dramatic action. No matter how fervently we pursue the common source of an indivisible action, we cannot ignore the fact that the body's energies organize themselves differently when vocal expression is conceived as paramount, and when it is not. True, there are times in opera when the voice is at rest and the body carries on. These can be important and even extended times, but they are not the operatic norm. In my opinion there is no hope for the survival of opera as opera without restoration of voice/ear primacy, and none for the resuscitation of the E-19 repertory without coming to grips with the forms of vocal expression pecu-liar to it. That is difficult for us for many reasons, some of which we will encounter soon, but the most important of these is our presumed distance from the narrative that generated those forms. Without the narrative, there's no need for those expressions. And without the expressions, there's no fulfill-ment of the narrative.

As I noted earlier, it is in the tensions between tonal and behavioral emphases that singing styles define themselves. Every technique aspires to an aesthetic ideal (a concept of beauty) and a behavioral model (a concept of virtuosity), and it is in terms of tonal aesthetics and virtuosic attainments that technique is most often scrutinized by both practitioners and devotees. In fact, these concepts apply to interpretation for both ear (how voices sound and behave) and eye (how bodies look and behave). But in a dramatic medium, technique's ultimate purpose can be neither aesthetic nor virtuosic. It must be dramatic. In a creatively thriving operatic culture, the aesthetic and virtuosic concepts form themselves around the dramatic narrative(s) the culture deems urgent, and cohere into a rhetoric. As the narrative evolves and elaborates, it develops its characteristic stylistic markers, which in time become conventions, and as it passes across ethnic, linguistic, and generational borders, the concepts and styles adapt. But the basic forms assumed by the rhetoric, and the techniques that support them, stay in place—that is, so long as the central tale remains culturally significant, generating vital new variations.

What happens to interpretation, though, when a narrative loses, or is thought to have lost, its cultural centrality? Opera's recent history teaches that the rhetoric becomes frozen. The aesthetic and virtuosic ideals become ends in themselves, detached from their dramatic purposes and inclining toward either the abstract or the patently imitative. Performers, no longer sensing themselves within the stylistic bounds that allow for instinctual, imaginative variations, are left to contemplate the gap between what seems to them authentic and true on the one hand (for the adaptations in the broader culture that alter their Sixth Sense for the "authentic" and "true" have continued to occur), and their rhetorical inheritance on the other. Since the relationship between interpretive and creative styles is symbiotic, the rhetoric now exerts an inertia on performance and creation alike. It is at this juncture that reformers, feeling the weight of the inertia, try to fight free of the rhetoric.

Rhetoric, according to Webster II's first definition, is "the art or science (well, Webster, which?—it's an ancient debate) of using words effectively in speaking or writing so as to influence or persuade." Further (definition 3), it is "the art of oratory; the rules that govern the art of speaking with propriety, elegance, and force." (For our purposes, "wordnotes" and "notes" must stand in for "words," "composing" for "writing," and "singing" for "speaking.") With respect to their rhetorical legacy, today's operatic performers meet two serious, often unacknowledged, difficulties. The first is that, as Webster notes, rhetoric takes two forms, spoken and written, and while the first of these, embodied in performance tradition, is more or less at the performer's disposal to adapt, the second, inscribed on the page, is not—and the written rhetoric of a musical score is far more explicit and prescriptive than that of a verbal text.

The second difficulty is that the past seven or eight decades have seen the fading not merely of E-19's rhetoric(s), but of rhetoric in general, of the very idea of rhetoric. Of course, there's no such thing as *no* rhetoric—that is, an absence of any sounded or written effort to "influence or persuade." But our fashions of persuasion are based on a profound distrust of all the devices and conventions of voice and body associated with older rhetorical traditions, which we have come to see as bombastic, manipulative and false—in short, inauthentic. For us, they tend to fit Webster's fourth definition: "artificial eloquence; showiness and elaboration in language and literary style." We ask, "If what you're saying is true, why the histrionics?" And we ask it whether the eloquence is of the pulpit, the rostrum, or the stage. Whereas forceful elaboration of the rhetorics was once taken for strength of conviction, it is now seen as the reverse, as a "putting on" to conceal a void at the core. At the same time, we want performance acts to seem spontaneous, inspired by the performance moment, as if there were no text. But there always is a text, and embodied in it is the rhetoric of the operawright's time, place, and personal style.

These developments return us to the question of belief, of trust in what is being said. They lie at the heart of what we think of as "good acting," and are the starting-point of the contemporary search for the authentic, true, and compelling. Wide as the gap is between our rhetorical sensibilities and E-19's, artists of modern means have on occasion bridged it.

FROM "*È STRANO*" TO "*RACHEL*" WITH THE MODERN SINGERACTOR (1966–2005)

Violetta's Pause is a good place to begin. It wasn't truly a stage pause, during which there is no physical or vocal action, but only the tense emptiness of whatever's going on inside the actors. In fact, it was a continuance of character action, of onstage life. But everyone called it a pause, because it entailed an unprecedented (and unwritten) interruption of the music, and thus produced in everyone present a momentary uncertainty. Something had gone wrong—the conductor'd had a stroke, Violetta'd gone up. Then, for us of actualist bent, it created a deeper thrill of recognition, an awareness of something happening that, despite its absence from either text or performance tradition, was so obviously what *ought* to happen that it constituted both a revelation and an embarrassment.

The "pause" occurred late in Act I on the opening night of a new NYCO production of *La Traviata* in October, 1966. I described it thusly in my original review:

> "Between the time the orchestra finishes off the departure of the guests and the time Violetta dreamily intones her first "*È strano!*", the following things happen: Patricia Brooks, the Violetta, thinks things over; two servants enter and remove the candelabras by the up center door; another brings Miss Brooks her shawl; Miss Brooks

thinks it over some more, sits on the couch, then lies back, thinks some more, sinking into reverie; and then: "È *strano!*"[1]

This activity took a little over a minute, a short time for all that had taken place, but very long for an unaccompanied pantomime inserted between the numbers of a middle-period Verdi opera. More important than the mundane household activities (logical and personal though they were) was the fact that we watched Violetta make a necessary but previously unremarked transition from her social persona to the private, emotionally charged state that generates her long, conflicted solo scene. How could we ever have tolerated the absurdity of Violetta showing out the last of the guests, turning around, taking a breath, and launching into the most intimate confessions of her soul? And of yet greater importance than this insightful directorial idea (for the repeated lesson of performance is that ideas are worth no more than the life performers can bring to them) was its embodiment by Brooks, a remarkable stage creature. Besides a lovely, strong lyric-coloratura voice and expert technique, she possessed not only unusual acting instincts and physical freedom, but thorough training and experience as an actress that established a common understanding with her director, Frank Corsaro. Because of that, the pause was not a pause, but a scene filled to bursting with Violetta's emotional and physical condition. We had always assumed, I suppose, that all that had to be there. But we had taken it on faith, one of our many routine concessions to operatic convention. We hadn't really seen it before.

The "pause" startled us in part because of its un-operatic nature. Little scenes of silent business are unsurprising in spoken theatre, as are sequences of accompanied pantomime in opera. But an event of any significance with no musical component at all violates the standard operatic compact. It forces the audience's attention toward the emotional logic of character action I spoke of above, and suggests that under certain rare circumstances, the reality of a character's ongoing physical life might even supersede the implied continuity of the score.* Yet once accomplished, it didn't seem a violation. That's why the "pause" became a kind of miniature icon for the reform-minded faithful.

---

* It also implied—unintentionally, I'm sure—that one of the greatest musical dramatists, Verdi, really ought to have supplied some music for this transition, as in his full maturity he might well have done (think of the passage that follows on Otello's "*Quella vil cortigiana che è la sposa d'Otello,*" at the end of Act III Otello/Desdemona confrontation—first the turmoil of the full-orchestra outburst, then the violins prickling upward with the little figure derived from it, and finally at the adagio, the double basses sliding sickeningly downward and subsiding into the opening of "*Dio mio potevi*"—a wrenching journey through Otello's viscera in the space of 18 bars. It's as if Corsaro's invention were pushing Verdi along toward the place that he (and all E-19 opera) were already headed.

Obviously, though, Violetta's Pause was not an emotional consummation. No "pause" could ever be. Such scenes can only point the way, knock down the brain barriers. They cement our empathies, bond us with the character, so that when the emotional peaks arrive, we are intensely with her. And there were two later moments in Brooks' Violetta that remain as vivid emotional memories for me. The first occurred in Act II, scene 2, at Flora's party, in the *"Scena della borsa."* You will recall that as the anguished colloquy between Alfredo and Violetta builds to the moment when she refuses his offer to leave in exchange for swearing to always "follow his footsteps," then forces herself to profess love for Douphol, he summons the guests to hear his accusations and witness that he has repaid in full all he had accepted from her. Carried forward by Verdi's genius, it's a powerful scene in any competent presentation. But this was something beyond that. In Corsaro's staging, Alfredo put Violetta on display, first raising her limp hand, then taking her by the chin and turning her face outward to receive his scorn and self-lacerating bitterness, and finally (at *"che qui pagata io l'ho!")* hurling his gambling winnings directly in her face. On the verge of collapse as the assemblage voiced its outrage at Alfredo, she staggered weakly away. Seeing this, he made an impulsive move to help her, but at his touch she wheeled on him like a cornered child and threw him off—both his action and hers entirely unanticipated by any veteran of *Traviata* performances, but exactly right as the behavior of two people *in extremis* with each other. Not before or since have I felt so deeply the pain and humiliation of these characters, the pathos of her feeble little call to him (*"Alfredo, Alfredo, di questo core"*), or the emotional depth of the ensemble finale. As with the "pause," the difference between our recognition of directorial choices as ideas and being swept into the life-situation lay with the performers—with Brooks' talent for letting devastation invade her face and body without appearing to demonstrate it for us, and with the slightly awkward, well-mannered sweetness of the young Domingo making Alfredo's reactions seem natural.

The second of the two episodes of emotional consummation I'm recalling for you differed from both the preceding one and the "pause" in two ways. First, it included a vocal contribution from the title character. (The "pause," by definition, had none, and in the *"Scena della borsa"* sequence only the chorus is singing.) Second, this was not the first time I had been abnormally affected by the moment. It's Violetta's final protest, when she realizes that, with the love and acceptance she has always longed for at last within her grasp, she hasn't the strength to go on living, and launches an outburst as impassioned as any in Verdi's oeuvre: *"Ah, gran Dio! morir si giovane"* ("Ah, great God! to die so young")—a propulsive allegro urged on by strongly plucked pizzicato. Like the party confrontation, it always makes an effect, short of the soprano losing her voice or bumping into the furniture. Once, though, nearly a decade earlier, I had been truly shaken by it, and that by the voice of Tebaldi, filled with feeling yet perfectly centered, beaming the phrases through me.* In Brooks' performance, the moment was equally powerful. But it was consummated by different means. Around Violetta's wrist was a rosary, whose precious meaning to her had been well established earlier in the act. As she launched into "*Gran Dio!*" (right on the downbeat of "*Di—*", if I recall correctly), she flung the rosary to the floor. Cheated by God!—A thrill-of-the-truth moment. Then, as her verse subsided and Alfredo's began, she sank to retrieve the rosary, kissing and fondling it like a beloved pet she'd kicked in anger.

The impact of these highly charged actions was the greater for occurring in ways that followed truthful character action beyond the indications of both text and performance tradition. But of equal interest here is the Brooks/Tebaldi comparison. Both artists left indelible emotional traces of the same moment. Each employed her full operatic self to accomplish this: Brooks was assuredly singing, Tebaldi was certainly acting, each inside the bounds of traditional stylistic expectations. Yet the sensory imprint is quite different. I still see Brooks; I still hear Tebaldi. And when I recall these two wonderful sopranos in a more general way, that is how they usually come through. Tebaldi's triumphs were of a traditional greatsinging kind, granted us in the last era when such triumphs were at all common. And as that era approached its end (in fact, the Brooks/Domingo *Traviata* came in the same season as the Tebaldi/Corelli *Gioconda*, the soprano's last big success), Brooks showed us a new route to emotional consummation.[2]

When I speak of a "new route," I do not mean that there had been no remarkable operatic acting, no striking interpretations of Violetta, before 1966. Nor do I mean that Brooks' performance was eye-led, ear-confirmed throughout—most of the time, it was not—or that her singing was at any point ineffectual.†

---

* Again in anticipation of remonstration: Violetta was the one of Callas's New York roles that I, unhappily, did not see, and very possibly the one I would have most liked. I have, of course, heard the recordings.

† Had it been that, moments like "*Gran Dio! morir si giovane*" would have been severely compromised no matter how inventive and committed the physical action. See, for instance, on a La Scala video, the Violetta of Tiziana Fabbricini, a lavishly gifted actress of both voice and body (and Italian, to boot), whose often involving performance is repeatedly undercut by her patchwork technique. Indeed, though Tebaldi and Brooks were both musically sensitive interpreters, and Tebaldi had at her disposal the great-voiced interplay of instrumental color that Hinton cited, neither was an "acting-with-the-voice" artist in the manner of Muzio, Lehmann, Callas, Scotto, et al.

I mean something more specific: the demonstration that through application of modern American acting technique, recognizable as such by a theatrically conditioned eye, a performer and director might together establish a physical characterization that could be tracked from beginning to end like that of a superb actress in a classical role of the spoken stage, and brought to the foreground (eye over ear) at any time with believable results; that at unexpected moments it could prove as intense and satisfying as the greatvoiced kind, though not always in the same places or with the same emotional quality (for neither replaces the other); and finally that all this could happen in a 19th-Century standard-repertory opera, and hold true in some degree for the production as a whole. Those were, truly, new findings.

And they were confirmed just a few months later by another Corsaro production, *Madama Butterfly*. Like the *Traviata*, it was thoroughly re-imagined. But because the re-imagining grew entirely from the emotional logic of characters' lives, even its more radical insights (the central one being Cio-Cio-San's Act II transformation into a Westernized Victorian wife, from which many powerful and moving developments unfolded) seemed to come from the gut of the work, not the head of an auteur. Again like the *Traviata*, this *Butterfly* enjoyed a vocally strong cast of dramatically engaged principals—Francesca Roberto, Domingo (as good a Pinkerton as any I've heard in the theatre), and Seymour Schwartzmann (whose large, warm voice was the best I've encountered for Sharpless since the young Mario Zanasi sang it at the Met)—and the solid, idiomatic conducting of Franco Patanè. Overall, these two productions, as performed by their original casts, remain the best I have seen of those operas in the ways that finally count the most: they were the most believable, the most moving, the ones that most fully realized the tragic potential of the operas. They also best exemplified the way past the aporia we thought we saw.[3]

In the time that has passed since we glimpsed that vision, as the flame of greatvoiced singing and the kind of "acting with the voice" that went with it has flickered, then guttered out, we have seen widespread change in how operatic performers present themselves onstage. The change reflects a general acceptance of the necessity of bending operatic material to a modern acting sensibility. It is broader than it is deep. In most instances it amounts to little more than an expectable generational adaptation—performers sensing the need to behave in a *manner* recognizable as "natural" according to contemporary social norms, so as not to appear old-fashioned—and merely eases the audience toward acquiescence. But in the hands of extraordinary performers, it sometimes bonds with the emotional potential of a role to achieve a fulfillment of the sort modeled by Brooks. Usually this has happened in operas already conceived with the modern acting sensibility in mind, like those of Janáček, culminating in the consummate ensemble stagecraft of Patrice Chéreau's *House of the Dead*. But it has on occasion connected with classical repertory roles—Mattila's Lisa or Eva or Amelia Boccanegra, Lieberson's Elvira or Didon, Netrebko's Gilda, to cite a few local examples of recent memory. For me, the most powerful proof of this bond since the Brooks Violetta (and one that, as it happens, affords the unusual opportunity for some comparison by eye and ear with a renowned greatvoiced portrayal) came only recently, in the form of Neil Shicoff's performance as Eléazar in *La Juive*.

Shicoff's Eléazar clearly benefited from a strong sense of personal mission. I took from it some of the same feeling conveyed by Treigle's Olin Blitch or Vickers' Peter Grimes: that something in the essence of the role struck into the performer in a place so perfectly aligned with his psychological stance in the world that keeping faith with it and expressing it fully was a matter of necessity, and the result was deep and true. For that reason we might be tempted to set it aside as an instance of role-of-a-lifetime dumb luck, in which subjective factors played too active a part to consider it a paradigm for singingacting technique. But that would be mistaken, for two reasons. The first is that Shicoff, like all the other performers named above, had shown enough on other occasions to assure us that though his Eléazar certainly represented something special in his body of work, it was by no means just an accident. He has a craft. The second is that it is precisely this psychological fusion of performer and character, this absorption of a character's circumstances and temperament into the subjective experience of the performer, that is central to the modern acting sensibility. Some say it has always been central to good acting. The extent to which that is or isn't true is one of the matters to be explored below.

In one way, Shicoff's achievement is more remarkable than Brooks'. For whereas her Violetta was the "right kind of good" by traditional standards, it would be hard to say that of Shicoff's Eléazar. In prospect, Shicoff would appear to stand no closer to the great interpreters of his role—or of French dramatic tenor writing in general—than does Hampson to those of the Verdi baritone parts. Yet, within his means, he gave a performance which, upon its arrival at the great Act IV scene by which this work is still remembered, proved emotionally overwhelming. To understand how that came about, we need some appreciation of the standards set by this extraordinary role's earlier exponents. And since *La Juive*, unlike *La Traviata*, has been a rare commodity for three-quarters of a century, some contextualization of both the piece and its performance history will not be amiss.[4]

Consider the operatic goings-on in the Paris of the early 1830s, particularly with respect to that fascinating and tragic figure, Adolphe Nourrit. The decade had begun with the Revolution of 1830, which installed the relatively liberal July Monarchy of Louis-Philippe, and during which Nourrit, already the idol of a decade, took to the barricades and rallied the crowds with his singing of *La Marseillaise.** In 1831 came the *succès fou* of Meyerbeer's audacious *Robert le Diable*, with its thrilling/shocking ballet of undead nuns led by Marie Taglioni and choreographed by her father Filippo. The principal singers: sopranos Dorus-Gras and Cinti-Damoreau, the wide-ranging bass Nicolas Levasseur, and, in the virtuosic and dramatically agonized title role, Nourrit. (Meanwhile, down in Lucca, was Duprez, wrestling into his new *acuti* for the Italian premiere of *Guglielmo Tell*.) In 1832 the Opéra saw the premiere of the original version of *La Sylphide*, danced and choreographed by the Taglionis, with scenario by Nourrit, based on a story by Charles Nodier—one of the signal events in ballet history. 1833 brought the premiere of Auber's *Gustave III, ou le bal masqué*, with Nourrit as Gustave. And now, in February of 1835 (less than a month after the premiere of Bellini's *I Puritani* over at the Théâtre-Italien, with Rubini as Arturo, and seven months before the reconstituted Duprez first hurled Edgardo's curse into the auditorium of Naples' San Carlo at the premiere of *Lucia di Lammermoor*), came *La Juive*, with new soprano rage Marie-Cornélie Falcon as Rachel, the well-established Dorus-Gras as Eudoxie, Nourrit as Eléazar, Levasseur as the Cardinal and, in the second tenor part of Léopold ("second" in relative importance, not range) a singer named Lafont. The Act I waltz and the extended Act III ballet and pantomime sequence were choreographed by Taglioni *père*. The opera was both a big and

---

* There is no equivalent today for the position occupied by Nourrit in the Paris of that time. If there were, it would be some mashup of Pavarotti, a movie star, and a rock star (say Bono, with his political activism)—with the proviso that this creature come forth at least once a year as leading man in a new work of lasting significance, in whose creation he had also been instrumental. Nourrit made his debut at the Opéra in 1821, as Pylade in *Iphigénie en Tauride* (his father was then the company's leading tenor), and over the next decade had created the principal tenor roles in four Rossini operas (*Le Siège de Corinthe*, *Moïse*, *Le Comte Ory*, and *Guillaume Tell*), as well as that in Auber's *La Muette de Portici*, in addition to sustaining roles in older repertory. He remained unchallenged at the Opéra through the premiere of *Les Huguenots* in 1836, after which the arrival of Duprez (as Arnold in *Tell*) sent him on tour in the provinces, then to Italy, and into the downward spiral that led to his suicide in 1839. Duprez, too, was much more than a trend-setting tenor. He wrote several operas and other music, and was extremely influential as a teacher, leaving volumes of memoir and vocal method. These were, to understate the case, men of parts.

enduring popular success and the cause of considerable debate, more for its social, religious, and political implications than its artistic merits. It was still making repertory appearances in Europe and the U.S. in the 1930s.

Halévy originally envisioned Nourrit as Léopold and the bass Levasseur as Eléazar. But Nourrit persuaded Halévy that he should take the part of the bitter, vengeful Jewish father rather than the archetypical leading-tenor assignment of the princely, heroic young Christian lover. And this unusual choice is pertinent to my present topic, for although Nourrit was clearly a singer of high accomplishment, his reputation (especially in contrast to Rubini's) was above all that of a great singingactor, or even "an actor who sings." He is sometimes considered the first "dramatic tenor," but the term applies to his interpretive skills and his passionate interest in physical characterization rather than to his voice type and technical set-up. For all the interpenetration of ballet with opera in his milieu, the idol of his youth was not a great singer or dancer, but Talma, the pre-eminent tragedian of the Parisian spoken stage.[5]

Having radically re-arranged the new opera's vocal distribution, Nourrit made a further crucial contribution to it. For it was he who conceived the Act IV scene and aria that came to define his role (if not the opera itself), and wrote, or at the least edited, the words for it.* We can be certain that throughout the score, but most especially in this scene, the writing was carefully crafted to the contours of Nourrit's voice and technique—though of course we cannot be certain that what appears on the page is in every instance what Nourrit sang.[†6] The layout of Eléazar's music is what I would term "upper-middle horizontal." That is, the lie of the role is fairly high, with a great deal of traffic from the middle C to the top A, and is at close intervals most of the time—there are relatively few gestures that cover wide stretches of range. Further, while there are passages that call for sustained *cantabile* (notably, the Passover Scene prayer and cavatina "*Dieu que ma voix tremblante*" and the famous Act IV air), and these are of great importance, most of the writing is declamatory, one syllable per note—there is little extended vocalizing on a

---

* It is well established that the idea of replacing an intended choral finale with this solo scene and double aria was Nourrit's. But whether the tenor provided or only "refined" (Diane Hallman's word) the lyrics, and whether his work applied only to the air itself, to the following allegro (whose rhyming couplets are entirely conventional and Scribesque), or to the entire scene, is apparently impossible to determine from surviving evidence.

† Neither Hallman nor Leich-Galland in his preface (see Notes 93 and 95) explores the musical and dramatic implications of the vocal setting. That's natural enough—it's not where their attention is focused—but it's a crucial question when it comes to the opera's actual effect in performance, and it would be interesting to know what alterations may appear at different stages in the working source materials.

single vowel, and little on passage work. But there is great stress on clarity of word and force of rhetoric, and with the presumption of unshakable security and dynamic control in the *passaggio*. There are many Gs, A-flats, and As, but only a scattering of phrases that carry higher. Thus, the latter stand out all the more.

I feel as safe as one can at this distance in inferring that with the exception of a few delicate moments, Nourrit sang everything up through A-natural in what we would recognize as "full voice." That is the habitual upper limit in the tenor writing of Handel, Mozart, and the "reformed" Gluck—and, of course, Wagner—and the presumptive point of departure for the falsetto/ *voix mixte/voce finta* extensions of the old-school bel canto singers. We must allow, as always, for the tuning differential, and that is of special relevance here, since whereas the tenors of Handel, Mozart, and Gluck sang at a pitch lower than our standard, those of Paris in the 1820s and '30s may have actually been at a slightly higher pitch than ours.[7] I also infer that these head-mix extensions were quite strong, for while some of the flights for the usage written by Rossini, Bellini, and Meyerbeer call for qualities of aristocratic sweetness, smoothness, and even a certain eeriness, others (including several in this role) are marked for strong dynamics and heavy accenting. A weak or cooing sound is not a plausible alternative, nor is a yodeling break every time the divide is crossed with any force. At the same time, in these climactic moments, the fact that these extensions pulled away from the hold of the chest-voice above A-flat or A would have given them a sensation of release— not the thrill of a ringing full voice like that available to a good "modern" tenor, but a different excitement of a sound still strong, but heady and suddenly unbound, "free." Audiences, unaware of the more visceral and impactful tones that were just around the corner, must have awaited such moments from a Rubini or Nourrit with high expectations.

Up until the *allegro* section of his Act IV double aria, which contains six B-flats and a C, Eléazar has seven written excursions above A-natural. One of them—a chromatic ascent to B-flat in ensemble (not unlike Arnold's famous climb to the C in *Guillaume Tell*, but a full step lower—pp. 149-50 of the Leich-Galland score), could easily have been written for a modern dramatic tenor voice. But the rest, in their selection of movement, accent, and dynamic, are extremely awkward, and in some cases virtually unsingable, for even a technically expert modern singer, and their choices of vowel ("*i,*" "*eu,*" "*Ô,*" the "*o*" of "*couronne*" or "*donne,*" and the nasal diphthong "*em*") are without exception the sort that encourage head-voice mixes. I will consider these gestures more closely in the comparisons below. First, it's important to understand, as best we can, the incorporation of this role into the later dramatic tenor tradition.

And this is a process that began almost immediately, for upon Nourrit's departure in 1837, the part was assumed by none other than Duprez. We must not assume that simply because Duprez had broken some ground with his famous high C, he sang everything above A "from the chest." He was of the culture of his time, and would have understood that many of the effects in the Meyerbeer and Rossini roles he undertook, and at least a few in this role, required oldstyle treatment. Nonetheless, Eléazar must have sounded rather different in his voice than in the one for which it was designed, Nourrit's. Everything in the writing and in what we can gather about the latter's technique suggests a bright, malleable sound set in a relatively high laryngeal position, with no weight thrown against its bottom fifth. (The role seldom descends below F#, and then only with the lightest of touches—it glances off D# in the pattery asides of the Act II trio with Léopold and Eudoxie, and starts the "*Chrétien, sacrilège*" trio on E, but *piano*.)*

Duprez, though, was clearly singing from a different adjustment with a deeper sound, darker and stronger overall, that comprised both a measure of *squillo* on *forte* high notes and his *voix sombrée* effects, and which (as I earlier observed) must have issued from a lower laryngeal position.[8] It's also reasonable to suppose that the unwritten high notes (sustained ones, launched from a fourth or fifth below) that became traditional among later tenors, including nearly all of whom we have aural evidence, originated with Duprez. The most common of these are the B-flat in the penultimate bar of the aria (in place of the indicated A-flat) and the B-natural at the end of the opera (instead of remaining on the written F). Both these are on the fat open "*a*" ("*c'est moi*" and "*La voilà!*"), the vowel of choice for fuller-voiced high notes.[†]

---

* For one of the few times it calls for any weight on the lower octave, see pp. 463-64.

† I stress that this is my supposition. The fact that the notes aren't in the score doesn't mean that Nourrit himself might not have sung them (though, given the circumstances of the role's creation, it strongly suggests it); nor is there any proof I know of that Duprez did. But they are exactly the sort of interpolation that would appeal to a tenor relying less on elegance and nuance, and more on a newfound proclamatory ring, and eager to establish himself in place of a great audience favorite. Hallman (see the note on pp. 184-85 of her book) reports that violin parts for Acts IV and V are marked "½ step lower for Duprez," but from her citation it's impossible to know exactly where the transposition was made. In the Brogni/Eléazar scene? That seems pointless for the tenor, and of no help to the bass. There would be no vocal need in "*Rachel, quand du Seigneur,*" but the allegro, "*Dieu m'éclaire,*" which was probably the crowning glory of the evening for an oldstyle tenor, is cruelly taxing for the new. Possibly Duprez, or the conductor, Habeneck—or Halévy himself—wished to preserve the relative minor/major key structure and avoid an awkward lowering of only the *allegro*, and so put the whole scene a half-step down. That would make Duprez an even more logical candidate for originator of the interpolations, for the resulting notes—at the Paris pitch, slightly sharp versions of A-natural, B-flat, and one B-natural—are meaty ones from a full-throated tenor.

These educated guesses about Nourrit and Duprez aside, there's no question about the direction the singing of Eléazar took. It's the direction all singing was headed. Like any change in performance style, this one happened gradually, against opposition, and with frequent exceptions. It was a time of shifting categories, when tonal expectations were not as set as they later became, and transposition was more acceptable. For instance, when *La Juive* arrived in London (in Italian) in 1850, Mario (the original Ernesto in *Don Pasquale*, though ten years earlier) sang Eléazar and Tamberlik (the original Alvaro in *La Forza del destino*, though twelve years later) Léopold. Viardot, one year after her creation of the contralto part of Fidès, was the Rachel— but then, she sang Amina, too. In any event, by the last decades of the 19th Century, with *La Juive* being performed everywhere from St. Petersburg to New Orleans, Eléazar was most often being sung by French dramatic tenors, Italians and Hispanics of the *robusto* type, and Germans of the *Helden* variety. The Metropolitan took up the work during its German seasons of the 1880s, and after one year with Anton Udvardy as Eléazar (judged too light for the role and the house), the part was taken by Albert Niemann, the leading Tristan and Siegmund of the era, with Max Alvary, a renowned Siegfried, as Léopold. Later, a number of performances were sung by the Polish tenor Julius Perotti (an Arnold, Raoul, Manrico, and even Siegmund), who evidently had a powerful voice with brilliant high notes.

After the German seasons, *La Juive* lay dormant at the Met for nearly thirty years, until the house revived it in 1919 as another in its series of French heroic assignments (following Samson and John of Leyden) for the mature Caruso. Eléazar proved to be his last new role, and the story of his triumph with it has been recounted often. When Caruso died, Martinelli assumed the part, and was invariable in it until *La Juive* dropped from the repertory in 1936. In those same years in Chicago, Eléazar was sung by Charles Marshall, the company's regular Otello, Samson and Tristan, until Martinelli briefly succeeded to his roles, also in 1936.

By the time Caruso was singing Eléazar, recordings were affording us multiple versions of "*Rachel, quand du Seigneur*," as well as a few other extracts from *La Juive*.[9] And by the time Martinelli was performing it, the earliest successful techniques for combining sound with film, the Vitaphone process, enabled movie-theatre presentation of operatic scenes and concert selections. So it is possible for us to piece together evidence at least somewhat stronger than that of report and hearsay, of the role's performance tradition as it stood when last heard from (except in concert and recorded form) before the Vienna production of 1999, with Shicoff. In fact, we can make direct audio comparisons between Martinelli and Shicoff throughout Acts II and

IV (which take in Eléazar's most important scenes), and a video comparison of Act IV. They entail major differences in sound and picture quality, and of course neither is a satisfactory substitute for live performance. Still, we can glean quite a lot from them, and much of that has to do with acting, since (as we saw in the last chapter) changes in vocality of the sort I have been discussing—from a Nourrit to a Duprez, from a Duprez to a Caruso, from a Martinelli to a Shicoff—go a long way toward determining both the basic performing personality and interpretive range of a given singingactor.

Since we are speaking at the moment of acting, we should look, from an actor's P.O.V., at the character to be interpreted. Hallman has an intriguing chapter on the literary ancestry of Rachel, *"la belle Juive,"* and Eléazar. She focuses especially on two Jewish single fathers with adopted daughters born Christian: Shylock and Jessica in the *The Merchant of Venice*, and Isaac and Rebecca in *Ivanhoe*, and is entirely persuasive on their influence.* But Hallman is concerned with these characters as Jewish literary stereotypes, and an actor must not think in terms of a stereotype. He must think of the events and circumstances of an individual life, the things that shape a particular person and account for the way he is. Then he must think no more, but only feel and do. Moreover, once on his feet, his character is no longer literary, and much as his parsing of text and background may have nourished him, it will not in itself solve one moment of stage life for him. In this connection, I often think of a television interview I once saw with the inimitable Peter Ustinov, all-round man of the theatre and one of the last century's great raconteurs. About to undertake the title role in *King Lear*, he began by observing that while tens of millions have read the play and millions more have seen it, only a relatively few (and he had come up with some shockingly low number based on *Lear*'s production history) have undertaken to play the part, and so be in a position to discover what's actually in it. Being a conscientious actor, and like any sensible fellow daunted by the assignment, he'd done his homework, squirreling about in historical accounts and scholarly commentaries, and had been duly impressed by their erudition and insights. Now he had to begin rehearsals, and he likened the moment to being on the deck of a ship casting off for a long voyage. At the pier, the

---

* Though I think we mustn't lose sight of Hugo's un-Jewish Triboulet and Blanche. Both Shakespeare and Scott were certainly à la mode, and the Christian/Jewish opposition is thematically vital to La Juive. But no one was more à la mode than Hugo. His play is surely an immediate antecedent, and operatically, the emotional power of the father/daughter bond and its musical expression does not depend primarily on religious identity. See n. 95.

monuments and towers of research and analysis loom imposingly. But as the vessel pulls away, they shrink to a little line along the horizon, and soon one is on open sea, no land in sight, with only oneself, one's plucky fellow voyagers, and one's *Doppelgänger,* "the character." Any literate person can do the homework. But to fairly evaluate an actor's performance, we must imagine ourselves on the voyage. We must adopt the P.O.V. of an actor of modern sensibility, who is also a tenor. That means that we must not only understand the content of a given moment, but feel our way inside the moment and sense how it generates the next, and establish some empathy with the performer's voice/body experience.

The first thing to be absorbed about any character is his or her backstory, and Eléazar has a powerful one, which we learn about in bits and pieces along the way. Many years before the start of the action, Eléazar had a family—a wife and two sons. That was in Rome—the "Widowed Rome" of the Avignon Papacy, a ruined and perilous place. For unspecified but presumably dubious reasons, his sons were torn from him by Christians and burned at the stake while he watched. Later, he was banished from Rome by a magistrate, Jean-François Brogni, apparently on a charge of usury.[10] But in a pillaging of the city by Neapolitan forces, Brogni's home was burned and everything he possessed was lost, including his wife and, he believed, his infant daughter. Actually, though, this daughter was saved from the conflagration by Eléazar himself. He received the child as a precious and profoundly ironic gift from God, delivered to him in replacement of his lost sons. He named her Rachel and, naturally, consecrated her to his faith. She is, as he sings in the Act I finale, his "beloved daughter," his "only blessing," his "treasure," and his "love," and before God he vowed to dedicate his life to her wellbeing. As for the magistrate Brogni, with nothing worldly left him, he gave himself over to God and became a priest.

The sequence of these events in the work's prehistory is by no means clear. What happened to Eléazar's wife? How long had she been dead? How old were the sons? Why, exactly, were they sent to the stake? If Brogni banished Eléazar from Rome, how is it that Eléazar was around to rescue the daughter? The actor's task is not merely to establish a coherent sequence of events, but to find the sequence that is dramatically the strongest, and above all to make the people and events involved emotionally alive and everpresent to him, as they are to the character. My own sequence is this: the wife died giving birth to the younger son. The sons were in their teens, just at the verge of manhood, when they were burned. (The exact cause requires further discovery—try to locate a vivid historical example connected to the persecution of

Jews, of which there should be no lack.) After several bitter years of life alone, profiting from his jeweler's trade and using some of the money to conduct a moneylending business on the side, the charge of usury is brought against Eléazar (false—he was charging only the legal 20%), and Brogni allows Eléazar a week to leave Rome. But on the very night that Eléazar is heading North into the Lazio, with a few precious stones he had saved from confiscation in a concealed moneybag, the Neapolitan raid takes place, and as he had seen his own sons perish in fire, he snatches the baby girl from the flaming villa of the Brognis. *La Juive* is a story of high melodramatic coincidences that touch off successive revelations. That is how its suspense is built, and how we arrive at its dénouement and final *coup de théâtre*. The higher the melodrama and the more extreme the coincidences, the more urgent that every nook and cranny of reality be filled in, so that the performer believes without reservation in his own story, and the audience sees a man who so believes.

Now, as the action begins, it is the year 1414, and we are in the Swiss city of Constance (Konstanz), by the big lake of the same name. Eléazar has prospered. He has a home and workshop with several employees, not in a ghetto but directly across an intersection from the town's main cathedral. It's early spring, the time of Easter and Passover, and more than usually festive because the Emperor Sigismund* has convened a grand church Council. The Council will debate church reforms and revisions of canon law, and decide how to proceed against the rebellious and heretical ur-Czech, Jan Hus. (As a matter of historical fact, Hus was executed in the following year, after having been granted a safe-conduct to defend his views before the Council.) But the Council's main purpose (which is eventually achieved—it lasted four years) is nothing less than bringing an end to the Western Schism, and consolidating the papacy in Rome. It's Opening Day (also the day of Passover Eve), and the town is jammed with dignitaries of church and state, their retinues and slaves. Among the dignitaries is Brogni, who has risen to the rank of Cardinal, and is in librettistic fact the President of the Council. Rachel is now a beautiful and devout young woman, as protective of her father as he is of her. She has entered into a liaison with a man she knows as Samuel, a co-religionist and a painter, but who is really Prince Léopold, married to the Princess Eudoxie, the Emperor Sigismund's niece. He's been away leading a successful campaign against the Hussites, but has this very day returned to publically receive his plaudits and privately pursue his affair with Rachel.

---

* The real-life Sigismund of Luxembourg, though at this time King of Rome and of Croatia and the son of a Holy Roman Emperor, did not himself assume that title until 1433. The libretto, however, identifies him as "Emperor."

All these psychologically loaded relationships are about to collide in a social atmosphere charged with anticipation, celebration, political fervor, and religious hatreds—as actors like to say, "the stakes are raised." Act I is set in the square between the Cathedral and Eléazar's house, where the public festivities around the opening of the Council are taking place. Three important events occur.* First, the crowd, incensed that Eléazar's shop is at work on a festival day and egged on by the City Provost, Ruggiero, menaces Eléazar and Rachel, but is pacified by Brogni, who preaches clemency. He even extends a hand of friendship to Eléazar, whom he recognizes from the Roman days, but Eléazar spurns the offer. Second, with the crowd temporarily gone, Léopold-as-Samuel sings his serenade, and is invited by Rachel to partake of that evening's Passover seder. With understandable nervousness, he accepts. Third, the returning crowd works itself up a second time on discovering Rachel and Eléazar on the steps of the Cathedral, and excitedly proposes throwing the Jews into the lake. But the advancing cohort is stopped on the orders of Léopold. In the ensuing finale, Rachel and Eléazar express wonderment at the mysterious authority exercised by their poor Jewish painter friend.

With the beginning of Act II, we are able to begin comparison of the performances of Martinelli and Shicoff. Since Martinelli's Act II survives only in audio format, let's start with some consideration of how these two Eléazars reach the ear, and through it the mind's eye, taking up the physical characterization when we come to evidence of it in Act IV. (For specification of the audio and video materials used, see n. 100.)[11] The second act begins at the Passover table. A brief orchestral entr'acte, with flute and harp prominent, sets the solemn mood: night, the interior of Eléazar's home. At the table are Rachel, "Samuel," and enough other celebrants to fill out a five-part mixed chorus (SATB, but the basses divide). Eléazar presides. Beyond this, the score has no scenic description at the top of the act, and the action will demand only two other elements: a door to the street, and another to the interior of the house. But the mind's eye envisions more, and fills in the scene as familiarity with the act grows. We are inside the shop-and-dwelling whose exterior we saw in Act I, and from which emanated the sound of anvils that had so aroused the Christians. So I see the workroom, the only room large enough

---

* I present these in skeleton form, since our comparisons do not begin until Act II. Interested readers will want to consult at least a more detailed synopsis (try some of the old "stories of the operas" books—the one in Grove's is quite inadequate for any real understanding), and preferably libretto or score. (Warning: the RCA recording of the Vienna production contains no libretto. The Philips studio recording has one, but it does not include any of the material cut from that version.)

to accommodate a gathering, cleared and cleaned of course, with all but the immovable tools (like anvils) put away, the table extended and set with its white cloth, silver, and candles.

Hallman informs us that an early version of the set design showed exotic Oriental decoration, and I think some of this is appropriate, to help lead us into the realm of Jewish private life, precious and concealed, and to contrast it with everything else in the opera's world. Hallman further notes that these early ideas about the set also included a small separate room on the street side, and that makes sense to me, too—the establishment's retail front, with more business-like décor, which can be closed off from the rest of the house by means of a door or portiere. I also see an upstairs level. I assume the celebrants include men in Eléazar's employ, with their wives and possibly a child or two, that some of these (perhaps those without families) might reside in the house, and that their quarters would be separate from those of Eléazar and Rachel. Finally, I see this interior setting contained within a surround. On one side is a bit of the street. Above and beyond the cathedral looms, and we catch glimpses of other buildings on the square, as in Act I, but now turned at a different angle. And the nighttime sky.

Eléazar intones a simple unaccompanied prayer with choral response, hushed in tone but with characteristic sudden changes in loudness, marked by liturgically suggestive harmonies and a vocal line not far removed from chant, asking God to send down His spirit and to keep the mysteries hidden from evil eyes. It's music that asks to be sung reverently and straight-for-wardly, showing only midrange sustainment and control of dynamics, but the difference between the voices of Shicoff and Martinelli (and consequently, in our first impressions of Eléazar) is immediately apparent. In format, the voices aren't comparable. Martinelli was a true dramatic tenor, trafficking by this time almost exclusively in roles like Radamès, Canio, Samson, Enzo, and even Tristan, with Otello just a year away; and as noted earlier, he was all core, without a trace of Easy Plush, his tone clear, rockribbed, and essentially bright even in the low range. Shicoff is a sturdy lyric tenor, comparable in format to Jan Peerce: an Alfredo and a Duke, a Hoffmann or Werther, with José or Manrico at the farthest stretch in terms of tonal weight. Though the voice is well balanced, its lower range inclines toward a right-column dark-ness and looseness, giving it some nice shadings but also a touch of shaki-ness. Martinelli's is the sound of an adamantine patriarch who is always in control. Shicoff's is more that of a strong family man who is, to again summon the term, vulnerable.

Before the prayer is even finished, we begin to encounter cuts. Some of these are of whole numbers, and a few represent choices between editions.

But the majority are internal (some of them truly tiny), and originated with conductors and singers. This first one is typical of the latter sort. Musically, such cuts undermine or foreshorten structure, but in acting terms their effect is to remove some of the dots the performer is trying to connect along his throughline—assuming of course that he's making that effort. In this instance, the last ten bars of the prayer are lopped off. Harmonically, this makes no difference: the transition from B-flat to G-minor (a movement of string chords) is the same in either case. The difference, in show-biz slang, is that with the cut, the number has no tag, or button. And the composer provided one. Instead of ending, as does the cut version, with one of the responses for Rachel and the chorus that segués smoothly into the strings' entrance, Halévy gives the assembly a final outburst in which Eléazar's attack stands out from the ensemble in both tessitura and movement, with a flashing little turn up to G before dropping quickly back down to *piano.* Then, in contrast to all the other response endings, this one stops abruptly. There's a single beat's rest, and then the soft, pregnant entrance of the strings. It's a very different feel—more active, not a smoothing-over but a sharp end to one action and a decisive switch into a new one. It sets Eléazar on a different track, bringing him out of the group prayer toward the more personally expressive solos that follow. In my mind's ear, I almost hear Nourrit sweeping through the turn up toward the top of his full-voice range with elegance and panache, perhaps accompanied by a Talma-esque physical gesture, quasi-balletic to our eyes. And who knows what a talented singeractor of our time, now embarked on Ustinov's lonely voyage, gazing about the table at his daughter, her strangely empowered suitor, at workers and family and other members of his small, precarious community, and carrying with him the events of the day and of his life, might be impelled to make of the moment?

If I were a conductor or musical scholar charged with the assignment of cutting *La Juive* in half, as was Artur Bodanzky for the Caruso revival of 1918-19,[*][12] and had already disposed of whole choruses and dances and Eudoxie's two arias without yet nearing my goal, I would congratulate myself on every redaction that saved thirty seconds without sounding brutal. But if I am Eléazar, mining the text for clues and opportunities, I resent the meddling with my role, the character that is my possession and my responsibility. I, not the conductor or the scholar, am Eléazar. It says so in the program. And if I'm a receptor, I have no way of knowing what the cumulative effect of these

---

[*]   Léon Rothier, the bass who sang Brogni in that revival and many subsequent performances, and who, having known the work well from his Paris days, collaborated with Bodanzky on the Met's edition, says that "The Metropolitan contemplated a version running from 135 to 150 minutes at a maximum."

dozens of internal cuts has been. Unless I'm unusually knowledgeable, I don't even know that cuts have been made. They are not always detrimental, but they do always change my experience.

Now the new beat begins. Eléazar sings: "If treason or perfidy should dare slip amongst us, great Lord, let fall your wrath." As with many such beats in this kind of opera, this one is built on repetitions of these words, with variations and emphases provided by the music. From an acting P.O.V., there are two points of interest in it. First: it offers an example of the kind of choice that makes no apparent difference to the audience, but which the performer must nonetheless make. Given the circumstances and what the audience knows, Eléazar's words could be heard as already indicating uneasiness about "Samuel," or just as easily as ritual invocation reflecting a more general fear and suspicion. Vocally and physically, the moment "reads" the same in either case (no one, not even Léopold, who must be gulping hard, can blow his or her cover at this point), but for the performer it's one of the many forks in the path that will affect the playing of everything that follows. So Eléazar must decide.

Second: this little section presents a rhetorical opportunity that neither of our tenors seizes—one that suggests something about Eléazar's attitude and manner, and about how some earlier tenors may have perceived the character. The page in question (p. 166 in the score) is laid out in horizontals that gradually climb the octaves between Gs; it's terraced, so to speak. As it approaches its peak, Eléazar repeats his plea for God's wrath *"sur le parjure/ ou sur l'impie"* ("upon the perjurer/or upon the impious") with forceful lines whose last syllables plunge from the upper F to the lower G, where they land on downbeats. Where should the emphasis fall? The music's layout and the normal word accent suggests those final syllables—*"sur le parJURE/ou sur l'imPIE"* (there's no way to sensibly render this stress in English). And, no doubt, the image behind the gesture is of heavenly punishment falling, like the voice, on the heads of transgressors. It's hard for a tenor, though, to project that emphasis while dropping down into his lower-middle range. (Caruso, or one of the good Heldentenors, might have managed it.) Shicoff and Martinelli both give a little kick to the short penultimate syllable, especially the first one (*"par-"*), with its plosive consonant. So the emphasis is created by taking off on the upbeat to hit what can be seen as the "meaningful" word, but against its accent: *"sur le PARjure/ou sur L'IMpie"*—an effect, certainly, but of what might be called the International Conventional type, and just a touch petulant.

Halévy has something else to offer. He's marked the *"sur"* and the *"ou"* with this instruction: *sfzp*. This means a *sforzando* attack followed by a quick pullback to *piano*. On the upper F, this would not even have to be loud to seize one's attention.* The *piano* would be of the held-in, suspenseful sort. The sudden drop would land more cleanly and with greater contrast. The second time, it would act as a springboard for the leap up to the outcry of "*Grand Dieu.*" Of these recitational choices, this offers the most intriguing set of possibilities, though it's technically harder—and there's the rub. It also gives us a hint of the old-time orator with his bag of rhetorical surprises, wagging an upraised finger as he proclaims, "*UPON* the perjurer/OR the impious," and then, suddenly: "*GREAT LORD!*" Like all such gestures in all good operatic writing, it's a bit of character description as much as a musical and vocal articulation—in fact, the character description is the reason for the articulation. Though neither of our tenors takes Halévy up on his suggestion, this page leaves no doubt that, as we would expect from an artist of his time, Martinelli is the more overtly rhetorical singer of the two: the format and timbre of the voice itself; the force of his attack; the relished rolling of the r's; and the emphatic *stentato* accenting of every syllable as the solo ends, are evidence enough.

Now Eléazar rises and, to a flowing melody that carries him a bit higher as he sings of God's promise to the children of Moses, distributes the unleavened bread, bringing us to one of the offenses that melodramatic convention regularly commits against our actualist sensibility: Léopold is supposed to fling away his portion, unseen by anyone save Rachel and us, and Rachel is supposed to exclaim, "What am I seeing!", unheard by anyone save us. Fortunately, it isn't our problem to solve and needn't detain us, since Eléazar has only to remain oblivious to it.† He proceeds directly into the lovely *cavatine*, "*Dieu, que ma voix tremblante.*" Except that in the San Francisco performance, he doesn't, for it's omitted altogether. So we must insert Martinelli's

---

* In the vocal score, this indication is marked in the accompaniment, as are most such throughout. In some similar cases, the voice is meant to hold steady against an orchestral effect, usually to make the point that the character is maintaining an outer cool while the orchestra tells us what's going on inside (like the famous "Orestes is lying" moment in Gluck's *Iphigénie en Tauride*. But that won't work here: unless horribly exaggerated, the string *sforzando* wouldn't register against the tenor's F strongly enough to tell us anything. I think the marking clearly includes the singer.

† But, to note the prerequisites for belief: Léopold cannot possibly throw away the bread—someone will find it later. He must deftly conceal it on his person, in a pocket or the costume equivalent. And Rachel must have a large enough voice and good enough technique to render "*Que vois-je!*" in a tensile mezza-voce that projects vividly but is credible as an aside.

1927 studio recording.* The *cavatine* is not quite a great hit tune like "*Rachel*" or "*Si la rigueur*," but it's an entirely respectable melody launched with an arpeggiated accompaniment in triplets that is set off by a nervous little figure for the violas. Eléazar prays that his voice may ascend so that an angered God may answer the cry for life from His unhappy people. In a contemporary family, even a devout one, it's the sort of speech that might have the rest of the family rolling their eyes as Dad holds forth—we haven't even eaten yet! Not this family in this time, though.

Both tenors sing the piece well and honestly, Martinelli containing his dramatic instrument to the point of squeezing the diphthong on "*Dieu*" and "*cieux*," with peculiar results, while Shicoff opens the same diphthong almost to "uh" and leans into his more lyrical voice for maximum authority. A telling contrast occurs in the *a piacere* bars that bridge back to the opening melody and tempo (bar 134, p. 171). Martinelli, after the ringing A-flat on "*vi-e*," brings the voice down to a longheld *mezza-voce* F (on the last syllable of "*irrité*") that melts into a perfect portamento down to middle C, then carries on without a new breath into the return of the main theme. The purity of tone and evenness of line, the absolute control of diminuendo and portamento, are marks of a greatvoiced master, and the unruffled smoothness with which the voice glides through the *passaggio* in either direction is due not only to his "gathered" treatment of vowels (shared by Shicoff), but to the presence of clear resonance—core—in the lower range. Thus, while the balance between registral families changes almost imperceptibly, no shifting of gears is required. The singer (and the character) is entirely, and seeming effortlessly, in charge of the impression he wishes to create.

Shicoff handles the same moment well in terms of his own vocal structure. But his darker, looser midrange adjustment translates into a trace of huskiness as he approaches these notes at restrained volume. He produces a sustained heady *piano* on the F, a lovely effect, though not the same as Martinelli's oldstyle *mezza-voce*. But then he breaks for the breath, putting a full stop to the phrase rather than leading on. His choice is perfectly legitimate. It can be defended as more modern, less "showy and elaborate in style," than Martinelli's. The stop can be heard as a dramatic pause. Had he executed the portamento and continuation, the effect would not have been the same

---

* This number, like Eudoxie's aria, was evidently dropped at the time of the premiere and, though subsequently restored by Duprez, did not make its way into the early published material. (See Hallman, p. 184.) The fact that Martinelli recorded it, and that it is included in the 1919 Fred Rullman libretto that the Met issued (as is "*Dieu m'éclaire*," but not Eudoxie's numbers or many other sections), would lead one to believe that Caruso and Martinelli sang it in their Met performances.

in any case, because the two voices' integration is not the same.* So his way is probably the right one for him. But Martinelli's, as rendered with his voice and technique, is the more transporting. It carries us farther into the grand opera realm where *La Juive* was meant to dwell.

But isn't this more ongoingness? Why is continuance right here, but not in the cut version of the prayer, or in Fleming's phrasing of "The Trees on the Mountain"? For three reasons: it is an acknowledged style element of the genre to which it belongs, especially at the bridge from a B section back to the return of A (the form of the *cavatine* is ABAB, with variants—this is a spot that earlier might have been marked by a flourish or even a mini-cadenza); it makes an active *event* of the transition; and it is executed with command by a greatvoiced artist, so it truly lands. It is continuance, but it isn't ongoingness.

At the end of the piece, both tenors interpolate one of the sustained open-vowel high B-flats mentioned earlier ("*à son pè-E-re irrité*"), both to good, though ever different, effect.

As the quiet postlude of the *cavatine* dies (and then the applause that follows), heavy knocking is heard. The terrified Jews scramble to extinguish the candles and hide all evidence of service. Voices off announce members of the imperial entourage. Eléazar orders Rachel and the others to leave the room, but detains "Samuel" for his "strong and courageous arm." Léopold retreats to a far corner, takes up his palette and brushes, and turns his back to the room. Fearfully, Eléazar opens the street door, to admit none other than the dazzling Princess Eudoxie, in search of a gift suitable for ceremonial presentation to her beloved, heroic, just-returned husband. "Who's that fellow over there?", she asks. Eléazar answers that he's a famous artist, expert with gold and vellum, whose talent he values. But if she'd like him to leave? "Not really. My visit's not a secret," she says, smiling.

And so begins a delicious *scène à trois*, whose effect rests on the interplay between, on the one hand, a charming, witty musical surface and a dramatic situation that would not be out of place in one of Halévy's many comic operas (like *L'Éclair*, which had its premiere over at the Comique a few months after *La Juive*'s), and on the other the far more consequential context in which it is played out here. The scene also raises intriguing, and potentially troublesome, acting possibilities for Eléazar. They have to do with archetype, stereotype,

---

* This is independent of the question of calibre. Think of Bjoerling, whose voice was certainly not of Martinelli's size, but was illuminated throughout with a clear sonority, a comparable purity of tone and vowel, evenness of line and vibrato, with a more liquid, elastic touch and greater timbral loveliness. Of course, in his day even these gifts would not have presumed to qualify him for roles like Eléazar.

and modeling. They arise immediately, with Eudoxie's entrance. Her smile enables Eléazar to relax a little. He smiles back. Nonetheless, he wonders, the emperor's valets, his livery—? "They're mine," she says. "I'm his niece."

"Heavens, what an honor for me! The Princess Eudoxie!" And (says the text) he prostrates himself. The Princess is actually a sweetheart—a casually patronizing one, perhaps, but still, a sweetheart: "Yes, yes," she says, smiling again, "Please do get up." And as he rises, Eudoxie gets to the point of this afterhours intrusion: "You possess, they say, a magnificent jewel." A rich customer! Eléazar is right into the sales pitch. Yes, a fabulous item, which he intended for a royal, a sainted relic once worn by the Emperor Constantine—once worn, I say, by Constantine himself! (I paraphrase, in the spirit of the music's emphasis.)

It's superb. We're talking about an item over 1100 years old that supposedly belonged to the very emperor who made Christianity the state religion. How gullible can this Christian girl be? And how gloatingly deceptive, how fawningly ingratiating, can the performer of Eléazar allow his behavior to be? Within the field bound by the given circumstances and the internal evidence of the text, there's a wide range of choice, from dignified and grudgingly correct to downright servile, that can be justified, artistically speaking. Certainly Eléazar has a tradeface, a manner he easily and instantly assumes when dealing with a customer. And certainly this must be different from the resistant public manner he shows in Act I and from the private one, with its humbly prayerful and oratorical facets, he has so far shown in Act II. In this moment, it is informed by the tension and fear and relief that have gone before; by anticipation of a big sale and a chance to trick the hated Christians; by discovery of the customer's rank; and by the rapid succession of all these—for manner is usually intensified when suddenly switched on.

But what *is* the manner? Since we are presently listening and only imagining the physical action (the act of prostration, for instance), we harken to what the voices may be sending us. In Martinelli's case, a fair amount. We surely pick up some of the tension in the orders he issues after the knock, and a nervous rapidity in the unaccompanied lines regarding the "famous artist." I don't hear much of the returned smile as he inquires about valets and livery, but there's a convincing outburst at "*Oh ciel—!*", and then a well-timed pause (not just a count of three beats, but time enough to get back to his feet) before his quiet "*et quel honneur pour moi! la princesse Eudoxie!*", which sounds sincerely respectful.

From Shicoff, what we get for most of this sequence is, literally, nothing, because a substantial cut is made, from Rachel's "*Oh, Je n'ose!*"* to Eléazar's "*Oh*

---

* ("Oh, I don't dare!") To open the window and look out, that is. So Eléazar must do it himself.

ciel! Quel honneur pour moi!" Again, there's no modulatory problem and nothing of any musical importance is excised. It's just a little scene to play. However,
this little scene includes: seeing who it is (the imperial escort); clearing the
room (with sufficient time to hurriedly do it); Rachel's under-the-breath line,
"I must speak with you this very instant, Samuel!" (because she's seen him
conceal the bread) and Léopold's thickheaded reply ("Ah, what great happiness!"); Eléazar's detaining of "Samuel"; Eudoxie's entrance as an unknown
personage and Léopold's horrified realization that the visitor is his wife; the
exchange about "the artist," highlighting his presence and Eudoxie's awareness of it; the exchange of smiles; and finally, Eléazar's surprise at her identity.
Everything that sets up the situation, in other words. Musically, the cut is piddling. Dramatically, it's disastrous. In the Vienna performance, Eléazar recognizes the Princess off the bat, as he would a neighbor dropping by for that cup
of sugar. Dots aren't just left unconnected, they're erased. When Shicoff does
sing, it's in purely informational tones—"what an honor for me!" could as well
be the pro forma opening of some remarks at a conference.

As Eléazar describes the "magnificent jewel," the differences in "approach"
between the two tenors become increasingly clear. But Renée Fleming's greatvoiced v. "highly detailed" comparison does not apply here, for Martinelli is
not only the one deploying a great voice, but the one offering far more interpretive detail. He's a "colorist reader." He differentiates between the bright
attack on *"une chaine incrustée"* and a subdued, reverential tone for *"une sainte
relique."* When he first utters the name of *"l'Empereur Constantin,"* he slows the
bar noticeably (the conductor, Gaetano Merola, and his orchestra accommodate easily) and leans into the nasal diphthongs of the emperor's name (*"on,"*
"an," and especially the final open *"in"*), which leads him into the exclamatory
repetition that puts the seal on his little presentation. It's been (to borrow a
term from the French Baroque) a *petit air*, a development of softer and louder,
faster and slower, and a distinct episode within the scene.

Shicoff does none of these things. He and his conductor (Simone Young) set
a quicker tempo, which they do not vary. (This affects the orchestral commentary, too—the pizzicato and the little woodwind figures seem less pointed.)
The touches of *portamento*, the variations in dynamics, tempo, and vowel colorations employed by Martinelli, are all absent. Shicoff renders everything
in firm tone and musicianly note values, and that's all. He would not in any
case be expected to inflect his wordnotes exactly as Martinelli did, or, with
his instrument, make exactly the same effect. But this is also clear: he is not
trying to do the same thing. The action of describing, by vocal means, the jewel's attributes as part of his "come-on" to a customer, which Martinelli took
as a singingacting given, is simply not a part of his strategy. Several things

about this difference come to mind—things relating to singer/conductor assumptions, to the desirability of description and of creating effects, to oral tradition, and to stereotyping—which I'll hold in abeyance for more general consideration. But we should make note that for the ear, Martinelli paints the far more vivid picture, one that arrests attention and lodges in memory.

The terzett develops as an alternation of brief, playful transactional events (inspecting the jewel, setting the price, signing and sealing the agreement, Eléazar promising to deliver the jewel to the Princess at the palace on the morrow) with more extended duet and trio sections in which the characters express their feelings. Eudoxie's are undisguised. To a tune of great charm, pointed by trills and flourishes, and finished with a little upward tail that carries a couple of beats past the expected phrase endings, she prattles along of her love and pride for a husband whose "heart beats only for me." She's all out there—first to Eléazar, then for any who may listen. The two tenors sing to themselves. Léopold, over in his artist's corner, picks up Eudoxie's melody, and some of her words, to lament the blow that is about to fall on this trusting soul, and to sing of his own pain and remorse. Eléazar sings that his fear and trembling has turned to joy at the thought of the "ducats of gold that I love" and the pleasure of fooling "these Christians—I hate them all, these enemies of God." He revels and gloats.

The last trio section, naturally, builds to a full-voice climax topped by Eudoxie's brilliant roulades and high Bs. Operatic ensemble convention allows us to accept that Léopold and Eléazar are not overheard by Eudoxie. But the singers are supposed to help us out by shading their voices in a way that lets us know they are singing to themselves. Once that's established, they can sing out more, and we'll go along with it. Still, it's good if a tint of the "to himself" remains.* Again, though, that is technically difficult. One imagines that Nourrit excelled at exactly this sort of nuance, and was able to "contain" the tone at the upper border of his full voice. Duprez probably brought his "*voix sombrée*" into play—but that works only if there is clear, secure positioning under it. The tensile *mezza-voce*, possibly shaded with a bit of the *sombre* if the singer can do that without losing tonal focus, is the answer. Shicoff, owing to the limited span of volume and color at his disposal, captures a modest suggestion of the situation with some sneakiness in his word inflection. Martinelli, with his fully extended dramatic tenor that shows no fleck of the *sombre*, and nine years along from his eloquent

---

* This is especially important for Eléazar, since he's in Eudoxie's immediate vicinity. His line is marked "*à part*" ("aside"), while Léopold's just reminds us that he's "*à droite*" ("on the right," as far away from Eudoxie as possible). That original design idea of a separate room "*à gauche*" would come in handy here.

midcareer recording of the *cavatine*, nonetheless possesses at least working remnants of the oldtime half-voice, as well as articulatory crispness, and gets some of the "aside" feeling while continuing to dominate the ensemble, into which Shicoff's voice sometimes retreats.* The scene ends with an exuberant orchestral postlude as the gleeful Eléazar shows the joyful Eudoxie to the door and (according to the stage directions) into the street, where he remands her to the imperial escort.

Rachel pokes her head into the room, and while Eléazar is seeing Eudoxie off, there is a quick, pained exchange between her and Léopold, in which he overrides her ever-stronger suspicions by swearing he will die if she refuses to see him later. Eléazar re-enters, and immediately senses the furtiveness between the two. In an episode cut from the Vienna/Met production and all the recordings (and absent from the old Met/Rullman libretto), Eléazar again detains Léopold to join in the evening devotions, which turn out to be a re-run of the act's opening prayer, with Eléazar's warning about treason and perfidy reinforced by a half-step's elevation, and Léopold given high, embellished (but still "to himself") lines to confide that the Jews' prayers trouble him, and that he fears that it is upon his impious head that their jealous God's wrath will fall. During the postlude, Eléazar, observing closely, sees Léopold to the door, kisses Rachel goodnight, and retires.

There follows Rachel's romance, which (as Germanically inclined critics of the early Nineteen Hundreds enjoyed pointing out) recalls Agathe's analogous solo scene in *Der Freischütz*. She voices her terror at what awaits with Léopold's return, and at thoughts of betraying her father and her religion. Opening the window, she also mentions the oppressive sense of an approaching storm. This suggests that the authors saw the act as a gradually developing Rossinian storm scene—not an interlude, as in *Barbiere* or numerous other instances, but in parallel with the onstage build-up of the characters' raging passions, as in *Rigoletto*. This aria, first sung by Falcon, must have left a deep impression in the hands of the great dramatic sopranos who were habitually cast as Rachel (in New York, Amalie Materna,

---

* Since these are both live performances (and apparently without any admixture of other sources—see Simone Young's essay on the edition and recording in the RCA booklet), the singers obviously move in and out of favorable mike range, and the newer recording, though "better" and less noise-beset, is not always the more favorable in this respect— Shicoff is seriously penalized, for instance, when he goes upstage to ask who's knocking. But there can't be much doubt that, whatever the differences in stage position and recording technology, they account for only a fraction of the difference in presence and calibre of these two instruments.

Marianne Brandt, Lilli Lehmann, Ponselle, and Lawrence; in Chicago, Rosa Raisa and Frida Leider).*

Léopold returns and, pressed by Rachel, confesses that he is Christian. After a long silence, she laments having given herself to him, thus disrespecting her father and her honor, and forgetting that she was also outraging a vengeful God. He replies that for his part, in loving her he forgot his destiny, fortune, and glory—that all these, and all his happiness, are now in her. But his Christian law, she points out, will condemn them both to death simply for being lovers (and, still unaware of his identity, she doesn't yet know the half of it). In one of those hyperbolic exchanges that would be taken as clear evidence of insanity in any world but that of *Novecento* Romanticism, Léopold sweeps them both off their feet with the notion that, Jew or Christian, their fates are one, and they must flee that very moment to some "obscure retreat" where a mutual destiny awaits them in the heavens.† They are about to do so when Eléazar re-enters.

Eléazar asks where Rachel and Léopold are going, and whether they suppose there's a place on earth where they can escape a father's curse. A brief "frozen by terror" terzett, unremarkable of its sort, ensues. Eléazar banishes Léopold from the house, and tells him that if he were not a child of Israel, he would strike him a mortal blow. Léopold defiantly reveals that he is a Christian, and Eléazar is restrained from stabbing him only by Rachel's intervention. It is here that the choice made early in the act concerning Eléazar's possible suspicions of Léopold (see p. 462) has its consequence, for both the bitterness with which Eléazar voices his sense of betrayal at the attempted flight ("*Et toi que j'accueilis*") and his outcry of "*Chrétien!*") have much more behind them if these offenses come as thunderbolts of surprise. Shicoff and Martinelli each inflect these lines with strong intent, with Merola's slightly

---

* In the San Francisco performances, Elisabeth Rethberg is the Rachel. It's a mark of how far we've come from the late-E-19 standard that when Rethberg first took the role in New York (after Ponselle, then Easton), she was considered good, but on the light side for it. With her beautiful soprano of full *jugendlich* calibre, firmly supported *mezza-voce*, total command of both range extremes and closely knit integration of everything in between, and the sense of easy authority granted by these attributes, she offers a substantially more complete realization than any of the estimable sopranos on the modern recordings. Oddly, her rendition comes across a bit better on an Eddie Smith LP (ANNA 1040—same performance, I'm sure) than on the generally superior Guild CDs.

† In the course of this duet, Rachel asks if Léopold does not hear "the storm that roars in fury in the flaming air?". This obviously is meant to carry a double meaning, and since Rachel is the only one to notice the storm, I suppose it is possible to interpret it as a purely subjective event. If so, it would be a first in the history of Romantic stagecraft. I think the moment at the window (see above) establishes that Nature, and not just human nature, is involved.

slower tempo always helping Martinelli to land the recitational events more firmly. "*Chrétien!*" brings another moment of rhetorical contrast. One might think that Martinelli would be content to let his voice do the work by simply singing the word on pitch (A-flats) *a piena voce* with his customary strong attack, while Shicoff might feel the need for some extramusical assistance. But it's Shicoff who just sings the notes, and Martinelli who explodes with a bit of unpitched theatrical declamation. I believe I would have preferred Shicoff's choice with Martinelli's voice—but one has to have been there to really know.

Now Rachel sings a melting plea, whose English horn obbligato prefigures, and seals a tone-color family bond with, her father's deepest emotional confession in Act IV. In her arioso's first verse, Rachel asks Eléazar to understand that her lover (she calls him "*mon époux,*" in fact) was not born into the laws of their faith, but that "his eyes may one day open to the light." In the second, always cut even though its argument is far more compelling, she invokes the mother's love she never knew, saying that she hears her mother's voice joining her prayer and telling her, "he shall be your husband!"

Think of the emotional complexity of this for Eléazar. He knows the woman of whom Rachel sings was not really her mother; the lifelong deception is there. But she *was* his beloved wife, the mother of his two dead sons, so the whole immensely sad backstory is also there. He hates all Christians, including the traitorous one standing before him, but he loves Rachel. And as with all things that move him for ill or for good, he believes her words are sent from God. In the little trio section that follows Rachel's solo, this complexity of high emotion produces one of the vocal flights conceived for Nourrit. "It's God who inspires her/her grief tears at me," sings Eléazar, except that in French there's a rhyme: "*C'est Dieu qui l'inspire/sa douleur me déchire.*" The setting is very characteristic of Halévy's ensemble writing throughout the score, with the solo voices taking turns at weaving figurations (Rachel and Eléazar often together, as if taking up the English horn's mournful patterns), meant to make the words of each stand out at some point. And on the second syllable of "*douleur*" (one of those heady diphthongs), Eléazar soars up and over the C and then, after returning to the middle C, takes the scale back up from D-flat to A-flat on the second syllable of "*déchire.*"

Throughout these four bars (p. 253), Eléazar is in effect singing "above" Rachel, near the top of the co-ordinations he is using, while she echoes his pattern, but comfortably within her upper-middle range. And while their note values are identical, the bar with his high grouping is phrased longer than hers, clearly implying that he carries through with a stronger impulse. Undoubtedly, Nourrit used his strong *voix mixte* for the high excursion—separating himself from, but not dominating, the other voices—then staying in

full voice for the run up to A-flat, making that the actual climax of the statement. It is probably needless to say that no postwar tenor attempts the high
figuration; Shicoff even declines the upward scale to A-flat. But Martinelli
takes it all on. He and Merola broaden the bar, and Martinelli launches a
clear, gleaming group with an on-the-button C, and then a contained ascent
to A-flat. The effect is startling, especially inasmuch as one would not have
supposed the Martinelli of 1936 at all comfortable with such a figure, and
it seems unlikely that Caruso would have established it at the Met, unless
he made use of the powerful falsetto he deployed for the D-flat in the "*Cujus
Animam*" of Rossini's *Stabat Mater*. This is surely not what Halévy and
Nourrit had in mind—the *voix mixte* would have preserved an ensemble feel,
and we would have heard Eléazar's C and Rachel's A-flat in balance, whereas
Martinelli takes possession of the moment undisputed. That's not all bad,
though. Eléazar's agony is the crucial reaction here: Rachel is only continuing with her plea, to repetitions of the same words, while Léopold is kept on
the inner line, saying for the most part that *he's* torn, too. Martinelli's voice,
with its irreducible core and sense of held-in compression, often suggests
emotion reluctantly pulled from the gut. Not least, the gesture is also that of
a great tenor accomplishing a feat, a performance excitation of the sort that
draws repeat customers and keeps a repertory opera alive. The feat is not
purely musical or virtuosic. It implies a character who, though not a romantic protagonist, has heroic stature. It touches on an archetype.*

The conclusion of this section gives us another contrast between a contemporary understanding of what's expressive and that of late E-19. Rachel
and Eléazar take a beautiful, slow upward turn together before settling onto
their final notes (an F for Eléazar, the tonic D-flat for Rachel, with Léopold
joining her an octave below). The Vienna threesome executes this with musicianly care and balance, with Shicoff sustaining a well-controlled, blendable
mezzo-piano. Then they cut off, as written, for the orchestral postlude. The
San Francisco singers, though, hold these notes right through the postlude
to the last orchestral chord, swelling and diminishing with the orchestra.
They also maintain excellent balance—but Martinelli glints through as these
larger-format voices swell. The effect is not as modestly pretty as Vienna's,
but it's far more satisfying, far more a consummation. It is born not of attentive obedience to the text, but of the oral tradition of greatvoiced singers.

---

* Of the Duprezian dramatic tenors on record, Slezak and Urlus are the only ones I can
imagine rendering this moment with something of the oldstyle effect. Escalaïs (for sure)
and Vezzani (possibly) could have provided thrills of the full-voiced variety, and with a
French linguistic set.

Rachel's plea proves irresistible. Eléazar cedes to her tears and hopes that, like him, Heaven will withhold its wrath and decree Léopold Rachel's husband. "Never!", answers Léopold, and after the appropriate shock-and-awe expostulations, Eléazar launches a crackling trio finale by pronouncing his anathema and God's everlasting curse on the erstwhile "Samuel," who protests that such a marriage is a blasphemy and that he mustn't be questioned further. He bids Rachel a final farewell, and all three take up the propulsive theme of Eléazar's anathema, starting at *piano* and building a continuous crescendo to the end, in best Rossinian manner. Léopold flings himself out the door into the street and Rachel, vowing to discover his true identity, seizes the cloak he has left behind and dashes after him, as Eléazar collapses in despair. This would be the natural moment for the storm to break in full power, the spectacle enhanced by the set's exterior surround, as the orchestra barrels through the anathema theme to some concluding E-minor chords. On this image of high Romantic melodrama, the Act II curtain falls.

In both the performances under consideration, this finale is redacted so as to deprive Léopold of his solo lines and shorten the development of the scene. Shicoff and his colleagues certainly sing through it with strong intent. But their attractive lyric voices (and the VPO's lovely, not-quite-urgent playing) do not lift us far enough above the feeling of a jolly number of the "What a predicament!" sort—Rossinian in the wrong sense. This is an ensemble not of comedic exasperation but of love-and-death conflict, and the Vienna performance leaves us to conclude that the music is a tad light—how seriously, really, can we take this? The San Francisco performance, for all its sonic deficiencies, more than suggests what's missing. All the voices are bigger, and they sound as if they're competing, not collaborating.* As we might expect, Martinelli is the most aggressive competitor. His vicious attacks on the A-naturals of the repetitions of *"blasphême"* are hair-raising. When Rethberg gets into the clear, her ascents to the top vault out as they must have in *Aïda* or *Ballo* (for there's no hint here of the whinnying quality that besets some of her high notes in Met broadcasts of the seasons immediately following this). But she's not in the clear very often, because Martinelli throws in an unwritten high B to double hers just before the start of *"Chrétien sacrilège,"* and another at the end. Unlike the earlier C, these notes are sustained, and as so often with the later Martinelli, their lack of vibrato gives them a howling

---

* I include even Hans Clemens, the Léopold, in this evaluation. In this country, he sang mostly secondary parts in German operas (the *Tannhäuser* Walter, David, Jacquino, et al.), and he clearly did not have the upper extension of the more recent Léopolds. But up through B-flat, he shows stronger tone, and at the important dramatic junctures, a more engaged emotional response, than any of them.

sound that suggests three things: a character in pain, an aging superwarrior making a courageous but arguably ill-considered, last stand, and a presumption of performer prerogative that has until quite recently attached to artists of established stature. These notes aren't pretty, they aren't collegial, and they aren't in the text. They leave a residue of excitement and disturbance, and, again, a touch of the heroic, as the act ends.*

Between the Act II finale and the point at which we can next take up our comparison, the following events occur:

· Rachel, who had evidently followed Léopold through the streets to the doors of the palace, gains admittance to Eudoxie's presence in the guise of a "humble poor girl, unknown, a stranger," and begs to be allowed to join the Princess's slave entourage. Eudoxie, baffled but compassionate, agrees.

· With the full court assembled in great pomp to honor Léopold's victory, Eléazar appears and, as promised, delivers the precious chain to Eudoxie, who is about to bestow it on her husband when "slave girl" Rachel, suddenly seeing the whole picture, bursts out with her denunciation of him, and confesses their affair. Amid an extended ensemble finale, Brogni pronounces official anathema on Léopold, Rachel, and Eléazar. Their cases will be laid before the Council.

· Eudoxie visits the condemned Rachel in the anteroom of the Council Chamber. The promise of her own life ended, she implores Rachel to recant her denunciation of Léopold, whom they both still love despite his betrayals.† Rachel at first bitterly resists, but at the sound of the drum that summons Léopold to the Council, she relents, and vows to plead for him.

· Brogni tells Rachel that he hopes her testimony will save both Léopold's head and her own. But she replies that hers alone will fall. Then, in a bit of "blood will tell" foreshadowing, Brogni says that in his soul a secret voice bids him to speak for her and defend her—what is this secret voice? She

---

* If you can pull your attention away from Martinelli's great yawps, you will hear that Rethberg is holding her own. Her voice would certainly dominate the contemporary cast, as Falcon's must have the original one, no matter what Nourrit may have done. In my judgment, the doubled B at the start is entirely appropriate, but the end of the scene should belong to Rachel.

† In the early planning of the scenario, Hallman says (pp. 226-227), a suicide aria for Eudoxie was envisioned. That went by the boards, but at the end of this scene Eudoxie hopes for "an early end to her misery." "Oh no! I shall die alone, farewell! Live in peace!", Rachel replies.

joins him in wonderment at this sentiment, and as the guards lead her away, he promises to watch over her. Brogni realizes that only one hope remains for the life of the young woman to whom he feels mysteriously attached. He summons Eléazar.

It is here (No. 21 in the score, p. 415) that the Vitaphone sequence begins. The sonics are atrocious, the cuts and simplifications even more egregious than on the latterday recordings.* Still, it helps us extend our knowledge of the last greatvoiced portrayal of Eléazar, and its earlier date finds Martinelli in somewhat springier vocal form. To continue with our mind's-eye, "acting-with-the-voice" impressions, I will first consider the audio-only versions of this crucial scene.†

Brogni tells Eléazar that his daughter is at this moment before the Council, which is about to pronounce her sentence. Then, in two pages clearly meant to show the virtuosic descriptive powers of a potent French deep bass voice, he says that only if Eléazar abjures his faith will Rachel escape a fiery death. "What are you proposing?" asks Eléazar, as a catchy rising-and-falling motif sneaks in underneath. "Renounce the faith of my fathers?" The tone of Eléazar's icy refusal is better conveyed by Martinelli, not through any interpretive merit, but simply by the power and rocklike timbre of his instrument. But Shicoff's version of the final *"Plûtot mourir!"* (after another silly two-line cut) at least allows him the indicated cadential run up to the A, which Martinelli ignores in favor of a plain ending in the lower octave.

There follows a brief theological exchange, in which Brogni points out that the vaunted God of Jacob seems not to have done too well by his children, and Eléazar answers that as He once empowered the Maccabees, He will soon again render his sons "free and triumphant." And on the first of these words (*"libre"*), there is written another Nourritian flourish—the first in a series of triplets, mounting to the high B-natural. The bar is *"a piacere,"* so singers have latitude to show us how these triplets carry Eléazar away into his dream of freedom and triumph. Nourrit could have taken advantage of the penetrating quality of the *"i"* vowel in his strong, "free" head-voice mix, perhaps taking a *tenuto* on the B-natural, then dashing through the remaining triplets, and/

---

* My assumption is that many of these were to shorten the scene for movie audiences or to accommodate the limited capabilities of Louis D'Angelo, the comprimario bass who takes on Brogni, and that they were not representative of the Met's performing version. Some of the cut material is present in the Rullman libretto.

† Fair warning to anyone who has ferreted out Eddie Smith's Asco LPs: Having transferred the Victor disc of *"Dieu que ma voix tremblante"* a half-step high, they now present the soundtrack of this scene a half-step low, with predictable results in both cases. The Encore DVD is correctly pitched, though with much hazy approximation.

or holding the next-to-last syllable of "*tri-OM-phants*" for a doubly conclusive effect. Duprez, I would suppose, took full advantage of the moment to pin back some ears with (given the tuning difference and his half-step transposition) a brilliant, full-throated, slightly sharp B-flat. Of all the opportunities for *forte* high notes, written and unwritten, afforded by what we have of his Eléazar, this is the only one Martinelli declines, probably because the vowel so easily constricts at that altitude in full voice. Both he and Shicoff latch onto the friendly overtones of "*i*" on G#, hang on a moment, then complete the triplets without much further ado (though Martinelli at least gives them some veristic emphasis).

The last syllable of Eléazar's "*triomphants!*" lands on a downbeat that kicks off a fairly extended marchlike duet. The section is invariably deleted, and is among the most understandable of the cuts, for it tramps along to a bedraggled little tune that does not bear repetition, yet will be repeated, inescapably, at the scene's conclusion. However, we must not ignore what this first statement of the duet is meant to convey. Eléazar welcomes the mounting flame as the means whereby he will fulfill his destiny, and he and Rachel will ascend to heaven. Brogni, though, trembles at the fate that awaits them, and prays that God will dispel Eléazar's fantasy of triumph and salvation.

The duet over, Brogni asks if Eléazar really means to die. "Yes, that is my hope!" is the reply. "But," Eléazar continues (and the rising-and-falling motif returns), "I want first of all to avenge myself upon some Christian—and that shall be you!" And now, in a recitative that gradually raises tension with pitch, and with pauses of varied length, he springs his emotional trap: "When the Neapolitans/invaded Rome/you saw your holdings pillaged/and your house prey to the flames/your wife dying/and your beloved daughter/ just given life/dying at your side. . ." Brogni bursts in, protesting the cruelty of this evocation of the time when all was lost to him. Eléazar presses relentlessly on. No, he tells Brogni, you did not lose all. For a Jew saved your daughter, a Jew lifted her living into his arms, and this Jew—is known to me! Brogni begs for the Jew's name and whereabouts, but Eléazar tells him he will never learn it.

This recitation, in which the balance of power in the opera's central conflict is abruptly reversed, is written to the strengths of the "first dramatic tenor." Eléazar's lines are marked "*récit,*" the bars lying empty beneath the voice except for a brief *ppp* comment in the strings each time Eléazar arrives at a downbeat. The actor, his sense of dramatic declamation built on the tradition of French classical verse plays, is in charge, with the impact of the passage determined by his inflectional subtlety, his timing of the pauses, his instinct for when to hold back or push ahead.* Brogni's interruption is "*mesuré*" (i.e., *a tempo*, conducted) and more fully accompanied, but after Eléazar's "*Non, vous n'avez pas tout perdu*" (marked "*à demi-voix et avec force*"—and how would that be accomplished save through the tensile *mezza-voce*?), the recitative resumes, the orchestral figure now nudged up to *pp*, and reinforced by a sustained low E from the horns.

In terms of mind's-eye characterization, this is one of Shicoff's finest moments—the moment, indeed, when he begins to exert a special sort of grip on the listener. Not that Martinelli is by any means ineffective; by the standards of traditional greatvoiced declamation, he is more so. As he begins to lay his trap ("*Un Juif avait sauvé ta fille*," etc.), he enlists his full inflectional stretch of open vowels and tangy nasal diphthongs, his full sinewy webbing of support, to build the suspense, and when he springs it ("*Tu ne le sauras pas!*"), the voice's leap to the upper G-sharp is electric. In the same passage, however, Shicoff shows how the lesser-voiced modern singeractor can create at least an equivalent emotional impact: straightened tone and an inward, less proclamatory dynamic that discloses less, that conveys the feel of something of heavy import being held back, of the coil before the pounce, so that the release at "*Tu ne le sauras pas!*" is, if anything, more devastating.

Brogni collapses at Eléazar's feet, and launches a quite heartrending plea of submission and supplication, its expanding and contracting halves divided by a cry of "*Ma fille!*", and concluding with despair-laden repetitions of "Say one word, or I die, I die before your eyes!" Eléazar takes up Brogni's melody, a fourth higher, to tell him that if he (Eléazar) can brave death, he can certainly resist his enemy's tears, and that his secret will die with him. The section is one of many in Romantic opera to present personal conflict as rhetorical disputation: one party takes up the other's theme and reproduces it almost exactly, but in order to top it (in this case literally, with raised pitch) and win the argument. We could almost call it repartée. Brogni's "*Ma fille!*" becomes Eléazar's "*Ta fille* (marked "*dolce*")," and Brogni's "And what, could it be that she breathes?" is now "Alas, it's very true, your daughter breathes" (but of course, she's Eléazar's daughter, too). Unfortunately, none of the principals on these recordings does much to convey the emotional depth and extremity of this exchange—they just sing on through with a kind of generalized energy. Martinelli's Eléazar is more triumphalist, Shicoff's more contemptuous.

---

* As in all good operatic writing, the notated time values, including those of the rests, are themselves derived from a sense of what an accomplished actor will do with the speech. Halévy was writing down what he imagined Nourrit was about to do. Or (it's entirely plausible, given what we know) Nourrit may have in effect dictated the passage, or even written it himself. Thus, if a "good musician" with clear French pronunciation sings it in strict time, he will get the idea across. An idea is not a fulfillment, however.

Now tenor and bass join in the repeat of their marchlike duo, and this time there's no deleting it, because the scene does have to reach an end. And had it been allowed its original sounding, we would now sense its structural purpose: a repetition between whose statements the relationship of the two characters has altered, and the psychological climate has changed. The second statement contains variations, though they probably don't register much with an audience until the few bars of coda at the end. More important, it has a different tone and is heard in a different light. This is especially true for Brogni. Eléazar is even farther into his exaltation compounded by vengeance and martyrdom. But the Cardinal is traumatized: "Oh God, if this isn't a dream, take pity on my unhappy fate", and his pleas reach a climax of desperation on repeated top E-naturals. But they are in vain, and Brogni departs for the Council's deliberations. Eléazar is left alone in the antechamber, to await his own turn before the judges.

During the duo, Eléazar has been oblivious to Brogni, and indeed to anything other than his date with Destiny and Heaven. Now, with the object of his hate no longer present, he apostrophizes: "God pronounce my death/my vengeance is certain./It is I who forever condemns you to wail!/I have brought upon you/the weight of my eternal hate/ and now I can die!" Then, with one of the two driving forces of his life fully vented, the other emerges: "But my daughter!. . . Oh, Rachel!. . . What horrible thought/comes to tear at my heart?/ Frightful madness, insensate rage, to avenge myself/It is you who are sacrificed to my fury!"

We can compare Shicoff with Martinelli only in the second part of this recitative, because the audio transfer of the Vitaphone performance jumps from the end of the duo to the lines *"J'ai fait peser sur toi,"* etc. And it seems that in this, the Vitaphone sequence is following the practice of the Met Caruso and Martinelli performances, for the Rullman libretto issued for them indicates the same cut, and it is taken on the Da Vinci recording as well.* Before proceeding, we must take a look at the implications of this excision, for they bear directly on our visualization of the dramatic progression, and Eléazar's behavior. To connect the dots from the actor's P.O.V. and account for what's on the page, we must back up to the end of the duo, Eléazar still rapt and exalted, Brogni an emotional puddle.

---

* When we come to consideration of the video, we shall discover that though it omits the brief orchestral introduction to the recitative (see below for further discussion on this), it begins earlier, with Eléazar's first words, *"Va prononcer ma mort."* It must have been Martinelli who advised Eddie Smith that "we always cut to here." The Vitaphone producers, though, recognized that a movie audience would need the preceding lines to clarify the circumstances, and that Smith would go so far as to snip them out of his audio release is one of his many inexplicable moves.

In some scores (and Hallman's synopsis), Ruggiero, the provost, now appears in the Council Chamber doorway and summons the Cardinal to preside over the trials. Brogni asks Eléazar one more time to relent, and when Eléazar refuses, promises that his sentence will be terrible. This little dialogue is not included in the Leich-Galland score or in any recording or performance I have been able to trace. It is both redundant and perfunctory, and breaks the tension of the scene. It does, however, get the Cardinal off the stage, and without it we are left to provide something credible for the mind's eye. We might envision Brogni dashing from the room in distress at his final sung notes, during the brief orchestral finish to the duo. But he cannot possibly let himself enter the Council in such a condition—he must somehow gather himself. Besides, these few bars are of a conventional ta-*da* sort, in no way related to Brogni's state. He is certainly still onstage, holding there during the applause for the duo, and must exit during the silence between numbers. So we can easily imagine an "*È strano!*" pause here: Brogni, shaken, rising painfully from his knees and, hurriedly dissembling as Ruggiero or a guard opens the Chamber door, proceeding with as much dignity as he can muster out of the room.

Perhaps Eléazar is so lost in fantasy that he does not even notice Brogni's departure, and with the beginning of the orchestral introduction to his solo scene is startled to find himself alone. Or (better, I think), perhaps he follows Brogni with gimlet eyes, tense and held-in, till the moment the door closes. In either case, the orchestra now sets the scene with seven bars of introduction. And a peculiar bit of writing this seems, at first glance or first hearing. It is marked *fortissimo* and *allegro*, scored for strings, and has a merry, skipalong quality. Further, this quick tempo, marked by forceful orchestral interjections, continues through Eléazar's first lines: "*Va prononcer ma mort,/ma vengeance et certaine!/C'est moi qui pour jamais/te condamne/à gémir!*" Only then does the tempo subside, and merely to *moderato*, for "*J'ai fait peser sur toi,*" etc.

The Vitaphone/Met cut is restored on all the "complete" recordings except the Da Vinci, and was possibly just another instance of Bodanzky moving a few seconds toward his unrealistic target.* It would also be a convenient

---

* A very few, however, on the Vitaphone performance, for there the *allegro* intro and recitative is replaced by a premonitory statement of the aria's main theme, so little if any time is saved. The Da Vinci performance, presumably modeled on Met practice, skips directly from the A major chord at the end of the duo to the C-sharp/D-natural alternation in the low strings at the *moderato*. I have a hunch Vitaphone's snippet from the aria was by way of reassuring a movie audience that the big tune was coming up. But it does also change the mood.

cut, though, for anyone who simply didn't know what to make of the apparent incongruity of the orchestral introduction. What might Halévy and Nourrit have had in mind? To me, their score suggests a pantomime of savage glee during the introduction—a pantomime which, given the traditions of bodily rhetoric of the French classical stage, and their cross-pollination with balletic carriage and movement, may even have been a dance—followed by quick, fierce, fist-shaking declamation in the recitative, simmering down with the *moderato* and slowly turning inward with Eléazar's thoughts of Rachel. That's a logical continuation of what's come before, an explanation of the otherwise puzzling tone of the intro, and a good fit with the reputed skills of Nourrit, which in our theatre would make him a champion "triple threat."

There are, certainly, practical reasons for ignoring the implications of this little section. Caruso was no triple threat; neither are most Eléazars. Visions of Jewish stereotyping, ugly or ridiculous—a prancing, chortling Tevye?—dance in our heads. Valid artistic reasons ("This is hard to get right!" not being among them) are scarcer, for the score's instructions are not at all vague. But Shicoff and Young do not heed them. Probably Shicoff is in the lead here as he starts his iconic solo scene, and he has a starkly different notion of the top of this sequence. Ignoring the *allegro*, he sets a slow, inward course from the start (at "*Va prononcer ma mort*"), giving us the feel of a man hoarding his emotional possessions as he would his material ones, savoring the single moment of fulfillment before all is ended. When he arrives at the *moderato* (now more of an *adagio*), the lines "*J'ai fait peser sur toi/mon éternelle haine*" ("I have brought upon you," etc.) land with baleful force, and while this can be described in rhetorical terms (the use, again, of straight tone, of a glaringly yellow coloration of the open "eh" vowels), the real achievement is that it does not sound like any sort of rhetoric. It sounds like the unedited, private relishment of triumphant hate.

So Shicoff has set his course for this segment of the voyage: he is ignoring the score because he has a strong feel for something quite different. The orchestral intro, however, is hung out to dry, and here Young and the VPO are of no help. They might at least have slowed the last three bars (where the skipping motion is replaced by a more proclamatory, portentous feel) to bring tempo and mood closer to Shicoff's choices. Instead, they zip through with a lilting, operetta-ish tone that leaves us wondering what the music can possibly be about, and (again) whether or not Halévy is really up to a moment of such gravity. I think he was, but only if interpreters seize upon his ideas, not avoid them.* When we arrive at our video inspection, we'll have a chance to see how Shicoff acts this moment. Till then, we scratch our heads.[13]

Apparently, Martinelli (and Caruso) never sang these opening lines, or had to decide how to interpret the music of the intro. But at the *moderato*, Martinelli is back in action, and we can follow both tenors through the rest of the recitative. Both are splendid, each in his way, and both follow the contours of the score with the exception of what we might term a Standard Tenor Deviation at "*Mais ma fille! O Rachel!*" Halévy/Nourrit wrote, in effect, anapaests: "*Mais-ma/FI-i-lle! O-Ra/CHE-e-elle!*". They could well have written "*MAI-AIS ma/fi-i-lle! O-O-O Ra/ch-elle!*", or have marked the "*mais*" and the "*O*" with a fermata or a "*ten.*". But they didn't. The bars are unaccompanied and surrounded by silence, so singers are free to play with them, and it's unlikely that Nourrit rendered them literally. But the rhetoric he at least sanctioned, if not wrote, is not the same as the rhetoric of our tenors. Expanding on the eighth notes of "But" and "Oh," is distinctly different from moving quickly through them to linger on the half-notes of the word "daughter" and the daughter's name. It's less personal and more suggestive of upper-note blo-viation. And this is true no matter what is done with the rest of these little exclamations: Shicoff and Martinelli both linger in both places, and do so feelingly, but the expressive weight has shifted. When Shicoff utters his daughter's name, there is a trace of the cantorial sob, the fleeting crack in the voice that conveys a sense of emotion that can't be contained.[†] As the recita-tive ends ("It is you who are sacrificed to my fury!"), it is again Martinelli, with his larger, steelier instrument, who allows the phrase to fade mourn-fully down, and Shicoff who gives it a punch on "*fureur!*"

Throughout this recitative, as in so much of the score, Martinelli creates the more convincing rhetorical effect. He has the more convincing rhetori-cal voice, and the firmer faith in the traditional rhetorical devices. He is the greater singer. Yet from the start, Shicoff's idiosyncratic reinterpretation holds us. It is based on neither a scrupulous rendition of the score nor a style-based notion received from oral tradition. It is derived from where he finds himself on his emotional voyage through the life of the part, and is of a piece with that. That is the way of the modern singeractor, whose priority

---

* On the Phillips recording, de Almeida and his orchestra (the Philharmonia) give a some-what more incisive reading. But no audio-only rendition can tell us anything about the acting during the orchestral intro, and while Carreras is responsive to the indicated pro-gression of feeling in the recitative, the performance still doesn't quite evoke the scene the writing suggests.

† Tucker does this, too, but somehow his—and I don't mean to imply any insincerity—sounds more like the practiced, "professional" cantorial sob. Shicoff's is closer to the true feeling beneath the convention.

is to make sure that an external effect does not precede an internal cause—indeed, that an "effect" does not appear as such. (Eléazar is not trying to make an "effect.") With his intense concentration and inner connection Shicoff leads us, tense and expectant, to the edge of the great double aria.

I don't go quite as far back with "*Rachel, quand du Seigneur*" as I do with "*Ombra mai fu*," but from my earliest hearings of it, it haunted me as few other arias do. I first met it in my early teens, through Caruso's recording, and his voicing of it, along with the accounts of his interpretation of the role in the early Caruso literature (Pierre Key's biography and Dorothy Benjamin Caruso's memoir), the photo of him in Shylockian gabardine, and the status of the singer, the character, and the opera itself as lost—parts of the legend of opera, rather than its present reality—set Eléazar in my mind's ear and eye for years to come. And for all that my experience of La Juive, Eléazar, and "*Rachel*" have broadened and deepened many times over, Caruso remains the inescapable reference. To anyone familiar with his recorded voice, he must always be there at any of the interpretive junctures we have examined. Admirable and impressive as Martinelli is, neither he nor any other tenor can offer anything like the combination of polychrome warmth of timbre, freely flowing legato, easy play of dynamics, and the ebullience and openness of personality that Caruso's singing affords.

Caruso's recording of "*Rachel*" is a high-quality late acoustical. On a good copy or transfer, there's no audible distortion, and little feel of high-note constraint. There are traces of labor in the singing, but they actually feed into the sense of a man at his emotional limits, and the overall tonal splendor is undiminished. His unique capacity for broadening the span of open vowels without endangering the technique (as at "*et c'est moi*," in preparation for the upward leaps to A-flat and B-flat) convey a bitterness, a rage at the tragic irony of his predicament, that is not accessible to other excellent tenors. Still, I think we can be sure that, powerful as this record is, it only suggests the impact of his live performance. Ponselle says (Drake, p. 102) that in performance ". . . he would use far more dynamics than what you hear on that recording. He would vary the tempo much more than he could on a record . . . when we made records, we had to take everything at a faster tempo. But onstage in La Juive, Caruso varied the tempo so that he could use more emotion . . ."

Apart from our present comparison, there are many recorded versions of "*Rachel*" that satisfy its general vocal requirements and edify us with respect to its several oral traditions. Among native French renditions, the blandishing timbre, flowing line and beautiful word-formation of George Thill and the meaty, gathered ring of Vezzani are good to hear. Escalaïs's version, with a few of his ever-exciting top notes, is somewhat compromised by traces of unwonted tremulousness and curt phrase endings—but no one should fail to hear him in "*Dieu m'éclaire*", one verse taken quite slowly and with several broadenings to allow the summoning of full resonantal forces, and capped by B-flats and a C that glitter like diamonds under light. It's the only modern-tenor voicing to render all thought of the old style superfluous.*

The pre-Nazi popularity of *Die Jüdin* in German-language houses is reflected in a number of interesting recordings of the aria, among which I find that of Jacques Urlus the most intriguing. His singing, always so smooth and freely emitted, so warm and rich in tone, combines the deep, baritonal set of the *Heldentenor* with a heady integration at the top that suggests earlier models. Indeed, he not only connects the B-flats "from the head," but takes the sustained A-flats both times in a full, round falsetto, presumably in emulation of former practices.†

Though *L'Ebrea* was certainly in the Italian repertory through the first three decades of recording, not much of compelling interest has come down to us in the way of Italian interpretation of the aria aside from Caruso and, of course, Martinelli. Which brings us back to our comparison, and to the question of how, with no greatvoiced candidates before us since the days of Tucker and Vickers, this extraordinary scene might find consummation. Its uniquely haunting quality has several components. First, the words are wonderful. Here's a translation, capturing none of the original's metric lilt, its word parallels ("*berceau/bourreau*"—"cradle/executioner") and other poetic

---

* His two versions of the cabaletta, one in French and the other in Italian, are both piano-accompanied, and both superb, but I prefer the Italian (Milan, 1905), whereon the language brings out more of the voice's color, and "*corona*" elicits an even better C than "*couronne*." Or perhaps I have simply heard the Italian in a superior transfer.

† It would have been fascinating to hear Urlus's solutions to some of the other high-note events in this role, which he evidently did sing, along with others (e.g., Raoul, John of Leyden, Masaniello) of similar vocal character. Even in heroic passages, he usually draws out his top notes from a "*sanft*," *messa di voce*-derived attack, from which they take on a beautiful late bloom. Rather surprisingly, though, in his recording of the "*Cujus Animam*" (Rossini, *Stabat Mater*), he declines altogether the high D-flat, whereon one would have assumed his falsetto would have rivaled Caruso's. The other great German-language Eléazar would have been Slezak, but I've always found his recording of the aria disappointing, despite some nice touches: the phrasing is clipped, the high notes rather thin and distant (the blasting-avoidance problem, I assume), and the translation sits awkwardly for him. The version of Max Lorenz, from his fresh-voiced days, is strong and straightforward—he certainly had the relevant vocal and interpretive gifts. Josef Schmidt captures the piece's mourning quality; but that lovely, soaring lyric tenor suggests not an Eléazar, but an exemplary Léopold. It's a shame that the young Melchior did not record "*Recha*," to go with his German-language *Africaine*, *Pagliacci*, *Otello*, and *Aïda* records. That would have been something.

33

nuances, or the sounds of its setting on the voice, but only its approximate meaning:

(A)
Rachel, when through the grace of the Lord
Into my trembling hands
Your cradle was vouchsafed,
It was to your happiness
That I consecrated my life.
And it's I who deliver you to death
["the executioner"].

(B)
But I hear a voice that cries out to me,
"Save me from the death that awaits!
I am young, and I cling to life!
Oh my father, my father,
Spare, spare your child!"

(Repeat A, with added repetitions and emphasis at the end.)

Second, there are the coloristic felicities of the accompaniment. They begin with the inspired stroke of English horns in thirds (the most commonly noted feature of the piece), and continue with such touches as the limping pizzicato that sets the song on its reluctant way, and the lovely flute entrance that first summons the voice of Rachel from an inner distance. But of by far the most importance is the tune. It, too, has its felicitous details—its davenning dotted rhythm; its pattern of triplets kicked off by sixteenths, alternating with responses in even eighths, etc.* But mainly, it's the F minor melody itself, the intervallic progression of the solo line, that hits the instant-memory button and which, when combined with even a general awareness of the situation ("A father must sacrifice his beloved daughter, who cries out to him from within"), opens Eléazar up to us. If Agamemnon himself had such a tune as he prepared to surrender Iphigenia, we would weep with him.

Martinelli, still in his prime in 1929, takes the first verse in great arcs at a slow tempo, the halves of each long phrase jointed by sad little glides; the "e's" of "c'est moi" opened in the Caruso manner (this would be unlikely from a

---

* The uneven patterns are often evened out or, at best, under-articulated, by singers, while the even ones get dotted. In fact, I've yet to hear an interpretation that I thought took full expressive advantage of these patterns.

French tenor, but is rather wonderful), each "*moi*" carried from D to E-flat on a wavelet of upward *portamento*; then the first A-flat ringing out like an alarm; and the final "*au bourreau*" drawn out long and soft. The last full measure of timbral beauty and warmth aside, this is a model of E-19 dramatic tenor singing in its perfectly drawn line, carriage of voice, command of expansive phrase shapes (undoubtedly closer to what Caruso did in the theatre) and finish of effect.

In the B section, one imagines Nourrit using his refinement of dynamics at the full-voice/*voix mixte* borderline and his elegance of inflection in his native language to differentiate Rachel's plea from Eléazar's "own" voice—that seems the point of the writing. No modern tenor really does this, but Martinelli does offer a superbly contained attack at "*sauvez moi*" and, after a rather uncomfortable time with the first B-flat at "ô *mon père*," another long-held, tender conclusion on "*votre enfant*" at the close. The repeat of (A) is more intimate-sounding than the first statement, the tone more blended and warm. When the string tremolando announces the brief *codetta,* Martinelli is able to call on his instrument's full resources to lean into the A-flat on the last syllable of "*Rache-el*" (with a vigorous lick to the "*l*" to bring the pressure right to the boiling point), then kick up into the climactic B-flat (a good one, this time) with a little bump from underneath, as if an *acciaccatura* were written—it suggests a man struck by a lightning bolt of realization. It's a tremendous traversal of the aria, masterfully controlled and strongly felt, whose effect in the opera house must have been quite overwhelming.

Martinelli's sound, with its ample format and its high degrees of compression and tensility, its unfailing clarity and longline sustainability, always implies an effort (usually triumphant) to surmount conflict, external or internal. Shicoff, whose sound is less rich in those properties, seems from the start more like a man struggling to get it out. This isn't due solely to inherent vocal qualities, or any unusual signs of vocal strain. It's because he doesn't go for the great arc, the magnificent carriage. In (A), he doesn't connect the halves of the opening phrases, but breaks for breath. There are no *portamenti*, of either the keening downward sort or the cresting upward type. He seems to need renewed strength for each short utterance, yet each is well completed. When the dotted rhythm of "*J'avais à ton bonheur*" is replaced by the even eighths of "*voué ma vie entiere*" (bars 71 and 75), he pulls back on both tempo and dynamic, giving each syllable an almost *stentato* feel, as though reminding himself, over and over, of his vow. His basic tempo is not much different from Martinelli's, and he certainly takes no longer at the cadential points; yet the aria's progress seems more halting. In (B), he secures a fine B-flat by choosing (as do most recorded tenors—but not Martinelli) to carry the voice up from below and into the high note on "*père*," rather than attacking it on the "*ô*." At the section's end, the last "*épargnez votre enfant*" is intense, inward, and soft to the point of disappearance (as if Rachel's voice were fading out), and so drawn-out as to bring the piece to a stop. As the repeat of (A) starts, we sense a singer at a verge that is both emotional and respiratory. To contain feeling is to control the breath, and when one breaks through, so does the other. Walking the verge—the tone turning husky, its support trembling or tightening—is a perilous passage, which is why its presence is usually signified by some applied affect of breath or vibrato, of timbral shading or musical emphasis. But Shicoff is really there, and we catch our own breath in response. In the brief silence after the A-flat at "*c'est moi*," there is an audible tremor of the breath. It bears no trace of "choice." The last repetition of "*moi*" is not sung at all, but whispered, before the singer gathers his forces for the final "*c'est moi qui te livre au bourreau!*" with its interpolated B-flat, the voice just bearing its limit of stress.*

We have on recordings a number of versions of "*Rachel*" that are, in traditional terms, "better" than Shicoff's—the voices of more satisfying calibre and quality, the techniques more authoritative, in a few cases the French recitation more authentic. But none quite takes us to the same place as Shicoff's—the place where the performer's danger is the same as the character's, and the response to it, though occurring in an opera, seems the same as it would be in life.

Listeners to most of the aria recordings and viewers of both the videos under consideration could be forgiven for assuming that the Great Scene, and the opera's fourth act, have just come to an end, which is to say that after a wrenching inner struggle during which he's heard the voice of his daughter pleading for her life, Eléazar has summoned the resolve to yield her to her executioners. His passion for a supreme act of revenge at his life's end has won out over his love for Rachel and his vow to protect her. Curtain. But that is not how the scene and act end. Eléazar's life-agony is about to twist him twice more within a few minutes' time. And here occurs the most

---

* On the occasion of receiving the title of *Kammersänger* at the Staatsoper (shown on the *Looking for Eléazar* video), Shicoff expresses his gratitude to the Viennese audience for its supportive ovation after his voice cracked under the pressure of contained emotion in this scene. I don't think it's just spin. As too few singers give themselves the opportunity to find out (again, actors are more familiar——but then, they have less at stake), there is a precise point at which genuine emotional contact puts the voice at risk. Once discovered, the point can be maintained under control by the technique, but given the excitability of singing itself, and the adrenaline-soaked heat of performance, there's always some peril in the presence of active feeling. If the feeling isn't active, it can't impregnate the sound. That's when a less talented performer will simply give a dull performance, and a more talented one will imitate the effect of emotion.

unforgivable of the Vienna recording's cuts, one that only the EMI/de Almeida version restores. For not only does the scene continue: it is meant to do so without interruption. "*Rachel*"'s last syllable ("*bour-REAU!*") is the downbeat of the first bar of an *allegro*, kicked off by a vaulting violin figure easily heard as an intensification of the one at the top of the scene. It's among the most thrilling moments in the score, as the realization floods in on Eléazar that just one word from him ("yes" instead of "no" to Brogni's conversion offer) can save the life of his child. "I abjure forever my vengeance," he sings. "No Rachel, you shall not die."

No sooner has he sworn this, however, than an offstage chorus of the gathering populace is heard: "Down with the Jews! Let them die! Death is owed for their misdeeds!" It is only with these lines that the Vienna production originally resumed, and that is what we have on the RCA CDs.* With this cut, we are deprived of half the scene's emotional violence—the wild swing first one way, then the other—and Eléazar's next decision ("You want our blood, Christians, and I was going to give you back my Rachel? No, never!") now makes no sense, since as of the end of "*Rachel*," he wasn't about to do that anyway. Further, we lose the score's clear mandate that each emotional swing be topped by the next. The ending of "*Rachel*" seems for a moment conclusive, but is immediately transcended by the leaping violins of the *allegro;* while the next swing back takes us into "*Dieu m'éclaire,*" which maintains altitude and excitement like nothing else in the role.

In this cabaletta, Eléazar returns to the ecstatic fantasy mode of the duo with Brogni. But now he must take it further. Its emotional intensity must be sufficient to overcome that of Rachel's outcry, even that of his determination of only moments earlier to save her. Otherwise, he will be unable to carry through with the sacrifice. Thus, he adds two fresh justifications to his earlier vision of a shared heavenly destiny. One is that Rachel will be reclaimed for Israel, fulfilling his dedication of her soul to the God of Jacob. The second is that by sending her to her death, he is giving her "the crown of the martyr," and that to prolong her earthly life would only delay her eternal one. Since even in his exaltation he cannot be sure that Rachel will receive his gift quite in the spirit in which it's intended, he asks her pardon for it—in fact, the scene comes to its true end with four feverish repetitions (including the ascent to C) of the words "*. . . pardonne s'il te donne/la couronne du martyre!*" That's the crucial thought, the crucial need, with which we are left.

---

* By the time the production was revived and the video accomplished, Shicoff, et al., were omitting everything after the conclusion of "*Rachel*," so that was the case when the production arrived at the Met. Whether this was from artistic conviction or because Shicoff was finding the continuation into "*Dieu m'éclaire*" too demanding, I do not know.

The delirious words evoke a hyperbolic musical setting, centered as it is around the high G and A-flat and sprinkled with its half-dozen B-flats and climactic high C, from whose stress Nourrit had the escape hatch of his reinforced falsetto, and Duprez (apparently) that of his not-quite-half-step transposition, both unavailable to any self-respecting, audience-fearing latterday tenor.

"*Dieu m'éclaire*" is not meant to be fast. After the *allegro* of Eléazar's vow to save Rachel, it is marked "*Moins vite,*" and at every cadential point, notated or latent, there is a "*colla voce,*" "*col canto,*" or "*senza rigore*" for the voice to assemble its full resonantal forces before returning to this "less fast" tempo. Nowhere is a quickening indicated. In both verses, the first utterances of the words "*la couronne du martyre*" are marked with a "*poco rall.,*" a legato phrase-mark, and the instructions "*vibrato*" and "*dolce,*" further underlining the significance of this component of Eléazar's vision. Between verses, Eléazar is egged on by the mob's calls, louder now. The scene builds to its end not with frenzied tempo, but with the summoning of progressively greater vocal force and color, the repetition of demanding patterns, and the surmounting of high tessitura, capped toward the close by the C.[14] And all of it—the entire No. 22, from the skipping orchestral introduction and Eléazar's "Go pronounce my death" to his final "... crown of the martyr!"—is intended to play through without a break.*

After their cut of the vow to save Rachel, and the severely redacted version of the reversal that follows (which nevertheless retains Eléazar's now-meaningless denial of the promise he hasn't just made), Shicoff and Young offer a single verse of "*Dieu m'éclaire.*" Despite the "*moins vite,*" they take it at a furious clip, almost a *presto*, easing only slightly at the obvious spots. This allows Shicoff to continue his extremely short-breathed phrasing ("*Dieu m'éclai-re/fill-e chère.*" etc.) without losing the continuity former tenors observed by longer-breathed, more carefully crafted phrasing. He does not attempt the C, but gets into superb B-flats, and these, together with the pell-mell tempo and favorable positioning vis-à-vis the mike, make for an undeniably exciting conclusion to the scene.

Still, it's a long way from what Halévy and Nourrit inscribed. It's not just that it's shorter. It displays a different concept of dramatic action and, at the end, a re-ordering of Eléazar's emotional priorities. According to the text, the

---

* I recall Robert Lawrence, conductor of the 1964 New York performances, telling me of persuading an initially skeptical Richard Tucker that he would "bring down the house" by taking no pause for applause after "*Rachel,*" but singing on through. "That's what I want," Tucker answered, and so he complied, demonstrating that even under concert conditions, the audience response to the aria can be controlled.

climactic line of "*Rachel*" has electrified Eléazar with the realization that he is contemplating the unthinkable. Everything up through his vow to save his daughter is part of the battle within him, of love vs. vengeance. But now the Christians are heard from, whereupon the battle has an external object. Eléazar's action is again suddenly reversed, impelling Verse I of the cabaletta, with its special caressing treatment for "the crown of the martyr."

The bridge between verses is Eléazar's answer to the threatening mob outside, and it is only here that he introduces the thoughts of Israel reclaiming Rachel, the ending of her earthly life in favor of the eternal one, and his consecration of her soul to the God of Jacob. These are modifications, elaborations, on his main theme, not the theme itself. That is the plea for his daughter's pardon, and it is reaffirmed with conclusive emphasis, literally topping everything that has come before, in the repeat of the A section. As his final A-flat rings out ("*du mar-TYRE!*"), Ruggiero and several guards again appear at the Council Chamber door, signaling him to follow them. Riding his wave of shared father/daughter heavenly glory, he rushes after them to give his defiant testament. *Now*: curtain.

I suspect that since the early days of *La Juive*, most tenors have sung only one verse of this cabaletta, when they have sung it at all. To the standard practice in treating such pieces (see n. 14), there is the consideration of the endurance demand placed on modern dramatic tenor voices, few of which have at their disposal the C to make it all seem worthwhile. In practical performance terms, the single-verse version is understandable, and if well sung certainly doesn't kill the scene.* Shicoff, however, also re-writes the ending. He rescues from the deleted bridge the words "*Israël la réclame!*" and, after omitting the bars containing the C and the repetitions of "*couronne du martyre*," uses the best of all his B-flats (the nice, fat "*a*" of "*réclame*") to conclude the piece. It's arguable, I suppose, which vision is more important to Eléazar's rationale: that of Israel reclaiming its own or that of Rachel in eternal splendor with her martyr's crown. But the score, at least as I read it, leaves little room for doubt as to what the creators thought.

Since both Shicoff's and Martinelli's video performances end with "*Rachel*," we cannot compare their physical characterizations in the rest of the Great Scene.† But we can watch what we do have of each, and so compare them not only with each other, but with the mind's-eye visualizations we have derived from their audio performances.

---

* It isn't surprising that the sole rendition we have of the complete scene, that of Carreras with de Almeida, is on a studio recording, with its opportunities for re-takes and rest breaks.

† And since this was true of Shicoff's performance at the Met as well, I am unable to give even a recollection-plus-notes report.

I am grateful to the participants of the Vienna/Met production. I believe they recognized *La Juive's* importance and meant well by it. Through their efforts we felt a good measure of the potency of a noble and neglected work. When I see a production I think is earnestly intended, I try to understand the obstacles the interpreters-in-chief have encountered. In the case of *La Juive*, some are concrete and external: the length and size of the piece; its musical unevenness; the difficulty of casting the roles; the unfamiliarity (to both audience and interpreters) of the opera itself and the genre to which it belongs, etc. In this case, though, the most important obstacles are not concrete and external. They belong to the collective mindset of the production team, to their "design matrix" and the attitude they have found it necessary to adopt toward the opera's world. And even though we are presently following the voyage of a single character, some attention to the production is necessary, for two reasons. First, the performer's work is done in interaction with it; either this interaction is mutually helpful, or not. Second, though the performer may ignore his surroundings and treat his own scenario as the only reality (the *sauve que peut* solution), receptors continue to observe both performer and surroundings, and will at some level sense whether or not they belong together.

In this *La Juive*, the physical setting is abstract and ideas-based. The attitude is contemporary and manipulative—like Zambello's *Lucia*, it imposes judgments, in this case on the opera's social, political, and religious milieu. But the principals' behavior ("*Personenregie*," acting) pursues a modern ideal of lifelikeness, which among other things disallows commentary on characters. So this isn't an actualist production. Its different parts propose different levels of reality, and ask us to leap the brain barrier between them. Consequently, the things I dislike about it all have to do with design and attitude, the things I like with the work of the principals, and the thing that ultimately frustrates me with the apparent indifference to the disparity among these elements. A brief word about each:

The set (a fixed unit that serves for all six locations, interior and exterior, private and public) is not fully revealed in the opening scene, which is played behind and before a wall of semitransparent panels far downstage. Once disclosed, it's a double-decker whose upper level is a brightly lit, severely raked ramp running across the stage. The Christian royals live up there. The lower is the stage floor, dimly lit and receding into gloom beneath the ramp, where dwell the Jews. *Lichtalben* above, *Schwarzalben* below, and in fact with just a little more curl in the ramp, this would be any of a hundred post-Wieland *Ring* sets. Later, the Jews are up and the Christian royals (oho!) are down. It is yet another metaphorical space, a sort of glorified Common Room, meant to be read as a single, simple idea: who's on top now? We're not to bother our heads about the logic of either time (i.e., history) or place. (For example, in Act IV, here staged as the first scenes of Act III, Rachel and Eléazar enter from and exit to the same door for their interviews with Brogni. But the place they're exiting to is the Council Chamber, to which they are successively remanded to testify. They can't possibly have *come* from there. But they do. Don't bother your head, and keep leaping.)

The attitude I don't like is conveyed largely through the "modern dress" costuming and the staging of chorus and minor characters. The Christians are all in white—Ironic White, of course—with the military looking faintly late Hapsburgian, the civilian royals white-jacket contemporary, and the populace vaguely *Zwischenkrieg*. In the opening scene the women of the chorus, seated as at a sporting match, wave tiny flags and do alternate-row side-to-side swaying drills. The men are in *Lederhosen* and shorts with suspenders—they look like enacters at an AlpsLand theme park. The Kaiser is an old dodderer. (The real Emperor Sigismund was a fierce veteran of campaigns against the Turks, in his forties at the time of the story.) The staging shows these Christians as stiff, sometimes silly people leading sterile, ritualized lives. They have a mean streak, no doubt, but are hard to take seriously. They are there to form our opinions for us and make sure we understand the director disapproves of them. The Jews are in plain, everyday black.

One other aspect of this updated attitude, a post-Holocaust consciousness, has more complicated implications, which I will touch on below.

Personenregie: This does not have the look of a production in which the performers have gone their independent ways. It gives every appearance of sympathetic collaboration between them and their director, Gunther Krämer. Three of the principals—Shicoff, Krassimira Stoyanova (Rachel), and Walter Fink (Brogni) offer textured, sincerely felt work (and this was true onstage in New York as well, where Soile Isokoski was the Rachel and Ferruccio Furlanetto the Brogni). This speaks to their own talents, of course, but has to owe its coherence in part to Krämer, who clearly wants complex, nuanced, "real" behavior from the characters with whom he sympathizes. Yet this same director has conspired with his designers to create a stage world divorced from realistic expectations, and has acquiesced in the removal of connective tissue vital to consistent character life. It's Krämer vs. Krämer.

The upside of updating—the ease it induces in performers wearing clothes like their own and acting like people they know—is also on view. But even this blessing is not unmixed. This Rachel might well open the door of any apartment in my Upper West Side neighborhood and make me comfortable with

tea and ruggeleh. That's not who Léopold has fallen for, though. He's not flee-
ing an uppity little bitch for a warm, understanding woman. He's entranced
by an exotic young beauty from the proscribed Levantine Other, for whom
he's willing to chuck his beautiful Tenth of the One Percent life, while she
is swept off her feet by his passionate, serenading, mysterious, artistic, glit-
tery self. That's the Protagonist Couple subplot, and its chemistry is out the
window with this sensible Jewish housekeeper and her quite ordinary suitor.

These decisions, which together constitute the production's "concept,"
affect the work of all the performers, all the time; they set the boundaries
of the field they may till. Within those boundaries, Shicoff works with commitment and clear intent—he has, in the modern actor's sense, a strong
throughline. He establishes it in the opening scene, despite the brain barriers
the designers have set in place: the aforementioned semitransparent panels,
the white-clad flag-wavers and Alpine boys, and lots of wooden chairs. We are
shut off from any imagining of place (the square with the Cathedral on one
side, Eléazar's house on the other) or of the variegated throng that occupies it,
or of any objects that might logically be found there. (A fountain, for instance,
might belong in the square but, absent a sidewalk café, wooden chairs don't.)
A space is not the same as a place. The production creates a space, and asks
us to leap the barrier. Which we do, but at the usual cost.

One of the reasons contemporary directors and designers like to think
this way is that it reduces the lifelike messiness of big scenes to two or three
focal points. They believe it simplifies and clarifies things for the audience,
and it certainly does that for their staging problems. Here, it encourages us
to focus quickly on Eléazar. And we are all too happy to do so, for it's clear
from his first entrance that Shicoff is on a purposeful track. The chairs play
a role. They would have no place in a place, but in a space they can be put to
use. A chorister sticks one out at Rachel, who must pretend to be helplessly
entrapped between its legs. That's no go, but now it's Eléazar turn, and Shicoff
makes the most of it. Jostled and thrown down by the crowd, he immediately
shows us his character's habitual response: to give them nothing, to maintain
his dignity no matter what. He does this in part through meticulous attention
to his clothes, neatening and dusting off his hat and coat, then composing
his tight, small frame and sitting, erect and imperturbable, down center, in
one of the chairs, amid the menacing melée. For all that we miss in this opening scene, we have learned about Eléazar that he can stand (or, rather, sit)
unflinching and quietly defiant in the midst of a threatening mob. We can
imagine him undergoing torture, even going to his death, without giving his

tormentors the slightest satisfaction. And we'll keep in mind his fastidious-
ness about his clothing.*

In the opening scene of Act II, Shicoff builds on the persona he has created, and this is fairly consistent with his audio characterization. Close in on
his face, we are made keenly aware of the muscular effort involved in stretching his voice over the frame of this role, somewhat lessening the pleasure
we take in the singing, but increasing our respect for the dedication to the
task—the singer's work and the character's struggle seem one and the same.
There is a nice touch in the staging when Eléazar, lost in the fervency of his
plea, wanders away from the table during "*Dieu, que ma voix tremblante,*" and
Rachel follows to gently lead him back to his place. The matzoh-droppings
episode is bungled pretty badly (and the camera close-ups exacerbate the
situation), but at least the bungling is in pursuit of lifelikeness.[15]

The scene of the jewel's purchase is a little inventory of what I find objectionable in the production, and in many contemporary productions that are
not blatantly adversarial. It tallies the price exacted, in terms of rounded characterization ("human interest," if you will) by the cuts, the mise-en-scène, and
the predilection of contemporary directors and performers for substituting
externalized, interpersonal exchanges for inner actions conveyed by voice—
or, to put it another way, their reluctance to deal with central operatic conventions because they can't figure out how to make them behaviorally credible.

Recall for a moment our mind's-eye vision of this scene, as evoked from
audio recording and text (see pp. 465-469). Recall in particular the omissions
necessitated by this production's cut at the top of the scene: Eléazar ordering
Rachel and the rest of the company out of the room, but detaining "Samuel"
for defense; the latter's identity as master artist, hiding in his artisanal activity; Eudoxie's ease and charm in dealing with Eléazar, with the "artist's"
presence, and with this unaccustomed locale at night; and the revelation of
her identity as the Emperor's niece—the conditioning circumstances of the
scene, in other words, that prepare us to accept the conventions of the *scene
à trois* as well as giving the performers chances to explore something beyond
the primary colors of their characters.

All that is gone. So now the scene starts quite differently. Rachel remains
in the room. The other Jews crowd into the shadows under the ramp and

---

* In the theatre, this was all clearer than it is on the video, partly because the staging
kept Eléazar central, but also because, with the freedom the theatre confers to watch
selectively, every glance at the surrounding activity returned us instantly to the only
interesting and believable option. On the video, the medium's congenital impatience
guarantees that we cannot follow any line of development for more than a few seconds.
So we get a moment of grooming, a glimpse of posture, a quick shot of Rachel brushing
off the coat, amid a welter of other stuff.

Léopold/Samuel, with nothing to do (for his artist identity goes unobserved), hangs out stage right. He needn't worry about being detected, because Eudoxie never enters the room. She stands at the lip of the ramp, up in the shining land of the Christian royals. Behind her, the festive table is set, and a crystal chandelier *à la moderne* gleams. At her side are a few smug-looking ladies-in-waiting, two guards, and, clutching her by the hand, two children, a boy and a girl of some ten to twelve years, who peer down curiously into the little *Nibelheim* below. Eléazar having already recognized the princess (does he frequent the palace?),* she launches immediately into "You have, they say, a precious jewel." Thus declaimed from above, with no personalizing moment having passed between her and Eléazar and constrained by the presence of family and court, this cannot appear other than imperious. Instead of a woman who comes down to his level, enters his shop leaving her escort outside, is at pains to make him comfortable, then enters into a private bargaining exchange with him, we have one who stays in her own elevated, quasi-public realm and deals with him from a distance. That's a premise for the scene that's not just different from, but opposed to, that of Halévy and Scribe.

As I noted in my ears-only discussion of this scene, the central convention to be observed is that of interior monologue, with the two tenors confiding feelings they are keeping hidden from the others—things they cannot say aloud—while Eudoxie sings out more openly about her emotions. The characters go in and out of this to-themselves mode, transacting the business of the scene between these episodes, during which physical stillness is necessary. Stillness draws the attention of the audience away from bodily actions toward vocal ones, and from outer to inner action. It helps the singers stay in touch with inner tensions, and with the technically difficult task of conveying them through voice. Motion resumes in the transactional passages. We go back and forth between levels of reality.

This inner material is of the kind conveyed by voice-over in film or video, and by the aside in old drama. In most contemporary theatre, we ask that actors suggest it via behavioral nuance (including tone of voice, this never becoming obvious enough to be picked up by the other characters) while the external action moves forward—as in life. Our theatre generally doesn't shift levels of reality in an overt manner, and doesn't suspend all outer action while characters express their deepest feelings through voice alone. And so Krämer, doubtless in quest of the believable, rejects the convention in favor of

---

* It is not inconceivable that Eléazar could know Eudoxie by sight. But the creators considered it more likely and more interesting that he would not. I agree with them. Another identity-recognition issue is created by Rachel's presence in the scene. If Eudoxie sees her here, how would she not know her when she comes to the palace to beg inclusion in the retinue? I know! We'll cut that scene, too!

a throughplayed staging of the scene. He directs it as if it belonged to a much later opera, a Twentieth Century one in which the structures and conventions of grand opera have been absorbed and concealed, or abandoned altogether.

Surely Shicoff, despite the narrow dynamic and timbral range at his disposal, has some means of suggesting a singing-to-himself tone, and of conveying what he's singing to himself about. But even if that were his particular genius, it would be incongruous in the scene as staged, for throughout the interior-monologue sequences he is bustling back and forth, attending to the particulars of the transaction. Rachel, now a participant in her father's business, assists him—something that is certainly unthinkable in the work's historical household, and not very likely in the updated one. She helps boost him up toward the ramp so he can stretch to hand the chain to Eudoxie (a Laurel and Hardy moment). She helps with the jewel-box, with entering the sale in the ledger, etc. She and Eléazar smile and nod at each other. Whatever Eléazar is singing, she is hearing. So to pretend that he is concealing his thoughts is pointless. No wonder we picked up so little from Shicoff by ear. And what *is* Eléazar saying, supposedly to himself? Redacting to isolate his thoughts:

> (I was fearing that this woman
> might discover all our secrets.
> And I was cursing in my soul
> all these Christians, whom I hate.
> But for me what pleasure now,
> and what a happy prospect—
> these good crowns that I so love
> will now return to me.
> Crowns, ducats, sequins, florins
> to me, to me, very soon will return!)

> [Repeat last 2 lines, with variation and emphasis. Further:]

> (What a joy, what a joy, to fool, to fool
> these Christians, fool these Christians!
> I hate them all, these enemies
> of my God and of my faith!)

> [Repeat with variation and emphasis.]

These words are often half-hidden in duet or trio passages, but all are in the clear at some point during the number. In this staging, though, they're just sung out while people go about their business, for all to hear. And that includes Rachel, who does not belong in the scene, and is made into a sort of tacit co-conspirator in this shady deal and her father's hate-speech. (We, of course, have empathy with Eléazar. But for Rachel to be privy to the crooked dealings and gloatings, with no room to incorporate what that would say about her, is another matter. Neither the character nor the actress should have to contend with it.)

Throughout the number, Léopold/Samuel crouches stage right in the shadow of the ramp, isolated in the space without a life to lead, no trace of concealment in his voice. Eudoxie sings her roulades out at us literally over the heads of the others. When the moment arrives for legalizing the deal, the kids zip paper airplanes down to the deck, where Eléazar smooths them out to affix his seal. Incredible, what the Krämers of our world resort to when they find themselves painted into a corner. The singers troupe on. Everyone is trying to be lifelike. But in the cause of showing us a throughplayed, "natural-seeming" sequence, recognizable not so much from life as from the kind of theatre we've grown comfortable with, only the basic plot point (Eudoxie buys a jewel from Eléazar for her husband) has registered, and it is but the tiniest fragment of the scene's content. The rest is lost in the shuffle, and this rich, delightful number is ruined.

With respect to the rest of Act II and Act III (wherein Eléazar is involved only in bringing the jewel to Eudoxie in the palace, then reacting to events in ensemble), there is much more that could be said about the production as an environment for acting.[16] But it would not alter the impression already made, of sympathetic direction of the principals in a framework that discourages exploration beyond a single facet of each character, the whole being dedicated to the comment the director wishes to make on the opera's relevance for us. And of all the concerns one might have about the work's viability, that is the most needless. What La Juive has suffered from for eighty years past (the suspected chief cause of its languishment, in fact) is not any lack of relevance, but a shaming excess of it.

In the Europe of the 1920s and early '30s, there was a vigorous operatic avant-garde that worked to transform traditional assumptions of production and acting. It was not without influence here, especially in the presentation of then-contemporary works. But in the American opera houses where Giovanni Martinelli sang Eléazar and his other grand-opera roles (those of New York, Chicago, and San Francisco), the directors and designers for such works just arranged the stage traffic, conjured the specified places and times, and dressed the performers accordingly. They were *metteurs en scene*, not auteurs. The Vitaphone films (for although the sequence is continuous and was doubtless shot in a single session, there are in fact two, each preceded by its written summary, for separate showing as theatre shorts) give us a glimpse, however fragmentary and compromised, of that world. They're shot on a little box set meant to represent the anteroom to the Council Chamber, with Brogni's desk plunked in the center. Our surrogate eye, the camera, is out here beyond the fourth wall, and it is fixed: after one cut near the beginning, the entire sequence is taken in a three-quarter-length two-shot from an angle of perhaps thirty degrees. The actors' movements are hemmed into the area around the desk, at which Brogni sits on one side while Eléazar stands on the other for their scene, and around which Eléazar circles during his aria. I see no evidence that the Eléazar/Brogni scene is anything other than an uninterrupted single take, and the same is true of Eléazar's solo scene. In a way, this primitive technique comes as a mighty relief after the viewing of contemporary opera videos, films and 'casts. No dollying and zooming, no intercourse among multiple cameras, no highlighting or isolating, no jumping from angle to angle, and above all no closeups—in short, no video director creating his Theatre of Continuous Interruption. There are only stage performers, doing as much as they can under cramped conditions, while their pictures are taken and their voices recorded. Like the records of acoustical times, the films impose severe restrictions, but within them report the truth about the artists' work.

The thing one notices immediately about the performance—especially if, as we have done, one has first listened to it in audio form—is how well the vocal interpretation holds up, and how poorly the visual. In listening, we have communed with the emotional power and recitational eloquence of Martinelli's singing and, to whatever extent the mind's eye has become involved, invested it with our own vision. But now, the ear's communion is shattered by the eye's scan of the spectacle. This is always true of film or video performance, but in this instance the eye is further transfixed by the nature of the behavior on display.

Anyone interested in material of this sort will watch with a sense of historical perspective, respect for the standing of the artist, and some indulgence for the difficulties of the circumstances and deteriorated quality of the picture. In my several viewings, I kept trying to imagine what the performance must have looked like at opera-house distance, with the staging at least at moments opened up, as I assume it must have been. The fascination of seeing even the faintest representation of a great tenor of a long-gone past in one of his most famous roles is strong, and so is his initial impression, with his fine carriage and convincing makeup and costuming—"in period," naturally, and similar to Caruso's. A presence, for sure. But if we are in search of physical behavior that could conceivably belong to life as we know it—or even as we fantasize having known it in Martinelli's time, or Nourrit's, or that of Eléazar himself, our mission is doomed.

The handiest reference for the acting style of these films would be silent-movie acting, and what is left of the mimetic stage traditions from which it was derived, like the exposition sequences of the classical story ballets, or the loving re-creation of French mime theatre in the Carné/Prévert *Les enfants du Paradis*. But it is also an operatic version of such a style, obligated to the music for its timing and expressive content, designed to complement the voice at a long throw and, unlike the best of silent-movie acting, unaccommodated to the camera and its potential (even in this fixed position) for intimacy and subtlety. Its language is one of large illustrative poses and gestures. Martinelli pantomimes each reaction, drawing himself up, pointing, flinging an arm across his chest, and so on. Upon the entrance of the rising-and-falling motif in the bass (and again, at its repetition), he looks about suspiciously in a half-crouch, as if confiding something that mustn't be overheard. But of course no one else is, or could be, in the room. He's not playing the reality of the situation, but miming the tone of the music. Throughout, one is also struck by the extent to which the gesticulating is rhetorical in the most literal sense, as if this deeply personal, highly emotional confrontation were a legal or political disputation to be won by being more impressive than the other fellow.

It's not that Martinelli has no acting talent. There's a pronounced theatrical flair to what he does. At times—as when he leans across the desk toward Brogni and, with admirable concentration and intent, declaims "*Un Juif avait sauvé ta fille*" (a spot we took note of in the audio-only version)—one picks up the tension of a moment, and imagines its spell in the opera house. Once past the recitative to the aria, wherein he pads about dabbing his forehead with his handkerchief and making little shows of dejection, he does better in the aria, where he can let his voice and presence carry more of the burden. In general, though, nearly all his behavior falls into the category of what modern actors call "indication"—demonstrative action that is decided upon and imposed, rather than derived from inner sources or an honest response to what's really happening. Martinelli's vocal rhetoric has retained its expressive validity. But his bodily rhetoric (what we habitually think of as "acting") has not. If we are to persist in searching for an operatic version of credible behavior, we will have to leave behind Martinelli, with his splendid voice and costume, in his little room with its improbably placed desk (which are, I must nevertheless point out, an actual room and an actual desk), and return to the present century and the Vienna/Met production.

Act IV of *La Juive* consists of three successive one-on-one scenes (Eudoxie/ Rachel, Brogni/Rachel, Brogni/Eléazar), culminating in Eléazar's solo scene with offstage chorus. In each of the one-on-one scenes, a Christian of high station pleads desperately with a lowly Jew. But since the Jews, though incarcerated, now hold *the upper hand*, they get an upgrade to the ramp, and the Christians are consigned to the deck, where they have at least brought rich-looking chairs with them. The dialogue must now be conducted across the higher/lower, upstage/downstage levels, and unless the newly abased Christians are to continually sing upstage and into the flies, the performers are obliged to play out front nearly all the time. So this contemporary staging is actually more presentational, more "stand and deliver," than that of the Vitaphone films—at least Martinelli and d'Angelo occupy the same room, as they would in reality, and sing at each other instead of at us.

Staging isn't the whole story, though, and because the Vienna/Met performers are talented and informed by modern acting sensibility, their behavior is much closer to our "true-to-life" model than that of the Vitaphone players. Stoyanova continues her excellent work, always in touch with herself. Walter Fink, the Brogni, who doesn't get much beyond stolidity in Acts I and III, here becomes quite moving in his desperation. And Shicoff is wonderful in the confrontation with the Cardinal. His body coiled around its inner charge of revenge on the brink of realization, he prowls across the ramp, spewing his contempt and triumphant denial down at Brogni. Vocally, he remains in Martinelli's shadow, but visually, he is far more persuasive. In the eye-led, ear-confirmed video medium, it's the visual that burns through. But in the theatre, too, Shicoff was powerful in this scene, a small, tense figure in a big, lonely space, who nevertheless gave off a concentrated energy that emerged with lean, spiteful force in his singing.

As Brogni staggers off, unbidden and unattended, at the conclusion of the duet, the orchestra plays the exultant *allegro* introduction. It has more pulse this time, but that doesn't matter, because Shicoff pays it no heed—he's on the line that will bring him to his way of beginning the recitative to his aria, at "*Va prononcer ma mort.*[*]

---

[*] We have a different conductor here, Vyekovslav Šutej instead of Simone Young. He has a heavier hand than Young's, and this is not to the good in episodes like the jewel trio. But in moments wanting weight or propulsion, it's an advantage, though in this case a wasted one. Think what different light would be thrown on Eléazar merely by requiring his performer to interpret two fragments I have discussed here: the opening of the jewel scene and this fleeting intro. That would not only introduce subsidiary colors in those places, but entail some re-thinking of the character throughout—the man playing out those snippets is not the same man as the one who doesn't. But here, the first fragment is excised, the second ignored.

With the arrival of Eléazar's solo scene, the attitudinal element whose consideration I have deferred till now, post-Holocaust awareness, moves front and center. To this point, it has been visible mostly in the costuming of the Christians, which connects them with the years leading up to the Third Reich, and in the modernish acting style, which brings the characters into our world, where such awareness is inescapable. It's inescapable anyway, as a matter of fact, because it's in us. We could not watch any kind of *La Juive* without it. But that is never enough for the contemporary directorial mind, which does not trust us to make even this inevitable connection, and does not trust the work to retain the peculiar, premonitory impact of one written out of a long history of persecution that had nevertheless not quite arrived at *this*. And so, it is not "merely" persecution, and not "merely" the tragedy of this father and daughter, but, specifically, the Holocaust that must be invoked. Nourrit's aria must be made to bear the weight of the ovens and gas chambers.

Without doubting the artistic sincerity of anyone involved, I find "manipulative" too weak a word for this sort of thing. So on my first encounter with the production, as the English horns intoned the melody (for it quickly became clear where we were headed), my first response was resistant and resentful. That changed almost immediately, though. Because I am myself attuned to the modern acting sensibility; because I will always look past a directorial idea to a performer's personal involvement if he or she gives me the chance to do so; because I had therefore been following Shicoff from the outset; and finally because the very element that tied the scene most tightly to the idea I didn't like was also the one that had the most personal resonance for me, I was able to put the idea on background and receive the scene.

As I have tried to indicate, the notion that "action" must be expressed in continuous physical behavior, must always find some outer object, does not invariably adapt well to the singing state-of-being or to certain operatic conventions. In fact, it's a plague on our current practice. Nonetheless, here we are with a substantial solo scene that is about Eléazar's feelings. Of course, it has an inner action: dealing with the feelings, trying to resolve them, trying to decide which should rule. And because Eléazar goes through this process and allows the feelings to surface, he arrives at a course of action. But "*Rachel*" is, in Operaspeak, an *aria d'affetto*, not an *aria d'azione*. The question of what to do while singing it is not an idle one. It could perhaps be answered with near-perfect stillness by an artist of special inner-communion gifts (like Lieberson's) or of extraordinary greatvoiced expressive ones (like Caruso's). Shicoff and Krämer answered it in a modern singingacting way.

One of modern acting's insights into lifelikeness, which one does not find much trace of in earlier acting styles, is that emotional crises do not necessarily put a stop to conditioned behavior. They may even reinforce it. One copes with the death of a parent while doing the dishes with particular care, or with a romantic breakup by re-arranging everything in the closet. Another article of belief is that a monologue is not a stopped-time moment, but a continuation of life's flow, and is addressed to oneself, not the audience. In much 20th-Century acting training (certainly in all that derived, however distantly, from the approach of Stanislavski and his followers), early technical exercises have to do with making believable the simple carrying-out of activities under various specified conditions, or with talking to oneself, or with combining the two. These are among the many ways that modern acting seeks to persuade through its resemblance to how people really behave, rather than through heightened histrionic constructs. Naturally, these techniques find their greatest fulfillment when an activity of special meaning coincides with a crisis of mortal proportion, and when talking to oneself engages deep emotional content.

A recurrent worry for directors and performers trying to create uninterrupted, lifelike behavior in opera is the instrumental introduction to an aria, especially when the time lapse from the end of the preceding recitative is long. The introduction may be very beautiful and atmospheric, but once the recitative has brought us to the brink of the aria's melodic expression, why doesn't the singer sing? What to do, that will not look like unmotivated filler (an old favorite is a long, slow cross when the character has no reason to go anywhere) or forced contrivance? It's the reverse of the "*È strano*" problem: whereas, from the P.O.V. of real-life behavioral logic, Verdi didn't write enough music, leave enough time, for Violetta to arrive at her moment, Halévy has written and left too much. When Eléazar finishes his conflicted recitative at "*. . . c'est toi qu'immole ma fureur!*", there follows first an exclamatory chord, then four beats of silence, then six bars of a winding-down *moderato*, ending with a held chord, that bring the tone down to that of the aria's beginning. Then comes the introduction itself—seventeen bars-plus of *andantino espressivo* led by those English horns in thirds, opening (as the aria does) with two statements of its mournful, long-phrased main theme, followed by little variations on its continuation. All told, about 1'45" (depending on the given tempo) elapses between utterances. Martinelli is aided by the big cut in the intro that was standard on 78 rpm recordings, but still is none too convincing with what is left. In full performance, one doesn't want to lose this half-page so full of ancient ache—musically, it sets up the piece perfectly. But if the pantomime is not persuasive, the mood vanishes—to close the eyes and listen becomes the receptor's only option.

Shicoff and Krämer found the perfect activity to carry them from the end of the recitative through the introduction and thence to the end of the aria in an unbroken arc. It provided them with the realization of their Holocaust association, but at the same time allowed for the playing of the scene on a purely personal level. The activity's intimate quality, and its very mundanity, intensified the poignancy of the moment, in the same manner as the kitchen-sink examples I cited above can. It embraced ritual and mourning. Its rhythms went hand-in-glove with those of the aria. And it brought to fruition the seed sown back in the first scene, with Eléazar's attention to his clothes.

This is one of the operatic moments when video/theatre tradeoffs are at least arguable. With the camera as our eye, we can get close-up with Shicoff's superb work. As "*Rachel*" winds on its keening way, he removes his coat and folds it. Then his vest, which he clasps to his chest—it could be, it is, the baby he plucked from the flames in Rome, so many years now past. He puts down the vest. Sitting on a chair, he takes off his shoes and sets them on top of the clothes. All this, with the care and precision of a man determined to die as he has lived, with dignity and identity intact, to use the preparation for death as a final statement of self-respect. All this, as either the song is generating the activity, or the activity the song. When the aria nears its climax, Eléazar stands in yarmulke, white shirt, and black trousers, clutching his life's final burden. We can now see, as well as hear, the singer's struggle to contain the emotional pressure, and the eye confirms that it is real. We are fearful that the voice may burst. But it doesn't, and as Shicoff comes down off this final assault on the full-voice heights, he drops his load and collapses beside it.

I cannot know to what extent the dots that I connected while tracking Shicoff's Eléazar were the same as the ones he connected. For all I know, the line from the clothes of Act I to the clothes of Act IV was drawn by sheer coincidence—I don't think so, but it's possible. The Holocaust references (smeared yellow Star of David on one of the Act I panels, the gathering of possessions and removal of shoes in "*Rachel*") cannot have been unintentional, and if there were any doubt on this point it is resolved in "Finding Eléazar," wherein the shoes (Krämer's idea)* are discussed, and Shicoff is shown heading for the stage in Act IV with his head swimming in images of the camps, strongly implying that these dominated his subtext. In honesty, I cannot even separate these references from my own response—my consciousness is post-Holocaust, too. I do believe though, that the scene's effect on me would have been equally powerful in its historical setting, with its relation to long-standing persecution left intact, and that if presented by talented, intelligent,

---

* Though it should be noted that a stage direction (p. 479 in Leich-Galland) specifies that when Rachel enters in Act V, she is "*vetue en blanc et les pieds nus*"—"clad in white and feet bare." So the thought of this state as a prerequisite for death by execution is present in the text.

and dedicated interpreters like Krämer and his collaborators, the work as a whole would have had greater artistic integrity in such a production.

Since "*Dieu m'éclaire*" and the wonderful bridge thereto is now deleted in its entirety, and is also absent from the old Vitaphone film, we have no opportunity to evaluate either tenor's enactment of that sequence. Shicoff lies on the ramp through his prolonged and merited ovation. Then, with the omission of the celebratory chorus that is meant to open Act V, and without any suggestion of a transition to the final scene's setting,* the music cuts directly to the funeral march meant to bring on Eléazar, Rachel, their guards, and groups of penitents. Shicoff rises and takes his place in the gathering. The transition "works" fine. Eléazar's interruption of the procession to ask Rachel if she wishes to save herself by converting, uninformed by the turnaround we would have seen in the cabaletta, is now unprepared, a spur-of-the-moment thought. Shicoff plays it well—no differently, I suspect, from the way he played it when the cabaletta was still in. Since late medieval punishments hardly make sense in this updated representation, Rachel is bum's-rushed off at the close by a gang in robes with peaked hoods—they could be Inquisitors, penitents, or the Ku Klux Klan. It's feeble and laughable.

I wish I had heard Caruso. I wish I had seen Martinelli in the opera house. I regret that I could not be in the Paris of the 1830s to witness its remarkable series of premieres, to hear and see for myself Nourrit and Duprez, and absorb the cultural truth of that time. But while I am sure I would have been overwhelmed by much and surprised by some, I am also certain that Shicoff's "*Rachel*," whose emotional impact was as deep and strong as anything in my operagoing experience, was, like Brooks' Violetta, an artifact of modern singingacting process, and peculiar to it. It revived in me my faith in that process as it applies to opera. At the same time, I observe that its realization in performance remains extremely rare, far rarer than the sort once provided by greatvoiced singers, and even by those specifically admired in their time as singingactors, "actors who sing," "actors with the voice," or "colorist readers." It is also clear that those artists, of whom Giovanni Martinelli is a late example, not only commanded vocal structures that gave them access

---

* "The stage represents a vast tent supported by Gothic columns, whose capitals are gilded. This tent overlooks the entire town of Constance, and we see the Great Plaza and the principal buildings. At the far end of the Great Plaza, an enormous brass cistern, heated by a flaming brazier; around the Plaza, the steps of an amphitheatre, filled with people."—Leich-Galland, p. 455. The opera's final moments are intended to show Rachel mounting the scaffolding over the cauldron as Brogni begs Eléazar one last time to disclose the whereabouts of his daughter, then being thrown into it as Eléazar exclaims "There she is!". Brogni collapses and Eléazar mounts the platform as the curtain falls.

to a broader range of dramatic effects, but that they had a stronger belief in the rhetoric(s) of those effects—a belief shared by opera's master creators, who mandated the vocal rhetorics in their scores and envisioned the bodily ones, along with the *mise en scène*, as they wrote. Our truth is our truth; we cannot relinquish it. But it is not the whole truth of the masterworks of our past. Consummation of those works will have to take into account both the modern acting sensibility and E-19's rhetorical one. As is always the case, respectful consideration of past practice will help us better define our own. It will also shed brighter light on other troublesome matters we keep encountering, such as archetypes and stereotypes, and the boundaries of interpretive freedom.

NOTES

1. See *Musical America*, Jan., 1967, pp. MA 6-7.

2. Some additional background on Brooks: She studied acting for four years with Uta Hagen, trained in both ballet and modern dance (Graham) techniques, and performed professionally as actor and dancer—I first saw her in the now-legendary production of *The Iceman Cometh* directed by Jose Quintero at the Circle in the Square, whose artistic director, Theodore Mann, she married. (For a personal recounting, see Mann's memoir, *Journeys in the Night* [Applause Books, NY, 2007].) Her City Opera debut was in 1960, and her first major assignment came a year later, as Abigail in the premiere of Robert Ward's *The Crucible*. Her command of theatrical skills gave her an extraordinary stylistic reach: she could respond not only to Corsaro's Method-derived techniques as Violetta, Gilda, and Mélisande, but to more choreographically conceived assignments like Stravinsky's Nightingale or Smeraldina in Giannini's *Servant of Two Masters*. Her salient quality was a constant emotional availability that informed both voice and body. ("Vulnerability," is the standard actorspeak for this. It should not be taken as a synonym for "fragility.") This quality appears "spontaneous" and "free," but cannot be consistently maintained without a mastery of craft.

   While Brooks was certainly one of the company's stars and had much more than a cult following, she was a particular favorite of opera-as-theatre believers—as David Alden has said, "She was our Schroeder-Devrient." (See the *Opera* interview previously referenced—p. 217, n. 19.) But partly because she was overshadowed by Sills in the matters of recordings and international réclame, and partly because her career was cut short at the halfway point by illness, she has left a sadly diminished legacy. To the best of my knowledge, no performance video survives, and her only studio audio recordings are of a Beethoven C-Minor Mass (which I have not heard) and her Abby in *The Crucible*. The VAI label, though, has released a CD taken from her New York recital debut in 1971. Neither this nor the *Crucible* recording is by any means ideal—the *Crucible*, recorded in 1962 by CRI, is in rather cramped sound, with the voices sometimes present and in good balance and sometimes not, while the VAI recital has some background hiss. Nonetheless, Brooks' Abby gives an idea of her natural-sounding delivery of text and, at moments, of her intensity. The recital shows the voice in its prime (it had gained in warmth and fullness in the intervening nine years) and the considerable musical and linguistic sophistication she had acquired across a broad stylistic range. Her operatic self is well suggested in three encores and in a compelling performance of "*Robert, toi que j'aime*" (*Robert le Diable*), in which her free, soaring top, her striking *subito piano* (with a touch of that old-style tensile feeling), and above all a good measure of the emotional directness and openness of which I just spoke, are on display. For those of us who saw her Mélisande, the Debussy songs also bring back something of her way with that role—stronger and more active than most, but still infused with the suggestive nuance required by the setting.

3. And for more on the operatic Corsaro: in the seasons immediately following that of his *Traviata* and *Butterfly* productions, he directed several more standard-repertory operas (*Cav/Pag, Faust, Rigoletto*) with the strong casts the NYCO could then offer, as well as some contemporary pieces and a couple of edge-of-repertory works (*Prince Igor, Pelléas et Mélisande*). He and Tito Capobianco—a director more inclined toward visual style and

choreographic integration, responsible for such fine productions as the famous *Giulio Cesare*, the Ginastera operas, and the Sills *Manon*—were very much the directorial stars of the City Opera's early Lincoln Center years, which, together with the late-'50s spring seasons of American opera, were surely the most exciting in the company's history. As with most directors, repeated exposure to Corsaro's work disclosed little personal pre-dilections (e.g., drunkenness as "justifying" behavior; sexual foreknowledge in the stead of sexual innocence; Little People) that did not always satisfy actualist expectations, and he experienced one fiasco with an ill-starred *Don Giovanni*. In these productions there could sometimes be sensed the incubation period of what has since become a full-blown directorial pandemic—not just the freedom, but the *obligation* to find the "original," if not subversive, ways of jumping brain-barriers for the sake of the contemporary sen-sibility. Nonetheless, these productions carried forward with general success the revi-talization of E-19 repertory. The *Pelléas*, in particular, was a notable realization, as were several Corsaro productions seen elsewhere during this period (the previously cited *La Bohème* adaptation at Lake George; the *Of Mice and Men* premiere in Seattle).

In the 1970s, Corsaro branched into multimedia (stage/film) projects, working with first-rate collaborators (most prominently the media designer Ronald Chase and costume designer Theoni Aldredge) on operas that had not achieved repertory status (Delius's *Koanga* and *A Village Romeo and Juliet*); Janáček's *The Makropoulos Affair*, and Korngold's *Die Tote Stadt*). These were imaginative productions of problematic works with little or no previous local history. *Makropoulos*, anchored by the singing and acting of another formidable soprano, Maralin Niska, and predating the Met's Janáček suc-cesses (the company had tried *Jenůfa* back in the '20s, but it didn't take), undoubtedly did more to establish that composer in New York than any other effort. So these were unquestionably successful undertakings. For those who consider visual imagery and auteuristic privilege the way forward for opera, they constitute Corsaro's "revolu-tionary" legacy. But there I disagree. For all that he was drawn to works redolent of dream and mystery (never mind Delius and Korngold—try Roland Boughton's *The Immortal Hour*) and to virtual-reality techniques, Corsaro's home style was one version of mid-20th-Century American realism; his greatest strength lay in working with indi-vidual performers and in deducing "concept" from character action; and his technical background was that of the Actors' Studio. The true revolution was his fusion of that style, strength, and technique with opera.

So far as I'm aware, not even video scraps of Corsaro's standard-repertory stagings remain. (Whatever one thinks of them, *Treemonisha* and the Maurice Sendak collabora-tions are not at all characteristic of his former work.) But for further biographical and artistic information, see Frank Corsaro: *Maverick* (Vanguard Press, NY, 1978), and the lengthy video interview with fellow director Lotfi Mansouri on the occasion of Corsaro's selection for NEA Opera Honors (accessible online). In both cases, try to overlook the occasionally pugnacious or exclamatory tone, selective artistic evaluations, and intima-tions of how awful things were B.C., and concentrate on the substance—his recapitula-tion of the thinking and working processes that went into his best productions. That's the part of the revolution worth saving.

4. In addition to the Pleasants books previously referenced (see p. 408, n. 8), I have drawn freely on three more recent volumes in my discussion of *La Juive* and its milieu. They are: Diana R. Hallman: *Opera, Liberalism, and Antisemitism in Nineteenth-Century France/ The Politics of Halévy's La Juive* (Cambridge Univ. Press, 2002); Marian Smith: *Ballet and Opera in the Age of Giselle* (Princeton Univ. Press, 2000); and Jennifer Homans: *Apollo's Angels/A History of Ballet* (Random House, N.Y., 2010). Hallman's is the most directly concerned with the opera's creation and reception; Smith's with the mixing and matching of performance techniques and styles in the grand opera, comic opera, ballet, and pantomime of the Romantic era in France; and Homans' with the place of those techniques and styles in the history of dance, with many reflections of occurrences

in other art forms. Hallman's and Smith's are somewhat more academically oriented than Homans', but all three are well written and highly recommended. Among them, they give us an excellent sense of the atmosphere and circumstances surrounding the first performances of *La Juive*.

5. François-Joseph Talma (1763-1826) was the foremost interpreter of the heroic roles in the tragedies of Corneille, Racine, Voltaire, and their imitators. The Talma of Nourrit's formative years—a former Revolutionary sympathizer, favorite of Napoleon's—is considered a forerunner of Romantic realism, and Nourrit emulated his attention to historical authenticity in physical characterization and costume. By the mid-1830s, though, in the time of the great French awakening to Shakespeare (Letourneur's translations, 1821; Stendhal's *Racine et Shakespeare*, 1823; the Paris triumphs of the English company led by Smithson, Kemble, Kean, and Macready, 1827) and of Romanticism's rise in the theatre (Hugo's *Hernani*, 1830; French translations of Schiller and Manzoni), Talma would have stood for a classicism that was on the verge of displacement.

6. All textual references in this discussion are based on the recent Bärenreiter edition: Halévy/Scribe: *La Juive*, vocal score by Karl-Heinz Müller, Alkor-Edition, Kassel, AE 340a, 2007, based on the full score edited by Karl Leich-Galland, first published in 1985. This is not an all-inclusive variorum edition, but an effort to arrive at a "composer's final wishes" version. The history of *La Juive*, both in score and in performance, is tangled. Hallman worked from original sources (see Hallman, pp. 118-19, n. 33), and on the "complete" recordings of the opera (all heavily, and variously, cut) one encounters snippets not found in the Bärenreiter edition. We still await a recording that even approaches completeness, to say nothing of an integral live festival performance. Since I am concerned primarily with the interpretation of Eléazar, and particularly with scenes in which "modern" and "greatvoiced" efforts can be compared, I will deal only with the cuts and variants that present themselves in those sections of the work. See also n. 12, below.

As to the final vocal distribution: *La Juive* is difficult to imagine without it. As Nourrit perceived, Eléazar badly needs something like the aria he suggested if we are to empathize with him at all, and since Nourrit conceived the scene for himself, it seems unlikely that anything similar would have been written for Levasseur. Without it, the original distribution leaves us with a bass father—Jewish, at that—whose vengefulness is unrelieved. Presumably, we would have had instead a big Act IV scene for Léopold (cavatina: despair, remorse; cabaletta: futile determination to intercede for Rachel? A marital confrontation scene for Léopold and Eudoxie?). And with Levasseur as Eléazar, who would have taken the role of Brogni? Possibly the baritone Labadie, the original Guillaume Tell, who wound up with the boilerplate recitative of Ruggiero?

Nourrit also would have understood that the Léopold/Eudoxie relationship has nowhere to go. In the opera's late scenes, attention has to focus not on the daughter and lover, with the father as antagonist, but on the daughter and father, with the Cardinal as antagonist. In his review of the Phillips recording (see *Opera Quarterly*, Vol. 7, No. 4, winter 1990), Roland Graeme points out that the dramatic situation is exactly that of *Rigoletto* (the nobleman who passes as commoner to seduce the daughter; the father whose vengeance on the lover costs the daughter's life), and that the literary source of *Rigoletto*, Hugo's *Le Roi s'amuse*, had premiered in Paris just as work on *La Juive* was beginning. (The disguised nobleman gambit had also just been played in Auber's *Gustave III*—the material later taken up by Verdi for *Un Ballo in Maschera*.) Of course there are important differences. To enumerate: Léopold is not a constitutionally licentious ruler, but a prince of the realm and military hero who has fallen in love and is haunted by remorse on both marital and religious grounds. Rachel is not a 15-year-old innocent but a strong grown woman in a consensual relationship of some standing (consummated, I think we must assume, before Léopold headed off on the Hussite campaign). Being a successful Jewish goldsmith and trader in jewelry in Switzerland is not the same as being a hunchback at an Italian court. In *Rigoletto* there is no figure like that of Brogni, with his determinative influence on the plot and powerful emotional involvement in its revelation. *La Juive* has a far richer and more complex backstory, and the surrounding social and political circumstances are entirely different.

Still, it's true that the essential triangle with its tragic resolution is identical. *La Juive* thus joins *Rigoletto* (and *Simon Boccanegra*, though that's more complicated), as one of the works in which the action is driven by the faydit romance, played out as an elaborate real-life game (Léopold even has a serenade, "*Loin de son amie*," whose sentiment could come straight from a troubadour's mouth), but moves aside as the center of emotional interest in favor of the father/daughter bond (see Backstory 3).

7. In an exhaustive study of concert pitch in European and English orchestras and opera houses, conducted through measurement of the tuning forks then in use, Alexander J. Ellis (see "On the Measurement and Settlement of Musical Pitch," *Journal of the Society of Arts*, London, May 25, 1877, pp. 664 f.) reported the following standards for three of the major Paris theatres in 1826: Paris Opéra, 445; Théâtre-Italien, 449; Opéra-Comique, 452 (later raised, he notes, to 455). Thus, though the Opéra's standard was the lowest of these, it was still a shade higher than ours—that 5 cps is just enough to be detected as a bit sharp by a good ear, and certainly enough to register physically with a singer negotiating high tessitura. This does not change my view of Nourrit's registral balances in this music (the only one that makes sense to me in terms of the vowels, dynamics, and accentings of the writing), but it does mean that the range he covered was certainly not lower than it appears in the score. It also means that all those legendary singers of the Théâtre-Italien (Pasta, Malibran, the entire original casts of *I Puritani* and *Don Pasquale*, including Rubini with his high F, et al.) were stretching yet higher for pitch, and those of the Comique, where lots of Auber, Boieldieu, et al. were done, higher still.

The push for higher pitch in search of brilliance (a general tendency during the Romantic era throughout Europe, the highest being found in England, the lowest in Germany and Austria, but with many variants) led to the first official effort to establish a standard—that of the French Commission, which issued its report in 1859. The Commission advocated A435, and specifically recommended this for the performance of the works of Meyerbeer, Halévy, Auber, Berlioz, Ambroise Thomas, and the later Rossini (not insignificant, since these composers were themselves members of the Commission), although Ellis contends that through mismeasurement (another issue), the "French normal," or "diapason normal," which did come into general acceptance, actually got no lower than 439. International conferences were held in Vienna (1885, with a follow-up in London) and London again (1939), eventually confirming A-440 as the standard modern pitch, though this has hardly stopped orchestras from tweaking it. For *La Juive*, the French Commission's target of 435 sounds to me like a really good idea.

This is a subject persistently addressed by Shaw, who is of course a lot more fun to read than the worthy Mr. Ellis. (See especially Laurence: *Shaw's Music*, Vol. I, pp. 277 f., and Vol. II, pp. 456 f.) Shaw points out that among singers, while sopranos and tenors favored a lower standard, contraltos and basses were less enthusiastic ("Astrifiammante [sic—the then-common Italianization for Queen of the Night] can only be relieved at the expense of Sarastro": Vol. I, p. 733). The "money notes" of the true contraltos and deep basses were at the bottom, not the top.

8. A word is in order on this question of laryngeal position, whose importance is perhaps mysterious to readers who are not voice professionals. Simply put: A high laryngeal position, necessarily associated with some lifting of the back of the tongue and usually with some widening of the upper vocal tract (the "smile" position), creates a shorter, wider acoustical environment that tends to favor a brighter timbre (shorter wavelengths, higher partials), with vowels inclining towards "*i*," "*e*" and the shallower versions of "*a*." A lower larynx, by creating a longer, more tubular space, tends to do

the reverse, encouraging a darker timbre and rounder vowels. Voices whose pitch-producing mechanics at their point of origin (i.e., the adjustments of the vocal cords for faster or slower vibration) are not in ideal balance will tend to stretch the laryngeal position in one direction or the other in an effort to reach the extremes of the range, in effect manipulating the acoustical environment of the tone to compensate for a problem at the point of origin. Because effective high notes are so desirable, problems associated with a laryngeal set that is "too high" are more frequently encountered than their low-larynx counterparts, but "too low" is no better than "too high," since both involve a strained relationship between the muscles that elevate the larynx and those that depress it—particularly if the position is fixed. The relationship between pitch mechanics and vocal acoustics, and of both these to the valve function that governs air compression at the upper end, with all their variations in individual cases, are much too complex to expatiate on here. But to clarify my view of the Nourrit/Duprez differential (and, by extension, the oldstyle vs. modern tenor models): Nourrit sang with a relatively high laryngeal position, in compensation for the fact that his pitch mechanics did not draw in enough Upper Family participation in the *passaggio* area. The tension created by such an adjustment demands relief by the time it arrives in the vicinity of A, and that gave rise to the array of sophisticated *falsetto* usages developed by the oldstyle tenors. Duprez, in his high-intensity search for a more heroic format (for I suspect that his primary concern in tackling Arnold was the smallness of his voice more than its range extension—otherwise, why could he not have carried on in the old manner?), forced the issue at the *passaggio* and brought down the larynx, thus eliminating the tensions of the lifted position and releasing the full-voice extension. His "high C from the chest" actually involved bringing "head" farther down in the range, with the tone's ring coming from vigorous laryngeal engagement, its volume and darkness from the roomier, longer pharyngeal space. And a note on "ring" or *squillo*, the "singer's formant": it comes from the bottom, not the top, of the resonance complex. For well-supported scientific discussion of this, see Vennard, pp. 89-90, who also reports the findings of Diday and Pétrequin (physicians, writing in 1840, three years after Duprez's Paris debut), who observed that while most singers allowed the larynx to rise with pitch, Duprez kept his low, and so created "a new type of singing voice." Also see *The Science of the Singing Voice*, by Johan Sundberg, a leading modern theorist (Northern Illinois Univ. Press, DeKalb, 1987, Chap. 5, and especially p. 121, on the relation of the "singer's formant" to laryngeal activation and positioning in the male voice. For a much earlier perception, see Manuel Garcia: *Hints on Singing*, E. Ascherberg, London, 1894, Beata Garcia, trans., p. 12: ". . . the ring or dulness [sic] of sound is . . . completely distinct from the open or closed *timbres* (Garcia's italics). The ringing and dulness are produced *in the interior of the larynx* (my italics), independently of the position, high or low, of this organ . . ." Note also that Garcia is not opposed to some mobility of the laryngeal position, depending on the timbral qualities sought, a tolerance much more common in the 19th Century than it is today. For a time I was taught by a teacher in the De Reszke line of descent to raise the back of the tongue, perforce lifting the larynx with it, while ascending into the upper range, a technique with which I came to emphatically disagree, just as I respectfully do with the contention of Jerome Hines that the larynx must be kept "as low as possible." (See many references in both his books, e.g., *The Four Voices of Man*, p. 175. He was a bass, after all.) Nonetheless, I think the view that the larynx may be allowed some vertical excursion, provided it is not extreme and does not become fixed, is worth some re-evaluation.

We should keep in mind that for roughly two hundred years after the dawn of operatic singing, technical theory was derived nearly exclusively from Upper Family models—the singing of the castrati, falsettists, women and boys, with gradual adaptations toward the necessity of a more complete male representation. So it's in no way surprising that the problem of fully developed male categories was not "solved" until the expressive requirements of E-19 opera made the issue inescapable.

9. Several pertinent versions of *"Rachel"* will figure later in my discussion. The only other excerpts to attract much attention on recordings are Brogni's (the *cavatine "Si la rigueur,"* which became one of the standards for deep bass, and the malediction, *"Vous qui du Dieu vivant."*). Most of the really impressive ones are in foreign languages (Italian, by Navarrini, Didur, or Pinza; or Russian, by Lev Sibiriakov), any of which will quickly show what is missing from contemporary efforts. But there is one of the *cavatine* in native tongue that should be heard—that of Paul Payan. His singing has the combination of splendid low notes, rich tone, superb line, and linguistic finish to fully realize the piece. Payan also recorded a liberally cut version of the Act IV Brogni/Eléazar confrontation with César Vezzani. Here, Payan's top notes don't quite do the trick. Like a number of basses from regions north of Italy and west of Russia, Payan went into a bass version of "pure head" around C#or D; the high notes were there, but in a relatively dry, colorless tone. Familiarity with the records of Jean-François Delmas helps us imagine a French-language consummation of the *cavatine* in key, as well as a scary malediction. There are good postwar versions of the *cavatine* by Siepi and Treigle, whereon the orchestral sound is, of course, much better.

Rachel's romance, *"Il va venir!"*, has never attracted much attention, which I find odd, since it's filled with dramatic possibility, and the role was taken by many greatvoiced sopranos. Ponselle's recording is beautifully controlled and musically expressive in her early classical manner, almost like a chip off her *La Vestale* block, which gives it great dignity but not much tension. One would assume that she sang it more expansively in performance, and that the voice's impact must have been significant (but see Drake, p. 127, for critical reservations that are not incompatible with what can be heard on the recording). Lotte Lehmann's rendition, in German, is expectedly expressive and very well sung. For Rethberg, see the main text. Otherwise, there isn't much outside the "complete" recordings—greatvoicewise, there's the impressive radio runthrough by Farrell (see p. 422, n. 30) and a version by Varnay, whose big, deep tone is welcome, but not the rather clumsy handling of the line or the shaved-off high notes she often summoned to sidestep heaviness. Anyone in search of stylistic and linguistic authenticity must hear the 1908 recording of Berthe Auguez de Montalant. She was primarily a concert singer, but her voice was operatically complete in range and format, and her guidance of it unerring. The timbre may strike us as closer to Eudoxie than Rachel—pure, clear, and bright—but the frame is strong, the low end present. It's a striking rendition.

The other roles were almost completely neglected for three-quarters of a century. So far as I can determine, not a note of Eudoxie's music was recorded aside from the Da Vinci "complete" recording (see n. 11) until Moffo sang the Bolero and the duet with Rachel (Martina Arroyo) on the 1974 RCA highlights LP with Tucker. Indeed, both the Bolero and the preceding air, *"Assez longtemps la crainte,"* were cut during the opera's premiere run (fly-on-the-wall fantasy: Dorus-Gras receiving the news in her dressing room), and do not seem to have been restored until the 1999 Vienna production. Of Léopold's lovely, stratospheric serenade I have traced only a single pre-LP recording, made in 1913 by Eugène de Creus. In many ways, it remains the model for all others: blandishing, crystalline tone, perfect poise on the tensile *messa di voce*, elegant but unfussed pronunciation, and an easy command of turns and other graces. He sings only one verse, plus the cadential ending, and at a slower-than-normal tempo, with many *ad libitum* easements, that captures the feel of the troubadourish plea far better than any other version. He slips smoothly in and out of falsetto for the high note on *"jour"* in the cadenza—which is, however, a C instead of a D, for he sings his piece a full step down, as must have been the widespread custom.

So we have only fossilized fragments. But if we string together Payan, De Creus, Montalant, Payan/Vezzani, and the *"Rachel"* (both sections) of Escalaïs, we do get the flavor of a well-cast original-language *La Juive*, in the years before WWI. And I should not fail to mention Georges Granal, who in 1910 recorded on four 78-rpm sides the entire

"*Rachel*" sequence, minus only the orchestral introduction and the second verse of the cabaletta, but including the bridge from "*Rachel*" to "*Dieu m'éclaire*" and the choral intrusions, with the resulting "change of heart" for Eléazar. These records, called to my attention by Will Crutchfield, are extremely rare, and the singer obscure except to highly specialized collectors, but this is a potent French dramatic tenor with a remarkably secure and powerful upper range. He's not the ultimate in terms of interpretive shading, but he sings a firm line, is in control of the dynamics, and introduces some interesting variants I haven't heard anywhere else. His version of this sequence broadens significantly our "performance practice" knowledge of the "*Rachel*" scene.

10. For helpful construal on the subject of usury and the Jews, and of resentful attitudes toward Jewish wealth in general, see Hallman, Chap. 6, and especially pp. 257 f.

11. Shicoff's performance is well documented by the CDs of the 1999 Vienna production (on RCA); the DVD of that production's 2003 revival (on DG, with important changes in cast and conductor); and the film *Finding Eléazar*, which I first saw during its brief New York theatre run, and is included as a bonus on the DVD. These are of course informed by my responses to the Met's presentation of that production in 2005 (with further changes in cast and conductor), which inspired my interest in the characterization in the first place. Of Martinelli's Eléazar, we have in audio form (on Guild CDs) the second act as broadcast by the San Francisco Opera in 1936, plus the cavatina "*Dieu, que ma voix tremblante*," which he had earlier recorded for Victor; and in video form, on an Encore DVD, the Vitaphone films that take in the Act IV interview with Brogni, the recitative "*Va prononcer ma mort*," and "*Rachel, quand du Seigneur*" (but not "*Dieu m'éclaire*"). There is also his 1927 Victor studio recording of the aria, not significantly different from the Vitaphone version. The audio portion of the Vitaphone sequence was made available over fifty years ago on a two-LP gatefold set by Asco, one of the several labels produced by the indefatigable Edward J. ("Eddie") Smith. The roar and crunch of background noise is formidable, but actually a bit less than that of the DVD, and the audio-only version at least enables the listener to focus one sense without squinting and blinking with the other through the film's sepia murk. The bass on the scene with Brogni, correctly attributed on the film, is Louis d'Angelo, a longtime Met comprimario. Smith, however, claimed it was the much more prominent (though seldom recorded) Virgilio Lazzari, apparently due to a dispute with d'Angelo over payment. The voices are just similar enough to make the deception plausible, and Lazzari did sing the role a number of times with Martinelli.

Three other tenors have recorded Eléazar at something approaching full length. Miklos Gafni sang it on the earliest "complete" recording (1961, on Da Vinci, another Eddie Smith label). Gafni was once a promising tenor (he recorded some Italian arias, and gave a well-received New York recital in 1947), but his effortful attempt at Eléazar is a write-off. There are two versions with José Carreras—a Vienna live concert performance and the Philips studio recording. He tackles the role courageously and not inartistically. However, it is a part for which his beautiful lyric tenor was unsuited even when in peak technical and physical health, some years earlier than this recording date. In a 1951 Frankfurt radio performance in German, the veteran Wagnerian Joachim Sattler (Furtwängler's Loge on the La Scala *Ring* of that same year) makes his way through a brutally cut version (no Act II *cavatine*, no repeats, and not even the B section and return to A in "*Rachel*") with neither dishonor nor revelation. His Rachel is Erna Schlüter, whose important dramatic soprano voice was nearing the end of its viability. She has some eloquent moments as the performance proceeds. The most satisfying work comes from the Eudoxie (Maria-Meta Kopp) and the Brogni (Otto von Rohr).

Richard Tucker demands more serious consideration. He is the one postwar tenor before Shicoff to try to bring *La Juive* back into the repertory, and aside from Vickers (who would probably have declined the role) or, at a stretch, McCracken, the one best equipped for it. He repeatedly pressed the Met management to stage the opera for him. That should have happened in the early '60s, when the company might have cast Crespin or Farrell, Moffo, Gedda or Kraus, and Siepi, Tozzi or Hines in the other roles, with Prêtre (or might they have lured Bernstein?) in the pit and Merrill and O'Hearn (or Zeffirelli?) as the production team. That, with a more inclusive edition than the one previously used, would have restored the work. The company finally got around to scheduling *La Juive* in the mid-1970s—but Tucker died, and the production with him. He did have one crack at the role during his prime singing years, in two concert performances (March, 1964, Carnegie Hall and the Brooklyn Academy) under the auspices of the Friends of French Opera, with Robert Lawrence conducting. These seem to have fallen through an historical crack, so for the record: Suzanne Sarroca was Rachel, Micheline Tessier Eudoxie, Jean Deis Léopold, Norman Treigle (Carnegie) and Chester Watson (Brooklyn) Brogni, and Spiro Malas Ruggiero. Tucker's vocalism was exciting, his temperament and commitment infectious. These performances first made me feel the power of the opera. I do not consider him at length in my comparisons for two reasons: there is no video to give us visual clues to his Eléazar; and as an actor he was always highly energetic but generalized, more about tenorial histrionics than any particular character. By the time he recorded the part (a London concert performance, 1973, and especially the Victor highlights disc, 1974) his voice, though in admirable shape for a sixtyish tenor who never stinted, had lost a measure of heft and richness. Nonetheless, the London Eléazar is a doughty effort that at times reaches the heights, and the Victor excerpts include some handsome singing from his colleagues. Tucker's 1967 recording of "*Rachel*" for Columbia captures a good measure of his singing's thrust and brilliance, along with some French that's rather shockingly bad, considering the number of Josés and Hoffmanns he sang.

La Juive devotees and doubters alike should search out the generous LP's worth of excerpts, cut for continuity like some of the *Grosser Querschnitt* German releases of the '50s and '60s, on the Philips label. Like no other recording, it boasts a highly capable all-French cast and conductor (Marcel Couraud), though the chorus and orchestra are those of the Karlsruhe Opera. Tony Poncet is the Eléazar. His performance is unsubtle and sometimes awkward. However, he is the owner of a genuine dramatic tenor voice, complete with on-the-button high notes right up through the C, and so offers otherwise-unavailable thrills at some of the score's most important moments. In addition, Jane Rhodes is the most interpretively compelling Rachel to be heard on any of these "complete" or extended-excerpts recordings.

12. Since this quotation is from another Eddie Smith source (the booklet accompanying the Da Vinci *La Juive* album) and thus open to question, I should note that it comes from an article under Rothier's name, recounting his long acquaintance with the work and his collaboration with Bodanzky on the Met version. One gathers that Gatti-Casazza felt the need for a shorter version than that used during the German-language seasons, when there was a substantial German-speaking audience base in New York. The German-English libretto published by Koppel for the Met season of 1884-85, and presumably in use there through the German-language seasons, includes Eléazar's Act II *cavatine* and both verses of his Act IV cabaletta, with choral interruptions, as well as the opening chorus of Act V, and the Act I scene of Léopold's return in disguise, which is not present in the Leich-Galland score. But it omits both of Eudoxie's arias, and the Eudoxie/Rachel scene from Act III—though on the first night the Eudoxie, Marie Schröder-Hanfstängl, inserted an aria from *Robert le Diable* at the top of the act. Altogether, this redaction does not look more than ten minutes longer than the one shown in the Rullman libretto for the Caruso/Martinelli seasons. In neither case, of course, can we be sure that the libretto accurately reflects what was actually performed.

Rothier speaks of "using the Paris cuts" (that is, those in use there around the turn of the 20th Century) as a starting point. I have no grounds for discounting his account, despite its provenance. For a diverting evocation of Eddie Smith's modus operandi, see

Robert Prag: "More EJS," etc. (*Opera Quarterly*, Vol. 17, No. 1, winter, 2001), a review of the second volume of the massive Smith discography by the Messrs. Shaman, Collins, and Goodwin (Greenwood Press, Westport, Conn., 1999), which sifts through the vagaries of pitch, the false attributions of names, places, dates, etc. All these notwithstanding, Smith was a pioneer of the opera underground and, for serious vocal collectors, a figure of unique importance.

13. There is still plenty of work to be done with respect to the performing traditions of this opera. I recently examined an old Choudens vocal score (undated, distributed in the U.S. by Peters) which corresponds to Hallman's description of the Schlesinger score published in Paris shortly after the premiere (lacking the Act II tenor *cavatine* and Eudoxie's Act III arias, etc.). The score had belonged to an unidentified tenor, apparently American, who sometime, somewhere sang the role of Eléazar, and is heavily marked in all the sections involving that character. The markings include beats, extensive articulations, alternative notes (e.g., A-flat instead of the C surmounted by Martinelli in Act II; the interpolated B-flat at the end of "*Rachel*," but remaining on F for "*la voilà!*" at the end of the opera, etc.); a few staging and "reaction" instructions, and cuts. These last are comparatively light—this tenor seems to have sung a fairly inclusive version of the role. At the top of Act II he has pasted in the sheet music of the *cavatine*, advertised as "*chanté par M. Nourrit*," though it apparently never was. Interestingly, the Brogni/Eléazar dialogue after the Act IV duo is not among the cuts. On the other hand, in the Met/Rullman libretto, the text jumps from the end of the duo to the *moderato* at "*J'ai fait peser sur toi*"—in other words, the entire little section I have been discussing, including the dancey instrumental intro and "*Va, prononcer ma mort*," etc., is omitted. Possibly it's again Bodanzky saving thirty seconds, or, conceivably, he just didn't know what to make of the music.

14. No doubt, "*Dieu m'éclaire*" is meant to be somewhat quicker than the *andantino espressivo* of "*Rachel*." Like most cabalettas in relation to their arias, it represents the launching of an action after an introspective monologue or intimate plea, often (again as customary) upon receipt of motivating information delivered by some functionary or the chorus. Sometimes the contrasts in tempo between aria and cabaletta are quite extreme and sometimes not, and sometimes set in motion by highly propulsive rhythms and sometimes not. But up to just about the time of *La Juive*, the up-tempo impression was almost invariably augmented by passages of written melisma and unwritten ornamentation, even when male voices were involved. Here, although the modest groupings at the return to the main theme ("*ton empire est vainqueur*," bars 196 and 246) offer the opportunity for embellishment that Nourrit could have taken, the effect of the piece is in no way dependent upon either ornament or velocity.

In later practice—extending into my own early operagoing years—such numbers were most often cut altogether or, at best, retained with a single verse plus codetta, Manrico's "*Di quella pira*" or Enrico's "*La pietade in suo favore*" being examples of the latter, and the cabalettas of Verdi's Duke, Alfredo, Germont, and *Trovatore* Leonora (Act IV) of the former. The tradition of omitting or shortening these pieces was not without reason. Musically speaking, it's true that, while some are genuinely exciting, others suffer from banal tunes, accompaniments that do nothing but chug along, and choral interjections that are only repeated asides or expressions of support. And with ornamental styles in disuse, the two-verse form relies entirely on greatvoiced presence and thrilling high notes. Dramatically, the second verse also poses the problem of what to *do*: having stated the life-and-death urgency of the action about to be taken, why does the character hang around to state it again? How, theatrically, is that to be represented? Too often, these pieces give the impression of being present solely to fill out a conventional form. And indeed, "*Dieu m'éclaire*"'s tune is perfectly commonplace, though it proves susceptible to convincing development. Dramatically, however, it is more playable than most two-verse examples, since the intervening cries of the approaching mob give the second verse an added impetus, an obstacle to play against. And a footnote: when even a shortened version of the overture is played (as here), if *"Dieu m'éclaire"* is omitted we are left with a theme drawn from the opera to follow that the composer worked up into an extended development and triumphal conclusion for his overture, but which never makes its reappearance in its dramatic context. Now it's just an ordinary tune, not especially in keeping with the drama, that is for some reason given pride of place and "symphonic" elaboration.

15. Here's how this little sequence goes in the present production: First, the director has seated Léopold right at Rachel's elbow, where she can't miss his tiniest tic. (The score's directions place them at opposite ends of the table, making it possible, in the dim candlelight, for Rachel to be not quite certain what she's seeing.) When the unleavened bread is distributed, Léopold makes an "E-e-ew" sort of face, as if unable to disguise this offense to his gourmet taste, and flings the partially masticated fragments to the floor, practically at Rachel's feet. Stoyanova's *"Que vois-je?"* has the same proclamatory tone as Isokoski's on the CDs. Krämer, recognizing the bread-on-the-floor difficulty, has Rachel pick it up when the celebrants disperse. This means that when Léopold returns later Rachel, rather than merely harboring a strong suspicion that she hopes will prove unfounded, cannot avoid knowing that something's off, Judaically speaking, with her mysterious suitor. And that in turn means that her questioning of him, her disbelief ("What am I hearing?") and shock when he finally admits his deception (twenty-seven bars of widely spaced pizzicato under held notes, *followed by* "a long silence"—this is of course shortened in modern performance) make her out as simply dullwitted. It's all so much less interesting than finding a plausible way of playing the situation as indicated.

16. One example is worth noting, since it represents such a departure from my text-and-ear, mind's eye visualization. During Rachel's aria, Léopold hovers over her on the ramp, almost like a stalker. His presence doesn't necessarily affect the artist's work, but it distracts us from her one chance to draw us into her fear and anticipation. "He will return," she sings, and we reply "Sure enough—there he is," and our attention is split. Instead of a woman in a closed-in place singing of the night, the silence, and the approaching storm outside that augments her inner state, we have one in an open space that also contains the absent lover. No lightning flickers, and no storm approaches to burst forth at the end of the act.

5

ONSTAGE III: RHETORICS

THE RHETORICS, ORAL TRADITION, AND THE MODERN ACTING SENSIBILITY

The rhetorics of voice and body were matters of intense interest during the E-19 era. Their sources were ancient. In his masterful *Orality and Literacy*,[1] Walter J. Ong traces the line from these sources down to the formal rhetorical studies of 19th-Century classical education. Ong's subject is the profound alterations in thought and perception that occur in the shift from an oral culture, with its purely memory-based ways of retaining and transmitting knowledge, to a literate one, wherein writing fixes and stores knowledge outside the mind, and then in the shift from writing to printing, whose exact replications fix knowledge yet more rigidly and disseminate it far more widely. Carrying forward his own previous work and that of several predecessors, Ong seeks to convey the mental habits of an oral culture, in which language exists only as sound, inherently evanescent.*

In a literate culture, words (and, in our context, notes and wordnotes) exist as visual symbols that refer back to sounded originals. But in an oral culture, only those originals exist—passing events sent by voice, received by ear. In the absence of inscription, nothing can be looked up. Knowledge consists entirely of what can be remembered: ". . . once acquired," says Ong, "it had to be constantly repeated or it would be lost." Thus, the forms assumed by recitations and enactments of such a culture's enduring wisdom (religious,

---

* Or, as he puts it, it's a "sound-dominated verbal economy," in which the "dissecting" eye plays a subsidiary role. Ong's formulations regarding the sensory properties of sight and sound are very close to those I have outlined earlier (Pt. I, "Eye and Ear," pp. 24 f.) See Ong, esp. Chap. 3, pp. 31-f.

mythical, epic-heroic) were shaped by usages that would leave deep and lasting imprints in the minds of both the reciters/enactors and their receptors. Ong identifies some of these, the mnemonic patterns that allowed transmission of long, elaborate tales, and which in great part constituted the shape of thought itself:

- They were formulaic and reiterative, using repetition to burn in key patterns.
- They were poetic, couched in "... heavily rhythmic, balanced patterns, in repetitions and antitheses, in alliterations and assonances ..."
- They strove for proverbial status, making frequent use of "... epithetic and other formulary expressions, in standard thematic settings ... patterned for retention and ready recall." (Ong, p. 34.)

As for the stories themselves, they had these properties:

- They were agonistic, conceived in struggle—which is to say, they were dramas.
- They were heroic, peopled by personages of vivid color and monumental action—easily recognized types, rather than characters in our modern meaning. (Ong calls them "heavy;" also "flat," as opposed to "round.")*
- In performance (by bard, priest, or shaman), they were rhapsodic, highly inflected, and songlike. To "rhapsodize," Ong tells us, means "to stitch songs together."
- They were unoriginal—even, we would say, clichéd (a term, by the way, that had its origin in a printing process—thus, in facilitation of multiple exact copies). The invention of new materials or of a previously unimagined P.O.V. was not the point. Virtue lay rather in finding striking ways of presenting and reinforcing familiar materials that carried important cultural meaning and served the objectives of social stability and continuity. In an oral culture, "Song is the remembrance of songs sung" (Ong, p. 142, in a lovely quotation from Berkley Peabody).

Writing, with its capacity for the retention of complex word or other notational constructions that can in turn generate fresh variations and extensions, its shift of word-perception from ear to eye, and its detachment of speech from speaker, began immediately to transform and expand human thought. But the practices of orality did not die, or even quickly fade, with its

---

* Ong follows E.M. Forster's application of this last term for a character that has a quality of incalculability, of surprise, as opposed to a "flat" character, which "delights by fulfilling expectations copiously." Ong, p. 148.

invention. A central figure in orality/literacy studies is Homer, whose inscriptions of the already-old, oft-told epics are much beholden to the formulas, themes, and metrical patterns of their oral progenitors in both language and structure. And a few generations after Homer, Greek classical drama, from which all Western arts of the act have sprung, gave us our first enactments of stories with through-line plots and characters whose public acts reflected inner lives, now tethered to a text, but all still heavily indebted to oral habit and all still memorized, recited, and sung.

The influence of orality's heroic tales and formulary devices proved tenacious for many centuries. Ong pursues it from the Greek and Roman poets, orators, and dramatists through medieval manuscription to the advent of printing; thence through the Renaissance, with its revival of Greco-Roman myths and arts, through the Enlightenment, and at last into the academic rhetoric of the 19th Century and the study of "Learned Latin," the Latin that served as the in-common Western language of church and state long after anyone acquired it as a first language or used it in everyday life. The persistence of these influences he illustrates through the Latin prosodic assemblages of the *Gradus ad Parnassum*,* with its readymade components of Latin phrases awaiting the more or less ingenious re-arrangements of schoolboy poets.

Classical education of the E-19 era sought to cultivate the eloquent speaker as much as the eloquent writer. Throughout the 19th Century—and, at least in the "better" schools, well into the 20th—rhetoric remained an essential subject for anyone seeking advancement, especially in the public sphere. Its pedagogy leaned heavily on Greco-Roman authority—on Aristotle and Demosthenes, Cicero and Quintilian, *et alia*. The eloquence of the sounded word had a bodily analogue, a vocabulary of gestures, poses, and facial expressions of sufficient profile and presence to tell (like the voice) at a distance, indoor or out. Both the vocal and gestural rhetorics developed sets of rules, duly codified in textbooks and taught in classrooms and studios. These codifications, of everything we would now classify under "tone of voice" and "body language", were extremely complex and detailed. Every nuance of vocal inflection, every flicker of variation in position and gesture, was presumed to signify a specific, narrowly defined affect, and to be necessary for its expression. And since reading aloud was still considered the best way to

---

* "Steps to Parnassus." Parnassus was the mountain assigned in Greek myth to Apollo and the Muses, and thus the seat of music and poetry. The phrase came into general use for any prescribed route toward perfection, as with sets of progressive exercises for musical or instrumental mastery.

realize a text's expressive potential, there were also rules governing written rhetoric, the means by which writers learned to build into their texts these same effects and nuances of expression, of performance, of presence (all the elements deconstruction seeks to expose and eradicate), so that even a silent, private reading would present them to the mind's ear and eye.

It is worth noting that behind these mighty efforts to "influence and persuade" with "propriety, elegance, and force" lies an argumentative presumption. As Ong points out, rhetoric is agonistic at its root. Opposition or resistance is always implied. That means it is a natural form of expression in our Western theatrical mode, the drama, wherein stage characters are perpetually engaged in overcoming opposing characters and forces, and performers in overcoming the skepticism of audiences, winning them over to unreserved belief. This has been the case for about three millennia now.

Rather like the musicological performance-practice pursuits of today, the vocal and gestural rhetorics of E-19 were mixtures of then-current performance styles with reconstructions of long-moribund usages, inferred from the evidence at hand. In spoken rhetoric, such evidence included texts of classical plays and poetic epics, and descriptions of oratorical feats and techniques in the writings of Greek and Roman authorities. In bodily rhetoric, the evidence lay in the poses, attitudes, and raiments of Greco-Roman sculpture and the recreations of classical history and myth in European art from the Renaissance forward.*[2] In both cases, the ancient representations were taken as models, as depictions of an authentic and superior life that had once existed and toward which mankind should once again aspire—a view easily conflated with Christian ones of art as elevation of the soul, of fallen mankind's ascent toward the divine.

The codifications of the rhetorics proceeded from the vast Enlightenment project of categorizing all human knowledge, and where possible systemizing it according to scientific, or even mechanical, principles. They were drawn from the practices of the most highly regarded orators of the time—of the church, legislative chamber, public platform, and above all the stage. As early

---

* Two (among many) characteristic observations: Colley Cibber in his famous *Apology* (1740), quoting with approval an admiring description of the acting of the Italian castrato Nicolini: ". . . every limb and finger contributes to the part he acts, in so much that a deaf man might go along with him . . . There is scarce a beautiful posture, in an old statue, which he does not plant himself in, as the different circumstances of the story give occasion for it." And, nearly a century later (1822), Macready on "the genius of Talma": "[It] rose above the conventionality of all schools. Every turn and movement as he trod upon the stage might have given a model for the sculptor's art, and yet all was effected with such apparent absence of preparation as made him seem unconscious of the dignified and graceful attitudes he presented. . . His object was not to dazzle or surprise by isolated effects: the character was his aim; he put on the man. . ."

as the 1770s, Joshua Steele, a trained musician and theorist, was embarked on creating a method of reproducing the spoken word in written score and was using it to notate the speech of David Garrick and other eminent speakers.[3]

Steele's book was unusual in proposing a notational system so closely tied to the scoring of music. But in other respects it was a typical product of the elocutionary movement of the 18th and 19th centuries, whose precepts, for all practical purposes, also constituted the acting theory of the time. Many erudite, meticulously observed volumes followed, all directed toward the maximization of rhetorical effect—toward the unanswerable argument, the ultimate portrayal. The degree to which any of these published systems may have directly influenced the work of particular actors and singers I am not in a position to assert. No doubt most of the practices they aspire to notate and codify were passed from older to younger, along with standard staging conventions, in the daily rough-and-tumble of rehearsal and performance. But there is no question that these systems *reflect* the prevalent beliefs and techniques of those performers. And while most of the works I have examined belong to the Anglo-American tradition of rhetorical instruction, it is abundantly clear that the basics of that tradition were embraced on the Continent, as well. Further, there is the family resemblance of the systems detailed in these books to that of François Delsarte, whose influence on theatre practice and direct connection to operatic acting have already been noted (see p. 51, n. 4). His method differs somewhat in emphases and vocabulary from those of the Anglo-American pedagogues, but is similar in its general approach and categorizations.

Apparent in the work of all these gentlemen is the same poignant paradox faced by modern operatic seekers: a unified action is sought, yet must be worked on and talked about in terms of its discrete elements. In discussing the unification of vocal and mimetic expression hoped for in his system, Delsarte said: "Persuade yourself that there are blind men and deaf men in your audience whom you must *move, interest, and persuade!* Your inflection must become pantomime to the blind, and your pantomime, inflection to the deaf." In other words, the performing artist must graphically *demonstrate*, with voice and body, the emotional and mental states of his character to the ear and the eye of the receptor. These states must be appropriate to the material at hand, and must be regulated by certain rules, whose formulation is the task of the master teachers. All the 19th-Century teachers of the rhetorics believed that the expression of emotion and meaning is a matter of compositional art, and that the rules governing such composition could be discovered and practiced. (For further on Joshua Steele's book, on the elocutionary movement and gestural rhetoric in general, and on Delsarte and his American champions Steele MacKaye and Genevieve Stebbins, see n. 3.)

Notwithstanding the authority of the presumably scientific rules and the proliferation of biomechanical exercises directed toward precision of illustration, the rhetoricians of E-19 insisted that genuine, spontaneous-seeming emotion must be present in the artist's work, and that this work should seem "natural." Robert Lloyd's delicious light poem *The Actor* (1760), whose citations in the literature of theatre and rhetoric were perhaps second only to Hamlet's advice to the players for over a century, begins: "Acting, dear Thornton, its perfection draws/From no observance of mechanical laws", and within a few pages is pleading, "To this one standard make your just appeal,/here's the golden secret; learn to FEEL." And a little farther along: "To paint the passion's force, and mark it well,/The proper action nature's self will tell."[4] The rhetoricians did not want expression to seem mechanical or forced, or for its elements to show. They sought a natural eloquence, and marked down any impression of the mechanistic or artificial to imperfect practice of their principles, not the principles themselves. Stebbins was at pains to counter the view that study of Delsarte's system would ". . .make one mechanical and elocutionary." And of MacKaye, one historian says: "He championed the Delsarte methods of *naturalism* [my italics] in acting."[5] The reference is casual, as though lower-case "naturalism" were the commonly acknowledged aim of Delsartian technique.

To us, the contradiction seems obvious. How is one to appear "natural," and to summon spontaneous-seeming emotion, from the welter of assumed poses, studied gestures, and mimicked facial expressions mandated by these systems? And how is one to "learn to FEEL"? To the first question, the rhetoricians' rejoinder would doubtless be some variant of the one always given by advocates of craft, as opposed to chance inspiration: "By mastering the technique so thoroughly that it becomes second nature"—a task that with these techniques seems to us both insurmountable and of dubious reward.

There's no doubt that in performance terms, "natural" for E-19 meant roughly what it still means today, that is, that the devices of expression be taken not for artifice, but as inevitable outcomes of expressive needs. However, there are at least three ways in which E-19's "natural" differed from our own, quite apart from the significant generational changes in customary comportment, both public and private, that go far toward determining what is accepted as "natural" in stage behavior. First, as we have already noted, the everyday uses of voice and gesture were, of necessity, more robust than ours. (Indeed, it is our technologically mediated usages that are "unnatural.") Second, to the practitioners and theorists of E-19, all artistic "isms," including "naturalism," were High Art categories. Artists were presumed to breathe the rarified air of at least the lower slopes of Parnassus, where "natural" had a special, elevated meaning. The great artist was the natural man in full, whose passion and grace were the consummation of Nature's intention for humanity. And pursuant to that, third: the rules of composition and expression were held to be rules of Nature herself, of the Natural Law so fervently sought and often proclaimed found, and which by definition would be inviolable. We still work to make artistic techniques compatible with, or extensions of, natural principles. But the old certitude has vanished.

As for how a performing artist might "learn to FEEL," there is at least an implication of how to go about this in Delsarte's system that corresponds to some later notions about it. By and large, though, freedom of emotional expression seems to have been taken largely as a matter of temperamental gift by the 19th-Century masters of the rhetorics. They do, on occasion, observe that sincerity of feeling must underlie the elaborations of vocal and gestural technique, but on the question of how to make this happen, they don't have much to say. The 20th Century would propose more methodic answers.

The great actors and orators of E-19 were not born of these rules; the rules were born of them. Of course, once rules are set down, their descriptive function becomes prescriptive, and we begin working backward, from rules to performance. Nonetheless, we can still read through the rules for their descriptive value, and implicit in these codifications is the individual performer's responsibility for every detail of interpretation. Nowhere in them is there talk of collaboration, either with a director (there was none, in our sense) or, more remarkably, with fellow performers. There is only the interpreter and the text, whose meanings and affects must be forcefully and eloquently set forth. The actor's imperative was to rise to the argumentative heights of confrontations, the revelations and conflicted emotions of soliloquies, the lyrical flights of transcendent and/or tragic endings. In short, he or she was dedicated more to the consummation of great effects than to contributing to an integrated whole. The "production" was assimilated to him or her, not the other way around. We also know that the texts of plays were often roughly treated—not only liberally cut but re-arranged, interlarded with other sources, given alternate endings—usually at the hands of the star actors themselves. In the performance world, texts, even those of revered authors, existed to serve the perceived necessities of specific performance situations. Their integrity was reserved to their literary existence.

The artistic drawbacks of the priorities I have just described are many and obvious. But those same priorities offer one undeniable advantage for drama constructed around defining moments in the lives of extraordinary individuals: they give the performers ownership of those lives, and freedom in the realization of those moments. However much else is neglected or distorted, the inescapable requisites of such works are placed in the hands of the only people who can, after all, meet them. In this valorization of the individual performer, in his or her elevated status and loose, proprietary relationship to text, more-than-vestigial remnants of an oral culture are evident.

Opera devotees will have no difficulty recognizing in their art the lineaments of an oral culture, notwithstanding that opera is, as developed, a highly literate form. The characteristics of orally transmitted art have been fundamental to opera, some from the time of its birth in the courts and academies of Late-Renaissance Italy, others by accretion in the decades and centuries that followed: formulaic, quickly grasped musical patterns (the eight-bar tune, the recurrent associative theme, the *Leitmotif*), often built on antithesis and recapitulation (as with the ABA structures of arias, choral numbers, or entire scenes) and simple repetition (twice-stated phrases, oft-repeated words); poetic verbal content whose rhymes, rhythms, and evocative sounds were more important than profundity or complexity of meaning; melodies easily caught and committed to memory; and of course the very notion of a rhapsodic recitation of stories. So were the stories themselves: mythic (often drawn, in fact, from myths originally perpetuated by the preliterate culture), agonistic, heroic, and replicated almost endlessly in slightly varied tellings.

Two more similarities between operatic and preliterate cultures should be mentioned. The first of these is opera's strong proclivity for archetypical (often stereotypical) characters (Ong's "heavy" characters), ranked in easily recognizable patterns, who function primarily as types and whose individualities are apparent only in the personalities of their performers. Their understood status is reflected in the vocal archetypes created for them, of which we have already explored a few. The very fact that a character is expressed through music, through the singing voice, takes it some distance toward the archetypical, idealized, even when it is individualized and "rounded"—in this sense, all operatic characters are "heavy." That is why they lose much of their stature, of their reality *as characters*, when the archetypical vocal demands are not met.

The second similarity lies with opera's oral tradition. It has two aspects, one in the transmission of interpretive tradition through generations of performers, the other in the relationship between works and audiences. As earlier suggested, in a preliterate culture the principal use of recited myths and stories is as generational social glue, the passing-down of in-common wisdom. To that end, reciters accomplish prodigious feats of memorization, holding at the ready many days' worth of tales in the traditional formulations learned from their predecessors. Nonetheless, these successive tellings incorporated time-and-place adaptations. As the explorers of orality have confirmed through observation of surviving preliterate cultures (see Ong, esp. pp. 59-67), the generational re-tellings accommodate to changed conditions by retaining the parts of collective memory that continue to serve social purposes, and discarding those that do not. These redactions are subconscious. The oral interpreters believe they are transmitting the old tales unchanged, when in fact they are presenting versions instinctively tailored to new circumstances and understandings—even to their sense of a particular audience on a particular occasion. Thus, in an oral culture, it is not only the way a thing is done (what we'd call "style") that changes, but the thing itself ("content"), however subtly and unintentionally. Paradoxically, the effect of this is not to contradict the traditional wisdom or even revise its meaning, but to preserve it by ensuring that it will continue to make sense. The presentation is really situational and adaptive, but to any given audience it re-affirms the apparently eternal relevance of the material.

A remarkable fact about operatic history is that these customs of oral transmission, of passing along a way of doing something and preserving a tradition, yet adapting it to accommodate a new style, have survived in the presence of writing and the fixity of printed scores. Indeed, much of what makes operatic performance live has always been transmitted just as it would be in a preliterate tradition, through emulation of "how things are done," conveyed through sensory impressions of the acts themselves, either as directly experienced or as described and demonstrated by mentors (retired singers, conductors, coaches). And so a measure of independence from text, a "remembrance of songs sung," has always been retained by operatic performers.

With respect to the audience, we might note that most of its members stand in roughly the same relationship to the works as did Homer's: they receive the works solely through performance. Some of them are musically literate to one degree or another, but except for professional musicians and scholars, they do not engage with the works through their texts. Even the engagement enabled by verbal literacy (reading the libretto) has generally been reduced to the in-performance semiliteracy of surtitles. Connoisseurship lies in superior knowledge not of text, but of how music goes and of "how things are done," have been done, should be done, by interpreters. It is orally transmitted, and endures in the mind's ear according to its memorability, as in the preliterate situation. Operas have scores, just as plays have texts, but while in a literate population the plays constitute a literature independent of performance, a broad operatic culture cannot survive as writing.

The 19th Century can easily be read as the conclusive triumph of literacy. Ong sees it that way, and he is not referring primarily to the democratization of reading and writing skills. He is speaking of the rise to literary dominance of the novel, with its tightly controlled narrative, its interiorized mind's-eye-and-ear mode of absorption, its rounded, increasingly antiheroic characters leading increasingly important inner lives, and its cultural saturation via print. All these, in the end, won the field from the previously dominant forms, poetry and drama, with their inevitable evocations of the sounds of recitation and performance. Ong focuses in particular on two kinds of novel that emerged for the first time in the first half of the 19th Century. One is the detective novel, with its taut, "pyramidal" plot whose revelations are under strict writerly control and are arrived at through the inner workings of the central character's mind. The other is the novel with a lengthy through-line plot (as opposed to an episodic structure), in which the inner lives of the principal characters, often hidden beneath their outer actions, engage much of the reader's attention and hold the central truths of the story. Ong credits much of this development to women authors (Jane Austen as Founding Mother), and points out that the women writers of the time, while highly literate and often superbly tutored in the arts, did not attend university, did not master Learned Latin, and did not practice rhetoric. They spoke in a different voice. He cites Dickens, with his sprawling episodic narratives and platform enactments, as orality's last-gasp holdout. Were Ong not the very model of an economical writer, he might have thrown the declamations of the rhetoricians and the effusions of great actors into the balance.

Except that Ong, for all his fascination with orality as the not-literature, is a literary man, not a musical or arts-of-the-act man. So perhaps he does not afford quite sufficient weight to the fact that while the 19th Century may not have marked a high point in Western drama, it was nothing if not theatrical. Like so many of the litcrit theorists, aestheticians, and philosophers we met earlier (and for whom he has little use—see Ong, Chap. 7), he does not take opera into account. And surely it was E-19 opera that, for a shining moment, seized the torch from orality's failing hand.

After what I think we may safely characterize as a post-Mozartean lull (lots of activity, much of which seemed important at the time, but of which only isolated works—a *Fidelio*, a *Freischütz*, a *Barbiere*—ultimately stuck), E-19 opera got going with a rush, as if it had suddenly discovered its mission. It grasped the medieval tale of the faydit poet and his lady and—riding a wave of nostalgia for a reconstructed time that was not quite preliterate, but pretypographical, pre-industrial, pre-Enlightened, and heavily oral—made it the new myth, the copious redundant narrative of its age. Even as the novel was declaring Mission Accomplished for the world of text (a private world of imagined presence, summoned by the eye's interpretations of inert symbols), opera revivified its public world of actual presence, of living communicative energies of both light and sound, but above all sound, and of sound above all of voice. It took full advantage of the technological advancements of literacy and industry to do this. But the cumulative effect was an apotheosis of orality that simultaneously overpowered and transfigured its audiences. At the very moment of literacy's decisive victory, orality found its champion in opera, whose own Parnassus was attained in orality's cause.

From the Renaissance on, the history of acting—at least the kinds of acting that work from dialogic text, as distinct from the scenarios of *commedia dell'arte* or the wordless enactments of pantomimic traditions—often reads like a cyclical repetition of shifts from something called "mannered" or "rhetorical" to something called "realistic" or "natural," with special attention paid to the progressive individuals or movements that represent these shifts. Garrick, for instance, was held to be naturalistic in his time, and we have already noted attribution of the same quality to the 19th-Century Delsartian Steele MacKaye. Certainly the generational adaptations in presentation and social custom noted above are involved in this, and by some are held to be the only thing that's ever really happened. But it does seem that beyond these recurring adaptations there has been a trend, a pressure, if not toward some absolute "real," then at least away from the idealized, the Parnassian—away from people and things as we think they should be, and toward people and things as they are. In any case, what we are dealing with here are the adaptations that have occurred since the end of E-19, particularly the ones that mark the fading of the high Romantic and melodramatic stage aesthetics of the late 19th Century and the fashioning of what I have been calling the modern acting sensibility.

That sensibility was coming into being just over a century ago. Since even the hardiest and most obsessed among us cannot boast a reliable and informed theatrical memory over more than two-thirds of that time, we must turn to documentation. That takes two forms, written and recorded, both more suggestive than conclusive. The written suffers the limitation implied above: terms like "mannered" or "elocutionary," "realistic" or "natural," are relative to contemporaneous custom; they appear to mean the same thing from one generation to the next, but in fact do not, as with the situational *glissements* of the preliterate storytellers. Written evidence is also impaired by our obvious inability to evaluate for ourselves the effect of the acting, even when reported by highly qualified observers. As Frances Donaldson has commented with respect to conflicting descriptions of Irving's acting by Craig and Shaw, "The difficulty . . . with detailed descriptions of acting is

that they tell us what was done but not how it was done ... In both these passages the miming might be of the highest quality or that of an old ham in a
Victorian melodrama."[6] Recorded documentation presents the difficulty that
during the period in question (that of the silent-movie/phonograph generation), our evidence is either of eye or ear, but never of both together. Further,
the eye-evidence is too technically primitive and scarce (only a few of the
notable old-school stage actors made it onto film, and much of that is lost),
and too compromised by the necessary emphasis on pantomimic technique,
to give us any confidence that we are seeing a close resemblance to theatrical
reality. We get glimmerings of personality and an awareness of heightened
gestural style, but not much more.

As to the ear, the technical inadequacies of early phonograph recordings
have already been described. But though they still apply, such problems as
restricted frequency response and high-note blasting are much less damaging to speech than to song, and one gets little sense that the oldtime actors
are much constrained relative to their stage recitational habits.* Since their
theatre was far more vocally centered than ours, and since we are considering their rhetorical practices relative to those of opera, I think we have more
to learn from the aural tracings than from the visual. Recordings of theatre
actors (I'm not including variety artists, vaudeville monologists, et al.) do not
afford the depth of field of those of singers. They are pretty much restricted
to major celebrities, and by no means all of those. Nevertheless, there is much
fascinating material. Starting in 1890, when Edwin Booth recited a fragment
of *Othello* onto a wax cylinder in a Chicago hotel room, we can hear the voices
of actors and orators steeped in the 19th-Century rhetorics. We can hear
Bernhardt and both Coquelins. We can hear Adolf Sonnenthal, longtime star
of the Vienna Burgtheater, and the much-revered Alexander Moissi, a principal of Reinhardt's troupe. We can hear the Italian tragedian Tommaso Salvini,
admired by all from Shaw to Stanislavski. From our Anglo-American tradition,
inevitably formed around Shakespeare, we have samples of Irving and Forbes-
Robertson, of Ellen Terry and Ada Rehan, the famous team of Sothern and
Marlowe, and a number of others.[7]

We mustn't suppose that these snippets do more than hint at how theatre
performance of around 1900 might have impressed us, let alone an audience

---

* The likeliest area of suspicion would be tempo—the possibility that side length may have
sometimes led actors to speed up their readings, as so often happened with singers. My
impression, though, is that this was usually handled by choice of material (often fragmentary) and/or internal cuts, which may or may not have reflected theatre usage. Recording
speeds and resultant pitch variations are also an issue, and are less easily resolved than in
the case of singers. I've heard it suggested, for instance, that Bernhardt's recordings must
be pitched too high, but know of no evidence for this other than our wish that she didn't
sound that way. I don't foresee this difficulty ever being definitively resolved.

of the era. It is with difficulty that even an informed mind's eye, supplemented by photographic evidence, glimpses the pictorial drops and flats and wood-wings and groundcloths, the architectural constructions, the costuming and makeup and footlighting, of the *fin de siècle* stage. The customary disposition of human figures in the stage picture and ways of arranging their movement are less accessible yet. Most importantly, the cumulative impact of the acting, and sustained pursuit of the elevated rhetorics by everyone onstage, often augmented by music, eludes us. We can imagine it, but we can't feel it or know what we'd think of it. There's enough, though, for us to gain an appreciation of how fundamental the change has been in what we expect of theatrical expression, especially if we can mate some of the more intriguing examples with informed commentary of the time. Here is a keynote quotation:

> "Walking about the stage, wrinkling the eyebrows, and gesticulating with the hands are not such wonderful things to do. A competent stage manager can readily train a novice in that sort of 'acting,' if it be worth his while. But the voice! That is where the great acting comes from. A voice that interprets while it charms is the best of all gifts. . ."

Those are the words of Lewis C. Strang, chronicler and critic of the New York stage in the late 1890s and early 1900s, and one of three writers I've chosen partly for the convenience of their collected observations and partly for the evidence in their writings of relevant knowledge and perception, as well as an awareness of the aesthetic shifts of the day. The other two are William Winter and Shaw.[8] In all three (perhaps a bit less in Winter than in Strang and Shaw), this insistence on the centrality of voice—voice with specifically theatrical strengths and aesthetic qualities—is evident.

I have heard only a single, noise-ridden example of the voice of Ada Rehan, the Irish-born, American-raised star of Augustin Daly's famous trans-Atlantic repertory company. Rehan was evidently a performer of nearly irresistible feminine appeal, which cannot have hurt her standing with male critics. But more particularly, she is repeatedly held up by Shaw as a model of stage speech, while Winter, in the course of a long appreciation, notes her "purity of enunciation that has seldom been equaled" and "the strain of fluent sweetness" with which she rendered "the melody of Shakespeare's verse." From her recording (of bits of Katherine in *The Taming of the Shrew*, one of her best-loved parts) we can extract almost nothing in the way of word meaning. But we can hear the rise and fall of a melodious, wide-ranged voice that commands both registral families and a considerable span of inflectional and timbral variety. And although to a contemporary ear her recitation sounds "vocal," by comparison with other actors of the time she is unselfconscious in her use of this equipment. (In a characteristically delectable passage of advice to the young, Shaw makes a distinction between Rehan and Bernhardt, whom he terms ". . . an *intentionally* musical speaker [my italics] of the highest class.")

This "intentional" musicality is present in greater or lesser degree in most of the representatives of the first recorded generation of actors, and in some instances pushes their recitation closer to song than to even the more formal sorts of everyday speech. The voices are all clearly cultivated for pleasing quality and for supported, resonant strength. Their owners frequently have recourse to precisely those elements that distinguish song from speech: wider pitch range (true of both sexes, but more noticeable with the women, since it carries them into Upper Family territory, and they don't belt); lengthened sustainment of tone, generally on long vowels or diphthongs, or on key words; variations of tempo, volume, color, and attack modeled on singing practices.

Ellen Terry, the most highly lauded English actress of the late 19th-Century, deploys the full panoply of these songlike usages—and fortunately her record-ings are clearer than Rehan's. One wants, really, Joshua Steele's system of notation (see n. 3) to specify the melodic rise and fall of the "Quality of mercy" speech, to pinpoint the sustained and vibrated stress of its key words and of diphthongs like "kings" and "crown," or the elevation into Upper Family color-ations at "*There*fore, Jew,/*Though* justice be thy *plea* . . ."; or to score the single syllable "*O-o-o*, (look! Methinks, etc.)" in Juliet's potion monologue, which flut-ters tremulously downward like a flock of tiny birds coming in for a landing. It is this manipulation of vibrato for emotional effect that is probably the most striking of all these effects to our ears, and the easiest to ridicule. We might suppose that it indicates mortal fear or terminal weakness, and so it some-times does. But Julie Marlowe starts us right off with it at the top of Katherine's final speech ("*Fie, fie!* Unknit that threatening unkind brow"), and gilds many a subsequent syllable with it ("*pa-ai-in*-ful labour", "the night in *sto-o-rms*", etc.); while Lewis Waller summons us once more unto the breach with it, and caps "'God for Harry, England, and Saint *Geo-o-o-rge*'" with a shuddering descending glissando that might have abashed Chaliapin or Bohnen.

Singing-actors of that ilk are called even more forcefully to mind by Moissi, with his powerful but sweeter, tenorish timbre, relished rolled r's, and liber-ally applied tremolo in heightened passages. His climactic flights (as at "*Ich bin der König von Ba-by-lon!*" in Heine's *Belsatzar*, a poem set in a very differ-ent reading by Schumann) take him into the vicinity of sustained F's and F-sharps—the *passaggio*, in other words, and in these moments he reminds us more of the tenor Leo Slezak than of any actor in memory.[9] *Tremolando*-ing is hardly ever absent from an emotional moment in Bernhardt (and most of her recorded moments *are* emotional), who drives it at mounting pitch as if to lash herself, and us, into a frenzy, and it is the thing that most clearly marks the Shakespearean soliloquizing of John Gielgud as Old School as late as the 1950s (he did not, of course, employ it in Pinter). It's clear enough, I think, that its use became a convention, applied in a generalized way whenever the actor sought to take us on a lyric or heroic flight. (See n. 9 for more on the uses of the tremolo.)

These actors belong to some world other than ours, where an entirely different belief system is in force. We can be impressed by their vocal and elocutionary skills, their ear for musicodramatic effect, and their commitment to an artistic ideal. But we cannot believe in the reality of their characters, and can admit only the barest possibility that we might have succumbed to their blandishments in the theatre. Yet Shaw, a founder of the modern drama, who repeatedly slated performers for melodramatic or rhetorical contrivance, and who could note of Victor Maurel's operatic Iago that it was "illustrative rather than impersonative," and impaired by "excessive descriptiveness," succumbed utterly to Rehan and Terry. Strang frequently pleads for acting that is "true" or "true to life." He praises simplicity and the "art that conceals art." He writes of Mary Sanders (a pupil of MacKaye's) that in contrast with the "insincerity, unhumanity, . . . sickening sentimentality" and "farcical kittenishness" of other actresses, she seemed spontaneous and expressed her relatively narrow range ". . . more *realistically* than any other actress in this country", and says of Maxine Elliott that she "acted as the great ones act, from within outwards . . .". Yet he also called the warbling Marlowe "the most satisfactory Juliet, the sweetest Rosalind, and the most perfect Viola of the English-speaking stage."

Or, consider the case of Tommaso Salvini. He triumphed around the world, especially in heroic or tragic roles. Here in New York, he alternated with Booth as Othello and Iago in mixed-language performances, and Winter, who evidently also saw him in Alfieri's *Saul* and Giacometti's *Morte Civile*, says of him:

> "His appeal was made chiefly to the feelings . . . and no auditor [sic—not "viewer"] of his acting could resist that appeal . . . the triumphant force of his delivery, and his sonorous speech—at imperial moments varied with a crashing outburst, like the roll of thunder,—could affect even nerves of steel. His most extraordinary endowment was his voice. In vocal force and variety combined he has not been surpassed on our stage, except by Edwin Forrest and Gustavus Van Brooke."

Shaw several times refers to Salvini as a paragon of vocal delivery, usually with respect to his force and passion, but with "the nobler side" of his Othello, for his "admirable artistic quietude and self-containment." In 1889, he termed him simply "the greatest actor of the day." The *Enciclopedia dello Spettacolo* also expatiates on Salvini's voice—"strong and melodious," or again "stupendous, of deep timbre, thundering and melodious"—but also portrays him as a modernist reformer of his time ". . . immune to the traditional vices of the Italian stage, he quickly declared himself for the modernization of recitation" and for the elimination of rhetorical excesses. In Naples early on, the *Enciclopedia* reports, he was not successful because "the method of recitation to which the actors of that theatre were accustomed was in exact contrast with his." (Again, my translations.)

But of all the assessments of Salvini's acting, the weightiest for us has to be that of Stanislavski, first among the founding fathers of the kind of theatre we now consider "real," "true," or "natural." There are four performers to whom Stanislavski most frequently refers in *My Life in Art* as he recounts his search for the in-common element of genius that might improve his own acting, and that would eventually lead to the way of working that became his System. Two are actresses of whom we seem to have no aural trace: Maria Yermolova and Eleonora Duse. The other two are Chaliapin and Salvini, to whose Othello he devotes (uniquely) an entire chapter. Of Chaliapin we have ample aural representation, but as Stanislavski himself noted, his acting was operatic, and thus not directly comparable to the others. In the single specimen of Salvini's recitation that I know (the dream speech from *Saul* beginning "*David, mio proprio figlio*"—an extended excerpt, and quite clearly preserved), we hear at once some of the modern actor's eschewal of the "laid-on" rhetorical effect (he foregoes the "tremor of the voice," for one thing) and the remarkable elocutionary gifts noted by his contemporaries: a powerful, rich baritone; beautifully finished classical Italian; and a wide inflectional range as to both pitch and force, capable of impressive outbursts of anger or lamentation, but of high, delicate, liquid intonations of musical quality as well. It is all mastered and contained, with never a suggestion of vocal strain. However "realistic" (as we would define it) Salvini's acting may or may not have been, the fact that its vocality was declamatory, formal, and aesthetically aware clearly did not disqualify it as truthful for Stanislavski.

There's a remarkable moment at Track 17 of F.C. Packard's Shakespearian compilation (see n. 7). By this time, we've passed through several exemplars of the earliest recorded generation, and on into the deep, rolling tones of Paul Robeson and Orson Welles, the velvet baritone of Gielgud, the penetrating second tenors of Olivier and Maurice Evans, and on past John Barrymore's sliding ascent to a Helden-ish A-flat with Hamlet's "O, vengeance!" And we have followed along in general agreement with the substance, if not the academic tone, of Packard's remarks on the gradual changes from the old rhetoric, with its "ranting and spouting," to what he, in 1959, heard as "naturalistic," if not "colloquial," but which we hear as still formalized and often obligated to histrionic effect. We have just listened to what Packard accurately calls Dame Sybil Thorndike's "diapason tone" in a bit of Lady Macbeth, recorded in 1935. Next up is Flora Robson in a 1942 redaction of the Sleepwalking scene. She is surely "speaking well," "honoring the words." But she is not declaiming for rhetorical effect. Unlike almost all other actors in this anthology (certainly all the earlier ones), she does not sound as if she thinks a charged-up intoning of words, a committed reproduction of the vocal *signs* of emotion, will make us believe in or empathize with the pity and terror of her character's situation. She truly sounds like a woman talking to herself in her sleep, in a walking dream wherein she vainly struggles to wipe away guilt and bring back lost comfort. Suddenly we're home, in a world of theatrical expression we recognize as our own.

The distance from Ellen Terry or Julia Marlowe to Flora Robson is a considerable one, traveled in a remarkably short time. How it compares with earlier stylistic adaptations, earlier redefinitions of "truthful" or "natural" or "real," we simply don't know. Acting teachers, and actors interested enough to have some sense of history, are fond of saying that the better old-time actors must have generated their grand rhetorical effects "from within" (translation: "good acting has always meant what we mean by it"). And I suspect (but that's the operative word: "suspect") that this is true in the sense that we would probably deem Garrick's acting closer to us than that of James Quinn or other older players of that time, or Salvini's than the orating Neapolitans', or that of MacKaye and his talented student Mary Sanders than that of many of their contemporaries. But I think we must grant that at least with respect to the adaptation of which we have evidence, however imperfect, we must acknowledge that a basic change took place. The actors of late E-19, and their critics and chroniclers, often use formulations like ours to describe their goals and methods. But they did *not* mean what we mean by them, and would in some important ways disagree with us on how to create theatrical truth.[10]

As always, the artistic movements I've been speaking of reflect developments in the broader society. And as usual, I believe it's more fruitful to deal with artistic issues and responsibilities as such, rather than surrendering them to the "tide of history" or the "changing times," which artists have in fact helped to shape. The modern acting sensibility, however, is usually defined by interested parties in extremely narrow and often quarrelsome terms: we are real, they were phony. Or: that was grand and noble, this is petty and squalid. Or we affix labels ("Romanticism," "Realism") which are not inaccurate, but do not in themselves bring much clarity. If we were to describe the nature of the change, and the essence of the modern acting sensibility, in artistic terms—through actors' eyes—but with some acknowledgement of social context to give us a perspective outside the intramural arguments, how would that look? Let me try.

First, I should clarify my use of the word "modern," since much of what it implies is recent only in the context of a long view, and is already seen as superannuated by some. My "modern" in acting begins with the changes in rhetorical practice outlined above. Its assumptions remain intact in most of what we think of as mainstream acting today, though there is already an "after," running along beside for the past thirty or forty years. In this book, we have encountered this "after" largely in the thinking of designers and directors, and the ways in which their P.O.V. has affected singingactors trying to do something else. But in *Einstein on the Beach* and *Bob*, we have seen acting that is itself based on different assumptions. That is not part of my modern. It is post-. Chronologically, my modern corresponds roughly with what we usually think of as "The Modern" in other arts, distinct from the Romantic and Classical ways of thinking and working that preceded it, and from the Postmodern or Poststructuralist ones that have followed.

There's no doubt that this modern acting is allied in both time and spirit with the theatrical styles we call Realism and/or Naturalism, and that these are in turn associated with ways of working exemplified by Stanislavski and his System, and his many successors with their diverse variations of "Method." But when I speak of a "sensibility," I mean to indicate an attitude toward theatrical truth that is broader than that. Flora Robson, after all, was first noticed for her childhood recitations, was trained at the Royal Academy of Dramatic Art, and learned her craft in a range of roles, including classical ones, on English stages of the 1920s. Whatever her habits of preparation and performance may have been, they were not learned from Method teachers. Yet she clearly shared this modern sensibility. With the expectable biographical variants, the same could be said of many actors over the past three-quarters of a century.

In view of the fact that actors have always sought truth and an appearance of naturalness, have tended to express these aspirations in similar terms, and yet have produced quite different versions of truth and naturalness, are there any things that can be said of the transition from the E-19 aesthetic to the modern one that describe not results, but actual intent? There is only one that I can think of that is so basic, and it has much to do with the rhetorics. It is that theatrical truth came to be seen not as a matter of composition—of predetermined vocal and physical actions which, when perfected and applied appropriately to a character and situation, will create a truthful and natural impression—but as a matter of ongoing contact with the inner life that all of us lead, and which generates our actions and determines the nature of our responses to others and to external events. It became a question not of "putting on the man," but of being the man. Or, to state it more abstractly, it became a problem not so much of form as of content. The sense in which Delsarte and MacKaye (for instance) could have been considered champions of "realism" or "naturalism" had to do, I think, with their models, which were drawn from the life that performers could see around them, rather than from statues and paintings and literary imaginings. The charts of emotional states that Lillian Nordica saw in Delsarte's studio and the remarkable "instant characterizations" for which he was noted, like MacKaye's "gamuts of facial expression" and "chromatic states of emotion" that he demonstrated in his lectures, were derived from close study of living behavior, and their plasticity led their students' attention away from fixed poses or attitudes, and toward a more lifelike flow. Nevertheless, these techniques, however appropriately and passionately used, remain means of studying and reproducing behavioral results. They are still refined ways of "putting on the man." They also assume that the expression of emotion is the central problem in acting.

If one is to be the man, there is no other starting-point than oneself. That is inescapable. But two questions immediately arise. Granted that the self is the starting-point, where is it going, and how does it get there? And: what is this self? How developed and capacious is it? What does it embrace? From attempts to answer the first question have flowed the key precepts of modern acting, among which the most important are new definitions of "action" and its interplay with emotion and with inner states of being, and of the relationship of actor to text. These attempts were successful. To claim the most for them: in our perpetual quest for truthfulness in acting, they made significant progress, recognizable as such then and now; they improved acting. To claim the least: they aligned acting with modern perceptions of truth and reality; they corrected for generational and situational movement in a particularly momentous time. I believe both things happened, but in any case these changes will not be rescinded. No acting will appear other than quaint that does not incorporate them.

On the second question, we have not done so well. Of the idea that acting (or any artistic endeavor) should expand the self into the art, not contract the art into the self—let alone the humanistic aspiration that "Natural" should mean "completed," "lifted to its highest level"—we have rather folded our tents. And in the great stage works of the past, no acting will appear other than inadequate that does not at least strive toward that.

Many paths can be traced on the journey to the modern acting sensibility, with the names of the reformers as markers along the wayside—in Italy, from the Riccobonis to Salvini to Duse; in France, from Talma to Delsarte to Antoine and the *Théâtre Libre*; in Germany, from the Meiningen ensemble to Brahm and the *Freie Bühne* to Reinhardt; and in our own Anglo-American tradition, from Garrick to Kemble and Macready to Irving, MacKaye to Booth to Gillette.* Theatre historians of these cultures could point to others, I'm sure. But if we're trying to define that sensibility in working terms, Stanislavski is still The Man. For anyone now alive, this is in large part because he wrote things down. Unlike other actor/director/teacher exemplars of the era (above all Reinhardt, who in his time was of at least equal influence), he committed his System to paper, at length and in detail. This material was never in his lifetime definitively organized, and was "unconcealed" (Heidegger's usage is in this instance decidedly right), only piece by piece. Nevertheless, it quickly became, and remains, the ur-text on the 20th-Century understanding of theatrical truth everywhere that the influence of Western drama is felt. Around it has grown an immense secondary literature of biography, hagiography and iconography, history, partial re-interpretations and revisions, teaching texts, and criticism. No other theatre interpreter, with the possible exception of Brecht,† has anything like this written presence. (See notes 12 and 14.)

---

* William Gillette (1853-1937) is sometimes cited as the first actor (at least in the Anglo-American tradition) to definitively break with the older rhetorical style. Packard so considers him, and on Gillette's single surviving recording, a scene from *Sherlock Holmes*, we do hear a conversational manner that would not be out of place in a contemporary production of such a piece. He's not doing Shakespeare, though, or any sort of classic or poetic work, and never did: he did plays (*Holmes* above all) of his own authorship, set in his own time, and by all accounts (Strang's among them) acted them with uncommon economy, simplicity, and a quiet, riveting presence that must, indeed, have "come from within." Ong would doubtless be gratified that this early example of fully rounded, internal characterization comes in an impersonation of the iconic novel detective.

† There's a vast literature on Brecht. But much of it deals, appropriately, with his creative output—his plays, librettos, and poems—and on his theoretical writings about the nature and purposes of theatre. His views on acting, while certainly important, form a relatively small portion of this *oeuvre*. I write "Brecht" advisedly, in full awareness of the disclosures about the contributions of others (his women) to his work. (As Harold Bloom observes in his *Dramatists and Dramas*, "'Bertolt Brecht'. . . was a brand name." This seems to have applied, though, more to the plays than to his other work, and to the writing-out more than to the ideas behind it. In any event, the author and the brand are co-extensive, and are called "Brecht."

This written System, however, would not only be of no consequence, but would not exist were it not for the fact that the company Stanislavski co-founded, and of which he was the guiding artistic personality, had not knocked people's socks off first in Moscow, then on European tours, and finally on its extended visit to America; and had he not further shown, through the work of his successive Studios, that the company could be sustained and refreshed by new generations of talent trained in evolving versions of the System; and, finally, had he not demonstrated that the System's sometimes rebellious spinoff companies—under Meyerhold, Vakhtangov, et al.—not only had vitality in themselves, but eventually fed back into the thinking of an always searching, always flexible artistic temperament. Stanislavski did the work first, then wrote about it. Had the work not opened people's eyes, no one would have bothered reading what he wrote.

And what he wrote was radically different from the formulations of even the progressive reformers of the elocutionary understanding. He created an entirely new vocabulary of acting elements. Terms like "Throughaction," applied either to a play (its "spine," or chain of logically connected actions, related to its governing theme) or to the actor's sequence of actions in pursuit of his objective; "Given Circumstances" (the dramatic situation as mandated by the script and/or production—also the more immediate situation of a specific scene or moment);[11] "Creative State" (three phases of preparation: inner or mental; outer or physical; and general—the two together); "Emotion Memory" (recollected emotional experience from the actor's own life, drawn on, consciously or not, in the course of his encounter with a role); or "Psychotechnique" (self-evident, I would hope) reflect a thoroughgoing redefinition of acting as art and craft.*[12] "Throughaction" and "Given Circumstances" imply scrupulous attention to the text and acceptance of the hierarchy of interpretation. "Creative State," "Emotion Memory," and "Psychotechnique" suggest immersion in the character's inner life, including all significant personal history, and the fusing of this with the actor's own.

With this change in P.O.V., we are clearly dealing with the actorly version of the novelization of character that Walter Ong wrote about—with the realization that the interior life, in all its richness and complexity, is not only important but is in fact the "real" life, of which all behavior, bodily and vocal, is the outgrowth. In a novel, the author can tell us directly about interior life,

---

* I have selected for illustration only a few key elements, adopting the terminology used in Jean Benedetti's translations, and adding my own variants on his thumbnail definitions. Some of these terms are slightly different in the long-standard translations of Elisabeth Reynolds Hapgood, and different yet in the re-interpretations of many later teachers. For further, see n. 14.

and we gain an understanding of a given character's actions, not shared by the other characters, because we are privy to that. Onstage, the presence of interior life had been handled by writing conventions like the aside or the monologue, or by whatever means the actor had of conveying his or her state, often in a way that would not pass undetected in real life, and so betrayed the unreality of the stage life. Stanislavski proposed instead that the actor live inside the character, wanting what the character wants, and from there respond to the situations presented by the text and by encounters with other characters. To this end, he sought to develop a technique for getting to that place, formerly accessed, as he saw it, by only a few actors of true genius, or fitfully by others when something happened to "hit" just right. In the search for artistic truth, this is a move away from philosophy and into psychology, from an objective stance to a purely subjective one. In acting terms, it's a rejection of the premise that one first locates necessary effects and impressions, then deploys close observation of appearances and highly developed rhetorical skills to arrive at those effects, and instead sets in motion a process whose realization is not predetermined, and of which the actor's skills are the servants.

Even in strictest observance of the boundaries set by the author, and with no conscious attempt at revisionist interpretation, this process often produces unconventional results. The non-conventional, the fresh take on a character that is itself not pre-determined (the actor does not begin by saying, "I will interpret the character *this* way") is in fact a particular virtue of this way of working. And though some interpretive conventions are virtually mandated by text, others belong to oral tradition. So, though the actor's exploration often leads in a direction that seems different from that suggested by a text, and may thus appear to belong to orality, it actually leads away from orality, from the delight in "fulfilling expectations copiously" that belongs to Forster's and Ong's "heavy," heroic types, and into the unpredictability of the fully rounded, "novelized" character.

Indeed, the actor's own process is in effect novelized, for it must begin with private imaginative engagement with the text, during which the actor provides for himself all that the novelist would give him—and more, for novelists leave things out, too.

Stanislavski's views on the role of emotion are also worth a brief mention here, since they are quite different from most of what came before, and some of what came after, his conclusions on this subject. He was as concerned as any actor or teacher with the truthfulness of emotional expression. But for him, emotion was the most important of all the results that must *not* be predetermined and then reproduced. Time and again, he enjoined his students never to work directly on the emotional content of a moment or scene, but instead to concentrate on the thing that goes before, on the physical and sensory life that leads the actor into the character's experience. Emotions will happen, as they do in life, not because we are trying to have them, but because they occur as our wants and needs come up against life's events. Thus, he casts aside not only the language of "painting" or "portraying" emotional states (the painter or the portraitist is, by definition, delineating from without), but, as well, any effort to pour rhetorical energy into the summoning of emotion. Despite terms like "Emotion Memory," "psychotechnique," and "subconscious," he also would not have been sympathetic to any process of drilling for feelings in a psychotherapeutic fashion, as if it were the actor, not the spectator, who must be purged through catharsis. In American actor training, a conflation of therapeutic with artistic concepts has sometimes led to sweaty labors on perceived deficiencies of personality, on "unblocking" and emotional release, as if "learning to FEEL" were the actor's central task. That isn't at all how Stanislavski saw it, save at a very early point on his own learning curve.

Our identification of Stanislavski with the theatrical style(s) we call Realism or Naturalism is certainly not wrong. A movement that had begun with "production values" (painstaking representationalism of time and place in sets and of class and social function in costume, the introduction of real or faux-real objects in place of generic theatrical props)[13] ended with the actor, and the productions of the Moscow Art Theatre, most particularly of Chekhov's plays, have been seen as emblematic of that transformation for over a century. Yet Stanislavski was fond of saying that his work was done not for the sake of naturalism, but for truth and belief, and his company mounted not only Chekhov, Turgenev, Gorki and Hauptmann, but Maeterlinck, Goldoni, Beaumarchais, Ibsen's *Brand*, comedies and farces and melodramas of many styles and nationalities—not always, to be sure, with equal success. It welcomed Gordon Craig for *Hamlet*. It spawned a musical theatre component (Nemirovich-Danchenko in charge) that did adaptations of Offenbach, Bizet, Lecocq, and Rachmaninoff's *Aleko*. For all his focus on creative states and the subconscious, Stanislavski was equally concerned with the development of the actor's instrument—with the strength and plasticity of the body, the range and power of the voice (he had a lifelong passion for opera and singing), with the tempo and rhythm of both, and their aesthetic finish. He paid meticulous attention to the "externals," to makeup and costume and the handling of properties. He believed that the most ordinary lives, the meanest and most squalid of conditions, must be given aesthetic shape, a kind of beauty, to qualify as artistic representation. He believed in art as a moral force. He was, after all, a man of the late E-19, and of a peculiarly Russian sort.

On both of the MAT's European tours (1906 and 1923) and its American visit (1923-24, with the Musical Studio following in 1925-26), the thing that elicited the most comment was the quality of ensemble playing. This was not because the MAT offered the first examples of integrated production. It was because the integration seemed to come from natural developments in the interactions of the performers rather than from on high. The MAT's "production values," never as impressive (as Stanislavski recognized) as those of Reinhardt or Belasco, were important insofar as they supported those interactions and established place and atmosphere for the audience, but no farther. The plays had been directed (in most cases by Stanislavski, who also acted in some of them), but the direction attracted little notice because it had in effect disappeared, its supervisory and thematic functions absorbed into the playing. The "staging" seemed to just happen.

This doesn't mean that the director had done nothing, or had functioned only as a traffic cop. Quite the contrary. It means, first, that much of the director's work had been accomplished over a period of years, during which the company had formed around a common understanding of the actor's responsibility for his or her interpretation and of the techniques for fulfilling that responsibility. And, second, it means that the director's primary task in any particular case lay not with the elements the audience would recognize as "the production," but with a process of guided exploration through the discovery period of rehearsal (a much longer period than is ever allotted in our theatre), incorporating some of the discoveries, discarding others, keeping them on track with the themes and ruling idea (as distinct from an auteurial "concept") of the play.*[14] The MAT was above all an actors' theatre, whose extraordinary ensemble quality rested not only on the personal intimacy and shared methods of a longstanding company (quite different from an induced "groupiness"), but on the fully developed agency of its individual artists as well. They shared not so much a style as a process.

Late in his life, Stanislavski was exploring two new directions, or, really, shifts in focus. One was the so-called "Method of Physical Actions," in which emotional recall and mental preparation were de-emphasized in favor of

---

* This is an especially hard point for audiences to appreciate, since it isn't recognizable in anything clearly attributable to the director. An elegant elucidation of it comes from Pavel Rumyantsev, who among other things sang the title role in *Eugene Onegin* in the Opera Studio: "Stanislavski's genius lay in his capacity to make everyone engaged in a production active co-creators with him in his directorial concept. All dividing lines were wiped out between what he himself suggested or demonstrated and what the actors did on their own creative initiative or because of the logical necessities inherent in their parts. This is the overriding significance of Stanislavski's method of work . . ." (*Stanislavski on Opera*, p. 374—see n. 14).

immediate physicalization, and would then be called on only as needed for purposes of "justification." This "just do it" approach (not so very different, after all, from Delsarte's admonition to Lillian Nordica that if she'd just go ahead, the feeling would follow, and the facial expression would reflect in the voice) is, I think, often misunderstood in a couple of ways. First, it assumes a highly responsive acting instrument, one that is emotionally and physically tuned—in other words, an extraordinary "natural" talent and/or a thoroughly trained one. (Stanislavski had always insisted that the techniques of the System were for use *as needed*, and that actors of genius might seldom need them. He hoped that the Method of Physical Actions might shorten rehearsal time, and accomplish as much as 50% of the actor's work. Still 50% to go!) Second, it doesn't mean physical action *in place* of emotional truth, but as a route into it. He had concluded that his rehearsal methods sometimes impeded actors' instincts, and that he should trust these more.

The second new direction, related to these conclusions, was a purification of his vision of an actors' theatre, giving the actor even greater centrality in the creative process, and placing production elements (and, indeed, the director) in a more strictly supportive role. (Set and costume design, for instance, was not to be fixed in advance, as a "matrix," but added as rehearsals progressed and the actors' work showed what was needed.)

The story of how Stanislavski's precepts took root here in America, first through colonization, then through appropriation and adaptation; of how these adaptations, herded together under a crudely lettered sign that reads "Method," came to exemplify the modern acting sensibility; and of how, largely through film, they established that sensibility in the popular understanding, has been often told, and does not bear repeating here.* A few observations about that story, from our now-longer perspective, might be helpful:

- It's often said that the MAT arrived in the U.S. at the opportune moment, when American theatre was "getting serious about itself" (O'Neill is usually cited here.) Yes, O'Neill was America's first great psychologically exploratory playwright, and most of what had been "serious" in our theatre had involved European plays—Shakespeare above all, but the moderns as well (the disturbing Ibsen, the provocative Shaw, et al.). But the MAT was foreign, too. Its plays and playing struck deep with us not

---

* Everyone interested in the theatre arts, though, should have some awareness of how this came to pass and what it means for our received wisdom about acting. Since in my experience most opera aficionados and practitioners have only the dimmest impressions on this matter, yet have stuck it somewhere in their file of presumed knowledge, I've compiled a selective, briefly annotated reading list. It is contained in n. 14.

so much because they were "serious" (Chekhov is not more "serious" than Shakespeare or Ibsen, Stanislavski than MacKaye or, in their way, Daly or Belasco) but because they were new in ways that fitted what was new about us in the way of psychology, politics, class and ethnicity, and because the company seemed separate from the commercial theatre, from theatre as a commodity. It was the MAT, the Moscow Art Theatre, and not MEPCO, the Moscow Entertainment Production Company. That—then as now—*was* serious, not to say desperate.

- Psychology: Stanislavski was a psychologist in the sense that gifted artists often are, i.e., he had a keen, empathetic interest in matters of the human spirit, in how people behave under life's "given circumstances." Of modern psychology as a discipline, however, he knew very little—bits and pieces from French sources, which he liked to cite for authentication about "human nature," and, later, something of Pavlov. If he had any awareness of Freud beyond the name-recognition level (something hardly encouraged in the Soviet days), evidence has yet to be disclosed. Here in America, though, the psychoanalytic culture exercised an ever-growing intellectual and therapeutic influence from the 1920s into the 1970s—one that penetrated well "down" into popular culture and everyday social transaction. The MAT's combination of an acting technique grounded in the inner lives, the struggles and dreams, of quite ordinary individuals, together with a quartet of great plays focused on the complexities of "the family romance," was bound to mesh almost seamlessly with that culture's theatre.

- Politics: By the 1920s, the MAT and its characteristic plays actually occupied the conservative, pre-Revolutionary corner of the Russian theatre scene. But because they burst upon us out of the energies of the young Soviet Union in the highly charged political environment of our Roaring, Bolshevik-scared Twenties, and because its "ensemble" aesthetic, set against the star- and personality-driven qualities of our commercial theatre (and, except for the fledgling Little Theatre movement, we had no other kind), seemed collectivist, the meld with the political Left was as mutually reinforcing as that with the Freudian consciousness. This alliance was reaffirmed by the Depression (the identity of the Group Theatre, seedbed of the American "Method," is inseparable from Depression politics), and continued to inform the stance of our theatre into the postwar era. It still does so, though now the politics tend toward Terry Eagleton's New Left triplet.

- Class and ethnicity: America being America, ethnic heterogeneity has always characterized our theatre scene. It was, however, a Northern European heterogeneity, and naturally enough soon assimilated to an Anglo-American model, High-Culture in tone if not often in substance. Now the vitality was coming from Greeks and Armenians, Southern Italians and Sicilians, Jews from Odessa and the Pale of Settlement, and in class terms it was coming from bottom up. Its populist rebelliousness carried with it no little resentment, a drive to exterminate the theatre of the *haute bourgeoisie* and the acting styles associated with it. Something like this occurred in British theatre a quarter-century later, in the days of the Angry Young Men, with much the same class component, but less of an ethnic one.

The neo-Stanislavskian movement was by no means the full story of American acting from the 1920s through the 1960s. But it gradually established itself as the dominant form of the modern acting sensibility, as the kind of acting most easily accepted as truthful and urgent. Most of what was best in American theatre happened when that sensibility encountered writing of similar psychosocial outlook, or when it was applied with revelatory effect to older work commonly associated with earlier styles. In that regard, though, it must be said that while modern actors have repeatedly shown us that yes, it is much better to have hold of the inner life and nothing else than to have something else but no inner life, that condition is still in the category of the necessary but insufficient. And while modern training programs (see n. 14) have always given mouth honor to the somethings else (to development of the mental and physical instrument), that work has not been pursued with the diligence accorded to inner technique—or has not been sufficiently integrated with it, or has replaced it as an alternate path, or (as has often been the case in my personal observation) has simply not been very good or very relevant to real acting situations. Thus, when it comes to classical material, compelling inner work is often betrayed by inadequacies of expression, while in colloquial contemporary plays, to say nothing of musicals, vocal expression is frequently so weak or aesthetically offputting or illshaped that one doesn't care whether it's "honest" or not. In practice if not in theory, the modern theatre is more one of physical action than of speech and its audience more one of watchers than of listeners. It's a theatre of "behavior," narrowly defined. Good modern actors, working from the inner lives of their characters, disclose only what they would disclose in their imagined real-life circumstances (though of course they theatricalize these disclosures in greater or lesser degree), and the audience is meant to sense the tension between what is withheld and what is disclosed—the more full and alive the former, the more meaningful the latter.

Yet, even when the modern actor fulfills his project of grounding his psychological, novelistic, rounded Man in himself, the question remains: doesn't Being the Man require transformation? It's perhaps the most divisive question asked of the modern actor, all the more aggravating for its implication that "self-expression" may not be enough, that there may have to be a giving-over, a change and growth beyond the comfort zone of the self. Why? To realize another self, the character's, and a different set of "given circumstances" which, as I tried to illustrate with the example of Eléazar, really means everything that has ever happened in the life of that character, brought with him into everything that happens in the course of the drama. This would pose the greatest challenge with characters that are far removed in period, social class, ethnic and religious cultivation, as well as those that have epic or archetypal size and weight, or are expressed through high poetic language. Or with those that must incorporate all these conditions into the reality of the singing person. That is where the modern acting sensibility and the rhetoric(s) of opera often seem truly incompatible.

Except that, in cases such as those of Brooks and Shicoff and a few others, these conditions do seem to connect from time to time. There is also the even more uncommon artist like Lieberson, who in her singing of Bach and Handel and Mahler sometimes seemed in communion with a source that cannot be analyzed or assigned to any technique, and from which must also have emanated the raw need that took her Elvira and Didon to levels unattained by other excellent artists. Duse was said to be like that, and Muzio—women who arrived at the theatre hours before curtain, shut themselves incommunicado in their dressing rooms, and inhabited another world for the duration of the performance. The trouble with even the splendid examples of Brooks, Shicoff, and Lieberson is, first, their extreme rarity and, second, the fact that they do not connect their remarkable interpretive capacities to the voice types that once regularly met the vocal and musical demands of the greatest roles in the greatest operas. We don't have a Brooks/Tebaldi gestalt, or a Shicoff/Martinelli, or a Lieberson/Stignani. It is as if the psychological conditions necessary to the organization of each of these sets of energies cannot co-exist. Did they, ever? If so, could they again? I will return to these questions. First, now that this look at modern acting has brought us back around to opera, let me conclude my overview of that encounter.

It should not surprise us that the first efforts to bring the modern acting sensibility and associated production techniques into opera occurred in Russia. It might even be said to have begun in the 1890s at Saava Mamontov's private company in Moscow, where the young opera aspirant Stanislavski had done some walk-on parts and Chaliapin was given the freedom to find his artistic identity as a new kind of singingactor. Certainly it was underway some ten to fifteen years later, when the directors Sanin and Lapitzki, both associated with the MAT in its early years, came to work in St. Petersburg at the Narodny Dom and then at the Theatre of Musical Drama, which so far as I can determine was the first opera company organized along theatre-ensemble lines.[15] After the Revolution, Stanislavski himself took over the artistic direction of the Opera Studio, at first associated with the Bolshoi but soon an independent training and production unit, which sought to integrate the System into operatic and song material.

None of this MAT-related operatic work came Westward. But by the time Stanislavski was in charge of the Opera Studio and a younger Russian generation was dealing with his influence, Max Reinhardt had already completed his fifteen years of work with his extraordinary Berlin company, whose leading actors were now scattered to the winds in search of gainful employment in the socioeconomic disaster zone of the post-WWI Germany and Austria, finding some in other established companies and some on the new happy hunting-ground of European and American film. Reinhardt was entering a new phase, collaborating with Richard Strauss and Hugo von Hofmannsthal to found (and direct at) the Salzburg Festival, directing new ventures in Vienna, and taking on projects at other theatres.

Despite the many writings about Reinhardt, and the considerable recorded and filmed legacy left by some of his actors and directors (most of which, however, postdates the Berlin years and reflects either the Expressionism of the Weimar era or Hollywood movie genres of the 1930s and '40s), and despite the fact that actor training programs were established in his name and with his initial guidance in Berlin, Vienna, New York and Hollywood, it is difficult to get a grasp on his views about acting technique—if indeed he held any consistent ones, beyond selecting the best talents he could find and then working intensely, inspirationally, with them. He had begun as an actor, and many of his associates and observers of his work emphasize that the actor was always at the center of his work, as Man was at the center of his *Weltanschauung*. Yet he is remembered as a master of industrial theatre techniques and a visionary of light and space, and for a kind of theatrical gigantism, with massive, populous productions of classic plays (e.g., Sophocles' *Oedipus*), the vast pantomimic spectacle of *The Miracle*, and his "Theatre of the Five Thousand." The productions that made his early reputation were noteworthy realizations of late E-19 Realism in the Meiningen-Brahm line of descent, but he soon moved into a wide range of stylized forms. So it is hard to identify him with any particular sort of actor except a serious, artistically committed one, or any particular way of working except a powerfully engaged, demanding one. The degree to which he ceded any real creative responsibility to his actors is especially elusive. I think we can say, though, that howevermuch Reinhardt valued the actor, both as individual and as ensemble participant, his was not a theatre wherein the direction disappeared into the acting (as in Stanislavski's vision) or in which design receded with the actor's entrance (as in Robert Edmond Jones'). It was a theatre of "production," a director's theatre. And though he would never have countenanced the sorts of conceptualization and auteuristic hubris we today associate with the term, and with full awareness that no one person accounts for a whole artistic mode, I believe it's not far off the mark to call him the Granddaddy of *Regietheater.*

Throughout his professional life, Reinhardt was involved with opera and operetta. Though he never had a permanent repertory opera company of singers molded by him, as he did of actors with his Berlin theatre company, his impact on the opera world—the original productions of *Der Rosenkavalier* and *Ariadne auf Naxos* (first version); the Vienna Mozart productions; Salzburg; reportedly brilliant stagings of Offenbach, J. Strauss, Lehár, etc.—was almost as great as that on spoken theatre, and his productions of plays usually had a significant musical component. It was often said of him that he had fulfilled the Wagnerian dream of incorporating all the arts of the act and their associated crafts into a unified synaesthetic event envisioned by a single artist who supervised all aspects of its realization. In Wagner's case, though, that artist was in fact the creator of the work, its true author, whereas in Reinhardt's it was a Second Interpreter-in-Chief—not, as with Mahler, the musical one, guiding rehearsal and performance from the pit, but the theatrical one, working from the matrix of a *Regiebuch* in which every mind's-eye, mind's-ear detail had been entered.[16]

Konstantin Stanislavski (d. 1938) and Max Reinhardt (d. 1943) were the two towering figures of 20th-Century theatre practice. Both concerned themselves with opera. It was Stanislavski whose definition of the modern acting sensibility became, with much amendment and redaction, the standard guide to the performer's process. But it was Reinhardt's production model that (again with much emendation) came to be adopted by our operatic institutions. It's not an easy fit.

THE "REALISTIC MUSIC THEATRE" OF WALTER FELSENSTEIN

After the war, tension between the creative agency of the performer and the prerogatives of the visionary director became the central issue in the work of operatic reformers. This is nowhere more evident than in what we can learn of the lifework of Walter Felsenstein.* The example of his Komische Oper of East Berlin remains unique: a permanent company of professional standing, buttressed by state subvention, devoted exclusively to the development and production of "unreservedly believable" opera, which for nearly three decades remained under the overall artistic supervision not of a Musical Director, administrative *Intendant*, or general impresario, but of a gifted, crusading dramatic director. During that time, the Komische Oper made East Berlin as much of a pilgrimage station for opera progressives as Brecht's Berliner Ensemble did for their theatre confreres. And while the work of St. Petersburg's Theatre of Musical Drama, of Stanislavski's Opera Studio, or of Reinhardt in opera and operetta—even of Corsaro in the New York City Opera's heyday—is almost as irretrievable as the recitations of the premodern elocutionists or the scenic realisms of the Bancrofts or Belasco, enough remains to us of Felsenstein and his company to repay close inspection.

Like Stanislavski and Reinhardt, Felsenstein began as an actor. But he moved into directing while still young. By 1947, when he was handed the ruined Metropoltheater by the Soviet occupation authorities, he was in his mid-forties, had been active in theatre, opera, and operetta for over twenty years, and had formed some strong ideas about opera as an art form, the state of operatic affairs, and the desirability of a new kind of "music theatre." Here are a few of them, in his own (translated) words, which I have selected for their centrality in Felsenstein's writings and pertinence to this discussion:[17]

> "Music theatre exists when a musical action with singing human beings becomes a theatrical reality that is unreservedly believable.†
> The dramatic happening must take place on a level where music is the only means of expression. The performer must not give the effect of being an instrument or a component part of music that already exists, . . . but that of being its creative fashioner."

> "What exists and is real? Certainly only the action, and the human situation that derives from it. This generates the state of the performer, which in turn produces his further action. This state is physical as much as emotional. *Therefore even singing belongs to it and is subordinate to it.*" [My italics—discussion below.] " . . . All technical elements of dramatic singing, such as breathing, intonation,

---

*   I say "what we can learn" to stipulate that I never saw a Felsenstein production live. What I have learned about his work, and how, will be clear from what follows.

†   Felsenstein used the terms "unreservedly believable" and "unconditionally plausible" interchangeably—or perhaps they are translators' choices.

and rhythmic flow . . . are an integral part of the emotionally conditioned physical action."

These thoughts are instantly recognizable as extensions of the modern
acting sensibility into the operatic sphere. They would find agreement from
any practitioner in the Stanislavski tradition, and probably from Reinhardt's
as well. Note that they focus on the performer, the "singing human being,"
not on production. What was revelatory in Felsenstein's work had to do
with the interpretation of character based on close scrutiny of the text, and
when he speaks of "*Konzept*" he means the view of a work so derived, not the
visual representation of ideas. He viewed himself as *in loco autoris*, working
within the boundaries established by creators, but with a fidelity and specificity that would make each work seem new. He considered even the most
familiar repertory operas to be unknown works, waiting to be revealed. With
the obsessive drive and thoroughness of the true missionary, Felsenstein set
these principles to work. He was not the only director to have a revitalizing
impact on the postwar opera scene, several of them with great international
influence—one has only to think of Günther Rennert and Wieland Wagner
in Germany, or of Visconti, Zeffirelli, and Strehler in Italy. Even at the Met,
where direction and design had lain fallow through the Depression and war
years, Rudolf Bing was importing established theatre directors, who for the
most part did thoroughly traditional or mildly revisionist work, but who still
elevated the general level of production, though seldom with any transformative effect on performers. There were others. But of them all, Felsenstein
alone made *Realismus* in acting the center of his work, and enjoyed conditions that gave it a fighting chance.

It is intriguing (and, I confess, a little eerie, for a then-young American who
followed European developments in real time, but from afar) to review the
documentation of Felsenstein's work in the pages of *Opera* through the 1950s
and '60s, as the Komische Oper solidified under his working methods and its
reputation as the home of "realistic music-theatre" spread.[18] The shock-and-awe
tone of nearly all these reports, from a selection of German and English critics,
leaves no room for reasonable doubt as to the impact of these productions—
something significant was taking place, particularly where the pursuit of truth
in physical action, the co-ordination of action with music, and the eradication
of received conventions of interpretation were concerned. Operas as stylistically unalike as Janáček's *Cunning Little Vixen* and Verdi's *Otello*, Offenbach's
Tales of Hoffmann and Britten's then-new *Midsummer Night's Dream*, were said
to be revealed as if previously unknown, and revivals of such long-abandoned
pieces as Paisiello's *Barber of Seville* and Offenbach's *Bluebeard* had success as

evenings of sharply-played music theatre. Wherever the Komische Oper traveled (Prague, Stuttgart, Schwetzingen, Moscow and Leningrad), its remarkable theatrical qualities were remarked upon. And when Felsenstein directed with other companies (always with a concession of extra rehearsal time), the results were described as transformational.

Running through even the most respectful and enthusiastic reactions, though, is a strain of uneasiness, of the feeling one has when nonplused by an airtight argument, but still sure that it's somehow not quite right. "*Aber etwas fehlt*," as one of the citizens of Mahagonny says. The *etwas*, in this case, has to do with an apparent working belief that the aesthetic properties of music and voice are enemies of truth, and must be kept strictly in the place assigned them by the director. Horst Koegler, a Komische Oper regular whose responses to Felsenstein over the years covered the range of possibilities, wrote of the *Hoffmann* (June, 1958) that while he had nothing but praise for the edition, the concept, the unity of elements, Rudolph Heinrich's designs, and the actors ("... everyone of whom [deserved] the main notice ... teamwork of hitherto unknown perfection!"), and vastly admiring "Felsenstein's genius as a 'producer,'"* he nevertheless wondered "... whether his place is really on the opera stage." Noting that he had never felt less carried away by Offenbach's music, he concluded with: "Felsenstein's realistic approach is a danger to all and everything which people like me love in opera!"

Just a year and a half later (Feb., 1960), Koegler, after a generally favorable review of a Komische Oper *La Bohème* directed by Götz Friedrich, went on to say that "This and every other German operatic event of 1959 was completely dwarfed by Felsenstein's own production of *Otello*." Here he chronicles felicities of acting, staging, translation (Felsenstein's own, as customary in his productions) and design (Heinrich again) that kept him "deeply and completely involved" in the stage action. "Overwhelming," "tremendous," "ravishing," "must be seen to be believed" are a few of the words he applies to successive episodes of Act I alone, and after remarking on what would normally be crippling vocal and musical shortcomings, the fellow who had only eighteen months earlier declared Felsenstein a danger to all he loved, now concludes with: "I must repeat that Felsenstein's *Otello* is the greatest operatic experience I have ever had in twenty years of operagoing."

And yet: even in this hot effusion from a normally sober evaluative mind, we again encounter a disturbing element. In this *Otello*, Koegler tells us, Iago's *Credo* and Otello's "*Niun mi tema*" "... have nothing anymore to do

---

* "Producer": British for "director." I think it's an inaccurate usage, but retain it when quoting from English sources.

with singing, here Felsenstein has arrived at the point where he liquidates the form of opera."[19] Fully acknowledging the reality of Koegler's epiphany, but wondering whether we (or he) are really in favor of this liquidation, we follow on through Wolfgang Nolter's rave review of a *Traviata* in Hamburg ("After Wieland Wagner's deplorable *Tristan,* Walter Felsenstein came to the Staatsoper to set things right again"—Apr., 1960); to Ralf Steyer's somewhat bemused reaction to the Paisiello *Barber* at Schwetzingen (again the theme that ". . . the artists were such good actors that . . . the distinction between the spoken and lyrical drama was virtually obliterated . . . a magnificent theatrical evening rather than a magnificent operatic performance"—Summer Festivals issue, 1960); and then to *Traviata* once more, a re-working of the Hamburg production (designs by Heinrich), but now at the Komische Oper itself, and now assessed by the eminent German critic, H. H. Stuckenschmidt (Feb., 1961). He begins by noting the dominance of ". . . visual elements . . . evident everywhere in Germany today" and the ascendancy of directors over conductors and singers, with the "stylization" of Wieland Wagner and the "complete realism" of Felsenstein as prime, opposed examples. He terms the Komische Oper ". . . in many ways . . . the summit of modern operatic art," and goes on to unreservedly praise all production aspects, including Heinrich's "brilliance of scenery and costume"; he is also impressed by Masur, recently installed as the company's Musical Director. He has serious reservations about the singing, though, and—uncommonly in these reports—the acting (see below).

After further highly laudatory reviews of *Rigoletto* in Hamburg and of *Bluebeard,* a *Hoffmann* revival, and *Jenůfa* at the K.O., we arrive at the first instance of serious backlash: "Encounter in Leipzig," by the English critic Charles Osborne (Feb., 1966). He had visited the then-East German city for a colloquium sponsored by the International Theatre Institute, and the event's Cold War context should be considered. The East/West frontier had been closed in August 1961. The Berlin Wall had gone up. In September of 1964, a Congress of East German composers and musicologists, with their Ministry of Culture, had issued a resolution which, to judge from translated extracts (Feb., 1965), might have come from Soviet sources in the 1930s: ". . . support [for] our West German colleagues who are trying to preserve the humanist content of art against . . . monopoly-capitalism, militarism and neofascism . . ."; ". . . a demand to place the socialist hero of our time . . . at the centre of the action," etc., etc. Now, at the colloquium, dominated by East-of-the-Curtain representatives, Osborne sat through "paeans of praise for the estimable Dr. Felsenstein" and repeated calls for a "realistic music theatre" that was both artistically and politically distinct from opera, before getting his first exposure to Komische Oper productions. He didn't much like the

Hoffmann, and hated the *Otello,* and not only for musical and vocal shortcomings. Perceiving a wide gap between Felsenstein's principles and his work, and judging him to be ". . . a fine producer with a very strong visual bias which frequently encourages him to work against the music," he refers to his performers as "browbeaten automata from the Felsenstein factory," "constipated, puppet-like," who are "drained of responsibility" and "do not act *with the voice.*" (There's that phrase—italics in the original.) He also described the interpretation of Iago as "wildly melodramatic."

These are extreme remarks, as extreme as Koegler's raptures, and undoubtedly fed in part by irritation at the surrounding atmosphere. But they echo some of Stuckenschmidt's reservations (acting that was sometimes "guilty of overstatement of gesture and expression," and that was "refuted by [Felsenstein's] own aesthetic theories"). Other strains surface over the years—of a bias toward critique of bourgeois style and class structure, and of a "Strindbergian" quality to some of the acting, along with much continued praise and acknowledgement of Felsenstein's importance as a reformer. In January of 1970, *Opera* devoted its cover and lead article to "The Road to Improvement," a translation of a lengthy interview with Felsenstein that had originally appeared in *Der Morgen,* a West German newspaper, containing his assessment of the operatic scene in the light of his principles.

Here I shall leave off this chronicle of productions and pronouncements, and narrow the discussion to what seems to me the nub of the debate. That comes down to two queries. Did Felsenstein actually do what he said he was going to do? And, since failures in execution do not necessarily invalidate principles, is what he said he was going to do right to begin with? In the absence of live full productions, I can't say I have conclusive answers. But I do have some fairly persuasive evidence: a description of Felsenstein's teaching methods from a perceptive, articulate student; my own report and recollections of Felsenstein's lectures, teaching/rehearsal demonstrations, and film showings in Boston, in 1971; and the films themselves, as restored and released in 2007.[20] In considering them, three sets of relationships should be kept in mind: between music (especially singing) and action, between interpreter and text, and between director and performer.

The Felsenstein student was a young English tenor named Charles Parker, who enrolled in an intensive role-study course with the master at the Vienna Music Academy, and wrote about the experience in *Opera* (May, 1964). His article well conveys the excitement of work with a dedicated, patient, demanding teacher who lifts the aspirations of his pupils and insists on taking nothing for granted, letting nothing pass. "The man is a fanatic," Parker says, "but very convincing." The pursuit of emotional logic and character action he describes would have been familiar to students of modern acting, but were startling to the operatic mentality of the time, and still would be to ours, if consistently followed through. Parker sweetly evokes the loyalty such a teacher can inspire: [the search for reality] ". . . seemed to matter to him so very much, and this made us all conscious of the great task before us."

Understandable as Parker's enthusiasm is, it's the place of singing in Felsenstein's schema that gives pause. When Felsenstein states, in the abstract, that all the elements of singing belong to "the emotionally conditioned physical action," we singingacting partisans second the motion, though some of us will have had our suspicions aroused by the subsequent "and subordinate to it." Parker gives us a graphic little sketch of how this principle worked out in a hands-on situation. He tells us that every detail of the score had to be scanned for its potential dramatic significance. Good! But it turns out that this also means that nothing not specifically marked may be introduced. No unwritten ritards or rallentandos. Metronome markings rigidly observed— "Even *rubato* has to go!" Further, the voice, as an opera-specific instrument, must be housebroken to music-theatre purposes. No tonal or technical thought must intrude: "The scorn poured on anyone trying to make a beautiful sound was withering. 'Singing' almost became a rude word!" So although we know that Felsenstein despised "recitation," it seems we might be left with exactly that, slavishly obedient to the text and bereft of any tone of voice not reflexively called forth by the interaction of the text with whatever state the singer's instrument happens to be in.

Felsenstein was extremely dissatisfied with the training methods employed in European conservatories, schools, and voice studios, and it is impossible not to sympathize with him in this regard. He was especially disturbed by (and does this sound at all familiar?) the separation of vocal technique from vocal expression. He inveighed against the enslavement of the performer by his or her obligation to ". . . purely technical vocalizing" and ". . . tone that does not signify or express something definite." He wanted voice teachers to devise ". . . expressive exercises [that would] contain every possible variety of feeling, in order to make it possible for every normal technique of voice production to adjust to any emotion."* The goal, says Felsenstein, is the creative independence of the performer. So we are back to the question of just what this creative independence would be—and how it might declare itself in a world of the text, all the text, and nothing but the text—as well as the question of the role of emotion in the singingactor's process.

---

* See *The Music Theater of Walter Felsenstein*, pp. 34-35, part of a lecture on working methods given in 1965.

The Boston visit, which drew an eager audience of opera professionals, left no doubt as to Felsenstein's dramaturgical grasp or his thoroughness in interrogating the musical and verbal text for its action content.* His lectures on training methods and the *Otello* backstory were penetrating, even inspiring. But the scene work and the films were disconcerting to someone hoping to see the penetration and inspiration prove their worth in practice. In some nine hours of work devoted to two scenic fragments (the recitatives and opening bars of Violetta's Act I scena—"*È strano!*", as it happens—and Iago's *Credo*) with two talented and willing young singers (Catherine Christensen and David Holloway) under conditions that felt more clinical than artistic, it quickly became clear that the performer's independence consisted of the freedom to arrive, in each and every moment and in every behavioral detail, at the result envisioned by the teacher, who was in fact functioning as a micromanagerial director. There was no real input from the respectful students, no adjustment to them by the director (though his manner was always considerate), and no progress that I could detect. When we viewed the *Otello* film, we saw that the sequence of moments Felsenstein had been trying to extract from Holloway was exactly that of the onscreen Iago. Moreover, the quality of the acting in this crucial scene was discouragingly close to the "wildly melodramatic" sort of Charles Osborne's description. It *was* closely related to musical events, and one could see the effort to create the illusion of the performer as the "creative fashioner" of the music. But the result was just high-toned mugging.

However, that would hardly be a fair generalization about the acting in the Felsenstein films. For one thing, its stylistic embrace is wide, from the remarkably uncartoonish forest creature characterizations of *Vixen* (ultimate vindication for all those Animal Exercise advocates) to the high human tragedy of *Otello*. For another, these *are* films, and of a special sort—television transmissions of Komische Oper performances or studio re-creations of productions in the K.O. repertory, enacted by stage performers under a stage director. Individual performances do not appear to have been toned down much for the camera, and on the whole don't need that as much as most operatic acting. One never suspects, as one often does with today's transmissions, that a performer has been cast with the camera, not the stage, in mind. (K.O. performers had to look reasonably "right" in the first place.) These productions need to be viewed with an awareness of the advantages and disadvantages endemic to all opera films, which we have already encountered

---

* For my original, more extended reactions, see *The Musical Newsletter*, Vol. I, No. 4 (Spring, 1971), pp. 22-24.

in the *La Juive* and other videos, and, since we are trying to get the feel of an evening at the K.O., an extra awareness of how these images translate to the stage perspective.

With these caveats in mind, I think it can be said that, though the "unreservedly believable" quotient varies considerably, an extraordinarily consistent effort to convey dramatic specificity and true-to-lifeness, as opposed to a general mood or a set of conventions, is evident. There's an unflagging pursuit, extending to the smallest roles, of strongly motivated action and of the interpretive logic that can emerge once the slate is wiped clean of received notions. Since a number of Felsenstein's principals, and many in his remarkably responsive choral ensemble, are real theatre talents, this pursuit can often sweep us along—yes, that's the scene, it's really playing!

But it's exhausting. In monologue sequences like the Countess's arias in *Figaro*, Desdemona's in Act IV of *Otello*, or the Forester alone in the woods in *Vixen*, Felsenstein's performers show an ability to convey inner emotion or a sensory state that is well beyond that of most opera singers. But elsewhere, the rule is externalization, the gestural and facial illustration of every musical event and every minibeat of verbal text, as if in fear that a moment pass by us unconstrued. There's no trust in the music, or in us. So a kind of cumulative fatigue, a browbeaten feeling, sets in, attributable only in part to camera closeness or the early point on the opera-movie learning curve. And although I think Charles Osborne's language of "puppets" and "automatons" was a bit strong, there is too often the sense of obedience to a pre-existing plan, and of the need to show us everything about the plan, rather than a free flow of action and emotion, the illusion of unplanned events.

Stylistically, too, Felsenstein's *Realismus* is a peculiar mix. Political facts have to be taken into account. If the Soviets handed you a theatre, and the government of Walter Ulbricht tolerated and subsidized your work, your "realism" had to at least pass muster as being of the Socialist variety. And it must be said that, with the exception of the tiresome "satire" of royalty in *Bluebeard,* there is very little in the way of political comment in these productions—perhaps some tone or emphasis here and there, but on the whole the characters are accorded their individual dignity, regardless of class.[21] Beyond politics or social critique, the effect of the physical acting is sometimes genuinely lifelike, and sometimes feverishly hyperexpressive. (That's what's meant, I'm sure, by the references to "Strindbergian" acting, though I don't think Strindberg is well served that way, either.) It's rather as if what we imagine of the Meiningen troupe had returned to be directed and filmed by Murnau. And those, along with Reinhardt, would after all be among the big influences of Felsenstein's youth.

And what of the singing—of vocalism itself, vocal interpretation, and their dreamt-of oneness with physical action? I believe not that Felsenstein was unmusical, but that his musicality was predominantly rhythmic, not melodic; that it was highly literate but not at all oral; and that it embraced a kind of anti-aesthetic that left no room for dramatic expression by the voice through purely musical means. For all his truly expert scrutiny of verbal and musical texts, he suffered from a blind, or rather, deaf spot right in the center of his singingacting vision. It's embedded in his formulation of sung action, with its subordination of singing to action. To re-formulate: it's not simply that "this state is physical as much as emotional." Emotion *is* a physical state. So is singing. Emotion can generate (or at least strongly condition) singing, but singing generates emotion, too—in the singer, as well as in the auditor. In opera, the "emotionally conditioned action" must originate *in the singing.* The relationship of such an action to character, to objectives and obstacles, to a throughline, to sensory states, and so on, is the same as it is in spoken theatre, but it must spring from the sung impulse. This doesn't mean that action is subordinate to singing. Nothing is subordinate to anything—it's all one, remember? But it does mean that bodily behavior is not the constant referent for "reality" or the "unreservedly believable" in opera. And it is opera we are dealing with. The term "music theatre," which in its operatic application began as an effort to break the semantic tyranny of musical aesthetics and remind us that we're dealing with drama, has become nothing more than an escape clause, a way of defining the artform down and avoiding its most perplexing challenges. The aspirations that Felsenstein so eloquently articulated—e.g., that actions must occur at a level that can only be expressed in music, that the performer must appear to be generating the music in the moment—cannot be achieved without locating singing at their source.

Further, this "singing" or "singingacting" must embrace something more than accurate declamation of the pitches, rhythms, and dynamics marked in the score, even when these are elaborate and can be "justified" by talented performers. The very act of singing belongs to orality. That means it includes a "remembrance of songs sung," which is to say an awareness of the unwritten, memorable modes of expression which, in our elaborated, high-culture artform we call "tradition" and "style." It must also include latitude for the performer's own creativity—the expectation that the singer, qualified by mindfulness of both the textual and oral materials, search out the character within him- or herself and bring forth the results. These elements of style and creativity are often the most immediate, personal means of conveying meaning, especially of the viscerally received, subliminally conscious kind.

Felsenstein wasn't a voice man. We wouldn't expect him to be—it's a highly specialized field of knowledge. But because his work process was so intimately bound up with vocal expression, his incomplete understanding of the interface between vocal function and interpretation constituted a roadblock on his performers' journey toward operatic truth. Such basic musical concepts as legato and portamento have a physical basis in the elasticity of tissue and the smoothness of its efficient use. The *messa di voce* is grounded in the preservation of respiratory poise. The guidance of musical line, its plasticity, its expansion and contraction and sense of destination—its melodic contour, in short—are also derived from our recognition of how energy flows and animates us. We call them beautiful and respond to them emotionally because of that recognition. The same applies to the registral checks and balances that extend and preserve the range of pitch, and to the resonantal properties of vowels. How voices work, sound, and endure, and how we react to them, are part and parcel of one another.

Felsenstein probably would not have argued with these propositions. But I don't think he understood their implications in working terms. I suspect that part of his annoyance with voice teachers arose from helplessly watching them putter and tinker in ways he didn't understand with the instruments he wanted solely at his disposal, not only because the results were sometimes bad, but because they were sometimes good in ways that didn't serve his purposes. He seems to have believed, as theatre people often do, that if one can just get rid of the complications of "technique" and let the voice respond "naturally" to the expressive demands of the music, the voice will find its optimum adjustment. There are grains of truth in this belief. Singers *are* often tied up with purely mechanical pre-occupations and obligations to effect, and it can be liberating to direct their attention to specific dramatic goals, to what's actually happening in a given moment, or out to a partner. Many have techniques that are patchy or laborious; identifying and easing the associated tensions can be at least Step One toward recovery.

By and large, though, an instrument must be complete before it can be played on. The aesthetic qualities and capacities for action I tried to describe in my earlier discussion of vocalities—the ones necessary for consummation of the great operatic scores—must be there, ready to respond to interpretive demands as they present themselves. They aren't "natural" consequences of the collision between a human and a score. In his highly laudatory review of the Felsenstein/Heinrich *Rigoletto* in Hamburg, Heinz Joachim notes that the leading voices sounded better than their usual selves as a result of being guided toward greater dramatic specificity and away from obligations to traditional effects. I believe him. However, the principals of this *Rigoletto* were

Mattiwilda Dobbs, Vladimir Ruzdak, and Arturo Sergi, all experienced singers with international track records, their techniques long since set.[22] How did the singers of Felsenstein's own company fare?

Stanislavski conceded that because singers of extraordinary talent would quickly move on to starrier venues, his Opera Studio would have to rely on competent vocalists dedicated to singingacting ideals. Felsenstein faced this reality as well, and in any case first-quality voices were spread quite thin among the German houses in the postwar years, even with the influx of Americans who had no place to sing at home. The political divide further drained the talent pool. And Felsenstein was looking for a special sort of artist. So the presence of only a few voices that afford any real pleasure is understandable—the level is far below what Corsaro was able to work with at the NYCO, or Rennert in Hamburg, to name a couple of companies with avowed "music theatre" aims. It's not even as good as that of the Opera Studio's direct descendant, the Stanislavski/ Nemirovich-Danchenko company of that time.[23]

But even modest voices and unfinished techniques are led toward or away from their expressive potential by the practices to which they are put. What I hear on these soundtracks is a determined stripping-away of anything that might help voices to bloom and the vocal line to claim its rightful place as the trigger for an action, the conveyer of intent, or the shaper of a mood. If Felsenstein believed that aesthetic qualities could convey dramatic truth, I do not hear it. If he truly wanted voices to "contain every possible variety of feeling" and "vocal production to adjust to any emotion," his singers succeed only within a "heightened speech" framework, and with an emotional range that tends to center on extremes of fear, anger, and petulance. Not only (as Charles Parker warned us) are there none of the easements that allow voices to create musically eloquent moments, to gather themselves, hold, then lead on in ways that keep us engaged, there is not even the sense of latent *sostenuto* behind recitative or declamatory passages to keep us in the world of musical expression. Everything that distinguishes singing from speaking, save for its greatly expanded pitch range, is scrubbed down till only the ineradicable traces remain. Parker tells us that in working with singers for text-obedience discipline, Felsenstein would say "This is not interpreting!" In the musical sense that appears to have been true, and he evidently considered it to his advantage. If vocal and musical aesthetics have no interpretive role to play, and if vocal effects are ruled out as dramatic acts, then any voice is suitable for anything so long as it reproduces the notated pitches and rhythms.

Then too, regardless of a work's language of origin, Felsenstein's singers were obliged to render it in German. Language-of-the-audience was standard practice in all but the international-level Continental houses at that time, and an article of faith for music-theatre proponents. It's often assumed that for those of us particularly interested in dramatic and theatrical values, the question of whether or not to translate is easily settled in favor of the affirmative—the audience must understand. Actually, it just generates more questions. Translate what, how, why, and for whom? The K.O. performances present these questions in the form of three arguable propositions: that these works (all of foreign origin) be translated into German; that they be translated by Felsenstein himself; and that in performance, the translations be rendered in a particular manner. Each of these steps represents a degree of alienation from the integrity of the original, justified or not by one's assessment of offsetting gains. To touch on them briefly, in order:

- The debate over translation (quite lively in English-speaking countries through the '60s and '70s) comes down to a matter of the immediate recognition of denotative verbal meanings (usually partial, usually off-kilter), plus the comfort of our way of saying things, vs. the sensory impact of vocal sounds—shaded chains of them intended for specific emotional affects created by their bond to the musical setting (see the earlier discussions in *Singingacting and Words, Eye and Ear,* and *The Enhancements*). But responsibility for answering this question is invariably sloughed off on the audience. Who are they? What can be expected of them? (Reading the libretto for instance? Learning something of a foreign language?) What level of experience of the work and performance are they capable of? What kind of understanding do we want them to have? And these questions are usually reducible to one other: will the audience come, and come back? We now content ourselves with the deceptive convenience of surtitles. The K.O.'s priority was word-recognition, reinforced by the company's mandate as a *comique*-style theatre, performing in a populist sociopolitical atmosphere.

- Felsenstein took great pains with his translations. He considered any departure from a line-by-line (if possible, word-by-word) matching of verbal meanings with note values to be betrayals of the originals, bits of the many interpretive distortions that had kept the truth of the works hidden behind a gauze of romanticization. This goal of wordnote literalism is, as he well knew, unattainable, if only for reasons of sentence structure and syllabic asymmetries. Still, by disregarding almost everything else normally taken into account by authors of singing translations, and occasionally smudging the line between his own interpretations and the absolute "original meaning," he achieved an in-the-moment accuracy ratio well above normal, and this story-line immediacy was no doubt an important value for his audiences. Among the factors he was obliged to ignore, though, were all those that might help his singers retain the musical feel of the setting through the aesthetic logic of its rise and fall or that would help them preserve some of the setting's expressive power by matching its sounds (brighter or darker, open or closed), to particular areas of range or phrase destinations, and so help Italian music sound Italian or French music sound French, even though sung in German. These, too, are ways of being faithful to the truth of an original, and ones that most translators try, with intermittent success, to take into account. Ironically, they are also ways of creating a world where "the dramatic happening [takes place] on a level where music is the only means of expression." But Felsenstein conceded little to them. (For more on Felsenstein's translations, see n. [24].)

- German is no one's idea of a hospitable second home for Italian or French musical settings. Whether in conversational exchanges, the conveyance of urgent information, or confessions of profound emotion, it's a radically different medium for self-expression and self-presentation. It takes a different stance toward the world. And because German culture is old and deep, German-language performers have also developed characteristic manners of musical and verbal delivery that often accentuate the differences. Non-Germanic operalovers have for decades—perhaps centuries—stood amazed at the AustroGerman tolerance for vocal signs of pain, distress, and derangement in whatever degree, so long as it's *echt*. All this notwithstanding, a half-century's worth of recordings preserves hundreds of examples of German-language artists who, despite sometimes unfelicitous translations, have rendered Mozart, Verdi, and Puccini; Gounod, Bizet, and Offenbach, with a fair measure of the music's original contours and temperament, and from time to time an awareness of timbral possibilities that opens up something in the music.[25] However, this involves musical interpretation, and acceptance of the fact that beauty is not always an unfortunate accident or an outright falsehood.

It isn't quite true that Felsenstein's singers don't act with the voice. In recitative, in conversationally set arioso (like most of *Vixen*), or in operetta patter songs, they often achieve a sharply pointed, "natural"-sounding (i.e., speech-like) rendering that is fresh and effective. The men can declaim with persuasive force, but in a particularly edgy sort of enunciation dominated by harshly closed vowel forms (special emphasis on the German "*i*," "*ee*," and "*eh*" spectrum and the "*ei*" diphthong) and tensely expectorated plosive and dental consonants—an exaggerated form of a fairly common tendency among German-language singers of the 1930s and '40s. It's wearying to listen to and tends to push even the good voices toward "character" status, but I suppose it has to be classified as "acting with the voice." It's when the music takes them into regions where the expression of action and emotion depends on exploitation of tonal quality, sustainment of line, technical finish, and the embrace of aesthetic effect—as it must in the great arias of the Mozart scores, the most fulfilling stretches of *Hoffmann,* and nearly all of *Otello*—that the K.O. artists don't act with the voice, either because they can't or mayn't. And this, unfortunately, is the territory where all of us who wish to believe with our ears search for our most intimate and meaningful contact with the masterworks of opera, and are dismayed to find it missing.

Despite these serious deficiencies, not all is lost musically, for out of the collaboration between Felsenstein and his music directors comes an unusual dramatic alertness—the feel of the orchestra as actor, about whose absence I complained earlier.* No one would suppose the orchestra of his Komische Oper to be on a par with the world's great pit ensembles, and in purely aesthetic terms, it probably wasn't. Nor will we find in its playing the expressive luxuriations that other orchestras and conductors sometimes provide, since its work must be of a piece with the textual discipline imposed upon the singers, which is in turn indebted not only to Felsenstein's predilections, but to the general atmosphere of German musicological scholarship and theatre practice of that time.

Given that framework, the orchestral playing on these recordings is nonetheless compelling. The level of execution is high and the dramatic involvement is unfailing. I'm not referring primarily to superb musical co-ordination with singers, or even to the co-ordination of musical gestures with stage action (certainly present, but sometimes an advantage and sometimes not), but rather to the realization of the dramatic content of the orchestral writing

---

* In the eye-led, ear-confirmed film/video media, it requires an unnatural re-adjustment of the synaesthetic balance to direct attention to the orchestral playing and hold it there. When these performances do achieve their versions of opera's sensory immersion (in fair stretches of the *Otello* and *Vixen,* and sometimes in the *Hoffmann* and *Figaro*), one is not really sure if the source of excitement is musical, or is in the visual rhythm, supported by the sound. But that's how these media are *supposed* to work, and it is almost impossible to avoid eye-dominance for more than brief intervals unless one looks away from the screen and just listens. That is what I have found myself doing, part of the time, on repeated viewings with the conductors who most interest me.

itself. It's a pity that there isn't more about this in the Felsenstein literature. In the essays contained in Fuchs's book and the Edition volume, and the video bonus materials, there is much edifying stuff on his collaborative approach with performers, designers, and dramaturgs, but only scattered and rather generalized comments on his way to working with conductors and orchestral musicians. And unless something is hiding behind a generic title, there is also very little to be found in the German-language literature referenced in the Edition's bibliography.

Some important conductors worked with Felsenstein. Klemperer conducted early performances of the 1949 *Carmen,* and though he declined the invitation to become the Komische Oper's Music Director, he considered Felsenstein "a producer of genius" (see Heyworth, Vol. II, p. 202). Vaçlav Neumann, known to Western record collectors for his operatic and symphonic recordings from Prague, was for a time the company's Music Director, and returned to lead nearly all the performances of the famous *Vixen* production. We have already noted Masur's four-year regime, and his subsequent disinclination to conduct opera under less rigorous circumstances. Carlos Kleiber was the conductor when Felsenstein directed *Der Freischütz* in Stuttgart. Fritz Lehmann, though less well known internationally, was a well-regarded Bach conductor. But how did the collaboration of these distinguished musicians with Felsenstein actually work? They obviously did not have the sort of interpretive authority over the pit and stage that a Mahler in Vienna or Toscanini at La Scala exercised, or even as much as the conductor of a new production in a well-run repertory house. Felsenstein maintained that all aspects of production should be under the guidance of either a highly musical director or a theatrically savvy conductor, and in this case it was the former. We do gather that, unlike the conductors caught up in the "design matrix" process described by Tom Sutcliffe, Felsenstein's were part of the team from the earliest discussions onward. From the occasional written comment or photo, we surmise that they were involved with staging rehearsals earlier and more intensively than is often the case. But beyond this, the role of Musical Director in the company, or of the conductor of a particular production, is left to the imagination. How much input did they and the rest of the musical staff have with respect to orchestral interpretation (quite successful, to judge by these performances) or vocal (not so much—did they simply acquiesce in Felsenstein's rhythmic ideas, his "uninterpreted" rendition of the vocal text?)? Did anyone in the company look after either the artistic prerogatives or the ongoing vocal health of the singers? And how were these matters negotiated when Felsenstein worked in other venues, as with his Verdi productions in Hamburg?* Given the wealth of explanation on all topics visual, the absence of information on this one is regrettable, and we are left to take it as indicative.[26]

So: did Felsenstein do what he said he was going to do? Yes, in several ways. He challenged all imitative convention and generalization, so that even today much of his company's work seems unusually fresh and specific. Though he was an eye man first and an ear man second, he at least trained his eye (and ours) on the right theatrical targets—the lives of the characters, and a stage world that drew us into those lives, not into visual representations of ideas about the works or critiques of them. He tried to honor the hierarchy of interpretation, and saw this as an ethical imperative. He also honored art as a calling, not as a vainglorious pursuit or business enterprise. He wrote and lectured on these matters with precision and considerable persuasive strength, and thereby lifted the level of operatic discourse. And his working theatrical expertise made all these qualities frequently evident in practice, not just in theory. As with Stanislavski, the fine words would not have gone far had not the work first set the opera pot aboil.

There were also important ways in which Felsenstein did not consistently do what he said he was going to do. It is vital that these be acknowledged, lest his surviving work be taken as exemplification of the effort to bond singing with acting, or opera with modern theatre. While his taste in acting did often induce genuinely lifelike, "unreservedly plausible" behavior, it inclined just as often to the flagrantly indicative, tinged with Expressionistic imagery—even at the time of their first showings, substantial sequences of his films looked like movies from the 1920s, not the '50s and '60s. His intention to stay within the bounds of the creator's field notwithstanding, he sometimes confused his interpretive logic with revealed truth. His rejection of celebrity culture and personal enrichment was entangled with Soviet views of art's place in society, and whether this is because he was a True Believer or a cunning survivalist is, from an artistic P.O.V., irrelevant. Above all, he does not seem to have accomplished his professed goal of artistic independence for the performer. For that, he would have had to concede that his own visions of interpretive detail, of the progression of scenes and the exact qualities of interpersonal exchange, however meticulously studied and brilliantly reasoned beforehand, were not necessarily the only ones or the best ones that creative performers

---

* Janos Kulka (*Rigoletto*) and Albert Bittner (*Traviata*) were the conductors there. Both were praised by *Opera*'s reviewers but only sketchily, following lengthy description of the production and brief ones of the principal singers.

might arrive at. He would have had to be content with establishing outlines for work, then sitting back watchfully while his performers set sail on their Ustinovian voyages, keeping them on course and guiding them toward port when the time came.

Further: is what Felsenstein said he was going to do right to begin with? The answer, again, is in many respects yes, assuming that one concedes the necessity of working toward some fusion of opera with the ways and means of modern acting. But his failure to recognize singing as the Unmoved Mover of the operatic action, and to acknowledge that independence for the performer would entail a measure of creative freedom not only with physical behavior, but with the music, undercut everything. If one does not begin with the *sung* action, and with opera as a theatre of sound first, sight second, one is truly on the way toward "liquidation of the form of opera." It is also important to recognize that Felsenstein's declaration of what exists and is real ("Certainly only the action, and the human situation that derives from it") fails to take into consideration the fact that the operatic sung action, particularly in all pre-modern genres of opera, often takes the form of lyrical description—something virtually banned from the modern acting vocabulary. The description may be of an emotional state or psychological space, a scene, or a narrative, or some combination of these. It is true that these descriptions are enfolded in character actions and that those actions are related to ruling objectives. It is among the advancements of modern acting techniques to insist on this perception. For the performer, though, while this awareness can keep him or her on course, the task of the moment is the description itself, with all the eloquence and force at his or her command. For practical purposes, it *is* the action. In opera, this must be accomplished principally by the voice, through the music.

Felsenstein, however, was trying to break opera down into music theatre, and in particular to eliminate its oral traditions, because he saw the many falsities commonly associated with the descent of these traditions into mere habits, and with a rhetoric that new generations of performers didn't know how to "get behind." Ergo, of the three ingredients always present in the vocal interpretive mix, namely, the ornamental, the prismatic, and the verbal, he heavily favored the least "operatic," the verbal. And of the singeractor's three interpretive resources, namely, the text, oral tradition, and interpretive creativity ("originality"), he embraced the first and proscribed the second. As for the third, he endorsed it and claimed it in the name of his performers, but in reality it was reserved for him, the director, the decoder of the text—and in the name of "authenticity."*

And so there remains the Parnassus problem, the still-open question of whether or not modern acting methods are compatible with anything we could properly call grand opera. In the writings of Felsenstein and the early productions of Corsaro, it seemed that this question was about to be engaged, that someone was going to summon the nerve to bring the neo-Stanislavskian techniques of Being the Man head-to-head with the high elocutionary rhetorics of E-19. But that has not happened in any integrated, consistent fashion. In his video interview with Lotfi Mansouri (see p. 506, n. 3), Corsaro is asked if he would ever stage *Aïda*. "Never!" is the answer, and except for Felsenstein's heroic stab at *Otello*, the answer so remained for both these humanizing reformers, not only for *Aïda*, but for any early Verdi or his quartet of late-middle masterworks; for all of Wagner; for the serious operas of Strauss; the serious operas of Rossini, Bellini, and Donizetti; any of Gluck's or Massenet's, or any from the French grand opera tradition.

No director should be forced to stage anything for which he does not feel a temperamental and stylistic affinity (though of course it happens all the time—directors need jobs, they need to step through any open door), and there is every reason why a "comique-style" company committed to a specific singingacting philosophy should be part of the operatic scene. Felsenstein was the first to acknowledge that many operas are not suited to music-theatre treatment. Fair enough. But if the unsuitable operas include all of the artform's large-scale, transcendent masterworks, we haven't really come very far.

Konstantin Stanislavski loved opera in all its poetic transcendence and grandeur. He venerated the great composers and their works, and venerated as well the great interpreters (like Chaliapin) whose voices and imaginations

---

* An important difference between Felsenstein and the American Methodists who essayed opera was in this matter of the text. Whereas Felsenstein's literalist fealty was in line with the dominant musicological attitudes of his time—and, as artistic director of his own company, he was in a position to impose it—the Americans brought from their theatre practice a much looser relationship to text that included an almost dismissive attitude toward specific interpretive directions. This gave performers more leeway, but since the Americans were also in rebellion against oral tradition, they were left in an often culturally uninformed creative space. The assumption was that from there, they would either miraculously find their way to stylistically appropriate choices, or be relieved of any questions of style, which would be declared immaterial and irrelevant. Of course, the American directors were generally working in companies that ceded them far less authority than Felsenstein enjoyed in such crucial areas as casting and the relationship between musical and dramatic interpretation.

could set free the spirit of those works. Though no one ever examined text more closely, he understood that this spirit, not the letter of the text, is the essence of artistic law, and that in the theatre's search for truth-in-life, something of the ancient bardic invention must survive. He believed that in even the meanest of realities, a spark of the ideal endures. He wanted to bring Parnassus into earthly purview, not blow up the mountain. He would never have put the actor, much less the singer, into a straitjacket, either of text or of directorial concept, and especially toward the end, saw that the task was not to tell performers what to do, but to furnish them with the intellectual, emotional, physical, and cultural wherewithal to do it themselves. For these reasons, and for his own generous, noble, and decidedly un-fanatical spirit (attested to by friend and foe), he looms, Anxiety-of-Influencelike, over all that has followed. The operatic reform movement to which we can loosely attach his name brought us lightning-flashes of achievement, and glimpses of future vistas. But except in the work of some individual performers, and occasionally in the production of a work of modern provenance, those visions have faded, displaced by others.

DOWN THE POST ROAD

Vsevolod Meyerhold was the brilliant, radicalizing unStanislavski of the interwar Soviet avant-garde. Then, for the twenty-five years following the murder of his wife and his own execution, he was among the most-once-famous of the many historically deleted victims of the Stalinist purges, his provocative ideas as forcibly repressed as the memory of his person. With The Thaw, the ideas, though not the person, were resurrected, and alongside Brecht he (or, rather, this ghostly idea-"he") became the brilliant, radicalizing unStanislavski of the European and Anglo-American neo-avant-garde. In the introduction to his splendid collection of writings by, to, and about Meyerhold,[27] Paul Schmidt calls his subject a "modernist" who was ". . . the first to insist on the primacy of the director's role, indeed the first to conceive it as a role . . .". I think we really must award that blue ribbon, if not to Stanislavski (or even to Daly or Brahm, or any of the other late E-19 pioneers of "integrated" production), then to Reinhardt. And it doesn't seem quite right to call Meyerhold a "modernist," except perhaps in his early Symbolist and Constructionist phases. He's more accurately defined, I think, as the theatre's first postmodernist director.

True, he did not banish narrative outright. Though he ". . . 'alienated' the staged plays in an extreme manner," observes Hans-Thies Lehmann in his keystone study of "postdramatic" theatre,[28] ". . . they were still presented in a cohesive totality." Meyerhold did, however, interrogate text, re-arrange it, critique it. He looked on classic texts as raw material for contemporaneous (avant-garde, Revolutionary) construal. He saw the director's function as "... a creative force as well, equal to the role of the playwright in shaping the theatrical experience" (Schmidt), who "... operated on the playtext in the modern sense: he wrote the text anew", and [quoting Barthes] "... crossed its writing with a new inscription." He was, in short, an auteur. Further, his "... conception of acting totally denies the idea of 'character,'" and his train-ing system of biomechanics "... structured gesture to present a possibility, a *virtuality*, an *idea*" (my italics).

All these are Schmidt's formulations, set down, like the Gospels, many years after the fact, and bits of what seems to me rather strenuous advocacy.[29] They are in agreement, though, with the general picture we can reconstruct of Meyerhold's work. Because Meyerhold's productions were "cohesive totalities" that still embraced some form of representation and invited some degree of empathetic response, he does not quite qualify as a "postdramatic" director. But he certainly prefigures the postmodern one. Take updating. Among New Theatre theorists and their followers, this is too piddling a matter to fuss over. For Lehmann, for instance, Peter Sellars doesn't make his list—an extensive one—of postdramatic theatre persons, for "... his productions [of *Ajax* and *The Persians*], like his original stagings of Mozart operas, were called 'post-modern' merely because he rigorously and irreverently brought classical material into the contemporary, everyday world (p. 25).* Let's avoid confusing a discussion of principle with personal reactions to a particular experience: there were many things I liked about Sellars's *Così fan tutte* and *Don Giovanni*, less about his *Nozze di Figaro* or Handel's *Orlando*, and less yet about his *Giulio Cesare* on video. But had I loved them all unreservedly, this would still be true: if one sets *Così* in the post-Vietnam U.S.A., and the Mesmer episode with text intact while presenting the disguised Despina as Dr. Ruth (pretty funny at the time, but on the video, Dr. Ruth is herself no longer topical enough, and the revised sequence is much less funny), one has accomplished the same displacement inherent in *Capriccio*'s discussion of the *guerre des bouffons* in WWII Paris, or the Robinson/*La Bohème*'s references to Guizot and Louis-Philippe in WWI Paris. One has "merely" detached the sense of the sung text from the time-and-place circumstances of its enactment, and so begun the unraveling of the performed work's integrity. And one has begun a more subtle, streaming incompatibility between text and performance—toward avoidance of the "doubling" of text by performance, and toward Bob's separation of elements. Isn't that obvious? And

---

* Since Lehmann was writing in the late '90s, his view didn't take on Sellars' subsequent work, like the *Tristan* collaboration with Viola. Would Sellars now make the "postdra-matic" cut, or at least the "postmodern" one?

significant? And all the more significant because, though obvious, it is now so seldom questioned?

Like Reinhardt, Meyerhold made music a crucial element in many of his productions of plays, and worked with it very much hands-on. Collaborating composers included Prokofiev, Shostakovich, Shebalin, and Asafyef, and he made use of Beethoven, Chopin, Liszt, et al., in the extensive musicalizing of some of his productions. He often defined scene sequences, acts, and even whole plays in musical terms, "scoring" them for their rhythmic and timbral correspondences, even when no music sounded.[30] Like both Reinhardt and Stanislavski, he also engaged with opera. During his time at the Imperial Theatres of St. Petersburg (1909-1918), he directed a highly successful *Orfeo* (Gluck, the Paris revision, with Leonid Sobinov in the title role, Golovin as designer and Fokine the choreographer), an innovative *Tristan und Isolde* (with Litvinne, Cherkasskaya, Yershov, and Kastorsky—there's a *Tristan* cast!), and an unsuccessful *Elektra*, while also staging a borrowed *Boris Godunov* with Chaliapin.[31] To read through his essay on *Tristan*[32] is to experience the intellectual excitement of encountering a visionary seized by a great subject, and keenly attuned to emergent artistic forces that might be brought to bear on it. The article contains something to contend with in every paragraph and is historically unreliable, but there is no gainsaying its insight and passion.

Many years later (1935), Meyerhold returned to opera with a production of *The Queen of Spades* at the Leningrad Maly. He was now in full auteur mode. Dissatisfied with the opera's libretto—particularly its genre scenes and its departures from the Pushkin source—he worked with the poet Valentin Stenich on a new adaptation in which, among other changes, the opera's period was updated; the character of prince Yeletsky became "a lucky gambler," with one new character, an "Unknown Guest," now singing his famous aria addressed to Lisa, and another, The Stranger, stepping forth in the last scene to disclose the fatal card; and the opening scene in the Summer Garden was eliminated, with some of its music cut ("the Quintet won't do," said Meyerhold) and the rest transferred to the card-playing scene at Narumov's that opens Pushkin's tale. (Listen to the Summer Garden music and ask yourself if it describes such a scene.) Some of the new libretto's words were retained from the original and others taken from various works of Pushkin and his circle. Understand: none of the changes are arbitrary, and some sound intriguing. A major theatrical mind is in charge. The production was a hit. But the highhandedness of the auteur and a privileging of the scenario over the music is evident, and, as is so often the case, clothed in a presumed nobility of purpose (here, a fealty to the great Pushkin, a contempt for decadent Imperial taste, and the eradication of *vampuka*, i.e., dead operatic convention, Russian style). Still a "cohesive totality" of a sort, and thus not yet postdramatic—but surely postmodern *avant la lettre.*[33]

Meyerhold's was, avowedly, a theatre of spectacle, a place where one went to see physical action, not hear texts, and except for his concern that line readings be exactly as his mind's ear heard them, he seems to have paid little attention to voice. We must in fairness remember that he never attempted a comprehensive codification of his rehearsal and training techniques, and that only a portion of the literature by and about him is available in English. Still, it seems telling that even in his substantial discussions of *Tristan* and *The Queen of Spades*, everything about acting is concerned with physical actions, movement, plasticity—with the performer as "actor/sculptor." This performer's relationship to the music is that of reactor to its rhythms (early on, through Dalcrozian eurythmic patterns) and, sometimes, to orchestral color; there isn't a word about melodic gesture, singing, or "acting with the voice," let alone of the sung action as germinal force. Meyerhold even speaks at some length about Chaliapin (the great exemplar for him, as for all his contemporaries, no matter their beliefs*) without a mention of that grand, multicolored instrument and its transformative interpretive uses.

It must have been a thrill, in the atmosphere of the early Soviet times, to be in the presence of one of Meyerhold's famous productions, to feel not only the cutting-edge exhilaration of an audacious avant-garde theatricalism, but the sense that it signaled the dawn of a re-made civilization. But on the question of the performer's creative responsibility, I think we must listen to Norris Houghton (see n. 14), who, unlike our more recent scholars, sat in on many hours of Meyerhold's rehearsals, spoke directly with him about his production and training techniques, and was able to place his work in the context of similar observations in other important Muscovite companies. Houghton does not for a moment challenge Meyerhold's genius or the impact of his work, and in fact devotes many respectful pages to the director's meticulous preparation methods and extraordinary inventiveness. He also calls Meyerhold ". . . in my

---

* Everyone lays claim to Chaliapin and Duse. Meyerhold, inveighing against acting techniques based on "authentic emotions" and psychology, even says this: "Only a few exceptionally great actors have succeeded instinctively in finding the correct method, that is, the method of building the role not from the inside outwards, but vice versa . . . I am speaking of artists like Duse, Sarah Bernhardt, Grasso, Chaliapin, Coquelin." (Braun, p. 199.) Methodists, of course, would be outraged at the appropriation of their revered Duse and (among those who know of him) Chaliapin as "outside inwards" artists—more evidence that these two must have been wonderful indeed. Braun notes (p. 245) that in Meyerhold's last triumphant production—"The Lady of the Camellias," starring Zinaida Raikh—Meyerhold ". . . openly admitted that his conception of Marguerite was based on the performance of Eleanora Duse whom he had seen in his early days in Petersburg."

opinion, the greatest actor in Russia today [1935]." This is based, though, not on any of Meyerhold's performances (Meyerhold, the original Treplev in *The Seagull* and Tusenbach in *The Three Sisters* at the MAT, had stopped performing many years since), but on the demonstration of actions and line readings for which he so frequently leapt from his chair onto the stage or rehearsal floor to insist—far into the night, if necessary—that his actors emulate to a T. "He is great," notes Houghton, "because he gives to his outward forms, which are superb, the inner spiritual meaning which his actors many times cannot give but which must be there if his theatre is to be of any dramatic force at all. The emptiness which so many of his performances have is because the soul of Meierhold [sic] is missing and only the body has been reproduced." Of his company's most renowned actor, Igor Ilyinsky, who seems to have been a sort of Russian Burt Lahr with extraordinary mimetic range, Houghton thinks that without Meyerhold's direction he ". . . would be only a very mediocre actor." He even compares Meyerhold's company to ". . . a collection of rubber balls. He throws them and they must be able to bounce; if they cannot, he has no use for them." And, since "An intelligent rubber ball is unheard-of nonsense; so is individual intelligence in the Meierhold Theatre." There's some figure-of-speech exaggeration in these words, no doubt, but unless we think Houghton is a hopelessly prejudiced observer, we must conclude that creative independence for the performer was not high on Meyerhold's to-do list.

In Moscow, in the 1920s and '30s, there was an inspiring theatre director who did not quite isolate the elements and did not quite dispense with narrative, but who in all other respects—especially in his anointing of director as co-author, his banishment of psychology and "character' from the acting process, his privileging of eye over ear, and his assumption of auteuristic, autocratic control over production as a whole—could make himself quickly at home in the intellectually respectable parts of today's theatrical and operatic worlds. We can draw jagged but distinct lines from Stanislavski to Felsenstein, Corsaro, et al., and from Reinhardt to at least the pre-Conceptualist *Regietheater* directors of the postwar Continental scene. But from Meyerhold we must take a little Skipover flight, from which we descend into the world of the more "advanced" productions we looked at earlier, and of those described in Sutcliffe's book. Sutcliffe tells us, in fact, that Peter Sellars's Harvard thesis was on "Meyerhold's concept of musical realism."* And Paul Schmidt's *Meyerhold at Work* is dedicated jointly to the director and playwright Timothy Mayer, who was Sellars' associate in the '80s, and to Robert Wilson. We are in the land of the posts.

"Post" as a prefix is like "neo" or "proto." These terms place something either before or after something else whose characteristics are presumed to be generally understood, and so imply that the post- or neo- or proto- thing is best understood in relation to that other something. "Post" isn't like "Classical," "Romantic," "Veristic," or even "Baroque" or "Rococo" or "Modern," all of which, though associated with time periods, have some descriptive function to anyone of moderate cultural awareness. "Post" assigns no characteristics. Either the thing it's trying to define has no characteristics of its own, or they are so diverse and nebulous that they can't be gathered into a meaningful form. And that is exactly the case—and embraced as the case by Postist thinkers, since anything that can be gathered would by definition be "cohesive"—with the "posts" we're involved with here.

Of course, the fact that a post-something comes after something else does place it in a linear progression from the other something, which is an odd way to name phenomena so insistent on nonlinearity. This spot in a succession also implies an advance, something that has evolved from a previous thing and is by way of replacing it with something more highly developed and better suited, as is evolution's way. The smarter Postists will deny this implication, but they're just dissembling—they think they're superior, and when it comes to opera their contempt for those left behind, stuck with narrative, character, drama, is unmistakeable. We must not let them forget the Devo Alternative, the distinct possibility that the after-something is de-evolutionary, not an advance but a regression or mutant.

A number of the posts—"postmodern," "poststructural," for example—have general cultural applications and have been sufficiently attended to via our meetings with the *philosophes* in Part II, Chap. 1 and Backstory 2. A couple of others, though, seem to have arisen directly from performance practice. They are Lehmann's "postdramatic," and "postpsychological." "Postdramatic"—at least in Lehmann's perception, which I take as being as close to definitive as this catch-all term can come—applies to the whole range of theatre events that have to do with, among other things, an end to narrative and to binary

---

* I don't know what the Meyerholdian "musical realism" is supposed to have been, or what it meant to the precocious Sellars at the time; the thesis might be an interesting read. Sutcliffe's reference suggests a shaky hold on musical and political events in the interwar Soviet—he's off by over a decade on the enforced closing of Meyerhold's theatre and his tragically brief rapprochement with Stanislavski.

oppositions; with non-linearity, with ambiguity, and with text presented as the inadequacy of language. Since such events are correctly designated not drama, they must of necessity lack whatever is constitutive of drama, which Lehmann proposes as an "excitability," with suspense as its core element, that produces a "dramatic quality." This seems a tad tautological (drama is whatever has a dramatic quality), but "suspense"—which, we recall, is the element we have identified as E-19's salient quality—is undoubtedly what he's getting at. Whence arises suspense? Uncertainty of outcome. "Bob" teetering at the lip of the stage had some suspense (will he fall?), and since Will Bond had enlisted us on "Bob's" behalf, and was himself a live performer conceivably in danger, we hoped he wouldn't. It was only a moment, though. As a totality, *Bob* had no suspense, and although it came to an end, it had no outcome. Things happened, but not en route to a destination. So there was no "arc," no "line" except for those drawn in space, and certainly that was part of the message—that life is just things happening, and that arcs and lines through time are illusions we impose upon it.

There are several possible rejoinders to this view, e.g., that while arcs and lines may be illusions, these illusions are indispensable for navigating life; or that while they may not even be necessary to life, they are necessary to art, etc. I have already suggested my own, namely, that arcs and lines through time are grounded in a biological perception of our birth-to-death destiny, which we experience as a trajectory and that presents itself to us as narrative, however much randomness and chaos may intrude en route. The fact that they are manmade does not make them illusions, but parts of the reality of being human in the world. In any case, the most common source of suspense would be conflict (those pesky binary oppositions), and while there can certainly be conflicts of ideas, thoughts, or opinions that can generate a kind of mild intellectual suspense, in drama (to again restate, for the present context) the most urgent conflicts are personal, sometimes of people against Nature or cosmic forces, but mostly of people against people, or of oppositions within a person. So a theatre that leaves drama behind, a postdramatic theatre, leaves conflict behind—especially personal conflict. Which brings us to "postpsychological."

I have always suspected that what's really going on here is the struggle to get out from under Freud and his immediate successors, with their patriarchal biases and their theories of sexuality and repression. So oppressive was the weight of their cultural authority that no room was left for discriminations, and so in the course of fashioning the postpsychoanalytic person, psychology itself had to get the heave-ho. That certainly comports well with strains of thought (though perhaps not the best thought) in important social movements of recent decades—feminism, gay liberation, and the counter-revolution within psychiatry. But there is no such thing as a person without a psychology, and since even the purest Postists surely know this, a postpsychological theatre must simply be one in which persons are not presented in psychological terms. That is another way of saying that we aren't going to get to know these persons, especially with respect to their pasts and to what's going on inside them. They aren't going to be rounded characters. Yet they won't be "heavy," heroic characters, either, striding memorably through their epic narratives. They won't be characters at all, but just embodied figures, possibly standing for an idea, a force, or some social or cultural stance, but possessing a psychology only insofar as we, the receptors, project one onto them. The acting of such a figure does not attempt to reveal the person at all, either from inside out or outside in. Postists think of this as "pure" acting (just committing actions) and as unmediated contact between the actor and the receptor, who is left "free" to interpret.

Actually, we are always free to do that. But as for the actor, if he or she is not trying to reveal, and is not dealing with a character, how are the actions to be selected? Most commonly, through signification, in its semiotic sense. A good summary of this thinking about performance is Jon Whitmore's *Directing Postmodern Theatre*.[34] This is a sort of syllabus for Postmodern Theatre 101. In his preface, Whitmore identifies "five systems of communication" and "twenty sign systems" that (to quote the backcover blurb copy) "can be manipulated by directors to bring about meaningful communication." After a brief stab at defining "postmodern" and a few introductory paragraphs on semiotics, he runs through the ways that the systems of communication and signs can be mixed and matched to control the medium and the message, with examples taken from the work of directors such as Wilson, Foreman, and Grotowski. As description, it's all pretty unexceptionable. Whitmore is fond of graphs, charts, and scales. One pair of bar graphs shows us Whitmore's estimates (hypothetical, but fairly accurate, I think) of the proportional weights assigned to the twenty sign systems in a postmodern production of *King Lear*, as opposed to a traditional one. Too late for Peter Ustinov to have positioned them amid his dockside towers of research, but in the almost inconceivable event of his having been cast in, and agreed to perform in, the postmodern *Lear*, he would have found that among his available systems, his three indubitable strengths ("Personality," "Voice [spoken word]," and "Facial expression") had been almost totally disallowed (indeed, the dialogue "would be severely cut"), and "Makeup and hairstyle" would also be minimized. "Gesture" and "Movement" would be his principal tools. These would not be his decisions in any case, those being the property of the director. "Music" and "Sound," however, which are figured at no more than fifteen and five percent, respectively, in the traditional *Lear*, are given very strong bars, up to eighty or so out of a hundred, in the postmodern one, nearly as high as "Smell" (do we have to go there?), and one is happy to see this, pending learning what sorts of music and sound are involved.*

As we see in the work of Barthes and other culture-critical semioticians, anything can be read for its signs. The whole point is to see through the artifact, strip it down to a sign, read through the cultural code. There's no question that understandings can be arrived at that way, to whatever extent one finds them useful. And any theatrical work or performance, even the most naturalistic and illusionistic, can be so analyzed, and thus laid bare for us all to see "what it really means," if for some reason one wants to mediate the theatrical experience that way. It's a legitimate critical method. Because the critical terminology operates at more than one level, Postists can testify, with straight faces and right hands raised, that signifying is always going on; that directors are always manipulating performers, and performers receptors; and that receptors are always interpreting codes in accordance with their cultural leanings. All true, and all meaningless—the question is how, and what sort of experience one is seeking. It's one thing to parse *King Lear* on the page as a meanings-deferred system of signifiers and signifieds. It's quite another to stage and perform some *Lear*-matter as a conscious manipulation of signs and systems, so that the audience is coerced into receiving it on those terms.

This is where Whitmore's *Lear*graphs touch on our operatic situation. As I remarked in regard to *Einstein on the Beach*, creative artists should be free to create as they wish. By all means allow them this (and anyway, what's going to stop them?—only money), and let them call themselves "post" if it makes them feel better. (Though let them also confess: that's an aesthetic sham. For a good half-century on, most theatre still has narrative, and characters,

---

* This all calls to mind the first *Lear* I ever saw. Orson Welles was the director and star, so Whitmore's bars would have been way up on "Personality," "Voice [spoken word]", and "Facial expression," but down nearly to zero on "Gesture" and "Movement," at least so far as the title role was concerned, since Welles, having broken an ankle or two in rehearsal, played the part from a wheelchair, trundling about with his customary flair. All this would place us in a "traditional" production. On the Postmodern chart, though, "Music" and "Sound" would have hit the top. In addition to the taped soundscape created by electronic music pioneers Otto Luening and Vladimir Ussachevsky, there was a five-piece pit band presided over from the harpsichord by Marc Blitzstein, who occasionally interspersed musical commentary with actors' speech, in the manner of an inventive continuo player. I don't recollect anything in the olfactory sign system, beyond the usual faintly musty, woolen-coat smell of the City Center's Second Balcony, c. 1956. As an actor, Welles should be placed on the cusp between the old-style elocutionary and modern sensibilities. But as a director, doesn't he belong among the precursors of the Postmodern?

and psychology, and drama, and most people still expect those things of it. "Contra-" or "sub-"dramatic would be more honest.) There is also nothing to prevent auteurs and their cohorts from treating legally available materials from the past as they see fit. Except—if I might suggest?—by declining to hire them, our grounds being that merely because creative artists must have creative freedom it does not follow that when they function as interpreters the same freedom must be granted them.

Although in the more rarefied forms of postmodern theatre there is indeed no psychological being onstage, no individual agency, and thus neither a personal past that would condition an action nor a future objective that would impel it (there is no time, really, except for an ongoing present), it is wrong to proclaim such theatre postpsychological. One psychology, one person, one character is not only before us but all around us: the auteur's. We might even say that a drama is being played out. It's a drama implicit in all creative work, but here in rawest form: the vision, the agenda, of the auteur vs. the indifference or opposition of the world. I felt this with considerable force on a visit to Foreman's Ontological-Hysteric Theatre for a piece called *Wake Up Mr. Sleepy! Your Unconscious Mind Is Dead!* The word on the rialto was that this was to be the final live production in the remarkable history of this enterprise,* and not having seen any of Foreman's work for some years, I felt I should get a final take on it.

There was certainly plenty to look at: an insanely detailed environment, with Foreman's characteristic divisions of space marked off with string; five live performers (Aviator, Girl in Pantsuit, et al.) who functioned as visual signifiers; film footage with a separate cast of Portuguese performers, and more. The program's cover offered a faux-naïf introduction about abduction to an alien planet, one insert that admonished us to relax and not try too hard to understand, and another explaining that Foreman wished to escape "... the tunnel vision of unified subject matter," and instead create "... a play about 'nothing' except the evenly distributed grid of all things at once," as well as a new self "no longer in need of the false 'kick' of events," but that will be content in "simply HOVERING over the field of total, evenly distributed 'multi-possibility.'"

I did feel such a self, and such a hovering. But it was Richard Foreman's self, hovering over me. I was reminded of the set description for Arthur Miller's *After the Fall*, which opens: "The action takes place in the mind, thought, and memory of Quentin." But Quentin, however much he may partake of Miller,

---

* It wasn't, and the program included an invitation to support future projects, with a new emphasis on film.

is a character we see objectively, in relation to the other characters, and inside his mind is a story with events, not an evenly distributed grid. So being inside his mind is very different from being inside that of Foreman, who is not a character yet is the only subject, the pan-protagonist, and who is not on his way anywhere, but hovering on his highly elaborated single plane of reality. Had I not foresworn the term "autistic," I would use it here to describe the quality of the experience.

As with *Bob*, the audience was avidly attentive, on the wavelength, many evidently nowhere happier than inside Foreman's mind, others not quite able to give up trying to understand, and possibly wondering just what they were doing there, enclosed in the clutter of someone else's obsessions and insights. Unlike my experience with *Bob*, I began to feel trapped, the way one feels with a domineering nonstop talker in whom one begins to recognize that behind the apparent self-confidence is an expiatory need or a terror of the void, and soon it does not matter whether the talk is interesting or not. While hoping to relax and hover, I contemplated the performers. I imagined they were not unhappy. They had jobs. Their most basic performer's need—to be out there—was being met. They were in a cool environment, and Foreman is probably a stimulating person to rehearse with. Beyond that, though, they were allowed none of the things that would make one want to be an actor to begin with. They had no more agency, or, in Houghton's term, "individual intelligence," than show-window mannequins. I admired their discipline, but could not sustain interest in them.

Wake Up, Sleepy! stands about as far from opera (as defined here) as theatre has so far been able to get, and in this country, at least, we haven't yet seen the postdramatic or even the postmodern brought into the opera house in their purest forms, since in opera as we have known it, it is impossible to definitively uncouple production and performance from verbal narrative and musical continuity. Wilson's *Lohengrin* gives it a good try, with its abstract setting and static or slo-mo signification that also dampens, however marginally, vocal and rhetorical energies, all coming close not only to separating aural from visual elements, but to "alienating" the story and obliterating character. Still, the action does bring us out somewhere and the music does unfold, though the impact of both is reduced. The damnable cohesiveness cannot be entirely eliminated. There is opera-related Posting going on in other venues, though, and in Europe some of it crashes the opera-house door, unadulterated.

In Lehmann's and Whitmore's books, there are forty-three unique listings of directors whose work, in whole or in part, is classified as postmodern. (See Lehmann, pp. 23-24, and Whitmore, p. 3.) The lists overlap, and both authors emphasize their incompleteness. Lehmann goes on to append the names of theatre companies or collectives whose work is collaborative or improvisational, or that falls into the category of happenings or installations, as well as those of a few writers. As we would expect, the majority of Lehmann's directors work exclusively or primarily in Europe, especially in the German-speaking theatres. Whitmore's much shorter list is focused on directors familiar in this country. Naturally these compilations don't include artists who have emerged only since 2000, or those who work exclusively in opera.

To the best of my awareness, I have seen live work by nine of these directors in theatre, opera or both,* and of several others on film and video. To make at least some further contact with the phenomena Lehmann has written about, I spent time on the internet, where biographies, descriptions and evaluations, interviews, and video clips pertaining to all these directors and their productions are to be found. It's impossible to learn much about any single artist or any single work by such means, but facts can be ascertained and impressions formed. Here are some, facts first:

With only a few exceptions, these artists were born between the mid-'40s and late '50s. A scattering come from the Low Countries, the U.S. or Britain, or the Southern Mediterranean region, but the overwhelming majority are from the former East Germany and Soviet bloc nations. Some of them came West before 1989, others not. Nearly half have their principal background in dance or movement, several more in design and visual arts. So far as I can determine, not more than two or three began as actors. Of those who started in spoken theatre in any capacity, a substantial minority were at the outset Brechtians—not surprising, since Brecht was Germany's pre-eminent dramatist and theatre theorist. Other influential figures of an older generation were Heiner Müller and, at least in his avant-garde youth, Peter Stein. Among those frequently involved with opera have been Christof Nel, Achim Freyer, Klaus-Michael Grüber, Silviu Purcarete, and Stein (and, of course, others better known here, like Peter Brook, Robert Lepage, and Wilson), but several others have at least approached the form in prominent venues: Hans-Jürgen Syberberg made a *Parsifal* film, Müller himself directed a Bayreuth *Tristan* (1993), and more recently Frank Castorf has staged a Bayreuth *Ring*. Among

---

* I may have lost track of some encounters. For instance, in the course of this trolling I became aware that I had seen Klaus Michael Grüber's very first professional foray, his design for Brecht's "The Trial of Joan of Arc at Rouen," at Strehler's Piccolo Teatro di Milano in 1968; also that the Goebbels (Heiner) whose *Aus einem Tagebuch* I heard at a Berlin Philharmonic concert a few years back is the same who has devised "scenic concerts," "stage installations," and cross-media "stage and video work" (these descriptions are Lehmann's, pp. 111-112). There may well have been other such instances, but they obviously can't figure into any evaluation here.

the kinds of work they are described and self-described as doing (and here I omit individual references to sketch the scene as a whole; translation from French or German is involved in a few instances) are "associative" pieces that "lack a cohesive story"; "stage happenings" and "interactive cross-media projects"; "exploded narratives"; work that "attempts to fill the space between theatre and opera left blank due to traditional genre borderline drawing"; setting that, "refusing all psychology ... is an estrangement of silent images" or that "introduces the idea of infinite waiting, suspending time"; work that will "offer the various sign-complexes of the receptors;" a *Walküre* that is "a masterpiece of ambiguity" and that "challenges all magical and mythological imagery"; an *oeuvre* that "combines Brecht's epic theatre with Wagner's aesthetics"; or one that seeks to "return to silence and use it as the basis of every encounter" and to "renounce the hegemonic position of the Western verbalist" and which declaims that "big scales and big gestures have become defunct once and for all."

These are selected quotes. Not all apply to any given director's work, and not all the directors would subscribe to any given statement. But collectively, they capture the mindset. I can pretty well guarantee that among these artists you will not find advocacy for more sharply drawn boundaries, for binding time into a clear narrative that leads to a defined outcome, for penetrating the inner lives of psychologically developed characters, or for encouraging the creative and intellectual independence of performers.

And a few impressions: the cultural attitudes and extracts of work on display are very much as Lehmann describes them, and while they share the general principles of Anglo-American postmodern theatre work, they are different in tone. Even in an American piece that is specifically directed at early-modern European artistic and psychological syndromes—i.e., Martha Clarke's *Vienna Lusthaus*—there is nothing like the dark, cold, ritualistic, affectless tint often encountered here, while on the other hand the notes of ironic whimsy in *Bob*, of bemused intellectual rummaging in *Wake Up, Sleepy*, or the abstract aesthetic loveliness of Wilson's visions are not much in evidence among the Europeans. What comes across in this skimming is damage, trauma, and disconnection, from which individual agency, psychological understanding and any sense of a thread through time have been released as burdens too heavy to bear, an insupportable *Sünden Last*. It feels at times like a willful destruction, at others like a surrender that is being welcomed.

In a personal sense, I don't feel permission to judge this mindset. It is born of the horrors and absurdities of two World Wars, brutal dictatorships of Right and Left, mass extermination, and the Generation of '68's violent disavowal of all these. I've lived in another part of the world, partaking at a remove of these same horrors (and a few, but lesser, ones of our own) and at times directly touched by them, yet never swallowed up in them. To the extent that a world of cultural and material ruination and fragmentation, of seemingly suspended time and detachment from all that has gone before, of feature-less landscapes with no borders, of the loss of will and the hopelessness of individual agency and even identity, is the world in which these artists have found themselves, they are simply depicting a reality, and that is part of the artist's imperative.

But, personal judgment aside, we are still allowed artistic inquiry, to ask in what spirit this reality is being shown. When Meyerhold devised his produc-tions, worked out his outside-in biomechanical acting technique, and sought to minimize the importance of individual psychology, it was in the name of a collectivist ideal that he saw as the future of not only theatre, but society itself. When Brecht wrote his epic-theatre plays and introduced an element of critical apartness into their styles of production and performance, he did so to clarify for us the ways of "human nature" under the assumptions of a capitalist system. We may disagree or oppose, or deplore the dominance of art by politics, but at the least these men worked from some vision of where humanity ought to be headed. And operatically, when Berg employed his adaptation of Schoenberg's "language of horror" to fashion his two lonely operatic masterpieces of that idiom, he told us stories (by Büchner and Wedekind) that still recounted E-19's protagonist-couple tale, but in distorted and de-valorized versions whose squalor and bleakness leave us in no doubt that we have arrived at a very bad place, and that this is no way for life to be. Or, when Shostakovich wrote into his symphonies, quartets and single mature opera all the personal and societal anguish of his time and place, with bits of the old triumphalism showing through, and the inner self, however suppressed and melancholy, still vibrantly and deeply alive, he left us feeling the full, tragic weight of oppression and violence, but with it the necessity of survival, a kind of redemption in survival.

The Postartists, though, want us to think we have passed through all that, and that having arrived at the end of narrative, of history, of psychology, it's now cool and smart to just hang out here among the fragments, aware of nothing but our own sensoria and immediate surroundings. We're supposed to *embrace* the PTS, and snuggle into the aporia. Further, I believe I detect in much of this a romanticization or fetishization of this syndrome, and since, as I write this, we are coming up on seventy years since the end of WWII, a half-century since '68, and even a quarter-century since the fall of The Wall, this feels artificial to me even from the children and grandchildren of those once fully entitled to their trauma. It's now been filtered through a couple of generations' worth of reification and intellectualization to become a fashion, of which the Stateside manifestations are distanced, aestheticized, and academized samples. Like all fashions, it presses in from all sides on the mentalities of directors and performers, invading what in other respects would be entirely conventional work (and thus replacing whatever re-creative element that might otherwise have had) and giving rise to nice theories which the intentionally unconventional can crib for program notes and interviews.

Castorf's Bayreuth *Ring* seems to have conquered the summit of pure Postist ambition: universal revulsion.[35] He was reportedly not the first choice for the job. Among those previously on the hook were Lars von Trier, and while I have no idea if he can even work in the theatre, I would have been intrigued by that notion, since he's shown (in *Melancholia*) a grasp of the tragic content of Wagner's music, tells stories, gets consistently wonderful work from his film actors (it's said he abuses them, but some of the best choose to work with him), and—and this is what really upsets people about him, I think—offers up not a scrap of redemption. However, von Trier backed out, and when Wim Wenders did also, Castorf became The Man. He was no pig in a poke, having been the longtime artistic director of Berlin's *Volksbühne*, where he is known for productions that "reject a narrative and conclusive interpretations," and in which "Psychological interpretation of character is anathema . . . and undisturbed acting [I assume this means complacently realistic acting] is right next to the trivialization of reality by art [and this I take to mean representational style, an imitation of reality] as an object of hate." His production of Schiller's *Die Räuber*, it is said, "unpacked the whole toolbox of Castorf's discontent," and I gather that his psychology (I bet he has one) harbors a deep well of anger that fuels his work.[36] (Stanislavskian actor's task for the role of Frank Castorf: what are the Given Circumstances, life history, and Super Objective of this character? Explore.)

So, it can't have come as a big surprise that this director who "destroys the work and leaves the public to pick up the pieces" cooked up a *Ring* that "left both sides [progressive and conservative] incredulous and incensed" and was really about "the moral downfall of East Germany" (Leipsic—for all these references, see n. 35); that sought to "tell his own story . . . absent *Personenregie*" (Shirley); that "cynically undercut the musical drama" (Tommasini); that is "bewildering . . . essentially non-Wagnerian . . . distinctly unmusical . . . works against rather than with the intentions of the composer" and involves "Rejection of basic dramaturgical principles" (Skramstad); or that calls into question "the point of having a Bayreuth Festival at all," not to mention "the future of the genre [opera itself]" (Apthorp).

I feel sure I would have shared many of these reactions. But it is far too late for such objections, for although Castorf obviously brought to his *Ring* his particular animus toward his own cultural heritage, he has only taken the postmodern, postdramatic P.O.V. to its perfectly logical endpoint. Once we have acceded to the propositions that the director is "equal to the playwright in shaping the theatrical experience" and may "write the text anew," that his work need not be cohesive or pursue the written narrative or seek to present characters, we have lost any ground from which to do anything other than squabble over which things we find neat and which not. Nothing can be called a violation, and even the most considered complaints are useless, because all thought of a theatre ethic, a hierarchy of interpretation, has been declared null and void in advance. Castorf understands and celebrates this. He cites as his reason for not having directed more opera the requirement to retain words and notes unaltered—indeed, he at first planned to revise and redact the libretto and music of the *Ring*. The conductor (Kirill Petrenko) dissuaded him on this point, but what, exactly, was his argument? All that amounts to is saying "Okay, destroy *The Ring of the Nibelungen*—leave me my notes and I'll accompany you." He didn't quit. The cast and orchestra didn't go on strike. And the audience (mostly) sat there till the end, when, to Castorf's immense satisfaction, they booed him to the echo while cheering his de facto accomplices, Petrenko and selected singers. But the "progressives" and "conservatives" may boo away till they all go hoarse—so long as they buy their tickets, Castorf has the better of them all, and the future of festival and genre both are well beyond being "in question."

In all the crime-scene reportage from our first responders, most of it devoted to the pros and cons of the design team's imposing sets and videos (there's a good selection of photos at wagneropera.net) or the more bizarre inventions of Castorf (copulating crocodiles), music and singing occupy their usual contemporary spaces. The writers for opera-dedicated magazines (Shirley and Leipsic) do their best to cram in brief characterizations, but even they find no room for specifics about vocal qualities, technical capabilities, or suitabilities for these great roles, or of where the singing, conducting, and playing might stand in relation to past standards. That's probably an honest reflection of the experience—but still. And except for the implications of the "absent *Personenregie*" comments, there's no consideration of where the boundaries of the performer's creative field are marked, where his or her prerogatives and responsibilities lie.

Where might we go in search of the anti-Castorf, the farthest remove from the limits of the Postdramatic sensibility? Southward, naturally. And down in Sarasota, on the sunny Gulf Coast of Florida, there's an opera company that performs in a lovely medium-size house with lovely medium-size acoustics. Its repertory is predominantly Italian and its approach to production is traditional—so much so, I am told, that directors (and by extension, performers) are contractually obligated to follow the stage directions indicated in the score. A few seasons back, I was glad to have the rare opportunity of seeing there a performance of Mascagni's *L'amico Fritz*, a happy-ending pastoral piece set on a Jewish farming estate in Alsace. It's sentimental and has a high atmosphere-to-action ratio, but in goodly stretches is engagingly written, and can be charming and touching when well performed. In my Sonzogno vocal score, musical markings—dynamics, articulation, variations in tempo, etc.—are abundant. In writing like this, much depends on a feel for *rubati* and *ritenuti*, when to hold back and when to go on, and Mascagni, perhaps in possession of a crystal ball that told him of Felsensteins to come, wanted to be sure his performers picked up on that. Stage directions, though, are minimal—entrances and exits, essential crosses, who's talking to whom in group scenes, an occasional bit of business. In the Sonzogno libretto included in the LP release of Cetra's wartime recording conducted by the aged composer, the set descriptions are much more complete, but the actual stage directions, though they show tiny differences, are no more extensive.

So the instructional priorities for Mascagni and his librettist, "P. Suardon,"* as inscribed in their texts, were: Musical interpretation—extensive and specific, but not extending to "acting with the voice" or "colorist reader" markings; sets—representational and specific, the detailed realism of the era; staging—skeletal; physical interpretation ("acting," behavior)—next to nothing. These last are up to the singers and their director, who in Mascagni's day would have done little beyond facilitating traffic and arranging the stage picture. What are the performers and their director to do? If they follow *only* the score's directions, they will be inactive most of the time, living no stage life in a work of lyricized naturalism. I'm afraid that's how much of Sarasota's musically enjoyable performance looked: constricted and stereotyped, with little sense of the inner lives of the characters, and little flow among them. And since the inflectional understandings that were second nature to Mascagni's singers are not instinctive for contemporary Americans, "acting with the voice" did not get much beyond a general effort to be "in style."[37]

But there was an oddity near the beginning of Act Two. As the curtain rose, sure enough, there was the farmhouse, the courtyard, the well, the wall,

---

* A *nom de plume* for Nicola Daspuro, abetted by others.

the cherry branches, all as per the libretto. It's dawn. Suzel, the very young, demure girl who the rabbi David will, at the happy end, succeed in marrying off to the confirmed bachelor Fritz, is alone onstage. At the opening, there's a stretch of descriptive music, but no stage directions. Suzel has a few contemplative lines: the cherries are ripe, Master Fritz must taste them. Then, a wordless, atmospheric offstage chorus of field workers, and an offstage solo oboe playing a wistful Alsatian folk tune. Now the offstage voices come closer, singing that if you don't seize hold of love when it first comes, it will never return again. Suzel has a few more lines: the field hands are going to work, for today the ripe barley must be harvested. There's another page of orchestral music, then the chorus, more distant, repeating its warning about love. Suzel now says the master will soon arrive; she wants to gather a bouquet for him. A little over seven minutes of stage time have elapsed before her first direction is entered.* It says: "gathering flowers."

Neither my memory nor my notes recall for me how the Sarasota soprano, Catherine Cangiano, spent this time, much less how Catherine Malfitano spent it in the only other *L'amico Fritz* I've seen, at the Manhattan School many years ago. But now came the oddity. As Suzel begins to put together her bouquet for Fritz, she sings a little song. It's a days-of-old folkish story, simply set as four short exchanges between a forest maid and a passing wifeless knight:

—Bel cavalier, che vai
  per la foresta . . .

—Che volete da me,
  cara figliuola?

—Bel cavaliere dalla
  faccia mesta . . .

—Cogliete fiori,
  allegra boscaiuola?

—Bel cavaliere, ti darò
  una rosa . . .

—Grazie, piccina,
  rose non ne vo'! . . .

—Fair knight, who passes
  through the wood . . .

—What do you wish of me,
  Dear child?

—Fair knight of
  face so sad . . .

—Are you gathering flowers,
  Merry forest maid?

—Fair knight, I shall
  give you a rose . . .

—My thanks, child,
  of roses want I none! . . .

---

* This is based on the timing of Mascagni's own conducting, often criticized as too slow, but in my opinion just right for finishing off his picturesque gestures—if they don't sink in, there's no point to this sort of writing.

—Bel cavalier, sarà	—Fair Knight, it shall be
per la tua sposa...	for your bride...
—Piccina, grazie:	—Child, my thanks:
la sposa non l'ho...	I have no bride...

Between each of these exchanges, set at a moderate, sustained tempo, there are eight bars of music that quickens and brightens before settling back into the song. To my astonishment, these interludes found Suzel rising from her chair to dance around the table, then back to the chair for the next brief verse. These excursions had a mechanical, hopping quality and bore no relation I could discover to the song, and while it's conceivable that a dreamy young woman might make some dancey moves while singing to herself, they could not be those moves. I felt embarrassed for the performer as she discharged this obligation, and held her blameless. I assumed that the episode was an awkward execution of something mandated by the score, which might in turn have recorded something invented by the first Suzel, Calvé, known as a powerful veristic actress by the standards of the day (1890). But I find no indication for it in score or libretto. It seems to have been a directorial inspiration, a forced response to the awareness that a long solo scene is in danger of dying, and that neither the text nor the interpreters' process is coming to the rescue.

I have sympathy for the Sarasota company's attitude. They aren't imposing "concepts." They are trying to honor the hierarchy of interpretation, and to rescind the auteuristic privileges that have been so widely abused. But at least in this production, they came no closer than Foreman or Castorf to restoring the performer's creative agency. Fidelity to the instructions encounters its own aporias.

Until the advent of the Postists, the great striving of theatre both spoken and sung was toward more powerful, truthful, and aesthetically satisfying means of presenting narrative and character. It was in that striving that Stanislavski was looking for shared understanding among his predecessors. In opera, it is what produced everything we would call progress, maturation, or reform. Narrative means: story, events in a sequence, or at least in a form whose cohesiveness becomes clear to the receptor. Character means: the theatrical representation of a person, and so, inevitably, of the psychology without which there is no person. Since the Postists reject both narrative and psychology, we must reject them. That is necessary. But it only returns us to the question of what performers and their directors are to do. To put this question in workaday terms: how are they to fill in all the blanks in *L'amico Fritz,* or the *Ring*, or any other work? To broaden it a bit: how can they find their artistic independence, their own range of invention, within the hierarchy of interpretation? How can they search out their individual truths and beauties while working within the boundaries of the creators' field and remaining faithful to their vision, insofar as it is inscribed?

These questions grow out of the more fundamental problem of renewal in an artform that has reached a crisis of purpose. If it forsakes the old meta-narrative and finds no successor to it, it has no means of generating repeatable, renewable works that can be gathered into a repertory. If it foregoes binary oppositions, it loses one essential element of drama—conflict—and the suspense it creates. If it declares narrative dead altogether, it loses another, story. And if it also eschews character, it loses the third. With the loss of all three, it must scavenge not only for nondramatic forms of theatre, but for any reason to sing.

That is the creative dead end to which our *soi-disant* progressives, the Postists, have led us, pronouncing at the rest stops en route that each of these irreparable losses is in fact a leap forward. With respect to new work, all the confusions about how it might be dramatically structured, what sort of music might arise from that, and how it could be sung, acted, and played, arise from these regressions. That is true for the singing, acting, and playing of old work, as well. To recapitulate: as the symbiotic dynamic between creation and performance that had always sustained opera, producing all the developments in those disciplines in the nineteenth and twentieth centuries I have touched on, began to founder owing to the failure to replenish the repertory, the task of renewal, the obligation of "originality," fell to interpreters. This meant at first the stage performers, the warriors of orality. But they did not have all the creative scope of the ancient bards, because of text. Ultimately, text gives far more than it takes away. But it does change, and in some ways limit, performers' responsibilities. It is not merely that text joins oral tradition and personal imagination as one of their resources and an object of reverent attention, but that it is also available to others to measure their work against and, as I suggested earlier, to act as a check on generational and situational adaptations. The remembrance of songs sung, that lingering in the mind's ear, fades with time; study, however diligent, is not the same. So it soon became apparent that renewal solely via singer-actorly interpretation, in the presence of text and the absence of vital new works, could not in the long run keep the artform afloat.

It happened that the late years of E-19, the last of plenteous masterly creation, were also the early years of fully integrated production under the supervision of Second Interpreters-in-Chief. Increasingly, the search for renewal and a semblance of originality devolved upon them—in the early days, often a conductor (Mahler and Toscanini fashioned the template)—but with the passing of time more and more often a director, who does not himself perform and is usually an eye-dominant artist even when not an auteur. When it finally had to be conceded that the revolution in musical language that was supposed to re-orient our hearing forever was only to take its spot as a patch in our tapestries, large or small according to temperament, and that it was not about to give us much in the way of operatic renewal, the quest for originality and "relevance"—to get down to it, some inducement for people to keep buying tickets—took on a very worried tone. Enter the auteur, and his life history and works to date, as described above.

In theatre, some actors of modern sensibility, working with some like-minded directors, found that despite the loss of certain prerogatives, the ideal of the integrated production gave them a creative field that was more fulfilling than the old actor-centered one. In opera, that has happened in fits and starts, but for the most part has been brushed aside by the Postist mentality. Operatic performers are not, generally, automatons or rubber balls, but their creative scope is severely restricted, both musically and dramatically. For the most part, they don't realize how far into the corner they've been pushed, having been groomed for the current system and being dependent on it. Even those who do sense their predicament don't see where or how they could begin to assert themselves, mark out their own creative clearings, and assume greater responsibility for the state of their art. (And after all, it isn't as if they don't have plenty on their plates already.) But since we cannot impose a metanarrative by fiat, the most constructive step we can currently take is to get on a better footing with the existing masterworks of the repertory, and only performers themselves can do that. I will offer some ideas about this in my final chapter. First, a short break to bring you the review I promised in my Introduction, along with a few updates.

NOTES

1. See Walter J. Ong: *Orality and Literacy: The Technologizing of the Word*, Routledge, 2002 (originally published by Methuen, 1982).

2. Cibber's *An Apology for His Life* has been reprinted many times, and is viewable online. The Nicolini description he quotes is taken from "the critical censor of Great Britain" in *The Tatler*, No. 115, here as cited in *An Anthology of Musical Criticism from the 15th to the 20th Century* (Norman Demuth, ed., Eyre & Spottiswoode, London, 1947, pp. 54-55). Macready's observations are taken from his *Reminiscences*, as quoted in A.M. Nagler: *A Sourcebook of Theatrical History* (Dover, N.Y., 1952, pp. 469-71).

3. See Joshua Steele: *Prosodia Rationalis; Or, An Essay towards Establishing the Melody and Measure of Speech, to be Expressed and Perpetuated by Peculiar Symbols.* (J. Nichols, London, 2nd Edition, 1779). Steele's system was entered on a five-line staff, subdivided to register quarter-tone intervals. His symbols indicated pitch, accent, and pulse, with sloping and curved lines and circumflexes to illustrate the sliding of inflection, and wavy lines to show the increase, decrease, or sustained evenness of volume. He displays two readings of "To be or not to be," his own and Garrick's, complete with musical tempo markings and bass accompaniment, observing ruefully that upon hearing Garrick's he realized that his own was " . . . noted in the stile of a ranting actor." Garrick's, he tells us, was " . . . delivered with little or no distinction of piano and forte, but nearly uniform; something below the ordinary force, or, as a musician would say, sotto voce, or sempre poco piano." There is much more in the book, including, in this second edition, lengthy exchanges with one Lord Monboddo, author of *Origin and Progress of Language*, mostly on points of correspondance with ancient authority.

   Later, Steele's system was taken up by the Rev. James Chapman in his *The Music, or Melody and Rhythmus of the English Language* (M. Anderson, Edinburgh, 1819). Chapman foregoes Steele's musical staff, since the "sliding" action of spoken voice (a concept derived from the ancients, which recurs throughout this literature) does not define pitches (and, no doubt, because Chapman was not a musician). But he appropriates many of Steele's symbols, and demonstrates their application to an extensive selection of passages in verse and prose. The musical properties of speech are repeatedly emphasized ("Melody and Rhythmus" : "tune and time"). A shift has occurred, though. Whereas Steele was hoping his notation would preserve the eloquence of great actors and orators, Chapman is almost exclusively concerned with a model for instruction.

   And it was with instruction that the Elocutionary Movement concerned itself. While the hundreds, if not thousands, of surviving tomes, manuals, and pamphlets include many fascinating ones of Continental origin (for instance, Claude-Joseph Dorat: *La déclamation théatrâle: poème didactique, Paris, 1767*; Johann Jakob Engel: *Idées sur le geste et l'action théatrâle, Paris, 1788-89*; Antonio Morrochesi: *Lezioni di declamazione e d'arte Teatrale, Firenze, 1832*), I will concern myself here with a few examples from the English-language literature, further to those of Steele and Chapman, that I think will give interested readers a good start into the field. A key work in this succession is the Rev. Gilbert Austin's *Chironomia, Or, A Treatise on Rhetorical Delivery* (London, 1806). Drawing primarily on the Greek and Roman ancients, but also on then-recent sources such as Steele's *Prosodia*, John Walker's *Elements of Elocution* (1799), the *Course of Lectures on Elocution* of the noted parliamentarian Thomas Sheridan (father of the playwright

Richard Brinsley Sheridan), Austin takes on all three of the classical divisions of rhetoric: Voice, Countenance, and Gesture. The greater bulk of this volume is of necessity devoted to gesture, since Austin had devised a highly elaborated system of notation for it, presented partly via symbolic lettering, partly by graphic representation of the direction and shape of each move, and finally by plates illustrating the ideal execution of the affects, based on that of admired actors (Kemble, Mrs. Siddons, et al.). Still, over two hundred pages are given to the voice and reading, with frequent reference to musical elements, and in the later chapters he attempts to show how the vocal, facial, and gestural codes are to be combined for maximum rhetorical effect.

In the U.S., the elocutionary cause was taken up by Dr. James Rush, with his *Philosophy of the Human Voice* (1827—I have worked with the Third Edition, 1855). As the title implies, Rush foregoes the facial and gestural aspects of the discipline to concentrate on the vocal. Though clearly grounded in the insights of the Ancients, and taking from them such important concepts as the "slide" of the voice, he nonetheless finds them inadequate for adaptation to modern English usage. In that regard, he acknowledges the efforts of Steele, Sheridan, and Walker, but sets out to correct and expand upon them. His book is a staggeringly thorough description and keen analysis of vocal movement and inflection, with notational systems proposed for every variation of rise and fall, of timing, and of emphasis. There is constant reference to singing practices and terminology, and even a concluding "Brief analysis of Song and Recitative."

Rush's work was followed by two more directly indebted to his: William Russell: *The American Elocutionist* (1844) and James E. Murdoch, William Russell, and James Webb: *Orthophony: Or, Vocal Culture in Elocution* (1845). The latter is actually designated as an introduction to the former, and is dedicated to Rush. It's best described as a simplification of Rush's opus (still coming to 336 well-filled pages) for use as a practical manual. Its three authors are each responsible for a distinct area of concentration—Murdoch for Orthophony and Vocal Gymnastics, Russell for Elocution, and Webb (a professor at the Boston Academy of Music) for an appendix on "Pure Tone." Russell's own book is a gathering of three of his previous volumes, based on his course lectures in enunciation, elocution, and gesture, the latter with suitable engraved illustrations of "attitude and action." It still follows Rush's definitions but, like *Orthophony*, with more emphasis on exercises and readings than on theory.

Taken together, these last three works can be considered a good summation of the American continuation of the concepts developed by the English rhetoricians, especially in regard to their vocal and elocutionary elements. Their principles were widely taught in institutions of secondary and higher education, and we can still learn from them, I think. The exercises and drills for vowel sonority, inflection, and articulation in *Orthophony*, for instance, along with the instructions for their use, I have found of more use than their equivalents in contemporary systems of speech and diction. There's considerable overlap between older and newer, but where there are differences, the older are superior. The Austin, Rush, Russell, and Russell/Murdoch/Webb volumes—though not all editions of them—are all available in inexpensive Nabu reprints.

When Steele Mackaye returned to America in the early 1870s after his period of intensive study with François Delsarte in Paris, he added to his considerable achievements as actor and playwright his ardent advocacy of the master's system. He took on private students, founded schools, and held forth hundreds of times with lecture demonstrations. Though the system had its detractors, Mackaye's stature was uncontested. In the histories, critiques, and stage memoirs of the late 19th Century, one comes across repeated admiring references to his high aspirations, his personal magnetism, and his wide influence. His own most fervent disciple was Genevieve Stebbins, and her book, *Delsarte System of Expression* (Edgar S. Werner, N.Y., 1885), is the best English-language source I have found on the Delsarte work. It opens with the transcript of a lengthy address given by Delsarte to the Philotechnic Society of Paris. Then, after an

Introduction in which Stebbins summarizes Delsarte's career and her own encounters with him, it works through the gamut of the system's exercises in "Decomposing" and "Aesthetic Gymnastics," with exacting instructions and exhortations, concluding with a substantial section on voice. It shares with the Anglo-American elocutionists a powerful belief in art as a moral—indeed, a Christian—force, but gives it a more specific theological tone derived from the concept of the Trinity. Thus, in every lesson or series of lessons on the actions of a body part, the "things to be known" are invariably three in number, unless, as in "The Affirmations of the Hand," the "Grammar of Pantomime," or the "Law of Altitude," they are nine (three threes). And of course the entire study of rhetoric is divided into three, concerning which the Delsarte system identifies the voice as "Vital," the gesture as "Moral," and the word as "Mental." From the High Protestant tone of the Anglo-Americans, we've moved into French Catholic mysticism, if not beyond into Masonic symbolism. The actual work, of course, can be considered independent of these beliefs, but it takes some sorting-out. Of all the works of the Elocutionist Movement, Delsarte's had the most direct impact on actors and singers. It is also worth noting that in America, Genevieve Stebbins cultivated a large following of women for her "Aesthetic Gymnastics," and so a set of disciplines that had been constructed and taught exclusively by men became one of female empowerment and vitalization, connecting to many of the developments in modern dance.

By 1872, Albert M. Bacon was arguing in his *Manual of Gesture* (S.C. Griggs and Co., Chicago—I have the Fourth Edition of 1881) that in the sixty-some years since Austin's *Chironomia*, while the rhetoric of voice had been thoroughly explored by Rush and his successors, the rhetoric of gesture had fallen by the wayside—hence his treatise. Bacon's *Manual*, avowedly derived from Austin's work and employing his notational system, is certainly the most complete and approachable volume on this branch of rhetoric, especially if one can find an original copy in decent condition, with its many superbly rendered cuts (steel-engraved, I believe), rather than a reprint. Beginning with the positions of the feet, distribution of weight, and incline of the body as basic Attitude, Bacon shows the three lines of gesture (descending, horizontal, ascending), each with four subdivisions (front, oblique, lateral, oblique backwards), to be identified by their initial letters (e.g., "d.o.=descending oblique," or more complexly, "b.h.d.f.p.=both hands descending front prone"). He arrives at a total of 56 gestures, plus 32 with the left hand, which are "admissable in some cases," en route to his complete "vocabulary of gesture commensurate with the realm of thought and feeling". To give a flavor of their expressive uses: "Both Hands Horizontal Front Supine" represents Earnest Entreaty with the body inclined forward, or Bold Challenge in retired position, "braced for resistance;" whereas "Right Hand Horizontal Backwards Prone" signifies "Remoteness in time or space, Superposition, repressive emotion," etc. There is a section on Special Gestures, as with the hands in isolation, another on the placement of gestures in relation to grammatical structures, and another devoted to readings.

Then there were the Readers, which instilled many of the elocutionary principles in elementary-school pupils. McGuffey's is probably the most widely remembered today, but a typical one I happen to know is *Franklin's Fourth Reader*, the "Fourth" designating the intended grade level (G.S. Hillard, 1882). Its progress through the elements of vocality and usage shows the command of the proprieties of verbal expression scholars were expected to attain at a young age, and its rather frightening illustrated description (lovely cuts again) of the seated attitude, approved way of rising to recite ("At the command, right face; at the command, stand; at the command, left face") and precision of posture while speaking are quick-lighting fuel for arguments about public education as the means of insuring strict regimentation of the young in the service of industrial capitalism and/or the military. On the other hand, the kids did learn to speak up.

Among all these, Russell's *Orthophony,* Bacon's *Manual,* and Stebbins' *Delsarte* will for most purposes cover the basics of the three rhetorical divisions of voice, gesture, and countenance that were so widely taught during the E-19 era. Even books confined to written rhetoric, like John S. Hart's *A Manual of Composition and Rhetoric* (Eldredge and Brother, Philadelphia, 1882), remind us of the assumed presence of sounded eloquence, of the voice, in all writing and silent reading. And the entire literature of the Elocutionary Movement recalls for us how pervasive were the concepts of performance technique as a mastery of physical and vocal composition and of idealized representation, within whose closely defined boundaries actors and singers were expected to locate truthfulness of emotional expression.

4. Robert Lloyd: *The Actor,* originally published in London, 1760, was reprinted in a lovely limited edition by C.W. Beaumont, London, in 1926. The edition includes a helpful introductory essay by Edmund Blunden and amusing engraved illustrations by Randolph Schwabe.

5. See John Anderson: *The American Theatre,* The Dial Press, N.Y., 1938, pp. 51-53. The book is interesting for its ambitious effort to embrace an overview of the American theatre's coming-of-age and to relate this to the emergence of the Hollywood film as an art form. There is an invaluable photographic section—some 230 pages of portraits, production shots, design renderings and completed sets (by Urban, Bel Geddes, Jones, Simonson, Gorelik, et al.), and more, covering both stage and film.

6. See Frances Donaldson: *The Actor-Managers,* Henry Regnery Co., Chicago, 1970 (originally published by Weidenfeld and Nicolson, London), p. 48. An informed and literate recounting of the English actor-manager tradition, from the Bancrofts to Du Maurier.

7. My primary sources have been: 1) "Styles in Shakespearian Acting." A private CD transcribed from an instructional tape for school use, compiled by F.C. Packard, Jr., who taught a course in the history of acting styles at Harvard. Twenty-five selections, from Booth in 1890 to Olivier in 1948. 2) "Actors and Actresses," Rococo #4003 (LP). Eighteen selections, all pre-WWI, of English, American, French, and German actors. There was an earlier "Actors and Actresses" disc, Rococo 4002, which I have not heard. 3) "Authors and Actors," Rococo 4014. Nine selections by six early English-, French-, and German-speaking actors, plus readings by four prominent authors. 4) "Stars on Broadway in the 19th Century," private CD from an unidentified source. Fifteen selections by twelve actors, from Jefferson and Terry on the early end to John Barrymore and Moissi on the later. 5) "In Memoriam," from DG 34011 (45 rpm). Four selections by three German-language actors (Moissi, Kayssler, Wüllner). 6) UORC-323, an Eddie Smith release whose second side is devoted to recitations by public figures (politicians, poets, composers, et al.) as well as actors. Twenty-four selections, of which the actors' are all quite early. 7) *"Goethe Interpretation im Wandel der Zeit."* From Christophorus CLX 75 435, part of a series devoted to German-language reciters. Eleven actors performing five selections, and thus interesting for its comparisons, e.g.: Kainz, Moissi, Wüllner, and Rolf Henniger all reciting *Prometheus.* I have supplemented these with online examples, especially of Bernhardt and Moissi.

In addition to the actors mentioned in the main text, these include some whose laying-on of inflectional affect sounds simply preposterous (Mounet-Sully), or whose material is shamelessly melodramatic to begin with (Tree as Svengali), to others whose power and sincerity are still evident. Among the German-speaking actors, we hear the same progression from florid, demonstrative vocalization to a more restrained, sense-oriented delivery as we hear in the Anglo-American tradition: from Kainz/Moissi/Wüllner (all quite different from one another) to Henniger in *Prometheus,* from Kayssler to Marks in *Grenzen der Menschheit,* even Bassermann to Westphal in *Der Schatzgräber,* the change is immediately apparent. Wüllner is of some special interest operatically, inasmuch as in addition to his high reputation as an actor and reciter, he had some success as a *Lieder* singer, and after a period of study with Georg Armin, founder of the *Stauprinzip* method, he actually undertook the roles of Tannhäuser and Siegmund. His puissant, overtly descriptive vocalizations of *Prometheus* and the Act IV monologue from Schiller's *Wilhelm Tell* suggest something closer to a bass-baritone than a tenor, but leave no doubt about the range and strength of the voice. For further on Moissi, see n. 9, below.

8. Strang's observations are taken from his "Famous Actors and Actresses of the Day" volumes, part of the Stage Lovers Series published around the turn of the last century by L.C. Page & Co., Boston. I have made use of his Second Series (1901 and '02), since as Strang notes, in the First "biography and anecdote were most prominent," whereas the Second focuses on criticism. While his critical standards are influenced by the style categorizations and moralizing outlook of the time, he is also clearly sympathetic to the emergence of a less rhetorical, simpler, more true-to-life approach to acting. He wrote a biography of Belasco, who he considered the greatest American director of his era.

    William Winter was a prominent New York theatre critic of long standing for the *Tribune*, among other journals. Near the end of his career, he published two weighty volumes of collected essays on actors and acting that take us some sixty years back in American theatre history (see *The Wallet of Time*, Moffatt, Yard & Co., N.Y., 1913). There are things to be gotten past in Winter. His belief in theatre as an instrument of moral instruction (especially powerful in his case) leads to a dismissal of Ibsen as a purveyor of unfit materials, and its Christian presumptions to an undisguisedly anti-Semitic ingredient in his comments on Bernhardt, or on the crassness of the new breed of businessman-managers whose monopolistic combines had driven the stock-company model and the older actor-managers from the field. His motivation was, at least in part, a defense of the theatre as a reputable profession (see "The Theatre and the Pulpit," in the Appendix of Vol. II, a spirited counterattack on the moral failings of clerics), and he writes eloquently on actors' deplorable working conditions at the very moment they were starting to organize against the new bosses. Regardless of motive, it remains often difficult to separate Winter's social prejudices from his legitimate critical evaluation. Much of the latter, however, is detailed and perceptive, and the sheer accumulation of observation makes *The Wallet of Time* an important source. Winter does not insist on the centrality of vocalism as persistently as Strang, so when he does give it extended attention, as with Rehan, Salvini, and Forrest (favorably) or E.H. Sothern (unfavorably—acceptable in comic roles like Benedick and Malvolio, but as Richelieu "hard, brittle, unsympathetic," and as Romeo "hard and dry"), we pay heed.

    The inclusion of Shaw, I hope, requires little explanation. No theatre critic since his time has matched his love of the verbal and his professional ear for voice, embracing a deep respect for rhetorical delivery along with a permanently activated fustian-and-bluster detector. ("As a critic," notes his biographer Michael Holroyd, "Shaw was primarily a listener rather than a watcher." See Holroyd: *Bernard Shaw: A Biography*, Random House, N.Y., 1988, Vol. 1, p. 343.) We must make some allowance for his propensity for hyperbole and self-dramatization, and of course for his complicated involvement with some of the actresses he wrote about. I think we can say that a prime requisite for a Shavian infatuation with a woman of the stage (Janet Achurch, Ellen Terry, Mrs. Patrick Campbell), or for his purely professional admiration (as with Ada Rehan), was that she possess a voice of extraordinary range, strength, and beauty, and use it to tell the truth as he heard it. For all that, the actress he considered the greatest was precisely the one for whom truth emerged unadorned by any glamorous asset of person or voice: Eleonora Duse.

9. Moissi is of particular interest, having been so highly lauded in a wide range of roles, and often taken as the quintessential Reinhardt actor. He also recorded prolifically (for an actor), and at late enough dates to produce discs of acceptable quality. As with

Bernhardt, we must remain aware that most of his recordings involve moments of extreme emotion, removed from their context and rendered "cold" in a studio. Often they have an ecstatic component, as with The Stranger's visionary description of Heaven at the end of Hauptmann's *Hannele*, complete with angelic cohort and musical accompaniment (ghastly, treacly stuff that we recognize as proto-Hollywoodian), or Faust's monologue (Act I, Scene 1, lines 735-784, with cuts), in which the sounds of bells and angels' voices save him from drinking from the poisoned chalice. In the latter, with its melodious, tremulous evocations and its back-to-earth, tears-in-laughter end, all the devices of poetic declamation are skillfully applied, and, in combination with Moissi's musical sensitivities, create an almost operatic impression. (Otto Klemperer, who was involved with the famous Reinhardt production of Offenbach's *Orpheus in the Underworld* in 1906, in which actors assumed all the roles, later recalled Moissi's singing voice as "wonderfully expressive"—see Peter Heyworth: *Otto Klemperer, His Life and Times,* revised edition, Cambridge Univ. Press, 1996, Vol. 1, p. 24.) Nevertheless, they are still technical devices, in the service less of character and circumstance as a modern actor would think of them than of a perceived obligation to elocutionary eloquence and poetic fulfillment. A lofty effect is produced, but it sounds "worked-up."

10. This tendency to search for authentication through reconstruction of a line of descent from an embattled minority of truthseekers is, I suppose, a natural one, but I think it can distort our perspective, and is often used by contemporary actors as an excuse for just going on "being themselves." In 1914, Stanislavski devoted time to sifting through the writing of earlier acting theorists, and was particularly excited by some observations in the *Reflections Upon Declamation* of Luigi Riccoboni (1676-1753), an important reformer of the Italian and French theatre. And indeed there are formulations in the *Reflections* that Stanislavski must have heard as companionable pre-echoes, e.g.: "We must however take care to distinguish the Difference betwixt an Alternation of the Features, in order to express the Sentiments of the Soul, and the Grimaces that attend a *Play of the Muscles* ... If a Man enter strongly into a proper Enthusiasm, and speaks in the Accents of the Soul, his Features will naturally form themselves into an Agreement with his Subject. . ."—and more in this vein. In his biography of Stanislavski, David Magarshak says that ". . . in 1737 [Riccoboni] was already propagating the type of acting which Stanislavski called 'living the part'." (See Magarshak: *Stanislavski: A Life* (Faber and Faber London, 1986, originally published by Macgibbon & Kee, London, 1950, pp. 336-337). But of course the "living the part" acting done by Riccoboni and his allies in his refreshment of the *commedia dell'arte* or his championing of Molière and Racine cannot have much resembled the acting of Stanislavski's company. They shared an aspiration and a distinction from other work of their times, but neither the processes nor the results can have been very similar. For those interested: Riccoboni's *Reflections*, printed early on in French and Italian editions, was translated into English by W. Owen, whose Second Edition (London, 1754) also embraced the author's *General History of the Stage* and *A Comparison of the Antient and Modern Dramas*, as well as an Introductory Discourse and critical footnotes by Owen. I have worked from the AMS reprint of that volume.

11. This term (*Predlagamemye Obstoyal'stva*), prevalent in modern acting training, apparently originated in its theatrical application with Pushkin. He, however, applied it to playwriting, as: "Authenticity of passions and verisimilitude in emotions *under given conditions* [my italics] are what our intellect demands of dramatic poets." (See *Russian Dramatic Theory from Pushkin to the Symbolists*, Laurence Senelick, trans. and ed., Univ. of Texas Press, Austin, 1981, p. 10. This volume is an invaluable resource for English-language readers interested in Russian theatre.) Stanislavski transferred the usage to the acting process. Whether for creator or interpreter, its meaning is the same.

12. The Benedetti translations of Stanislavski, all published by Routledge, are: *My Life in Art* (2008); *An Actor's Work* (2008, comprising the two volumes formerly called *An Actor Prepares* and *Building a Character*); and *An Actor's Work on a Role* (2010, formerly *Creating a Role*). There is no question that for an English-language reader wishing to go as far into Stanislavski's work as possible (the Russian-language *Collected Works* run to eight volumes), the Benedetti editions are the ones to work from. They are more inclusive than Hapgood's, sequence the materials more logically at some points, and read a bit more gracefully. (There is nothing to be done with Stanislavski's pseudo-Socratic way of presenting the acting lessons—it's clunky, but we may as well take it for charming and try to imagine ourselves in a Moscow studio one hundred years ago.) I cannot vouch for the new versions' improved precision of expression, but that has been generally acknowledged in critical assessments. There are helpful contextual contributions by Declan Donnellan, Anatoly Smeliansky, and Benedetti, plus a glossary and endnote references. All this said, if one is simply looking for a basic understanding of Stanislavski's principles and practices, it can be found in the Hapgood versions, now also taken up by Routledge and available in relatively inexpensive paperbacks. And though lacking much of Benedetti's apparatus, Hapgood does include an index, making it easier to search than the Benedetti, which, maddeningly, does not.

    Benedetti has also written several other books on Stanislavski. Among them are a biography, which I have not read, and *Stanislavski and the Actor* (Methuen, 1998), a thoughtfully designed working handbook whose priorities are in accordance with latterday findings, complete with exercises and examples drawn from English plays rather than the E-19 Russian works used by Stanislavski, which are unfamiliar to most students. (It should be said, though, that anyone willing to work through Stanislavski's comments on scenes and roles with the play texts at hand—as, for instance, with the extended analysis of the classic part of Chatski in the Griboyedov play we call *Woe from Wit*, or *Woe from Wisdom*—will be well rewarded as to both acting and cultural enrichment.) Finally, Benedetti has also produced *The Art of the Actor*, a historical survey of acting theory from Aristotle up to the dawn of the auteur. He touches on the Greco-Roman rhetoricians and their post-Renaissance descendants (English Division), and of course devotes considerable space to Stanislavski. He includes substantial excerpts from the writings of his exemplars, highly selective but intelligently so. He makes clean distinctions between Stanislavski's system and The Method as developed by Lee Strasberg, and offers good perspective on the Stanislavski/Brecht polarization of the 1950-90's. If the book has a weakness, it is its inattention to modern American teachers and writers—but then, that is amply compensated for elsewhere (see n. 14, below). Overall, Benedetti's has been an enormous contribution, synthesizing the piecemeal work of many others, and bringing to a comfortable resting-place the project of some sixty years past of enlarging our picture of modernity's greatest acting teacher and correcting the distortions that historical accident had created in our view of it.

13. We have already noted the attention paid by Talma and Nourrit to historical accuracy in costume, and the representational detailing of setting in *La Juive* and other grand opera productions of the 1830s. In England, John Kemble had shown a similar concern, and this was expanded into other areas of production by Macready. (See Alan S. Downer: *The Eminent Tragedian/William Charles Macready*, Harvard Univ. Press, 1966, esp. Chap. 6, "Regisseur," and most particularly pp. 224 ff, "The Beginnings of Modern Theatre Practice.") Macready dispensed with the use of generic stock pieces to fashion a set; insisted that actors act in rehearsal (as opposed to merely reciting and marking the blocking); and worked with supporting actors to bring them into the action as artistic partners rather than walking cue cards for the star or perpetrators of the shopworn "business" associated with their stereotyped positions in the distribution. A generation later, the Bancrofts (see Donaldson, *The Actor-Managers*, Chap. 1), building on the example of Mme. Vestris, brought into their repertory of domestic comedies and dramas (chiefly

those of J.W. Robertson) the accoutrements of their "cup and saucer" theatre—actual rugs, furniture, ceilings, and (especially noticed) doorknobs, and for their revival of *School for Scandal* produced period furnishings and rooms with real china, chandeliers, oak bookcases, etc. based on exhibits at the British Museum. Not to mention a "real Negro page." They also emphasized ensemble playing and, under Robertson's influence, the de-stereotyping of "stock" parts.

All these were innovations, carried forward into the practice of later English actor-managers and, in the U.S., of producers like Wallack, Daly, Belasco, and Frohmann. They were concerned mostly with the stage picture—its completeness, unity, and authenticity, what Macready called "the perfect image." The acting done from within this realistic *mise en scène*, though certainly increasingly influenced by the development of ensemble, the democratization of subject matter, and the presence of detailed sets, real props, and time-and-place-specific costumes (for all these affect, sometimes profoundly, the actor's feel of self in character and environment) was still Old School, and taught largely through illustrative demonstration on the part of the actor-manager or producer-director. It only gradually extended to the assumption of individualized lifelikeness, by everyone onstage, on his or her own creative responsibility.

14. First, for the readers who may be unfamiliar with the development of modern acting practice in general and who desire some context, I would recommend a couple of relatively recent titles:

Richard Brestoff: *The Great Acting Teachers and Their Methods* (Smith and Kraus, Hanover, N.H., Vol. 1, 1995, and Vol. 2, 2010). And:

Arthur Bartow (ed.): *Training of the American Actor* (Theatre Communications Group, N.Y., 2006).

Brestoff's volumes consist of concise, fair descriptions of the principal extant "schools" of acting. They cover much of the territory explored in Benedetti's *Art of the Actor* (see n. 12, above), but with more evaluative description and less direct citation, and with a much fuller accounting of American developments. After introductory chapters that give a onceover of premodern practices (including some attention to Quintilian, the rhetoricians, and to Delsarte and MacKaye), Vol. 1 moves on to the children of the Russian and American (acting) revolutions (conveying, along the way, the essence of Stanislavski through an imagined encounter with Thespis, fortunately handled with a light touch), and then to Spolin, Brecht, Grotowski, and Suzuki, and ends with brief profiles of major training programs. Vol. 2 focuses on French modernists (Antoine, Copeau, St.-Denis), American realists (Kazan, Hagen, Mamet), and finally edges into postmodern territory with Anne Bogart and Keith Johnstone. A good all-round orientation.

Bartow's book is an anthology of pieces written by representatives of most of the influential contemporary American techniques. Each section is therefore a bit of advocacy, but by and large straightforwardly done, and accorded some placement by Bartow's introduction. A solid single-volume view of what's out there.

Those in search of an economical but thoroughly researched telling of Stanislavski's development out of the 19th-Century Russian theatre; of the growth of American acting theory up to 1925 (a somewhat different perspective from that of McTeague's *Before Stanislavski*); and of the impact of the former upon the latter, should seek out:

Christine Edwards: *The Stanislavski Heritage* (New York Univ. Press, 1965).

It is long out of print, and obviously doesn't cover events that postdate its publication. But by that time its story was essentially complete, and it is well related by an author who understood its substance and significance. In that same connection, also see:

Tulane Drama Review: *Stanislavski and America* (*TDR* Vol. 9, Nos. 1 and 2, Fall and Winter, 1964).

These superb issues embrace some 25 contributions from practically everyone then prominently involved with the subject, from Strasberg and Kazan to Brecht and Meyerhold. Issued at a time when American adaptations of Stanislavski had taken firm hold and were beginning to generate the reactions that would inform academic critique and postmodern response, they contain much informative commentary and bear all the battle scars of their time and place.

And to complete this background:

Harold Clurman: *The Fervent Years* (Alfred E. Knopf, 1945, with several subsequent editions that include epilogues).

The story of The Group Theatre, in its social and artistic context, recounted by a moving-force participant who was a well-regarded director and critic. Clurman's several other books also repay attention.

Then there are the many additional books that deal directly with Stanislavski and his work. A complete list would be overlong, a selective one rather arbitrary. There is considerable overlap among them, and much of their substance is subsumed in Benedetti's *oeuvre*. Here, I will mention just three that I find to be of special interest:

Pavel Rumyantsev: *Stanislavski on Opera* (Elizabeth Reynolds Hapgood, trans. and ed., Theatre Arts Books, 1975).

Vic Schneierson (trans.): *Konstantin Stanislavski, 1863-1963* (Progress Publishers, Moscow, 1963).

Vera Gottlieb (trans. and ed.): *Anton Chekhov at the Moscow Art Theatre* (Routledge, 2005).

Rumyantsev, a baritone, was a member of the Opera Studio from its early days, when Stanislavski was personally in charge. His book consists of the extensive notes he took during the study and rehearsal periods on several opera productions, plus work on individual arias and songs. He was a keen and sensitive participant/observer, and his volume gives us not only a vivid picture of Stanislavski's work with operatic material, with its stress on musicality, verbal beauty and clarity, and rhythmic movement, but perhaps the most comprehensive of all the memoirs left by those who studied and performed under his guidance.

Schneierson's translation, compiled by three Russian editors, is a kind of centennial *Festschrift*. Divided into three sections ("Man and Actor," "Stanislavski and the World Theatre," and "Stanislavski's Letters"), it includes a number of contributions still otherwise unavailable in English. Some are brief personal tributes, but others are longer and artistically substantive. As we would expect from a Khrushchev-era book from the U.S.S.R. (the Soviets, warily, preserved Stanislavski the way they preserved *Swan Lake* or their traditional productions of *Boris* or *Onegin*), some of the commentary reflects mental gymnastics attempting to reconcile theatrical art with the Revolution's notions of its uses, though it's no less fascinating for that. But there is plenty of penetrating artistic thought, and the range of response from great figures of the 20th-Century world theatre is staggering.

No lover of theatre and acting should stay unacquainted with Vera Gottlieb's book. It is a beautiful reproduction of a photographic journal (198 pictures in all) created by Nikolai Efros, the first literary manager of the MAT. Originally published in 1914, it presents sequences of scenes and moments from original productions (or very early revivals) of all five major Chekhov plays, plus studio portraits of the actors in various roles, of Chekhov himself, of scenic models and renderings, etc. Not all the photos will be unfamiliar to students of the subject—some have been reproduced often. What is unique here are the production sequences, which in several cases allow an almost moment-to-moment tracking of complete acts of the plays. There are also full-color renderings (on the back flap) of four of Viktor Simov's settings, which enable us to sense the life in the boxy interiors and leafy woodwing exteriors we usually see in black and white. Included is Efros's original essay, which conveys much about Chekhov, the plays, and the productions (which he had of course seen multiple times) from an insider perspective. A good introduction and informative notes by Gottlieb. No other work brings us so close to being in the presence of the company—a magnificent volume.

Two books by Norris Houghton give us our best sense of the MAT in its late prime in the context of other developments in the Soviet theatre and how these played out in the postwar years, as seen by an American of extensive theatre knowledge and sharp critical perception: *Moscow Rehearsals* (Harcourt, Brace & Co., 1936, reprinted by Grove/Evergreen in 1962); and *Return Engagement* (Holt, Rinehart and Winston, N.Y., 1962). Houghton, active in the theatre as director, producer (he co-founded New York's Phoenix Theatre with T. Edward Hambleton) and educator for over half a century, spent five months in Moscow in 1934-35, not only attending the theatre virtually every night, but by day sitting in on rehearsals, attending classes in the schools attached to several of the most prominent theatre companies, and talking at length with actors, students, directors, designers, technicians, and administrators. He gives the companies of Stanislavski, Vakhtangov, Tairov, and Meyerhold the most in-depth attention, and, without disguising his own preferences, writes with understanding on the philosophies and working methods of all of them. Twenty-five years later he returned to Moscow for a shorter but still extended and intensive stay, and wrote with equal understanding about the continuities and changes he found. In both instances, his clear, graceful writing conveys a strong cultural and artistic empathy for his subject (and envy for the working conditions in the Russian theatre and its place in Soviet society), but with an unturned head with respect to artistic distinctions and the political surroundings. When combined with the observations of Sayler, these volumes give us a vivid, though obviously incomplete, American view of the Russian theatre from the eve of the Revolution into the late Soviet era.

My final little grouping is from the literature (again extensive) of American directors, teachers, and critics who were directly or indirectly influenced by Stanislavski. It is with no intention of slighting the émigré actors and teachers who injected Stanislavskian plasma into the American bloodstream (Boleslavsky, Michael Chekhov, Soloviova, et al.) or the Americans most closely identified with The Method (e.g., Strasberg, Meisner)—all of whom anyone with an acting appetite will consult—that I restrict this list to a few I find germane to my arguments:

Robert Lewis: *Method—Or Madness?* (Samuel French, Inc., 1958).

Barry Paris: *Stella Adler on Ibsen, Strindberg, and Chekhov* (Alfred A. Knopf, 1999), And: *Stella Adler on America's Master Playwrights* (Alfred A. Knopf, 2012).

Uta Hagen: *Respect for Acting* (Macmillan, 1973). And: *A Challenge for the Actor* (Charles Scribners Sons, 1991).

In 1957 Lewis, an alumnus of the Group Theatre (as were Clurman, Adler, Strasberg, Meisner, Kazan, and many excellent actors and writers) and co-founder of the Actor's Studio, presented a series of eight weekly lectures to a professional audience at New York's Playhouse Theatre, seeking to clear the air with respect to the debates over The Method; they are gathered here. Witty and lucid, they are still the best summary of the American neo-Stanislavskians' ideals. The extent to which these ideals were put into practice is, naturally, another matter.

It was Adler who, returning to the Group in 1934 after several weeks of work with Stanislavski in Paris, reported that its understanding of his views were at best partial and at worst distorted, thus creating a schism in the Church of Methodology that was never healed. I think she was bound to set her own course anyway, in part as an assertive, talented woman in a company of assertive, talented men, and in part as a member of an illustrious acting family whose patriarch was the leading tragedian of New York's then-flourishing Yiddish theatre, a theatre of heightened emotion and passionate rhetoric. She left writings on technique, and they are fine, but I think these selections of transcribed lectures on plays and characters are more inspiring and entertaining, especially for nonprofessional readers. I like them for their insistence on the expansion of the actor's embrace, of growth into the character and the playwright's vision, with its implied comprehension of time-and-place social and cultural circumstances as well as the immediate, psychological ones. "It's not about you", she says more than once.

In some ways, Uta Hagen stands even farther apart from the rest of the Methodists. She had no connection to the Group Theatre. She is the only one of these teachers to attain and maintain a position among the distinguished actors of the American Stage. Born into a Northern European, high-culture family (her Danish mother was an opera singer, her Welsh-German father a musicologist and art historian instrumental in the start of the 20th Century Handel revival at Göttingen), she cites as positive influences and models Eva LeGallienne, the Lunts, Laurette Taylor, Albert Bassermann (ex-Reinhardt), Clurman (as director), and above all her longtime husband and teaching partner Herbert Berghof, whose own mentor was Reinhardt. Yet she thoroughly absorbed Stanislavski's principles, and in her books presents them, in combination with the lessons of her own extensive experience, with thoroughness and clarity. These *are* books about technique, but in a broad human context. I like the first one for the simplicity with which it presents the exercise work, but the second is in some ways richer, and touches on the developments of the intervening years.

Lewis, Adler, and Hagen were distinct personalities, whose teaching differed with respect to emphasis and priorities. What I think sets them off a bit from many others is their insistence that while the actor must indeed be grounded in his or her own self leading his or her life in the real here-and-now world, he or she must then reach out and up to become many selves, including those that live in the worlds of the great artworks. That is where the modern acting sensibility begins to rub up against the words and actions of the characters who inhabit the classical plays of all traditions—and, of course, the ones who sing their ways through four centuries' worth of operatic drama.

15. See *The Levik Memoirs*, esp. Chap. 11.

16. See "Reinhardt in Rehearsal" by Heinz Herald, in Sayler's *Max Reinhardt and his Theatre*; also quoted in J.L. Styan: *Max Reinhardt* (Cambridge, n.d.), pp. 122-123, who prefaces by noting that Reinhardt ". . . worked out all the details of a new production in his head long before rehearsals began . . ." and ". . . would write down every movement and gesture, every expression and tone of voice . . .". Quoting Herald: ". . . the atmosphere of every scene, of every conversation in that scene, of every sentence in that conversation. Expression, intonation, every position of the actor, every emotion, the indication of every interval, the effect on the other actors—all these details mapped out in clear, concise words." Doesn't sound like a lot of leeway for the actor. On the other hand, Styan also cites the testimony of the designer Norman Bel Geddes, who reports that Reinhardt was endlessly patient and open to actors' interpretations, and that he spoke gently and quietly to individual actors, not in front of the others.

There are also reports from some of Reinhardt's devoted performers and other observers concerning his willingness to incorporate their ideas in rehearsal (see "How Reinhardt Works with His Actors," by Gertrude Eysoldt, and the reports of others in Sayler, Chap. IX), and of Jarmila Novotna in Rasponi's *The Last Prima Donnas*, all of whom seemed to have felt reasonable freedom in working with Reinhardt. Finally, there is this from Bel Geddes: "When an actor's work was unsuccessful, Reinhardt had a few words with him and the actor became receptive through awareness of his own limitations." Now, when an actor is in trouble, he or she surely appreciates the perspective of a good director, who will always be guiding performers toward his overall vision of the work. But everything here depends on the definitions of "unsuccessful" and "limitations," and it rather sounds as if "unsuccessful" means "Not arriving at the precise result indicated in the great *Regiebuch*," while "awareness of his own limitations" would mean "humble acknowledgement of failure to foresee the correct result." Theodore Hoffmann said of Stanislavski (see TDR 25, p. 15): "The System depends on an unwritten compact whereby the actor discovers on his own what the director wants him to." In the sense that this means the actor must arrive at a result *of which the director approves*, and which now belongs to the actor in a way that a dictated result cannot, this could be said of any healthy director/actor relationship. The question lies with how much the creativity of the performer can contribute to the process, and at what level of micromanagement the director seeks to control the outcome. We can only take educated guesses at what the interactions between Reinhardt and his actors (or Stanislavski's and his, for that matter) were really like; doubtless they varied from one case to another. But there doesn't seem much question that Reinhardt's working method was much more pointed toward directorially predetermined results.

17. See *The Music Theater of Walter Felsenstein*, Peter Paul Fuchs (ed. and trans.), W.W. Norton, 1975, Chap. 2, pp. 15 and 17. Aside from the materials included with the film release (see n. 20 below), this volume is by far the best English-language source on Felsenstein's thinking, which is otherwise scattered through magazine articles and anthologies. In addition to a generous selection of writings and interviews by Felsenstein himself and several of his followers, there are a helpful Foreward and annotations by Dr. Fuchs, a devoted editor with working knowledge of the issues involved. Felsenstein's formulations on the problems of opera as theatre (in Part I of the book) are brilliant and precise—still stimulating to read—and his essays on specific interpretations (Part II), while more open to argument, are always grounded in the works and closely reasoned.

18. Unless I've miscounted, there were 21 substantive entries during the years 1953-1971. Of course, *Opera* was not the only source of running commentary on Felsenstein. *Opera News* published intermittent reviews and reports, and a particular champion was the Berlin-based American critic Paul Moor, who called Felsenstein ". . . one of the few authentic theatrical geniuses of our time" and ". . . the German Democratic Republic's dominant cultural personality"—which, given Brecht's passing, was probably not an exaggeration. (See "The Legacy of Walter Felsenstein," *High Fidelity/Musical America*," Feb., 1976.) *Opera*, however, provided the most consistent and, in general, most knowledgeable coverage.

19. Koegler is an instructive and poignant case: a critic always mindful of the vocal and musical heights to which traditional operatic performance could carry him, yet also susceptible to the theatrical consciousness-raising that Felsenstein and others were working on. Or, rather, susceptible and resistant at once, because always aware that, whichever approach was winning him over at the moment, something vital was missing. Thus, after a generally negative stance toward Felsenstein early on (at one point he had his press privileges revoked by the Komische Oper), by 1958 he had contributed to *Der Monat* an enthusiastic appreciation of Felsenstein's achievements in operatic realism that wound up in Dr. Fuchs's volume. It's an endorsement, however, that omits any mention of singing and musicmaking.

20. The *Walter Felsenstein Edition* (ArtHaus Musik, 2008, 12 DVDs), comprises his seven complete films along with many extras (interviews, speeches, rehearsal snippets, and brief clips from earlier Felsenstein productions). The DVDs are accompanied by a set of scenic and costume renderings and a hardbound book, in German and English, that includes articles by and about Felsenstein and about each opera and production; many photos, renderings, manuscript reproductions, etc.; a timeline biography; and an extensive

bibliography. Altogether, the Edition is one of which an American can only be envious—envious that such a legacy exists in the first place (our NBC-TV opera productions of the 1950s and '60s might be a very rough equivalent, but of course nothing has been done with whatever materials may still be extant), and envious that it has been so reverently treated. The audio and visual restoration is superb, the book and renderings beautifully printed on high-quality papers, and the whole enclosed in a box built to last. Some of the DVDs have been released singly. For brief assessments of the films, see n. 26, below.

21. Perhaps some of Felsenstein's productions that didn't make it to video, like the *Traviata*, contained elements of social critique that could be interpreted as political commentary or not, depending on who needed convincing. Moments that point up class-based social ritual, like the promenading procession in the *Figaro* Act III finale, can be read that way. But there is no trace for instance, of cheap shots at the Count, which one has seen taken in non-Socialist productions in the vain hope that they will prove funny. I think Felsenstein protected himself mostly through what he said and wrote rather than by what he put on the stage. In the informative introductory essay in the book that accompanies the films, Jens Neubert tells us that from the time "Socialist Realism" was declared the official aesthetic of East Germany (1950), "Felsenstein and his dramaturges preceded the phrase 'music theatre' with the adjective 'realistic,'" and that "Felsenstein's struggle to survive in a totalitarian state forced him to adopt the stance of a realistic dialectician." (We are reminded of the position the Soviets accorded to Stanislavski, whose "realism" made him fit for veneration, while the true revolutionary, Meyerhold, was exterminated for his artistic defiance.) And so, in his trenchant manifesto "The Approach to the Work" (see Fuchs, Chap. 6), Felsenstein insists that *The Magic Flute* ". . . is not mythology; it is politics"; we find the Brechtian term "culinary" popping up to describe the accepted condition of opera, etc. There is no reason to doubt the sincerity of his contempt for the international opera "business," its catering to superficial entertainment values, and its lazy production methods. Though often clothed in Marxian language ("bourgeois decadence", etc.), such views could have come from a high-minded European artist or intellectual of any political persuasion. I have found no clues to Felsenstein's personal political sympathies.

22. See *Opera*, Oct., 1962, p. 675. This is clearly the review of a true believer, but it argues the case and offers a full bill of particulars, including this one: "Each participant seemed to have reached the fulness of his or her personality for the first time, not only as a performer, but also, surprisingly enough, as a singer!", and he characterizes the vocal improvement of each of the principals. The production, "thrillingly designed by Rudolf Heinrich," was given ten weeks of rehearsal, and was mounted at a time when the political tensions were at their highest.

23. I base this on the recordings of the S/N-D company with which I am familiar (*Bethrothal in a Monastery, Katerina Ismailova*) and the single performance I saw at that theatre in 1968, a *Così fan tutte*. (Another recording, of Rimsky-Korsakov's *Mozart and Salieri*, employs the S/N-D orchestra and chorus, but this seems to have been a recording convenience: I doubt that its principals, Bolshoi luminaries Alexander Pirogov and Sergei Lemeshev, ever sang with the company.) The men of the company were especially strong, and while there were some relative individual weaknesses, the overall level was several notches higher than the K.O.'s. The *Così*, with all *secco* recitative played as spoken dialogue, was the best-played I have seen—witty, believable, and relaxed in a way that seems to have eluded the K.O.

24. Felsenstein urged those interested in translation problems to compare his with older ones and with the originals, to verify his claims of greater faithfulness to creators' works. Unfortunately, the otherwise exemplary Felsenstein Edition (see n. 20) does not

provide them, and they are not listed in the Edition's bibliography. The *Otello* transla-tion is in fact in print (Reclams Universal-Bibliothek No. 7727, Stuttgart, 2008), so an extended comparison between it and Max Kalbeck's original German translation (Ricordi, n.d.), traditional in German-language houses for many years, could be made. I will not undertake that. But a tiny example is presented by the Edition's editors, and it's of a fragment we've already met: the recitative into Iago's *Credo*. Felsenstein speaks of it in an interview in the bonus material, and it's referred to in the Edition book's essay on the opera by Marcus Heinike. The book also reproduces the scene's first page in Kalbeck's translation in vocal score, showing Felsenstein's revisions in his hand above the vocal line. Brief though it is, this sample, selected by Felsenstein himself, will serve to give us one small test of Felsenstein's efforts to uncover the truth of an "unknown" original. Indeed, the sense-and-sound problems are so tightly packed in this little pas-sage that we glance at them only to confirm their insolubility. This insolubility isn't anybody's fault. It's in the nature of the project.

If you are familiar with *Otello*, you will recall that the preceding dialogue between Iago and Cassio, built over variations on the orchestral introduction's pulsating triplet motif in the strings, ends as Iago sends the demoted Cassio off with a slap-on-the-back "*Vanne!*" to plead for Desdemona's intercession with Otello. "*Vanne*," Iago now repeats, but in a quite different tone. And here we should look at the original Italian of the recitative, along with my own guilty-with-explanation, non-singing English version. Though elaborately accompanied, the recitative proceeds in typical one-word-per-note fashion, with short note values. My slur markings show the ties that make the Italian an uninterrupted rolling-forward of liquid vowel sounds, something that no German or English translation can duplicate, and a part of what the original "means." Italics show syllables that are assigned longer note values, which may in turn be further extended by the singer.

Vanne; la tua *me*ta già vedo.	Go now; your destination I see already
Ti spinge‿il tuo dimone,	Your demon drives you onward,
e‿il tuo dim*on* son io.	and that demon is myself.
E *me* trascina‿il *mi*o, nel	And my own drags me on, in
qua*le*‿io‿*cre*do	whom I believe,
in*e*sorato Idd*io*.	inexorable Godhead.

Notes:

Vanne: "Go then" is the most common English choice, and a perfectly sen-sible one, given that a two-syllable solution is needed. I choose "Go now" partly for its sound, and partly because we need the repetition of what Iago's just said to Cassio, which carries an implication of "this is the moment!" time urgency. In an "in period" translation (worth considering, I think) there would be such options as "Go thou!" or "Hence, then!"

Ti spinge, &c.: Literally, "Pushes you your demon." But it needs the force of "drives." "Demon" should be understood as "daemon," or dark driving spirit. I've seen "evil genius," which is O.K. for sense, but wouldn't work on the notes.

E me, &c.: Note the heavy, dragging sensation created by the alternation of shorter and longer values, as the line drills forward into the fermata and "*Iddio*," the set-up for the orchestra's thunderous voicing of the Credo theme, like a wall that shuts out everything in its surroundings.

Now for the German versions, again with my translations. Keep in mind that theirs are constrained by note values, while mine are for sense only. The italics will be explained below.

KALBECK

Geh nur, ich erkenne dein Ziel schon.	Just go, I discern your destination already.
Denn dich regiert dein Dämon,	For your demon rules you,
Und dieser *bin ich selber,*	and that is me, myself;
mich *reisst* der *meine* Fort,	my own pulls me onward,
an *den* ich *glaub'* als meine furchtbare	in whom I believe as my dreadful
*Gott*heit.	Godhead.

FELSENSTEIN

Geh nur, deinen *Weg seh* ich Vor mir!	Go now, your path I see before me!
Denn dich regiert dein Dämon,	For your demon rules you,
Und dieser *Dä*mon, ist in mir.	and this demon is in me.
Er *reisst* mich *mit* sich *fort,*	He pulls me with him onward,
Ich glaub an *ihm* als mein erbittliche	I believe in him as my inexorable
*Gott*heit.	Godhead.

Let's look at these choices, first with respect to sense and faithfulness, and then with regard to sounds and likely vocal outcomes.

"*Geh nur*": My translation, "Just go," is very approximate, but is the closest I can come, and is agreed to by the subtitles of the film. In the filmed interview, we encounter "Go there." Neither really captures the feel of "*Geh nur*," which in turn is no more than an approximation of "*Vanne*," notwithstanding which both K. and F. settle for it. But they part company in the remainder of the line. Neither of their versions sits "naturally" on the Italian scansion, particularly at the end. For faithfulness, though, Kalbeck wins on two points: F.'s "path," or "way" ("*Weg*") is not the same as destination ("*Ziel*"), which is closer to Boïto's "*meta*"; and Kalbeck's "*schon*" retains the thought of "already" ("*già*"), which is dropped by Felsenstein.

F. retains K.'s words in the next line, even though being "ruled," or even "led," ("*regiert*") is not the same as being pushed. Note that the German "*dämon*" is closer to the sense of "*dimone*" than is the English "demon." Now comes a departure of some significance. To say that "this demon is in me" (F.) is not at all the same as saying "I *am* this demon" (K., my italics). The latter is in fact how Boïto has it. Felsenstein's preference is based on an interesting perception. He proposes that Iago needs to keep the demon separate from himself in order to blame the demon for his actions—a ball-park equivalent of "the devil made me do it." That is entirely plausible. We're always looking for an external cause to evade responsibility for questionable behavior, and we all have demons. Now, I don't agree with this interpretation, because I believe the whole point of the *Credo*— the reason Verdi and Boïto stuck it in there, and thereby lifted this scheming, nasty noncom to the level of Cosmic Force of Evil—is precisely that Iago *does* take responsibility. He proclaims himself a demon, embraces evil and nurtures hatred in the manner of many an affectless, conscienceless psychopath. He invents a cruel God to worship, and announces all these facts to us in a direct-address monologue. If the words of the *Credo* (which, Felsenstein tells us, "is no Credo at all"—but what is he talking about?) did not fully convince me of this interpretation, the music would more than suffice. In performance terms, all that really matters is the belief of the performer. As with some of Eléazar's choices in *La Juive*, it makes no difference to the audience if the performer feels one or the other more strongly, provided it plays out through the role's progression. The thing to recognize here is that Felsenstein *is* interpreting, and should, like Iago, take responsibility for that.

In Boïto's original, Iago, having declared himself Cassio's evil spirit, now acknowledges his own, who is his god. There are two points of interest. First, by specifying that this demon/god "pulls me *with him* onward," F. reinforces his picture of an evil force separate from Iago—an emphasis missing in K.'s version, which is closer to Boïto. Second, F. unquestionably has the better of it, meaningwise, with "*erbittliche*". K.'s "*furchtbare*" is far too general to do justice to Boïto's "*inesorato*". This is the only spot in the recitative where Felsenstein is truer to the original than Kalbeck; otherwise, either they are identical, or Kalbeck's is more the faithful. This is certainly a small, and perhaps unrepresentative, sample, but more than once Felsenstein got himself into trouble with musicologists and critics over his habit of claiming authenticity for what were really interpretive directorial decisions. (See Winton Dean, *The Musical Times*, Nov., 1965, and *The Musical Newsletter*, Vol. III No. 4 (1973), on Felsenstein's collaboration with Fritz Oeser on the latter's critical edition of *Carmen*, and my own *The Mouth-Honored Prophets* in *The Musical Newsletter*, Vol. V No. 4 (1975, previously referenced), which discusses Felsenstein's views on both *Carmen* and *The Magic Flute* in the light of his assertions about authenticity.

Now for a quick look at these word choices for their sound values, and how these tend to push interpretation in one direction or another. My italicizations in the German versions and the italicized longer notes in the Italian will, I hope, help to clarify the differences. I'll proceed line by line, with Kalbeck's choices first, then Felsenstein's:

· *erkenne* vs. *Weg*: Kalbeck gives the sole sustained note (a quarter, amid sixteenths) to the second syllable of *erkenne*, with its open "*e*" leading into the sounding "*nn*," while F. allots it to *Weg*, a naturally short, clipped word (closed "*e*," then the hard "*g*," that begs to be cut off before its time.

· *Ziel schon* vs. *vor mir*: pretty much a wash. Neither scans "naturally," since the normal vocal inflection of both would be short/long (an iamb), whereas the Italian "*vedo*" is long/short (a trochee), with the first syllable landing on the downbeat. However, K. does end each short word with a sounding consonant, while F. twice gives us the quick-tongued "*r*."

· *bin* vs. *Dämon*: while *Dämon* has the more open vowels, their sounding potential is compromised by splitting the original's quarter note into two eighths. So the shorter word, K.'s *bin*, makes the longer effect.

· *selber* vs. *in mir*: again in K., an open "*e*" leads into a voiced consonant ("*l*") and then into a neutral end syllable often rendered almost as "*sel-bar*" in older renditions, whereas F. chooses two narrow words on the "*i*" vowel. Here, the *selber* also has its natural trochaic scansion, while the normally iambic *in mir* is forced to comply. Of course, this last can be "justified" by the singer as an interpretive emphasis.

· *der meine* vs. *mich mit sich*: a major contrast—K's open "*e*," "*ei*" diphthong, and neutral vowel ending, as against F's three consecutive little "*i*" words with atonic endings, and on the long note, K's "*ei*" vs. F.'s "*mit*."

· *glaube* vs. *ihm*: a sonorous diphthong rounded off by its "*u*" against yet another "*i*"-word. To be as even-handed as possible: in the Italian, each of these last two examples are also on an "*i*"—the second syllable of "*trascina*" and the first of "*mio*," on these longer notes. Yet the singing effect is quite different, with the first leading into the sounding "*n*" and the second morphing into "*o*."

· *furchtbare* vs. *erbittliche*: F. wins on meaning, but at the cost of a particularly shallow and pecky-sounding series of syllables—"*furchtbare*" fills out these longer-held notes much better, building into the fermata on D for the first syllable of "*Gott-heit*."

The pattern is unmistakable. Kalbeck attempts to mitigate the unsuitability of his native tongue for Italian music by selecting, when possible, words with a greater potential for rounded, open-throated sonority and continuity of sound, while Felsenstein pushes relentlessly toward bitten-off little units, usually sounded on some version of the closed "*i*" vowel and bound off by unvoiced consonants, tiring to the ear and unfriendly to any singer hoping to resound. It's part of a rejection of a rhetoric of musical and vocal fulfillment in favor of one of rasping speech. It continues into the opening bars of the *Credo* itself, where Verdi leads the singer to a sustained E-flat on the final syllable of "*simile a se*" ("like unto him"), knowing that any well-structured baritone voice will make a potent effect there with the Italian "*e*." Kalbeck gives the singer the second syllable of "*erzeugt*," which German baritones have rendered quite closed and dark (emphasizing the "o" of the "oi" diphthong), or open to the point of verging on "*erzeigt*," or somewhere between, depending on their techniques. Felsenstein sticks the voice with the second syllable of "*erschuf*," denying any possibility of an open sound. True, much depends on the singer. If Felsenstein's translation were sung by a Schwarz or Bohnen or Scheidl or Hotter or Schöffler, it would sound less snippy and more imposing. But of course he would not have chosen such a singer, and such singers would probably not have chosen the Komische Oper.

This inspection of minutiae of sense and sound may strike some readers as a picking of nits. But look at the density of them in this sliver of *Otello*, multiply by the length and breadth of the score, and consider the cumulative effect.

The goal of faithfulness to an original is admirable, but claims to the transmission of unaltered meaning fall in the same category as that of the transparent orchestra that just conveys The Music. Besides: faithfulness to which aspect of the original? Verdi created a musicodramatic entity of which Böito's text is an element. This entity is itself a text, which the Second Interpreters (singeractors, musicians, conductors, directors, designers) must bring to life. But in this and similar cases, another interpreter, the translator, is interposed between the First and Second—let's call him 1A. What is 1A's notion of faithfulness, of "authenticity?" Does he believe in the closest possible rendition of note-to-note denotative meanings, as Felsenstein professes? Or does he think a more figurative language, more loosely tied to the musical structures, is actually truer to the intended impact of the original? Or does he believe an eloquence of sound, the play of vocal color, a luring *away* from the effort to follow the verbal progression, is his highest responsibility? Does he want to bring the language into the here-and-now of the audience, or to pull the audience toward the there-and-then of the work?

The only "true," "authentic" *Otello* is an original-language one, and then only when powerfully performed by stylistically informed artists and received by an audience of more than casual acquaintance with it. Its verbal content, while important and deserving of meticulous attention, is far less crucial, dramatically, than the music and the stage action. In Felsenstein's time and place, the question of whether or not to translate was predetermined by a combination of Continental custom and his *Muskitheater* ambitions. For the loyalists in his audience, his translations undoubtedly achieved their just-the-facts storytelling aims much of the time, and kept them involved on that level. For us, the question has been rendered moot by the original-language-with-subtitles dodge, whereby we "follow" the performance by reading the jottings of Second Interpreter 1B, the Titleist. I'm loath to say it, but in some instances, a good singing translation might well be preferred to that.

25. Among innumerable examples from the '00s through the '50s (after which original-language performance began to penetrate the local cultures, first on recordings, and soon after in the theatres), I'll mention just a few drawn from the works represented in the Felsenstein Edition: Meta Seinemeyer or Frida Leider in the Countess's arias, and the latter in Donna Anna's *Rache Arie*; Torsten Ralf in Otello's excerpts, with Tiana Lemnitz in the Act I duet, and the Melchior *Otello* extracts discussed earlier; Joseph Schwarz in Iago's *Credo* (and for an interesting contrast between two more "modern" baritones, you might try the same aria with Hotter—one of his best early-prime discs—and Mathieu Ahlersmeyer, a powerful "character baritone" who later sang the Count with

Felsenstein); Lotte Lehmann in the Willow Song; Richard Tauber in Hoffmann's arias, Josef Metternich in Dappertutto's, and Lehmann or Sena Jurinac in Antonia's song. On the many recordings of complete or condensed operas taken from German radio transmissions from the '30s and through the '50s, you can encounter dozens of singers who show that much of the tonal beauty, sustained line, and dramatic eloquence asked for by the music can be maintained despite the linguistic unease and the occasional brutal outburst. A case in point is the *Traviata* (Berlin, 1942) with Cebotari, Rosvaenge, and Schlusnus. Cebotari is a thrilling and touching Violetta, and Schlusnus a lyrical paragon of a Germont. Rosvaenge was unquestionably one of the important singers of the interwar and wartime period, a long-ranged essentially lyric tenor with enough ring and thrust to fulfill spinto and *Jugendlich* roles. The honing of his *"i"* and closed *"e"* vowels was especially sharp—he seems to have used them to center the voice, keep it *schlank*, and this tendency was becoming exaggerated around this time, as the voice threatened to thicken. As Alfredo, he displays his mastery of line, of dynamic and timbral control, in the *"Un di, felice," "De miei bollenti,"* and *"Parigi, o cara"* (their German equivalents), but in the accusation scene resorts to unmusical ranting of a disturbingly military quality.

26. Here are particulars on the films contained in the Edition, followed by notations on matters discussed in the main text. These are selective credits, especially on the technical side. For complete information, see the listings and essays in the Edition. In chronological order:

- Beethoven: *Fidelio*. Black and white film, 1956. Felsenstein, dir., scenario by Felsenstein in collaboration with Hanns Eisler. Vienna Symphony and Vienna State Opera Chorus, Fritz Lehmann, cond. Separate acting and singing casts for most roles, Claude Nollier (Leonore) being the most prominent of the actors, and Magda László (Leonore), Richard Holm (Florestan, singing and acting), and Heinz Rehfuss the most important of the singers. Not a K.O. production.

- Janáček: *Das Schlaue Füchslein* (The Cunning Little Vixen). Studio production adapted from the K.O. staging. Black and white, 1965. Felsenstein, dir.; Rudolf Heinrich, des.; K.O. orchestra and chorus, Vaçlav Neumann, cond. Irmgard Arnold (Vixen), Rudolf Asmus (Forester), Manfred Hopp (Fox), Herbert Rössler (Harasta), Werner Enders (Dog and School Master), et al.

- Mozart: *Don Giovanni*. Live transmission from the Komische Oper. Black and white, 1966. Felsenstein, dir.; Reinhart Zimmermann and Sylta-Maria Busse, des.; K.O. orch. and chor., Zdeněk Kösler, cond. Klara Barlow (Anna), Any Schlemm (Elvira), György Melis (Giovanni), Asmus (Leporello), et al.

- Verdi: *Otello*. Studio production adapted from the K.O. staging. Color, 1969. Felsenstein, dir.; Heinrich and Helga Scherff, des.; K.O. orch. and chor., Kurt Masur, cond. Christa Noack (Desdemona), Hanns Nocker (Otello), Vladimir Bauer (Iago), et al.

- Offenbach: *Hoffmanns Erzählungen* (The Tales of Hoffmann). Studio production adapted from the K.O. staging. Color, 1970. Felsenstein, dir.; Heinrich and Scherff, des.; K.O. orch. and chor., Karl-Fritz Voigtmann, cond. Melitta Muszely (Stella/ Olympia/Antonia/Giulietta), Nocker (Hoffmann), Asmus (Lindorf/Coppélius/Dr. Miracle/Dappertutto), Enders (Andreas/Cochenille/Franz/Pitichinaccio), et al.

- Offenbach: *Ritter Blaubart* (Bluebeard). Studio production adapted from the K.O. staging. Color, 1973. Felsenstein, dir.; Wilfried Werz/Paul Lehmann and Scherff, des.; K.O. orch. and chor., Voigtmann, cond. Schlemm (Boulotte), Nocker (Bluebeard), Enders (King Bobèche), Asmus (Popolani), et al.

- Mozart: *Die Hochzeit des Figaro* (The Marriage of Figaro). Live transmission from the Komische Opera. Color, 1976. Felsenstein, dir.; Reinhard Zimmermann and Eleonore Kleiber, des.; K.O. orch. and chor., Geza Oberfrank, cond. Magdalena Falewicz

(Countess), Ursula Reinhardt-Kiss (Susanna), Jószef Dene (Figaro), Uwe Kreyssig (Count), Asmus (Bartolo), et al.

Even the least recommendable of these videos (those would be the *Fidelio* and the *Don Giovanni*, and I won't comment on them further) serve a historical documentation function with respect to singers, experimentation with onscreen opera, Germanic text literalism (if you're tired of appoggiaturas and ornaments and of dallying recitatives in Mozart, these readings will correct that, and then some), and other matters of time-and-place interest. In all of them there are ideas about scenes and characters that, whether convincingly carried through or not, will intrigue anyone concerned with operatic interpretation. In lieu of a thorough critical examination of all of them (I know of none), I will rest my case here with some attention to the two I find most recommendable (*Vixen* and *Otello*), along with a few additional observations on performance.

Vixen: This famous production premiered in 1956; the filming was done just after its last repetition, while the K.O. was closed for restoration. Though it bears its age visually and aurally despite the expert technical refreshening, it is perhaps the most consistently successful of all these films as a realization of Felsenstein's stated goals. It introduces us to the ensemble feel of all the company's work, put to the best possible use: the tiniest roles as thoroughly studied and meticulously rendered as the leads, the forest-creature pantomiming intimately observed and accurately executed, the performers all at home with one another. It also acquaints us with several of Felsenstein's favorite performers, including three who had participated in every repetition of the production's run: soprano Irmgard Arnold, bass-baritone Rudolf Asmus, and character tenor Werner Enders. The evocation of life on the forest floor is lovely; indeed, the animals fare better than the humans in character roles, whose exaggerated mug shots are held well past shelf life. In the title role, Arnold gives a behaviorally remarkable performance, and Asmus is splendid as The Forester. All the good acting work, however, suffers at points from the general Felsenstein flaw of showing it all, all the time. Even in old two-dimensional black and white, Heinrich's sets and costumes (here quite naturalistic) retain some of the magic they must have summoned in the theatre, with their muted colors, dappled lighting, and the depth of the stage. Vocally, Arnold is an expressive singeractress, but the incessant pressing on the brassy lower-middle conversational range is clearly frazzling the balance of her voice. She was, right around this time, taking on Violetta—hard to imagine how that worked. Asmus is, as usual, pleasurable to hear, and the Harasta, Herbert Rössler, sounds good in his song. Neumann and the K.O. orchestra do involved, detailed work and play well. A spot comparison with Neumann's Prague recording of a few years earlier shows these same virtues, plus greater warmth and relaxation—something also true of Asmus, who is singing there in the original language (his own) and, one suspects, with rather more leeway to sing. The difference in recording venues is surely responsible in part for the difference in sound.

Otello: Here is the greatest of all the challenges Felsenstein took on—not much of the *comique* about *Otello*, and for all its adaptability to the modern sensibility, it is also inescapably an E-19 grand opera. In the theatre, Felsenstein extended the apron out over the pit to give the K.O.'s relatively small stage more depth, and Heinrich used lots of wood in his sets to help launch voices into the auditorium. The production was ten years old by the time it was adapted for film, and was considerably reworked for that medium. (Among other things, Felsenstein had to overcome his aversion to what he saw as the falsifications of color, preferring the grittiness and the light-and-shadow contrasts of black-and-white. Perhaps he should have been among the film noir emigrés.) It's not hard to see why Koegler was bowled over by Act I. The opening storm sequence must have made a terrific impact. Instead of trying to depict its tempest scenically, Felsenstein aimed to show its effect on The People. He took his chorus to a wind tunnel to practice fighting the fearsome gale. On camera, we're much too close to all their synchronized responses, whose style was old-fashioned even then: The People throw up their hands, gape, bug their eyes, fall down and struggle up, etc. However, they do so with wonderful discipline and willingness, and as their work meshes with Masur's drive through the scene and with the expert shot selections and editing rhythms, the grip of the work starts to take hold despite laughable moments. To walk into an opera house in 1959 and be blindsided by this, at theatre-seat distance, must have been stunning. The little Iago/ Roderigo scene is wonderful, closed-in and intense, better-acted than I've ever seen it in either opera or play. "*Fuoco di gioia*" is a tour de force, the ensemble action filled out with little relationship scenarios and the expert camera tracking coming close to convincing us that the aural is actually giving birth to the visual. The Brindisi and fight are also beautifully built to Otello's second entrance (though inebriation, real and feigned, is too much too soon), and when Otello and Desdemona are left alone, their simple and deep pantomiming over the immortal cello introduction to the love duet gives us the second "unreservedly believable" moment of the act. I will not detail the rest of the performance. In sum, the Otello/Desdemona relationship plays well, which means that in acting terms it fills its quota of pity and terror. The Iago is an alert, talented performer, but carries the greatest burden of Felsenstein's silent-movie closeups and mandated illustrative reactions of face and body. The Emilia, Cassio, and Roderigo are all excellent, vocally and theatrically. The video staging falls to pieces, literally, in the Act III concertato (interior monologue closeups and serial floating heads), and the great scene is ruined. Act IV is movingly enacted.

Masur and the K.O. band are tremendous. The reading sweeps us through with impetus, pointed instrumental commentary, and a perfectly gauged tension that eases, but never relaxes, for the lyrical tenderness of the love duet or the inner suspense of "*Dio mi potevi.*" Its tonal palette, though, is not one I associate with this conductor. Apart from the fact that this was recorded in the studio, not in the theatre with its partially covered pit, the audio restoration, worked up from aged and sometimes damaged materials, has striven for clarity, "brilliance," and "vividness." Surely the live performance had more warmth and weight.

And the singing? The title role is taken by Felsenstein's longtime *primo tenore assoluto*, Hanns Nocker. Felsenstein loved him, and why not?—a sturdy tenor voice of sufficient range and listenable quality that could navigate roles from Paisiello to Offenbach to Verdi, whose owner was willing to pledge himself to F.'s way of working! Within the limits of Felsenstein's "no interpretation" approach, his Otello is an impressive achievement. It doesn't have all the line or tonal expansion of a great voicing, but it meets the proclamatory challenges and brings effective dynamic control to the love duet and death scene. As the vocal expression of a committed physical characterization, it ranks with Asmus's *Hoffmann* villains as the closest we come on these films to a meld of operatic with music theatre satisfactions. One wishes the same could be said for Christa Noack, an honest and sensitive actress whose visual performance is truly lifelike and touching, but whose pale lyric soprano, while never ugly, is really sufficient for only the quieter midrange moments of the music. As Iago, Bauer shows a light baritone of utterly nondescript quality, a voice one might cast as Dancaïro or in a character part like The Doctor in *Wozzeck*. He uses it effectively in recitative passages and shirks nothing—he's in there pitching with the hiss-the-words-and-forget-the-voice commandment—but the instrument just doesn't meet the music. Even on film, the Truth of Verdi would have to include a soprano and baritone of basic Verdian command.

For all its weaknesses, this performance does burrow into a masterpiece, and leaves its mark.

Of the remaining films, the *Hoffmann* is the most interesting. In many ways, the work was a natural for Felsenstein and his designers, with their inborn understanding of the source materials and their love of the grotesque, very brilliantly realized by Heinrich (sets) and Scherff (costumes) and their filmic collaborators. Every scene has captivating atmosphere, every character a sharp visual profile. When Koegler entered his *Hoffmann* protest eleven years earlier, he professed admiration for Felsenstein's redaction, but one of the reasons he wasn't carried away by the music is that lots of it is missing, and much of the continuity here has the start-and-stop feel of a play that suddenly switches into a hypereality with the music. At times we wish some experienced theatre musician of the kind we often call hack (Ernest Guiraud, for instance) would come along and write some well-designed recitatives. The big musicological findings on *Hoffmann* lay just ahead. We still haven't figured out how to best make use of them, but Felsenstein was trying to get back to *comique* dimensions, and did get The Muse in on the act, which was an innovation at the time. Nocker's well-fed physique and *tabula rasa* face, which worked out well for Felsenstein's ideas about Otello, are less suited to Hoffmann, and while he carries out his tasks well enough, who the fellow is and what he wants remains vague. Muszely, Felsenstein's Violetta in Hamburg, isn't glamourous of face or voice, but she's a capable artist who succeeds "beyond her means" with her formidable assignment. Vocally best suited to Antonia, she is surprisingly interesting as Giulietta. Asmus is arresting in all his roles, and there is fine work by several supporting players—the Crespel, Andrej Wroblewski, is about the best I've seen, and here is Bauer well cast as a striking Spalanzani.

To fathom the tremendous success of the *Bluebeard* production (29 years in K.O. repertory, visits to many other important stages, 369 performances in total, all highly acclaimed) will require a great deal more investigation than I have found an appetite for. The score is pleasant but never captivating—around Offenbach's twelfth best, I should judge, among his operettas. The wordplay is alleged to be witty and the satire keen, but it all seems pretty obvious to me, and the production (handsome to look at) pushes it relentlessly in our faces. The Edition book's essay by Dr. Georg Mielke, the TV director and screenwriter, will get you started on what they were up to, but I suspect you had to be there, then, and of a certain politico/theatrical inclination. Schlemm and Nocker locate some sly moments, and Asmus is professional as always, but since the characters don't develop, the performers have nowhere to go.

The *Figaro* was the last of Felsenstein's K.O. productions, and the filming was done after his death. I've quite enjoyed watching it, partly because it is the most consistently well sung of these videos, but also because the playing seems somewhat freer. Falewicz, the Countess, finds a moving interiority in both her arias, and the Susanna, Reinhardt-Kiss, seems in touch in "*Deh, vieni*"—in both cases, getting under the skin instead of showing us everything. Asmus is expert and entertaining. During the overture, the camera takes us around the gorgeously restored old K.O. auditorium. That does more for the music, and our anticipation of the event, than any staging.

I can't help reflecting on the music-theatre fates of some of the K.O.'s good voices. A few of the more important instruments belong to short-timers or guests, like the Hungarian baritone György Melis and the American soprano Klara Barlow (and odd that two Americans, Barlow and John Moulson, brother of Robert, creator of Floyd's Lennie, found themselves in East Berlin in the 1960s). But I'm thinking of K.O. regulars, who dedicated themselves over extended periods to the company's system of role preparation, rehearsal, and performance. In terms of technique, I detect two patterns: among the men, one of the lighter engagement with support that the quest for a "natural" conversational singing level tends to encourage, and which adversely affects the firmness and core of a voice; among the women, the resort to a lower-middle mix that the same quest brings out, especially among lighter voices trying to punch the sound out into the auditorium, and which tends to limit access to the top. (The effects of Felsenstein's preferences with respect to the German language and its interpretive uses on voices of all types have already been suggested.) Thus, both Nocker and Asmus have voices of strong format and good quality, and both deal well with the adjustments of Felsenstein's approach—Asmus is, in fact, a master of parlando shadings. But in the more excitable moments of his Leporello or, more damagingly, in his one test of long-lined, legato singing (the "*Scintille, diamant*" in *Hoffmann*), his warm tone turns quivery. No doubt he would have dispatched Lindorf's couplets brilliantly had they not been cut. Nocker sounds capable of a good Hoffmann. To achieve it, however, he would have to pay a great deal more attention to suppleness of line and arc of phrase, and find some other way of negotiating ascending passages than simply barging through. In a couple of Puccini arias that can be heard online, his top is secure and the lower octave a shuddery mess. Among the women, the very talented Arnold is Exhibit A (that lower-middle adjustment, almost a "belt mix," has projective strength and verbal clarity, but there's no way it can release into a full, attractive top), but the equally gifted Schlemm isn't far behind: though she manages Bulotte quite cleverly, her Elvira is harsh and ungainly. She sounds markedly better on away-from-K.O. recordings. The same distortions of balance turn up to lesser degrees in the Zerlina and the Cherubino, especially in recitative.

Now, I have no way of knowing what might have become of these voices if there had not been a K.O. and a Felsenstein, or what outside advice they were getting while working there. None of them has anything to apologize for in terms of music-theatre artistic achievement. But patterns are patterns, and one can't help but wonder how much more these fine voices might have shown with guidance that, however strong its theatrical bent, might at least not have put tonal beauty, rubato, and technical balance under erasure.

To conclude, a few fidelity-to-text notes. I am not disputing all of these departures, some of which may have had purely practical causation, and I note them only in the light of Felsenstein's claims to authenticity. I omit "standard" cuts, such as the Leporello/ Zerlina scene, the *Otello* ballet, or the arias for Basilio and Marcellina.

- In *Don Giovanni*, "Ah, pietà signori miei" is cut. This not only banishes a good number, but makes Leporello's escape in II, 2 even more difficult to play credibly.

- In *Vixen*, the important role of The Fox is transposed from mezzo-soprano to tenor (to be more visually "real"? to avoid suggestion of same-sex romance?). In Handel or Monteverdi there are plausible arguments for such transposition. Here, the practice only pushes the scenes of flirting and wooing toward operetta routine.

- In *Otello*, the Act II scene of Desdemona receiving the loving tributes of The People is hacked off at the stump. We lose the children with their mandolin song, the mariners with their pearls and corals, the women scattering fronds and flowers, and the full ensemble at the close. I am told that this used to be a standard cut in German houses, but from the Discloser of the "true *Otello* of Verdi and Boito," it's particularly puzzling.

- In *Nozze di Figaro*, the order of the Act IV arias for Figaro and Susanna is reversed. Da Ponte and Mozart's story is not quite the one Felsenstein wants to tell.

- There is no "true" *Hoffmann*. This one has the least music of any I know. I have not consulted the other Offenbach score, *Barbe-Bleu*, or any scholarly exegesis on it, so I can't comment on that adaptation.

27. See: Paul Schmidt, ed.: *Meyerhold at Work* (Carcanet New Press Ltd., Manchester, 1981; originally published by Univ. of Texas Press, 1980). Schmidt was a distinguished theatre scholar, author of highly regarded translations of Chekhov and others, and an occasional actor. His book comprises an edifying selection of Meyerhold's production notes, letters to and from collaborators and important cultural figures (e.g., Ilya Eherenburg, Boris Pasternak), bits of memoir (by Sergei Eisenstein, the actors Ilya Ilyinsky and Mikhail Sadovsky, and others), and more fascinating material. Each of its seven thematically grouped sections opens with a concise and pointed introduction by Schmidt, who also contributes many of the translations.

28. See Hans-Thies Lehmann: *Postdramatic Theatre* (Routledge, 2006, Karen Jürs-Munby, trans. & Introduction; first published, in German, by Verlag der Autoren, Frankfurt-am-Rhein, 1999). Lehmann coined the term "postdramatic," and his presentation of the background and manifestations of the kinds of theatre he groups under it is clear and through. Some of his concepts will figure in the main-text discussion.

29. I don't object to taking sides, but Schmidt is rather sneaky about it: Stanislavski thought "only" this, whereas Meyerhold "knew" that; the concept of "character" arises from "19th Century bourgeois individualism"; Stanislavskian "realism" has somehow been hegemonic for several generations, yet is "untenable," etc. There are also some rather breathtaking pronouncements that can slip past because they're so appealing to theater lovers: "To believe in books is to believe in things that last; to believe in theatre is to know better." I understand what he's getting at, but gosh—as to Statement One, some things do last, and I do believe in them, since they're there, and as to Statement Two, it once was true of theatre, but not anymore—it's mostly virtual now, not here but in the Cloud, and I don't quite believe in it. Schmidt is really trying to devalorize those classic texts, so that it will be O.K. for directors to "cross them with new inscriptions." *Meyerhold at Work* is a valuable book, but the Introduction should be read advisedly.

30. See Schmidt, Chapter V, as well as the letters to Vissarion Shebalin (pp. 192-198), the music director for Meyerhold's production of *Camille*.

31. These productions are described in Braun (see n. 32 and 33, below), with extra cast details taken from Levik, *Memoirs*, pp. 458-460. Litvinne I have already discussed. Cherkasskaya would have been a soprano Brangäne, as indicated by the score. Her recording of Lisa's Act II romance in *The Queen of Spades* indicates a pure, centered voice with a strongly etched line; Levik recalls "a beautiful, rich voice with an almost mezzo-soprano fullness in the middle." Yershov was, by all accounts as well as the evidence of his recordings, the greatest of the Russian dramatic tenors, fully comparable with the best Western singers of that category, and apparently a powerful actor as well. Braun states that Yershov later sang at Bayreuth, but this is inaccurate. The voluminous *cantante* voice of Kastorsky must have made for an eloquent Marke. Levik is not high on the Meyerhold opera productions: "I was unable to see any musicality in Meyerhold's productions . . . [he] attempted to establish on the stage, the impressionism advocated and employed by him in the straight theatre but his method got in the way of his intentions"—etc. It's interesting that Levik refers to Meyerhold's style at that time as "impressionism"—not a manner most writers associate with him, and possibly just Levik's way of saying it wasn't realistic. He does however, recognize him as a reformer, about whom "real opera lovers were forced to think," and that while such efforts might not work, "one must have a go." Both he and Braun report that after the brief *Boris* encounter, Chaliapin declined to work with Meyerhold in Dargomizhsky's *The Stone Guest* (he would have sung Leporello). Of course, Levik was a singer, and on the other side of most of these aesthetic, singing-acting debates from Meyerhold. Possibly that's why I tend to trust his P.O.V. and his unacademic, sometimes unpolished voice.

32. See Edward Braun: *Meyerhold on Theatre*, Hill and Wang, N.Y. 1969, the cornerstone collection of Meyerholdiana in English, with informative critical commentary by Braun that carries us through the life and career. The *Tristan* essay occupies pp. 90-98, but do not overlook Braun's introduction to the section (pp. 75 ff.), which summarizes all of Meyerhold's operatic work for the Imperial Theatres.

33. The essay on *The Queen of Spades* is in Braun, pp. 278-89.

34. See Jon Whitmore: *Directing Postmodern Theatre*, Univ. of Michigan Press, 1994. So far as I can ascertain, Whitmore's career has been entirely within academia, as teacher and director early on, administrator more recently. His main interest, stated at the outset, is

in "... how theories can be applied to a problem or how theories can be used to improve the actual practice of a profession."

35. The reviews consulted on the Castorf *Ring* are: Hugo Shirley (*Opera*, Oct. 2013); Jeffrey A. Leipsic (*Opera News*, Nov. 2013); Martin Kettle (*The Guardian* online, July 28, Aug. 1, and Aug. 2, 2013); Anthony Tommasini, *NYT*, Aug. 1, 2013; Per-Erik Skramstad, *wagneropera. net*, n.d.); Shirley Apthorp, *Financial Times* online, Aug. 2, 2013; Alex Ross, *The New Yorker*, Aug. 26, 2013; "J.J." (James Jorden), *parterrebox.com*, Aug. 23, 24, 26, and 29, 2013; Christine Lemke-Matweg, *zeitonline*, Aug. 1, 2013; Mike Roddy at *classicalite.com*, Aug. 2, 2013; Clive Paget at LIMELIGHT, July 31, 2013; and an interview with Castorf by Hans Christof von Bock on *Deutsche Welle*, July 24, 2013. I will leave it to readers to decide how much critical weight should be given to the online fan sites vis-à-vis the established professional sources. At the least, they represent the real-time reactions of engaged opera lovers, and in this case their efforts to wrestle with what Castorf is up to result in a more mixed response to the confusion he has created. In the von Bock interview, Castorf expressed his wish to present his *Ring*stuff in montage, rather than the pokey linear progression of Wagner's libretto and score. As Skramstad points out, that takes us back to Eisenstein. And Eisenstein takes us back to Meyerhold, of whom Eisenstein was a student and life-long admirer. It seems quite a distance from Meyerhold's rewrites of *Queen of Spades* to Castorf's dismemberment of the *Ring*—but slippery-slopewise, it's not, and here we are at the bottom.

36. These quotes are all from the portrait of Castorf on the Goethe Institut website. This substantial and thoughtful entry, signed by Till Briegleb, is generally admiring of Castorf and the Volksbühne, though Briegleb also notes that "In recent years, his work seems to have increasingly run out of control."

37. To get a sense of what I mean here, you might compare two modern performances of the next scene (the "Cherry Duet," the score's best-known excerpt)with one or all of several earlier ones. The modern versions are those of Pavarotti with Freni (on the complete recording conducted by Gavazzeni) and Alagna with Gheorghiu (from a duet disc), all in youthful prime condition. The older ones are: Lucrezia Bori/Miguel Fleta; Rosetta Pampanini/Dino Borgioli; Mafalda Favero/Tito Schipa; Magda Olivero/Ferruccio Tagliavini; Pia Tassinari/Tagliavini (on the complete recording conducted by Mascagni); and Rosina Carteri/Cesare Valletti (on a RAI broadcast complete performance conducted by Vittorio Gui). Of these, the Bori/Fleta is a late acoustical, and offers only the latter half of the scene, beginning with Fritz's "*Tutto tace.*" The rest are electrical and complete, starting with "*Suzel, buon dí.*"

   Now, there is nothing to quibble over in the luscious singing of Freni and Pavarotti, and Gheorghiu and Alagna are easy listening, too. All these voices have the rounded warmth that is characteristic of the best of postwar Mediterranean singing, and they benefit from modern stereo recording. Among the older performances, the Bori/Fleta is the most distinctively different from the more recent ones, and in some ways my favorite. The other sopranos, via different routes and at different points, all succeed in suggesting through inflection Suzel's youthfulness and an innocent shyness of expression that does not always conceal the beginnings of feminine guile—an evocation of girlhood out of fashion now, but not so then. Bori conveys this in the very sound of her voice, a pure, centered timbre that would strike us as not yet mature were it not for the light but firm Lower-Family grounding at the bottom, and some surprising strength, with a touch more movement in the tone, as the voice ascends, both of which signal the emerging woman. Bori also recorded Suzel's Act 1 aria, "*Son pochi fiori,*" where the same qualities are evident, the song's incipient sentimentality forestalled by an utter naturalness of expression. And in the duet, she is partnered by Fleta, whose voice is of lyrical guidance but *spinto* format. While all these tenors have means of controlling the ascending *pp* phrases at the end of the scene prettily, Fleta and Borgioli are the ones most able to achieve the effect of a strong sound shaved back under perfect control—the tensile mezza-voce.

Of these older performances, the Favero/Schipa version is the most prized by connoisseurs. Favero is surely delightful, and Schipa, as was his wont, is ingenious in engaging us with the immediacy of his *pronuncia*, intimacy of tone, and sure guidance of the line. At the time of recording, though, his always-slender voice had withered close to the ultimate acceptable dryness, and if we want a Fritz of *leggiero* format, Valletti offers more freshness and color. In all these pairings, we hear bright, young tone and manner from the women (with a prominence of vibrato from Olivero and Pampanini that won't be to all tastes), a variety of expression among the tenors, and inimitable qualities in the exchanges of both partners that are marks of singers who "live in the style," and so are free to vary it in subtle but distinctive ways.

PART V

A REVIEW AND
SOME UPDATES

Perhaps it is misleading to call the following essay a "review," since it luxuriates in an allotment of space never granted to newspaper or magazine pieces so designated, is subject to no editorial restrictions but my own, and is written against no deadline but my own. But as distinct from my earlier commentaries on aspects of productions and performance, it tries to do what reviews are meant to do: consider all elements of a performance event, prioritize these elements in accordance with the reviewer's beliefs, and measure them—and the effect as a whole—against the standards he or she has developed. And to report accurately, give as truthful an account of the event as possible, a matter of both journalistic and critical ethics. The subject has been selected over other events that have presented themselves toward the end of my process on the book for its convenience in extending discussions already begun with respect to auteurship, radically altered views on the integrity of a "work," the upending of opera's synaesthetic balance, and the remarkable extent to which these have won acceptance as a matter of course.

1

PRINCE IGOR AT
THE MET

(Feb. 24, 2014)

I f we were to search among works of the past for the opera most suited to
auteurial production, *Prince Igor* might well be it. Left far from finished
by its composer and already spruced up by others to bring it to performable condition, it has always seemed a misshapen beast, with head far out of
proportion to rump, even as its musical and theatrical blandishments have
earned it an honored place in the Russian canon. With its many pages of
unpublished, unperformed materials, some of them shifted back and forth
between this and other works, constituting a rich soil for musicological till-
ing ever since Pavel Lamm's intrepid spadework in the 1940s, it has always
posed legitimate questions of inclusion, redaction, and sequence beyond
the standard performing edition of 1890. Of course, the fashioners of that edition (principally, Rimsky-Korsakov and Glazounov) were themselves highly
accomplished composers, close friends and colleagues of Borodin's with an
intimate knowledge of the music as it came from his pen and a more complete
understanding of his dreams for it, a more passionate concern for their shared
project for Russian opera and music, than anyone outside their famous little
circle can possibly have had from that day to this. So a reluctance to replace
their decisions with those of latterday interpreters and scholars, and a dash
of humility about it all, might behoove us. Still, if in the light of fresh discoveries and with our much longer perspective, it seems that the piece might
actually be helped—made more satisfying and powerful—there is no artistic
excuse for not trying to do so and no reason that a smart, talented director

should not contribute to the effort. If there were ever a case for a guiding auteurial hand, this would be it.

The hand in this instance belongs to Dmitri Tcherniakov, and he scored a hit. His Misshapen Beast 2.0 sold the house out and generated an astoundingly acquiescent critical (well, that's not the word) response of a sort you'd expect from collaborationists greeting an occupying force.[1] That some thoughtful people might find things to like in his work is not in itself terribly disconcerting. But that this takedown of a production and sadsack performance should stir not a whiff of dissent, not a scrap of controversy, is a mark of a dead artform.

One depressing aspect of this unanimous acclamation is, yet again, its failure to characterize the singing, measure its impact, or demonstrate any familiarity with the standards by which to evaluate it at one of the world's great opera houses, or to even acknowledge it as the primary "sign system" an opera is supposed to be ensnaring us in. And though *Prince Igor* has a wealth of orchestral vitality and color, ample theatricality, an outrageously entertaining choral dance episode, and more "action" than it's often given credit for, it is very much a singer's opera. Borodin was a captivating melodist with a fine feel for vocal setting that would bring out the best in characteristic Russian voice types and choral groupings. He followed the song-based path marked out by Glinka and the Dargomizhsky of *Russalka* and the Romances, not the speech-based one Dargomizhsky took in his *Stone Guest* or that Mussorgsky struggled along in parts of his great operas and all of his not-great ones. Borodin was writing a numbers grand opera for bigtime singers, and for it to approach consummation, it must be met on those terms. So I'm going to give performance pride of place, with all the alluring matters pertaining to edition and production to follow. There was a time when the following sixteen paragraphs, and the review, would have ended like this: "Maestro Noseda conducted with admirable attention to the score's exotic colorations, if not always to the proper apportionment of its dramatic weights and tempi. The eccentric staging and décor were by Dmitri Tcherniakov." I'll try to do better than that. But singing and playing first, and the ear before the eye.

Those of us who love the recordings that take us back almost to the time of *Igor*'s premiere dream bootless dreams of legendary casts—of Yuzhina or Cherkasskaya (or, for that matter, Litvinne) as Yaroslavna, of a contralto like Onegin for Konchakovna, of Sobinov or Smirnov as Vladimir, perhaps Baklanoff or the Latvian Josef Schwarz as Igor, Chaliapin as Galitzky and some thunderous bass with plangent low notes (like Sibiriakov) for Konchak. We muse on the presence of Amato and Didur in the only previous Met presentation, or on the dozens of international artists who could have met the requirements of these roles in the intervening decades. But to give us easily available comparisons and lessen the proportion of mind's-ear reconstruction, I will restrict recorded references to postwar singers. Two recordings will make repeated appearances throughout the review. One is the 1951 Bolshoi performance led by Alexander Melik-Pashayev, in which every role is taken by a singer who is either arguably or inarguably the best among all those considered. The other is the DVD of a 1998 Maryinsky performance under Gergiev, populated by singers who have become thoroughly familiar to us in recent seasons; it also represents contrasting choices of edition and, especially, production "concept." I will supplement these with references to other artists who can be heard in modern recorded sound, with preference to those I have heard in person. Among them, these should give us a good sense of where the bar might reasonably be set for these roles in a major international house.[2]

The four principal male roles of *Prince Igor* are not better written or more important than the two female ones, but they contain the music that has attracted the most attention from outstanding singers, thus becoming familiar and so creating expectations. Borodin, acting as his own librettist, based his opera on a poetic epic, the anonymous *Song of Igor's Campaign*, c. 1187,[*] and on a scenario drawn up from it by Vladimir Stassov. Since he was writing to the epic scale, the vocal expectations are first of all of the "heavy," archetypal sort we want to be "copiously fulfilled." But it was also Borodin's considerable achievement to vividly personalize these characters in his words and music, cutting Galitzky from whole cloth and tailoring the others from the fragmentary portraits found in his source. They require artists who can take over the stage with both voice and personality. Since it's the low-voiced parts that, aside from the Polovtsian Dances, boast the opera's most famous excerpts, I'll start with them.

Prince Galitzky and Khan Konchak are the twin antagonists of *Igor*, one undermining our hero on the home front, the other opposing, then trying to recruit him, on the distant battlefield. Both roles are relatively short (Konchak

---

[*] See *The Song of Igor's Campaign*, Vladimir Nabokov, trans. (Vintage, N.Y., 1960). My understanding of the epic itself and of its relation to historical events is based largely on the extensive commentary that accompanies Nabokov's translation, and on G.P. Fedotov's *The Russian Religious Mind/Kievan Christianity: the 10th to the 13th Centuries* (Harper Torchbooks, N.Y. 1960, originally published by Harvard Univ. Press, 1946), especially Chaps. X and XI, "The Ancient Chroniclers" and "The Tale of Igor's Campaign." The epic is considered a foundational document of Russian literature, sometimes compared to the *Chanson de Roland* or the *Nibelungenlied* in other national literatures, and bears many characteristics of oral tradition.

especially so when Act III is omitted*) but rich; it's crucial that they make indelible impressions. Galitzky, unmentioned in the epic, is a remarkable act of imagination on Borodin's part. It's helpful to understand the relationships. Yaroslavna (Euphrosyne in the poem) is Igor's second wife, daughter of Prince Yaroslav of Galich; their union joined two of Kievan Russia's important houses. Vladimir, historically only twelve years old at the time of the campaign (1185), is Igor's son by his first wife. Borodin, whom we would nowadays term a strong womens' rights advocate, thought about the perilous predicament of the princess left behind to preside over the little court in Putivl, and by inventing Galitzky, a dissolute, ambitious brother of Yaroslavna's apparently banished from his home court into the care of the upstanding Igor, was able to create not only a rapacious bully with a certain craftiness and a famous song, but the heart-rending little chorus of pleading for the defenseless women of the court, the fine confrontation between Galitzky and Yaroslavna, and the dramatic tensions of potential usurpation. The role is written for a powerful high bass with the ability both to dominate with declamatory utterance and to shade a sustained line in his upper range. All the important effects of his writing—the forte E-naturals, Fs (even an F-sharp and touched-on G-flats) of carousing or defiance, the sensuous *piano* phrases of the B section of his song, the mocking and wheedling ones of his scene with Yaroslavna—lie near the upper range limit. Yet this is a bass role, not a baritone.

Borodin did not have to start quite from scratch with Konchak, who is sketched in the poem. He is certainly fierce, and turns particularly so in his Act III aria. But he is also politically shrewd and endowed with an opportunistic bonhomie, like an LBJ of the steppes.† He is meant for another powerful

---

* All references in this review to page and act numbers, and to the sequence of scenes, are based on the full score published by M.P. Belaieff, Leipzig, in 1890. Departures from that in the performances under review will be noted where relevant to the discussion. A score based on the recent Maryinsky version has apparently been published in Russia, but I have not seen it. I am unaware of any plans to publish one based on the Met's version. Although for convenience I will continue to refer to the standard version as "Belaieff," I think it's important to remember that it is the "Three Composers" or "Borodin and Friends" edition, while the Met's is the "One Composer, a Director, and a Conductor" version.

† In the poem and in Act III of the opera, Konchak is contrasted with the utterly undiplomatic Khan Gzak, who has ravaged Putivl. After Igor's escape with Ovlur, the other khans want to kill Vladimir and the Russian prisoners, but Konchak opts for the marriage of Vladimir to his daughter, Konchakovna. Historically, Kievan princes sometimes allied with khans in their quarrels with one another, and intermarriage did occur. Nabokov tells us (in his n. 856) that according to one of the main historical sources, the Ipatiev Chronicle, Vladimir and Konchakovna were indeed married during Vladimir's captivity, and that they and their child subsequently returned to Novgorod-Seversk in 1187 and were remarried according to the Christian rite. How this reconciles with Vladimir's date of birth (1173) is not addressed.

bass, but a low one. Except for a couple of optional high notes, the writing sits a step lower than Galitzky's, and its most memorable effects occur toward the bottom—the slow descent by half-steps to the low F as he describes his death-dealing sword, and the B-flat that ends the Act II aria, which is usually sustained beyond its notated value to cut like a buzz-saw through the jangle of the orchestral conclusion. These roles are often doubled on recordings, and sometimes in the theatre, but though a greatvoiced bass can score a coup thereby, it's a bad idea—the sonorities and personal auras should be distinct.

It is one of the joys of the old Bolshoi recording that these parts are taken by two of the pre-eminent Russian basses of the Soviet times, Alexander Pirogov and Mark Reizen. Both men had been before the public for over thirty years, their voices still potent and their artistry fully matured. Pirogov had recorded Galitzky's scene with Yaroslavna several years earlier (Dzerzhinskaya the soprano, bumpy of voice but touching at the scene's end), and by the time of the complete version there are touches of greying and loosening in the timbre. But everything's there. As exciting as the forte top notes are, it's the technical capacity of a voice of this size and weight to touch lightly and purl suggestively that is most impressive—the passage wherein he first finds Yaroslavna's anger sexually arousing, then insinuates that, so young and beautiful, she must have taken a lover in Igor's absence ("*Nu, polno, perestan*," etc.) could come from the lips of a memorable Don Giovanni.

Reizen's was one of the most complete bass instruments of the 20th Century. A voice of extraordinary length in both range and time of effective service, it embraced the right-column attributes of plush beauty and a dark softness, and the left-column ones of stonelike core and flashing brilliance. He could sustain cantilena in the best Italian fashion, but Konchak's writing has more to do with wordplay and shifts in pulse, and Reizen makes a banquet of the aria, which can be either a showpiece or an overextended bore. A shame that the third act is cut in the 1951 performance; he could have made us rethink its value.

In the opera, Igor himself is a much-ennobled, idealized version of the figure we meet in the *Song* or in history. There, he undertakes his ill-omened mission mostly out of envy of the earlier successes of his older cousin, Svyatoslav III, and upon his ignominious defeat and capture is chastised by the poet and chroniclers for the woe he brings upon his people. His escape and return is lauded only because for the Russian land to be without its prince "is [as] bad as it is for the body/to be without head." Borodin did not actually change this story line, but in keeping with the nationalistic tone of his opera, he raised Igor to heroic stature. The part is written for a dramatic baritone of noble timbre, projective thrust, and introspective colorings. In the extended, wide-ranging Act II monologue, "*Ni sna, ni odtikha*," which stands with those of Boris and Susanin as a brooding cornerstone of the Russian literature, he turns the poet's laments into self-recognition of darkest hue, and it is this scene that has lured important singers to an otherwise unremarkable role. The Bolshoi recording's Igor is Andrei Ivanov, whose voice has both the weight and bite in midrange and the command of the top (he is a splendid Rigoletto on a 1949 Moscow recording), as well as expressive comfort in the idiom, to stand as our exemplar, though he has some significant competition.

Vladimir is the most conventionally conceived of these roles, his function restricted to that of the ardent tenor required for the romantic subplot in what is otherwise an atypical E-19 conformation. He is, however, given some extremely pretty ardent-tenor music in his aria and duet with Konchakovna, and while the part seldom gets the benefit of a star's presence, a first-rate lyric tenor who can strike some sparks with his mezzo partner will be well rewarded. And as with all stage characters, an interesting interpreter can make a big difference. The role has been taken by all kinds of tenors, from white-voiced lyrics to spintos or even dramatics (e.g., David Poleri, who sang it in Chicago in 1959, or Vladimir Atlantov, who took it on a later Bolshoi recording), but responds best to strong, flexible lyric voices with some ping at the top and a connected mezza-voce—Fritz Wunderlich or Nicolai Gedda would be representative of this type at the high end. In the '51 Bolshoi version we do get star casting in Sergei Lemeshev, who stood alongside the more idiosyncratic Kozlovsky as the Soviets' leading romantic tenor. In the impassioned climactic phrases of the duet, his highest notes cloud just a bit with constriction, but his blandishing timbre and liquid line are perfectly suited to the music. His lovely rendition of the aria could be improved only by a little more solidity at the bottom.

Of these four juicy roles, three were seriously undercast, and the fourth somewhat so, by the Met. Mikhail Petrenko, an innocuous Hunding Lite and modest Pimen in earlier seasons, was brought back for the higher and more demanding assignment of Galitzky, his smallish, greyish voice establishing no vocal presence and his untroubled tallness no physical one. I thought at first that he was shooting for an insinuating undertone, but that turned out to be his vocal limit. In material of this sort, a Chaliapin or Pirogov or Ghiaurov can insinuate; small voices have to just sing out. Even less adequate was the Konchak, Stefan Kocan. His nondescript instrument registered little when he was down front, and faded out of earshot when he moved a few steps upstage. Sent forth in a hideous yellow-mustard uni, bald dome, and pencil-line moustache that made him look like a Chiang Kai-shek re-enacter, he was given some silly locker-room shoulder punches in place of the Khan's wonted aura of at-ease intimidation. As Vladimir, the Met proposed a previously unfamiliar singer, Sergey Semishkur. He offered a clean, narrow sound that might be sufficient for an operetta lead in a smaller house, provided that he summon a lot more charm and ardor than he showed. These three singers did not meet the elementary requirements of vocal calibre and quality for these roles, and offered no feats of musical or dramatic imagination in partial compensation. Their casting by the Met—on whose recommendation, and with whose approval?—is hard to comprehend.

Ildar Abdrazakov, the Igor, was better than that. He has proven himself a reliable, adaptable artist in a range of assignments and here, on native ground, did so again, with a pleasing medium-weight bass-baritone that is technically sound and always under musical guidance. His farewell to Yaroslavna in the Prologue ("*Molis za nas, golubka*" was touchingly shaded, and he threw himself into the aria interpolated into the final scene (more on this below) with admirable commitment. Still, the voice is limited in size, weight, and color for writing of such scale and gravity; one appreciates the work without feeling quite satisfied.

Yaroslavna is the heart of *Prince Igor*. She has the most to sing of any of the principals: two extended arias; the sequence of scenes with the maidens, Galitzky, and the boyars; and her reunion duet with Igor. We are told that some of her music inspired by Euphrosyne's Incantation late in the *Song* (and her only appearance in it), was the first to be set by Borodin, and is thus in a sense the musical germ of the entire work.* Her greatly increased stature, and with it the elevation of the theme of personal love and loyalty to at least equal standing with the political and military ones, is the biggest single change in emphasis from poem to opera. (In the *Song* Euphrosyne weeps on the ramparts, but there's nothing reciprocal for Igor, and their reunion goes unmentioned at the close.) Despite this centrality, the role has difficulty holding its own against the splashier and more immediately alluring music given the other characters. Her arias, both laments, are beautiful, deep, long, and difficult. Contemplative monologues concerned with interior thoughts and feelings, they rely almost entirely on eloquence of wordnote and phrase, along with any visual and behavioral help the physical setting can provide.

---

* This was, apparently, part of her Act II arioso. I wonder if this might suggest that the flowing melody we think of as belonging to Igor in his Act II monologue (at "*Ti odna, golubka, lada*"), later echoed by Yaroslavna in her Act IV lament, and so becoming a shared call of longing in their separation, actually originated with her, and was transferred into Igor's aria in its rewritten version, the one we know now (see below). With the exception of the song of the Polovtsian Maidens at the start of the Dances (the "Stranger in Paradise" tune), it is the most memorable melody in the opera, and its total of five full iterations, not counting its uses in the overture, make sure of that.

The writing calls for a dramatic soprano (she must face down Galitzky, soar above the choral and orchestral clamor of the Act I finale, and strongly animate her apostrophe to the river in the Act IV aria), but one under strict technical control, able to keep wide upward intervals—many to a sustained, swell-and-diminished upper Fsharp (a tough note), which becomes a keening tone in the second aria—in perfect balance and to hold out a high B, preferably taken at mezza-voce or else attacked forte and then diminished, at the aria's close. The arias have seldom been recorded separately, and the role has not been very well treated on integral recordings. But Evgenia Smolenskaya, the soprano of the Bolshoi performance, is equal to all the demands outlined above. Her voice may not strike many listeners as outstandingly lovely. It's at the high end of what was then a common Russian soprano voice type, strong but lean, without much plush around that bright core, but it is firm and authoritative, and interpretively she is alert and sensitive. The role's profile is well established.

Konchakovna, like all operatic Other Women, is a great deal more fun. Dripping with deepvoiced Oriental allure, free of Yaroslavna's princessly duties and goodwife constraints, she gets a sinuous, torchy contralto aria, a sexual-intoxication duet with the tenor, and the propulsive lead in the Act III Escape Trio. She also gets to strike a gong and land her man. It's a terrific role, and while the disappearance of the true contralto leaves an aspect of it not quite fulfilled (just as it does with Arsace or La Cieca or Erda), several of the mezzos we can hear on recordings have been effective in it. Of them all, the finest is Vera Borisenko, the wonderful low mezzo of the '51 *Igor* and several other Bolshoi recordings of the late '40s and '50s. Her expansive, humid sound winding through the lowlying melismas and her sense of passionate destination take us on a sensuous trip. Again we regret the absence of the Act III material.

In the Met performance, the female roles certainly fared better than the male. While neither singer showed all the vocal format or technical authority of our best exemplars, they at least brought with them some basic goods. Of all the principals, Anita Rachvelishvili, the Konchakovna, had the most to offer in size and quality of voice—a bit hectic and bright for the writing, not quite ideally settled and solid, but able to embrace this role in this house. The Ukrainian soprano Oksana Dyka was the Yaroslavna. She sang capably and expressively with a voice of medium weight and rather icey coloration, the first aria under good command, the second traversing some frazzled moments.

The conductor was Gianandrea Noseda, who in addition to Met assignments like the *Forza* mentioned earlier, has worked extensively at the Maryinsky, mostly in Italian repertory. The Met's orchestra played superbly for him, all choirs tonally resplendent and polished, sonorities in perfect balance, solos exquisitely intoned and phrased—and while they weren't really diving in like the Bolshoi under Melik-Pashayev or Gergiev's Maryinsky, they weren't coasting. When these virtues coincided with the more successful imagistic events Tcherniakov had devised, as at the opening of the Polovtsian scene, some magical moments ensued. This magic was of a detached, aesthetic sort, because the onstage happenings were not those for which the music had been conceived, but they were fleetingly effective.

That all this fine orchestral work did not, could not, more than sporadically dramatize the music was not directly Noseda's fault. His error, like Kirill Petrenko's with Castorf, was to assent to the collaboration in the first place—with a director/designer intent on using the music to underscore his counternarrative, and with singers who in large part could not realize the dramatic gestures of their music. To swell into the expansive lyricism of Vladimir's cavatina; to contrast the alternation of Igor's broad, arching phrases of longing for his wife with the dark declamations of his shame or the outbursts of his plea for freedom; to animate the shifting episodes of Konchak's aria, each a musical impulse born of a change in tactic; in short, for the players' response to at any point be lifted by the crescive leadership of a singer—all these presume voices and temperaments that set radically different proportions in the stage-podium-pit relationship. Without that, the orchestra retreats to a discreet version of whatever's on the page. Accordingly, Noseda and his players pushed unobtrusively along through the Act II sequence until the brief scene with Ovlur, which, though very slow, did convey its dramatic point.

At that, the ever-refined Met band always seems to require a Gergievish jolt to quite get there in Russian music. This was demonstrated anew in the fall of 2010, when in a new *Boris Godunov*, again with the original orchestrations that had fared so miserably under Bychkov, and in a substantially longer version, the music snapped to attention with a good measure of the visceral penetration always claimed for Mussorgsky's scoring.*

Gergiev is also the conductor for the 1998 Maryinsky performance. I think enough has been said here on the differences between the Met and Maryinsky orchestras, and on Gergiev's general characteristics as a conductor, that it suffices to note that both are typically represented by the *Prince Igor* comparison. The Maryinskys have an unfair advantage, though, for they are playing to a visual scenario that at least roughly corresponds to the one indicated by the words and music. They are also playing on a DVD, whose sound levels are under

---

* True, Gergiev had some voices to work with: Pape, Semenchuk, Antonenko, Ognovenko, Nikitin—sometimes *parlando*ing too much and singing too little, but vital enough to hold their own.

one's personal supervision. I am nagged by the blurred recollection of the Maryinsky *Igor* during the '98 Met visit, when the efforts of these same musical forces were not enough to overcome the unrelieved dreariness of the spectacle.* Same opera, same year, same orchestra and chorus and conductor, some of the same singers—radically different experiences. Cross-media queasiness.

Without shaking that condition completely, I feel secure in comparing the Met and Maryinsky casts. With the single exception of the Vladimir, Yevgeny Akimov, whom I had not heard since the '98 season, all the Maryinsky principals (Gorchakova, Borodina, Putilin, Aleksashkin, Vladimir Vaneyev) have sung more recently (and in the cases of Borodina and Putilin, frequently) at the Met, as has the Yeroshka, Nicolai Gassiev. Their imprints are fresh. If we're tracing the curve from the '51 Bolshoiskis to the Maryinskis of '98 (taking each group as, with an argument here and there, the best of its time), there's a pronounced downward bend. A mere 16 years from there to the Metsies of '14, the bend veers toward the vertical, with much less room for argument. But let me not pass over the things that could be argued. Between '98 and '51, one *could* prefer Gorchakova to Smolenskaya, since the former's tone is lovelier and fuller-bodied. Smolenskaya has a narrower but more plaintive sound I find appropriate, and a touch of edge and of well-engaged chest that I assume cut through in the theatre in a different way than Gorchakova's more voluminous but less grounded one. She is musically and technically the more finished artist, but if you were to say, "I'd sooner hear Gorchakova," I'd understand. Perhaps you'd also make a case for Borodina, with her undeniably beautiful timbre and an observance of dynamics and *espressivo* phrasings that is more detailed than Borisenko's. But the latter's voice is bigger and warmer, her manner more unbuttoned and released, and having on several live occasions been left hungry by Borodina's polite, thought-out-sounding traversals of roles like Laura and Carmen, I'd go for Borisenko without hesitation. Among the men, I hear no room for debate. The '98 Maryinsky cast is to the '51 Bolshoi's as today's most presentable *Bohème* lineup is to the Tebaldi/Serafin performance (see p. 297, n. 8).

If looking back from '98 to '51 is deflating, looking forward to '14 is more so, the only consolation being the assumption that this was not the best the Met could have done. Again, to the short menu of discussable issues, which

---

* Although dating from the same year as the present DVD, this was a different production, scenically halfheartedly "modern" in a uselessly abstracted way, and acted with numbing conventionality. The Igor and Galitzky (Putilin and Aleksashkin) were the same as those of the DVD, and Gorchakova was the Yaroslavna of most of the performances, though not of mine. The admirable Gegam Gregorian was the Vladimir, and Tarassova the Konchakovna, rather light for the music but enjoyable. Gergiev conducted.

number three: 1) If one were to argue that Rachvelishvili is a hotter, though less polished, performer than Borodina, I wouldn't dissent. 2) It could also be said that Abdrazakov is at times a more sensitive interpreter than Putilin, and so suggests more of Igor's "roundedness," and that his voice ascends to the baritone top more easily than Putilin's. But the gains are peripheral: Putilin consistently gratifies the expectation of solid, steady dramatic baritone presence and toothsome elocution, and Abdrazakov's top has only its easiness to recommend it—the music just goes on by. 3) Akimov, no more than adequate as Antonio in the '98 *Betrothal in a Monastery*, is only marginally stronger than Semishkur as Vladimir. On a CD or DVD, Semishkur might come off better. With these few minor and questionable exceptions, the Maryinsky cast meets the bedrock vocal demands—the ones we want met before we get finicky about the niceties—better than the Met's, in the cases of the bass parts by a wide margin. In the house, these differences would be magnified, not lessened. Of course, all visual aspects of interpretation have yet to be considered, and cannot be outside the boundaries set for them by edition and production choices. So let me turn to those now.

From the reviews of the Met's production, and the information made available in connection with it, one would assume that all of the many changes from the Belaieff score were made by Tcherniakov, with the collaboration of Noseda and the musicologists Elena and Tatiana Vereschagina, who had worked with him on previous projects. But there was precedent for several of the most important of these departures, which were in fact incorporated in the Maryinsky production that premiered in 1993. The first, and most noticeable, is the transposition of the first two acts, so that after the prologue with the departure of Igor's host and the warning sign of the eclipse, we are taken with Igor and Vladimir directly to their country–club captivity in the Polovtsian camp. Now the original Act I scenes with Yaroslavna and Galitzky, Skula and Yeroshka, and the victimized maidens assume a "Meanwhile, back in Putivl . . ." function, and the (standard) Act I finale, with Khan Gzak's marauders at the gates, fits the timeline better.* This arrangement also separates the two Polovtsian acts, which has always seemed desirable. Act III now seems less egregious in its recycling of musical materials and has more chance of registering its dramatic impact, with the striking of the gong like an answer to the tocsin back home.

---

* That is: the Polovtsians' incursion is now seen to occur only *after* Igor has rejected Konchak's offer of an alliance. Evidently no one has yet thought of performing the Prologue and Act I, Scene 1 as a unit, then going to the Polovtsian camp for Act II, then back to Putivl for Act I, Scene 2. In terms of timeline, buildup of suspense, and keeping up with developments on both ends, that would make even more sense.

The Maryinsky production retains Act III, though with cuts (see below) and one important addition, a second monologue for Igor. In Act IV, it brings the opera to a close by reiterating the *"Slava!"* chorus from the opening of the Prologue, thus bracketing the narrative with a departure-and-return framework and lending uplift to the end. The transposition of acts and the inclusion of the second monologue and of some material for Galitzky and his rebellious retinue (again, see below) are the changes from Belaieff that Tcherniakov has taken over from the Maryinsky version. There is certainly a case to be made for all these changes, though there's a danger in them as well, namely, that nearly all the hit tunes and the exotic ballet spectacle—which the standard sequence places farther along, closer to its traditional late-evening, wake-'em up grand opera position—are over and done with before the show is half over, and the late scenes (the ones least fleshed out by Borodin before his death) are apt to leave a playing-out-the string feel. That's one reason Act III is often omitted. And so it was in Tcherniakov's production, except for the Escape Trio. Displaced to the last scene, it was heard and seen in a new context. But then, so was everything else in the production.

Tcherniakov is an advanced case of auteurial Postitis. He has striking creative gifts, but they are of the interpretive order. He doesn't write librettos or compose music, so according to the chain-of-interpretation ethical code, it's not his prerogative to decide what a work shall be, what clearing it's going to make for itself in the world that will belong to it and to no other. Yet he has beliefs, opinions, feelings of his own, with which he wants to make personal artistic statements. They belong to him, here and now, so they must be more important than those that belonged to them, there and then, including those that once belonged to the originators of works, the artists formerly known as authors. So he has decided (with plenty of cultural approval) that it's not only O.K., but something along the lines of a moral imperative, that he get these personal statements out there via the words and music of those who have gone before. Naturally, this will involve gross misrepresentation of their creations. But it's vital that you understand: he's not here to represent them, but only himself. And if that's true *vis* à *vis* Mozart/Da Ponte and Wagner/Wagner (Tcherniakov has directed *Don Giovanni* and *Tristan*), why wouldn't it be true with these remnants of poor old Borodin?

These convictions, along with Tcherniakov's visual bias, were made clear from the outset, when instead of a piece of music we were given a piece of writing. The music would have been the overture. (And let's not forget: Maestro Noseda's compliance was required for this and many other changes.) It's "by" Glazounov, meaning that he fashioned it from thematic materials already included in the opera by Borodin, and it sails along rather like Glinka's for *Ruslan and Lyudmilla*, which would have pleased Borodin. Like the *La Juive* overture (only better), it includes music from numbers often deleted in performance, i.e., from Act III. It's not the *Meistersinger* Prelude, but it's a rattling good curtain-raiser. Tcherniakov didn't want rattling good, with its ear-whetting anticipation of onstage excitements and uplift at the end. He wanted to cross that promise with a new "writing," an adversarial one. So instead of engaging our ears and feelings, he caught us by the eye with a silent-movie title, as if we were about to hear nothing at all, or maybe a piano in the pit with strung-together scraps cribbed from the classics. The writing said: "To unleash a war is the surest way to escape from oneself."

I have no critically dignified language with which to express my resent-ment at this sort of instruction, the sort that tells me how to interpret what I'm about to see and hear and curries my favor by telling me something I'm presumed to already believe, and that this something is both wise (I actu-ally heard approving "Um'"s and "Ah'"s around me) and brave, as if Dmitri and I were saying it directly to Putin or W. If there'd been time, I might have been gladdened by the realization that this was not to be a postpsychological event. It was going to be about someone's psychology, ostensibly Igor's. But there wasn't time, for now the curtain was up.

And now that it's up, a brief procedural digression: from here on, we'll be comparing the Met production directly with both the Belaieff score and the Maryinsky DVD, not in great detail, but in terms of the crucial choices that add up to "concept" and how the performance is taken in. One such choice has already been made: overture v. title. The former, peppily played on the DVD by the Maryinskis without any staged distractions, put me in a good anticipatory mood for what was to follow. The latter left me in the frame of mind just described.

But now the scene is disclosed. It is a slightly opened box set, an interior in grey-white, a plaster-over-concrete look, and so lit, with high windows at the back and a mezzanine running around the sides. The commoners of Putivl are crowded into this mezzanine, and as they begin their chorus in praise of the valiant Russian princes, Igor's troops file into the grand floor of the hall and stand at attention in rows perpendicular to the audience—an impressive tableau. We have already learned from the opening title that we are to take the people's cries of "Glory!", Igor's urgings to battle for God and country, and the boyars' excited recounting of Igor's earlier victories with irony if not con-tempt. We're way ahead of you, poor Putivlin peasants, boyarish popinjays and drillhall conscripts! Of course, while Kurt Weill might have written such an attitude into this scene, Borodin did not, so his sturdy, festive music now sounds hollow, and we only observe, not share, the propitious atmosphere Borodin was trying to create. We also now learn that we'll be watching a 700-year update, for this building is no ruin of the Kievan Rus, and these uniforms are either late Imperial or early Red Army (the former, I think—they look expensive). We begin the now-familiar process of streaming dissociation, the detachment of what's being sung from what's being shown, and the mental exercise of providing our own substitutions instead of fully, directly receiving an integrated sound/sight event. For instance, for the Polovtsian khans, invoked in the opening chorus: they can't really be khans, so would they be the '05 revolutionaries, or the Japanese? The Whites? Or, since dates don't matter and it's really about now, the Afghan Mujahedeen of the Soviet times or the Iraqis with their in-the-cloud WMDs? The Chechnyans? It will never reach an end, the garland of faux relevancies Tcherniakov is stringing between *Igor* and us, which we can sniff while contemplating the unedifying sight of Igor pacing up and down straightening troopers' collars, since the director/designer has boxed himself in and there's quite a bit of music to get through.

What do the score's directions say so far? They say: "A public plaza in the city of Putivl. The troops are on the point of departure for war. The people. At the rise of the curtain Igor, accompanied by the princes and boyars, enters in great pomp from the cathedral." That's all until the beginning of the eclipse, when "All gaze with astonishment at the heavens." So in terms of stage directions this is more like *L'amico Fritz* than *La Juive*: there's no guidance concerning the placement of the cathedral or other buildings, the positioning of populace and soldiers, or the style of buildings or costumes. All would have been based on period research and on the requirements of the action. Eye-confirmation of things heard in words and music would have been taken for granted. It's very unlikely that these directions originated with Borodin. Either Rimsky or Glazounov inserted them, or they are based on the St. Petersburg premiere production. They aren't Holy Writ, but they convey two points of some importance. One (speaking of Holy Writ) is the religious motif—that the defense of Orthodox Christianity is seen as an important theme, incorporated into the set and the first onstage movement. The second is that we're outdoors, not indoors.

These scenic directions are followed in the Maryinsky production. Like the *Mazeppa* brought to the Met, it's retro in design, with sets and costumes uncredited but presumably based on the originals. And as with the *Mazeppa* DVD, the sets, especially the exteriors, don't read very well on video; they undoubtedly looked better in the theatre. As ever, the camera cannot begin to capture panoramic scenes or the effect of mass movements. Throughout, too many longheld closeups of heavily madeup but otherwise blank faces, too many choristers on idle till it's time to sing, too much token gesturing, etc., etc. However, we *are* in period; there's magnificence in the costuming; there's a cathedral; and we are outdoors, where such an occasion has to have taken place. This soon becomes of practical importance. The eclipse is the central event of the Prologue. It functions much the same as Monterone's curse in the first scene of *Rigoletto*, laying an air of foreboding over everything that follows. In both cases, we are much more inclined to feel its power if we have been taken to a time and place of superstitious belief in omens and curses. Besides, the sun going under out of doors is quite different from a room getting dark. Besides again, Vladimir has a specific line—an iconic one, actually, taken from the poem—telling us that the sun is like a sickle in the sky, and the chorus sings of stars appearing at midday. These are things we need to see that the actors can see, and we need to see them ourselves. The sun like a sickle, stars at noon, suspenseful music—even today, there's something creepy there. The room getting dark, not so much.

Probably you're waiting to hear about the poppies. They're coming right up. But we have to get there first. Not an easy trip. From Putivl, some 120 miles northeast of Kiev, Igor's army heads southeast into the steppes, toward the Don. Historically, according to Nabokov, it took nine days' mounted march to the river Donets (but that was from Igor's seat in Novgorod-Seversk, a bit to the north of Putivl), and then farther southward beyond the junction of the Donets and the Oskol, where battle was joined. It was May.

On the Maryinsky video, we follow theatre custom. The curtain goes down on Putivl, the curtain comes back up, and we are in the encampment of the marauding Orientalish nomads. Tents, dusk, all looking rather murky and tacky on video, like something out of the Classic Comics *Arabian Nights*. (In the Belaieff score, there's nothing on the setting.) A Polovtsian girl, seconded by a chorus of maidens, sings a haunting little song with a melismatic English horn obbligato: the flower, blasted by the heat of day, withers and droops, but with the coming of the night and the dewfall it revives. The girls, led by tambourine and a prancing clarinet, perform a short, quick dance that builds up a fair head of steam. These numbers are in atmospheric preparation for the emergence from her tent of the lovelorn Konchakovna to invoke the aid of night as she awaits an unnamed lover—the beginning of the sequence of arias and duet that will lead, almost opera-seria-like, to the choral ballet that ends the act. (For a synopsis and imagined staging of this act in its standard, complete sequence, see n. 3.[3] Some readers may prefer to consult this, to "get it straight," before reading on.)

But by this time, Tcherniakov has taken us on a very different route, with a new set of associations. During the scene change, a procession of black-and-white stills shows the fate of Igor's troopers, increasingly fearful and then prostrate and bloodied, Igor himself and Vladimir among them. I've heard and read of Eisenstein in connection with this slide show, I guess because it's b&w and shows faces. But though that would in one way be appropriate, since as we've seen (and here comes my first association), Eisenstein was a student of Meyerhold, the founder of the auteurism Tcherniakov is practicing, it's an unfortunate comparison: Eisenstein's *Ivan* closeups, even when borderline campy to our eyes, are tremendously effective; Tcherniakov's, not. But wouldn't this be part of the anti-heroic takedown, the *de-valorization*? As you please. Either it's clunky by way of adversarial re-interpretation, or it's just clunky. In any event, it was compromised in two ways. First, it was unaccompanied by music, and opera audiences get really shifty these days when either eye or ear is addressed in isolation. Second, in order to avoid infuriating malingerers, the Met decided to let them in while the slide show was in progress. Unfair to Tcherniakov! I missed several images altogether, and several more in part, amid whispered "Sorry . . . excuse us . . . very sorry"'s.

But now came the poppies, and the magical moment I alluded to earlier. They looked great, an expansive field of vermilion backed by a royal blue sky, and their Sovcolor amazingness was most welcome after the dirty white drear and black-and-white stills. With the Polovtsian maiden's song prettily sung by Keo Deonorine (unseen, a disembodied voice and English horn floating out into the theatre), it was a heart-catching couple of minutes. There was no surprise factor. The poppies had beseeched us from every promotional site, including bus-stop shelters, for weeks. But if anything, they exceeded expectations, and like the flowers themselves, associations ran riot now. Afghanistan for sure, both the Soviets' campaign and our own, and the sticky economic fact of opium as cash crop. Then again, "In Flanders' fields the poppies blow," and WWI, and gradeschool English class, and wearing a poppy bought from a vet on Armistice-now-Veterans' Day—and have you heard Britten's *War Requiem* lately, or Butterworth's *Shropshire Lad* songs or Vaughan Williams' *On Wenlock Edge*, or read Housman or Owen or Sassoon?— and, as a woman with me in the elevator asked as we headed for the coat room, I to retrieve something, she on her way out at the intermission: "So—we get *Kismet* and *The Wizard of Oz?*" And on, along the potentially infinite chain of connections, some fragrant and touching, some amusing or absurd, yours and mine overlapping here, separating there, the only characteristic common to them all being that they lead us away from the possibility of experiencing *Prince Igor* as an integrated work—that is, as a work whose stage events correspond to the ones that gave rise to the music.

During the music that was written for the Polovtsian Maidens' dance, we are shown more dead soldiers, but before long, Igor's head pops up among the blossoms of Free Donets/Afghanistan/Flanders/Oz. He gazes dazedly about, and we soon realize that all the events of this act are to be understood as happening inside Igor's traumatized head. We don't know whether he was taken prisoner or simply left to die on the field. This is a hoary Postist dodge, but ingenious. It relieves the director of any obligation to the creator's vision and allows him to substitute his own in the guise of Igor's subjective, even subconscious, experience. It keeps us asking mindgame questions (is Vladimir already dead? Does Igor imagine that Konchakovna is singing her cavatina to him? Does she even exist? Since we saw Konchak/Chiang Kai-shek in the slide show, he must exist, but is he here for real?, etc.) instead of taking events at face value and going on from there, further into them. It dumps everything into a playpen with two favorite Postist playmates, Ambiguity and Ambivalence.

The poppy field, which at first looked solid, is soon seen to be traversed by narrow horizontal paths, like the corn mazes that spring up every late summer as downrent kiddie attractions in New England, and perhaps elsewhere. The action, such as it is, will all take place along these rows. I have already indicated the undersung, ineffectual nature of the act's numbers,* and there is little to add except to note that except for Konchak, everyone is dressed in dirty whites, slates, and duns, and that there is no environment for acting or dancing, since all are standing in their appointed rows waistdeep in fake poppies, whose allure is fading fast.

I don't quite know what to say about the Polovtsian Dances. According to the skimpy synopsis in the Met program, they represented "a vision [of Igor's] of the overwhelming joy of living life to the fullest." Is that what that was? What I saw was perhaps a score of possibly capable dancers hopping up and down and along the aisles of the maze, watching out for the poppies and occasionally lifting their arms like baseball fans doing a sloppy version of The Wave with the game out of reach. Igor stood among them and lifted his arms, too, like the guy who has to be reminded. The men wore chest hair and white pants; the women wore shapeless white smocks that made them look bulky, with forbidding bony protruberances. The scene was palely lit. Absolutely none of the exotic color, the macho male savagery or alluring feminine sensuality of the music was realized. Ambiguity, Ambivalence, and

---

* Musically, only one cut is made in the act. This is No. 10, referred to in the helpful comparison of editions made available by the Met's press office as "Brief recit with Konchakovna and the Russian prisoners." It *is* fairly short, but its choral development is well beyond the "recit" category. For my view of its function, see n. 3.

Androgyny: three qualities very much not at home in E-19. The chorus sang from the side boxes next to the proscenium, saving Tcherniakov the problem of integrating them into the stage action.* As depressing as the spectacle itself was the realization that I had been returned to the Age of Aquarius, and that the antidote to violence and hubris is still Flower Children making love, not war. Tcherniakov wasn't born till 1970, but this is the freshest insight he's got.

The Maryinsky DVD is at its least persuasive in this first Polovtsian act. The set and lighting elements come up poorly on the video, and most of the stolid, conventional acting does not bear camera examination, though Putilin and Vaneev have strong presences and present the basic characteristics. And it's hard to squint back to whatever may have been fresh and arousing in Fokine's choreography, even if it were better lit, more imaginatively shot, and more excitingly danced than it is here. Still: the events are shown as realities, not flitting virtualities in a passing dreamscape; the singing is strong enough to establish them in the ear; and the conducting and playing have dramatic thrust.

In both productions, the action now moves back to the court at Putivl. In these two scenes (the Belaieff Act One, its first scene set in the courtyard of Galitzky's house, its second in Yaroslavna's quarters of the princely palace) the Maryinsky performance comes into its own. The Galitzky house is a massive log structure, its courtyard enclosed by a stockade and open to the sky. Yaroslavna's apartment is in a palace, also of log, but decorated and furnished, open at the back to a view of the town and river. Both sets, lit for day, look a great deal better than the night encampment on the steppes. Skula and Yeroshka, the scamp followers of Galitzky, are given their identities as gudok-playing rabble-rousers. We aren't asked to think about anything, free-associate with anything, except the events of the scenes, the qualities of the performances.

Much is owed to Sergei Aleksashkin. He does not quite belong to the line of great Russian singing basses, but he's much more than what we'd normally think of as a character bass—a solid, sizable voice, a vivid personality that's adapted itself deftly to a broad range of characters (Mendoza, Kochubei, The General in Prokofiev's *The Gambler*). He wakes up the show from his first entrance, and nails every moment opposite Gorchakova's strongly sung and played Yaroslavna. Since they're actually in a representational room, they

---

* This solution was adopted by Corsaro in his 1969 NYCO production, too. But he had a smaller chorus with which to make sonic impact, and a smaller stage space to clear for the dancing.

can act like they belong in one. Thus, when Galitzky complains that his sister might at least offer him a drink, he can head for the table, grab a goblet, and pour one for himself. Almost like life.

At the Met, the order of these two scenes was reversed—or, rather, the bulk of the scene at Galitzky's was inserted into the middle of the one over at Yaroslavna's. This meant that the quarrel between the two of them preceded Galitzky's introduction and song, and the chorus of girls pleading for Yaroslavna's intercession came before we had seen anything of their plight.* This ordering involves a second scene change, back to Yaroslavna's court, and since in the vision of cinematic flow shared by Tcherniakov with many other contemporary directors, even one scene change is undesirable, a second is surely to be avoided. So for both locations we saw again the walls from the Prologue, now become a space so anonymous that any and all events might occur there with equal implausibility—another Common Room. There are no objects to be at home with, no activities, and no Nurse.

You may recall that in *Mazeppa* I objected to the insertion of Lyubov into the scene of Kochubei's torture, in part because it introduced a comforting presence and released all the steam from his opening monologue. But the situations are different. Lyubov doesn't belong in the dungeon at any point. The Nurse, however, though her entrance is not specified till later in Belaieff, is a natural presence in Yaroslavna's chamber, and Seeking Comfort could well be the action label for the scene. In the Maryinsky version, she is present at rise, working on some weaving as Yaroslavna gazes out over the river through the *adagio* orchestral introduction, and Yaroslavna plays much of her monologue in close contact with her, sharing her emotion with an old intimate companion. In Tcherniakov's staging, on a spare platform in the drillhall, we certainly get the idea of a lonely woman in a bleak place. As with the poppies, it works as an image, but now what? Paradoxically, if we want a close-in feeling, a glimpse of distance is helpful; if we want to convey the yearning after an absent beloved, the presence of a next-best substitute, comforting and unfulfilling at once, only sharpens it; and if we need to establish the emptiness that hangs in a familiar room, we do it better not by showing an empty room, but by showing all its familiarities, missing the one most wanted, and with some of the others distorted through misuse. (How does Yaroslavna feel when it's her off-the-rails brother, not her absent husband, who helps himself to a drink?) Oksana Dyka sang capably and dealt professionally with her empty space. But the image burns away, and short of greatvoiced singing

---

* Meaning that not only is the logic of dramatic events changed, but that of the music, too— we hear fragments of Galitzky's musical signature before it's been stated in his song.

(Litvinne?), mystical emotional presence in the voice (Muzio?), or some unusual combination, as with the primetime Mattila (Northern ache in the timbre, a gift for opening herself up to us), the scene cannot keep its grip.

The reason Tcherniakov and Noseda found it necessary to alter the sequence of these scenes was that they wished to insert some of Borodin's unused material, showing Galitzky's crowd in open rebellion. So they devised their scenario of Yaroslavna alone, then Yaroslavna with the girls, then Yaroslavna/Galitzky; then over to Galitzky's for his song and everything else in the standard Scene One; then back over to Yaroslavna's for the first part of the scene with the boyars, the invasion of the palace by the rebelling mob, and finally the ringing of the tocsin and the finale, now augmented by the presence of the rebels.

Dramaturgically, there's not a thing wrong with this progression. It could even be said to raise the stakes, with Putivl now visibly in revolt just as the Polovtsians arrive. It also offers a chance to account for Galitzky's disappearance from the story. He and Vladimir are two oft-complained-of pieces of Borodin's unfinished business, and now he can be shown to have been killed off in the act-ending mêlée. Rimsky and Glazounov could certainly have chosen this ordering in the first place. But they didn't. I credit them with three reasons. First: since these were among the scenes most clearly defined by Borodin, requiring only the orchestration of several numbers, and with much bigger problems to be solved later on, they saw no reason to dishonor their friend and colleague's choices here. Second would have been that additional scene change, back and forth with the time required for representational sets, and for the sake of rather short scenes. Of course, the present-day Met could accomplish this very efficiently, and the sight of the mob bursting into a set that actually resembled Yaroslavna's palace would have had some theatrical shock value. Instead, visual monotony and anonymous space. Third, and most important: Rimsky and Glazounov, composers, recognized that the music Borodin had left for a possible rebellion scene was not very interesting—well below the rest of Scene Two—and that it was of a sort the audience had already had plenty of at the end of Scene One, where it is sung by secondary characters usually not too easy on the ear. Not seeing where it would be comfortably accommodated, they instead filled out the blueprint of a strong, tight act whose well-paced progress toward its finale does not ask to be interrupted by the tiresome rebellion stuff.

Two things that can be convincingly depicted on film and powerfully invoked by music, but are hard to show onstage: chaotic crowd scenes (the *Meistersinger* Act II riot) and collapsing buildings (the *Samson* temple). Even when expertly solved, they are problematic on repetition, when the mechanics begin to show and (unless a Felsenstein is on hand) individual assignments tend to loosen. Tcherniakov tried both at once, and of course your falling building can't land on your cast. So, although he is certainly meticulous with staging and masterful with tech, the rebellion was still only another baseball fight—both benches emptied, but no punches landed—and the collapse of the drillhall was a front-yard fireworks moment while selected pieces descended from the flies to land in selected places. Not badly done, but still no match for the eye with what the music is doing, and all made necessary only by the director's scenario.

We have arrived at Act III, or not. Musically, it is very spotty. In the Belaieff version, it contains two numbers that are effective if powerfully performed: the Khan's second aria and the "Escape" trio. It has some "We have won! We are mighty!" choral writing that is serviceable, and some that is superfluous, and a drunken guards' dance that requires a generous concession to convention to move the plot along. It also begins with the Polovtsian March, once a common "classical pops" item, which now inhabits the same glade of faded amiability as Victor Herbert's "March of the Toys." Much of the act's thematic material is recycled from Act II, often in bits and pieces that try to serve a *Leitmotif* function, but really are merely reminders of catchy tunes. It isn't hard to see why directors and conductors would as soon not be bothered.

However, things do happen in Act III. The Polovtsian raiders under Khan Gzak return to camp with their plunder from Putivl, which they literally throw at the feet of Igor and Vladimir. Konchak, spurned by Igor in Act II, is in an if-you-can't-join-'em, lick-'em mood, his aria full of boastful snarling. Russian prisoners, so well treated in the earlier scene, are now threatened. They report the sacking of their towns and the raping of their women, and urge Igor to escape. When Ovlur reprises his Act II music with the news that horses are waiting (one musical repetition that is effective), Igor is ready to comply. He flees, but Vladimir does not and—as is implicit in the text and explicit in the Maryinsky staging, he becomes a prince of two realms, as son of Igor and husband of Konchakovna.

So, despite the musical weaknesses, Act III assists materially in terms of dramatic clarification and resolution. The answers to the musical problems are, in ascending order of importance: judicious cuts, convincing staging, and terrific performances. The Maryinsky version makes cuts, but they aren't all judicious. The Polovtsian March (as entr'acte), the opening chorus, and the Khan's aria are all included, but from there a huge cut is made to a number not included in Belaieff. This is Igor's "second" monologue, *"Zachem ne pal ya,"* which, the scholars report, was originally intended for Act II, but was set aside by Borodin in favor of the familiar one. That was certainly the right decision. "*Ni sna, ni odtikha*" is far more compelling musically, and embraces the theme of Igor and Yaroslavna's mutual longing, which Borodin had decided was to be an important one in his opera. "*Zachem ne pal ya*" focuses entirely on Igor's guilt and shame over the fate of the Rus. It struck me at first as labored and workaday, but after several hearings I find it a solid piece, with some intriguing harmonic and orchestrational colorings and a repeated ascending figure that is effective. Its inclusion is, I think a case-by-case decision. It does give Igor more to sing, but whether or not that's an advantage depends on who's singing it. It boosts the shame-and-guilt quotient over the love-and-loyalty one—a possible interpretation, though Borodin was obviously looking for a balance of these elements. Its strengthening of Igor's motive for escape is not needed if Act III is included, yet this second captivity scene is the only logical place for it. And here is the logical place to specify the remaining differences between the Maryinsky and Belaieff editions, especially since by the time the DVD was made, the Maryinsky was making cuts in its own version. For that, see n.[4]

From here, the Maryinsky redaction proceeds to the scene with Ovlur and then, out of nowhere, to Konchakovna's striking of the gong, and thence to the act's end as in Belaieff. Only a fragment of the trio is left, and almost nothing of Vladimir's anguish of choice, though we do at least see the outcome. From the Khan's song on, this is literally a cut-to-the-chase edition, serving the bare necessities of plot, with the inserted monologue for Igor standing in for all the excised numbers. This does save some time, and puts a substantial piece for the title character in place of several others that are, musically, only competent workups in the service of what can seem an outmoded theatricality. This is where convincing staging and terrific performances are supposed to come in. Personally, I can do without the Polovtsian March and wouldn't mind some internal cuts in the choruses. But in an opera of epic proportions, I don't believe we help a relatively short, scrappy act by making it shorter and scrappier. And if quaint theatricality and music that doesn't stand very well on its own are disqualifications, we can safely eliminate not only hefty chunks of 19th-Century opera, but most of 19th-Century ballet—yet when great singing or dancing and passionate relationships are on offer, we still find ourselves transfixed. The Council of Khans, quite brief, *if well sung and acted*, helps maintain an atmosphere of suspense and threat, and establishes this group for its role in the finale. The falling-down-drunk guards could be an embarrassment, and their music will never haunt you, but if sharply sung, cleverly staged, and performed by adept character dancers (presumably they are on hand), it could set up the sneaky little recitative for Ovlur and Igor very well.*

I can't say that all these numbers belong in, since I've never seen anything approaching a complete Act III, let alone one performed at the level required to overcome the stretches of moderate musical interest. In the Maryinsky performance, Vaneyev and Putilin sing strongly in their arias and Borodina dispatches the little that is left her. The playing and choral singing have plenty of spirit, along with some sloppy moments and scratchy tenor throats toward the end. Needless to say, many details of commission or omission can be argued, and it would take something on the order of the Bolshoi '51 cast, thoughtfully staged and well acted and danced, to fully realize the act.

As already noted, Act III is omitted altogether from the Met production, except for No. 23, the "Escape" duo-trio, now inserted into the final scene. According to Belaieff, this scene takes place at the city wall of Putivl, with a public square also visible, fronted by some dwellings and dominated by the citadel. One gathers from the text that the citadel has held and the city itself is largely intact. It is the surrounding countryside that has been devastated, its villages burned and many inhabitants killed, its fields laid bare, the joyful songs of the young no longer heard. From a terrace high on the rampart, Yaroslavna sings her lament and describes the scene. A passing chorus of peasants sings that all has been laid waste by the ruthless Khan Gzak. These numbers are of surpassing musical beauty, filled with loss and hopelessness. Next (says Belaieff), Yaroslavna spots two distant horsemen, and fears they herald the returning Polovtsians. But they are Igor and Ovlur, and there now follow the reunion duet, the couple's entry into the citadel with boyars and elders, the terror of Skula and Yeroshka at the sight of the returned Igor, and their reinvention of themselves as loyalists and their ringing of the bells to summon the townspeople. Finally, the happy-end ensemble, with all (say the stage directions) in suitable finery, and the townsfolk with the traditional offerings of bread and salt. The Maryinsky performance follows this script faithfully in musical terms, with no cuts or re-arrangements except for the repeat of the "*Slava*" chorus at the end, as noted earlier. For some reason (limitations of the retro set arrangement?), it keeps the peasants' chorus offstage, and does not bring Ovlur to his new Christian home. Heavily reinforced at

---

* It would do less well as the lead-in to Igor's monologue—it strains credulity too far to have him roaming among the sleeping guards while voicing it. Including the monologue almost mandates cutting the chorus and dance. At least at some phases of his work, Borodin was envisioning a dance-heavy entertainment like *Ruslan*, harking back to French ballet-opera models, and if we include all the dancing specified in Belaieff (and without knowing if any further dance music was left on the cutting-room floor), we have something approaching that. Tcherniakov reduces this element as much as possible.

the close is the understanding, quite different from that left by the poem, that with the head restored to the body, the Slavic Rus will reassemble its forces, sally forth once more, and this time be victorious. This is certainly what Borodin and Friends meant us to understand.

Tcherniakov is not a Castorf. He's not even postdramatic. He doesn't seek incoherence or the repeal of all dramaturgical law. He works with narrative and character. But as an adversarial auteur, he seeks not to further and strengthen the understanding of the creators in their place and time, but to lecture them from ours as viewed from (must I write these words once more?) the eve of WWI. He wants to teach Igor a lesson. So, after the love-not-war delirium of the poppy field, he must return Igor to real time and bring him down so that he may discover his new, humbled, communitarian self, helping to rebuild his hometown among the common folk. I would say this is just a new piety in place of an old one, except that there is nothing new about it. Call him Comrade Igor.

And of course lots of parts don't fit, beginning with the set. Tcherniakov takes us back to once more the drillhall, now a heap of rubble. Again we're indoors, not outdoors, and again it makes a difference, especially for Yaroslavna, again on watch across an impossible distance. It is the sight of distance from her overlook that gives rise to her thoughts. The words of her lament are full of winds and waters, birds and arrows, sun and clouds. Its central section is an apostrophe to the far-off Dnieper. Its music is made of empty space and far horizons. And once again Tcherniakov's match of music and image is momentarily compatible, until the aboutness of the singing detaches one from the other.

From the end of Yaroslavna's lament to the end of the opera, the Met's version makes substantial alterations in the sequence of numbers, necessitated by Tcherniakov's concept. In productions that omit Act III, like the '51 Bolshoi recording or the '69 NYCO production, the hole in the plot is customarily papered over by a brief exchange in the reunion duet: Yaroslavna asks Igor how he got back, and he tells her. Vladimir goes unmentioned.* It's pretty feeble, and contributes to the hurried, patched-together feel of the final act. Tcherniakov cleverly folds this problem into his notion of accounting for

---

* At the NYCO, Corsaro dealt with the Vladimir problem by showing him killed while trying to escape—as I recall, his arrow-pierced body was flung at Igor's feet at the end of the Polovtsian Dances. John Stewart, the Vladimir of that production, hazily recollects that "Eddie Villella [in the role of a Polovtsian Chieftain—not too shabby a lead dancer!] did me in." That does give us news about Vladimir, and further motivation for Igor to overcome his noble scruples and escape. But really, nothing fills in for Act III except Act III.

everything between the Prologue and the concluding couple of numbers as artifacts of Igor's trauma. To do this, he snips off Yaroslavna's recitative after the lament at her description of the devastation, leaving out her narrative of the approaching horsemen and the arrival of Igor with Ovlur. Instead of that, he inserts the Escape Trio from Act III, now sung as a dream episode amongst the ruins, Konchakovna pleading from atop a heap of fallen ceiling. The sequence then vaults over the reunion duet (Igor, still traumatized, has picked his way over the rubble, unrecognized) to the drunken song of the gudok players—*sans* gudok—about Igor's ignominy, and their discovery of his return. The ringing of bells becomes banging on exposed pipe. Now the sequence flips back to pick up the first part of the reunion duet, as Yaroslavna comes upon the dazed Igor. This is cut short, though, before she can inquire about her husband's return, and before he can sing of rallying the princes and the people to vanquish the khans. As Meyerhold would have put it, all that wouldn't do.*

Tcherniakov decided that after the stillborn reunion, the time had arrived for Igor's second monologue. So, very late in this determinedly dolorous evening, we were treated to seven minutes of self-flagellation among the white-grey, whitely lit remains of the same space we'd stared at for a couple of hours already. If I'd had the forethought to bring a white flag with me, I'd have waved it. As it was, I sat through a truncated version of the choral finale, the one that has never seemed quite enough to cap off the opera, which is why—in addition to its framing function—the Maryinsky version repeats the much stronger one from the Prologue. The End? No such luck, for here came some more music, making its debut appearance in *Prince Igor*. It was written by Borodin for an unrealized collaborative project, *Mlada*,† to describe the flooding of the River Don—a rather sluggish flood, one gathers, spreading out slowly across

---

* In his review of the production for the *New York Review of Books* Geoffrey O'Brien observes that "The music they [Igor and Yaroslavna] sing together after they are reunited in the last act cannot compare to the mournful power of what they sing alone." There is some truth in that (those monologues are so eloquent), but a great deal more if, as here, you hack off the part of the duet where a good baritone and soprano can really soar together. The scene is structured the same way as the Vladimir/Konchakovna duet: the partners fling lots of quick, overlapping wordnotes at each other, as if raining kisses, before settling into some real singing. But Tcherniakov cannot allow either the words or the musical lift of this section, since it doesn't accord with his adversarial interpretation of the opera. So out it goes.

† This was to be an epic/mystical work of mythic origin, with sections composed by Cui, Borodin, Mussorgsky, and Rimsky-Korsakov. But the project was dropped, and except for Cui, none of the composers got much beyond the sketch stage. Rimsky later returned to the material for his gigantic opera-ballet of the same name, which has some stunning passages (at least for the susceptible), but hasn't held the stage.

636 · OPERA AS OPERA

the wide valley. I regret having to confess that I can't tell you much more about this piece, except that in my fully numbed state, it was not interesting enough to nudge my attention back to my ear from my eye, which was busy deciphering Tcherniakov's revisionist ending for the opera: the chastened Igor bestirs himself to start the cleanup, and some of his subjects follow suit.

This, then, was the way that one of the world's foremost operatic institutions chose to lay before its public, after nearly a century of neglect, a cornerstone work of the Russian repertory. This is the production for which critics have exhausted their vocabularies of wonderment but found no words for argument, or even inquiry into its musical and dramatic representation, its uses of scholarship,* its interpretive principles, or simply what's neat and what's not, for all is neat. For some particulars, see the foregoing. As to the principles: if *Prince Igor* is indeed an auspicious test case for the privileges of auteuristic subjectivity, if it gives us an ideal opportunity to ask ourselves if there is ever an instance in which the director's function is "equal to the role of the [operawright] in shaping the theatrical experience," the answer is "no."

---

* Both the Met and Maryinsky versions are buttressed by well-informed and, I am sure, highminded musicological support. The Met's notations make much of the fact that most of the "new" music is by Borodin, and most of the redacted by his composer colleagues. So, as with Felsenstein, "authenticity" is apparently a Good Thing. A crooked-shaped authenticity, though, that will not only reverse some of Borodin's last thoughts, but will (in the case of the Met version) put the whole, significantly cut and re-arranged, at the service of a dramatic "concept" that flagrantly contradicts that of the operawright(s)— the one that gave rise to the music.

NOTES

1. Here are the articles that have been consulted: In print: Anthony Tommasini: "A Blazing Folk Tale Spliced With Grainy Sorrow," *NYT*, 2/8/14; Alastair Macaulay: "A Rare Opera Whose Dance Is In Step With Its Drama," *NYT*, 3/18/14; Geoffrey O'Brien: "A Great 'Prince Igor,'" *NY Rev. of Books*, 3/20/14; James Jorden: "*Prince Igor's* Triumphant Return," *NY Observer*, 2/17/14; and the reviews by John Allison in *Opera* (Apr., 2014) and F. Paul Driscoll in *Opera News* (May 2014). Online: Justin Davidson: "'Prince Igor' Marches an Army Back Into The Met," *NY Magazine's Vulture*, 2/10/14; Wilborn Hampton: "A Stunning Revisionist Staging of Borodin's 'Prince Igor,'" *The Huffington Post*, 2/16/14; David Patrick Stearns: "Met Tries Conceptual Approach in Rich, Confounding 'Prince Igor,'" *Operavore*, 2/7/14; Eric C. Simpson: "Borodin's original [sic] 'Prince Igor' shines, dark yet brilliant, at the Met," *NY Classical Review*, 2/7/14; Leslie Kandell: "Met's *Prince Igor* An Exotic Romp Amid the Poppies," *Classical Voice North America*, 2/18/14; Raymond Stults: "A Profound Prince Igor From Met Opera," *Moscow Times*, 2/20/14; Barry Bassis: "After A Century, 'Prince Igor' is Back at the Met," *Epoch Times*, 2/17/14; Martin Bernheimer: "Prince Igor, Met Opera"—review, *FT.com (Financial Times)*, 2/9/14; Laura Genero: "The Met's 'Prince Igor,' A New Production at War with Itself," *American Spectator*, 2/16/14; David Rubin: review *CNY Café Momus*, 3/9/14; Manuela Hoelterhoff: "'Prince Igor' Marches Into Met Led by Great Director," Bloomberg, 2/10/14.

   As the titles suggest, nearly all these reviews are raves, with minor qualifications having to do with one or another individual performance or some aspect of the sequence or scenic investiture the reviewer finds questionable. Bernheimer's could be read as mixed with strong reservations, and Rubin's cites some, too, but seems to attribute most of them to the opera itself. The only generally negative review among these 17 (and that of the direction and design, not the actual performances) is Genero's—she called it "A depressing psychodrama and a joyless evening," the work "crippled by another one of the Met's bizarre, experimental productions." Several of her objections are in the same areas as mine. None raises any issue of principle or interpretive ethics, or questions the director/designer's auteuristic privileges. These are now beyond challenge.

2. I'll take the roles in the same order as in the main text. Discographic completeness is not the goal here; I'm only trying to guide readers whose familiarity with the opera is limited toward examples that will give them an idea of how it can sound with major voices. All the examples are from studio recordings. With respect to the bass roles, I must flout my postwar-only rule, since it's impossible to bypass Chaliapin as Galitzky, preferably in the 1911 acoustical rendition—the perfect voice, technique, and vocal personality for the part. He recorded Konchak's aria, too, and it's superb. But 78 side limitations (and, I assume, his own preference) necessitated deleting a chunk that includes the lowest notes—Levik notes that Chaliapin was a ". . . basso cantante of an even, velvety timbre with rather weak low notes and free top ones," and that "He would transpose some of Konchak's notes." (Levik, pp. 347-348.) Hear it anyway, for its demonstration of interpretive intent always conveyed through musical tone and tightly bound line.

   Among the other basses on integral recordings, Christoff handles both roles with relish, the Galitzky especially good (no Act III, though, for his Konchak). Ghiuselev is also a potent Galitzky, and on the same recording Ghiaurov, though past his prime, shrewdly gets most of what's to be gotten from Konchak, with Act III included. On the Maryinsky

CDs we have Vladimir Ognovenko (Galitzky) and Bulat Menjilkiev (Konchak), both strong. As for separate recordings of the arias, there is the younger Ghiaurov in both (Galitzky and Konchak, Act II)—something of a put-on interpretively and recorded with such ludicrous reverb it make the voice sound smaller than it really was, but still terrific singing; and on one of his superb early discs, the Bulgarian bass Raffaele Ariè dives into Galitzky's song with tremendous appetite and burnished tone. For versions of Konchak's Act II aria, I would strongly recommend those of Maxim Michailov, Ivan Petrov, and Boris Gmyrya. The first was a contemporary and formidable rival of Reizen and Pirogov, the second and third the most prominent successors to them, though Petrov the more favored and, one gathers, the more vital theatrical presence. Three stupendous voices, all plausible alternatives to Reizen, and the differences among them only matters of taste: Michailov's the deepest and most calmly authoritative, Petrov's the brashest and liveliest, Gmyrya's the plumpest and most orotund.

Apart from Ivanov, one Igor stands above the others on the complete recordings: Dusan Popovich, who sings the role on the Belgrade recording under Oscar Danon. He seems to have slipped through the cracks, for although he sang the roles of Igor, Onegin, Yeletzky, Shaklovity, Andrei (*War and Peace*), Mizgir (*Snegorouchka*), and Shchelkalov on widely circulated recordings and was the leading baritone of the Belgrade company for many years, he does not even rate an entry in the *New Grove Dictionary of Opera* or the Kutsch and Riemens *Concise Biographical Dictionary of Singers*. But to judge from these recordings, he was a baritone of major vocal calibre, tonal richness and color, and technical stability, and his Igor, while not especially illuminating from an interpretive standpoint, is very satisfying to hear. Two versions of the Act II monologue should be sought out: Pirogov's and George London's. Like Reizen's, Pirogov's big basso swept commandingly up over the G-flat, and could linger on a restrained F. In terms of phrasing and nuance, his reading is the most interesting of any I know. London recorded the aria in 1951. With its deep bass-baritonal hue, his voice, amply powerful in the declamatory bars, also possesses a blandishing lyrical tenderness in the apostrophe to Yaroslavna. Finally, there is a version in his native language by the fine French baritone Michel Dens that is well sung, thoughtfully interpreted, and extremely well recorded.

After Lemeshev, the notable Vladimirs on complete recordings are Atlantov and Gregorian, the former's singing strong and secure with well-drawn line, the latter's somewhat less powerful but with greater wordnote nuance and shapings of phrase. Among modern recordings of the excerpts, there's a good one of the aria by the lyrico-spinto Sergei Larin and a nice one of the duet with Gedda and Kerstin Meyer. But the classic references would be Björling (in Swedish, at least three versions) and Kozlovsky. The former's sheer vocal glamour is unparalleled, but the latter's rendition is the one we could term definitive. This extraordinary singer is always fascinating to hear, with his unique vocal set-up (a highly refined, almost precious-sounding lower octave rising into a ringing extended top), his splashy virtuosity, and superb *messa di voce*. Every phrase, every shading (his readings are highly detailed) has musicodramatic direction, and of course Russian is the language for the role. He recorded both the cavatina and the love duet, the latter with Maria Maksakova.

As indicated earlier, there is less choice with respect to the female roles. Between Smolenskaya and Gorchakova, Stefka Evstatieva is easily the best Yaroslavna—a roomy, beautiful voice, stylishly handled. As heard on the Maryinsky CD, the voice of the very capable Gorchakova has a touch more freshness and core than on the later DVD release. I know of no compelling modern recordings of the arias. The delightful Israeli soprano Netania Devrath recorded both in the '60s, and as always sang expressively, but with a voice much too light for the music.

The only Konchakovna who really bears comparison with Borisenko is Melanie Bugarinovich, on the Belgrade recording with Popovich. (These two, along with the bass Miro Changalovich, make some of the recordings in this series worth seeking out.) She has the deep, rich timbre and settled position for the music. Obraztsova certainly has the equipment for the part, but the singing is rather hectic and fierce, missing the necessary allure, and really satisfying only in Act III. There's a fine version of the cavatina by Podles—some mighty peculiar vowels in that lower-middle tessitura, but the unique color of that blend suits the music, and the melismatic gestures are second nature to her.

3. Act II is often complained of as a "concert in costume," and it's true that its succession of numbers is not bound together in a through-composed, organically developed manner. But if the director, designer, and performers are really working to render the conventions of grand opera as inevitable-seeming as possible, there's no reason the act can't build its plot-lines and conflicts in a perfectly coherent, "modern" way. The *mise-en-scène* is crucial: the royal compound of the Polovtsian camp, within a guarded perimeter. Konchak's own tent would be here, though not necessarily shown. So is that of his daughter, Konchakovna, and the one assigned to the most honored hostage, Igor. Their exact positions, and their relation to what is visible of the whole encampment, depends on stage practicalities—the more Romantic-realistic, historically suggestive detail, the better, to show the exalted status of this part of the camp and suggest the life that goes on in it.* The maidens, gathered at sunset before Konchakovna's tent, engage in whatever domestic activities seem best as they sing in response to their soloist's song. Their dance. Konchakovna's smoldering song; the women, in on her secret, again respond. (In the Maryinsky staging, Konchakovna now gives the solo Maiden a ring to carry to her lover as summons; The Maiden, grinning, brandishes it to show it to the other girls, and to us, before running off—a nice, helpful little bit.) Now, in a scene cut by Tcherniakov for several likely reasons (it's too obviously something that takes place in real time and space rather than in Igor's fevered imagination; it would entail an onstage choral contingent, amidst the poppies; it no longer has an Act III counterpart), a group of Russian prisoners enters, under guard, after their day's forced labor. At Konchakovna's behest they are offered food and drink by the maidens, for which the prisoners give thanks. Next, Konchakovna and her retinue exit as a Polovtsian patrol makes its rounds, singing of the night watch. (This splendid little chorus, full of the constant alertness to danger, is retained by Tcherniakov, but, like all other Act II choral music, is sung from offstage.) The patrol exits, its last lines sounding from the distance.

It is now night, and the only figure visible is that of Ovlur, who takes up his guardpost on the perimeter, awaiting his moment. The lover to whom Konchakovna addressed her cavatina now makes his way among the shadows toward her tent. It is none other than Igor's son Vladimir, who sings of the warm Southern night and his passion for the khan's daughter, who now re-enters from her tent. Their duet and mutual declarations of love. But there's an obstacle: while her father will welcome their union, his won't, and Vladimir now senses activity in Igor's tent. (A sliver of light would do it. The moment is reminiscent of Walther and Eva as Sachs bestirs himself in the workshop.) Over her protests, he leaves; she returns to her tent in frustration. For a moment, the stage is again empty save for Ovlur. Chords of great somberness, anchored by the deep woodwinds and trombones—it is Igor, unable to rest. His great, tormented monologue. As its despairing final lines fade into its postlude with thumping pizzicatos in the low strings and Igor is

---

*   In Act III, Konchakovna is supposed to initiate the Escape Trio by coming to Vladimir's tent to question him about the plot of Ovlur, which, in a logical staging, she would have sniffed out at the end of the Igor/Ovlur exchange. But here in Act II, some distance is necessary between Konchakovna and Vladimir—the progression of their arias of longing, their duet and hurried separation, makes no sense if their tents are in close proximity. So the sets for the two Polovtsian scenes cannot be exactly the same. The arrangements for Act II shown on the Maryinsky DVD seem plausible enough, though quaint in execution. With a stage as deep as the Met's and modern scenic techniques, such a setting could be visually entrancing and a constant support for the action.

about to return to his tent, another theme is introduced—an insinuating, shifty one for flute and clarinet. This is Ovlur's Motif, one of my favorite inspirations in the score. It weaves its way downward over a bed of strings as Ovlur, leaving his guardpost as the first grey of dawn is faintly visible, approaches Igor. His voice, written in high-baritone range but best cast with a tenor, doubles the instrumental line. Repetitions and slight variations of this figure are all he will sing, since he, a Christian convert, wants only to help Igor escape and to go with him. He has swift horses. But Igor, treated as a royal guest by the khan, has given his word that he will not try to escape, and he holds to this even though Ovlur points out that an oath not sworn upon the cross is not binding. Ovlur returns dejectedly to his position as his theme trails off. A longheld chord.

Dawn is brightening. Igor again heads toward his tent, but now another of my favorite moments: barely two bars of an easy, calm movement in the low strings. It is Konchak, and this brief introduction tells us he needs no fanfare—he's simply, suddenly there, fully in command. (Perhaps it also suggests the camp beginning to return to life—possibly Ovlur is relieved, possibly women pass upstage with jugs of water, etc. Fleeting bits that help us keep on track without pulling focus from Konchak and Igor.) Konchak asks what's troubling the prince, and launches into his long, colorful aria. He flatters Igor with praise for his bravery and his refusal to ask for quarter—allied, they would sweep all before them. He boasts of his own bravery and past triumphs. He offers Igor the pick of his many slave girls—the sultry one from the Caspian. He even offers Igor his freedom in exchange for an oath to never again take up arms against him. When none of this works, Konchak orders the dances to commence. I think it's important to understand the function of this sensational sequence, so often detached from its context and, since *Kismet*, incorporated into the popular culture. In his review of the dance portion of the production, Alastair Macaulay, while conceding that the poppy maze is rather restricting and there isn't much actual dancing going on, finds much to like in the choreography of Itzik Galili. "I admire them [the dances] as an inextricable part of a compelling whole," he writes. "Seldom in opera does dancing intensify the central drama, but that happens here." In a sense he's right—the prancing in the maze *is* part and parcel with Tcherniakov's concept. But if one sees that not as a "compelling whole" but as an offensive, hubristic distortion, inextricability is not a recommendation. Macaulay reads into the male and female figures "multiple abstractions of Igor and Yaroslavna, or just Man and Woman . . ." A big inference, I think, but assuming we grant it, precisely part of the problem. We want multiple Polovtsians, not multiple abstractions, and identifiable men and women, not Man and Woman. The drama of *Prince Igor* is not abstract or symbolic. But Macaulay's favorite movement image from this act is that of Yaroslavna standing upstage of Igor during the latter's monologue, extending her arm toward him as he sings, then lowering it as he sinks back into the poppies. It's kind of a Bob Lite moment, and is specifically unoperatic, part of the damnable auteurish fixation on rendering visible and objective what the music is keeping invisible and subjective. What's touching is Yaroslavna's *absence* as a great dramatic baritone voice pours out Igor's heart to her, and Igor's absence when, to the same theme, a sumptuous spinto soprano sends Yaroslavna's tears to him from her watchtower in the final act—in both instances, the unbearable longing for an unseen beloved, invoked by sung melody. The more striking the visual image, the more the music recedes. We are no longer in the ear-led, eye-confirmed world of opera.

Back in the Three Composers *Igor*, what goes on is this: as Konchak and his suite (including Konchakovna, Igor and Vladimir) are set up in prairie magnificence and his subjects gather, dancers, Polovtsian and slave, enter, some with musical instruments. As some of the women begin an undulant dance, those of the chorus commence their haunting song—a sad one, speaking of the luxuriant Southern land of their birth. As it dies, the men start a fast, savage dance. When it has come to a wild climax, a new, vaulting movement begins, with a thunderous chorus in praise of the khan, leading directly into a dance for the female slaves. Here Konchak points to the girls from beyond the Caspian, and repeats his offer to give Igor his choice of them. Young boys dance, then alternate with the men; the women of the chorus re-enter with their song, and from here to the end, these groups and their musics intermix, the chorus lauding the khan, who is compared in glory to the sun. And indeed it is now brilliant, burning daylight on the steppe. The picture as the curtain falls: Konchak in triumph, Igor unmoved, Vladimir caught been his father and lover, these last three betraying nothing. It's not a dream. It's for real.

4. As seen on the DVD, the big jump from Konchak's brief recitative after his aria, wherein he orders the horn calls that will summon the council of khans, takes in No. 20b, in which the khans gather to discuss whether or not to undertake further predations; No. 20c, in which Igor and Vladimir question the Russian prisoners, and its continuation when the Polovtsian boys and men display more of their booty and taunt Igor and Vladimir; and No. 21, the Chorus and Dance in which the guards get drunk and pass out. In Belaieff, this last is meant to set the stage for No. 22, the dialogue for Ovlur and Igor, but in the Maryinsky version, Igor's monologue is inserted here, with Ovlur's moment following it, after which No. 23, beginning with Konchakovna's discovery of the planned escape, her pleading with Vladimir to either stay or take her with him, Igor's re-entrance and the tug-of-war trio, is all omitted up to Konchakovna's sounding of the alarm, leaving only the brief recapitulation of its main theme at the beginning of No. 24, the finale.

However: in The Philips CD recording of the Maryinsky version, made in 1993, the cuts are not so drastic. The Chorus of Khans and the drunken dance are still out, but the first part of 20c (Igor, Vladimir, Russian prisoners) is in, and so is all of 23—particularly desirable musically. Earlier, the CD recording also includes the invasion of Yaroslavna's chamber by Galitzky and his retinue, and the boyars' loyalist response, from the Act I (now Act II) finale. With Ognovenko a biting Galitzky, it comes off better when we don't have to see it, but I'm still not convinced there's a strong case for its inclusion. The CDs also have the advantage of a superb accompanying booklet. Both it and the DVD offer the essay by another musicological duo, Marina Malkiel and Anna Barry, which is the best single rundown I have seen of the problem posed by the sources. (For a solid understanding of the situation prior to these recent reworkings, see Richard Taruskin's entries on Borodin and *Prince Igor* in the *New Grove Dictionary of Opera*.) But the CD booklet also contains a number-by-number accounting of everything in the Maryinsky version, with the dates of Borodin's work on the material and indication of who did what to it subsequently—plus a bibliography and the complete libretto in English and transliterated Russian. However one feels about the relative merits of any of these versions (Belaieff, Maryinsky, the Met), it's a shame that the DVDs don't present the complete Maryinsky one, as originally produced. The complete Act III according to Belaieff is performed on several previous recordings, among them the Belgrade performance under Danon, the second Bolshoi recording under Ermler, and the Sofia under Tchakarov. None offers an especially compelling performance, but at least the music's there.

2

SOME UPDATES

I think often about the developments I would have to define for myself to extend my Backstory 1 (q.v.) into the present century. But as yet I find it difficult—well, no, impossible—to put together anything resembling a coherent ordering of them. I gain moments of clarity about aspects of them, sometimes through insight into my subjective experience and my efforts to deal with them in my teaching or critical practices, and sometimes from the writings of authors who address them from one or more of the common points of engagement—brain/mind/ scientific, philosophical/humanistic, media-technological. Currently, my favorite such authors—the ones who make me feel I'm getting a grasp—are Jaron Lanier and Astra Taylor, but there are several others, too.[1] However, since the very nature of these developments is fragmentizing, virtual, disruptive, "liquid" (Zygmunt Bauman's term[2]), I feel no confidence in arranging them even for my daily use, let alone for critical purposes. Only one thing about them shines through with ever-intensifying luminosity. That is opera's extreme incompatibility with them, and the necessity of setting opera forth not as a manifestation of them, but an alternative to them.

On the New York scene, two big institutional changes have occurred—the death of the New York City Opera and the regime change at the Metropolitan. One fears that both are symptomatic. The NYCO sank from sight with all hands after many distress signals and some jumping up and down of onlookers on shore, but no response at all from any of the entities, private or public, that could have helped.[3] The direction of the Met has been assumed by a man who has doubled down on the visual, the technological, and the promotional, on production and what he thinks of as innovation. If these were the guarantors of the operatic future, we would have no worries, for all have reached their zenith in 21ˢᵗ-Century America. But as I write this, the Met has just squeaked past its worst financial crisis since the Great Depression, thanks to cutbacks on everything and everybody associated with it—even some of its bankable stars. Unlike the NYCO, it is too big to let fail, and when the time comes, will receive its publicly funded bailout like any other major tourist attraction.

The travails of both these companies are clearly related to the survival concerns of the live performing arts throughout the West, among which I can casually call to mind the evidently still-widening gap between inflation and artistic productivity;*⁴ the stagnant state of the economy as a whole; the weakened presence of artistic appreciation and skills among the young in home and school; the obliterative presence of the popular culture; and a vertiginous demographic swing in the potential audience and patron pool. So they can't be attributed wholly to local artistic policies. Yet it is also impossible that there is *no* case-by-case cause/effect relationship between what is on offer and what is, increasingly, insufficiently supported. Forty years of artistic decline, with an uptick here, a downturn there, preceded the City Opera's death throes. The Met has not sustained excitement in its core repertory for many years, and with its most widely acknowledged calamity, the new *Ring* cycle, it got an ironic comeuppance: having succeeded in directing everyone's attention from performance to production, it was excoriated for production when performance was the more fundamental problem.

Inasmuch as it has been several years (in some cases, over a decade) since I wrote here on certain aspects of production and performance, there have been many occurrences in these areas that might be profitably examined. Some loom large in the moment, and for a performance critic it's very tempting to keep the record going. But most of them, however momentarily arousing, do not materially add to the arguments already presented or furnish any fundamental challenge to them. For this little update section I have chosen just a few that do seem to me to afford some refreshment of the discussion. And so, in order of their first previous appearances, further to:

Eye and Ear. This topic, with all that it implies for the underlying circumstances of operatic communication—its sensory balance, its focus and duration of attention—seems to me more important than ever to be clear about. We have to get our sensory priorities straight. Two recent pieces of writing, a book and

---

* In Astra Taylor's book (see n. 1) I encountered the first reference I've seen in a number of years to Baumol and Bowen's cornerstone economic analysis of the performing arts, in which the structural factors that account for the worsening of this predicament (the "productivity lag") over time were first presented. I will touch on the subject in the epilogue.

an article, lend furtherance to what I've already written on the topic, though neither is directly concerned with opera. The book is *The Universal Sense—How Hearing Shapes the Mind*, by Seth S. Horowitz.[5] The article is "Losing Our Touch," by Richard Kearney.[6] Intriguingly, both Horowitz (a neuroscientist and sound designer) and Kearney (a philosophy professor and author) use the adjective "universal" to describe one of our senses, but don't agree on which one it is. They do agree, though, that it isn't sight, and their common ground here is that unlike sight, hearing and touch are "always on."* I'm not here to referee that debate, but when it comes to opera, hearing is clearly the winner. In any case, Horowitz's "universal" extends well beyond the "always on." He observes that while a number of species have no sight and/or are very limited in other senses, "all animals with backbones hear," have some means of detecting a range of vibrations and translating these into auditory experience to help them determine their own location in space and the location and distance of other objects.

Hearing's "universality" doesn't necessarily mean a lot to our specific concerns, though the notion does buck us up in a culture whose sensory attention is monopolized by sight. But I'm gratified to see that with respect to all the distinctions made earlier with respect to sight/sound reception, Horowitz lends expert substantiation. He's not saying (nor am I) that hearing is superior to sight, or that it is or should be the dominant human sense. He is only identifying the particular advantages of hearing in relation to sight, especially its greater quickness of sensory input (or, more accurately, the shorter lag between input and recognition) and its direct, visceral response to vibratory signals. He notes that familiar sounds are processed faster than unfamiliar ones (hence the importance of repetition, the laying down of sensory tracks—Ong would nod); that the universal meanings of many sounds are independent of their verbal comprehension; that sounds that have evoked a strong emotional response are more easily remembered than those that haven't (though I assume this applies to sights and other sensory experiences as well?); and that music and sound sneak in "under the cognitive radar." Horowitz also writes about attention, both the "goal-directed" kind (when we *decide* to "pay" attention) and the "sensory-directed" sort (when our senses convey something, internal or external, that is compelling enough to temporarily decide for us.) With some notable exceptions, it is goal-directed

---

* But Kearney fudges on this. "Even when we are asleep," he notes (he's glossing on Aristotle's *De Anima*), "we are susceptible to changes in temperature and noise." Noise? That would be hearing, would it not?

attention that we're involved with in performance, audience members shifting focus by intention, though under the suasion of interpreters.*[7]

Kearney is writing mostly about love and sex, touch in its most literal sense, but about its metaphorical meanings, too (being "in touch;" the skin as sensitive organ, as in "thin-" or "thickskinned"). He uses the splendid term "excarnation" to describe where he's afraid the digital media and the cyberfuturists are leading us (a "more and more fleshless society"), and "optocentrism" (synonymous with my "ocucentrism"—take your choice) to define the sensory order that has reigned in the West ever since Plato anointed sight as the highest sense, precisely "because it is the most distant and mediated." Short of turning opera into "Huxley's "the feelies," or running wild with Jon Whitmore's bottom-most "theatre communication system" (the tactile), opera's in-touchness will continue to depend first on the body's response to sound vibrations, and second on the brain's mediation of lightwaves. The ear-led, eye-confirmed model is constitutive of opera as opera. Its obverse, currently ascendant, is inimical to it.

Enhancements and Secondary Oralities: Checking Out Another "New Art Form." Yes, I'm hearing the claim on behalf of the HD theatre videocasts, just as we did with radio opera and TV opera. And as with those adventures, until a body of work exists that is created specifically for the medium and is strong enough to demonstrate its artistic viability, it's just another technological enhancement of our transmission capacity. That is by no means an insignificant thing, but it's not an artform. In theory, there's no reason original operatic work conceived for the specifications of the big screen cannot be written. But since, at the very least, an economic practicality equal to that of the arthouse film would have to be demonstrated for someone to take a flier on it, I have a hunch we'll be waiting for a while.

As for what we do have, it took me a couple of seasons to avail myself of "Live! In HD." The Met's Saturday afternoon transmissions conflict with my teaching schedule, and repeat screenings slip past my goal-directed attention on cocktail hour and other afterwork pursuits. But in December of 2010, a weekend off in the Berkshires coincided with the showing of the Met's new production of *Don Carlo*, at the Clark Art Institute in Williamstown. Moreover, I already held a ticket for the in-house performance on the following

---

* Possibly nourishing food for further thought: as receptors, particularly of music-related artforms (music, dance, opera) isn't a big part of what we're seeking (the "fix") the moment when our goal-directed attention is overwhelmed by the sensory-directed one? We "pay" attention in order to surrender it. For reference to more on attention in a more philosophical/humanistic context, see n. 7.

Wednesday, with only one cast change. So the opportunity for my favorite kind of close comparison was at hand.

In terms of basic sight/sound reception, there is not a lot of difference between the home audiovideo experience and the theatre-HD one, at least for someone with good equipment and an acoustically decent room. My normal viewing and listening distance at home gives me about the same relationship to picture and sound as my seat halfway back in the Clark's balcony, though at a different angle. Still, the sheer bigness and vividness of it all, the electronic aura charging so much larger a space, kicks the experience into a higher gear. Further, I'm now in public, with both the pleasant sense of sharing the event with likeminded people and the constraints on manners and mobility that that entails. And in exchange for waiting for the DVD to be issued—and, for about the same modest investment, purchasing it for playing at leisure—I have surrendered control over the start and finish and the breaks in between, over the volume of sound or the brightness and contrast of picture. I have purchased admission to a single performance, which I do not own and cannot reproduce. Of course that's true of live performance, too. But this is only a chunk of secondary orality, and with that I'm used to having my property do my bidding. No breaks for commercial in either circumstance, except for the infomercial that is the intermission feature, which I'm at liberty to skip.

I intensely dislike the artificial, compartmentalized misrepresentation of operatic reality at the heart of this experience. It's no good saying that it must be received on its own terms. Its own terms include taking away not only the flesh-and-blood presence of live performance, and not only the aforementioned privacy and control of the home experience, but the imagined performance of the audio recording, as well. It sets in their place a puffed-up engine of image and sound that mercilessly magnifies all the inherent distortions of transmission. For the ear: the current fashion in broadcast mixology, each singer in his or her own acoustic, bumped up or down for fair and balanced debate with other voices and with orchestra and chorus, the whole in a sort of interwoven mat whose sheer presence in the auditorium, it is hoped, will override its synthetic quality. For the eye: relentless cutting from closeup to closeup, faces and upper bodies only; terror of long shots or of holding the camera still for more than four or five seconds; nervous and often seemingly arbitrary shot selection; and the hopelessness of capturing groupings of characters or the feel of an ensemble, of taking in simultaneous visual events bound together by music, all so vital to a work like this one. The quality of both audio and video is fine, per se—the Clark's system is a good one. These problems are from the source, and if they are even more troublesome here than in the better home video or film examples, there's a good reason: "Live!" means no second chances, not just for the performers, but for the video director and colleagues as well. There's no slo-mo replay, no alternate shot selection after the fact, and no postproduction palliative care. This is boots-on-the-ground conflict resolution between parties not meant for close proximity.

Between the "Live!" and live-in-actuality performances there were of course similarities, especially in the overall impression conveyed of the production (Nicholas Hytner, dir., Bob Crowley, des., lit by Mark Henderson) and of the conducting (Yannick Nézet-Séguin), both of which seemed concerned with making a weighty, deep, long work seem less weighty, deep, and long. However, I'm not writing about the similarities, but about the differences, the relative advantages and disadvantages of these ways of coming to *Don Carlo*. This production was a fair test, for while the sets had a flat, somewhat flimsy born-to-travel feel,* it wasn't of the kind that seems calculated to look better onscreen than onstage, and while for performers camera readiness is now almost a professional entrance requirement, there wasn't much reason to think the Met would or could have done anything radically different on the casting front, either.†

In my comparison, one thing fascinated me and a second dismayed me. The fascination lay with which individual performance came across the strongest. The HD transmission was my first encounter, by either ear or eye, with Marina Poplovskaya. I'll just quote, with a bit of writerly re-arrangement, from my notes: "P. comes off best, though it is obvious that the span of voice [for the role] is not there, and she's pushing on air. Doubt it will last. At first, didn't like her much—the face is hard, with a squared-off jaw, not actually attractive. But she gradually grew on me. Farewell to Countess of Aremberg very touching; Act V aria [*"Tu che la vanità"*] and last duet absorbing. Good performer for this medium: she has the continuity of involvement, understanding of moments, of receiving the camera [letting it read her]. Can keep her attention on an interior object. So she registers as involved and sensitive, with singing that is pretty and [on mike] adequate to augment the images." I awarded Second Place to Furlanetto, even though at times he got a little pushy, as if not quite trusting the authority of his voice.

---

* The production originated at Covent Garden, and was further shared with the Norwegian State Opera and Ballet.

† The one couldawoulda: in London, the Eboli was Elina Garanča, a deft and comely performer, and she was initially announced for the New York cast. But she withdrew, and probably wisely—as cleverly as she navigates her Modern Mezzo voice, I would not relish the thought of her charging the breastworks of the Garden Scene trio or "*O don fatale*" with it at the Met.

To the house. Again, I'll quote myself: "Onscreen, the one performance that worked for me was Poplovskaya's. In the house, it's Furlanetto's. [He has] the only voice and presence of grand-opera, Verdian possibility, though the voice is greying and sometimes shaky, and the line falls short of real grandeur. He's Italian and experienced, [native to] the dialogue moments and declamatory effects, how to project them with economy. By no means a great Philip, but a Philip, sometimes impressive and always to be respected.

"She, on the other hand, creates little impression. Voice much too small and narrow for the music, straining after the big moments and grand phrases. The subtleties of both physical and vocal expression, so engaging at times on camera, not often detectable. She holds it together, doesn't do anything 'bad'— but it simply doesn't register. [It's an] entirely different understanding of what an operatic characterization is. She's a movie actress, does know how to create involvement with mike and camera, with a pretty voice of not much substance."

And the dismay? I *preferred* the HD transmission. At the Clark, some measure of this masterwork's stature came through; at the Met, very little. Sheer aural and visual presence is *sine qua non*, even when we don't like it, and at times the screen-and-speakers override kicks in to take us on the trip, whereas in the Met's auditorium the combination of clear, tidy-up playing, light production values, and serious undercasting* doesn't even get us aboard. I have seen some bad performances of *Don Carlo* over these sixty-some years—sloppy playing, shoddy staging, wrecked voices, worn-out sets—but never before one so distanced and ineffective, and so contentedly so.

A clue to this last surfaced in one of the HD enhancements, the intermission feature. Like several of her colleagues, Deborah Voigt has become a personable backstage hostess. The content of these excursions is not above the level of daytime TV celebrity chit-chat, containing nothing that would actually help the audience with the work in question, but she does it well. She had a brief interview with Nézet-Séguin, and sure enough he toed the party line about the wonders of "making chamber music together." Yes—for themselves. In *Don Carlo*. It's beyond tiresome, this pose.

I glanced at the subtitles—not often, but often enough to confirm the presence of that deadly, prosaic syntax that pulls us down into the world of "information," and to note, incidentally, that "Mahomet" has been censored from the Veil Song and that Elisabetta's magnificent last aria, in which she

---

* To be clear: Anna Smirnova, the Eboli, does have a voice of appropriate calibre. But except for an occasional note at either extreme of the range, it's too messy to shape the music. And the voice of Alagna, the HD Carlo, would certainly have impinged more than that of his in-house replacement.

apostrophizes the statue of Carlo's grandfather, the Emperor Charles V,* is no longer an apostrophe but a sort of tour guide or classroom tidbit. "*You*" [my emphasis] who have known the vanity of the world," says the libretto. "Charles understood the vanity of the world," say the titles, their third-person impersonality (and the analytic tone of "understood" in place of "have known," "knew," or even "recognized") coldly discarding the sense of connection, of a final shared understanding of experience, invoked by the "*Tu*," to say nothing of the lofty, sculpted tone of the music.

If I am able to extract from *Don Carlo* more of what I know to be in it from its HD simulacrum than from the thing itself, and for one-fifth the price, why would I—let alone someone less experienced, less devoted, or with less ease of access—choose the live-in-actuality option? In my case, sheer stubbornness. In the other, one-time curiosity or, perhaps, the need to impress someone.

Here and Now. The search for repeatable, renewable new operas continues to yield meagre results, but it is not for lack of trying. In the seasons that have passed since I addressed the topic in Part II, Chapter 4, I have encountered eleven recent† English-language operas in professional productions. They are: *A View from the Bridge* (Bolcom/Weinstein/Miller, from Miller's play), *Dead Man Walking* (Heggie/McNally), *American Tragedy* (Picker/Scheer, from Dreiser's novel), *Lysistrata* (Adamo, from Aristophanes), *Dr. Atomic* (Adams/Sellars, Act I only), *Claudia Legare* (Ward/Stambler, from Ibsen's *Hedda Gabler*), *A Quiet Place* (Bernstein/Wadsworth), *The Seagull* (Pasatieri/Elmslie, from Chekhov), *The Tempest* (Adès/Oakes, from Shakespeare), *Two Boys* (Muhly/Lucas), and *The Death of Klinghoffer* (Adams/Goodman, Act I only). I've checked in with several more on TV, DVD, or CD, and have also sat in on a couple of "work in progress" performances, which by definition aren't ready for fair evaluation.

These pieces are not of an experimental, "what is this?" sort, or of a musically challenging, "must get my ear accustomed" kind. They are all hoping for the approval of mainline opera companies and their audiences. For me, two or three fall into the category of pieces I'd be willing to give a second try under

---

* This is the very same Charles, you'll recall, who stepped out from Charlemagne's tomb to proclaim, in a *voce terribile,* "*Carlo Quinto, o traditor!*" in *Ernani,* then proceeded to apostrophize his ancestor in an ensemble finale of reconciliation ("*O sommo Carlo*"). He is now apostrophized in turn at his own monument, and will soon emerge again, this time silently, to take grandson Carlo under his wing. Has anyone ever thought, I wonder, of a pairing of *Ernani* and *Don Carlo* productions in which the appearance of Carlo Quinto's spirit at the end of *Don Carlo* reproduces in detail (of costume, age, attitude) the *Ernani* moment?

† "Recent": The Ward, Pasatieri, and Bernstein works are of an age to have been included in an earlier grouping, but had not previously been produced here, and *Klinghoffer* is not brand-new (1991).

extremely promising auspices, the rest not. None seems a candidate for long-term repertory status. I found *A View from the Bridge* the most successful of them, for although the prosification and impassionisation questions I raised in regard to some of the earlier operas are writ large here (expositional conversation is set very awkwardly, and key confrontations, like that between Eddie and Catherine, turn from singing to yelling*), there are also several affecting scenes, and passages of lyrical writing that lend some point to an operatic adaptation of one of Miller's strongest plays. That strength is a built-in advantage for the opera, as it is for Ward's setting of *The Crucible*. As in that case, though, the play itself is still viable, and about the best one can say for the opera is that it adds a new color in places and does not entirely vitiate the play's power.

In terms of musical language and dramaturgy, *View* could nestle quite comfortably amidst the postwar "Here and Now" operas. With *Two Boys*, I got the feeling of something newer—an uneasy feeling that started with an odd mating of story and score. A toiler in the vineyard of contemporary opera with whom I've exchanged thoughts thinks that one difficulty with many current efforts is a television mentality, both in the selection of subject matter and in the scenic progression of the writing, which prevents the work from ever arriving at the level of sung drama. The libretto of *Two Boys*, which is by the skilled and experienced playwright Craig Lucas and is based on an English murder case from 2001, would seem to fit this description: as several commentators have pointed out, it moves along like a noirish police procedural episode. In opera, though, it is the music that finally determines a work's character, and as *Two Boys* got past its establishing moments I began to suspect that I was having my first experience with an opera conceived and nurtured entirely within an internet mentality. It was not just that the protagonist inhabits the world of the internet more than he does that of physical reality, or that the plot involves unraveling chatroom secrets. It was that the music sounded like surfing, complete with surfing's attention span, and the characters (even the "real-life" ones) had the anonymity of internet acquaintances.

Muhly certainly has a command of orchestral resources, which he uses to create many short-lived events. Sometimes these events seem to have onstage equivalents or counterparts, but more often not, and at last this does not matter because each little unit vanishes without a trace, with no sense of thematic function or of one gesture bearing a relation (continuous or intentionally discontinuous) to another. We end up with an extensive, complex sound

---

* These passages are mandated in the score, as indicated by three varieties of *Sprechstimme*-derived notation. As in earlier examples, the composer builds intensity with the pitch level of the naturalistic dialogue rising till it can go no further, then breaks off into shouting.

environment of unrelated occurrences, all of equal importance whether large or small, with no lasting imprint or causative purpose—just chatter that begs for attention for a moment, then jumps to something else.

It could be argued that yes! That's the internet! And so it is. But can it be an opera? Anything to sing about? Not that I could hear. As with much contemporary writing, the score sounds constructed upward from the orchestral bedding, with a vocal line laid on top, consisting of boilerplate responses to whatever comes next. The characters have neither the vocal individuality of "rounded" ones nor the weight and numinosity of "heavy" ones. Act I was a musical desert with one nice choral oasis. Act II was marginally better, with the plot coming to a head and predatory sex stirring things up for a few minutes, until a doleful attempt at a final summation from the detective on the case.

The production, directed by Bartlett Sher, simply surrendered to the work's limitations. On a stage dominated by projections of fuzzy early-internet scannings and security-camera video (Michael Yeargan, des., visuals by 59 Productions), figures entered into pools of light, stood and sat, and recited their wordnotes. Behaviorally, this bore a close resemblance to the presentational style of the Adams operas and, ironically, to the most unrepentant park-and-bark stagings of bad opera tradition—minus wonderful arias and greatvoiced singing.

Even in cyberspace, something more than that needs to happen.

There and Then. This is in part an update on updates, occasioned by the unusual coincidence of two Shakespearean events, one a time-forwarded production of the operatic *Falstaff* at the Met, the other an in-period *Twelfth Night* (the play) from London's Shakespeare's Globe, with performance-practice elements we often encounter in music and opera, but seldom in our spoken theatre. The contrast was sharp. The *Falstaff* (Robert Carsen, dir.) did at least bypass the eve of WWI, only to land us in the 1950s. Beyond having come to feel we almost always lose more than we gain with updates, I found this one particularly unproductive. It had the potential advantages of all such displacements—those of underlining social distinctions for the audience and of encouraging more recognizably "natural" behavior from the performers. Less work for all. The first of these, though, is for this opera a solution without a problem: when, in any performance of *Falstaff*, have these distinctions been unclear? The lot of the sorry but sympathetic remnant of nobility fallen amongst the rising mercantiles is baked into the piece. Indeed, that element *loses* force in an updated setting.

As to naturalness of behavior, here are a few things that Carsen causes to happen in Act I, Scene 1: Right at the top, at the entrance of Bardolfo and

Pistola, the former blunders into a table, knocks it over, and sends plates scattering, thus initiating a Three Stooges sequence of improbable actions with no consequences (all ignore the scattered plates); Bardolfo and Pistola hop into bed with Falstaff; Falstaff tweaks Bardolfo by the nose and Bardolfo does a prancey little-step routine till Falstaff lets go; Bardolfo and Pistola cavort on a tabletop to laud Falstaff; Falstaff sings much of the Honor monologue while walking away from Bardolfo and Pistola, as if singing to himself (this is really absurd—the speech doesn't play unless there's constant interplay among the three); and to bring the scene to a riotous, rollicking close Falstaff chases B. & P. from the premises by discharging a hunting piece into the ceiling (twice!), bringing down bits of debris.

That's the mentality at work throughout the production. It's one of phony "comic" theatricality, and it doesn't matter a whit that the men wear suits and the women gather in a '50s middleclass kitchen. That's only an overlay to make us think it's all about us. Your response to this sort of thing depends, I guess, on whether you think that this opera, which must certainly rank with *Le nozze di Figaro* and *Die Meistersinger* as one of the three greatest and deepest of operatic comedies (*Don Giovanni* not being a comedy in the same sense), is best performed as a series of farcical routines and bits of focus-pulling shtick taken from low-comedy stage convention, or as a representation of actions (with consequences) that persons might actually undertake in the situations and relationships they have created for themselves—the whole point being, I would argue, that Verdi and Boïto, working with, yes, time-honored theatrical materials, went far past them, filled them out and lifted them up to the real-life level of sad, sweet, silly humanity. This production took the former route. Its musical performance had some modest virtues, but they fell well short of the redemptive.[8]

Twelfth Night, directed by Tim Carroll and brought into the Belasco Theatre in repertory with *Richard III*, represented the opposite choice. It attempted to place all aspects of physical production and presentational framework (the music, the pre-show) as close as possible to historically authenticated Elizabethan practice, but to play the piece as a well-spoken helping of the modern acting sensibility. The set (a re-creation of the sort of hall with oak screen often used by Shakespeare's company for indoor performances), the costumes, and the seven-piece original-instrument consort afforded delightful sights and sounds, from the pre-show on to the final dance and Feste's closing song, which releases us back to the here and now. The costumes especially intrigued me. Even though we had watched their outer layers being donned during the pre-show, they still "popped," with a richness and depth surpassing those of even the well-built period dressings we often see at the opera. After the performance, as per my custom I read the extensive program note (in a Broadway *Playbill!*) by the designer, Jenny Tiramani. In it, she details the painstaking, labor-intensive search after the now-rare materials and artisanal methods (alum-tawed deerskin from Montana, hand-woven silk velvet from Genoa; hand-stitching and cutting to the old patterns, hook-and-eye fastening, etc.) that went into the multiple layers of Elizabethan dress and accessories. One result of these efforts—the effect on the wearers' postures and movements—can be at least approximated by good reproductions. It was the other, the visual aura, which I sensed and to which I felt drawn from the outset, that was unique in my experience.

The production's last "authenticating" element was the assumption of female roles by male actors. This stopped short, though, of asking boys to take on the parts of Viola, Olivia, and Maria. These actors were grown men of ponderable talents and experience, and there were no falsettoed speeches (inflectional, but not registral, obeissances to feminine usage) or campy flouncings-about. All the felicities of set, clothing, and music would have remained incidental if the acting could not be taken seriously, and acting is the practice that can't be really authenticated—it must incorporate the now-many generational adaptations that have transpired since c. 1600, and even as each performer elaborately and openly "puts on the man," he must also be the man, even when he's a woman.

I would not always want to see Shakespeare performed this way, if for no other reason than that I like to see women on the stage. This was not at all points the most touching or the funniest *Twelfth Night* I have seen. But it was the clearest, the most sharply defined, and drew me the farthest into what felt like the world of the play. The audience response, and that of everyone I've spoken with who saw it, was ecstatic—a festive air surrounded its extended run. I do allow for the "This is a smash, and we're here!" momentum that regularly affects Broadway audiences at prestige events with star actors (in this case, Mark Rylance), but there was no doubt about the genuineness of the enthusiasm. Somehow, sold-out houses that included many young playgoers received this 400-year-old deeply shaded comedy, in a production that ran as far as it could from the pleadingly relevant sort typified by the Met *Falstaff*, as a piece of hot, immediate entertainment.

There and Then; The Flight from E-19. The more I encounter Skipover works and performances, the more it seems to me that the flight from E-19 is also a flight from tragedy—not tragedy as a category, but as an experience. I thought about this while spending some time with two works previously unfamiliar to me, the *Médée* of Marc-Antoine Charpentier and *Atys*, by Jean-Baptiste

Lully. It's odd to think of these operas this way, since both are examples of the *tragédie lyrique*, and are serious dramas in which one or more of the characters we're meant to empathize with meet gruesome deaths. It also happens that in both the deaths are perpetrated by mezzo-ish women possessed of infernal magical powers which they use to wreak vengeance on the male protagonists who have spurned them in favor of lyric-soprano lovers; and if we throw in one or two more nasty-sorceress tales (e.g., *Armide*), it begins to appear that what this genre is actually dealing with is male sexual paranoia in the form of terror of possessive-Mother females, rampaging unchecked through the court of the Sun King. These creators had their own little meta-narrative, generating a tidy bunch of operas for their time and place: *tragédie lyrique*, or, The Undoing of Men.

Médée I met in a performance by the Chicago Opera Theatre. My first shock was the venue. From everything I had known of the company's repertoire and personnel, I had assumed it played in a chamber-opera space, perhaps a neo-Rococo jewelbox like the Pabst up in Milwaukee. So I was bemused to find myself descending through stacked, fluorescent-lit foyers and over open gangways into a vast, sharp-angled hall of catwalks, ducts, and grids, and that my front-row-center balcony seat was quite a throw from the stage. This is important: the volume of the space conditions everything about the performance, especially in a piece so dependent on inflectional details of word-setting and the instrumental articulations that are the orchestra's equivalents. It's not that singers and players couldn't be heard. All could be heard, but little was immediate, and as the performance struggled to life with the scuttling, sawing sounds of the strings-and-recorder-dominated orchestra and the lower-midrange declamations of the singers, the heart sank. I leaned forward and tried to extend my ears.

The cast, headed by the English mezzo Anna Stephany, was for the most part capable. The musical preparation and execution were at a high professional level. The staging, of the choric, ensemble-and-stage-picture sort, was intelligently conceived, admirably detailed, and well blended with expressive, nuanced lighting. The costuming was vaguely contemporary ("timeless"), which in my experience invariably succeeds more with the women than the men—anything gracefully cut will look good and move well on a shapely female body, whereas the men have to do some variation on the modern suit, which leaves them wondering how to carry themselves and takes the whole proceedings down a peg. The set was simple and abstract: a plank deck that curled into jagged ends upstage, suggesting perhaps the ribs of the Argo, the ruins of Corinth, or just a broken-up cradle for the drama. There were also some transparent plastic or Plexiglass cubes, at times practical and at others decorative, that didn't always work out for the best; but on the whole, the physical production conveyed a mood and supported the action.

I specify these aspects of production and performance to make clear that they were by no means so inadequate as to cheat the piece, or the entire genre it represents, of its basic effect. The distancing problem of the venue, though, might come close to doing that, and so I turned to the recording by the designated torchbearers of the French Baroque, William Christie's Les Arts Florissants. On CD, the immediacy of voices and instruments is assured. And much as I had admired Stephany's work, the ears prick up whenever Lorraine Hunt Lieberson comes within earshot. Further, these *are* the specialists. Still, I found my engagement with *Médée* traveling the same trajectory it had in Chicago: the first ninety minutes or so a slog, then a heightening of interest that sustains fairly well till an abrupt end. In a way, I love the end. Médée, with the help of her Hellish contacts and magically poisoned dress that activates at her touch, has driven to insanity Créon, who has murdered Oronte, then killed himself; has sent Créuse to an excruciating death with the aforementioned dress; and finally murdered her children, whom Jason had fathered. Now, with Jason on his knees and the vengeful Thessalians approaching, she just leaves town—no triumph aria, no final duet or lamenting chorus, and certainly no god or goddess descending to restore sanity, resurrect the dead, and receive the praises of the multitudes. Just a few agitated, swirling bars in the strings, and the show's over, with a rather stunning flatness. It's not only a tragedy, but one that refuses any gesture toward transcendence or "closure."

Yet, *Médée* doesn't feel like a tragedy. It has aesthetic pleasures (many of them to be found in the *divertissements*), and evokes the feelings we associate with those, which are mild and temporary—the infernal spookiness is fun for a while, and the death of Créuse brings on a quite enjoyable sort of melancholy. We are brought only to the edge of true dramatic engagement, of deep empathy or horror. We acknowledge the artistically intelligent representation of all these, and a frequent eloquence in telling the story of a tragedy, but not the shattering power, the confrontation with mortality that is the experience of tragedy.

Atys is one of the earlier *trágedie lyriques* of Lully, the man who established the form, albeit with much Italian precedence. Its production by Christie's company, and the production's restoration thanks to the patronage of a wealthy admirer, is legendary in devotee circles, and presented as such by the DVD release.* No business suits here: everyone parades forth in full Louis Quatorze court costume, bewigged in cascades of ringlets, and follows the director's take on the presentational conventions of the period. It's a great, if sombre, look, even if we do expect the men to burst into "When I, good friends, was called to the bar" at the next little chorus. Everything about the production bespeaks devotion to the project and fastidious preparation, presumably according to the understanding that if the circumstances and manners of the place and time are brought to life, the aesthetic and dramatic portals to the work will open, and we can enter in. (Christie & Co. are careful to disclaim "authenticity" or "re-creation.") We who argue for creators' rights and the hierarchy of interpretation can hardly complain about that. Still, even when it is genuine rather than affected, the fascination with a loving reproduction of the antique, along with the savoring of its aesthetic and even our well-earned admiration for the craftsmanship entailed by its pursuit, still leaves us at a remove from the direct impact of the drama. They leave open the question of how a piece is to be sung, acted, played, and danced, these many generational adaptations later.

I have not been steeped deeply enough in the stylistic specifics of French Baroque music and theatre to make declarations on period performance practice or court custom, especially with respect to dance and instrumental music. As presented here, it all looks and sounds plausible to me, and I don't feel intruded upon by *Columbo* associations or The Tumbler.† So any quarrel I have with the dancing and playing is over not its authenticity, but its effect. For me, the interest of the dancing, which is tightly woven into the ensemble as a whole, *is* that of its historical aesthetic, rather than of any urgent emotional involvement or revivifying distraction. The orchestra executes on a very high level. It afforded me many moments of enjoyment, and some of dramatic point, and to those for whom its range of timbres and gestures do not wear down as quickly as they do for me, I'm sure these are multiplied.

As for the singingacting, this form presents the reverse of the *opera seria* problem. Instead of worrying over how to enact thirty virtuosic ABA arias separated by recitative and occasionally relieved by a duet, a brief chorus, or an instrumental *ritornello*, in the *tragédie lyrique* we confront scenes

---

* A flossy presentation, whose many supplements offer some good background on the opera itself, but direct your attention mostly to the production. Nothing substantive in print, of course, that one can contemplate, refer to, consider in one's own time and sequence—you're supposed to catch it all on the fly. Interesting thoughts from conductor, director, designer, choreographer. Not represented: the stage performers.

† Actually, there *are* tumblers, *commedia* types intrinsic to the genre, though if I ask myself "What are the tumblers doing? What is their function?", my only answer is "Well, they had tumblers then."

constructed from dramatically declaimed recitative, interspersed with airs of relatively modest range whose effect relies on clarity of tone and word, and precision in tiny ornamental movements. In *Atys*, there is significant choral participation, always welcome, and in this instance a prolonged sleep-and-dream episode, famous among the initiated, that is extremely lovely and on first encounter had its desired effect—I nodded off and had to go for some refreshment, then re-start the chapter. As with Monteverdi's operas, this layout would seem to be more compatible with the modern acting sensibility than is the *opera seria* structure; it's more like a play with songs and musical interludes. So an operatic equivalent of the Shakespeare's Globe's *Twelfth Night* is not unthinkable. The obstacles are two. One is vocal/rhetorical, and for that see below, under Singing I. The other is behavioral. The key dramatic moments build up their intensity toward a *tirade*-like pitch out of the recitative, in the manner of French classical drama, and without a strong acting craft based on inner technique or the presence of a Luigi Riccoboni* to warn them that the task of the tragedian is to persuade spectators that ". . . they who speak and act are not *Players*, but real *Heroes*," who "were Men like us," performers will tend to simply work up an emotional lather, rather than staying with themselves or each other. That sometimes happens here, and the staging solution is to send people pacing furiously about in choreographed patterns, doing their ultimate to stay sincere under the artificial circumstances. The best moments tend to be quiet ones, or the more quotidian exchanges. As with *Médée*, these unsolved (or partially solved) problems are present, but with all the accomplishments of the performance they don't keep us from getting a fair sense of the opera's character.

We must somehow arrange for an Ovidian festival in which we can alternate *Atys* with Strauss's *Daphne*.† They're a gender-mirrored pair. You'll recall that in *Daphne* the heroine, trapped by the unwanted advances of Apollo, escapes a fate worse than death by becoming a presumably immortal tree, her earthly suitor, Leukippos, dying by the god's hand. And here the hero, similarly trapped by the unwanted attentions of the Mother Goddess Cybèle, is also made into a tree, his worldly beloved, Sangaride, dying through the goddess's machinations. In both cases, the hero/heroine is made to feel responsible for the beloved's death, and it is the vengeful deity who, in a fit of remorse, effects the metamorphosis. This telling is obviously reductive and does not account for differences; but still—that's what happens. In *Daphne*,

---

* Who, as it happens, was born in the year of *Atys'* premiere, 1676.

† I'm not forgetting old Marco da Gagliano and his *Dafne*, which might seem a logical pairing. But that's no fun—Strauss is much the wilder choice.

the death of the mortal lover and final transformation take place before us, and the closing pages are carried by Strauss's magical orchestra and Daphne's wordless voice, floating out from the leaves and branches of her new being. In *Atys*, the death of the lover and Atys' fatal self-wounding occur offstage, though he makes it back on for a death scene. After an air of mourning for Cybèle, she summons the wild, crested, ecstatic drummer-dancers of myth, the Corybantes, who in this version are several gentlemen of the court who perform some stiffbacked, decorous steps, coattails swishing about, to Lully's brief start-up, die-down movements. Then Cybèle proclaims: "*Que le Malheur d'Atys afflige tout le monde*" ("Let the fate of Atys afflict all the world"), and the chorus builds the concluding ensemble on her words.

All this is very solemn and dignified. We are respectful, as at any funeral, as Cybèle, perpetrator and bereaved in one, maintains her game face throughout the ending sequence. But even less than *Médée* does *Atys* feel tragic. Certainly it's all a shame, especially about the innocent Sangaride. But we don't see her die; there's no Liù-moment or Manon-moment, or even a Leukippos-moment, to bring up a tear or two. As for Atys himself, his human life is done, but after all he's a tree now, a sacred evergreen at that, forever part of the Life that continues. That's a touching thought, but as presented here not a touching stage event, and as the fine concluding chorus (not quite up to Handel's Top 100, but on the way) progresses, we realize that though its words are of mourning, the music is actually turning towards a modest sort of transcendence—we're at one of those Celebrate The Life memorial events, and we leave feeling a bit of virtuous uplift, doubtless due in part to being released from staying the course, but surely in part to the effect of these last scenes as well.* So although *Atys* is in form a tragedy (the hero and his beloved die), it consoles us with transformation, even a suggestion of resurrection. (The story of Attis and Cybèle is in fact frequently classified as a resurrection myth, though obviously not of the Christian triumphalist sort.)

---

* It *is* essential to keep in mind the influence of production choices. The decision to forego the work's pastoral elements; the decision to set all the action in a royal apartment rather than to represent, in any style, the indicated locations of Quinault's libretto; the decision to costume the characters in court dress of solemn hues, as if in mourning from the start; the decision to treat the characters choreographically in several crucial scenes, etc.; and here, at the end, the decision to not show us Atys's arborial transformation and the universal homage rendered to it (which, I should think, accounts for that final chorus's tone), but to instead create a candlelit tableau of Cybèle in mourning over the body—these all affect, quite radically, our visual reception of the work. But whether we agree with one choice or another or not, these aren't adversarial. They're all trying to support the work, as were the very different ones of the Chicago *Médée*. And so, unlike those of Wilson's *Lohengrin* or Tcherniakov's *Prince Igor*, they do not dislodge our understanding of the basic nature of the piece, which can still come through, wobbly, via words and music.

However, the most important reason it is hard for us to receive *Atys* as tragedy is the infinitely greater power of E-19 tragedy and the performing energies associated with it. Anyone who has truly engaged with the sad-ending works of Verdi, Wagner, Bizet, Puccini and the verists, and early Strauss, knows that wherever one may rank individual works in relation to one another or in neo-Aristotelian categories, and whether or not they emit the incense of transcendence, they have in common a cathartic pity-and-terror impact far greater than those of Lully or Charpentier, or of other nominally tragic earlier works. And it isn't just a matter of adjusting one's aesthetic to gain access to an analogous experience. Even granted that a magnificently performed, brilliantly produced *Atys* or *Médée* might be enthralling and moving to a degree, it will still bear nothing like the emotional weight of a competent rendering of not only an *Otello* or *Tristan*, but a *Tannhäuser* or *La Traviata*. Or a *La Juive*. That's a different order of "being moved," unavailable—to anyone—in the *tragédie lyrique*. The form simply had not yet developed the musical and dramatic means or indeed the intention, of doing that, and it's an evasion to pretend otherwise.

Now, a tragedy isn't the only thing an opera can be, or the experience one always wants to have. Nor do magical-thinking transformations, unearned happy endings, or narrative closures of dubious permanence foreclose experiences of great beauty, dramatic suspense, and emotional depth. But the enactment of our mortal fate, of all life's promise brought to an end through irreconcilable conflict or a "fatal flaw" embedded in our very humanity, has been drama's highest aspiration from the start. For the past two centuries, opera has provided the most complete fulfillment of that aspiration, but we have now drawn back from it. The *appearance* of tragedy is still allowed. It may be represented, but not deeply felt, and the *tragédie lyrique* is a perfect vehicle for that. It makes it possible for us (depending, always, on performance) to contact the dark side and a tragic tone, yet finally without much consequence. The not-exactly-happy ending may be redemptive or transformative, and may be morally instructive. In any case, it lifts us back up. We can say we've seen a tragedy, but in fact we're off the hook. Real tragedy doesn't do that. It makes us feel that the individual lives of the characters are of supreme personal significance, like those of our loved ones, and does not try to console us for their loss.

This experience of individual mortality as tragic and irretrievable, ameliorated where not ignored by the Skipover mentality, is opera's alone among the large-form musical arts of E-19. It surfaces in the artsong, especially of the German variety, and could occasionally be said to have the final word in chamber or solo instrumental pieces. But in the extensive literature created for symphony orchestra—symphonies, concertos, tone poems, concert over-tures, themes-with-variations—that is almost never the story being told. We encounter, again, the tragic *tone*, along with profound contemplations on mortality and agonizing conflict. But inevitably the joyous, the celebrative, the transcendent, and/or the outright triumphal returns to overcome, if not in a prankish, dancey third movement, then surely by the rousing coda of a fourth. It isn't until Tchaikovsky's last symphony (1893) that any of these major orchestral works ends darkly, and not until their later-yet late sym-phonies that even Mahler or Sibelius forego some variation on victory or transcendence in their finales. E-19 ballet, too, seems to always pull us back just in time from its moments of aching melancholy (the right people getting married in the end), and while some entrancing scores were written to its scenarios, they do not come to grips with mortality with anything like the weight and depth of the operatic masterpieces.

I'm not complaining. I'm never happier than when at a good orchestral concert, or watching a good evening of ballet. But it seems odd to look across the classical music landscape and note that only opera takes on, and thrives on, the sad-ending task. Its loneliness is mitigated if we look to the remaining art of the act, the spoken drama. There we find during the E-19 era an abundance of sad-ending plays from the likes of Schiller and Hugo; Sardou, Scribe, and Rostand; Pushkin and Chekhov; Ibsen, Hofmannsthal, Belasco, and more, along with a continuing repertory of earlier plays that included many with deathly conclusions. (And what an advantage for the operawright, to be able to work with pre-theatricalized words!) Some of these aspired to tragedy in the strictest sense, some tried to define that sense more broadly, and others were happy as high melodrama. They provided the librettistic material for the majority of E-19 operas, the melodramas among them frequently lifted to tragic stature by the music.*

In the opening chapter of this book, I said that although all the ways of defining opera that I can trace would lead us to classify it as a form of theatre, and that it needs to be rescued from the habit of claiming it as a form of music, I believe it's most productive to think of it not as a form of anything else, but as itself, opera as opera. If, however, one were to insist on categoriz-ing opera as theatre, one would have no stronger evidence than this intimacy at its tragic peak with the spoken stage, and its simultaneous divergence from the major musical forms at their own time of highest development.

Tragedy or triumph: now we ascend to neither.

---

* The principal exceptions would be the operas of Wagner, hewn from legendary/historical or mythical matter (though written in what he considered play form before being set to music) and a minority of pieces drawn from novelistic, Biblical, or other literary sources.

Singing I. The coincidence of Skipover singing in contemporary operas (e.g., those of Adams, Adès, Muhly) and in *tragédie lyrique*, plus its increasing encroachment on even the grandest standard repertory works, provokes some further thoughts on vocality. In all the varieties of Skipover usage, it's the first syllable of "wordnote" that bears the stress. The presence of the word, and the development of a singing style reliant on word clarity and meaning, is paramount, especially in contrast to E-19 practices. As I have previously observed, this demands a technique founded on the theatricalized speaking voice, and is especially treacherous for female voices (higher, lighter ones most of all) because their optimum speaking range falls on or near the junction of the upper and lower tonal families. Thus, a tough, durable binding of the registers, with exceptionally clear vowel profile, is essential, and to achieve this without limiting the reach and quality of the voice requires true mastery. We have seen some of the results of less-than-masterful solutions among the talented singers of Felsenstein's company, and we hear it frequently on Broadway.

I had an early epiphany in this connection during the New York visit of the Comédie Française in 1956. They played the Broadway Theatre, then the largest legitimate house in New York apart from the City Center, with a repertory of Molière, Marivaux, and Beaumarchais. I sat far up in the balcony. Throughout the run, but especially in *Le Bourgeois gentilhomme*, I was struck by the easy presence and clarity of the voices; especially among the women and most especially in intimate conversational mode. In those pre-enhancement days, we certainly had strong-voiced actresses in our own theatre, and comprehensibility was seldom a problem. But this was different. When these voices were raised, there was no hint of straining upward in a strident "belt mix," and when they were not, we heard melodious, feminine sounds uttered with unforced lightness, yet carrying easily to the farthest seats in a large theatre.[9]

Recalling this experience during the Chicago *Médée*, it struck me that the voices, though pleasing, were upside down for the demands of the writing. The actors of Molière's own troupe, performing their *commedia*-derived versions of his *comédie-ballet* collaborations with Lully, must have declaimed vigorously with a clear, open technique founded on the lower end of the range, and a few years later the singers of the early *tragédie lyrique* must have worked with a musically extended version of that model. The contemporary singers of this repertoire, however, for the most part display "down from the top" techniques, peaking an octave or so above the "optimum pitch" areas of their speaking voices. It's a scaled-down version of the right-column, Easy Plush structure, often yielding rounded, warm tone, but lacking a sturdy undercarriage. Though the women suffer the most from this, the men also lose some of the core and flash needed for lower-to-midrange declamation, whether of speech or recitative. While it's true that registral integration (which is the necessary precursor to well-aligned vocal acoustics, and hence of strong word formation) is sealed from high to low, from soft to loud, from "head" to "chest," this presumes a well-developed lower family to begin with. "Down from the top" isn't of much use if there's nothing to come down to.

In the examples of their writing encountered in this book (*Platée, Médée, Atys*—and while I suspect this is true across the board, I don't want to generalize beyond them, because I haven't scoured the repertoire for internal evidence), the composers of the French Baroque respected the low ceiling implied by the theatre-declamation structure, and kept the tessitura of their vocal setting middle-ish. The appellation *"haute-contre"* for their proto-tenor protagonists may appear to indicate an exception, but I think at most it's a partial one. These were not castrato parts, or predominantly falsettist ones. Allowing for even a conservative interpretation of time-and-place tuning difference, they extend no higher than many later Franco-Italian tenor leads (e.g., Faust, Nadir, Ernesto, Fernand) and not as far as the high-extension ones of Bellini, Rossini, et al. As for tessitura, Platée, a *travesti* role and thus a special case, lies very high in our tenor range, with a clear allotment of defined Upper Family (i.e., female) notes. Of the two heroic roles, Charpentier's Jason sits fairly high, Lully's Atys quite low, the technical difficulty (especially for Jason) being that so much of the writing on the upper side of the *passaggio* is talky. This was undoubtedly handled with shadings of *voix mixte*, relieving the voices of some air pressure and the oppositional tensions that go with it, and so easing the enunciatory task—a from-the-ground-up structure not so different from the later pre-Duprezian kind, limiting vocal power at the top, but preserving oratorical vigor down below. That's quite different from calibrating the entire range to the weights of a head-derived blend.

Of the two tenor heroes on the recordings, one is highly effective, and the other has admirable solutions. The Atys, Bernhard Fischer, with a voice of typical Mozart/Handel configuration that does not suggest "countertenor," has enough strength in his lower octave to declaim with precision and force, and the occasional higher forays have some fire. Mark Padmore's distinctly headier instrument negotiates Jason with stylistic expertise and inflectional acuity, but is not able to hint at the heroic. I have not heard either of these voices live.

In most kinds of word-centered vocal writing, some loss of tonal splendor and entrancing musical effect (brilliant floridity; ravishing line; thrilling *acuti*) is tolerated for the sake of verbal clarity and nuance and of declamatory eloquence. From Monteverdi and Lully to Debussy and Janáček, we accept the tradeoff when the writing accomplishes that goal and has other musicodramatic fascinations. In the best of Britten we find a unique combining of the virtues. But in the Adams, Adès, and Muhly works, we heard singing whose aesthetics ranged from dull and bland to actively irritating, and nevertheless could not be understood: among the men, squealy-voiced tenors who sounded as if they were singing a third higher than they actually were and muzzy-voiced high baritones of indistinguishable format and color; among the women, gentle-sounding modern mezzos of modest calibre, the occasional light soprano, or croaky low "character" voices that didn't project. All were "dictionizing" feverishly, and all were incomprehensible, because just as "down from the top" is no good without a bottom, so "diction" is no good without the range of harmonics provided by full-throated tone—vowels are resonance, and vice-versa. Thus, while the program synopsis for *Klinghoffer* told me that at one point in Act I Mahmoud sings of the night, of the music he hears on the radio, and of his memories, and that at another he sings of the freedom of migrating birds, I have to answer that no, he did not. He sang of nothing, partly because the music is so generic that one passage could be about the other or about many other things, and partly because the singer could not render intelligible wordnotes in the required tessitura. At the other end of the spectrum, the solo of the Austrian Woman remained a mystery owing to vocal weakness in the lower range, where most of it was set. The examples are chosen for their purity, but are not unrepresentative.

We could hold the singers responsible, and wouldn't be wrong altogether. Indeed, during these performances I found myself recalling the many artists I have heard singing in English in our opera houses and making the words not only comprehensible but vibrantly present, even when the writing was difficult, and wondering how much difference it could make if Detective Inspector Anne Strawson of *Two Boys* had been sung by Irene Dalis or Regina Resnik or Blanche Thebom, or the Captain of the Achille Lauro by Theodor Uppman or John Reardon or (to go all the way) Sherrill Milnes. Certainly the casting of such pieces at either the NYCO or the Met in the 1950s or '60s would have encouraged us to at least pay attention and stay with the stories, and the sense of personal ear-contact with the performers would have provided some substitute for the lack of character in the writing.[10]

So yes, the singers are at fault. But it's a writing/casting vicious circle. The Met would have had to squander Stephanie Blythe on the role of the detective, and Keenlyside, I suppose, on that of the Captain (and why would either consent?) just to achieve the denotative level of word meaning, and it wouldn't have been enough to make the music interesting. The composers write faceless stuff in ranges unlikely to yield the verbal clarity they say they want, then are given singers whose strengths lie elsewhere or, operatically speaking, nowhere.

A much more productive way of thinking about vocal setting, and musical dramatization in general, is advanced by *Written on Skin*, with music by George Benjamin and libretto by Martin Crimp. Where I'll finally settle with this piece I don't know,[11] but as heard on CD it's intriguing, and with respect to narrative technique is at once odder and more plausible than any other I've heard lately. The piece returns us to the time and place of the faydit story—Provence in the 1200's—and even sets up a debased version of the courtly love triangle: a woman (Agnès) married to a powerful landowner (the Protector) is drawn into a liaison with an artist (The Boy) who produces an illuminated book that encodes their forbidden passion. Things don't end well. The husband murders the artist and serves the deceased's heart to his wife for dinner; she says it tastes great, then jumps off the balcony. There's more to discover, worth it if you can tune into the weird wavelength.

The music of *Written on Skin* still seems more orchestrally than vocally generated, but it gets round to the dramatic point of each scene, of each character's drive through the story. Three aspects of the word/music relationship are of interest in the present context. One is the setting of lines in the third person (The Boy sings: "This—says The Boy—is a work of Mercy"; The Protector sings: "But the Protector takes the page ...", etc.). On the surface this is a distancing device, but by reminding us constantly of the telling of the story (and doing so by ear, not by eye) it maintains suspense, especially in combination with the second aspect, which is the held-back pace of the musical progression, with broken words we have to wait on for completion (another suspense device) and epithetic repetitions, so that the effect is of simultaneous enactment and bardic recitation. In Agnès's final defiant solo, this technique is set aside, and she sings from the purely subjective P.O.V. of most dramatic characters. The third aspect is the care taken in selection of pace, instrumentation, and tessitura to give the words a fighting chance. Timewise, there is usually space around the wordnotes, so that they register, except when there is deliberate overlap for a particular dramatic point. The orchestra, which achieves considerable mass and intensity when taking the lead, is kept to discreet underscoring in most of the dialogue scenes. With one exception, the tessitura of the vocal writing is kept within acoustical reason, and the performers take good inflectional advantage of this. The exception, as one might suspect, is in the big confrontation toward the end, especially in the writing for Agnès, with its wide intervallic leaps and phrases to be

punched out at both range extremes. Barbara Hannigan, who in E-19 categorizations would be called a *Hochsopran*, gives what sounds like a terrific performance. But in a piece that has been at pains to establish that the words are
crucial, it's too bad to lose some of them at the top, and to direct a voice of this
type into perilous-sounding pushing at the bottom, even for brief stretches—
as if Mélisande were suddenly asked to scream high D's and declaim in chest.

While many Skipover voices could use a post-Duprezian booster shot even for
their own purposes in their own venues, their modest formats and amiable
timbres, if allied with the appropriate musical and linguistic gifts, can carry
out their customary artistic missions well enough. But too often, their attributes are being taken for adequacy in the grand opera context, and voices
so developed are making the rounds in major E-19 roles. In the 2014 Met run
of *Meistersingers*, we had two instances: the Beckmesser of Johannes Martin
Kränzle and the David of Paul Appleby. Kränzle does not sing Skipover repertory. Many of his parts have fallen on the lyrical side of the standard canon,
but he's also taken on not only Wolfram and the *Figaro* Count (I would judge
him to be 2/3 of a Hermann Prey, already on the light side for those roles),
but Gryaznoi (*Tsar's Bride*—a dramatic baritone part) and Alberich. Appleby
came through the company's Lindemann Young Artist Development program, and aside from character roles his repertory has centered on Mozart.

The question isn't whether or not these are good artists. I could tell that
both were pursuing a welter of artistic minigoals, and perhaps scoring a fair
percentage of them. But I had to infer much of that. Kränzle's Beckmesser had
two virtues: his voice was not ugly, and he did his best to avoid caricature.*
But if a singer elects to forego the comic behavioral clichés and the "character
voice" deformities often encountered in the part, he must replace them with
a domineering officiousness of manner and desperation of purpose in his
pursuit of Eva to make him a ridiculous but formidable antagonist, and these
must be made present of voice and body throughout the hall. Kränzle seemed
to be working intelligently toward the sort of rendition that earns critical
approval for being "like that of a Lieder singer," forgetting that the artists that
have made such an approach work (Hans Hotter, in such roles as Wotan and
Sachs, is a go-to citation) have done so with voluminous grand opera instru-

---

* When I say he did his best, I mean that his instincts were in that direction. He and all the
other principals were saddled with the often pointless comings and goings of the production's original blocking, as transmitted 21 years later by the assigned staff director.
In Beckmesser's case this included repeatedly traversing the steps of the Act II set, one
at a time, to show "mounting" frustration during Sachs's "*Jerum, jerum!*", and pretending
the stair railing was his lute during his workshop scene delirium. Dumb ideas, and to
judge from his half-hearted execution of them, he seemed to agree.

ments. Kränzle's narrow baritone is well-balanced and well-tuned; he probably brought off many nice moments as miked for HD or radio. In the house, they did not impose even when detectable. It would have taken a voice of Fischer-Dieskau's format and color range to make this approach tell. F-D sang Kothner, and later Sachs, but he would have been the Beckmesser for the ages.

I had looked forward to Appleby's David. I thought that, apart from one strange-sounding high excursion that could have been an anomaly, he had handled the thankless writing of *Two Boys* admirably, and his grainy, medium-sized lyric tenor had a warmth and flexiness that sounded apt for this important and challenging role. In *Meistersinger*, when he sang out—especially in Act III—that proved to be so. But that's two intermissions past his own obstacle-strewn Act I trial song. The episode is brilliantly written, and at *"Der Meister Tön' und Weisen"* briefly offers a highly ingratiating, vocally rewarding melody. But what a hard scene! Ten minutes spent describing infinite varieties of rigidity and fustiness while we wait for the action to move forward—we need a fine singer with a captivating personality. Melchior, whose recording of Walther's excerpts constitute the touchstone for the opera's tenor lead, declined to ever sing that role, by reason of its unremitting tessitura, with no chance to renew the voice's grounding. David lies just as high, and calls for two emphatic phrases topping off on the high B natural and positioned as the climactic statements of his big scene. Along the way, the singer encounters trills, crush notes, little runs (of wordnotes, not vocalise), and nuanced high phrase endings that suggest a virtuosic bel canto tenor. So a lighter, more flexible voice than Walther's is clearly implied. Yet David, shoemaker's apprentice and the intended of Magdalene, is a sturdy young man in a Wagner opera, and the success of the many subtle effects is in direct relation to the calibre of the voice. Appleby, obligated to the kind of scampery busy-ness that seeks to illustrate everything he's telling us about, literally chased about the stage in pursuit of a mastertone here, another there, but keeping most of them to himself. Both assaults on the Bs were undertaken in a spread reinforced falsetto, so that the elaborately constructed edifice was never topped off.

The casting of these roles (and, on this particular evening, a couple of others as well) resulted in long stretches of what a conductor friend of mine used to call "great mental singing," by which he meant singing that shows recognition of appropriate effects, but not their actual accomplishment. In terms of artistic effort, this is a step up from singing that shows no such recognition to begin with. But it doesn't satisfy.

And no, it's not my admittedly ancient ears: solo instruments, small orchestral groupings playing at *p* or *pp*, came up to Balcony Row C very nicely.

Singing II. From the ranks of tenor contenders mentioned earlier (see p. 326), a new one of unquestionable artistic significance has emerged. I mean, of course, Jonas Kaufmann, and I say "of course" in full confidence that not many readers were about to name someone else. Kaufmann can actually sing, at a level that would give him standing among the leading tenors of the 1950s and '60s. And in terms of acting for the eye, he is superior to any of them. His Cavaradossi in April, 2010 brought the best singing of a romantic tenor role I'd heard since the primes of Pavarotti and Domingo, and his Werther in March, 2014 had only Shicoff's Eléazar to match it as the most compelling male performance over an even longer span.* When a performer stands out this way among others who, at least under certain conditions, can sing and/or act quite well—and when sheer vocal splendor is not of itself responsible—it is because of some unusual combination of virtues, frequently including an oddity or two. So it is with Kaufmann. Readers will by now anticipate that the virtues unexpectedly combined in his work have to do with fusing a modern actor's instincts with those of a premodern singer's, and that the outstanding oddity has to do with vocal technique. I'm going to focus on Kaufmann's performances in the opera house, where opera is opera, and where the unexpected has its full, not-to-be-doubted impact. But his recordings (very few, compared with those of any major tenor of the LP or early CD era) can afford some supplementary reference, and his video presence will allow further consideration of what lives in the theatre, what on camera and mike, and why.

The unexpected initially arises from simply clearing what we used to consider the lower bars. From his first few minutes onstage in *Tosca* hopes are raised: the voice's intonation seems untroubled! His upper range has a clear, gathered ring! He's shaping phrases, controlling the line and the dynamics, *interpreting the music!* This much is evident by the end of "*Recondita armonia*," with its stunningly graded final diminuendo on the F at "*Sei tu!*". (Carlo Bergonzi made this effect, too. But we expected it from him.) Upon the conclusion of the Act I love duet we've relaxed, safe in the hands of someone who is in charge of his performance. His vocal and musical competence will no longer be unexpected. From here on out, we can turn our attention to his artistic choices, in the happy awareness that he has some.

---

* I should give a nod to Rolando Villazon's Met debut as Alfredo, which within its more purely lyric framework accomplished almost as much. But his misfortunes have not permitted him to fulfill the great promise. Among women undertaking standard repertory roles, I can think only of the very best of Mattila (Lisa) and Netrebko (Gilda) as equivalent artistic achievements.

A second source of the unexpected is this: Kaufmann's technical set-up is unconventional, especially in the context of Franco-Italian tenor writing, and we don't expect it to work as well as it does. The peculiarity is related to the one already identified as a trend among postwar tenors—either an overall darkening, or a darkening of the lower range that the singer hopes will not preclude *squillo* at the top, but whose pharyngeally dominated resonance and right-column looseness don't sound solid enough to hold such a structure together. It's especially unexpected that this framing would serve well for a voice that, like Kaufmann's, is not of dramatic calibre. It's lyric with a dash of spinto in size, but because of this peculiarity, not characteristically lyric in quality—we don't associate that darkness with the voice type. So far, however, Kaufmann has made highly effective use of this set-up.

I'll return to the technical question below. First, to Kaufmann's Werther. For an artist not averse to digging beneath the surface, this is a much more interesting role than Cavaradossi. Cavaradossi is romantic and courageous. He fights bad guys, but has no battle with himself, whereas Werther is nothing but inner struggle. Stopped at the first bend on his protagonist-couple pathway (he cannot even induce Charlotte to join him against the world), he can do nothing with his faydit passion but turn it in on himself. The inevitably tragic standoff between engulfing emotion and social containment is what generates the protagonists' music, the darkest Massenet ever wrote, and accounts for the work's uniquely haunting quality. And here's the always-hoped-for, but now most unexpected thing of all: Kaufmann understands the suffering romantic soul—"understands" it as a visceral connection—and can make us feel that in the opera house.

Vocally, Werther is a perfect fit with Kaufmann's strengths. The penumbral velvet of his lower range, which at softer dynamics threatens to turn to cotton but never quite does, is a sombre cloak for the moments of suppressed despair, and provides the *messa di voce* basis for the crucial shaded dynamics of many phrases on and just above the *passaggio*. From there, he's able to rise without a glitch on the graduated arcing ascents into the upper range at full voice that carry the poet's passion to its anguished heights. (Kaufmann never opens the tone in the upper-middle area in the once-typical Italian manner, but also has no need to "cover," since the voice is already "turned over." He stays on a gleaming, centered track until an occasional widening at the very top on open vowels.) Among the great variety of tenors who have had special success with Werther—and they range, in light-to-heavy ranking, from Schipa to Kraus to Gedda to Thill to Corelli—Kaufmann commands the role's defining gestures with an intriguingly different mix of colors and weights. Further, we are almost never in the moment aware of gestures and colors and weights as such, or even the peculiarity, but only of the expression of a life that hangs by a thread.

This last, naturally, is bound up with the embodiment. In *Tosca* we saw a handsome man of Mediterranean aspect (despite his origins) and almost ideal physique, in his natural element onstage, always focused on the intent of the moment and able to convey intensity and commitment without gesticulations related only to the effort of singing. The effect of these attributes, useful in any role, are multiplied in that of Werther. And they are eminently suited to the video situation, as can be verified by the 2010 DVD of the Opéra Bastille production: the physical centering, the organization of singing energies and elimination of peripheral ones, the concentration on his partner when with her and on his inner state when alone—all these read tellingly on camera. Nothing's in our way. Still, this is all on video. Had I seen the DVD first, I might have entertained concerns about its opera house impact. But in fact I bought the DVD because I'd found Kaufmann's performance moving in the theatre. I also hoped it would quiet an ominous feeling I'd gotten from the only other Kaufmann video I'd seen, a Covent Garden *Carmen*—namely, that when we got close up we'd find nothing much going on. (For more on the *Werther* video, see n. 12.) In the theatre, I had been excited to see a visual analogue to my long-ago experience with the voices of the Comédie's women: physical acting that partook of no grand gestures or demonstrative significations but which, when united with a sufficient vocal presence, sustained dramatic tension and drew me in, as so many others of late had not. Thus, a small behavioral moment, like his greeting of the children in the first scene, held and left a mark because of its fullness. Unsentimental, it suggested not only an adult-to-child tenderness, but a grave respect and identification with the innocence of the very young. And the rare incidents of more overt physicalization, sudden then quickly contained, struck home as disruptions of a powerful inner life.

Kaufmann's Werther set a paradigm for contemporary performance of this and other agonized romantic protagonists: the voice pours forth what the body may not show. Under less favorable circumstances, this contained, modern rhetoric of the body can read as cool, even diffident, and can leak over into the singing, as well. By "less favorable circumstances" I mean roles that lure Kaufmann into some of the easy modes his technique allow him to enter (i.e., an over-reliance on very soft singing and on an ongoingness of phrase), and/or unhelpful productions. To date, I've seen these dampening factors at work twice, in *Faust* and *Parsifal*, and while it's not always possible to disentangle them, since the former can be at least in part a response to the latter, we can consider them in juxtaposition and set down our impressions. First, to be more specific on matters of voice and technique, including the peculiarity:

As I have noted, Kaufmann's instrument is not of dramatic calibre. If you've read of its thrilling power or house-filling size (I've even seen it likened to Del Monaco's), forget it. I would love to see Kaufmann in his *Jugendlich Heldentenor* roles (Walther, Lohengrin, Erik), but in relation to the best postwar singers of that repertory (Kónya, Thomas, Heppner), his voice is the next size down. In my light-to-heavy lineup of Werthers above, it falls between the mature Gedda and Thill, but probably closer to Gedda (I know Thill only from records), which puts him in the vicinity of Shicoff, to whom he is most closely comparable. But all these comparisons are deceptive, owing to the peculiarity. The dark wrap on Kaufmann's lower range gives an impression of heft that is different not only from the lean clarity of a Kraus or Gedda, but from the *oscura* heard in dramatic voices like Del Monaco's or Merli's, which was always informed by the *chiaro*, by core. Yet it isn't bulky, like Vinay's or McCracken's, and mustn't be confused with weight. It's the sort of loose, pliable structure we might anticipate hearing from a good *Lieder* baritone (of the modern type, that is—a Prey, not a Schlusnus), and the *mezza-voce* effects Kaufmann obtains higher up are also similar to those such a voice might give us. Because it's a low-compression adjustment, it puts no drag on the transition notes, and allows the upper range to ring freely. It is not, however, the strongly braced platform from which *tenor di forza acuti* can be launched, and if more compression were summoned within it (in quest of heavier repertory, for instance), it could become weighty. This is an altogether unique balancing of registral and resonantal elements. How he arrived at it (for it represents a major re-tooling of his earlier technique) is a story he has sketched in interviews, and makes for the sort of debate that voice professionals find endlessly stimulating.[13]

With one vocal caveat, Faust should be an excellent role for Kaufmann. He's within the style, sings that sort of line and handles that sort of tessitura well, and should be able to locate a dramatic key in the character. Though capably sung, it didn't turn out very well at the Met. The vocal caveat has to do with the peculiarity. Because he doesn't sing open vowels in the *passaggio* (quite a contrast with the Crooks/Jobin/Di Stefano succession of the '40s, and with the better-balanced Thill and Björling, too), he can't bring much life to upper middle phrases whose emphasis relies on an open sound (two examples from the opening scene: "*Pourquoi trembles-tu dans ma main?*" and "*la jeunesse, et la foi!*", both on F, both pleading for an opening-out). Such moments are important, but they do pass. More bothersome was the withdrawal of great portions of the Garden Scene into a half-voice of the easy-does-it kind, offering us the condiment in place of the entrée, and a demeanor that suggested the scrupulously dutiful rather than the urgently engaged.* Parsifal is a different case, a role that lies much lower, offers none of the lofting line that carries a strong lyric voice out and up, and realizes many of its climactic gestures directly on the passaggio notes. Kaufmann sang through the more proclamatory passages solidly and securely, but without the extra impassionisation that might compensate for the midsized tonal presence. In the Good Friday scene, where I thought his *mp*-to-*mf* shadings would give us a rare benediction, he offered only a pretty softness that sounded disconnected when it could be heard at all.

In the notes he provides for his CD of Verdi arias, Kaufmann addresses the half-voice question, unsurprisingly in the context of the final high B-flat of "*Celeste Aida*":

> "On no account should this note be blasted out. If tenors nonetheless do so, this is usually because they are worried that audiences will think that they are crooning or perhaps that they are not sufficiently masculine. This macho complex is unfortunately widespread. Yet such a *piano* sound requires at least as much power as a tremendous *forte*, for physically speaking, the singer should be able to turn up the volume at any moment and transform this *piano* into a *forte*."

Having already discussed the male *mezza-voce* at some length, I wouldn't re-open the subject were it not relevant to the work of a superb artist whose use of it can be experienced today in the theatre as well as on recordings. Three observations:

1. Yes, the *Aïda* marking is notoriously unobserved, and there is that lovely subdued postlude. In my in-house experience, the *pp, morendo* has been best indicated by Bergonzi, who sang a perfectly controlled *mp*, and by Corelli, who attacked at *forte* and then brought off a long, even *diminuendo*, giving us both the macho and the *morendo*. Otherwise, every tenor I've seen as Rhadames has sung it *forte*, including some fine ones I would hesitate to call inartistic. Then there's the long line, from Björling back to Caruso and beyond, of recorded versions. Nothing wrong, I think, with a

---

* Full disclosure: I cut my evening's losses at the end of Act III, Kaufmann being by far the least of my problems with the proceedings, so if anything startlingly unlikely occurred thereafter, I missed it. When professionally assigned, staying the course is my duty. On my dime and time, the choice is mine. N.B.: I love *Faust*.

ringing high note that shines like the sun ("*un trono vicino al sol*"). See my earlier remarks on the end of "*O de' verd'anni miei*" (*Ernani*).

2. "Macho complex?" Maybe. More often, I think, lack of that particular technical skill, or confidence in its reliability. Or, simple tenor joy in bringing down the house.

3. Kaufmann's last sentence is correct, and is exactly the point. Sometimes I hear that swell-and-diminish latency in his soft singing, and sometimes not. Two possibilities have occurred to me: either the overall "relaxed" engagement of his voice makes it problematic to add in the tensile, held-back quality of the operatic mezza-voce, or he doesn't realize the extent to which his floaty *pianissimi*, which sometimes do sound like crooning for the mike, let us slip off the hook. In any case, that high B-flat—which on the recording he begins with what sounds like a supported *piano* that would be convincing if longer held, but quickly passes over into a delicate head- voice—will carry; the E-to-G phrases of *Karfreitagszauber* not really, and since in other music he makes wonderful effects with a more sup-ported half-voice in his tessitura, it's exasperating. See the remarks on Vickers and apply the two-to-three ratio.

I mentioned unhelpful productions. Star singers are seldom open about this, even in a generalized way, and substar singers simply can't be. But in a 2012 interview with Marie D'Origny,[14] Kaufmann speaks of it. In response to her observation that he always seems confident that his sense of a character will survive the staging, he concedes that this is "... sometimes very difficult," citing the disruptive departures of auteuristic productions and the "constant fight" between a conductor who is not interested in "... the story, the sets, the singers, or anything [but the orchestra]" and a director who "... believes it's an all-visual thing." His workaround: "As long as you've done a traditional production ... you have that in your head. No matter what goes on around you, you just create this moment for yourself." Probably that's the best a per-former can do in this now-normal *sauve qui peut* situation (where, though, would he or she have done this "traditional production?"). But where does it leave the rest of us? We're watching someone trying to sing and act what's in his head, while everything that "goes on around" him either has nothing to do with it or is in opposition to it. The best we can hope for is that some in the audience have also seen "traditional" productions (that is, ones that at least roughly honor the creators' indications) or have constructed compat-ible mind's eye versions, and can on an occult plane hang in there with the performer in contradiction of everything they're seeing, hoping that at some point the singing will transcend. Perhaps it will, at some point.

We are back to the hierarchy of interpretation, to actualism, to the "creative independence of the performer," and to horror of the literal. Indeed, Kaufmann tells us that when he questions why he's asked to do something when everything in the story, in what's being sung, and in what the music is saying is different, the answer that comes back is "Don't be so literal." There speaks the dis-integrative postmodern mentality, enemy of coherent art. Kaufmann: "I believe that when all arrows are pointing in the same direction, then this is a reason why you should probably go there." Yes, but not if you're not following those arrows, or aiming for that target.

In my experience with him so far, Kaufmann always stays on track. Whether a role is exactly right or not, whether a production aids or detracts or just leaves him alone, even whether or not he's in his best form (in the *Faust*, he was just coming off an illness), he maintains vocal and bodily integration. That's why he can have a superstar's career. But I also believe that "production" (direction and design, rehearsal process) is a powerful determinant of when he can or can't render full justice to his remarkable talent.* And I believe that is true for many performers—most of all those with strong lie-detector instincts—and at a literally organic level. Caught up in the streaming contradiction between what he or she is being required to sing—to whom, for what reason, under what circumstances, in what sort of environment—and the truth he or she feels strongly is there and must be expressed, there are just two options: sell your artistic soul by diving into the nonsensical, or pull back in, stay on track, and hope it reads. However deep inside the shutdown occurs, the artist always knows: "This isn't the truth." In *Tosca*, the production (Luc Bondy, dir., Richard Peduzzi, des.) had some bizarre aspects, but in terms of the basic character relationships and activities involving Cavaradossi was not seriously obstructive, and granted a receptive, participant partner (Patricia Racette), Kaufmann was free to give a performance. In *Faust*, the world of the production had been pulled so far away from that of the words and music that an air of general discouragement settled in quite early, and the two appropriately cast principals, Kaufmann and Pape, fell back on a tucked-in professionalism. In *Parsifal*, the *Personenregie* was such that people sang for and to themselves most of the time, Kundry and Parsifal turned away from each other for long stretches of their pivotal Act II scene. The only

---

*   In the Covent Garden *Carmen* (Francesca Zambello, dir.), for example, he spends most of his time doing nothing but staying on track, not because of an ideas-based concept, but because of a welter of ill-chosen physicalizations that keeps the two talented leads careening from one tortured invention to the next. He sings very well, but on video this disappears in the behavioral scrum.

character for whom that works is Amfortas, and accordingly Peter Mattei gave the one performance that exerted a grip.

The Met's *Werther* (Richard Eyre, dir., Robert Howell, sets and costumes) was of a kind customarily called "traditional" or "conventional," by which is meant that it has a representational look, seeks to hang together as a drama, and is not ruled by conceptual ideas. It has revisionist aspects, though. It moves the action forward a century to the composer's era, perhaps on the same reasoning that underlay the Peter Brook/Rolf Gérard *Faust*—that this sounds like French music of the latter 19th Century, not German music of much earlier. It's Massenet's tone, not Goethe's. I think Massenet threw himself back in time with great success, and that the work's early Romantic pattern of effusion and repression, with its strong religious undertone, plays better in that context, provided it is visually specified for us with atmosphere and detail. I also would like my mind's eye, not the director's, to be the one at work during the prelude and interludes. The music is more powerful and evocative than even a sensitive acting-out of the family backstory, of the dance, of the fatal shot; and this heard-but-not-seen life is quintessentially operatic, and Romantic. And for me, Albert returning in military uniform instead of his quotidian bourgeois mufti is the wrong kind of explanation. Still, this is a relatively compatible update, and the pantomimed sequences are at least efforts to sustain a narrative. Kaufmann was able to incorporate the changed perspectives, the qualities of new moments, without losing the arc and emotional commitment he had already established for "his" Werther. As with the quite different Bastille production (see n. 12), I got the sense that there had been productive interchange between the director and performers.

In Jonas Kaufmann I see and hear an extraordinary artist with a singing technique unusual enough to make him distinctive, an equally unusual melding of vocal and theatrical attributes, and perhaps a little too much faith in the modern actor's belief that if a thought or feeling is full, it will carry to the edges of the universe. In the prevailingly unfriendly artistic environments of contemporary opera productions, he always survives and from time to time releases something close to the fullness of his talent. In moments of idle dreaming, I see him as the leading tenor of the New York City Opera of the 1960s, performing all his compatible roles with those singers, directors, and designers, and an occasional guest or two from the old Komische Oper. Not much money, not enough rehearsal, and little bouts with American provincialism, but I think he might have felt at home.

Acting. A recent book, Olga Haldey's *Mamontov's Private Opera*,[15] helps us fill out the story of the Russian beginnings of opera as modern theatre. We've known about Saava Mamontov and his company from the memoirs of Chaliapin, Stanislavski, and Levik, and a few other references. But this is the first book-length account in English of the history, artistic standing, and impact of this remarkable enterprise. Mamontov, a railroad magnate and aesthete turned impresario and director, established his opera company in Moscow in 1885, and maintained it, with some interruption, into the first years of the 20ᵗʰ Century. During that time, it gave the premieres of several of Rimsky-Korsakov's operas and performed an ambitious repertory mix of Russian and Western European works. In competition with the state-sponsored Bolshoi, it represented a decidedly more progressive aesthetic, with emphasis on the fusing of all elements into a unified theatrical event. And unlike the Theatre of Musical Drama up in St. Petersburg, Stanislavski's opera studio, or Felsenstein's Komische Oper, the Mamontov Private Opera did not have to make do with a modest level of vocal accomplishment—even aside from Chaliapin, some of Russia's important singers were regulars with the company.

Haldey colorfully describes the confluence of artistic cross-currents that became the Mamontov production style, and the influences of that style on the projects of Stanislavski, Diaghilev, and ultimately Meyerhold and other avant-gardists of the Russian theatre, where we pick up the traces of the developments described earlier. She makes a strong case for Mamontov's company as the first to organize opera production along theatre-ensemble lines, with the dramatic director in charge. But, while Mamontov was assuredly a lover of singing (he had studied the art, and had evidently reached an advanced amateur level in it), and while according to Chaliapin's account he had the sense to recognize a great, new kind of talent and allow it to grow in his company's soil, his concept of integrated production had design at its center. He was a bold and discerning connoisseur of the fine arts, and into his Circle and theatre he brought many of Russia's best and most innovative painters, several of whom (the Vasnetsov brothers, Konstantin Korovin, Mikhail Vrubel) became the set and costume designers for most of his productions. He wanted a " . . . *powerful*, talented performance of the *drama*,* and as stage director worked painstakingly to get it. What he did not do was seek to develop the creative independence of his performers. Like so many before and after him, he visualized and demonstrated—often, no doubt, to good effect—but the ideas were his, and the integration was that of performer into the pictorial effect, often choreographically conceived or related to pantomimic or other stylized forms of expressive gesture. It was Stanislavski's perception, early

---

* See Haldey, p. 131. It is this Chapter Five, "Opera as Drama," that most closely examines Mamontov's directorial involvement with performance.

in both men's formation as dramatic artists, that Mamontov's magnificent physical productions and interesting conceptual ideas were useless without a developed acting craft and coherent staging that led him to the realization that what was needed was a theatre centered on the performer's own creative process.* That's a very different interpretation of the "integrated production" ideal, fitfully raised in opera ever since the short-lived efforts of the Theatre of Musical Drama, and quickly squelched on each reappearance. Mamontov's place in our Pantheon, I think, is as early Champion of The Design Matrix.

---

* See *My Life in Art*, pp. 72-74 (Benedetti edition).

NOTES

1. See Jaron Lanier: *You Are Not a Gadget* (Alfred A. Knopf, N.Y. 2010) and *Who Owns the Future?* (Simon and Schuster, N.Y., 2013), and Astra Taylor: *The People's Platform*, Metropolitan/Harry Holt, N.Y. 2014). Lanier was a pioneer in the field of virtual reality and all internet-related matters, and so writes from inside the subject at a high level of expertise, his early enthusiasms still intact but tempered by later insight into the social, cultural, and economic impact of digital technologies and the social media. He confronts ethical problems and is not afraid of radical proposals, like his system of nanopayments to everyone for everything they contribute to the net—an idea I suspect he borrowed from the residuals and royalties structure of the recording, publishing, and film-TV industries (he's a musician). Taylor is a less quirky writer whose previous subjects (as author and film documentarian) have included contemporary philosophy and the Occupy Movement. She sorts through the twisted promises of internet democracy and openness, and such related issues as its exacerbation of economic inequality and the denial of the value of individual creativity (authorship, copyright, etc.) with surprising clarity and coolness for someone who is herself caught up in the predicaments. I have also found Andrew Keen's *The Cult of the Amateur*, Lee Siegel's *Against the Machine*, and Robert Levine's *Free Ride* informative and reinforcing, as I have many articles and columns (haven't yet got round to their books) of Evgeni Morozov, Nicholas Carr, and Sherry Turkle. Read any of them, and think of the implications for opera and high culture in general as you do so.

2. See Zygmunt Bauman: *Liquid Times*, Polity Press, 2007.

3. R.I.P. New York City Opera, b. 1944 (first performance) as a component of the New York City Center of Music and Drama, *as a civic enterprise* under the administration of Mayor Fiorello La Guardia, to provide high quality performances at popular prices;* m. 1966 to Lincoln Center for the Performing Arts; div. 2011; d. 2013 under the administration of Mayor Michael Bloomberg with his moving eulogy entitled "Their Business Model Doesn't Seem To Be Working." The story of the company's birth out of the spirits of the WPA and the Austro-Hungarian *Volksoper* is recounted in Martin Sokol's *The New York City Opera/An American Adventure* (Macmillan, NY, 1981), which carries the history, with annals, up to the year of publication.† The company's populist mission, and its years of greatest artistic importance, have been misunderstood in more recent references. While the City Opera always sought out items of repertoire (the neglected, the contemporary, the American) to help mark off some territory vis á vis the Metropolitan, the majority of its evenings (except during the Ford-subsidized American spring seasons) were taken with bringing the *Fausts* and *Carmens* and *Hoffmanns*, *Traviatas* and *Rigolettos*, *Figaros* and *Giovannis* and Puccini Big Three to The People at People-friendly prices. And while

---

* The NYC/City Center deal, as amended after the company's solvency crisis of the mid-'50s, was: the city will give you a long-disused albatross, the Mecca Temple on 55th Street, for a buck a year. Keep tickets cheap. Not unlike Felsenstein's bargain for the Metropol four years later.

† Also see Jean Dalrymple: *From the Last Row* (James T. White, Clifton, N.J., 1975), a more personal view of the events by a longtime participant in them.

it also sought a theatrical freshness to set against grand-opera conventionality, it was the freshness of a homegrown singingacting ensemble whose artistic coin of realm would be more, not less, accessible to The People. It did not assemble stars, but stars grew within it, and helped secure The People's loyalty. Unless I missed some newsworthy demonstration, at no point in the NYCO's seven-decade history did The People rise to demand yet-more-obscure repertory, yet-feebler new operas, or yet-more-transgressive productions of canonical works, at least in sufficient numbers to sustain a repertory house in an expensive venue. Many factors were involved in the company's decline and demise, but the effort to re-cast "The People's Opera" as caterer to such rarefied tastes was surely among them.

4. William J. Baumol and William G. Bowen: *Performing Arts: The Economic Dilemma*, Twentieth Century Fund, N.Y., 1966.

5. Seth S. Horowitz: *The Universal Sense* (Bloomsbury N.Y., 2012).

6. Richard Kearney: "Losing Our Touch," *NYT*, Aug. 31, 2014.

7. See *The Hedgehog Review*, Vol. 16, No. 2 (2014). I am fond of this journal for its focus on a single topic per issue, e.g., "The Fate of the Arts" (Vol. 6, No. 2) or "Humanism Amidst Our Machines" (Vol. 13, No. 2). In this case, the subject is "Minding Our Minds," with particular attention to attention. Essays by four authors with philosophical, sociological, ethical, and cultural P.O.V.s plus, as usual, a bibliographical essay that cuts across all of them. *Hedgehog* always has other thoughtful material as well, often on education, religion and morality, etc.

8. In this cast, there were two matches of voice and personality to role that were fully satisfactory. These were the Nannetta (Lisette Oropesa, her song beautifully and tenderly wafted out) and the Pistola (Christian Van Horn). The rest of what we used to call The Distaff Side (Angela Meade, Stephanie Blythe, and Jennifer Johnson Cano) was perfectly acceptable, but in a soft-grained, casual way (no Italian core or bite), and frequently partaking of the Levinian ongoingness (see below). But the men! Unfortunately, the Falstaff of my performance was not Ambrogio Maestri, who was scheduled when I bought the ticket and about whom I was hopefully curious, but his alternate, Nicola Alaimo, who did a professional job of stepping into an elaborately stagey production and making some idiomatic points with tolerably good cheer. His voice had reasonable presence when used fully in the midrange, but otherwise did not impinge—nothing disgraceful, but not enough to charge up the goings-on. The Ford and Fenton simply fell far short in terms of vocal quality and presence. Levine, pluckily returning after his prolonged physical ordeals, ran into something virtually unprecedented: reserved reviews, owing to sloppy ensemble. The night I was there, there was a moment of messiness in one of the womens' ensembles, though I couldn't be sure where the fault lay. But the score was certainly better played than Levine's last time through it (see p. 154). There was a warm timbral enclosure, some delicate textures, transparency that was sometimes suitable, and a logical progression of tempos. There was also the old Levine problem of episodes not defined and dramatic moments smoothed over. We just chug contentedly along till we get to the end.

9. The pit band for *Bourgeois gentilhomme*, twenty-some-odd strong, played an arrangement by André Jolivet of numbers from Lully's score. Though severely redacted from the original, it still included songs, dances, brief radio-style entr'actes, and even occasional underscoring. The production was recorded by Vega that same year from a live performance (presumably in Paris), so the actors are playing at full theatre energy. In the Dorimène of Hélène Perdière, with her natural-sounding interplay between "chest" and "head" and charming subtleties of inflection, something of what I'm speaking of with regard to the women's voices can be heard. Jolivet's modernized instrumentation, old-timey enough to theatregoers of the '50s, falls strangely on the ear now. A more

extended, period-instrument rendition of the Act IV Turkish masquerade has been recorded by Marc Minkowski and the Musiciens du Louvre.

10. Apart from the many American and English works in its repertory, the NYCO of those years customarily performed Mozart in English, along with Russian works (*Love of Three Oranges, Flaming Angel, Katerina Ismailova, Golden Cockerel, Golden Slippers, Boris Godunov*), operettas (*Fledermaus, Gypsy Baron, Merry Widow*), and unfamiliar works like Orff's *The Moon* or Strauss's *Silent Woman* and *Ariadne*, etc. So, although original-language standard repertory accounted for a majority of performances, a great deal of English was sung by the company. At the Met, too, we heard it with some frequency. Again, all Russian works (*Khovanshchina, Boris, Onegin, Queen of Spades*) and operettas (*Fledermaus* and *Gypsy Baron, La Périchole*), the English-language operas (*The Rake's Progress, Vanessa, The Last Savage, Antony and Cleopatra, Mourning Becomes Electra, Peter Grimes*), some Mozart (*Così, Flute*), and unfamiliar or "difficult" works (*Wozzeck, Arabella, Martha*[!]). For a time, we even had alternate Italian/English *La Bohèmes*. Readers may consult the casts of these productions, on my assurance that though of course we didn't catch every word and some singers fared better than others, we could follow the show, and there was nothing like the general unintelligibility of the recent efforts. This is not because the older singers had better "diction," but because they had better voices— larger, more resonant and theatrically energized, with more distinct vowel profile. Note that at the Met, a number of foreign singers were involved. Hilde Gueden, Victoria de los Angeles, Nicolai Gedda, and Herman Uhde, among others, sang clearly and expressively in our language.

11. That is to say, on first meeting it casts a spell, and opens a clearing for the uses of techniques we would normally classify as postmodern at the service of a cohesive dramatic progression. But pending deeper acquaintance, including a live performance of quality, I'm not yet sure how important my preliminary reservations will prove. They would include a tendency to woman-as-chattel preachiness, which the music seems to transcend but which might go either way in performance; the setting of The Boy for male falsettist, which takes us beyond the Octavian/Cherubino convention into the realm of a potentially unpalatable woman/boy coupling; and the layering in of a contemporary framework, including brief scenes with present-day characters, doublecast with supporting singers in the main plot.

12. The Opéra Bastille *Werther* seen on the Decca DVDs originated at Covent Garden in 2004, with a different conductor and a cast from which the Albert, Ludovic Tézier, is the only holdover. Directed by the French film director Benoît Jacquot (joined for the video by Louise Narboni), it was scathingly reviewed for *Opera* by Max Loppert, an experienced and perceptive critic. The DVD set was no more joyously received seven years later by Rodney Milnes. I see some of what Loppert was objecting to in the physical production, which has an austere, empty look that only gestures at the social setting. It's very beautifully lit, though, and since the predominantly closed-in, hothouse feel of the piece is as close to camera-appropriate as opera can get, the visual atmosphere is more supportive than it may have been in the theatre. Stage-to-video devices I often find obtrusive (skycam shots during scene changes, backstage glimpses as performers prepare entrances, etc.), and which had me worried at the outset, actually work into the musical narrative effectively as we go along, and the musical responsiveness of the visual rhythms and moods seems to me well above video norm.

In any event, it's not production, but performance, and those aspects of direction that closely affect performance, that count in the end. And these performances (I speak of the two leads, who have the big challenges) are wonderful. I think a great deal depends on how one watches acting, and what one expects of it. Both Kaufmann and his Charlotte, Sophie Koch, have learned to live onstage as their characters would in life, containing extremes of desire and disturbance within what they believe it is allowable to show (until, finally, they can't), and letting us read that the way an intimate would sense it in life. But of course a lot of this doesn't look like "acting," the whole point being that the work not show, and other performers might present the identical surface aspects with no life at all underneath. (Tézier reads that way to me at times. But Albert's a hard assignment.) It's up to the viewer to be the intimate, to pick up the vibe. These are two fine stage talents, on a wavelength with each other. They are doing the work, they know how to generate the moments and events, keep them alive between them, and let the music guide them. However, it would be most unlikely that they do this without the participation of the director. At the very least, he (or she—it's unclear what role Narboni played) has abetted and encouraged them, and set up the shots. There are, for sure, things I don't like in the design/direction department, at least on first viewing. Charlotte's room looks like a historic preservation exhibit, not a place someone lives. This captures a desolate, overly ordered feel that is at moments striking, but gives the singer little to draw on—Koch winds up on the apron, dealing with the *Air des Lettres* as a direct-address aria. She copes, but it's not ideal. She also wears the same long white dress season in, season out, indoors or out. I infer that this has to do with Werther's vision of an utterly pure, even angelic Charlotte; but we have to watch the real one. In the crucial Act III scene, physical grappling is too much too soon (this happens in the Met production, too—it's a disease). Johann and, especially Schmidt, are a bad vaudeville drunk act. Unfortunate things, but exceptions to a thought-out, felt-out performance that keeps us zeroed in on the central relationships. It is conducted with deep sympathy by an old *Werther* hand, Michel Plasson.

Koch was also Charlotte at the Met, and there her performance, so involving on the video, did not translate as well as Kaufmann's. It could be that she felt less comfortable with the production, but she seemed engaged as an actress, and I think the problem was mostly a vocal limitation, the technical aspect of which gives us one more look at some of the current issues of female vocality. We once again meet a singer—a mezzo, at that—who wants almost nothing to do with the Lower Family, a/k/a chest voice. She rarely touches on that quality, and then gently on the very lowest pitches. It's a "relaxed"-sounding voice, of considerable beauty but not much command at either range extreme. The difficulty with this for Charlotte is not so much that she needs intense chest notes (only a few seem called for, though more could be chosen, depending on the singer's gauge of the emotional temperature), but that without enough of the lower function to draw on, the whole lower octave lacks the strong, clear blend required by much of this writing. Once she has arrived in the vicinity of the G-sharp or A above middle C, Koch's voice takes on a round, plush timbre, warm but not brilliant, that suggests a voluminous, right-of-center mezzo voice. Yet it isn't voluminous. In a house like the Met, it is of the Siébel/Stephano/Nicklausse/Cherubino calibre, but darker and more feminine than is customary in those parts. Since it's the vocal presence and the "acting with the voice" that draws us into the intimacy of the physical acting, this is not quite enough to convey the concentrated internality and bond with her partner with which Koch succeeds on the video.

Because of the role's low center of gravity and its upper limit at A-natural, we have been accustomed to hearing mezzos as Charlotte. Contraltos have sung it, beginning with the formidable Marie Delna, as have Italian dramatic mezzos like Simionato, and Tassinari in her late mezzo adjustment. Rita Gorr made a tremendous effect with it. In a grand opera venue, such voices make sense. But like Carmen and Mignon, Charlotte was written for the type of *comique* vocalist patterned by Galli-Marié. Probably the closest we come to the original vision of the role is in the voice of Jeanne Marie de L'Isle, a famous Carmen and Mignon, who recorded two excerpts from *Werther* in 1904-05. (The *Werther* discs of both de L'Isle and Delna are contained, with much else, on Marston 52056-2). She called herself a mezzo, but as heard on these early acousticals, her voice sounds like that of a firm, technically balanced lyric soprano, and while she and similar *comique*-style artists would have usually sung in smaller houses, during *Werther*'s first half-century Charlotte was often sung by sopranos, even in grand-opera settings. Mary Garden made it one of her many Chicago triumphs, and at the Met the first two Charlottes were Emma Eames and Geraldine Farrar. The two most emotionally compelling recordings of the *Air des lettres* known to me are those of Lotte Lehmann (in German) and Maria Callas. On the opera's first complete recording (1931, superbly sung with a now-vanished unity of style), the Charlotte is the cherishable Ninon Vallin, a lyric soprano. How is it, then, that sopranos, and not of the dramatic variety, once projected this music effectively in big houses, while presumably better-suited lyric mezzos don't? The answer is that the issue is not how a voice is categorized, but whether or not it is well bound in the lower-middle range, strong and clear throughout, and capable of the dynamic and color span with which a sensitive artist can inflect the phrases; and that vocal techniques have changed so that neither sopranos nor mezzos, except for a few of a dramatic calibre not ideally suited to this role's range of expression, possess these attributes. Koch succeeds with it on video through her vocal and physical attractiveness, her concentrated internality, and her bond with her partner. In the opera house, it's the vocal presence, the "acting with the voice," that draws us into the physical acting.

I look forward to seeing and hearing more of Kaufmann, live and recorded. On his Verdi CD, I hear a bit more compression in the sound, and further darkening that is beginning to affect the clarity of open vowels. These lend added starch at places that seem to suggest the plausibility of roles he is evidently contemplating (Alvaro, Otello). He would no doubt be absorbing in these great parts. But the album was recorded nearly a year before the Met *Werther*—the voice is still the voice, and not really meant for those battles. Meanwhile, there are superb snippets online, e.g., a riveting *Lamento di Federico* (the perfect vocal and temperamental fit for him), and a fine closing scene of *Don Carlo* with Harteros, which also answers my earlier question about the opera's end, for in this staging a fairly youthful Carlo Quinto in full armor strides on, just as he would have emerged from Carlo Magno's tomb in *Ernani*. Good thinking there.

13. This gives us another instance, more current than those of Domingo and Gedda, of a tenorial structural change undertaken with a career already underway. The only example I have found of Kaufmann's singing before the change is an online video of *"Un' aura amorosa"* (*Così fan tutte*) from a Milan performance of 1998. His voice here is attractive and clear, but in a shallow way—it hasn't the "deep clarity" I spoke of earlier. The *passaggio* is already smoothened, and the voice bends over the A's at *"un dolce ristoro"* without difficulty. But the color range is restricted, and the arrangement doesn't sound like it will bear much pressure—there's a slightly fragile, "walking on eggshells" feel. Since there's no behavior here—just a handsome youth posing in a pretty costume in a pretty setting—the performance is a blank. Sensing trouble (by his own account, the voice cut out on him a couple of times in performance), Kaufmann sought out technical advice. The teacher he found was an American baritone, Arthur Rhodes, who had settled in the German city of Trier, on the Moselle, where he sang and taught.

I first heard the tale of Kaufmann's re-tooling from my longtime colleague Peter G. Davis, who had learned of it in an interview with Kaufmann. (In an online thread, Davis relates the story, and his own fortuitous connection to it, exactly as he told it to me.) Kaufmann describes the process with Rhodes as being primarily a matter of learning to relax into his lower range, allowing the voice to settle where it belongs rather than holding it in a higher "placement." Possibly (see our earlier discussion about Duprez) this involved some lowering of the laryngeal position, or a lengthening of the pharyngeal stretch, or both. In terms of pedagogical influences on Rhodes, Kaufmann mentions Giuseppe de Luca, but according to Davis's knowledge of Rhodes's teaching, the principal one was Douglas Stanley. Stanley was an outlier whose writings exude an undisguised contempt for the mainstream vocal theories of his interwar era. (His *Your Voice: Applied Science of Vocal Art*, 3rd Ed., Pitman, 1957, presents his final statements on technique.) From the "Establishment" P.O.V., his technical views are disturbing enough, especially inasmuch as they came from an obviously serious investigator with superior scientific credentials. His ideas on registration—including the assertion that loudness, not range, is the governing factor, and that "chest" (yet another puzzling idea of what is meant by this term) should be carried as high as possible in the female voice, beyond which the other register (he called it the "falsetto") would rule for one octave, and on resonance, which waved away ideas about "forward placement," were truly subversive. Even more scarifying was his use of "The Manipulations"—hands-on, instrument-aided pressures applied to habituate the tongue, jaw, hyoid bone, and larynx itself to optimal positioning in the act of singing. For most of us who work with voice, this effort at external governance is not the preferred way to proceed; but the goals themselves were, I think, on the whole desireable. Stanley's contemptuous attitudes and *en masse* put-downs of hallowed contemporaneous singers (unidentified—you're supposed to guess) made him easy to dismiss, and he and his "school" remained on the cultish margins of the pedagogical community.

As I have previously suggested, I am congenitally suspicious of attributions of techni-cal influence, unless one can present in-person, longterm observation backed by at least some audible evidence. What was the condition of the singer's voice before studying with a particular teacher? How well did the singer incorporate the teacher's advice? What other influences were at work, before, during, and after? Can the teacher's approach be identified in other singers, so that we hear something in common among them, and is that something in line with what we know of the teacher's theoretical principles and aes-thetic tastes? Stanley offers a clear example of this difficulty. His best known pupil was Nelson Eddy, a good singer who belongs in the higher, brighter grouping of American baritones. If I had to search out another voice of the same model, in the manner of Lauri-Volpi's *Voci parallele*, I would pick that of John Charles Thomas—a greater instru-ment, certainly, but the same lean, manly tone (*very* similar timbres), dead-steady (to the point of straightness at times), the same gathered-but-not-covered approach to the upper range. If I were speculating on influences, I would set the odds not too long that Eddy and Thomas had worked with the same teacher. Eddy did study with Stanley, though exactly when and for how long I haven't quite figured out, but he had at least two principal teachers earlier on, and had already established himself professionally. His tonal set does conform well with Stanley's preferences, but we don't know the extent to which that was already present, or how Stanley changed it or added to it. Thomas, too, had early vocal grounding and was highly successful in Broadway operettas and proto-musicals before heading to Europe, where during his several seasons with the Monnaie in Brussels he studied (on and off, I gather) with Jean de Reszke—who Stanley goes out of his way to revile. Similar voices, similar techniques, different paths.

Second-generation influences are trickier yet. Even if a teacher sets out to transmit unaltered the "method" of a previous master, he or she will fail in that no matter how well they have absorbed the teaching—the same unconscious adaptations seen in the recounting of oral-culture storytellers will soon creep in. Besides, no talented teacher does that, though some will seek to boost their cred with claims of handing down "the Lamperti Method," "the Garcia Method," or—"The Stanley Method." All this by way of preface to saying that I hear in Kaufmann's singing very little that accords with what I infer about Stanley's teaching. He would no doubt have approved of the more settled position and the overall gain in volume. But he would surely have worked for far more "chesty" laryngeal engagement in the lower voice, resulting in more brightness and core in the tone. He would have disapproved of Kaufmann's *pianissimo* as "crooning *falsetto*," and his derivation of the *messa di voce* from it as "mixed registration" (in Stanley's vocabulary, a negative term). This isn't to denigrate the work Rhodes did, which seems to have done much to enable the artist we have in Kaufmann today. It's just to restrain what I see as a widespread bad habit of drawing conclusions about "schools," "methods," etc., through mere association.

P.S.: Rhodes can be heard in the few lines of Oreste's Tutor on the (wonderful) 1949 NY Philharmonic broadcast of *Elektra* (Mitropoulos, cond., Varnay's best in the title role, in well-restored sound on the Guild label). Certainly little can be gleaned from these few midvoice phrases; it sounds like a firm, clear baritone, with a touch of tremolo on the one or two more sustained notes. As for de Luca: I know nothing of his teaching, and to my knowledge he left no writings. He was in New York at least part of the time in the immediate postwar years, so Rhodes could well have sought him out. Who wouldn't want to hear this great singer's advice, on matters of both technique and finish of style, and who wouldn't be pleased to cite him as an influence? P.P.S.: It's just a curiosity, but De Luca, the baritone, sang the bright vowels "open" a half- to full-step higher than Kaufmann, the tenor, and had more of the old tensility in his perfectly graded *mezza-voce*.

14. See Marie d'Origny: *The Tenor on the Stage: An Interview with Jonas Kaufmann, NYRB,* Apr.26, 2012.

15. Olga Haldey: *Mamontov's Private Opera/The Search for Modernism in Russian Theatre,* Indiana University Press, 2010.

PART VI

EPILOGUE

1

DREAM ON, AND A NOTE ON ONE LAST SHOW

(April, 2013–August, 2015)

Here we are. Beyond the uneasiness imparted by the liquid times, which undercuts any effort to sum up, there is also the sense of end times hovering about opera and classical music. That's less true of theatre and, I believe, dance, since they still generate new creation that sometimes rises above the popular culture, yet connects to an audience that can fill at least a roomy niche. But with opera, it's hard to avoid the beating of wings in the air, and hard to resist a conclusion that partakes of eschatology: either the Four Horsemen are just now riding into town or a Second Coming is imminent. Since I have written, with as much evidentiary support as I can muster, that opera is stumbling about in an unfriendly aesthetic environment that neither nurtures new creation nor refreshes and honors its canon of masterworks; that without a metanarrative it gropes for something to sing about amongst whatever's trending in the *Zeitgeist*; that its interpretive elements have been weakened and/or distorted in fundamental ways; and that its very biology of sending and receiving has been interfered with, a tacked-on happy ending would be as unearned as it is in some of those early operas, and with no music to give it cover. Yet I'm not quite ready for the riders, either.

The feeling of lateness is not opera's exclusively. Opera reflects the more general problem of disentangling what will advance us from what will destroy us, and the overarching question of whether we want to go on being human, and if so, how. Technofuturists foretell that we will soon be taken up into the transhuman Singularity, there to dwell in a kind of virtual, excarnated realm, and that we must celebrate this. Not all of us do. Even among secularists, there are some who do not believe that technology, or even science, is ever going to answer all the questions, satisfy all the cravings, that religion and philosophy, the arts and humanities, try to address. We even get a little tired of being hectored about STEM, not because we dispute its importance, but because we think the arts and humanities belong on at least an equal footing. As in my interpretations of the *Ring* and *Lohengrin* (see Backstory 3), we aspire to ascend not to the godly or the transhuman, but to a full humanity. For myself, though I know it's heretical, I just don't think Silicon Valley is going to bring us the New Jerusalem, or that we shall all be changed thereby in any salvific way. (And if you find these religious references overblown, take a look at how these prophets present themselves.[1])

However late it may feel, artists must, as always, seek to create a clearing for themselves wherein they can confront the artistic lateness on their own terms, and work toward a real-world renewal. That is what I feel the end of this book must be about. And it's an odd sensation, this awareness that though I have chosen to write about certain events in place of others, and have given guidance to the development of certain themes instead of others, I feel as if the events and themes have been leading me. They have presented themselves; I have responded. And the last two to have flagged me down are the longing for a place where important artists like Jonas Kaufmann could fully realize their talents, and the life story of a railroad baron/aesthete who underwrote a private opera under an imperial regime. We need a company. Artists need it, a certain audience needs it, and as devotee, I need it. Also, it needs to be paid for.

Two visits to the City Center stirred these thoughts up. The first was to the NYCO production of Rossini's *Mosé* in April, 2013, and the second, a little over a year later, to a staging of Pushkin's *Eugene Onegin* by the Vakhtangov State Academic Theatre of Moscow. The *Mosé* turned out to be my last encounter with the City Opera, and while a part of me suspected this might be the case, another part still found it unthinkable that this troupe, with which I had begun my operagoing life in the fall of 1946, would just slip away. In any case, after their long residency at the State Theatre here they were, wandering minstrels back where they'd started, and here was I once more in the Second Balcony, basking in Mecca teal and gold. Some of my thoughts were, naturally, of the past. But mostly, I thought about money— or, more exactly, value—and while when we talk about the economics of the performing arts we customarily speak of the plights of institutions, it might not be a bad idea to glance at the other end: what's the experience worth to the potential ticketbuyer? As ticketbuyer, I am not in the bull's eye of the demographic target. But I am definitely part of the core constituency. If opera can't hang onto me and others like me, the jig's up. I was quite pleased, value-wise, with my *Mosè* purchase. I was in the second row of the Second Balcony, toward the side but with excellent sightlines. This felt like about half the distance from the stage of a Balcony seat at the Met, and with the forward overhang I was closer than I'd been for the Chicago *Médée*. The sound comes right up at you here. I had paid forty bucks, and knew from time-of-purchase inquiry that the Second Balcony had been scaled within an inch of its life: a few seats over, the price jumped, and then at center jumped again. Further back, I could have gone cheaper, but above the cross-aisle things do start to feel remote.

This was a good deal, I thought. I was paying about a third of the cost of that Met balcony ticket. Granted, that was still about double, in real dollars, what I'd paid for a comparable seat in the mid-1950s. But that only reflects costs that have risen faster than inflation. What rental, I wondered, was the company paying the City Center? I rather doubted it was the inflation-adjusted equivalent (about $10) of that '50s dollar per year. At this price in this location, I would be happy to attend several times a season, wouldn't mind taking a flyer on a new piece or a production of dubious provenance, and wouldn't put quite so much weight on such matters as (in the case of *Mosè*) the edition selected, the production choices, the casting of a couple of major roles, or the barely sufficient numbers in the choral and orchestral ranks. I was getting a chance to see a rarely done Rossini opera of considerable musical and theatrical stature, performed at a solid professional level by forces resembling those called for. There weren't any Sillses or Brookses or Treigles or Curtins on hand, but this was a reasonable facsimile of the original New York City Opera compact, and despite some important reservations, I didn't feel cheated.

For the Vakhtangov *Onegin* I paid $127, near the box-office price you'd pay for a Broadway play, to sit in the front section of the First Balcony (now called the Grand Tier). A fine seat—good perspective, good sense of contact with the stage. In money's-worth terms, this was so good an evening it left me both excited and depressed. I had never seen anything like it, and realized I never will in our theatre, commercial or nonprofit—it's an economic impossibility. This was a high-concept theatricalization of Pushkin's verse novel by the company's Artistic Director, Rimas Tuminas. It embraced dialogue and narration, naturalistic acting, mime, and dance, and lots of music. The onstage company numbered about thirty-five. The physical production was sophisticated and elaborate.

When I say I'd seen nothing like it, I'm not speaking of my opinion about this or that in the production or performances, or even of whether or not I agreed with the whole idea. I am speaking of the utter competence of everyone onstage. Every performer was capable of fulfilling his or her assignment with precision and commitment across this broad stylistic "lateral cut," with full awareness of his or her function in a scene or moment, yet with the appearance of individual agency, too. The movement capacity and physical command of the actors had clearly reached an athletic level, and the vocal the elocutionary. Neither was taken to that pitch often. But when they were the effect was startling, yet seemed a natural outgrowth of the more everyday key. It occurred to me that my resistance to productions in mixed styles may owe mostly to never having seen one taken to its actualistic consummation, and I had the feeling that had these performers been called upon to sustain a production in any one of the modes on display (Chekhovian "panpsychism,[2] choreographic stylization, etc., they could have done so. Except for the music and a few special effects, there was no aural enhancement that I could detect, and that took me back to the days when the City Center's own drama company and others from here and abroad (the Brattle from Cambridge, Mass., the Comédie on subsequent visits, the Old Vic, the Hamburg Staatstheater, etc.) played Shakespeare, Shaw, Molière, Goethe, et al. in this same auditorium on the presumption of verbal strength and clarity. When an actor failed in that, the inadequacy was deemed his, not the auditorium's.*

For the *Onegin*, there were English subtitles, to the side where they did not enter the visual field unless invited. I glanced over at them from time to time, especially during long narrative speeches. In this I was almost alone, for this was a New York Russian audience, worrisomely loud and unsettled before the show, voluble at intermission, and silent with the curtain up—for nearly four hours, not a beep or a peep, or the rustle of a program.

An accomplishment like the Vakhtangov's *Onegin* is not possible without a resident company—an ensemble of selective membership that trains, rehearses and performs together over a period of years, developing the shared aesthetic, understanding of process, and personal trust that take root under only these conditions, all of which in turn cultivate unique audience intimacy

---

* The pre-renovation City Center was in fact acoustically more difficult than the present configuration. The back wall at the orchestra and balcony levels has been moved forward and about 300 seats lost, with the Second Balcony the only level not affected. It's still a big, wide auditorium, seating nearly 2,700, and with balcony overhangs that put two-thirds of the orchestra and much of the First Balcony in under. Recent experiences with amplification there have ranged from the abysmal (the New York Gilbert and Sullivan Players) to the blaringly mediocre (the Encores! *Most Happy Fella*).

and loyalty. Two things are necessary for that: energetic leadership that defines what sort of theatre the company is and isn't, and massive, ongoing underwriting. Opera is in dire need of such a company now. Of course, whenever I begin to describe such an enterprise, and what form it might take, the eyelids of whoever is giving me the courtesy of listening begin to droop, and I hear some version of "dream on." Fine, let's do that. Why shouldn't we say what we want, especially since without it, opera's prospects are not inviting?

THE DREAM-ON COMPANY

1. Some Principles and Policies.

What sort of company would this be?
- A company that confronts the core Mozart-through-Strauss repertory, which has become a performance-practice problem as surely as are the works of Lully or Monteverdi, but has not been addressed as such, and which is being so poorly served by the major international companies that feed on it.

This means:
- A company dedicated to the ideas, wisdoms, and intuitions of the past that created the masterworks of that repertory, and to the testing of those ideas, wisdoms, and intuitions in the context of the present.
- To that end, a company that seeks the union of the modern acting sensibility with the full rendering of the written vocal, verbal, and musical rhetorics inscribed in the scores, resulting in a new mode of operatic expression.
- A company that will, within this new mode, make the oft-posited "creative independence of the performer" a reality.
- A company that will place production in the service of performance, and not the other way around.
- A company that people of modest means can attend with regularity, and will want to because the masterworks are being brought to them familiar yet renewed—a source of satisfaction like no other.

But fantasies are no good unless they seem plausible, so before I elaborate on the artistic identity of this Dream Company, I'm going to stay a little longer with the matter raised by my $40 *Mosé* ticket and my references to "economic impossibility" and "massive, ongoing underwriting:" money, the dreamiest subject of all. And for the moment, I'll stay with the P.O.V. of the ticketbuyer, not the ticketseller—or, if you prefer, with demand, not supply.

Actually, I thought my *Mosé* ticket was slightly underpriced. I would have paid ten or fifteen dollars more and still found it fair. And relative to New York theatre ticket prices in general—even nonprofit and off-Broadway offerings—my *Onegin* seat was an unheard-of bargain for the size and quality of the production. But then, I thought: "Well, the City Opera is in big trouble. It needs to sell every seat at *some* price. Although this performance is quite well attended, there are a few empty spots in these side sections. My seat is excellent, but many people don't understand that, and it might have gone unsold if I hadn't jumped at that low price. Hard to guess where to draw the line. As to *Onegin,* it's an international showcase touring production from a state-subsidized company, which also has a local sponsor [the Cherry Orchard Festival], with a near-guaranteed sellout audience for its four performances. That has nothing to do with our normal theatre economics." *Onegin* did not appear to incur what economists call an "artistic deficit," i.e., a noticeable compromise in size or quality because of money constraints. But *Mosé* did—as was often, and progressively, the case at City Opera after its first dozen or fifteen years at Lincoln Center.

I sometimes read that opera (you may substitute any performing art) is in competition for my entertainment dollar. Since everything is in place of something else, I suppose that is true, in a sense so broad as to be meaningless. But if all I'm looking for in opera is entertainment—the pleasurable passing of time in a mode I'm attracted to—it's going to lose out as often as not. I'm a baseball and tennis fan. There are circuses, amusement parks, caper movies, Broadway farces (smart, like *One Man, Two Guv'nors,* or dumb, like *Boeing-Boeing*), all of which I can enjoy when in the mood, and for less money than a decent seat at the opera. There's reading of the beach and bathtub varieties. On current TV, there are the sports I love, political satire, old movies and TCM, and Congressional antics on C-Span. And on home video there's *Columbo, Fawlty Towers,* Eddie Murphy trying to cross the highway in *Bowfinger,* and much else—all not quite free, but very cheap.

I need entertainment from time to time. But these pastimes are not substitutes for the deeper, richer, more intense engagement I seek from art, and my usual problem with entertainment is not access to it, but fending it off to leave a clearing for what I really care about, without turning into a hermit. It's not my entertainment dollar that opera has at stake; it's my High Arts dollar. And there, opera does have some competition. I'll give you an anecdotal comparison. The Met's pricing has recently adopted the same value relativity (they're calling it "dynamic pricing") as the other Mets', the baseball kind, according to which the home team vs. the Milwaukee Brewers on a Tuesday is notably less expensive than vs. the Washington Nationals on a weekend.

So my three most recent Met Opera excursions showed a price differential of about 30%.* At the top was Verdi's *Macbeth* with Anna Netrebko; next came Wagner's *Die Meistersinger* with no luminaries of Netrebko/Kaufmann wattage; and at the bottom was Adams' *Death of Klinghoffer*. The average price per ticket of these three was (rounding off) $126.50. And a couple of other recent events I attended:

Albee's *A Delicate Balance* on B'way, prominent actors, prime seat: $155.-

Takács Quartet with guest artist Joyce Yang at Alice Tully Hall, playing Haydn, Debussy, and Dvořák; prime seat: $80.-

Always, I am aware that for the price of my Met Balcony ticket, I can also have a choice place for the American Ballet Theatre or the New York City Ballet, or hear the New York Philharmonic or another of the world's great symphony orchestras at either of our major concert halls. Or, for that matter, that this Sunday I can see whichever movie I choose (there are three that interest me at the moment) at the neighborhood arthouse, the Lincoln Plaza, for $10. These, also, are not substitutes for one another. They satisfy different parts of my cultural appetite. And although I have a personal hierarchy, established by first love and sustained by professional involvement, that gives preference to opera, I desire all of these—they are all vital to my cultural life, and each, for me, is in some way unfinished without the others. So in a strictly practical sense, there is an element of competition among them in my allocation of time, money, and energy, which is why arts economists consider them substitutes for one another.

I can be swayed, too. If I feel I have derived more nourishment from seeing Albee's play or hearing and watching the Takács than from any of my operatic encounters (as indeed I did, since only in the final scene of *Meistersinger*, which cannot fail if the chorus sings and the drums play, and the Sleepwalking Scene of *Macbeth*, in which Netrebko's eloquence and insight compensated for the less-than-dramatic calibre of her soprano, did those three evenings approach consummation); or if, based on experiences like the *Don Carlo* comparison, I decide I might do better for less money at "Live! In HD" than in the opera house, my hierarchy might start to re-arrange itself.

---

* For all three I held Balcony locations, within two rows and a few seat numbers of one another. (And for anyone unfamiliar with the house, I should specify that the Balcony is the fourth tier above Orchestra level, with the Family Circle ascending behind it.) To control for other factors: all were on weeknights (Tues.-Thu.); neither *Macbeth* nor *Meistersinger* was a new production, whereas *Klinghoffer* was new to the house. These prices represented a 20%-30% increase from the previous season's (2013-14).

I'm aware that other devotees' hierarchies and allocations are different from mine. My long history with and active participation in the performing arts makes me somewhat unusual. But we all have some system of taste and preference, and some system of assigning whatever disposable income we have. Together we make up an audience. (The same is true, not at all incidentally, for the much larger group who do not make up the audience.) I am aware, as well, that opera is by a wide margin the most expensive of the stage arts to produce, irrespective of efficiencies of management. We cannot expect *Meistersinger* for anything close to the ticket price of the Takács (on a cost-reflective basis, we'd be nearing four figures for prime seats). In fact, given a comparable level of artistic quality, we can't expect *La serva padrona* for the price of the Takács, if we're asking it to pay for itself. Hence the question, "How on earth, in the here and now, can we pay for opera?", and the related one, "How can we attract and shape an audience?" With these questions, though, we move to the ticketseller's side, and we can't do that until we have a clear and complete picture of our company, the thing tickets are being sold for. Since this fantasy is simply a description of what is needed for a healthy operatic culture, the fantasy is in fact a reality check: face it, this is what has to happen. Then comes the money talk.

2. But Who?

As to the further question of who could or would develop a company of the sort I'm envisioning, I think the answer is, performers themselves. They must organize and take artistic responsibility for it. They are the only ones who can figure out what their creative independence actually entails, and thereby generate a performance preparation process that puts their own work in its rightful (central) place, and all other production elements in theirs. They must begin by agreeing on a few principles, subject to refinement. Here are mine:

- Singingacting is the matrix.
- All work will be directed toward discovering the inner coherence of the material, and reflecting that in performance and production.
- The performers will adhere to the code of artistic ethics proposed for the Interpreters-in-Chief (see p. 244).

I'll elaborate below.

Some performers, individually or in small companies, *are* struggling to set things in motion, largely to create work for themselves, but sometimes with an artistic vision in mind. On the individual level, it's the time of the petit entrepreneur. The young man or woman who has just been to school (see pp. 395 ff.) is now urged to become the artist as self-promoter, self-representative, and efficient, innovative small businessperson. The best-intentioned and best-informed advice urges her or him to master the knowledge and skills required by that identity.[3] And given the conditions, one cannot dispute the validity of such counsel. I am frequently in awe of the drive, inventiveness, and persistence of young artists trying to find a place for themselves. Two difficulties, though: 1) all the resources (time, energy, cash) spent on grooming the artist as businessperson (the part of him or her just like other ambitious, smart young people) are resources not spent on grooming the artist as artist (the part not like everyone else), and for that grooming to approach completion, it demands attention 24/7, 365, while swimming against the tide. 2) The mindset, the bent of the successful young businessperson is not the same as that of the valuable artist. Those are different temperaments, different sensibilities, and while they may co-exist at a high level in some individuals, those cases are, I think, very much the exceptions. So a milieu that favors the entrepreneur is apt to disfavor many promising talents, and give us instead the bright young singer who is on top of everything, remarkably together in the conduct of his life, and even well organized in his preparation of text, but simply waiting for instructions when he steps onstage. And in fact the entrepreneurial model is a terrible one for singers. I say again, they need a company, a home.

And speaking of companies, I am again often filled with admiration for those who found and sustain the smaller operations that give performing opportunities to young performers, develop their own modest constituencies, and somehow survive. Here in New York, there are enough of them to make up a fringe scene of some vitality. However, in terms of our Dream-on Company, they face the same Catch-22 that trips up the young performer in search of a job or representation: you can't put on a good show—a show we want to see on its artistic merits, not because of personal connection or because we're feeling charitable—without real money, and you can't attract real money without a good show. We must, from the outset, leapfrog their subworld.

And to that end, in my Dream-On world, the call has gone out. Among the ranks of experienced professionals—singers of good reputation with their peers and, in some cases, with the public—the sense of artistic frustration and disenfranchisement has reached such intensity with so many that they have overcome their natural-born reluctance to organize. Belatedly realizing that they in fact hold life-or-death power over their art, they have decided to go beyond their individual complaints and assert that power. In addition to their artistic disgruntlement, many are also unhappy with respect to lifestyle, sick of constant displacement and "entrepreneurship" and of wrangling over contracts and perks, and tired of trying to make their professional and personal lives fit together. However, their *artistic* restlessness and helplessness is the key. The awareness that their craving to perform is again and again being twisted into tortured, dishonest shapes can no longer be suppressed, and has become intolerable. They know they are not fulfilled, that their artistic selves are being squeezed dry, and that their art is being betrayed. As Kaufmann more than hinted in his interview with Marie d'Origny, even a superstar can long for something better. Certainly the company also needs the energy of young, relatively inexperienced performers (the less "written on" the better, in fact), with their willingness to think afresh and to innovate—provided they understand that what they're innovating is their own process for coming to grips creatively with the mandatory challenges of the masterworks. That is far harder than improvising to "get comfortable" and "see what happens," or "devising" something from the material, just as the assumption of creative responsibility is far harder than acquiring the adaptability of the "protean" performer. These young performers will carry the company forward in the future. But to supervise the development of the process and to establish instant credibility for the enterprise, the company's founding nucleus must consist primarily of artists who have already learned the lessons, positive and negative, of their profession as it presently exists.

So the first step is the formation of this nucleus of artists who decide to start working together to find out how to put their principles into practice. I confess to knowing of no precedent for this. Perhaps the old Theatre of Musical Drama in St. Petersburg came close, but even it owed its existence to a single obsessed visionary.[4] Opera companies have been established from the top down, whether the top is a king or czar, an alliance of wealthy socialites and civic-minded people, a persuasive and well-connected impresario, or some combination of these with a mayor who has an unused theatre building on his hands. The artistic director is usually a conductor, less often a stage director, rarely a singer.

In theatre, though, there is some precedent. I'm not referring to the old stock company model* or the latterday vestiges of the actor/manager tradition, like Eva LeGalliene's Civic Rep or Orson Welles' Mercury Theatre, but companies that began simply with actors foregathering to work. I can think of two American ones that proved to be of artistic significance: New York's Group Theatre and Chicago's Steppenwolf Theatre. The Group began with summer retreats for reform-minded theatre people inspired by the visits of

---

* Originally, that meant a company in which the members held stock.

the Moscow Art Theatre, and uninspired by the commercial Broadway scene. From the beginning, it had a vision of a particular kind of actor-centered theatre, and a strong political leaning. It was a powerful but shortlived force, whose influential afterlife included the founding of the Actors' Studio. Steppenwolf was a now-classic instance of young actors getting together to do something, however and wherever possible—literally the old church-basement startup. It just happened that they were unusually talented and a little pugnacious, attracted support and favorable attention early on, quickly graduated several members to theatre, cinema, and television fame, and made the transition to major cultural institution with a state-of-the-art theatre, still thriving at age 39 as of this writing. In both these cases, the answers to the questions of who would take on leadership roles and who would fulfill certain functions emerged from the artistic process and personal interactions, which were often indistinguishable. In its first decade, Steppenwolf even had a rotating artistic directorship, drawn from the acting company. And in both cases, despite many differences, the founders set out to do something different from what they saw around them—something they believed to be more authentic, more truthful.

There are several possible reasons why nothing comparable to The Group or Steppenwolf has happened in opera, but at street level the most important is that opera is a lot more complicated. Actors require nothing more than one another and a room to begin work. Singingactors require one another, a room, a piano, and a musician. As the work approaches realization in production, these musical complications, their associated numbers (in personnel, time, dollars), as well as their relative artistic weights, multiply. So operatic preparation generally begins with the musical complications in place, their weights already assigned, and their methods of preparation taken for granted.* Even at the training level, it also starts with people in charge, people who are not themselves the embodiers, the Ustinovian voyagers. Given its stated goals and principles, our fantasy company must begin its work the other way around. Someone is organizing and co-ordinating things, but artistically no one is yet in charge. Each performer is in charge of him- or herself.

---

* My musical friends and colleagues will undoubtedly be amused to see their work classified as "complications." No slight intended, believe me. One can of course think of the musical elements all set (as in a concert performance), with theatrical "complications" added later. Indeed, if one adds to the concert performance a pinch of behavior, a projection or two, and some indication of costume, one arrives at the ghastly pretense of the "semi-staged" performance. It's not a question of which is more important—music or theatre—but of how to work.

3. Day One and The Discovery Phase.

On Day One the founding members gather in an atmosphere of high excitement. They know that they now belong to a true company, and that the company has a mission. It also has a working space, centered on a good-sized
room that is a theatre or can take on that conformation, but that also includes
practice rooms large enough to accommodate the same stage dimensions.
The spaces are equipped with basic platform, stair, and door units for use in
scene work. There is a well-stocked properties closet. In or near the building
are living accommodations for members who have relocated to join the company, until they find permanent quarters. This need not yet be the company's
final home (though that would be nice), because the company is not yet going
into production. Instead, it is entering into what I'll call a Discovery Phase of
intensive exploratory work—a minimum of six months, I should think, five
or six hours a day, six days a week. (Actually, a year would be more like it.
But as I said, this is a plausible fantasy.) The company numbers somewhere
between forty and fifty, plus the organizer/co-ordinator(s), and eight or ten
pianist/accompanists. In this initial phase, all participants are receiving a sti-
pend, modest but not token. In 2015 dollars, that would be somewhere in the
vicinity of $1,250 per week, which is approximately 20% to 25% higher than
the rate paid by our richer regional theatres. From the earliest audition-and-
interview steps, certain members have been seen as likely principals, others
(mostly among the younger group, but perhaps including two or three experienced "character" performers) as more likely associates, forming the basis
of a choral and supporting-role ensemble. This has been openly discussed
with them, and is subject to revision as work proceeds. But for now, everyone
is on the same playing field, artistically and financially.

The questions of voice type, preferred repertory, levels of musical, linguistic, and theatrical skills have also been taken into consideration so that relative weaknesses can be addressed. But this is an advanced working group,
not a remedial class. It includes some who have had teaching experience,
some who are open to trying their hands at directing, and some who know
about movement and dance disciplines beyond the beginning level. Given the
nature of the E-19 culture, it would be splendid if the group included some
Europeans. Whatever their mix of talents, all are performers above all.

Everyone has prepared something in advance, singly or with partners, and
on Day One they offer it, by way of introduction. Then the work begins. Its
primary goal is to place the singing actor entirely in command of him- or
herself in relation to the material. He or she must learn how to assume
total responsibility for character development and scenic action in all its

aspects—vocal, musical, behavioral. Only then can collaboration with a conductor or director assume the right relationship. The work is a mixture of scene study and exercise, not in accordance with a sequential syllabus, but all mixed up so that each participant gradually integrates the elements through a combination of work and observation. At this stage, no one directs anybody. The performers rehearse their chosen material, deciding how the scene is laid out, what to wear, how to approach the action and each other. There is no staging as such, only the interaction that develops between partners, or the action that emerges from dealing with the solo self.

The pianists have been chosen for solid technique, responsiveness to singers, and stylistic awareness of a range of E-19 work. They may have coaching expertise and/or conductorial aspirations (indeed, we hope that conductors will emerge from this process), but for the moment their input is minimal, and not of an instructive sort. They are present to explore with the singers, and learn along with them. Of course, all are free to make suggestions and offer observations, so long as no one tries to take responsibility for another's work.

Exercises! The mere thought is enough to give professionals the heebie-jeebies or send them into high dudgeon. But if we're trying to invent a process, we can't afford to feel above them. I would propose inventions that fall into two broad categories: exercises for mining the text, and exercises for freedom from text. By "mining" I mean exploring all elements of the text, verbal and musical, independently and in combination, for all their levels of meaning and sound values, and to account for everything on the page. Superficially, this is a category of exercise that singers are already familiar with, since close attention to text is part of every good musical education. But I think, first, that this attention is more honored in the breach than in the observance, especially when performers begin to think of themselves as old pros, which sometimes happens surprisingly early; second, that when honored, it is often in the form of mere obedience; and third, that it is seldom translated into vocal and physical action with enough commitment—exaggeration, even—for performers to discover how it might really serve them. So these exercises will be taken as cues for performance impetus, as a good-faith effort to "get behind" everything the creators have set down, whether it be Verdi's copious articulations, Strauss's rhythms and note-value pointillisms, the often extended stage directions of Wagner and his amanuensis, Mottl, or Schoenberg's bar-by-bar affective instructions, all taken as Gospel. The goal is never to answer questions about meaning in an intellectual sense or to "set" a "definitive" interpretation, but to find out what feeds the performers, and what doesn't. Thus, for these exercises a Beckmesserish *Merker* will be on hand to be sure nothing has been ignored, but each exercise will be evaluated for what it has done to animate, specify, and individualize the performer's work.

In the scene work, stress will be laid on grasping the full implications of "given circumstances," which, as I tried to illustrate through the example of Eléazar, include everything that has formed the character as well as the dramatic situation of the moment; on sensory work and its influences on both vocal and bodily interpretation; and on specifying the event of a scene or aria in relation to the arc of a role. Yes, there might be written assignments. Every performer his or her own dramaturg—no outsourcing of the artist's precious findings and unique, personal construal of them, which is to say ownership of the life of the character. This is also by way of "mining the text," not only to extract everything that is there, but to contemplate what isn't, and the necessity of completing the picture in a way that is logical and compelling to the performer.

Exercises for freedom from text will cover the two remaining sources of interpretive choice: oral tradition and the individual creative imagination. For the former, the accumulated knowledge of all participants—singers, accompanists, the co-ordinators—will be drawn on, as will recordings, to explore what is of value in even the most exhausted traditional effects—the ones "good musicians" studiously avoid—and to see how it feels to "get behind" the inflectional inventions and departures from text of the great actors with the voice, with their extremes of interpretive choice within a given stylistic framework. And for the latter, as well as for much of the scene work, some of the techniques of modern acting will be summoned, particularly those that are designed to release the performer from all preconceptions and obligations of both text and oral tradition, so that all decisions about tempo, dynamics, accent, color, and physical behavior are derived from the inner sources of emotion and action and/or close attention to what is passing between partners.

Certainly there must be exercises in the area of movement, pantomime, and dance. They would have several purposes:

· To improve presence and what we used to call "comportment".*
· To explore traditional dance vocabularies for their possible adaptabilities to operatic situations.
· To build on the sensitivities all our performers already possess to their bodies' responsiveness to music, since in opera all action is musically conditioned.

---

* Most singers have decent basic posture, but I am frequently shocked by their apparent obliviousness to the necessity of heightened bearing as a basis for bodily rhetoric in all works of Romantic or Classical influence. Sometimes this is a misapprehension of what it means to seem "natural," or a belief in turning the heroic into the anti-heroic. But The Company doesn't share that belief.

- To investigate the values of musically expressive body language independent of singing energies, and so create a freer interplay between the two.
- To explore means of dealing with the many pages of operatic music that
are parts of the scenic action, yet involve no singing.

Except for the minority of these last that can be credibly filled with naturalistic action (such as the interludes in the domestic scenes of *Louise*), these
range from lengthy introductions to arias (the mini-violin concerto that precedes "*Marten aller Arten*," the mini-clarinet concerto that precedes "*O tu che
in seno agl'angeli*") to highly charged Wagnerian "pauses" (Tristan and Isolde
face off, Act I, Scene 3) to pantomime sequences verging on dance (Salome at
the cistern) or breaking into dance (Salome with the veils, Elektra at the end),
or many shorter passages of all descriptions and styles. The goal here is to
enable performers to approach each problem on its own musical and physical terms, and leave no moment of stage time blank or mechanical. As the
sessions move along, these exercises will be extended to include ensemble
and choral extracts.

Finally, there will be exercises in the spoken text. Many coaches and teachers
already make such recitation part of the preparation process, and it is always
useful for getting a better grasp on the sense of a passage and sharpening
awareness of how far the composer's treatment has departed from the spoken
norm, and to what purpose. These exercises, however, will be derived from the
elocutionary principles of E-19, so much closer to the vitality and musicality
of opera and song than our own. Theatrically heightened, poetically elevated,
attentive to the emotive effects of the sheer sounds of language, then taken
across the edge into music, these must be among the most important exercises for a company in search of finding a new fusion of the modern acting
sensibility with the written rhetorics of the masterworks. They will also be
a component of the more general effort to encourage greatvoiced vocalism,
within the bounds of each singer's voice and technique. E-19 "performance
practice" must start with singing itself. In that regard, some of these elocutionary exercises will combine with some of the movement-based ones to
locate the vocal gesture as wellspring of the physical action.

The relationship between exercises and actual rehearsal is fluid and indirect.
Performers select which exercises may be of use in which circumstances, and
eventually the exercises function mostly as a consciousness each artist brings
into the room at the outset, to be resorted to only when an element seems
missing. They simply help develop the awareness of where one must go, and
augment the performer's toolkit. To further the assumption of responsibility
and command of materials, and to bring some perspective to the otherwise

subjective work, interested participants will have the opportunity of taking charge of a session and offering first thoughts on the work. Critiques will be directed solely toward the usefulness of an exercise or scene in working toward the company's goals—nothing personal, no attacks or defenses, no penalty for disagreements.

As work swings back and forth between fealty-to-text and freedom-from-text, and each participant begins to discover the relative importance of all these elements to his or her own process and artistic identity, the company will need to sort out a new procedural hierarchy to add to the Chain of Interpretation's ethical code. The obvious challenge to the code's insistence on remaining within the boundaries defined by the creators is that of finding room for the performer's own creativity, and not everything in the text is of equal importance. So this hierarchy will have to do with assigning the relative weights of the instructions given by the text and by related materials. Here's a proposed ranking, in descending order of importance:

1. The basic "given circumstances" of the work. These would include the time and place of the action, the identities of the characters and their relationships, and the overall progression of scenes.

    Giving these instructions primary importance does impose certain strictures on the production team. "Time" means observance of the indicated period, not because updating or pandating can't ever "work" in some rough sense, but because it never does in a more demanding, particular one. It *always* undermines a work's integrity to some degree. "Place" means observance of the indicated locations, for the same reasons. It doesn't mean that a designer has no leeway in rendering "A town square in front of the cathedral" or "A room in the castle," but it does mean that even if abstraction is involved, the feel of such a square or room is unmistakably present, and that the staging practicalities of these places have been preserved. It means there will always be a place, not just a space. Character "identity" includes the ages, occupations, and general temperamental traits of the *dramatis personnae*, where these are stated at the outset or clearly revealed by the verbal and musical text.

2. The general layout of the score (its structural units), and the words and notes themselves. The latter comprise, obviously, key signatures, metres, and tempo relationships, but also such orchestral technical indications as *"col legno," "pizz.", "sul pont.", "con sordino,"* etc., which are basic to the

execution of the music. "Tempo relationships" refers to the close interpretation of *relative* quickenings and slackenings, since "tempo" is never an absolute. Metronome markings, and their musicological authentications, are carefully considered, but are never solely determinative. Included here would also be broad indications of affect, such as "*marziale*," "*pomposo*," "*wie ein Wiegenlied*," etc., that govern an identifiable episode in the score.

These first two categories are inviolable in all cases.

3. Dynamic markings, including all gradings of loudness or softness, as well as *cresc.* And *dim.* articulations.

4. All other articulations, including accents, fermatas, cadential observances, easements or momentary shifts of rhythm and tempo.

These two categories remain under strong textual admonishment. They are still in the purview of written rhetoric and the performer's serious obligation to it. So interpreters must strive to understand the musical and dramatic implications of these markings, and render them to the best of their abilities. However, interpreters' personal responses, and their findings of what works most powerfully for them, will carry the results well beyond what appears on the page, and these findings are only made through allowance of great freedom in the early stages of work. With No. 4, the lessons of oral tradition begin to have important influence.

5. Specific instructions to singers, whether affective ("*tristamente*," "*con gioia*," etc., or coloristic ("*cupo*," "*squillante*," etc.

6. Moment–to–moment stage directions and detailed set descriptions.

Nos. 5 and 6 are very much the property of interpreters, who have again explored what is meant by the indications, and now make use of what they can. But this is where the changes in rhetorical practice and theatrical technique—the generational adaptations—are so marked that the text can no longer be the absolute determinant.

By "items immediately outside" the text I mean things found in the work's source material (play, novel, epic poem, historical event), things found in other works of the composer and librettist and in their artistic life stories, and things found in the course of research into the period, the milieu, and cultural context of the work. Any of these may prove a key to an individual characterization, to envisioning a scene, or even to the dominant atmosphere of a whole production. But none must be privileged over what is in the text, or allowed to distort it. After all, the creators knew about these things, yet chose not to incorporate them into the work.

This hierarchy is more fluid than the Second Interpreters' code of ethics, because the understanding of the relationship of text to performance varies so much from period to period, style to style, composer to composer, that it must leave room for case-by-case adjustments. But it gives the company a guide to priorities, a court of appeal.

As the work begins to resemble a process with the singingactor at its creative center, new elements will be added. Solo instruments (a violin for "*Salut, demeure*," a 'cello for "*Morrò, ma prima in grazia*") will participate in scenes from the first discussions forward. Accompanists will, in selected cases, begin to function more like coaches or assistant conductors. Company members with directorial inclinations or design ideas will volunteer or be assigned to work with the performers on developing scenes. After more time has passed, some of the sessions will be opened to outside auditors from within the profession—conductors, directors, designers, and even other singers who are curious about the work. Their observations will be solicited and discussed, and their possible future interest noted.

The overall effect of the Discovery Phase has been to reverse the trend of the century past, which has been to narrow the performer's field of responsibility and to shift its boundaries from those set by creators to those who would "write the text anew." This does not mean a return to the willful misuses of interpretive freedom that egocentric singers of the past sometimes fell into—the checks and balances of our collaborative search for fully integrated production will prevent that. It simply gives performers a process by means of which they can more fully own their work. I know people (musicians and critics) who do not believe singers are capable of doing that. The Dream-On Company will quickly prove them wrong, and audiences will just as quickly feel the difference between presentation that originates with performers' own impulses and insights and that which, however skillfuly, "justifies" the expressive needs—often as perverse, and far more damaging, as the most arrogant singer's of bygone times—of someone else.

It may seem that in giving greater creative freedom and responsibility to performers, we have granted less to conductors, directors, and designers. Not really. It is true that we have proscribed auteurial subjectivity and interpretation-as-criticism. We have insisted that integration be approached collaboratively, not autocratically, and that everyone abide by our code of artistic ethics. The Second Interpreters-in-Chief are free to use the same resources available to performers: the text, performance tradition, and artistic imagination, and to assume the great responsibility of co-ordinating everyone's work into a cohesive whole, of which they are indeed in the end in charge. Those whose creativity is released by this understanding will flourish in the company. Those who cannot imagine how to proceed without a predetermined interpretation, an external concept, or a "design matrix" will not.

In the late stages of the Discovery Phase, a winnowing-out will have occurred. Ideas that seemed promising but have not in fact proved productive have been discarded. Others, suggested in the course of the work, have been tested and, perhaps, incorporated. Some scenes will have reached the point of being fully staged, with at least rough design elements, and conducted, possibly with modest instrumental ensembles such as those that accompany the doughty Mom-and-Pop companies mentioned earlier. A few have grown into sequences of scenes from the same work, including skeletal choral elements. And of these, the most exciting, the ones that most clearly suggest the fruitful union of these performers and this way of working with these operas, will be candidates for the first productions of the Dream-On Company, which is now ready for its first production cycle.

4. The Launch.

The company moves into its permanent quarters. These consist of a theatre seating some 1,600-1,800 patrons, the centerpiece of a complex comprising ample rehearsal and storage spaces—ideally, the spaces used during the Discovery Phase. The conformation is that of a modified amphitheatre, the orchestra level rising on a gentle rake from the edge of the pit—which, owing to the generous stage-to-auditorium ratio, can seat up to the full Wagner/Strauss orchestral complement. This room is somewhat larger than its seating capacity might indicate, since the upper tiers—a mezzanine and balcony—have shallow overhangs and abnormal floor-to-ceiling dimensions—no ticketbuyer will cower in a lowering tunnel where a third of the sound is cut off. The mezzanine, being shallow all around, will have a limited seating capacity, but the center section of the balcony, which is also shallow toward the ends of its arc, will extend up and over the ample lower lobbies to accommodate many more.

Everything in the public areas of the house will be designed with two ends in mind: to suggest that the past is alive in the present, and to prepare the audience for an ear-led, eye-confirmed experience. The look and feel of the spaces will be classic, as we apply that term to clothing or furniture—shapes and colors and textures that endure, and that avoid the fashionable or any particular period identity. There will be nothing futuristic, or industrial, or cool. Simple, but not pointedly "functional"; dignified, but not grandiose. Decorative elements of homage (portraits and prints, busts, etc.) will focus on the great creators of the artform, and perhaps some of the interpretive artists of the past who could be considered as among the company's artistic ancestors. The lighting will be warm and even. Outside the auditorium, sound- absorbent materials will keep the noise level down—no bounce off stone or metal. The eye will be encouraged to contemplate, the ear to open up, the insides to settle. Not a revving-up, but a calming down, a heightening of receptivity. People will still talk as they talk, behave as they behave. But there will be an influence.

In the common areas at all levels there will be bar and light snack service, with a higher-than-usual barista-to-patron ratio. Out of respect for both the scenario structures of our repertory (see below) and the comfort of the audience, the company will be taking more frequent, but shorter, intermissions than has become the custom, so at neither the bars nor the restrooms can there be long lines. Each level will also have secure lockers, accessed for a small fee, for coats and other belongings.*

There will be an exhibition gallery. Its exhibits will concern the performance histories of operas currently in repertory, perhaps augmented by some visual materials on the preparation of The Company's productions, and will change with each production cycle. As years pass, The Company's own performance history will be folded into the displays. There may be audio and video aspects to the exhibits, but if so they will not be promotional, and will be set up for individual viewing and listening, rather than imposed on everyone in the gallery. In the gallery, too, will be a kiosk where the production cycle's complete program booklet can be bought. This will contain non-self-promotional commentary by directors, designers, and performers, substantive critical essays on the operas, photos and renderings, performer biographies, possibly an article on some more general artistic issue, and the acknowledgements of financial support that make up the bulk of so many programs of nonprofit companies. It need not contain the librettos, since these will have been made available gratis, in print and online, to all ticketbuyers. The latter will be urged to read them, since there won't be any surtitles. On the night, ticketholders will receive a minimal program, a folded folio with basic

---

* This sensible system is in use in some modern theatres, including the Circle in the Square here in New York. It obviates the tips and lines (particularly on exiting the theatre) of the standard coatcheck.

performance information, for all who don't wish to pay the modest price (four dollars?) of the program booklet. The kiosk may also have for sale the company's yearbook (as soon as there has been a year) and a few books, CDs, and videos, narrowly targeted to what's playing.

These thoughts of low-end commerce naturally raise the question of ticket prices. Notions about this cover a wide range. At one dream-on end, the bareknuckle capitalist: "It should pay for itself. Set prices high enough to cover it. Who cares if they're all rich people? Rich people are just as deserving as anyone else. If they come, great; if not, fold the tent." At the other, the public-good moralist: "It should be free, or by voluntary contribution. All are deserving, none should be excluded. It's a civil responsibility, to be funded through a highly progressive tax system." In between: the real-world formulas that the business managers, development directors, and in-house economists of real-world companies strive to concoct. I'll touch on those later. For the moment, I'm sticking with the ticket-buyer's personal P.O.V., and with the value of the experience in relation to potential substitutes. And I'm not thinking of that value in terms of attendance at a single performance, but at many performances (at least one of each production throughout the season, for instance), because that is what I would want to be able to do as a devotee of this exciting company in this beautiful venue, and because I would be trying to cultivate such devotees if I were helping to run the company.

Even for top price, and even in 2015 in New York City, there's something about three figures that dims my passion for frequent attendance. My awareness of opera's costs and my sense of fairness are not involved here. It's purely a matter of my wish to attend often, and of not having to assign all my high-culture dollars, to saying nothing of my entertainment dollars, to this one favored pursuit. So I'm hoping for a top price of $95. Since there are no really poor seats, the house is scaled relatively high, let us say down to $40 for the uppermost balcony rows, with only two prices at each level, so the average is closer to the top than the bottom, while the mean is farther down. I don't plan to subscribe. I want a flexible plan whereby I could, if my exchequer is full, purchase the whole season in advance, but with mixed locations and price levels. (Others, of course, will have the more usual subscription plan available to them.) Ideally, I'd like an advance-payment FlexPlan: I deposit a given amount, spend it as I go, sitting where and when I like subject to availability, and refreshing the pot when necessary. This ties me closer to the company than single-ticket purchase, yet allows me leeway with time and money, and gives the company some cash up front.

Although the house is scaled toward the upper end of this very reasonable price range, many seats, at all price levels, will be discounted, since the company very much wants to hang onto senior devotees (moderate discount) and to lure students from at least middle-school age on up (heavy discount). It will also be seeking ways of identifying and helping others who simply don't have much money. That's harder. In time gone by a lot could have been done through the unions, and perhaps that's still the place to start—the performers' unions obviously, but especially the teachers' union. We want the teachers there, every night, in force, and of the union we ask no quid pro quo except the enthusiastic promotion of the program to its members.

Since the auditorium's seating plan is not yet determined, we can't yet know exactly how many seats at which prices will be put on sale. But we can get a rough figure for the likely take on a sold-out performance. Let's say our full-price average has turned out at $72, and let's say further that the company's economic realists have pushed the house capacity to 1,800 seats. Of these, one hundred aren't for sale (press—I guess we have to do that—company members, comps to distinguished artistic visitors, etc.). This leaves us with 1,700, but we must allow for our generous discounting policy. So let us now say that seven hundred of our tickets have gone at half-price. Thus:

$$1,000 \times 72 \quad - \quad \$72,000$$
$$700 \times 36 \quad - \quad \underline{25,200}$$
$$\$97,200$$

Just a guesstimate for a Dream-On Company sellout, calculated from the ticket-buyer's P.O.V. All the ticket-buyers—the students, the teachers, the seniors, the wealthy taking advantage of our pocket-change tariffs (you're welcome; come often), and the everyday, middleclass folks paying our full popular prices—are now in the auditorium. Here, they see that the atmosphere of understated, unfashionable elegance still prevails, and that the seating arc on all levels stops well short of the horseshoe. There are no partial-view seats or extreme viewing angles. They also see that beyond the curved apron there is a proscenium. That is because the company will be designing for opera as we have known it. Conformational adaptability is of small use for this repertory, and adds greatly to mechanical complexity. And while we want a well-equipped stage with respect to scenic capacity and lighting, cinematic flow is not a goal for this company, since (and here is the reason for those extra intermissions) with very few exceptions the works we are presenting were written for a theatre of bound-off segments of space and time. Closed scenes, closed acts, structured for such closures in linear progression, were presumptions of creation and production. When continuity between segments was desired, it was provided by music, directing the audience back to ear reception, ear understanding. A few of these interludes have mandated visual components, usually where some conception of a space-time continuum or travel between realms is involved (*Parsifal, Das Rheingold, Frau ohne Schatten*), but others are meant simply to keep us engaged during changes of scene (*Pelléas et Mélisande*—and note, in all these instances scenes are connected, but acts are not). These must be addressed in actualist terms, as must our repertory's many scenes of spectacle and magical transformation. Nothing must be cheated. But we aren't after visual amazingness per se. We are trying to follow the aspirations of Robert Edmond Jones (to create "an environment in which all noble emotions are possible," then cede the stage to the performers) and Rudolf Heinrich (to "meet the internal requirements of the work itself"). Therefore, our capacities will be used with restraint; the feel will be relatively low-tech. Here's another quote from Jones:

> "The trouble with our modern theatre is that it is mechanically perfect. It is far too perfect: its perfection has become tiresome. Interlocking dimmer boxes, stereopticon lenses, false prosceniums, revolving stages, sliding stages. The theatre is like a great throne; a throne with no king."[5]

In the years since Jones wrote those words, the "too perfect" has perfected itself many times over and the throne has blown itself up to Brobdingnagian proportion, nowhere more so than in opera. We won't be playing this game of thrones. We're going in search of kings—and queens, of course.

At first glance, the company that now begins rehearsing is not very different from the group that gathered for the Discovery Phase. Perhaps there has been some discontinuance and replacement from the waiting list, but for the most part these are the same people. They already had the talent, experience, and skill to meet professional standards, via the customary rehearsal and production route. They haven't undergone sci-fi mind melds or personality implants. Yet they have changed, some a little, some a lot, in at least two important ways. First, they have come to know one another as people do when they work intensively together for a significant amount of time, especially in an artistic context, with all emotional, mental, and physical energies bent toward a common understanding. They have found out what can be counted on from whom, where sparks are struck, how to deal with one another. They know they will be continuing together, not heading off to something else. Even the inevitable disagreements and antipathies belong to the Dream-On Company's world, and not some other. All this is of itself quite different from the norm. Second, through the exploratory work all of them will have experienced, at least at times, the transformative sensation of actually fashioning the music and the action, rather than reproducing them, and of creating specific expressions of character and action that are theirs alone, yet belong to an inherited understanding. They will have found in themselves their "creative independence," and now bring it with them to the first rehearsals.

As envisioned from the outset, everyone now signs new contracts. They are for two years, to guarantee stability at this early stage, and involve increases from the initial wage. Thinking again in 2015 dollars and allowing for an economically challenging environment like New York City's, this would need to reach the vicinity of $2,000 per week, though now there would be some separation between principals and associates. Included will be health insurance and fixed-benefit retirement plans, toward which the members will contribute. The goal is a structure for long-term employment that treats everyone fairly and transparently. Perhaps the permanent, top-level staff (Artistic Director, Dramatic Director, Musical Director, Administrative Director) will receive a premium over the principal performer salary, but otherwise no one will be paid above this level. There will be modest over-time provisions, something on the order of time-and-a-quarter, which will probably favor the technical staff and stagehands more than anyone else. It will have to be understood that with respect to stagehands, orchestra, and chorus, the company is not in competition with the commercial theatre, the major symphony orchestras, or the Metropolitan Opera.

After the first two years, contracts will be renewed with automatic increases keyed to a predetermined percentage over the local inflation rate, with no negotiation and no distinctions on merit. If the artist has proved good enough to continue and wishes to do so, he or she is re-signed under the same condi-tions as all other artists. If not, the contract lapses after careful consideration by the artistic staff in consultation with an artistic committee elected from among the membership at the quarterly company meetings. There will be some paid vacation, probably in the form of a portion of the company's one or more annual production shutdown periods. There will also be provision for an artist taking unpaid leave to perform elsewhere. But this will have to coincide with a production cycle, and will not kick in till after these first two years, during which all hands must be on deck. Outside artists—performers, conductors, directors, designers—who have interest in the company's way of working will be invited to participate on a guest basis. They must commit to a complete production cycle, and in all respects, including remuneration, will be treated as company members during that time.

No one will get rich. Fair pay for hard work. Everyone is crucial, no one is special. Opera loses money, in great tranches, and it is absolutely necessary that everyone understand that nonprofit status, with its draw on public monies, involves acceptance of certain limitations. These limitations may be quite significant in comparison to what an international star can command, and for that reason the company may from time to lose an extraordinary performer it has developed. So be it. We need not share all of Walter Felsenstein's cosmic socialist disdain for the globetrotting, fee-grasping star, or ever cease wondering why a great artistic talent is not worth a hedge-fund manager's weight in gold, to see that the atmosphere of wealth and social glitz that envelops opera on the international level is seriously misleading with respect to the artform's economic realities. In any case, only a few of the company's artists would realistically face such a choice, and they can always come back as guests for a production cycle or two.

I keep using these terms, "production cycle" and "repertory," and should clarify what they mean for the company. As I observed in the Introduction, only our ballet companies now offer versions of the repertory system that used to exist in opera, wherein not only works (repeatable, renewable ones, of necessity) but different casting combinations rotated through the course of a season, and much of the lure to return lay in the mixing and matching of singers. There are two reasons, one positive, one negative, why this system has died in opera. The positive one is integrated production, which implies a cast and conductor that stay together through rehearsal and a run of performances. The negative one is the scarcity of singers with the voices and temperaments to arouse any genuine anticipation, and it is largely because of this scarcity that the search for renewability of the masterworks has come to focus on production. The Dream-On Company seeks to reset that focus.

A production cycle, for our purposes, is a period during which a group of works is rehearsed and placed into repertory performance. At least at the beginning, these works will number only two, the two that have come closest to readiness in the Discovery Phase. This readiness is the only criterion of selection. It implies that the principal roles have proved particularly suitable for company members, and that in the musical and dramatic interchanges that have occurred, showers of sparks have flown off. These might be any two works, but suppose they are *Don Giovanni* and *Elektra*. These two canonical masterpieces will be the repertory of the first production cycle, which lasts eight weeks—five of rehearsal and three of performance. Both are challenging operas. But then, every opera is challenging if it is taken seriously, and these have the advantage for our initial offerings of being relatively light on chorus. And here is how chorus and orchestra will work into the company system:

During the Discovery Phase, some of the artists now under contract as associates—perhaps even some who are now principals—will have stood in as chorus during the work on ensemble scenes, like the Act I finale of *Don Giovanni*. And as mentioned earlier, solo instrumentalists, and even small orchestral groupings, have been introduced late in the work on some scenes. These singers and players have fully participated in the musical and dramatic development of these scenes, and are privy to the unique binding of vocal, instrumental, and physical elements into units of dramatic intent that has been sought. They now set the template for the company practice of requiring the attendance of choral and orchestral section leaders at the staging rehearsals from the first day forward, and soliciting their contributions to the work. Then, as fuller choral and orchestral forces are involved, they function as associates of the conductor and chorus master, helping to convey phrase-by-phrase, action-by-action expressive intentions, and conducting separate sectional and small-scene rehearsals as needed. The conductor and director are thus able to concentrate more freely on the unification of the broader musical and dramatic concept, and no player or chorister is left without a precise understanding of each moment and its place in the progression. Since this will all be new to the singers and players who will now make up the company's full chorus and orchestra, and will take time to settle in, it eases matters if these first two shows are not heavy choral ones like, for instance, *Carmen* and *Lohengrin*.

Giovanni and *Elektra* do have dance components—nothing like the formal ballets of the *grand opéra* and earlier forms, but very important for the fulfillment of the key scenes. The dances in *Don Giovanni* are not in themselves demanding, and are to be executed not as professional dancers would, but as the real-life participants would, some socially cultured, others with rough gusto and true ineptitude. That is by no means easy. The production is in period, so the dances must be also.

Elektra is a different case. Only one performer is involved: Elektra herself. But her wild, ecstatic death dance is the apotheosis of the opera, and is foreshadowed in her opening monologue. Further, Elektra (our director has decided) must have the dance latent in her body from beginning to end. This must be kept under, because her scenes with others are played realistically, but we must sense that it is waiting to burst forth. And the style of the dance must be within the culture of the work; that is, adapted from the forms of movement being developed among dance and pantomime progressives of Strauss and Hofmannsthal's era in Germany, Austria, and Switzerland, with its perceived connection to primal sources and to female empowerment. Again, not easy—it's a style easily parodied, and until the final two pages, the singer's breath management must be preserved. But the dance can't be just indicated. It has to happen, truly and fully, and if we did not have in the company two sopranos (the Elektra and her alternate) with the background and capability of developing the death-dance element far beyond what one usually sees, we would not be undertaking this opera.* For both *Giovanni* and *Elektra*, it's possible that we already have someone in the company—probably the principal co-ordinator of the movement exercises—who can collaborate choreographically with the performers. If not, interested outsiders will be brought in pending appointment of a permanent overseer of the company's dance requirements.

I mentioned an alternate. With only two operas in repertory, even our relatively light performance schedule (see below) will, in some pairings, put heavy demands on the vocal, emotional, and energetic resources of principal singers. Exactly how much can reasonably be asked of them we will discover only when we come to know the performers well, so the need for alternates will vary from production to production, cycle to cycle. In the Cycle I example of *Don Giovanni* and *Elektra*, the demands are severe—and if you think *Elektra*'s an obvious case but *Giovanni* is "only" Mozart, take a good look at the length of the latter's roles, including the ensembles, and bear in mind that we're shooting for E-19 usages, not Skipover ones. From the "shared cover" P.O.V., the pairing is actually advantageous. One soprano could, with generous and supportive preparation, cover both Anna and Elektra, another both Elvira and Chrysothemis, a third Zerlina and one of the Maids or the Overseer. One of the baritones or basses standing by for the Don or Leporello and/or Masetto and the Commendatore (we might double these last two, as in the original distribution—a rugged bass Masetto) could do the same for Orest. Even Aegisth and Ottavio might have the same alternate, since the company wants a strongvoiced Ottavio and an Aegisth who can actually sing, however extreme his characterization. Klytemnestra will require her own, unshared alternate, as will whichever of the lowvoiced *Giovanni* males is not also the standby for Orest.

These alternates will be well beyond the usual "cover" or understudy level. They are other principals of the company, who might well have been cast as

---

* I was too young, and my eye too untrained, to have any sharp recollection of Astrid Varnay's solution for the dance, though I remember a brooding, prowling presence. In Inge Borkh, however, I saw at least a close approach: an intense actress with a strong, flexible body and clear acquaintance with the physical language. And sure enough, she started as an actress, then studied dance with Grete Wiesenthal, an important figure in the early 20th-Century modern dance movement. More recently, Martha Graham's technique would be a relevant point of reference. We're looking for a Patricia Brooks with an Elektra voice.

first choices for their roles. Their competitive spirits are simmering at not having been so designated, at not receiving quite as much rehearsal time toward the end as the first cast, and not getting the mainstream reviews. But they know their time will come, for in some production soon the first/alternate situation will be reversed. Meanwhile, they are going on well prepared, and earning the same money as their colleagues. Owing to the performer-generated nature of the company's process, with its insistence on the living dynamics of character interactions, many interpretive differences will have emerged from the alternates' rehearsal collaborations. Most of these will be by way of nuances of phrase and inflection, of behavior or rhythm. But others may entail changes that are, within the boundaries of the overall musical and dramatic concept, quite radical, extending to shifts in staging and lighting, orchestral tempos and dynamics, etc., and giving a distinctly different look and sound to scenes and moments. The company's process and scheduling make it possible to incorporate even these substantive changes at the alternates' performances to a much greater degree than is usually the case in a repertory situation. Behind the alternates, of course, must be a second line of "covers" in the usual sense, capable of stepping into a true emergency (*both* the Chrysothemis and Elvira are sick) and allowing the show to go on, albeit with some artistic deficit.

Within a production cycle, the performance schedule will depend on the company's best assessment of two things: performer energies and the market. A five-performance week would be ideal—three performances of one opera, two of the other. If one opera is projected as noticeably stronger box office than the other, it can be scheduled as the three-performance show in all three weeks, for a nine-to-six split over three weeks. Or the middle week can reverse the split, for an eight-to-seven balance. Here's a possible schedule for the premier production cycle, assuming an eight-to-seven split, and with alternates' performances designated:

	Mon.	Tues.	Wed.	Thu.	Fri.	Sat.	Sun. (mat)
Week 1:	DG	—	El.	DG	DG (alt)	EL.	DG
Week 2:	—	El.	DG	DG (alt)	El.	DG	DG (alt)
Week 3:	El.	DG	—	El.	DG	DG (alt)	El.

As you can see, alternates (possibly not all of them—the Elvira or Leporello, for instance, may be fine with consecutive nights) have appeared in four of the *Don Giovanni* performances, on different days of the week. The *Elektra* cast has always had two nights' sleep between shows, and the *Giovanni* first cast at least one, sometimes two. Both operas have been made available at least once on each day of the week, and the dark nights (in addition to Sunday, which is always dark following the matinee) have been scattered among the early weeknights. We will hope that Friday night's Donna Anna alternate is not faced with an indisposed Elektra on Saturday, and will have had to exercise best judgment regarding the physical and technical resources of our sopranos to foresee whether or not separate alternates are necessary for those roles. The scheduling of the alternates, and the accommodation of their interpretive choices, will introduce a bit of the old repertory excitement into our integrated-production model. Fans will report their performances to one another. The critical press, or whatever still passes for it, will be given reason to return. And the company will have begun to lead its audience toward the realization that though its physical productions will be attractive and interesting, performance itself is what makes the crucial difference.

This last will be true of all the company's productions, beginning with those of the second cycle, which happen to be *La Bohème* and *Pelléas et Mélisande.* Like the *Giovanni* and *Elektra* productions, these have grown from seeds sown by the performers themselves during the Discovery Phase, brought to fruition through collaboration with the production team. In all these cases, the perfomers' work has produced the concept, not a concept the production. We would only have selected an opera as familiar as *Bohème* (however popular) upon seeing that some of our workshopping performers, exploring the dynamics of all the character relationships in the time and place specified by the creators, had come up with something revelatory about them. And we would choose a piece as enigmatic (and unpopular) as *Pelléas* only upon learning that we had in our midst a few performers (especially for the female title role) with the unusual instinctive connection to the material that allows us to actualistically investigate this unique masterpiece for what it is: a Symbolist music-drama of the occult. These conditions being met, we are able to schedule a Cycle II that is also convenient from a Human Resources P.O.V. The works draw from another side of the company's range of vocal and stylistic talents, and in Act II of *Bohème* begin to bring fuller chorus into the proceedings.

5. Going On.

There will always be a Discovery Phase. As Cycle I enters full rehearsal, the advanced scene work on the operas chosen for Cycle II intensifies. These productions are ready for full rehearsal as the Cycle I performances begin, and will complete their five-week rehearsal period with *Sitzprobe,* tech and dress rehearsals during the two dark weeks between cycles. As they do so, the Cycle I performers, most of whom are not cast in Cycle II, return to the workshop spaces for participation in the development of later productions. There, they are joined by some new faces—not an entire new company, but some eight or ten new singers who join under Discovery Phase agreements, and are now doing their scene and exercise work, attending rehearsals and performances, and working their way into the company culture. They don't have the advantage of six months' pure R&D,as did the founding group, but they do have the compensation of a process that has defined itself, and colleagues who are working within it. For the most part, they will have to await attrition to become full company members, like minor league ballplayers waiting for the established major leaguers to move on or fall aside. But they'll be on tenure track, and can be promoted at the discretion of management and members. This renewal will happen every year, depending on slots foreseeably available.

Under this particular imagining, each cycle occupies five weeks—three performance weeks, and two dark weeks for final rehearsals. So there could conceivably be as many as ten cycles, twenty productions, and one hundred and fifty performances per calendar year. Some regional theatre companies (Steppenwolf is an example) do perform year-round. But even the largest of these is far smaller than any full opera company, and with far fewer seats to fill. They also benefit from economies of scale, with the initial costs of fewer productions spread over much longer runs in any given season, and with no expectation of rotating works through an ongoing repertory. Besides, in The Company's case, everything about the physical production—sets, costumes, lighting, staging—has been derived from and is tied into performance discoveries. It makes no sense to detach one from the other. This further limits economies of scale, since much greater-than-normal trouble must be taken with revivals in future seasons (keeping the original cast together, thoroughly re-rehearsing and tweaking, working any new principal in painstakingly), and co-productions with other companies will not be likely.*

Ten cycles, occupying fifty weeks of the year, are clearly too many for both The Company and its audience. For that matter, the whole structure of five-week, 15-performance cycles has been up for debate in The Company's often-contentious organizational meetings. Some members have argued that

---

* Someday, perhaps, there will be another company in the U.S. or abroad whose principles and practices are close enough to The Company's that an exchange of productions, or a sharing of artistic personnel for particular purposes, might be possible. That would be exciting. And of course The Company as a whole might be invited to take one or more productions to another venue. We would gladly accept, so long as it did not involve serious disruption of the home season.

at the outset, each cycle should have only two weeks of performances ("We're going to try to sell seven *Elektras*, six performances of *Pelléas*, in an 1,800-seat house? Are we crazy?"). Some have said that to really set a precedent for "repertory," at least three operas should be put into rotation from the start, possibly spread over four weeks. Some have plumped for six-performance weeks, whether in two- or three-week cycles. Some have suggested that The Company begin with a much shorter season, or perhaps two or three short performance periods, hoping to build up to more extended schedules in the future. And some have maintained that market considerations should, especially at the start, play a more determinative role in programming—proven box-office draws, with care to avoid too much head-to-head competition.

Here is how the ultimately victorious faction replied: "You raise legitimate questions. Perhaps time will prove you right about some or all of them. But our overall sense of them is this: We have our facility. We have the financial backing to carry us through anticipated early struggles. (See below.) We know what we're about, and we think it is vitally important that we establish this with the public from the get-go: that we are offering an artistic experience, unavailable anywhere else, that has the look of something old but is actually something new, and that it is here full-time and for the long haul. Yes, two-week performance cycles might be more prudent. Perhaps *Pelléas* will sell miserably. (It usually does.) Maybe even *Don Giovanni* will. Operagoers think they know what these experiences are. They have also learned what the efforts to make them new and "relevant" amount to, so telling them that this is new in a more emotionally meaningful, intellectually honest sense won't impress them. They have to be shown, word has to get out, both in relation to a given production and to the enterprise as a whole. The same goes for the people who aren't operagoers. They think they know what they're missing, and they don't mind missing it. Bringing them in, one by one and couple by couple, is a generational project. If *Pelléas* sells to half-houses but gets good word-of-mouth and some interesting critical response, that's a success for us. We can build on it.

"We think three productions per cycle at the beginning is too big a strain for our way of working. It's not probable that our Development Phase work will generate that much repertory at one time that meets our standards, especially as the season progresses. The same goes for six-performance weeks—not enough space around the shows, not enough time and availability for brush-up and tweaking, for a rhythm of rest and preparation. No doubt everyone will feel driven by schedule, pushed to open before ready, to show up though exhausted. We all do, always. But the reality is that in this company, those factors must be mitigated to keep us relatively fresh and sharp.

"Short spurts obviously don't work with our company model of full-time employment, or for developing the inescapable presence and audience loyalty we seek. And of course the market will influence us—we're not idiots. But we don't know what our market will turn out to be. We only know what the depleted soil of other markets has been, because we haven't yet had a chance to shape ours. That'll take a few years. All the works we do are masterworks. They should be before the public the way we can do them, in the order they come to readiness.

"Of course, all this is subject to revision. We live and learn."

And so the first season of the Dream-On Company, exemplified by the two production cycles already described, has been set at eight cycles totaling forty weeks, of which twenty-four are performance weeks, resulting in 120 performances. This implies up to sixteen productions, all new—a staggering undertaking that can be contemplated only because of the initial Development Phase and the continuing process shaped by it. It is also assumed that at least two or three of the productions mounted during the season's first half will have been successful enough to bring back during the second, thus reducing the number of new productions. In subsequent seasons, some of these first-year offerings will belong to a gradually accumulating repertory, still getting plenty of attention, but cutting back from season to season on made-from-scratch productions.

These considerations, and many more, must find their places in The Company's longterm vision. Since we can't yet know what we don't know, this is necessarily a plan with some areas that are sketched in, some that are provisional, some that are TBA. But moving forward requires that it exist as best as it can be imagined, not only for the survival and advancement of The Company, but of the artform itself in our capitalist democratic republic.

6. The Future.

If The Company's production cycles occupy forty weeks of the year, twelve weeks remain. They might be distributed in any of several ways, with all taken over the summer (there might some day be a festival residency in a bucolic venue), or some in the relatively dead weeks following December holidays or even in a longer Fall/Spring split, with performances extended into the summer. In any case, these twelve weeks will be used for a combination of the paid vacation time all company members receive and intensive Development Phase work. All principal and associate performers; all conductors, coaches and instrumentalists; all directorial, design and choreographic associates; and all administrative staff continue on full employment. So do the orchestral and choral first chairs and section leaders, who continue to participate in the scene work as they did in the initial Development Phase, and who have the function of conveying the findings to their choirs. The rest of the orchestra, which numbers around 80, and the chorus, about 60-strong, might fairly be handled by putting them on half-salary with the freedom to accept other employment. Something comparable may be needed for stage crew and some other technical personnel.

The ballet presents a similar situation. Given The Company's repertory, this will be a very active and artistically crucial unit, with some work to do in many of the shows and a full 19th-Century complement needed for some. However, ours is not a joint opera/dance venture (though that's another possible model), but an opera company. We probably justify no more than four principal dancers plus a small core of the corps. The core will function in the same manner as their orchestral and choral counterparts, helping the choreographic associates in working with the full corps when it is required, and lending their skilled pantomimic presence to large non-dance scenes. The full corps, which will usually be needed for four or five productions in a season, will have to be hired on a per-production basis, with some of the regulars ready to be admitted to the core when openings arise. In time, it may be that ballet evenings can be offered, with programs drawn from operatic ballet sequences, some of which will have been in The Company's repertory and are familiar to operagoers, some musically familiar but almost never done, and some of great rarity—there is a wealth of material in Russian and French grand opera, to say nothing of neglected Verdi and Donizetti suites, and with the right choreography,* some highly pleasurable evenings and surprise hits, some incorporating singers and chorus, might be derived from it. Similarly, the orchestra and chorus might be involved in oratorio and concert performances, where again the E-19 era has much to offer that has fallen into sometimes-unmerited disuse. Taken all together, these activities could eventually further extend employment for the orchestra, chorus, and ballet, so long as they do not in the slightest compromise The Company's main mission. Speaking of which:

By my calculations, there are in the E-19 repertory between sixty and seventy Category One works—operas that are either of great general appeal or of high reputation among opera professionals and critics. And there are as many more that belong in Category Two—operas that have definite strengths, that

---

* As in all The Company's work, the ballet will be seeking to honor traditional stylistic markers of its material while aligning these with the modern acting eye, which often finds the dancing unconnected to dramatic motivation and the pantomime little more than pure signaling.

some aficionados love and no one hates, and that have shown that despite certain weaknesses can give great satisfaction in the hands of inspired interpreters. I won't list either category here, because beyond the Top Forty or so that will only trap us into fruitless bickering. But if you create your own list, I predict you will finish with numbers close to mine. Then there are the few operas of our Little American Canon and others like those in Group One of "Here and Now" (see pp. 111-121), to which the Dream-On Company feels some obligation, and a handful of other 20th-Century pieces which, though not strictly of E-19 descent, are of high quality and clearly amenable to The Company's way of working.* And we might reach back to the proto-E-19 reform operas of Gluck, believing that our talents and methods can more completely realize the high drama and musical beauty of those pieces than any other approach on offer.

So there are somewhere between 150 and 200 operas that the Dream-On Company can plausibly consider putting into Development Phase work as candidates for production, without counting the hundreds of E-19 operas that lie beyond Category Two, and which may from time to time present something worth looking at. As experience teaches us about our market, our market will certainly be a factor in our decisions, but not to the exclusion of seemingly unlikely projects about which some members are enthused. A market (or, rather, its extrapolators) predicts on the basis of past performance. If something surprises it, its basis of predictability, its supposed wisdom, is suddenly different. No artistic enterprise of any integrity allows "the market" to rule all other considerations, and The Company less than most.

Since The Dream-On Company is the world's only dedicated E-19 company, it must forego the musical glories and scenic amazingness of all the works of the French and Italian Baroque, including those of the mighty Handel. To pre-occupy ourselves with their thespic and dramaturgical peculiarities, their frequently ornamental aesthetics, the distraction and costs of the amazingness, and vocal usages that do not buttress those we are trying to encourage, would only blur The Company's identity with the public and make no sense for its personnel. Ideally, there will be a Skipover Company of superior quality in our metro region that can assume responsibility for those vast and rich territories and for some of the modern and postmodern scores

---

* Remember that E-19 is defined more by its narrative, by plot and character, than by musical style. Taking Britten as an example: *Peter Grimes* is a full-fledged E-19 grand opera. His other unquestionable masterpiece, *The Turn of the Screw*, is neither grand nor E-19 (unless we consider the ghosts our protagonist couple). But its dramatic and musical qualities are Company-friendly, and our auditorium, though not a chamber-opera venue, is intimate enough for our artists to register the work's overwhelming effect.

that are, from the Skipover P.O.V., compatible with them. Frankly, I doubt that such a company could sustain full seasons, especially in the presence of one that is repeatedly demonstrating in full the tragic pathos and comedic wisdom of opera's maturity. But if it could come even close to that, it would round out the healthy operatic scene we should have.

By the end of its first decade, The Company may have mounted as many as seventy or eighty productions. But since some will be fresh views on works already done, and we cannot anticipate many long-running shows like Felsenstein's *Vixen*, as few as fifty different operas may have been presented—less than a third of all those within The Company's purview. Naturally, the operas that are most readily adaptable to modern acting techniques and modern dramaturgy will have made up much of the repertory. But those based on early Romantic conventions (*Guillaume Tell, Der Freischütz*, etc. etc.) cannot be shirked; they must be solved. Work such as those sworn off by Corsaro (*Aïda*) and avoided by Felsenstein (Wagner, R. Strauss, all of grand opera except *Otello*) will have been tackled, because without those no claim to represent E-19 is sustainable. The first Dream-On *Ring* will surely have been produced. By the third or fourth season, when chorus and ballet have been thoroughly incorporated, *Prince Igor* may have been revealed for what it actually is. And over this time, the production cycle model may well have loosened to allow more programming variety within any two- or three-week period, or to accommodate the mixing in of revivals or Category Two operas that are unlikely to sustain box-office intensity. Perhaps the whole repertory format will have changed. However these matters are arranged, it will take an operagoing lifetime to work through the playlist while keeping the most renewable, repeatable masterworks in the rotation. The E-19 canon is in fact inexhaustible. Whether or not it is imperishable depends entirely on performance.

Because of this last fact, The Company's success or failure will be measured not by how many or which operas it has produced to some approbation, as by whether or not it has indeed forged a tough new alloy from the metals of the old rhetorics and the new sensibility—by whether or not it has spawned such creatures as a Brooks/Tebaldi, a Lieberson/Stignani, or a Shicoff/Martinelli, and enabled them to find their "creative independence." My assumption is that the equivalent of such creatures did at one time exist, that is, that the confluence of written rhetorics with the beginnings of modern stage aesthetics of voice and behavior did result in great singingacting, as then defined, from some of the advanced artists of those times. But I do have to assume this; I don't really know it, since I did not experience in the theatre what the records and written descriptions suggest.* Further, stage aesthetics have changed. The new compound, this alliance of the Duprezian and Stanislavskian revolutions, would be quite different from theirs.

This is going to take a while. The founding members of The Dream-On Company have been selected because they have the ambition and talent to become such artists, and are already on that road. Once into the Company's process, they can certainly acquire ways of thinking and working that will very quickly set them off from the run of gifted operatic performers, and give audiences the taste of a new/old experience they will recognize as something they've been longing for. However, most of these artists are well past their training and early professional years, and from the vocal standpoint there are limits to how far an underlying technical structure, the functional frame-work that accounts for the calibre, dynamic range, and color spectrum of the instrument, can be responsibly pushed. It may be tweaked, but must remain essentially intact and stable for the singer to continue with consistency and confidence. There are, therefore, limits at the visceral, bioenergetic[†] level, at Ground Zero for the generation of the sung action, to what can be demanded of the first generation of Dream-On singers. That is why The Dream-On School must be established immediately.

7. The School.

The School will seek to identify and attract potential operatic artists at an early stage of development, in some cases as early as the middle-school years, but in all cases before they have become enmeshed in the university/regional complex. This is necessary for guidance in two crucial areas of artistic and personal development: voice itself, and cultural background. With respect to voice, it is important that the students begin as early as possible not only on

---

* Chaliapin is the pre-eminent exemplar—a singer whose outsize vocal, musical, and rhetorical accomplishment is attested to, though not fully conveyed, by his recordings, and whose dominant presence, embodiment of character, and mastery of makeup are so thoroughly documented from credible written sources and pictorial evidence that we cannot doubt his standing as a great singingactor of his time. The failure of his only film, *Don Quixote*, to bring us much of this cannot cast that seriously into question. I am sure that among the many others who "make us see" via their recordings and held high reputations as actors for the eye, at least some justified those reputations. But of artists who combined greatvoiced singing with physical characterizations that contained elements of the older rhetoric along with modern acting awareness, I can testify only to Jon Vickers, Maria Callas, and Tito Gobbi, of whom I cannot say I saw the latter two at the height of their powers.

† "bioenergetic": I employ this term in its generic, lower-case meaning, referring to the flow of energies within, or emanating from, the body, and not in reference to the particular theories and practices of the therapeutic discipline called Bioenergetics.

formal vocal study directed toward E-19 requirements, but on everyday habits of speech that lay down the neuromuscular tracks of the pre-enhancement/ public speaker's voice. "Cultural background" has two meanings. The first is narrow, taking in everything that has to do with opera itself—acquaintance with classical music and drama, with the lives and times of operawrights and interpreters, with the legacy of exemplars, and so on. The second is broad, embracing primarily European history, literature, philosophic and religious thought, and above all languages themselves. In both meanings, it involves sharpening the appetite for the past and curiosity for how things used to be and why, for what is really still the same and what different, and for an awareness that those things and people are "relevant" not because they were just like us, but because they became us. Attention will be insistently directed away from the popular culture and toward the higher one, away from entertainment and toward art, toward the cultivation of taste.

At first, The School will be small and loosely organized, a network of teachers (Company members, Development Phase instructors and co-ordinators, others who share the Company goals) who meet with the students singly or in very small class groupings, with each student's program individually structured according to what he or she already knows, has a special feeling for, or is getting adequately from other sources during these secondary school years. The réclame surrounding The Company's launch, including announcements about this mentoring program, may well have attracted the interest of a number of families whose children have shown an early passion for opera, and of school teachers who have identified such children in their classes. These will be unusual children, representatives of a tiny minority. But The Company isn't looking for numbers; it's looking for special cases. Children of The Company's own members might make up most of the group in the early years. The program will be free to all who qualify.

Always, The School will be seeking collaboration with the middle and high schools the students are attending for their general education. Perhaps close co-ordinative ties can be established with one or two such schools. They will most likely be private schools, with their enrichment programs and select student bodies, but The Company will always be hoping to connect with public schools as well, to share in their advocacy for funding for arts programs, and to locate students from less privileged circumstances who nevertheless have promise. It's just that even a Dream-On Company must be chary of the energies and salaried time of its personnel, and of fundraising that does not go toward its core mission.

Throughout their time in the program, the students will feel a strong Company connection. As their schedules and interests allow, they will attend performances, watch rehearsals and Development Phase sessions, and develop relationships with Company members. As they approach high school graduation, far ahead of their peers in vocal, linguistic, and theatrical skills and in cultural knowledge that is germane to opera, they will have a number of options. We hope that some of the most talented will proceed directly into Development Phase work with the company. There may occasionally be one (probably female, due to the age differential in vocal maturation between the sexes) who can already qualify for associate company membership, either skipping further formal education altogether or putting it on a slow part-time track that does not compromise her professional status. Others may continue as they have, fitting their Company training into the early years of a liberal arts college program. The Company cannot allow the pipeline to become clogged toward the end, but it will be especially patient with the men, since some kind of affirmative action initiative for male singers is desperately needed in the profession. Some students, of course, will decide to enter a conservatory or university music school, go off to another company's apprentice program and then sink or swim, or quit opera altogether. With time, The School will expand a bit with The Company's reputation, possibly attracting funding that would not be made available for another purpose. Given that a realistic yield for The School is one or two Company artists per year, and that no results can be expected for the first four or five years, The Company should nonetheless acquire six or seven artists from The School by the end of its first decade, with more coming along each year. Because they have been nurtured in E-19 ideals and crafts, forsaking all others, from an early age, they will carry The Company to higher levels than even its founders achieved. By the time a second generation is fully in place—joined, as always, by gifted and motivated performers from other sources—the Dream-On Company will enter its prime, and the masterworks of opera's greatest years will be fully unconcealed.

Wonderful as all this will be, there will still remain the problem of creative renewal, of new work. It is not really the problem The Company is meant to solve. Before we can build anew, we must stop the practice of bombing the village to save it, stop denying the past while living off it. That's what The Company will do. In so doing, it will restore coherence to the artform; clarify for lots of bewildered people (who include our potential composers and librettists) that coherence, not incoherence, and integration, not disintegration, are quite useful practices; and that consummation in performance, not brilliant ideas and concepts, is the stuff of opera as opera. Everyone who works in The Company will come to understand this more deeply, more organically, with each passing day. Among them will undoubtedly be, from time to time, someone with the operawrighting itch. In daily working in The Company's process, discovering and re-discovering what makes the masterworks of sung drama tick in the theatre, in front of audiences, and inspired by some story that feels hot and immediate, indeed of mortal urgency, and is yet more than his or her pet virtuous cause,* may start to set some wordnotes down on paper. If the wordnotes begin to take performable shape, The Company will certainly provide space and time and people to try them out, in the hope that an opera worthy of the repertory may emerge. But The Company will not devote resources to endless workshopping and "development," and will never commission work from composers who have not shown that they can write music of specifically operatic qualities.

It may be that the Postists are right—that there is no meta-narrative, and that's the point. We wouldn't know, being part of it. In any case, there are subjects, there are sources. And meanwhile, one of the great bodies of work for the stage will be before us, resembling itself.

8. Money.

Back in the day when I and a few other refugees from the worlds of performance and/or arts journalism and criticism found ourselves involved in that of development and philanthropic support for the performing arts, Baumol and Bowen's *The Performing Arts: Economic Dilemma* was our Bible. Certainly there were other sources we turned to for some self-education in those expansionary times, such as the Rockefeller Panel Report, insider books on the pioneering launch of the Guthrie Theatre, and a bit later, The American Assembly's anthology of assessments, along with the steady stream of articles, conference speeches, and newsletters that kept the discussion churning.[6] But it was to Baumol and Bowen's book, the first comprehensive effort to collect reliable data on the performing arts economy and then apply disinterested expert analysis to it, that we turned for a realistic perspective on what the field was dealing with. That was bracing, even though their findings didn't give grounds for much optimism.

Baumol and Bowen's most famous observation was that the financial woes of the live performing arts—particularly in the nonprofit sector and most particularly in the "high-culture" segment of it—were due not to the oft-cited proximate causes (poor management, unreasonable labor demands, etc.) but to something more fundamental, which owing to its nature was bound to worsen over time. This factor, known to this day as "Baumol's Disease," they

---

* I have one: the tragic and/or redemptive fate of a protagonist couple or lone artist, struggling for humanity as the age of the robotic transhuman dawns.

identified as a productivity lag, resulting in an ever-widening income gap. By "productivity lag" they meant this: while in most industries technological advances enable productivity gains (more units of output per man-hour of labor) to offset rising costs and thus hold prices down, the performing arts are relatively impervious to these gains. They may benefit around the margins, but in their central function they experience no increase in productivity—it takes just as many man-hours to perform a Schubert string quartet or a Shakespeare play as it did two or three hundred years ago. The labor of the players produces no external good—it is itself the "product," and even when held below the standard of other areas of the economy, is by far the single biggest item on the expense side of the balance sheet.

This relative stasis of productivity makes the arts a "stagnant" industry, along with other labor-intensive ones (education and health care are commonly mentioned). The problem for such industries is that their costs for equipment and services are rising in sync not with their own rate of productivity, but with that of the economy as a whole, where the productivity gains made possible by technological advances operate to keep prices more or less in line with the general rate of inflation. The living expenses of all their employees rise in like manner, so their wages must also keep step, however modest their relative position. Yet arts enterprises of the labor-intensive, high-production-cost sort we are discussing, of which opera is the foremost representative, have over time found it impossible to raise prices commensurate with their increased expenses, for two reasons: 1) limits on what the market will bear (for, important as they are to their devotees, they are not necessities like food, housing, or transportation), and 2) moral reluctance. Even if it were possible to sell out the Metropolitan Opera House a couple of hundred nights a year at a scale of, say, $1,000 per seat down to $250, which is approximately what it would take to eliminate the company's income gap, that would negate the primary social purpose of any artistic effort, and make opera into what it is often perceived to be, a self-referential diversion for the one percent. Ergo the income gap, which, owing to the ever-quickening pace of technological advancement in economically determinant industries, is destined to widen in the future. (It should be underscored that "income gap" describes the difference between total expenditures and *earned* income. In the nonprofit arts, it is presumably covered by unearned income, i.e., contributions.)

Much has changed since Baumol and Bowen published their pioneering study in 1966, even aside from the real-dollar adjustments that need to be made in all their nominal figures. Indeed, much has changed even since the appearance of Heilbrun and Gray's *The Economics of Art and Culture* in 2001.[7]

This fine volume brings forward and expands on Baumol and Bowen's work, and with many references and attributions takes into account the information and arguments offered by others over the intervening years. Among many carefully supported observations, Heilbrun and Gray note that the increase in the income gap forecast as imminent by Baumol and Bowen did not occur at the near-catastrophic level they predicted. The main reason for this is that over the ensuing ten or fifteen years, the overall standard of living rose sufficiently to leave a large portion of the population with more disposable income. In consequence, ticket prices could be raised faster than the rate of inflation without significant loss in attendance, thus restraining, at least for a time, the growth of the income gap.* However, this only mitigated, not eliminated, the effects of productivity lag. (Costs in some areas, in fact, rose even more rapidly than these ticket price gains.) And it was temporary. Though the diagnosis of "Baumol's Disease" has been refined since 1966 and occasionally challenged,[8] it remains an underlying condition of the performing arts and other "stagnant" industries. With this background in mind, let me turn back to the situation of the Dream-On Company. This is the reality part of the fantasy. Artistic folks must dream, but not idly.

Earlier, I projected income from a sold-out performance with a $95 top price at $97,200. And I proposed an initial season of 120 performances, which would yield in a year of sellouts a total of $11,664,000. Of course it's possible that in our ongoing debate between pragmatists and idealists the pragmatists have scored a small victory and raised the prices to the following scale:

Top:	$110
Bottom:	45
Full-price avg:	82
Avg. 50% discount:	41

Allowing our same estimate of 1,000 seats sold at full-price and 700 through our various generous discounts, the sold-out house now brings in

---

* Drawing on studies by the Ford Foundation and by Samuel Schwarz and Mary J. Peters, Heilbrun and Gray report that the relative income gap for American opera companies fell slightly in the late '60s and remained stable through the 1970s. They also reproduce a table compiled by Marianne Victorious Felton (p. 158), which shows a continued slight decline between 1981 and 1991. Two caveats: Felton's table excludes the Metropolitan, I assume because its size might distort the averaging of the 24 companies included (I don't think it would have made much difference). And that word "relative," referring to the *proportion* of earned income to expenditures, can be deceptive. The *absolute* figures, and thus the actual number of real dollars to be raised from contributions, continue to rise. I will be leaning on both Baumol/Bowen and Heilbrun/Gray throughout the rest of this chapter, without specific citations.

$110,700, and a season of sellouts $13,284,000. But we will not have a season of sellouts, or anything approaching that. Perhaps toward the end of the first decade we can work our way up to a percentage of capacity the Metropolitan would consider disastrous (75 or 80 percent), but in our first year we should consider something like 50% of capacity as more likely, and with a higher proportion of discount tickets in the mix. That's not a failure. That means that around 100,000 people who don't have to be wealthy to qualify have come to see and hear great art. However, it also means earned income of around 5.5 million or 6.6 million for the year. We will hope for more (two-thirds of capacity, for instance, would yield approximately 7.8 million or 8.9 million—we'd be delirious), but half seems a prudent first-year goal. There will also be some ancillary income from concessions, exhibition gallery sales, possibly an occasional recital or small concert on a dark night, etc. But it will be very modest, hardly worth predicting in this rough outline.

Now let's look at expenses. This will be rougher yet, since we aren't attempting a complete company budget. But we have some guidance from the economists' findings that on average, between fifty and sixty percent of an opera company's expense is incurred by the wages of its artistic personnel. It isn't evident just where the line is drawn between artistic personnel and others—I assume that a lighting or costume designer counts, but that lighting technicians, seamstresses, and fitters don't, but I could be wrong. It is also not immediately clear how the Dream-On Company compares with others. There are no megastar salaries; on the other hand, all are compensated fairly. In the first year, all productions will be new, so material costs, stagehand overtime, etc., will be abnormally high. Still, we can't go too far wrong in taking the average as a measure, staying at its lower end (50%) to allow for high production expense, start-up costs, etc. So let me tot up our estimated artistic salaries:

The company is starting with forty principal solo artists earning $2,000 weekly, plus ten associates at $1,750 weekly year-round. Annualized:

Principals	:	$4,160,000
Associates	:	910,000
TOTAL SOLOISTS	:	5,070,000

In our orchestra, there are ten principals, earning $1,800 weekly for the forty full-wage weeks, and $900 for the twelve summer weeks. The remaining seventy players earn $1,700 and $850, respectively. We must also allow augmenting the numbers by ten players for two of the season's shows, for the five weeks of each production cycle, at the regular company salary. Making the necessary multiplications:

Principals, 40 wks	:	720,000
Principals, 12 wks	:	108,000
Players, 40 weeks	:	4,760,000
Players, 12 weeks	:	714,000
Augment, 10 weeks	:	170,000
TOTAL ORCHESTRA	:	6,472,000

The chorus has eight principals (one for each of the SSAATTBB sections) and fifty-two regular choristers, paid at the same wage scale as the orchestra. Again, we must count on augmenting in the same numbers for the same durations for two operas (possibly not the same two—for instance, for *Götterdämmerung* or *Frau ohne Schatten* one might supplement the orchestra but not the chorus; for *Otello* or *La Juive*, the reverse). Thus:

Principals, 40 wks	:	576,000
Principals, 12 wks	:	86,400
Choristers, 40 weeks	:	3,536,000
Choristers, 12 weeks	:	530,400
Augment, 10 weeks	:	170,000
TOTAL CHORUS	:	4,898,800

Next, we need to account for all the artistic personnel who in most companies would be considered interpreters-in-chief, but in ours are termed artistic associates or co-ordinators with areas of production responsibility. (I will save the multiplications till after the descriptions.) In overall artistic command is The Company's Artistic Director, either elected from among the company members or appointed with their approval. As I mentioned above, he or she is paid a slight premium over everyone else on the artistic side. Only his or her counterpart on the business side, the General Manager, also selected with full approval of the members, is of equal standing. This Artistic Director's salary is $2,200 weekly, or $114,000 per year. Working closely with the Artistic Director are the Musical, Directorial, and Technical Directors. The first two will no doubt themselves be the conductor and director of one or two productions per season, but their main function is artistic supervision and the setting of standards in their respective departments. Each of these three is paid $2,000 weekly, year-round.

On the musical side, there are, immediately under the Musical Director, four conductors (two for the current production cycle and two for the next), with the Musical Director's participation creating from time to time a floating conductor who can rotate back to Development Phase work or whatever else seems necessary. Each conductor is paid $1,800 per week. There are also eight assistant-conductor/coaches, in charge of musical preparation, rehearsal accompaniment, and Development Phase work, at least two or three of whom could assume conductorial responsibility in an emergency. They earn $1,700 per week. All conductors and assistant conductors are fulltime employees, since their participation is required for project development and classes during the dark weeks. Finally, there is a Chorus Master, who is paid $2,000 weekly year-round, and a Choral Associate, earning $1,700 for forty weeks and $850 for the dark twelve.

To the production side. It is organized along the same lines as the musical, but embraces more functions. So in addition to the Dramatic Director there are four resident directors ($1,800 weekly year-round) and five stage managers (one floats), at $1,700 for forty weeks and half that for twelve. We also need four Assistant Directors, two per cycle. Like most ADs, these are young aspirants gaining their first professional production experience, and hired season by season. They are paid $900 weekly for the forty production weeks.

Design is more complicated, since it takes in the artists of sets, costumes, and lights, all of whom are ultimately answerable to the director. We probably don't need an overall Design Director, since we aren't seeking a house style, and any unifying decisions would be under the Dramatic Director's jurisdiction. Design time is distributed differently than in other areas, since much advance work is required, but only maintenance once a production opens. Further, some directors assume one or more design functions themselves, so although it is unlikely that our internal process will breed many director/designers, we cannot foresee how show-to-show requirements will play out. Nonetheless, we must make an estimate to cover the category. So let us say that the Company employs five set designers, compensated at $1,800 per week, and four each of costumes and lights, at $1,700. Because of their involvement in development from a very early stage, they are year-round employees.

Two categories of artistic personnel remain: teacher/evaluators, and guest artists. While all The Company's interpreters-in-chief will participate in Development Phase workshopping as time allows, there will need to be four who are dedicated fulltime to that work. In the long view, they are among the most valuable company members with respect to artistic improvement, and are paid accordingly, in line with the Musical, Dramatic, and Technical Directors, at $2,000 weekly. Guest artists are distinguished professionals—conductors, directors, designers, and teachers—who are intrigued by The Company's talent and way of working, but cannot make season-long commitments, and whose participation will stimulate our artists and broaden their P.O.V. The Company may not have guests the first season or two, while it consolidates its processes and builds enough reputation to attract them. But there should be room in the budget for them, so we will allow two positions in each of the four above functions. Since they are hired for one production cycle only (i.e., eight weeks, including preliminary rehearsal) and do not benefit from the pension and retirement program, they are paid at the top rate: $2,000 weekly.

It is likely that all this is an underestimate. In many companies, for instance, there is a job called Production Co-ordinator, responsible for liaison between the musical and production sides with respect to rehearsal time and other matters. It may be that the costume and lighting assistants, the construction and running crews, and other functions will fall into the budget as artistic personnel; I haven't counted them as such. But with what we have, calculating and annualizing:

DIRECTORS

Artistic	:	114,400
Musical	:	104,000
Dramatic	:	104,000
Technical	:	104,000
		426,400

MUSICAL

Conductors	:	374,400
Asst conds	:	707,200
Chorus Master	:	104,000
Choral Assoc	:	78,200
		1,263,800

PRODUCTION

Directors	:	374,400
Set Des	:	468,000
Cost Des	:	353,600
Light Des	:	353,000
Stage Mgrs	:	391,000
ADs	:	144,000
Teach/Ev	:	416,000
		2,500,600

GUESTS

Conductors	:	32,000
Directors	:	32,000
Designers	:	32,000
Teach/Ev	:	32,000
		128,000

TOTAL CHIEFS : 4,318,800

And adding that to our previous totals:

TOTAL ARTISTIC PERSONNEL : 20,759,600

If we add to that a modest contingency allowance of five percent, we are over $22,000,000, and I'll round it off at that. It's strictly a preliminary Dream-On projection. But even if it's wildly off, by fifteen or twenty percent, it gives us the general idea. It is very much my hope that it actually represents over half the expense total, meaning that everything in the categories of administrative, material (production and other), fund-raising, audience development/advertising/ publicity, plant maintenance, front-of-house services, insurance, pension and health costs, and who knows what-all I'm forgetting, can be held well below that figure. But if we follow the guideline the economists have given us, and conservatively take our 22 mil as 50%, we must multiply by two and arrive at a first-season budget of $44,000,000. As you can see, at our proposed price scales and attendance estimates, we are projecting earned income as somewhere in the low to midteens as a percentage of total expenses. Even the more optimistic projection of two-thirds of capacity brings us up to only 20%, at the higher price scale. Not a good business model here.

And of course, these are only the running costs. They do not contemplate the construction or acquisition of the Dream-On theatre/rehearsal hall/ storage/housing complex, and they do not figure the expense of the initial Development Phase, which yields no income at all. Many, many millions more are needed there, and there is no unused New York City Center or war-ravaged Berlin Metropol for some municipality to fork over (they would be inadequate anyway), nor a Soviet government finding it convenient to not only underwrite Art for the People but to support artistic R&D, as it did for Stanislavski in his later years. We anticipate that as The Company thrives, it will bring its earned income/expense ratio up, and perhaps (though history tells us this is unlikely) it will find a way to keep costs in line so that their increases stay even, in real dollar terms, with ticket prices.[9] All that notwith-standing, our percentages will be well below the levels usually considered minimal for consideration by funding sources public or private, and between thirty and thirty-five million constant dollars per year will have to come from somewhere. As economic impossibilities go, The Dream-On Opera Company leaves an American Vakhtangovish Theatre in the dust.

Yet *this is an entirely reasonable plan.* It merely proposes the establishment of a company of sufficient but by no means excessive size, in a pleasant and comfortable but not lavish theatre of appropriate dimensions, whose artists may count on steady lower-to-middle-middle-class employment and inte-gration into their community, to renew and sustain a body of artwork that should always be before the public of any civilized Western nation. True, it also insists that to "be before the public" means being economically open to all, which should go without saying in any democracy. Its only unusual demand is that it be granted freedom to explore promising new artistic pathways, which does in part require an easing down on the assembly line. But that is simply an artistic necessity, without which The Company has no *raison d'être*.

I love the story of the founding of the Theater of Musical Drama, St. Petersburg, 1912, as recounted by Levik.[10] Its Artistic Director, a dreamer named Joseph Lapitzky, had raised some seed money from interested individuals (inves-tors—this was no nonprofit, but a joint-stock company), but now needed a much larger sum to adapt the Great Hall of the Conservatory to operatic use. He approached a rich factory owner named Neischiller, who grilled Lapitzky on finances, then asked him what gave him his confidence. The answer: "I've been ruined three times with theatrical enterprises and know the reasons for my failures." After a little vote of confidence from the Conservatory's director (Glazounov), Neischiller pulled out his checkbook and signed over the impressive amount. The Theatre of Musical Drama was launched.

There are many Neischillers about, and if we dream on into delirium we can imagine one of them clicking through a transfer to fund the whole Development Phase, and a consortium of a few more throwing in the land acquisition, design, and construction costs of our theatre. Our fever soaring, we think we see an Opera Angel, or flights of them, guaranteeing our deficits for the decade to come, and setting up a billion-dollar endowment for the more distant future. In exchange, they ask only that their names be graven in The Great Book of Angels on permanent display in our Exhibition Gallery. The Dream-On Company now resembles a commercial for-profit enterprise that loses tons of money at the outset, and tons more once in operation, from

year to year, like a Broadway show that closes having lost its entire investment (a regular occurrence) or several newspapers one could name.* And in
time gone by, many an opera company was organized with the expectation
of making money for some impresario, or at least breaking even on behalf
of a court, municipality, or group of wealthy directors and boxholders. The
Metropolitan Opera itself did not begin to turn from the last-named arrangement till its formation as an Association in the early Depression years, in
part to avoid the entertainment tax and gain access to foundation funding.[11]

But Lapitzky's audacious enterprise lasted only a few years, as did
Mamontov's and Oscar Hammerstein's and many another, and the days when
the Kingdom of Naples allowed Domenico Barbaja to run gambling rooms in
the lobbies of its opera house to defray production costs and megastar fees
are presumably gone. (The Reno/Las Vegas Grand Opera, with Netrebko,
Kaufmann, and Bocelli? It's a paradigm.) The artistic goals of the Dream-On
Company, which are what seem so improbable to my patiently listening
friends and colleagues, are achievable. The financial needs are insoluble
under current cultural and political conditions.

The elephant in the Dream-On room is public funding, the very thought of
which implies a status that opera does not have in our society. Opera is not
widely recognized as a public good. Its case for public support is therefore
quite weak, even among those who grant that there are such things as cultural goods held in common, whose value goes beyond that shown on the
balance sheet. We do have indirect means of public funding for the arts and
other nonprofit undertakings, in the form of our tax code. It provides, first,
that as the Met observed back in the Thirties, the proceeds of institutions that
can get themselves classified as "educational" will not be taxed, and second
that contributions to such institutions from any source (private foundations,
corporations and their foundations, individuals) constitute tax deductions.†
This made up, at least in part, for the fact that the vast industrial fortunes
were no longer income tax-free. It gave the wealthy a practical incentive to
continue their support of the arts, especially while a highly progressive tax
scale was in place, and got a broader spectrum of American society involved

---

* I'll name just one. As I write this, owner Mortimer B. Zuckerman has just taken *The New York Daily News*, once the country's largest-circulation paper, off the market. Losses for the most recent of many consecutive red-ink years: $20,000,000. Yet, for the *pro tem* and for whatever combination of reasons, he continues to publish, and there are several potential buyers in the wings.

† We also have unemployment insurance which, more or less accidentally, allows thou-sands of performers to hold their fraught lives together and "stay in show biz."

in support of the arts. It also tended to classify the arts as "charities" in the public mind, and to compel arts organizations to devote much of their energy, time, attention, and money to the cultivation of financial support.

This system of private plus indirect public subvention worked tolerably well for much of the Twentieth Century, especially when paired with the introduction of some direct public support—not so much for the latter's sheer amounts, which were never large relative to the needs of the field, but for the simple acknowledgement of high culture as a public good, and its catalytic effect on private giving.[12] Sometimes it seems to me that it has worked better than we operaphiles had any right to expect—you mean that this scheme of tax benefits for corporations and citizens has, among other things, kept our tottering old Eurocentric artform from collapsing in a heap for nearly a hundred years, through good times and bad? Astonishing. But it all depends on your standard of measurement. If, like me, you feel that the flourishing of at least some twelve to fifteen Dream-On companies in our major metropolitan areas, within striking distance of everyone from sea to shining sea, is a sensible baseline from which to calculate, it's much less than astonishing. Besides, the income gap continues to widen, for a time more slowly, now again more quickly. The tax code is no longer highly progressive. Collapse of what we have is not unthinkable.

And how puny these amounts are. That depends, again, on your P.O.V. In the high-cultural world, an income gap of thirty million (or, for all fifteen companies nationwide, some four-and-a-half billion), with the prospect of only slight improvements in future, is very large indeed. But that is only because the arts sector as a whole, of which opera is but a segment, is of such small economic significance. Arts advocates are forever emphasizing the economic importance of their enterprises for fundraising purposes, and to be sure, their arguments are sound in many localized or even regional instances. But in the macro sphere, where such matters as government funding or major foundation support are decided, the argument from economics is a feeble one, and recognized as such. Forego it, friends of art. Another common set of arguments, based on comparisons with defense budgets, agricultural subsidies, or oil depletion allowances, does serve to underline disparities—it's the "Please, sir, we have so little, drones have so much" gambit—but puniness is hardly a sound reason for support. Forego that, too.[13]

The rationale for public support of the arts is cultural. It doesn't have to do with material necessities, public safety, or the survival of the republic. It has to do with richness of life, depth of understanding, satisfaction of aesthetic hungers, and a longing for something beyond economic measure—not with whether or not we can be a great and powerful country, but a great and memorable civilization. That rationale has been eloquently articulated in one strain of American political thought from the Founding Fathers' time to this. It was drawn upon for the establishment of our mechanisms of direct support—the National Endowment for the Arts under Presidents Kennedy and Johnson; its working model (rather as "Romneycare" in Massachusetts more recently served as model for President Obama's national program), the New York State Council for the Arts under Governor Nelson Rockefeller; and *its* model, the British Arts Council, under John Maynard Keynes, no less. It is implied in the sober marshalling of for-and-against arguments by our economist exemplars (see Baumol and Bowen, Chap. XVI, "On the Rationale of Public Support," and Heilbrun and Gray, Part Four, "Public policy toward the arts").

However, this has been far from the only strain of thinking on the subject in the history of our democracy, and here in America we have never felt comfortable with the notion of significant governmental subvention for the arts—especially from the federal government, and especially for the arts of the high culture. Or, to put it as positively as I can, we believe it's healthy to have as wide a diversity of sources, a coming-together of as many interests public and private as possible, in recognition of the arts as a common good.

Yet it is clear that the "massive, ongoing underwriting" I mentioned in relation to the Vakhtangov company will never be forthcoming without much stronger political leadership. This would mean (dreaming on) direct funding support in multiples of the present allocation at all strata, a panpartisan lockbox to ensure stability, and much more vigorous advocacy to keep awareness of the arts *as an affair of state* constantly alive.

I think we must concede that democracy and high culture have an uneasy relationship. This is often framed as an elitist v. populist quarrel. Michael Straight, the first Deputy Chairman of the NEA and a thoughtful chronicler of the times (see n. 14, below) identified it as the pull between the Jeffersonian and Jacksonian visions of a democratic republic, between the guidance of a highly educated minority shaped by the European Enlightenment on one hand, and that of a socially equalized populace on the other. It is well illustrated by the twisted, irony-soaked saga of public arts support in 20th-Century America. That began during the Great Depression with the Works Progress Administration (WPA), which as part of its vast undertaking of government as employer of last resort established programs in theatre, music, and dance, and commissioned projects for fine artists, architects, and writers. The WPA enabled the survival of thousands of artists in their disciplines, and left a bounteous legacy of notable careers and works. As a major component of FDR's New Deal, it also went far toward associating the arts (including some of high-culture ambition) with a populism of the left, and giving that the sanction of official policy. As such, it generated a powerful political backlash, and set a pattern of support for public arts funding from the left and the Democratic party, opposition to it from the right and the Republicans.

That pattern was still operative in the 1960s, when two Democratic Presidents and a coalition of influential Democratic Senators and Congressmen with a few moderate Republicans managed to embody public arts funding in an agency which, with true Dream-On imagination, they called an Endowment. Then came a couple of odd turns. One was taken by President Richard Nixon. Instead of (as we had all assumed upon his election) sharply cutting back or even killing off the Endowments, he gave them his full backing and presided over substantial increases in their appropriations. His political reasoning was that, with so much rage directed toward him and "The Establishment" from the intertwined antiwar and pro-racial-integration movements, he could offer some pacification in the form of backing for a traditionally progressive cause. The other turn came from the New Left, which now considered high culture an expression of The Establishment—not as a treasury to be more democratically distributed, but as a horde to be looted for whatever might be of use to the counterculture, and otherwise disposed of as decadent and oppressive. The budget slashings, political correctitudes, and folkish bias of the (Democratic) Carter administration were of scant help, and however personally genial toward the arts and artists men like Reagan and Clinton may have been, there has been progressively less evidence of any Presidential vision of the place of the arts in society in the decades since. The few but effective Congressional champions of the arts have passed from us, along with the spirit of comity and cultural optimism into which the Endowments were born.[14]

Public funding programs are put in place from above. Politicians must decide to install them, and where there are no powerful arguments of economic gain, public safety, or material necessity to compel them, there must be a component of belief held in common, of values acknowledged even when not held personally dear, to supplement the inevitable calculation of gain or loss with a given constituency. While it is true that in a democracy it's no good blaming the politicians since the buck stops in the voting booth, there remains the question of which politicians are actually made available to the voters, of what sorts of persons they are and which values (if any) they do hold dear. I suspect that even in Richard Nixon there was, in addition to his sharp political instinct, precisely that acknowledgement of values that enabled him to overcome his temperamental antipathy toward aspects of the artistic and intellectual worlds when it finally came to his influence on public policy. We don't have Sun Kings or Medici or Mad Ludwigs, and we cannot expect that more than a small fraction of our legislators will themselves be acolytes of the Muses. It is the acknowledgement itself, at one time shared by a working majority of our representatives, that we need. If it's lacking in our politicians now, it's probably because it's lacking in our citizenry.

All the sources of wisdom I have been able to tap into—subjective observation, the evidence of economic studies, and common sense—tell us that two factors above all others influence active interest in the arts. They are education and income level, of which education is the more determinative.* Familiarity breeds appreciation. One cannot develop a taste for something without exposure to it, and without early exposure one is unlikely, later on, to expend time and money acquiring the taste. People hate being told they don't know what they're missing, but that is quite literally the case. So if we wish to cultivate a taste for the arts among our citizens, and thence among our political deciders, we must widen the childhood experience of such exposure. The classical arts will always be a minority taste, like anything requiring sustained attention and an aesthetic sensibility. But the minority can be expanded, and the standing of the arts as public goods strengthened.

"Education" means everything that is learned, and in childhood much of what is learned originates in the home and in the immediate social environment, of which the early grades of formal schooling are only a part. But what goes on in formal schooling is, I think, crucial. That is where the groundwork for all the elements I mentioned in connection with the Dream-On School's mid-school and high school training program is laid. Those same elements, in age-appropriate form, are what awaken the sensory awareness of the adult audience members-to-be, the parents-to-be whose homes will nurture the next generation, the constituency-to-be that will demand more of more receptive politicos-to-be.

There have been, and still are, initiatives to make arts education a matter of public policy.[15] They have always foundered over arguments on the mechanics of distribution and the standards to be employed, concerning which the High Culture has become an antidemocratic bogeyman. These days, the arts are also consigned to the rear echelons of the math/science/technology offensive, and what advocacy there is for them generally takes the form of trying to demonstrate they are of use to brains being shaped for that onslaught. It's depressing. Nonetheless, let's pretend that marvelous things have happened. Arts awareness, appreciation, and participation have doubled, tripled,

---

* With respect to the economic factors, Chapters 3 ("Audiences for the arts") and 17 ("Innovation, arts education, and the future of the arts and culture in the United States" of Heilbrun and Grey are especially pertinent.

and the High Culture bogeyman has been revealed to all as a wise, kind elder. This new/old awareness has, through democratic means, given us a few enlightened politicians and exerted a firm, gentle pressure on some others. These leaders have not only inspired greater support from the private sector, but have installed a Department of Cultural Affairs, complete with lockbox, at cabinet level, through which markedly increased public funds are disbursed. Similar marvels have occurred in municipalities, regions, and states throughout the land, and a co-ordinative structure among all these strata has been devised.[16]

It is in such an environment that the Dream-On Company might actually come into being. The theatre complex would be a municipal responsibility, through new construction, renovation of existing facilities, or a combination of both. Either ownership of the complex and/or land would then be transferred to The Company, or the municipality would extend a longterm lease at token rental. The Development Phase and much of the first season would be capitalized by one or more Neischillers, in combination with private giving featuring a major crowdsourcing campaign and, in view of the credentials of The Company's members and leaders, some public funding through local instrumentalities. As The Company consolidates its position as an artistically vital, quality-of-life necessity, public funding at higher levels will be increased, and as it comes to be recognized as a national good, a substantial portion of its budget will come directly from The Department of Cultural Affairs. This will be general support, not targeted at a particular project, and will not be tapered over time to shift its responsibility back to the private sector. The rationale for its continuance will depend not on some specified percentage of earned income, but on the true democratic measure of public interest: attendance. Since income level is second only to education as a factor affecting participation in the arts, it is upside-down to set an earned income requirement (thereby pressuring ticket prices upward and discouraging attendance from lower income groups) as a test for use of public monies.

Does all this seem no more than a fantasy in our real political world? I'm afraid it does. Yet to anyone who believes in the value of the arts to society, in art as what the economists term a "merit good," it is, like the Dream-On Company itself, entirely reasonable, no more than we should expect from any advanced nation. I like the attitude of the Russian film director Alexander Sokurov. I've seen only two of his many films, *Russian Ark* and *Alexandra*, very different in style and subject, and found them both fascinating and humanizing.* Speaking of Russia's troubled times, Sokurov says, "We're not irrevocably fated to be civilized . . . every time, we have to prove it, we have to pass the exam that we can be civilized."[17] That's right, I think. That's the task, and it's not Russia's alone.

A NOTE ON ONE LAST SHOW

In the *Updates* chapter I wrote briefly on my first encounter, on CD, with *Written on Skin*. I have now had the chance to solidify my impressions of this extraordinarily successful work, which since its premiere in Aix (2012) has already been performed at several other stops on the international Upper Circuit and is scheduled for many more, though sometimes only in concert or for a single performance. Its composer and librettist have been commissioned for a new opera by Covent Garden. A new piece can hardly do better than that. *Written on Skin* came to the Koch (State) Theater of Lincoln Center for three performances in August, 2015, in the same production seen at Aix, with two of the same principals (Barbara Hannigan as Agnès, Christopher Purves as The Protector) and the same orchestra (The Mahler Chamber Orchestra), but a different conductor (Alan Gilbert). The performance confirmed my opinion that this is the smartest, most intriguing new opera to come my way since—well, I can't remember the last smart, intriguing new opera I saw. It's full of original thinking and masterly craftsmanship, both musically and theatrically. It is a modernist, not postmodernist, work—that is, it has a coherent narrative, the nature of which its words repeatedly keep before us and which its music seeks to clarify, shape, and animate. Its musical language, intense and filled with pointillistic detail, also belongs to modernism. Our attention does not often stray far from these materials, from how it's made. It is a fully integrated actualist piece that stays true to itself, and the production, directed by Katie Mitchell, designed by Vicki Mortimer, and lit by Jon Clark, is also integrated with itself and the work. In the theatre, the self-narrative device combines with the production's visual framing to create a curiously ambivalent effect. The former draws the ear into the story while keeping it aware of storytelling. The latter—literally a frame, with the observing Angels occupying spaces around the central room as they might hover in the margins of an illuminated manuscript, and at a couple of junctures invading the room to participate in the story—shows

---

* Operatic connections: the final sequence of "Ark," famous for its single-tracking-shot technique, shows the Grand Ballroom of the Hermitage in full, aristocratic swing with Gergiev leading the mazurka from "Eugene Onegin"; in "Alexandra," Galina Vishnevskaya plays an old woman making her way to Chechnya to visit her grandson who is on the front lines of the war there.

the eye a contemporary perspective on the ancient narrative while reminding us that theatre life is a made-up life. Thus, the principals inhabit their
roles with a modern, true-to-life ferocity; the surrounding does not inhibit
them. But for us, while their work does at times take hold, we stay one layer
removed from sustained involvement. The opera's techniques try to evoke in
us the feel of being told a childhood tale, and in a way they do. The trouble
is, we're adults now. We don't enter the story as would a child, but can only
look on. *Written* is yet another tragedy that doesn't feel tragic. We don't see
Agnès' end—it is abstracted in the narration, and as the principals ascend
a staircase, presumably to join the Angels in the margins, the music bears
neither tragic weight nor transcendence.

This opera and this production didn't belong in this theatre. Much of
Written is rendered at a hushed level. This did have the salutary effect of
enforcing audience silence. But some of the orchestral intimacies didn't
quite hold, and it would not have helped to bump them up, because sung
narrative would have been lost—which returns me to my earlier point of
interest, the word-setting relative to voice types. This is chamber opera, and
in this house only Purves, a bass-baritone, had a voice of sufficient size and
color to fill out the space in the bigger moments, and remain inflectionally
distinct in the many small ones. His voice's format and sympathetic timbre
suggest a good Wolfram or Amfortas, possibly a Holländer or Boris, but he
seems drawn mostly to Skipover repertory or character parts (Alberich in
Rheingold—why not Wotan?). Hannigan is a first-rate modern singeractress
whose physical performance was compelling, and she can summon the
strength for the high-range climaxes. All the good work she does in the lower
octave would register better in a smaller venue. With The Boy we encounter
again the falsettist problem, and in a crucial role, taken here by Tim Mead.
(On the recording the part is sung by Bejun Mehta, with a somewhat deeper
set and duskier sound that connects better with the prevailingly low tessitura.) But the problem is more basic than a particular performer. It is the
choice of vocality, and is well beyond the Marschallin/Octavian convention.
Dramatically, we hear a liaison between a grown woman and a prepubescent boy—and much as we empathize with Agnès' desperation, that's really
unsettling. Musically, we hear an instrument drained of color and projective
ease—not a voice of gold, silver, bronze, or even fabric, but a voice of milk.
The character simply has no agency in the music, and the physical characterization (Mead did it well) only serves an ear/eye incongruity. There's a
vocal category called tenor . . .

Written on Skin is an opera for the intelligentsia. I consort with that class
from time to time, and find the piece altogether superior. It isn't a repertory

opera; it hasn't enough popular appeal. But it's an admirable effort, and I look forward to that Covent Garden Commission.

And how fortuitous it is for my E-19 faydit thesis, that for this acclaimed international hit, composer and librettist have been drawn back to its origins and, in their sophisticated, somewhat detached way, have sung that tale yet one more time.

The End

September 23, 2015

NOTES

1. Lanier is wonderful on this. See, for instance, Chapter 2 of *You Are Not a Gadget* ("An Apocalypse of Self-Abdication"), in which he explores the "cybernetic totalist culture" as a new religion, or the Sixth Interlude of *Who Owns the Future?* ("The Pocket Protector in the Saffron Robe"), on Apple stores as temples. As I write this (and there's something every week), I can peruse Megan Eustad's "The Church of TED" (NYT, Mar. 15, 2015) or Sue Halpern's "How Robots and Algorithms Are Taking Over," an essay review of Nicholas Carr's *The Glass Cage: Automation and Us*, (*NYRB*, Apr. 2, 2015) especially its concluding paragraphs on automation, AI, and some belatedly dawning premonitions in the techno community. And where are the semioticians when we need them? Barthes would have had a field day with Steve Jobs unveiling the latest doodad for the adoring faithful.

2. "Panpsychism": the word is Leonid Andreyev's, invented to define more precisely the famous "mood" of the MAT's Chekhov productions, with their development of a psychologically defined inner action (and a relative absence of more externalized "acting") that pervaded the air among the characters and extended to heightened awareness of objects, sounds, and time. See his "Letters on the Theater," in this connection specifically the Second Letter. These virtuosic essays, originally written in 1911-14, are contained in Senelick: *Russian Dramatic Theory*.

3. See the Perspectives Series (Opera America, 2005-2008, 4 vols.), a series of guides for aspiring singers based on advice from a wide range of professionals. The volume entitled *Building and Managing Your Network* addresses the present topic most directly; see, in particular, Chapter 3, "Working With Other Professionals." I keep a set of these guides at my studio, and urge students to familiarize themselves with them. They describe the world we're living in, and how the gatekeepers of that world look at things. The homeless must turn into entrepreneurs or live on the street. What we really need, though, are more homes.

4. See: *The Levik Memoirs*, Chap. 11, which is devoted to the history and accomplishments of this company.

5. See: *The Ideal Theater: Eight Concepts*, The American Federation of the Arts, New York, 1962, p. 9. This is the catalogue for an exhibition of designs and models by eight of the leading designer/architect teams of the time. Jones's words are cited by the exhibition's installer, Peter Larkin. He does not specify their source, but mentions material sent to him by Jones, who died in 1954.

6. See: The Rockefeller Panel Report, *The Performing Arts: Problems and Prospects*, McGraw Hill, N.Y., 1965; Tyrone Guthrie: *A New Theatre*, McGraw Hill, N.Y., 1964; Bradley G. Morison and Kay Flier: *In Search of an Audience*, Pitman, New York, 1968; and W. McNeil Lowry, ed.: *The Performing Arts and American Society*, Prentice Hall, Englewood Cliffs, N.J., 1978.

   By way of disclosure: during the period 1968-1980 I was for five years an associate of The Martha Baird Rockefeller Fund for Music, evaluating and administering grants to both individual artists and organizations, primarily operatic; for another five or six years a field evaluator of opera companies for the firm contracted by the National Endowment for the Arts to gather such information; and briefly in the same capacity for the New York State Council on the Arts. I also served on the boards of two important service organizations, Affiliate Artists (nine years) and The National Opera Institute (four years). All this did not make me into a mover and shaker, but it did give me a good grounding in the business side of the nonprofit performing arts and the problems of development and survival of artistic enterprises that I could not have otherwise acquired.

7. See James Heilbrun and Charles M. Gray: *The Economics of Art and Culture*, 2nd Edition, Cambridge Univ. Press, N.Y., 2001. Chief among the relevant developments since that date would be the general worsening of the economic climate, with its negative effect on funding sources both in the U.S. (largely private) and Europe (largely public), and the ever-increasing pace of technological advancement. The latter remains only peripherally useful to opera companies, except for the boost given to a few of the largest from the net proceeds of their HD movie-theatre transmissions, whose longterm effects have yet to be determined.

8. Online, for instance, is *Why I Do Not Believe in the Cost Disease*, by Tyler Cowen, an economist at George Mason University (from the *Journal of Cultural Economics* 20, Kluwer Academic Publishers, The Netherlands, 1996). But his arguments conflate live performance with electronic reproduction (as if both rendered the same "musical service") in the name of claiming increases in artistic productivity. (In terms of "consumption output," true; in terms of monetary returns to artists and artistic organizations, scarcely, as Heilbrun and Gray demonstrate.) He also extends his definition of live music to include contemporary non-classical commercial music. This simply has nothing to do with the predicament of the high-culture nonprofit arts being analyzed by Baumol/Bowen and Heilbrun/Gray, and under consideration here.

9. There are three routes to an improved income/expense ratio: 1) Ever-increasing ticket sales. We count on that. 2) Decreasing numbers of new productions. That's bankable also. 3) Through experience, better cost control. This is unlikely to yield much, especially since my projections are probably low to begin with. But the first two could markedly improve the look of the balance sheet, without approaching the 50-50 standard (of earned to contributed income) set by the Met.

    Won't the wages of artistic personnel rise from year to year? Individually, yes. In the aggregate, I don't know, because it's hard to predict the rate of turnover. All Dream-On wages are indexed to the local rate of inflation. However, those aren't raises—they're just cost-of-living adjustments that keep the wages from falling behind in constant dollars. So in addition, each member will receive a real raise, determined in advance and universally applicable, upon the signing of each new contract. It will be modest—as a beginning talking point, I would suggest 7½% every two years, with the directorial personnel who are on longer contracts for necessary continuity accorded such raises in midcontract. Still no one getting rich, but as you can see, anyone staying with the company for an extended period will be steadily improving his or her standard of living, and adding to their pension or thrift-plan holdings. There would need to be a cap on these raises after a number of consecutive years, to be determined. If we retain a majority of members over long terms (which we hope to do), this will gradually drive up the personnel costs. However, new members, added only to replace departing ones, will begin at the inflation-adjusted equivalent of the beginning salary, so it will take a few years to get a good handle on the rate of increase.

10. See Levik, *Memoirs*, pp. 421-425.

11. See Martin Mayer, *The Met, One Hundred Years of Grand Opera* (Simon & Schuster, N.Y., 1983), pp. 169-179, esp. pp. 175-176. Of the Met's three major histories, Mayer's devotes the most detailed attention to financial matters.

12. Heilbrun and Gray (pp. 293-294) caution that evidence for this catalytic effect is lacking, since there is no way to determine that private contributions raised through the matching grant mechanism are in fact "new money." Repeated personal testimonials from the managers of opera companies and other musical organizations to the effect that "money we never would have gotten" was in fact raised because of tangible interest at the national level left me convinced that the catalytic impact was considerable, at least during my time of involvement.

13. Often, I think, arts advocates are convinced of their own arguments, and present them ingenuously. But ingenuous or not, they tend to cook the books in a couple of ways: by expanding the boundaries of the arts economy, and by failing to account for substitutability. By definition, it is only the nonprofit arts sector that is eligible for public funding, direct or indirect. Granting that in some areas only estimates can be made and that their own totals may well be on the low side, Heilbrun and Gray arrive at a figure (as of 1997) of 0.218% (approximately two thousandths of a percent) of Gross National Product for the entire nonprofit arts sector, including museums as well as all live performing arts. So one wonders how Jane Alexander (see n. 14, below), at her confirmation hearing as chairwoman of the NEA heading into fiscal 1994, would have substantiated her claim of "an arts economy of about 6 percent of the gross national product." This has to have included not only the commercial theatre (tiny), probably rock concerts and maybe circuses, but something major like movies and/or television. On that basis, the figure may approach accuracy—I don't know. But it has nothing to do with the case for public funding.

"Substitutability" is the word for the economic activity that would take the place of lost spending. By way of illustration, consider the NYCO's demise. This certainly entailed the loss of many jobs and of business for the company's suppliers and service providers, as well as ripple effects elsewhere in the arts community (for instance, among independent voice teachers, coaches and accompanists, et al.—hard to measure). City Opera audiences spent money on meals at restaurants, transportation to performances, babysitters, and other incidentals. Within the arts economy these losses, especially of jobs, were real and calamitous, for nothing takes up the employment slack when a large company with an extended season leaves the scene. And they are ominous indicators, portending even greater disasters to come. For the broader economy, though, the net loss was probably slight (it would present an interesting case study). Some of the company's employees may have retired, moved out of the region, been thrown back into the less-secure free-lance life, or left the profession. But most have taken other work of some sort. "The Economy" doesn't care what sort. The theatre has found alternate bookings, and the audiences for those are buying meals, paying babysitters, etc., just as the City Opera's did. No doubt there have been net losses to some people and businesses. Perhaps they outweigh net gains for others. But overall, the economy of city and region doesn't appear to have taken much of a hit. That's not where the wound is.

This isn't to say that in some towns and regions, like the arts-favored, industry-bereft Berkshires of Western Massachusetts, the non-profit arts do not make a substantial net economic contribution. (For a recent instance, see: Tony Dobrolowski: "Stellar performance at two renowned theatres help [sic] sustain Pittsfield economy," *Berkshire Eagle*, Aug. 29, 2015.) The article's evidence, backed by a regional study by Americans for the Arts, is strong, and though the figures do not take substitutability into consideration, as one long familiar with that scene, I think I can vouch for what the economic substitutes would be: nothing, or close to that. And such evidence should certainly be cited in fundraising. But it should not be skewed or puffed.

14. For anyone interested in tracking the history of public arts funding in the United States into the early years of the present century, I would suggest chronological perusal of these accounts: 1) Michael Straight: *Nancy Hanks, An Intimate Portrait* (Duke Univ. Press, 1988);

2) Livingston Biddle: *Our Government and the Arts: A Perspective from the Inside* (American Council for the Arts, 1988); John Frohnmayer: *Leaving Town Alive: Confessions of an Arts Warrior* (Houghton Mifflin, 1993); Jane Alexander: *Command Performance* (Public Affairs, 2000); and Bill Ivey: *Arts, Inc.* (Univ. of Calif. Press, 2008), supplemented by the relevant chapters in Heilbrun and Gray. Bear in mind that this history is concerned with direct support of the nonprofit sector, and does not present a complete picture of American arts activity or of all public assistance to it (Ivey presents a more inclusive summary on *Arts, Inc.*, pp. 238—*still* puny). For those interested in appropriations levels, beware the nominal figures. For instance, the NEA's highwater mark of about $176 million in FY 1994 would equal roughly $281.6 million in 2015; the amount is actually $146 million. The pioneering New York State Council on the Arts in its breakout year of 1971 had a budget of $20.1 million, or approximately $120 million in 2015 dollars. The real total is not quite $44 million. Money isn't everything, but the trend in public interest, as expressed in conveniently fungible form, is pretty clear.

15. For the promising beginnings and sad ending of Congress's initiative on arts education through the Title programs of the Elementary and Secondary Education Act (ESEA) in the late 1960s, see Straight, pp. 93-94. He also recounts the history of the NEA's Artists-in-the-Schools program of the 1970s (pp. 250-257). As I write, there are murmurings of revived Congressional discussion on the ESEA, but what action may be taken, and in what direction, is unclear.

16. The default mode of reasoning about the mechanisms of distribution goes something like this: the start-up money for any artistic enterprise must be largely private, though often with civic energies behind it. After it has demonstrated viability through community interest expressed in paid attendance and the ability to attract donated monies for a given amount of time, it becomes eligible for increased funding from local government, the state Arts Council, and regional entities (corporations, foundations) with a mandated interest in the area's development. Upon further growth and some evidence of national reach, it may qualify for federal support.

All along the line, difficulties have centered on the politics of qualification: who decides how public monies are distributed, and on what grounds? The elitist/populist antagonisms, as well as those activated by religious, moral and "community standards of decency" considerations, have had a seriously constrictive effect on the peer-panel recommendations and administrative decisions of the process. One suggestion I have always found of some interest (and I regret not recalling where I first heard it) is that artistic evaluation be removed altogether, along with any concession to other sensibilities, so long as laws are obeyed. If a nonprofit arts entity meets some version of the survival tests sketched above, it qualifies for progressive levels of public support at predetermined portions of its budget, and it continues to qualify so long as it meets those tests and provides audited proof of due diligence in business practices. Under this system, there are no panels, no evaluators. Government is entirely out of the highly subjective, easily politicized business of passing on the worthiness of art, and the bureaucracy is radically reduced, freeing those salaries, honoraria, and travel chits for the program itself. There would need to be a cap on the total percentage of any company's budget coming from the co-ordinated levels of public support. Perhaps 50%? In that event, even the Dream-On Company, with its modest percentages of earned income, would find its fundraising needs much more manageable, and its expenditures on them at least somewhat reduced. Yet the private sector would remain significantly involved. Of course, all this presupposes tax dollars made available in unprecedented, though still comparatively moderate, amounts.

17. See Rachel Donadio: "Reflecting on Art and War, and on Russia's Relationship With the West," *NYT*, Sept. 3, 1915.

PART VII

THE BACKSTORIES

1

A CHRONOLOGY OF EYE AND EAR PERFORMANCE MEDIA

1900–2000

Note: This ordering of twenty-five-year eras, with key developments placed at the beginning of each, will arouse suspicions of patness. And of course the dates are slightly imprecise: the first radio broadcast, for instance, was in 1920, the first sound movie 1927, the debut of the long-playing record 1948, etc. Each innovation took time (but in all cases, very little) to take hold as common experience. What is striking, though, is how close the tolerances are (two or three years) from a neat, quarter-century, single-generation pattern. Though the "formative years" of most lives overlap the divisions, we can with some accuracy speak of a phono/silent movie generation, a phonoradio/sound movie generation, a TV generation, and an audiovideo generation, each of which incorporated the habits of the preceding ones, but was defined by the innovation(s) associated with it.

We should begin by reminding ourselves that the performance media were introduced into an environment in which voice-to-ear communication was habitually more muscular than in our own, on both the sending and receiving ends. This was true in daily life as well as in art, and thus presumptively true. For performance, this suggests the acceptance as "natural" of a more highly energized theatre of the ear. The implications of this for opera are obvious, but they extend to spoken theatre as well, in the heightened uses of the voice and the often elaborate employment of live music.

The early years of this chronology also coincide with the electrification of theatre lighting. Over time, this generated all the possibilities for the definition of space, the flow of transitions and sequencing of time now assumed in staging and design. This enhancement for the eye had no ear counterpart, and thus constituted a gain for eye over ear.

The capture and preservation of sights and sounds from other places and times constituted true miracles, mesmerizing in effect almost without regard to content.

1900-1925

For the ear: The acoustical phonograph. Ear-only, mind's-eye.

- Essentially private; social only in the domestic sense.
- Reproduction at will is the essence of the experience. The receptor is also the producer of the performance, choosing its circumstances and controlling its progress. As consumer, he purchases the instrument of performance and owns the objects (records) that comprise it.
- The performance is fixed and mechanically contained. It will change only through depreciation.
- In setting and tradition, the engagement resembles and extends that of home music-making, which it gradually but substantially replaces. As is often noted, this marks a change from an active, literate engagement to one that is passive and vicarious.

For the eye: The "silent" movie. Eye-dominant, ear-confirmed, but with sound (music) in a strictly accompanimental position, not necessary for the performance or integral to it. All important information is received and interpreted by the eye, including the verbal (through the reading of titles, of lips).

- Essentially public, therefore social. Attendance at a single, transitory event is the essence of the experience. The receptor is part of an audience, with choice of circumstances and control of performance in the hands of the presenter. As consumer, he purchases a ticket and incidental comestibles.
- The eye portion of the performance is fixed and mechanically contained, and will change only through depreciation; the subservient ear portion, however, is live, changeable, sometimes improvisatory. The whole is reproducible, but is not at the will of, nor the property of, the receptor.
- In setting and tradition, the engagement resembles and extends that of theatergoing, which it in some measure replaces.

1925-1950

For the ear: The radio, the electrical phonograph. The introduction of radio coincides with the most important single step in phonographic development: the changeover (1925) from acoustical to electrical transmission.* In all other aspects, the conditions of phonographic listening remain as described above.

- Like the phonograph, the radio is ear-only, mind's eye. It demands the same aural concentration, and helps to sharpen this as a skill.
- Again like the phonograph, radio is essentially domestic and private, not public.
- The receptor is not the producer of the radio performance. He may select the program and adjust the appliance, but otherwise has no control over the timing, progress, or duration of the performance. Duration is of special interest: for the first time, it is determined by the presenter for reasons related not to artistic needs, perceived audience tolerance, or mechanical limitation, but to scheduling convenience (i.e., an ordering of saleable segments). These segments, artistically arbitrary in length, are themselves subdivided by commercial intrusion. As consumer, the receptor purchases the performance appliance and, presumably, some of the advertised products. The real price paid, though, is the agreement to accept performance in arbitrarily limited, frequently interrupted seg-ments.† That new agreement, and the receptor's new awareness of belong-ing to a vast, unseen audience, are the essence of the experience.

---

* The only other candidate would be the advent of stereophony, in the late 1950s. But in terms of opening the ear to the full presence and power of music, even this does not rival the acoustical/electrical switch. This is especially true of music involving massed forces and complex textures; solo voices and instruments were quite faithfully rendered by the acoustical process at its best, but larger ensembles were not. Of course, electrical recording also opened the door to sounds whose power is disproportionate to their human sources, a fact quickly exploited by record producers and quickly detected by critics and connois-seurs, who complained regularly of pushed, overblown sound even while acknowledging the obvious advantages of early electricals—see, for instance, the comments of Hermann Klein around this time (*Hermann Klein and the Gramophone*, William R. Morrow, ed., Amadeus Press, 1990). It also paved the way for all subsequent techniques for the manipu-lation and alteration of sounds, for the control of the outcome by non-performers and the substitution of technical for artistic standards. From this point on, changes in sound quality are ameliorative, not basic (some extension of frequency range, improved signal-to-noise ratio, etc.), and most other improvements have to do with convenience and exten-sion of listening time (the record changer, the LP, the CD).

† Classical music events—especially live opera and symphony orchestra concerts—have always been among the few kinds of programs exempt from this segmenting. Their privileged position has implied an acknowledgement of worth, of social value, whose measure is not fully taken by the commercial yardstick. This remains true of such programming as remains. However, it seems incontrovertible that three generations' habituation to the saleable segments of radio and television have assisted in reduction of attention span, expectations of accelerated pace, acquiescence in art as packaged product, and progressive narrowing of the niche for classical music in the media.

- In setting, the engagement resembles and extends that of phonographic listening. But in other respects it is closer to public performance traditions.

For the eye: The sound movie. Another first: sight and sound emanate from a common source in a mechanical medium. Still eye-dominant, ear-confirmed, though the two are brought closer to equality.

- The sound element is now fixed, and integral to the performance. Verbal information is received the way it is in life or theatre: directly and instantaneously.
- As in phonographic reproduction (and for the same reason: electrical transmission), all sounds—voices, music, sound effects—are projected with unprecedented range, color, and impact. Midway through this period, a visual analog for this is found: color photography.
- Its new impact and its moments of sensory dominance notwithstanding, the music of movie dramas has no formal integrity, no structure independent of its service to the eye narrative. By comparison with the simple-minded vamping or traveling music of vaudeville and music hall (which also served most silent-movie purposes), sound-movie scoring is rich and subtle. But by comparison with the musical practices of serious theatre (think of the scores of Lully and Purcell, Beethoven and Schubert, Mendelssohn and Bizet and Grieg, with their complete overtures, entr'actes and intermezzos, songs and dances, their sequences of *mélodrame* and underscored pantomime), it is strictly subordinate. (See commentary below.)

In all other respects, the movie engagement remains as described above.

1950-1975

For the ear: Audiotape. On the receptor's side, it facilitates widespread home recording, with its possibilities of storage and retrieval of sound materials from radio, phonograph, and live sources. These materials are now reproducible at will, with the receptor acting as researcher, engineer, and producer. Audiotape also becomes an alternative to the record (in reel-to-reel form, superior in quality but inferior in convenience, and as *objet*; in cassette form, a handy convenience only) in the distribution of commercial recordings.

- Some of the ameliorations and conveniences alluded to earlier: for the phonograph, the LP and stereophony; for radio, FM and FM-Multiplex (stereo) broadcasting. Though these are improvements more in degree than in kind, their cumulative effect, combined with advances in the quality of listening equipment and healthy economic conditions, created the high-fidelity boom of the 1950s and '60s, the high-water mark of ear-only home performance.

For the eye: Television. Eye-dominant, ear-confirmed. The sight/sound relationships of the sound movie, integrated into the private setting.

- This engagement resembles and extends that of radio in its degree of receptor choice and presenter control; its non-reproducibility; its segmenting of duration; in the consumer's role; and in the nature of the agreement between the presenter and the dispersed audience. But it differs from radio in two related aspects: it replaces the mind's eye with the outer eye; and it markedly loosens the aural concentration of the phonoradio engagement.
- Because of the poor quality of television sound, and its failure to keep pace with improvements in video quality, plus the small screen's limited capacity for handling the eye relationships of opera, television's operatic use is limited during this era.

1975-2000

For the ear: Nothing that changes the terms of phonoradio engagement as described above in any substantive way. However, in the category of conveniences and ameliorations (the former indubitable, the latter dubious): the CD.

- Indubitable convenience: Maximization of storage space; lessened wear (depreciation); ease of handling, including remote control and programmability.
- Dubious amelioration: Noiselessness. The proposition that even the better CDs represent any advance in actual sound quality over the better stereo reel-to-reel tapes and LPs of the 1960s is still a matter of debate, with many devotees taking the negative. Noiselessness, though, is a digital fact and must be reckoned a mechanical gain. Whether or not it is an artistic gain depends on its alliance with recording and postproduction (including editing) techniques.
- And an indubitable inconvenience: The severe physical reduction of the illustrative and literary materials to accompany recordings that flourished during the LP era, thus degrading them both as scholarly apparatus and as eye confirmation.

For the eye: Video. Videotape and its associated equipment, used professionally since WWII, made widely available for home use. Eye-dominant, ear-confirmed. All the functions of audiotape (see above) realized for eye materials. Complete sight/sound recorded performance now retrievable and reproducible at will.

- Ameliorations:
  - Cable or satellite reception
  - Larger screens with higher resolution
  - The laser disk, CD ROM, and DVD

These constitute improvements in both the video and audio quality of video materials. The disc formats also reinstate the functions of accompanying booklets (translation, commentary, illustration), though in different format and to different effect. In addition, they increase the receptor's power to manipulate artistic content.

And a few observations:

Records and broadcasts isolated, for the first time, the aural element of performance. By doing so, they placed this element in an unnaturally exalted position relative to the live experience, and made possible two new kinds of engagement: ear-only and ear-text. The fact that the ear-only engagement requires the reception and interpretation of sounds, the following of sound narratives, without any visual cues whatever has two important effects: it draws the listener into an intimacy with aural detail and nuance, and it opens the mind's eye while placing the outer eye on background. Because the mind's eye is now free to roam without dictation, and because in this private engagement the receptor's response is free of social constraint, the situation invites a peerlessly subjective absorption in the performance. This absorption can be sensorily abstract (drifting with images, colors, etc.) or meditative. But in opera this is not often the case. Opera evokes a more active visualization: the theatre of the mind's eye. This can extend to a sense of participation in the drama, of generating its sounds and actions and melding with the characters or performers—the classical equivalent of the lip-synching teenager or the karaoke star. There is no eye equivalent for this immersion in a mind's-eye world stimulated by sound vibrations.

The ear-text engagement is beloved of critics and teachers, some professional musicians, and advanced devotees—a tiny but influential minority. It extends and enriches the curious listener's tapestry. It partakes of a connection to the music otherwise known only to practitioners, though obviously lacking its fulfillment in performance. It has its own intensity, for a new ear/eye confirmation is in place: the listener sees the music he is hearing. This coalescence of patterns seen and heard, the scanning of structures and textures and metrical layouts, the arrival in the ear of something spotted ahead—these create their own thrills, their flashes of recognition and illumination, unique to listening with the score. However, this form of eye confirmation involves a tradeoff of serious consequence for opera. With the outer eye re-activated, the inner one retreats. Opera's theatrical component is expunged, even in its vicarious incarnation. The text is now the visual component of performance. It serves as the engagement's standard of judgment and court of appeals, and tends to replace effect as the measure of authenticity. The confirmation of music seen as well as heard is also an invitation to inspect structures and techniques, all the materials of composition and the "how" of performance. Intimacy with nuance and detail easily turns into a pinning-down that exaggerates the importance of small events. This mode of reception is thus inclined toward analysis and objectification, quite unlike the participatory subjectivity of the ear-only phonoradio encounter.

By making possible an integrated audiovisual home performance, video ended the isolation of the aural element. It did not end the ear-dominant engagements, for phonoradio listening survives. But it brought into the domestic setting the eye/ear relationships of the sound movie, thus completing the gradual subjugation of the ear by the eye; in the course of this little history, concentration is initially sharpened and lengthened, then slackened and abbreviated; the mind's eye is summoned to life, then killed off.

Audiovideo performance mimics with some accuracy the sound/sight confirmations of live performance, and its state of art is such that given domestic tranquility and good equipment, it can bring home a fair measure of opera's impact. But with regard to the nature and quality of attention, its sensory balance is the reverse of opera's. It is necessarily eye-led, because the visual element is senseless if the receptor does not follow the camera on its journey. The rhythms of this journey are more restless than those of either theatre or music. This is also necessary, partly because of the monotony inherent in a contained, mechanical, two-dimensional image, and partly because of the eye's need to shift, rest, and re-focus—a need not shared by the ear, whose span of unforced attention is longer.

And to a musically responsive person the outer eye, as herded and funneled along by its surrogate, the camera, is no match for the mind's eye launched in flight by the music.* Savvy video and movie directors can force the balances toward moments of conformity with opera's natural condition, or provide ingenious distractions. But they cannot overcome the imagocentric nature of their medium, with its inherent itchiness of rhythm, tempo, and P.O.V.

Onscreen, rhythm and P.O.V. (point of view) come down to the same thing, for shifts of P.O.V., with all their variants of shots and edits and cuts, *are* the visual rhythms, the scoring and phrasing for the eye. (Only within a given shot can performers exert an influence, and that severely limited by directorial and editorial control.) This mobility of physical and psychological P.O.V., the freedom to roam space and time and levels of reality and to control rhythm visually, is the source of screen liberation and power. The surrogate eye becomes an omniscient narrator, with the receptor as unseen companion.

The stage cannot offer the screen's freedoms and privileges, nor the strange intimacy (the closeup, the whisper) that is the essence of its realism. The stage's freedom is that of the *Mazeppa* performance—to decide what merits attention in a living, three-dimensional world held constant before us, with psychological P.O.V. left to our discretion, and with rhythms determined not by visual flights, cuts, or pans, but by onstage action. Most of the time (except in mime theatre), these are essentially rhythms of the ear, of words or music. And stage realism is dependent precisely on the only P.O.V. life actually affords: our own. It is fixed. We are stuck with the characters in the dramatic situation, in which every action has an unavoidable consequence for what follows. We cannot leap oceans, fly over continents, or nuzzle into an actor's neck. Our stage eyes are not omniscient.

The omniscient narrator is much more a device of literary fiction than of the spoken stage. Opera has one, though: the music. Music fulfills the functions of description, of physical and psychological P.O.V., of commentary and authorial voice, that are assumed onscreen by the camera and in literary fiction by the word's evocation of the mind's eye. It adds to them the layering of texture, the simultaneity of conflicting actions and emotions, made possible by music's vertical dimension. I think it would not be too much to suggest that the history of opera's development (in close parallel with that of the novel) has been its progressive discovery of itself as omniscient narrator for the stage.

So far as opera is concerned, the electronic media are creatively inert; they remain transmission devices for stage works. Thus, the contradictions

---

* The death of the mind's eye accounts, I think, for the failure of video opera to emulate the wide, rapid sweep of the audio-only variety.

between stage and screen freedoms, between the omniscient narrations of ear and eye, can be palliated but not resolved, and the only remaining issue of any artistic import is the effect of media conditioning on the live engagement. Among devotees, the effect is on their expectations—of their mind's-eye fantasies and ear-text elucidations, or for historical performance standards. Devotees either stay home, where these expectations can be met, or carry the expectations with them to the theatre, where they become part of the "new audience demand."

Beyond the devotee circle are the potential devotees and Nams, the seekers with nameless hungers—customer candidates all—that are of such interest to our artistic institutions. They are used to eye dominance, eye explanation, eye tempo, to casual mastery and ownership, and their ears are indolent. Can opera find a way among these children of the audiovideo culture to re-assert the freedoms and realities of the stage, of the ear? To reveal to them its own expectations, rather than simply catering to the ones they already have? In my view, these are questions for which opera must find answers bespeaking a greater clarity of belief, a stronger faith in its own authenticity, than that represented by the enhancements.

2

A BIBLIOGRAPHICAL ESSAY

The following refers in its entirety to Part III, Chapter 1. Its purpose is fair play: since the subject of this chapter falls outside the author's field of expertise, it is only proper to inform any interested readers as to the sources consulted, and help them judge whether or not the ideas under discussion have been sufficiently considered for the arguments at hand. It should be borne in mind throughout that the intention here is not to help opera chime in with the various academic discourses. On the contrary, it is to weaken the hold of those discourses on performance, and to re-direct the operatic conversation back where it belongs, to the musical and theatrical realization of dramatic values. To do this, however, it is necessary to recognize the nature of the discourses, and define the intrusive roles they are playing.

There is by now a considerable body of work that seeks to apply semiological and poststructural insights to the Arts of the Act, including opera, and some readers may ask why I have not sought to engage the discourses through that literature. My principal reason is that so far as I can determine, that literature has originated none of the governing ideas involved, and in its efforts to bend them to its own uses, presents them twisted and piecemeal. This being the case, I have thought it preferable to explore these ideas on their home terrain. Opera devotees with a serious curiosity about the influences on what they're seeing and hearing will, sooner or later, find themselves in this same territory—they have only to follow the bibliographies. My necessarily brief and selective comments on the volumes listed here may also further clarify some of my own views.

Since my goal has been to grasp apposite problems in accurately drawn outline, much of my attention has gone to reputable secondary sources—that is, to critical overviews and anthologies intended to put the field in perspective, with enough crosschecking and reference to individual works to ensure that such perspective did not conceal unrecognized bias. Major figures are missing here, and major works of those included. That is only because exploration of operatic issues has not led me to them. Like everything else in this book, my encounter with these ideas arises directly from questions raised in performance. Where foreign-language originals are involved, they have been read in English.

Among the overview and anthology volumes consulted, two have been familiar to me for a number of years: *Deconstruction: Theory and Practice*, by Christopher Norris (Methuen, 1982) and *An Introductory Guide to Post-Structuralism and Postmodernism*, by Madan Sarup (Univ. of Georgia Press, 1989). Both are clearly written, responsible presentations. Norris begins with a chronological background chapter that runs from Kant through the births of structuralism, semiotics, and the New Criticism, then focuses at some length on Derrida and Nietzsche, the crosscurrents between deconstruction and Marxism, and the work of important American respondents to deconstruction as of the book's time. Sarup sees linguistic theory of the deconstructive variety as one of three fields of study whose intersecting developments have generated postmodern thought, the others being psychoanalysis and social science; he therefore gives equal consideration first to Lacan, Derrida, and Foucault, then to such post-s and post-m thinkers as Lyotard and Deleuze. In each case, he presents careful summaries of the significant critical counter-arguments. Both Norris and Sarup include copious references and notes for further reading.

A very useful volume is Terry Eagleton's *Literary Theory, An Introduction* (Second Edition, Univ. of Minnesota Press, 1996) though most of the text is intact from the original issue, 1983). He covers much the same ground as do Norris and Sarup, but in the context of a brilliantly concise synthesis of the literary, linguistic, and philosophical background, and with a concluding chapter on political criticism, with which he is much concerned. Eagleton is a sharp, engaging writer of reasoned polemics, who always argues his case; I have also found stimulating his *The Illusions of Postmodernism* (Blackwell, 1996).

A helpful anthology is *Postmodernism—Philosophy and the Arts*, Hugh J. Silverman, ed. (Routledge, 1990). This comprises four essays on "problematics" (all interesting—I especially liked Donald Kuspit on "The Contradictory Character of Postmodernism"), then nine more on "sites" (individual arts). Two of the live Arts of the Act—theatre (Fred McGlynn) and dance (David Michael Levin)—are among the latter, but except for some general comments in Silverman's introduction, nothing on music or opera. I found Brian Seitz on television and Gail Faurschou on fashion suggestive for my own line of thought. Also of some interest here is that the entries on literature (Gerald L. Bruns) and film (Wilhelm S. Wurzer with Silverman) are heavily involved with Heidegger. The extensive bibliography on postmodernism by Helen Volat-Shapiro is a prime reference, particularly for its listings of articles in books and journals.

Another good collection is *Directions for Criticism: Structuralism and its Alternatives*, Murray Krieger and L.S. Dembo, eds. (Univ. of Wisconsin Press, 1977), which as its title and date imply, stands at a much-contested fork along the litcrit road. For me, Hayden White's essay on "The Absurdist Moment in Contemporary Literary Theory" was especially illuminating, along with Krieger's Introduction. (Introductions and Prefaces, with their stock-taking and summarizing, are often most useful to wandering Pure Fools like myself, in quest of the right question.) Other essays by Edward Said, Hazard Adams, René Girard, and Ralph Freedman.

If we're not at the aporia, we're in the dialectic—through all these volumes runs a Marxian vein, either because the author's viewpoint is, at least broadly and implicitly, Marxist, or because the tensions between Marxist and post-modernist thought are the subject at hand. Marxism continues to afford a critical vantage point on both the mainstream capitalist and postmodern cultures. It shares with the latter the goal of radically undermining the former, and there is much interpenetration of semiotic, structuralist, deconstructive, and Marxist language and insight. On this matter the work of Fredric Jameson is instructive, and I have had frequent reference to his essays collected under the title *The Ideologies of Theory*, Vols. 1 and 2 (Univ. of Minnesota Press, 1988). The learning is impressive, the writing always trenchant, and while he only occasionally touches on matters of immediate concern here, his perspective on the political, social, and the cultural issues that lie in the operatic background is valuable—see, for instance, his "Reflections on the Brecht-Lukács Debate" or "Marxism and Historicism," both in Vol. 2.

In opera, while what we might loosely call the Marxist-Deconstructionist nexus has been far more influential on the other side of the Atlantic than on this, both creatively (e.g., Henze, Nono, Berio) and interpretively (most aggressively in Wagner, but in most other standard-repertory productions as well—the Folkoperan *Carmen* is by no means unrepresentative), it has certainly had echoes here, perhaps most obviously in the contemporized class-warfare parallels of Sellars' productions. Though postmodernists think of themselves as living in a post-Marxian world—one that has incorporated Marxism's Greatest Hits and then moved on—contemporary Marxism views much in the postmodern as regressive. This is due first to its willingness to serve as a chic, co-opted alternative to the capitalist/bourgeois mainstream. (The productions of the Postmodern Lite can easily be seen this way—a Lookism of Difference, a window display of mock-revolutionary emblematics.) And it is due second to what Marxists see as a retreat from the core problem of oppression and exploitation through modes of production to a group of real but secondary issues (what Eagleton calls "the class-race-gender triplet") that are regarded as substitutive. (For our subject, this substitutive quality recalls the straining-for-relevance sameness of the newer efforts of the Here and Now.) Eagleton and Jameson are strong on this; see also John O'Neill's "Postmodernism and (Post) Marxism" in Silverman, and Faurschou on fashion in the same collection, distinctly in Walter Benjamin's line of descent.

On matters of aesthetics, I have referred to two recent anthologies: *Aesthetics: The Big Questions*, Carolyn Korsmeyer, ed. (Blackwell, 1998) and *The Routledge Companion to Aesthetics*, Dominic McIver Lopes and Berys Gaut, eds., (Routledge, 2001). The former groups its reprints (ancient to contemporary, with a multiculturalist/feminist predilection among the latter) into six categories of enquiry ("What is Art?", "Can We Learn from Art?", etc.), while the latter embraces 46 original contributions on aesthetic history, theory, issues, and the individual arts, all from well-credentialed writers. Both books offer reference lists and "further reading" notes. In them, there is (to put it in deconstructive syntax) the overbearing presence of an absence: opera. In Korsmeyer, indeed, there is nearly perfect avoidance of performance altogether: a few pages on Greek tragedy as literature and philosophy, one brief contribution on dance that is really a post-m anthropological commentary, and, on music, one ethnomusicological piece by Bruno Nettl that moves from Blackfoot Indian to Persian classical to Mozartian examples (opera does get a brief mention here)—solid and interesting, but awfully peculiar as the single selection on the Big Questions of musical aesthetics. In Gaut/Lopes (more to my purpose for its balanced evaluations of major controversies and figures, there are three performing arts chapters (music, theatre, dance), but none on opera; nor is there any consideration of opera in the good essays on music (Mark De Bellis) and theatre (James R. Hamilton), though of course relevant issues are raised. (As they are in Graham McFee's dance entry—see especially his section "Performer's vs. critic's interpretation," very close to distinctions insisted on here.) A few citations by way of example in Alan Goldman's entry on "The Aesthetic" is as close as opera comes to status; in neither of these volumes does the subject even make the index.

Think of it: in two fat, current volumes intended as overviews of the field of aesthetics, opera does not exist. It apparently has no aesthetic properties or implications, either of its own, as a "branch" of something else, or as a gathering of somethings. Further, its absence goes unacknowledged; the editors feel no need to explain its non-inclusion. They must assume we'll understand—we don't speak of it, though we all know it's there. This is some sort of pure prejudice, but what could account for it? Phonophobia? The old literary intellectual's contempt for the "exotic and irrational entertainment?" I suspect these, but more, an utter confusion and sense of helplessness in approaching the form. Opera cannot be contained within any system of aesthetics of music or theatre (though on its face it actually appears more compatible with the latter). It needs its own. Since an aesthetics of opera would have to begin by accounting for its basic elements (music, words, action) in a performance context, it would immediately remove the form from the domains of both the music theorists who have historically controlled the discussion and the litcrit *philosophes* who have recently invaded it. It would dispense with some pet contemporary assumptions, such as the dismissal of music as representation. It would also dispose of the notion that opera is something that can be looked down on by "pure-art" aesthetes, and even raise the possibility that it is something that should be looked up to. (See, for instance, the "registers of perception" arguments on film of Christian Metz, noted in the next entry. Their equivalents have long been common coin among opera devotees.)

Given all this, it's perhaps understandable that opera doesn't make the cut with the anthologizers. It's still not forgivable, however.

The final anthology I must mention is *Film Theory and Criticism, Introductory Readings* (Third Edition, Oxford Univ. Press, 1985, Gerald Mast and Marshall Cohen, eds.) This now-classic omnium gatherum (852 pages) contains cornerstone pieces of film criticism from its founding fathers on, in coherent thematic groupings. It includes those cited here by James Spellerberg ("Technology and Ideology of the Cinema," referring to Baudry and Oudart in regard to parallels with Lacan and specularity), Christian Metz ("Identification, Mirror," from *The Imaginary Signifier*), and Andrew Sarris ("Notes on the Auteur Theory in 1962," to be read in conjunction with Pauline Kael's response, "Circles and Squares"). Among many stimulating entries, André Bazin ("Theatre and Cinema," from *What is Cinema?*) and Susan Sontag ("Film and Theatre") elaborate interestingly on aspects of issues considered here. Bazin addresses "presence" in language that at once recalls Benjamin's discussion of the "auratic" and prefigures Derridian constructs. With respect to the arts, this all still seems to me to come down to a matter of live on one hand, mechanical on the other; of human energy here, electronic energy there; of the in-the-moment and mutable versus the caught-in-time and immutable. Bazin speaks of "pseudopresences" and "an intermediate stage between presence and absence." Yes, good, but where does it leave the movies with respect to presence? In Limbo, I should say. And theatre, opera, that aspires to cinematize itself?—the landfill of Limbo, the tag sale of Limbo.

Metz draws heavily on Freud and Lacan in his substantial and intriguing excerpts on specularity and perception. Cinema is seen here as the new *Gesamtkunstwerk*, granted a "numerical 'superiority'" over the other arts. According to Metz, the registers of perception afforded by literature, the visual and auditory arts, and music each lack an important perceptual element. (I don't at all agree. Literature and visual arts *do* lack the auditory register, but anyone who thinks that music lacks the visual has not attended many musical events.) Cinema is "more perceptual" because it mobilizes more "axes of perception." It does, in other words, exactly what opera does, with these three differences: 1) Opera is ear-led, eye-confirmed, while in film the case is reversed. 2) In opera, the registers are closer to being in balance, the ear only occasionally dominating the eye as completely as the eye customarily does the ear in film. 3) When opera is permitted to be itself (i.e., live and played on its own field), it may put you in Heaven or in Hell, but will never take you to Limbo.

Metz naturally overlooks opera, as do all filmists. Ocucentrism of course, but also the fact that so much of their work has been by way of validating and valorizing, *justifying* their artform, providing it with intellectual respectability, a history and mythology (Sarris, in 1962, could speak in archaeological and apparently unironic tones of "ancient" films to be unearthed). For opera, these matters have been on the back burner for two or three centuries. But the aporia has changed all that.

Now for notes on a few more specific authors and works, presented in approved unhierarchical order, i.e., alphabetically:

Barthes, Rolland: It was this author's *Mythologies* (Hill and Wang, 1972, selected and translated by Annette Lavers) that introduced me to semiological analysis in a structuralist vein (as Barthes relates in his preface to the 1970 French edition, he had just read Saussure). I have always found him enjoyable—witty and pithy, his quirky playfulness never just a tone, but the outcome of observation from an acute angle—and this collection of short pieces remains an inviting route into his thinking. Although I had certainly encountered the principle in previous readings, I believe it was *Mythologies* that also first set me at unease about at least one implication of the semiological project, namely, that since the thrust of this project was the pursuit of signs as items of social discourse, and since for this purpose artworks were at once highly convenient but of neither greater nor lesser value than just about anything else (and, finally, since this pursuit clearly yielded some valid and seductive insights), it was not only possible but inevitable that art would come to be seen as having *only* such purpose and value, and to be critiqued accordingly.

Barthes is exceptional among the modern *philosophes* in his passionate engagement with classical music (Edward Said is the only other example I can think of). He even studied voice with the fine recital baritone Charles Panzéra. Another of his books, *Image/Music/Text* (Noonday Press, 1988, selected and translated by Stephen Heath) contains two of his pieces on the subject, "Musica Practica" and "The Grain of the Voice." The first is concerned with the disappearance of a practicing musical culture in favor of a listening one, the second with the juncture between language and musical tone in the human voice. Though their *aperçus* will seem less remarkable to musical practitioners than to others, these are neat little essays, replete with Barthean virtues. They also illustrate some of the mutual frustrations of opera and the discourse. Barthes would like to be rid of adjectives, first in criticism, then in musical inscription itself. Then he would like to be rid of dramatization, and with respect to singing he is quite precise on this: "Opera," he says, "is a genre in which the voice has gone over in its entirety to dramatic expressivity, a voice with a grain that little signifies." It is this signifying "grain," allegedly canceled out by dramatic expressivity, that is exclusively prized; in Barthes' ideal singingacting event (the death of Mélisande, unless *Pelléas* is "sung badly—dramatically"), "nothing occurs to interfere with the signifier." Let us admit that adjectives are often badly used and that much dramatization is false. Barthes appears to be arguing, beyond this, for the elimination of any critical description that might evoke the affective properties of music or performance in the receptor; then for any musical instruction that might guide the performer toward such properties in the music (he is not objecting, as I have with Schoenberg, to the imprisonment of performer by creator); then to any personalized dramatization whatever, false or true. The stance is specifically anti-operatic.

Image/Music/Text also includes "The Death of the Author," which together with Foucault's (q.v.) "What Is an Author?" constitutes the most concise and accessible presentation of the eponymous line of thought, with all that it excuses.

Baudrillard, Jean: The Baudrillard references in the main text are to his *Simulacra and Simulation* (Univ. of Michigan Press, 1994, Sheila Faria Glaser, trans.). I'm not happy that so many of the insights generated by his thinking on "cultural materialism" intuitively seem right to me, but they do. Though Baudrillard does not apply them to opera, they are instantly recognizable in that context. Thus, his proposals on the "precession" of simulacra and the hyperreal ("The map precedes the territory. . . It is no longer a question of imitation, nor duplication, nor even parody. It is a question of substituting the signs of the real for the real."); of "proving the real through the imaginary" (e.g., "the proof of theater through antitheatre; the proof of art through anti-art;" etc.); of the obliteration of meaning by information (the exponential increase of information does not produce a surplus of meaning; its actual purpose is the end of meaning); of the "nostalgia for a lost referential," the last moments of the real before the traumatic conversion to an era of simulacra; and above all, of all these illusionistic purposes being carried out while posing as their opposites—these, and others, unfortunately seem to me in perfect accord with the operatic spectacle and its broader cultural context.

Bloom, Harold: The quotation in the text is from the Introduction to *The Anxiety of Influence* (Second Edition, Oxford Univ. Press, 1997—this edition includes a valuable new preface). Any exploration of the influence of our greatest dramatist considered almost purely as poet on the page, and of his successors among poets but not among playwrights, will never feel complete. But unlike Mozart, Wagner, and Verdi, Shakespeare *can* be so interpreted with coherence, and in Bloom's case with the richest of imagination and erudition. For his insistence on the transcendent nature of individual genius and the centrality of character, and for his tireless wrestle with the angels of French intellectual fashion and their cherubim (the "Resentful historicists of several persuasions—stemming from Marx, Foucault, and political feminism—[who] now study literature essentially as peripheral social history", or again, the ". . . certain more or less recent Parisian speculators [who] have convinced many (if not most) academic critics that there are no authors anyway"—this from the opening essay in *Shakespeare/The Invention of the Human*, Riverhead Books, 1998), we must remain ever grateful.

Culler, Jonathan: "The Mirror Stage" referred to in the main text is Chapter Eight of *The Pursuit of Signs* (Augmented Edition, Cornell Univ. Press, 2002), which along with the works of the Yale Derrideans (Paul de Man, Geoffrey Hartmann, J. Hillis Miller) is a focal text in American deconstructive criticism. Among its further contents are lucid reviews of the development of semiotics and structuralism, and assessments of such figures as Bloom, Stanley Fish, and Michael Riffaterre. The rather forlorn preface to the Augmented Edition suggests a significant lowering of semiotic expectations since the book's first appearance in 1981.

Danto, Arthur C. and *Kuspit, Donald*: I am reluctant to drag yet another field's discourse into this discussion, especially one whose inapplicability to arts of the act I have been insisting upon. However, art criticism does at the least influence design, and design has in turn been accorded an unprecedented interpretive position in opera. It happens that recent volumes by these two eminent commentators (Danto's *The Madonna of the Future*, Farrar, Straus & Giroux, N.Y. 2000; and Kuspit's *The End of Art*, Cambridge Univ. Press, N.Y., 2004) can stand as poles of the contemporary artcrit universe—indeed, although I assume, given the New York journalistic provenance, that the sinister "K" referred to in Danto's preface is Hilton Kramer, on most of the key issues it could as well be Kuspit. Danto and Kuspit agree on one thing: that the developments of the past half-century have brought us beyond previous definitions of art, with their aesthetic and psychological components and their histories, into a postartistic region. The difference is that Danto welcomes this and Kuspit does not. Danto is a philosopher by training and an elegant writer and logician of broad learning, who navigates well beyond the usual culturecrit shallows. He is fond of locating certain works as the endpoints of their histories, points past which nothing further in a given line is possible. (In music, similar claims were being made with regard to harmony and melodic tunefulness a hundred years ago.) His pursuit of the challenges to our definitions of an artwork raised by Duchamp, Warhol, Twombly and others leads him to conclude that ". . . progress from this point on is philosophical progress, progress in the analysis of the concept." He actually states a belief that though art-making may go on, ". . . in terms of self-understanding . . . it can take us no further." He goes on to assert the triumph of the "unlimited lateral diversity" of art (contemporary, multicultural) over any vertical understanding (through time, within a cultural history): ". . . the heterogeneity today is of so high a degree . . . that a next lateral cut will be strictly unpredictable. All that one can predict is that there will be no narrative direction. And that is what I mean by the end of art." (My translation: "Things are such a mess right now that we've lost all sense of direction.") Danto, at first depressed by this insight, has now recovered, and accepts the artworld as a "model of pluralistic society." But then he adds, parenthetically, that he has "no use for pluralism in philosophy." I'm flummoxed. Danto *is* both philosopher and art critic, and claims that art *is* henceforth philosophy. How can pluralism, no good in philosophy, be OK in art, now that art and philosophy are the same thing? I would share his initial depression if I shared his habit of assigning endpoints and breakthroughs. But I don't, anymore than I share the view that *Tristan* pointed to the end of tonality, or that Sophie's *"Ist ein Traum"* was the last usable tune, or that there will be no more narratives.

Kuspit has a different take on these same matters. He argues for art as an aesthetic and sensual experience. (Danto: "Art is a mode of thought, and experiencing art consists of thought engaging with thought." Kuspit: "Pure intellect is a poor defense against the traumatic ugliness of life compared to art, for ugliness has to be defended against with the whole psyche not simply a part of it . . ." [He does not mean that there is no place for the ugly in art, but that in art the ugly is aesthetically transformed.]) Danto quotes the modernist painter Frank Stella disparagingly, Kuspit approvingly. Both quote Hegel, to entirely different purposes. For Kuspit, the postart world Danto has reconciled himself to is a wasteland: ". . . the end of art . . . does not mean works of art will not be made, but that they will have no important human use: they will no longer further personal autonomy and critical freedom . . ." (*The End of Art*, p. 14, construing Stella). He argues that postart keeps one "suicidally attached" to the ephemeral, futilely chasing after serial excitements that offer no stability or durable value. Duchamp (especially his readymades) and Warhol, who between them dramatized the notions that any object could be both art and non-art, that two objects could be identical yet one art and the other not, and finally that no boundaries can be drawn between art and non-art—are special bones of contention between these authors, Danto viewing these dramatizations as breakthroughs, Kuspit as breakdowns.

Throughout these volumes the disagreements are continuous but the descriptions of the postartistic scene virtually identical, testifying to the pervasiveness of the theories under discussion. As with the analogous litcrit theories, where one stands on them with respect to their home arts is one thing, but their uses in arts of the act another. One could at least hypothetically side with Danto, yet concede the non-transferability of his ideas to stage design, with the exception of works created according to those same theories, or works about them. Operatically, this would to date confine us to a handful of joyless pieces, for these theories have had minimal creative impact. Interpretively, however, they are justification for many of the abuses committed by designers and design-oriented directors. If anything from anywhere in the "lateral cut," regardless of its aesthetic properties, its place in a cultural history, or even its standing as art or non-art, may cross the boundary into the work, where its function is to mean something independent of the work's narrative, then critical sanction has been granted for the work's infanticide. Just as a Shakespeare sonnet will continue to survive for Bloom irrespective of critical violence visited upon it, so will a Caravaggio or Vermeer or Turner for Danto, and all of us. Not so for a Shakespeare play or a Wagner opera, when the critical violence claws from within.

A thought: for the thoughtful pure, the purely thoughtful, it is desirable that art find its end in thought—that *everything* end in thought—for that is their playing field, where games are played according to their rules. Shall we let them govern our responses to art, and define art's future?

Deleuze, Gilles: I have read nothing by Deleuze. Instead, I have relied on *Gilles Deleuze*, by Claire Colebrook (Routledge, 2002, in the Critical Thinkers series), on the assumption that it fairly summarizes his views, along with those of his frequent collaborator, the psychoanalyst Félix Guattari. With its direct, clear, but not simplistic language, its sidebars on related thinkers and concepts, its end-of-chapter summaries and list of works, this seems to me an admirable volume. It's Deleuze on film that connects here. Deleuze takes cinema as a paradigm; he locates in it a "movement-image" and a "time-image," through which the "disinterested" camera frees us toward a machinic, virtual/actual "becoming" (his extension of the concept of Being, evidently much influenced by Bergson's ideas on creativity and time) in the flow of time and life. Roughly put, he sees liberating vision where Baudrillard sees entrapment in illusion. I cannot resolve the philosophical difference, but for reasons hinted at in Backstory 1, I am temperamentally closer to Baudrillard. Deleuze insists on the specificity and independence of his artform—that cinema is not a secondary form of *literature* (emphasis added). But surely it's the theatre, not literature, that cinema isn't secondary to, and from which, in its early days, it needed to differentiate itself. And surely the main point of difference between film and live theatre is very close to the distinction between virtual and actual, however defined. Also: Deleuze's entire description of the time/space orientation within which our becoming must go on (at least as represented by Colebrook) rests on the eye as the sole channel of sensory perception. In other words, the two usual biases (literary and ocular) are present.

Derrida, Jacques: *Of Grammatology* (Johns Hopkins Univ. Press, 1976, Gayatri Chakravorty Spivak, trans.) is central to the Derridean *oeuvre*. The translator's preface by Spivak is a model of all such, guiding the reader through Derrida's important concepts and techniques and his primary antecedents, and to his position among his contemporaries. The book itself presents Derrida's main contentions on the nature of language and "writing," on the privileging of "speech" in Western thought. The arguments are subtle and elaborate; they cannot be summarized here. Of greatest interest from the operacentric P.O.V. is Part II, "Nature, Culture, Writing," throughout which Rousseau, seen as the great transmitter of the phonocentric bias via the Enlightenment into modernity, is the constant predecessor/antagonist. In particular, "Genesis and Structure of the *Essay on the Origin of Languages*," wherein Rousseau's musical thoughts (e.g., the precedence of song over speech, the valorizing of melody vs. harmony in the dispute with Rameau, the lifegiving South vs. the death-dealing North, etc.) are closely examined. In terms of music history, training the Weapons of Mass Deconstruction on Rousseau may seem merely quaint, but Derrida clearly sees a necessity in it. There's also a brief chapter on "The Theorem and the Theatre," again in engagement with Rousseau.

Most of *Deconstruction in a Nutshell* (Fordham Univ. Press, 1997, edited and with a commentary by John C. Caputo) consists of Caputo's exegesis on issues raised in a 1994 roundtable held at Villanova University, and its interest is confined to its home field. Besides its annotated bibliography of recent Derridean literature, though, it does offer the transcript of the roundtable itself, which allows the more informal and personal tone of conversation with the man. In this regard, I also enjoyed the sly documentary film *Derrida*, by Kirby Dick and Amy Zieging Kofman. (We know we are in sly hands when the long opening tracking sequence arrives at a section of metal fence whose strappings form the sign for *sous rature*, "under erasure," adapted by Derrida from Heidegger to indicate a word that is both necessary and inadequate.) The film incorporates many little tropes of this sort, proposing itself as a bit of glissing deconstructive pursuit. I was taken with Derrida's own concern with the artificiality of the situation on the movie/TV shoot, with the wish for authenticity while avoiding the confessional. It boils down again to the matter of presence, and I reflected that presence (in its literal, physical sense) can cut both ways: on the page, Derrida's brief discussion of the "*qui ou quoi?*" of love (is it the person herself, for herself, that one loves, or something about the person that meets a particular need or desire of one's own?) would no doubt assume a quite imposing aspect. In (virtual) person, it takes on the air of a bull session with a bright but puzzled roommate. Presence (as here, as in performance) can quite undo the defenses and presentational constructs of literature and offer something else instead. Perhaps *that's* their problem with it. I was also beguiled by the fact that although Derrida's wife, Marguerite, is a psychoanalyst (Lacanian or not unspecified), analysis is for Derrida himself "*absolument excludé*." An interesting household.

Foucault, Michel: Apart from the discussions in overview volumes, my main reference has been *The Foucault Reader* (Pantheon, 1984, Paul Rabinow, ed.), a selection of extended excerpts from his writings, concluding with an interesting interview conducted shortly before Foucault's death. Once again, a fine introduction by the editor well summarizes the recurrent themes of the writer's work, which cluster around the unexamined assumptions underlying the uses and misuses of power (hence: limitation, control, oppression, and—though Foucault would not employ the Marxist term—"false consciousness") in Western society. "What Is An Author?" is here, and its context as well—the more general enquiry into the (human) subject, and hence the individual, the self, character (see Bloom, and contemplate the chasm). The entry on Foucault by Robert Wicks in Gaut/Lopes (see above) focuses on his artistic analyses (all visual-literary), a subject absent from Rabinow. Foucault's extensive and provocative explorations into sexuality and the body as battlegrounds for control have served as entry point for some of his ideas (however simplified and even misapprehended) into opera criticism and production itself, chiefly through writers and directors of gay/lesbian/feminist orientation.

Heidegger, Martin: "The Origin of the Work of Art" first took the form of a lecture delivered in Freiburg (1935), expanded for another lecture in Frankfurt the following year. This essay, based on the expanded version, appears in *Martin Heidegger: Basic Writings* (HarperCollins, revised and expanded edition, 1993, David Farrell Krell, ed., trans. various). The book contains eleven readings from Heidegger, proceeding chronologically from "Being and Time: Introduction" onward. Solid background and orientation is provided by Krell's General Introduction and his prefatory notes to each reading. Simon Glendinning's Heidegger chapter in Gaut/Lopes, which led me to this volume, is helpful construal of Heideggerian aesthetics.

In any attempt to engage a fundamental question like this one, there are bound to be assumptions that invite challenge. I will mention here only the two that touch the operatic sensibility most closely. The first concerns artistic materials. I quote from the essay: "When a work is created, brought forth out of this or that material—stone, wood, metal, color, language, tone—we say also that it is made, set forth out of it." And then: "All this comes forth as the work sets itself back into the massiveness and heaviness of stone, into the firmness and pliancy of wood, into the hardness and luster of metal, into the brightening and darkening of color, into the clang of tone, and into the naming power of the word." How can we fail to object to this account of "material(s)", to note that the first three do not belong in the same category with the last three, and particularly the last two? How can we overlook the fact that "clang" (an interesting choice of descriptive noun to represent music*) and "naming power," whether apt or not, are not equivalent to each

---

* Perhaps this nuance should not be attributed to Heidegger, but to the translator, Albert Hofstadter. The usual English rendering of *"Klang des Tones"* would be simply "the sound of tone;" the English "clang," however homonymous, rather forces the issue. Possibly Hofstadter's sense of the passage is that Heidegger, in search of primitive qualities to illustrate the earthy origins of artistic materials, intended something like "clang" or "ring," and that this justifies the stretch. Neither interpretation, however, affects my point about the forced equivalencies of these "materials."

other or to the qualities of the other "materials?" That the writer or composer has no raw material to work with in the sense that a sculptor works stone or metal, creates form from matter, but works instead with fluid, symbolic components already transformed by human imagination (musical tones, words), conveyed by equipment of human invention (musical and writing instruments, paper, even—to postdate Heidegger—recording devices and computers)? Or finally (and most significantly for this discussion) that stone, wood, and metal represent energy trapped in matter, whereas sounded language and tone represent energy released from matter, which is also the physical difference between fine arts and arts of the act?

And the second assumption to mark: In the essay's third part, "Truth and Art," Heidegger arrives at this: "*All art*, as the letting happen of the advent of the truth of beings, is as such, *in essence, poetry*." (Emphasis in original.) Again: "Art, as the setting-into-work of truth, is poetry." Once more: "The essence of art is poetry. The essence of poetry, in turn, is the founding of truth." Of course Heidegger intends "poetry" in the broadest sense. Still, there is, again, the literary presumption as the very essence of all art.*There is, also again, the non-distinction between poetry seen (intrapersonal, its energy trapped) and poetry heard (interpersonal, energy released), poetry silently read vs. poetry recited, contemplation of the object vs. reception of the active. Heidegger's artistic metaphors, and his examined samples—a Van Gogh painting, a Greek temple, a few German poems—are all visual/literary, and this leaves us with no choice but to assume that the non-distinction masks the usual bias. Heidegger also asserts that only great art is under consideration without offering any means for defining great art. (His few examples do not, I think, make up a case.) This seems a peculiar lacuna in such a determined effort to bring problems of art to philosophic ground.

"The Origin of the Work of Art" remains an essential reading on its subject.

Lacan, Jacques: So far as I am aware, Lacan's theories have had far less impact on therapeutic practice here than in his home country. But particularly in their fusion of psychoanalytic with linguistic study, they have exerted a strong intellectual influence in the international academic community. His paper "The Mirror Stage as Formative of the Function of the I," referenced in the main text, can be found in *Écrits: A Selection* (Norton, 1977, Alan Sheridan,

---

* Could we not substitute "music" for "poetry" in each instance, with equal claim? Or even "opera?" Heidegger sought to rescue Greek thought and art from what he saw as modern misinterpretation. But were not the Greek poetic epics recited? Were not the Greek plays (Heidegger mentions Sophocles' *Antigone*—but in "best critical edition") performed, and "operatically," at that?

trans.), which is in turn drawn from the French-language original (Éditions de Seuil, 1966).

Lyotard, Jean-François: This author's hypotheses on the nature of knowledge, language games, and (especially) delegitimation of the metanarratives of modernism have virtually defined postmodernism for many. Two closely related volumes, *The Postmodern Condition: A Report on Knowledge* (Univ. of Minnesota Press, 1984, Geoff Bennington and Brian Massumi, trans., foreward by Jameson) and *The Postmodern Explained* (Univ. of Minnesota Press, 1993, trans. various, afterword by Wlad Godzich) present his piquant thinking succinctly, in prose that is clear and direct. Printed in both volumes (though in different translations) is his article *"Réponse à la question: Qu'est-ce que le postmoderne?"*, which presents thoughts on realism, the function of the avant-gardes, and other artistic matters. Lyotard argues the necessity of abandoning efforts to construct new (or reconstruct old) metanarratives in favor of a "legitimation by paralogy," a "war on totality." He wants art to bend its techniques to ". . . present the fact that the unpresentable exists." But his "unpresentable" is that which can be conceived but not made *visible* (my emphasis). His artistic references are drawn exclusively from painting and literature (all modern, at that, and all French, at that, except for Joyce). *Toujours la même chose*: Anything that cannot be apprehended by the eye, the analytic eye, is dumped into the category of the "unpresentable."

Sontag, Susan: I include Sontag here because her famous essay *Against Interpretation* remains an admirably pithy presentation of the modernist privileging of form over content. (*"Against Interpretation" and Other Essays*, Farrar, Straus & Giroux, 1965, is now in paperback from Picador USA, 2001.) Fed up with the endless mining of artworks for subtextual meaning, and convinced that the presumed presence of content as critical imperative blocks our reception of art as sensory experience, Sontag prods our attention toward form in the hope of silencing ". . . the arrogance of interpretation," to see ". . . *what it is*. . . rather than to show *what it means*." She dismisses as a ". . . fancy that there really is such a thing as the content of a work of art," and calls "highly dubious" the theory that ". . . a work of art is composed of items of content." This was a characteristic modernist challenge: we can see that this box, say, is of a certain shape and made of a certain material—that much we can define—but since when we turn it upside down and shake it no "items" fall out, it must not have any content.

We must keep in mind that Sontag was writing about critical focus, about Third Interpreters. She wasn't advocating (at least explicitly) the installation

of form and material as the central concern of creative and interpretive artists. But that is the turn modernism took, and it is essentially a critical move,
for to give "how" primacy over "what" is to tend not only from the representational toward the abstract, but from the inspirational toward the analytic.

Ironically, in opera (with which Sontag was little concerned) the kind of
criticism she deplored (". . . prompted . . . by an overt contempt for appearances. . . that excavates, and as it excavates, destroys. . .") has come to
dominate not only criticism itself but performance—the *interpretive artists*
excavate and destroy, either by erecting ". . . another meaning on top of the
literal one" (Sontag) or by loading into the work a surplus of information that
". . . exhausts itself in the act of staging communication. . ." and ". . . dissolves
meaning. . . in a sort of nebulous state dedicated not to a surplus of innovation, but, on the contrary, to total entropy" (Baudrillard). As I have noted with
respect to Bloom's complaint (see above), in the Arts of the Act such "destruction" is not figurative, but literal: while works like *Lohengrin, Tannhäuser,* or
Die Frau ohne Schatten; *Lucia di Lammermoor, Il Trovatore,* or *La Bohème* may
on "appearances" have a content from which a "literal" meaning could be
derived, they can actually be made to contain anything and mean anything,
and so, nothing. In that view, they have no integral content, content they can
call their own.

It would never be my wish to pound on France. I love her language, her culture, her thought—even some of the thought I've glanced at here. But owing
to the ascendancy of that thought, no country illustrates quite so starkly
the collapse of creativity and interpretivity into criticality—and by the very
rules of the critical game, we are not even permitted a triumphal Arch of
Deconstruction. I close with this from Rousseau, as cited by Derrida:

> "Thus, as soon as Greece became full of sophists and philosophers,
> she no longer had any famous musicians or poets. In cultivating the
> art of convincing, that of arousing the emotions was lost."

I don't know if it happened just that way in old Athens, but it has certainly
occurred in the France of our time.

3

THEMES AND VARIATIONS:
A SAMPLING

Themes and variations (I call these last "diversions," not because opera-wrights used them to deliberately distract us from what happens, but because for us that is often their effect) are mixed up together in E-19, and that is how I shall sample them here, some under one heading, some under the other. Of the themes discussed in the main text, the first two ("Marriage, and the alternative;" "Fathers, mothers, and inheritance") are ubiquitous and nearly always undisguised, and so require no example. For the remainder, I shall avoid as self-evident the *ur*-faydit operas (see p. 206). While by the end of this chapter and Backstory most standard-repertory operas will have been touched on, I have not attempted all-inclusiveness. Any interested reader can easily compile his or her own *catalogue raisonée*.

Among the diversions, a favorite of mine (it goes to such lengths!) is the switched-positions telling, wherein the characters begin in reverse-faydit conformation and must be maneuvered into their proper places. *Don Pasquale* and *Eugene Onegin* offer fine, contrasting examples. *Pasquale* opens in the reverse mode: the man, Ernesto, stands to inherit wealth, while young widow Norina is in modest circumstances. But because he refuses an arranged marriage, Ernesto is cast out by Uncle Pasquale. Now Ernesto is the dispossessed faydit, but Norina not yet the elevated lady. Get that inheritance!—but how? We might suggest that Ernesto use his wanderings in *lontana terra* to find a job. But although *Pasquale*, for all its *commedia* derivations, is an "advanced" generational comedy of its day, it is not quite advanced enough to suggest that its hero go "into trade"—end of romance, for sure. Another way must be found: the enactment of a courtly-romance playlet with real-life consequences. And there is a particularly piquant set-up for this, especially if we keep in mind Donizetti's other lovely comedy, *L'Elisir d'amore*. Norina's introduction is nearly identical with Adina's in *Elisir*: they are both reading courtly romances whose plots and sentiments they are about to appropriate for their own purposes. Adina, in fact, is reading a version of the Tristan legend, and her opera goes on to recount a low-key, country-village takeoff on the story. Norina, breaking off her recitation of "the cavalier Riccardo's" avowal to his lady, lets us know that her own familiarity with feminine sorcery will be used to ensure that things do not turn out the same this time. And in a way they don't (this *is* a comedy), but in a way they do, for in order to bring about the happy end, the old plot must be enacted. In the masquerade-comedy marriage, Norina becomes the wealthy wife of her lover's uncle and mistress of his house, while Ernesto is the suppliant troubadour, complete with off-stage serenade and clandestine garden tryst. Just as in the Tristan tale, the betrayed uncle, who thought he'd married the perfect woman, discovers the awful truth with the dawn.

At the end of *Onegin*'s opening scene, it seems impossible that the faydit romance can emerge. The woman is an ingenuous, dreamy young daughter of country gentry, the man an urban social insider pointedly uninterested in her life. The remainder of the plot shows the elaborate series of moves whereby the characters wriggle free of this apparent checkmate to play a proper faydit endgame. It stipulates that the man first spurn the girl's passionate avowals, then kill his best friend in a pointless love-triangle charade, and finally return after *Wanderjahren* to find the girl a princess in manner and in fact. Now she is married and elevated, he alone and rootless. The hopeless drama may begin, its high emotion crammed into the fevered final scene. Yet it ends without granting us either of E-19's customary emotional gratifications: Tatyana, having outgrown the story, rejects both the happy-end illusion and its sad-end alternative. So we must forego both, as well, and are left to ask ourselves whether or not we are satisfied. As we saw with *Mazeppa*, Tchaikovsky, the ultimate romantic, loves to disappoint romantic expectations.

A second diversionary preservation tactic—and one that yields some of E-19's richest rewards—is to shift the faydit story a bit to one side while another character (usually a father) moves to the emotional center. In both *Rigoletto* and *Simon Boccanegra*, for instance, the most highly developed character is that of the baritone/father, and a father/daughter relationship lies at the heart of the work. (Mothers are dead or unmentioned. But they haunt.) Both, too, present the theme of a curse or oath as Destiny. In each case, the

oath is sworn by a second daughter-bereft father. It pursues the baritone/
father, and we suspensefully await its fulfillment, signaled in *Rigoletto* from
the first bars of the prelude. So strong is its coloring, and so central the
father/daughter bond, that we may easily mistake either for the force that
drives the action.

But in neither case is this so. The action of *Rigoletto* is driven by the Duke's
pursuit of Gilda. That is the first thing we learn of in this inverted Court of
Love where women, though addressed in courtly language, are at the mercy
of rapacious men. In Scene Two we meet the disguise stratagem for counter-
ing an upside-down class difference. The Duke assumes the identity of a poor
student so that the daughter of his jester may become his exalted lady. In most
such cases (*Luisa Miller* and its happy-end cousin *Linda di Chamounix, Barbiere
di Siviglia, Cenerentola*) the purpose of the false identity is pure, intended to
effect a genuine life alliance. *Rigoletto* tells a bad-faith version of the tale, and
pulls us into the perspective of the character who, as patriarchal impediment,
would normally be its antagonist. But it is still the spine of the action.

In *Simon Boccanegra* the story is told in two overlapping versions, and
the faydit circumstance cast in triplicate. The opera's complex plot, source
of much handwringing and amused condescension among Anglo-American
critics, becomes instantly clear if it is recognized as the faydit tale twice told,
passed from one generation to the next. In the first telling (contained in the
Prologue) Simon, corsair and plebeian, aspires to the daughter of a great patrician family, the Fieschi. But the death of this daughter and the disappearance
of the baby she has had by Simon call down the father's oath of enmity. In the
second telling Simon is himself ruler and father, and his own rediscovered
daughter (the disappeared baby of the first telling) is aspired to by Gabriele,
tenor/lover of the now-disempowered patrician faction and hence the new
faydit. Paolo, the political ally and friend responsible for Simon's rise in
the first version, is now for his misdeeds cast out under *another* terrifying
father's curse, and thereby becomes the second telling's antagonist and the
opera's third (albeit unsympathetic) faydit. Throughout both tellings, the
action is impelled by the romantic undertakings of the faydit of the moment:
Simon's alliance with Maria; Gabriele's with Amelia, leading to defiance and
regicidal rage; Paolo's abduction escapade and poisoned drink. Also throughout, Fiesco and his oath lurk, awaiting the moment of vengeful disclosure.
Finally, Faydit No. 3 carries out the father's vengeance on Faydit No. 1, while
Faydit No. 2 attains ruling status and the hand of his lady. Thus, though the
first telling dominates and Simon's death lends a tragic cast to the close, the
second arrives simultaneously at its happy end: the father's curse has been
turned into another father's benediction, and Gabriele will rule. Momentous

political changes have occurred (nothing less than the conciliation of long-standing factional strife and the peaceful succession of power), but the personal has determined the political throughout.

As we approach the time of late-19th-Century realism, we find the tale set contemporaneously and the status of knight and lady often re-defined, so that we scarcely recognize them. This diversion accomplishes at once the purpose of our own production updatings—to make the plot and characters seem fresh and "relevant"—and that of disguising the fact that the old story is still being told. The mother of all such tellings is *La Traviata*.

Its heroine, Violetta, reigns over an indubitable Court of Love, with its own elaborate etiquette. She has neither title nor marriage, but may role-play at both due to an elevation she has earned, though by means that haven't much to do with the commonly lauded virtues. Into her sophisticated and licentious milieu comes a passionate, earnest young man from (sure enough) Provence. He is ready with his drinking song, his declaration of fealty, his serenade from the street below. When he kneels at the feet of his lady centuries fall away, and no game is being played.

But the relative cultural positions of the Languedoc and the Ile de France have been reversed since courtly times: Alfredo's South is rural and conservative, a land of old customs and values. There, there is a father. Germont's position is complicated, for he has both a son and a daughter. If he had only the son, the question would be painful but simple: disinherit him or not. But the daughter must marry, and such are the mores of time and place that the prospective groom (a "loved and loving youth," according to Germont) will not enter into the marriage unless his brother-in-law-to-be renounces his scandalous liaison and returns to "the bosom of the family." These and other arguments (that Alfredo will stray when Violetta's beauty fades; that without Heavenly blessings their union will not outlast the tedium of marriage) are so readily acknowledged by Violetta, despite their emotionally devastating consequences, that they carry the force of old truths she has been hiding from. Besides, she harbors her Illness-as-Destiny, whose progression is clearly tied to that of her fateful love bond. And so there cannot be a happy ending. Except, of course, that down in Provence the unseen daughter's wedding will doubtless go forward, and the venerable social order will be sustained.

Then there are cases wherefrom an element appears to be missing. The stories of Tristan and Isolde or Pelléas and Mélisande, or of Romeo and Juliet or Paolo and Francesca in any of their versions, for instance, do not contain the element of dispossession in its original, literal sense (deprivation of title or property). But the presence of a powerful family taboo and the standing of the young hero in relation to the impedimental character (an older sibling, an uncle/father figure) serve to put the protagonist couple in the faydit bind, and allow the tale to proceed.

Or, consider the Shakespeare operas of Verdi. The tragedies, *Otello* and *Macbeth*, have in common that the protagonists are already married to each other and apparently secure in their elevated situations. But as the drama unfolds the man is manipulated into an outsider position and into extreme, ignoble faydit responses. Macbeth commits a series of horribly distorted chivalric deeds as if eternally in need of winning his lady, returning to himself only when released from his need by her death. Otello's marriage is destroyed by the lightest of touches on its most vulnerable point—his inner conviction that he is always an outsider, and that nothing he does will win him true acceptance from his lady or her society. Like Violetta's, his resistance collapses instantly, and for the same reason: he cannot believe he is worthy of the bond. Hence, the most towering and deadly of all E-19's accusatory rages.

In the comedy, *Falstaff*, the setting is thoroughly bourgeois, with a community-and-family ethic to the fore. The merry wives are already wives, and the young hero aspires to none of them. Nor is he dispossessed; he is merely not rich. The title character, though, is a fallen knight, a parody of noble powers and courtly graces. He acts out fantasies of troubadour romance with the wives of the wealthy burghers while a sweet, Lite version of the lovematch-vs.-arranged-match *commedia* (the real engine of the action) plays in little fits and starts, well to the background. A misunderstanding husband works up a convincing accusatory rage, but the clever women solve it all by means of a masquerade comedy, and all celebrate fugally if ruefully: we are, of course, fools. Note that it is not our beloved hero-buffoon who gets married, any more than it is Don Pasquale in his opera, Hans Sachs or Beckmesser in theirs. In these comedies, as with the happy-end aspects of those tragedies that have such (like *Boccanegra*), the problem being solved is that of accommodating choice in love with succession and inheritance, and for this purpose the older-generation impediment must be moved aside—gracefully if possible, but by death, banishment, or humiliation if necessary.

These elaborations that tend to divert us from what happens are infinitely variable. The foregoing examples should suffice. Bearing in mind that most operas incorporate several of the selected themes, let me cite one or two that present each of the remaining ones with special clarity.

There can be no better demonstration of the workings of the Low End of Destiny than *The Queen of Spades*. It is the operatic apotheosis of the concept that life must be lived as a game but will, literally, collapse like a house of cards when the hero tries to beat the odds. The atmosphere of the tacky occult that proves true, which pervades *Ballo* and to some extent *Forza*, and the notion of the hero-as-gambler (e.g., Alfredo and Des Grieux, jobless like Ernesto and so forced to the table) also get definitive treatment here. Ghermann does have a job, that of ill-paid military officer. Not in a hundred lifetimes will it lift him to the rank of the Prince on whose arm Lisa appears in Scene One. Here is the outsider's Catch-22: a legal union with Lisa would gain him rank and wealth, but rank and wealth are the prerequisites for the union. And so he feels the faydit rage at being deprived of something rightfully his, now seen as simple human equality, full social participation based solely on the fact of his existence. He is the ultimate modern faydit, unless that be his successor Alexei of *The Gambler*, an intellectual caught in a decadent world of inherited rank and privilege where only chance offers hope of redress.

I think the Manon story best exemplifies the theme of the meeting, the bond, and trust. This is true in both the Puccini and Massenet versions, but particularly the latter, which also shows with unusual transparency the opportunistic, invented-of-necessity nature of its "romantic destiny." The meeting of the lovers is truly an unprepared, chance encounter. But because it is an intersection on Roads of Life they do not wish to travel, it becomes their Destiny. It takes place at a literal intersection: the inn at Amiens, a transfer and rest point on coach routes. Manon—not yet sixteen, alluring, high-spirited—is on her way to the convent. Her cousin Lescaut, charged with seeing her on her way, has left her alone in the courtyard. Filled to bursting with the wide world's call and dazzled by the example of fashionable worldly women, she tries to put her longings to rest: "No more dreams," she tells herself. As she reaches this uneasy composure, she senses someone coming—another coach has arrived.

It is the Chevalier. We hear his theme, a falling instant-melody-meme intoned in the strings, confident on the surface but with a hint of undertow. He, too, is hiding an unease: en route to re-uniting with his father, he feels oddly hesitant. His theme repeats as he lectures himself about how splendid the paternal meeting is going to be, and it finally calls in instrumental reinforcements to buck him up. But just as it swells to a climax, it fragments and breaks off into a suspenseful violin vamp.* He has spotted Manon, and

---

* This theme, so strong, so quickly dissolved, appears twice more: at the opening of Act II, the final moments of the lovers' idyll in the little Paris apartment, where several slightly varied restatements of it combine with a scampering little figure we associate with Manon to construct the introduction; and briefly again at the act's end, a fleeting fragment in the bustle of his abduction. After that, this marker of identity is gone; Des Grieux is lost to himself.

the moment hangs, breathless. Des Grieux sings that his life is either beginning or ending in this instant, that an iron hand is leading him down another road in spite of himself. Abandoning song for the musicalized speech of *mélodrame*, he declares himself no longer his own master; that though he sees her for the first time, he somehow knows her; and (returning to song) that he must know her name. Within another two minutes, he has proclaimed her an enchantress and mistress of his heart and has promised to save her from the convent and give her his name. Throughout, her responses are encouraging but modest, appropriate to an innocent young lady receiving her first courtly compliments. She even enters initial reservations about living together, about stealing Guillot's coach. This could almost be Marguerite meeting Faust at the fair, save for the fact that she has let slip that in her family she is sometimes accused of loving pleasure too much, and that the coach *is* available.

This entire drama of romantic destiny, complete with all its genuine passion and real-life consequences, has been whipped up on the moment by two people on journeys they don't want to complete: she really doesn't want to go the convent, and he really doesn't want that meeting with his father. "Destiny" is the unspoken contract between these two very young, mutually attracted persons, giddily defying the fathers.

The reader will doubtless recognize "the political is the personal" as the inversion of the slogan that achieved such wide currency in the Sixties, whose meaning was that there is no act one can commit—public or private, by choice or default—that does not have a political ramification. The operas of E-19 do not dispute this, but they view it from the other end of the telescope, by insisting that all political acts, however great their magnitude and public repercussions, are personal and private in their origins. They arise from the psychology of relationships. This is another theme present in so many E-19 operas as to require little elaboration. (*Simon Boccanegra* has already been cited. *Don Carlos, Boris Godunov*, the Donizetti "Queen" operas, would be other clearly illustrative cases.)

What is remarkable, especially for such politically involved creators as Verdi and Wagner, is how often the political is kept to the background or is absent altogether, even when its implications are vast—not how central it is in their works, but how tangential—and the degree to which it is seen as effect, not cause. That is why efforts to render their works "relevant" by emphasizing their political resonances are so often partially successful at best, destructively tendentious at worst.

A number of works could with profit be examined in light of the artist/faydit theme. In its most despairing form—that of the poetical youth rejected by his ladylove, forever shut out from the warmth of domesticity and doomed to wander, isolated and morbid, through town and country—it is best shown in the song cycles of Schubert, Schumann, and Mahler. *Werther*, with its pure faydit triangle transplanted to an 18th-Century bourgeois setting, but set in 19th-Century accents, and its hypersensitive hero obsessed with the poems of that faux-medieval chivalric invention, "Ossian," is the operatic prototype. Of greater interest, though, is a more complicated case like *Lohengrin*.

Wagner himself viewed *Lohengrin* as a parable of the artist, descended from the mythical stories of gods who long for union with humans.[1] About the latter connection there is not much room for question, but we are under no compulsion to follow the artistic metaphor. In fact there is nothing in this Christian legend dangling from the Grail matter that clearly points in that direction. It is a private attribution, a piece of personal subtext that second interpreters ought approach warily and that receptors are free to weave into their tapestries, or not. If the parable is in the work, it is well-hidden. And that's curious, since Wagner treated the subject of the faydit artist, his connected lady, and the community quite openly in *Tannhäuser* (sad ending) and *Die Meistersinger* (happy ending). Indeed, since the story of *Lohengrin* is in most essentials identical to that of *Der Fliegende Holländer*,* one may well ask why one is about an artist and the other about the Wandering Jew, and decide we are better off without either.

Still, since the very theme being considered here is the one Wagner concealed in this work, and Bob's "What-Is-It" production of the same opera launched the present enquiry, it's only natural to ask what *Lohengrin* tells us if we follow it as the story of an artist. In such a reading, the Grail—mystical source of light, sustenance, and renewal, revealed to only a chosen, tested few under special conditions—would stand for Art itself, or at least the power of artistic inspiration. This Art is seen as a righteous force from which its servants draw magical powers to overcome evil, reveal justice and truth, and reinforce the civilized order. The sources of artistic genius are mysterious. Their secrecy must be protected, or they lose their power. Thus, the artist must keep deep within himself what is most himself, and others—even intimates—must understand that he is not to be questioned in the matter.

---

* At their simplest, deepest plot-and character level, they are one and the same: an otherworldly man arrives in dramatic, mystical fashion to unite with a woman of the everyday world who has already dreamt of him. To keep him in the human world, her unquestioning acceptance is required. It doesn't work out. Upon revealing himself he returns whence he came, she dies, our everyday world resumes as before, and it all seems a pity.

Lohengrin is not, like Tannhäuser, torn between the sensual and the saintly. Nor is he an outsider from a world of the accursed, like the Dutchman, but rather an outsider from a world of the blessed. And unlike Stolzing, he is no mere stripling knight with unformed songs to sing and many lessons to be learned. He is fully evolved, select, a dedicated and unswerving Knight of Art supremely confident of his mission in the world.

Yet he is incomplete. The artist is also a man, and like all men longs for connection and inclusion, for the comfort of the quotidian, and above all for the love and trust of another. (And though Lohengrin descends from his world into ours, he—like the Empress in *Frau*—can complete himself only among us. As with the *Ring*, this is a story of an attempted *ascent* to humanity.) As usual, it is marriage that holds out these possibilities, and in *Lohengrin* a marriage is actually solemnized. A high affair it is, this union of the Knight of Art with the woman who is the temporary link in Brabant's line of descent, and who has sworn her oath on the intuitive knowledge that knows nothing outside itself. For once, a tale of blind trust does not stop short of marriage— not quite, for this one carries us into the first hours of the wedding night. After the celebrative festivities, the ceremonial pomp, and the acceptance into the nuptial folkways of the community, Lohengrin and Elsa are like any other couple alone in their bedchamber, where knowledge of each other begins to be necessary. And here Elsa cannot keep her promise, elicited as it was under circumstances both ecstatic and coercive. We may be inclined to blame Elsa, and the work can seem to encourage this. If only she had been stronger! "Oh, Elsa! Just one year at my side," mourns Lohengrin afterwards. Then all would have been revealed, all healed. But how was she to know? "*Never* must you ask"—that is what he made her swear, following his own imperative to keep art's secrets till its work is done. And in addition to Elsa's natural curiosity about her husband's nature and identity, there is the fear and suspicion sown by practitioners of old, discredited arts, who with some reason see themselves as the true faydit couple of the story.

The portrait of the artist that emerges from this reading is not easy to own up to. The artist as tortured blasphemer whose inner goodness is finally recognized by God through female intercession (*Tannhäuser*), or as untamed genius who at last learns about artistic form and respect for tradition (Stolzing), or as all-wise, self-abnegating People's Artisan-Poet (Sachs, the ultimate fantasy of the artist's social position)—these are identities fit enough for romantic sympathies. But Superartist, descending from a realm of the Perfect to wield magical powers in combat and prophecy, to decide affairs of state, to claim the privilege of full non-disclosure while soliciting compassion for his longing for inclusion, all the while putting on airs of Christian nobility: this is less appetizing, particularly if viewed as self-portrait. If a parable about the artist is hiding behind the Christian legend (itself a screen, in Wagner's own view, for pre-Christian myth), it asks not only what it might take for common humanity to accept the artist, but what it might take for the artist to become fully human. Its tragedy is that it has no answer: the artist will return to his little brotherhood of isolates, and the world will go its barbaric way without him. .

I think not only of Wagner, uncharacteristically bashful behind these veils, but of "Bob," with his anguished diagonals, Mercerized hands, and enigmatic Grail of milk, and of Bob himself, with his abstracted, slo-mo beauties, his refusal to discuss meaning, and his alleged non-interpretation of the same tale of the hidden artist. Close to the bone, it would seem; yet (and here's the beauty part) who can ever say?

But we are trying to keep our eye on what happens. And all the foregoing notwithstanding, what finally happens in *Lohengrin* (joyful tears amid the cries of woe) is that patrilineal propriety is, once again, restored. The boy Gottfried, rightful heir, abducted and bewitched by a sorceress, is now Duke of Brabant.

The last of these themes, transcendence, is central. More than any of the others, it is the enabler of E-19's greatest music. In its guise as exaltation of emotion, of life in a realm of emotion as the only true thing, it is always what is being sung, and the cause of singing that way. Thus, it is constitutive of E-19 opera. Its migration through works of Wagner, Verdi, and Bizet, and its fate at the close of E-19, is given attention in the main text. Here, I should like to examine the entanglement of transcendence with the theme just discussed, that of the artist as faydit. The Artist Transcendent was E-19's great, though fleeting, dream. The shift of transcendence from old religion to new is seen at a glance in the contrast of the Faust settings of Gounod and Boïto with Offenbach's *Les Contes d'Hoffmann.*

What the Faust settings show is that when an old man, full of learning and up against its limitations, is granted his fondest wish, he will choose to enact the drama of courtly romance. It's life itself to E-19 Man, valued above wealth or power. The enactment, for all its real-life fallout, is clearly presented as such: we are led into it by the Demon and extracted from it by the Heavenly Host; it is an episode in their eternal war, which is finally what is real: both operas end in full-blown Christian triumphalism proclaimed in mighty choruses.

Given the textual confusions of Offenbach's opera, it must be admitted that few assertions about it are beyond challenge. But in any version, its title character is a serial faydit-artist and his progression (stipulating only that

Giuletta's act follow Antonia's, which is now the customary sequence) is both courtly and Faustian: it collates the extractions from Goethe made by the Faustian operawrights. That is, Hoffmann loves first an illusion presented in marvelous fashion, then a dreamy young woman in a domestic setting (both as in Gounod), and finally a celebrated beauty at a court of love (as in Boïto, hinted at in Gounod). In each of these adventures he is thwarted by a demonic rival who is both indigenous to the scene (i.e., an insider) and of a type inimical to the spirit of romantic art: mechanical engineer, quack doctor, seafaring man of action. Each of these antagonists pretends to take the poet's part while actually undermining him. This trio of flashback, otherworldly tales is bracketed by a fourth, set in the opera's present and at the very bottom of the everyday world—the tavern beneath the opera house. This tale is complete with its own elevated but empty illusion of femininity (the literal prima donna, La Stella) and its own anti-romantic demon, the old bureaucrat Lindorf. It ends the same as the others, and on that account can be said to draw conclusions about the faydit artist's place in society that are as discouraging as *Lohengrin*'s. But Hoffmann comes to recognize himself, to understand that his place is in the world but not of it. Hoffmann will never be rid of his Muse or his Demon; they are parts of him. God-the-Father, though, has vanished, for Art has replaced Religion as the counterforce to the demonic, and Art does not pretend to be other than of and by humankind. For the poet, there is only the call of the Muse and one more stiff drink down here in the cellar, and this victory of the romantic spirit is the bitter new transcendence.

NOTES

1. See Dieter Borchmeyer: *Drama and the World of Richard Wagner* (Princeton Univ. Press, 2003), Chap. 5, for a good summary of *Lohengrin*'s mythical derivations.

ACKNOWLEDGEMENTS

I should probably begin with some words about people who have been instrumental in helping me develop my thoughts about the present subject over a lifetime of engagement with it. First among these would be the dedicatee of this book, who first taught me, largely by example, that opera and singing are things that deserve both love and critical attention. Next would be the editors of several publications with which I've had ongoing connection, who have given me the latitude to pursue my interests in print, as well as guidance on how best to do that. They would include Roland Gelatt, Peter G. Davis, Kenneth Furie, James Oestreich, and Shirley Fleming at *High Fidelity/Musical America*; James Oestreich again at *Opus* and *The New York Times*; Frank Merkling, Robert Jacobson, and Brian Kellow at *Opera News*; John Higgins at *The Financial Times*; Patrick J. Smith at *The Musical Newsletter*; and Sedgwick Clark at *Keynote*.

It was Margaret Carson, publicist extraordinaire, who first suggested that one of my articles for the Sunday *New York Times* be expanded into a book on the state of the operatic art. That didn't happen right away or perhaps in quite the way she'd envisioned, but her idea planted the seed. Among those who encouraged and advised me in the early stages of the writing were Walter Lippincott, then of Princeton University Press, and my daughter Lauren, then of Farrar, Straus & Giroux, who also added some sage advice on contract negotiation later on. Stephen Rubin, Jeannie Williams, Charles Affron, and Peter Bloch offered similar support toward the end, and Joel Friedlander gave me invaluable help in his capacity as consultant. In addition to compiling the extensive Index, my sister Suzanne contributed invaluable proofreading backup along the way.

Two long-valued colleagues, Will Crutchfield and Peter G. Davis, did me the considerable service of reading the entire manuscript and offering much supportive but clear-eyed feedback. Others who read and commented helpfully on sections of the book included Gene Scheer, Steven Blier, Ralph Hammann, Kenneth Furie, Austin Pendleton, and Peter Bloch. I also consulted Reinhard Mayer, Michael Sargent, Marc Scorca (Opera America), Hedi Siegel, Cantor Joel Gafni, Sally Murphy, Matthew Lau, Peter Clark (Metropolitan Opera), and Eric Halfvarson on specific questions relating to their areas of expertise.

Throughout the entire writing process, Stephan Kirchgraber directed my attention to, and in many cases furnished me with, materials both printed and recorded that might otherwise have escaped my attention. Will Crutchfield shared with me his extensive audio files of vocal rarities, as well as some of the preliminary results of his own research into the history of singing. Richard Slade also lent me useful materials, especially concerning *La Juive*. And again from beginning to end of the book's gestation, David Zimmerman rendered invaluable assistance with word processing and technological trouble-shooting. The names of those directly involved with the book's production will be found on the Credits page.

Finally, I owe immeasurable gratitude to my beloved wife, Molly Regan, who in addition to her unfailing personal support has read and responded to every chapter in real time, has researched and followed up on countless issues—procedural, technical, legal, and others—that have presented themselves along the long way, often taking time and energy from her own personal and professional projects to do so. Without her, my book would be much farther from the finish line, and I myself much closer to it.

CREDITS

Interior design and production: Marin Bookworks

Jacket Design: Kelley Rich

Index: Suzanne Osborne

Front cover artwork: Yael Saiger

Author photo: Ralph Hammann

Publicity: Kathryn King Media

Website development: Alison Cheeseman (http://birdhive.com)

INDEX OF NAMES AND TITLES